HISTORY+ FOR EDEXCEL

DEMOCRACIES IN CHANGE:
Britain and the USA in the twentieth century

HISTORY+ FOR EDEXCEL A LEVEL

DEMOCRACIES IN CHANGE:
Britain and the USA in the twentieth century

ROBIN BUNCE
PETER CLEMENTS
VIVIENNE SANDERS
NICK SHEPLEY

Every effort has been made to trace all copyright holders, but if any have been inadvertently overlooked, the Publishers will be pleased to make the necessary arrangements at the first opportunity.

Although every effort has been made to ensure that website addresses are correct at time of going to press, Hodder Education cannot be held responsible for the content of any website mentioned in this book. It is sometimes possible to find a relocated web page by typing in the address of the home page for a website in the URL window of your browser.

Hachette UK's policy is to use papers that are natural, renewable and recyclable products and made from wood grown in sustainable forests. The logging and manufacturing processes are expected to conform to the environmental regulations of the country of origin.

Orders: please contact Bookpoint Ltd, 130 Milton Park, Abingdon, Oxon OX14 4SB. Telephone: (44) 01235 827720. Fax: (44) 01235 400454. Email education@bookpoint.co.uk Lines are open from 9 a.m. to 5 p.m., Monday to Saturday, with a 24-hour message answering service. You can also order through our website: www.hoddereducation.co.uk

ISBN: 978 1 4718 3768 5

© Peter Clements, Vivienne Sanders, Nick Shepley and Robin Bunce 2015

First published in 2015 by

Hodder Education,

An Hachette UK Company

Carmelite House

50 Victoria Embankment

London EC4Y 0DZ

www.hoddereducation.co.uk

Impression number   10   9   8   7   6   5   4   3

Year   2019   2018   2017

All rights reserved. Apart from any use permitted under UK copyright law, no part of this publication may be reproduced or transmitted in any form or by any means, electronic or mechanical, including photocopying and recording, or held within any information storage and retrieval system, without permission in writing from the publisher or under licence from the Copyright Licensing Agency Limited. Further details of such licences (for reprographic reproduction) may be obtained from the Copyright Licensing Agency Limited, Saffron House, 6–10 Kirby Street, London EC1N 8TS.

Cover photo vector_master – Fotolia

Illustrations by Integra Software Services

Typeset in 10/12.5pt Bembo Std Regular by Integra Software Services Pvt. Ltd., Pondicherry, India

Printed in Dubai

A catalogue record for this title is available from the British Library.

In order to ensure that this resource offers high-quality support for the associated Pearson qualification, it has been through a review process by the awarding body. This process confirms that; this resource fully covers the teaching and learning content of the specification or part of a specification at which it is aimed. It also confirms that it demonstrates an appropriate balance between the development of subject skills, knowledge and understanding, in addition to preparation for assessment.

Endorsement does not cover any guidance on assessment activities or processes (e.g. practice questions or advice on how to answer assessment questions), included in the resource nor does it prescribe any particular approach to the teaching or delivery of a related course.

While the publishers have made every attempt to ensure that advice on the qualification and its assessment is accurate, the official specification and associated assessment guidance materials are the only authoritative source of information and should always be referred to for definitive guidance.

Pearson examiners have not contributed to any sections in this resource relevant to examination papers for which they have responsibility.

Examiners will not use endorsed resources as a source of material for any assessment set by Pearson.

Endorsement of a resource does not mean that the resource is required to achieve this Pearson qualification, nor does it mean that it is the only suitable material available to support the qualification, and any resource lists produced by the awarding body shall include this and other appropriate resources.

CONTENTS

	Introduction	v
	Note-making	ix

Paper 1 Britain transformed, 1918–97 — 2

Theme 1 A changing political and economic environment, 1918–79 — 2
- 1a: A changing political landscape — 4
- 1b: Responding to economic challenges — 25
- 1c: Change and challenge in the workplace — 42

Theme 2 Creating a welfare state, 1918–79 — 57
- 2a: Provision of social welfare — 58
- 2b: Public health — 68
- 2c: Education and widening opportunities — 80

Theme 3 Society in transition, 1918–79 — 94
- 3a: Class and social values — 96
- 3b: The changing role and status of women — 106
- 3c: Race and immigration — 118

Theme 4 The changing quality of life, 1918–79 — 130
- 4a: Changing living standards — 132
- 4b: Popular culture and entertainment — 141
- 4c: Leisure and travel — 155

Historical interpretations
What impact did Thatcher's governments (1979–90) have on Britain, 1979–97? — 169

Paper 2 The USA, 1920–55: Boom, bust and recovery — 232

Key Topic 1 Boom and crash, 1920–29 — 234
- Section 1: The 1920s' economic boom — 234
- Section 2: Causes of the Wall Street Crash — 241
- Section 3: Changes in society — 246
- Section 4: Cultural changes in the 1920s — 252

Key Topic 2 The Depression and the New Deal, 1929–38 — 264
Section 1: The spread of the Depression, 1929–32 — 264
Section 2: Hoover's response to the Depression, 1929–32 — 269
Section 3: Roosevelt and the First New Deal, 1933–35 — 274
Section 4: The Second New Deal, 1935–38 — 283

Key Topic 3 The impact of the New Deal and the Second World War on the USA to 1945 — 296
Section 1: The New Deal and the economy — 296
Section 2: The impact of the New Deal and the war on ethnic minorities — 302
Section 3: Social and cultural changes — 308
Section 4: The war and the economy, 1941–45 — 313

Key Topic 4 The transformation of the USA, 1945–54 — 322
Section 1: Economic transformation — 322
Section 2: The end of post-war euphoria — 326
Section 3: Cultural change — 332
Section 4: The changing status of minorities — 336

Paper 2 The USA, 1955–92: Conformity and challenge — 352

Key Topic 1 Affluence and conformity, 1955–63 — 354
Section 1: Urbanisation and affluence — 354
Section 2: Cultural conformity and challenge — 361
Section 3: The civil rights movement — 367
Section 4: Kennedy's New Frontier — 374

Key Topic 2 Protest and reaction, 1963–72 — 386
Section 1: Civil rights — 387
Section 2: Johnson's Great Society, 1964–68 — 395
Section 3: Protest and personal freedom — 400
Section 4: Reactions to the counter-culture, 1968–72 — 409

Key Topic 3 Social and political change, 1973–80 — 422
Section 1: The crisis of political leadership — 423
Section 2: The impact of economic change on society — 428
Section 3: Changing popular culture — 433
Section 4: The extent of progress in individual and civil rights — 438

Key Topic 4 Republican dominance and its opponents, 1981–92 — 451
Section 1: New directions in economic policy — 452
Section 2: The Religious Right and its critics — 457
Section 3: Cultural challenge — 463
Section 4: Social change — 470

Glossary — 486

Index — 500

INTRODUCTION

History+ for Edexcel A Level: Democracies in change: Britain and the USA in the twentieth century supports Edexcel's Route H. Specifically, it supports the following papers:

- Paper 1H: Britain transformed, 1918–97
- Paper 2H.1: The USA, c1920–55: boom, bust and recovery
- Paper 2H.2: The USA, 1955–92: conformity and challenge

About the course

Your overall A level History course for the Edexcel Specification includes three externally examined papers and coursework. If you are studying AS History, there are two externally examined papers. The papers are:

- Paper 1: Breadth study with interpretations (AS and A level)
- Paper 2: Depth study (AS and A level)
- Paper 3: Themes in breadth with aspects in depth (A level only)

This book covers the breadth study with interpretations 'Britain transformed, 1918–97' and two depth studies of which you must study one: 'The USA, c1920–55: boom, bust and recovery' or 'The USA, 1955–92: conformity and challenge'.

How to use this book

This book had been designed to help you develop the knowledge and skills necessary to succeed in Paper 1 and Paper 2.

The book divides into three main parts, dealing with Paper 1, Paper 2.1 and Paper 2.2 respectively. The structure of each part parallels the structure of the specification. Therefore:

- Paper 1 has four themes, each divided into three chapters, and a final section dealing with the historical interpretation, again divided into four chapters. Each theme and historical interpretation begins with the Big Picture, setting the scene for the material which follows.

- Paper 2 starts with a big-picture overview of the whole period and then is divided into four chapters dealing with the four key topics of the specification.

Each chapter begins with an overview of the theme, topic or interpretation discussed to set it in context, and ends with a chapter summary to help with revision of the key points included in the chapter. Summary diagrams at the end of chapters should also help with revision.

Our features throughout the book with help to aid your understanding of the period and develop your essay-writing skills.

Essay-writing skills

Essay technique sections at the end of chapters help develop essay writing skills. These include how to:

- focus on the question
- structure your answer
- deploy detail
- analyse
- create and sustain a balanced argument.

Where necessary, they also show how to approach the sources and extracts that accompany some exam questions.

Practice questions provide exam-style questions so that you can practise answering questions related to the different topics and themes that you study.

Help with note-making

On pages ix–xi there are a series of note-making styles, which you can use as you work through the book. These are designed to ensure that your note-making is clear, and set you up to revise for the exam.

Note it down activities appear throughout the book, to guide your note-taking. They sometimes refer back to the note-making styles outlined at the beginning of the book.

Work together

The book also contains Work together activities. These consist of activities designed to help you work together to check your understanding of the topics as you go along.

Extended reading

In addition to the traditional textbook narrative, this book contains four specially commissioned essays from practising academic historians. These address the historical interpretation and are designed to introduce you the historical debate in a way that is contemporary historiography directly related to the exam.

Recommended reading

You can find recommended reading sections throughout the book. These are designed to point you in the direction of both classic works on the subject and examples of more recent historical writing.

About the exam

The A level exam

The A level comprises three papers and coursework. Paper 1 and Paper 2 are examined at the same time, as part of the same route. Paper 1 is worth 30 per cent of the total A level and Paper 2 is worth 20 per cent. Paper 3 is examined separately and is worth 30 per cent, with the coursework making up the final 20 per cent of marks. This section looks at Paper 1 and Paper 2, as these are the papers this book supports.

Paper 1

The Paper 1 exam paper is divided into three parts: Section A, Section B and Section C. The different sections will test different skills and aspects of the history you have studied.

Sections A and B test your knowledge of the period 1918–79. The questions test your breadth of knowledge of four key themes:

- A changing political and economic environment, 1918–79
- Creating a welfare state, 1918–79
- Society in transition, 1918–79
- The changing quality of life, 1918–79.

Section C tests your depth of knowledge regarding a historical interpretation.

Sections A and B

Sections A and B test the breadth of your knowledge, and each section requires you to write an essay. In both Section A and B you have to answer one question from a choice of two.

Section A of the exam paper contains two questions, of which you are required to complete one. Questions in Section A will test the breadth of your knowledge by focussing on at least ten years.

Section B of the exam paper also contains two questions, of which you are required to complete one. Questions in Section B will test the breadth of your knowledge by focussing on at least one-third of the period you have studied, about twenty years.

Neither Section A nor B requires you to read or analyse either sources or extracts from the work of historians.

Section A and B questions require you to deploy a variety of skills. The most important are focus on the question, selection and deployment of relevant detail, analysis and, at the highest level, prioritisation.

Questions in Section A and B will focus on one of the following concepts:

- cause
- consequence
- change/continuity
- similarity/difference
- significance.

Therefore, the questions will typically begin with one of the following stems:

- How far…
- How accurate is it to say…
- To what extent…
- How significant…
- How successful…

Section C

Section C of the exam paper is different to Sections A and B. While Section A and B test your own knowledge, Section C tests your own knowledge and your ability to analyse and evaluate interpretations of the past in the work of historians. Therefore, Section C contains two extracts from the work of historians. Section C of the exam contains one compulsory question.

Section C focusses on an interpretation related to the following controversy:

What impact did Thatcher's governments (1979–90) have on Britain 1979–97?

It looks at the following aspects of the potential crisis:
- the effect of Thatcher's economic policies
- the extent to which state intervention and the public sector were 'rolled back'
- the extent of political and social division in Britain
- the effect of Thatcherism on politics and party development.

Section C tests your ability to analyse and evaluate different historical interpretations in the light of your own knowledge. Therefore, it tests a variety of skills including:

- identifying the interpretation
- writing a well-structured essay
- integrating own extracts with own knowledge
- reaching an overall judgement.

Paper 2

Paper 2 is a depth paper. This means that the questions will test your knowledge of short periods of history.

The USA, c1920–55: boom, bust and recovery's key topics are:

- Boom and crash, 1920–29
- Depression and the New Deal, 1929–38
- Impact of the New Deal and the Second World War on the USA to 1945
- The transformation of the USA, 1945–55

The USA, 1955–92: conformity and challenge's key topics are:

- Affluence and conformity, 1955–63
- Protest and reaction, 1963–72
- Social and political change, 1973–80
- Republican dominance and its opponents, 1981–92

The Paper 2 exam is divided into two sections. Section A is a source question while Section B requires you to write an essay from your own knowledge.

Section A

In the A level paper questions in Section A require you to analyse two primary sources. They will typically be phrased in the following way:

How far could the historian make use of Sources 1 and 2 to investigate [x]?

You are required to use the sources, your own knowledge and the information given about the sources. You might consider the following:

- What the sources would tell the historian about the topic.
- How nature, origin and purpose could give the historian more information about the critical stance of the author, as well as some evidence about usefulness.
- How you can use your knowledge of the historical context to support or develop inferences made from the sources, and to either confirm the accuracy or limitations of information within them or to note limitations and challenge the accuracy of the sources.
- What you could say about the two sources in combination.

Section B

You should answer questions in Section B in the form of an essay. The questions could focus on the following concepts:

- cause
- consequence
- change/continuity
- similarity/difference
- significance.

The questions could begin with the following question stems:

- How far…
- How accurate is it to say…
- To what extent…

The AS level exam

The AS level comprises two papers. Paper 1 is worth 60 per cent of the total A level and Paper 2 is worth 40 per cent.

Paper 1

The AS exam tests all of the same content as the A level exam, and is structured in exactly the same way. However, there are differences between the two exams:

Sections A and B

There are three key differences between the A and AS level in Sections A and B.

- **Wording:** the wording of AS level questions will be less complex than the wording of A level questions. Specifically, there are likely to be adjectives or qualifying phrases in the question. For example:

A level-style question	AS level-style question
How far does the economic effect of The Second World War explain Britain's relative economic decline 1945–79?	How extensive was welfare provision by 1939?

- **Focus:** Section A questions can focus on a more limited range of concepts at AS than at A level. Specifically, at AS level Section A questions can only focus on **cause** and **consequences** (including success and failure), whereas A level questions can focus on a wider variety of concepts.
- **Mark scheme:** the A level mark scheme has five levels, whereas the AS level mark scheme only has four. This means that full marks are available at AS for an analytical essay, whereas sustained analysis is necessary for full marks at A level.

Section C

Section C of the AS exam focusses on the same aspects of the same debate:

What impact did Thatcher's governments (1979–90) have on Britain 1979–97?

As in the A level exam you have to answer one compulsory question based on two extracts. The AS level exam is different from the A level exam in the following ways:

- **The question:** the AS level question is worded in a less complex way than the A level question. For example:

A level-style question	AS level-style question
In the light of differing interpretations, how convincing do you find the view that Thatcher's economic policies led to 'a positive improvement in the trajectory of the British economy'? To explain your answer, analyse and evaluate the material in both extracts, using your own knowledge of the issues.	Historians have different views about whether Thatcher's economic policies benefited Britain. Analyse and evaluate the extracts and use your knowledge of the issues to explain your answer to the following question. How far do you agree with the view that Thatcher's economic policies were positive in that they halted the long-term trend of economic decline?

- **The extracts:** at AS the extracts will be slightly shorter and you may get extracts taken from textbooks as well as the work of historians. In this sense the extracts at AS level should be slightly easier to read and understand.
- **The mark scheme:** The A level mark scheme has five levels, whereas the AS level mark scheme only has four. This means that full marks are available at AS for an analytical essay, whereas sustained analysis is necessary for full marks at A Level.

Paper 2

The AS exam tests all of the same content as the A level exam, and is structured in a similar way. However, there are differences between the two exams:

Section A

Section A of the AS exam is structured in a different way to the A level exam. In essence, Section A at AS tests the same skills as Section A at A level, but over two questions rather than one.

The AS Section A is divided into part (a) and part (b).

Part (a)

Part (a) contains one compulsory question related to a single source. Part (a) asks you to consider how the source is of value to a historian who is engaged in a specified enquiry.

The question requires you to reach a judgement about the ways in which Source 1 is valuable. In that sense the question is not primarily about looking for the ways in which the source is unreliable. Examiners are looking for the following skills:

- detailed contextual knowledge that explains the meaning of relevant points made by the source
- valid inferences
- an overall judgement about the value of the source related to valid criteria.

Part (b)

Part (b) contains one compulsory question related to a single source. Part (b) asks you to consider how much weight to give a source for a specified enquiry. Therefore, part (b) requires you to consider the value and the limits of the source.

Part (b) tests your ability to:

- comprehend and analyse source material
- use historical knowledge to weigh the value of the source
- reach a judgement, based on valid criteria, about the value of the source.

Section B

Section B of the AS exam tests the same content knowledge as Section B of the A level exam. Section B comprises three questions, of which you must complete one.

Paper 2 Section B questions are very similar to Paper 1 Section B questions (see page vi). The key difference relates to the period on which the question focusses. Paper 2 examines your knowledge of depth. Therefore Section B questions can focus on a single event or a single year. Alternatively, they might focus on the whole chronology of the course.

NOTE-MAKING

Good note-taking is really important. Your notes are an essential revision resource. What is more, the process of making notes will help you understand and remember what you are reading.

How books work

Most books are written as clearly as possible. Therefore, writers use a variety of techniques to help you learn.

Authors often break up their work into key points (the most important ideas and themes) and supporting evidence (the details that support the key points). Key points are usually general statements. For example, a key point might be 'The immediate cause of the Liberals' decline were the actions of David Lloyd George', while the supporting evidence might be a list of detailed examples that indicate the key point is correct.

How to make notes

Most note-making styles reflect the distinction between key points and supporting evidence. Below is advice on a variety of different note-taking styles. Throughout each section in the book are note-making activities for you to carry out.

Hints and tips

The important thing is that you understand your notes. Therefore, you don't have to write everything down, and you don't have to write in full sentences.

While making notes you can use abbreviations:

Full text	Abbreviation
Liberal Party	LiP
Labour Party	LP
Lloyd George	LG
General Election	GE

You can use arrows instead of words:

Full text	Arrow
Increased	↑
Decreased	↓

You can use mathematical notation:

Equals	=
Plus, and	+
Because	∵
Therefore	∴

Here's an example:

Text	Notes
During Lloyd George's six years as prime minister (1916–22) he sold 1,500 knighthoods and nearly 100 peerages. The scandal did immense damage to his credibility.	K'hoods + peerages = scandal ∴ LG's credibility ↓

Note-making styles

There are a large number of note-making styles. You can find examples of four popular styles below. All of them have their strengths so it is a good idea to try them all and work out which style suits you.

The examples below are of notes taken from Chapter 1 on pages 4–5.

Style 1: Bullet points

Bullet points can be a useful method of making notes because:
- They encourage you to write in note form, rather than in full sentences.
- They help you to organise your ideas in a systematic fashion.
- They are easy to skim read later.
- You can show relative importance visually by indenting less important, or supporting points.

1 Scan the section before you read it in depth. Identify headings (points of explanation). Significantly, you should try looking for the key points in the first sentence of each paragraph. On your page of notes, set the key points out in sections
2 Now read carefully through the section. Write supporting points or points of evidence under the relevant headings.

The end result should look like this.

The Liberal Party in 1918

- Free trade; limited role for government; social reform
- Appeal to trad. voters ↓
- Divisions: power of state; coalition = split (LiP vs Coalition LiP)

Style 2: Spider diagrams

Spider diagrams or mind maps can be a useful method of making notes because:

- They will help you to categorise factors: each of the main branches coming from the centre should be a new category.
- They can help you see what is most important: often the most important factors will be close to the centre of the diagram.
- They can help you see connections between different aspects of what you are studying. It is useful to draw lines between different parts of your diagram to show links.
- They can also help you with essay planning: you can use them to quickly get down the main points and develop a clear structure in response to an essay question.

1. Draw a circle in the middle of your piece of paper. It should be large enough to contain the section title.
2. Scan the section and identify headings. Draw lines out from your central circle – remember to leave plenty of room between them so that you can fit in all of your notes.
3. Read through the section carefully. Write supporting points or points of evidence under the relevant headings.

The end result should look like this.

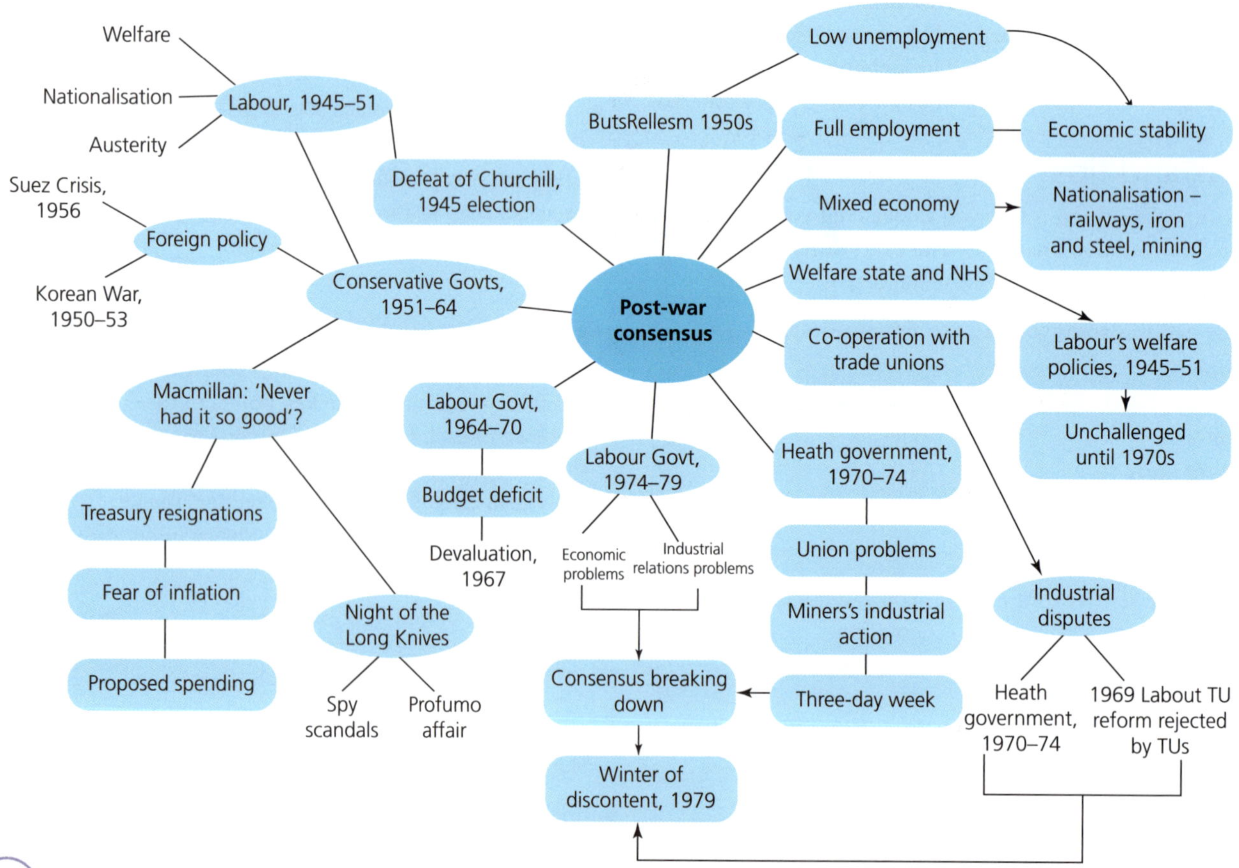

Style 3: The 1:2 method

Divide your page as in the example below:

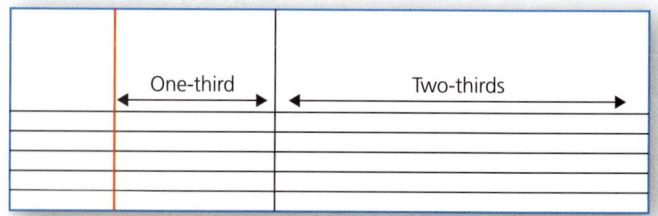

1. Write the key points in the left-hand section.
2. Write the supporting detail in the right-hand section.

The end result should look like this:

Key points	Supporting detail
The decline of the Liberal Party, 1918–22	Divisions in the party – GE 1918 split into two
	Credibility of LG ↓ ∴ sale of k'hoods; Turkey
	Rise of LP ∴ Rep. People Act 1918
	1922 GE – LiP collapse

Note-taking

Style 4: Index cards

> Index cards are particularly useful when you are revising for your exam, or when you are planning your essays.
>
> ### Revision
> Index cards are small, and therefore they encourage you to prioritise, by forcing you to note down only the most important information.
>
> ### Essay planning
> You can use index cards to help plan essays in the following way. First, select all of the cards that are relevant to your essay. Arrange the cards in order to develop a structure for your essay. Rearranging the cards can also help you work out the best structure for your essay.

1. Scan through the section. Identify either themes or important sub-sections. Use a different index card for each sub-section. On one side of each index card write:
- the title of the main section in the top left corner in one colour
- the title of the sub-section that you are currently reading about in the middle of the index card, in another colour.

2. Now read the section carefully. On the back of each index card write bullet points for the relevant notes.

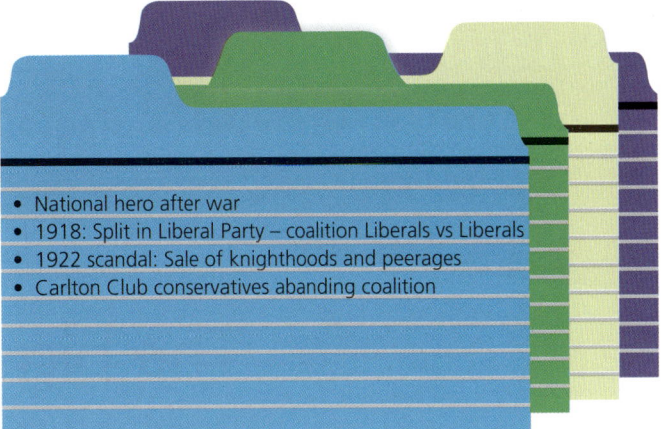

- National hero after war
- 1918: Split in Liberal Party – coalition Liberals vs Liberals
- 1922 scandal: Sale of knighthoods and peerages
- Carlton Club conservatives abanding coalition

3. You can punch a hole in the corner of the cards, and tag-tie the cards for each section.

Note-taking 1

Paper 1 Britain transformed, 1918–97

Theme 1 A changing political and economic environment, 1918–79

The big picture

This first theme examines the political and economic changes that took place in Britain from the end of the First World War in 1918 to the election of Margaret Thatcher in 1979. It was a period when the basic assumptions of how the state, society and political parties worked and interacted together fundamentally changed.

From 1918 onwards millions of working-class male voters were enfranchised, alongside women over 30 who met property qualifications. In 1928 all women over 21 were enfranchised on the same terms as men, and Britain became a mass democracy. This extension of the vote to working-class men, and eventually women, helped the development of the Labour Party, which formed its first government in 1924. As the Labour Party developed as an electoral force, the Liberal Party went into terminal decline, never forming a government after 1922 for the rest of the twentieth century.

The interwar years saw a series of minority governments or coalition National Governments dominate politics. This was closely related to the other main feature of the period: the economic problems that Britain was encountering in the aftermath of the war.

When the Second World War broke out in 1939, a national coalition government made up of Conservative, Labour and Liberal ministers united to win the war. After the end of the war a broad consensus about the role of the state, the management of the economy and the relationship between the government, industry and the trade unions emerged.

Both Conservative, Labour and Liberal politicians broadly agreed on economic and social policy throughout the 1950s and 1960s. The goal of full employment and the involvement of trade unions in pay negotiations were accepted by all parties.

But as economic performance declined at the start of the 1970s, and the number of working days lost to strikes and industrial protests increased, this political consensus began to change.

During the 1970s Britain was gripped by major economic crises. The consensus that had existed since the end of the Second World War broke down. Rising inflation led to waves of trade union unrest, which neither the Conservative or Labour governments were able to defeat.

By 1979 the election of Margaret Thatcher indicated an end to the post-war consensus and the its rejection by much of the population.

In this theme you will consider the following:
→ **A changing political landscape:** how the fortunes of the Liberal, Conservative and Labour parties changed 1918–31, how they worked together as a National Government 1931–45, and the rise of consensus politics and challenges to it, 1945–79.
→ **Responding to economic challenges:** the post-war boom and depression 1918–39, the creation of a managed economy 1939–51 and the economic challenges of 1951–79.
→ **Change and challenge in the workplace:** the reasons for changing industrial relations 1918–39, changing working opportunities and conditions 1939–79, industrial relations 1939–79 and the reason for their breakdown in the 1960s and 1970s.

TIMELINE

1918 February	Representation of the People Act
1918 November	Armistice signed with Germany, end of the First World War
1919–20	Post-war boom followed by slump
1922 October	David Lloyd George resigns; Bonar Law becomes prime minister
1923 May	Conservative government formed, led by Stanley Baldwin
1924 Jan–Oct	First Labour government formed, led by Ramsay MacDonald
1924 November	Conservative government formed, led by Stanley Baldwin
1926 May	The General Strike
1928	Representation of the People (Equal Franchise) Act
1929 June	Second Labour government formed, led by Ramsay MacDonald
1929 October	The Wall Street Crash
1931 August	Fall of Second Labour government; establishment of National Government; height of Great Depression
1934	Introduction of the Means Test
1935 June	Ramsay MacDonald resigns; Stanley Baldwin becomes prime minister
1936	Abdication crisis
1937	Neville Chamberlain becomes prime minister
1939 September	Outbreak of Second World War
1940 May	Establishment of wartime coalition government, led by Winston Churchill
1945 July	Labour landslide victory; Clement Attlee becomes prime minister
1946	Nationalisation of major industries begins
1951 October	Defeat of Labour government; Conservative government led by Winston Churchill
1955	Anthony Eden becomes prime minister
1956 Oct–Nov	Suez crisis
1957 January	Harold Macmillan becomes prime minister
1957 July	Macmillan makes his 'Never had it so good' speech
1963	The Profumo scandal
	Alec Douglas-Home becomes prime minister
1964 October	Defeat of Conservative government; Labour government led by Harold Wilson
1970 June	Defeat of Labour government; Conservative government led by Edward Heath
1974 Jan–Mar	Edward Heath is forced to introduce a three-day working week
1974	Labour win two elections under Harold Wilson
1976	James Callaghan becomes prime minister
1978–79	Winter of discontent
1979 May	Defeat of Labour government; Conservative government led by Margaret Thatcher

Theme 1 A changing political and economic environment, 1918–79

1a: A changing political landscape

Overview

Between 1918 and 1979, the political landscape of Britain changed significantly as a result of the challenges it faced from war, economic and technological changes and the desire for greater social equality. While the period from 1918–45 saw the decline of the Liberal Party and growth of Labour as the second major party, it also saw the Conservatives in government for most of time, whether in their own right or as part of a coalition.

In the years after the Second World War a political consensus developed in which the major parties tended to agree on principles such as economic intervention and the maintenance of social welfare. This may have been fading by the 1970s but was finally ended by the election of the Conservative government of 1979, which greatly supported the movement of free market forces.

This chapter explores the changing political landscape of Britain in the twentieth century and how the country's political parties attempted to deal with the external and internal challenges that faced them through the following sections:

1. Changing party fortunes, 1918–31
2. The National Government, 1931–45
3. The rise of consensus politics and political challenge, 1945–79

1 Changing party fortunes, 1918–31

Britain emerged from the First World War victorious but economically damaged. During the war Britain amassed £3.2 billion of war debts, mainly to the USA. This, together with the loss of world markets due to disruption to British trade, and the growth in the USA's economic power would present British governments with serious economic problems, which would in turn shape the course of British politics.

This section explores the fortunes of Britain's three political parties: the Liberal, the Conservative and the Labour Parties.

The political landscape in Britain was changed by the First World War (1914–18) and in the two decades after the end of the conflict the Liberal Party, which had been dominant before 1914, went into decline. The demise of the Liberals coincided with the growth in the popularity and size of the Labour Party. This new political party, which had emerged from the **trade union movement**, was based on working-class votes. The Conservative Party, which had been part of the wartime **coalition**, was electorally the most popular party of this period forming the government for much of the 1920s and dominating a **National Government** coalition during the 1930s.

> **Note it down**
>
> In this section your notes should focus on how the fortunes of the parties changed during the interwar period. You could use bullet points (see page ix) to make notes on:
> - the status of the three main political parties in 1918
> - how the Liberal Party declined in support and influence
> - how the Labour Party developed
> - the work of the first Labour government and the reasons for its collapse
> - the reasons for Conservative domination between 1924 and 1929
> - the changing political landscape between 1929 and 1931.

The Liberal Party in 1918

The Liberals believed in **free trade** and a limited role for government. They were a party of social reform. From 1906 onwards they had implemented state pensions, unemployment relief and the beginnings of state-provided healthcare (see page 68).

In the decade before the First World War the Liberal Party had dominated British politics, and had faced growing unrest over the issue of **Home Rule** in Ireland, the **women's suffrage movement** and an increasingly militant trade union movement. All three growing conflicts were interrupted by the outbreak of war, preventing the Liberal government from being overwhelmed by them. However, after 1918, not only did the problems of Ireland and trade union unrest return (see page 43), but the appeal of the Liberal Party to its traditional voters, the **middle classes** and the **artisan working class**, began to decline. Even though the party had introduced major social reforms in housing and national insurance (see pages 58–9), the perceived party of social reform in Britain became the Labour Party.

The experience of the war had deeply divided the Liberals:

- Many opposed the growth in the power of the state, particularly on the issue of **conscription**.
- The war had resulted in a coalition with the Conservative Party from 1915 onwards. In 1916, when David Lloyd George became prime minister, many Liberal MPs believed he had abandoned the principals of the party and had become too close to the Conservatives.
- In the election of 1918 Lloyd George campaigned against the many members of the Liberal Party who stood in independent opposition to him. This split the party's vote (see Table 1, page 6) and they were never to recover.

The Labour Party in 1918

The Labour Party had evolved from the Labour Representation Committee of the **Trades Union Congress (TUC)**, which the TUC set up in 1900 as the main organising body of the trade union movement. As a result, the party was closely tied to the unions who saw it as a useful tool in advancing working men's pay and conditions through getting union-backed MPs into Parliament. In 1906 the Labour Party had nearly one million **affiliated members**, and returned 29 MPs to Parliament.

The party had 40 MPs after the 1910 General Election and after 1911 it became much easier for working-class politicians to be elected to Parliament when the Liberal government allowed wages for MPs. This meant that politics was no longer solely an activity for people who were already independently wealthy. The Representation of the People Act in 1918 saw the British electorate triple in size from 7.7 to 21.4 million, leading to a dramatic expansion in the party's voter base.

The Conservative Party in 1918

The Conservative Party had been associated with the landed gentry in the nineteenth century, but electoral reform had forced the party to change and attract new supporters. By the end of the First World War the Conservatives presented themselves as a party of the middle classes and those members of the working classes who aspired to 'better' themselves through property ownership.

> ### Voting rights
> The extension of voting rights had been ongoing throughout the nineteenth century with Reform Acts in 1832, 1867 and 1884. Pressure for full democracy increased in April 1917 when the USA joined the war. US President Woodrow Wilson had made spreading democracy a specific war aim and this put extra pressure on the government to extend the franchise. They did so in March 1918 with the Representation of the People Act. It ensured that:
>
> - Nearly all British adult men over the age of 21 had the vote.
> - Women over the age of 30 were enfranchised if they owned property or were a member of a **local government register** or married to a man who was.
>
> The Representation of the People Act was followed by another in 1928, when women over 21 were given the vote on the same terms as men. Finally, in 1969, a further Representation of the People Act extended the vote to everyone over eighteen years of age.

The Conservatives had been part of David Lloyd George's wartime coalition from 1915 to 1918 and continued to support him as prime minister until 1922.

After 1918 a large proportion of their votes came from newly enfranchised property-owning women and the party actively encouraged their engagement with Conservative ideas.

The decline of the Liberal Party

In 1918, at the end of the First World War, the Liberal government had been in power since 1906. However, within four years of the end of the conflict the Liberals were a politically spent force and would never again form a government in the twentieth century.

Elections

The two elections in 1918 and 1922 were important events in understanding the decline of the Liberal Party.

By 1918 Liberal leader and prime minister, Lloyd George, had effectively split the party. The election of 1918 was fought between the ruling Liberal–Conservative coalition and the Labour and Liberal opposition parties. Table 1 on page 6 shows the outcome.

Theme 1 A changing political and economic environment, 1918–79

Table 1: United Kingdom general election results, 1918

Party	Votes (millions)	Share of the vote (%)	Seats	Increase in seats
Coalition Liberal	1.4	12.6	127	0*
Conservative	4.14	38.5	332	+60
Labour	2.25	20.8	57	+15
Liberal	1.39	13.1	36	–235
Other	1.61	14.9	105	–

* This was the Coalition's first election so while it appears as if they had not lost seats, the Liberals overall had experienced huge losses.

Source: House of Commons Library, UK Election Statistics: 1918–2012

The Liberal–Conservative coalition won a landslide victory. However, the Conservatives within the coalition were by far the more popular political party, with over three times as many votes cast for them than for the Coalition Liberals. The effect on the opposition Liberals was catastrophic. They experienced a collapse in their vote, partly caused by the popularity of Lloyd George's coalition and the promise of social reform, and partly as a result of the rise of the Labour Party (see page 7).

David Lloyd George

The immediate cause of the Liberal's decline were the actions of David Lloyd George.

In 1918 Lloyd George was a national hero. He was credited by much of the country as the 'man who won the war', and as the tough negotiator who would be able to represent Britain at the **Paris Peace Conference**. He was a man of humble origins from north Wales and had made it clear that he was an enemy of privilege and no friend to the House of Lords, an unelected body of hereditary peers that sat at the apex of Britain's class system.

Consequently, the news in June 1922 that he had been involved in a scandal selling **knighthoods** and **peerages** was deeply shocking. In the past, titles had been sold by government ministers to their supporters in industry for large donations, but it was done in a discreet and largely unnoticed fashion. Lloyd George's trade in titles was run from a private office he established, and knowledge of the operation was widespread. During his six years as prime minister (1916–22) he sold 1,500 knighthoods and nearly a hundred peerages.

Several titles were freely given away to Fleet Street newspaper magnates, such as Lord Beaverbrook, so that they would turn a blind eye and not report the practice. When the 1922 **honours list** was announced there were several people on it who had criminal convictions for fraud and the press finally published the story. Lloyd George himself called the honours system corrupt, but the scandal did immense damage to his credibility. His decision to go to war with Turkey, if it sought to revise the terms of the peace treaty it had been forced to sign in 1918, further dented his credibility; his Conservative coalition partners disagreed with the policy. They decided that the looming crisis with Turkey was their opportunity to act.

A secret meeting of leading Conservatives was held at the Carlton Club, a private members club used by London political elites. At the meeting it was decided to abandon the coalition with the Liberals. As a result, the election of November 1922 was a disaster for the Liberals (see Table 2).

Table 2: United Kingdom general election results, 1922

Party	Votes (millions)	Share of the vote (%)	Seats	Increase in seats
Conservative	5.5	38.5	344	+12
Liberal	2.67	18.9	62	+26
Labour	4.24	29.7	142	+85
National Liberal	1.47	9.9	53	–74
Other*	0.51	3.6	14	–91

* No longer included MPs from Southern Ireland

Source: House of Commons Library, UK Election Statistics: 1918–2012

Those led by Lloyd George (now the National Liberal Party) were reduced to 53 MPs, and while those opposition Liberals led by Herbert Asquith saw their share of the vote grow to give them 62 MPs, it was still too small an increase to prevent the party from further decline.

Lloyd George's personal unpopularity by 1922 was partly the cause of the Liberals' decline, but the growth in the popularity of the Labour Party had a much greater, long-term impact.

David Lloyd George, 1863–1945

David Lloyd George was a leading figure in the pre-war Liberal government elected in 1906, and held the office of chancellor of the exchequer from 1908 to 1915.

He grew up in Llanystumdwy, a small village in a remote part of north Wales. As a Welsh politician from reasonably humble origins he felt himself to be an outsider in British politics. He believed that by capturing public opinion and being popular with voters, he could make up for his lack of wealth and connections.

During the First World War (1914–18) Lloyd George became prime minister following Herbert Asquith's indecisive leadership. He was widely credited with holding together the coalition government that he ledg and successfully managing relations with allies such as France and the USA until the armistice in November 1918.

Following his political downfall in 1922 Lloyd George continued to play an important role in British politics. He became the leader of the Liberal Party in 1926, even though the size of the party continued to dwindle. He spent the 1920s and 1930s attempting to find new political and economic solutions to the problem of unemployment. He was so unpopular with the Conservatives who were in office during 1924–29 and 1931–45 (as part of a National Government) that there was little possibility of him returning to office. He died in 1945.

The rise of the Labour Party

Labour would win office twice in the 1920s, but the two Labour governments of the era were to prove disappointments to many of their working-class voters, who had huge expectations of what could be achieved.

Labour in government

The first Labour government was led by Ramsay MacDonald in 1924. It was a minority government and its election was seen as a deeply alarming development by many of the Conservative-supporting newspapers like *The Times*. The party was committed to parliamentary democracy and went to great lengths to demonstrate how moderate it was. Nonetheless, Labour's opponents in the Conservative Party and the media liked to compare it to the repressive regime in Soviet Russia and suggested that there might be Soviet sympathisers among the cabinet.

One of the main problems that MacDonald and his government encountered was strained relations with the National Executive Committee of the Labour Party itself. MacDonald was forced to make harsh economic choices that affected the poorest voters and had to manage the threat of industrial action. As prime minister he had to compromise, but the party was critical of him for not being more radical. Because he was the head of a minority government, dependent on Liberal support, any attempt to introduce a more radical programme would have resulted in a withdrawal of this support and the collapse of the government. The government lasted for nine months, too short a time to introduce much legislation.

Measures that were passed included the Housing (Financial Provisions) Act 1924, which increased the amount of money available to local authorities to build homes for low-income workers.

Ramsay MacDonald, 1866–1937

Ramsay MacDonald was the first British Labour prime minister. He led three governments between 1924 and 1935. He was born in Lossiemouth in north-east Scotland in 1866 and as a young man moved to Bristol and London where he became involved in radical socialist politics. He was elected as a Labour MP in 1906 and was on the left wing of the party until the end of the First World War. Throughout the First World War MacDonald was a pacifist but he visited France and witnessed the fighting first hand. He moved away from the radical left of the party after 1918 and became very suspicious of communism after the Russian Revolution. When he became prime minister in 1924 he was the first ever working-class leader of Britain.

Government collapse

MacDonald's government collapsed in the autumn of 1924 following a **motion of no confidence** which MacDonald only narrowly won. The motion against Labour came about following the decision of the Attorney General Sir Patrick Hastings to drop charges of **incitement to mutiny** against a socialist newspaper, the *Worker's Weekly*. The newspaper had published an article by John Ross Campbell which broke the law by demanding that soldiers:

> Refuse to shoot down your fellow workers! Refuse to fight for profits! Turn your weapons on your oppressors!

On 6 August, under pressure from backbench Labour MPs, the prosecution against Campbell was withdrawn and MacDonald was accused by both Liberal and Conservative parties of having secret communist sympathies. The case coincided with his attempts to normalise relations between Britain and the **Soviet Union**. A second motion was passed against the government, calling for an official inquiry into the withdrawal of charges against Campbell. MacDonald was forced to resign and call an election.

The General Election, October 1924

Labour's election campaign was marred by the publication of a damaging story in the *Daily Mail*. The Conservative-supporting newspaper claimed that a letter from the Russian communist revolutionary Gregori Zinoviev to the British Communist Party had been discovered. The letter, a forgery, appeared to be an incitement to revolution, telling British communists to prepare to overthrow the government. The *Daily Mail* hoped it would dissuade people from voting for Labour or any other left-wing party.

Although the Labour vote didn't collapse (see Table 3), it lost the election and the Conservative Party, under Stanley Baldwin, was able to form a majority. This election was a defining moment for the Liberal Party as a declining force in British politics; it saw a 12 per cent decline in its share of the vote and a loss of 118 seats. The Conservatives were the clear beneficiaries, taking seats from both the Liberal and Labour parties. First-time Labour voters in the previous election who were now disappointed with Ramsay MacDonald switched to the Conservatives, as did Liberal voters who had lost faith in the ability of the party to revive itself.

Table 3: United Kingdom general election results, October 1924

Party	Votes (millions)	Share of the vote (%)	Seats	Increase in seats
Conservative	7.85	47.2	412	+154
Liberal	2.93	17.6	40	–118
Labour	5.49	33.0	151	–40
Other	0.37	2.2	12	+4

Source: House of Commons Library, UK Election Statistics: 1918–2012

Conservative dominance, 1924–29

The new Conservative government formed by Stanley Baldwin presented itself as an alternative to the Labour Party and the 'threat' of socialism in Britain. However, Baldwin wanted to be seen by the country as a moderate politician who could appeal to all social classes. He believed that the rhetoric of 'class war' that had emerged during the brief MacDonald government was deeply damaging to Britain and he discouraged the Conservative Party from attacking Labour as secret agents of the **USSR** (which had been alleged in Conservative-supporting newspapers during MacDonald's administration). When he was confronted with a **general strike** in 1926 (see page 44–5), and defeated it, he attempted to be conciliatory to the strikers, saying:

> Our business is not to triumph over those who have failed in a mistaken attempt.

Reform to Labour's funding

Despite Baldwin's appeals to his party for peaceful coexistence with the Labour Party, many Conservative MPs still believed that the government should use all methods at its disposal to weaken it and the trade unions. In 1925 a **private member's bill** to prevent the Labour Party from receiving a **political levy** from the trades unions, which would have financially crippled it, was opposed by Baldwin in the House of Commons and subsequently failed. He was more concerned with political stability than political conflict between the parties.

Baldwin's conciliatory approach could not be sustained in the long run. Following the General Strike (see pages 44–5) he yielded to pressure to introduce laws reducing Labour's funding from the unions. In the 1927 amendment to the 1906 Trade Disputes Act the political levy on union members could no longer be automatically deducted from their union membership and passed to the Labour Party; instead, members had to agree to pay it. Over one-third chose to opt out, causing the Labour Party's finances to decrease by 35 per cent.

A changing political landscape, 1929–31

In March 1929 Baldwin held a general election. Although the Conservatives won the largest share of the popular vote, this did not translate into an overall majority of seats (see Table 4). MacDonald returned to power but his government would not prove strong enough to weather the economic storms that were to break later in the year (see page 29).

Table 4: United Kingdom general election results, 1929

Party	Votes (millions)	Share of the vote (%)	Seats	Increase in seats
Conservative	8.66	38.2	260	–152
Liberal	5.31	23.4	59	+19
Labour	8.37	37.0	287	+136
Other	0.31	1.4	9	–3

Source: House of Commons Library, UK Election Statistics: 1918–2012

Social reforms

MacDonald had much more ambitious reforms planned in his second ministry than his first. His lack of an overall majority once again made him dependent on the Liberals to pass legislation, though he had a largely co-operative working relationship with them. As a result, the government was able to pass some social reforms:

- The 1930 Housing Act cleared three-quarters of a million slum houses and replaced them with modern homes by 1939.
- The Coal Mines Act of 1930 attempted to ensure better pay for workers and more efficient pits, but the weakness of the legislation ensured that the mine owners could ignore it.
- MacDonald amended the Unemployment Insurance Act, giving the government powers to create **public works schemes** to alleviate unemployment. It was funded with £25 million of government money.

The government was also limited in what it could achieve by the growing economic crisis. MacDonald referred to the next two years of crisis in Britain as an 'economic blizzard', and it had significant political repercussions as well.

Economic problems

During the summer of 1931 there were rumours that the forthcoming budget would be unbalanced – meaning that the government had plans to spend more than it could afford – leading to an increase in borrowing. This caused the banks in America to engage in panic selling of the pound, exchanging it for other currencies, and the pound slumped in value. In order to reassure financiers that their investments were safe, the government proposed spending cuts and tax hikes, the main measure being the introduction of a 10 per cent cut in unemployment assistance. This would keep the value of the pound stable, but caused hardship for many of Britain's poorest. The threat of this cut split the Labour Party and MacDonald's cabinet, leading the government to resign on 24 August 1931. After negotiating with the other main political parties, and at the urging of King George V, MacDonald formed a National Government from the three main parties with himself as prime minister. Both MacDonald and his chancellor of the exchequer, Lord Philip Snowden, were viewed as traitors to the Labour Party, which passed a motion expelling them. They formed a new National Labour Committee which was designed to sponsor Labour parliamentary candidates who supported the National Government.

MacDonald and the American banks

The second Labour government under Ramsay MacDonald struggled to finance its spending commitments and, by 1931, came under intense pressure from international banks, particularly in the USA. The banks did not want the British government to spend large sums on welfare, even though unemployment in Britain was rising. These banks had significant power over Britain as they held large **currency reserves** of the British pound, due to the amount of debt Britain had accrued by borrowing from the USA to finance the war.

These banks could lose millions at a stroke if the value of the pound went down and so did not want to see economic policies introduced that might cause that to happen. A high-spending government would either have to tax or borrow, both actions that would reduce the pound's value and cause the **Gold Standard** (see page 29) to be readjusted.

2 The National Government, 1931–45

Following the government's collapse in August, MacDonald called an election in October 1931. He did so reluctantly, fearing it would destroy the Labour Party, but the Conservatives in the National Government insisted on one.

The National Government won the election by a huge majority but it was the Conservatives within it who won the vast majority of the seats. MacDonald continued as prime minister, though only as a figurehead. The share of the vote for the Labour Party slumped as many voters believed the party was putting its own interests and those of the unions before the national interest. By expelling MacDonald and Snowden the Labour Party appeared to be rejecting a coalition of national unity on party political grounds The National Government presented them as 'running away' from difficult decisions. The National Government was to last until 1945, although various elections during this period showed shifting support for the different parties, as shown in Table 5.

> **Note it down**
> Using a spider diagram (see page x), make notes on the following topics:
> - The experience of the National Government during the economic crisis (see also pages 30-32).
> - The problems faced by The National Government over rearmament.
> - The role of the National Government during the Second World War.
>
> In this section you will see that there are all related to one another. You should try to show these connections in your spider diagram. Evaluate which issues presented the National Government with the greatest challenges.

MacDonald's premiership, 1931–35

MacDonald's premiership was dominated by the economic challenges caused by the **Great Depression** (see pages 29–30) and attempts to alleviate it and effect an economic recovery. The government made some moves to rearm, given the increasingly threatening situation in Europe and the rise of fascism there. At the same time it had to deal with the threat of fascism at home.

Economic policy and its effects

The National Government implemented the spending cuts which had caused the previous government's downfall. Public sector pay cuts of 10 per cent were felt to be so harsh that they led to a mutiny in the Royal Navy at the naval base of Invergordon.

In addition to the spending cuts the National Government was able to introduce a limited number of **tariffs**. By 1933 the end of the Gold Standard and low **interest rates** had begun to stimulate an economic recovery (see page 31). The National Government's popularity increased, even though MacDonald became increasingly isolated in the government and was replaced as prime minister by Stanley Baldwin in 1935.

Labour Party opposition

The Labour Party managed to reorganise itself throughout the first half of the 1930s and become the official opposition to the government. Under its new leader, Clement Attlee, it managed to gain 154 seats at the 1935 General Election, demonstrating that the Labour vote was rapidly recovering from the slump in votes in 1931.

The growth in extreme political ideas

Throughout the 1930s there was in increase in support for extreme ideas on both the far left and far right. Communist and **fascist** parties saw an increase in their membership as

Table 5: United Kingdom general election results, 1931-45, showing numbers of seats only

Election	Labour	National Labour	Liberal	National Liberal	Conservative	Others	Government
1931	46	13	33	N/A	470	5	National Government
1935	154	8	21	33	387	11	National Government
1945	393	N/A	11	12	210	25	Labour victory

Source: House of Commons Library, UK Election Statistics: 1918–2012

more people became convinced that liberal democracy no longer had the answers to the economic crisis.

- By 1934 the British Union of Fascists had 50,000 members.
- In the same year the Communist Party of Great Britain only had 9,000 members but throughout the 1930s organised the National Unemployed Workers' Movement, which some historians have argued represented hundreds of thousands of unemployed men.
- Many intellectuals on the left, including **Fabians** Sidney and Beatrice Webb, visited the Soviet Union, believing that communism was an economic success. This had an impact on Britain from the 1930s onwards as these influential figures argued convincingly in favour of state planning.

Oswald Mosley, 1896–1980

One charismatic and forceful Labour MP, Oswald Mosley, was inspired by the seemingly dynamic economic policies of Mussolini's Italy. In Italy, since 1922, a fascist one-party state had established itself under the charismatic dictator Benito Mussolini.

Mosley, frustrated at the National Government, resigned and set up his own organisation – the New Party – in March 1931. Mosley's New Party put forward a manifesto for change, titled the 'Mosley Memorandum', which temporarily attracted support from both the right and left. It demanded a co-ordinated national economic plan to deal with the economic crisis. Moderates from the Conservative and Labour parties who had supported him soon withdrew their backing when Mosley established his own group of violent enforcers called 'Biff Boys', who were given the task of attacking his opponents.

In 1932 Mosley drew all the fascist organisations in Britain together with the New Party to form the British Union of Fascists (BUF). The union's impact on the political system overall would prove to be negligible, but it briefly presented a challenge to law and order. The National Government passed the Public Order Act in 1936, banning groups from wearing uniforms and requiring permission for marches and demonstrations. Mosley never became a threat to the National Government and his movement began to decline after 1936.

Even though his movement dissipated after 1936, Mosley's BUF demonstrated that there were significant numbers of people (the movement had 50,000 members at its height) who did not believe the existing political system of parliamentary democracy was capable of working at the height of the depression.

▲ Oswald Mosley addressing a fascist audience in the 1930s. What impression does this picture give of him?

Disarmament and rearmament

From 1933 onwards many British people began to take a much more active interest in world events. The appointment of Adolf Hitler as chancellor in Germany caused public opinion to divide between **rearmament** and **disarmament**. With traumatic memories of the previous war, hundreds of thousands of people were attracted to organisations such as the Peace Pledge Union, and the **League of Nations** Union that supported peaceful resolution to conflicts.

> ### The Peace Ballot and Pledge
>
> In 1934, millions of householders were asked their opinions on war and security. This Peace Ballot was organised by the League of Nations Union. The 11 million people who answered the questions made it clear that they supported the idea of '**collective security**'.
>
> The Peace Ballot was followed by the Peace Pledge Union, organised by Father Dick Sheppard, the Cannon at St Paul's Cathedral. Over 100,000 men and women sent Sheppard postcards pledging to oppose war.

By the early 1930s, the idea that Germany had been solely responsible for the First World War was rejected by most British politicians and civil servants. Instead a different view prevailed, one which blamed arms races and secret treaties. The government negotiated with other powers to disarm at the World Disarmament Conference, which ran for two years between 1932 and 1934. However, the conference broke down in 1933 when Germany withdrew, expressing its right to rearm to levels equal to France, Britain and the USA. Following Germany's exit, Baldwin argued not for disarmament but for agreements limiting arms so that nations could have 'parity'.

Britain started to rearm from 1934 onwards:

- The RAF was increased in size to 40 squadrons, a recognition of the importance of air power in future conflicts.
- The British Army was reorganised.
- The Royal Navy was expanded
- The munitions industry was developed in partnership with private capital.

Stanley Baldwin's premiership, 1935–7

By 1935 Ramsay MacDonald was very unwell and was forced to step down. He was replaced by Baldwin who became prime minister for a third time and called a general election in October that year. In his manifesto he pledged new houses, jobs and government help for the most economically deprived parts of the country. He also pledged to improve Britain's defences, although there was little desire among the public for rearmament.

Labour and collective security

Throughout Baldwin's premiership and Neville Chamberlain's which followed, the opposition Labour Party continued to be divided on the question of peace and security. The left of the party believed that rearmament made war more likely, not less. The centre of the party, led by Clement Attlee, argued that collective security would make war impossible, and therefore

> ### The abdication crisis
>
> In January 1936, when King George V died, a constitutional crisis began that was to dominate political events that year.
>
> After George V's death his eldest son Edward VIII inherited the crown. Edward was a handsome and popular monarch, his glamorous playboy lifestyle as heir to the throne had made him popular with the public. His many affairs with married women were known about by the government but the details were hidden from the general public by self-censoring newspapers. Public attitudes towards sexual morality in the 1930s were very conservative and an heir to the throne behaving in such a manner would have brought the monarchy into disrepute.
>
> In the months after his coronation rumours circulated about a relationship with an American divorcee, Wallis Simpson. In November 1936 he informed Baldwin of his intention to marry her and Baldwin replied that the marriage would be seen by many in Britain as morally unacceptable. The British cabinet and the **Dominions** rejected even a **morganatic marriage** and presented him with three choices: abandon the marriage plans, marry and risk a constitutional crisis with the government, or abdicate. He chose the final option on 11 December 1936, making way for his brother, George VI.
>
>
>
> ▲ Edward and Mrs Simpson

rearming unnecessary. However, world events made collective security seem more and more difficult.

> ### World events
> 1935: Italian invasion of Abyssinia
> 1936: Hitler reoccupies the Rhineland
> 1936: Outbreak of the Spanish Civil War
> 1937: Japan invades China
> 1938: Hitler annexes the Sudetenland and Austria

In 1936 when Hitler broke the **Treaty of Versailles** by reoccupying the Rhineland, Labour opposed the threat of economic sanctions against Germany but the National Government was divided between taking action and backing down. Harold Nicholson, a National Labour MP and a former diplomat who attended the Paris Peace Conference, summed up the situation in 1936 in his diaries. He believed that any threat of action against Germany would result in a general strike in Britain. The British and French governments did nothing following Germany's actions but Baldwin continued with rearmament.

Chamberlain's premiership, 1937–40

Stanley Baldwin resigned in 1937 due to ill health, making way for his chancellor, Neville Chamberlain, to become prime minister. Chamberlain was prime minister during a period of economic recovery, falling unemployment and stable prices (see page 31).

The main problem that the National Government under Chamberlain, and Baldwin before him, would face was that the breakdown of international order made war increasingly likely, but the antiwar movement in Britain was growing in strength, a factor which made rearmament more difficult.

Due, in part, to a desire for peace among the electorate, the National Government allowed a series of concessions to **Nazi Germany**, as Hitler continued to tear up the Treaty of Versailles.

Neville Chamberlain, 1869–1940

Neville Chamberlain was the son of Joseph Chamberlain, one of the most high profile and successful political figures of the Victorian and Edwardian era.

Chamberlain became Lord Mayor of Birmingham in 1915 and served as Director of National Service in 1916, administering conscription in Lloyd George's government. He stood for Parliament in 1918 and as an MP concerned himself with public health and social reform. He sat on the Unhealthy Areas Committee and understood the problems of inner-city slums. By 1923 Chamberlain was chancellor of the exchequer in Stanley Baldwin's first administration and the two men maintained a strong political allegiance for the next twelve years. He became chancellor of the exchequer in the National Government, before succeeding Baldwin as prime minister in 1937.

He is often associated with the policy of **appeasement** of Hitler; on three occasions he went to Germany in 1938 to try to prevent an outbreak of war by negotiating with Hitler. The Munich Agreement of September 1938 granted nearly all of Hitler's demands and allowed him to annex the Sudetenland of Czechoslovakia. Chamberlain returned to England promising 'peace for our time'. When Hitler attacked Poland in September 1939 Chamberlain declared war on Germany.

After a failed military expedition to Norway in April 1940, Chamberlain resigned, having lost the support of many MPs. He died later that year.

Chamberlain has been characterised as weak, vacillating and naive following his dealings with Hitler, but to see him in such a simplistic light can be misleading. Chamberlain had written several times throughout the 1930s that Hitler could not be trusted, that he was a grave threat to international peace and that war with Germany ultimately might be necessary. Chamberlain had also argued with Baldwin that rearmament should have been made the central feature of the 1935 General Election, showing that he was more committed to the possibility of war than some historians have suggested.

As chancellor and prime minister he misjudged the scale of military spending required. He increased military spending by £120 million in 1934, believing that this figure would cover the next five years of expenditure. By 1937 the figure had increased to £1.5 billion, but two years later when war began, this was still an underestimate of the total amount required.

Chamberlain replaced

Following the declaration of war in September 1939, the British Expeditionary Force was mobilised to France. There followed a seven-month stand-off during which little action ensued. The 'Phoney War', as an American journalist christened it, ended in April 1940 with a bungled British attempt to save Norway from German invasion and Norway's subsequent occupation by Germany.

In the resultant Norway debate in Parliament on 7 May, Chamberlain faced the full fury of both opposition and government benches for the incompetent handling of the war. He narrowly won a vote of no confidence but recognised it in real terms as a defeat. On 9 May Chamberlain attempted to form a new coalition government but the Labour Party refused to serve under him, leaving either Lord Halifax or Winston Churchill. Halifax realised he could not run the war from the House of Lords and stepped aside to give the job of prime minister to Churchill who came to power the day of Germany's invasion of France.

Churchill's wartime cabinet was a mix of Conservative, Labour and Liberal politicians. Churchill included Labour politicians mainly from the centre and right of the party who he believed were ready to place the national interest above party politics.

Churchill's premiership, 1940–45

On 13 May, as the situation deteriorated in France, Churchill made his first speech as prime minister to the House of Commons offering 'blood, toil, tears and sweat'.

By the end of the month the situation had worsened. As the German Army swept through France, the British Expeditionary Force withdrew to Dunkirk, trapped on the beaches and awaiting evacuation. German successes brought about a new political crisis in government as some ministers considered whether or not to make peace. On 25 May Halifax proposed a negotiated settlement with Germany, clashing with Churchill. Churchill called a meeting of the whole cabinet arguing that Britain would be a 'slave state' if it agreed to German terms. Much of the popular view of Winston Churchill, his stoicism in the face of adversity, was formed during this debate and subsequent speeches to Parliament.

Churchill's wartime cabinet served under him until the war ended in May 1945. At the end of the Second World War, social, cultural and political changes were accelerated by the pressures of **total war** that had affected every part of society.

Winston Churchill, 1874–1965

▲ This statue of Winston Churchill stands in Parliament Square, Westminster.

Winston Churchill was born into the aristocratic Marlborough family. He stood as a Conservative MP in the 1900 election but when the party proposed to abandon free trade he crossed the floor to the Liberals, becoming a close political ally of Lloyd George.

During the war he served as First Lord of the Admiralty and was in charge of planning the Gallipoli Campaign against Turkey, which ended in a humiliating disaster, costing thousands of British, French and Australian lives.

After the war Churchill returned to government but lost his seat in 1923 and stood as an independent MP in 1924, returning to Parliament and joining Baldwin's government as a Conservative. He served as chancellor of the exchequer, controversially returning Britain to the Gold Standard (see page 29) and was part of the government until 1929, when the government was defeated.

Churchill became politically isolated for ten years. During this time he sat as a Conservative MP but was not invited to join the cabinet of the National Government. He was unpopular with MacDonald and Baldwin for the following reasons:

- India: Britain's control over her largest imperial possession, India, had declined to the point where Home Rule seemed inevitable. Churchill opposed Home Rule but had very little support outside his own small circle of political allies.
- Support for Edward VIII: Churchill believed that Edward should remain king (see page 12) and even proposed forming a new 'Kings Party' to oppose Baldwin.
- Disarmament: As former First Lord of the Admiralty and briefly a colonel in the First World War, Churchill was instinctively supportive of military spending. He also opposed the policy of appeasement.

He returned to office in 1939 and served as prime minister until the end of the war in 1945. Churchill was prime minister again between 1951 and 1955, when he resigned due to old age and ill health. He died in 1965 and was honoured with a state funeral.

3 The rise of consensus politics and political challenge, 1945–79

The post-war period between 1945 and 1979 saw the rise and the decline of a particular style of party politics. The term 'consensus' has been used to describe the broad agreement between both parties on the running of the economy and the development of the **welfare state**. Both Labour and Conservative parties up to the early 1970s believed in:

- attempting to achieve **full employment**, even though this might allow a degree of **inflation**
- a **mixed economy**, with **heavy industry**, railways and other parts of the national infrastructure in state ownership
- a welfare state and a national health service
- co-operation between the government, industry and the trade unions in managing wages and prices.

In economic terms, the consensus was to the **moderate left** of the political spectrum, with policies devised by Labour following the party's landslide victory in 1945 being continued by the Conservatives when they came to power, specifically a commitment to full employment. Equally, both parties endorsed a foreign and defence policy which sat comfortably to the right of the political spectrum, with Britain confronting the USSR in the **Cold War** and investing in nuclear weapons.

This section explores the gradual decline of this consensus and the political polarisation that occurred by 1979.

Note it down

In this section the key theme is the political consensus that existed between the two parties for much of the post-war period.

1. Make notes using the 1:2 method (see page x) on what made politics consensual and why this consensus came to an end.
2. There are several different Labour and Conservative governments mentioned. Using a spider diagram (see page x) make notes on:
- the areas that both parties agreed on
- the problems and challenges that both parties faced after the war
- the areas that both parties disagreed on.

The 1945 General Election

In May 1945, following the defeat of Nazi Germany, the Labour Party signalled its intention to withdraw from the coalition. In July 1945, a general election was called.

Churchill believed that he would be rewarded by a grateful British public for his wartime service, and his manifesto focussed heavily on foreign policy. There were bitter memories of the Conservative pre-war governments and economic hardship, not helped by Churchill's rather crass claims that a post-war Labour government would rely on a '**gestapo**' in order to police its planned social reforms. The Labour manifesto, 'Let us face the future', promised action on housing, jobs, social security and a national health service, and resulted in a landslide victory, as Table 6 shows.

Table 6: United Kingdom general election results, 1945

Party	Votes (millions)	Share of the vote (%)	Seats	Change in the number of seats
Conservative	9.97	39.7	210	–219
Labour	11.97	47.7	393	+239
Liberal	2.25	9.0	12	–9
Other	0.91	3.6	25	+14

Source: House of Commons Library, UK Election Statistics: 1918–2012

The Labour Government, 1945–51

Labour achieved a considerable amount in its first five years of government and its social reforms were popular with much of the country. The main reforms were:

- the establishment of a National Health Service (see pages 71–2 for more details)
- the National Insurance Act (see page 63 for more details)
- the National Assistance Act (see page 63 for more details)
- the Housing Act 1949 which extended local authority's powers to build public sector housing for all income groups.
- the implementation of the Education Act 1944 (see pages 82–3 for more details).

After its landslide win in the 1945 election, the Labour government went on to win another election in 1950, which saw its majority slashed to just five seats (see Table 7 on page 16), despite polling over one and a half million more votes than the Conservatives.

Theme 1 A changing political and economic environment, 1918–79

Table 7: United Kingdom general election results, 1950

Party	Votes (millions)	Share of the vote (%)	Seats	Change in the number of seats
Conservative	12.12	42.9	297	+85
Labour	13.20	46.8	315	−78
Liberal	2.62	9.3	9	−3
Other	0.28	1.1	2	−19

Source: House of Commons Library, UK Election Statistics: 1918–2012

Reason for decline in Labour's vote

Some of Labour's lost seats in 1950 were due to the 1949 House of Commons (Redistribution of Seats) Act, which reduced the number of Labour **safe seats** by redrawing constituency boundaries. But it was also the decline of its popularity with middle-class voters that saw Labour gain fewer votes. In addition to this, the overall size of the working class was shrinking, with 78 per cent of British society identifying themselves as being working class in 1931, and only 72 per cent viewing themselves as working class in 1951. More people considered themselves to be living middle-class lifestyles as the 1950s began and they were less inclined to vote for the Labour Party or be a member of a trade union.

The main causes of dissatisfaction with Labour were:

- Rationing: wartime food and fuel rationing continued after the war, with some items such as bread that were not restricted during wartime becoming rationed in peacetime (see page 135).
- **Austerity**: the Labour Party seemed unable to revive Britain's struggling economy in the immediate post-war years (see pages 32–3).
- Taxation: the standard rate of taxation in 1949 was nine shillings in every pound (45 per cent), and the top rate of **marginal tax** for high earners was 90 per cent.

The 1951 General Election

Following the 1950 election, Prime Minister Clement Attlee found it increasingly difficult to control the Labour government. By 1951 he was exhausted by five years of government and many of his most able ministers fell ill or died in office. When Foreign Secretary Ernest Bevin died in 1951, the party lost one of its most able and talented ministers. In addition to this, the party had become divided over budget cuts. Labour's chancellor Sir Stafford Cripps had resigned in October 1950 due to ill health, depriving Attlee of two of his most experienced ministers in just over six months of each other.

In 1950 Britain became involved in the Korean War to protect South Korea as part of the new **United Nations** force. The war resulted in a huge increase in military spending and the new chancellor Hugh Gaitskell announced an 'austerity budget' in 1951. This involved the introduction of prescription charges for glasses and dentistry, and resulted in the resignation of Aneurin Bevin, the minister for labour and the pioneer of the National Health Service. Attlee had previously been skilled at defusing feuds within the party but, by 1951, he lacked authority. He called an election in October 1951 and lost to the Conservative Party (see Table 8). Although Labour gained more votes it won fewer seats because of the nature of the constituency structure in Britain and the **first-past-the-post** system. Labour voters tended to be concentrated in fewer, mainly urban, constituencies. Indeed Labour votes outnumbered Conservative votes by 250,000. However, the Conservatives won 26 more constituencies and so formed the next government.

Table 8: United Kingdom general election results, 1951

Party	Votes (millions)	Share of the vote (%)	Seats	Change in the number of seats
Conservative	13.72	48.0	321	+24
Labour	13.95	48.8	295	−20
Liberal	0.73	2.6	6	−3
Other	0.2	0.9	3	−1

Source: House of Commons Library, UK Election Statistics: 1918–2012

Not only was the Labour Party exhausted and divided, but the Conservatives offered to preserve the main features of the welfare state, and also to return the country to prosperity.

Conservative dominance, 1951–64

For the next 13 years the Conservative Party would dominate British politics and win two further general elections in 1955 and 1959. The main thrust of their policies were not much different to those of Labour, so much so that in 1954 *The Economist* used the term 'Butskellism' – a mixing of the names of the Conservative chancellor between 1951 and 1955, R. A. Butler, and Labour shadow chancellor Hugh Gaitskell – to describe the economic and welfare policies associated with the **post-war consensus**.

Winston Churchill returned to Downing Street for four years, just as the final wartime rations and restrictions came to an end. Churchill was 76 years old when he returned to power and many of his cabinet colleagues observed that the dynamism and drive he had exhibited during the war years appeared to have gone. Instead, Churchill acted more as a 'caretaker' prime minister, while the ministers within his government gradually came to prominence.

Eden's government, 1955–57

Even though Churchill suffered a stroke in 1953, he still managed to remain in office until retiring in 1955. His replacement was Anthony Eden, a relatively young and popular politician with an impressive wartime record as Churchill's foreign minister. He called a general election in May 1955 to ensure that he had a strong mandate. The election results indicated that the British public approved of the Conservative Party's management of the economy (see Table 9). By July 1955 Britain had the lowest unemployment figures in its recent history, with only 215,000 people out of work, accounting for just over 1 per cent of the workforce.

Table 9: United Kingdom general election results, 1955

Party	Votes (millions)	Share of the vote (%)	Seats	Change in the number of seats
Conservative	13.29	49.6	344	+23
Labour	12.41	46.4	277	–18
Liberal	0.72	2.7	6	–
Other	0.35	1.3	3	–

Source: House of Commons Library, UK Election Statistics: 1918–2012

Within a year, however, Eden had become embroiled in a foreign policy disaster that forced him from office.

The Suez Crisis

Britain had maintained a presence in Egypt since the nineteenth century to protect the Suez Canal (part owned by Britain and France), which was its route to India. After Indian independence in 1947 the canal was used as a means of shipping oil to Britain, Europe and America.

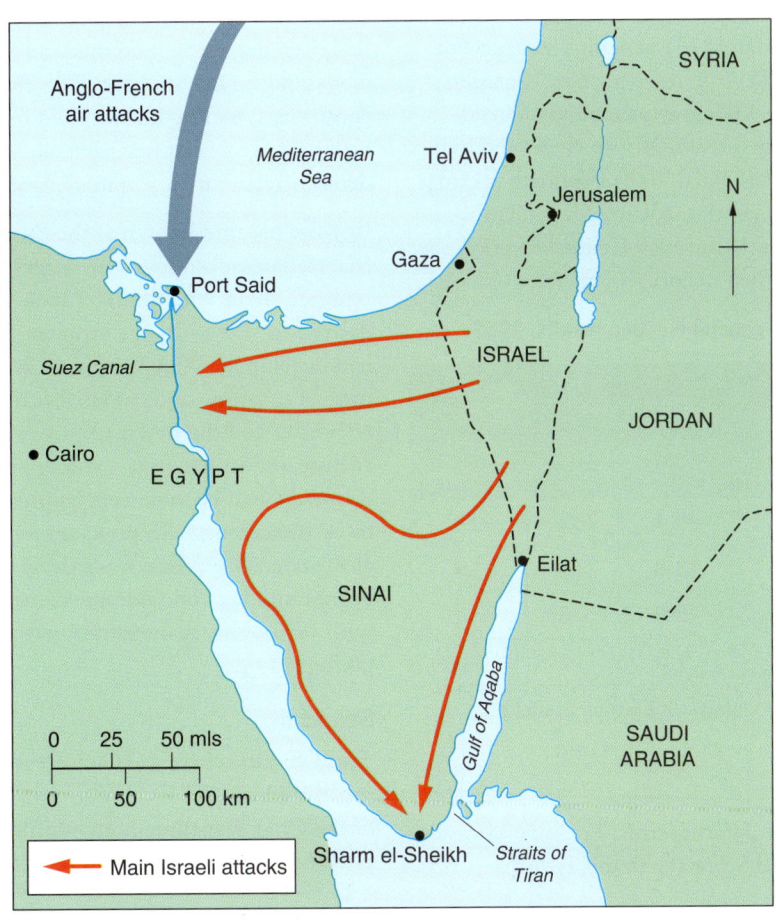

▲ Egypt and the Suez Canal

The nationalist president of Egypt, Gamal Abdul Nasser, stated that the canal should be in Egyptian hands and that he would be willing to pay British shareholders a fair price for it. Eden reacted with suspicion and hostility and, when Nasser occupied the Canal Zone on 26 July 1956, his close relationship with the USSR convinced the British that the canal would soon fall into Soviet hands.

When France and Israel invited Britain to take part in an invasion of the Suez Canal Zone, Eden agreed in secret to participate. He was motivated by a desire not to be humiliated by Nasser and knew his standing in the Conservative Party depended on presenting a strong image as an international statesman.

When the invasion began on 5 November 1956, US President Eisenhower, who had not been consulted on Britain's intentions, reacted angrily and felt deceived. He threatened to sell America's reserves of British currency and collapse the value of the pound. Faced with the possibility of economic crisis, Britain was forced to withdraw and Eden resigned in January 1957. The outcome of Suez was a significant reduction in British world power and a recognition that it could no longer act independently without seeking US approval.

Macmillan's Britain, 1957–63

Eden's replacement was Harold Macmillan, his chancellor of the exchequer. A mixed economy (see page 34), rising living standards (see page 137), low unemployment and declining social inequality (in 1957 British wages and living standards were at their most equal in the twentieth century between the rich and the poor), made the Macmillan government very popular. In the 1959 General Election the Conservatives increased their majority (see Table 10).

Table 10: United Kingdom general election results, 1959

Party	Votes (millions)	Share of the vote (%)	Seats	Change in the number of seats
Conservative	13.75	49.4	365	+21
Labour	12.22	43.8	258	–19
Liberal	1.64	5.9	6	–
Other	0.26	1.0	1	–2

Source: House of Commons Library, UK Election Statistics: 1918–2012

Dissent on the right

In 1959 Chancellor Peter Thorneycroft, Treasury Minister Nigel Birch and Financial Secretary to the Treasury Enoch Powell all resigned. The three men believed that Macmillan's government was spending too much and storing up economic problems for the future. They were convinced that inflation, not unemployment, posed the greatest threat to the economy; these were views different to those held by most economists and politicians in the late 1950s. They proposed spending cuts, tax rises, an end to subsidies to nationalised industries, and other measures to take excess money out of the economy that they claimed was the cause of inflation. The resignation of the three men was an embarrassment to the government, but during a period of low unemployment and relatively low inflation, their exit made little impression on the wider public. In the next two decades inflation would become one of the most fundamental issues in British politics and economics and their ideas would come to enjoy far wider support in the Conservative Party.

'Night of the Long Knives'

By 1962 the popularity of the Conservative Party was declining. Macmillan's privileged background and the large number of upper-class cabinet members (there were 35 former **Etonians** in his government) meant that many people perceived the Conservatives as out of touch. The Labour Party under Gaitskell, and then Harold Wilson, argued that privileged aristocratic Conservatives who had risen due to their connections, not their ability, were holding Britain back. The dramatic increase in consumer spending had resulted in a series of unforeseen economic problems (see page 34) and Macmillan needed to demonstrate that he was in control of his government.

In what became known as the 'Night of the Long Knives', Macmillan sacked seven ministers from his cabinet and replaced them with younger men. Part of his reason for doing this was an image problem that the Conservatives had developed. They were seen as ageing and privileged, instead of young and **meritocratic**. In the early 1960s television and the newspapers were dominated by youth culture and in America a young president, John F. Kennedy, had become very popular. Youth was thought to be in keeping with popular feelings among the electorate. Macmillan was briefly perceived as ruthless, but the sudden and widespread sackings proved popular with the public, demonstrating that he was capable of taking action.

Scandal

Another area where the Conservatives were starting to be mistrusted was the issue of national security. At the height of the Cold War three high-profile spy scandals rocked the government (see box, page 19).

Spy scandals

1 John Vassall

Between 1952 and 1962 John Vassall, a naval attaché at the British embassy in Moscow, was blackmailed by the KGB – the security agency for the Soviet Union. He passed on large quantities of top-secret information on the British Royal Navy and was caught when Soviet spies defected to the West and gave **MI6** Vassall's name.

2 Harold 'Kim' Philby

In January 1963 one of Britain's most senior intelligence agents, Kim Philby, defected to the USSR. He was the head of British Counter Intelligence and had been under suspicion of spying for the USSR since the early 1950s. As Foreign Secretary in 1955 Macmillan had publicly announced that he had investigated Philby and exonerated him. It was hugely embarrassing to Macmillan when it was revealed that Philby had defected to the USSR. Because of the **Official Secrets Act**, it was not revealed until 1968 that Philby had held such an important office within MI6.

3 John Profumo

Less than six months later, in June 1963, the government's secretary of state for war, John Profumo, admitted to having had an affair with Christine Keeler (see page 99). He had previously denied the affair to Macmillan, who had believed him. When it transpired that she had also had a relationship with a Russian attaché, Yevgeny Ivanov, the press focussed on the spy angle to the story (though it is doubtful there was any security risk).

Sir Alec Douglas-Home

Ill health and the stress of mounting problems forced Macmillan to resign in October 1963. His replacement was Sir Alec Douglas-Home. Home was regarded by most of his party to be a skilled administrator and an astute politician, but he suffered from an image problem that would damage the Conservatives' chances in the next election. Home was a member of the House of Lords and had the title of Earl (which he renounced when he became prime minister). Satirists on television and in magazines like *Private Eye* ridiculed Home for his aristocratic manners.

Wilson's government, 1964–70

Harold Wilson had been the leader of the Labour Party for a year by the time he won the general election of 1964. He presented the party as meritocratic and classless, comparing it to public perceptions of the Conservatives. During the election Wilson effectively used the television to present himself as the face of modern Britain. However, despite the problems that the Conservatives faced, Labour won by a slender majority of four seats (see Table 11), meaning that if Harold Wilson wished to bring about major policy changes, a new election would have to be called.

Table 11: United Kingdom general election results, 1964

Party	Votes (millions)	Share of the vote (%)	Seats	Change in the number of seats
Conservative	11.98	43.3	303	–62
Labour	12.21	44.1	317	+59
Liberal	3.10	11.2	9	+3
Other	0.37	1.4	1	–

Source: House of Commons Library, UK Election Statistics: 1918–2012

Wilson's plans, Wilson's problems

Harold Wilson and his chancellor, James Callaghan, discovered within their first few days of office that Britain's economic problems were far worse than they had previously thought. The previous chancellor of the exchequer, Reginald Maudling, had delivered generous tax cuts and spending promises in the Conservatives' last budget and left the country with an £800 million **budget deficit**. This presented Wilson with a dilemma. He had promised to improve pensions and build half a million new homes a year. In addition to this Wilson was determined to maintain Britain's military presence overseas, which accounted for over one-fifth of all Britain's spending in the 1960s.

Wilson did not wish to abandon his commitments to either social reform or Britain's prestige. The only other option to lessen the pressure on the economy was to devalue the pound. This would have allowed the British government to pay off its debts more easily and aided exports but Wilson was unwilling to do this. He did not want Labour to be seen as the party of devaluation. However in 1967 he was forced to devalue the pound anyway (see page 37), which was a huge embarrassment for the government and led to the resignation of Callaghan as chancellor.

Wilson's achievements

In 1966 there was a second general election. Wilson got the majority that he needed (see Table 12, page 20).

Table 12: United Kingdom general election results, 1966

Party	Votes (millions)	Share of the vote (%)	Seats	Change in the number of seats
Conservative	11.42	41.9	253	−50
Labour	13.07	47.9	363	+46
Liberal	2.33	8.5	12	+3
Other	0.45	1.7	2	+1

Source: House of Commons Library, UK Election Statistics: 1918–2012

Table 13: United Kingdom general election results, 1970

Party	Votes (millions)	Share of the vote (%)	Seats	Change in the number of seats
Conservative	13.15	46.4	330	+77
Labour	12.18	43.0	287	−76
Liberal	2.12	7.5	6	−6
Other	0.48	3.2	7	+5

Source: House of Commons Library, UK Election Statistics: 1918–2012

Wilson's government achieved significant social and educational reforms in its six years in office:

- A series of new universities and polytechnics were built (see page 88).
- The Open University was established (see page 88).
- The laws on abortion (see page 113), homosexuality (see page 102) and the death penalty were liberalised.

However, much of this was undermined by the economic problems that were endemic in Britain throughout the decade (see page 34). The sense of optimism that dominated British politics and influenced public opinion in 1964 was all but gone by 1970, and instead there was a widespread feeling that the promises of the Wilson years had gone unfulfilled.

Wilson and his cabinet

Harold Wilson's government declined in popularity towards the end of the 1960s as unemployment began to steadily grow and the number of days lost to strikes increased. Wilson became increasingly suspicious of government ministers who were popular in the party or with the trade unions, believing they might replace him as prime minister. Roy Jenkins, James Callaghan and Barbara Castle were all seen as possible contenders for Wilson's job. The decline in morale in Wilson's cabinet that resulted from his mistrust of his ministers had serious consequences. In 1969 legislation to curb the numbers of **unofficial strikes** was proposed by Barbara Castle at Wilson's behest (see page 50), but Wilson feared that Callaghan, a union loyalist, might use the confrontation that would ensue to replace him. The legislation was never enacted and partly as a consequence of this, Britain endured a decade of rising strikes and union unrest. In 1970, despite predictions that Labour would win a third term, the Conservative Party under Edward Heath defeated Wilson (see Table 13).

Heath's government, 1970–74

Edward Heath attempted to bring about a radical political change from 1970 onwards. He sought to break with the post-war consensus on the size of the state and the commitment to full employment.

Prior to the 1970 election Heath and his shadow cabinet met at the Selsdon Park Hotel and planned a new manifesto. Following his election victory Heath's government began to introduce the policies from the Selsdon meeting. Heath referred to the change in direction that he wanted the country to take as a 'quiet revolution'. He believed that by removing the state from people's lives they would become more enterprising. A first budget from Chancellor Anthony Barber featured tax cuts and government spending cuts (see page 36). Heath ended Wilson's incomes policy, believing that wages should be set by the market, not by government.

The Barber budget (referred to by the press as the 'Barber Boom', because of the large tax cuts) failed to cure Britain's growing economic problems and fuelled inflation. Heath was forced within eighteen months of taking office into a U-turn in policy and had to increase intervention in the economy over the next two years of his time in office.

Heath's biggest problem was the government's relationship with the trade unions (see page 51). By 1974 Heath's government had endured two miners' strikes and he faced criticism from both the opposition and his own party. Wilson accused Heath of attempting to strip away union rights, but his critics within the party on the right saw Heath as a 'traitor', betraying the promises made in 1970 at the Selsdon Park meeting. Several Conservative MPs, including Keith Joseph and Nicholas Ridley, formed the 'Selsdon Group' within the party, which was dedicated to introducing free market policies and reducing state intervention.

Edward Heath, 1916–2005

Edward Heath, like Margaret Thatcher who would succeed him, was one of the few Conservative prime ministers of the twentieth century not to come from wealth and privilege. His father was a builder from Kent and his mother a chamber maid. He attended Balliol College in Oxford on a scholarship and had a successful military career during the Second World War, rising to the rank of lieutenant colonel. Heath stood for Parliament in 1950 and during the election campaign supported Margaret Roberts (later to be Margaret Thatcher). When Home lost the 1964 General Election he resigned and was replaced by Heath. Edward Heath's personal style earned him few friends; he was described by colleagues as blunt, impersonal and humourless. Heath was passionate about forging closer links with Europe and eventually secured entry into the European Economic Community (**EEC**) in 1973.

The Conservative Party defeat in a second general election in 1974 led to a challenge being mounted for Heath's leadership. Margaret Thatcher, Heath's former education secretary, challenged Heath and won. She led the party from 1975 to 1990.

Following the second miners' strike over the winter of 1973–74, which resulted in Heath declaring a **state of emergency** and a three-day week, he called a general election in February 1974. He wanted the election to be a referendum on union power and asked the question to voters in an election broadcast 'Who runs Britain?' Heath was defeated, reflecting a lack of confidence in his ability to manage the unions, inflation and economic decline. However, the defeat of Heath did not result in widespread success for Labour either. Wilson was elected with a minority government and was forced to rely on the Liberals (see Table 14).

Table 14: United Kingdom general election results, February 1974

Party	Votes (millions)	Share of the vote (%)	Seats	Change in the number of seats
Conservative	11.83	37.8	297	–33
Labour	11.65	37.2	301	+14
Liberal	6.06	19.2	14	+8
Other	1.8	5.8	23	+16

Source: House of Commons Library, UK Election Statistics: 1918–2012

Labour government, 1974–79

When Harold Wilson returned to office in 1974 the widespread sense of optimism and energy among the public and the Labour Party that had existed in 1964 was no longer present. Wilson was older, in poorer health and had little of the modernising zeal that he had once possessed. The **hung parliament** meant that he needed to call a second election in 1974. In October, he managed to win a slender majority of three seats (see Table 15), a result that was weaker than his first victory in 1964.

Table 15: United Kingdom general election results, October 1974

Party	Votes (millions)	Share of the vote (%)	Seats	Change in the number of seats
Conservative	10.43	35.7	276	–21
Labour	11.36	39.3	319	+18
Liberal	5.35	18.3	13	–1
Other	1.96	6.7	27	+4

Source: House of Commons Library, UK Election Statistics: 1918–2012

The third Wilson government, 1974–76

The first priority of Wilson's third government was to end union unrest by repealing the Industrial Relations Act (see page 51). Instead, it attempted to return to the **corporatism** of the mid-1960s by developing a policy called the 'social contract'. In return for the unions agreeing not to pursue excessive wage claims, the government would offer subsidies to the cost of living. Wilson attempted to present his government as conciliatory towards the unions, as opposed to Heath, who Wilson claimed was confrontational. In the short term, Wilson's government ended the miners' strike, but the new policy of the social contract did nothing to deal with the underlying cause of the strikes, which was inflation.

Wilson's party was divided between three factions:

- A centre right of which Wilson, Callaghan and Denis Healey were members. They held ideas that were still very similar to the moderate left of the Conservative Party. Chancellor Healey went further in 1975 and embraced **monetarism** (see page 38) as an economic philosophy. He abandoned the post-war commitment to full employment.
- A 'soft' left led by Michael Foot. Foot was a pro-union politician, but did not back Tony Benn's radical economic ideas (see below).
- A 'hard' left led by Tony Benn, who shifted towards more extreme left-wing thinking throughout the 1970s. He believed that Britain should become a '**siege economy**' in response in the 1976 **IMF** crisis (see page 37).

Wilson resigned in 1976, having become less interested in and concerned with the running of government. He was succeeded by James Callaghan.

Callaghan's government, 1976–79

Following Wilson's decision to resign, Callaghan became prime minister. He was from the centre right of the Labour Party and along with his chancellor, Denis Healey, began to abandon key aspects of the post-war economic consensus. He was a pragmatist and did not follow policies out of ideological reasons. This caused him to clash with Tony Benn at cabinet meetings.

Callaghan did not think that the British government could continue to spend its way out of difficulties and believed that Britain must 'pay its way' in the world. He thought that Britain had used borrowing to live beyond its means for decades and this had resulted in a loss of confidence in Britain and the pound on the international currency markets. Benn proposed leaving the EEC and believed that Britain could effectively cut herself off from the global economy. He proposed a 'siege economy' to protect state spending on welfare from the influence of international banks and currency traders. Benn became an increasingly marginal figure within the cabinet, his economic arguments being seen as unworkable and extreme.

Despite these internal divisions, however, Callaghan remained personally very popular with the electorate as opposed to Conservative leader Margaret Thatcher, who, in 1978, had low opinion poll ratings. It was widely believed that Labour would be victorious at the next general election, but a winter of strikes (see page 52) caused Callaghan's poll rating to slump. In March 1979 one poll found 69 per cent were dissatisfied with the government's performance, but still only 45 per cent of those polled thought Mrs Thatcher was performing well as leader of the opposition.

Nevertheless, the 1979 General Election saw the Conservatives win with a sizeable majority and Margaret Thatcher became prime minister (see Table 16).

Table 16: United Kingdom general election results, 1979

Party	Votes (millions)	Share of the vote (%)	Seats	Change in the number of seats
Conservative	13.70	43.9	339	+63
Labour	11.51	36.9	268	–51
Liberal	4.31	13.8	11	–2
Other	1.71	5.4	17	–10

Source: House of Commons Library, UK Election Statistics: 1918–2012

Work together

1 Look at the following key questions:
   a) Why did the Liberal Party decline after the First World War and the Labour Party grow in power?
   b) What made politicians fearful of revolution in the 1920s?
   c) Why did the Labour Party win a landslide victory in 1945?
   d) Why was there a post-war consensus on the economy and the trade unions until the 1970s?
   e) Why was Margaret Thatcher elected in 1979?

In pairs look back at your notes for this chapter and decide on the facts and arguments you need to answer the questions. Then rank these, with stronger evidence scoring higher than weaker evidence. A powerful reason for the fall of Ramsay MacDonald's 1929-31 Labour government, for example, is the impact of the economic crisis, which might get a number one ranking. The reason for giving an importance ranking for your evidence is that you will have to evaluate the relative importance of evidence in your essays.

2 Consider the question:

   How far did the political landscape change between 1918 and 1979?

   Using your notes work together to prepare a plan to answer the question. Your plan should include paragraph headings and a summary of the contents of each paragraph.

Chapter summary

- In 1918 Britain saw the extension of the franchise. This radically altered the political landscape in Britain. The main beneficiary of this change was the Labour Party.
- The war had elevated Lloyd George to the office of prime minister but the coalition he led unravelled in peacetime. Lloyd George was eventually deposed by a meeting of the Conservative Party in 1922 which voted to end the coalition.
- Labour had governments in 1924 and 1929 but both were minority governments, making it difficult for them to legislate effectively.
- The Liberal Party went into decline in the 1920s, eclipsed by Labour who took on the mantle of social reform.
- Between 1924 and 1929 Stanley Baldwin's Conservative Party dominated British politics.
- Ramsay MacDonald's second administration was split over the question of welfare cuts in 1931 and the government fell. MacDonald and Snowden formed a National Government dominated by the Conservatives but led by MacDonald.
- Fascism and communism failed to take hold in Britain.
- Until 1938, most British people were keen to avoid war with Germany, having traumatic memories of the First World War. The Peace Ballot and the Peace Pledge Union were clear signals to politicians that aggression would not be popular. Nevertheless, Britain did rearm from 1934 onwards.
- When war broke out with Germany in 1939, Neville Chamberlain presided over a failed military expedition to Norway that saw his government fall in May 1940.
- Chamberlain's replacement was Winston Churchill, a unifying figure who led Britain to victory in 1945.
- From 1945 to the mid-1970s a consensus existed in British politics which favoured nationalisation, full employment, an acceptance of a certain degree of inflation and a conciliatory approach to union disputes.
- In 1945 the Labour Party introduced the most far-reaching social reforms to health, education, housing and the workplace that Britain had ever seen.
- By 1951 an inability to end rationing led to the end of Labour rule and the start of 13 years of Conservative dominance.
- Throughout the 1960s inflation and strike days steadily increased.
- By the 1970s both Conservative and Labour governments were facing huge challenges from the unions.
- Edward Heath attempted to shift to the right and break the consensus in 1970 but was ultimately unable to do so.
- Margaret Thatcher finally moved the Conservative Party to the right in the mid-1970s and won the general election in 1979.

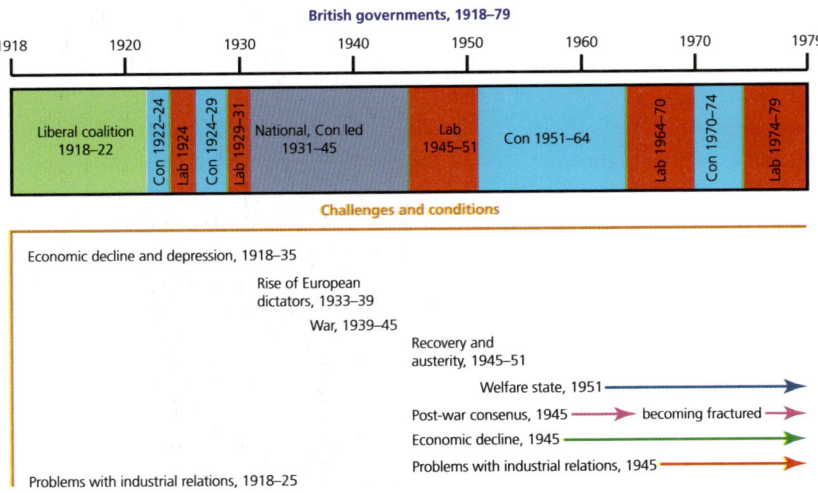

▲ Summary diagram: A changing political landscape

Essay technique: Understanding the question

Section A and B questions require you to deploy a variety of skills. The most important are focus on the question, selection and deployment of relevant detail, analysis and, at the highest level, prioritisation. The introduction to this book (page v) gives more detail about Section A and B questions.

Section A and B questions for AS level are different from that of A level, and some guidance about this is given on pages v–viii. However, you will need to develop very similar skills for the AS exam, therefore the activities will help with the AS exams as well. There are also some AS-style questions to practise at the end of chapters.

In order to answer the question successfully you must understand how the question works. Below is a sample question.

The question is written precisely in order to make sure that you understand the task. Each part of the question has a specific meaning.

Overall, **all** Section A and B questions ask you to make a judgement about the extent of something, in a specific period. In order to focus on the question you must address all three elements. The most common mistakes come from misunderstanding, or ignoring one of these three elements.

'How accurate is it to say', like other stems such as 'How far' indicates that you are required to evaluate the extent of something, rather than giving a yes or no answer.

How accurate is it to say that there was a **fundamental change in the fortunes of Britain's main political parties** in the years 1918–39?

This sets out the subject that you must address.

The dates define the period that you should consider.

Activity: What should a good answer look like?

Having read the advice on essay questions on this page and in the introduction (page v), complete the following activity:

1. Make a bullet point list of the skills that you need to do well in this type of essay.
2. Number the skills in order of their difficulty, so the easiest skill to demonstrate is 1, and the hardest 4.
3. Try to work out what a good essay would look like. Specifically, note down your thoughts about:
   - Roughly, how many paragraphs should the essay have?
   - Which skills should you deploy in which sections of the essay?
   - How should you structure the different types of paragraphs?

Work together

Having completed these activities, swap them with a partner.

1. Did you agree on which skills were easiest to demonstrate and were hardest? How did you make this judgement?
2. Did you agree on the number of paragraphs in the essay?
3. How did you both make the judgement about the number of paragraphs you should write?
4. If you had different reasons for the judgement, whose reasons were better and why?
5. Did you agree on where the different skills should be used?
6. Were your reasons for locating skills in different parts or throughout the essay as good as your partner's reasons?
7. Did you agree on how to structure each paragraph?
8. Can your partner justify their thoughts on how to structure a paragraph?

Use this discussion as a basis for further notes on how to approach the question. For advice on the structure of the essay see page 41.

1b: Responding to economic challenges

Overview

There are two main views of British economic history across the twentieth century, one of decline and the other of diversification. Between 1918 and 1979 Britain had undergone a period of relative economic decline compared to other industrialised nations, but by the end of the period her economy had also been transformed. Britain was still the seventh largest global economy in 1979, but many traditional industries such as mining, ship building and steel production were no longer able to compete with foreign rivals.

The two recessions of the interwar period, 1920–21 and 1929–34, saw Britain's heavy industries and the regions they support hardest hit. In contrast, new industries based on light manufacturing such as electrical consumer goods and the automobile industry flourished in the 1930s, indicating that some aspects of the British economy escaped the depression.

The impact of two world wars on the British economy was profound. Not only did the British lose market share for manufactured goods to America and other rivals, but also accumulated enormous war debts. The other major effect of the world wars was the growth of the role of the state in British economic affairs. The British government took on a greater role, co-ordinating industry and distributing goods in order to gain victory. This trend continued after the Second World War. The post-war Labour government nationalised key industries in order to promote economic growth and protect the rights of workers. However, from the 1950s underinvestment in nationalised industries such as coal and rail led to the view that state ownership was inherently inefficient. Governments between the 1940s and the mid-1970s maintained a commitment to full employment even though some economists believed this led to the ever-higher levels of inflation.

Part of the reason for Britain's economic woes in the 1970s was related to its shift from being a great power; it was more vulnerable to economic 'shocks' the less power it had in determining global events. The oil crisis of 1973 which led to crippling inflation and shortages is a prime example of this. From 1979 onwards, Margaret Thatcher's governments proposed a revolutionary solution to Britain's economic problems – the embracing of free market economics and the end of the post-war economic consensus.

This chapter examines the economic challenges of the period through the following sections:
1. Post-war boom, crisis and recovery, 1918–39
2. Creating a managed economy, 1939–51
3. The response to economic challenges, 1951–79

1 Post-war boom, crisis and recovery, 1918–39

Britain emerged economically damaged at the end of the First World War. Several factors accounted for this:

- The British government had not expected the war to last as long as it did and to command so much of the nation's resources.
- America's banks on **Wall Street** had loaned Britain large sums of money to enable it to continue the unexpectedly long and expensive conflict.
- Britain had been cut off from many of its most valuable export markets by German **U-boats**, which sank 40 per cent of British **merchant shipping**. In 1914 Britain's exports accounted for one-third of its total wealth, but by 1918 it had declined to one-fifth.
- Britain's industries had been forced to switch to war production instead of supplying export markets.
- By 1918 the country had lost over three-quarters of a million men, many of whom were essential to its economic output.
- The total financial cost of the war was £3.25 billion.

The British continued to import the same pre-war level of goods from abroad, but the decline in exports meant that the country experienced a negative **balance of payments** throughout the 1920s. The debts that Britain had incurred (amounting to 136 per cent of the country's entire annual economic output in 1919) and the damage to its trade left it greatly weakened. By 1920 the total British debt was £8 billion. In that year, the government's annual budget came to £800 million, but £300 million went directly on debt repayment. In 1908 the standard rate of income tax had been one shilling in a pound (5 per cent), but had risen to five shillings (25 per cent) by 1924. Much of this increase was necessary to repay the nation's debts.

After a brief post-war boom from 1919–20, caused by consumer demand for scarce goods that had been rationed during the conflict, the interwar period was characterised by two **recessions**, 1920–21 and 1929–34, which hit Britain's **heavy industries** and the regions they supported hardest. Even during boom times Britain's overall level of unemployment remained high, on average it remained at approximately 10 per cent of the working population between 1921 and 1938; this figure was double the average unemployment rate of the period 1870–1913.

Both recessions were followed by periods of recovery (1921–29 and 1934–39). In the mid-1920s consumer demand gradually increased and unemployment declined across much of Britain, however in declining industrial areas such as south Wales and Tyneside, it stayed persistently high. Between 1934 and 1939 **rearmament** and new **light industries** in the south east and the Midlands developed as a result of growing consumer demand, but heavy industry continued to decline. In some parts of the coal-producing south Wales valleys it stood at over 80 per cent of the adult population.

This section considers the post-war boom, economic crises and recovery, looking particularly at how different governments responded to try to alleviate suffering and bring the country out of recession.

> **Note it down**
>
> As you read through this section, make bullet points (see page ix) on the following aspects of post-war boom, crisis and recovery. This will help you to complete the table in the Work together activity towards the end of this chapter (page 38).
> - Why were there problems with the speculative post-war boom?
> - Why was there a post-war recession?
> - How successful were the attempts to solve the economic problems of 1921 to 1924?
> - How significant was the reversion to the Gold Standard in 1925?
> - What was the impact of the Great Depression and how successfully did the government deal with it?
> - How successful was the recovery from 1934?

Post-war boom

The end of the war in 1918 was followed by a short-lived economic boom in Britain that ended in a recession in 1920.

Because of wartime restrictions and rationing, both individuals and businesses had been unable to spend and had accumulated considerable savings in cash and bonds. Throughout 1919 consumers and businesses spent their savings. Individuals bought luxury items that had been rationed during the war such as coffee, soap, clothes and cigarettes.

There was a huge **speculative boom** as businesses issued new shares for traders, investors and other businesses to buy and more money poured into the London stock market than at any other time previously in British history. The total amount of new shares issued dramatically increased from £65 million in 1918 to £384 million in 1920. Investors were keen to buy British shipyards, cotton mills and coal mines, but these were all poor investment choices. The monopoly that Britain had over these industries had vanished during the war and Britain now had new competitors in the USA, Japan and South America. In addition to this, these industries had become outdated and had received little investment throughout the war years, making them uncompetitive. In the case of shipping, there was an assumption by investors that global trade would quickly resume to pre-1914 levels and merchant ships would be in demand. Not only did this resumption of trade not happen as quickly as desired, but by 1919 there was a global surplus of ships.

British wartime industries still in the process of returning to civilian usage could not keep up with the level of demand. Goods in short supply became excessively expensive and, as a result, demand declined and the boom came to an end.

Recession, 1920–21

The recession that followed was one of the most severe slumps experienced by Britain prior to 1929. Unemployment levels rapidly increased to 12 per cent of the working adult population.

By 1921, 2 million workers were unemployed and areas of the country like south Wales and Tyneside were deeply depressed as old industries like coal and ship building collapsed. The crisis in the coal industry led to a wave of strike action (see pages 43–4). The cost of living had increased by 25 per cent between 1918 and 1920 and wages stagnated, meaning that unions were far more likely to strike to secure higher living standards for their members.

This recession was caused by a range of factors.

Deflation

The government cut spending by 75 per cent between 1918 and 1920. In addition, in order to return the value of the pound to its pre-war levels, the Bank of England raised the interest rate to 7 per cent. This meant that it suddenly became very expensive to borrow money. These two factors drained available money for spending from the economy. Both the Bank and the government took these measures to try to repay Britain's wartime debts, but by the end of the decade debt had risen from 120 per cent of GDP to 160 per cent.

Loss of export trade

The global economy had been transformed by the war. It was no longer dominated by Britain. There were several new foreign manufacturing and financial competitors who had taken advantage of the disruption to British trade during the war. One example of market loss was in textiles. Japan began to supply India and South East Asia with cotton and silk during the First World War, causing the textile industry in the northwest of England to decline.

Underinvestment

British industry suffered from long-term underinvestment and by the 1920s this had begun to cause serious problems. In the steel industry, output throughout the interwar period was lower than that of Britain's rivals. By 1920 a growing number of British manufacturers were importing American steel because of its superior quality and price. By 1937 British steel foundries were producing 83,000 tonnes per year, but American foundries were producing 210,000 tonnes and Germany was producing 125,000 tonnes.

Industrial relations

In order to prevent a **general strike** in 1919 Lloyd George had bought off British workers in the main industries (coal, rail, docks) with generous pay and working hours. These workers, many of them former soldiers, were unwilling to lose these conditions when times became tough. The creation of an eight-hour working day (48-hour week) resulted in a 13 per cent decrease in working hours, but no increase in productivity during the hours worked. Wage rates also stayed high, meaning that products remained overpriced and uncompetitive.

Attempts to solve economic problems, 1921–24

Lloyd George believed that there was little choice but to wait for the economy to improve on its own. He was anxious to appease middle-class voters who were experiencing financial hardship after 1920, many of whom wanted to see tax cuts and less government spending. He advocated a policy of spending cuts known as retrenchment.

The Geddes Axe

In 1921 Lloyd George appointed Sir Eric Geddes to implement greater cuts in public expenditure. High taxes were blamed on high spending and Lloyd George hoped tax cuts would stimulate the economy. Geddes recommended £87 million of cuts in the 1922–23 budget. Most of these came from the government's military budget, but the health, welfare and housing budgets were reduced from £205.8 million in 1920–21 to £182.1 million in 1922–23.

Tariffs and free trade

One of the most important economic questions of the interwar years was that of **tariffs**. For most of the previous century Britain had adopted **free trade**. Table 1 shows the advantages and disadvantages of free trade and protectionism.

Table 1: The advantages and disadvantages of free trade and protectionism

Policy	Advantage	Disadvantage
Free trade	Free trade means that domestic industries have to compete with foreign competitors. • There are no import taxes on foreign goods so British manufacturers have to make sure that their products are sold at the lowest possible prices in order to attract customers. • British businesses can trade in other countries without the threat of protectionist tariffs being imposed.	Free trade means that more competitive foreign businesses can out-compete British ones and force them into bankruptcy. This can lead to unemployment and poverty, particularly in areas heavily dependent on one industry.
Protectionism (tariffs)	Protectionism is the policy of adding tariffs to certain goods that are imported into a country. It helps to protect domestic industries that are struggling from competition by making the goods more expensive. This protects the profits of domestic manufacturers.	The downside to protectionism is that it prevents consumers from having access to cheaper goods and it can result in other countries applying tariffs to British exports in retaliation.

Stanley Baldwin, 1867–1947

Stanley Baldwin, unlike many Conservatives of his generation, was the son of an industrialist, not an aristocrat. His family had become wealthy in the iron and steel business during the Industrial Revolution. Baldwin was an experienced businessman before he entered politics.

Shortly after the Conservative Party came to power in 1922, the new prime minister, Andrew Bonar Law, was diagnosed with terminal cancer and Baldwin was chosen by King George V to replace him. In December 1923 he was forced to call a general election over the question of protectionism.

Many Conservatives demanded the imposition of tariffs, but Baldwin did not believe he could introduce the policy without first having an election as he had been appointed to office, not elected. The Conservatives were divided on the issue of protection and lost the election to the Labour Party as a result.

Baldwin returned to government in the 1924 General Election and was prime minister until 1929.

Baldwin was often criticised as aimless or directionless by his cabinet colleagues and much of the day-to-day administration of policy was carried out by Baldwin's chancellor of the exchequer, Winston Churchill, and his minister of health, Neville Chamberlain. Chamberlain already knew a great deal about public health and welfare, but Churchill had no knowledge or experience of finance and made a catastrophic error in returning Britain to the **Gold Standard** in 1925 (see page 29).

Baldwin joined the **National Government** in 1931 and became prime minister again when Ramsay MacDonald fell ill in 1935. Baldwin retired in 1937, his age and ill health forcing him to leave active politics and hand over the office of prime minister to Neville Chamberlain.

Because of the depth of the post-war recession, many members of the government began to consider introducing tariffs in order to protect British industry and prevent further increases in unemployment. Lloyd George had always believed in free trade and had opposed tariffs. When he left office in 1922 some in the Conservative Party sought an election victory that would give them a mandate to impose tariffs on imports and protect industry (see box above). This divided the party and led to the establishment of the first Labour government.

Ramsay MacDonald and the economy

MacDonald had campaigned on the issue of unemployment, criticising Baldwin's failed attempts to bring the numbers of jobless down. However, when MacDonald became prime minister he was unable to make any real improvement to Britain's economic fortunes. He blamed this on the complexities of government, stating that:

> what seems to be a simple thing … becomes a complex, and exceedingly difficult, and laborious and almost heartbreaking thing.

MacDonald lacked a parliamentary majority with which to carry out major economic measures to deal with unemployment. He was unable to increase spending and taxation to help revive the economy or create jobs, but he was also reluctant to do so. He wanted to present Labour as a moderate party, one that was 'fit to rule', not a party of radical **socialist** ideas. He wanted the other two political parties, the largely Conservative-supporting press and Britain's upper and **middle classes** to feel that they had nothing to fear from a Labour administration.

Between 1921 and 1924 unemployment had declined from 12 per cent to 6.5 per cent, but started to climb again throughout MacDonald's year in office and rose to 8 per cent in 1925. One positive side effect was the dramatic fall in inflation from 15 per cent in 1920 to just under 1 per cent in 1924. This was not the result of economic strategy however. Inflation fell because spending had collapsed due to unemployment.

Baldwin's second administration, 1924–29

Stanley Baldwin's chancellor of the exchequer was Winston Churchill. He had never held the post of chancellor before, and presided over one of the most catastrophic economic blunders of the decade. By reintroducing Britain to the Gold Standard it has been argued that the economic slump was prolonged.

The Gold Standard

Before the war the value of the pound had been decided by a fixed exchange rate called the Gold Standard. Being on the Gold Standard meant that the prices of British exports stayed high, which made sense when the economy was booming, but made life very difficult for manufacturers when the economy was struggling.

The war had led to the suspension of the Gold Standard, but Churchill reintroduced it in his 1925 budget for two reasons. First, a pound that was decreasing in value was bad for British prestige and second, Churchill believed that a competitive economy could not be built by the government simply making things easier for manufacturers.

The exchange rate in 1925 was £1 to US $4.85 (the economist John Maynard Keynes believed that the value of the pound was fixed 10 per cent too high). In order to make the pound nearly five times as attractive to foreign investors, interest rates had to be kept high. This meant that foreign investors were attracted to Britain and put their money in British banks, but it also meant that the cost of borrowing money was equally high. As a result businesses found it more difficult to borrow money in order to expand and take on new workers, which added to Britain's problems with unemployment.

Many businesses wanted to come off the Gold Standard to make their exports cheaper so they could sell their products across the world, and compete with the cheaper imports flooding into the country. The higher costs of British exports were offset by employers through reducing wages or moving workers on to **short-hour contracts**. This meant that for many people paid employment often resulted in almost as much financial hardship as unemployment.

In September 1931 the Bank of England was forced to concede that it could no longer keep the pound in the Gold Standard. Interest rates were already at 8 per cent and would have to dramatically increase in order to prop up the value of the pound. That month a decision was taken to withdraw the pound from the Gold Standard and devalue; a measure that enabled the British economy to recover more quickly from the depression than many other countries.

Depression, 1929–34

In October 1929 a stock market crash on Wall Street in the USA sent shock waves through the US economy, resulting in economic depression. The USA had replaced Britain as the world's largest importer of overseas goods and the financial crisis had consequences for nearly every other country in the world. Global trade contracted by 66 per cent over the next five years. Britain's exports declined by 50 per cent. They were worth one-third of the country's Gross National Product (**GNP**) and the collapse in trade was catastrophic for several key industries:

- coal
- dock work
- cotton
- iron and steel
- ship building.

In addition to these industries, the shops and markets where miners, dock and mill workers spent their wages were also seriously affected. Unemployment, which had stood at 1 million in 1929, leapt to 2.5 million in 1930. The increase in unemployment put additional pressures on the government – tax revenue declined, but the number of people applying for financial assistance rapidly increased. In 1931 the British economy shrank by nearly 5 per cent, but despite these problems the government's main priority was keeping the pound in the Gold Standard system and supporting its value through spending cuts and high interest rates.

The Labour government's response

Britain's huge debts, along with her rising level of unemployment, led to a debate within the new Labour government. The chancellor of the exchequer, Philip Snowden, believed that unemployment relief should come from taxing the wealthy and from corporate profits. However, as these profits slumped, and private, wealthy individuals with money were anxious to protect or conceal it, the cost of providing for the unemployed became unsustainable.

The economist John Maynard Keynes suggested government spending on public works, such as new roads, to create jobs, but Snowden refused. He knew that the bankers in New York and London had little patience for further spending, as the value of British government bonds they had purchased during the war would decrease. The only part of the economy that the government invested in and created jobs in during the depression was the defence industry.

During the summer of 1931 there were rumours that the forthcoming budget would be unbalanced – meaning that the government had plans to spend more than it could afford, leading to an increase in borrowing. This caused

MacDonald and the banks

The second Labour government under Ramsay MacDonald struggled to finance its spending commitments and by 1931 came under intense pressure from international banks to limit the amount that was spent on social welfare. These banks had significant power over Britain as they held large reserves of the British pound, due to the amount of debt Britain had accrued by borrowing from the USA to finance the First World War. The reserves were normally in the form of bonds (a government-issued IOU), which had been exchanged for cash during the war when the British were desperate for funds. The bonds were redeemable at a later date but could also fluctuate in value, depending on whether the currency they were issued in (the pound) continued to be valuable or not.

These banks could lose millions at a stroke if the value of the pound went down and so did not want to see economic policies introduced that might cause that to happen. A high-spending government would either have to tax or borrow; both actions would reduce the pound's value and cause the Gold Standard to be readjusted.

the banks in America to engage in panic selling of the pound, exchanging it for other currencies, and the pound slumped in value. In order to reassure financiers that their investments were safe the government proposed spending cuts, the main measure being the introduction of a 10 per cent cut in unemployment assistance. This would keep the value of the pound stable, but caused hardship for many of Britain's poorest. The threat of this cut split the Labour Party and the government resigned on 24 August 1931 (see page 9).

The National Government's response

The National Government (see page 10) implemented the public spending cuts which had caused the previous government's downfall, primarily through cutting public sector workers' pay by 10 per cent and the **means test** for unemployment assistance (see page 59). Alongside cuts it tried to give direct assistance, through the Special Areas Act, to those areas most hard hit by the depression.

The Special Areas Act

In 1934 the government introduced the Special Areas Act, a measure that identified Tyneside, south Wales, west Cumberland and Scotland as regions in need of direct government assistance, but only a trickle of investment came to them. A new steel works in Ebbw Vale brought some jobs to the depressed south Wales valleys, but it was too little too late. King Edward VIII visited Dowlais in Wales in 1936, stating rather belatedly when he saw the unemployment and poverty that 'something must be done'.

Hunger marches

The desperation of workers and their families in the most deprived parts of the country from 1921 onwards had led the Communist Party of Great Britain to establish the National Unemployed Workers' Movement. The organisation, which was boycotted by the Labour Party because of its links with communists, organised a series of marches to protest the means test throughout the 1930s, which quickly came to be christened the hunger marches. The protesters were unemployed men from the depressed regions of Britain who walked to London, encountering both support and opposition along the route. The most famous of the marches was from Jarrow in Tyneside in 1936, called by the marchers the Jarrow Crusade.

The northeast of England felt particularly forgotten and ignored by the far wealthier southeast and London, and the marchers sought to bring to the attention of the government the scale of the deprivation and poverty in which the region was mired.

▲ Unemployed men from Tyneside and Yorkshire march to London in May 1931, refusing to 'starve at home' and demanding a 'seven-hour day'. How useful is this to a historian investigating the phenomenon of hunger marches in the 1930s?

Recovery, 1934–39

The depression did not last as long in Britain as it did in other countries such as America. On average between 1932 and 1937:

- real incomes rose by 19 per cent
- industrial production rose by 46 per cent
- GNP rose by 23 per cent
- exports increased by 28 per cent
- unemployment fell from 17 per cent to 8.5 per cent.

Economic growth averaged 4 per cent a year between 1934 and 1937 as the decision to remove Britain from the Gold Standard enabled the following economic measures:

- A cut in **interest rates**. Borrowing for businesses and individuals became cheaper, which enabled more spending and job creation. It also made it less attractive to save money so people investing their wealth bought property instead. This fuelled a housing boom in the southeast and Midlands in the second part of the decade as more people could afford to buy houses and the number of new houses built dramatically increased (see Table 2). The cut in rates was referred to as a 'Cheap Money' policy. The total value of **mortgages** taken out in 1930 was £316 million, but by 1937 it was £636 million, with an extra half a million borrowers buying new homes.

Table 2: House building

Year	New homes built
1931–32	133,000
1934–35	293,000
1935–36	279,000

- The government was able to allow a degree of inflation by the end of the decade. Instead of trying to prevent inflation completely (therefore protecting the value of the pound and its place in the Gold Standard), the National Government stimulated spending, which had the consequence of letting prices rise slightly. For example, the government spent money on road building, which in turn stimulated the car industry (see pages 161–162).
- The devaluation of the pound made British exports cheaper and more competitive.
- Banks became more willing to spend again.
- The national government also stimulated economic growth by restructuring British war debts, ensuring they cost the country 25 per cent of its tax revenue, as opposed to 40 per cent.

2 Creating a managed economy, 1939–51

Like the government during the First World War, Winston Churchill's government took control of war production and developed specific ministries for controlling the wartime economy:

- The Ministry of Aircraft Production
- The Ministry of Supply
- The Ministry of War Production
- The Ministry of Food
- The Ministry of Labour and National Service.

All ministries were given extensive legal powers to intervene and, if necessary, take over the running of essential war industries. The most fundamental difference between the British wartime and peacetime economies was the role of market forces. In peacetime, production was determined by prices for goods and profits; during wartime, production levels were decided by the government. The managed economy was to a large degree maintained by the post-war Labour government, particularly through the **nationalisation** of key industries.

> **Note it down**
>
> This section explores how a very different type of economy emerged in Britain as a result of crisis. In your notes you need to show a clear difference between the pre-war economy and the way the government managed the nation's resources after 1945. An effective way to do this is to use the 1:2 method (see page x). Use the following headings:
> - Military expenditure
> - Economic aid
> - Post-war austerity
> - Nationalisation.

Military expenditure

Britain had managed a degree of rearmament before the war, however by 1939 there were still significant shortages in military equipment. In 1940, when Britain appeared to be losing the war, the growth of state intervention resulted in a huge increase in war production and military expenditure (see Table 3, on page 32). Britain produced 15,000 aircraft in 1940, rising to 47,000 in 1944 and between 6,000 and 8,000 tanks per year.

Table 3: Government military expenditure, 1939–45

Year	Military expenditure (as % of national income)
1939	15%
1940	44%
1941	53%
1942	52%
1943	55%
1944	53%
1945	51%

Aircraft production

A British Spitfire plane

One example of the efficacy of Britain's centralised control of the economy during the war was the rate of aircraft construction during the **Battle of Britain**. Lord Beaverbrook was appointed to head the new Ministry of Aircraft Production, applying quotas for fighter aircraft. In the six months before his appointment, of the nearly 3,000 aircraft built only 638 were the badly needed fighters to defend British airspace. In the following four months 1,875 were built, tripling British output. The rate of **Luftwaffe** losses and Germany's slower rate of replacement meant that the RAF could win the fighter war of attrition.

Economic aid

Between 1939 and 1941 the USA offered Britain considerable economic help, despite the fact that the USA was neutral. The 1939 American Neutrality Act initially allowed the British to buy supplies with cash only, but by December 1940 Britain's cash and gold reserves were spent. Winston Churchill arranged a credit agreement, known as the **Lend-Lease Agreement**. America would supply Britain with the resources it needed but the bill would be paid after the war.

Equally as important were American 'Liberty Ships' – large cargo vessels full of oil, coal, timber, foodstuffs and essential raw materials for the war effort. These provided Britain with an economic lifeline throughout the war as German U-boats in the Atlantic prevented British merchant ships from bringing goods to Britain.

Post-war austerity, 1945–51

By the end of the Second World War Britain had accumulated over £4 billion of debt with the USA. Repaying this and the mounting interest cost £70 million every day.

Once again, British trade had been seriously disrupted and damaged by the war. The British economy had contracted by one-quarter and trade had declined by two-thirds. Not only had British shipping been sunk by German U-boats, but many of the countries in Europe and Asia which had previously bought British exports were devastated by war. American wartime aid to Europe and China helped US manufacturers dominate post-war markets with their products. Brands like Hershey's chocolate and Studebaker cars now competed with Cadburys and Morris.

The economist John Maynard Keynes visited Washington in August 1945 to negotiate an emergency loan for Britain. He believed it should be a non-repayable gift in recognition of Britain's wartime efforts, but the **US Congress** did not see it in such terms. Britain's bleak situation was underlined by an arctic winter in 1947 that saw rationing reintroduced and parts of the country experiencing food shortages (see page 135).

Britain's expensive world role

In 1948 George Marshall, US Secretary of State, proposed offering extensive loans to war-ravaged Europe. He believed that unless America acted and helped the continent to recover it might fall to **communism**. Britain was one of the biggest recipients of this Marshall Aid in 1948 (receiving up to £2.7 billion in loans).

Britain failed to use Marshall Aid to reinvest in industry and used it instead to pay for general expenses at home and overseas. The end of the war brought about a reduction of Britain's international commitments, but not a complete end to them. Britain continued with the policy of national service until 1965 and was involved in conflicts in Greece, Korea, Malaya and Kenya throughout the 1940s and 1950s. Britain also had a large army based in Germany and the responsibility of keeping civilians in the **German zone of occupation** fed and supplied.

By 1950, even after the establishment of a National Health Service (see pages 71–2), Britain's investment in infrastructure stood at 9 per cent of GDP, whereas Germany's was close to 20 per cent. Japan, too, poured huge efforts into building up its infrastructure; by the

1950s and 1960s both countries exported cars, electrical and consumer goods to Britain and the rest of the world.

Nationalisation

Perhaps the most important economic change to occur under the new Labour government in 1945 was the advent of nationalisation, with the state taking control of coal, power, railways, ship building and banking. It was hoped that nationalisation would give the government the ability to create **full employment** in the economy: nationalised industries that were financed by the government would not have to shed jobs during economic downturns. The main priority of Labour and later Conservative governments was not to return to an age of mass unemployment as in the interwar years.

During the first Labour ministry a series of nationalisation acts brought large sections of industry under government control.

- The Coal Industry Nationalisation Act 1946
- The Bank Of England Act 1946
- The Transport Act 1947 (nationalising the railways, road haulage and buses)
- The Electricity Act 1947 (nationalising electricity production and the national grid)
- The Gas Act 1948 (nationalising the gas industry)
- The Iron and Steel Act 1949 (nationalising the iron and steel industry).

The shareholders of the industries taken into public ownership were compensated by the government. For example, the private rail companies were bought from their owners for £1 billion. The total bill for nationalisation exceeded £2 billion, which left little money for the important modernisation needed and stored up economic problems for the future.

> ### Labour's economic record, 1945–51
> Labour's economic record after 1945 was strong in most regards:
> - Labour's first priority, full employment, was achieved in a four-year period between 1947 and 1951. The total number of unemployed reduced dramatically from 1930s' levels to just under 300,000.
> - Britain began to boost its world trade and reduce its balance of payments deficit. The percentage of world trade dominated by Britain grew from 17 per cent in 1939 to 20 per cent in 1950. Exports grew by nearly 80 per cent (though this figure can be explained by the fact that the war had reduced British exports significantly).
> - The economy grew dramatically, by 4 per cent each year after 1948.

3 The response to economic challenges, 1951–79

While the immediate aftermath of the war saw a greatly weakened and impoverished Britain, within a decade a combination of economic factors saw the beginnings of a boom that would last until the 1970s. This boom needs to be viewed in a wider global context. There was a huge expansion in the world economy during the 1950s and 1960s as a global recovery from the war occurred and the new technologies invented during the war were applied to civilian industries.

Although Britain experienced this consumer boom (see pages 137–138), it also experienced relative economic decline. This meant that as personal expenditure rose and consumer demand fuelled the economy, Britain as a whole was spending more than it earned, which resulted in a series of recurring economic problems which each government attempted to address:

- balance of payments problems
- devaluation
- inflation
- union disputes (see pages 49–52)
- unemployment in the 1970s.

> ### Note it down
> In your notes create a spider diagram (see page x) to help you answer the following questions:
> - What were Britain's economic problems between 1951 and 1979?
> - What did politicians do to try to solve them?
> - Why did many of these solutions fail to work?

The Conservatives and the post-war economy, 1951–64

In 1951 the Conservatives were returned to power by middle-class voters who switched from Labour. They were opposed to further nationalisation and wanted an end to wartime rationing and controls over the economy. By 1954 all rationing was over and an economic boom was under way. The political consensus between the Conservative and Labour parties over the economy led to the Conservatives prioritising:

- A commitment to full employment. The government was quick to use Keynesian-style **public works schemes** when unemployment began to rise. Throughout the period unemployment averaged 500,000, with lows of 300,000. There was no return to the mass unemployment of the 1930s.
- A **mixed economy**. The Conservatives had pledged not to increase the level of nationalisation, but they had no plans to reduce it either.

During the thirteen years of Conservative rule Britain retreated from her world role. Decolonisation and the end of its empire in Asia and Africa reduced vast expenditure and an influx of hundreds of thousands of new workers from the Caribbean and South Asia brought new energies and skills to the British economy (see page 122).

> ### The end of empire
>
> In 1918 Britain had the largest empire in the world, but by the 1950s it was in decline. In 1947 India, Britain's largest and most important imperial possession, was granted independence. In the next three decades British colonies in Africa and Asia also gained their independence:
>
> - Ghana (1957)
> - Jamaica (1962)
> - Uganda (1962)
> - Kenya (1963)
> - Malaysia (1957).
>
> One of the main motivations for abandoning colonies was the realisation by the British treasury that they cost far more to govern and administer than they were worth in trade, especially since foreign rivals now dominated trade to Britain's colonies.

'Stop-go' economics

The key feature of the period 1954–64 was the growth of consumer affluence and the ability of people in Britain to borrow and spend more on consumer goods than they had ever before. The government encouraged this new spending, but also struggled to deal with its consequences. It relaxed the laws surrounding **consumer credit** and borrowing, but had to employ a strategy that critics described as **stop-go economics**. The Conservatives allowed the consumer economy to grow, but excessive spending tended to result in a growth in inflation. It also resulted in an increase in imports which led to balance of payments problems. In order to counter this, Macmillan, while serving as Eden's chancellor of the exchequer, deliberately slowed the economy down by raising interest rates and taxes. This led to exports becoming less competitive and resentment from taxpayers. It demonstrated that controlling unemployment *and* inflation at the same time was impossible. Commentators referred to this policy as 'stop-go', meaning a failure of the government to develop consistent policies to ensure growth. The government tended to increase taxes and raise interest rates to make it difficult to borrow money for investment in order to slow things down when the economy grew too quickly. Then they would reduce them again after the slowdown to make money easier to borrow and facilitate an acceleration.

Managing the economy, 1957–64

Despite the rising living standards in Britain, the comparative difference between British economic performance and the output of her competitors was alarming for the government. West Germany and Japan had recovered from the devastation of war and their economies had dramatically grown. Japan experienced growth of 12 per cent in 1960 whereas Britain managed just over 4 per cent growth in the same year.

Macmillan believed in 'one-nation' Conservatism, where a united Britain, irrespective of social class, could work together to solve common problems. He decided to experiment with **corporatism** to try to arrest the economic decline. Corporatists believed that by uniting labour, management and government, economic goals could be planned and achieved. In 1962 two organisations were set up to achieve this.

Harold Macmillan, 1894–1986

Harold Macmillan was a moderate, aristocratic Conservative. He was part of the Macmillan publishing dynasty and, as an MP in the 1930s, spoke out against government inaction on unemployment. His parliamentary constituency was in Stockton-on-Tees in the northeast of England, one of the most depressed parts of the country. When Macmillan became prime minister in 1957 he believed in the goal of full employment and a mixed economy with a degree of nationalisation. His memories of high unemployment in the 1930s made him determined not to risk this in Britain again. Throughout his term of office he benefited from favourable global economic conditions, but he was aware that inflation could be the consequence of the economic boom. Macmillan's period in office is seen popularly as an era of affluence.

In 1957 he said that 'most of our people have never had it so good'. He also included an element of caution into his speech adding that: 'What we need is restraint and commonsense – restraint in the demands we make and commonsense on how we spend our income.'

NEDDY (The National Development Council and Office)

NEDDY was an institution where management and unions could discuss the development of the economy and co-operate with one another. It was assumed that they would want to work together because both would benefit from long-term economic growth. NEDDY was unable to enforce any legal control over either industry or unions, and the government hoped that both sides would come to voluntary agreements with each other.

NICKY (the National Incomes Commission)

Throughout the 1950s the number of working days lost to striking gradually increased (see page 49) and the level of pay rises demanded by workers grew. The Conservatives were chiefly interested in keeping unemployment down, but some ministers in the treasury feared that inflation could eventually get out of control unless pay rises were controlled. NICKY was purely an advisory council assembled from economists and industry experts. Its role was to give guidance to employers and unions on what the government considered 'reasonable' pay increases. It could not enforce any of its decisions. Unions for the most part ignored NICKY's calls for wage restraint. The union bosses were mindful that their members wanted improved living standards and greater spending power. The new **consumerism** of the 1960s was attractive to union members and they wanted to participate, so ignored appeals for wage restraint.

Economic problems by 1964

By 1964 the government was encountering serious economic problems:

- Unemployment in 1963 grew to its highest level (878,000) since the end of the war.
- Increased consumer spending increased demand for foreign goods and Britain experienced a balance of payments problem, causing a threat to the value of the pound.
- In August 1961, the government refused to devalue the pound, instead borrowing £714 million from the **IMF** in order to support it.

The Wilson government and the economy, 1964–70

Harold Wilson came to power in 1964 with a stated aim of modernising the British economy. He talked about making the economy more egalitarian, which would result in growth by allowing the most talented people in the country, irrespective of class, to have opportunities. He also believed that the economy could be transformed through technology, although he rarely went into specifics when he discussed modernisation.

Prices and Incomes Act

Wilson's government experienced similar economic problems to previous governments, with recurring balance of payments deficits, gradually increasing inflation and the failure of voluntary wage restraint. In response to the latter it created an incomes policy that gave the government legal powers to limit pay claims.

The National Board on Prices and Incomes (NBPI) was created to regulate pay settlements. It was accompanied by the Prices and Incomes Act 1966 which forced a statutory wage freeze for six months to curb inflation. The following year the Prices and Incomes Act 1967 allowed wage increases in companies that could prove they were increasing productivity and output.

Technology

Wilson's belief in technological improvement in British industry saw the creation of the Ministry of Technology in 1964, headed by Tony Benn from 1966 'to guide and stimulate a major national effort to bring advanced technology and new processes into industry'. The ministry grew to be one of the largest bodies in government. One of its main achievements was in the aviation industry with the creation of the supersonic passenger plane Concorde.

The IRC

Another aspect of government intervention to drive efficiency was the Industrial Reorganisation Corporation (IRC). The corporation promoted efficient practices in industry and offered loans to companies who wanted to implement new efficiency measures. It also promoted mergers between businesses where it was thought that there could be greater economic efficiency through combining them. Many of the mergers proposed by the IRC ended in failure, the most high profile being British Leyland, the car giant formed in 1968 by the merger of Leyland Motors and the British Motor Corporation. A £25 million loan was offered to fund the cost of the merger, but the car company that emerged was not able to compete with European and later Japanese imports. Throughout the 1970s British Leyland cars were synonymous with poor quality and the company operated at a loss, continually requiring subsidies.

Devaluation

In 1967 Wilson was forced to admit that devaluation would help ease deep-seated problems in the economy and allowed the pound to be devalued. It was reduced in value from $2.80 to $2.40, a decrease of 14 per cent. He claimed to the British public that the 'pound in your pocket' would be unaffected. The decision to devalue led Wilson's chancellor, Callaghan, to resign in protest.

The Heath government and the economy, 1970–74

In 1970 when Edward Heath became prime minister he intended to reject corporatism and embrace free market ideas.

One of the first organisations to be axed by Heath was the IRC. In 1970 Heath believed, as Wilson had, that modern techniques and practices in industry could revive the country's fortunes. However, unlike Wilson, he argued that it was the role of private businesses to provide that modernisation and that it could not be effectively imposed by the state. His pre-election Selsdon Park meeting (see page 20), where he devised a manifesto that was a break with consensus politics, led to major economic changes following the election.

Cuts to state spending were introduced in the following areas:

- cuts to subsidies to council houses
- cuts to free school milk for children
- raising charges on prescriptions.

Heath believed that cuts in spending and reducing the tax burden on the public would stimulate economic growth. In total, his government's first budget made cuts of over £330 million. Heath assumed that a natural spirit of entrepreneurship would result from the cuts. He abolished the NBPI set up by Wilson, ending the government's ability to control or influence prices and incomes. However, Heath had not counted on several problems:

- mounting inflation across the world as the global economic boom slowed down
- Britain's own problem of inflation, which was 15 per cent after eighteen months of Heath's leadership
- unemployment, which had risen from 2 per cent at the end of the 1950s to 6 per cent in the early 1970s.

In 1972, Conservative Chancellor of the Exchequer Anthony Barber attempted a 'dash for growth' in his budget with massive tax cuts and forecasts of low borrowing. The result was a huge spike in inflation, which was followed soon after by price rises caused by the **1973 oil crisis**. Barber tried to cool the economy down with public sector pay cuts, which led to union unrest and confrontation with the National Union of Miners (see page 51).

New economic thinking

The most significant economic problem that dominated the Labour government from 1974 to 1979 was inflation. By the mid-1970s prices were rising faster than wages, dramatically reaching over 30 per cent by 1975. Appeals by the government for restraint in wage demands were ignored by the unions who saw the standards of living of their members eroded by the constant increases in prices.

By 1975 Labour Chancellor Denis Healey had begun to challenge Labour's commitment to full employment. He believed that pumping money into the economy to stimulate employment was pointless, because it simply led to ever greater levels of inflation.

The IMF loan

By early 1976 the confidence that international banks and currency traders had in the British economy rapidly declined due to the rate of inflation and the likelihood of further strikes. This meant that the value of the pound slumped and the British government once again was forced to accept a loan from the IMF. The loan was agreed by September that year, by which time the value of the pound had declined by nearly 20 per cent from $2 to the pound to $1.63. The IMF loaned Britain just under £4 billion, but the money came with conditions. Britain had to prove it was capable of repaying its debt and was forced to agree to £3 billion of spending cuts. When Healey announced the deal at the Labour Party conference he was denounced as a 'traitor' by the left of the party, which accused him of selling out Britain to the interests of international finance. Healey argued that the left of the party was hopelessly unrealistic and that Britain was living far beyond its means.

The left of the party, led by Tony Benn, proposed an Alternative Economic Strategy. It argued that the welfare state needed to be protected from cuts imposed by the IMF by:

- using trade barriers to keep out foreign imports
- making Britain economically self-sufficient by government investment in industry and increased nationalisation
- withdrawal from the **EEC** (see page 22).

Benn called his proposals a '**siege economy**'. Callaghan dismissed Benn's arguments as unworkable and unrealistic. In supporting Healey, Callaghan indicated that the Labour Party had moved away from the post-war Keynesian consensus and had embraced monetarist thinking.

Monetarism

The Centre for Policy Studies (CPS), co-founded by Margaret Thatcher's economic guru, Keith Joseph (see page 65), argued that control of the money supply in an economy was one of the most important roles of government.

This philosophy, known as monetarism, stated that a tight reign on the money supply would eventually prevent inflation, even though it might cause unemployment. This was a price worth paying, however, because as the experience of the 1970s had shown, inflation eventually led to unemployment anyway.

In addition to proposing limits on the money supply, principally by cutting state spending, the CPS and Joseph also argued for a dramatic change to the economic consensus that had dominated Britain since the end of the war. Free market or neo-liberal economics were proposed, which meant:

- a dramatic reduction of the state's role in the economy
- privatisation of all state-owned industries and utilities
- the deregulation of industries that struggled with excessive bureaucracy (particularly the financial sector)
- the promotion of free trade.

By scaling back the role of the state, Joseph, and later Thatcher, believed that the energies of the free market would be unleashed. It was not the first time during the decade that these ideas had been mooted either. Most of the proposals put forward at the end of the decade by the CPS were contained in the 'Selsdon Manifesto' (see page 20), although most proposals had to be abandoned due to union opposition and Heath's weakness against the TUC (see page 52).

Work together

1. There are two main views of economic history during this period:
   - Britain was in unstoppable decline after the First World War.
   - Britain was not so much declining as transforming into a post-industrial economy.

   Use the following table to assign the evidence to these two different views using the notes you made throughout the chapter. With a partner decide which view you most agree with and why.

2. Look back over this chapter and decide which five events you think are the most important in the period 1918–79. Your partner will score you out of 15 for each event using the following criteria:
   - Details of the event (what happened) 1–5
   - Significance of event (how it shaped later events) 1–5
   - What evidence is there of its importance? 1–5
   - Overall score out of 15.

Years	Unstoppable decline	Economic transformation
1918–39		
1939–51		
1951–79		

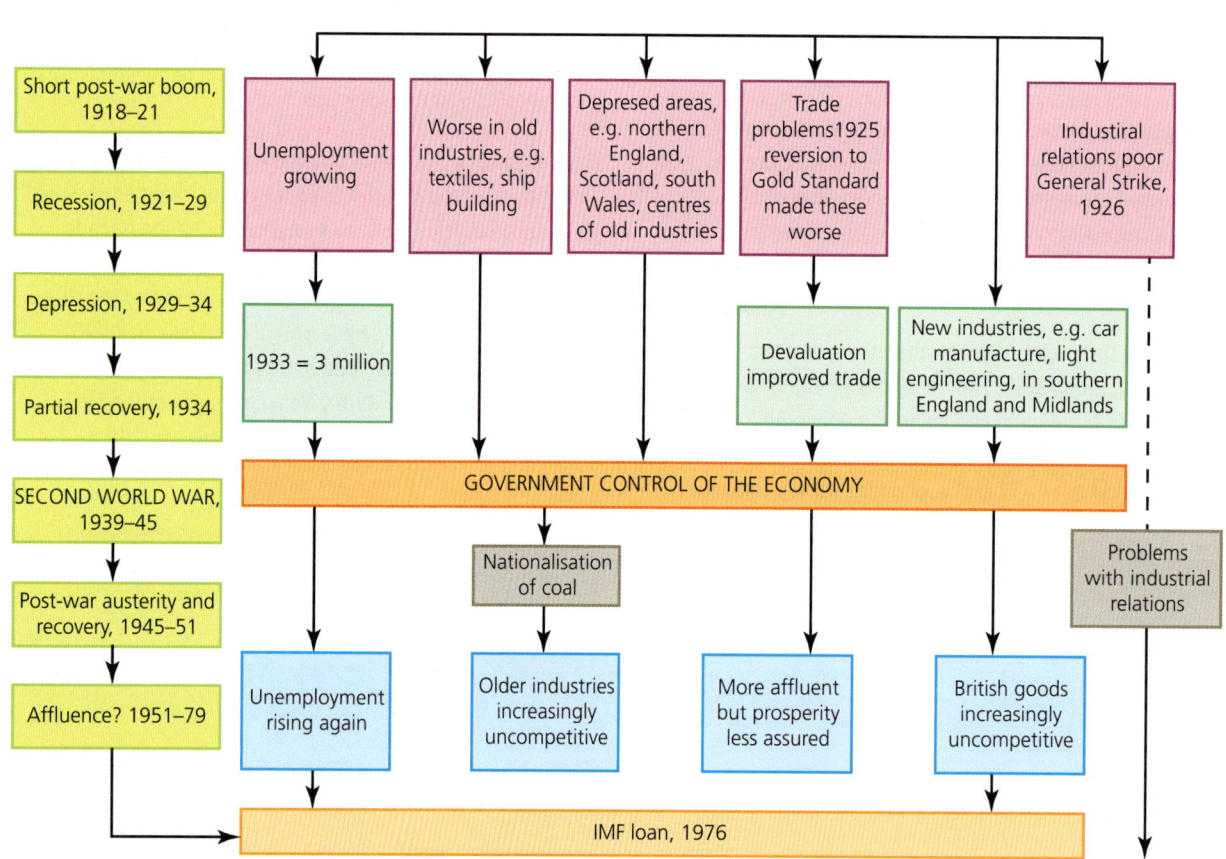

▲ Summary diagram: Responding to economic challenges

Chapter summary

- After a brief post-war boom, a devastating economic slump led to a huge increase in unemployment and poverty from 1920 to 1921.
- The Conservatives hoped protectionism and tariffs would revive the economy but this was electorally unpopular.
- The hardest hit areas in Britain were the regions associated with heavy industry, the south Wales coal fields, the shipyards of Tyne and Clydeside and the mining areas of northern England.
- Following the Wall Street crash in the USA, Labour's spending plans in 1929–31 came under immense pressure because of Britain's struggling economy.
- During the 1930s the depressed regions suffered disproportionately to the rest of the country. The National Unemployed Workers' Movement organised several hunger marches, protesting against poverty and the means test.
- In more affluent parts of the country the 1930s were a time of growing living standards, jobs and consumer goods.
- The government took control of large sections of the British economy during the Second World War.
- The Labour Party wished to continue government intervention in the economy after the war and pursued a policy of nationalisation.
- From 1950 to about 1975 the world experienced a global economic boom that Britain benefited from.
- During the same period both Labour and Conservative parties had a broad agreement over the management of the economy, with a commitment to full employment, nationalisation and tolerance for a degree of price inflation.
- A retreat from empire and mass immigration not only reduced government expenditure overseas but also resulted in new skilled workers and low-cost labour in Britain.
- The 1950s saw a relaxation in consumer credit and an increase in new products available to buy, leading to a dramatic increase in consumer spending.
- In the late 1950s the first sign that the consensus on the economy was being challenged came from within the Conservative Party when senior treasury ministers resigned, arguing that Macmillan should adopt monetarist policies.
- Macmillan hoped that people would be sensible in their spending and unions would show restraint in their pay claims, but this was naive.
- Throughout the 1960s inflation began to gradually increase and by the 1970s so did unemployment.
- Harold Wilson's attempts to modernise the British economy were undermined by his high spending plans, his refusal to devalue and relative economic decline.
- By 1970 Edward Heath planned to introduce monetarist and free market policies, but trouble with inflation and the unions prevented this.
- In 1976 Britain applied for a loan from the IMF and was forced to adopt neo-liberal policies, which included cuts to state spending and free market reforms.

Essay technique: Focus and structure

All of your examined essays will be judged on how far they focus on the question, and the quality of their structure. The better your focus and the clearer your structure, the better your chance of exam success.

Focus of the question

First, you must identify the focus of the question. Imagine you are answering the following question:

> How far does the economic effect of the Second World War explain Britain's relative economic decline 1945–79?

The question has two parts:
- The economic effect of the Second World War
- Britain's relative economic decline, 1945–79.

Essentially, the question asks you to explain Britain's economic decline in the post-war era, and questions the extent to which the war is to blame. This means you need to evaluate the relative importance of a range of causes.

Structuring your essay

Your essay should be made up of three or four paragraphs, each addressing a different factor which helps explain Britain's post-war economic decline. One of these paragraphs has to address the factor stated in the question: the effect of the Second World War. Therefore your essay plan should look something like this:

Paragraph 1: [Stated factor] *The effect of the Second World War*

Paragraph 2: *Lack of investment*

Paragraph 3: *Corporatism*

Paragraph 4: *The refusal to devalue*

It's a good idea to deal with the stated factor first, otherwise you may run out of time and then miss the opportunity to deal with this important part of the question. Once you've dealt with the stated factor, deal with the other factors in order of their importance. Write about the most important factor first.

In addition to your three or four main points, you should begin your essay with a clear introduction and end with a conclusion that contains a focussed summary of your essay (see pages 92–3).

Different kinds of question

The example above is a causation question, which asks you to consider how far a stated factor caused a specific process. Significantly, not all questions deal with cause, and not all questions have an obvious stated factor. Nonetheless, you will need to consider a range of themes in any essay your write. Therefore, you should always begin by thinking of the three or four main topics you want to discuss, and these should be the basis of your essay.

Writing a focussed introduction

Having made your plan it is important you write a focussed essay. One way of doing this is to use the wording of the question to help write your answer. For example, the first sentence of your essay could look like this:

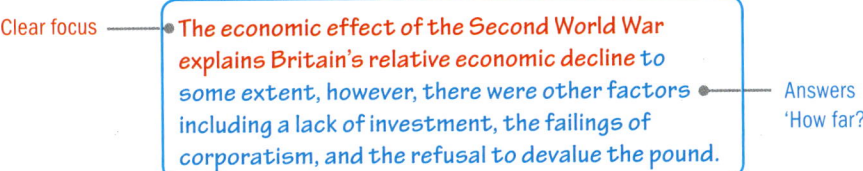

Clear focus — The economic effect of the Second World War explains Britain's relative economic decline to some extent, however, there were other factors including a lack of investment, the failings of corporatism, and the refusal to devalue the pound. — Answers 'How far?'

This sentence begins with a clear focus on the question by addressing 'how far' the economic effect of the Second World War explained Britain's relative economic decline. In this sense, the first sentence provides a focussed answer to the whole question.

Focus throughout the essay

A second way of maintaining focus is to begin each paragraph with a clear point, which both refers to the primary focus of the question and links it to a factor.

For example, you could begin your third paragraph with the following point:

Introduces a new factor — Corporatism was another reason for Britain's relative economic decline following the Second World War. — Maintains focus on the question

This sentence clearly introduces a new factor: corporatism, while maintaining focus on the question.

Summary
- Work out the primary and secondary focus of the question.
- Plan your essay with a series of factors that focus on the question.
- Use the words in the question to formulate your answer.
- Return to the primary focus of the question at the beginning of every paragraph.

Question practice

Having read the advice on how to write a structured and focussed essay, use your notes to plan and write the first sentence of the following questions:
1. How far was Labour policy the main reason for economic decline in the period 1945–64? **AS**
2. How accurate is it to say that the years 1945 to 1970 were a period of political consensus between the Labour and Conservative parties? **AS**
3. How effectively did Conservative and Labour governments address Britain's economic problems between 1945 and 1970?

1c: Change and challenge in the workplace

Overview

Throughout much of the twentieth century, millions of British workers were represented by trade unions. They used strike action and other forms of protest to force the government and employers to guarantee fair rates of pay, safe working conditions and protection from arbitrary sacking.

By the end of the 1970s Britain's industrial conflicts had come to define it in the eyes of the international community. Union unrest and strike action in the winter of discontent of 1978-79 appeared to have caused Britain to come close to a state of anarchy.

This chapter explores labour relations from 1918 to 1979 and examines why the trade union movement was able to exercise such power over politics by the end of the period. It also examines how working opportunities changed in Britain as the country's economy underwent a transition from heavy industry to a service sector economy. It does this through the following sections:

1. Changing industrial relations, 1918-39
2. Changing working opportunities and conditions, 1939-79
3. Industrial relations, 1939-79

1 Changing industrial relations, 1918–39

In 1871 the Trade Union Act gave legal recognition to trade unions. A series of large 'new' unions developed that catered not only for the artisan or skilled working classes, but also for the far greater number of unskilled workers who were often more radical and less likely to see their interests best represented by the Conservative or Liberal parties. In 1900 the **Trades Union Congress (TUC)**, a body which represented the unions collectively, established a Labour Representation Committee (LRC) to pursue parliamentary representation for the newly enfranchised working classes (see page 5). This became the Labour Party. Throughout this chapter the changing and often antagonistic relationship between the TUC and the Labour Party will be crucial to understand.

The period between the two world wars began with a high level of union unrest. A brief post-war boom (see page 26) in 1919–20 led to an increase in labour disputes – as factories took on large numbers of men, the leadership of the TUC realised it was in a position to extract concessions from employers. This was followed by a slump and continued hardship throughout the 1920s for many working-class people, which weakened the unions as their membership decreased. In 1926 a **general strike** occurred, but it was an aberration in the period 1921–39, which actually saw comparatively low incidences of industrial action.

Note it down

The unrest that Britain faced at the end of the First World War from the trade unions had direct political and economic causes. With your partner, create a timeline of events from 1918 to 1939 and place on it not only the events relating to union activity but those economic and political changes in Chapters 1a and 1b that you think are relevant.

Once you have done this look at the two major periods of unrest:
- 1919-20
- 1926.

Using your timeline try to explain the economic and political factors that made these outbreaks of unrest occur.

Reasons for industrial change

Much of British industry after the First World War had not really moved on since Victorian times. It was still based in the centres of iron ore and coal in the north of England, south Wales and southern Scotland. It was still overwhelmingly **heavy industry**, which may have made Britain wealthy during the previous century, but now was often antiquated with old machinery, old methods of production, underinvestment and an inability to compete with foreign competitors such as the USA. It was in these areas of heavy, older industries that most industrial unrest took place during the interwar years.

There were, however, newer industries centred in the Midlands and the southeast. The most noticeable were motor vehicles, mainly adopting the mass production techniques of companies such as Ford in the USA (see page 236). There were also more light engineering factories producing consumer goods and household appliances for the domestic market such as washing machines and vacuum cleaners. These factories were often light and airy, and although unions often didn't penetrate the work force, wages were good.

'Two Englands'

Contemporary observers and historians have often spoke of 'two Englands' in the interwar years and differentiated between those in the older and newer centres of industry. Cotton, mining and ship building each lost one-third of their workforce while other industries saw increases:

- Those making electrical appliances increased their workforce by two and half times.
- Those working in the building industry increased their workforce by 33 per cent.
- Service industries such as hotels and holiday camps increased their workforce by 40 per cent during the 1930s. This is a reflection of the fact that more people could take holidays – in 1939 11.5 million people were awarded holiday pay for the first time.

Nevertheless, most people still worked in the older industries where industrial relations could be a significant problem.

Industrial relations, 1918–21

During the First World War Prime Minister David Lloyd George had negotiated with the **trade union movement** to keep strikes to a minimum, as the wartime economy had required a high degree of labour discipline. Even so, there were wartime strikes, for example, in 1917 there were 48 strikes across Britain that involved over 200,000 workers and, by 1918, the relationship that the government had with the workers was deteriorating. In 1918, following the **armistice**, there was an enormous wave of unrest across the country as not only workers but soldiers and even the police went on strike as resentments and perceived injustices that had developed during the war were unleashed at the end of the conflict.

As factories took on large numbers of men, the numbers of strikes declined. New jobs, many of which were well paid, satisfied unionised British workers. In 1919 there were 32 million days lost to strikes but the following year, at the height of the boom (see page 26), the figure had fallen to 25 million. A year later, as unemployment soared and the workers who were in jobs saw their wages slump, strikes grew once more, reaching 84 million days lost.

Many of the grievances of the strikers were based around repressed wages, rising prices and food shortages, but a minority of strikers expressed more political and ideological grievances. The government was able to contain the strikes by offering concessions. This suggests that while the *perception* may have existed that Britain was close to a revolution, in reality there was not much chance of one occurring.

Red Clydeside

In 1919 the epicentre of union unrest in Britain was Clydeside, in Glasgow. The Clyde workers had been involved in actively protesting against the First World War in 1914 and a May Day protest in 1918 calling for the end of the war attracted tens of thousands of workers.

In response to growing unemployment in the depressed former ship-building industry, the Glasgow Trades Council proposed to reduce the working week from 54 hours to 40. This was intended to give surplus hours to unemployed men, many of whom were ex-servicemen.

Matters came to a head on 31 January 1919 when 90,000 demonstrators filled George Square demanding the 40-hour week, raising the **socialist** red flag. At a time when governments across the Western world were very nervous about the possibility of revolution breaking out (Allied intervention was still ongoing in the **Russian Civil War** to 'strangle Bolshevism in its cradle' as Winston Churchill put it) the raising of the flag was an incendiary act. It is unclear if the police acted first, but by the end of the day pitched battles had taken place between protesters and police, with tanks and soldiers being quickly transported to Glasgow from England and other parts of Scotland in order to put down any organised revolutionary violence. The scale of the violence and the potential for greater bloodshed from the Army shocked union leaders who called on protesters to halt the rioting. The 40-hour week was never obtained by the workers.

The miners' strike, 1921

In 1921, it was the turn of the miners to strike. The Miners Federation of Great Britain (MFGB) was the largest union, with over 900,000 members. Wartime government control of the coal mines had been popular with the miners who looked upon the pit owners as lazy, greedy and incompetent.

Once the government's control of mines ended in March 1921, and they were returned to private industry, wages were cut and hours lengthened in order to compete with foreign coal imports. The high levels of unemployment in 1921 enabled mine owners to reduce wages, knowing that the miners did not have other work to go to if they left their existing jobs.

The MFGB, the National Transport Workers Federation (NTWF – representing dock workers) and the National Union of Railwaymen (NUR) had discussed the possibility of united strike action to protect wages if a post-war economic slump occurred. A miners' strike could easily be broken by the importing of foreign coal, but if dock workers refused to unload it and rail workers refused to move it across the country the strike could be potentially crippling and might quickly become a general strike.

When union leaders refused to accept pay cuts mine owners **locked out** their workers on 1 April and the government used the **Emergency Powers Act** to send troops to south Wales in anticipation of unrest and violence.

Black Friday

The miners' attempts to strike in 1921 were sabotaged by the other two branches of the 'triple alliance' abandoning their cause. On Friday 15 April (referred to in the **labour movement** as 'Black Friday'), the NUR and the NTWF both decided not to go out on strike in solidarity with the miners. The miners' leaders had made a crucial error in asking for support from the other unions but refusing to allow them to be part of the negotiations. This made members reluctant to strike and union leaders wary of the potential consequences of involving their members. The miners went on strike between 15 April and 28 June, but were eventually forced to end the walkout, realising they could not beat the mine owners alone. The miners were forced to accept pay cuts that left their wages 20 per cent lower than in 1914.

Black Friday left the miners with a lasting sense of grievance towards the rest of the union movement and a hope that the election of a Labour government might change their fortunes. However, the fall of the first Labour government in 1924 without achieving any of its core goals (see page 8) meant that union militancy once again became the primary means of bringing about change. The decision of the Baldwin government to return Britain to the **Gold Standard** (see page 29) left mine owners' profits depleted. Their default response was to cut miners' pay, resulting in a strike by the MFGB, led by a popular and radical union organiser Arthur Cook. His slogan, 'Not a minute on the day nor a penny off the pay', had great resonance with the miners who had no sympathy with the mine owners' predicament.

The general strike, 1926

The government, fearing a general strike, established an enquiry into miners' conditions and offered a subsidy to the mine owners that would maintain miners' pay until 1 May 1926. The mine owners, knowing that the subsidy was coming to an end, told the miners they would have to accept pay cuts and threatened a lockout unless they agreed. In March 1926 a government enquiry, the Samuel Commission, recommended a 13.5 per cent pay cut for the miners with the withdrawal of the subsidy. On 1 May 1926 a million miners across Britain were locked out of their workplaces for refusing to accept the new lower wages.

The TUC announced that a general strike would begin on 3 May, knowing that abandoning the miners again would be catastrophic for both them and the prospects for a future Labour government.

> **Arthur Cook**
>
> Arthur Cook was a Somerset-born miner, trade unionist and Baptist lay preacher. He was imprisoned for three months during the First World War for **sedition** after speaking out against **conscription**. He became the leader of the South Wales Miners Federation in 1921, but his radical left-wing views left him isolated and distrusted by much of the rest of the TUC. He was a leading figure in the **National Minority Movement (NMM)**, and hoped that the union movement would become revolutionary.

Government response to the strike

The government, knowing the strike was coming, was far better organised than the TUC, publishing its own propaganda paper, the *British Gazette*, and using the new BBC to broadcast radio messages in support of the government position. The Labour Party distanced itself from the strikers and the TUC only authorised unions to strike who could claim to have common interests with the miners to strike – miners, railwaymen, dockers, iron, steel, transport workers and printers.

An anti-union group of volunteers, the Organisation for the Maintenance of Supplies, was founded to do the work that the strikers refused to do. Its members manned buses, trains and telephone exchanges during the strike. The strike collapsed when it transpired that the 1906 Trades Disputes Act that gave unions legal immunity from damages claims for loss of profits from businesses would not apply. Union members began to return to work and the TUC appealed to the government not to victimise the strikers. Baldwin told the unions he could not guarantee the rights of workers who returned to work and many were singled out as trouble makers. Wages for the miners were slashed and the industry lost 30 per cent of its jobs; the strike had been a catastrophic failure for the miners. A new Trades Disputes Act in 1927 prevented **sympathetic strikes** and **mass picketing**.

Changing industrial relations, 1929–39

Union activity throughout the 1930s was significantly weakened by the aftermath of the General Strike. With the advent of the **Great Depression** and the resulting mass unemployment (see page 29), union revenues were depleted and membership declined from its height of 8 million in 1922 to 4.5 million in 1932.

The exception was the Communist-Party-backed National Unemployed Workers' Movement (NUWM) which grew in size during the depression but was still small compared to unions like the MFGB.

By the eve of the Second World War, while most of Britain had seen an economic recovery, the heavy industrial heartlands now in terminal decline were still the most poverty-stricken and deprived parts of Britain. Union action had been unable to alleviate the conditions in the Clyde, south Wales, Yorkshire and Tyneside coal fields or the Merseyside docks.

▲ Police protection for volunteer bus drivers during the General Strike. Why is this photograph useful to a historian investigating the General Strike of May 1926?

2 Changing work opportunities and conditions, 1939–79

Between 1939 and 1979 the availability and the type of work on offer in Britain changed dramatically. The 1950s and 1960s saw almost **full employment** which gave employees more choice as to their occupation, but the 1970s brought a downturn and the ending of government commitment to full employment.

> **Note it down**
>
> Produce a spider diagram (see page x) to show the changing work opportunities and conditions between 1939 and 1979. In the middle put the title 'Work opportunities and conditions', with legs labelled as:
> - Second World War
> - Full employment in the 1950s and 1960s
> - Growth of unemployment in the 1970s.

The Second World War

The Second World War brought considerable changes to employment in Britain. The movement to war production brought full employment and the deployment of large numbers of women into factories and jobs previously designated for men. Factories that may have lain idle during the 1930s were fully operational, building weapons and munitions. By 1944 it was estimated that 33 per cent of the civilian population was involved in war work, including 7 million women.

This meant that during war time working opportunities for many people in Britain improved. Not only did the mass unemployment of the 1930s virtually disappear, but the working conditions, wages and benefits that unions could negotiate were improved.

Wartime employment

Minister of Labour Ernest Bevin had issued an Essential Work Order in March 1941 which tied people to jobs considered essential for the war effort and made it difficult for employers to dismiss them. Even so there were a shortage of skilled workers, for example in engineering and ship building, and the September 1939 Control of Employment Act was used to allow semi-skilled workers to undertake formerly skilled jobs. Skilled workers in essential war industries were also exempt from military service.

> **'Bevin Boys'**
>
> One controversial policy, which began in December 1943, was the conscription of 10 per cent of young men into the coal mines rather than military service. The mines had lost 36,000 of their workforce and were replaced by 'Bevin Boys', many of whom resented this enforced alternative to joining the armed forces.

Working conditions in factories often improved. Bevin insisted that employers as far as possible provide medical centres and canteens to feed their employees; crèches were also introduced for working mothers. He established the popular radio programme 'Worker's Playtime' and ensured that munitions workers knew that they were a vital part of Britain's eventual victory. Wages also increased. Hours, however, were long.

Full employment

Between the 1940s and 1970s, both parties maintained a commitment to full employment. This was in part possible due to favourable economic conditions throughout much of the 1950s and 1960s. Unemployment rose to above 2 per cent in only eight of the years between 1948 and 1970. Record levels of low unemployment had a direct impact on industrial relations. Employers needed to keep skilled workers in their workplaces and had to use attractive wages and working conditions to prevent them from leaving for another job. With little worry about long-term unemployment workers were more mobile and more likely to leave a job that didn't suit them. This was especially common in regions and cities where particular industries were based, such as the textiles industry in Nottingham. One could leave one firm and easily find similar work in another. For this reason, employers often offered benefits to their workers such as cheap canteen facilities, sports and social clubs, subsidised works outings and social functions.

Employment opportunities

Employment opportunities developed, too. With better education and an economy that remained buoyant despite its problems, people had more choice and could be more flexible in how they were employed.

Previously children often followed their parents into the same occupation, be it in a textile mill or coal mine. Now expectations rose. As technology developed, there were more white-collar and technological jobs in electronics, light engineering and the provision of consumer goods. More managers were required. Unsurprisingly, surveys showed that those in professional and white-collar jobs tended to gain more satisfaction from work than those in manual jobs. There was a growth, too, in the service sector, in tourism (see page 160), shops and restaurants.

Work in factories

Many people worked in industry and factories. The car industry became a major employer. By 1956 over 500,000 people were directly employed in the production of motor vehicles or components.

One continuing problem with factory work was its tedium. Many employees spent their days doing repetitive work often tied to the speed of a conveyor belt in deafening noise. As automation developed, this aspect worsened. It was difficult to make production lines interesting. The benefit was pay. Average weekly earnings for men doubled from £8.30 per week in 1951 to £15.35 a decade later. They had doubled again to £30.93 by 1971. While retail prices rose by 63 per cent between 1955 and 1969, weekly wage rates went up by 88 per cent. When overtime is taken into account this figure rose to 130 per cent. People could buy more with their money as well – as technology and mass production developed, the cost of consumer items such as TV sets fell in real terms

Growth of unemployment in the 1970s

Full employment began to decline before governments actually abandoned their commitment to it. As industrial problems began to bite, unemployment rose to 1 million in 1972 and ideas that had existed since the late 1940s about job security began to fade against a new reality of joblessness. The decline in heavy industry meant that unemployment was more acute in industrial parts of Britain such as the north, south Wales, the Midlands and Scotland.

In the west Midlands so much of the industry was geared to motor vehicle production and related components that problems in motor vehicle production could have massive knock-on effects – for example a downturn in the car-producing factories led to short-time working in headlight manufacture.

In these areas, where often there was little alternative to jobs in mines and factories, the downturn bit hard as places of employment closed.

By 1976 the Labour government had conceded that the working opportunities that had existed since the end of the Second World War were no longer possible. It abandoned the commitment to full employment and accepted that market forces would have a greater role in determining who worked and who did not.

3 Industrial relations, 1939–79

In the period 1939–79 the relationship between the trade unions and the government underwent a period of transition.

During the war, unions and the government worked closely together and in the 1950s and 1960s an era of 'consensus' and policies of **corporatism** (see page 34) gave unions a role in industrial policy and wage setting alongside businesses. During the late 1960s and 1970s the relationship between the trade unions and the government became progressively less co-operative and more antagonistic, resulting in a series of confrontations between them. In 1974 this resulted in the fall of Edward Heath's Conservative government and in 1979 contributed to the defeat of James Callaghan's Labour government.

> **Note it down**
>
> From 1969 to 1979 the unions defeated every attempt to control them or limit their powers from both the Conservative and Labour parties. How did they exercise such power? As you read this section note:
> - long-term causes of union strength in the 1970s
> - long-term causes of union militancy in the 1970s
> - short-term causes of Conservative weakness
> - short-term causes of Labour weakness.
>
> Then, with a partner, evaluate the strongest causes of the unrest, 1969–79.

The war years, 1939–45

In May 1940 the support of the Labour Party enabled Winston Churchill to form a new National Government (see page 14). From a union point of view the most important member of the new cabinet was Ernest Bevin, the minister of labour and national service. Through the Emergency Powers (Defence) Act (1939) Bevin had almost complete control over the British workforce.

Bevin had been the leader of the Transport and General Workers Union (TGWU) and was seen as a safe pair of hands by Churchill because he had repeatedly preached moderation and co-operation, hoping that workers and bosses could find compromises between themselves. He fostered joint production committees in factories between workers and management to explore efficiency-saving new techniques and offered **piece-rate** bonuses to more efficient workers. Skilled workers and union **shop stewards** became powerful during the war because of labour shortages and the high demand for quality work.

> ### Ernest Bevin, 1881–1951
> Ernest Bevin was a working-class Labour politician and trade unionist. He was born in Somerset and worked as a lorry driver and labourer, before becoming involved in labour politics. He was on the right of the Labour Party and suspicious of **communism**. He participated in the General Strike of 1926 but believed it was a mistake. After his wartime service as minister of labour and national service he became foreign secretary and was regarded by the civil servants who served under him to have been one of the most talented statesmen to have held the post. He died in 1951.

Wartime strikes

A popular but largely inaccurate view of the war years is one of relative social peace and unity in the face of the Nazi threat. The problems that the war created – long antisocial hours, lack of recognition for workers and changeable pay packets – led to numerous strikes and protests over wages and working conditions. In 1940 the government introduced Defence Regulation 58AA banning strikes and lockouts.

Miners

In 1942 at Betteshanger in Kent, miners went on strike illegally. The government took over the running of the coal industry from its private owners and initially chose to prosecute 1,050 miners, fining most of them between £1 and £3. The miners in other pits downed tools in solidarity, forcing the Home Secretary to drop the charges and improve wages.

Often younger miners or 'Bevin Boys' (see page 46) who were conscripted to work in the mines went on strike because they were angry about the lower rates of pay they received, compared to the older more experienced mine workers. In the south Wales coal fields alone there were 514 strikes between 1939 and 1944.

In the spring of 1944, 100,000 Welsh miners went on **unofficial strike** for better wages (by 1944 the average daily rate for miners working underground was just £5 per day, whereas the average wage in manufacturing was £6.10s a day). The government quickly relented to their demands. Britain's miners found that the war presented opportunities for improved pay that peacetime had not offered.

Industrial relations, 1945–51

Throughout the war, union leaders had been appointed to numerous government bodies on wages, industry and social policy and this continued after 1945. It meant that union leaders had more access to decision making than at any point in their history and their views were frequently heard within government. In 1939 union leaders sat on twelve government committees, but by 1949 they sat on 60. In 1945, 120 Labour MPs were sponsored directly by the unions of which 26 became ministers and six sat in the cabinet, including Ernest Bevin. Between 1945 and 1951 the TUC and the Labour Party shared similar views on economic and social priorities

Labour repealed the 1927 Trades Disputes Act imposed after the General Strike, restoring the union movement much of its power in industrial disputes.

> ### The Industrial Charter
> In 1947 the Conservative Party carried out a review of its policies and published the Industrial Charter. The pamphlet was a clear indication that the party recognised that growing union membership and a widespread desire for a welfare state and fair treatment at work meant they had to adopt Labour's pro-union approach. The Charter expressed a desire by the party to see large unions that democratically represented the will of their members. The Conservatives argued that a 'human relations' approach to dealing with workplace disputes was better than strike action. By considering the feelings and opinions of workers, the party believed the discontent that could be used by socialist agitators could be avoided. A **paternalist** approach to running businesses would ensure that the interests of all parts of industry from the boardroom to the shop floor could be protected.

Industrial relations, 1951–64

The 1950s was an era of high employment and high trade union membership, and union membership grew throughout the 1960s and 1970s (see Table 1).

Table 1: Trade union membership, 1940-80

Year	Membership in 000s
1940	6,613
1945	7,815
1950	9,289
1955	9,741
1960	9,835
1965	10,325
1970	11,179
1975	11,656
1980	12,636

Source: Department of Employment Statistics Division (1892–1974); Certification Office (1974–2012)

A new prosperous union leadership emerged whose lifestyles were often far removed from their poorer members. TUC general secretaries, like Vic Feather and Len Murray, lived comfortable, affluent lives, though they worked long hours in the interests of their members. A more important difference between men like Feather and Murray and the rank and file of the unions was a difference in expectations. Both men had begun their union careers in the 1930s and 1940s, during periods of depression, war and **austerity** and had not been heavily influenced by post-war **materialism**. Many younger union members were keen to participate in the consumer boom of the 1950s and wanted the wage rises that would enable this to happen.

This meant that many members saw themselves having more in common with the more militant and unpaid shop stewards. Some stewards were able to build power bases within certain factories and called strike action long before a decision had been made by senior union management. These stewards had no constitutional right to call strikes and often staged walkouts before any negotiation with management could take place. The growth in the power of the stewards would lead to more aggressive confrontational unions in the 1960s and 1970s. This new attitude was less to do with the success of socialist ideas among the workers and more a product of the success of the new **consumerism**. Working-class men and women wanted pay rises in order to be able to participate in the consumer boom of the 1950s and 1960s, and with a decline in **deferential** attitudes throughout the period (see pages 98–9) they were less content to ask politely for them.

Unions and strike action

Unions were democratically organised bodies, they had constitutions, elected leaders and their members were able to vote on important issues that affected the union and their industry. Most strikes were supposed to be undertaken only after a national ballot of members had occurred, but there was no legislation that guaranteed this. By the mid-1960s the numbers of official and unofficial strikes being called without a ballot was rising, and by 1970, 10 million working days were lost to strike action. Often disputes were caused by factional feuds between different unions within the same factory. Walkouts could be caused by trivial disputes that had nothing to do with the actions of the management.

Deterioration in relations

Walter Monckton, the Conservative minister of labour, attempted a conciliatory policy with the unions but relations between the TUC and the Conservatives deteriorated. In the decade 1945–54 there were approximately 1,751 strikes per year involving just over half a million workers, but from 1955 to 1964 the number of strikes jumped to 2,521, involving over 1.1 million workers. The unions were often blamed by middle-class observers and newspapers such as *The Times* for Britain's relatively weak economic performance during the boom of the 1960s, but the figures suggest that this may not be entirely fair. They became a convenient excuse for deeper economic troubles (see page 35) and a source of resentment to many in Britain's middle class. There was a growing perception among the British public of unionised men being lazy, obstructive and too powerful.

I'm Alright Jack

In 1959 a hit comedy film, *I'm Alright Jack*, unexpectedly became the most successful movie of the year, even watched by the Queen and Prime Minister Harold Macmillan. It satirised British industrial relations by presenting a union shop steward, portrayed by Peter Sellers, as a pompous, incompetent bully, forcing the factory that employs him to go on strike over the tiniest, pettiest of issues. The fact that this film was so popular suggests that there was much about it that seemed familiar to viewers. The film's other main protagonist was another familiar figure - the incompetent recent graduate and new employee - played by Ian Carmichael.

Industrial relations, 1964–69

In 1964, thirteen years of Conservative political rule was swept away by the Labour Party, with a leader who understood the national mood (see page 19). Harold Wilson would preside over one of the most fateful periods in trade union history, when there was the opportunity for the government to fundamentally alter relations.

Wilson's public persona – beer drinking and pipe smoking, wearing a mac and holidaying on the Scilly Isles – was consciously designed to project an image that would be popular to the unions, but by the end of the decade he was proposing legislation that would curtail union power to a greater extent than any previous Labour prime minister had proposed.

Wildcat strikes

Throughout the 1960s wildcat strikes, those that were not officially sanctioned by the unions or the TUC, increased steadily. Wilson was reluctant to intervene but the image of the shop steward as a jumped-up Napoleon figure was becoming more and more accepted by the public who associated the actions of stewards with the wider union movement as a whole. It was a serious political problem for Labour who were seen as sympathetic to the unions due to their shared history. The potential for voters to react against the Labour Party as a result was clear to Wilson, but as 90 per cent of all strike action was unofficial, the leadership of the TUC were seemingly unable to control their members. An average of 3 million days were lost each year to strikes throughout the 1960s, but in 1968 that leapt to 4.7 million, causing *The Times* to call it 'the year of the strike'.

> ### The Girling Brake strike
> In 1968 a wildcat strike began at the Girling Brake Company, which had factories in Cheshire and Monmouthshire. The dispute began when the Amalgamated Union of Engineering and Foundry Workers (AEF) protested about a worker from another union using an oil pump that only AEF members were allowed to touch. The walkout stopped the manufacture of brakes for the British car industry. It led to 5,000 workers across the industry being temporarily laid off and millions of pounds in orders being lost.

Causes of militancy

The cause of increased militancy was less to do with the men satirised by *I'm Alright Jack*, and more the result of creeping inflation that had risen throughout the 1960s. The growth in affluence throughout the decade only benefited the professions that were rewarded with above-inflation pay increases and most unionised professions, particularly the miners, were frequently exempt. For many people, pay increases were cancelled out by inflation between 1967 and 1969 and the prosperity of the late 1950s and early 1960s appeared to be sliding into reverse.

'In Place of Strife'

Wilson's relationship with the unions while he arranged national wage increases to match price rises had been very close. The leadership of the TUC had been invited to 10 Downing Street for meetings and 'beer and sandwiches'.

The Conservative opposition under Edward Heath proposed union reform in 1968. Wilson, aware that it could be a potential election winner for them, decided to steal their thunder and create a policy of his own. In 1969 Barbara Castle, one of the rising stars of Wilson's cabinet, was tasked with the job of creating new laws to prevent wildcat strikes and limit union power. She was passionate that the unions must be forced to change, even though striking resulted in only 0.1 per cent of all working days being lost. She compiled a **White Paper** called 'In Place of Strife'. It proposed that:

- The government could order a strike ballot before official industrial action took place if a strike was deemed to threaten the economy. Castle knew that a majority of workers in most situations would prefer to remain at work and a ballot would reduce the power of the union bosses.
- Workers in unofficial strikes led by militant shop stewards could be ordered back to work by the secretary of state for employment for a 28-day 'cooling off' period.
- When unions fought one another in the workplace the dispute would go to an industrial board who would hand down a legally binding verdict.
- A strike that broke these rules could be declared illegal and the union could face stiff fines and its members could even be imprisoned.

There was widespread public support when the White Paper was published in January 1969 but the unions were opposed to it. The Labour Party was divided and when James Callaghan, Wilson's home secretary, opposed it, Wilson feared for his job and the planned legislation was scrapped. This victory for the unions would all but doom Edward Heath's attempts to reform them when he came to power in 1970.

Industrial relations, 1970–74

Heath's Industrial Relations Act (1971) attempted to introduce all the measures that Castle had proposed. In a time of soaring inflation this legislation proved ineffective because the TUC now refused to comply or co-operate, threatening expulsion for any union that did. Illegally striking shop stewards could now face jail but Heath's government hesitated in enforcing its own new rules. The group that would bring Heath to his knees was the miners.

The miners' strike

Miners had been consistently underpaid and undervalued throughout the 1960s; their wages were 3 per cent lower than manufacturing workers by the end of the decade and many of the high expectations of **nationalisation** (see page 33) had not been fulfilled. During a period of rising living standards, home ownership, overseas holidays and mass consumerism, thousands of poorly paid miners felt they had been excluded from the nation's prosperity. Rising prices caused by inflation during the late 1960s and early 1970s made strike action more likely, as the miners saw their living standards decline.

Throughout the 1960s the British coal industry had shrunk, the National Coal Board (NCB) had closed over 400 pits and 420,000 miners had been made redundant. The only way the National Union of Mineworkers (formed from the MFGB in 1945) was able to keep the NCB from closing many of the pits in poor parts of the country like south Wales was by making low wage claims. As a result many miners felt their wages were falling below those of other industrial workers.

However, in 1970 the union voted for a 33 per cent pay increase, which would increase miners' wages so they were more on a par with those of other industrial workers. The NUM leadership voted for strike action but it required a two-thirds majority and just over 50 per cent agreed to strike. Despite this, a wave of unofficial strikes broke out across the north of England and south Wales. The Heath government had imposed a pay policy that restricted possible pay rises to 8 per cent and in December 1971 a second ballot (now with changed NUM rules that meant only a 55 per cent majority was needed for a strike to be called) was successful and a strike began in January 1972.

'Flying pickets'

The most high-profile union member during the dispute was Arthur Scargill, leader of the Barnsley Area Strike Committee. He developed a new tactic of 'flying pickets' using a group of 1,000 miners to quickly blockade power stations and coal depots. In 1972 this reduced electricity output to 25 per cent. Scargill had 40,000 miners picketing 500 separate sites across the country. Heath feared widespread violence and loss of life if the striking miners were confronted directly.

Unlike the Baldwin government in 1926 (see page 8), Heath had not sufficiently planned for the strike and had no available resources to beat it. When Scargill succeeded in shutting down the west Midlands gas board's Saltley coke depot in Birmingham, the government capitulated, offering a huge 27 per cent pay rise.

Arthur Scargill, 1938–

Arthur Scargill was a Marxist trade unionist on the left of the National Union of Mineworkers (NUM). He believed that the struggle against the Heath government in 1973 was more than a fight for better wages; he believed it was an attack on the capitalist system. He was popular with large sections of working-class people during the dispute, but during the 1980s would be seen as a far more divisive figure (see pages 201–2).

'Who governs Britain?'

A second strike in the winter of 1973–74 was called by the NUM who, realising that the oil crisis of 1973 had left the country dependent on coal, saw it as an opportunity to gain fresh pay increases from the government for its members. The strike meant that coal-fired power stations began to run short on supplies of coal, and electricity production declined. This led to power cuts, causing the government to declare a **state of emergency** and order a three-day working week between January and March 1974. All businesses were supplied with electricity for three days a week and employees were forced to stay at home for the rest of the time.

In 1974 Heath went to the polls with the slogan 'Who governs Britain?', asking the voters to back him against the unions. The Conservative's subsequent defeat showed that the public had no confidence in their ability to deal with the unions.

Industrial relations, 1974–79

The new Labour government repealed Heath's Industrial Relations Act and negotiated a new policy with the unions called the 'social contract'. The social contract was created as a voluntary code to prevent the need for a formal incomes policy with specified limits for pay rises, but it rested on the assumption that union bosses could persuade their members to accept pay restraint. Not only were union bosses becoming less influential compared to union shop stewards, but it was difficult for them to ask their members to stick to single 6 per cent pay rises during a period of 27 per cent inflation.

In 1975 the TUC agreed to pay increases of £6 per week to workers earning less than £8,500. They accepted further limits in 1976 and rejected a motion at the 1976 TUC conference to end the social contract and return to free pay bargaining

When Wilson resigned in ill health in April 1976, he was succeeded by Callaghan and in 1978 the prospects for Labour in the next general election seemed good; the unions had complied with Callaghan's call for pay restraint and had he called an election in mid-1978, he would probably have won.

'The winter of discontent'

James Callaghan and his chancellor Denis Healey made tackling inflation a much more important economic priority than former Labour leaders (see page 36).

By 1977, Denis Healey believed that inflation was being brought back under control and that the social contract had run its course. He believed that free bargaining could return but warned against 'greedy' unions demanding too much. The following year he was forced to backtrack as inflation soared once again and he enforced a strict 5 per cent pay increase for low-paid workers. This resulted in a winter of strike action in 1978–79, known as the 'winter of discontent', that the government was powerless to prevent.

Ford pay negotiations

Ford, the car manufacturing giant, attempted to enforce the government's pay policy; in response 15,000 auto workers went on strike on 22 September. The strike was unofficial when it began but by 5 October the TGWU had endorsed it, causing other Ford workers to strike, with the total number of workers refusing to work rising to 57,000. Ford offered a rise of 17 per cent which meant they incurred government penalties, but it also showed that the social contract was unenforceable.

The left of the Labour Party also sabotaged the social contract, voting through a motion at the party conference in October that the government stop intervening in pay negotiations between workers and management.

Haulage strike

The government now had no way of enforcing pay restraint and the unions seized the opportunity to gain pay increases. In December 1978 lorry drivers began an overtime ban, demanding a 40 per cent pay rise. Callaghan was reluctant to declare a state of emergency as Heath had done, even though it would have enabled the Army to drive lorries and oil tankers. The TGWU picketed oil refineries, meaning that petrol could not reach petrol stations and heating oil could not reach schools, hospitals and homes. The situation was exacerbated by one of the longest, coldest winter since 1947.

Public sector strike

The next group to go on strike was Britain's public sector workers. On 22 January 1979 millions of low-paid public employees went on strike as public sector unions, such as the National Union of Public Employees (NUPE), tried to ensure that their members got the same pay rises as employees in the private sector. More than one-third of public sector employees took home £40 a week and public sector unions demanded it rise to £60. The nurses' union, the Royal College of Nursing, demanded a 25 per cent wage rise for nurses. Public sector unions began to lose control over their members, who declared strike action in vital services such as the ambulance service and 999 emergency telephone lines. The British press reported that cancer patients had to use the London Underground to get to hospital appointments. In January Liverpool's grave diggers went on strike, and while the numbers of striking men were small (just 80), the newspapers printed full-page stories of mortuaries filling with unburied bodies and the possibility of having to bury people at sea. Another visual example of the chaos strikes had brought to Britain was the mountains of rubbish in city centres caused by refuse collectors going on strike.

The government offered public sector strikers an 11 per cent pay rise. They attempted to negotiate directly with the unions, but gradually realised that the unions themselves had lost control over their members. Union bosses were unable to end strikes directly, instead they gradually decreased as strikers either got the pay increases they wanted or decided to return to work anyway.

▲ Rubbish piling up during the winter of discontent. What impression does this photo give of the winter of discontent?

Shifting public attitudes

The main consequence of the winter of discontent was a dramatic shift in public attitudes against the trade union movement. Whereas a decade earlier in 1969, 60 per cent of people said they had positive views of the unions, in 1979 only 20 per cent did. There was dissatisfaction about the power of unions coming from within the union movement itself. When Margaret Thatcher was elected in 1979, promising to curtail union power, one in three trade unionists voted for her.

> ### Work together
> The attitudes of the public, the government, the rank and file of the union movement and the union leadership were slowly drifting apart during the 1960s and 1970s. Why? What factors were causing this to happen? Debate in pairs and place the following factors in order of importance:
>
> - government policy
> - union strikes
> - union members' expectations
> - actions of shop stewards.

Theme 1 A changing political and economic environment, 1918–79

Chapter summary

- The short post-war economic boom in 1919–20 led to an increase in Labour disputes, which decreased in times of economic hardship from 1921.
- The failure of Ramsay MacDonald's Labour government led to increased militancy and the General Strike of May 1926.
- The failure of the strike led to a decrease in union power throughout the late 1920s and 1930s, further weakened by mass unemployment.
- The relationship between government and labour changed during the war as the government once again took control over the economy; strikes were illegal but that did not prevent them happening and the government was generally conciliatory.
- The experience of wartime controls of industry raised workers' hopes for full nationalisation after the war.
- The 1950s and 1960s saw mass union membership and high employment, though resentments towards union attitudes were growing. Strikes were increasingly the result of militant shop stewards.
- Wildcat strikes by 1969 had become a major political problem for the government, though they were less of an economic problem than they appeared.
- Barbara Castle was tasked with the job of drafting union reform legislation and she produced 'In Place of Strife' in 1969. The proposals had widespread public popularity but union opposition. Wilson eventually abandoned the proposals, fearing for his own position.
- Edward Heath's government passed the Industrial Relations Act (1971) but met with opposition from the unions who refused to co-operate.
- A miners' strike over pay paralysed Heath's government in 1972 and when they went on strike again in 1974 they brought down the Heath government.
- In the late 1970s the unions went on strike again causing the 'winter of discontent', giving Margaret Thatcher a mandate for her policies of union reform in the 1979 election.

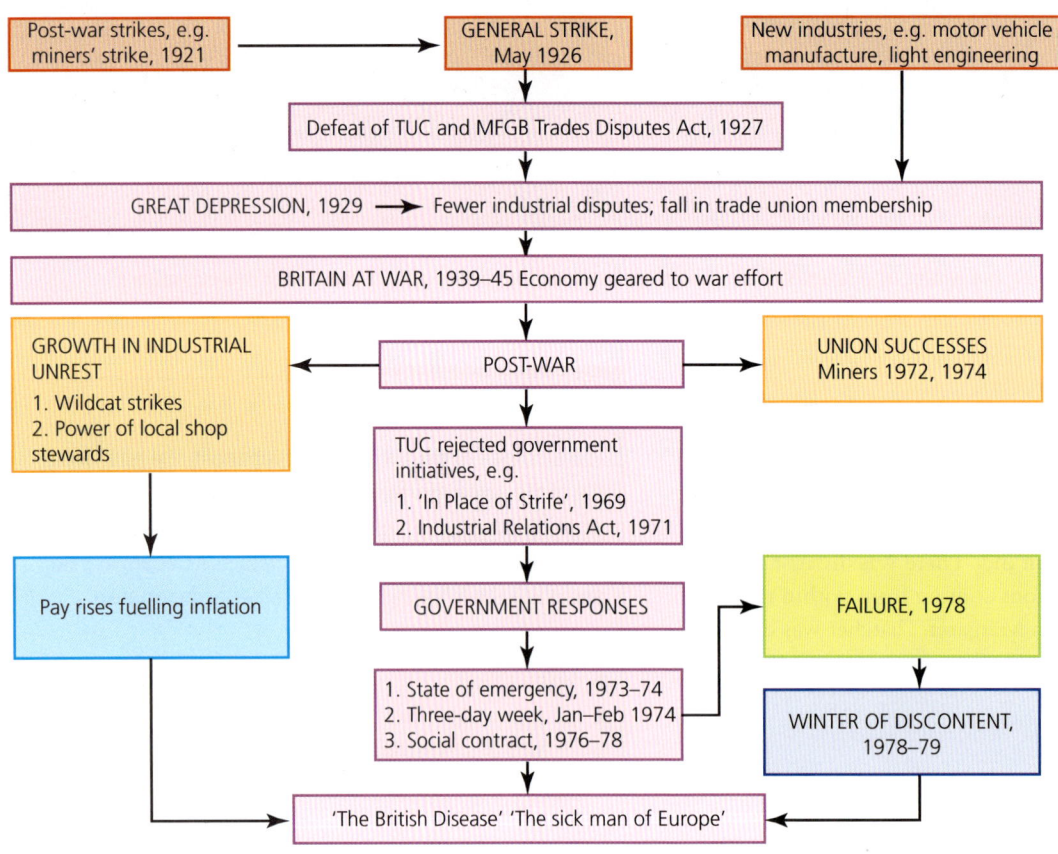

▲ Summary diagram: Change and challenge in the workplace

Recommended reading: A changing political and economic environment, 1918–79

P. Clarke, *Hope and Glory: Britain 1900–2000* (Penguin, 2004). An excellent and accessible overview of British political, economic, social and cultural change throughout the twentieth century.

M. Dintenfass, *The Decline of Industrial Britain: 1870–1980* (Routledge, 1992). An accessible study guide to the transformation that the British economy underwent in the twentieth century from an industrial to a post-industrial society.

R. Floud, J. Humphries and P. Johnson, *The Cambridge Economic History of Modern Britain: Volume 2* (Cambridge University Press, 2014). This is a very thorough history of Britain's post-industrial history, presenting several different arguments and perspectives from historians on Britain's economy in the twentieth century.

C. Howell, *Trade Unions and the State: The Construction of Industrial Relations Institutions in Britain, 1890–2000* (Princeton, 2005). A skillful examination of the developing relationship between the trade union movement and the state and how legislation has been used to mediate it.

D. Kynaston, *Austerity Britain, 1945–51* (Bloomsbury Publishing, 2007). A detailed and in-depth examination of Britain in the six years after the Second World War. Political, economic and social history is covered in depth.

D. Kynaston, *City of London: The History* (Vintage, 2011). A thorough and authoritative history of Britain's financial industry and its role in shaping Britain and the world economy.

M. Pugh, *The Making of Modern British Politics, 1867–1939* (Wiley-Blackwell, 2002). A very clear account of the evolution of Britain's three main political parties and the impact of war and economic crisis on politics.

C. Wrigley, *British Trade Unions since 1933* (Cambridge University Press, 2002). A comprehensive history of the trade union movement in Britain since the Great Depression, focussing on the changing relationship between the unions and British public opinion in the post-war era.

Essay technique: Deploying detail

So far we have looked at how to structure your answers with a clear line of argument (see page 41). This is essential, but you also need to ensure that your paragraphs are sufficiently detailed. Vague or imprecise statements will weaken your essay.

What is detail?

Essentially, correct dates, proper names and statistics are all examples of detail. You can also increase the level of detail in your essays by using the correct technical vocabulary: words or phrases like 'corporatism' or 'social contract' that you have learned while studying this unit.

How to use detail

You should use detail to support the points that you are making. The main points provide the overall structure for the essay. The details help prove the points that you are making. Imagine you are answering the following question:

> **How successfully did British governments manage the problems of industrial conflict, 1945–79?**

You might decide to argue that initially they were successful but by the 1960s and 1970s industrial conflict became almost impossible for governments to handle. You might support this line of argument by referring to the following:

- numbers of strike days lost in the 1960s and 1970s
- percentages of pay increases demanded
- specific policies that were attempted (corporatism, social contract, the 1971 Industrial Relations Act).

Activity: Adding detail

Here is a plan in answer to the question above:

- **Paragraph 1:** Broadly successful – Labour's relationship with the unions, 1945–51
- **Paragraph 2:** Successes and failures – corporatism and compromise, 1950s and 1960s
- **Paragraph 3:** Short-lived success – Wilson and Callaghan and the social contract
- **Paragraph 4:** Failures in the 1970s – Heath and the miners, Callaghan and the 'winter of discontent'

Using your notes, find at least three pieces of detail to support each of these points.

Try to select a variety of types of detail: if possible make sure you use statistics, dates, the names of people and organisations, and technical vocabulary.

Question practice

1. Was economic depression the main reason for union unrest in the period, 1918–39? Explain your answer. **AS**
2. How far did the government's relationship with the unions change in the period, 1964–79? **AS**
3. How far did British governments manage to resolve the country's economic problems, 1945–79?

Paper 1 Britain transformed, 1918–97

Theme 2 Creating a welfare state, 1918–79

In this theme you will consider the following:
- **Unemployment benefit and poor relief:** the extent and nature of social welfare provision, 1918-39; the impact of the Second World War and the Labour government and consensus, 1939-64; and the reasons for increasing challenges to state provision, 1964-79.
- **Public healthcare:** health provision, 1819-45; the creation and impact of the NHS, 1945-79 and the challenge of medical advances.
- **Education and widening opportunities:** education policy, 1918-43; the significance of the Butler Act, 1944 and the development of comprehensive education; the growth and social impact of university education, 1918-79.

The big picture

Between 1918 and 1951 successive governments created a comprehensive welfare state. Building on the foundations laid by reforming governments prior to the First World War, governments in the 1920s and 1930s began building new welfare institutions. While the political parties disagreed over the extent of welfare provision, following 1918 there was a new consensus. It was widely agreed that government had a duty to provide welfare in terms of unemployment benefit, some kind of healthcare and education. Put another way, welfare was perceived as a right, an entitlement for British workers.

The 1945–51 Labour government took welfare provision to another level. Keen not to repeat the mass unemployment and widespread poverty that followed the First World War, Labour ministers introduced comprehensive welfare provision, designed to support British workers from the cradle to the grave. The National Health Service was, perhaps, the most radical aspect of Labour's welfare state. It provided world-class healthcare to all in need and was free at the point of delivery.

Labour's welfare state was supported by all mainstream politicians during the 1950s and 1960s. However, in the early 1970s the political consensus began to break down. Politicians associated with the New Right argued that social welfare, including unemployment benefit, trapped people in a culture of dependency. Moreover, they argued that growing welfare bills were diverting resources from economic growth and therefore undermining Britain's long-term economic performance. There were concerns that hospitals were poorly managed and that education was failing to equip and discipline students.

TIMELINE

1911	Unemployment Insurance Act
1918	Education Act
1919	Ministry of Health established
1920	Unemployment Insurance Act
1921	Unemployment Insurance (Amendment) Act
1926	Hadow Report
1929	Local government Act
1931	National Economy Act
1934	Unemployment Act
1935	Pioneer Health Centre opened in Peckham
1939	Evacuation began
1939	Emergency Medical Service created
1940	Food rationing introduced
1942	Beveridge Report published
1944	Government White Paper on health
1944	'Butler' Education Act
1946	National Insurance Act
1946	Industrial Injuries Act
1946	Family Allowances came into effect
1948	NHS created
1959	Mental Health Act
1959	Crowther Report
1962	Macmillan's Hospital Plan
1963	Newsom Report
1963	Robbins Report
1967	Abortion Act
1970	National Insurance Act
1971	First students enrolled in the Open University
1973	NHS Reorganisation Act
1975	Child Benefits Act
1976	Education Act

2a: Provision of social welfare

Overview

By 1918 it was widely accepted that government had a part to play in ensuring individuals had a basic level of social security. While the extent of welfare benefit was contested, all parties used government power to provide benefits for the poor.

During the 1920s and 1930s there were a variety of different benefits available to the poor. However, there were important debates concerning who should qualify, and how far the British economy could afford to pay for public welfare. On the right politicians argued that welfare should be a minimal safety net, funded entirely through the contributions of workers. On the left, by contrast, politicians argued for a more extensive system that would help to address the long-term inequalities in British society.

The 1945–51 Labour government was a turning point in the provision of social welfare. Labour politicians were determined to use state power to ensure that the mass poverty of the interwar years was not repeated. The National Insurance Act and National Assistance Act created new welfare rights to guarantee that everyone was able to afford basic goods and services, even in times of unemployment.

During the 1950s and 1960s Conservatives and Labour governments remained committed to this essential vision. However, by the late 1960s there were increasing concerns that social welfare had failed to improve the opportunities of the poor. Moreover, economic difficulties meant that there was pressure to cut welfare spending. Consequently, the cross-party consensus that had supported the welfare state began to breakdown during the 1970s.

This chapter explores the extent of social welfare provision in Britain in the twentieth century and the factors that influenced it through the following sections:

1. Social welfare provision, 1918–39
2. The impact of the Second World War
3. The Labour government and consensus, 1939–64
4. Challenges to welfare provision, 1964–79

1 Social welfare provision, 1918–39

This section considers the growth of welfare provision in the interwar period. It deals with the key changes in welfare, and debates over welfare provision. Specifically, it deals with:

1. Welfare provision in 1918
2. The growth of welfare provision, 1918–39

Note it down

Using bullet points (see page ix) make notes on the key features of welfare provision, 1918–39. Make sure that you note down:
- the causes of change
- the key changes
- detail that demonstrates the nature and impact of those changes.

When note taking, it is a good idea to group your bullet points into themes so that you can see how change occurred throughout the period. The major themes in this section relate to: the goals of welfare provision; the impact of the depression on welfare provision; and the effectiveness of welfare provision.

Welfare provision in 1918

In 1918 government provision for the poor was based on:

- the **Victorian Poor Laws**
- Liberal welfare reforms of the early twentieth century.

Many of the **welfare institutions** of the Victorian Poor Laws remained in place until 1930. Poor Law **guardians** levied a poor rate on local landowners or businesses, to support the system of **workhouses**.

In addition, some unemployed men were entitled to unemployment benefit. The pre-war Liberal government introduced **unemployment insurance** in 1911. The scheme provided them with seven shillings a week

Workhouses

Workhouses had originally been designed to house impoverished families but, by the twentieth century, they had become homes for the sick and the destitute; some had evolved into hospitals. The workhouse system was in decline after the First World War, and was abolished by the Local government Act of 1930. In spite of the abolition of the workhouse in 1930, many stayed open as **public assistance institutions**.

unemployment benefits for up to fifteen weeks in a year. This was a relatively low payment as in 1911 average wages were around twenty shillings a week. Women workers were also covered by the scheme. Moreover, women covered by the scheme, including the wives of working men, were entitled to a maternity allowance. Significantly, the scheme covered only around 10 per cent of Britain's total working male population. The money had to be collected from **labour exchanges**, also set up by the Liberal government, to ensure that men looked for work while they claimed.

Between 1900 and 1918 there was a major shift in the political consensus about welfare provision. Until 1914, most welfare had been administered by a patchwork of local, voluntary and charitable organisations. This reflected the Victorian view that private charity was the best way of helping the poor. However, in the early part of the twentieth century it became widely accepted that the state had a much bigger part to play in poor relief. This view was influential in the development of welfare in the interwar period.

The growth of welfare provision, 1918–39

One measure that significantly enlarged the state's role in welfare provisions was the Unemployment Insurance Act of 1920, which extended social welfare in the following ways:

- National insurance was extended from the 4 million workers covered in 1919 to 11.4 million in 1921.
- Benefits were increased to 75p for unemployed men and 60p for unemployed women. These payments were still low compared to average earnings. Low-paid workers such as bus drivers earned about £3 a week.

The state's role became significantly larger than originally envisaged. In 1911 Lloyd George assumed that insurance would be **self-financing** as payments were based on contributions from employers and employees. However, the 1920 Act covered millions of non-contributors who had been affected by mass unemployment. Indeed, the Act created a state funded **'dole'** which was available to the unemployed without a **means test**. This extension of state spending was justified by:

- the need to support the unprecedentedly high levels of unemployment (see page 26)
- fears that extreme and widespread poverty might lead to revolution as it had done in Russia in 1917

- the popular desire to support soldiers who had fought and risked their lives for Britain in the First World War.

Nonetheless, as unemployment receded during the 1920s, there was no reduction in the state's commitment to welfare provision.

Welfare in the 1930s

The size of the welfare budget became controversial in the early 1930s due to the state of the British economy. The chancellor, Philip Snowden, proposed a 10 per cent cut in unemployment benefit. Arthur Henderson, the foreign secretary, led a cabinet revolt against the proposals which brought the government down (see page 9). As a result, Labour leader Ramsay MacDonald was forced to form a **National Government** with the Conservative Party.

The National Economy Act, 1931

MacDonald's National Government reformed welfare provision significantly. The National Economy Act of 1931 introduced a means test for unemployment benefits in order to limit the overall benefits bill. The result was a policy that was detested in the most deprived parts of the country and that exacerbated hardship for many of the most vulnerable.

First, the means test disqualified 'short-time workers'. This dramatically affected men who worked occasional days in collieries or shipyards but were dependent on welfare payments the rest of the time. The impact was most keenly felt in the most deprived parts of the country such as Tyneside and south Wales, where most workers worked reduced hours. The disqualification from benefits meant that unemployment made more economic sense than work. This created a sort of poverty trap in which if someone went to work benefits would stop and they would be worse off.

Second, the Act changed the system so that benefits could only be claimed for six months. After this people needed to reapply.

Finally, the Act introduced 'transitional payments' that were designed to support unemployed people after the first six months. In order to get transitional payments, claimants were required to register at a local labour exchange. The payments could be authorised by the local **Public Assistance Committee**, which would investigate the claimant's circumstances to make sure

Theme 2 Creating a welfare state, 1918–79

they were not trying to abuse the system. All forms of household income were taken into account when assessing what rate of relief a claimant was entitled to. It required recipients of relief to have exhausted all savings and to have sold all valuables before they gained a meagre weekly amount to survive on.

The change in the system had significant consequences for working families. Many low-income families relied on the incomes of all the adults in the family to survive. Now, unemployed parents with working children would lose their benefits if their children lived with them, even though their children's wages would not provide for the needs of the whole family. Consequently this measure forced some children of working age to leave the family home.

The means test became the single most unpopular piece of legislation passed by the National Government throughout the decade. Its measures resulted in protest marches from the poorest parts of the country to London (see page 30).

The Unemployment Act, 1934

The 1934 Unemployment Act built on the changes introduced in 1931, continuing the distinction between short-term and long-term unemployment. First, the Act reversed the 10 per cent cut in benefit for the short-term unemployed, restoring benefit payments to their 1930 level for the first six months. After six months, the long-term unemployed could apply to the newly created Unemployment Assistance Board for further benefits. Means testing of the long-term unemployed continued, but payments were made at a lower rate than those provided between 1931 and 1934.

The cut in long-term benefits led to large public protests. For example, 300,000 people demonstrated against the cuts in south Wales alone. Consequently, in January 1935 the government introduced 'standstill regulations' which suspended the cut. The 'standstill' indicates the extent to which popular pressure protected welfare provision in the 1930s.

By 1939 the worst of the depression had passed and unemployment had dropped sharply, falling from 3 million in 1933 (20 per cent of the adult working population) to just under 1.4 million in 1939 (9 per cent of the adult working population). Crucially, during the 1930s all of Britain's major political parties had accepted that the state had a significant role to play in providing unemployment benefit.

2 The impact of the Second World War

The Second World War greatly enlarged the role of the state. The government became responsible for directing the economy in order to ensure that troops and workers were supplied (see page 31). The state also took on powers to ensure the welfare of the population and state provision of welfare increased significantly. Specifically, the state co-ordinated large operations such as evacuation and rationing. In December 1942 the Beveridge Report was published, offering a blueprint for a more socially equal post-war society.

> ### Note it down
> Write bullet points (see page ix) in this section about the impact of the Second World War on welfare provision. Your bullet points should address the following issues:
> - How far did evacuation and rationing make people feel they lived in a more equal society?
> - What was the significance of the Beveridge Report?

Evacuation and rationing

During the Second World War, the government took control of people's lives more than at any previous time. Children were evacuated often from poor urban centres to safe areas in the countryside. This had the impact of bringing together sectors of society that might never otherwise have met. Rationing meanwhile made people feel more equal in that they were all suffering hardship for the war effort – and yet food rationing, with shortages of unhealthy foodstuffs, made people generally healthier.

Evacuation

Evacuations moved children out of the cities to the countryside in order to protect them from bombing. The first evacuation in 1939 relocated 1.5 million children. However the evacuation authorities, led by Home Secretary Sir John Anderson, did not cater for the needs of the evacuees. Rather, Anderson assumed that families or private charities would provide. Private charity was not sufficient to meet the needs of evacuees and in the initial evacuations children from poor homes were transported to the country without spare clothes, bedding or food. Later evacuations were substantially different. The government learned from its mistakes and ensured that children were provided with the essentials. Social workers were also made available to help children who were distressed.

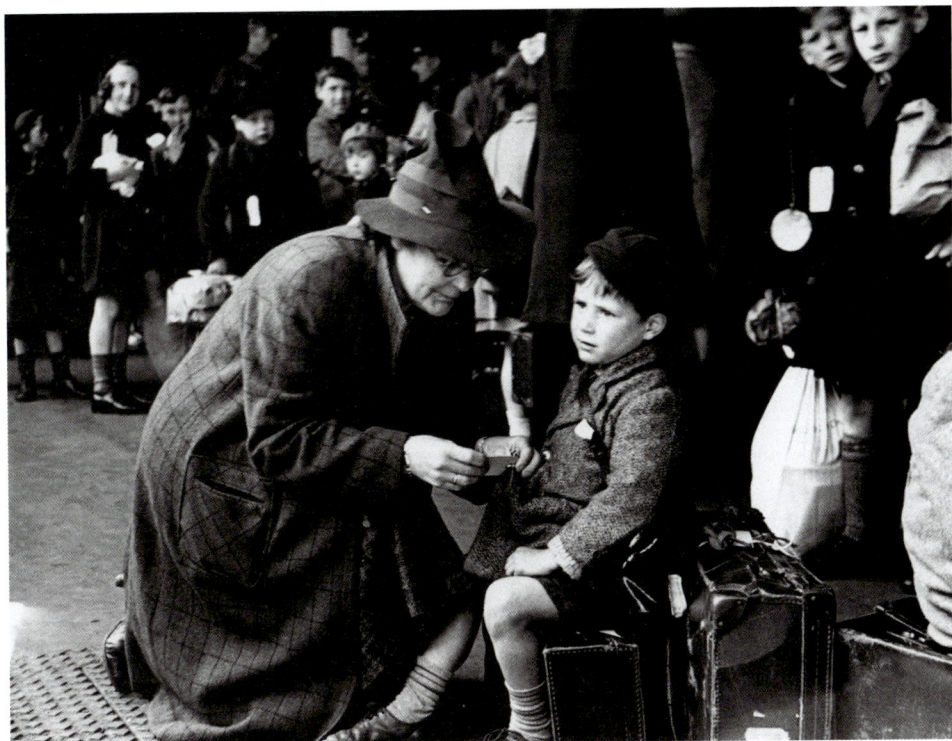

▲ A woman checks the details of a child waiting to be evacuated, 1942.
What impression does this photograph give of the process of evacuation?

Rationing

As early as January 1940, the government introduced food rationing, not least because surveys showed the public welcomed it. The first items to be rationed were products such as bacon, butter and sugar, which British people consumed in prodigious quantities. Items such as cooking fat, meat, tea, jam and eggs followed over the course of the next year. A complex points system was introduced so people could buy items such as biscuits, tinned fruit and fish each month to add more variety to their diet. Many food items such as bread were not rationed and people grew vegetables in great quantities.

Nutritionists tend to agree that the British diet improved as a result of rationing because less healthy foods tended to be unavailable and were supplemented by healthier foods. As a result people were generally healthier. Alcohol and tobacco, while not rationed, were often in short supply – the price of a pint of beer doubled from 3p to 7p between 1939 and 1942.

Clothes

Clothes were rationed from June 1941 with a yearly allowance per person of 66 coupons – a lady's dress usually took about 11 coupons. Utility clothing was introduced based on simple styles to save on material. Some commentators remark that the quality of pre-war clothing was so good that people could continue wearing it; it wasn't until the end of the war that it took on a shabby appearance. Washing was more problematic with restrictions on coal and fuel for heating, exhortations to only have shallow baths and soap rationed to a measly three ounces per month. Commentators say crowded spaces could be rather smelly!

Effects of rationing

While there was a thriving **black market** and many items were available for a price which only certain sections of the population could afford, there was a genuine feeling that rationing equalised society and enhanced the feeling that everyone was making a sacrifice for the war effort. The mood when rationing continued when the war was over darkened and people grew more resentful – but during the war years themselves people generally accepted it and made the most of what they had.

Improved diet

The state also used its power to improve the diet of British people. The government's Food Policy Committee, chaired by Clement Attlee, the Labour leader, authorised subsidised milk and heating fuel for mothers with small children.

Theme 2 Creating a welfare state, 1918–79

The war years, therefore, were actually a period in which one-third of the population who had been unable to eat enough during the depression, found their standards of living improve, even during a period of rationing.

The Beveridge Report, 1942

The Beveridge Report set out a vision of post-war Britain in which state welfare conquered the five evils of squalor, ignorance, want, idleness and disease. It was written by the social reformer William Beveridge in 1942 as part of broader attempts by the government to plan the reconstruction of Britain after the end of the war.

The report advocated a new relationship of co-operation between the state and the individual. Beveridge was not suggesting that the state should take over responsibility for the running of people's lives. He was keen to provide welfare, but also to preserve the independence of the British people. He argued that government action:

> should not stifle incentive, opportunity, responsibility. In establishing a national minimum, it should leave room and encouragement for voluntary action by each individual to provide more than that minimum for himself and his family.

The report advocated **universal benefits**, rejecting the means tests introduced in the 1930s (see page 59). In essence, Beveridge argued for flat rate of contributions from all wage earners to pay for welfare benefits and a flat rate of benefit irrespective of individual circumstances.

Reactions to the report

Beveridge's vision was extremely popular. Indeed, it sold several hundred thousand copies. It was also used as propaganda. British troops stationed overseas were sent copies to encourage them to fight for a better Britain. The Beveridge Report seemed to articulate the hopes of most Britons of a Britain free of poverty. The **Ministry of Information** monitored public opinion and found the report to have support from all elements of society. It was well received by all of Britain's newspapers, too, including *The Times* and *Telegraph* which traditionally supported small government and low taxes.

The government decided not to implement the recommendations immediately. Prime Minister Winston Churchill spoke out against introducing excessive welfare provision after the war. It became clear, however, that the post-war general election would be fought over the recommendations in the report and the Conservative, Liberal and Labour parties all adopted the report to differing degrees.

3 The Labour government and consensus, 1939–64

In 1945, Labour argued that state planning should continue in order to rebuild Britain and solve the problems of deprivation and unemployment. Labour politicians such as Clement Attlee, Herbert Morrison and Stafford Cripps had been senior ministers in the wartime National Government, and had been involved in government planning. They argued that the methods that had won the war should be used to win the peace.

The 1945 Labour manifesto, *Let Us Face the Future*, made the connection between social welfare and economic success. It argued that economic success was necessary to pay for welfare. However, it also claimed that welfare could promote economic growth and efficiency. Healthy, better-educated workers would be better equipped to work productively in a modern economy. In this sense, the Labour Party assumed that welfare would aid national efficiency and therefore the economic benefits of welfare would justify large welfare bills. Its landslide victory in 1945 resulted in a dramatic change in the nature and role of the welfare state in Britain.

Note it down

This section is concerned with how far the Labour government created the modern welfare state. There is a lot of legislation to remember so a spider diagram might be most appropriate (see page x). The spider's body should be labelled 'Creation of a welfare state' and each leg a piece of legislation:

- The Family Allowances Act, 1945
- The National Insurance Act, 1946
- The Industrial Injuries Act, 1946
- The National Assistance Act, 1948.

In each case you need to consider the significance of the Act.

Finally draw a leg to consider how far there was a consensus of welfare provision in the period 1945-64.

The modern welfare state

The post-war Labour government is credited with the creation of the modern welfare state. A plethora of laws were passed embracing social security and welfare, housing and healthcare, which changed the face of Britain and led to the idea that the state would care for its citizens 'from the cradle to the grave'. This became a crucial factor in the **post-war consensus** (see page 15).

The Family Allowances Act, 1945

The Family Allowances Act created child benefits for the first time. From August 1946, the Act gave an allowance of five shillings (25p) a week for each child (with the exception of the family's eldest child). Significantly, the benefit was payable to the mother, rather than the father. Therefore, the Act also led to an improvement in the status of mothers who did not work outside the home, because they had a small income that was independent of their husband.

The National Insurance Act, 1946

Labour's National Insurance Act:

- levied a 4s 11d (25p) weekly charge on the wages of all workers
- made unemployment benefits and sickness benefits available to all workers
- paid a state pension to all men over 65 and all women over 60. Pensions were £1.30 a week for a single person and £2.10 for a married couple.

One of the guiding principles of the Act was that of 'universality', meaning everyone, irrespective of wealth, would be covered. The creator of the Act, Labour MP James Griffiths, said that everyone 'from the barrow boy to the field marshal' would be covered and would be required to make contributions. In this sense the Act abolished means testing.

Health minister Aneurin Bevan had initially hoped that pensions would be gradually phased in over a twenty-year period, but Griffiths argued that many people already of pensionable age were poor and had lived long hard-working lives. Griffiths believed they were entitled to pensions, even though they had not contributed to the scheme. Both Griffiths and Bevan were influenced by the harsh experiences of the 1930s and the poverty experienced by Britain's working classes.

One major flaw with the Act was the fact that the amount British people paid into the scheme was the same, whether they were rich or poor. This meant that poor people paid a much larger percentage of their income in national insurance than the rich.

The Industrial Injuries Act, 1946

The Industrial Injuries Act extended welfare by giving workers the right to compensation for accidents and injuries in the workplace. The national insurance fund paid this out. An average of 2,425 people were killed each year at work in the 1940s. Mining was particularly dangerous, accounting for over one-quarter of the total number of deaths and injuries in the workplace.

The National Assistance Act, 1948

The National Assistance Act offered welfare to those who were not covered by national insurance as they did not work. The homeless, disabled and unmarried mothers were all able to claim, as were pensioners living in poverty. The Act abolished the unpopular Public Assistance Committees and replaced them with a centralised National Assistance Board. The Act delegated many responsibilities for social welfare to local authorities, for example requiring them to find suitable accommodation for people in need, promoting welfare of the handicapped and encouraging voluntary groups to provide facilities and help.

The National Health Service

Perhaps the major achievement of the welfare state legislation was the creation of the National Health Service in July 1948, which will be dealt with the next chapter.

The welfare consensus, 1939–64

From 1939 to 1964 there was a broad agreement between the major parties over the role of the state and the provision of welfare. The centre and left of the Conservative Party saw welfare as an essential ingredient of modern Britain. Harold Macmillan was an early advocate of Conservative welfarism. In 1938 he wrote *The Middle Way*, a book advocating government action to regulate private enterprise, and end social deprivation through welfare. As Conservative prime minister from 1957 to 1963, Macmillan wanted the government to ensure that there was no return to the poverty and deprivation of the 1930s. He believed that the upper and **middle classes** had a moral responsibility to help provide for the poor. Moreover, he also knew that cuts to welfare would be unpopular, and therefore make the Conservatives unelectable. Macmillan's style of Conservatism proved very popular. Radicals in the Conservative Party, such as Treasury Minister Enoch Powell, who advocated cutting welfare were in a minority in the Conservative Party in the 1950s and 1960s.

In spite of the consensus Britain spent less on welfare throughout the 1950s and 1960s than France and **West Germany**. However, during the 1950s the cost of social welfare as a percentage of total **GDP** rose from 3 to 4 per cent, with pensions taking up a further 3 per cent.

Significantly, welfare spending did not end poverty. Notably in 1965 the **Child Poverty Action Group** claimed that 720,000 children were living in poverty. The increasing welfare costs and the persistence of poverty led to a debate over the effectiveness and desirability of the welfare state. Indeed, by 1970 the Conservatives began to reconsider their commitment to high levels of welfare spending.

4 Challenges to state welfare provision, 1964–79

One of the main reasons that the welfare state was put under pressure between 1964 and 1979 was Britain's economic decline (see page 35), which made it seem unaffordable to many right-wing thinkers and MPs who increasingly posed challenges to welfare provision.

> **Note it down**
>
> This section is involved with challenges to the welfare system. Use the 1:2 system (page x) to make notes in answer to the following questions:
> - How far did economic decline lead to problems with welfare provision?
> - How persuasive were the right-wing challenges to welfare provision?
> - How far did the welfare policies of 1974–79 illustrate the problems with welfare provision during this period?

Economic decline

As part of the 1964 General Election campaign Labour promised to increase welfare spending. However, when Labour won the election, the new prime minister, Harold Wilson, discovered that Britain had serious economic problems that had been hidden by the previous Conservative chancellor Reginald Maudling. Wilson and his chancellor James Callaghan discovered an £800 million **budget deficit**, the result of Britain's overspending on its military and welfare system, and of too many imports entering the country during a period of mass **consumerism** (see pages 137–138).

Wilson's advisors suggested that he cut welfare benefits in order to rescue the economy. Wilson refused, due to his commitment to the welfare state, and his desire to win the next election. Wilson's decision to stick to his commitments on expanding welfare provision meant that throughout his time in office there were successive economic crises. His government was forced to pay for a growing welfare state in the 1960s by increasing levels of taxation. This growing pressure on individual taxpayers inevitably led to a growing resentment against the cost of welfare. By 1966 social welfare costs had risen to 5 per cent of GDP and were continuing to grow.

The National Insurance Act, 1970

In 1970 Edward Heath led the Conservative Party to victory. Not only did he inherit mounting inflation and trade union problems from Labour (see pages 50–1), but also a welfare bill that many in his party thought was unsustainable.

The manifesto pledges that were discussed before the election at the Selsdon meeting (see page 20) were described within the party as a 'quiet revolution', as they broke with many of the economic ideas that had underpinned the post-war consensus. Union reform, ending subsidies for national industries and ending state control of wages and prices were all proposed, but the manifesto actually pledged to increase spending on the welfare state and pensions. It stated that:

> The next Conservative government will take urgent action to give some pension as of right to the over-eighties who now get no retirement pension at all. We will improve the benefits payable to those who are seriously ill or disabled, and introduce a constant attendance allowance for the most seriously disabled. We will improve the present situation where a woman who is just over fifty when she is widowed gets a pension but a widow just under fifty gets nothing.

Shortly after the election Heath introduced a generous package of welfare benefits in the National Insurance Act. The Act extended welfare in the following ways:

- It gave pension rights to 100,000 people who had not been covered by the 1948 National Assistance Act.
- It introduced an **attendance allowance** for people who needed long-term care at home.
- It established invalidity benefit.
- It increased the child allowance given to mothers.
- It made rent subsidies available for low-income families in private accommodation.

Right-wing challenges

During the 1970s right-wing Conservatives such as Sir Keith Joseph argued that the welfare state was leading to a reduction of individual freedom. Inspired by the writings of the Austrian economist Friedrich Hayek, Joseph made the following argument. First, he argued that the state was the enemy of individual freedom, therefore that any growth in the welfare state would always lead to a restriction of individual freedom. Specifically, advocates of the welfare state assumed that the government had a right to take money from citizens in order to improve the lives of poor citizens. What is more, Joseph claimed that politicians like Wilson would, as time went on, take more and more money in taxes to fund an ever larger welfare state. The growth of the state and increased taxes restricted the freedom of British citizens and therefore should be stopped.

> ### Keith Joseph, 1918–94
> Keith Joseph was a Conservative MP who had served in the Second World War. He was deeply concerned with the welfare of Britain's poor and as secretary of state for social services in Heath's government he actually spent more on social welfare than any of his Labour predecessors. In 1974 his views shifted away from welfare and he came to believe that the welfare state actually perpetuated poverty. Cutting welfare, in his view, was the only way to help poor people to escape a cycle of poverty and dependency.

Welfare and efficiency

Joseph, and right-wingers at the **think-tank** Institute of Economic Affairs, also opposed welfare spending on the grounds that it led to economic inefficiency. Again, inspired by Hayek, they argued that the government would always spend money less efficiently than private business. First, Joseph claimed that private businesses were run to make a profit, therefore business would always spend money in the most efficient way. The government, by contrast, did not want to make a profit, and therefore had no reason to spend its money efficiently. Second, Joseph argued that the more money the government spent, the more inefficient the economy would be. Indeed, he argued that one of the reasons for Britain's economic problems was that since 1945 governments had been spending large amounts of money on welfare. Therefore, the Conservatives should seek to cut government spending in order to make the economy more efficient and Britain richer.

Welfare and inflation

Another reason why right-wing Conservatives opposed welfare spending was the relationship that they claimed between welfare and inflation. Joseph argued that welfare spending required high levels of government borrowing. This increased the amount of money in the economy without increasing the amount of goods available. The consequence was too much money chasing too few goods, which led to inflation: a general rise in the level of prices. Worse still, as inflation rose governments tried to make things better with increased welfare spending, which in turn led to even worse inflation. The only way to break the cycle, according to Joseph, was to cut government spending, particularly in areas such as welfare.

Welfare and dependency

A final reason why radicals in the Conservative Party sought to limit welfare spending was the supposed link between welfare and dependency. Towards the end of the 1970s radical Conservatives argued that the welfare state created a dependency culture. In essence Conservatives MPs like Margaret Thatcher and Keith Joseph claimed that welfare payments encouraged people to live on benefits rather than get jobs. This 'culture of dependency' had two consequences. First, it promoted economic decline, as more and more people gave up work and therefore contributed nothing to the economy. Second, it perpetuated relative poverty, because people preferred to live on relatively small handouts rather than earning a decent wage.

According to the Conservative right, the dependency culture also resulted in moral problems. Welfare, they claimed, robbed recipients of the self-respect that people gained through hard work. Moreover, it robbed people of their initiative and independence. In essence, welfare created a class of people with no aspirations, goals or self-respect who contributed nothing to society but demanded ever larger handouts from the state.

An end to consensus

The consensus on welfare came under increasing strain following Heath's failure to win the election of 1974 (see page 21). Following Heath's defeat, his critics on the right seized the opportunity to replace him as Conservative leader with Thatcher – a right-wing candidate who was less sympathetic towards the welfare state. Thatcher led a new generation of Conservatives who no longer believed in the post-war consensus and felt that cuts to welfare would encourage people to be more self-reliant and less dependent on the state.

Welfare policies, 1974–79

The new Conservative leadership attacked Wilson's Labour welfare policies. These policies included:

- a 25 per cent rise in pension rates and a freeze of council house rents in the budget of 1974
- Invalid Care Allowance, 1975
- Universal Child Benefit, 1975, for all children including the firstborn; the number of children under its remit doubled.

Wilson sought to pay for these policies by taxing high-income earners and people who had an income from investments and property.

James Callaghan, who had succeeded Wilson as Labour prime minister in 1976, continued to develop welfare policies including new pension rights in the Supplementary Benefits Act, 1976.

> ### Monetarism
> Part of the reason for the government's need to continue extending welfare benefits was the growing problem with inflation throughout the decade. As prices rose, real wages consistently fell and benefit payments were unable to keep pace with the rate of price inflation.
>
> The Conservatives argued that these policies were counterproductive. The solution that was proposed by the new leaders of the Conservative Party was to rein in the money supply. The economic theory of monetarism argued that it was excessive state spending and too much money in the economy that led to both inflation and unemployment. One immediate target for cuts was the welfare budget.

IMF cuts

Also in 1976, the first major cuts began as the International Monetary Fund (**IMF**) insisted that the government cut its spending in return for a loan of $4 billion (see page 37). The partial loss of control over social spending that the fund's conditions required was summed up in a secret memorandum to the cabinet from Energy Secretary Tony Benn:

> They would involve cuts into public services so deep as to endanger their basic function and cuts in social benefits that would put at risk the Social Contract.

The government made £2.5 billion in cuts. Housing and education budgets were cut but pensions and other benefits were largely unaffected.

The opponents of welfare

Antiwelfare-state thinking during the 1970s was not confined to the Conservative Party. Much of the press, particularly the *Telegraph*, *The Times* and the *Financial Times* became increasingly critical of what they saw as excessive welfare spending. Within Britain a growing number of affluent working-class and middle-class people began to see welfare as a problem, not a solution, and looked to politicians who shared these views.

More generally, the 1970s saw the beginning of a generational shift which had an impact on attitudes to welfare. The generation that had grown up during the 1960s and 1970s were less inclined to endorse the **collectivist** ways of thinking that had emerged from the depression and the Second World War. Large sections of the working class were 'aspirational': their goal was to grow rich, rather than to defend the rights of their class. Consequently, many had less time or sympathy for policies that meant higher taxes. Thatcher appealed to this new generation and the **C1s** – the new working class who wanted lower taxes and less welfare spending. The Conservatives entered the 1979 election presenting welfare as bad for the recipient, bad for the economy, bad for society and a burden on the taxpayer. By 1979 the welfare state lived on but the consensus that sustained it was dead.

> ### Work together
> First go through your notes together. Take two large pieces of paper.
> - On one write all the reasons you can find in favour of the provision of a comprehensive welfare state – for example the need to maintain basic living standards.
> - On the other write all the reasons opposed to this provision, for example the cost and the growth of welfare dependency.
> - Which arguments do you find the most convincing?

> ### Question practice
> 1 Was the poverty of the interwar years the main reason for the introduction of the welfare state in the years following the Second World War? Explain your answer. **AS**
> 2 How extensive was welfare provision by 1939? **AS**
> 3 To what extent were the provisions of a welfare state already in place before 1945?

Chapter summary

- By 1918 governments accepted responsibility for a basic level of social security for its citizens based on the Victorian Poor Laws and early twentieth-century legislation.
- Measures were strengthened in the 1920s through developments in unemployment insurance.
- The Great Depression led to greater demands for welfare provision which governments could not afford; one response was the introduction of the means test.
- The role of the state was extended during the Second World War and measures such as evacuation and rationing helped equalise society, with people feeling they were all making sacrifices for the war effort.
- The Beveridge Report of December 1942 created a blueprint for extensive social security and welfare.
- The post-war Labour government implemented many of the recommendations of the Beveridge Report to create a welfare state caring for citizens 'from the cradle to the grave'.
- Although there was broad consensus on the desire for the welfare state, critics began to question its cost as economic conditions worsened during the 1960s.
- Welfare spending continued to increase, however, and provision was extended, for example by the Conservative Government's National Insurance Act of 1970.
- Increasingly right-wingers challenged the welfare provision with arguments on the grounds of cost and the growth of welfare dependency.

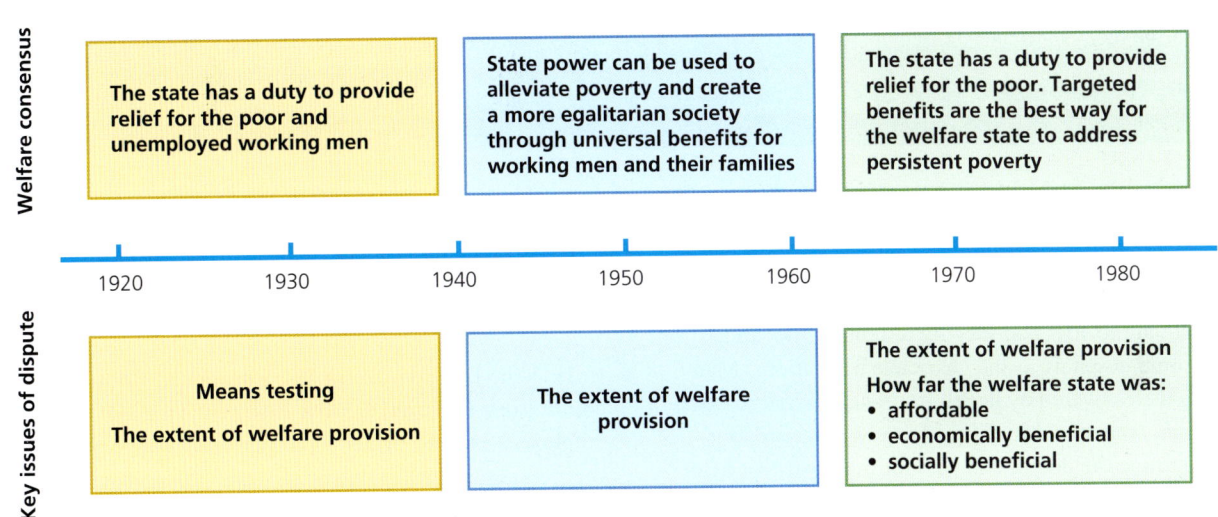

▲ Summary diagram: Provision of social welfare

Theme 2 Creating a welfare state, 1918–79

2b: Public health

Overview

This chapter examines the changing role of the state in the provision of public healthcare and changing attitudes towards public health. The creation of a National Health Service (NHS) in 1948 is widely regarded as one of the major achievements of the British state in the twentieth century. It was a bold experiment, quite different from other Western healthcare systems as it was funded from taxation rather than insurance and free at the point of delivery. It reflected the universalist aspirations and faith in state action of policy makers following the Second World War.

The creation of the NHS was part of a longer process of change that dated back to before the First World War. From 1906 onwards, the state had gradually taken on a greater responsibility for the provision of healthcare. Doctors and policy makers assumed that medical science would continue to advance and the government should play a role in stimulating medical progress. During the 1920s and 1930s governments played a co-ordinating role, trying to manage a patchwork of local authority, voluntary and private hospitals. During the Second World War the government organised the Emergency Hospital Service, which, in many ways, became the pattern for the post-war NHS.

The NHS led to a dramatic improvement in physical health. However, this improvement was not even. The NHS tended to favour already privileged groups, so middle-class people and men did better than working-class people and women.

From 1948 to 1964 the NHS broadly kept up with people's expectations. However, as expectations increased, treatments diversified and the population aged, the NHS came under increasing pressure to do more. Therefore, although budgets and staffing increased and medicine became more sophisticated the NHS was continually pushed to meet the ever-growing demands of the British public.

This chapter examines public health through the following sections:

1. Health provision, 1918–45
2. The National Health Service, 1945–79
3. The impact of the NHS to 1979
4. The challenge of medical advances, 1945–79

1 Health provision, 1918–45

Healthcare provision during the interwar years was patchy. Local health authorities had varying responsibilities and operated some hospitals, as did charitable institutions. Many employees were covered by health insurance, although often their families were not. Much healthcare was private; one paid to go to see the doctor and paid for the treatment he or she recommended. As a result, although healthcare overall seemed to be improving, there were many areas, particularly in less affluent areas, where this was not the case.

Note it down

This section focusses on the provision of healthcare throughout the early part of the twentieth century. Use a spider diagram (see page x) to make notes on this. The spider's body should be labelled 'Healthcare provision, 1918–45'. The main legs should be based on the following headings:

- The position of healthcare in 1918
- How far healthcare improved in the years 1918–39
- How far the Second World War impacted on healthcare.

Healthcare in 1918

By 1918 significant steps had been taken towards providing healthcare to the nation:

- In 1911 the Liberal government introduced a system of compulsory **national health insurance** for low-paid employees earning under £160 per year. They and their employers paid into the scheme which provided sick pay and free medical treatment. However, the Act only applied to wage earners and the unemployed and families of wage earners were not provided for under the scheme.
- There were numerous private charitable and philanthropic groups that paid the costs of healthcare for the poor.
- The **Poor Law** provided for some degree of medical care with Poor Law Hospitals.
- **Workhouses** often had their own infirmaries and many of them converted completely into hospitals once their use as effective prisons for the poor became obsolete (see page 58).

Healthcare, 1918–39

The period 1918–39 was important for the development of healthcare for two main reasons. First, a consensus emerged between medical professionals and policy makers about what was wrong with the existing system and about the goal of reform. Second, there were significant government reforms.

Healthcare consensus

In the interwar years, there was a widespread consensus that the government should play a leading role co-ordinating provision, and that more money should be spent on healthcare.

It was widely agreed, among Western nations, that important medical advances had been made during the nineteenth century. Additionally, it was assumed that medical science would continue to grow, and that further research would lead to better healthcare. However, treatment for serious illnesses was still mainly palliative, concerned with making the patient as comfortable as possible. Illnesses such as cancer were still usually fatal.

It was also widely believed that the government had a role to play in encouraging medical advance. Specifically, there was a consensus that the government should:

- invest in research
- invest in medical training
- organise a national network of hospitals
- play a role in rationing healthcare.

There were, however, disagreements over the exact nature of the government's role:

- The **Fabian Society** advocated centralising healthcare provision before 1918. The Fabians believed that centralised, state-planned healthcare was the only way to significantly improve healthcare for all in Britain.
- In 1919 the Labour Party became the first British political party to advocate a free and comprehensive national health service.
- The **British Medical Association (BMA)** advocated a regional system of healthcare, co-ordinated by central government.
- In 1920 the government commissioned a study into the organisation of health services. The resulting Dawson Report recommended a network of state-funded and state-organised hospitals.
- The 1926 Royal Commission on National Health Insurance also recommended a regional, rather than a national, structure for healthcare. The commission recommended a compulsory health insurance scheme to fund a unified national health insurance service.
- During the 1930s private hospitals and voluntary hospitals lobbied, unsuccessfully, for government funding.

> ### Voluntary hospitals
> Voluntary hospitals were charitable organisations that treated immediate or life-threatening conditions. They fell into three main categories:
> - university or medical school hospitals
> - specialist hospitals for particular illnesses such as tuberculosis
> - cottage hospitals that served small rural communities.
>
> Many of the doctors and surgeons worked voluntarily, having other paid work or independent sources of wealth.

- The Voluntary Hospitals Commission of 1935 argued that the government should merge voluntary hospitals and local authority hospitals in order to bring together expertise and finance.
- The 1937 *Report on the British Health Services* by the **think-tank** Political and Economic Planning, also recommended a regional model, but based on central government planning and greater funding.

Generally speaking, there was a consensus in favour of government planning and co-ordination of a series of regional health services, although there were groups on the left that advocated a truly national healthcare system.

Government reforms, 1919–29

The role of government in healthcare provision expanded significantly in the decade following the First World War. In 1919, the government established a new Ministry of Health. The ministry was responsible for co-ordinating health at a regional level. Additionally, it administered funds raised by the national health insurance scheme. Christopher Addison, the first minister of health, was an academic and medical doctor who had played an important role organising medical care for troops on the western front in the First World War. He was a strong advocate of regional health services.

Tuberculosis

The most serious public health problem in the immediate aftermath of the First World War was the deadly disease tuberculosis (TB). Before the war, the government had set up TB sanatoria funded by national insurance in order to slow the spread of the disease. The Ministry of Health Act, 1919, also created the Medical Research Council (MRC), which was established in order to research the causes of TB, led by Lord Richard Haldane. The council was an official, publicly funded body but independent of government control – ministers had no power over the MRC's medical or scientific findings. The Tuberculosis Act of 1921 made the provision of TB sanatoria by local authorities compulsory. As a result of co-ordinated action the number of cases of TB declined in every year between 1920 and 1938.

Local government Act, 1929

The Local government Act steered through Parliament by Minister of Health Neville Chamberlain was the most important medical reform of the 1920s. The Act:

- passed responsibility for Poor Law hospitals to county and borough councils
- allowed county and borough councils to convert Poor Law infirmaries, which only served the poor, into public hospitals
- gave local authorities responsibility for other areas of public health such as the running of venereal disease clinics, child welfare, dentistry, school medical services and school meals.

Chamberlain's Local government Act led to the reorganisation of healthcare on a regional basis. It created a single health authority that co-ordinated healthcare in each county or borough. This was a vital moment in the history of healthcare in Britain; it enabled local authorities to provide medical services to the entire population of the area. However, it did not lead to cheap, modern healthcare for all.

Healthcare in the depression

In spite of the healthcare reforms of the 1920s less than half the population was insured against illness in 1929. Affordable health services for the poor increased in importance following the onset of the **Great Depression**. Uninsured people were forced to rely on private health insurance, which in many cases did not pay out enough to cover medical costs. In the most deprived parts of Britain, extreme poverty and hunger led to higher incidences of illness and, in some cases, premature death.

The depression focussed the debate on the best way to provide healthcare. During the 1930s there was a new consensus that existing provision was inefficient, varied widely in terms of quality, and failed to meet the medical needs of all patients. Healthcare professionals and ministers continued to favour a regional approach to these problems, rather than creating a national service. Nonetheless, at a local level, individual hospitals provided innovative care.

Innovations in healthcare

During the 1930s there were a number of innovations in healthcare. Partly as a result of what had been learned about diet and fitness when training troops in the First World War, new advances in **preventative healthcare** occurred. The Ministry of Health's priority was hospital funding, but local authority hospitals began innovative experiments in preventative health, focussing on improving diet and hygiene.

The Pioneer Health Centre and Finsbury Health Centre

The Pioneer Health Centre in Peckham, established in 1935, is one example of the experiments with preventative health. Local residents paid a subscription of 1s (5p) a week to join the clinic and received an annual health checkup and access to leisure facilities. Around 950 local residents signed up to the scheme.

The Finsbury Health Centre is another example of innovative 1930s healthcare. When it opened in 1938 it was the most technologically advanced and modern public health centre of the era. It addressed the problems of the deprived local community, including lice, poor hygiene and TB. It had a wide range of facilities including a solarium and a lecture theatre. The Finsbury Health Centre was highly influential, and inspired wartime planners and the architects of the NHS.

Healthcare by 1939

Between 1929 and 1939 public health seemed to be improving. Key indicators such as **infant mortality** were in decline. Indeed, infant mortality in England and Wales dropped from 14.3 in every 1,000 between 1906 and 1910 to 12 per 1,000 between 1936 and 1938.

However, in areas afflicted by extreme poverty the picture was quite different. For example, during the 1920s and 1930s **maternal mortality rates** were 50 per cent higher in low-income groups than among the middle class. Equally middle-class men lived on average twelve years longer than working-class men, while middle-class women lived nineteen years longer than working-class women. Indeed, at the end of the decade, Political and Economic Planning, a think-tank established in 1931 to monitor health policy, argued that British healthcare lagged behind other developing countries. Compared to healthcare in parts of the British Empire such as Australia and New Zealand, it argued that overall British healthcare provision was inefficient, poorly co-ordinated, and badly regulated. It pointed to the failure to organise a co-ordinated response to a typhoid outbreak in Croydon in 1937, which lead to the deaths of almost 50 people.

By 1939 the Ministry of Health was discussing plans for regional health boards centrally managed by government. Additionally, the medical journal *The Lancet*, began to advocate a national system of healthcare. However, it would take the radicalising experience of war to create the consensus that led to the creation of the NHS.

The impact of the Second World War

The Second World War resulted in the establishment of a nationwide emergency healthcare system, and the emergence of a new consensus. The threat of air raids, which planners in the mid-1930s predicted would lead to millions of casualties, resulted in detailed planning before the war about how to care for the wounded.

The Emergency Medical Service

In 1939 the Emergency Medical Service was founded, to provide first aid and casualty clearing stations for people wounded in air raids. It allowed the government to dictate a hospital's activities, a power it had never previously possessed. During 1939 and 1940 an entire national service had been created in anticipation of German attacks.

The Emergency Medical Service resulted in pooling resources, skills and expertise, and the creation of a national system. Very quickly, government planners adopted the national framework as the basis for plans for a post-war healthcare system.

War also led to a change of attitude within the medical profession. Previously many doctors and hospital administrators had preferred to stay independent of government. However, the central organising power of the state, along with additional funding, proved to be attractive. Consensus in favour of a national state-run system did not emerge immediately, but in 1941 Medical Planning Research, a group of 200 doctors, endorsed provisional plans for a nationwide health service.

Negotiations, 1942–44

The creation of a post-war health system required intense negotiation between doctors, represented by the British Medical Association (BMA), and managers of local authority, private and voluntary hospitals. All groups were willing to collaborate but were also concerned about the loss of autonomy that a national state-run health system required.

Negotiations during 1942 and 1943 resolved many of the major issues. Consequently, the government published a **White Paper** on health in 1944 recommending a new national system paid for from general taxation. By the end of the Second World War a huge shift in thinking about health had taken place. All three main parties committed themselves to state-provided, centrally funded healthcare.

2 The National Health Service, 1945–79

In 1945 there was a clear political consensus behind the creation of a National Health Service (NHS). Both the Conservatives and the Labour Party had promised to create one in their manifestos prior to the general election.

When the new Labour prime minister, Clement Attlee, formed his cabinet he gave the position of minister for health to the Labour **left-winger** Aneurin Bevan. Between August 1945 and July 1946 Bevan devoted himself to the creation of the National Health Service Act (England and Wales) with a separate Act for Scotland the following year.

Between the founding of the NHS and the election of Margaret Thatcher in 1979, both main parties remained committed to providing a National Health Service.

> **Note it down**
> This section focusses on the creation and development of the NHS. You could use bullet points in your note-making (see page ix). Your bullets should address the following issues:
> - How were the aims of the NHS achieved?
> - How did the early NHS develop?
> - What successes did it enjoy and what challenges did it face in the years 1948–79?

The National Health Service Act, 1946

The Act established a National Health Service based on the following principles:

- Healthcare would universal, available to all.
- Healthcare would be comprehensive. The NHS would offer:
  - curative and preventive care
  - mental and physical healthcare
  - hospital care, general practice surgeries, dental care and other specialist services such as opticians.
- Healthcare would be free: patients would not pay for the care they received **at the point of delivery**. The NHS would be paid for by **direct taxation** rather than insurance.

In order to achieve this, Bevan created a nationalised but regionalised system.

- All existing hospitals were nationalised: local authority, voluntary and private hospitals were merged into one unified system.
- NHS hospitals would be run by regional hospital boards managed by executive committees, with local health authorities providing services such as ambulances, vaccinations and community nursing.

Until the foundation of the NHS in July 1948, Bevan struggled to get the co-operation of doctors. In order to win their support, he agreed to a series of compromises:

- Consultants were allowed to continue working privately and were allocated beds in hospitals for private patients.
- GPs were able to avoid becoming local authority employees and therefore subject to local authority pay controls.
- Regional health boards were appointed, not elected, and were dominated by consultants who tended to be upper middle class.

As a result of these compromises, the BMA agreed to support the universality of the service. However, it meant the NHS was run by privileged groups from the outset. Nonetheless, Bevan achieved much of what he intended.

Health clinics

Section 21 of the National Health Act called for the establishment of health clinics where GPs, consultants and nurses would carry out all kinds of healthcare from preventative health advice to acute care, much like the Pioneer Centre in Peckham (see page 70). This was opposed by the BMA who thought that it would downgrade the status of doctors. Because doctors' practices were private businesses, the BMA feared that the changes would affect each doctor's ability to earn. By 1958 only ten of these health clinics had been built, showing how powerful the BMA was in deciding the fate of healthcare in Britain.

The early NHS

Initially, the NHS was a tripartite system, meaning that it comprised three tiers:

- Hospital services: accident and emergency services and in-patient treatment for serious illnesses.
- Primary care: GPs, dentists, opticians and pharmacists all operated as independent contractors (private businesses, not run by the NHS but who sold their services for a profit).
- Community services: health visitors, vaccination services, health education, midwives and ambulances were all managed by local authorities, not directly by the NHS.

The creation of the NHS did not lead to equal provision across the country. The NHS inherited the existing **infrastructure**, which was distributed unequally across the country. In 1948 it was made up of 3,100 hospitals, with 550,000 beds, employing 360,000 staff.

The development of the NHS

During the period 1951–79 the NHS was reformed under successive governments.

- Macmillan's Conservative government introduced the Hospital Plan in 1962. It led to:
  - the creation of 90 new hospitals
  - the redesign and modernisation of 134 hospitals
  - the refurbishment of 356 hospitals.
- Sir Keith Joseph, Conservative secretary of state for social services 1970–74, introduced the NHS Reorganisation Act (1973), which introduced a new management structure to the NHS. This led to a significant growth in management costs between 1974 and 1979.
- Dr David Owen, Labour minister of state for health 1974–76, established the Resource Allocation Working Party. It identified areas of health deprivation, allocating additional resources to reflect the need of different communities.

NHS spending

Spending on the NHS increased under both Labour and Conservative governments. The Conservatives, who were more traditionally associated with limiting public expenditure, maintained Labour's level of health spending and during the early 1960s significantly increased it. Between 1949 and 1979 health spending mostly grew as a percentage of **GDP**, as shown in Figure 1.

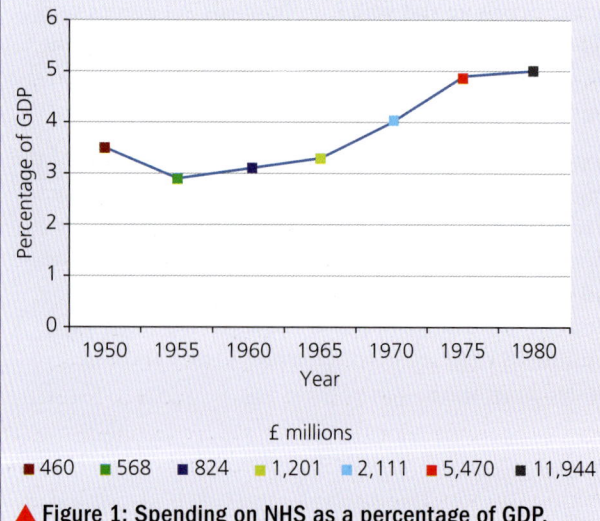

▲ Figure 1: Spending on NHS as a percentage of GDP.

3 The impact of the NHS to 1979

The NHS proved to be remarkably effective at improving the physical health of the nation. This is reflected in the declining mortality rate throughout the period. However, NHS treatment tended to reflect the inequalities in society. In this sense, middle-class people received better treatment than working-class people, and men received a better deal than women. Improvements in mental health were also less obvious than improvements in physical health.

> **Note it down**
>
> This section focusses on the impact of the NHS on people's lives. Use the 1:2 system (page x) to address the following issues:
>
> | Impact on public health | How successful was the NHS in the area of public health? |
> |---|---|
> | Health and class | How far did more affluent classes benefit from the NHS in comparison to poorer groups? |
> | Impact on women | How far have women specifically benefited from the NHS? |
> | Impact on mental health | How successful had the NHS been in the treatment of mental illness? |

Impact on public health

Between 1948 and 1979 there was a general improvement in the health of the nation. Life expectancy increased from 65.8 years for men and 70.1 years for women in 1948 to 71 years for men and 77 years for women in 1979. This was due to the combination of better healthcare and increased affluence (see page 137). In addition to improved life expectancy the NHS also had a large impact on the attitudes of British people towards healthcare and the role of the state, and on educating people about public health.

However, the improvement was not uniform. The Merrison Report (1979) argued that hospitals received around 70 per cent of NHS funding, whereas other services, including GP surgeries and preventative health programmes, received much less. Additionally, within hospitals, surgery and general medicine received much more money than services dealing with mental illness, and geriatric medicine. Moreover, investment in hospitals tended to create regional inequalities. For example, a lot of the investment in hospitals introduced in the 1962 Hospital Plan was spent in London.

Health and class

The middle class tended to benefit more from the NHS than the working class. Investment in working-class areas lagged behind investment in middle-class areas. In largely working-class areas 80 per cent of GP surgeries were built before 1900, whereas in middle-class areas 50 per cent of surgeries were build after to 1900.

Research conducted in the 1950s indicates that budget allocations in the 1950s favoured middle-class areas. According to one study, hospitals in some middle-class areas received an annual budget of £4.98 per head, whereas in working-class areas budgets were set at £3.19 per head. This problem persisted into the 1970s. A similar study conducted in 1972 found that middle-class areas tended to have per capita budgets that were 24 per cent higher than working-class areas.

The Black Report, published by the Department of Health and Social Security in 1980, indicated that the gap between working-class and middle-class healthcare grew between 1949 and 1972. By the 1970s the gap between the richest and the poorest meant that:

- Working-class women were twice as likely to die in childbirth compared to middle-class women.
- Unskilled working men were twice as likely to die before reaching the age of 65 as middle-class professionals.

> **The inverse care law and middle-class privilege**
>
> One important piece of research published in 1970 argued that there was an inverse relationship between medical need and the availability of treatment under the NHS. GP Julian Tudor Hart, described this as the 'inverse care law.' Hart compared the availability of medical care in a south Wales mining community with the availability in middle-class areas of London. In Wales where working miners had regular and often serious medical needs related to their jobs, healthcare was difficult to access due to the relatively small number of GP surgeries. However, in London where middle-class professionals had relatively few medical needs healthcare was widely available.
>
> Social researcher Richard Titmuss' 1968 study *Commitment to Welfare* argued that the middle class tended to get more from the NHS than the working class. In essence, he argued that middle-class patients understood how to get the most out of the system, and therefore received better treatment than working-class groups.

Impact on women
Reproduction

The introduction of the NHS tended to give women greater control over their fertility. This led to a decline in birth rates. Whereas women born in 1920 had, on average, two children, a woman born in 1966 had 1.3 children. While free contraception was only available from the NHS from the 1970s, education provided by the NHS in earlier decades, and the contraceptive pill introduced in 1961, led to women having fewer babies.

However, the availability of the pill also had drawbacks:

- Early contraceptive pills had side-effects such as an increased risk of stroke and some types of cancer.
- The availability of the pill meant that men tended to take less responsibility for contraception.

Abortion

The 1967 Abortion Act had a mixed impact on women's reproductive rights. The right to terminate a pregnancy was dependent on the approval of two, typically male, doctors. Moreover, medical staff were given the legal right to refuse to participate in terminations. In practice, access to abortions were controlled by medical professionals, and therefore provision reflected the beliefs and prejudices of doctors. Between 1968 and 1978, 1.5 million terminations were carried out. Around 58 per cent were performed in the private sector, to women who paid around £200 for the procedure. In this sense, abortions were more easily available to middle-class women. Additionally medical supervision of abortion was often poorly regulated in the NHS. As a result 86 people died during a legal abortion between 1968 and 1978, and 72 died as a result of NHS surgery.

Childbirth

The NHS made childbirth in hospital the norm for British women. In the 1950s only 60 per cent of women gave birth in hospital. By 1978 that figure had increased to 97 per cent. How far hospitalisation benefited women during this period is disputed. One survey recorded that between 70 and 90 per cent of women who gave birth in hospitals were given an **episiotomy** in order to assist the birth. This procedure led to pain when sitting in 68 per cent of cases and longer recovery times. Moreover, the procedure was often carried out without the consent or knowledge of the woman.

More generally, feminist writers have argued that the medicalisation of childbirth shifted power away from women to men. Doctors, who between 1948 and 1979 were predominantly men, controlled birth.

Women and work

The NHS created greater opportunities for women in the workplace, although it did not create full equality of opportunity between women and men. The expansion of health and social services created a state-funded 'caring profession'. According to traditional stereotypes women were naturally more caring than men, and therefore women were able to find jobs in these new professions. For example, in 1948 the government attempted to recruit 54,000 female nurses. A significant minority of female nurses were recruited from the Caribbean (see page 123). In general women were restricted to the lower paid and lower status jobs in the 1950s and 1960s. The experience of black women was even worse. Not only was promotion extremely rare, but they were also subjected to racial harassment.

Impact on mental health

The NHS was explicitly created to treat physical and mental health. However, by 1957 there was concern at the top of government that the NHS was not treating mental illnesses effectively. Specifically, the 1957 Royal Commission on Mental Illness and Mental Deficiency argued that patients with mental illnesses were routinely stigmatised, that their personal rights were not respected and that mental health hospitals operated more like prisons than hospitals. The 1959 Mental Health Act addressed this by:

- Introducing new terminology. Patients were referred to as 'mentally ill' rather than insane.
- Removing judges from the process. Decisions to force treatment on people with serious mental health problems would be made by mental health tribunals rather than judges. These tribunals had a responsibility to protect the liberty of patients.
- Introducing an open door policy, so that most patients could attend voluntary treatment sessions in daycare centres, rather than being compelled to stay in hospital long term.

The 1959 Act marked a move away from residential care towards out-patient or drop-in care. This was confirmed by the 1962 Hospital Plan, which proposed a 50 per cent reduction in hospital beds for people with mental illness by 1975.

However, the 1959 reforms did not have the impact that was hoped. By 1974:

- only 15 per cent of the daycare places needed were available
- only 33 per cent of the hospital places needed were available.

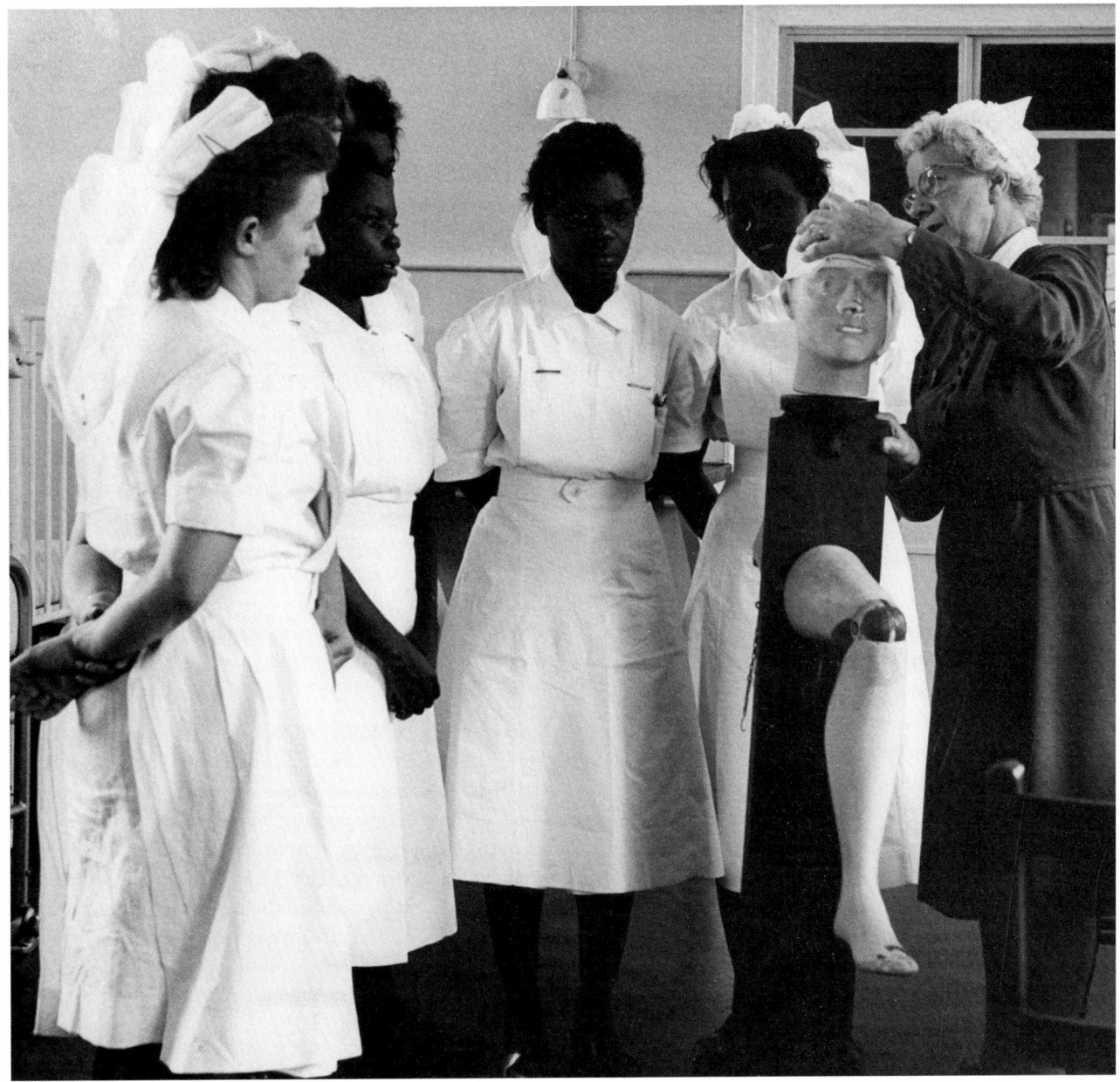

▲ A group of student NHS nurses learning how to bandage a head properly at Milford Hospital. How valuable in this source to a historian investigating the training of nurses in the 1960s?

As a result patients with mental illness tended to be admitted to non-specialist hospitals.

Moreover, the stigma attached to mental health issues had not disappeared. At Ely hospital in Cardiff, the *News of the World* newspaper reported that 'cruel and inhumane' treatment was meted out to residents. A report into the abuse was commissioned, along with a much wider enquiry into all of Britain's NHS mental health hospitals. As a result of this enquiry, long-stay psychiatric hospitals where people had been incarcerated, often for decades, began to close. The report also recommended the practice of introducing hospital inspections. Between 1967 and 1981 there were 25 separate enquiries into misconduct and abuse at psychiatric hospitals across the UK. This demonstrated that the provision of healthcare for the mentally ill was in need of improvement.

Two White Papers, one published in 1971 and another published in 1975, recognised ongoing problems, but no major reform happened until the early 1980s.

Theme 2 Creating a welfare state, 1918–79

4 The challenge of medical advances, 1945–79

Between 1945 and 1979 advances in medical science and changes in society created challenges for NHS provision. To an extent, the NHS was a victim of its own success:

- The effectiveness of NHS hospitals led to increasing expectations.
- Longer lives led to an ageing population with more complex health needs.
- Medical advances meant that the NHS could perform new procedures.

In this sense the NHS was under increasing pressure to deliver more services and cutting-edge medicine. Consequently, although NHS resources increased, demands on the service rose faster.

> **Note it down**
> Choose which note-making method (see page ix) you think best suits this section. Whichever method you choose, you need to ensure you have addressed the following issues:
> - To what extent did the range of treatments expand?
> - How significant were the challenges facing the NHS?
> - How far was the NHS in crisis?

Expansion of treatments, 1948–64

Demand for NHS services grew rapidly from 1948. This is clear from the number of prescriptions issued, and the amount spent by the NHS on prescription drugs:

- Free healthcare led to a significant increase in demand: in June 1948, the last month before the NHS was introduced, 6.8 million prescriptions were dispensed by chemists. By September 1948, that figure had risen to 13.6 million.
- Between 1949 and 1964 there was a 'pharmacological revolution'; more and more medicines became available. This led to increasing NHS drug costs. Setting aside inflation, the NHS spent 250 per cent more on drugs in 1964 than it did in 1951. This was largely due to the fact that drugs themselves became more expensive.
- Vaccinations also increased the scope of NHS provision. Prior to 1939 the only vaccine given routinely was for smallpox. By 1964, vaccines against diphtheria, TB, poliomyelitis, whooping cough and tetanus were all available universally.

In addition to the increased prescription of drugs, the NHS also expanded in terms of the services that it offered.

In 1959, as a result of the Younghusband Report, the NHS began to offer chiropody services.

By 1964 the NHS had proved to be an extremely cost-effective way of improving public health. Although there were shortages and inequalities the NHS was rarely a major political issue. In general NHS patients felt that NHS provision was far superior to pre-war medical provision and were therefore prepared to tolerate shortages, and the dilapidation of many NHS hospitals. However, public attitudes changed in the later 1960s and 1970s as the challenges of provision grew.

The challenge of medical advances, 1964–79

By 1964 there was a broad public consensus in support of the NHS. However, there were also serious problems. From 1948 to 1960 there had been little investment in modernising NHS hospitals, and little had been done to tackle the inequalities of provision. During the 1960s and 1970s governments tried to modernise the NHS and deal with long-term inequalities in provision. Additionally, during this period there was an increasing demand on NHS resources, and new treatment possibilities.

Consequently, spending on the NHS increased at rates higher than those predicted in the 1950s. During the 1950s the National Institute of Economic and Social Research predicted that NHS spending would increase by 3 per cent a year from 1960 to 1975. In reality spending grew by an average of 4.5 per cent. The greater increases in funding reflected the greater demands being placed on the service, and the underfunding that had taken place between 1948 and 1964. However, higher funding rates took place in the context of weaker economic growth and, during the 1970s, economic crisis.

Treatment and staffing

Increasingly high-tech medical equipment led to new challenges for the NHS. High-tech medicine tended to require specialist staff to operate new technology. For example, from the 1960s, the NHS was able to provide:

- kidney dialysis
- catheters
- organ transplants.

These procedures required expensive technologies and an expansion of specially trained staff. Therefore, numbers of consultants and nursing staff increased by 66 per cent from 1964 to 1979. At the same time the numbers of technical staff increased by 300 per cent. In total, NHS staffing increased from around 407,000 in 1951 to just over 1 million in 1979.

Thalidomide

The use of thalidomide is an example of how medical developments can go horribly wrong. Thalidomide was developed by a West German pharmaceutical company, Grunenthal, as an antibiotic in the 1950s. However it was noted that side-effects included drowsiness and prevention of morning sickness in pregnant women. It was successfully relaunched as a drug to aid women through pregnancy; thousands took it and, as a result, 10,000 seriously deformed babies were born. It had not been properly tested. After a long press campaign and criminal trial, Grunenthal offered DM 100 million and the government of West Germany a further DM 320 million as compensation to victims in 1968. Ironically, thalidomide is widely used today for its original purpose as an antibiotic, being particularly effective against leprosy and various AIDs-related illnesses.

An ageing population

As the population aged demands on the NHS increased, because older people tend to have more health needs. In 1951 there were around 7 million people of retirement age. That had risen to 9 million by 1971. In the 1970s hospitals began offering hip replacement surgery, a treatment designed for elderly people. In 1979 the NHS performed 24,000 hip replacements, an operation that was impossible in 1960.

Major surgery

Advances in surgery also increased demand for NHS services. Between 1964 and 1979 there were important advances in organ surgery. In 1979, the NHS performed:

- around 800 kidney transplants a year
- around 5,000 heart bypass operations.

These operations were time-consuming and expensive and required lengthy periods of aftercare.

Contraception

The Family Planning Act of 1967 also increased the scope of NHS services. From 1968 the Act made family planning advice available to all women, regardless of medical need or marital status. The policy was reversed by the Conservatives in 1972, but reinstated by Labour in 1974. By 1979 around one-third of women of childbearing age had received free advice on family planning.

Crisis in the NHS?

During the 1970s the NHS was facing a series of issues that could amount to a crisis. First, there was a growing demand for NHS services due to an increase in the number of treatments available and the growing age of the population. Second, there was a recognition that the NHS had failed to deal with health inequalities. Third, economic crises made large increases in funding unlikely. Fourth, the period 1974–79 saw a collapse in economic confidence; it was no longer taken for granted that economic growth would continue and support ever-increasing spending on healthcare. Nonetheless, the NHS was protected by a widespread public consensus that viewed it as an indispensable part of British national life.

Work together

In pairs discuss how far the NHS was a victim of its own success and in crisis by 1979. This means how far had its many achievements, such as more varied treatments and greater life expectancy, led to a drain on resources and increased costs that it could not sustain?

You need to go through your notes together to consider the following:

- How extensive was healthcare provision before the NHS?
- How successful had the NHS been by 1979?
- What problems did it face between 1948 and 1979?

Then discuss together how far the NHS was in crisis.

Chapter summary

- By 1918 there had been steps to improve people's health through measures such as the introduction of national health insurance in 1911, but the overall picture was patchy.
- During the interwar years there was an overall consensus that the government should take an active role in the provision of healthcare, but disagreement as to what forms this should take.
- The 1929 Local government Act led to the reorganisation of healthcare on a regional basis with the creation of local health authorities.
- The 1930s saw innovations in preventative medicine, for example at the Pioneer Health Centre in Peckham, south London.
- In 1939, the creation of the Emergency Medical Service laid the foundation of a national health service during wartime.
- In July 1948 the National Health Service was created as available to all and free at the point of delivery; the opposition of powerful medical groups such as the BMA having been overcome.
- In the post-war era, healthcare and life expectancy improved dramatically.
- As provision increased alongside medical advances and people's expectations, costs increased enormously.

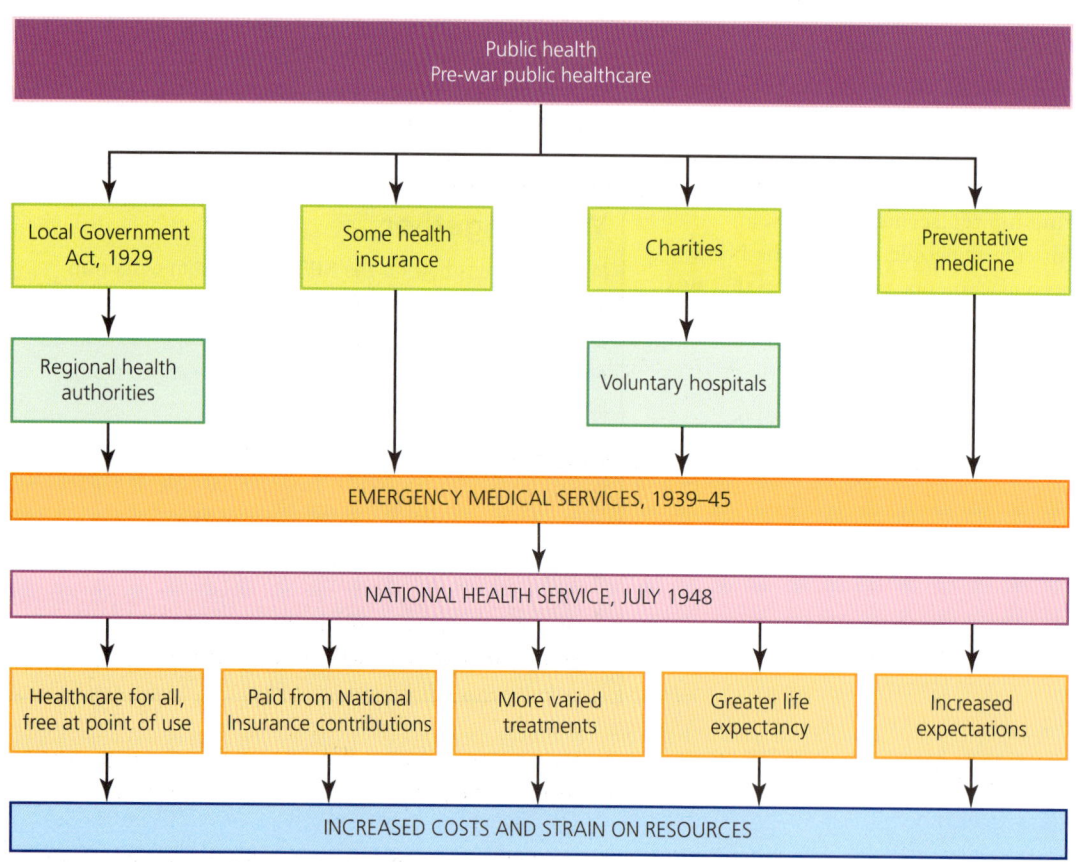

▲ Summary diagram: Creating a welfare state, 1918–79

Essay technique: Analysis

In Section A and B of the exam your essays are judged on their focus and structure (see page 40), the extent to which they include relevant detail (see page 56) and the extent to which they are analytical. Therefore, having made a relevant point, and supported it with accurate detail, you should conclude each paragraph with analysis.

Analysis is a term that covers a variety of high-level skills including explanation and evaluation. In essence, analysis means breaking down something complex into smaller parts. Therefore, a clear structure, which breaks down a complex question into a series of paragraphs, is the first step towards writing an analytical essay.

The purpose of explanation is to account for why something happened, or why something is true or false. Therefore, an explanatory statement requires two parts: a **claim** and a **justification**. For example, imagine you are answering the following question:

> How accurate is it to say that there were radical improvements in healthcare in the period, 1918–39?

You might want to argue there were radical improvements in some areas of London. Having made this point, and supported it with relevant detail, you can then explain how this answers the question. For example, you could conclude your paragraph like this:

Claim — **Clearly, there were radical improvements in healthcare in some London areas** because developments such as the Pioneer Health Centre in Peckham and the Finsbury Health Centre made cutting-edge, affordable healthcare available to everyone in the area. — Justification

Relationship

The first part of this sentence is the claim, the second part justifies the claim. 'Because' is a very important word to use when writing an explanation, as it shows the relationship between the claim and the justification.

Activity: Claim and justification

Here is a plan in answer to the question above:

- **Paragraph 1:** Radical improvements in some London areas, e.g. Peckham and Finsbury Park
- **Paragraph 2:** Radical improvements in treatment of some conditions, e.g. TB
- **Paragraph 3:** Improvements not radical – government unwilling to tackle healthcare on a national level, or bring different providers together, therefore typhoid outbreak in Croydon
- **Paragraph 4:** Improvements not radical – improvements uneven, health improvements benefit middle class more than working class. Some areas still have limited access to healthcare; Peckham and Finsbury Park are exceptional.

Using your notes from this chapter
1. Write a paragraph about the government's unwillingness to tackle healthcare on a national level. Make sure the paragraph:
- begins with a clear point that focusses on the question
- develops the point with at least three pieces of accurate detail
- concludes with explanation: a claim and a justification.
2. Write a conclusion to the essay in which you weigh up at least two factors and reach a judgement about how far there were radical improvements in healthcare in the period, 1918–39.

Don't forget, in order to get the highest marks you will need to address what 'radical' means.

2c: Education and widening opportunities

Overview

This section explores the development of education in twentieth-century Britain and how successive governments in periods of peace and war made changes to how children and adults were educated. Throughout the period 1918–79 the question of how schools should be organised and in what ways children should be taught attracted fierce controversy. The development of mass education in the 1920s and 1930s; the comprehensive system and the decline of grammar schools in the 1960s; the development of the progressive education movement; and growth in new universities in the 1960s and 1970s not only widened access to education but changed the way in which people in Britain learned.

This chapter examines education and widening opportunities through the following sections:
1. Education policy, 1918–43
2. The 'Butler Act', 1944
3. The development of comprehensive education, 1944–79
4. University education, 1918–79

1 Education policy, 1918–43

Education policy between the wars was dictated to a large degree by economic conditions and cost. The 1918 Education Act devolved significant responsibilities to local educational authorities while providing them with funding. As a result there were a variety of different systems, with some authorities maintaining elementary schools to cater for pupils throughout compulsory education, and others transferring pupils to secondary education at age eleven. Most provided grammar schools for the brightest pupils but these charged fees or accepted scholarships. The quality of education was very variable and its inadequacies were highlighted in the poor educational attainment and skills of many military personnel during the war.

Note it down

This section focusses on educational policy between 1918 and 1943. Write bullet points (see page ix) to address the following issues:
- What was the significance of the 1918 Education Act?
- Why was it so difficult to reform the educational system?
- What were advantages and disadvantages of grammar schools?
- How far did the war highlight the need for educational change?

Education before 1918

Education for most children in Britain by 1918 was provided by local education authorities (LEAs), which had been created in 1902 by the Balfour Education Act. Local authorities paid teachers' wages, provided free school meals to children from poor families, ensured the upkeep of school buildings and monitored teaching standards and qualifications.

Educational reform, 1918–39

In the aftermath of the First World War, the government embarked on ambitious educational reforms. The Education Act 1918 was passed based on the Lewis Report which was compiled during the war. The report recommended:

- a school-leaving age of fourteen
- a new tier of county colleges to provide vocational training for school leavers up to the age of eighteen. Employers were obliged to release their young employees to attend, normally one day a week. In practice this didn't always happen because of cost.
- the curriculum to be divided between 'practical instruction' for less able children to prepare them for the workplace and 'advanced instruction' for more able children.

Most of the costs of education were transferred away from the LEAs to central government, making the 1918 Act a watershed moment in the history of British education, as control over school financing was centralised. This process of centralisation would continue throughout the century. It resulted in an improvement in teachers' salaries and pensions, which the government hoped would improve school standards.

Educational provision

There were 328 authorities which provided two types of schools:

- Elementary schools – providing children with a basic education to the age of fourteen.
- Secondary and technical schools – educating children to the age of sixteen.

Different LEAs had different provisions, however. The 1926 Hadow Committee into education provision not only lamented the incomplete records kept by LEAs but reported 'there was the widest diversity of educational provision in different areas'. Its report recommended:

- the abolition of elementary schools and the division into primary and secondary schools with children transferring at the age of eleven
- the raising of the school-leaving age to fifteen.

Its recommendations were not adopted both because of cost and because the responsibility for education had been devolved to local authorities. Some authorities only provided elementary schools of variable quality. Sometimes class sizes were huge, often reaching 50 and on occasion as many as 60; the only possible form of education was learning by rote in these classrooms. Elementary education was, however, free. Some authorities provided secondary or technical schools to which children transferred at eleven, although the quality of education in these was variable. Given the financial constraints the emphasis was generally on frugality.

Secondary education

Overall, secondary schools were the preserve of middle-class children; from 1918 to 1944 education was compulsory only up to the age of fourteen. Even on the eve of the Second World War only 13 per cent of working-class children aged thirteen and above were still in school.

The uneven nature of educational provision can be shown in the following figures. In 1931 there were 5.5 million children in elementary schools and 600,000 in some form of secondary education; the university population was 30,000. Put differently, the figures show that only 20 per cent of children were in some form of secondary education – and many of these would leave at fourteen.

▲ A school outing in the interwar period. What does this photograph suggest about life in school in the interwar period?

Theme 2 Creating a welfare state, 1918–79

> **Grammar schools**
>
> The 1918 Act also created another kind of secondary education – grant-funded grammar schools, sometimes called central schools, and often operated by the local authorities. They charged fees, but brighter children could be awarded scholarships. The schools often used entrance exams to select pupils. Many grammar schools offered an academic curriculum based on that of fee-paying public schools and provided an excellent education; places were highly sought after. However, the system was based on wealth as much as equality of opportunity as poorer parents often could not afford to keep their bright offspring at school beyond the age of fourteen, even if they did get a scholarship – they needed them to earn a wage to help support the family.

Changes in education, 1939–44

By the outbreak of the Second World War it was recognised by civil servants and social reformers such as the **Fabian Society** that there were major variations in the provision and quality of education across Britain. There were huge inequalities and these were believed to be key factors in reinforcing Britain's class system (see page 96). The poor were unable to access the education that the children of the **middle classes** enjoyed and as a result they remained stuck in cycles of poverty. While grammar schools increased the number of free places they offered to poor but able children, the other costs associated with sending children to grammar school such as transport and uniform made it unaffordable for many working-class parents.

The impact of the Second World War

The Beveridge Report of 1942 identified ignorance as one of the great 'evils' that affected Britain (see page 62). Indeed, many branches of the armed services had to teach basic literacy and numeracy to the lower ranks. The Second World War required educated troops as the technological complexity of modern warfare had dramatically increased. An educated civilian workforce and a **civilian defence** and **auxiliary service** was also required, not just during the war but after it as well. As the tide of war turned against **Nazi Germany**, Britain approached a new and uncertain world of **superpower rivalries**, one in which it could not afford to be complacent.

2 The 'Butler Act', 1944

The Education Act 1944 and the later Scottish Education Act 1945 were both major extensions to working-class children's access to education. State secondary schools would no longer charge fees and the cost of mass education would be paid for out of general taxation, making schools, like healthcare, the responsibility of central government. Compulsory education was extended to the age of fifteen.

LEAs were obliged to provide 'instruction and training as may be desirable in view of their different ages, abilities and aptitudes'. However, both Acts created an education system that reflected, and critics argued perpetuated, Britain's rigid class structure.

> **Note it down**
>
> Note-making in this section would lend itself to a spider diagram (see page x). Label the spider's body 'Education Act, 1944' and draw each leg to represent one aspect: grammar schools, secondary modern schools, technical schools. In your notes give at least one advantage and disadvantage of each.

A tripartite system

The Education Acts were created by Richard 'Rab' Butler, the education minister, and they established a 'tripartite' system of schools for secondary education, closely matching Britain's class system: grammar schools, secondary modern schools and secondary technical schools.

Grammar schools

Grammar schools were intended to make an academic curriculum open to all children who could pass an 'eleven-plus' exam and, particularly in less affluent areas, were to provide a route into greater opportunity for many working-class children.

Secondary modern schools

Secondary moderns tended to educate the majority of **lower middle-class** and working-class children and generally received fewer resources and had less well-qualified teachers. Having said this, the best secondary moderns offered innovative curricula appropriate for their intake and developed close ties with local colleges so pupils could transfer onto vocational courses and embark on work placements.

Seventy-five per cent of children went to secondary moderns in the post-war period; in 1964 only 318 of their total intake were entered for 'A' levels.

Paper 1 Britain transformed, 1918–97

Technical schools

The technical schools were intended to educate the middle classes for a life in scientific or engineering work; to create a **technocratic class** who could help the country to adapt in an age of high technology and nuclear power. However, the reality was that few were ever built because of the cost. Their intake was never more than 3 per cent of secondary school students.

> **The eleven-plus exam**
>
> In order to determine which secondary school a child eventually attended they sat the eleven-plus exam which had three sections: academic, technical and functional. Initially, the drafters of the Butler Act had intended for the exam to filter children to the three types of school:
>
> - academic ability: grammar schools
> - technical ability: technical college
> - functional ability: secondary modern.
>
> Technical ability was eventually left out and instead of the test being a means of channelling pupils to schools that suited them, it became a test to decide whether pupils could enter grammar school or not. Critics argued that it was impossible to tell how a child would intellectually develop at the age of eleven. Opponents of grammar schools in the Labour Party argued that the Act deepened class divisions by sending the majority of working-class children to secondary moderns.
>
> Butler did not anticipate how few technical schools would be built. The majority of children who did not pass the eleven-plus exam found themselves joining secondary modern schools instead.

The effect of the Butler Act

For the first time millions of working-class children had a free and compulsory secondary education and girls, who had previously been excluded from secondary education, were able to attend school. Social change in the 1960s and 1970s was in part the result of the 1944 Act, as it enabled more children than at any other time in the nation's history to become educated.

3 The development of comprehensive education, 1944–79

Between 1944 and 1976 (when a new Education Act was introduced) the Butler Act determined how most of Britain's children were educated. The Conservative Party and the right of the Labour Party saw the three tiers of the education system as a way of effectively providing for the economy's needs, but the Labour left viewed it as socially divisive.

The left of the Labour Party had hoped for comprehensive schools, which would have seen children of all class backgrounds attend the same schools with no eleven-plus exam, but they were disappointed. Just as the Attlee government struggled to break the power of vested interests in medicine (see pages 71–2), so did it fail to really tackle divisive issues of class in education.

By the early 1960s, as thirteen years of Conservative rule came to an end, a popular anti-elitist sentiment was present in politics and the media (see page 99). The **Etonian** backgrounds of Prime Ministers Harold Macmillan and Alec Douglas-Home were seen by voters as hopelessly anachronistic and from an era of deference that was long gone. Most developed countries in Europe, Canada, Australia and Japan had abolished their selection practices, leaving Britain appearing to lag behind.

In this context, the issue of selection in schools was high on the agenda and Harold Wilson's new Labour government of 1964 was finally able to address the issue. It felt that if the grammar schools were so good, they ought to be available to every child. This marked the development of comprehensive schools, which were intended to offer what Labour's Wilson called, 'grammar schools for all'.

> **Note it down**
>
> Write notes on the development of comprehensive education. Choose the form of notes that you prefer (see page ix), but make sure you address the following questions:
> - What was the significance of the 1959 Crowther and 1963 Newsom Reports?
> - What was the purpose of comprehensive schools?
> - Why was the 1976 Education Act passed?
> - How widespread and successful was progressive education?
> - What were the concerns about education by the late 1970s?

Early comprehensives in the 1950s

Throughout the 1950s there had been a growth in comprehensive schools in mainly Labour local authorities; the first purpose-built comprehensive opened at Kidbrooke in 1954. By the end of the 1950s opinion over the selective school system was divided, with some people (those who tended to benefit from selection) seeing it as fair and rational, and others seeing it as unfair and arbitrary.

Comprehensive schools included all children, regardless of ability. It was felt they could offer equality of educational opportunity and prevent children being stigmatised at the age of eleven. It was found, moreover, that the eleven-plus examination could be inaccurate in predicting future potential because the brain matures at different times. Comprehensive schools would give pupils the opportunity to transfer between streams of attainment and different courses. They would not only be more flexible but, in taking greater numbers of pupils, would be able to offer a greater variety of courses with more resources.

Reports into education provision

In 1959 and 1963 the Conservative government commissioned two reports into education provision – the first looking at education for young people aged fifteen to nineteen (the Crowther Report), the second at the provision for average or less able children aged thirteen to sixteen (the Newsom Report). These reports were a precursor to the expansion of comprehensive education in the 1960s.

The key feature of both reports was that they focussed on the realities of education in the late 1950s and early 1960s and sought to work with and improve conditions for young people. They also added fuel to the movement toward comprehensive schools as the best way to ensure equality of educational opportunity.

The Crowther Report, 1959

The Crowther Report was commissioned because the government was conscious of 'the changing social and industrial needs of our society, and the needs of its individual citizens', and therefore changes in the type of education required. British society had undergone a transformation since 1954. It had become more **meritocratic** and less **deferential** (see page 99), with greater opportunities for education and **social mobility** for the working classes. The report was based on a recognition of these changes and made a series of recommendations:

- raising the school-leaving age to sixteen
- creating county colleges for post-sixteen education and creating more technical colleges
- attracting sixth-form teachers of the 'highest intellectual calibre'
- widening the number of sixth-form courses from the purely vocational to subjects such as art and the humanities; this would reflect the large number of students accessing sixth-form education for the first time
- preparing highly able pupils for university while not treating less able pupils as second-best in the classroom
- enabling all pupils who were capable of taking O levels to do so
- facilitating a large influx of teachers into the profession in order to bring these changes about.

> **O levels and A levels**
>
> In 1951 the General Certificate in Education was introduced, divided into an Ordinary level taken at sixteen and an Advanced level taken at eighteen. The vast majority of pupils who took them were either in grammar schools or in private education.

The Newsom Report, 1963

The next major education report after Crowther was the Newsom Report, which had a working title of 'Half Our Future'. The report examined education provision for low-ability children, stating that it would:

consider the education between the ages of 13 and 16 of pupils of average or less than average ability who are or will be following full-time courses either at schools or in establishments of further education.

The report found some serious failings in the provision of education in poor areas. In some inner-city schools there was a high turnover of teachers, leaving already disadvantaged pupils with little continuity in their education.

Newsom recommended the following:

- There should be a new focus on researching teaching methods to help children who struggled at school.
- More attention should be paid to teaching deprived children personal and social development; and sex education was essential.
- A working party in Parliament should be set up to examine the links between deprivation and poor educational attainment.
- More practical subjects should be provided for lower ability pupils and schools should not make pupils sit exams where it was thought to be inappropriate.

The development of comprehensives

In the Labour Party's 1964 election manifesto it clearly articulated its intention to:

> get rid of the segregation of children into separate schools caused by 11-plus selection: secondary education will be reorganised on comprehensive lines.

In the year of the election there were 3,906 secondary moderns, 1,298 grammar schools and only 195 comprehensives, meaning that the Labour Party had an enormous structural change to make if it planned to stick to its manifesto pledge. Labour's new education secretary, Anthony Crosland, who privately pledged to destroy the grammar school system said:

> The whole notion of a selection test at this age belongs to the era when secondary education was a privilege of the few.

Labour informed LEAs that it expected to see them dismantle selection, but it never forced them to do so. The government hoped that gradually, more and more authorities would adopt comprehensive schooling, and that as new schools were built they would instinctively make them non-selective. The number of comprehensives did grow, but no policy to force the issue was ever created. It was planned for introduction if Labour had won the 1970 General Election, but as Wilson lost to Heath (see page 20), the full comprehensive policy was lost.

Comprehensives under Heath

The development of comprehensive schools and the decline of grammar schools from the 1960s onwards was one of the most divisive and controversial issues in post-war British education. Both parties created comprehensive schools and abolished grammars, despite many members of the Conservative Party being fiercely opposed to the policy.

The Heath government's education secretary, Margaret Thatcher, instructed that no more requests from LEAs for mergers of grammars and secondary moderns would be considered. She also increased funding of **direct grant schools** and spoke out in favour of the right to choose private education.

However, by the time she had left the Education Department she had authorised more comprehensive mergers than any other secretary. Between 1970 and 1974 she was presented with 3,612 comprehensive schemes and approved 3,286. The number of comprehensive schools had more than doubled from 30 per cent of secondary schools in 1970 to 62 per cent four years later.

The Education Act, 1976

When the Labour government returned to office (see page 21), the opponents of selection hoped that finally the opportunity to abolish it had arrived.

Wilson knew that ending funding for non-comprehensive schools would be popular with the **left wing** of the Labour Party. He proposed ending funding for direct grant schools and making them comprehensives, even though they offered half their places free to working- and lower-middle-class families with academically able children. The National Union of Teachers supported the government, claiming that it would take elitism out of education. In many cases, however, the opposite happened. As direct grant schools lost their funding, they were forced to charge fees and become private schools instead, meaning that low-income pupils would no longer be able to afford to attend.

Despite the hopes of many in the cabinet, there was little enthusiasm from either Wilson or Callaghan to finally abolish all grammar schools and in the 1976 Education Act selection survived. The Act simply reiterated the 1965 demands for LEAs to submit proposals for making their schools comprehensive, but did not compel them to act. Both prime ministers realised that Britain's middle classes were opposed to abolition and neither wanted to become unpopular over an issue that was not a central part of their political agenda.

Nevertheless, by 1979, comprehensive schools were the main form of secondary education in much of England

Table 1: Different types of secondary schools in England and Wales

Year	Secondary modern	Grammar	Technical	Comprehensive
1955	3550	1180	302	16
1960	3867	1268	251	130
1965	3727	1285	172	262
1970	2691	1038	82	1145
1975	1216	566	29	2596
1980	445	224	17	3297

Source: Education: Historical statistics, found at www.parliament.uk/briefing-papers/sn04252.pdf

and Wales. Meanwhile others sought alternative forms of education both within and outside mainstream schools, and in the 1960s and 1970s progressive forms of education became more accepted.

Progressive education

During the 1960s and 1970s new and unconventional methods of teaching were pioneered in some of Britain's comprehensive schools, attracting immense controversy in the press. In Britain's teacher training colleges, older ideas about teaching, such as **rote learning**, were replaced by a new concept: '**child-centred learning**'. This was partly as a result of a government paper – the Plowden Report – in 1967 that recommended:

- banning **corporal punishment**
- giving children much more freedom within the classroom (instead of forcing them to sit on chairs for long periods of time)
- encouraging teachers to help and advise, rather than lecture pupils.

Academics who supported progressive education believed that if schools were friendlier, less strict and more welcoming, then educational attainment would improve, especially in deprived areas where children were disadvantaged by poverty.

A small minority of teachers saw progressive education as a means to introduce overtly political ideas into the classroom. Within the National Union of Teachers, a group of radical left-wing teachers, the Rank and File group, which had over 2,000 members in 1975, saw it as an opportunity to undermine Britain's class system.

William Tyndale School

One school in particular attained national notoriety, William Tyndale School in Islington. The school removed all rules and allowed pupils to decide what they wanted to do, including watching TV or leaving the classroom. Parents withdrew their children from the school in protest. An official government enquiry was held about the failings of the school, which concluded that the teachers had placed their own revolutionary **socialist** views ahead of their commitment to teaching pupils. Schools like William Tyndale were the exception to the rule, even among those schools that adopted progressive educational ideas. However, the national press interest in the case and the widespread concern about how children were being taught shows that there were deep-seated anxieties and fears about change in education throughout the 1970s.

Some schools that practised progressive education had outstanding educational results. They combined allowing children to have more freedom in the classroom and more of a say in how the school was run with extra planning and organisation. Other schools produced chaotic classrooms where very little was taught, and even though they were a small minority of Britain's comprehensives, the press publicised the most extreme examples of educational failing and ideological interference.

The Black Papers

The first major negative reaction to progressive education was published in 1969. Two academics, Brian Cox and Tony Dyson, published a series of essays called the 'Black Papers', criticising the decline in the teacher's authority in the classroom. Yet neither man advocated returning to the strict and repetitive learning that was common in the 1950s. They were joined by a North London headmaster, Dr Rhodes Boyson, who was a tough disciplinarian and an outspoken opponent of progressive education.

Yellow Book

When James Callaghan became prime minister he ordered a report into Britain's education system, which was published in October 1976. The findings of the report, titled the 'Yellow Book', were damning, suggesting that progressive education methods had caused immense harm to teaching. It stated that:

- school discipline had declined
- many school curricula did not prepare pupils to take up productive roles in the economy
- the government and the public had too little say over what went on in schools.

Ruskin speech

Based on the Yellow Book's findings Callaghan delivered a speech at Ruskin College (he chose Ruskin because it had been founded to educate working-class men, and Callaghan believed that it was the working classes who were most negatively affected by progressive education). In the speech he suggested that:

- Progressive education had some merits and achieved good results when in the hands of skilled teachers, but failed when it was applied incorrectly.
- He did not wish to return to the rote learning of the 1950s.
- There should be a national curriculum that all schools should follow.
- Teachers should be more closely scrutinised and inspected.

The Ruskin speech initiated a 'great debate' on education, which called for education to provide school leavers with the skills they would need in an increasingly technological and competitive world. Many felt that comprehensive schools were often too large, impersonal and failed too many pupils. It was argued that they didn't offer relevant curricula or prepare students for the modern world. It was felt that many teachers had too much autonomy over what they taught and how they taught it. Progressive educational methods were particularly vilified. Many spoke of the need for greater control over the curriculum and methods of teaching. The debate set the path for educational reforms, including the introduction of a National Curriculum in the 1980s.

4 University education, 1918–79

Britain's universities in 1918 were some of its oldest institutions, many having been founded in the Middle Ages, and were used to being autonomous from the government. However, in an age of **total war** and global economic competition and an era where the role of the state massively expanded, universities would be forced to make radical changes. By 1979 they would experience the effects of mass education, mass affluence and a decline in deference that were to mark the era.

> ### Note it down
> Use the 1:2 method (page x) to develop notes about university education in the period 1918–79.
>
> | | |
> |---|---|
> | University education in the 1920s and 1930s | How far did university education grow during the interwar years? |
> | Percy and Barlow Reports | How influential were these reports? |
> | University expansion during the 1960s and 1970s | How far did higher education expand during these decades? |
> | Social impact of university education | How far was society affected by the growth of higher education? |

Universities in the 1920s and 1930s

British universities in the second half of the nineteenth century became far more accessible to Britain's middle classes and to women, meaning that by 1918 there was a diverse and expanding university education provision. While Oxford and Cambridge remained largely for the privileged, provincial universities increasingly took on more middle-class and bright working-class students. These were funded mainly through grants and scholarships offered by LEAs and charities. Some LEAs were far more generous than others but all such grants were fiercely competitive. One more common route, particularly for bright working-class students, was through government-funded teacher-training grants. Here, recipients known as 'Recognised Students in Training' (RSTs) agreed to follow their degree with postgraduate teacher training with a commitment to teaching for varying periods thereafter. Many families saw the value of higher education in enabling their offspring to have a better future and memoirs tell of all sorts of family sacrifices and ways of earning money, such as taking in washing and lodgers, to enable them to go to university.

University funding

From 1919 onwards universities became directly funded by the government, coming under the control of the treasury. During the 1920s a deputation of universities, including Oxford and Cambridge, appealed to the government for increased funding to help cover their growing costs. The government increased the levels of grants to universities but also increased its scrutiny of how universities were managed. Three commissions throughout the 1920s examined and improved universities' governing institutions, and by the end of the decade the role of government funding in the university sector was established. In general, however, the government did not overly interfere with the working of universities and the amount of financial aid offered normally amounted to about one-third of university funds. The rest came from fees, endowments and so on.

Even though the universities had been partly nationalised at this point, they were not a central part of government policy until after the Second World War. Most governments of the 1920s and 1930s considered universities as irrelevant to their overall goals. It would take a government in 1945 with a far broader vision for social transformation to draw universities into the centre of government policy.

The Percy and Barlow Reports

The Second World War demonstrated the needs for large numbers of science graduates – innovations like radar, code breaking, jet technology and computing had developed during the war and in the post-war era there was still a huge demand for such skills.

The 1945 Attlee government believed that universities should become centres for science and engineering, creating the technologically skilled generation that would run the country's economy in the 1950s and 1960s. In the same year a government paper, the Percy Report, recommended that:

- the privileged position of classical education (Latin, the classics) in university curricula be challenged in favour of science and engineering
- universities be dramatically expanded to cater for the large numbers of students that would be created as a result of the Butler Act, 1944 (see page 82).

The following year a second paper, the Barlow Report, confirmed that there were far too few scientists and engineering students and also argued for a government-funded expansion of universities.

Despite these recommendations, by the 1960s there were still far too few science courses and many universities prioritised arts subjects, indicating that universities were institutions that were resistant to change.

By 1961, despite the huge increase in school pupils and the recommendations of Percy and Barlow, only 15 per cent of applications to university were successful. However, over twenty new universities were opened in the 1960s and by the end of the decade a revolution in British university education appeared to have taken place.

University expansion

In 1961 the government set up the Robbins Committee; two years later it produced some dire warnings for the government. Britain was being overtaken by other countries in terms of university performance and the only option was to guarantee a university place for all who were eligible to attend. The committee's report recommended a goal of five times more student places by 1980, and stated that university education should achieve four main goals:

- Universities must give 'instruction in skills' to make sure the country had a competent workforce.
- Universities must develop in their students 'general powers of the mind' to make sure that they were broadly well-educated.
- Teaching academics should still continue to carry out research because 'the process of education is itself most vital when it partakes of the nature of discovery'.
- Teaching also had a social role and should impart 'the transmission of a common culture and common standards of citizenship'.

The University of East Sussex opened in 1961, just as the Robbins Committee met. It was described as a 'plate-glass' campus because of its modern buildings and architecture. A similar university, Kent, at Canterbury, opened in 1965 and both institutions adopted a multi-disciplinary approach to learning, enabling students to experience a number of different subjects instead of just one. This was the result of Robbins' recommendations, encouraging learners to have a rounded education and a sense of common culture and citizenship.

By 1970 a further eleven universities were established and both Labour and Conservative, keen to show how egalitarian, progressive and modern they were, agreed that the welfare state should be expanded to pay for tuition fees and student grants. In addition 32 'second-tier' institutions or polytechnics were founded, focussing on scientific subjects and vocational courses. This was designed to counter the trend in established universities of focussing on the arts.

The Open University

The final university innovation that was planned during the 1960s and began in 1971 was the Open University, established by the Wilson government under Arts Minister Jenny Lee in 1964. The Open University was an institution based almost exclusively on distance learning, where people could study degrees at home. It ensured that people of any age who had missed out on higher education could become qualified and it was a key part of Wilson's modernising and democratising goals. When Edward Heath came to power in 1970 he considered cancelling the Open University, but decided against it, fearing the political fallout.

Universities in the 1970s

Education Secretary Margaret Thatcher advised Heath against abolishing the Open University. In addition to this, she heavily invested in Britain's university sector, despite the country facing a bleak economic outlook between 1970 and 1974 (see page 36). She spent more than any of her predecessors on university and polytechnic funding, increasing grants by 40 per cent throughout Heath's government.

Both Conservative and Labour governments throughout the decade began to reduce targets for the numbers of students going to university and the funding available for them. By 1979, there had been a slowdown in the increase of numbers enrolling at universities, but not an overall decline. The target that the Heath government set for 1981 was three-quarters of a million students in higher education, and even though this was missed by over 100,000 the overall increase in student numbers was enormous. Table 2 shows the number of students who passed a first degree. The data do not show the total numbers of those who took a first degree but may have failed or dropped out of study, nor those taking postgraduate study. Nevertheless they show a significant increase in the numbers of students earning degrees between 1920 and 1980.

Table 2: Number of first degrees awarded in the UK

Year	Number of first degrees
1920	4357
1930	9129
1950	17337
1960	22426
1970	51189
1980	68150

Source: Education: Historical statistics, found at www.parliament.uk/briefing-papers/sn04252.pdf

Social impact of university education

The expansion in state-funded university education throughout the twentieth century has had a far-reaching impact on society and social mobility. The emergence of working-class and lower-middle-class British prime ministers such as Harold Wilson, Edward Heath and Margaret Thatcher (all of whom were Oxford graduates) was only possible because of state subsidies available to universities. In addition to high-profile political figures, large numbers of men and women from modest backgrounds were able to obtain qualifications that enabled them to join professions such as law, engineering, medicine and finance, which before would have been the preserve of the better-off.

The large increase in student numbers was only possible because of the increase in the number of institutions. By 1971 there were 53 universities and 30 polytechnics, and by 1974 there were half a million students in higher education.

Student funding increased from the 1950s onwards, enabling students not only to pay tuition fees to universities but also to live on grants that covered the basic costs of food and accommodation. The lack of financial risk to the student involved in studying for a university degree was another powerful incentive for many people from working-class backgrounds to study.

Elitism

Despite the increase in equality in higher education throughout the twentieth century, social class remained a controversial issue. Pupils from private schools, especially Britain's top public schools such as Eton and Harrow, were over-represented at elite universities such as Oxford, Cambridge and St Andrews.

While participation in higher education increased dramatically, there was still a sense of elitism in British education and alumni from traditional universities and public schools had influence way beyond their numbers. Many would argue that with the demise of local authority grammar schools, this influence increased rather than diminished. While the educational system may be based on equality of opportunity, this was not necessarily the case in practice and educational success that leads to opportunities at the highest managerial and professional levels were still dependent far more on privilege and position.

> **Work together**
>
> A major theme in this chapter has been how fair the educational system was in terms of equality of educational opportunity. Read through each other's notes. Prepare a plan for the following essay based on your partner's notes:
>
> **To what extent was equality of educational opportunity achieved in Britain through educational reforms 1918–79?**
>
> When you have completed this, discuss how straightforward it was to follow each other's notes to complete this activity. If you found it difficult, how could the notes be improved?

Chapter summary

- The 1918 Education Act saw education funded by central government but organised by local education authorities (LEAs).
- Provision varied according to LEA but most ran grammar schools funded by fees or scholarships for bright pupils.
- The onset of the Second World War and the Beveridge Report of 1942 highlighted shortcomings in educational attainment in Britain.
- The 1944 Education Act introduced a tripartite system of grammar, secondary modern and technical schools, based on selection, often through the eleven-plus examination.
- Grammar schools were often excellent but secondary moderns, taking up to 75 per cent of the yearly intake, were often poorly resourced and staffed, and comparatively few technical schools were ever built.
- The 1959 Crowther and 1963 Newsom Reports highlighted the unfairness of the current system and low attainment of less affluent pupils.
- The 1950s, 1960s and 1970s saw the growth of comprehensive schools to promote equality of educational opportunity more effectively.
- The Education Act 1976 shied away from the complete abolition of selection but cut funding to direct grant grammar schools which had taken many bright working-class children.
- Progressive education based on child-centred learning developed both in mainstream schools and outside the formal system.
- Concerns with the overall quality of education led to the Black Papers and the 1976 Ruskin speech, initiating a 'great debate' which saw the advocacy of schools becoming more accountable to government and parents.
- More middle-class and working-class students went to university during the interwar years.
- The Percy and Barlow Reports highlighted the need for more science and technology-based university education.
- The Robbins Report of 1963 led to the rapid expansion of university education in the 1960s and 1970s.

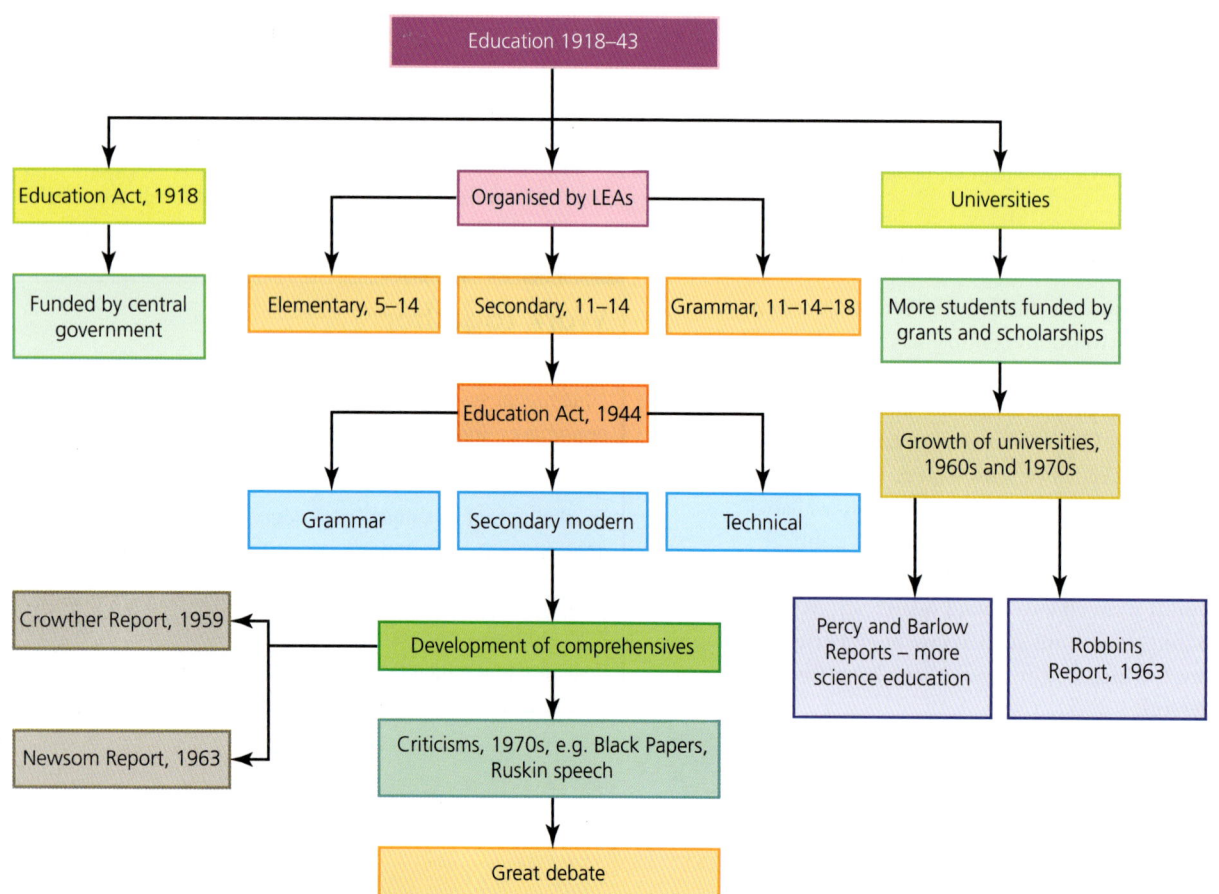

▲ Summary diagram: Education and widening opportunities

Paper 1 Britain transformed, 1918–97

Recommended reading: Creating a welfare state, 1918–79

S. Braster, F. Simon and I. Grosvenor, *A History of Popular Education: Educating the People of the World* (Routledge, 2013). A series of essays about twentieth-century education internationally, but with Chapters 9 and 10 devoted to educational change in mid-twentieth-century Britain.

A. Hardy, *Health and Medicine in Britain since 1860* (Palgrave Macmillan, 2000). A thorough history of the development of healthcare in Britain and the development of medicine throughout the nineteenth and twentieth centuries.

M. Jones and R. Lowe, *From Beveridge to Blair: The First Fifty Years of Britain's Welfare State 1948–1998* (Manchester University Press, 2002). A detailed exploration of the history of the welfare state, housing, education, health and social services throughout the post-war era.

R. Lowe, *The Welfare State in Britain Since 1945* (Palgrave Macmillan, 1998). This is a thorough analysis of changes to all aspects of welfare, health and education provision in Britain since 1945.

M. Sanderson, *Education and Economic Decline in Britain, 1870 to the 1990s* (Cambridge University Press, 1999). This book explores the relationship between Britain's education system and its economic performance, arguing that educational standards have been part of, but not solely the cause of, relative economic decline throughout the century.

N. Thomas-Symonds, *Nye: The Political Life of Aneurin Bevan* (I.B. Tauris, 2014). A critically acclaimed and expertly researched new life of Aneurin Bevan, founder of the NHS.

N. Timmins, *The Five Giants: A Biography of the Welfare State* (HarperCollins). An accessible and detailed guide to the history of the welfare state, with a very clear discussion of the Beveridge Report.

Essay technique: Overall judgement

In addition to focus and structure (see page 40), the level of relevant detail (see page 56) and analysis (see page 79), your exam essays will be assessed on how far you reach a supported overall judgement. The clearer and better supported your judgement, the better your mark is likely to be. The mark scheme distinguishes between five levels of judgement (this is a summary – the full mark scheme can be found on Edexcel's website):

Level 1	No overall judgement.
Level 2	Stated overall judgement, but no support.
Level 3	Overall judgement is reached, with weak support.
Level 4	Overall judgement is reached, and supported.
Level 5	Overall judgement is reached, and supported by consideration of the relative significance of key factors.

This section looks at reaching and supporting an overall judgement. Dealing with the relative significance of key factors is discussed at the end of Chapter 4c (see page 167).

Reaching an overall judgement

The conclusion of your essay should reach an overall judgement. This judgement should reflect the overall argument of your essay. Imagine you are answering the following question:

> How far did the development of comprehensive education widen equality of opportunity in education in the period, 1954–79?

Your essay plan might look like this:

Paragraph 1: The goals of the comprehensive system compared to the tripartite system

Paragraph 2: The extent of implementation, 1954–79 – comprehensive education is never available universally

Paragraph 3: The successes of comprehensive education

Paragraph 4: The problems of the comprehensive system – Black Papers, Ruskin speech

This essay focusses on the extent to which comprehensive education increased equality of opportunity. In order to answer it successfully, you'll need to consider both the successes of the scheme and the ways in which it failed. For example, Paragraph 2 considers the extent of success through examining the extent to which the policy was implemented, and Paragraphs 3 and 4 deal with the successes and failures in comprehensive schools where the policy was implemented. Having focussed on the success or failure of the policy throughout the essay you will also need to evaluate the extent of success in your conclusion.

Your essay might argue that from 1954 comprehensive schools were intended to promote equality of educational opportunity as a result of the failures of the tripartite system, for example through the inadequacies of many secondary moderns and the failure to build technical schools. However, critics in the 1970s drew attention to continuing problems with educational attainment so they were only partly successful. This argument should be reflected in your overall judgement. Therefore, the first line of your conclusion might look like the one below.

- Establishes that you are reaching your overall judgement → **In conclusion,** the development of comprehensive education was never able to ensure complete equality of opportunity in education in the period 1954–79. ← The words of the question are used to answer the question – ensuring a clear focus

- The conclusion mentions the successes of the system → Clearly, comprehensive schools did succeed in some ways.

- The conclusion mentions the failures of the system → However, they failed in others. Therefore, although there was some advancement in equality of opportunity, the system failed to create equal opportunities for all in the period 1954–79. ← The conclusion reaches a judgement that reflects the balance of the paragraph

Supporting your overall judgement

The example on page 92 is a good start, because an overall judgement has been reached that reflects the argument of the essay. But so far the overall judgement only has weak support.

In order to get into the higher levels it is important to support your overall judgement. This can be achieved by backing up your judgement with a summary of the key points of your essay. For example, the overall judgement you have just read on page 92 could be improved by adding the following summaries of your argument:

Establishes that you are reaching your overall judgement	**In conclusion**, the development of comprehensive education was never able to ensure complete equality of opportunity in education in the period 1954–79. Clearly, comprehensive schools did succeed in breaking down the old tripartite system, which tended to help middle-class children more than working-class students. However, the implementation of comprehensive education was never universal and therefore in some areas the divide between grammar schools and secondary moderns remained. Also there were concerns that comprehensive schools failed to open up opportunities to students because of alleged poor discipline and curricula that failed to equip students with the skills needed for the modern world. **Therefore, although there was some advancement in equality of opportunity, the system failed to create equal opportunities for all in the period 1959–79.**

- The words of the question are used to answer the question – ensuring a clear focus
- The conclusion considers the successes of the system
- The conclusion considers the failures of the system
- The conclusion reaches a judgement that reflects the balance of the paragraph

This conclusion is an example of high-level work because it reaches an overall judgement and supports it with material that reflects the rest of the essay.

Activity: Writing an overall judgement

Below is a plan in answer to the question:

How accurate is it to say that schools and universities failed to provide genuine equality of opportunity for students in the years 1964 to 1979?

- **Paragraph 1:** Comprehensive schools – successes
- **Paragraph 2:** Comprehensive schools – failures
- **Paragraph 3:** Universities – successes, e.g. expansion and Open University
- **Paragraph 4:** Universities – failures, Robbins Report and its impact, continuing elitism especially in the top universities

Using your notes from this chapter:
1. Write a summary sentence that states an overall judgement about how far schools and universities failed to improve equality of opportunity for students in the period 1964–79.
2. Support this with a summary overview of the successes and failures of education growth in terms of accessibility, in both schools and universities.
3. Write a final sentence that summarises your judgement.

Paper 1 Britain transformed, 1918–97

Theme 3 Society in transition, 1918–79

The big picture

This theme considers how far Britain changed in relation to class, social values, gender and race between 1918 and 1979.

Society moved from a rigid class structure in the interwar years to greater flexibility in the years following the Second World War, but particularly during the 1960s. Commentators speak of a decline in deference, which not only manifested itself in more assertiveness among the middle and lower classes but also a greater readiness to criticise the Establishment, particularly after the 1963 Profumo affair. The 1960s saw legislation to reform previous restrictions in personal lives such as the legalisation of homosexuality and abortion and greater freedom in the media. This provoked a reaction from critics such as Mary Whitehouse and her supporters.

Women fought for more equality, although they discovered that winning the vote on equal terms with men in 1928 did not necessarily lead to greater opportunities. Their role in political life remained comparatively small, and whereas they faced enhanced employment opportunities during the wars, these were rescinded by the return of peace. Although the government passed equal pay legislation and made sexual discrimination illegal in the 1970s, women still often faced discrimination. Second-wave feminism emerged as a reaction to continuing inequalities and morphed into a greater awareness of unfair treatment within the family. Women's groups, meanwhile, took the initiative in the fight against issues such as domestic violence and rape.

The period saw Britain become a more multi-racial society, although black and Asian people often faced discrimination in all walks of life, especially in the interwar period and into the 1950s when an unofficial colour bar operated. However, the need for cheap labour in the post-war period saw a massive rise in the numbers of immigrants from the new Commonwealth along with legislation in the 1960s and 1970s to outlaw discrimination. Many black and Asian people took the initiative to fight against unfair treatment and assert their right to be treated as equals in practice as well as in law.

In this theme you will consider the following:
- **Class and social values:** class, social change and the impact of the wars, 1918–51; the emergence of the 'liberal society' and its opponents, 1951–79.
- **The changing role and status of women:** the right to vote and political advancement, 1918–79; changes in family life and the quest for personal freedoms, 1918–79.
- **Race and immigration:** immigration policies and attitudes towards ethnic minorities, 1918–39; the impact of the Second World War and new Commonwealth immigration; racial controversy and the impact on race relations and immigration, 1958–79.

TIMELINE

1918	Representation of the People Act
1919	Sex Disqualification (Removal) Act
1920	Alien Orders Act
1925	Special Restrictions (Coloured and Alien Seamen) Act
1928	Representation of the People Act
1936 October	British Union of Fascists march in the East End of London
1937	Matrimonial Causes Act
1948	British Nationality Act
1948 August	Arrival of *Empire Windrush*
1958 August	Notting Hill riots
1957	Wolfenden Report published
1959	Obscene Publications Act
1960	*Lady Chatterley* trial
1961	The contraceptive pill introduced for married women
1962	Commonwealth Immigration Act
1963 March	Resignation of John Profumo
1965	Race Relations Act
1965	National Viewers and Listeners Association (NVALA) founded
1967	Sexual Offences Act
1967	Abortion Act
1968 April	'Rivers of Blood' speech by Enoch Powell
1968	The Dagenham sewing machinists' strike
1968	Race Relations Act
1968	Commonwealth Immigration Act
1970	Equal Pay Act
1970	*The Female Eunuch* by Germaine Greer published
1971	Immigration Act
1973	First Rape Crisis Centre opened
1974	National Women's Aid Federation established
1975	Sex Discrimination Act
1976	Race Relations Act
1976	Domestic Violence and Matrimonial Proceedings Act

3a: Class and social values

> ## Overview
> It is clear that by 1979 the way much of the population felt about key areas of public and private life had changed beyond recognition since 1918. The two world wars had to some extent led to a change in attitudes towards class and authority, including a decline in deference. This change became more pronounced during the 1950s and 1960s. The 1960s and 1970s also saw the emergence of a 'liberal society' with a new openness about sex and challenges to existing ideas about sexuality, marriage, abortion and homosexuality. Some groups opposed this greater permissiveness and changes to social values, greeting them with fear, suspicion and hostility.
>
> This theme examines these changes in attitudes and values through the following sections:
> 1. Class, social change and the impact of the wars, 1918–51
> 2. The emergence of the 'liberal society', 1951–79
> 3. Opponents of the liberal society, 1951–79

1 Class, social change and the impact of the wars, 1918–51

At the beginning of the twentieth century, social class largely determined a person's status and place in society. The British class system was organised into four main groups whose occupations and values can be generalised as follows (see Table 1).

Table 1: British class system

Social class	Description
Industrial working classes	People who worked as manual labourers or skilled craftsmen in factories, mines, docks and on the railways. Lived predominantly in tight-knit communities The skilled or artisan working classes were craftsmen who had specialised skills, earning more and often identifying with and aspiring to join the middle classes.
Lower middle classes	Workers in semi-skilled clerical jobs; small business owners who tended to own their own homes.
Middle classes	Professionals (doctors, lawyers, bankers, civil servants), who did highly specialised tasks.
Upper classes	Families who had inherited wealth, land and titles, often represented in the House of Lords. Natural supporters of the Conservative Party. Most senior army officers who fought the First World War were upper class, as were a significant number of ministers (25 out of 59 cabinet posts) in Asquith and Lloyd George's wartime cabinets.

There was a tendency for those in the higher social classes, in positions of power, to be treated with deference by those in the lower social orders. Those in power were generally respected and trusted to lead the country's institutions. However, although in the years preceding the First World War there were some challenges to the existing status quo, it was the impact of the First World War (1914–18) and then the Second World War (1939–45) which led to more notable social changes.

> ### Examples of challenges, pre-1918
> - The suffragette campaign. In the years before the war, women protesting the vote had adopted increasingly violent tactics such as window smashing and arson. This shocked many who had perceived women as docile and quiescent.
> - Trade union militancy. Radical syndicalist unions threatened a **general strike** in 1914, believing it would bring about revolution. This questioned the perceived deference of working people towards 'their betters'.
>
> Both examples convinced many conservative figures that the world was changing for the worse as former certainties about the position of people in society were challenged.

> ### Note it down
> This section focusses on how far people's attitudes to class changed as a result of the two world wars. Using a spider diagram (see page x), make notes on the following topics:
> - the impact of the First World War
> - class and social values between the wars
> - the impact of the Second World War.
>
> The emphasis should be on how far attitudes changed during this period.

The impact of the First World War

In 1918, social class still very much determined status, but there were changes which were impacted by the First World War.

Decline in deference

The high death toll (704,803 men from Britain were killed) shook the confidence the working classes had in the upper-class generals who led them. Moreover, life in the trenches had often resulted in working- and middle-class men interacting on a more even basis (sharing dangers and what comforts there were). Both these factors led to a decline in the deference in which the upper classes and middle classes were held. This was to decline further throughout the twentieth century, particularly after the Second World War in the 1950s and 1960s.

Decline in the upper classes

The death toll among Britain's upper classes was disproportionately high in the First World War. In 1914 alone six peers, sixteen baronets, six knights and 261 sons of aristocrats lost their lives. Many families were forced to pay death duties for those killed. Death duties themselves, introduced in 1894, were instrumental in what many historians such as David Cannadine have called 'the decline of the aristocracy'. Elder sons often had to sell their land or stately homes to pay these. Before 1914 less than 10 per cent of those working the land owned it; by 1930 this had risen to 33 per cent.

Many aristocrats could not afford to maintain their grand homes. Some were sold to the National Trust; others were sold as schools or hotels; some fell into disrepair as owners could no longer afford to live in them. However, one should not over-exaggerate the impact; the Duke of Portland owned eight grand houses in 1914 and despite straitened circumstances still maintained four in 1939.

Greater equality

The experience of war had resulted in a more democratic society, with the passing of the 1918 Representation of the People Act (see page 5). People in work could improve their living standards in the interwar years and even in the worst years of the depression prices fell faster than wages. As a result many people felt more equal. They had surplus income and could aspire to more affluent lifestyles than their parents.

> **Housing**
>
> One indication of improving living standards was a growth in the construction of houses for owner-occupiers. The number of owner-occupiers rose from 750,000 in the early 1920s to 3,250,000 by 1938. They were particularly evident in growing suburbs where increased car ownership and the extension of the railway network made it possible for more people to travel to work. The term 'Metroland' was coined for an area of north London serviced by the growth of the Metropolitan Railway and developed with houses built speculatively by builders who anticipated a ready market.

Class and social values, 1918–39

Although some commentators at the time, particularly in the immediate years after the war, feared open class revolt, these changes did not lead to social barriers and conventions significantly breaking down.

In 1919 the British government feared open revolt in some parts of the country, such as Clydeside (see page 43). Much of this was the result of long-term economic factors, but it also suggested that working-class attitudes towards other social groups had changed. In 1926, at the time of the general strike (see page 44), *The Times*, a newspaper that tended to represent the views and concerns of Britain's middle classes, attacked the strikers calling them unpatriotic class warriors. Middle-class volunteers organised to break the strike, identifying with what they believed was the national interest.

These examples of 'class conflict' were, however, rare. In the mid- to late 1920s strikes were actually in decline and the Conservative Party continued to enjoy widespread working- and middle-class support in general elections, suggesting that there was far less class conflict than commentators at the time originally thought. The experience of the **Great Depression**, instead of bringing the country to the point of revolution, actually served to undermine working-class solidarity. Union membership rapidly declined due to unemployment and, while some regions like south Wales and the northeast were badly affected, there was a growth of new jobs and affluence in the Midlands and southeast. Unions in affluent areas were unlikely to strike in solidarity with poorer unemployed workers, irrespective of how sympathetic their members may have been.

In 1939, then, the class system and society was not so different from 1914. The Second World War and the years that followed were to see greater changes.

Theme 3 Society in transition, 1918–79

The impact of the Second World War

The social research organisation, Mass Observation, reported frequently throughout the war that working-class people interviewed by researchers expressed a desire for a more equal Britain after the war, but were unsure about what shape this equality would take. Many onlookers at the time were sure that the experience of the war would make Britain a classless society. Some historians in the post-war era have argued that a social revolution took place. Evacuation, the experience of being made homeless through bombing, and the hardships of rationing caused people of all social classes to co-operate and interact in ways that they had never done before and this, it has been argued, caused class barriers to diminish.

However, Mass Observation studies suggest that actually very little social change happened during the war and that class distinctions remained, sometimes reinforced by wartime experiences. For example, in many instances, wartime evacuation of working-class inner-city children to more affluent rural homes reinforced class prejudices instead of diminishing them. Child psychologists Susan Isaacs and Anna Freud both reported in 1939 the widespread phenomenon of bed wetting (a clear sign of children in emotional distress from the stresses of evacuation) being blamed by host families on the poor standards of inner-city working-class families.

Post-war attitudes

The 1945 General Election at the end of the Second World War saw both parties campaigning on a platform of greater state intervention in society, suggesting that attitudes towards the role of the government had changed. The establishment of a Labour government committed to nationalisation and a welfare state dramatically changed the role of the state in people's lives. Despite these changes, brought about by the experience of war, ideas about social class seemed not to have shifted dramatically.

Britain's class system, privilege and deference remained largely intact. Some Labour ministers believed that institutions such as the House of Lords and the elite public schools Eton and Harrow should be abolished, but the Attlee government had not been elected to carry out such radical policies. The Labour landslide victory was less a revolt against the class system and more a recognition that the hardships of the 1930s were not to be repeated.

The bigger changes in social values and deference based on class were still to come with the advent of a more liberal society in the 1950s, 1960s and 1970s.

2 The emergence of the 'liberal society', 1951–79

The period from the 1950s to the early 1960s saw an unprecedented increase in affluence, leisure time and consumer choice for British people (see pages 137–138). Throughout this period of rising living standards and spending power, attitudes towards the class system, deference and authority changed. Not only were ideas about class called into question but also notions of propriety and morality as established ideas about sexuality, marriage, abortion and homosexuality were challenged. The period was one of unprecedented reform of laws which had restricted private lives and the development of a more liberal and tolerant society in which differences between people were no longer suspect and not only tolerated but actively celebrated.

While many people enjoyed the new prosperity and liberalism, some commentators voiced deep-seated anxieties about the pace of social change, and the growth of materialism and consumerism.

> **Note it down**
>
> This section deals with the emergence of a more liberal society in the post-war era. Use a spider diagram (see page x) to frame your notes here. Label the body of the spider 'The emergence of the liberal society, 1951–79', and label the spider's legs:
>
> - Decline of deference
> - The liberal society
> - Sexuality and the state.
>
> Your emphasis again should be on how far attitudes changed.

Decline of deference

An end to rationing in 1954 and the relaxation of consumer credit enabled working-class households to enjoy a level of prosperity they could scarcely have dreamt of a decade earlier (see page 138). It also meant that traditional ideas about community, social class and social mobility became increasingly challenged; people began to question the class system not from a position of poverty, but from a place of prosperity, surrounded by the comforts that consumer capitalism could afford them.

Television and cinema exposed audiences to satirical entertainment which ridiculed ideas about social class, while writers and filmmakers questioned the class system, and tabloid newspapers exposed scandals involving the ruling classes.

The 'satire boom'

One of the clearest examples of a decline in deference came with the 'satire boom' of the late 1950s and early 1960s. In 1960 a subversive and popular stage show 'Beyond the Fringe' starring among others Peter Cook, Dudley Moore, Jonathan Miller and Alan Bennett, played to packed audiences. It attracted fierce controversy for making fun of Britain's establishment: the government, Army and the upper classes.

One sketch titled 'The Aftermyth of the War' poured scorn on Britain's war effort, even though for most people the war was a recent memory and a victory of which to feel proud. The success of the stage show led to a satirical TV programme 'That Was the Week that Was', starring David Frost, which combined satirical humour with interviews of leading politicians. It was the first time that the British public had seen elite political figures on the television being questioned rigorously by journalists, and it represented a clear change in public attitudes to authority.

'British New Wave'

A generation of writers and filmmakers also articulated Britain's changing attitudes towards the class system in a movement that was loosely termed the 'British New Wave'. The late 1950s and early 1960s saw a profusion of novels about working-class men and women coming to terms with the end of the old working-class world of the pre-war era and the birth of new prosperity. One example is the Alan Sillitoe novel *Saturday Night Sunday Morning* (1958), which became a film starring the actor Albert Finney in 1960. It featured an angry young working-class man, Arthur Seaton, who has contempt for his bosses, the authorities and even his own community. Arthur is an amoral character who is desperate to escape his background, but who enjoys all the benefits of the new consumerism. Far from being a left-wing working-class hero, he is a product of the affluent society. Both the book and the film were very popular and indicated that working-class ideas about respect for authority and the older generations were in decline.

In this extract from the novel Arthur Seaton explains his frustrations with authority:

Once a rebel, always a rebel. You can't help being one. You can't deny that. And it's best to be a rebel so as to show 'em it don't pay to try to do you down. Factories and labour exchanges and insurance offices keep us alive and kicking – so they say – but they're booby-traps and will suck you under like sinking-sands if you're not careful. Factories sweat you to death, labour exchanges talk you to death, insurance and income tax offices milk money from your wage packets and rob you to death.

Sex scandals

In early 1963, an unprecedented sex scandal engulfed the British establishment and shocked its citizens. To an extent the revelations resulted from the growth of satire, itself a mark of decline in deference – so the scandal both developed and resulted from changing social attitudes.

Rumours began of sex parties regularly held at Cliveden, a stately home owned by the wealthy Astor family, featuring important establishment figures. The satirical magazine *Private Eye* was particularly important in reporting these rumours but the rest of the press latched onto them, especially when it was alleged that Minister of War John Profumo was sharing a nineteen-year-old sexual partner, Christine Keeler, with a Soviet attaché, Yevgeny Ivanov. While there was no evidence Profumo had divulged any state secrets (or indeed that Ivanov had in fact ever slept with Keeler), the potential for blackmail was evident.

Prior to the Profumo scandal the sexual indiscretions of politicians, the royal family and other establishment figures were routinely ignored by Britain's powerful press barons. However, in 1963 the Profumo scandal was featured on the front pages of the *Mirror*, *News of the World*, *Daily Express* and *Daily Mail*.

People were shocked by the revelations of sexual activity, especially after Profumo at first vehemently denied such behaviour then later admitted to it. Profumo resigned in March 1963 and some commentators believe that the scandal led to the defeat of the government, by four seats, in the 1964 General Election.

This scandal was significant in the decline of deference in British society. People were shocked not only that members of the establishment had been indulging in seedy practices but that they routinely lied about such involvement until caught out. This marked a watershed when people realised their leaders were not necessarily paragons of virtue and didn't deserve people's trust purely by virtue of position.

The liberal society

During the mid-1960s some newspaper journalists and writers argued that a **sexual revolution** had taken place. By the end of the decade the government had taken decisive steps to make the law more liberal towards male homosexuality and abortion, but that did not necessarily translate into widespread changes in public attitudes.

1950s attitudes towards sex

In the 1950s the view that the state had a role in regulating private sexual behaviour, particularly homosexuality, was widely accepted. By 1949 less than one-tenth of the population had received any kind of sex education and there is little evidence that parents discussed sex with their children. A popular view from foreign observers and contemporary commentators in the 1950s was that the British were reserved and sexually repressed. This seems unlikely.

- Cases of venereal disease were high in Britain until the discovery of penicillin, and prostitution flourished during the Second World War.
- A 1950s survey concluded that one-fifth of women born between 1894 and 1904 had experienced pre-marital sex and half of all women born between 1924 and 1934 had sex before marriage.
- From the 1930s onwards there was a growing demand for advice books about sex. Eustace Chesser's 1941 book *Love Without Fear*, which explained that both men and women could enjoy sex, had sold 3 million copies by 1964.

This shows that there was a big difference between what British people in the 1950s said about sex and what they actually did. Looking at these statistics, it might be possible to argue that Britain did not experience a sexual revolution in the 1960s but that sexual behaviour had been steadily changing throughout the century. If any revolution took place among the British public it was a revolution in how open or explicit they were willing to be in discussing sex.

1960s attitudes towards sex

Statistical evidence gathered in the 1960s tends to suggest that the popular image of the decade, one of decadence and sexual exploration, is misleading. Michael Schofield's *The Sexual Behaviour of Young People*, published in 1965, was based on interviews with 2,000 teenagers and uncovered the following:

- One in three boys and one in six girls between sixteen and nineteen had had sex.
- Nearly all of those that had were in established relationships and were not promiscuous.

The swinging sixties

▲ Carnaby Street, considered the heart of 'Swinging London', in 1967.

In popular mythology the 1960s saw new freedoms in terms of behaviour, dress and attitudes. This was particularly related to sexual behaviour where it was believed that ideas around premarital sex and having multiple sexual partners became widely accepted. The atmosphere of lively music, dance and often provocative clothing is exemplified by the London of the mid-1960s with trendy boutiques such as Biba, exciting nightlife, the ready availability of narcotics including the mind-bending drug LSD, and above all the celebration of youth.

Many ideas were provocative. The American musical 'Hair', for example, showed full nudity on stage when it opened in Britain in 1968. The musical 'Oh Calcutta', which opened in London in 1970, went even further in its celebration of sexual activities and ran for 3,900 performances.

Many conservatives reacted strongly to what was perceived as the lack of morality of the swinging sixties. When band members of the Rolling Stones, Mick Jagger and Keith Richard, were briefly imprisoned for possession of narcotics in 1967, *The Times* newspaper castigated the establishment for over-reacting. Nevertheless there was a real feeling of a 'generation gap' in which the elders could no longer understand or empathise with the young.

Another study, conducted five years later, by Geoffrey Gorer came to similar conclusions. In this survey attitudes towards sex before marriage, homosexuality, infidelity and contraception were very similar to popular attitudes in the 1950s. Gorer's study suggests that attitudes had not particularly changed at all by 1969.

The media

Nevertheless, there was an increased openness in talking about sex in the 1960s. Britain's newspaper industry played an important role in the dissemination of sexual ideas. During an age of mass consumerism advertisers paid to place their advertisements in the tabloid press, knowing they would reach a wide audience. Tabloid sex scandals and the discussion of sex in news articles and features not only captured a large readership but associated sex with celebrity and consumerism. For example many advertisements featured sexual allure as a sales technique to sell products.

Shatter the rules in Terlenka. Invade the stuffiest men's preserve in this gay, young creation of St. Honoré.

The bold belt and yoke effect is beautifully accented by white piping.

And, of course, Terlenka means it couldn't be easier to care for. Colours include Navy, Peach, Saffron, Red and Dove Grey. About £6.

▲ An advertisement for a polyester dress, c. 1969. What message is this advert trying to get across?

> ### The Lady Chatterley trial and its impact
>
> When Penguin Books published D.H. Lawrence's *Lady Chatterley's Lover* in 1960, the story of an aristocratic woman who has an affair with her working-class groundsman, the government decided to prosecute the publisher under the Obscene Publications Act 1959. The Act had actually been introduced to relax censorship, enabling a jury to consider 'literary merit' when deciding if a book was obscene.
>
> The jury decided that *Lady Chatterley's Lover* had sufficient merit and found in favour of Penguin. The publicity surrounding the case caused sales of the book to soar. The case demonstrated to the public that the laws surrounding obscenity were outdated and Britain's attitude towards sex and morality was changing. Many historians regard it as the start of Britain's 'permissive society'.
>
> One result of the Lady Chatterley trial and the end of censorship of books and magazines that contained 'obscene' material was the growth of the pornography industry. Areas of cities such as Soho in London became synonymous with shops selling pornography. Pornography was still illegal but the Obscene Publications Act was so ambiguously worded that prosecuting sellers and publishers was very difficult. Low printing costs and corrupt policemen in the Obscene Publications Squad of Scotland Yard enabled the industry to flourish.

Newspaper reportage of scandals like Profumo (see page 99) and the Lady Chatterley trial polarised British public opinion on sex between those who were shocked and alarmed about the rise of 'permissive' attitudes and those who embraced the new openness.

The poet Philip Larkin seemed to capture the mood of the early 1960s when he wrote in his poem *Annus Mirabilis*:

> Sexual intercourse began
>
> In nineteen sixty-three
>
> (which was rather late for me) –
>
> Between the end of the 'Chatterley' ban
>
> And the Beatles' first LP.

Sexuality and the state

In 1957, following pressure from church groups and moral campaigners, the Macmillan government published the Wolfenden Report. The report said that there had been a decline in 'morality' since the war and that family life had been weakened. Lord Wolfenden believed that the law against prostitution should be made harsher, but that homosexual activity between consenting adults over the age of 21, in private, should be decriminalised. Wolfenden believed that prostitution was a public display of 'immorality' whereas male homosexuality was at least hidden and took place behind closed doors. This meant that the state could police public acts of sexuality but it had no right to regulate private life.

The Sexual Offences Act, 1967

In 1958 the Homosexual Law Reform Society (HLRS) was founded. This followed a letter to *The Times* calling for a reform to the law, signed by the former prime minister, Clement Attlee, the intellectual Isaiah Berlin and historian A.J.P. Taylor among others. The HLRS was active in campaigning for a change to the law and in lobbying the government to implement the Wolfenden recommendations.

From 1960 to 1966, there were various attempts to introduce a Sexual Offences Bill based on the Wolfenden Report and finally, in 1967, the Labour MP Leo Abse's **private member's bill** was passed by a narrow majority. Home Secretary Roy Jenkins gave the bill parliamentary time, even though he had quite conservative opinions on sexual morality. Jenkins believed that homosexuality should be decriminalised because criminalising aspects of private life was 'uncivilised'. Jenkins also allowed parliamentary time for the MP David Steel's 1967 Abortion Act. Parliament passed the Act, which legalised abortion of a pregnancy up to 28 weeks.

Neither move was particularly popular, showing that despite the new affluence of the 1960s some attitudes towards private life had not changed. Of those interviewed by Schofield and later Gorer, 85 per cent disapproved of homosexuality and half believed it should be punished more severely. Even though most people in Britain during the 1960s had not experienced the glamorous hedonism of 'swinging' London, had lived lives of conformity and normality and were not part of the 'permissive society', a reaction against much that the 1960s seemed to stand for began towards the end of the decade.

3 Opponents of the liberal society, 1951–79

For most people in Britain, the sexual revolution was something that featured in the newspapers, but was not experienced personally. By the end of the 1960s most people's attitudes towards sexuality and their lifestyles were conservative. The sensational reports of celebrity scandals in Britain's newspapers gave their readers a misleading picture of the nation's attitudes towards sexuality.

Other newspaper stories portrayed sexual liberation as having shocking consequences. When the Moors murderers Myra Hindley and Ian Brady were convicted of killing three children in 1966, the press focussed on the fact that the two were unmarried and in a sexual relationship, creating a connection between this and their violent crimes. The fact that their relationship status had no bearing on their actions was often overlooked by newspaper readers who were shocked by the crimes and alarmed by what they believed was a rapid decline in 'moral' standards.

Sensational stories of upper-class sexual behaviour were accompanied throughout the 1960s with articles about the behaviour of British teenagers. Sexual behaviour was linked in tabloid stories to teenage crime, vandalism and hooliganism, fuelling a moral panic about the state of Britain's youth.

A conservative reaction to the perceived decline in moral standards was led by campaigners such as Mary Whitehouse, Malcolm Muggeridge and Lord Longford.

> ### Note it down
> The focus in this section is on opposition to greater liberalism. Choose the form of note-making which best suits you (see pages ix–x) to examine why there was such opposition and how effective it was. In developing your notes, focus on the following issues:
> - How significant were the campaigns of Mary Whitehouse?
> - How influential was the NVALA?
> - How significant was the Festival of Light?

Mary Whitehouse

In 1964 a school teacher with devout Christian values, Mary Whitehouse, launched a campaign group called Clean Up TV. She believed that television was the most corrupting medium in modern life and was introducing un-Christian ideas to British youth. The rapid popularity of Whitehouse's new organisation indicated that many people agreed with her. At the first meeting of Clean Up TV over 70 coaches full of campaigners filled Birmingham Town Hall and most of their criticism was directed against the BBC. Not only did Mary Whitehouse condemn scenes of a sexual nature on television, but also images of drinking, criticism of the royal family and references to crime and lawlessness. Her views were often far more extreme than those of her supporters. She believed that television and consumerism were eroding faith in God in Britain and that her task was to bring the country back to what she believed were its original Christian roots.

The NVALA

In 1965 Whitehouse co-founded the National Viewers and Listeners Association (NVALA), which attracted campaigners from the general public, senior Church of England bishops, chief police officers and MPs. Not only was the NVALA opposed to sex, violence and swearing on television, but its members associated permissiveness with what they believed was a creeping 'socialism' in Britain. Mary Whitehouse condemned 'Marxist, humanist' ideas and many of her members believed that Christianity was under threat from a mixture of socialism, consumerism and television. Even though these ideas were dismissed by most of the population as absurd during the 1960s and 1970s, the fact that Whitehouse claimed NVALA had attracted over 100,000 members after its formation shows that fears about 'moral decline' in Britain were widespread.

> ### Secularisation
> The post-war period in Britain saw a decline in organised Christianity. Although this was particularly noticeable in the Church of England, all denominations were affected and the Methodist Church even looked for a merger with the Church of England. The number of people who took holy communion in the Church of England fell from 3 million to 2.5 million between 1935 and 1945 and dropped to 2 million by 1970. It seemed that most people only used the Church for special events such as weddings and funerals. Even here there was a decline: the number of Roman Catholic marriages fell from 46,480 in 1960 to 17,294 some 30 years later. While some churches, particularly evangelical denominations, grew in popularity, most local church authorities would have been delighted with regular congregations in the hundreds. The reality was that for most people Christianity had become something at best peripheral but more likely irrelevant to their lives.

The NVALA was made up predominantly of people from outside London who lived in the Midlands, the northwest, Yorkshire, the northeast, Scotland, Wales and Northern Ireland. Many activists looked at London with suspicion and disgust, associating it with the 'swinging' sixties, promiscuity and pornography. The organisation's impact, however, was limited. It is possible that Whitehouse and her supporters exaggerated its membership from the start and there is little evidence that the media ever really took it seriously. The NVALA made a lot of noise and gained a lot of publicity – but its influence on TV and radio programming was minimal.

Successes

On a wider level the NVALA may have influenced legislation banning child pornography with the Protection of Children Act of 1978 and indecent advertisements with the Indecent Displays Act of 1981. In terms of specific successes, its efforts were instrumental in getting the movie *Deep Throat* banned in Britain and in 1976 it was involved in efforts to get a Danish filmmaker who wanted to make a movie about Christ's sex life banned from Britain. Perhaps the most famous campaign was to initiate a successful blasphemy trial against *Gay News* for what was perceived to be a heretical poem about Christ.

The Festival of Light

One leading figure of moral conservatism by the late 1960s was the journalist Malcolm Muggeridge. He founded an organisation called the Festival of Light, along with Whitehouse, the pop star Cliff Richard, Labour cabinet member Lord Longford and Christian missionaries Peter and Janet Hill. The organisation's aims were to:

- prevent the sexualisation of television
- promote Christian teachings.

Nationwide events organised by the festival in 1971 included the lighting of beacons on hill tops, which attracted over 100,000 people to take part. However, it did little to change the content of TV programmes or to alter public attitudes towards sex. The overtly evangelical approach of the Festival of Light alienated many people who shared their concerns but who were not church-going Christians.

Malcolm Muggeridge

Muggeridge had been infamous as a drinker and womaniser for much of his adult life but underwent a religious conversion during the 1960s. He became critical of the new affluence and materialism the 1960s brought with it. In 1968 he argued that Britain would suffer the fate of the Roman Empire and collapse because of decadence and immorality.

Lord Longford

Lord Longford, a devout Catholic, funded his own report into pornography and visited the sex industry in Copenhagen to investigate the effects of an end to censorship. He concluded in 1972 that the Obscene Publications Act 1959 had made it easy for pornography to be published and called for new censorship against materials that 'outrage contemporary standards of decency or humanity accepted by the public at large'.

Work together

One common theme in this chapter has been the question, 'How far did attitudes change?' Go through your notes. Then, with a partner, get two large pieces of paper. On one jot down all the evidence that suggests attitudes changed significantly. On the other find evidence that suggests they didn't change much. The work of Mary Whitehouse and her supporters might feature significantly here.

When you have completed the task, discuss together how far attitudes to class and social values changed during the period 1918–79.

Question practice

1 Was the experience of the Second World War the main reason why society become less deferential in the 1960s? Explain your answer. **AS**
2 To what extent did a 'liberal society' emerge in the years 1951–79? **AS**
3 To what extent did attitudes towards sexual behaviour change in the period 1945–79?

Chapter summary

- At the beginning of the twentieth century, class largely determined one's status and place in society.
- One effect of the First World War was the decline in deference, through the decline of the aristocracy and the growth of more assertive middle classes.
- The Second World War led to claims for greater social equality, although class distinctions remained into the post-war period.
- The 1960s saw more liberal values as exemplified by the 'swinging sixties'.
- Factors such as TV, satire, British New Wave writing and sex scandals led to a decline in deference.
- The widespread growth of sexual freedoms was largely a myth, as most people's attitudes remained conservative.
- More liberal laws were introduced in the 1960s with homosexuality and abortion being legalised.
- Opposition grew to perceived promiscuity and immorality in society, as exemplified by Mary Whitehouse.

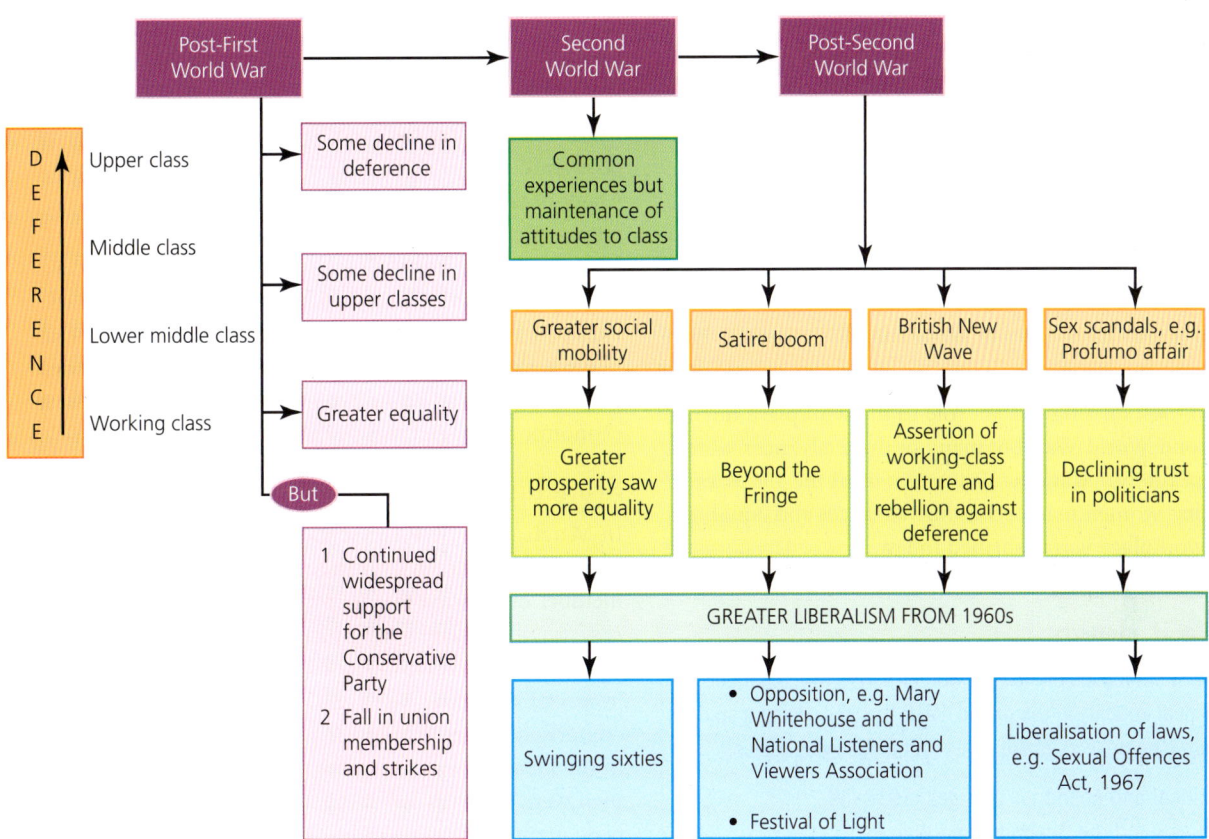

▲ Summary diagram: Class and social values

3b: The changing role and status of women

Overview

Throughout the twentieth century groups and individuals struggling for women's rights and equality confronted gender discrimination in three main fields:

- political
- economic
- social.

Women gained equal voting rights and political equality in 1928, although the number of women represented in Parliament and local government remained low. However, it was not until the 1960s that women's economic and social status began to change and move towards a greater equality with men.

This chapter examines how, why and to what extent women's role and status changed, through the following sections:

1. The right to vote and political advancement, 1918-79
2. Changes in family life and the quest for personal freedoms, 1918-79

1 The right to vote and political advancement, 1918–79

Women gained the right to vote first at the age of 30 in 1918 and at the age of 21, on equal par with men, in 1928. However, they failed to gain a significant political voice in the sense that there were comparatively few women MPs throughout the period and political parties tended to use them in subordinate capacities such as delivering leaflets and organising functions.

Women took on a significant role in the workplace during the Second World War, but many of these advances were lost once the war was over. It was not until the 1960s and 1970s that women made economic advances and equality in the workplace was enshrined in law.

Note it down

This section focuses on how far women's lives were changed by political equality in the period 1918 to 1979. Using a spider diagram (see page x), make notes on the following topics:

- Political and economic changes, 1918-39
- Women and the Second World War
- Economic advances, 1945-51
- Political advances, 1945-79
- Economic advances, 1951-79.

The emphasis throughout should be on 'how far' the lives of women were changed.

Political and economic changes, 1918–29

In the decade after the First World War political and economic change shaped the lives of women in Britain. Many became accustomed to new political rights and employment opportunities, and were able to enjoy leisure time and **consumerism** (see page 138). However, work opportunities were still highly **gendered**, and the experience of women in the workplace was often one of low wages, low-skilled jobs and long hours. This section explores how women in Britain interacted with the new economic and social realities they encountered.

Franchise

In March 1918 the Representation of the People Act enfranchised women over the age of 30 if they were a member or married to a member of the **local government register**, a graduate voting in a university election or a property owner. This meant that only educated and 'respectable' women were enfranchised; however they comprised 43 per cent of the electorate (8.4 million voters) in the December election that year. In the same Act, all men were enfranchised at the age of 21 and had women been granted the same rights they would have made up the majority of the electorate due to the high losses of men during the war. Britain's working-class women did not receive the vote until 1928 when all women rate payers were enfranchised on the same terms as men in the Representation of the People Act (1928).

Employment opportunities

The First World War enabled many women to make considerable gains in the workplace as the entire civilian population was mobilised for war work. Thousands of women also worked as auxiliaries, drivers, telephonists, signallers and nurses on the western front.

In 1914 there had been a large female industrial workforce with 200,000 employed in the metals and chemicals industries. By 1918 there were over 1 million in these two fields alone. In Britain's main cordite factory at Gretna, 11,000 women worked to create explosives. Women also took roles in public life that had always been the preserve of men, such as working on the railways and trams.

The decade after the war saw many of the gains that women had made overturned as a result of the harsh economic realities Britain faced after 1918. Wartime employment was only required as long as the conflict continued. In addition the return of fighting men from the First World War forced many women out of the workplace. The government had introduced a 'dilution' agreement with the trade unions in 1914, meaning that skilled workers who went to fight in France could be replaced by semi-skilled labour, including women workers, on two main conditions:

- Their employment lasted only as long as the war did.
- The new workers would not be able to profit from the war and would not be paid higher wages than the men whose jobs they were filling.

Consequently the numbers of employed women returned to 1914 levels when the war ended (approximately 5.7 million).

The return of men to the workplace and the home seemed to herald a return to the traditional ideas about gender that had existed before the war. When women did work they returned to their traditional occupations such as service or clerical work.

'Woman's work'

In the first three decades of the twentieth century, working in service as a maid, cook or cleaner was the largest source of employment for working-class women. In 1918, 1.25 million women were 'in service'. The work was unpopular and most women who experienced it were keen to find other employment if possible. However, opportunities were limited because of prejudice, the lack of educational opportunities for women, and also because of prevailing ideas about what was 'woman's work'.

In the 1920s there were clear gender roles in employment. Employers hired women for factory work or service if they were working class or clerical work if they were educated (often this meant that the **artisan working class** or the **lower middle class** filled these roles). Clerical work was the biggest growth area for female employment in the 1920s with over 1 million employed as typists or clerks by 1921 and a further 300,000 ten years later.

The only other opportunities for working-class women to earn a living was through sweated labour in the new **light manufacturing** that had developed after the war. Much of the available work was poorly paid and as unemployment benefit for women was set at a lower rate than for men (see page 59), there was no incentive for employers to offer better rates of pay.

Two-thirds of all work done by working-class women was done from home. Baking, brewing, sewing '**piece work**' was combined with household tasks and caring for children.

Middle-class women

The suffrage campaign that resulted in the Representation of the People Act 1918 had been carried out by educated middle-class women, many of whom were interested in the franchise being extended to women who owned property. The idea that uneducated working-class women might have a say in the running of the country was popular only among the more radical fringes of the suffrage movement.

For middle-class women between the wars there was some gradual improvement in opportunity for advancement as universities began to accept women. This change was a result of the Sex Disqualification (Removal) Act 1919, preventing the barring from a career in law or the civil service on the basis of gender. The Act gave women greater opportunities when applying for work in these fields and there is some evidence to suggest that male attitudes were gradually starting to change.

However, one should not over-emphasise the point about improvement in opportunities. In 1931 there were 3,000 female medical practitioners and 180,000 nurses, 21 female architects out of a total of 6,000 and two structural and two civil engineers. The civil service was open to women, particularly at the more clerical levels, but no women were posted overseas. Teaching was a common career for educated women but until 1944 they had to leave the profession if they married. In 1931, 84 per cent of the female workforce was single, divorced or widowed. Married women, especially if they were middle class, were expected to stay at home to be supported by their husbands.

Ivy Williams

Ivy Williams, the first woman to be called to the **English Bar**, in 1922, had first qualified as a lawyer 20 years earlier, when the *Law Journal* described her ambitions as 'futile'. In 1922 however, the *Journal* had changed its editorial opinion and called her appointment as a barrister 'one of the most memorable days in the long annals of the legal profession'.

Women in politics

Women faced prejudice in politics during the interwar period when never more than 5 per cent of MPs were women and the number of women MPs peaked at 15 in 1931. They had to face petty restrictions, such as not being able to use the Commons dining room. One Labour MP, Edith Summerskill, said it was 'like a boys school which had decided to take a few girls'. The Labour Party, as the proponent of women's enfranchisement and promoter of social reform, attracted more women than the other parties – 150,000 joined between 1918 and 1924. Even so, many Labour activists felt women should stay at home and only nine women served as Labour MPs in the interwar period. The other parties tended to cast women in a subservient role such as delivering leaflets and organising fundraising events. Neither encouraged women to become MPs.

At a local level, women were more influential, although by 1930 less than 15 per cent of elected local councillors were female. Many were focussed on social issues such as education and welfare. Nevertheless it was often a grounding for national office. Thelma Cazalet-Keir, for example, served as a Conservative councillor in London between 1924 and 1931 before becoming an MP in October 1931.

Women and the Second World War

As with the First World War, the demands of **total war** meant that there was an increase in opportunities for women, and they engaged in a wide range of military and civilian roles between 1939 and 1945.

- By 1944, 80,000 women worked on farms, often far from home, for the Women's Land Army.
- Munitions factories, aircraft construction, parachute packing and uniform manufacture required a predominantly female workforce.
- The Women's Voluntary Service supported the civil defence forces and offered shelter and comfort to bombing victims.
- Women had non-combat roles as drivers, cooks, intelligence analysts, clerks, radar plotters and mechanics in all three of the auxiliary services (Air Force, Army and Navy).
- Women cryptanalysts and translators worked to break enemy codes, and a small number of British women spies carried out wartime intelligence work.

Despite the hardships caused by rationing, the war years brought practical benefits to the lives of many women.

- Many were better paid as a result of their employment.
- They acquired new skills and confidence in their abilities.
- Many reached levels of importance and seniority that were not available to them in civilian life.
- Overseas postings and relocation gave women opportunities and experiences they had never had before.
- The opportunity to work alongside men towards the defeat of Germany, Italy and Japan gave many women a sense of participation and contribution that they found missing in everyday civilian life.

Economic advancement, 1945–51

At the end of the Second World War the government hoped that the social upheavals it had caused would not result in social change, and that women who had worked throughout the war would resume their roles at home as wives and mothers. They offered few inducements in terms of pay or working hours to encourage women to remain in the workplace.

Those women that remained in employment worked in fields that were almost exclusively reserved for women: 86 per cent of working women in 1951 were in industries such as nursing, teaching, factory work, waitressing and clerical work. Before 1944 most women were required to give up work once they were married and in the majority of industries a 'marriage bar' was applied. From 1946 onwards major employers began to remove the requirement for women to leave their jobs when they got married. The practice ended in:

- the teaching profession, 1944
- the civil service, 1946
- the Bank of England, 1949.

Throughout the 1950s and 1960s it was gradually removed from most businesses, but the attitudes of women recorded by **Mass Observation** in the 1940s and 1950s show that many were ambivalent about working life. Some analysts believed that working women who anticipated their jobs ending when they got married had inherited the values of previous generations. A 1948 study of 100 women in three different locations found:

- a widespread desire to end work after marriage
- the need for extra income as the main motivation for working
- that most women interviewed didn't define themselves by their work or see it as an important part of their identity.

The minority of women who wanted to build careers for themselves were often seen to be unusual and were often thought to have failed in some way to fulfil their primary role of 'home maker' and mother.

Economic advancement, 1951–79

The end of the marriage bar meant that in the three decades after the war, more and more women worked for longer with 50 per cent of married women retaining their jobs by 1972. Until the late 1950s, in nearly all workplaces unequal pay was an established norm for women, who received, on average, 40 per cent less money than their male counterparts. In 1958 the civil service introduced equal pay for all employees, along with the education system and the NHS, but there was no government legislation on pay until the Equal Pay Act of 1970.

The Equal Pay Act, 1970

In 1959 the Labour Party made a manifesto commitment to equal pay and in 1965 the TUC also agreed that it would give 'support for the principles of equality of treatment and opportunity for women workers in industry', but it took until 1970 for these pledges to become law. One reason the Equal Pay Act was passed was the fact that equal pay was a pre-requisite for joining the European Economic Community (EEC). The law, which made pay discrimination between men and women illegal, came into effect in 1975.

The Sex Discrimination Act, 1975

In 1975 the Labour government established the Equal Opportunities Commission as part of the Sex Discrimination Act to ensure that fair employment practices were observed and that women had legal protection against discrimination in education and employment. It established tribunals to deal with workplace sexual harassment and also recognised the everyday sexual discrimination women encountered when visiting doctors and banks, going shopping or hiring tradesmen.

Although legislation made discrimination more difficult, women still faced prejudice in political life and the workforce, which they had to fight hard to overcome.

The Dagenham sewing machinists' strike, 1968

In 1968 management at the Ford Motor Company's car factory at Dagenham decided to pay the female sewing machinists who made car seat covers 15 per cent less in wages than men doing equivalent jobs. The female machinists went on strike for three weeks and Secretary of State for Employment and Productivity Barbara Castle intervened in the dispute. She and the strikers negotiated a pay deal that increased wages by 7 per cent. A court of inquiry eventually ruled against the women, however, and equal pay was only established by a further strike in 1984. The long-term significance of the strike was that it significantly raised the issue of unequal pay and was one of the main causes of the Equal Pay Act, 1970 (see page 110).

▲ The picket line of the machinists' strike

Many people still believed their primary role was as wives and mothers and paid employment should be secondary to this – that they worked only for 'pin money'. It was due to the failure of political equality to effect meaningful change in women's lives that **second-wave feminism** (see page 113) was developed.

Political advancement, 1945–79

Women did not progress significantly in terms of political advancement, as Table 1 shows.

The number of female MPs stayed constant at between 20 and 30 with dips in 1951 and 1979 despite an upward trend of candidates. This was due to prejudice and the widespread belief that women would be too busy with domestic duties to fulfil the role of MP. Margaret Thatcher was one of the most high-profile victims of this prejudice. Although she frequently stood way above the abilities of her male rivals, she found it difficult to be chosen by local Conservative Associations in winnable constituencies because of her gender. She twice stood for election in the safe Labour constituency of Dartford before finally being selected against fierce opposition for the more winnable seat of Finchley in the 1959 General Election.

Table 1: Number of female MPs and candidates in general elections, 1945–79

Election year	Female MPs	%	Candidates
1945	24	3.8	87
1950	21	3.4	127
1951	17	2.7	77
1955	24	3.8	92
1959	25	4	81
1964	29	4.6	90
1966	26	4.1	81
1970	26	4.1	99
1974 (Feb)	23	3.6	143
1974 (Oct)	27	4.3	161
1979	19	3	216

Source: http://www.ukpolitical.info/FemaleMPs.htm

Women in Parliament rarely were selected for cabinet posts; one or two was the norm. In local constituencies they were still expected to fulfil the same subsidiary roles as before the war.

2 Changes in family life and the quest for personal freedoms, 1918–79

Political and economic advancements, including the Representation of the People Acts, the Equal Pay Act and the Sex Discrimination Act had brought political and economic equality in law for women – ultimately leading to changes in their role and status in society. Likewise, changes in family life and personal freedoms brought about by campaigners and changing social values also impacted on their role and status.

Note it down

The emphasis in this section is on how far family life and women's personal freedoms changed in the period 1918-79. Use the 1·2 method (page xi) to make notes, using the following table as a guide.

Family life and personal freedoms, 1968–79	How far did family life and personal freedoms change?
Family life and personal freedoms, 1939–68	How far were women stereotyped as wives and mothers during this period?
The struggle for new freedoms, 1968–1979	How effective was second-wave feminism? How far did women take control of their own lives?

Family life and personal freedoms, 1918–39

In the period 1918–39 women's role and status in society remained largely unchanged. Women were seen as homemakers with the husband as the head of the household. There were a few gains in giving women more control over their family life, particularly with changes to the divorce law, access to birth control and freer self-expression. However, access to these greater freedoms was generally experienced by middle-class women, with little positive change for working-class women, who suffered in particular during the **Great Depression.**

Divorce

The first major Act enabling women to obtain divorce was the 1857 Matrimonial Causes Act, and further reforms to divorce law followed throughout the nineteenth century. In 1934 the issue was revisited, first in the guise of a satirical novel, *Holy Deadlock*, by the lawyer A.P. Herbert, in which he pointed out the absurdities in divorce law.

- An unhappily married couple could not obtain a divorce based on mutual consent; there had to be instances of adultery or violence.
- This meant couples often had to perjure in court to obtain a divorce. If one spouse had been unfaithful a divorce was granted, but if both had been unfaithful the court could refuse.

The attempt to prove adultery was often farcical, with private detectives finding evidence of unfaithfulness or, sometimes, paying females to meet errant husbands in hotel bedrooms to be photographed in compromising positions.

Herbert became an independent MP in order to campaign for divorce law reform; he succeeded with the 1937 Matrimonial Causes Act. This allowed for divorce if either partner had been unfaithful, as well as for desertion after three years. The Act was opposed by the Church of England and the Catholic Church but had widespread public support. Before this reform, the average number of divorce petitions was below 4,800 per year. By 1951 it was 38,000.

In 1936 the issue of remarriage took on national significance when King Edward VIII sought to marry the American divorcee Wallace Simpson (see page 127). Public attitudes towards divorced women became very clear during the subsequent **abdication** crisis. Wallace Simpson was portrayed in the popular press and in popular discussion as a scheming, manipulative gold digger.

Birth control

The issue of divorce was not the only ethical battleground for women in the interwar period. Birth control also became a question of public morality. In 1921 Dr Marie Stopes founded the first birth control clinic in London. Health workers who directed women towards Stopes' clinic were sacked, though the demand for birth control advice saw clinics spread across the country throughout the 1920s.

In cities such as Salford and Cardiff senior clergymen condemned the clinics as 'filthy' and 'unnatural', and many doctors were equally critical. The Labour Party in 1927 voted for a resolution at their conference against allowing local authority funding for birth control clinics. By 1930, however, many local authorities were arguing that it was essential that they were allowed to fund the clinics. The government decided in 1930 that it was acceptable for clinics to advise mothers who already had one child and for whom a second pregnancy would seriously damage their health.

Dr Marie Stopes

Dr Marie Stopes was a botanist who became converted to the idea of birth control in 1915. In 1918 her book *Married Love* was published and was one of the first widely available books for couples about sex and contraception. She believed that women should be freed from the 'cycle of births' and that sex should be enjoyable. She also believed in **eugenics**, arguing that 'wastrels' should not be allowed to breed. She advocated contraception for the poor, arguing that only people who could contribute to society should have children. Her ideas were popular among the **Fabian Society** but fell out of favour in the 1930s.

In 1930 the Church of England allowed married members of their congregations to use birth control methods, but the Catholic Church remained staunchly opposed.

In 1930 the General Medical Council allowed doctors to give contraception advice, only to married couples, for the first time. Working-class women who were not covered by **national health insurance** schemes did not benefit from such advice and instead relied on help from local birth control clinics and advice from friends and neighbours. Contraceptive caps, condoms, pessaries and other methods of birth control could be bought from barbers, chemists and hygiene stores.

Self-expression

The advances in legal and political rights for women were mirrored in the way they expressed themselves. Because of the large number of young men killed in the First World War, many young women lived single lives in the 1920s and found new freedoms as a result. The growth of new clerical jobs for women enabled young single women to enjoy the consumerism of the interwar years.

Many young women rejected the fashion of the Edwardian era to cover the entire body and wore shorter skirts, others preferred shorter haircuts and exotic fashions, creating what was known as a '**flapper**' look. Newspaper articles dating back as far as 1907 had mentioned 'flapper' girls, so it was not a phenomenon purely of the 1920s, but clearly grew as a social trend after 1918.

Flappers

Flapper girls enjoyed dancing, jazz music and social freedoms that would have been unheard of before the First World War. In the popular press their lifestyles were portrayed as both glamorous and promiscuous, though there is no evidence to suggest that their attitudes towards sex were any different than the majority of women of their age group in the 1920s. Smoking and drinking were also habits associated with 'flapper' girls, two activities that were considered 'un-ladylike'. The fact that many did smoke and drink was seen as an indicator that they lived independent lives and were not dictated to by men (tobacco companies realised this and quickly associated the idea of 'freedom' with female smoking). The growth of cinema as a leisure activity also had a profound impact on 'flapper' culture, as actresses such as Clara Bowe and Coleen Moore were presented as attractive role models for women.

These new pursuits were conditional on having a good income and plenty of leisure time and, as such, were seldom experienced by working-class women, many of whose family lives and personal health suffered during the Great Depression.

Family life during the Great Depression

The grinding poverty of the Great Depression had a disproportional impact on women. As the primary carers for children, women in the poorer parts of the country frequently ate less so their husbands and children could have meals. Because household roles were divided along gender lines with the man being the primary wage earner, mothers were often expected to go without food when there was not enough money to provide for the whole family. In 1933 the Hungry England enquiry, set up by an economist A.L. Bowley, reported that in some instances women were starving to feed their families.

Women with poor families often had large numbers of children (in parts of the East End of London in the 1930s, families with nine children were not uncommon) and depended on unemployment relief which after 1934 became **means tested** (see page 59). This condemned many to live below the **poverty line** and unable to provide the minimum amount of food for their families.

Family life and personal freedoms, 1939–68

The Second World War involved the majority of Britain's adult female population in war work or active service (see page 108). Women who did not serve in the armed forces or who were not working in the munitions industries still experienced rationing and many saw their families split up by evacuation and the enlistment of their husbands into the Army. This fragmentation caused by wartime experiences meant that in the immediate post-war period many were happy to return to their primary role of 'home maker' and mother. However, by the late 1950s surveys were starting to show a different picture, with women feeling isolated and becoming increasingly discontent with their role and status in society. The 1960s and 1970s saw the rise of women's groups and movements to challenge the existing status quo.

Isolation of the 1950s housewife

One study in the late 1950s showed that 40 per cent of women interviewed were content with their lives at home, but the remaining 60 per cent admitted to feelings of boredom, frustration and loneliness. Possible explanations for these changes in attitude from the late 1940s to the late 1950s are the rapid growth of a consumer society (see page 138), the expansion of leisure time, and the improvement in educational opportunities (see pages 82–3), presenting women with far greater choices than they had previously known.

Advertising and consumerism helped to shape the perceptions and expectations of women at home. The 'housewife' was portrayed in newspaper and television adverts as the controller of the domestic sphere, utilising modern technology to run the kitchen. The role of the woman was not simply to cook and clean but to be the decision maker in day-to-day purchasing decisions (though men normally made big purchases such as cars or televisions). As a result advertisers and product makers in Britain's consumer boom were keen to market their goods to women. Labour-saving devices like washing machines and vacuum cleaners, it was suggested by advertisers, would leave more time for a woman to focus on her family and pleasing her husband.

In 1960 a journalist for *the Guardian* newspaper, Betty Jerman, wrote an article that highlighted the frustrations of many women who lived at home. In the article 'Squeezed in Like Sardines in Suburbia' she presented domestic life for middle-class women as dull and suffocating, stating that:

> *this example of suburbia is an incredibly dull place to live in and I blame the women. They stay here all day. They set the tone. Many of them look back with regret to the days when they worked in an office … I cannot help wondering what effect the mental atmosphere will have on our children.*

One reader Maureen Nichol responded to the article, suggesting that:

> *Perhaps housebound wives with liberal interests and a desire to remain individuals could form a national register, so that whenever one moves, one can contact like-minded friends.*

The Housebound Housewives Register was created as a result, and was subsequently re-named the National Housewives register. It was the first organisation to cater for isolated women at home.

The struggle for new freedoms, 1968–79

Commentators often describe two waves of feminism between the end of the nineteenth century and 1979. The first wave featured the suffrage movement and the campaign for political equality. Second wave feminism developed from the mid-1960s onwards, also known as the **'women's liberation'** movement. It was concerned with equal conditions at work and issues such as:

- birth control and other reproductive rights
- domestic violence
- sexism in the workplace
- pornography and the objectification of women
- the stifling effect on women's confidence and mental health of a male-dominated or **'patriarchal'** society.

The women's liberation movement raised consciousness of these inequalities and the period saw far-reaching changes in family life and women's personal freedoms, particularly as regards to reproductive rights, marriage and support for victims of domestic violence.

Birth control and abortion

In 1961 the contraceptive pill was introduced but doctors were only allowed to prescribe it to married women, fearing that it might encourage promiscuity among unmarried women. This showed the extent to which doctors were seen (and saw themselves) as guardians of public morality. Within a decade a million women were using the pill, demonstrating its popularity and the needs of many women to limit the number of children they had. The pill offered women sexual freedoms that had been unknown and was seen by conservative critics as a cause of Britain's 'permissive society'. Women were now able to enjoy sex without the fear of an unwanted pregnancy.

Previously it was common for men to consider themselves in charge of contraception, either by 'natural' methods such as avoiding ejaculation or purchasing condoms. The pill gave women the ability to control their own fertility and was far more effective than other contraceptive devices. By the end of the 1970s more women were having fewer children and having their first children later. In 1971, 47 per cent of women had their first child by the age of 25, a figure that fell to 25 per cent by the end of the century. Instead they were able to focus on careers and education, which resulted in more skilled women entering the workforce.

In 1967 abortion was decriminalised by an Act of Parliament proposed by Liberal MP David Steel. While many supported this measure as unknown numbers of back-street and illegal abortions could harm or even kill unknown numbers of women, others worried about the ever-increasing numbers –149,746 per year by 1979.

Marriage

Social researchers who studied family life in the 1960s began to see a change in the roles of men and women at home. Research showed that many families had become less patriarchal and married couples shared housework more equally. This 'partnership' marriage was different from traditional ideas about gender roles in the home.

Impact of the women's liberation movement

From 1969 onwards, partly as a result of the Dagenham sewing machinists' strike (see page 109), a women's liberation movement developed in Britain. Throughout much of the post-war era, feminism had been seen as an old-fashioned concept, associated with the suffragette movement. Within both political parties it was treated as an irrelevance that only interested extremists. In 1968 the most prominent female politician in Britain, Barbara Castle, refused to discuss the legacy of female suffrage at the Labour Party conference.

A new wave of feminist activists began to associate the struggle for economic equality with the far wider issue of social inequality in society. Sheila Rowbotham, who had been a writer for the radical magazine *Black Dwarf*, helped to organise the first National Women's Conference at Ruskin College in February 1970. The attendees were mainly young, middle class and university educated, and they gathered to discuss feminist politics and history.

Within twelve months the number of women's groups in London had grown from four to over 50. A new movement, the Women's Liberation Workshop, emerged from this growth in activism. The movement held consciousness-raising workshops where women could openly express their experiences. The purpose of this was to enable group members to identify everyday experiences of sexism as oppressive and to develop a group **political consciousness**. Activists like Rowbotham hoped that a new political awareness would spread within the women's movement.

Growing activism

In 1970 protest groups staged demonstrations at the Miss World Beauty Contest, storming onto the stage at the Royal Albert Hall and throwing flower bombs at the all-male judging panel. The BBC outside broadcast unit sent to cover the pageant was attacked by the **anarchist** terrorist group the Angry Brigade (the two incidents do not appear to have been co-ordinated), who were also protesting against the role the Miss World contest played in the 'oppression of women'.

The Female Eunuch

Germaine Greer, a feminist activist, wrote *The Female Eunuch* in 1970, and the book had a lasting influence on the feminist movement. Greer argued that men's control of women had led women to become trapped into suffocating gender roles, to become self-loathing about their bodies and to compete with other women.

Women, in Greer's view, had been cut off from their own sexuality by the institution of marriage. In an article 'Opinions That May Shock the Faithful' in the *New York Times* on 22 March 1971, she said:

Women have somehow been separated from their libido, from their faculty of desire, from their sexuality. They've become suspicious about it. Like beasts, for example, who are castrated in farming in order to serve their master's ulterior motives – to be fattened or made docile – women have been cut off from their capacity for action. It's a process that sacrifices vigor for delicacy and succulence, and one that's got to be changed.

Spare Rib magazine, published by feminist writers Rosie Boycott and Sheila Rowbotham, captured the ideas of the movement from 1972 onwards. *Spare Rib* linked the feminist movement to **socialist** politics, arguing that there was a link between capitalism and women's subjugation. A generation of novelists such as Angela Carter, Doris Lessing, Iris Murdoch and Margaret Drabble articulated the experience of women throughout the 1970s.

Refuges for victims of domestic violence

The early 1970s saw women activists set up refuges and centres for victims of domestic violence and their children. The most famous of these was established in Chiswick by Erin Pizzey. She did not identify herself as a feminist and argued that women could also be violent, but the network of domestic violence refuges that grew from Chiswick Women's Aid (eventually becoming the domestic violence charity Refuge), developed within the context of 1970s feminism. In 1975 the Labour MP Jack Ashley said in the House of Commons:

The work of Mrs Pizzey was pioneering work of the first order. It was she who first identified the problem, who first recognised the seriousness of the situation and who first did something practical by establishing the Chiswick aid centre. As a result of that magnificent pioneering work, the whole nation has now come to appreciate the significance of the problem.

The problem of domestic violence was not unknown at all and Erin Pizzey didn't *identify* it, but was able, because of the changes in women's politics at the time, to allow it to be addressed in public for the first time.

In 1974 the National Women's Aid Federation was established, uniting over 40 independent women's refuges into one national body. The federation was able to campaign throughout the 1970s for legislation against domestic violence. In 1976, the Domestic Violence and Matrimonial Proceedings Act was passed, which provided courts with the power to impose **injunctions** on individuals who had assaulted their spouses, resulting in jail terms if they were breached.

Rape Crisis Centres

In 1973 the first Rape Crisis Centre was opened, partly as a result of the consciousness-raising workshops that were popular in the Women's Liberation Movement. Many participants in the workshops revealed their experiences of sexual violence and the failures of the legal system. The few rape cases that came to court were often conducted in a manner that was highly advantageous to the accused. Female victims were cross-examined about their own sexual history and made to feel as if they were on trial. Within a decade of the first Rape Crisis Centre opening, there were over 60 across the UK.

Abortion

In 1975 James White, the MP for Pollok, sponsored the Abortion (Amendment) Act, believing that unborn foetuses were being aborted at stages of development where they could survive if they were naturally born. The time limit on abortions was reduced to 20 weeks as a result. In protest the National Abortion Campaign was established to protect abortion rights in Britain. A further bid by MP John Corrie to amend the Abortion Act came in 1979, after widespread tabloid press reporting of women and girls abusing the abortion laws and using abortion as contraception. The reality of this was quite different; of the 112,055 abortions carried out in 1978 in England and Wales, 95,688 were deemed to be for medical grounds, suggesting that most abortions were not frivolous. The Corrie Bill proposed limitations on the grounds that abortions could be granted. Over 80,000 women marched through central London to protest against the Act.

Conclusion

The 1960s and 1970s saw significant changes in family life, with women gaining more control over birth control and abortion. The development of second-wave feminism and the work of feminists such as Germaine Greer saw women becoming more assertive, demanding more respect as equals to men but also in terms of their own gender and sexuality. The work and influence of activists such as Erin Pizzey led to women demanding more control over the issues of domestic violence and rape. However, the fact that these things still occurred meant that there was still some way to go on the route to true sexual equality.

> ## Work together
> The big issue in this chapter was how far women's lives changed between 1918 and 1979. Debate the following question.
>
> **'Despite all the legislation between 1918 and 1979, women still faced discrimination in all walks of life.'** How far do you agree with this statement?

Chapter summary

- In 1918 women over 30 gained the vote in the Representation of the People Act and a second Act in 1928 gave them equality with men in voting at 21.
- Women's gains in the workplace in the First World War were largely overturned by the return to peacetime.
- Women's roles in the professions were limited due to prejudice and being expected to stop work once they married.
- There were few women MPs in the period 1918 to 1979.
- Although women undertook jobs previously reserved for men during the Second World War they were not encouraged to keep them at the end the war.
- During the 1950s the role of women as wives and mothers was emphasised by the media.
- The 1960s saw women gaining more control over their bodies through birth control and abortion.
- Second-wave feminism emphasised equality for women in personal relations as well as in the public sphere.
- Women became more assertive in campaigning against issues such as domestic violence and rape.

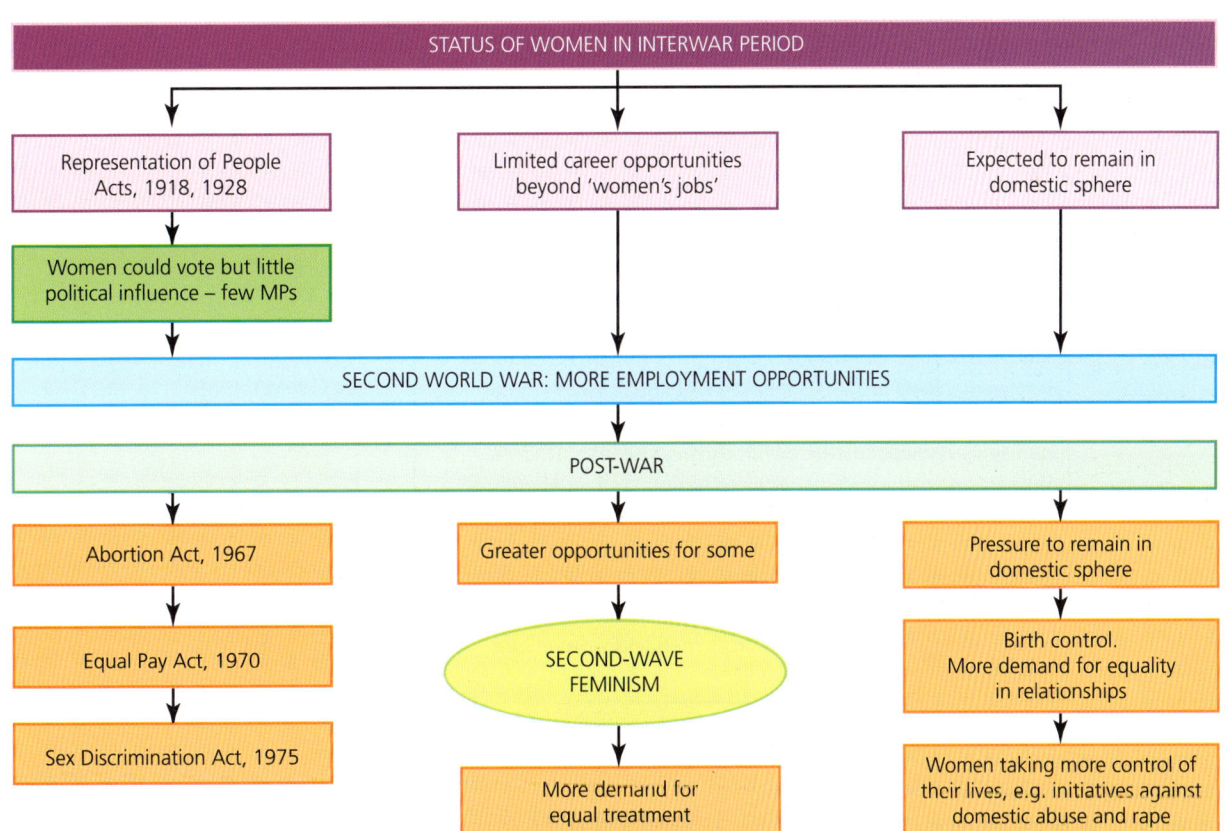

▲ Summary diagram: The changing role and status of women

Theme 3 Society in transition, 1918–79

Essay technique: Argument

Essays that develop a good argument are more likely to reach the highest levels. As you know, your essays are judged on the extent to which they analyse (see page 79). The mark scheme distinguishes between five different levels of analysis (this is a summary – the full mark scheme can be found on Edexcel's website):

Level 1 (LOW)	Simplistic or no analysis
Level 2	Limited analysis of key issues
Level 3	Some analysis of key issues
Level 4	Analysis of key issues
Level 5 (HIGH)	Sustained analysis of key issues

The key feature of the highest level is sustained analysis: analysis that unites the whole of the essay.

High-level arguments

Typically, essays examine a series of factors. A good way of achieving sustained analysis is to consider which factor is most important.

Consider the following question:

> How accurate is it to say that government policy led to major advances in women's equality in the years 1945–79?

The following introduction addresses the question, without developing an argument:

Introduction 1

Clear focus on the question — There were some major advances in women's equality in the years 1945 to 1979. The welfare state, introduced between 1945 and 1951, improved the lives of women through free access to healthcare and benefits such as family allowance. Moreover, during the late 1960s Wilson's government introduced legislation on abortion targeted at improving the lives of women. Additionally, the government passed the Equal Pay Act in 1970 and Sex Discrimination Act in 1975. However, many prejudices remained unchanged. Indeed, a great deal of welfare provision reflected the view that men and women had different roles. — Considers a wide range of factors / Addresses both sides of the question

This introduction could be improved by the introduction of an argument. An argument is a type of explanation. Therefore, an argument is a claim supported by a reason. A good way of beginning to develop an argument is to think about the meaning of the words in the question. For example, what is meant by 'major advances in women's equality'?

Introduction 2 on page 117 is an example of an introduction that begins an argument.

Introduction 2

The argument begins with a claim: distinguishing between improved rights and 'advances in equality'.

Government policy did lead to some major advances in women's equality in the years 1945 to 1979. However, while women gained greater rights throughout the period, the major advances in equality tended to come from the late 1960s onwards. First, the welfare state, introduced between 1945 and 1951, improved women's right by giving them access to better healthcare and benefits such as family allowance. However, social security payments did not always advance women's equality because they were designed on the assumption that men would work and women would stay at home. Second, in the 1960s, governments introduced legislation such as the Abortion Act of 1967, which reflected a genuine concern with women's equality. Third, the Equal Pay Act of 1970 and Sex Discrimination Act of 1975 were advances in women's equality because they established legal sexual equality in the workplace. Finally, government policies did not deal with other spheres, such as violence in the home and, even in terms of abortion rights, male doctors still had a significant say in women's rights to a termination. Therefore, from 1945 to 1979 women did gain new rights and there were even some major advances, but government policy did not lead to major advances in all areas of women's equality.

The claim is supported by a series of factors that examine actions that improved rights, actions that lead to equality, and areas in which the government failed to act.

The introduction concludes with an argument about how far genuine equality was achieved.

This introduction focusses on the question and sets out the key issues on which the essay will focus. However, it also sets out an argument that can then be developed throughout each paragraph and rounded off with an overall judgement in the conclusion. It also introduces an argument about which aspect of the movement towards female equality was most significant. Therefore, Introduction 2 is of a higher level than Introduction 1.

Activity: Developing an argument

Look at the following question:

How accurate is it to say that government policy consistently advanced sexual equality in the years 1945–79?

Using your notes from previous chapters.
1. List the areas of women's lives in which government policy had not advanced equality.
2. Write an introduction that clearly answers the question.

- Begin with a clear claim about the extent of political equality.
- Justify this with reasons based on your understanding of political equality.
- Make an argument about the aspects of women's lives in which they did not have full sexual equality.

TIPS:
- Remember the laws say what should happen in practice but are not always matched by reality.
- Sexual equality only covers limited aspects of women's lives.

3c: Race and immigration

Overview

From 1918 to 1979 Britain became an increasingly multi-cultural society. Since the seventeenth century Britain's global empire led to migration from Africa, Asia and the Caribbean to port towns such as Bristol, Southampton and Cardiff. Migration led to economic growth and social and cultural change. However, anxieties over jobs, housing, and the loss of empire, combined with deep-seated prejudices, led to ongoing patterns of discrimination and periodic explosions of white racist violence. Nonetheless, from the late 1940s hundreds of thousands of migrants made Britain their home.

Racism, controversies over immigration and the government's own 'race relations' policies led to an immigrants' movement determined to win the full rights of citizenship.

This chapter examines race and immigration through the following sections:

1. Immigration and attitudes towards ethnic minorities, 1918–39
2. The impact of the Second World War and new Commonwealth immigration
3. Racial controversy and the impact of government policies, 1958–79

1 Immigration and attitudes towards ethnic minorities, 1918–39

By the end of the First World War Britain's black and Asian communities had grown, partly as a result of seamen, labourers and soldiers being stationed in the British Isles during the war. Over one-third of Britain's manpower during the First World War had been made up of black and Asian colonial troops and labourers, including:

- a million Indian soldiers fighting in Europe and the Middle East
- around half a million locally recruited troops in Africa
- West Indian volunteers in labour battalions on the western front.

Following the First World War there was an increase in white racist violence as white workers attempted to stop black and Asian workers taking 'British jobs'. Widespread discrimination indicates that white people tended to view black and Asian people as inferior, un-British and not entitled to equal rights. At the same time, immigrants worked to defend and extend their rights. This section explores both of these developments.

Empire, nation and race

Attitudes to minority ethnic groups in Britain in the years 1918 to 1979 were influenced by ideas that had taken root during the rise of the British Empire. From the seventeenth century, the Empire placed Britain at the centre of a global network of colonies. Recent historians have stressed the racists ways of thinking that became established during this period.

People at the heart of the great European empires saw themselves as white, civilised, advanced and superior to the 'coloured' people they colonised. For example, Edward Long, a white British philosopher and historian, who was considered an expert on 'the negro people' in the eighteenth century, described black Jamaicans as 'a people certainly very stupid and very brutal. In many respects they are more like beasts than men'. The black British eighteenth-century philosopher Ottobah Cugoano, nicknamed Long, and his followers 'the orangutan philosophers' due to Long's view that 'the orangutans and some races of black men are very nearly allied'.

The view of white superiority which justified slavery was part of a broader worldview that placed white people at the top of the racial hierarchy, black people at the bottom, and people from Asia and Ireland in the middle. While slavery was abolished in the nineteenth century, racist attitudes persisted.

The period of empire was also crucial in forming attitudes towards ethnic minorities because of its impact on British nationalism. Due to imperialism, Britishness became bound up with whiteness. Consequently, 'national' institutions such as national insurance, national unions and even the National Health Service were conceived as serving British people, and therefore white people, rather than black or Asian people.

> **Note it down**
>
> Make notes on this section using a spider diagram (page x). Label the body of the spider 'Attitudes to ethnic minorities, 1918-39'. Each of the spider's legs should consider:
> - Working rights
> - 'Alien workers'
> - Anti-imperialism and antiracism
> - Education and health.
>
> In each case the focus should be on attitudes, in terms of how far they were racist and how far they were trying to break down racist attitudes.

Working rights

Between the wars attitudes to migrant workers were a barrier to their rights as workers. In essence, unions, law makers and the police considered minority ethnic groups as non-British and therefore not entitled to the same rights as white British workers.

'Alien' workers

In 1919, following the **demobilisation** of much of the British Army, there was an explosion of racist violence across Britain. In Cardiff, Newport, Glasgow, Salford, Hull, South Shields and London, angry mobs of unemployed white Britons attacked black and Asian people that they considered foreign, and therefore not entitled to jobs in Britain.

- In Limehouse, an East End district of London, black people were attacked in four days of white rioting.
- In Cardiff white violence led to three deaths, and over £3,000 of property damage.

> **The 'colour bar' in the 1920s and 1930s**
>
> In theory, all British citizens had the same rights to work and use public facilities regardless of their ethnicity. However, in practice there was a colour bar: black and Asian people were excluded from employment, or refused service in theatres, hotels or restaurants. The colour bar was based on:
> - widespread prejudice
> - unions and businesses working together to deny the rights of black and Asian people
> - police indifference to racism
> - the absence of government action to end racism.

National unions also fought for the 'right' of white workers to take the jobs of 'coloured' workers. For example, the National Union of Seamen (NUS) demanded that the jobs of 'non-white' sailors should be given to white seamen. Local branches of the union took action to force black workers out of jobs. For example, in 1919 white workers in Liverpool went on strike in protest at working alongside black workers. The strikes and white violence led to the sacking of 120 black workers.

NUS campaigns led to two laws which placed all black and Asian people under the threat of deportation.

The Alien Orders Act, 1920

The Alien Orders Act required migrant workers (or 'aliens') to register with the police before seeking work. 'Aliens' who failed to comply would be punished by deportation. In reality, the police only applied the law to black and Asian people. Moreover, many of those branded 'alien' were British citizens, or citizens of the British Empire. However, their rights were ignored as police assumed that black and Asian people were automatically 'aliens'. In this sense the Act placed all black and Asian people under suspicion and under threat of deportation.

Special Restrictions Act, 1925 (Coloured Alien Seamen Act)

This Act forced 'coloured' seamen to prove their British citizenship to immigration authorities or face deportation. The Act assumed that 'coloured' seamen were non-British unless they could prove their status as citizens.

Discrimination

Wage rates were weighted in favour of white workers. For example, a report presented in the House of Commons in 1919 by MP Neil Maclean stated that Asian chefs were paid £5 a month while white chefs were paid £20 a month.

Equally, in the 1930s, black people were more likely to be unemployed than white people. In the year 1934–35, the **League of Coloured People** reported that 80 per cent of black and Asian men had been unemployed for a prolonged period, compared to just 30 per cent of white men.

Racist action continued in the 1930s, particularly in areas of economic depression. In Cardiff a race riot erupted in 1935. The local police collaborated with white workers to prevent black British sailors from working on ships, declaring them non-British under the Aliens Orders Act.

Anti-imperialism and antiracism

During the 1920s and 1930s there were a number of groups fighting for the rights of black, Asian and Jewish workers. The most influential were the Communist Party of Great Britain (CPGB) and the International African Service Bureau (IASB). Both groups linked the fight against white domination in the Empire with the fight against white domination in Britain.

The Communist Party of Great Britain

The CPGB played a significant role in leading the fight against racism in the 1920s. The party, founded in 1921, had a very high proportion of members from minority ethnic groups including people from the Caribbean, India, Ireland, as well as Jews. Equally, the party was relatively unattractive to the majority of white workers. In this sense the CPGB represented many radical immigrants, including Shapurji Saklatvala, an Indian-born radical who played a leading role in the movement.

One of the CPGB's major campaigns involved the defence of the rights of Arab seamen. In 1930 the NUS tried to force Arab and Somali seamen out of their jobs in South Shields in South Tyneside. The CPGB, working with groups representing the Arab and Somali seamen, organised regional strikes against the union's racist policy. White workers in South Shields, Liverpool and Stepney struck against the NUS. While the action was unsuccessful, it did show that some white workers were prepared to support antiracist campaigns. Moreover, it demonstrated the extent to which immigrants were prepared to fight for their rights.

Finally, the CPGB organised campaigns against the British Union of Fascists (BUF) in the mid-1930s (see page 11). The BUF attempted to incite anti-Semitism in London's East End, leading to fire bombings and 'Jew-bashing'. The local Jewish People's Council (JPC) and the CPGB organised a demonstration of over 10,000 people to stop the BUF march. The two marches led to the Battle of Cable Street, a series of fights between the BUF and antifascist campaigners, which forced the BUF to abandon the march.

The International African Service Bureau

The IASB was another group dedicated to fighting imperialism and racism. It was established in London in 1937 by the Caribbean intellectuals C.L.R. James and George Padmore. The IASB established a newspaper *International African Opinion* which encouraged readers to lobby their MPs for black rights. Specifically, they lobbied for black and Asian people to have equal access to healthcare and shopping facilities.

Education and health

Racist attitudes towards immigration were also evident from the way black and Asian people were treated in colleges and hospitals.

Britain's universities played an important imperial role, educating people from British colonies. In the interwar period around 50 people from West Africa, 150 from the Caribbean and a similar number from India were educated in Britain's top universities. British policy makers hoped that young men from the colonies would come to Britain, receive an excellent education and then return to the colonies to serve the Empire as senior administrators. Significantly, students from the colonies were not expected to stay in Britain and work in elite positions within the British government, however good their education. Harold Moody, for example, was born in Jamaica and moved to Britain in 1904 to study medicine. Choosing to stay, he was repeatedly refused employment in British hospitals. As a result he established his own medical practice in London.

Black and minority ethnic students routinely experienced racial discrimination during their studies. Therefore, they established groups to campaign for equal rights. The League of Coloured People (LCP), was established by Harold Moody in 1931 to support immigrant students to gain equal rights. The LCP:

- worked to expose the colour bar, and therefore end white ignorance of the extent of discrimination
- started campaigns to ensure equal access to facilities for all black and Asian people in Britain
- campaigned to gain equal access to healthcare.

2 The impact of the Second World War and new Commonwealth immigration

The Second World War, and the period 1948–58 saw a step change in patterns of migration. During the war British policy makers looked to the Empire to provide the resources and the manpower to ensure British victory. However, successive governments rejected migration as a solution to the problems of reconstruction after the war.

Mass migration, as it became known, fundamentally changed British culture. However, the impact of immigration tended to reflect the prejudices of the white majority. During the war and in the decades afterwards Britishness was still associated exclusively with whiteness by the majority of Britain's white population. By and large, black and Asian migrants were expected to perform the menial, low-paid and low-status jobs, regardless of their education and skills. Indeed, trade unions, employers and the police worked together to exclude the new migrants from well-paid jobs on the basis that they were not white and therefore not British.

The impact of the war

The Second World War had a series of important consequences for government policy, the British economy and British society.

The war effort

First, by 1945 the government had recognised that migrant workers and soldiers had been crucial to the war effort. Indeed, some in government recognised that Britain's victory had depended on the support of the colonies. Many of the Empire's subjects thought of Britain as benign – 'the mother country' – and in need of their aid. Others joined up in order to escape grinding poverty – armed service might have entailed risks and hardship, but it also offered steady pay and prestige.

> **Note it down**
>
> The emphasis in this section is on the influence of the Second World War and post-war immigration. Use bullet points (see page ix) to work through the section, addressing the following issues:
> - How influential was the Second World War on attitudes towards race in Britain?
> - How significant was the impact of post-war immigration from the new Commonwealth?
> - How significant were racist attitudes during this period?

Around 1,200 men from across the Caribbean were employed in factories in Lancashire and Merseyside. Other men joined the armed forces.

- Between 6,000 and 10,000 Caribbean men joined the RAF.
- Around 500,000 black African men served in the British forces.
- By 1945 the Indian Army numbered 2 million men. It was the largest multi-ethnic volunteer army the world had ever seen.

Ongoing racism

Second, the war exposed ongoing racism. Early in the war there was still official prejudice. Government propaganda encouraged white men from Australia and New Zealand to help the war effort. However, it discouraged men from the Caribbean. For example, in mid-1940 the government rejected an offer from a Caribbean shipping company to pay for 2,000 Jamaican workers to travel to Britain to carry out war work. While government discrimination disappeared as the war went on, many West Indian soldiers found that they were marginalised and workers faced discrimination from white factory managers and unions on arrival in Britain.

- Some Caribbean workers were refused work in factories due to 'cultural differences' with white workers.
- Promotions for black and Asian soldiers were rare.
- There was considerable social pressure against black men marrying white women.

British racism was complicated by the arrival of the American military from 1942 onwards. The US Army was racially segregated, black and white soldiers lived in different accommodation, and fought in different battalions. American authorities tried to enforce this segregation in Britain, seeking to prevent black American troops from mingling with unsegregated British colonial troops. Additionally, some British businesses used the US Army's desire for segregation as an excuse to enforce a colour bar. For example, the renowned cricketer Learie Constantine was refused accommodation in London's Imperial Hotel in 1944 on the grounds that white American guests did not want to stay in a hotel that served black people.

New opportunities

Third, the war opened up new opportunities for black and Asian people in Britain. For example, education and training was offered to all ex-servicemen after the war, and many recent immigrants made full use of this provision. Also, the British state, while refusing to outlaw discrimination, did at least publicly reject it. Indeed, government officials welcomed Learie Constantine's legal victory against the Imperial Hotel, a victory that established black Britons had the same legal rights as white Britons.

'New Commonwealth' immigration

Following the war there was a serious labour shortage. This provided an opportunity for migrants from across the Empire to earn money. Additionally, government policy made it easy for imperial subjects to gain entry to Britain. The British Nationality Act (1948) created a new legal right for all people in British colonies to enter the UK. Together, the British Nationality Act and the labour shortage led to waves of migration, which significantly increased the proportion of black and Asian people living in Britain. The arrival of the *SS Empire Windrush* in June 1948, bringing 492 Jamaican people to Britain, is often celebrated as the beginning of mass migration.

The impact of mass migration, 1948–58

Immigration changed the population of Britain as Asian and Caribbean communities grew from tens of thousands to hundreds of thousands (see Table 1).

> ### Commonwealth and 'new Commonwealth'
>
> The Commonwealth is an international organisation created in 1949. It is largely made up of countries that were once part of the British Empire. Unlike the imperial colonies, Commonwealth countries are regarded as 'free and equal'.
>
> The phrase 'new Commonwealth' became popular in the 1960s and 1970s. The phrase introduced a distinction between two types of Commonwealth country:
>
> - The 'old Commonwealth': countries formerly part of the British Empire with a predominantly white population, such as Australia, New Zealand and Canada.
> - The 'new Commonwealth': countries formerly part of the British Empire with a predominantly black or Asian population, such as Jamaica, Ghana or India.

Table 1: Estimated migrant population from the 'new Commonwealth', 1939–59

Migrants from	Population in 1939	Population in 1949	Population in 1959
The Caribbean	8,600	133,000	173,000
India and Pakistan	9,300	64,000	462,000

▲ Jamaicans on board the *SS Empire Windrush*, June 1948. How useful is this photograph to a historian studying post-war immigration from the new Commonwealth to Britain?

Opportunities

As the British economy grew in the 1950s, the new immigrants found opportunities to make money. There were lucrative opportunities in the entertainment business. The Guyanese entrepreneur, Dr Mooksang, opened nightclubs in London. Another person who gained fame in the 1950s was the Jamaican DJ Wilbert Augustus Campbell. He played Jamaican ska and reggae under the stage name Count Suckle in nightclubs such as Paddington's Q Club and the Roaring Twenties in London's West End. Frank Crichlow, who moved from Trinidad to Britain in 1952, established El Rio in the late 1950s – one of the first Caribbean restaurants in London. More generally, new migrants found work in the Post Office, on the railways and in the NHS. Indeed, the NHS recruited 3,000 nurses from the Caribbean between 1948 and 1954.

Government reaction

Neither Labour nor Conservative governments welcomed the new immigration. Indeed, Prime Ministers Attlee and Churchill actively tried to discourage immigration from the 'new Commonwealth' by putting pressure on governments in the Caribbean, Africa and Asia to restrict the availability of passports. Labour and Conservative governments all considered policies such as limits on 'coloured' immigration and **repatriation**. They were rejected for fear of damaging Britain's international reputation.

Racist reactions

Letters to MPs record widespread concern among white people about the consequences of the new immigration. White people objected to black and Asian people:

- buying houses
- claiming welfare benefits
- getting jobs
- committing crime
- behaving in ways that reflected 'cultural differences'.

Fundamentally, the complaints were based on the assumption that only white people were British and therefore only white people had the right to national benefits and housing. Significantly, letters to MPs did not express concern about immigration from Australia, New Zealand or other 'white colonies'. Concern about immigration was almost exclusively related to black and Asian people.

MPs also received letters from recent immigrants complaining about discrimination. White racism was discussed by the cabinet, but no action was taken. Lord Salisbury, leader of the House of Lords, argued that action against discrimination would make Britain more attractive to 'coloured' immigrants and therefore the government should not intervene to combat racism.

The colour bar in the 1950s

Historian and sociologist Satnam Virdee argues that in the period following the Second World War, unions, employers and the government worked together in an unprecedented way to enforce the 'colour bar'. During the 1950s unions and management in businesses such as Ford Dagenham, Vickers and Tate and Lyle enforced a quota system, whereby 95 per cent of jobs had to go to white people. There were similar agreements in the transport industry. Indeed, in 1955 white transport workers went on strike due to the breach of the 5 per cent rule in Wolverhampton.

White violence

Mass immigration was also accompanied by white violence against new immigrants. There were many causes.

- Black and Asian men who dated or married white women were often subject to beatings by white men.
- Anger at the loss of Britain's colonies (see page 34) was expressed by violent actions against black and Asian people, who were perceived as representatives of the people who had rejected British rule.
- Black and Asian people were blamed for social and economic problems.
- Police officers were more likely to prosecute crime against black and Asian people.

Notting Hill riots, 1958

The Notting Hill riots of 1958 are the most notorious mass violence against black people in the 1950s. The riots took place in late August and early September. Over several nights mobs of between 300 and 700 white men armed with iron bars, knives and heavy leather belts beat the black residents of Notting Hill, as well as attacking their homes and businesses. The crowd shouted slogans such as 'We will kill the blacks' and 'Keep Britain white!' Police did little to stop the attacks, and therefore the black community organised its own defence.

3 Racial controversy and the impact of government policies, 1958–79

Between 1958 and 1979 the government took a series of steps to restrict immigration and outlaw a variety of forms of racial discrimination. During this period there were several political trends and related debates over immigration, 'race relations', and racism.

- Conservative and Labour politicians attempted to win votes by proposing policies to restrict immigration.
- A minority of politicians 'played the race card': they tried to win votes or political advancement by appealing to popular racism.
- Other politicians began to advocate 'multi-culturalism'.
- A number of black rights groups were founded to lead the fight against racism in Britain.

> **Note it down**
>
> This section follows government policies between 1958 and 1979. Use whichever note-taking method (see page ix) that best suits to note down the main points about each of the following:
> - immigration policy, 1958–79
> - consequences of immigration Acts
> - race relations Acts
> - white backlash.
>
> The section contains a lot of legislation. You might find it useful to write down the details of each piece of legislation on a card, which you can keep for ease of reference.

Immigration policy, 1958–79

In the period 1958–79 there was a series of government initiatives designed to restrict immigration.

Legal restrictions

There were a number of factors that led to the introduction of restrictions on immigration from 1962:

- widespread public concern about 'racial tensions'
- government reports that blamed black and Asian people for crime, the rising costs of welfare and overcrowding.

Macmillan's 1962 bill was the first of many which were designed to restrict immigration from the 'new Commonwealth'.

Commonwealth Immigration Act, 1962

This Act was designed to end large-scale immigration. In that sense it was designed to prevent the creation of a multi-cultural society. People from former colonies could obtain an entry voucher for two main reasons:

- They had a job waiting for them.
- They had specific skills that the British economy required, for instance a member of the medical profession.

The Act did, however, allow families to be reunited, so the spouses or children of people living in Britain still had entry rights.

Commonwealth Immigration Act, 1968

Labour's 1968 Act tightened the rules further.

- Children of migrants living in Britain who were over seventeen years of age were denied entry to Britain.
- Children with only one parent living in Britain were denied entry to Britain.
- Entry required a connection to Britain: new migrants had to prove that a parent or grandparent lived in Britain.

The Immigration Act, 1971

The Immigration Act of 1971 introduced two, largely racial categories into British law.

- Partial: People born in the UK, or whose parents or grandparents were born in the UK. This category tended to apply to white British people, and white people from Australia, New Zealand and Canada. There were a very small number of people from the 'new Commonwealth' who were in this category.
- Non-partial: People who were born outside the UK, and whose parents and grandparents were born outside the UK.

Partials were not subject to any restrictions. Therefore, most white people from the Commonwealth could come and go freely.

Non-partials were subject to strict controls. They had no right of entry or residence and those who had lived in the UK for less than ten years could be repatriated.

According to opinions polls all three of the Acts had widespread public support (see Table 2).

Table 2: Support for the Immigration Acts

Act	Level of support
1962	62%–76%*
1968	72%
1971	59%

* Figures based on several opinion polls.

Controversy

The 1968 Act led to widespread controversy. The Act effectively denied Kenyan Asians, who were fleeing persecution, entry to Britain. As a result it was attacked by the press and student radicals.

The consequences of the Acts

The Acts to restrict immigration had an impact on mass migration, multi-culturalism and the radicalisation of black rights groups.

Mass migration

The 1962 Act was designed to end mass immigration. However, it had radically different consequence. It led to the creation of a multi-cultural society in four ways.

1. In order to beat the ban, large numbers of black and Asian migrants moved to Britain before the Act came into force. As a result the black and Asian population in Britain doubled between 1960 and 1961.
2. The Act led many black and Asian migrants who had planned to leave Britain to stay, for fear of being denied re-entry as a result of the Act.
3. The Act allowed the immediate families of migrants to enter Britain. Therefore, once one member of the family had decided to stay the rest of the family moved to Britain.
4. Between 30,000 and 50,000 work vouchers were issued each year between 1963 and 1979, therefore migration continued at historically high levels (see Table 3).

Table 3: 'New Commonwealth' migration, 1956–61

Date	'New Commonwealth' migration
1956 (peak 1948–60)	46,050
1959	21,600
1961	136,4000

Radicalisation

Changes in government policy also led to the radicalisation of black rights groups. Until the early 1960s black and Asian people tended to vote Labour. The Labour Party's opposition to the 1962 Immigration Act, and the Conservative Party's slogan, 'If you want a nigger for a neighbour vote Labour' during the 1964 General Election in the Smethwick constituency cemented the link between Labour and black and Asian voters. However, Labour took an increasingly hard-line attitude to immigration between 1965 and 1968, therefore many young black radicals rejected mainstream politics in favour of Black Power – an ideology that had emerged in America in 1966. From the late 1960s black and Asian people formed radical groups to fight for their rights.

- In 1968 the Nigerian-born playwright Obi B. Egbuna formed the British Black Panther Party.
- In 1971 Jamaican-born radical Olive Morris founded the Brixton Black Women's Group.
- In 1974 Trinidad-born radical, intellectual and writer Darcus Howe founded the Race Today Collective, the most significant black rights organisation of the period.
- In 1975 a group of Asian teenagers founded the Asian Youth Movement in response to the murder of Gurdip Singh Chaggar.

Black, 'coloured', 'negro'

During the early part of the twentieth century, it was common to refer to black people as 'coloured' or as 'negro'. In the late 1960s, black radicals rejected these terms in favour of the word 'black'. 'Negro' was associated with slavery, and 'coloured' was associated with segregation in the US and the 'colour bar' in Britain. Therefore both words implied that black people were inferior to whites. Black radicals claimed the word 'black', which they argued implied independence, power, and absolute equality. Even so, white politicians and journalists continued to use the word 'coloured' into the late 1980s. During late 1960s and early 1970s radicals used the term 'black' to refer to all black and Asian people.

Roy Jenkins and multi-culturalism

Multi-culturalism has never been formally defined in law. Nonetheless, Labour's policies in the late 1960s and through the 1970s often reflected Home Secretary Roy Jenkins' vision of a multi-cultural society, when speaking in 1966 he:

- rejected the goal of **cultural assimilation**: he argued that immigrants should be under no obligation to adopt 'English customs'
- argued that there should be a common commitment to equality of opportunity for all
- wanted Britain to become a country of cultural diversity, where people from different background sought to understand each other and respect each other's customs.

During the 1970s the **Black Panthers** and the Race Today Collective proved extremely effective at organising to challenge racism.

- In 1971 Darcus Howe and Althea Jones Lecointe, leader of the Black Panthers, forced the first official acknowledgement that there was 'evidence of racial hatred in the Metropolitan Police'.
- In 1974 Darcus Howe and the Race Today Collective helped organise the Imperial Typewriters strike. The strike forced predominantly white unions to support Asian workers.
- Between 1974 and 1976 Darcus Howe and the Race Today Collective helped organise the biggest squat in British history to ensure the Bengali population of Tower Hamlets had access to safe housing.

Race Relations Acts

In addition to the Immigration Acts of the 1960s and 1970s, Labour governments introduced three Race Relations Acts to outlaw various aspects of racial discrimination (see Table 4). The Acts were motivated by a series of issues:

- pressure from black and Asian people to deal with racism in Britain
- government concerns that poor 'race relations' would lead to widespread rioting; indeed, British policy makers were worried by riots in US cities in the 1960s
- a political commitment to multi-culturalism.

The consequences of race relations law

The ban on inciting racial hatred led to a number of prosecutions. However, the law was often used against black radicals. For example, Michael X, the leader of the Racial Adjustment Action Society, was the first person to be convicted of inciting racial hatred for a speech he gave in Reading in 1967. Also Roy Sawh, deputy chair of the Universal Coloured People's Association, holds the record as the person with the most arrests under the 1965 law.

White backlash

The new laws also created a backlash. The most famous example of this was Enoch Powell's 'Rivers of Blood' speech. The speech, given on 20 April 1968, addressed Labour's 1968 proposal to introduce a tougher race relations law. Powell's speech argued:

- Mass migration and antiracist laws meant that black and Asian people had more rights and privileges than white people in Britain.
- White Britons were now 'strangers in their own country'.
- Multi-culturalism would lead to segregated communities and violence.
- The government should give grants to black and Asian people to encourage 're-emigration'.

Powell's speech reflected a new kind of 'post-colonial racism'. It acknowledged that the British Empire was dead, but also advocated keeping Britain white.

The speech led to widespread condemnation. He was sacked from the Conservative shadow cabinet. However, according to an opinion poll 74 per cent of Britons agreed with his ideas. Three days later a march of 1,000 dock workers expressed their support for Powell, carrying placards that read 'Don't knock Enoch'.

Powell's speech reflected a widespread view among white Britons that black and Asian people had no right to express their own culture in Britain. This view was at the heart of the National Front, a new political party founded in 1967.

Table 4: Race Relations Acts

Act	Provisions of Act
Race Relations Act, 1965	Outlawed the colour bar – it became illegal to deny people access to services and public places on the basis of race. Outlawed incitement of racial hatred. Established the Race Relations Board (RRB) to monitor the enforcement of the law. The Act did nothing to end racial discrimination in housing.
Race Relations Act, 1968	Extended the 1965 provision by: • outlawing racial discrimination in housing and employment • establishing the Community Relations Commission (CRC) to promote multi-culturalism through education.
Race Relations Act, 1976	Led to further protections from racial discrimination. **Indirect discrimination** was outlawed: discrimination that was not based primarily on ethnicity, but affected some groups in a detrimental way was banned. Combined the CRC with the RRB to create the new Commission for Racial Equality.

The Notting Hill Carnival

In 1976 there were extremely aggressive attempts by the Metropolitan Police to close down the Notting Hill Carnival. The carnival had been created by immigrants predominantly from Trinidad, and grew steadily during the 1960s and 1970s. Aggressive policing led to violent clashes during the 1976 carnival. Similarly, police officers attempted to close celebrations of African Liberation Day held in Notting Hill in 1977. Black radical Darcus Howe responded by performing a **citizen's arrest** on local police officers. His actions were later upheld in court.

Work together

The main focus of this chapter has been on how far attitudes to race changed in Britain over the period 1918–79. Work together to design a chart as follows:

1918--1979

Attitudes   Attitudes

Identify key events in the change of attitudes between 1918 and 1979 and plot them on your chart.

When you have finished discuss how far you think attitudes to race have changed over the period.

Assimilation or multi-culturalism

Jenkins' vision of a fully multi-cultural society did not emerge in the 1960s and 1970s. Indeed, policies designed to force immigrants to assimilate continued. One example was the policy of dispersal, which took place in some British schools. In essence, some local governments had a policy that students from an Indian or Caribbean background were not allowed to make up more than 30 per cent of a school population. Therefore in some areas of Yorkshire and London students were bussed to schools to ensure they were dispersed. The policy was opposed by parents' organisations and political groups such as the Race Today Collective. Consequently, by the late 1970s it was abandoned. Nonetheless, it reflected an ongoing desire for immigrants to assimilate, and popular white unease about the emergence of 'black schools' which rejected the principle of cultural diversity at the heart of multi-culturalism.

The three Race Relation laws did create the beginnings of an official commitment to cultural diversity. For example, the 1976 law was used to uphold the right of Sikh boys to wear turbans to school following the 1982 court case *Mandla* v. *Dowell-Lee*.

Conclusions

Between 1962 and 1976 government policy pointed in two directions. First, increasingly racist immigration laws sought to restrict the number of migrants from Africa, the Caribbean and Asia, while protecting the rights of white migrants. Second, the Labour Party tried to outlaw discrimination and lay the foundations for a multi-cultural society. Neither policy was wholly successful. Immigration laws failed to stop mass migration and race relations laws failed to create a multi-cultural society. Yet, alongside the history of government action is a history of local activists who defended the rights of their communities, and in so doing began to create a genuinely multi-cultural society.

Chapter summary

- Between 1918 and 1979 immigration created opportunities and controversies.
- For most of the period white Britons believed that only white people could be truly British and in the early part of the century the British government passed laws to restrict the rights of immigrants from Africa, Asia and the Caribbean.
- By the Second World War the government explicitly rejected racial prejudice.
- Post-war Conservative governments hoped that new immigrants would assimilate.
- The majority of British citizens were happy to tolerate black and Asian people as long as they accepted low pay and low-status jobs.
- Pressure from immigrants, and a commitment to end racism from Wilson's Labour governments, led to the creation of laws that were designed to end racial discrimination.
- These laws led to a backlash from people who wanted to keep Britain white, which found a voice in Enoch Powell's 'Rivers of Blood' speech in April 1968.
- Immigrant groups were determined to make Britain their home and claim the full rights of citizenship.

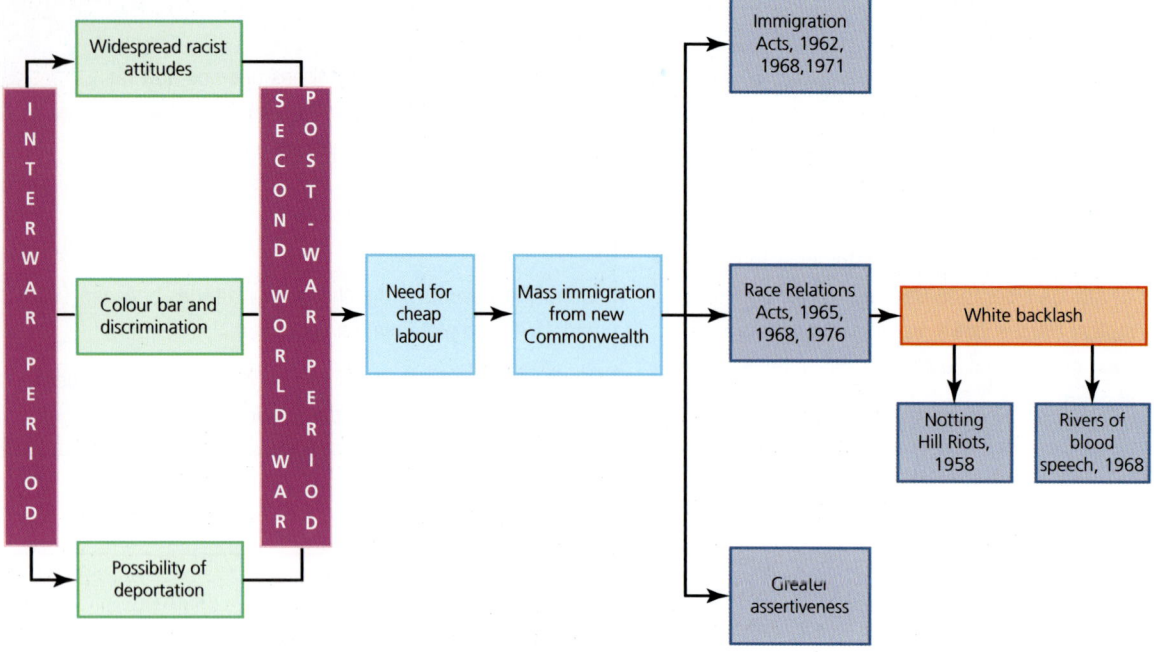

▲ Summary diagram: Race and immigration

Recommended reading: Society in transition 1918–79

S. Bourne, *The Motherland Calls: Britain's Black Servicemen and Women, 1939–45* (The History Press, 2012). An history of the role that black servicemen and women had during the Second World War.

D. Cannadine, *Class in Britain* (Penguin, 1998). A thorough account of changing social attitudes in Britain in the twentieth century.

P. Fryer, *Staying Power: The History of Black People in Britain* (Pluto Press, 2010). A comprehensive history of black immigration and politics in Britain.

G. Greer, *The Female Eunuch* (Harper Perennial Modern Classics, 2006; first published 1970). Germaine Greer's seminal 1970 exploration of patriarchal society.

P. Horn, *Flappers: The Real Lives of British Women in the Era of The Great Gatsby* (Amberley, 2013). A study of the lives and aspirations of women in the 1920s, and how changes to women's lives were interpreted by the media.

J. Purvis, *Women's History: Britain, 1850–1945: An Introduction* (Routledge, 1995). A comprehensive social history of British women from the industrial revolution through to the Second World War.

A. Marwick, *British Society since 1945: The Penguin Social History of Britain* (Penguin, 2003). A comprehensive history of social change in Britain since the end of the Second World War.

I. R.G. Spencer, *British Immigration Policy Since 1939* (Routledge, 1997, pages 8–20). The first major analysis of the development of British immigration policy.

S. Todd, *The People: The Rise and Fall of the Working Class, 1910–2010* (John Murray, 2014). A social history of Britain told from the perspective of the working class.

A. Spry Rush, *Bonds of Empire, West Indians and Britishness from Victoria to Decolonization* (Oxford, 2011, pages 117–147). The book examines the relationship between Britain and former British colonies in the Caribbean. Very useful for a discussion of the relationship and perceptions of Britishness.

S. Tuck and H. Gates, *The Night Malcolm X Spoke at the Oxford Union: A Transatlantic Story of Antiracist Protest* (University of California Press, 2014). The history of American Nation of Islam radical Malcolm X's visit to Britain and its effect on racial politics in the UK.

S. Virdee, *Racism, Class and the Racialized Outsider* (Macmillan, 2014, Chapter 6). Virdee's book examines the impact of racism and anti-racism on the British class structure, considering the central role played by generations of immigrants on British politics, economics and culture.

Essay technique: Counter-argument

Essays that develop a good argument are more likely to reach the highest levels, because argumentative essays are more likely to develop sustained analysis (see page 79).

You can set up an argument in your introduction, but you should develop your argument throughout the essay. One way of doing this is to adopt an argument–counter-argument structure. A counter-argument is an argument that disagrees with the main argument of the essay. Setting up an argument and then challenging it with a counter-argument is one way of weighing up, or evaluating, the importance of the different factors that you discuss. Essays of this type will develop an argument in one paragraph and then set out an opposing argument in another paragraph.

Imagine you are answering the following question:

> **How far did British governments fight racial discrimination in the period 1918–79?**

You could write an essay in which the first two paragraphs set out the arguments as in the example below.

These two paragraphs could be developed into the beginning of a high-level answer. However, you will need to resolve the tension between the argument and the counter-argument (see page 153) and write a conclusion that weighs up the different aspect of the essay (see page 154) in order to write a full essay.

Paragraph 1: Argument	British governments publicly opposed racist attitudes but did not pass any significant laws to eradicate them in the interwar period. Indeed, laws such as the Alien Orders Act of 1920 made it easier to deport foreign nationals.
Paragraph 2: Counter-argument	However, from the mid-1960s governments passed laws to fight discrimination in three Race Relations Acts of 1965, 1968 and 1976. Initial laws were quite limited and sometimes used against black radicals, rather than white racists. The 1976 law did contain some important rights for black and Asian people.

Activity: Relative importance

Imagine you are answering the following question:

How far was racism a dominant feature of British society from 1958 to 1979?

Using your notes from the previous chapters:
1 Draw the following diagram:

2 Write the following factors on cards or sticky notes and place them on the line, according to their importance in how far black and Asian people were treated as equals in the period 1945–79.
- The Colour Bar
- Immigration policy, 1958–71
- Race Relation Acts, 1965, 1968, 1976
- Work of black and Asian organisations
- Multi-culturalism

3 Now write a short argument justifying the relative importance of each factor.
   TIP: Remember, your argument must contain a statement and a reason.
4 Reverse the order of your first and second most important factors.
5 Write two sentences that explicitly argue that your second most important factor was actually the most important factor. This is your counter-argument.
   TIP: Remember, your counter-argument must contain a statement and a reason.
6 Use your original argument and counter-argument as the basis for writing two paragraphs in answer to the question.

Paper 1 Britain transformed, 1918–97

Theme 4 The changing quality of life, 1918–79

The big picture

By 1979 the quality of life that most people enjoyed in Britain had dramatically improved. By the 1970s most British people experienced a level of consumer choice that had never previously existed and rising wages and available credit gave them spending power to purchase consumer goods in ever greater quantities. They also enjoyed access to more leisure time and travel than in previous generations.

A generation earlier, between the 1920s and 1940s, the experience of many people in Britain was different: instead of affluence they encountered economic hardship, wartime rationing and post-war austerity. The economic circumstances in which this generation lived had shaped very different attitudes to spending, saving and consumerism than that of their children who grew up during the post-Second World War boom.

The quality of life in Britain was transformed, in part, by popular culture and the development of new media throughout the century. Popular culture in British life was nothing new, but the availability of radio and television transformed it. Some historians have referred to Britain as a TV nation in the post-war era, meaning that the widespread availability of television and the range and quality of programmes on offer transformed British cultural and social life. In many homes both radio and television became the focal point.

Cultural change in Britain has not always been greeted with approval and in the 1950s and 1960s there were growing anxieties about the pace of cultural change and fears that Britain was being 'Americanised'. Music, film and TV programmes from the USA were hugely popular, but Britain also retained much of its own cultural distinctiveness and exported its culture back across the Atlantic.

Car ownership, the availability of affordable holidays and increased leisure time also had a widespread social and cultural impact. Foreign holidays enabled many British people to encounter different cultures, climates and foods for the first time. Overseas travel was partly responsible for changes to British tastes in food, drink and culture. Increased car ownership and the development of the motorway network enabled greater mobility for most British people throughout the period. More affluent families were able to live further away from where they worked because cars enabled them to commute. In addition to this, as car ownership became available to lower-income families, more British people were able to holiday in and travel around the British Isles.

Changes in personal affluence, consumer choice, leisure time and the kinds of popular entertainment available transformed the lives of millions of people.

In this theme you will consider the following:
- **Changing living standards:** the impact of boom, crisis and recovery and regional differences 1918–39; the effects of total war and austerity, 1939–51; the growth of consumer society, 1951–79.
- **Popular culture and entertainment:** the impact of mass popular culture including cinema, radio and music, 1918–79; the influence of television from the 1950s; youth culture 1955–79.
- **Leisure and travel:** the growth of spectator sports from the 1920s; increased leisure time and the development of mass tourism from the 1930s; the impact of car ownership and other travel developments.

TIMELINE

1922	First BBC radio broadcast
1927	Cinematograph Films Act
1930	Road Traffic Act
1933	Walthamstow Stadium opened
1934	Mersey Tunnel opened
1934	Road Traffic Act
1937	BBC began to broadcast live from football matches
1939	Great North Road opened
1940	Creation of the Ministry of Food
1944	Housing and Temporary Accommodation Act
1946	New Towns Act
1946	Bread rationing introduced
1951	Opening of the Festival of Britain
1959	M1 motorway opened
1963	Beeching Report published
1966	Housing charity Shelter founded
1966	World Cup final
1967	Radio 1 first broadcast
1972	Sports Council of Great Britain established

4a: Changing living standards

Overview

The period 1918–79 saw an overall rise in living standards but this was uneven, particularly during the interwar period when there were significant regional differences. The centres of older industries in the north, Scotland and south Wales faced continual economic hardship worsened by the onset of the Great Depression, while centres of newer industries often enjoyed high employment which led to a consumer boom. Rationing and austerity continued after the Second World War, but by the 1950s the economy developed. There ensued a prolonged consumer boom, fuelled by full employment and readily available credit – although there remained pockets of deprivation and hardship.

This chapter examines changing living standards through the following sections:
1. The impact of boom, crisis and recovery, 1918–39
2. The effects of 'total war' and austerity, 1939–51
3. The growth of a consumer society, 1951–79

1 The impact of boom, crisis and recovery, 1918–39

The government hoped for a consumer boom after the First World War to revive the country's struggling economy. It initially assumed that the end of wartime shortages and the lifting of rationing and other controls would work. Indeed, Britain did experience a two-year boom, ending in 1920 (see page 26).

The short-lived boom failed to generate the levels of high employment needed to absorb the large numbers of men demobilising from the Army. This caused an economic crisis and a decline in living standards, which was to be exacerbated by the **Great Depression** of the 1930s. Not all regions experienced the same economic hardships however, with some faring much worse than others. Towards the end of the 1930s, as government spending increased to prepare the country for war there was an economic recovery.

Note it down

This section deals with how far living standards rose during the interwar period. Use the 1:2 method (see page x) to complete the following table:

Boom, 1918–20	How far were living standards increased in the immediate post-war period?
Economic crisis in the 1920s	How far did this impact on living standards?
Regional differences	How evenly were improvements in living standards spread?
Improvements in living standards in the 1930s	How far did living standards improve in the 1930s?

Boom, 1918–20

As the war came to its conclusion, Prime Minister Lloyd George's promise of 'a land fit for heroes to live in' seemed initially to be achievable. There was a post-war boom in which firms recalibrated for peacetime production, prices continued to rise and government did little to regulate production. Initially demobbed soldiers returned to work and it seemed that living standards would rise and that families had money to spend.

Economic crisis in the 1920s and 1930s

As we have seen the boom was short-lived and by the end of 1920 there were 1 million unemployed, one-third of them ex-servicemen. Beggars began to appear, often with medals.

The growth in unemployment led to cuts in living standards in many areas. While unemployment never fell below 1 million during the 1930s, the picture was not uniform across Britain. New industries were emerging and unemployment was not so severe in these areas (see page 43). In 1932 approximately 12 per cent of those engaged in electrical appliance manufacture were unemployed compared with up to 70 per cent of those engaged in ship building.

Other factors were noted, too. Often young women could maintain employment as teachers or nurses, and many people resented their being able to buy what were considered fripperies at the counters of Woolworths while men were unemployed.

Regional differences

The decline of **heavy industry** such as ship building, and the production of coal, iron, and cotton had a huge impact on living standards in the areas where they were concentrated. As a result of the decline of traditional industry, the disparity between living standards in the poorest and wealthiest parts of the country widened in the 1920s and 1930s. At the height of the Great Depression in 1932 London and the southeast faced unemployment rates of 11 per cent compared to almost 40 per cent in Wales. Areas such as the south Wales coal fields, the ship-building regions of the Clyde and the Tyne and formerly busy ports like Liverpool slumped.

Hunger

Hunger was a persistent factor in the lives of many unemployed families in these depressed areas. A survey in 1933 concluded that unemployment benefits were insufficient to provide a minimum diet recommended by the Ministry of Health. It was only during the 1930s that a real scientific understanding about the effect of nutrition shortages emerged and the causes of **deficiency diseases** like rickets were understood. For many families in depressed areas meat was a rarity, as, often, were fresh vegetables.

On average far more working-class women went hungry than men when there was insufficient food to go round. Mothers would ensure their children ate first and men as the primary bread winners would eat too, meaning that women's health suffered disproportionately. Staples like bread, margarine and tea made up most meals. Because most money was diverted towards food, there was little left for anything else, meaning that homes, clothes and possessions became progressively more worn and shabby and were irreplaceable if they were damaged or lost. Many poor working-class families managed to make ends meet by getting '**tick**' from the local greengrocers and in poorer areas the local pawnbroker enabled families to borrow money.

However, the popular picture of the depression years being a time of poverty, hunger and hardship for all is misleading, as some areas of the country saw living standards rise. After 1933 '**light industries**' such as the production of household appliances grew in the southeast of England and these more prosperous areas experienced a consumer boom.

Migration for work

The 1931 census showed a movement of people to London, whose population rose to 8 million. However, many commentators have shown that there was no great wholesale migration to areas where work could be found. This was due to uncertainties. In an age when people were far less mobile than today, many were reluctant to move away from families to a new area where there was no guarantee of a job.

Improvements in living standards

As the economy recovered from depression, living standards improved overall for those in work, although there were still pockets of poverty in depressed areas.

The consumer boom

Household electrical appliances such as washing machines, electric cookers and vacuum cleaners, often purchased on credit, filled the homes of middle-class families throughout the 1930s. In 1930, there were 200,000 vacuum cleaner sales a year, a figure that had risen to 400,000 eight years later. In addition to this there was a 300 per cent increase in the sale of electric cookers between 1930 and 1935.

This growth was due to the greater number of homes that were electrified, many being built in new suburban housing estates (see page 97), and indicates that electrification of homes had a significant effect in improving living standards. It also shows that before the consumer boom of the 1950s (see page 138) there was a growing market for consumer goods. These consumers were being supplied by new chains such as Marks and Spencer and Sainsbury's and the advertising and public relations industries helped to create growing consumer demand for new products.

The beginnings of 'teenage' culture (though the term was not used at the time) can be seen in the 1930s with young people spending money on clothes, records and enjoying themselves at dances and on day trips.

Food

There was a wider variety of foodstuffs such as fresh fruit imported from abroad which led to improved diets – although some believed fresh fruit was harmful to children and most fruit still came in tins to be accompanied by evaporated milk. Prices for basic foodstuffs such as tea, sugar, vegetables and milk fell. Even for the less affluent, food improved. It is estimated that by the late 1920s, there were 20,000 fish and chip shops in Britain; with fish at less than 2p and chips at 1p, it was an affordable treat.

Housing

Many moved from overcrowded terraces in inner-city areas to council houses in the suburbs – of the 1.1 million council houses built during the interwar period, 90 per cent were on new estates. The number of owner-occupiers increased, too – in 1914, 10 per cent of the population owned their own homes and by 1938, 32 per cent. Increasing home ownership was a result of government policy (see page 31). Decent new houses could be purchased from £450 in the London region and outside London a small bungalow cost as little as £250. Older houses could be purchased for £125 in less affluent areas – less than the cost of a new small car.

Theme 4 The changing quality of life, 1918–79

2 The effects of 'total war' and austerity, 1939–51

During the Second World War the government intervened directly in the supply of food, clothing and other essential items. Germany's sinking of British shipping and the need to divert resources away from the civilian economy to the Army, put pressure on the standard of living in Britain through rationing.

Living standards were also adversely affected by the bombing of British cities, where many homes were destroyed. However, people had better employment prospects and pay during the war years. The immediate post-war years saw a period of austerity as Britain struggled to recover from the devastation of the war.

> **Note it down**
>
> This section considers living standards in the war and immediate post-war period. Use bullet points (see page ix) to address the following issues:
> - What was the impact of rationing?
> - How did working conditions improve?
> - Why did austerity continue?
> - How far did the quality of housing improve in the post-war period?

Rationing

Rationing had a direct effect on standards of living. It ensured that the vast majority of the population had the same limited access to food and resources, irrespective of how much or how little money they had. The creation of a Ministry of Food in 1940 involving 50,000 administrators meant that nearly all foodstuffs, from meat and fish to dairy products and luxuries like coffee and chocolate were allocated by ration cards.

Every ration book holder was allocated points that they could use each month on whatever they wanted, meaning that they still had a degree of choice in what they bought. Not only was food rationed but other essential items such as clothing, soap, paper, fuel and kitchen utensils were controlled by rationing until the end of the war.

The restrictions in the availability of food were accompanied by a government public information campaign which emphasised thriftiness and a 'make do and mend' mentality, along with ideas on how to make food go further and what to eat from the available food that was most nutritious and healthy. Substitutes for normal foodstuffs were often unpleasant and unappetising. The lack of white flour led the government to introduce the National Loaf, a grey-looking type of bread which was generally agreed to be unpleasant to eat. Only one out of seven consumers preferred it to normal bread.

In 1942 restaurants also became subject to rationing controls. This was, in part, to prevent resentment from working-class households who saw wealthier Britons getting round the rationing restrictions and eating well. Restaurants were restricted in how much food they could serve and only a very limited amount of meat or fish was available.

Some evidence now suggests that while many people in Britain may have felt their standards of living decline during the war, their health actually improved. This was because food was supplemented with vitamins and minerals by the Ministry of Food. The level of infant mortality (a major indicator of levels of public health) fell during the war years, which might account for the post-war baby boom (see page 50).

Working conditions

The large number of new jobs created during the war for civilian munitions workers offered good standards of pay and working conditions as a result of negotiations with the trade unions (see page 48). Average pay for British workers increased during the war, even though the money they earned could buy only as much as their rations would allow.

> **A weekly ration**
>
> This might include:
> - 4 ounces of margarine and bacon
> - 1 egg
> - 2 ounces of butter and tea
> - 1 ounce of cheese
> - 8 ounces of sugar

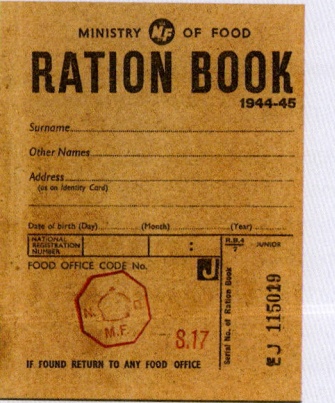

In order to allow women munitions workers freedom to work, crèches were established in the factories of many essential war industries. The first were set up in November 1941 and within six months there were 667 crèches that were either open or in the process of being set up.

Housing

Mass bombing during the war resulted in the deaths of 40,000 people and the destruction of around 2 million homes in towns and cities. Rural countryside areas were not directly affected. In the post-war era the destruction of the city centres of Coventry and other cities gave town planners and architects the opportunity to rebuild along what they believed were appealing modern lines. They followed the pre-war Taylor-Walters Report which specified minimum space and number of rooms, and restricted building to twelve houses per acre. People moved into homes with bathrooms, kitchens and modern appliances – and, most importantly, gardens to cultivate.

Austerity, 1945–51

Some rationing lasted long after the end of the war. The Labour government had been forced to introduce bread rationing between 1946 and 1948, a move described by the *Daily Mail* as 'the most hated measure ever to have been presented to the people of this country'. Other non-foodstuffs remained rationed: clothing was rationed until 1949, along with wood. Furniture produced during and after the war (1942–52) was designed to use as little wood as possible. It was called 'utility furniture' and was restricted to newly married couples or people who had been 'bombed out' during the war.

The Labour government had little choice but to continue rationing as Britain was bankrupted by the war:

- Fifty-five per cent of British food was imported but Britain did not have the foreign **currency reserves** to pay for all the imports that were needed.
- The USA ended Britain's wartime financial lifeline in 1945, the **Lend-Lease Agreement** (see page 32).

Raising the standard of living in the immediate aftermath of the war was therefore very difficult. In addition other overseas spending commitments such as feeding parts of Germany that were under British control, keeping men fighting in Greece and re-establishing British control in Asian countries like Malaya, impacted on spending at home. Expensive British defence commitments grew again in 1950 with the start of the Korean War, diverting resources away from the civilian consumer economy and into **rearmament** (defence spending was 23 per cent of **GDP** in 1950).

The winter of 1946–47

During the winter of 1946–47 extremely heavy snow exposed the extent of Britain's post-war economic fragility and had a significant effect on the quality of life for British people. From December 1946 to March 1947 the country was partially paralysed by snow and ice. This would normally not have been such a problem, but because coal stocks had been depleted by the war it led to coal shortages for Britain's homes. Families who relied on coal to heat homes instead used electric fires, placing an increased strain on the national grid.

Electricity supply to industry and homes was cut by the minister for fuel and power, Emmanuel Shinwell, to nineteen hours a day. This resulted in cold homes, factory closures and unemployment. The government feared that it would start to run out of food. One-quarter of all Britain's sheep were lost, root vegetables were frozen into the ground and food reserves declined to such an extent that Canadian and Australian citizens began to post food parcels to British families.

A planned economy

The Labour government believed that a planned economy would eventually result in raised standards of living. In Labour's 1950 manifesto it accepted shortages in food and other essential items and luxuries as an inevitability, stating:

> There can be no advance without planning. Exports must be sold in the right markets at the right price, and imports arranged according to our needs. Only by price control and rationing can fair shares of scarce goods be ensured.

And

> many Tories still cry 'Scrap controls'. Nothing could be more disastrous.

The Conservatives campaigned to end rationing as quickly as possible, and although Labour won the election that year, it was with a greatly reduced majority (see page 16), indicating that it had seriously misread the public mood. The electoral defeat of Labour in 1951 was partly attributed to the failure of the government to ensure food and energy distribution.

Housing

The huge problem of homelessness caused by the destruction of homes in the war was dealt with by building wooden **pre-fabricated homes** that could be quickly and cheaply assembled.

Pre-fabricated housing

In Catford, southeast London, the Excalibur Estate was built between 1945 and 1946. It was the product of the 1944 Housing and Temporary Accommodation Act, passed in anticipation of post-war housing needs. The pre-fabricated homes were small two-bedroom bungalows that were designed to last for a maximum of ten years (many are still standing today in 2015), and had wooden walls and flat roofs. Despite the problems the prefabs had with damp and cold, many of their owners recorded immense satisfaction and happiness with life on prefab estates and were often reluctant to eventually leave.

Other pre-fabricated homes, made out of pre-cast concrete frames, were nicknamed 'Airey houses' after the industrialist Sir Edwin Airey whose company built them. As with the other types of prefab, the Airey houses had persistent problems with cold and damp.

Blocks of flats

Blocks of flats appeared to be an easy solution to the loss of large numbers of working-class houses in the inner-city areas. In 1951 the Lawn Flats were built in Harlow, Essex. The Lawns was the first of a generation of 'point' blocks, where all the flats were accessible from a central landing and elevator. The flats were given official approval by the Festival of Britain and were seen as an attractive, modern and scientific solution to Britain's housing needs.

Another housing development with close connections to the Festival was the Lansbury Estate in Poplar, an area of east London that had been heavily bombed. The estate was planned in 1943 and work began in 1949. It was designed so that the neighbourhoods within it would have close access to their amenities (schools, shops, social clubs), which would help to create communities. Frederick Gibberd, who designed the Lawns Flats, also created the Lansbury Estate's own indoor market at Chrisp Street, which was included in the Festival of Britain.

▲ Exterior of the Chrisp Street market at Lansbury Estate in Poplar.

The Festival of Britain

In 1951, Britain celebrated the centenary of the **Great Exhibition** of 1851. A 'Festival of Great Britain' was held in order to help boost exports and to showcase British manufacturing and science after six years of post-war austerity.

The government hoped that the festival would raise morale and act as 'one united act of national reassessment, and one corporate reaffirmation of faith in the nation's future'. The festival took three years to plan between 1948 and 1951, and events were held across the country.

The focal point of the exhibition was London's South Bank, a former warehouse district that now featured a modern new riverside embankment and gardens. This reshaping of the South Bank of the Thames was meant to showcase what housing would look like in the Britain of the future, when modern new towns would be built and Victorian slums would be cleared away. The displays along the South Bank also showed the cutting edge of British architecture, science, engineering and design. Even though the festival came three years before the end of rationing and the start of mass consumption it suggested that Britain's economy and consumer confidence were recovering.

New Towns Act, 1946

In the immediate post-war era and throughout the 1950s, governments invested in housing in large part because of the homelessness caused by wartime bombing but also because of a belief that governments had a social responsibility to improve the standard of living in Britain. They were particularly keen to improve working-class living standards.

The most important piece of housing legislation passed by the post-war Labour government was the New Towns Act, 1946. It created fourteen new towns across Britain. These were designed to relieve the overcrowded working-class districts of big cities such as London and Birmingham. New towns like Stevenage, Telford and Cumbernauld were designed using modern architecture and town planning. For many working-class families who had lived in crowded slums before the war, they represented a considerable improvement in living conditions. It was the first time that many working-class people had lived in suburban estates.

As housing conditions improved and **full employment** appeared a reality, the post-war period saw the development of a consumer society.

3 The growth of a consumer society, 1951–79

The post-war decades in Britain saw the longest sustained improvement in living standards in British history. This was often known as the '**Affluent Society**', a period when more people achieved living standards their forebears could not have imagined, as their spending power rose. Even during the 1970s when inflation reached double figures (see page 36), the overall standard of living improved.

This rapid growth in living standards was based on several key factors:

- a global economic boom throughout the post-war era
- Britain's welfare state, which ensured a basic standard of living for most of the population
- relatively low energy prices – until the early 1970s
- a commitment by Labour and the Conservatives to full employment
- strong trade unions, able to negotiate high wages for their members
- the increasing availability of consumer credit
- the rise in average wages since 1945.

In 1957 Prime Minister Harold Macmillan famously declared that 'most of our people have never had it so good'. Macmillan's statement reflected the fact that a decade earlier there were still food shortages but by the late 1950s the economy had recovered. The statement also reflected how Britain's **mixed economy** (a welfare state, NHS, free education and booming private industry), successfully provided for most of the population's material needs and luxuries, ensuring a long period of improvement in living standards. However, there were exceptions to this picture of overall growth and problems still remained for some areas of society.

Note it down

This section considers the growth of a consumer society in the comparatively affluent period beginning in the 1950s. You should choose the type of note-making (see page ix) which best suits you to address the following issues:
- What was the impact of the growth in consumer spending?
- What was the impact of new towns?
- What was the impact of 'Admass'?
- How widespread was affluence? How far did pockets of poverty remain?

Consumer spending

In 1957 Britain spent just over £1 billion on consumer goods rising to £1.5 billion by 1960, showing that the rate of consumption of luxuries dramatically increased in a short space of time. Wages in 1959 being on average twice what they were in 1950, there was far more spending power.

Money was spent on labour-saving devices in the home such as vacuum cleaners, washing machines and fridges. The ownership of household labour-saving devices dramatically increased throughout the 1950s and 1960s. For example, in 1955 only 17 per cent of homes had a washing machine, but eleven years later the figure had risen to 60 per cent. This growth in consumption of labour-saving devices took much of the drudgery out of women's household chores and helped change the role of women in the home (see page 112). Household chores that would normally fill a week could be done in a matter of hours. Married women were portrayed in adverts and TV shows as 'housewives', in charge of the kitchen with the help of modern consumer products. Advertisers and manufacturers were particularly keen to appeal to women, who were often the managers of the household budget.

Consumer credit

One factor that allowed working-class families to buy consumer goods such as household furnishings, televisions, fitted kitchens and cars was the relaxation of the rules surrounding **consumer credit** in 1954. Being able to borrow in order to afford luxuries increased at a rapid pace in 1955 (the demand for television sets rose by 10 per cent). Shopkeepers selling electrical goods announced delays of up to three months while new stock was ordered.

In the interwar years, buying on credit had been popularly seen as far less morally acceptable, particularly in working-class communities; 'respectable' people lived within their means and did not borrow. The 1950s saw an inversion of this idea and respectability often came through the ability to purchase new and desirable products.

Consumer choice

The economic shocks of the 1970s (see page 36) seemed to do very little to slow down consumer spending or the expansion of consumer choice. Throughout the decade British tastes for foreign food and drink rapidly grew, partly as a result of cheaper travel and access to overseas holidays (see page 60), and partly to the rapid growth of supermarket chains providing low-cost foods and choice.

New towns

In the 1960s further new towns were created, indicating the success of the 1946 New Towns Act. Between 1961 and 1964, Runcorn, Skelmersdale, Redditch, Washington and Livingston all became new towns and, in 1967, a final series of towns was created, including Milton Keynes. Inner-city families who moved to the new towns were able to do so because of an increase in affluence. Prices remained stable and real wages rose by 130 per cent between 1955 and 1969. Architects and critics tended to view the new towns as artificial and lifeless, but this does not reflect the experience of most people who moved to them. The availability of central heating, hot water, gardens and green spaces, and access to shops and amenities made life in the new towns very attractive.

'Admass'

In the 1950s and 1960s the new prosperity was enjoyed by many, but there were also anxieties about the growth of the new consumer society. The writer J.B. Priestley invented the term 'Admass' to describe the new society of mass consumption and advertising, which in his view encouraged superficiality. As American brands like Ford, Hoover and Heinz dominated the market there were fears about the 'Americanisation' of British culture.

A 1953 study of the habits of teenage girls notes 'the amazing extent to which the minutiae of the clothes and hair arrangements of an American actress may affect the spending habits of a girl in a mining village in Durham or a girl in a tenement in central London'. The former US public servant Harry Hopkins went one step further in 1964, calling Britain just 'one more offshore island'.

Poverty

Despite the improvement in the quality of life for millions of people, there were still pockets of deep deprivation in Britain throughout the period. In 1966 the housing charity Shelter was founded in order to help the 12,000 people nationwide who were homeless and the tens of thousands of people who were living in temporary accommodation.

People living in poverty were unable to enjoy the new **consumerism** and instead were forced to struggle in order to survive. In 1967 it was revealed that 7.5 million people were still living beneath the **poverty line**, often in cold, damp, dirty homes. In 1963 Manchester still had 80,000 slum houses without running water, heating or inside toilets. Most of these homes were overcrowded, depriving their residents of any chance of privacy.

The most vulnerable residents in these run-down neighbourhoods were the elderly. In 1965, 1.5 million elderly people lived alone, many on small pensions. Their quality of life in many instances was poor due to dirty, insanitary living conditions, poor diet and loneliness. Their plight was rarely discussed in national or local newspapers, which were focussed on attracting young audiences with disposable incomes.

High-rise flats

During the 1960s new 'system-built' high-rise flats were created to replace terraced housing in inner-city areas. Two architects, Jack Lynn and Ivor Smith, described the new tower blocks as 'streets in the sky'.

The flaws with system-built flats became clear to their residents shortly after they were built. Cold and damp affected thousands of homes. In 1968 an explosion at Ronan Point flats in London, killing three people, brought the scandal to national attention. When investigators examined the building for the cause of the gas leak, they found that the builders had used old newspapers instead of concrete in certain parts of the build and in some places the flats were structurally unsound. While Ronan Point was a high-profile case resulting in fatalities, scores of other high-rise housing projects across the country left families stranded in cold and draughty concrete flats on estates that suffered from rising levels of crime.

Conclusions

The post-war era saw improvements in living standards across society which would have been almost unimaginable to many in the pre-war period. However there were still many pockets of poverty, particularly in the inner cities. Nevertheless many in Britain enjoyed a consumer culture in which goods were readily available, often on credit, and living standards improved dramatically, fuelled by low unemployment and rising wages. Many of the problems, for example with high-rise flats, would surface to a greater degree later in the period when the affluence which many had assumed was permanent, came under threat.

Park Hill, Sheffield

Lynn and Smith created a huge complex of tower blocks in Sheffield called Park Hill, which was built on the former site of back-to-back terraced housing. The doorways of flats opened out onto wide corridors and faced the front doors of neighbours in a bid to maintain the community feel of the original Park Hill neighbourhood. Families were rehoused in flats near their old neighbours and, when the complex opened in 1961, it was greeted by politicians, the press and public with enthusiasm.

Throughout the 1960s and 1970s conditions at Park Hill declined, poor noise insulation and a growth in violent crime caused residents to apply to move away. However, this decline in living standards cannot be blamed exclusively on the flats. Park Hill had a long history of violent crime dating back to the 1930s and as incomes rose in the 1960s and 1970s many people became more socially mobile and chose to move away from their communities.

Work together

Check each other's notes to ensure they cover this chapter thoroughly. Then write a list of factors you need to consider in order to discuss the following question:

How far did living standards improve between 1918 and 1979?

Having agreed the factors, use your notes to produce evidence for each one.

Chapter summary

- Britain enjoyed a short boom after the First World War but, by 1920, the number of unemployed never fell below 1 million in the interwar years.
- The depression was, however, regional, largely concentrated in the areas of the old industries while new industries developed in the Midlands and southeast.
- Many poorer people suffered illness through malnutrition.
- Those in work saw their living standards improve with a rise in consumerism.
- Over 1 million council houses were built, often on estates outside the cities, while owner occupiers grew from 10 per cent to 32 per cent of householders.
- The Second World War equalised society by guaranteeing minimum standards.
- Rationing and austerity remained in force in the immediate post-war years.
- Prosperity returned in the 1950s with the development of the 'Affluent Society'.
- Consumer spending grew, often fuelled by credit.
- Pockets of deprivation remained where residents could not share in consumerism.

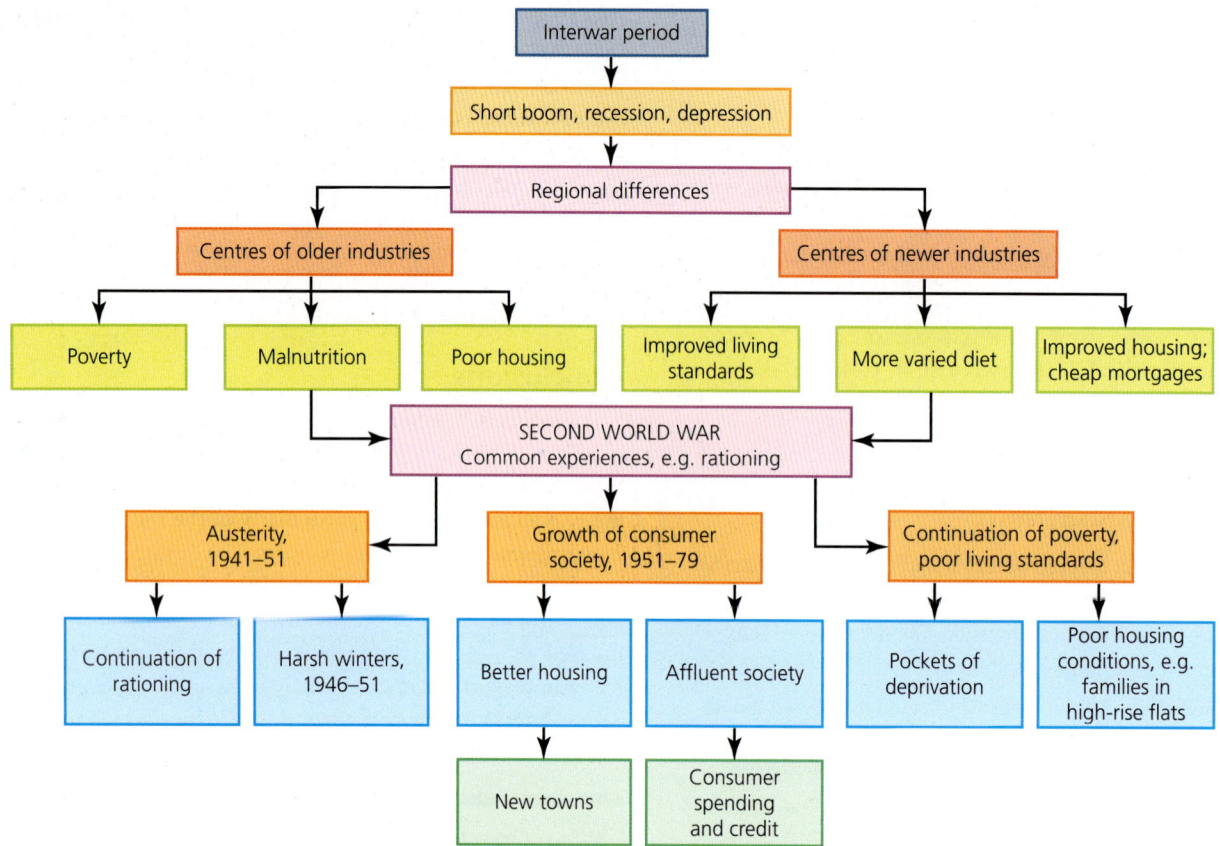

▲ Summary diagram: Changing living standards

Question practice

1. Was the creation of the welfare state the main reason for improved standards of living in the period 1945–79? Explain your answer. AS
2. To what extent did living standards improve in the years 1918–39? AS
3. How accurate is it to say that the living standards of the working class improved significantly in the years 1945–79?
4. How far did housing and welfare improve during the years 1918–39?

4b: Popular culture and entertainment

Overview

Between 1918 and 1979, popular culture changed dramatically. The mass production of radios, gramophones, record and cassette players brought popular music to a much wider audience than had been possible in the previous century. New technology brought moving images to mass audiences for the first time. From 1918 to 1979 cinema developed into a national industry in Britain, followed by television in the post-war era. In general the development of British popular culture coincided with an improvement in living standards, apart from the economic downturn in the 1920s and 1930s when cinema attendance continued to grow, as did the market for popular music. The growth in spending power of much of the population combined with an increase in leisure time in which to enjoy popular music and film. The post-war era saw a growth in the numbers of young people anxious to create their own identities and culture, which fuelled a ready market for clothes, music and gadgets.

This chapter examines changing living standards through the following sections:
1. The impact of mass popular culture, 1918–79
2. The influence of television
3. Youth culture, 1955–79

1 The impact of mass popular culture, 1918–79

By the end of the First World War there was already a widespread audience for mass popular culture in Britain. Cinema and spectator sports such as football were popular with the working class. Middle- and upper-class people, seeking to distinguish themselves from those they considered their social inferiors, often looked upon mass culture as vulgar. By the end of the period, in 1979, these attitudes had changed significantly, with cinema, television and popular music being enjoyed by all social classes.

This section looks at this growth of mass popular culture, particularly examining the impact of cinema, radio and music on people's lives.

Note it down

This section considers the impact of mass culture during the period 1918–79. Use the 1:2 method (see page x) to complete the following table:

Cinema, 1918–39	How significant was cinema during the interwar period?
Cinema, 1945–79	Why did cinema decline 1945–79
Music	How important was music during the period?
Radio	How significant was radio during the period?

Cinema, 1918–39

In the 1920s cinema was by far the most popular medium of entertainment. Working-class music hall stars such as Charlie Chaplin transferred the acts that had made them popular onto the big screen. In the 1920s the British film industry came under pressure from the much larger and more powerful American industry based in Hollywood (in 1914 one-quarter of all films shown in Britain were made by British film companies, but just over a decade later, in 1925, this had fallen to 5 per cent). Whereas in the nineteenth century British audiences might have enjoyed books about the adventures of British imperial heroes by H. Rider Haggard and Rudyard Kipling, in the early twentieth century they were much more likely to enjoy American films about cowboys and gangsters. In 1927 the British government passed the Cinematograph Films Act, ensuring that 7.5 per cent of the films shown had to be British, rising to 20 per cent in 1935. It was also in this year that 'talkies' – films with spoken words – were first produced.

In the popular press, many cinemas in the immediate post-war period were depicted as 'seedy' and dirty places to go. Throughout the 1920s, cinemas became more gentrified, 'respectable' places to visit. In the 1920s and 1930s hundreds of elaborate 'picture palaces' were built and attracted affluent middle-class audiences.

Cinema in the 1930s

Cinema ticket sales grew during the post-war slump of the 1920s and again during the **Great Depression**. By the 1930s, 18 to 19 million cinema tickets were sold every week. The cinema offered unemployed men and women one of the few opportunities for escapism from the mundane realities of unemployed life. In London a study in 1931 showed that unemployed people tended to watch films on average 2.6 times a week, normally daytime showings because of the cheaper tickets. In Glasgow 80 per cent of the city's jobless saw a film once a week during the depression, indicating that visiting the cinema had become an important part of life for people caught in long-term unemployment and deprivation. In the south Wales valleys, the area of highest poverty in the country during the early 1930s, improvised cinemas were created in the **miners' institutes**. Some institutes only charged what out-of-work miners could pay for tickets.

Cinema remained the most popular form of entertainment throughout the 1930s. Between 1937 and 1939 cinema provided more than 50 per cent of all tax revenues on entertainment. In 1937 the tax on cinema tickets yielded the government £5.6 million, whereas the tax on football tickets yielded £470,000. In 1938 there were 978 million admissions to the cinema.

Films reflecting social issues

Most of the output of British film studios between the wars were films that provided entertainment and escapism for their audiences. Romances, thrillers, crime dramas and history pictures dominated. Some films, however, had a clear social commentary which reflected the experiences of everyday life in Britain. One example of this is *The Pleasure Garden* by Alfred Hitchcock.

Films reflecting life issues

Other silent melodramas of the period reflected social issues such as divorce and loveless marriages. In the 1928 film *The Firstborn*, an unhappy wife with an unfaithful husband longs for a child. She adopts her unmarried hairdresser's baby, saving the hairdresser from shame and stigma and placating her husband by giving him the heir he desires. Issues such as the shame of an 'illegitimate' child would have been clearly recognisable to a 1920s audience.

One of the earliest talking films to use sport as its main plot line was *The Great Game* (1930). The film reflected the centrality of football in many working-class people's lives. It features a conflict in a football club about whether to bring in professional players or to stick with the local amateur team.

> ### *The Pleasure Garden* and *London Love*
>
> *The Pleasure Garden*, released in 1925, is a silent movie about two chorus girls at a seaside show. The film begins with two female friends living together independently of husbands or parents. It follows their journey as relatively independent women to find love and happiness, as they meet and marry men and experience infidelity and jealousy in their relationships. This narrative reflected the changes that were taking place in the lives of young women in the 1920s (see pages 111-112).
>
> A similar silent film of 1926, *London Love*, also shows an empowered female figure. The heroine Sally Hope becomes a famous film star to raise money to pay legal fees for her fiancé. He has been falsely accused of a crime and is dependent on her to help him.

Films that explored working life, ambition and the day-to-day experience of the modern urban world were also popular. In the 1932 musical *Love on Wheels*, a bus conductor helps a commuter to find love with an anonymous female passenger. In the course of his romantic courtship the protagonist also finds himself with a dream job in advertising, a highly aspirational role in an era of increasing **consumerism**.

Cinema during the Second World War

Cinema was important for morale during the war years. At first there was a short-lived attempt to close cinemas in case of bombing, but popular demand kept them open, and it was recognised that they had a value in taking people's minds off their problems, if only for a few hours. Despite the war the British film industry managed to produce over 500 films during the war years. Films which encouraged patriotism were popular such as Noel Coward's *In Which We Serve* and Laurence Olivier's cinematic version of Shakespeare's play *Henry V*, which coincided with the invasion of northern Europe. The moment when comic actor George Formby smacked Hitler in the 1940 release *Let George Do It* was alleged by **Mass Observation** to be one of the highest morale-raising boosts of the entire war. The **Ministry of Information** also found cinemas useful to promote ideas such as how not to waste food via short films.

Cinema, 1945–79

In the immediate aftermath of the Second World War, Britain's film industry produced a series of immensely popular comedies from the Ealing film studios. Between 1947 and 1957 the 'Ealing Comedies' entertained but also explored the changing quality of life in a Britain still struggling with the economic aftermath of the war.

Ealing Comedies

In 1947 *Hue and Cry*, a film about a group of school boys who thwart a criminal gang, was filmed amid the ruins and bomb craters of the East End of London. The villains in the film were loosely modelled on the wartime black marketeers, with which some Britons would have been familiar.

Another film that dealt with the aftermath of the war and reflected the difficulties of post-war **austerity** was *Passport to Pimlico*. The film told the story of the residents of Pimlico, London, who find they have a legal right to declare the district independent of the rest of Britain. The newly independent Pimlico no longer faces rationing restrictions and suddenly becomes a haven for black marketeers and eventually the new nation (having discovered buried treasure) offers a loan to bankrupt Britain. The film satirised the harsh economic conditions that Britain found itself in at the end of the war and reflected popular dissatisfaction with post-war rationing.

Later Ealing Comedies examined other aspects of people's lives. In *Meet Mr Lucifer*, a television set that seems to be cursed is passed from owner to owner, causing chaos wherever it goes. The film was made in 1953, the year that television ownership in Britain grew dramatically (see page 148), and in a humorous way discussed unspoken anxieties about how TV might change society.

War films

As austerity ended and Britain's world role also declined, a generation of war films in the late 1950s and early 1960s served to reassure cinema goers about Britain's war record. For many British people this was important because relative economic decline, the loss of world power status, the end of empire and the growth of immigration left them with a sense of uncertainty. As the defeated nations, Germany and Japan, became economically powerful once more and began to outcompete Britain (see page 34), a positive sense of Britishness could be derived from memories of the war.

Many of the films featured stories of near disaster and failure, however. David Lean's *Bridge on the River Kwai* (1957) shows Alec Guinness as an obsessive British officer, captured with his men by the Japanese, and co-operating with them to build a bridge in Thailand, unaware that the Allies plan to destroy it. The Japanese are ultimately thwarted at the end of the film as the bridge is blown up and Guinness dies, realising his mistake. The tragic ending mirrored the feelings that many British people had about the war, that it had perhaps been a noble but ultimately fruitless endeavour. Other, more patriotic war films included *The Dam Busters* (1955) and *Sink the Bismarck* (1960).

Spy films

▲ Sean Connery as James Bond.

Britain's most successful film franchise, the James Bond movies, reflected the improving living standards of the 1960s. In the Bond films, starting with *Dr No* (1962), Sean Connery's 007 enjoys expensive cars, clothes, drinks and international travel. Movie watchers enjoying the economic boom of the early 1960s could relate to the Bond films as exciting spy dramas but also as aspirational fantasies.

In another spy film of the same period, *The Ipcress File* (1965), the hero, Harry Palmer, is not a former public school boy like James Bond, but a working-class Londoner played by Michael Caine. Palmer does not lead an exciting jetset lifestyle and resents his upper-class bosses who run **MI6**. The film represented popular egalitarian ideas that were widespread in the early 1960s, with a working-class character responsible for the security of the nation, often denigrating his upper-class superiors.

Social realism

During the 1950s and 1960s a 'new wave' of filmmaking called social realism produced dramas based on the everyday experiences of Britain's working classes. The film version of John Osborne's play *Look Back in Anger* (1956) and Shelagh Delaney's *A Taste of Honey* (1961) both told the stories of the passions, desires and ambitions of everyday people.

In the film *Saturday Night, Sunday Morning* (1960), directed by Tony Richardson and starring Albert Finney, the main protagonist is a working-class man called Arthur Seaton, who is resentful of his class status. He looks around at his community in Nottingham and dreams of better things. He is materialistic and enjoys spending his weekly wages on smart clothes and drinking in the city's pubs. The portrayal of a working-class man with access to more money, leisure time and consumer products than his parents' generation represented the experience of mass consumption for many newly affluent working-class people in Britain.

Darker visions

At the start of the 1970s, as Britain's economic problems grew (see page 36), several films reflected the changing quality of life, presenting dark visions of British society. Fears of rising crime and the 'permissive society' (see page 103) were represented in two films in 1971, *Get Carter* and *A Clockwork Orange*.

Get Carter (1971)

In *Get Carter*, Michael Caine portrays a gangster seeking revenge for the death of his brother. The film was much darker and more pessimistic in tone than many other crime dramas of the 1960s. A relaxation in film censorship meant it could include scenes of drug abuse and prostitution. The film's bleak portrayal of Britain as a seedy and corrupted place reflected popular concerns over the quality of life in the early 1970s. The film's screenwriter, Michael Hodges, wrote *Get Carter* to be a 'crime story as an autopsy on society's ills'.

A Clockwork Orange (1971)

Another dystopian vision of Britain in the 1970s is Stanley Kubrick's *A Clockwork Orange*. The film is a vision of a future Britain where gangs of violent young men kill and rape for enjoyment. Many viewers found the graphic scenes of violence shocking. Violent crime had gradually increased throughout the 1960s and the film mirrored many popular anxieties about 'hooliganism' and lawlessness. It was quickly withdrawn from cinemas by Kubrick after several violent crimes, including murder, were blamed on the film.

These darker visions of society reflected fears of a decline in the quality of life, but the reality for most people in Britain was that standards of living continued to rise throughout the 1970s.

Cinema in decline

During the 1970s, British cinema went into a temporary decline, with soft porn comedy films such as *Confessions of a Window Cleaner* and TV series spin-offs such as *On the Buses* among its most popular productions. James Bond movies apart, there were comparatively few successful blockbusters. As funding drained, the industry's most talented personnel either moved to the USA or switched to working in TV.

Music

Popular music throughout the twentieth century has been integral to the lives of much of the population. Changes in music tastes between 1918 and 1979 have reflected changes in the lifestyles of millions of people. Popular music has been closely associated with fashion trends and consumerism, as British people selected types of music and performers who they felt reflected their lives and aspirations.

Music, 1918–45

British popular music in the twentieth century is part of a longer tradition of popular entertainment that dates back to the nineteenth century. The most successful recording artist in Britain in the 1920s was Ivor Novello. The Cardiff-born songwriter wrote the song 'Keep the Home Fires Burning' during the First World War, which was still popular in 1918. It appealed to families who had a loved one stationed overseas, reflecting the fears and sorrows of separation and wartime hardship. Novello became famous instantly and his success demonstrated to many other entertainers after the war that music could be immensely lucrative. Novello was paid £15,000 by his record company (just over £1.5 million in today's money) as a result of the popularity of 'Keep the Home Fires Burning'. He continued to be a successful songwriter and movie star until his death in 1951.

Jazz and swing

The 1930s saw the first major introduction of American music into Britain with the success of jazz and swing music. There were some 20,000 dance bands in Britain by 1930 according to the magazine *Melody Maker*, demonstrating the immense popularity of the dance hall during the decade. American music only grew in popularity. British dance bands were influenced by

American jazz band leaders like Duke Ellington and Count Basie. American artists came to Britain during the Second World War, and the US Army and Air Force and American Forces Radio (AFN) broadcast jazz and swing music across the UK. The BBC, which had previously broadcast little music, created the Light Programme in 1945 to broadcast light entertainment and music. This ran as a station until 1967 when it was replaced by Radio 2.

Rock 'n' roll

In the late 1950s and early 1960s American rock 'n' roll music found an enthusiastic following in Britain. American performers like Elvis Presley, Buddy Holly and Chuck Berry reinvented black blues music and popularised it for a youth audience, and the market for American records grew. A home grown style of rock 'n' roll, **skiffle**, was also extremely popular. The most successful skiffle artist, Lonnie Donegan, was the biggest selling British performer throughout the 1950s, with 31 top-30 singles and three number ones by 1962. At this time new groups like the Beatles, the Kinks, the Rolling Stones and the Who replaced skiffle and American blues with their own rock sound and, from 1963 onwards, 'invaded' America, making British pop music world famous.

Beatlemania

The Beatles formed in 1957 and had their first major commercial success in 1963. The following three years of their career have been described as 'Beatlemania'. Their fourth single 'She Loves You' (1964) sold 750,000 copies in just under a month. Records by the Beatles sold millions and merchandising such as Beatles wigs earned huge profits for companies such as Seltaeb. The four members of the group were greeted by screaming fans at their concerts and eventually stopped touring for good in 1966, exhausted by the popularity they had achieved. The enormous appeal of the Beatles should be seen within the context of rising living standards in the early 1960s. Their music between 1963 and 1966 was cheerful, optimistic pop music, which seemed to capture the times.

▲ The Beatles and their fans. How useful is this source for a historian investigating the popularity of the Beatles?

Theme 4 The changing quality of life, 1918–79

Mod music

One pop music genre in the 1960s that had a close relationship with consumerism and fashion was Mod music. Bands like the Who, the Kinks and the Small Faces attracted mainly working-class fans who spent their wages on acquiring the Mod 'look' (see page 150). In many music subcultures of the 1960s and 1970s consumerism, which was only possible through rising living standards, played an integral part. Being able to buy the right clothes or accessories became as important to fan subcultures as the music itself.

Glam rock

By the 1970s music had become a means of expressing and challenging ideas of gender identity. Glam rock stars like Marc Bolan and David Bowie often appeared to be androgynous and made statements about their sexuality. This was both shocking to an older generation and fascinating to their younger fans who saw them as radically different and subversive. Some historians of popular culture have argued that the increased interest in recording artists who challenged existing ideas about gender and sexual identity was the result of improved living standards in Britain. As teenagers had more disposable income and greater leisure time, some sought out new ways of distinguishing themselves from their parents. Increased wealth enabled some teenagers and young adults to assert their own identities in ways that would not have been possible a generation earlier.

David Bowie

David Bowie (born David Jones), found fame in 1969 with his song 'Space Oddity', which was inspired by the moon landings that year. He created an alter-ego 'Ziggy Stardust', an androgynous cross-dressing alien messiah. His first appearance on Top of the Pops in 1972 as Ziggy Stardust brought him to a mass audience which reacted with both fascination and shock. His hair, makeup and 'camp' mannerisms were a deliberate rejection of male heterosexuality. Bowie became one of the most influential recording artists of the next two decades.

Reggae

Immigrants from the Caribbean in the 1950s brought with them the sounds of Trinidad and Jamaica. Traditional calypso music had developed into reggae and by 1969 two record labels, Island and Trojan, imported reggae records, selling them to both a black and white audience. The first ever reggae song to hit the number one spot in the charts was Desmond Dekker's 'The Israelites' in 1969. The fact that it reached the top of the charts shows that already, by the end of the 1960s, the appeal of reggae had crossed over from small black audiences into larger white ones.

Roots reggae

Reggae music reflected the changing ethnic makeup of Britain, but it also began to articulate the experiences of black immigrants dealing with racism, police violence and inequality in work and housing. One particular style of the reggae genre that developed was roots reggae, which was closely associated with Rastafarianism. Roots described the experience of black people living in Britain and called for resistance against racism. The most popular album of the genre was Linton Kwesi Johnson's *Dread Beat an' Blood* of 1978. One song on the album, 'All Wi Doin' Is Defendin', reflected widespread anger among Caribbean immigrants in Brixton and other parts of Britain against the National Front and allegations of police brutality (see page 127). As well as being a musician, Johnson was a political activist. As a young man he had been part of the Black Panther's Youth league, and in the mid-1970s he joined the Race Today Collective (see page 125). Both groups consciously used pop culture to present their political message. The Panthers collaborated with hippy writers who produced magazines such as *Oz*, *Time Out* and the *International Times*, and therefore these pop magazines also carried stories about campaigns for racial equality. Similarly, Darcus Howe, founder of the Race Today Collective, worked with film maker Horace Ove to make the documentary *Reggae*, which set out the political roots of the music. For black radicals like Johnson and Howe pop culture was a valuable way of influencing public opinion and exposing racism.

Ska

Another variant of reggae music was Ska. In Britain, Ska was adapted by black and white musicians into a harder, more aggressive sound than reggae called two tone.

The sound of two tone drew much from punk (see below). The most popular Ska/two-tone performers of the 1970s were a Coventry group called the Specials. Jerry Dammers of the Specials wrote music that clearly reflected the lack of opportunities for both black and white young people in the 1970s.

Punk

During the last years of the 1970s a new subculture, punk, developed in Britain, having first originated in New York. The angry music of bands like the Sex Pistols, the Clash and the Buzzcocks captured the mood of the decade as punk fans tore their jeans, wore piercings and spiked their hair in order to appear shocking and offensive.

Several commentators between 1976 and 1979 in the popular music paper the *New Musical Express* directly linked punk's appeal to declining living standards. The growth in youth unemployment throughout the decade led to punk being labelled 'the music of the **dole** queue'. It articulated, for some, the anger and frustration they felt at their decline in living standards and job opportunities. This argument is quite valid, but it must also be considered that the audience for punk music in the 1970s was extremely small. Tastes throughout the 1960s and 1970s tended to be quite tame. Throughout the 1970s for example far more people enjoyed the disco music of the Bee Gees than listened to the Sex Pistols. In the 1960s the top-selling UK album was the Beatles' psychedelic *Sergeant Pepper* album, closely followed by the family-friendly soundtrack to the film *The Sound of Music* with Julie Andrews.

The most popular recording artist of the 1970s was Elton John who had sixteen top-50 albums between 1970 and 1979, four of which were number ones. Similarly, the rock group Queen sold 19 million records in Britain between 1975 and 1977. The audiences for artists like Elton John, Queen and the Bee Gees were much larger than punk or Ska audiences. The 'feel-good' pop music they produced had a wide appeal to different age groups.

Radio

Throughout the period 1918–79 radio played an important role in British people's lives. The growth of a mass radio audience from the 1920s onwards was due to the relatively low cost of radio sets. British listeners were able to access news, drama and advice programmes on gardening and cooking. Radio grew in popularity after the Second World War as listeners experienced greater affluence and a new market for popular music developed. Pirate radio stations and eventually the BBC catered for new tastes in pop music and a close relationship between radio, the music charts, record producers and stars developed.

BBC Radio, 1918–39

In the years immediately following the First World War, the government was suspicious of the possibility of a public radio service that could transmit information to the public. Fears about the possibility of revolution or a **general strike** made ministers and civil servants apprehensive about the power of radio broadcasting.

The inventor of modern radio technology Guglielmo Marconi found the government to be obstructive when he proposed setting up a radio station, but eventually it allowed the British Broadcasting Company to form in 1922. It was licensed by the government and so, right from the start, the organisation that would become the British Broadcasting Corporation (BBC) had a close relationship with the state. This would often have an impact on the way news, music and entertainment was transmitted, first as radio and later as television programmes. This close relationship meant that radio programmes often reflected the values of the government and the BBC, not necessarily the interests of the listener. As a result, BBC broadcasts often did not reflect the quality of life experienced by many British people throughout the 1920s and 1930s.

In 1927 the Corporation was given a royal charter and effectively became a publicly owned state broadcaster, though it retained its independence over its editorial content. John Reith became the first director general.

> ### John Reith, 1889–1971
> The BBC's mission as set out by Reith was to 'inform, educate and entertain', and throughout the 1920s and 1930s the BBC broadcast lectures, concerts and programmes thought to be beneficial to ordinary people and to improve their understanding of the world in which they lived. Reith claimed that the BBC should 'give the public slightly better than it thinks it likes'.

Theme 4 The changing quality of life, 1918–79

Pirate radio

It was not until the advent of American forces radio in Britain during the war that radio began to change and entertainment became more of a priority. After the war three channels, the Home Programme, the Light Programme and the Third Programme, broadcast programmes but by the 1950s and 1960s they began to lose ground to unlicensed and illegal broadcasters. The BBC had the only licence to broadcast in the UK but 'pirate' radio stations based on ships moored just outside British territorial waters broadcast immensely popular programmes. Radio Caroline had an audience of 10 million people in Britain by 1964.

The problem for the BBC and the government was that there was no effective way of stopping the broadcasts, which gained a huge teen audience because they were playing the latest music. Because of a post-war baby boom and growth in affluence, the large teenage market had more disposable income than ever before and were a keenly sought-after demographic that the BBC did not want to lose. The impact of pirate radio was significant; as millions of people tuned into pirate broadcasts to enjoy music they could not hear elsewhere, it forced the BBC to broadcast pop music as well.

In 1967 pirate radio resulted in the reorganisation of the Light, Third and Home Programmes into Radio 2, 3 and 4 respectively, and a new Radio 1 was launched that focussed exclusively on catering towards a youth market by broadcasting pop music. Many of the pirate radio DJs were hired by Radio 1 and became national celebrities.

Commercial radio

In 1975 licences for commercial radio stations were granted and the BBC lost its monopoly on broadcasting. Commercial stations could appeal to more niche audiences and sustained themselves through selling airtime to advertisers.

Impact of radio

The impact of radio on British culture and society has been far-reaching. Radio has delivered news, particularly during the Second World War, far more rapidly and with far greater impact than print newspapers did. During the post-war era it was an important component of the development of popular culture, the shaping of music fashions and trends, and the development of a collective experience among audiences. The BBC and later commercial radio became part of the way in which people in Britain related to one another and interacted, though its importance was eventually eclipsed by television.

2 The influence of television

Television has probably had the greatest impact of any media since the end of the Second World War in changing the quality of life for families in Britain. By the mid-1960s, sociologists were describing Britain as a 'TV nation' with television becoming an essential facet of family life. Television has had a profound impact on British people's entertainment, education and view of the world. It has helped to shape attitudes, consumption habits and behaviours, and has changed the way people in Britain have related to one another and understood the lives and experiences of different communities within the UK.

> **Note it down**
>
> This section discusses the significance of television during the post-war period. Write bullet points (see page ix) from this section to address the following issues:
> - How did television develop during the 1950s?
> - How significant was television both as a form of entertainment and in highlighting societal issues in the 1960s and 1970s?
> - How influential was television in the post-war period?

Television in the 1950s

The BBC's first television broadcast was in 1936, but due to the high cost of television sets, the audience was small. In 1939, only 20,000 viewers were affected by the switching off of the BBC's broadcast signal to prevent it being used by German bombers as a homing beacon. Television really developed as a medium after the war and particularly after the end of the austerity that continued until 1954.

In 1953 the coronation of Queen Elizabeth II attracted massive audiences. The BBC's television service, which had previously been seen by director generals of the corporation as something of an inconvenience, filmed the event live and broadcast it to nearly 8 million viewers, proving that television would be the dominant medium for news and entertainment in the post-war era. Following the coronation broadcast the number of TV licence holders doubled to 3 million (many people had rented a television to see the coronation and decided to purchase one as a result). Television ownership was an important part of the post-war consumer boom and without this growth in affluence, the BBC would have been a much smaller, far less important broadcaster.

Television in the 1960 and 1970s

By the early 1960s the BBC had established itself as a national institution and was seen by many commentators as an expression of Britain itself, a 'mirror' to British people's values and a communicator of tastes.

Director General Hugh Carlton Greene, appointed in 1960, decided that the values of the BBC needed to change – the rather elitist tone of many BBC programmes were seen by many as old-fashioned and outdated. In a decade where class and elitism were under greater scrutiny and criticism than ever before (see page 101), Greene decided that the BBC had to present a more egalitarian face. He was aware that traditional ideas about deference were in decline and championed new programmes like *That Was The Week That Was*, which challenged the establishment and ridiculed snobbery. Other programmes that reflected changing attitudes towards class were *Steptoe and Son*, a comedy about a rag-and-bone man (scrap dealer) and his pretentious son. The BBC also broadcast dramas about social issues such as homelessness and illegal abortion in plays such as *Cathy Come Home* (1966) and *Up the Junction* (1968). The BBC's innovative new programmes proved to be popular. *Doctor Who* was first aired in 1963, and became a national sensation due to the impact of the Daleks. Dalekmania, a craze that lasted from 1963 to 1966, led to two spin-off films and merchandising of toy Daleks and models of the Tardis. The programme became increasingly popular in the late 1970s following the casting of Tom Baker as the show's hero.

Television grew even more popular in the 1970s as the vast majority of households gained licences. It was an age particularly of variety shows where former music hall acts like Morecambe and Wise, who had been popular on TV during the 1960s, acquired more sophisticated sets and budgets so their shows became massively popular. With only three channels, artistes often had a captive audience. It is estimated that over 20 million people watched the Morecambe and Wise 1977 Christmas special. It was also a time of classic comedy with *Dad's Army* and *Fawlty Towers* retaining their popularity into the twenty-first century. However some critics would argue that the decade saw TV playing safe. The innovatory broadcasts of the 1960s such as *Cathy Come Home* were not widely replicated. It was believed that audiences preferred escapism.

Television's influence

Television brought about subtle but far-reaching social changes; within ten years (1953–63) it had taken up an ever-increasing share of people's leisure time at home and became a fundamental aspect of family life. The price of TV sets dramatically decreased and television was no longer a pleasure for a minority. Instead, Britain was increasingly defined by its choice of programming. Some intellectuals believed that television of all varieties, commercial and non-commercial, was destroying traditional working-class life in Britain. Family meal times and home life in general, it was feared, were forever changed by the existence of TV in the home. However, the huge popularity of television meant that if these changes were taking place they were actually as a result of choices made by Britain's working- and middle-class families who wanted television to have a role in their daily lives. The most successful programme on ITV was *Coronation Street*, which began broadcasting in 1960. It was not the first British soap opera; the BBC had already been broadcasting *The Archers* on The Light Programme for ten years by this point.

Commercial TV

In 1954, just a year after the BBC's coronation triumph, the government passed the Television Act which allowed for a commercial rival to establish itself. The following year ITV was established and was financed not as the BBC was, through a licence fee, but through commercial advertising.

ITV offered a different type of broadcasting from the BBC, one which attempted to be more classless and modern. It did not try to impose values on the viewer that were thought to be good for them, but offered entertainment that the viewer wanted. The result was that within five years the company was so financially successful that its advertising revenues were greater than all the major national newspapers put together.

ITV was made up of a consortium of regional TV broadcasters and the station had a predominantly working-class audience that enjoyed the quiz and variety shows it broadcast. The station imported American sitcoms to Britain for the first time, which were immensely popular but attracted criticism from some commentators that they were enabling the Americanisation of British culture. Middle-class viewers tended to prefer the BBC and look upon ITV broadcasts as 'vulgar' or 'common', demonstrating that in the nation's TV watching, class distinctions and elitist attitudes were developing.

3 Youth culture, 1955–79

In Britain as elsewhere in western Europe and the USA, there was a so-called 'baby boom' at the end of the Second World War as forces personnel returned home and family life re-established itself. In Britain the post-war period saw between 900,000 and 1 million births per year compared to about 700,000 to 800,000 in the early 1930s. There were more young people in Britain and, towards the end of the 1950s, these 'baby boomers' – those born in the mid to late 1940s – were becoming teenagers. Many had jobs and all provided a new market based on American influences in terms of films, music and clothing. Until this new market was created young people had largely dressed like their parents and listened to the same kind of music, often bland and non-threatening.

In this way, the post-war period saw the development of a distinct youth culture throughout the Western world, driven by distinctive clothing and music. While much of the 'look' of the era may have disappeared, the music remains, a soundtrack to the period that is still listened to today.

> **Note it down**
>
> This section deals with youth culture after the first generation of baby boomers became teenagers. Choose which form of notes to use (see page ix) to address the following issues:
> - What was the significance of the growth of teenagers?
> - What forms of youth culture emerged during the 1960s and 1970s?
> - How far did young people seek to be different from their parents?

Teenagers

Teenagers developed as a new phenomenon between childhood and adulthood during the 1950s. Previous generations had tended to leave school at fourteen and go to work; often their income was needed to supplement that of their parents. The school-leaving age was raised to fifteen in 1947, but many more stayed on to sit exams and, from the 1960s onwards, to go to university (see page 88). National service, or **conscription**, had been introduced in 1948 and at its peak took 160,000 boys every year for two years' military service. In 1960, as Britain's military commitments lessened, this ended.

With **full employment** and plentiful apprenticeships, teenagers had time and money to spend on what their parents might have considered luxuries and waste. Goods aimed at teenagers, such as the latest fashions or gadgets such as transistor radios, were effectively marketed to be seen as essential. Television shows were developed aimed specifically at teenagers, either generally, such as *Top of the Pops*, which began in January 1964, or at specific youth cultures such as *Ready Steady Go!*, which was aimed at mods. Parents were often glad when the programmes were over for another week.

> **Ready Steady Go!**
>
> *Ready Steady Go!* was broadcast from August 1963 to December 1966. It featured a studio audience dancing to live (or mimed) performances from current popular pop acts. Both the audience and the presenters, especially Cathy McGowan, were dressed in the latest fashions. The audience was in fact largely selected from teenagers in trendy London nightclubs or seen in areas such as Carnaby Street which housed fashionable boutiques. The audience at home copied the dances and bought the clothes. The programme was hugely popular and also hosted special editions such as the Rave Mod Ball in Wembley, April 1964, where rockers tried to disrupt proceedings by revving their motorbikes outside.

Youth culture

As the baby boomers grew, they wanted to be different from their parents, to create an identity that was entirely separate. Hence in the mid-1950s Britain saw the teddy boy gangs with slicked back hair and Edwardian-style suits who listened to rock 'n' roll. They were replaced by rockers, with leather jackets and powerful motorbikes, whose listening tastes were the largely white American-based harder-edged rock and rollers such as Eddie Cochran. Others became mods, dressed in fashionable Italianate suits and riding sleek Vespa or Lambretta motor scooters from Italy. They listened to a new kind of musical import – largely black-inspired rhythm and blues from the USA. In the early 1960s more British bands such as the Beatles based in Liverpoool and the Hollies in Manchester developed their own versions of this rhythm and blues to create the hugely successful British popular music which enveloped the world as the decade progressed.

As the 1960s progressed, mods morphed into skinheads with short hair, braces and a working-class arrogance whose reggae and ska-inspired music often came from the Caribbean. The later 1970s saw punks with torn clothing, chains and Mohican hairstyles. Both these cultures involved a sort of minimalism, based on simplicity of style. However, they were just as commercially targeted as their predecessors had been. Skinheads often wore expensive Abercrombie overcoats, Ben Sherman shirts and Doc Martin bovver boots. The styles may have been simple but the prices weren't.

Young people and violence

During the post-war period many people were afraid that young people, and particularly the cults to which they belonged, were associated with violence. Teddy boys were accused of wrecking cinemas when films featuring rock 'n' roll hits such as Bill Haley's *Rock Around the Clock* were shown. This fear grew worse after May 1964 when gangs of mods and rockers descended on seaside resorts to commit acts of vandalism and fighting, sending holidaymakers scurrying for safety. There were 51 arrests in Margate and 76 in Brighton.

It grew worse still with the widespread outbreaks of football violence, particularly among gangs of skinheads, which lasted into the 1980s and beyond. Sociologists often explained it in terms of territorial defence; a major objective was to capture the part of the ground where most home supporters stood. However this was little consolation to those caught up in street battles or ravaged trains as gangs of supporters travelled to games. Hooligans themselves were more prosaic in explaining their behaviour. As one explained to the BBC programme *Panorama*, 'All we are going for is a good game of football; a good punch up and a good kick up.'

It should be remembered, however, that most young people were not violent and simply wanted to 'hang out' with the friends with whom they shared common interests. They listened to music, went to the cinema and attended dances, just as their parents had. They just listened and danced to different music and wore different clothes. They still joined the Scouting movement, attended youth clubs and did charity work. Indeed, in 1945 the various Scouting movements including Girl Guides, Cubs and Brownies claimed 471,000 members; by 1970, admittedly after the baby boom, this had risen to 539,340.

▲ A mod's Lambretta

Some young people became hippies or supported an alternative culture, often rejecting societal values of **materialism**. For the vast majority however this was a transitional phase until the need to earn a living imposed itself.

Many commentators noted the generation gap and how different young people seemed to be from their parents. This was noted also in songs such as Cat Stevens' *Father and Son*, which takes the form of dialogue between father and son.

Youth cults had two things in common:

- Their proponents wanted to be noticed, perhaps to shock their elders.
- They were exploited by successful businesspeople who often created their styles and then marketed them very successfully. Hence the punks, while espousing the desirability of anarchy, were heavily influenced by Malcolm McLaren whose boutique SEX on the King's Road sold clothes by Vivienne Westwood and developed into a multi-million pound business.

Work together

This chapter particularly lends itself to extra research. Work in groups of three to research one of the following:

1. The impact of mass popular culture, 1918–79
2. The influence of television
3. Youth culture, 1955–79.

You should aim to present a multi-media display, addressing the question in each case of *impact*:

- How significant was the growth of popular culture?
- How significant was the growth of TV?
- How significant was the development of youth culture?

When you have completed your presentations, discuss together how significant the development of entertainment and popular culture was on society as a whole.

Chapter summary

- There was a widespread audience for mass popular culture in Britain, such as cinema and football, before the First World War.
- Cinema remained hugely popular during the interwar years, even in areas of economic depression.
- Cinema was a huge morale booster during the years of the Second World War.
- Cinema went into decline as a result of television and the 1970s were a particularly bleak period.
- Most popular music in Britain until the early 1960s was American-based and often bland.
- British popular music from the 1960s onward was innovative and hugely popular throughout the world.
- Television's popularity grew in the 1960s and programmers often risked controversy with programmes such as *Cathy Come Home*.
- During the 1970s TV shows became more elaborate and sophisticated but largely lacked the controversy of the previous decade.
- Youth cults and gangs such as mods and rockers developed in the 1950s.
- Although youth culture was often associated with violence, this was exaggerated.

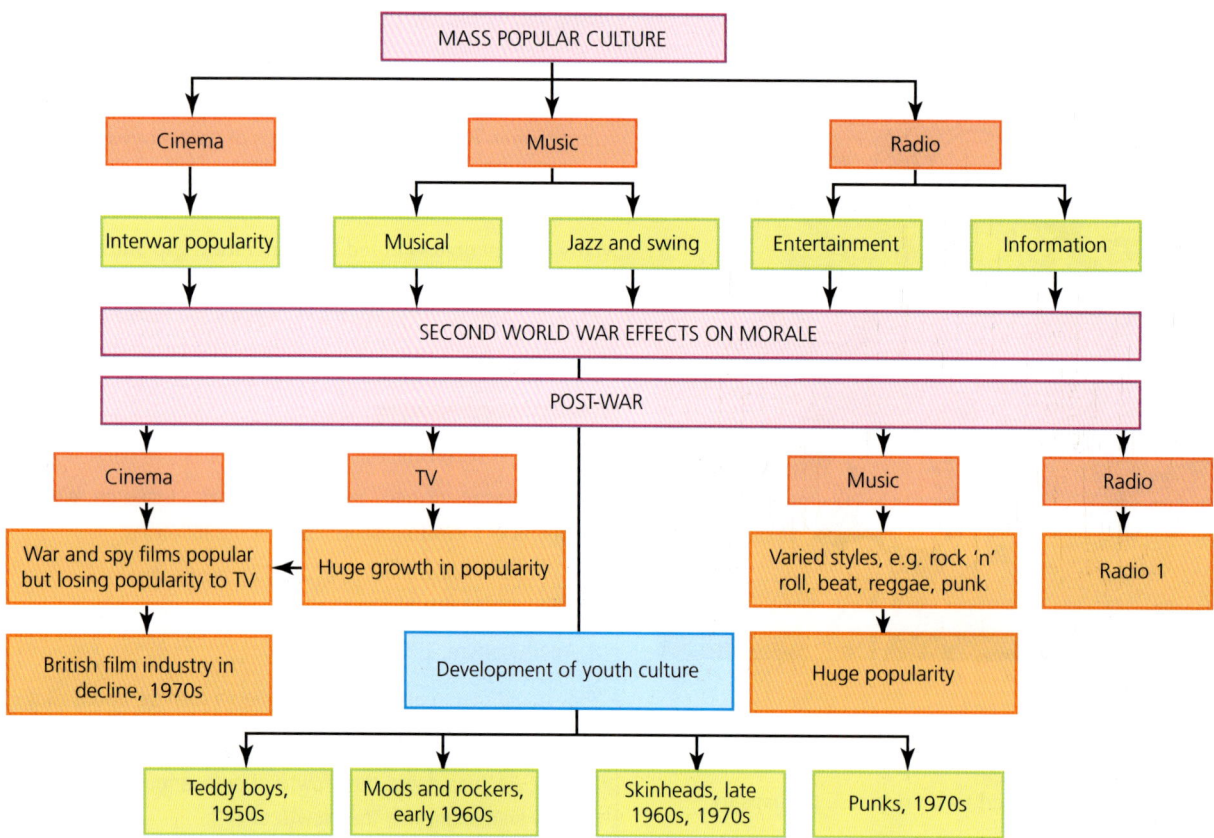

▲ Summary diagram: Popular culture and entertainment

Essay technique: Resolution

The highest marks on Section A and B of the exam are available for sustained analysis. One way of achieving this is to write an essay that develops a clear argument (see page 116) and counter-argument (see page 129).

Having set out an argument and a counter-argument you should resolve the tension between the two. One way of concluding an essay is to resolve the debate that you have established between the argument and the counter-argument.

Imagine you are answering the following question:

> **To what extent was popular culture a major influence on social change in the 1960s and 1970s?**

Your essay plan could look like this:

Paragraph 1: Argument	Popular culture did influence social change in the 1960s and 1970s. Reggae, Ska and punk challenged authority and racism. Glam rock helped challenge stereotypes about gender and sexuality. *A Clockwork Orange* and *Get Carter* presented bleak visions of Britain and social realism challenged established beliefs about the fairness of British society.
Paragraph 2: Counter-argument	A great deal of popular culture did not influence change. Escapist television programmes such as *Dad's Army* reflected established values and did little to challenge convention or provoke change.
Paragraph 3: Counter-argument	There were other important causes of social change such as the women's movement and black rights groups.
Paragraph 4: Relevant detail	Black rights groups and women's groups used popular culture to get their message across. For example Linton Kwesi Johnson was a member of the black rights group, the Race Today Collective.

This essay has one clear paragraph arguing that popular culture was an important influence on social change, two paragraphs countering this, and one that radical groups used popular culture.

You can resolve the tension by weighing up the argument and counter-argument in the conclusion. In so doing, you can reach a supported overall judgement. For example, your conclusion could look like the one on page 154.

The conclusion begins with a clear focus on the question

It summarises the counter-argument

It reaches a final judgement based on weighing up the argument and counter-argument

> **In conclusion popular culture clearly played a role in challenging convention and therefore creating social change.** Reggae, for example, challenged police racism, glam rock helped undermine traditional gender roles, and films such as *Get Carter* undermined perceptions of Britain as a country that was at peace with itself. However, a lot of popular culture was escapist. James Bond films glamourised traditional gender roles as well as traditional perceptions of Britain as a great country. Similarly, *Dad's Army* and *Morecambe and Wise* lacked any kind of radical edge, and therefore tended to reinforce convention. Black rights groups such as the Race Today Collective and the Black Panther movement were much more vocal critics of racism than television or film. Similarly, women's rights groups and activists campaigning through magazines such as *Spare Rib* were far more consistent in their advocacy of sexual equality than pop culture. Nonetheless, many radicals saw the potential of pop culture to change society. Indeed, reggae artist Linton Kwesi Johnson used his music to advocate change. Therefore, although popular culture was not consistent in advocating change, it did contribute to it, particularly in the hands of radicals like Johnson who were committed to promoting equality by all means necessary.

It summarises the argument in favour of popular culture being a cause of social change.

It considers the overlap between radical groups and popular culture

TIP: The process of evaluating the argument and the counter-argument is helped by the use of words like 'however' and 'nonetheless' which indicate that the paragraph is weighing up contrasting arguments.

Activity: Resolving tensions

Imagine you are answering the following question:

How accurate is it to say that the development of youth culture in the period 1945–79 was primarily due to social change?

Here is a possible plan:

Paragraph 1: Argument	In the post-war era most young people joined different groups because they wanted to be different from their parents and established culture.
Paragraph 2: Argument	Young people formed a new market and businesspeople were anxious to market goods to them by emphasising that they were for the young.
Paragraph 3: Counter-argument	The majority of young people only joined youth movements briefly and were never intending to rebel or effectively be different from the older generation.
Paragraph 4: Counter-argument	The majority of young people just wanted to be with people their own age with whom they shared common interests such as clothes and music. They simply followed fashion.

1 Write a plan in answer to the question:
- Include at least one argument and counter-argument in your planning
- What are the flaws in the weaker argument?
- Decide on what your overall judgement will be to resolve the argument(s) and counter-argument(s)

2 Having answered these questions, write a conclusion that weighs up the argument and the counter-argument in order to reach an overall judgement.
   TIP: Use the words 'however', 'nonetheless', and 'therefore' to structure the paragraph.

4c: Leisure and travel

Overview

The interwar period saw the growth of spectator sports despite the onset of depression. Football in particular was popular, with crowds in the tens of thousands. For those in work, mass tourism developed with the growth of holiday resorts such as Blackpool, and the opening of holiday camps. After the Second World War foreign travel became more possible for greater numbers of people, and the domestic holiday industry had to adapt to compete. More people owned cars and more roads were built to accommodate them. The result was a decline in rail transport as exemplified by the Beeching Report of 1963, which cut over 5,000 miles from the network. However, far more people travelled and went farther afield – which explains a huge growth in air travel.

This chapter examines leisure and travel through the following sections:
1 The growth of spectator sports from the 1920s
2 The development of mass tourism
3 The impact of car ownership and other travel developments, 1918–79

1 The growth in spectator sports from the 1920s

In the twentieth century, football, rugby and other spectator sports have had an important social function as central institutions in British life, culture and identity. An increase in leisure time, enabling working-class supporters to attend matches, and the development of teams of players from local communities created a close affinity in the minds of many supporters for their teams. Audiences for sporting events grew rapidly with the introduction of television and radio broadcasting, changing how people spent their leisure time and how they experienced spectator sports.

> **Note it down**
> This section is focussed on the development of spectator sports during the interwar period. Use bullet points (see page ix) to make notes on the following issues:
> - How far did watching and listening to sport grow during the interwar years?
> - What was the significance of sport during the war years?
> - How far did spectator sports develop in the period 1945–79?

Spectator sports, 1918–39

As sport developed mass spectator audiences throughout the century it gradually became more profitable for the participants and hosts of sporting events. During the 1920s and 1930s it was possible to see major events such as horse races for free. At Epsom, Aintree and Derby race courses, large free areas attracted crowds estimated to be between 200,000 and 500,000 strong. Throughout the 1920s and 1930s, on average 22 million people a year attended professional football. Statistics suggest that there was probably a similar-sized audience for amateur football as well.

During the **Great Depression**, football, rugby and cricket clubs in the most deprived parts of the country struggled to continue. Many found declining ticket sales and cheaper tickets made it difficult to survive financially. For example, nearly all rugby league clubs outside Yorkshire and Lancashire closed due to low attendance, and the only matches that had over 50,000 spectators were held after the worst of the economic crisis had passed. In contrast, other sports enjoyed large, mainly middle-class audiences

> **Greyhound racing**
>
>
>
> After football, the next largest spectator sport during the interwar period was greyhound racing. In June 1927 White City Stadium, one of the largest athletics arenas in the UK, became the biggest greyhound track in the country. In 1933 Walthamstow Stadium opened. On busy race nights up to 100,000 people would attend to bet on their favourite dogs. The development of major arenas for sporting events suggests that spectator sport as a means of leisure had become central to many people's way of life.

between the wars: tennis, show jumping and golf all attracted large audiences, with 50,000 people paying to see the Ryder Cup (golf tournament) in 1933.

Mass sporting events added to spectators' quality of life by providing entertainment at an affordable price. However, in most instances, the audience was almost exclusively male, so these sports had little impact on women.

Broadcasting

By 1936 the BBC had begun to broadcast live from football matches, which concerned the Football Association (FA), which believed that people would simply listen from home and not attend matches. However, the opposite occurred; the radio broadcasts helped to strengthen and increase mass participation in football and enabled it to develop its audience, ensuring that it transformed into a national spectator sport. As the mass media helped to extend sporting events across the country and create a national spectator culture, the amount of money that sport could generate began to increase.

Sport during the Second World War

Initially sports stadia were closed during the war due to fear of mass casualties should they be bombed. As with cinema, however, the effect on morale and demand from the population led to their reopening. There was obviously a cessation of normal league competitions due to many of the professional sportsmen joining the armed forces. However the military were able to form highly talented teams. Often spectator sport took the form of games between the forces in aid of charity – in May 1943, 55,000 attended a football match at Chelsea which raised £8,000 for naval welfare charities. Successful cricket matches were staged between the British Empire XI and the London Counties XI. One match at Lords in July 1944 between the RAF and the Army was temporary delayed as a V1 bomb landed nearby. An FA Services football team even played France and Belgium in their capital cities in September 1944 shortly after their liberation, winning 5-0 and 3-0 respectively. Allegedly, the terraces had to swept for mines beforehand.

Military personnel and civilians were encouraged to keep fit through organised sport and it was generally seen as important for the boosting of morale.

Spectator sports, 1945–79

After the Second World War British newspapers devoted more coverage to sport than to any other topic. Despite the later dominance of football, in the late 1950s the nation's

Cricket

Cricket experienced an enormous surge in popularity after 1945; by 1948 the Ashes test between England and Australia attracted as many spectators as the London Olympics that year. By the 1960s there was a gradual decline both in the numbers of people attending cricket matches and the number of matches held. In 1955 there were 3,473 matches, but ten years later this had declined to 2,268. The popularity of football, the power of television and the wider choice of leisure activities available all contributed to cricket's decline. The sport was also associated with Britain's imperial past and its class system, and was seen to be out of step with the Britain of the early 1960s. West Indian and Asian immigrants were among the most passionate cricket fans in the 1960s and beyond, particularly when their native countries were playing against England or the other major cricketing nations.

favourite game was county cricket, but a decade later this seemed to represent all that popular culture in the 1960s rejected; it was perceived as a sport of the upper and **middle classes**. Football had far fewer of these alleged pretensions.

Developments in technology increased British television audiences' access to sporting events around the world. The televisation of international sporting events such as the Football World Cup and the Olympic and Commonwealth Games enabled viewers to support British teams and sportspeople competing around the world. During the 1966 World Cup final, 32 million viewers watched England defeat West Germany.

A direct benefit of the development of a national sporting culture was increased government investment in sporting facilities during the 1960s and 1970s. In order to help British athletes and sportspeople compete internationally and win the events and tournaments that so many British spectators were tuning in to watch, the government developed the Sports Council of Great Britain in 1972. This was designed to promote sport both among elite athletes and the public as a whole, with the motto, 'Sport for All'.

Football

In 1948 41 million tickets were sold for Football League matches, a figure that had fallen to approximately 30 million two decades later. The economic hardships of the austerity years and the post-war boom might possibly explain this surge and decline. Football spectatorship offered an escape from post-war austerity, but as the British economy boomed in the 1960s and living standards grew, football had to compete with other pastimes for people's attention. Another reason for the decline of ticket sales was the growth in the availability of sport on television.

A further reason that alienated many from attending football matches was the growth in violent clashes between rival supporters. Ordinary fans witnessed the game they enjoyed being overshadowed by news headlines of violent disturbances.

2 The development of mass tourism

In the nineteenth century tourism, and especially foreign tourism, was a luxury reserved for the aristocracy and the upper middle classes. In the twentieth century this changed with sufficient leisure time, money and cheap travel costs to turn tourism into a mass industry. By 1925, 1.5 million working-class employees had access to paid holidays and bank holidays as a result of Liberal and Labour social reforms. This legislation created opportunities for the tourism industry to expand. Previously it had catered for middle-class tastes and interests but now working-class families with leisure time represented a huge opportunity.

As standards of living rose in the decades after the Second World War, the degree of consumer choice regarding leisure time and holidays also grew. Holidaymakers began to adopt new holiday experiences when presented with alternatives to boarding houses, Butlin's camps or poor customer service. A vast growth in foreign travel meant domestic venues had to adapt to maintain their custom.

Affluence allowed the tastes of the British public to change and not everyone shared the same outlook and aspirations. There was a shift away from older, more collectivist ideas (especially in the case of the working class), to more aspirant and individualistic values.

> **Note it down**
>
> This section is focussed on the development of mass tourism during the period 1918–79. Create a spider diagram (see page x). Label the spider's body: 'Development of mass tourism'. Use the legs to address the following issues:
> - How important was tourism for the wealthy in the interwar years?
> - How far did tourism for the working classes grow during the 1930s?
> - What was the significance of the growth in foreign travel on the domestic tourism industry, 1945–79?
> - What new forms of tourism developed, 1945–79?
> - How did customer service improve?

Football hooliganism

▲ An injured Millwall supporter, third from right, is led to treatment during violent clashes between fans and police at the Millwall v Ipswich game, March 1970.

From the 1950s onwards, football became synonymous with ever-increasing outbursts of violence on the terraces as supporters and fans engaged in bloody clashes and riots. This is a phenomena that is most associated with the 1970s and 1980s but research suggests that it began much earlier. Violence was almost exclusively contained to football; other sports that attracted mass audiences such as rugby, cricket or boxing were unaffected. There have been a number theories as to why violence became part of the 'national game'.

One interpretation has suggested that as the crowds at football matches were almost exclusively working class, violence was the result of the conditions of poverty that many of them lived in. This, however, is countered by the fact that most working-class fans throughout the post-war era were becoming progressively better off. Older men, who might have exerted a calming influence, attended matches less and less frequently as they were able to afford leisure time away from the football terraces (gardening, holidaying, DIY). The restraining influence they had went with them.

Tourism for the wealthy

Before 1918, few working-class people had been able to take holidays. As a result most tourist facilities were geared towards the wealthy, such as expensive hotels in seaside and spa resorts, and leisure facilities such as golf courses. Sailing was popular among the wealthy both off the coast and in inland areas such as the Norfolk Broads. Many people went to seaside resorts for the good of their health and brochures often featured their health-giving qualities. Few people went abroad and those who did tended to go to exclusive locations such as the French Riviera or for tours of art galleries and museums in Italy and Greece. This continued throughout the interwar period. Many followed guidebooks such as the German-produced Baedeckers, which concentrated on the most expensive hotels, art and cultural pursuits and gave advice on how much to tip staff:

> *For opening a church door, cloak-room services etc. a fee of 30-50c is enough, for uncovering an altar piece, lighting candles etc from 50c to 2l (Italian cents and lire). No reward should be given for unasked services.*
>
> Source: *Baedecker's Guide to Southern Italy*, 1930

Indeed it was often the increasing popularity of resorts that led more affluent tourists to find alternative venues:

> *Not so many years ago a holiday in Norfolk meant almost invariably a holiday at Cromer, Sheringham, Yarmouth or afloat on the broads; but with the greatly increasing popularity of these places alternative accommodation was sought and found elsewhere.*
>
> Source: *Ward Lock Red Guide to North Norfolk*, 1947, page 9

Tourism in the 1930s

The growth in the affordability of cars throughout the 1930s (see pages 161–162) led to the development of tourism across Britain that was not reliant on train travel to seaside resorts. In 1936 coaches transported 82 million passengers to rural parts of Britain, and by 1939 there were 2 million cars on the roads. Scotland, the Lake District and north Wales were the most popular destinations for caravanners, campers and hikers, with 72,000 people a year visiting the Lake District during the 1930s. Cheap hiking holidays were made easier by the growth in the Youth Hostel Association, which offered dormitory rooms and breakfast. The attraction of the Lake District grew in the 1930s with the publication of Arthur Ransome's *Swallows and Amazons* novels between 1932 and 1936. A better educated population resulted in more visits to places of important cultural and historical significance, such as Stratford-upon-Avon for the annual Shakespeare Festival and Hampton Court Palace.

Nevertheless, holidays to seaside resorts remained popular, and in the 1930s the number of boarding houses and holiday camps grew in these resorts to accommodate the growth in tourism.

▲ **The Lake District**

The boarding house

For many seaside holidaymakers, hotels were too expensive, so a cheaper option was a stay in a seaside boarding house. By the 1920s there were 4,000 boarding houses in Blackpool and many families returned year after year to the same establishment. Many boarding houses were run by single 'spinsters' or widows (often they were women who had lost their husbands or a chance of marriage as a result of the First World War). As the disposable income of holidaymakers gradually increased, boarding houses became less attractive: guests were not given keys of their own and were not able to stay out after certain hours. Many landladies operated strict rules of behaviour and while many offered a 'home away from home' experience, others were considered overbearing.

Butlin's

Day trips to Blackpool, Bridlington, Weston-Super-Mare, Morecambe Sands and Southend became familiar experiences for working-class families in the 1920s and early 1930s, but mass working-class tourism changed with the creation of holiday camps. The businessman Billy Butlin imported the idea of the holiday camp from Canada, building the first one at Skegness in 1936, promising 'a week's holiday for a week's wages'. Traditionally, landladies at British seaside resorts were inhospitable and unfriendly. Butlin knew that if he offered cheap holidays in chalet accommodation with activities and entertainment whatever the weather and three meals a day, they would be popular. He was correct, and his holiday camp empire grew for 30 years. It was the creation of the cheap package holiday that ended Butlin's domination of the working-class leisure market. In 1939 his Skegness and Clacton camps were providing holidays for 100,000 visitors a year. By the 1960s six more holiday camps had been built but visitor numbers across the Butlin's empire began to decline in the early 1970s.

▲ A typical Butlin's resort entrance c.1950s

One of the main aspects of Butlin's that began to be less and less appealing to holidaymakers from the late 1960s onwards was the regimented nature of their time there. The holiday camp, with its chalets, communal dining areas and loudspeaker system broadcasting updates on the day's entertainment felt similar to an army camp to some guests. As tastes gradually changed as a result of rising living standards, holidaymakers began to demand more individual holiday experiences. However, the main factor in Butlin's decline was the growth in foreign holidays.

In order to arrest the decline of its holiday camps, Butlin's changed strategy in the late 1960s. Instead of offering holidays exclusively to families, the company recognised that teenagers and young adults had more disposable income (see page 150). They marketed holidays to teenagers, but the results were disastrous. Tabloid stories of vandalism, drinking, teenage sex and antisocial behaviour caused damage to Butlin's family-friendly reputation.

The rise and gradual decline of Butlin's shows how changes in income and consumer choice shaped spending habits. It also shows how important newly empowered teenage consumers had become to businesses in Britain during the 1960s and beyond.

Customer service

Attitudes towards customer service in Britain, particularly in the hotel and tourism industries, experienced a transformation in the 1960s and 1970s. Service became more personalised. Hotels, for example, offered a wider choice of menus and developed leisure facilities such as bars and gyms, which meant they almost became a resort in themselves. Increased spending power from customers, wider access to overseas travel and greater expectations on the part of consumers meant that the standard approach to hotel guests that had existed since the 1930s would no longer be tolerated (hotels in seaside resorts would frequently lock the front door at 9pm, close the bar early, ask guests to leave during the day or simply provide abrupt or unhelpful service). Similarly, holiday camps became more comfortable with chalets being updated, more elaborate entertainment, including top acts, and more health and leisure facilities.

Foreign tourism in the 1950s to 1970s

During the 1950s the affordability of holidays meant that they became a central feature of life for many families, instead of being seen as a rare luxury. Almost all businesses in Britain offered at least a fortnight's annual leave to employees by the early 1960s, and for many working adults, holidaying was an opportunity to rest from the strains of everyday working life.

The beachfronts of Spain and Portugal, once home to tiny, sleepy fishing villages, were transformed throughout the 1960s as high-rise holiday apartment blocks and hotels, bars, cinemas and restaurants were built. The combination of cheap accommodation, cheap flights and hot weather for most of the year proved immensely attractive to large numbers of British holidaymakers who now had the income to afford foreign travel. The gradual increase in British holidays to the Mediterranean in the 1960s (1 per cent of all British holidays in 1968 to 8 per cent in 1971) helped to finance these developments and encouraged tour operators to find similar overseas locations.

During the 1960s the government, keen to keep the value of the pound high, prevented Britons from taking more than £50 out of the country per year. This limited the scope of holidaymaking and the number of holidays people could take. The decision to allow holidaymakers to take £25 per trip caused a boom in holiday travel. In 1971 British people took 4 million holidays abroad, rising to 13 million a decade later.

▲ Benidorm Bay, Spain – an example of the high-rise holiday resort

Changing tastes

The experience of foreign travel for many was exciting and exotic, but a common experience for many new travellers in the early days of mass tourism was overcrowded planes, half-built hotels and stomach upsets. Cautious British holidaymakers, suspicious of foreign cuisine, found restaurants, bars and hotels that cooked 'British' food, set up either by ex-pat Brits or local businessmen who understood how to cater to British tastes. Gradually, as foreign holidays became more popular, British tastes for foreign food became more adventurous and many holidaymakers returned to Britain with a taste for wine and pasta. The growth in overseas travel enabled many British people to experience foreign countries in a way that would have been impossible a generation earlier. The rising living standards that enabled this also brought about changing tastes and attitudes towards European countries and a gradual change in the often insular attitudes of British people.

The expansion of leisure time and affluence were enjoyed at home as well. Family life in many working-class and middle-class homes changed as men spent more time with their families. Traditional escapes from family life such as the working man's club and the pub declined in popularity as home ownership increased and television became part of family life. In addition, pursuits like gardening and DIY increased in popularity largely as a result of home ownership; home owners became more interested in keeping their properties attractive in order to maximise their value.

New forms of tourism

New forms of tourism developed in popularity during the post-war period, although they had often predated it. Here we consider two of them.

Caravanning

One of the most popular means of travelling Britain and enjoying the countryside in the 1960s was the caravan holiday. Caravanning had developed as a leisure activity in the 1930s; in 1934 there were over 90 models of caravan available to the buying public. As living standards rose in the decades after the Second World War, the ownership of caravans increased as many families who would once have visited a Butlin's camp instead adopted a less communal type of holiday. Caravanning was possible because of an increase in car ownership and a growth in suburban living with more homes having driveways. It appealed in particular to people who wanted to be independent on holiday and not tied to schedules from tour operators or organised activities in holiday camps.

Caravan holidays accounted for 20 per cent of all holidays taken in the 1960s and over half the population had participated in a caravan holiday by the 1970s. This in turn created a large market for domestic tourism within Britain.

The 'Hippy Trail'

Rising living standards and levels of education led to the development of alternative ideas about travel in the 1970s. Young people who searched for a more 'authentic' experience and rejected the overt **materialism** of the 1960s travelled a route to Nepal and India known as the 'Hippy Trail'.

The actual numbers of people taking this journey, compared to those who went to Majorca or Ibiza on holiday, were exceedingly small. Most went by car, van or train across Europe, Turkey, Iran, Afghanistan and Pakistan to India and Nepal, with some travelling on to Thailand. All countries along the route, before the late 1970s, were allied to Western countries and were largely safe places to travel for adventure-seeking Western tourists. Most travellers were in their twenties and many were attracted by the availability of hashish and opium in Afghanistan and Nepal. The existence of the Hippy Trail demonstrates that as living standards changed, attitudes towards leisure and travel were exceedingly diverse. Some young, university-educated people had different ideas and expectations of life and this was reflected in their choice of holiday destination. Not everyone found the package holiday to be an attractive option.

Leisure and class

Notably, there were still significant inequalities in the sphere of leisure. By 1965 **full employment** and broader rights for workers meant that 60 per cent of working adults had two or three weeks of paid holiday a year. However 25 per cent had no paid holiday entitlement. In terms of holiday entitlement, the working class in the 1960s were clearly better off than they had been in earlier decades. However, whereas around one-third of the middle class took regular holidays abroad in the 1960s, only around one-fifth of the working class could afford to go overseas on holiday. Foreign holidays became more common in the later 1960s and early 1970s. Around 1.5 million people holidayed abroad in 1951 compared to 8.5 million in 1972. Numbers declined again from 1973 due to the rise in prices.

3 The impact of car ownership and other travel developments, 1918–79

The relationship between British people and car ownership has closely mirrored changes in affluence throughout the twentieth century. The development of Britain into a car-owning society has seen dramatic transformations in the country's transport infrastructure and urban environment, with thousands of miles of motorways being built over the course of the century.

Towns and cities have been redesigned and remodelled to accommodate cars and the vehicles themselves have been advertised and marketed as aspirational possessions. Since the birth of the British auto industry, cars have been presented as status symbols or expressions of individuality, success and sex appeal. The growth of car ownership however has seen a decline in public transport. The development of foreign holidays meanwhile has seen a huge growth in air travel.

> **Note it down**
> Choose whichever form of note-making you prefer (see page ix) to address the following questions:
> - How did the car industry and car ownership grow during the interwar period?
> - How far did car ownership fuel the post-war consumer boom?
> - What was the relationship between car ownership and road building?
> - What was the impact of greater car ownership on the railways?
> - To what extent did air travel grow?

The interwar car industry, 1918–39

Throughout the 1920s and 1930s there had been a dramatic shift away from the use of horse-drawn carriages (there were over 200,000 in Britain in 1923 and 12,000 in 1937). There was also a rapid decline in tram usage as town and city councils switched to buses instead. The effect of this was to transform the environment of inner cities – horses and trams were part of a disappearing Victorian and Edwardian world. By 1934 there were nearly 2.5 million cars on British roads, of which half were privately owned.

Most cars produced in the 1920s were prohibitively expensive. The Rover 10/25 cost £250 in 1929 (approximately £11,000 today) and was far beyond anything most families could afford. By the early 1930s, however, car prices had fallen considerably. An Austin

Seven (a small family car) cost £125 and the Morris Minor SV was the first £100 car, going into production in 1931. Car ownership in the 1930s was overwhelmingly the preserve of the middle classes – these prices were affordable to middle-class motorists, but still beyond the reach of most working-class families. However, there were numerous secondhand car sellers who would sell at anywhere between £40 and £70 for those whose budget wouldn't stretch to a new car. Some working-class families formed syndicates where they shared the cost and usage of the car. The development of mass marketing and **consumerism** made cars a desirable and sought-after possession.

Road building

The rapid growth in car ownership led to an expansion of Britain's road network in the 1930s. Many new tarmac-covered roads were built on pre-existing highways, but new roads, often cutting through Britain's most scenic countryside, were also built. Major civil engineering projects such as the Mersey Tunnel (opened in 1934) and the Great North Road (finished in 1939) were the result of increased car ownership, but there were very few major roads in Britain by the eve of the Second World War.

> ### The Road Traffic Act
>
> In 1930 the Road Traffic Act removed speed limits from all but the most dangerous stretches of road, because the original 20 mile per hour speed limit was almost unenforceable. Without sophisticated methods of ascertaining speed, the police were unable to bring effective prosecutions. The 1930 Act did contribute to road safety in other ways, however. It introduced:
>
> - compulsory third party insurance
> - the Highway Code (the rulebook for pedestrians and motorists)
> - powers for local authorities to control traffic with traffic lights, roundabouts and one-way streets.

Road deaths

Between 1926 and 1930 there were 124,000 car crashes in Britain, resulting in over 4,800 deaths. Motorists caused 80 per cent of deaths. In 1934 this figure had risen to 7,343 deaths and 231,603 injuries. As a consequence, in 1934 a speed limit was reintroduced in a new Road Traffic Act. It reduced the speed limit to 30 miles per hour in built-up areas and introduced pedestrian crossings. Most importantly it required drivers to take tests before they were given licences to drive

New industries

A new industry of car workshops, garages and petrol stations developed in order to provide motorists with everything they needed to keep a car running. Car engines had become progressively more reliable by the 1930s and therefore consumers increasingly looked to cars as a better way of travelling than rail travel.

Driving also became a leisure activity in its own right. Travel guides for drivers with detailed maps and ideas about places to visit and stay became popular. Cars were used for day trips and weekend excursions and a new market emerged for books on rural Britain.

Cars and the consumer boom

Car production in Britain was interrupted by the Second World War as production lines were used to build fighter aircraft. The war also placed restrictions on the amount of petrol motorists could use and rationing of petrol continued until 1950.

After the war many of the models that came off the productions lines were plagued with problems and faults. A combination of poor labour relations in car factories such as Ford's Dagenham plant (see page 109) and Morris Motor's factory at Cowley and autocratic management styles in most of Britain's major car companies resulted in a weakened car industry. By the 1970s the British car industry was becoming synonymous with faulty and poor-quality cars. When Prime Minister James Callaghan ordered two new ministerial cars from Rover they had to be returned with 34 faults, including faulty windows. British consumers responded to the decline in quality of domestic cars by increasingly choosing imports.

> ### The Mini
>
>
>
> In 1959 the most iconic British car of the post-war era was manufactured. The Mini, built by the British Motor Corporation (an amalgamation of the Austin and Morris car companies), was extremely popular and sold nearly 1.2 million vehicles in Britain and around the world. The car was small, fashionable and affordable in the early 1960s but actually made a loss on every vehicle sold.

As British average wages continued to rise throughout the 1960s, car ownership increased: 2.2 million cars were registered in London alone by the end of the decade, as many as there had been in the entire country three decades earlier. By 1972 there were 13 million drivers on Britain's roads and they were increasingly buying better made and cheaper cars from overseas, particularly Japan and Germany. One-third of cars were imported in 1975 (up from just under 1 per cent at the end of the 1940s) and half of them by 1979.

British consumers bought millions of Volkswagen Beetles and later Golfs, and the small reliable and cheap Japanese car the Datsun Sunny. The failure of the British car industry had little overall impact on the living standards or driving habits of motorists in the UK; most demonstrated that they were not loyal to a particular British brand and simply went with price, quality and reliability.

Significantly, car ownership was not spread equally across the nation. As early as the 1950s middle-class families often owned two cars. As a result, middle-class men were able to commute to work, and therefore new villages, such as Tewin Wood in Hertfordshire, were constructed on the fringes of cities which became almost exclusively middle class. Working-class families in the northeast were least likely to have cars. Consequently, working-class children from these areas were much less likely to travel far away from home, even when they left home to go to university.

The rise in car ownership however saw a decline in journeys by bus and coach. These had grown significantly with the growth of holidays, and by 1952 accounted for 42 per cent of all journeys at 92 billion kilometres. By 1969 this had fallen to 286 billion kilometres. Car travel meanwhile increased from 58 billion to 286 billion kilometres in the same period.

Roads and motorways

The development of Britain into a car-owning society resulted in a dramatic expansion of the road network from the 1930s onwards. The most significant period of road development was in the 1960s and 1970s.

In 1958 the Preston bypass road opened – the first eight-mile stretch of motorway. This was followed a year later by the M1 motorway between London and Birmingham. Throughout the 1960s and 1970s motorways were gradually completed. The development of these major new high-speed roads had a significant impact on the quality of life for much of the population. Environmentalists complained about the loss of green space and habitats for wild animals and home owners close to motorways felt the impact of noise and traffic on their lifestyles.

The Beeching axe

The rise in the popularity of cars as a means of passenger transport did not in itself result in a decline in the use of the train network. Figures tended to hold up between 1955 and 1965 at 994 and 865 million **passenger-kilometres** respectively, with a peak of 1,100 million in 1960. It was more that rising operating costs, including wage levels, meant the nationalised railways ceased making a profit at the start of the 1960s and by 1962 had made a £104 million loss – about £300,000 per day. Dr Richard Beeching, the Head of the **British Transport Commission**, decided to prioritise the road network. In his 1963 report *The Reshaping of British Railways*, he recommended a dramatic reduction in the rail system and removed 5,000 miles of railway despite widespread public opposition. At the end of the 'Beeching axe' Britain had half its pre-war railway capacity. Many people in Britain in remote areas who did not have access to car transport relied on the railways to connect them with nearby towns and cities. Other people looked upon Britain's railway system with nostalgic pride, knowing how important it had been a century earlier in the industrial revolution.

Most commentators and historians in the years after 1963 have looked upon Beeching's decision as a catastrophic error, causing irreversible damage to the railway network. One result was an increase in pressure on Britain's road network, which became increasingly congested throughout the 1960s and 1970s. While railway usage may not have fallen before the Beeching axe, it certainly did later and by 1982 passenger-kilometres had fallen to 31 billion.

However, some historians argue the cuts would have come without the Beeching axe – 3,000 miles had already been cut in the 1950s and between 1948 and 1961 the number of railway staff fell by 26 per cent. Some lines, for example that from Thetford to Swaffham in Norfolk, recouped only 10 per cent of their operating costs. The industry simply couldn't continue as it was – and Beeching did recommend investment in profit-making intercity services and modernising the freight services through the use of containers rather than wagons. While demand for rail transport has since increased, it was widely believed at the time that the future lay with road transport – and the politicians acted accordingly.

However, people became more mobile and found it easier than ever before to travel across the country. Motorways also made it easier for people to commute, to relocate for work and to live further away from the communities they grew up in.

International travel

We have seen that international travel grew significantly in the 1960s with the advent of cheap foreign holidays (see page 160). Until the advent of roll-on roll-off ferries in the early 1960s, taking a car abroad could be an expensive and time-consuming process, involving loading the vehicle aboard using a crane; now it became far more common. For journeys further afield, however, people preferred air travel.

The first international air service began in August 1919 when Air Transport and Travel flew one passenger from Hounslow near London to Le Bourget near Paris for a fare of £21. Soon other companies were plying this route, often using converted wartime aircraft. Demand was low, however, and most companies were short-lived. Private companies found it difficult to operate without the types of subsidies offered by the French government to their firms.

In 1924 the four major British companies amalgamated into Imperial Airways with government subsidies to encourage the development of air routes to countries in the Empire. By 1932 it was possible to fly to Australia using British colonies as refuelling stations. The interwar period was a glamorous age for air travel, with flying boats plying the Atlantic and comfortable seatings in planes. Demand however remained low; 1937 saw fewer than 250,000 passengers and even by 1955, when direct flights to the USA were possible, aircraft flew fewer than 1 million passenger journeys. However, the advent of cheap holidays led to growing demand and by 1970 this had risen to 14 million. One factor was the development of cheaper flights pioneered by Laker Airlines, which began operations in June 1966. Laker Airlines were charter-only so they were booked in advance by holiday companies as part of a joint holiday resort and transport package for their customers. Laker Airlines were the precursors of modern 'no frills' airlines.

Conclusion

The period 1918–79 saw many developments in transport in keeping with increased demand. Far more people found independence in car ownership although the offshoot has been overcrowded roads and often underfunded alternatives. The development of charter flights made cheap air travel possible and more people gained experience of domestic and foreign travel.

▲ An Imperial Airways flying boat, 1931.

Chapter summary

- Spectator sports continued to grow during the interwar years, although many clubs in less affluent areas struggled to survive during the depression.
- BBC broadcasts brought sport into many people's homes and thus helped develop a sense of common interest among people.
- During the Second World War although competitive leagues were halted, sport was an important morale booster.
- During the post-war period television helped to make sport more international in scope.
- As a spectator sport football was marred by hooliganism during the 1960s and 1970s.
- During the interwar period tourism grew among those in work with holidays in resorts such as Blackpool, the growth of holiday camps and healthy pursuits such as walking and camping.
- The period after the Second World War saw a huge growth in foreign tourism.
- Holidays such as caravanning became very popular as people preferred to organise their holidays independently from tour operators.
- Car ownership developed during the interwar period although it was overwhelmingly the preserve of the upper and middle classes.
- The significant development in car ownership gave people more independence but led to overcrowded roads.
- The decline in the railways led to the Beeching axe, which saw 5,000 miles of railway closed.
- The growth in foreign travel led to a large increase in air travel facilitated by charter flights and cheap airlines.

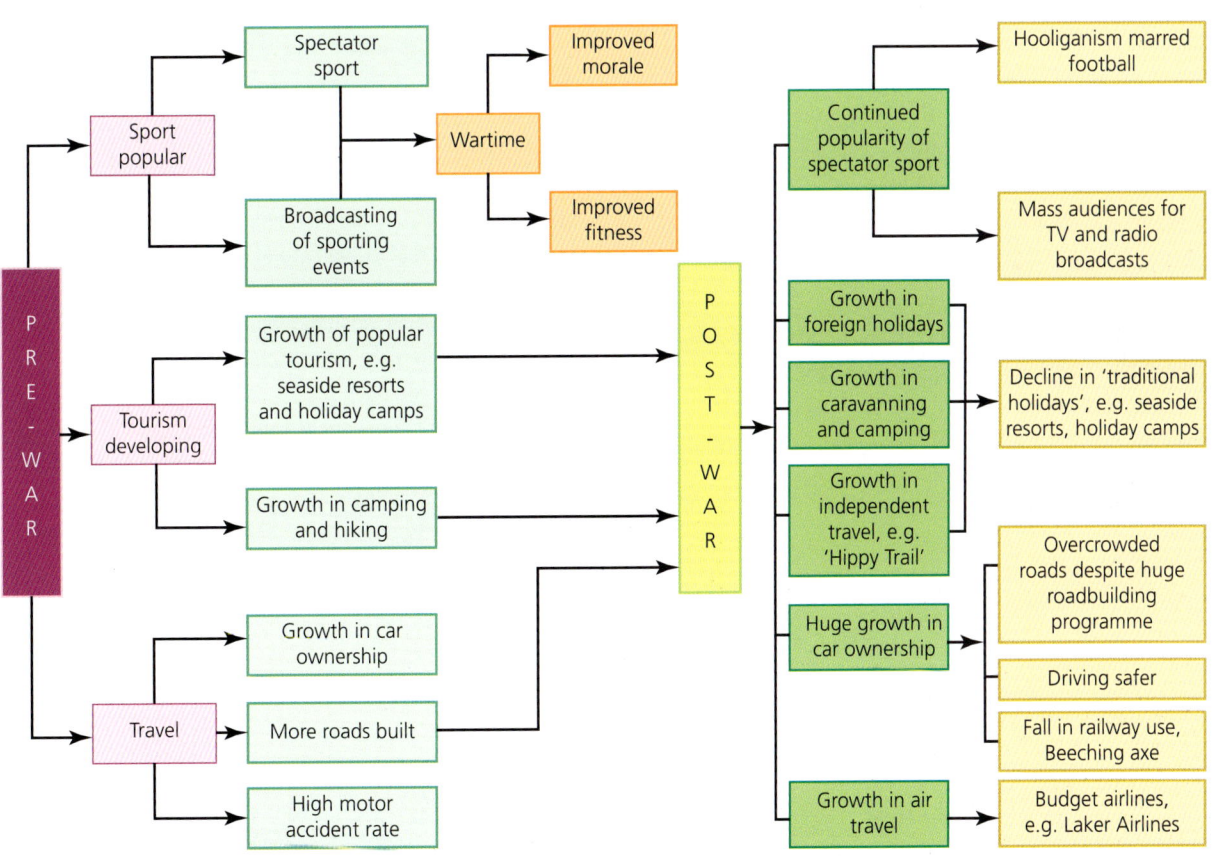

▲ Summary diagram: Leisure and travel

Theme 4 The changing quality of life, 1918–79

Recommended reading: The changing quality of life

P. Doggett, *The Man Who Sold The World: David Bowie and the 1970s* (Vintage, 2011). A new biography of Bowie's musical and cultural significance during the 1970s.

M. Hilton, *Consumerism in Twentieth-Century Britain: The Search for a Historical Movement* (Cambridge University Press, 2003). An overview of changing patterns of consumerism and tastes throughout the twentieth century.

K. Jeffreys, *Sport and Politics in Modern Britain: The Road to 2012* (Palgrave Macmillan, 2012). A history of British sport and society in the post-war era.

H. Kureshi, *The Faber Book of Pop* (Faber, 1995). An anthology of pop cultural writing from Britain in the twentieth century.

J. Moran, *Armchair Nation: An Intimate History of Britain in Front of the TV* (Profile Books, 2013). A detailed social history of television in Britain and the relationship that British people have had with TV in the post-war era.

S. O'Connell, *The Car in British Society: Class, Gender and Motoring 1896–1939* (Manchester University Press, 1998). This book explores driving and its cultural significance before the age of mass motoring and the Second World War.

J. Savage, *Teenage, The Creation of Youth: 1875–1945* (Pimlico, 2007). A history of the development of youth culture in Britain. The exploration of the growth in mass culture in the inter-war years is particularly detailed and well-researched.

Work together

You have reached the end of the themes part of this unit. This is a good moment to check through your notes and make sure they are complete. In this final 'Work together' activity you will do this with one twist – you will check each other's notes. Together, go through the specification and this book. Create a table with the following features:

1. In the first column write the big topic, for example 'A changing political landscape'.
2. In the second column write the names of the sub-sections, for example, 'Changing party fortunes, 1918-31'.
3. Head the third column 'Notes' and the final column 'Revision'.
4. Now swap folders and complete the following tasks for your partner:
- Put the notes in order.
- In the 'Notes' column, tick if your partner has a good set of notes on a sub-topic. Leave it blank if they do not have notes or if they are incomplete. You can also use this column to record the type of notes, for example class notes, index cards, independent reading.
- Leave the 'Revision' column blank. As your partner revises they can then use this column to tick off the sub-topics as they go.
- Now swap your folders again. This should highlight any strengths and weaknesses in your notes. You can fill in the gaps with further notes, diversify your notes by creating more index cards, doing more reading or making different types of notes. Then you can move on to revision!

Essay technique: Evaluation and relative significance

Reaching a supported overall judgement is an important part of doing well in Section A and B essays. One aspect of reaching the very highest level is to reach a supported overall judgement by evaluating the relative significance of different factors, in the light of valid criteria. This section examines how to evaluate and how to establish valid criteria.

Evaluation

The purpose of evaluation is to weigh up and reach a judgement. Therefore, evaluation needs to consider the importance of two or more different factors, weigh them against each other, and then reach a judgement. Evaluation is a good skill to use at the end of an essay, because it helps support your overall judgement.

For example, imagine you are answering the following question:

> **To what extent did the living standards of the working class improve significantly in the years 1945–79?**

Clearly, there was an improvement in living standards for the working class in the period 1945–79. However, the best essays will take the issue of 'significance' seriously. It is up to you to come up with a valid criteria. Criteria can be very simple. The following criteria are often useful:

- Duration: which factor was important for the longest amount of time?
- Scope: which factor affected the most people?
- Effectiveness: which factor achieved most?
- Impact: which factor led to the most fundamental change?

The conclusion on page 168 compares absolute and relative improvements and argues that relative measures were more significant, because of the continuing and considerable inequalities that remained. Therefore, the conclusion is an example of high-level work because it reaches an overall judgement and supports it through evaluating the relative significance of different factors in the light of valid criteria.

In this example the evaluation is helped by using a series of words that help to weigh the significance of the improvement in living standards. 'Clearly', 'however' and 'therefore' are useful words as they can help contrast the importance of the different factors.

The first sentence focusses on the question

The paragraph summarises the counter-argument: in relative terms there was still a significant gap between the middle class and the working class.

> In conclusion, clearly, living standards improved in absolute terms from 1945 to 1979. For example, the welfare state provided free healthcare, social security provided a variety of benefits, housing programmes built millions of new homes, and full employment and regular wage rises meant that take-home pay went up during the whole period. However, compared to the middle class there was still a significant gap. For example, working-class families tended to holiday in Britain, attending destinations such as Butlin's holiday camps. Middle-class families, by contrast, could increasingly afford to travel abroad. Equally, middle-class families were more likely to own cars than working-class families. Therefore, while living standards improved for the working class in the period 1945–79, for many they did not improve significantly because there were still considerable differences between the standard of living of working people and the more privileged middle class.

The paragraph opens by summarising the absolute rise in living standards that took place between 1945 and 1979

Having weighed absolute and relative improvements, the paragraph concludes by reaching a judgement, which considers the meaning of the word 'significant'.

Activity: Weighing up the factors

Here is a plan in answer to the following question:

How accurate is it to say that Britain became a truly affluent society in the years 1945–79?

- **Paragraph 1:** Absolute increase in standards of living among working class and middle class
- **Paragraph 2:** Development of a consumer economy
- **Paragraph 3:** Persistent inequalities between middle and working class
- **Paragraph 4:** Groups that were excluded from prosperity, e.g. immigrants

1. Decide on the criteria that you are going to use to judge how 'truly affluent' Britain became.

    TIP: You could start with how far car ownership grew and its relationship with the consumer boom.

2. Having established your criteria, write a sentence that summarises the extent to which Britain became truly affluent in the period 1945–79.
3. Support this by writing three or four sentences that weigh up at least three of the factors mentioned in your plan.

    TIP: Be explicit about the relative significance of the different factors in reaching your judgement.
    TIP: Use words such as 'however' and 'nonetheless' to weigh contrasting points.

4. Write a final summary sentence that explicitly weighs the different factors in terms of your criteria and reaches an overall judgement.

Historical interpretation

What impact did Thatcher's governments (1979–90) have on Britain, 1979–97?

Margaret Thatcher attracts admiration and criticism in equal measure. She was one of the pivotal figures in recent British political history. This chapter focusses on exploring her legacy in Britain, including the impact of her policies on the governments of her successors, John Major and Tony Blair. Most historians agree that the 1980s was a decade of major political, economic and social change in Britain. However, the extent to which Thatcher and her governments were responsible for or capable of bringing about such a radical transformation is a matter of intense historical debate. The chapter is divided into four main topic areas. Each considers the interpretations of historians regarding the extent of Thatcher's impact on Britain.

1 The effect of Thatcher's economic policies

Thatcher's approach to the economy was radical. Whereas past prime ministers had trusted the state to play a big role in the economy, Thatcher believed that Britain needed to return to the free market. Some historians argue that Thatcher's free market policies helped reverse Britain's relative economic decline. Other historians suggest that Thatcher's economic polices did little to change Britain's long-term economic performance. Finally, others view Thatcher's economic policies as largely negative, fundamentally weakening British industry, and creating an unbalanced economy with radical inequalities of wealth.

2 The extent to which state intervention and the public sector were 'rolled back'

Another area of debate about the legacy of Thatcherism is the extent to which she 'rolled back' the public sector that had grown throughout the twentieth century. Some historians suggest that Thatcher ultimately failed to prevent the state from growing throughout the 1980s and cite the increased cost of welfare and law and order as evidence of this. Another view is that the state intervened less in the economy and in people's lives than it had done in previous decades and allowed market forces and individual freedom to determine whether industries succeeded or failed.

3 The extent of political and social division in Britain

Thatcher entered office promising to bring harmony and hope. However, some historians argue that by the end of the 1980s there were deeper social divisions than there had been since the Second World War. Riots, industrial conflict, protest movements and controversy over section 28 and AIDs: all of these are indicative of the social divisions which emerged in Britain and came to public attention in the 1980s. The extent to which Thatcher's policies were the cause of these social divisions is debated by historians. Certainly, statistics suggest that Britain was a less equal society under Thatcher than it had been in the 1970s. Some historians argue that her economic policies were responsible for growing divisions. Others argue that social division was the result of longer-term economic and social changes.

4 The effect of Thatcherism on politics and party development

Some historians argue that Thatcherism led to transformation of the Conservative and Labour parties. Clearly, her ability to win three successive general elections demonstrated that her style, ideas and policies struck a chord with a considerable portion of the electorate. Some historians argue that her electoral success shaped the Conservative Party, as well as leading to splits, debate and reform in the Labour Party. Throughout the 1980s and 1990s the Labour Party went through a series of ideological transformations. British politics, which had been highly polarised in the early 1980s, reached a new post-Thatcher consensus. The Labour Party moved from the left to the political centre ground. By 1997 the party had embraced many of Thatcher's key economic principles. Not all historians agree that this transition was due solely to Thatcher's influence. Some see a shift away from left-wing politics and economics during the 1970s; others believe it began with the publication of Anthony Crosland's *The Future of Socialism* in 1956.

1 The effect of Thatcher's economic policies

> **Overview**
>
> Thatcher's premiership lasted eleven years. Following her victory in 1979 she led the Conservative Party to two further victories in 1983 and 1987. She finally lost the leadership of the Conservative Party in 1990 due to a combination of unpopular policies and economic problems.
>
> Between 1979 and 1990 the British economy underwent a profound transition. Thatcher's goal was to revive the British economy by allowing the free market and the spirit of enterprise to flourish. This would require reducing state control and interference in the economy to a minimum. For Thatcher this was the only way to save Britain from terminal economic decline.
>
> Thatcher's initial policies were designed to control inflation through large cuts in government spending. Over time, her emphasis changed and 'privatisation' became the centrepiece of her attempt to revive Britain's economic dynamism. Finally, her chancellor Nigel Lawson tried to sustain stable growth through a monetary policy which linked the value of the pound to the value of the German currency. During the period heavy industry and manufacturing declined, and the service economy grew.
>
> This chapter considers the extent to which Thatcher's economic policies succeeded in addressing Britain's economic problems, and looks at historical interpretations of her success in tackling inflation and unemployment. It also considers historical debate over the impact of privatisation.
>
> It does so through the following sections:
> 1. Thatcher's beliefs
> 2. Economic change, 1979–90
> 3. The consequences of Thatcher's economic policy, 1979–97

> **Note it down**
>
> This chapter focusses on Thatcher's economic policy and its changes over time. Create a spider diagram or a flow chart to show the different stages of the economic initiatives. You could use different colours for different periods.

1 Thatcher's beliefs

In order to understand the impact of Thatcher's policies it is important to understand her beliefs and values. Thatcher took ideas seriously, and her ideas were radically different from mainstream conservative ideas. Her willingness to discuss ideas, and their radical nature, led to the emergence of the term 'Thatcherism'. Thatcherism is rarely described as a coherent ideology, but it was a series of essential ideas or principles that inspired Thatcher throughout her premiership.

Conviction politics

Fundamentally, Thatcher was a conviction politician. She believed that politics should be rooted in the fundamental beliefs of political leaders, rather than in consensus and compromise. In this sense, Thatcher was unlike previous Conservative leaders such as Macmillan, Douglas-Home and Heath. Indeed, Thatcher rejected consensus politics, believing that sticking to principles was more important. From Thatcher's point of view finding consensus meant abandoning principles, which she viewed as morally wrong. More specifically, she believed that one of the main problems with post-war politics was that politicians had sought consensus rather than doing the right thing.

Thatcher's rejection of consensus reflected the recent history of the Conservative Party. She believed that the main problem that afflicted the Conservative Party in the 1970s was Heath's willingness to compromise, to abandon his 'Selsdon Man' programme (see page 20) and move to the centre ground of politics.

Thatcher's economic outlook

Thatcher had strong economic convictions. To some extent it is easier to describe what Thatcher rejected rather than what she wanted. She was against dependency, high levels of tax, debt and powerful unions. At heart Thatcher's economic ideas reflected her essential moral principles, which she believed reflected basic common sense rather than a sophisticated ideology.

- First, Thatcher believed that everyone should work hard in order to earn a living. Put another way, she did not believe that anyone, except the most vulnerable, should depend on the state to live.

- Secondly, she believed that hard work should be rewarded. Therefore she wanted low income taxes as she believed that tax prevented people benefiting from the money that they had earned.
- Finally, she believed that the key to economic growth was individual enterprise, and therefore she wanted to help foster a new generation of entrepreneurs, creating room for individual creativity by scaling back the state's economic role.

At a more complex level, she also believed in the importance of economic efficiency. She argued that private companies were more efficient than government agencies, as private companies had to make a profit and, therefore, every penny counted. Governments, by contrast, could be wasteful as they did not aim to make a profit.

As a result of these basic economic ideas, Thatcher and many on the right of the party believed that government spending had to be cut as it required high tax and led to the growth of inefficient government agencies at the expense of efficient private companies. She was also highly critical of unions who, she argued, interfered with the free market, also making industry less efficient. Inefficiency, the result of growing taxation and growing union power in the post-war period, she believed had led to low economic growth and high rates of inflation.

Over the years, Thatcher's beliefs led her to advocate a variety of policies. These policies reflected a consistent belief in the benefits of free markets and private enterprise.

The rule of law

Thatcher was a passionate believer in the rule of law. For her, British law was central to politics as it was the result of a democratic process and defended individual rights. As a result, she believed British people should obey the law, trusting that it would protect their rights.

Thatcher was suspicious of radical forms of protest such as marches, occupations and strikes. She believed that reform should come about through elections rather than by direct action – laws could be changed democratically as all citizens had a right to vote. She believed that radical forms of protest were undemocratic as they used force to change things rather than democratic debate. Moreover, she viewed them as a kind of lawlessness, or at the very least as likely to degenerate into violence. She also rejected these forms of protest because they tended to be used by unions, feminist groups or black rights groups to advance **collective rights**, such as black rights or women's right. Thatcher believed that individual rights alone deserved to be protected.

This view of the importance of law and order and the importance of democratic methods informed her approach to the unions and other forms of political protests.

Nationalism

Thatcher was a firm believer in the virtues of Britain and Britishness. She believed that Britain had fundamentally civilised values of individual rights, hard work and democracy and that British people should celebrate their culture and rights. She was very suspicious of black rights groups that accused organisations such as the police of **institutional racism**, or feminist groups who campaigned for **women's liberation**. Thatcher believed that these groups were fundamentally misguided as, under British law, freedom and justice were guaranteed for all.

She was also a nationalist in the sense that she opposed interference in British affairs from other countries. As the 1980s went on she became increasingly concerned about interference from Europe.

Margaret Thatcher

Margaret Thatcher came from a relatively humble background. Her father was a shopkeeper in Grantham and a member of the local Conservative Association. She attended a grammar school, and studied chemistry at Oxford University during the Second World War. While at Oxford she read the works of an Austrian economist Friedrich Hayek, who profoundly influenced her thinking.

Thatcher became an MP in 1959, and joined Edward Heath's cabinet in 1970. Heath's defeat by the National Union of Miners led Thatcher to believe that breaking union power in Britain was a crucial task for the next Conservative government. She believed that Heath's refusal to stick to his manifesto pledges and a reluctance to confront the trade unions was morally wrong.

Thatcher successfully challenged Edward Heath for the leadership of the Conservative Party in 1975, becoming the first female party leader, and only the second Conservative leader of the post-war era who was not an aristocrat.

2 Economic change, 1979–90

The eleven years of Conservative rule from 1979 to 1990 have been described by many commentators as a 'revolution'. From this perspective Thatcher was revolutionary because she overturned the economic policies that governments had relied on since 1945. Moreover, she was revolutionary because her policies were underpinned by new economic assumptions. The impact of her policies led to significant changes in the economy by 1997. However, Thatcher's economic policy evolved over time.

Monetarism, 1980–82

Thatcher's early economic policy was a break with the economic consensus that had dominated British politics from 1945. It reflected a new approach to economics known as **monetarism**, which introduced a new economic priority and therefore required new economic policies.

Thatcher's new economic priority was controlling inflation. This was a significant break with the past, as previous governments had prioritised keeping unemployment low, and were therefore willing to allow inflation to rise in order to preserve jobs. Thatcher's initial measure included tax rises and spending cuts.

Geoffrey Howe, Thatcher's first chancellor, set out the plan to control inflation in the Medium Term Financial Strategy, which accompanied his 1980 budget. The document set out targets for reducing the amount of money in circulation in order to control inflation.

Monetarism and inflation

The principal economic objective of the first Thatcher government was to bring inflation down. Economists tend to describe inflation as the product of too much money chasing too few goods. From this point of view inflation occurs when there is an increase in the amount of money in the economy which is larger than an increase in the goods and services that can be bought.

Thatcher and Howe believed that years of excessive state spending and large pay rises for industry had resulted in too much money flooding into the economy. Inefficient industries produced too few goods and the result was price rises, as consumers with excess cash bid for scarce goods and services.

Inspired by the economist Milton Friedman, Thatcher adopted a monetarist policy designed to measure and reduce the amount of money in the economy in order to reduce inflation. The aim of the budgets from 1979 to 1982 was to drain excess money from the economy.

Taxation

Thatcher's first policy to tackle inflation was to change the tax system. Howe raised VAT from 8 per cent to 15 per cent. At the same time as raising indirect taxes he lowered direct taxation, cutting the **standard rate of income tax** from 33 per cent to 30 per cent, and the **top rate** from 83 per cent to 60 per cent.

Thatcher reasoned that as income tax went down there would be more incentive for people to work hard. The shift also had other consequences. Increasing VAT hit poor people harder than the rich. VAT is a tax on spending, and therefore it targeted poor people who spent a higher proportion of their income than rich people. Cutting income tax helped the rich who had higher incomes than the poor.

Spending cuts

Thatcher was much more radical from 1980 to 1982. During this period she focussed on public spending cuts. Public spending dropped from £11 billion in 1980 to £9 billion in 1981. This was designed to rebalance the economy so that the government did less in order to encourage the private sector to do more. It was also a monetarist policy designed to control inflation.

Thatcher's 1981 budget was a turning point. Against conventional wisdom the government raised income tax in the middle of the **recession**. New taxes were introduced on North Sea oil and a one-off windfall tax was imposed on the banks. In total, taxes went up by £4 billion. At the same time she introduced cuts in education and health and benefit increases were downgraded. This was a **deflationary** budget at a time when the economy was shrinking and unemployment rising. This was a complete change from the past decades when governments increased spending in a recession to boost growth and safeguard jobs.

The government's budget was so unconventional that 364 economists wrote a letter to *The Times* protesting at the policy. Even within the Conservative Party there was concern. Labour's shadow chancellor branded the policy 'sado monetarism', due to the pain it would cause.

Thatcher's policy softened in the middle of 1981. A cabinet rebellion in July 1981 rejected a further £5 billion of spending cuts, which they feared would make the recession even deeper.

North Sea oil

By the mid-1980s North Sea oil had become a major source of income for Thatcher's government. From 1983 to 1985 the government received over £41 billion from North Sea oil, double what the government received from the North Sea in Thatcher's first term. This revenue helped to finance many of the government's policies, including paying for large amounts of unemployment benefit and tax cuts.

Historical interpretation: the significance of the 1981 budget

Historians have disagreed over the significance of the 1981 budget. Historian Richard Vine argues that it was a political turning point, but that it masked the abandonment of Thatcher's early economic principles. Political biographer and former minister Jonathan Aitken agrees that it was a moment of great political significance, but also sees it as an economic turning point, the moment at which Thatcher and her ministers saved the British economy.

> **Extract 1** From Richard Vinen, *The Politics and Social Upheaval of the Thatcher Era*, 2013.
>
> The 1981 budget provoked muttering on the Conservative back benches. Two professors of economics drew up a letter stating 'the present policies will deepen the depression, erode the industrial base of our economy and threaten its social and political stability'. The letter was signed by 364 economists.
>
> But the British economy did not collapse. In fact it began to recover soon after the 1981 budget. It was portrayed as 'the turning point in post-War British economic management': a moment when a small, determined group defied conventional wisdom, held fast against apparently impossible odds and consequently began to reverse decades of economic decline.
>
> The government's critics disputed all of this. Some of them believed that the economic recovery was 'below trend' and would have been more pronounced if the government had pursued different policies. Others attributed recovery to the fact that the government's monetary policy became increasingly loose as time went on.
>
> The storm over the March 1981 budget helped to conceal another important economic turning point, which came in a cabinet meeting of July 1981, where some of Thatcher's most loyal ministers resisted public spending cuts.

> **Extract 2** From Jonathan Aitken, *Margaret Thatcher: Power and Personality*, 2014.
>
> The 1981 Budget was a major turning point in the reputation of the government and of Margaret Thatcher. It did not look that way at the time, for it received one of the worst receptions of any budget in modern times. Yet seen with the wisdom of hindsight, this was the political event that confirmed beyond doubt that 'The lady's not for turning' on economic strategy. It crushed the wets in the cabinet, and marked the end of Britain's long and dismal record of economic decline since the early 1960s. Also it demonstrated that the Prime Minister and her Chancellor of the Exchequer deserved recognition for political courage. For it was the time they stood alone against the prevailing opinion of the pundits, the political elite and the general populace, but they were proved right.

Having read Extracts 1 and 2:
1 Summarise the argument of Extract 2 in one sentence.
2 Write a paragraph arguing either for or against the argument in Extract 2. Use your own knowledge and Extract 1 to justify your claim.
3 Swap paragraphs with a partner. Write a counter-argument to your partner's argument.
4 Having read the arguments and counter-arguments, discuss how far you agree with Extract 2.

Nationalised industry, 1979–82

Thatcher was suspicious of state-run industries. First, she believed they were inherently less efficient than private industries, as they did not have to make a profit. Secondly, she believed that government money should not be used to keep failing industries afloat in the long term. To try to reduce government spending on nationalised industries she appointed Sir Keith Joseph, a fellow supporter of free markets, as secretary of state for industry in 1979.

Joseph allowed some of Britain's national industries to decline. For example, he allowed that the government would no longer support the loss-making British Steel. Therefore, British Steel made 53,000 workers redundant in 1979. However, the policy led to further government payouts to the steel industry to finance the redundancy settlements. Between 1979 and 1981 Joseph authorised over £1 billion of payments to British Steel, more than Labour had paid in the last years of the 1970s. In spite of the job losses, British Steel was still making a loss of over £450 million by 1981. Joseph also invested £990 million of government money in the loss-making car manufacturer British Leyland. In spite of these setbacks, the long-term vision was clear: Thatcher wanted to end government subsidies for nationalised industries. Therefore timetables were set for industries to become more efficient and start making money. In all cases this meant laying off large numbers of workers to cut wage bills. Indeed, Joseph was only willing to invest government money in the nationalised industries in return for guaranteed job losses. British Leyland, for example, promised to lay off 30,000 workers in 1981 in return for the government's investment.

Supply side economics, 1982–87

Thatcher's economic policy shifted at the end of 1982. In essence ministers admitted that it was impossible to measure the money supply, and therefore monetarism was largely abandoned. Nonetheless, as inflation was back in single figures Thatcher believed that the policy had done its job.

From 1982 to 1988 Thatcher embraced a free market policy, known as 'supply side economics'. The policy, which was designed to stimulate production in the private sector, included tax cuts and privatisations.

Tax cuts

Throughout the 1980s the government cut income tax and **corporation tax**. Income tax was cut in 1982 and 1983. Chancellor of the Exchequer Nigel Lawson continued this strategy from 1984. He cut the standard rate of income tax from 30 per cent to 27 percent in 1987.

Breaking even

Thatcher continued the industrial policy of ensuring that nationalised industries became more efficient. She had originally set targets that most nationalised industries should break even by 1982. However, even with large job losses, this failed to happen, so the target was revised to 1985. Redundancies, restructuring and investment led to a turnaround in the fortunes of Britain's nationalised industries. Whereas in 1984 the government was subsiding nationalised industries by around £1.1 billion, by 1988 they were making a profit of £1.3 billion. The government still gave grants to some nationalised industries that were struggling, but these fell from £3.8 billion in 1984 to £335 million in 1987. Making these industries profitable again led to large-scale job losses. British Steel, for example, shed 95,000 workers between 1979 and 1983. Similarly, in 1984 Ian MacGregor, head of the National Coal Board, announced a plan to close 75 pits and make 64,000 coal miners redundant. Notably, reviving nationalised industries was only a first step. Once industries were profitable they tended to be privatised.

Privatisation

Privatisation was another aspect of Thatcher's economic policy. It was a process whereby state-owned businesses were sold to private shareholders.

The policy fitted well with Thatcher's convictions, because it decreased state involvement in the economy and therefore allowed more room for private initiative. Thatcher believed that returning companies to the private sector would make them more profitable and efficient, as they would be forced to make profit. Indeed, by 1979 many nationalised companies were running at a loss, requiring government subsidies to keep going. British Airways, for example, made a £544 million loss between 1981 and 1982. Moreover, nationalised companies tended to be inefficient. For example, in 1979 nationalised companies employed 25 per cent of British workers, but only produced 10 per cent of GDP.

Privatisation under Thatcher was also a distinctive policy because the government tried to encourage ordinary people to buy shares. In this sense the policy was an attempt to create 'popular capitalism', in which a larger proportion of society owned shares and felt the benefits of the free market. Therefore, privatisation was accompanied by large advertising campaigns designed to appeal to ordinary people. The 'Tell Sid' campaign, which accompanied the British Gas sale, stressed how easy it was to buy shares. The £40 million campaign was a big success and 4.6 million people bought shares in the company.

Buying shares was popular because the government tended to sell shares below the market rate, therefore purchasers would see the value of their investment increase quickly. To some extent this policy worked. In 1979 only 7 per cent of the country owned shares, but by 1990 that figure had leapt to 25 per cent: one-quarter of the entire population were now part of Thatcher's 'share-owning democracy'. She argued that privatisation had been a way of 'returning power to the people'.

Thatcher began privatisation on a small scale during her first term, but the policy became a centrepiece of her government during the mid-1980s. In the four years between 1982 and 1986 the Conservative government privatised:

- the remainder of British Aerospace and Cable and Wireless
- car manufacturer Jaguar
- British Gas
- Britoil
- British Telecom.

The sale of British Telecom in 1984 was a step change. The sale brought £3.7 billion into the Treasury and was accompanied by a major advertising campaign to promote share ownership. The apparent success of the policy convinced most of the Tory 'wets' that privatisation would revitalise the British economy.

Historical interpretation: the significance of privatisation

Historians have considered different aspects of the consequences of privatisation. Anthony Seldon and Daniel Collings in Extract 3 focus on the economic motives and the political consequences, particularly the creation of 'popular capitalism'. Claude V. Chang in Extract 4, by contrast, focusses on the economic consequences of the initiative.

Extract 3 From Anthony Seldon and Daniel Collings, *Britain Under Thatcher*, 2014.

Privatization was a crucial ingredient of Thatcherism. She argued that whereas nationalized companies were controlled by politicians and the civil service, the widespread share ownership resulting from privatization left companies under the control of many individuals – 'the state's power is reduced and the power of the people enhanced'. The government's coffers were welcome beneficiaries of these sales of assets to the private sector. Privatization moreover could be justified on grounds of economic efficiency as nationalized companies, being supported by the state, had little chance of going bankrupt and thus little motivation to ensure they operated efficiently.

The most significant privatization in Thatcher's early years was British Telecom, 50.2% of which was sold in November 1984, raising £3,916 million. The privatization bandwagon was now given a tremendous push. 'Popular' capitalism had become the vogue: now the 'ordinary' British voter could own not just his house, but also shares: a revolution was seen to be underway and set to continue throughout Mrs Thatcher's time in office.

Extract 4 From Claude V. Chang, *Privatization and Development*, 2014.

The sale of public assets at below market valuation to be sure provided a handsome profit to the original purchasers of fixed-price share offerings. In 1987, indeed, Rolls Royce shares, for example, gained 70 per cent on the next trading day.

Despite objections from trade unions and others who saw the process as asset stripping, the programme was largely successful. The re-election of Mrs Thatcher to a third term served to validate her policies. Hence, 42 businesses employing over 900,000 workers were privatised by 1990. British Telecom, privatised on 20 November 1984 has proven criticism to be premature, prices came down, waiting lists for telephones vanished in the early 1980s and never reappeared, most faults were cleared quickly, and even public telephones began to work, once the industry regulator cracked his whip.

Read Extracts 3 and 4 and write a brief answer the following questions:

1. How does Extract 3 define 'popular capitalism'? How does it support its definition?
2. What is Extract 4 referring to when it mentions 'the sale of public assets at below market valuation'?
3. How far do the two extracts agree about consequences of privatisation?

Having answered these question share your answers with a classmate. How far do you agree? Where you disagree, can you resolve your disagreements referring to the interpretations of the extracts and the information in this chapter?

Lawson boom and bust, 1987–90

After a third election win in 1987, Thatcher was confident that her economic vision for Britain was working. From the mid-1980s the economy started growing again, inflation remained low and unemployment began to decline. On average, the economy grew at around 4 per cent a year from 1985 to 1988, levels of growth that exceeded anything since 1960. Popular capitalism was also winning converts. Millions of people had applied to buy their own council houses (see page 133) and privatisations became popular. The late 1970s had been an era of pessimism. The mid-1980s, by contrast saw the emergence of a 'loadsamoney' culture and London became associated with yuppie culture. Yuppies ('young upwardly-mobile professionals') were associated with stock market trading, and, according to popular stereotype, wore sharp suits, drank champagne at lunch and used a new super-sized gadget known as a mobile phone. The stock market became fashionable: *The Times*, for example, launched an ongoing lottery-style game based on the stock market. Players, who received a free portfolio card from *The Times*, checked the value of their stocks on a daily basis to see if they had won a prize.

By 1987 the economic atmosphere in Britain had been transformed. Whereas Thatcher's first years had been devoted to ending Britain's supposed economic crisis, the mid-1980s were about consolidating and sustaining the economic upswing.

Chancellor Nigel Lawson attempted to keep the boom going with a series of measures designed to continue curbing the state and setting the market free.

Deregulation

The **deregulation** of the City of London began in 1986 under Nigel Lawson, the same year that the 'Lawson boom' began. Lawson permitted the relaxation of credit controls, allowing people with lower incomes to borrow large sums of money. At the same time he decreased interest rates from 14 per cent in 1985 to 7.5 per cent in 1988. This made borrowing cheaper.

He also deregulated London's financial markets. The 1986 Financial Services Act made the trading of stocks and shares easier in an attempt to attract foreign investment. The deregulation took place at the same time that the stock exchange began computer trading. Together the two measures were known as the 'Big Bang'.

Controlling inflation

Lawson abandoned monitoring the money supply in 1985. From then on he used interest rate policy to control inflation. Lawson's plan was to raise interest rates when inflation began to rise, and cut interest rates when inflation was low. Higher interest rates would decrease spending as people with debts would have to pay higher interest on their loans, and people without debts would want to save more. Lawson believed that this would help control inflation.

Crash and bust

Rather than leading to a prolonged boom, Lawson's policies led to a stock market crash on 17 October 1987. The crash, which became known as Black Monday, wiped £50 million off the value of shares. Fearing that the stock market crash would lead to an economic crash, Lawson introduced a series of measures to keep the economy going:

- He cut interest rates to 7.5 per cent.
- His 1988 budget cut the top rate of income tax from 60 per cent to 40 per cent, and the standard rate was cut from 27 per cent to 25 per cent.

Rather than protecting the economy, deregulated credit, low interest rates and historically low taxes led to rising inflation. To control inflation Lawson, and then his successor John Major, increased interest rates. This hit everyone who had borrowed money in the mid-1980s due to Lawson's deregulation of credit. As a result the economy went into recession and unemployment started rising again. However, the policy succeeded in reducing inflation. John Major, Thatcher's last chancellor, welcomed the rising unemployment, with the phrase 'if it's not hurting, it's not working'.

> ### Lawson, Major and the ERM
>
> Nigel Lawson believed that inflation could be controlled by joining a fixed exchange rate system (similar to the Gold Standard, see page 39) with other European countries: the **Exchange Rate Mechanism (ERM)**. He was overruled by Margaret Thatcher on the advice of her chief economic advisor, Alan Walters. Lawson resigned over his differences with Thatcher and Walters.
>
> John Major, Thatcher's third chancellor, was also convinced that Britain should join the ERM. He held the office of chancellor for less than a year, but during that time he persuaded Thatcher that Britain should join. The importance of joining the ERM for both Lawson and Major was that other methods of fighting inflation such as high interest rates and spending cuts had only temporarily halted it, at the cost of massive unemployment and economic hardship, meaning that another solution was necessary.

Conclusion

Thatcher's economic policy was a radical attempt to revive the British economy by freeing the market. Allowing unemployment to rise meant that the government could control inflation and return nationalised industries to profit. Tax cuts, deregulation and privatisation meant that by 1990 the government played a much smaller economic role than it had in 1979. Between 1985 and 1988 Thatcherism seemed to be working: unemployment fell, economic growth rose and inflation remained low. In the southeast there was a boom, and a new loadsamoney culture. However, the boom was shortlived and economic problems returned in the recession of 1989 and 1990.

3 The consequences of Thatcher's economic policy, 1979–97

Thatcher's policies certainly transformed the nature of the British economy. However, the extent to which they transformed the performance of the British economy is disputed.

Inflation

Thatcher's prime economic goal was controlling inflation. In this aspect of her economic policy her achievements were mixed.

Initially, she enjoyed some success. Inflation was running at 13.4 per cent in 1979 and jumped to over 18 per cent in 1980. However, inflation fell in the early 1980s and stayed relatively low from 1983 to 1989. From 1992 to 1997 inflation also remained relatively low. Significantly, British inflation tended to be higher than inflation across Europe. Indeed, in the period 1979–97 British inflation ran ahead of the European average in all but five years (see Table 1).

Moreover, historically, Britain enjoyed prolonged periods of low inflation before Thatcherism. Between 1954 and 1969, for example, inflation rarely grew above 5 per cent. In this sense the period 1983–97 could be interpreted as a return to long-term trends rather than a dramatic improvement.

Economic growth

Controlling inflation was part of a broader economic goal. Thatcher wanted to increase the growth rate of the British economy and end Britain's relative economic decline. In general terms, Thatcher failed to achieve this.

The British economy grew at an average of 4 per cent a year in the mid-1980s. However, over the long term there was little change in Britain's growth rates (see Table 2).

Table 2: Growth, 1979-97

Years	Average growth (%)
1960–73	3.3
1974–83	1.1
1983–92	2.5
1993–97	2.8

From Table 2 it is clear that Britain's economic performance under Thatcher was better than the period between the beginning of the Heath recession and the end of the late 1970s–early 1980s recession. However, compared to longer-term trends, Britain's growth under Thatcher was weaker than it had been under Macmillan and Wilson in the 1960s. Moreover, growth rates under Thatcher averaged a little over 2.5 per cent, and therefore were comparable to the average growth rates for the whole period 1960–97, during which growth averaged around 2.5 per cent.

Thatcher's policies were unable to halt Britain's relative economic decline. In 1950 Britain was ranked sixth in the world in terms of GDP per capita. But by 1973 it had fallen to eleventh and by 1997 the fall had continued to fourteenth. In this sense Britain continued to decline in relative terms, in spite of Thatcher's economic policies (see Table 3 on page 178).

Table 1: Inflation, 1979-97

	Yearly inflation rates (%)									
Year	1979	1980	1981	1982	1983	1984	1985	1986	1987	1988
UK	13.4	18.0	11.9	8.6	4.6	5.0	6.1	3.4	4.2	4.9
Europe	9.7	12.6	11.6	10.3	7.9	6.7	5.8	3.3	3.4	3.6
Year	1989	1990	1991	1992	1993	1994	1995	1996	1997	1989
UK	5.2	9.5	5.9	3.7	1.6	2.4	3.5	2.4	3.1	5.2
Europe	5.1	5.6	5.2	4.0	3.2	2.8	3.0	3.0	1.9	5.1

Table 3: Global ranking by GDP, 1950-97

Global GDP per capita ranking			
	1950	1973	1997
Germany	13	6	5
France	11	7	2
Japan	17	14	4
UK	6	11	14
USA	1	2	2

Unemployment

Unemployment was never Thatcher's top priority. Nonetheless, she hoped that it would decline as the private sector expanded. The initial impact of Thatcher's economic policies was a huge growth in unemployment, which peaked at 3.2 million in 1985. Unemployment began to fall from 1986 onwards, but unemployment rates remained historically high. In that sense one of the major changes brought about by Thatcherism seems to be relatively high rates of unemployment (see Table 4).

Table 4: Average unemployment percentage, 1960-97

1960–73	1974–79	1980–90	1991–97
1.9	3.4	9.1	8.5

The state and the economy

Rebalancing the economy was another of Thatcher's key economic aims. She wanted to reduce the state's role in the economy and increase private sector involvement. In this aim too it seems that she failed.

In terms of the relationship between public expenditure and GDP the state's role in the economy grew between 1979 and 1997 (see Table 5).

Table 5: Public expenditure as a percentage of GDP

1979	1989	1997
37	39	44

The growth of public spending as a percentage of GDP is initially perplexing, as Thatcher privatised large parts of industry and cut taxes. However, various areas of government spending grew significantly under Thatcher. The rise in unemployment led to a rise in spending on social security. Indeed, under Thatcher social security spending grew by 9 per cent. Equally, spending on law and order increased by 36 per cent. In addition, large increases in military spending in the mid-1980s followed Thatcher's pledge to increase military spending by 3 per cent a year and buy the US nuclear weapons system Trident.

Productivity

Thatcher wanted to improve the efficiency of the British economy by improving labour productivity. Again, she succeeded in improving productivity compared to the 1970s, but international comparisons show that Britain was still lagging behind other countries. In 1979 British workers were around 50 per cent as productive as US workers. By 1997 the gap had closed and British workers were around 77 per cent as productive as those in the US. In addition to lagging behind the US, British workers still less productive than workers in France, Germany and Japan in 1997.

Industry and finance

Even in the good years, economic growth under Thatcher was uneven. Financial services expanded greatly, boosting the economy of London and much of the southeast. Investment in this sector rose 300 per cent during the Thatcher years, compared to just an 8 per cent rise in manufacturing investment. Industrial production declined. During the 1960s Britain's industry had produced around 40 per cent of GDP; by 1997 this had almost halved to 21 per cent. As a result, UK manufacturing exports declined. The **balance of payments** of manufactured goods declined from a £5 billion surplus in 1979 to a £20 billion deficit in 1989. The decline of industry, brought about by the closure of coal pits, car plants and steel mills, led to disproportionately high levels of unemployment and poverty in the north.

Conclusion

Thatcher undoubtedly changed the nature of the British economy. Under her premiership large sectors of the economy that had been state-owned were privatised, direct taxes were cut and indirect taxes rose, and relatively high levels of unemployment became the norm. However, the performance of the economy continued much as it had since the 1960s. Long-term growth rates and inflation continued at much the same rate they had since 1960. Productivity rose, but Britain still lagged behind its competitors. The most significant change brought about by the Thatcher government was a long-term increase in unemployment.

Historical interpretation: Thatcher's economic legacy

Thatcher's economic legacy has provoked debate among historians. In Extract 5 Elliss Wasson outlines the view that Thatcher was a saviour of the British nation, saving Britain from decline and creeping socialism, much as Churchill saved Britain from Hitler during the Second World War. Wasson counters this view by considering the ways in which Thatcher failed to achieve her own aims. In Extract 6 Earl Aaron Reitan considers Thatcher's failures in a broader sense. Both historians discuss the extent of regional and class inequality created by Thatcher's policies (these are discussed in Chapter 3, pages 199–213).

> **Extract 5** From Ellis Wasson, *A History of Modern Britain*, 2009.
>
> For some, Thatcher was a figure of Churchillian stature, a savior who altered the course of Britain. She took command of a derelict wreck, ready to sink, and guided it not just to safe harbor but to repair, relaunching, and a new beginning. Her accomplishments were prodigious, and she led her party to three electoral victories. Her privatization policies took a dramatic turn, the sale of state assets tripled the number of owners of stock between 1979 and 1989. This strategy and war with the unions decisively reshaped the class structure of Britain. 'Thatcherism' split the working class into winners and losers.
>
> However, Thatcher was actually more cautious than she sometimes seemed and less effective in putting many of her ideas into practice than one might expect. She abandoned her initial economic program in 1981 when it clearly was not working. The frontiers of the state, outside the sale of assets, were not rolled back. Welfare and expenditure on healthcare expanded during her tenure.

> **Extract 6** From Earl Aaron Reitan, *The Thatcher Revolution: Margaret Thatcher, John Major, Tony Blair, and the Transformation of Modern Britain, 1979–2001*, 2003.
>
> Under Major and Blair the shortcomings of the Thatcher Revolution became clear. The Thatcher economic policies did not lead to the burst of entrepreneurship that she anticipated. Development of the economy was highly uneven with financial services doing well and manufacturing sluggish despite large numbers of unemployed people available to work in factories. When the crisis of the recession and 'Black Wednesday'* had passed, the Major and Blair governments adopted tight fiscal and monetary policies that stifled public investment in infrastructure, education, health and other requirements of an advanced country.
>
> The greatest failure of the Thatcher Revolution was unemployment, poverty, and the waste of human resources that these entailed. Thatcherism brought a period of strong economic growth, but it did not raise all boats. Not enough attention was given to regional differences.
>
> * 16 September 1992, when the government was forced to withdraw sterling from the European Exchange Rate Mechanism (ERM).

Having read Extracts 5 and 6:
1. Summarise the key argument of the two extracts.
2. Select three details from your own knowledge which support the argument of Extracts 5 and 6. Write these down as a list under your summaries.
3. Swap your summaries with a partner and discuss lists:
- Which summary best captured the argument of Extract 5?
- Which summary best captured the argument of Extract 6?
- Which details most precisely supported the argument of Extract 5?
- Which details most precisely supported the argument of Extract 6?

Extended reading: The effect of Thatcher's economic policies

Margaret Thatcher's politics were based on her economic beliefs and economic policy was central to her premiership. Historian Dr Scott Anthony explores the impact of her economic thinking.

The long-term impact of the economic policies pursued by the Thatcher governments was the rise of finance over industry, of self-employment over the unionised worker, of exchange over production.

If 'Thatcherism' equates to the key policy decisions taken by Margaret Thatcher's governments it can be understood as a turn away from Keynesian demand management, the abolishing of capital controls and the privatisation (or de-nationalisation) of significant national industries. Income tax was cut, while at the same time the powers of trade unions were curtailed, in the belief that greater inequality of income was necessary to foster an entrepreneurial society. The expansive social and economic functions of the post-war state were to be rolled back.

Rhetorically 'Thatcherism' fused a theory of human nature (self-interested) and recent history (a great nation hampered by over-regulation) with a theory of reason (markets distribute goods more efficiently than states). Although eighteen years of 'Thatcherite' Conservative rule came to an end in 1997, the reluctance of the incoming government to repeal their marquee economic policies led Thatcher herself to declare New Labour 'her greatest achievement'.

However, both the success and popularity of economic 'Thatcherism' is debatable. Control of the money supply was the central plank of the government's economic policies, but by abolishing rate controls and increasing indirect taxes (to help pay for cuts to income tax) inflation increased to 18 per cent by 1980. Large cuts in public expenditure eventually brought it down but only at the price of mass unemployment (which reached 3.3 million by 1983, a return to inter-war levels of worklessness) consequently public spending on social security continued to rise. This was not the short-term impact 'Thatcherite' economics promised.

Over the longer-term, the percentage of GDP consumed by taxation and state 'interference' in the economy would remain stubbornly high – privatised industries necessitated quangos and regulatory authorities. The state had been reconfigured rather than rolled back; bigger central government proved essential for both creating new markets and introducing market mechanisms into the public sector (although the power and influence of local government was greatly diminished).

Despite the vigor of Margaret Thatcher's public pronouncements her governments' policies were not always 'Thatcherite'. Arguably their defining policy success stood in opposition to the governments' core economic rationale. From 1980 council tenants were offered the opportunity to buy their own homes at a discounted rate and by 1990 owner occupation had risen from 55 per cent in 1980 to

Activity

Having read the essay, answer the following questions.

Comprehension
1. What does Anthony mean by the following phrases:
   - 'entrepreneurial society'
   - 'Thatcherite'
   - 'the reluctance of the incoming government to repeal their marquee economic policies led Thatcher herself to declare New Labour "her greatest achievement".'

Evidence
2. Make a list of the examples of Thatcher's economic successes and failures that are listed in Anthony's essay.

Interpretation
3. Identify the passage in which Anthony explains why, in his view, Thatcherism failed to achieve its economic goals.
4. Summarise Anthony's interpretation in 25 words or less.

Evaluation
5. Using your own knowledge, write a paragraph explaining how far you agree with Anthony's interpretation of the effect of Thatcher's economic policy.

67 per cent. Tax relief on mortgage interest payments rose sharply to £7 billion: an expensive state subsidy that by 1987 was already nearly double the national budget for public housing.

The electoral performance of the Thatcher governments thus does not correlate strongly with either the success or popularity of 'Thatcherite' economics – the Falklands War in 1982 and the emergence of the Social Democratic Party (1981–1988) which split the anti-Thatcher vote explain more. 58 per cent of the electorate voted against Thatcher in 1983 and 1987.

Equally, the overwhelming triumph of 'Thatcherite' economic ideas in the political sphere is far from clear: a large rump of her first cabinet violently disagreed with her economic policies. This first band of 'wets' (such as Jim Prior, Peter Walker and Sir Ian Gilmour) was succeeded by a new generation of Conservatives (Chris Patten, William Waldegrave and John Major) less impressed by 'Thatcherite' convictions. When Labour came to power in 1997 they did not repeal anti-union laws, or rehabilitate the idea of the state enterprise, but they governed (and were elected) to reinvest in the public sector.

International developments such as the end of **Bretton-Woods**, responses to the inflationary '**Oil Shocks**' of the 1970s, and the rise of the '**Washington Consensus**' also weighed heavily on the economic policies of the Thatcher governments and those that have followed. As did membership of the European Economic Community. Global trends towards liberalising global capital flows and shrinking the role of National Governments were central to institutionalising the economic policies now coterminous with 'Thatcherism'.

Over the second half of the twentieth century Britain essentially transformed from a country that imported food and energy to export goods, to a country that sold food and North Sea Oil to pay for imported goods. The economic strategies adopted by the Thatcher government meant that Britain emerged from this transition as a low inflation economy, bolstered by a revitalised finance industry, with its companies recording record profits in a single European market. These policies also structurally entrenched unemployment, destroyed industrial capacity and resulted in the UK running ever-widening balance of payments deficits.

Scott Anthony specialises in modern economic history and the political, cultural and iconographic legacy of industrial change. He has recently published Public Relations and the *Making of Modern Britain*, and is based at the History Faculty of the University of Cambridge.

Work together

Having completed the activity on page 180, swap your notes with a partner. Consider:

1. Did you both spot the same evidence in Anthony's essay?
2. Has your partner missed anything?
3. Did you agree on which passage contained the interpretation? If not, who was right?
4. What was good about your partner's summary of Anthony's interpretation?
5. Can you learn anything about Anthony's interpretation from your partner's summary?
6. How far did you both agree with Anthony's interpretation?

Use these questions to feedback to each other and improve your analysis of the debate.

What impact did Thatcher's governments have on Britain, 1979–97?

Essay technique: Identifying the interpretation

Section C of the exam paper is different to Sections A and B. Unlike Sections A and B it contains two extracts from the work of historians. Significantly, Section C tests different skills.

In essence, Section C tests your ability to analyse different historical interpretations. Therefore, you must focus on the interpretations of the extracts.

Interpretations and evidence

The extracts will contain a mixture of interpretations and evidence. The mark scheme rewards essays that focus on the *interpretations* offered by the extracts more highly than essays that focus on the *information or evidence* mentioned in the extracts. Therefore, it is important to identify the interpretations.

- Interpretations are a specific kind of argument. Like all arguments, they tend to make general claims such as 'Thatcher's economic policies transformed the British economy during the 1980s'.
- Information or evidence tends to comprise specific details. For example: 'By 1982, 3 million people across Britain were unemployed but by 1983 inflation had begun to decline.'

Imagine you are answering the following question:

> In the light of differing interpretations, how convincing do you find the view that Thatcher's economic policies led to 'a positive improvement in the trajectory of the British economy' (Extract 1).
>
> To explain your answer, analyse and evaluate the material in both extracts, using your own knowledge of the issues.

In Extract 1 the evidence and the interpretations have been identified for you.

> **Extract 1** From Terrence Casey (ed.), *The Social Context of Economic Change in Britain*, 2012.
>
> On numerous measures Britain's relative performance since 1979 has been on a par with – and in some respects even superior to – that of other G-7* economies. Improved relative performance has not been sufficient, however, to close the absolute gaps in income and productivity arising from decades of decline. The long-term trend of economic decline bottomed out under Conservative economic stewardship, but the Tories were unable to reverse the process. Even if the Conservatives did not meet their stated goals, halting the process of decline was a major feat. The period of Conservative rule thus represents a positive improvement in the trajectory of the British economy.
>
> Indeed, the Conservatives' economic legacy would probably be more widely praised had it not been for the 1990–92 recession, which seriously marred an otherwise favorable record. Hard won economic gains, particularly on inflation and employment, evaporated – which critics took to indicate the shallowness of the economic improvements. In reality the economy was allowed to overheat in the 1980s, but the supply side improvements were real.
>
> * Group of the world's seven most industrialised economies (Canada, France, Germany, Italy, Japan, UK, USA).

Evidence — (blue text)
Interpretation — (orange text)

Extract 2 From John Eatwell, *Global Unemployment: Loss of Jobs in the '90s*, 1997.

> We can now take stock, and look at the whole period since Mrs Thatcher came to power in the context of the entire postwar period. As a result of Mrs Thatcher's famous policy of 'creating the conditions for stable growth', Britain had the slowest growth rate of the postwar era. The counterpart of that slow growth was a rise of unemployment to previously unimagined levels – punctuated by an unsustainable consumption-driven boom of the late 1980s.
>
> Slow growth and increasing unemployment were accompanied by a rundown of the productive strength of the economy. Investment in manufacturing reached postwar lows, and the declining competitiveness of Britain's manufacturing industry led to a persistent deterioration in the balance of payments.
>
> The true legacy of Mrs Thatcher's policies is unemployment around the 10 per cent of the labour force, which by 1997 must be regarded as the new norm.

Activity: AS-style question

Historians have different views about whether Thatcher's economic policies benefited or harmed Britain. Analyse and evaluate the extracts and use your knowledge of the issues to explain your answer to the following question.

How far do you agree with the view that Thatcher's economic policies were positive in that they halted the long-term trend of economic decline?

Activity: Identifying the interpretation

1 Identify the following aspects of Extract 2:
- the argument
- information or evidence that supports the argument.

2 Having identified these, share your answer with a partner.
- Did your partner correctly identify the interpretation?
- Did you both spot the same information in the extract?
- Has your partner missed anything?
- Did you miss anything that you should note down?
- What can you learn from your partner's approach?

Use these questions to feedback to each other and improve your analysis of the extract.

2 The extent to which state intervention and the public sector were 'rolled back'

Overview

Thatcher's governments were publicly committed to 'rolling back' state intervention and reducing the size of the public sector. The famous phrase, about 'rolling back' the state came from her 1988 Bruges Speech, in which she argued:

We have not successfully rolled back the frontiers of the state in Britain only to see them re-imposed at a European level, with a European superstate exercising a new dominance from Brussels.

This section of the speech made two important claims. First, Thatcher argued that in the past nine years her government had succeeded in rolling back the state in Britain. Second, she claimed that this success was in danger from the European Economic Community, which wanted to reintroduce all of the state control that Thatcher had abolished.

This chapter focusses on the first of these claims, evaluating the extent to which Thatcher succeeded in her aim of 'rolling back the state' and reducing the public sector. Historians disagree on the extent of Thatcher's success. Some agree with Thatcher's own assessment, arguing that she 'rolled back the state' by ending Keynesianism, abolishing corporatism, and reducing the public sector through initiatives such as selling off council housing. Others, however, claim that while Thatcher rolled back the state in some areas she rolled it forward in others, introducing new legislation to strengthen law and order and defence, and centralising control of local government. Finally, other historians argue that Thatcher's own policies led to the growth of the state. Mass unemployment led to a rise in welfare spending and, for pragmatic reasons, Thatcher increased spending on popular public services such as the NHS.

This section considers:
1. Thatcherism and state intervention
2. Thatcher and the public sector.

1 Thatcherism and state intervention

Thatcher's view of the state was more complicated than her comments on 'rolling back the state' in the Bruges Speech indicate. Andrew Gamble, historian of political thought, argues that Thatcher wanted to create 'a free economy and a strong state'. In that sense she was committed to strengthen some aspects of the state while 'rolling back' others. Crucially, Thatcher believed that a free market and a strong state were essential to preserve the liberty of British citizens:

- The free market would ensure economic liberty.
- The strong state would protect political freedom.

In essence, Thatcher wanted to ensure economic liberty by creating a free economy. This entailed 'rolling back the state' in four areas, which Thatcher believed were essential for creating a free market that would end inefficiency and inflation as well as boosting economic growth. These were:

- end Keynesianism – to end the state intervention and management of the British economy
- end **corporatism**
- cut government spending on welfare
- cut direct taxes.

At the same time, Thatcher wanted to strengthen the British state. Significantly, she believed that in some ways a strong state was necessary to protect political and economic freedom, which was threatened by:

- The Soviet Union – a communist superpower that wanted to dominate Britain. Therefore a strong state with a powerful army and state-of-the-art nuclear weapons was necessary to protect British freedom from Soviet domination.
- Powerful unions and vested interests who wanted to use undemocratic methods to force up wages. Therefore a strong state with new powers was necessary to protect British citizens from undemocratic unions.
- Terrorists, hooligans and muggers who threatened people with violence. A strong state with a large police force and security service was necessary to protect citizens and their property from criminals.

Note it down

As you read this chapter, use the 1:2 method (see page x) to make notes on the different meanings of state intervention and Thatcher's different policies for dealing with it. Then write a paragraph evaluating how far Thatcher rolled back state intervention.

State intervention

State intervention has at least two meanings:
1. First, it can refer to government intervention in the economy. Since 1945 governments had intervened in a Keynesian way to promote growth and protect employment in periods of economic difficulty. Since the 1960s, economic intervention had also taken the form of corporatism. However, economic intervention can also take other forms such as manipulating interest rates and introducing laws to regulate industry.
2. Second, state intervention can also refer to other policies, which the government uses to influence politics or society.

Thatcher's willingness to use the state to intervene reflected two debates that had been taking place in the 1970s. First, on the right wing of the Conservative Party, senior Conservatives, such as Sir Keith Joseph, believed that state economic intervention in the form of Keynesianism and corporatism was destroying the free market and therefore leading to economic decline. Second, there was concern across the political spectrum that Britain was becoming 'ungovernable'. From this point of view, unions had brought down the Heath government in 1974 (see page 51) and had brought Britain to a standstill during the Winter of Discontent (see page 52). Additionally, the government seemed unable to deal with terrorist groups such as the IRA.

From Thatcher's point of view, these two 'problems' required different solutions. To revive the economy the government needed to intervene less. However, reasserting government power required a stronger state. Therefore during the 1980s Thatcher 'rolled back', or at least changed, the form of economic intervention while strengthening the powers of the state in order to ensure that Britain could be effectively governed.

Corporatism

Corporatism was an aspect of state intervention that Thatcher rejected. Traditionally, corporatism was used as a descriptive term for a style of economic management in which the government negotiated with representatives of business and unions in order to create a common policy on pay, prices or industrial development. However, Thatcher and her ministers politicised the term. Norman Tebitt, one of Thatcher's key allies at the top of the government, argued that corporatism was undemocratic and a key characteristic of **fascist** governments. Thatcher, too, used the term politically, arguing that corporatism stifled innovation and economic growth by giving the government control over crucial sectors of the economy.

Thatcher effectively abandoned corporatism from 1979. As soon as she was elected the government abandoned prices and incomes policies. This was a dramatic break with the policy approach that had dominated government since the 1960s. Moreover, the government effectively stopped negotiating with the major unions regarding economic policy and the Department for Trade and Industry was reorganised specifically to break its links with the Confederation of British Industry (CBI).

The abandonment of corporatism meant that the government gave up an important tool of state intervention. From 1979 the government increasingly left prices, wages, investment and production to the free market.

Keynesianism

Between 1945 and the late 1970s governments had used Keynesian policies to intervene in the economy – traditionally cutting taxes and increasing spending to stimulate the economy during periods of low growth. Thatcher rejected Keynesianism believing that it led to high inflation rates and that it interfered with the natural rhythms of the free market.

Nonetheless, the government did not give up all forms of economic intervention. Geoffrey Howe's budgets cut spending in order to try to reduce inflation. Nigel Lawson also cut taxes and manipulated interest rates in order to stimulate growth and control inflation. In that sense, the end of Keynesianism did not mean the end of economic management. Rather, the government intervened in different ways, using monetary policy, rather than taxation and spending, to influence the direction of the economy.

Union policy

Rather than negotiate with the unions, the Thatcher government tried to control them. This required a significant extension of state power, as the government passed laws allowing it to control aspects of union activity. government control over the unions was extended through a series of laws:

- The Employment Act (1980) criminalised **secondary action**, including **secondary picketing**.
- The Employment Act (1982) changed the law so that union leaders could only impose a **closed shop** in an industry if they had the backing of a majority of their members in a secret ballot.

What impact did Thatcher's governments have on Britain, 1979–97?

- The Trade Union Act (1984) forced unions to call a secret ballot and win a majority of support prior to starting strike action.

Extending government power in this way weakened British unions. The government's commitment to confronting powerful unions was evident during the miners' strike of 1984–85 (see page 203).

Defence

Thatcher was committed to defending British interests through strengthening the state's defence policy and resolve to act powerfully when challenged by other nations. This was evident throughout her time in government:

- In 1979 she confirmed that she would allow US cruise missiles to be stationed on British territory. She believed that this would deter military aggression from the Soviet Union and its allies in eastern Europe.
- In 1980 she bought Trident, a new generation of nuclear weapons, from the USA. Buying, installing and maintaining Trident would cost the government £7.5 billion a year for the first 15 years alone. Thatcher believed that this would deter a Soviet invasion or a Soviet nuclear strike.
- The 1981 Defence Review, entitled *The Way Forward*, committed the government to increasing defence spending by 3 per cent a year every year throughout the 1980s. Increases in spending were introduced largely to pay for Trident.
- In 1982 Thatcher approved a complex military operation to retake the Falklands Islands from Argentina.
- In 1986 she gave permission for US bombers stationed in Britain to carry out bombing raids in Libya.

As a result of these factors defence spending rose by 20 per cent in real terms between 1979 and 1986. Thatcher's commitment to maintaining high levels of defence spending indicates that she was not committed to rolling back the state in all areas.

Thatcher began to reduce defence spending in the mid-1980s as the costs of Trident were far greater than initially estimated:

- Between 1984 and 1986, 18,000 troops were made redundant.
- Plans to buy a new RAF fighter plane were scrapped in 1986.
- The Navy was reduced in size and the Chatham dockyard and the Royal Dockyard in Gibraltar were closed.

Overall, defence spending fell by 7 per cent in real terms from 1979 to 1989 due to cuts in **conventional forces**. Defence budgets continued to fall between 1990 and 1997. Major continued Thatcher's approach of protecting spending on nuclear weapons while cutting Britain's conventional forces. As a result defence spending fell by 12 per cent in real terms between 1990 and 1997.

Law and order

Thatcher significantly extended police powers, and allowed extensive use of existing powers.

One of the first indications that Thatcher was prepared to sanction aggressive policing was the introduction of Operation Swamp '81, in which police used 'sus laws' to stop and search black people in London, particularly in Brixton. The police justified the campaign by arguing that most muggings were committed by black people, and therefore the police had a duty to target the black community. For ten days police operated a continuous policy of stop and search in Brixton. Black people living there at the time liken the operation to the introduction of **apartheid**. The aggressive policing led to the Brixton Riots, which the government argued, in turn, was evidence that the police needed more powers. Consequently, it passed a series of laws to enlarge police powers:

- The Police and Criminal Evidence Act (1984) expanded police stop-and-search powers, giving them new rights to search cars and enter properties.
- The Public Order Act (1986) gave police new powers to arrest and charge people involved in demonstrations and pickets. It created a new offence, 'disorderly conduct', which allowed police to arrest people using insulting words.
- The Criminal Justice Acts of 1982 and 1988 introduced shorter prison sentences for young offenders, but also tough conditions. The policy was known as the 'short, sharp, shock'.
- The Prevention of Terrorism Act (1989) extended police powers of stop and search.

In addition to these new laws the government authorised the upgrading of police equipment, particularly riot shields, plastic bullets and CS gas.

> ### 'Sus laws'
> 'Sus laws' were a nickname for part of the Vagrancy Act of 1824, which gave police the power to:
> - stop and search people who they believed to be acting suspiciously
> - arrest people they suspected of intending to commit a crime.
>
> In the 1970s and 1980s the laws were used disproportionately against black people.

> ### Mugging
> Mugging is a type of crime in which a victim is robbed in a public place, sometime violently. Mugging became a cause of serious public concern in the early 1970s. The phrase comes from the US. Stuart Hall, a sociologist, argued that the British media routinely linked 'mugging' to young black men, to stereotypes about violent inner-city life, and to popular fears about lawless immigrants who lived criminal lives rather than working for a living. Moreover, he argues that in the 1970s and 1980s there were periods of moral panic about mugging.

Policing the free market

Some historians argue that harsher policing was a necessary part of the creation of the free market. According to this view, Thatcher's free-market policies created mass unemployment and widening social inequality, which in turn led to more crime. Therefore, the state responded by increasing police powers to control the discontent that the new economic policies had created.

Secret state and civil liberties

Thatcher was committed to using government power to protect traditional freedoms. Specifically, she was concerned that traditional liberties could be undermined by Russian-organised communist infiltration. However, Thatcher was prepared to limit some freedoms in order to protect others. This was clear from her approach to the government Communications Headquarters (GCHQ) and from her handling of the 'Zircon affair'.

GCHQ

GCHQ is responsible for providing the government with secret intelligence through intercepting and monitoring communications. In addition it is responsible for keeping top-level government communications secret.

In 1984 the government banned workers at GCHQ from belonging to a union. The ban was introduced in response to strikes at GCHQ in 1981, which had threatened the government's control of secret information. The government argued that strikes at GCHQ threatened national security and should therefore be illegal. However, it also seems to have other motives for introducing the ban. During disputes between the **TUC** and the government about the ban, Thatcher claimed that she viewed union members as part of an 'enemy within'. In essence she argued that unions were socialist organisations and therefore sympathetic to the communist Soviet Union. Therefore, she used state power to ban union membership at GCHQ in order to protect the country from unpatriotic socialists.

The 'Zircon affair'

The 'Zircon affair' was another controversy in which the government used its powers to restrict traditional liberties in order to 'protect the national interest'.

The Zircon affair relates to the banning of a television documentary relating to secret spy satellite codenamed Zircon. In 1985 Duncan Campbell, a Scottish investigative journalist, had uncovered evidence that the government were planning to launch a satellite that would intercept transmissions from across Britain, Europe and the Soviet Union. During 1986 he worked with the BBC producing a documentary about the satellite, its expense and its surveillance capabilities. The government remained committed to keeping the satellite secret. Therefore it put pressure on the BBC not to broadcast the programme. The BBC finally agreed not to show the documentary in late 1986.

However, Campbell was determined to expose the secret Zircon project. Therefore he gave the story to the *Observer* newspaper. In response police raided Campbell's BBC office and confiscated his research. Additionally, the government gained a court order legally banning Campbell from writing or speaking about his research.

Crucially, the government even kept the project a secret from parliament. According to constitutional convention the government had a duty to inform the Public Accounts Committee – a senior committee of MPs – of all major spending projects. However, Thatcher viewed the project as too sensitive to tell even senior MPs.

The Zircon affair exposed the government's willingness to interfere with the media and ignore the constitution in order to protect secret security projects.

Media interference

The Zircon affair was not the only instance when the government used its power to interfere with the media:

- *Spycatcher*, a memoir of a former MI5 officer, was banned in England and Wales in 1985. Press coverage of the book's contents was also banned in England and Wales. The book was available in Scotland, and widely covered in the Scottish press.
- In 1988 the government banned the broadcast of interviews with members of the IRA, the Ulster Volunteer Force and **Sinn Fein**.
- The government put broadcasters under pressure to drop programmes on the SAS and the conflict in Northern Ireland.

What impact did Thatcher's governments have on Britain, 1979–97?

A 'crisis of civil liberties'?

Government ministers defended the suppression of secret information. However, the government's critics claimed that state intervention was being used to take away traditional rights to free speech. Significantly, newspapers were unable to challenge the government successfully in English courts, as English law, at the time, did not guarantee freedom of speech or publication.

The European Court of Human Rights did overrule government bans. Indeed, it ruled that the government had breached the European Convention of Human Rights by banning press coverage of *Spycatcher*. The pressure group Charter 88 was formed in 1988 to campaign for greater protection of civil liberties in Britain.

Expansion of law and order

Thatcher clearly increased the powers of the state in terms of law and order. As a result:

- the law and order budget increased 36 per cent between 1979 and 1989
- the prison population rose from around 42,000 in 1979 to 48,000 in 1989 – the highest per capita prison population in Europe.

Policy remained broadly similar in the 1990s. The prison population continued to grow, reaching 60,000 by 1997.

Historical interpretation: Thatcher and the state

Historians have disagreed on Thatcher's view on the state. Andrew Gamble, in Extract 1, presents Thatcher as an ideologically driven politician who was committed to the creation of a free economy and a strong state. Jeremy Black, in Extract 2, on the other hand, argues that Thatcher was partially committed to 'rolling back' the state. He also argues that she was pragmatically willing to maintain high levels of expenditure on the health service in order to remain popular.

Extract 1 From Andrew Gamble, *The Free Economy and Strong State: The Politics of Thatcherism*, 1994.

In her 1979 manifesto Margaret Thatcher claimed that the balance had been tilted too far in favour of the state at the expense of individual freedom. The 1979 election, she wrote, was the last chance to reverse this process.

The Thatcher government believed that it knew how to turn the country around. It set itself five main tasks:

1. To restore the health of the economy and social life
2. To restore economic incentives
3. To uphold Parliament and the rule of law
4. To support family life
5. To strengthen Britain's defences.

The first two of these tasks involved the creation of a free economy – that marked a break with strategies associated with Keynesianism and corporatism. The other three involved the creation of a strong state to provide the institutions that would support a free economy.

Extract 2 From Jeremy Black, *Britain Since the Seventies: Politics and Society in the Consumer Age*, 2004.

Thatcher sought to roll back the state in the interests of free-market participation and competition. She was committed to the view that state intervention in the economy was not a benefit and, instead, that the independence of the free market was constructive. The role of the state in Conservative thinking declined dramatically from the mid-1970s. The neo-liberal, anti-corporatist and anti-collectivist rhetoric, attitudes and policies of the Conservative Party under Thatcher ensured that it looked more to the USA than to the Continent for its models and parallels.

In practice, as with other politicians, there was much compromise, especially in her early years. Thatcher was not the most Thatcherite politician: intuition and self-confidence, as much as ideology and doctrine, were central to her leadership. Indeed, there was to be criticism that her rhetoric of 'rolling back the state' was misleading, especially in healthcare where the NHS remained in a dominant position. Furthermore, government expenditure did not fall as anticipated.

Having read Extracts 1 and 2:
1. Summarise the key argument of the two extracts.
2. Select three details from your own knowledge that support the argument of Extract 1. Write these down as a list under your summaries.
3. Swap your summaries with a partner:
- Which summary best captured the argument of Extract 1?
- Which summary best captured the argument of Extract 2?
- Which details most precisely supported the argument of Extract 1?

2 Thatcher and the public sector

Thatcher wanted to end much of the work done by the public sector. Her speeches attacked the public sector in a variety of ways. She presented her government as:

- anticollectivist: it prioritised individual freedom and individual wellbeing over policies designed to promote the welfare of the whole of society
- antistatist: it claimed that state action tended to be counter-productive, and was inferior to the action of private companies and individuals.

In some areas, such as housing and local government, Thatcher introduced policies that led to a reduction of the size of the public sector. However, she never intended to abolish it. Indeed, for pragmatic reasons, she supported the NHS, claiming that it was 'safe in my hands'. Moreover, in spite of her speeches she did little to limit welfare spending.

The public sector

The public sector is the part of an economy which provides government services such as healthcare, education, policing and defence. The size of the public sector can vary. In the 1970s, for example, it provided electricity, gas, water, transport, council housing and telecommunications. By the mid-1990s, all of these services, except some council houses, had been sold to the private sector.

Note it down

This section deals with Thatcher's approach to the public sector. First, skim the section and note down the various aspects of the public sector that Thatcher attempted to reform. Use these as headings in a note-making style of your choice, and record Thatcher's different policies under each heading. Make sure you also make a note of how effective these policies were.

Housing

One area where Thatcher clearly reduced the size of the public sector was council housing. Traditionally, Labour and Conservative governments had invested in housing. However, house building was expensive and therefore, with the return of economic problems in the late 1960s, Wilson's Labour government cut house-building budgets. The Labour governments of the 1970s went further, giving local authorities the right to sell council houses to tenants. Thatcher went further still, shifting large numbers of homes and the responsibility for building into the private sector.

Thatcher and the 'right to buy'

From 1975, Thatcher and the Conservative Party began to advocate giving all council house tenants the right to buy their homes. Thatcher advocated this policy because she believed in:

- A property-owning democracy: Thatcher believed that owning property gave people a stake in society, and therefore gave people a reason to behave responsibly.
- Property and freedom: Thatcher believed that property ownership was an important aspect of freedom. She believed that owning property meant that people were independent of the state, whereas people who lived in state-owned houses were dependent on the state.
- The superiority of the private sector: Thatcher believed that the private sector would build better houses. Therefore, she wanted to end public-sector involvement in house building.

Thatcher's housing policy

Thatcher's housing policy greatly extended council tenants' right to buy. The 1980 Housing Act gave council house tenants who had lived in their houses for more than three years the right to buy their houses at a 33 per cent discount from the market rate. Tenants who had lived in their council houses for more than 20 years could buy their houses at a 50 per cent discount.

The consequences of the policy

The policy proved to be extremely popular. Around half a million people bought their council houses every year from 1980 to 1989. Between 1990 and 1997 the rate decreased to about 160,000 a year. Nonetheless, the Housing Act had a profound impact on the public sector. Between 1980 and 1997 over 5 million state-owned houses were sold to private tenants. The proportion of state-owned houses in Britain fell from 31.5 per cent in 1979 to 23.6 per cent in 1989. The proportion of **owner occupation** increased from 50 per cent in 1971, to 55 per cent in 1981 and to 78 per cent in 1989.

Thatcher believed the policy was a huge success. Speaking in 1982 she claimed that it was 'the largest transfer of assets from the state to the family in British history'. She also claimed that the policy was an attack on the dependency culture (see page 65) which council housing had created.

At the same time, council budgets were reduced, and the 1988 Housing Act explicitly banned local authorities from spending the money earned from the sale of council houses on new building projects. As a result the number of new council houses being built declined. By 1997 the state was effectively no longer building new homes.

Nationalised industry

Another way in which Thatcher successfully rolled back the frontiers of the state was through privatisation. Privatisations began in Thatcher's first term (see page 174), but became a key feature of government policy following the privatisation of British Telecom in 1984.

Privatisation clearly reduced government ownership, and shifted the balance of the economy away from the public sector towards the private sector. Moreover, there was sufficient public support for privatisation to ensure that the policy continued after Thatcher's fall.

The civil service

Thatcher did not trust or like the civil service. While she believed that a small number of civil servants were necessary for running the state, she thought that the civil service did nothing to help create wealth, that it was inefficient and that it should be reduced in size. Moreover, she believed that it was a powerful elite with its own vested interests that needed to be placed firmly under government control.

Thatcher attempted to cut the civil service down to size in the following ways:

- the establishment of an Efficiency Unit to find ways to make the civil service more efficient
- the introduction of the Management Information System to monitor and reduce civil service costs
- the commissioning of the *Next Steps* report, leading to a new management culture in the civil service. Following the report, civil service departments were required to set targets, evaluate how far they had met these targets and publish reports on their progress.

By 1989 the government had achieved more than £1 billion worth of efficiency savings, and the number of civil servants had been reduced by almost 25 per cent.

At the same time, Thatcher changed the culture of the civil service. She believed that the civil service was determined to stand in the way of reform. Therefore she promoted civil servants who were prepared to find ways to make her ideas work, rather than those who would point out the problems. When promoting civil servants she routinely asked 'Is he one of us?'

Thatcher's distrust of civil servants meant that she employed more policy advisors, and relied less on the civil service for advice.

Local government

'Rolling back' the public sector required reducing the size of local as well as central government. Thatcher was concerned about the size of local government for two reasons. First, local government was responsible for 28.1 per cent of total government spending. Second, as Thatcher cut back central government services some local authorities were trying to expand their services. Thatcher's government believed that some local authorities were using their power to introduce 'socialist policies', which she viewed as a threat to individual freedom. As a result, Thatcher's government took on new powers to try to

Local government and the Labour left

During the 1980s there were at least three different strands within the Labour Party:

- The Old Left: From 1983 to 1989 Labour's leadership was dominated by the Old Left. Labour leader Neil Kinnock remained committed to traditional Labour policies such as nationalisation, Keynesianism and corporatism.
- The New Left: The Labour leadership in London was associated with a new view of socialism. Ken Livingstone and Labour councillors on the Greater London Council (GLC) believed that the Labour Party should fight for the equality of all people. Therefore they supported initiatives to advance women's liberation and gave money to groups campaigning for different rights (see page 204). In addition, the GLC campaigned for nuclear disarmament and began a dialogue with the Irish nationalist group Sinn Fein.
- Militant Tendency: This was a Trotskyite organisation that believed in the overthrow of capitalism in Britain and the establishment of a revolutionary socialist government. Militant's strategy was to infiltrate local Labour Party groups and to get their members elected as official Labour Party candidates. This proved to be a success and enabled the organisation to control Liverpool City Council under Militant member Derek Hatton.

The right-wing press labelled the GLC and Militant 'the loony left'. Significantly, the two groups had little in common. Specifically, Livingstone and the New Left were not Trotskyites and Militant had little interest in black rights, LGBT rights or women's rights.

ensure that local government was also rolled back. This led to a series of battles between central government and local authorities. By the late 1980s local government spending had been cut and some of the most left-wing councils had been abolished.

Reducing spending

Thatcher tried a series of methods to reduce local government spending:

- Between 1979 and 1984 the government cut funding to local authorities. In 1979 it provided £44 million of local government funding; by 1984 that had been cut to £39 million. Thatcher assumed this would lead to a reduction in local government spending, but instead local authorities responded by increasing rates (local taxation).
- In 1981 Michael Heseltine, who was responsible for local government, introduced a policy of 'targets and penalties'. Local government was set maximum targets for spending and those that exceeded these targets had their central government allowance reduced. The policy failed, as local authorities responded to the penalties by increasing rates.
- The Rates Bill, passed in 1984, gave the government the power to impose a cap, an upper limit, on local taxation.
- The Local government Act of 1988 forced councils to buy in (or contract-out) services from the private sector rather than provide them directly. The Act also gave the government the power to force local governments to accept the most competitive offers in order to keep costs down.

Significantly, each step in this process extended the power of the state. In this sense, rolling back the size of local government was only possible by strengthening the power of central government.

Rate capping

A number of Labour local authorities organised a campaign against the Rates Bill and the government's 'rate capping' policy. In 1984 Liverpool Council, led by Derek Hatton, who was part of Militant Tendency, openly defied the government by setting an illegal rate. In 1985–86 the government announced plans to cap the rates of eighteen councils – sixteen Labour and two Conservative. The campaign against rate capping continued into 1987, but in the end all eighteen councils set a legal rate. The campaign against rate capping fell apart for four main reasons:

- The government was prepared to compromise and allowed six of the councils to set higher rates.
- The sixteen Labour councils were not united. There were big divisions between the Old Left, Militant and the New Left.
- The right-wing press carried out a sustained campaign against the 'loony left'.
- Labour's leader publically criticised Liverpool's council for setting an illegal rent.

The Greater London Council

The Greater London Council (GLC), created in 1963, administered the inner city and the outlying boroughs of London, making it the largest single local authority in the country. Following the GLC elections of 1981 Ken Livingstone (nicknamed 'Red Ken') and the New Left councillors of the GLC's Labour Party managed to take control of the council. Livingstone's GLC introduced a series of policies in order to create 'urban socialism', including:

- subsidising travel on the London Underground in a campaign titled 'Fare's Fair' – the policy reduced traffic and pollution in the capital by reducing fares
- giving financial support to LGBT groups, women's groups and groups fighting for the rights of black and Asian people such as the Race Today Collective – for example the GLC spent £300,000 on grants to gay and lesbian groups and a further £750,000 to create a London Lesbian and Gay Centre
- spending budget that was designed to prepare London for a nuclear attack on a campaign against nuclear weapons
- opening up government cafes to the public so that all Londoners could have access to subsidised meals
- establishing the London Ecological Unit which set up ecological gardens in London in order to protect wildlife habitats.

Thatcher believed that these collectivist and left-wing policies represented an unacceptable expansion of state power. In addition to these economic policies the GLC initiated a number of political programmes that Thatcher believed were dangerous:

- Livingstone published the government's secret plan for dealing with a nuclear strike, revealing that the government planned to surround London with the British army to stop Londoners escaping from the capital in the run-up to a nuclear strike and in the aftermath of an attack. The government believed that the population of the capital were unlikely to survive for more than two weeks after an attack and therefore it would be better for them to die in a confined area.

- The GLC endorsed the anti-apartheid campaigner Nelson Mandela while he was still viewed as a terrorist by the British government.
- Livingstone invited Sinn Fein leader Gerry Adams to speak in London, and arranged a meeting between Adams and the black rights activist Darcus Howe.

Thatcher's response was to abolish the GLC. She claimed it was responsible for high taxes, high public spending and collectivist policies. In that sense the abolition of the GLC was part of her desire to roll back the state. Livingstone argued that the move was politically motivated, but in 1986 the Council was abolished as a result of the Local government Act 1985.

The poll tax

Thatcher's final and most controversial local government reform was the introduction of the community charge, which quickly became known as the 'poll tax'. The poll tax was designed to replace rates as the system of taxation to fund local government. Rates were based on the value of property, therefore there were problems with the system. For example, two houses of the same size in the same street would have the same value and therefore the owners would pay the same rates. However, the income of the two households could be radically different. The community charge was designed to address the problem by ensuring that all adults paid the same tax. Thatcher also argued that this would make local government more accountable because by making all citizens community-charge payers it would mean that all citizens had an interest in ensuring their local councils spent money wisely and kept costs down.

However, the poll tax was a flat rate tax and therefore not related to income. This meant that rich and poor would all pay the same rate. As a result the tax was highly controversial. The new tax was introduced by the Local government Finance Act of 1988. The community charge was introduced in Scotland in 1989 and in England and Wales in 1990.

The unpopularity of the community charge was one of the reasons for Thatcher's fall. It was replaced by the council tax in 1993 (see page 219).

Rolling back local government

Thatcher's local government reforms were radical. However, her record on rolling back local government spending was mixed. Local government spending increased by 15 per cent in real terms from 1979 to 1989. It did start to shrink following 1990, but, by 1997, it was still almost 14 per cent higher than it had been in 1979. Measured against GDP Thatcher's reforms were marginally more successful. In 1979 local government spending accounted for 10 per cent of GDP. That figure dropped to 8.7 in 1989 and 8.3 per cent in 1997.

In addition, by abolishing the GLC Thatcher was able to remove Ken Livingstone and in so doing end local government efforts to use government power to protect the rights of minorities and the environment. In this, and in London at least, she did succeed in rolling back the state.

NHS

The NHS was one of the most radical measures introduced by the 1945–51 Labour government. In many ways it represented everything that Thatcher rejected: it was a huge public sector institution, funded by tax which supported the collective good. Nonetheless, the NHS was extremely popular. Therefore, Thatcher did not propose privatising the NHS or significantly reducing its funding.

Thatcher began the process of NHS reform in 1983, appointing Sir Roy Griffiths, head of the supermarket Sainsbury's, to advise on how to make the health service more efficient. Griffiths introduced a new layer of management into the NHS. More radical reforms were introduced in the mid-1980s when NHS hospitals were required to buy in services from the private sector.

Thatcher's final NHS reforms, introduced following the 1989 White Paper *Working with Patients*, created an internal market in the NHS. Rather than funding hospitals directly, the new system gave government money to district health authorities which would buy services from local hospitals. Thatcher and her ministers argued that this system would be more efficient because it would force local hospitals to compete with each other for district health authority money.

The reforms and continual search for efficiency did not stop costs rising. Indeed, government spending on the NHS grew by 35 per cent in real terms from 1979 to 1989.

Social security

Social security spending increased under Thatcher due to the large rise in unemployment (see page 172), which meant a large rise in unemployment benefits the government was bound to pay. The 1986 Social Security Act tried to stop the rise in social security costs, by introducing **means testing** to some universal benefits, and making it harder to claim some existing benefits. While these measures increased poverty among the poorest fifth of Britons it did not lead to a long-term reduction in the social security bill (see Table 1).

Table 1: Government spending on social security as a percentage of GDP

1960	1979	1984	1989	1995
6.0	10.6	13.0	11.1	14.6

Pensions

Thatcher's goal was to increase uptake of private pensions, and therefore reduce dependence on state pensions. As a result she changed the State Earning-Related Pension Scheme (SERPS), set up by Labour in 1975, to make it less attractive and to encourage people to opt out of the scheme into private schemes. In spite of this, government spending on pensions stayed almost exactly the same, falling from 6.7 per cent of GDP in 1979 to 6.5 per cent of GDP in 1990.

Education

Thatcher's major school reforms took place in her third term. In order to address concerns about the quality of British education she strengthened central state control of schools, introducing a national curriculum focussing on maths, English and science. Thatcher also introduced standard tests at the ages of seven, eleven, fourteen and sixteen. The results of these tests were published in league tables, allowing parents to evaluate which schools were the best. Finally, Thatcher allowed schools to become 'grant maintained': they could opt out of local authority control and receive funding direct from the government. This allowed the government to break up local educational authorities, such as the Inner London Education Authority (ILEA), which it believed was run by dangerous socialists.

The strengthening of central control did not lead to a sustained reduction of spending (see Table 2).

Table 2: Government spending on education as a percentage of GDP

1960	1979	1984	1989	1995
3.5	5.2	5.2	4.8	5.5

John Major took further steps in the 1990s to improve education. In 1992 he established the Office for Standards in Education, Children's Services and Skills (Ofsted), to monitor the performance of schools. Ofsted reports, like school league tables before them, were intended to help parents make informed choices about local schools.

Conclusion

Thatcher's claim that she 'successfully rolled back the frontiers of the state in Britain' did not mean that she wanted to reduce every aspect of the state. Thatcher was committed to rolling back some aspects of the state's economic power, while strengthening other aspects of state power. Moreover, in terms of local government and public services such as the NHS it would be more accurate to say that Thatcher's policies changed the way the state worked, rather than reducing the size of the state.

Thatcher's legacy was profound. The direction she set in terms of the relationship between the public and private sector and in terms of state intervention in law and order influenced policy throughout the 1990s.

Extended reading: Rolling back state intervention and the public sector

Thatcher believed that the state stifled individual initiative and freedom and was determined to 'roll it back'. However, the extent to which she achieved this is questionable. Professor Peter Dorey explores the extent to which the state was reduced during the 1980s.

One of the main objectives of the Thatcher governments was to reduce the role of the State, and in so doing, increase individual freedom and allow the private sector to expand. According to Margaret Thatcher and those who shared her philosophy (Thatcherism), the State in Britain since 1945 had become too large, too costly and interfered far too much in people's lives.

The State had taken many industries into public ownership (nationalisation), ran much of Britain's education system and the National Health Service, and provided a comprehensive welfare state which aimed to support people financially from 'cradle to grave'. In effect, millions of people were educated by the State, cared for by the State in times of illness and often worked for the State.

Thatcher firmly believed that the private sector was inherently more efficient and innovative than State-owned industries and public services, and that the pursuit of profit, along with wealth-creation, were to be admired and encouraged. By contrast, the public sector was often a bottomless pit into which ever increasing sums of tax-payers' money was poured and wasted each year.

These criticisms resulted in the Thatcher (and Major) governments privatising most of Britain's State-owned industries and introducing 'the market' into services such as education and the National Health Service, in order to force them to operate more like private companies; for example, different types of schools, university fees to create a 'market' in higher education and the 'internal market' in the NHS. More recently, private companies have become increasingly involved in managing or providing some of these services, resulting in allegations of creeping privatisation – which Ministers always deny.

These reforms were presented as 'rolling back the State' and 'setting people free'; the less the State did or provided, the more people could do for themselves, and the more that services were opened up to 'the market', the more choice people would have. This would raise standards in education and the NHS, for example, because schools and hospitals would have to compete with other schools and hospitals to attract pupils and patients.

However, many academics have challenged this view of the State, with Andrew Gamble defining Thatcherism as 'free economy, strong state'. This was not a contradiction, he argued, because the State has to be strong and active in order to remove obstacles to 'the free market' and the private sector. Hence, while Thatcher(ism) was boasting of 'rolling back the State', it was introducing the National Curriculum in secondary education, and creating OFSTED to conduct regular

Activity

Having read the essay, answer the following questions.

Comprehension
1. What does Dorey mean by the following phrases:
   - 'rolling back the state'
   - 'free economy, strong state'
   - 'the public sector was often a bottomless pit'.

Evidence
2. Make a list of the examples of Thatcher's successes and failures in 'rolling back the state' mentioned in Dorey's essay.

Interpretation
3. Identify the passage in which Dorey explains, in his view, the extent to which the state was really rolled back.
4. Summarise Dorey's interpretation in 25 words or less.

Evaluation
5. Using your own knowledge, write a paragraph explaining how far you agree with Dorey's analysis about the extent to which Thatcher 'rolled back the state'.

inspections of schools to measure standards – as defined by government Ministers.

Meanwhile, in the NHS, the creation of an internal market has resulted in a massive increase in bureaucracy, due to the need for many more accountants and managers to administer it.

Many public service professionals increasingly complain that they are spending too much of their time providing statistical data, and preparing for/participating in repeated audits and inspections ordered by governments, instead of focusing on serving the public or their clients. For example, many police officers complain that they spend more time at their desk filling-in forms or ticking boxes than they do out 'on the beat' tackling crime. Similar complaints about time wasted on paper-work, box-ticking and an endless cycle of 'strategic reviews' or 'business plans' are routinely made by nurses, probation officers, social workers and teachers.

Finally, the regime of inspections and targets in the public sector, in response to government objectives or priorities, means that professionals now have to do their jobs in a way demanded by the State (such as how teachers actually teach) and can be measured, rather than using their own expertise and judgement. This can mean that they are sometimes unable to act in the best interests of their pupils, patients or clients, because they have to do their job in a specified way, or hit certain targets by a particular date. For example, in many hospitals, nurses are told to spend only 20–30 minutes with each patient, so that they can see more patients each day, and show that they are being efficient or 'productive'.

For many public sector professionals, therefore, the regime established by Thatcher and her successors, far from 'rolling back the State', has made the State far more interventionist, intrusive and obsessed with measuring, monitoring and micro-management than ever before. Governments continue to justify relentless public sector reform on the grounds of improving efficiency, but refuse to acknowledge that it is the State itself which is frequently causing the public sector to be inefficient. As such, every time there is another major failure or scandal in education, the NHS or social work, there is another bout of State-imposed reform.

Peter Dorey is Professor of British Politics at Cardiff University, and the author or editor of thirteen books on British politics and public policy. He has written extensively on the Conservative Party, and his 2011 book *British Conservatism: The Politics and Philosophy of Inequality*, published by I.B. Tauris, won a 'best book of the year' prize from the Political Studies Association.

Work together

Having completed the activity on page 94, swap your notes with a partner. Consider:

1 Did you both spot the same evidence in Dorey's essay?
2 Has your partner missed anything?
3 Did you agree on which passage contained the interpretation? If not, who was right?
4 What was good about your partner's summary of Dorey's interpretation?
5 Can you learn anything about Dorey's interpretation from your partner's summary?
6 How far did you both agree with Dorey's interpretation?

Use these questions to feed back to each other and improve your analysis of the historiography.

Essay technique: Structuring your essay

In order to do well, your essay needs to focus on the interpretations of both extracts. Although there are only two extracts, your essay may have to deal with several interpretations, as each extract might contain an argument and a counter-argument.

Your essay structure should allow you to:
- analyse all of the interpretations effectively
- deal with the different interpretations in turn
- deal with the different interpretations in a logical sequence.

Therefore, your essay should be structured around the key interpretations contained in the extracts.

Analysing the extracts

In order to deal with the different interpretations in a logical sequence, you should look for the ways in which they support and challenge each other.

Imagine you are answering the following question:

> **In the light of differing interpretations, how convincing do you find the view that Thatcher's policies led to 'hollowing out the state' (Extract 1)?**
>
> **To explain your answer, analyse and evaluate the material in both extracts, using your own knowledge of the issues.**

A suggested plan for this essay can be found on page 197.

Extract 1 From Peter Kerr, *Postwar British Politics: From Conflict to Consensus*, 2001.

> Throughout their first two terms the Thatcher governments had experimented with several ways of reforming both the public sector and the welfare state. These experiments, though, had mainly led to only minor and certainly ad hoc changes. In the third term however, some of these former initiatives were combined with previous measures such as contracting-out and privatisation, and with ideas which had been tried in other countries, in order to create a more determined and effective strategic mutation that took shape and evolved throughout this phase of 'radical Thatcherism'. The resulting process of 'reinventing government' or 'hollowing out the state' manifested itself in a wholesale reform of the basic system of welfare provision and the public sector in general, following publication of the Next Steps report. Building upon the previous Social Security Act (1986), the Conservatives introduced the Education Reform Act (1988), the Housing Act (1988), and a wider reform of the NHS following the publication of the 1989 White Paper, Working for Patients.

Extract 2 From Earl A. Reitan, *The Thatcher Revolution – Margaret Thatcher, John Major, Tony Blair, and the Transformation of Modern Britain*, 2002.

> The GLC, led by 'Red Ken' Livingstone, was Thatcher's thorn in the flesh. From 1981 to 1986 Livingstone increased GLC expenditures by 170 percent. He greatly expanded the number of employees and other dependents and made generous grants to activist groups. He claimed to be creating 'urban socialism' as the people's alternative to Thatcherism. He hung red flags on the GLC building across the Thames from the houses of Parliament, invited foreign revolutionaries to the council chambers, and posted a banner listing the figures for unemployment. In 1981, the GLC cut fares on the London Underground by 32 percent, a popular step, and raised the rates to make up the difference. The government intervened and London Transport was nationalized.
>
> Thatcher's answer to urban noncompliance was a demonstration of raw power, fuelled not a little by anger. In 1985, the Thatcher ministry proposed abolition of eighteen urban councils whose fiscal management was regarded as irresponsible. Labour controlled all but two. The list included the six metropolitan counties established by the Heath government plus the GLC.

Planning your essay

In order to plan your essay, you need to analyse the two extracts, that is to say, you need to break down the extracts into the different arguments, counter-arguments and pieces of evidence they contain.

While you are doing this, look for:
- contrasting arguments between the extracts – these can be the major sections of your essay
- aspects of the extracts that support each other.

For example, a plan for an essay in answer to the question on page 196 could look like this:

Extract 1		Extract 2
… because of the 'wholesale reform of the basic system of welfare provision and the public sector'	(1) [ARGUMENT] Thatcher's policies hollowed out the state	Thatcher ended GLC initiatives designed to create 'urban socialism'.
State intervention grew: • Education Reform Act (1988) • Housing Act (1988) • Reform of the NHS (Working for Patients).	(2) [COUNTER-ARGUMENT] However, she also created a strong state.	Thatcher used the state's 'raw power' against her opponents: Nationalisation of London Transport, abolition of GLC.
• Contracting-out and privatisation • Contrast between first two terms and third term.	(3) [RESOLUTION 1] Thatcher's 'hollowing out' of the state was primarily economic and occurred later in her governance.	
	(4) [RESOLUTION 2] Thatcher was also prepared to strengthen the state in order to protect citizens from 'socialist' initiatives.	GLC's 'socialist policies': • GLC expenditures rose by 170 per cent. • GLC greatly expanded the number of employees. • GLC made generous grants to activist groups.

Activity

> In the light of differing interpretations, how convincing do you find the view that Thatcher's governments succeeded in 'rolling back the frontiers of socialism' (Extract 3)?
>
> To explain your answer, analyse and evaluate the material in both extracts, using your own knowledge of the issues.

Using the guidance on page 197, plan an answer to the question above, by following the steps below:
1. Read both extracts (Extracts 3 and 4).
2. Analyse them by looking for:
   - the main arguments
   - counter-arguments
   - evidence.
3. Look for contrasting arguments between the extracts.
4. Look for aspects of the extracts that support each other.

TIPS
- Your first main paragraph should analyse the interpretation set out in the question.
- Your second paragraph should analyse the interpretation that contrasts most strongly with the interpretation in the main paragraph.
- Other paragraphs should deal with other arguments that the extracts put forward.
- Try and use both extracts in each paragraph.
- Overall, you can try and achieve an argument–counter-argument–resolution structure.

Work together

Having completed the activity above, consider the following question w/a partner:
1. Did you both identify the same arguments and counter-arguments in the extracts?
2. Did you agree about which aspect of the extracts was the biggest contrast to the main argument of Extract 1?
3. How was your partner's plan different to your own?
4. Did you miss anything that you should note down?
5. What can you learn from your partner's approach?
6. Which plan better answers the question and why?
7. Use these questions to feed back to each other and improve your analysis of the extracts.

Activity: AS-style question

Historians have different views about the impact on Britain of Thatcher's governments in the years 1979–97. Analyse and evaluate Extracts 3 and 4 and use your knowledge of the issues to explain your answer to the following question.

How far do you agree with the view that Thatcher's governments 'rolled back the frontiers of socialism' (Extract 3)?

Extract 3 From Andy McSmith, *No Such Thing as Society: A History of Britain in the 1980s*, 2011.

> Since 1945, the UK had edged towards becoming more 'socialist', with free medicine, free schools, state pensions and more than 40 per cent of the country's industrial capacity owned by the state. Mrs Thatcher, however, was determined to 'roll back the frontiers of socialism', which she succeeded in doing. Though her economic legacy is highly controversial, no government has attempted to undo it. The Thatcherite mix of privatized utilities, low taxes for the highly paid and restrictive trade union legislation survived even thirteen years of Labour government.
>
> More change and more conflict were crammed into the 1980s, particularly the first half of the decade, than any other decade in the second half of the twentieth century. Out of political chaos, Britain arrived at a settlement that lasted, for better or worse. The way we live now follows directly from the tumultuous events of the 1980s.

Extract 4 From James Obelkevich and Peter Catterall, *Understanding Post-War British Society*, 1994.

> The Conservative government headed by Mrs Thatcher between 1979 and 1990 was committed to rolling back the frontiers of the state. Although it failed to reduce government expenditure as a proportion of the gross national product until its later years, it succeeded in removing many nationalised industries from public control, as well as producing a fall in the proportion of households living in council houses from 31 per cent in 1981 to 21 per cent by 1992.
>
> Furthermore, the period since 1979 has also challenged the claim that governments were unable to introduce new policies because of the opposition of vested interests. The legal immunities of the trade unions have been challenged successfully, and the opposition of the strongest union of the 1970s – the National Union of Miners – to the reduction in the coal industry has been overcome.

3 The extent of political and social division within Britain

Overview

One of Thatcher's first acts as prime minister was to speak to the press as she entered Downing Street. Speaking on the steps of Number 10 she said,

Where there is discord, may we bring harmony. Where there is error, may we bring truth. Where there is doubt, may we bring faith. And where there is despair, may we bring hope.

The statement, which she attributed to the mediaeval Saint Francis of Assisi, points in two directions. On the one hand, Thatcher committed herself to creating harmony. On the other, she wanted to correct error. In office, Thatcher tended to prioritise the truth, as she saw it, over harmony.

Significantly, the fact that Thatcher entered office promising to restore harmony clearly indicates that in 1979 Britain was a country already experiencing political and social divisions. Divisions between Catholics and Protestants in Northern Ireland, divisions between employees and employers in industry, and divisions between immigrants and those seeking to continue white dominance were nothing new. Britain was a divided society in 1979 and continued to be divided until 1997. Thatcher did not create divisions in society, but some historians argue that she made them worse.

Traditional 'One Nation Conservatives' had tried to use government power and policy to heal social divisions by forcing employers to be responsible and by ensuring an improving quality of life for the working class. Thatcher also wanted to create harmony around a common set of values. However, she was also prepared for conflict. Thatcherism is often presented as an economic doctrine, but it was also a set of moral convictions. For Thatcher, rejecting socialism meant not just reforming the economy; it also meant rejecting the permissive society. In practice she wanted to strengthen monogamous heterosexual marriage, and curb political groups that challenged her basic assumptions about British society. Thatcher's moral crusade led to a series of confrontations with a variety of groups who represented values that Thatcher rejected.

Moreover, Thatcher was concerned about the emergence of a diverse society. She believed that a diverse society could not be united. She argued that people feared immigration because 'people are really rather afraid that this country might be swamped with a different culture'. She was concerned that people living alternative lifestyles would lead to 'a weakening of the bonds which hold us together as a people'.

Whereas Thatcher undoubtedly shifted the economic consensus to the right, she was far less successful at combating permissive Britain. She prevailed in her battle against the National Union of Miners. However, groups of black, LGBT, Asian, and women activists, often working with the media, shifted the social consensus to the left. Tolerance of racism, sexism and homophobia all decreased during the 1980s and 1990s, paving the way for new minority rights legislation that was introduced under Tony Blair.

This chapter explores support and opposition for Thatcher and the polarisation of politics and society in the 1980s, as well as its consequences for John Major, through the following sections:
1 Thatcher and 'class war'
2 Thatcher's 'colonialism'
3 Thatcher and sexuality
4 Thatcher and feminism.

1 Thatcher and 'class war'

Thatcher was dedicated to restoring the power of the government and ending socialism. One aspect of this was her desire to replace class division with national unity. She hoped that all people would embrace 'British values' of hard work and independence, rather than 'foreign' or 'socialist values' of welfare dependency.

> **Note it down**
> This section requires three different kinds of note-taking:
> - First, make a timeline of the important events in order to ensure you have a secure chronology of the period.
> - Second, draw a spider diagram of the ways in which class conflict either increased or decreased in the period 1979–97.
> - Third, note down key words and their definitions – you might want to use index cards for this purpose.

National unity

Thatcher's attempt to create national unity was evident in her approach to foreign policy. She repeatedly encouraged national unity in her speeches about the threat of Russian communism. It was also apparent during the **Falklands War** of 1982. Thatcher presented the Argentinian invasion of the Falkland Islands as an affront to the British values of democracy and to the rights of British people. Moreover, she initiated a complex and difficult military operation to take back the islands, in order to defend national honour. The Falklands War created a sense of national unity, with nationalistic headlines in the tabloid press and a surge of support for Thatcher's government.

The problem of class

Thatcher viewed class politics as a problem because it undermined national unity and the 'British values' of hard work and self-reliance. Moreover, she believed that the unions were undermining national unity by putting the interests of the working class above the interests of the nation. This was evident in her confrontation with the National Union of Miners (NUM) (see below).

Thatcher's battle with the NUM was not the only example of class conflict during the Thatcher years. Indeed, some historians argue that Thatcherism increased class conflict by increasing inequality. On this account the more unequal a society, the less harmony. Equality gives people a stake in society, and therefore a reason to be loyal. Inequality, by contrast, leads to the emergence of an **underclass** who have no property and a very limited income. In this position they have no reason to feel part of society, or to respect its laws or customs. Indeed, one explanation for growing Scottish and Welsh nationalism was the fact that while the southeast prospered under Thatcher, Scotland and Wales did not. Therefore, Scottish and Welsh voters increasingly voted for nationalist parties, as they felt that the Conservative government no longer represented them or their aspirations. Thatcher rejected arguments of this kind, arguing that citizens had a moral duty to obey the law regardless of their economic circumstances.

One key example of a policy that created class conflict was the sale of council houses (see page 189). This policy opened up a gap within the working class between those that could afford to buy and those who could not. Moreover, it left the poorest people with very limited choice about where to live. The right to buy effectively took the right to rent decent affordable housing away from the poorest in society.

The miners' strike

Thatcher's battle with the miners is a useful case study for assessing the extent to which she created political and social division within Britain. Her conflict with the NUM was one of the most divisive conflicts of a troubled period. Even some Conservatives thought that Thatcher went too far in her battle with the union. Peregrine Worsthorne, editor of the *Sunday Telegraph* and sympathiser with Conservative **wets** (see page 216) acknowledged that the war with the miners was something new: 'Old-fashioned Tories say there isn't any class war. New Tories make no bones about it: we are class warriors and we expect to be victorious.'

The conflict with the miners had deep roots, going back at least as far as the fall of the Heath government.

Long-term causes

Margaret Thatcher was elected with a mandate to reform the unions, but it was not until her second term that she felt able to confront the NUM. The miners' union was one of the most powerful in the country. Indeed, it had brought down the Conservative government in 1974 (see page 51). In that sense, Thatcher's battle with the NUM had historic roots: she wanted to succeed where Heath had failed and show the miners that the elected government, rather than the unions, ran Britain.

The 1978–79 'winter of discontent' (see page 52) turned public opinion against the trade union movement. Therefore, Thatcher felt she had public backing in adopting a tough anti-union position.

In 1978 Nicholas Ridley, one of Thatcher's closest supporters, prepared a strategy for dealing with the NUM, arguing that the following measures needed to be put into place:

- a law against secondary action
- the development of alternative sources of power, such as gas or nuclear energy, so that the country was not overly reliant on coal
- the development and reserve of coal stocks so the country could not be held to ransom.

Short-term causes

In the short term, conflict with the NUM was triggered by Thatcher's determination to reform British mining and union rights. The coal industry was nationalised in 1946 by Clement Attlee's Labour government. As a result, the government controlled the British Coal Corporation.

Thatcher appointed a Canadian businessman, Ian MacGregor, as head of the National Coal Board, in order to reform the industry. Thatcher was determined to reduce the state subsidies to the mining industry – she believed that taxpayers' money had no place propping up unprofitable pits. The reduction of the subsidy meant that pits would close; this would be devastating to mining towns in south Wales, Scotland and the north of England where the majority of adult men were employed in the industry.

Thatcher was also aware that she would have to deal with Arthur Scargill, who was elected president of the NUM in 1981. Scargill, a well-known left-winger, had masterminded the defeat of Heath's government in 1974. Like Thatcher, Scargill was determined to fight and win any battle over the future of British coal.

Initially, MacGregor announced a plan to cut subsidies to the British Coal Corporation and therefore close twenty pits. Scargill claimed that MacGregor was concealing the real scale of government plans; that he really intended to close 70 pits – the vast majority of Britain's mines. Cabinet papers released 30 years later have confirmed Scargill's claim. Scargill responded to the threat of pit closures by announcing a strike.

The ballot

Prior to the confrontation with the NUM, Thatcher's government had introduced a series of laws that took away some of the traditional rights of the union movement (see pages 185–6). Significantly, the 1984 Trade Union Act required that all unions conduct a secret ballot of their members prior to announcing a strike, and the strike had to be approved by the majority of members.

Scargill suspected that he might lose the ballot because some miners in pits that were not closing needed to go to work to earn a living. Consequently, he chose not to hold a ballot. The lack of a vote undermined Scargill's claim that the strike was legitimate and it would eventually prove to be a fatal weakness in his strategy.

The strike

The strike began in May 1984. Scargill quickly organised **pickets** from pits on strike to protest at pits that had stayed open. Another mining union, the National Association of Colliery Overmen, Deputies and Shotfirers (NACODS), chose not to strike and as a result there was immense anger and resentment towards their members who went to work.

As the strike was illegal the government was able to confiscate some NUM funds. The government also employed MI5 officers to infiltrate the NUM to find out its strategy and therefore stay one step ahead of the miners.

Tens of thousands of police officers from all over Britain were sent to Yorkshire and to other major coal-producing areas to police the strikes, but in some instances their presence provoked confrontation with mining communities. The police were equipped with horses, riot shields and truncheons. Some miners argued that the police were an **army of occupation**. Throughout the summer of 1984 there were several violent clashes with the police, such as the one in Orgreave, near Rotherham.

The Battle of Orgreave

The Battle of Orgreave refers to a conflict between police and miners that took place in Orgreave, South Yorkshire on 18 July 1984. Around 5,000 miners and 5,000 police clashed when the steel plant was picketed by the NUM. The police led horseback charges against the miners, who responded by throwing bricks and stones at the police. Over 100 miners and police were injured and dozens of miners were arrested. The incident shocked the country and the following day Margaret Thatcher used the violence as an opportunity to present the miners as an undemocratic mob:

I must tell you ... that what we have got is an attempt to substitute the rule of the mob for the rule of law, and it must not succeed. It must not succeed. There are those who are using violence and intimidation to impose their will on others who do not want it. The rule of law must prevail over the rule of the mob.

Public opinion and the strike

The strike polarised public opinion. Radical groups supported the miners:

- Black radicals in the Race Today Collective (see page 125) organised support for the striking miners. Members of the Collective, led by Leila Hassan, met with the wives of miners to express their solidarity with the strike.
- Women Against Pit Closures (WAPC) organised a series of rallies in London in support of the miners' strike. WAPC was formed by Arthur Scargill's wife, Anne Scargill, and fostered collaboration between miners' wives and feminist groups such as the Spare Rib Collective (see page 114). WAPC also organised soup kitchens for striking miners.
- Lesbians and Gays Support the Miners, founded by Mark Ashton and Mike Jackson, organised marches and fundraising in support of the striking miners.

The Labour Party was split by the issue of the strike. The right wing of the party believed that union power was out of hand and therefore that Thatcher's new union laws were justified. Moreover, they refused to support Scargill's illegal strike. The Labour left supported the strike, arguing that Scargill was defending jobs across an entire industry. Labour leader Neil Kinnock tried to compromise, but was unable to come up with a position to unite the party.

Most of Britain's tabloid and broadsheet press opposed the strike, were critical of Scargill and claimed that the miners were attempting to bully the country. Opinion polls showed that the majority of the British public disapproved of Scargill's methods. Moreover, there was a surge of support for the government during the strike, indicating that Thatcher's action was broadly popular.

The end of the strike

Scargill had hoped that the strike would starve the British economy of coal and therefore bring industry to a standstill. However Ridley's strategy of stockpiling coal before the strike, relying more on gas and nuclear power and importing coal meant that the economy kept running. Crucially, power stations continued to function so there were no power cuts. The NUM began to run low on funds and mining communities experienced extreme hardship as striking miners were unable to provide for their families.

Scargill's failure to call a national ballot weakened support for the strike among miners in some regions. In Lancashire and north Wales, miners were far less interested in industrial action than in south Wales or Yorkshire. A new union, the Union of Democratic Mineworkers (UDMW), was founded in December 1984. UDMW went back to work in early 1985, demonstrating the divisions that existed within the movement.

During late 1984 and early 1985 some strikers returned to work and in March 1985 the NUM voted to call off the strike, defeating Scargill who argued that the union should fight on.

The impact of the strike

The strike was a turning point in British industrial relations. Trade union militancy that had been a feature of the 1970s was decisively defeated. Moreover, the government had shown it was committed to enforcing its new union laws. Therefore, practices such as calling strikes without a secret ballot and **secondary picketing** died out. The NUM, once one of the most powerful unions in Britain, was also hit hard. Between 1985 and 1990 it lost 84 per cent of its members.

Thatcher's success against the miners allowed the government to continue to attack union rights. Laws introduced in 1988, 1989, 1990 and 1993 further reduced the rights of unions. In 1988 union members were given legal protection for crossing picket lines, and in 1993 John Major's government introduced a law forcing unions to conduct strike ballots by post, as well as forcing unions to submit their voting process to independent scrutiny. The reduction in union power went hand in hand with a reduction in union membership. Between 1979 and 1997 union membership declined by almost 40 per cent.

Public support for Thatcher's anti-union policy also led to changes in the Labour Party. From 1985 Labour leaders took steps to distance the party from the unions. The decisive break happened in 1993, when Labour leader John Smith rejected the union block vote (see page 222).

The defeat of the strike also allowed the government to reduce the size of the mining industry. Between 1985 and 1990, 94 pits out of a total of 170 were closed.

The strike was extremely significant in terms of political and social division because it demonstrated that the government was prepared to deal with opposition in an uncompromising manner. Between 1951 and 1964 Conservative governments had been prepared to work with big unions, such as the NUM, in order to preserve political and social unity. Thatcher, by contrast, chose outright confrontation. What is more, she was rewarded for her hardline approach by public support and heightened authority within her party and her government. Thatcher's support during the strike demonstrated the appeal of what historian Stuart Hall described as Thatcher's 'authoritarian populism'. Hall argues that Thatcher's willingness to use government power to break the power of the unions showed that a significant proportion of the working class supported her emphasis on self-reliance and individualism.

Historical interpretation: Thatcher and the NUM

Historians have disagreed about Thatcher's approach to the NUM and the miners' strike. Richard Viven in Extract 1 argues that Thatcher sought to crush the miners. In this sense he implies that she increased social and political tensions for her own political purposes. However, David Howell in Extract 2 argues that Thatcher was prepared to behave more cautiously and that her victory over the NUM was not a central part of her policy.

Extract 1 From Richard Viven, *Thatcher's Britain: The Politics and Social Upheaval of the Thatcher Years*, 2009.

On 5 March 1985 Britain's miners, or at least those who remained loyal to their union, returned to work, a year after they had gone on strike. No one was fooled. The miners had been crushed. They had gone on strike to prevent pit closures. After a year of grinding poverty, they had got nothing. The NUM had lost members and money: legal action had rendered it technically bankrupt. The miners were divided. About half of them were working by the time the NUM gave up the fight. The membership of the NUM, which stood at almost a quarter of a million during the strike, had dropped to fewer than 100,000 by the end of 1987.

The very fact that parts of the Left had invested such symbolic significance in the miners meant that their defeat was all the more resonant. Ever since Thatcher's election as leader of the Conservative Party, her supporters had feared that union resistance might destroy her economic policies. This fear was laid to rest in 1985. Norman Tebbit wrote that Thatcher had broken 'not just the strike but a spell'.

Extract 2 From David Howell, *Defiant Dominoes: Working Miners and the 1984–5 Strike*, 2012.

Privatisation and the fragmentation of the union accorded with Thatcherite ambitions but the route by which they came about did not follow a preconceived agenda. Probably no one in government expected a year-long strike in March 1984. The strategy of incremental closure without serious confrontation was working effectively. NUM branches had responded with verbal opposition to specific closure proposals followed by acquiescence. In this context the response of the majority of NUM members to strike was remarkable for its solidarity and longevity. It cannot be reduced to the imposed priorities of Scargill and his supporters. The motivations of the strikers were complex: loyalty to union and community; a desire to protect a way of life in an increasingly insecure world; an appeal to some sense of moral economy against the destructiveness of the market.

For the government, there were several acceptable outcomes. An early end to the dispute would have meant a return to the strategy of incremental closures faced by a chastened union. In the event, it obtained a much more thorough victory.

Having read Extracts 1 and 2:
1. Summarise the argument of Extract 2 in one sentence.
2. Write a paragraph arguing either for or against the argument in Extract 2. Use your own knowledge and Extract 1 to justify your claim.
3. Swap paragraphs with a partner. Now write a counter-argument to your partner's argument.
4. Having read the arguments and counter-arguments, discuss how far you agree with Extract 2.

2 Thatcher's 'colonialism'

Colonialism usually refers to a form of government in which an imperial power (such as the British Empire) rules over people who have become part of that empire. Colonial rule tended to be exploitative and resulted in white colonial masters having greater power and privilege than black or Asian colonial subjects. From the 1960s radicals used colonialism to explore new kinds of relationships between ethnic minorities and the government of Britain, arguing that the British police acted like a colonial army in places such as Brixton, Notting Hill or Southall which had large black or Asian communities. Republicans in Northern Ireland also saw British forces as operating a colonial policy in Northern Ireland.

Thatcher deliberately used nationalist language. She spoke of the importance of 'Anglo-Saxon heritage' and 'the remarkable qualities of the British people'. Thatcher's commitment to 'the survival of our way of life' led to her concern about the social and political divisions she believed were caused by immigration.

> **Note it down**
>
> This section requires three different kinds of note-taking:
> - First, make a timeline of the important events in order to ensure you have a secure chronology of the period.
> - Second, draw a spider diagram of the ways in which Thatcher's policies toward black and Asian people and the IRA either increased or decreased division in the period 1979–97.
> - Third, note down key words and their definitions – you might want to use index cards for this purpose.

The black rights movement

Between 1918 and 1979 millions of people from across the world made Britain their home. During that time a variety of groups emerged to fight for the rights of black and Asian people who faced discrimination from racist police, landlords or employers (see page 119). During the 1980s a series of important battles were fought to establish the rights of black and Asian people. The rise in black and Asian protest reflected a number of factors:

- Continued racist discrimination, particularly in housing, employment, education, and institutions such as the police.
- Thatcher's stress on the importance of cultural uniformity, and her emphasis on the need for black and Asian people to assimilate: to adopt 'British values' and 'British customs'.

> **The Race Today Collective**
>
> The Race Today Collective was one of the most effective groups fighting for black rights during the 1980s. The Collective had been founded in Brixton in 1973. It published a monthly magazine *Race Today*, and helped local groups organise campaigns to advance the rights of black and Asian people. One of the leading members of the collective was Darcus Howe (see page 125) who, along with the radical journalist and historian Tariq Ali, created the Channel 4 current affairs series *The Bandung File*, which focussed on issues relating to black and Asian people. It ran for six years (1985–91). The media success of Howe and Ali is indicative of a cultural shift that took place in the 1980s. It indicates that there was a growing willingness, at least in the media, to ensure that the concerns of black and Asian people were addressed. In this sense it was a recognition of the right of black and Asian people to participate fully and as equals in British society.

- The impact of Thatcher's economic policies, which disadvantaged black and Asian people to a far greater extent than white people, as they affected sectors of the economy in which black and Asian people tended to work.
- Thatcher's willingness to support police initiatives that targeted young black people.

The New Cross fire

The New Cross fire was one of the early sources of tension between the government and the black community. On 18 January 1981 a fire swept through a house in New Cross Road, in an area of southeast London. A party attended by black teenagers was in progress, and thirteen partygoers were killed. The local black community believed the fire had been a racist arson attack by the **National Front**. As a result the fire quickly became known as the 'New Cross massacre'. Within a week a public meeting attended by 1,000 local members of the black community led to the establishment of a New Cross Massacre Action Committee.

Thatcher's government issued no statement in response to the New Cross fire. This was in stark contrast to events which were to take place a few weeks later in Ireland, where the deaths of white teenagers partying in Dublin led to official letters of support from the Queen, the British parliament and the British government. What is more, the parents of the victims believed that the local police had mishandled the investigation. The police had apparently made no attempt to follow up reports of witnesses of arson.

The Black People's Day of Action

In response to the lack of government action and the inadequate police investigation, the New Cross Massacre Action Committee, led by Darcus Howe, organised the Black People's Day of Action. On 2 March 1981, 20,000 people from across the country marched through London to demand justice for the dead. The Day of Action is the largest black protest held in Britain to date. It forced the government to acknowledge what had happened. Moreover, historian Paul Gilroy argues that the march represented 'a symbolic defeat' for the police as they were unable to prevent the march from taking place and it alerted the media to the inadequacies of their investigation. In this sense the Black People's Day of Action exposed ongoing social divisions, highlighting the indifference of the police and the government to racism.

Stop and search

Relations between the police and black communities in London had been problematic for many years. Darcus Howe accused the police of acting like a colonial army of occupation in Noting Hill and Brixton. Police used 'stop and search' powers extensively against young black people throughout the 1970s and 1980s (see page 186).

Immediately following the Black People's Day of Action, the Metropolitan Police introduced Operation Swamp '81, a mass stop-and-search campaign aimed at black people in London. Black MPs such as Bernie Grant and academics such as Paul Gilroy believe that the operation was designed to reassert police authority after their 'symbolic defeat' on the Black People's Day of Action. Swamp '81, however, led to mass riots in which the police lost control of Brixton.

The 1981 riots

After two weeks of Operation Swamp '81 rioting broke out in response to rumours that a black teenager, Michael Bailey, had died in police custody. Around 300 black and white youths clashed with over 1,000 police officers. By the end of the riot 299 officers were injured, and 70 members of the public were also hurt. Over 100 cars had been destroyed and 28 shops and homes had been burnt to the ground with over 100 more looted. Three months later more riots broke out in some of Britain's most deprived inner-city areas, all with high ethnic minority populations: Moss Side in Manchester, Southall in London, Handsworth in Birmingham, Toxteth in Liverpool, and Hyson Green in Nottingham. There were also disturbances, though not full-blown riots, in Wolverhampton, Southampton, Leeds, Leicester, Halifax, Bedford, Gloucester, Coventry, Bristol and Edinburgh. In nearly all cases, racial tension and alleged police discrimination were causes of the disturbances.

The Scarman Report

The Day of Action and the riots forced the government to re-examine the role of the police in the black community. As a result the government commissioned the Scarman Inquiry. Lord Scarman's inquiry found:

- clear evidence of disproportionate and unnecessary use of stop and search against young black and ethnic minority men
- that 'complex political, social and economic factors' such as poverty, unemployment, poor housing and discrimination were key factors in causing the riots.

Scarman recognised the significance of social division in Britain, and urged the government to do more to address inequality.

Ongoing social division

Thatcher rejected the idea that poverty and discrimination were a cause of rioting, stating that, 'nothing, but nothing, justifies what happened'. Scarman's proposals were not implemented and there was little improvement in urban areas in general or in conditions for urban black communities throughout the rest of the 1980s. Rioting broke out again in 1985 on the Broadwater Farm housing estate in north London following the death, in two separate incidents, of two black women Cynthia Jarrett and Cherry Groce. Cherry Groce was shot by armed police during a raid and Cynthia Jarrett died of a heart attack during a police raid on her home.

Changing attitudes

The Thatcher and Major years were a time of changing attitudes. British society became increasingly multicultural, and black and Asian people became better represented in British society. During the 1980s there was a significant increase in the number of black and Asian MPs. In 1987 Diane Abbott, Bernie Grant, Paul Boateng and Keith Vaz became MPs. Black and Asian people were also becoming better represented in journalism and the media. Channel 4, created in 1982, had a specific responsibility to provide television programmes for minority groups. Farrukh Dhondy, editor for multi-cultural programming at Channel 4, commissioned television programmes from leading black and Asian writers and journalists, such as the current affairs programme *The Bandung File* and the situation comedy *Desmond's*, which stared a predominantly black cast. Acid house (see page 220) saw black musicians and DJs from across the country leading a new cultural movement. Black writers and journalists Dotun Adebayo and Steven Pope set up X-Press and had a publishing hit with the novel *Cop Killer*. In terms of high art, the Nigerian-born author Ben Okri won the 1991 Booker Prize for his novel *The*

Famished Road, and British politicians, particularly from the Liberal Democrats, rallied to support the British Indian novelist Salman Rushdie when he was placed under a *fatwa* for his 1988 novel *The Satanic Verses*.

The response to the murder of Stephen Lawrence in April 1993 is an indication of the extent to which social attitudes had changed. Lawrence, a young black man from southeast London, was stabbed to death in Eltham, a London suburb. Whereas the New Cross fire led to no immediate reaction from the government or the mainstream media, the government and the media immediately condemned Lawrence's murder. Moreover, when the police mishandled the investigation it led to the Macpherson Report, which officially stated that the Metropolitan Police was 'institutionally racist'. Lawrence's murder demonstrates that social divisions, including racism, still existed in British society and the British police twelve years after the New Cross fire. However, the response to his death shows that John Major's government was much more willing to address racism than the Thatcher government had been – indicating the change of attitudes that had taken place between 1979 and 1997.

Historical interpretation: Thatcher and immigration

Historians have different approaches to Thatcher and the issue of immigration. In Extract 3, Bunce and Field point to Thatcher's willingness to use anti-immigrant rhetoric and its impact on social and political division. Schofield in Extract 4, by contrast, emphasises the way in which Thatcher was prepared to include immigrants in British society, as long as they were prepared to adopt 'British values'.

Extract 3 From Robin Bunce and Paul Field, *Darcus Howe: A Political Biography*, 2014.

The early 1980s were a turning point in British politics. The post-war consensus, which had been under strain for some time, finally gave way to political polarisation and the politics of confrontation. The Tories had overtaken Callaghan's government in the polls soon after Thatcher's 1978 interview for Granada TV's World in Action. The interview tackled the subject of immigration head on. Speaking to Gordon Burns, Thatcher made a point of seeking to address the purported grievances of those driven to voting National Front. Thatcher said she understood 'that people are really rather afraid that this country might be swamped with a different culture' and declared that she would not allow 'false accusations of racial prejudice' to stop her from tackling the 'problem' of immigration. Clearly, the politics of race played a significant role in Thatcher's victory.

Those on the Tory Right with a track record of opposition to immigration were emboldened by this climate. On 2 January 1981, right-wing Conservative MP Jill Knight was reported as calling for 'noisy' West Indian parties to be banned … A veteran member of the Far Right Monday Club, which advocated voluntary repatriation of immigrants and defence of white minority rule in South Africa and Rhodesia, Knight appeared to suggest that local whites would be entitled to take direct action to stop such parties.

Extract 4 From Camilla Schofield, 'A Nation or No Nation?' Enoch Powell and Thatcherism, 2012.

The message on a Conservative political campaign poster of 1983 is yet another strategic approach to nationality within Thatcherism. It certainly breaks with a Powellite vision of the nation. The poster, which came in two varieties, presents a photograph of a black man or an Asian man in a suit, with the line: 'Labour says he's Black, Tories say he's British.' For Powell, race in Britain in the 1970s and 1980s produced an insurmountable identity politics. As a solution, this poster promises to wash away history and identity. The poster provoked resentment, because 'it misunderstood the wish of many to retain their own identity, to be both British and black'. But the poster also nicely reflects on what it means to be British within Thatcherism. Britishness is expressed in their shared suit. The man, as Paul Gilroy has noted, looks ready for a job interview: 'isolated and shorn of the mugger's key icons – a tea-cosy hat and the dreadlocks of Rastafari – he is redeemed by his suit, the signifier of British civilisation'.

Having read the two extracts, write a paragraph by following these steps:
1. Identify the main differences between Extract 3 and 4.
2. Explain why Extract 3 and 4 appear to be arguing different things.
3. Evaluate the extent of the difference between the two extracts – are there any important similarities between the two?
4. Working in pairs, swap and read each other's paragraphs. Discuss which most clearly identifies and explains the difference. Which paragraph contains the most effective evaluation?

Thatcher and Northern Ireland

The Thatcher government inherited an ongoing conflict in Northern Ireland. One of the Conservatives' key manifesto pledges was to restore law and order and to defeat the **Irish Republican Army (IRA)**. Thatcher's attitude to the IRA was uncompromising, like her attitude to the unions. She believed that there could be no negotiation with the IRA or their supporters, and that the only way of dealing with the IRA was the deployment of force.

Thatcher's attitude to Northern Ireland was part of her broader view of social and political division. Rather than seeing social and political division as the product of complex situations or competing demands, she saw them in terms of right and wrong. As she saw Northern Ireland in terms of a moral battle, she was unwilling to compromise, rather she saw it as her role to provide uncompromising moral leadership regardless of the consequences.

The death of Bobby Sands and the Brighton bombing were two of the most divisive episodes in the troubles of the 1980s.

Bobby Sands

Bobby Sands's death in 1981 showed just how far Thatcher was prepared to take her refusal to compromise with the IRA. Bobby Sands, one of Britain's highest profile IRA prisoners, had been sentenced to fourteen years in prison in 1976 for his part in the IRA bombing of Dunmurry. Sands returned to the headlines in 1981 when he led a protest in prison against the repeal of the 'special category status' that prisoners convicted of terrorist offences had been granted by the Conservative Home Secretary William Whitelaw in 1972. Sands and other IRA members went on hunger strike in 1981, demanding the return of the following privileges:

- the right not to wear a prison uniform
- the right not to do prison work
- the right of free association with other prisoners, and to organise educational and recreational pursuits
- the right to one visit, one letter and one parcel per week.

IRA members believed that they were political prisoners, not ordinary criminals, but Thatcher and her government refused to recognise them as such. The hunger strike resulted in lots of negative publicity for the British government. Senior figures in parliament, such as leader of the Labour Party Michael Foot, urged Thatcher to compromise with Sands in order to save his life.

Moreover, Sands was able to embarrass the government further by standing as a member of parliament in the **by-election** for the seat of Fermanagh and South Tyrone, narrowly winning the seat. Sands died on 5 May 1981 as a result of his hunger strike, less than a month after being elected as an MP. Following his death another nine IRA prisoners died on hunger strike and Britain was widely condemned internationally, as the popular perception of the hunger strikers' deaths in Europe, America and much of Asia was that the Thatcher government had 'let' the strikers die.

The Brighton hotel bombing

Three years later, on 12 October 1984, the IRA detonated a large bomb inside the Grand Hotel at Brighton. Their target was Margaret Thatcher and her cabinet and their motivation was revenge for the death of Bobby Sands. Several Conservative MPs, party members and their wives were killed by the bomb, but Thatcher and her cabinet survived.

For Thatcher the bombing was yet further evidence that she was engaged in a struggle between democracy and terrorism. The bomb strengthened her resolve to continue fighting without compromise. Indeed, the Conservative Party conference continued the next day in spite of the bomb as a symbol of her refusal to surrender.

Miscarriages of justice

In the mid-1970s the IRA carried out a bombing campaign on the mainland of Britain. Among the many attacks perpetrated by the terrorist group were the detonation of bombs in crowded pubs in Guildford and Birmingham in 1975. In the immediate aftermath of the attacks, a public desire for retribution and pressure from the Home Office for speedy arrests led to the wrongful arrest of innocent Irish men and women living in England. Three groups of wrongly convicted friends and family members, the Guildford Four, the Birmingham Six and the Maguire Seven spent between fourteen and sixteen years in prison.

Throughout the 1980s several campaign groups in Britain, Ireland and America demanded that the convictions be overturned; the TV programme *World in Action* cast doubt on the Birmingham Six convictions in 1985. By 1988 Home Secretary Douglas Hurd referred the case of the Birmingham Six to the Court of Appeal, which ruled the convictions to be sound, but three years later it decided against this ruling, accepting that the accused men had been beaten and coerced into signing statements and that evidence had been suppressed. When the Guildford Four and the Maguire Seven were freed after their convictions were found to be 'unsafe', the presiding judge Lord Lane concluded of the police who investigated the bombings in 1975 that: 'The officers must have lied.'

3 Thatcher and sexuality

Thatcher's government wanted to promote family values. By this it meant the promotion of heterosexual monogamous marriage. As part of this family values agenda, Thatcher passed laws to stop the 'promotion' of homosexuality in schools. These policies were part of a wider concern about the emergence of a 'permissive society' which was leading to 'moral decline'. Thatcher's concern with 'liberal' sexual attitudes was that they were part of a wider breakdown in self-discipline.

Thatcher's attitude to sexuality was complex. She worked closely with gay colleagues and did not want to recriminalise homosexuality. Nonetheless, she did not want homosexuality promoted for fear it would lead to an 'erosion' of moral standards which would lead to 'moral anarchy' in which British citizens lost, once and for all, their ability to tell right from wrong.

Thatcher's attitude led to political divisions. LGBT activists argued that homosexuality did not reflect 'moral decline'. Moreover, they argued that the government should not use its power to stigmatise homosexuality.

Note it down

This section requires three different kinds of note-taking:
1. First, make a timeline of the important events in order to ensure you have a secure chronology of the period.
2. Second, draw a spider diagram of the ways in which Thatcher's policies toward the LGBT community either increased or decreased division in the period 1979-97.
3. Third, note down key words and their definitions – you might want to use index cards for this purpose.

HIV and AIDS

In 1981, doctors diagnosed the first case of the disease **HIV** in Britain and over the next decade the illness became associated with gay men. Initially there were high incidences of HIV and AIDS in the gay community but by the 1990s more heterosexual people were being diagnosed. Widespread public ignorance about the disease resulted in an increase in anti-gay attitudes; in 1987 three-quarters of people surveyed on their attitudes towards homosexuality believed that it was 'always or mostly wrong'.

AIDS was one area where the Thatcher government was prepared to compromise. Rather than suggesting sexual abstinence, the government threw its weight behind a safe sex campaign, promoting the use of condoms. The campaign was promoted in schools and in the media, and indicates that the government was prepared to act pragmatically.

Section 28

During the early 1980s press campaigns demanded that children should not be exposed to material about homosexuality. As a result the government passed two controversial laws effectively banning discussion of homosexuality in schools:

- Section 46 of the 1986 Education Act specified that sex education should promote 'the value of family life'.
- Section 28, also known as Clause 28, of the 1988 Local government Act outlawed the promotion of homosexuality or the publication of 'material with the intention of promoting homosexuality'. It went further than the 1986 Act by outlawing any educational activity designed to 'promote the teaching in any maintained school of the acceptability of homosexuality as a pretended family relationship'.

These laws were, in part, a response to right-wing press campaigns against books such as *Jenny lives with Eric and Martin*. The book was used to help young children understand and adapt to living with same-sex parents but was described by the *Daily Mail* as 'homosexual propaganda'. Conservative MPs believed that left-wing councils were actively promoting homosexual lifestyles to children, but there is no evidence that this was ever the case.

The passing of the Local government Act and Section 28 led to several protests by gay and lesbian groups, including the 'invasion' of the BBC Six O'Clock News studios. It also led to the gay community in Britain becoming more politicised. Famous actors like Ian McKellen and activists like Peter Tatchell and Michael Cashman, formed the gay rights group Stonewall in 1989. It campaigned for the repeal of Section 28, the recognition of violence against gay, lesbian, bisexual and transgender people as hate crimes, and the repeal of the ban on homosexuality in the armed forces.

LGBT rights campaigners argued that Thatcher's promotion of 'family values' was divisive. Rather than recognising that people choose different ways to live, Thatcher used government power to promote one vision of family life and to discourage discussion of alternatives. In so doing, they argued, she created division.

Historical interpretation: Thatcher and morality

Historians have disagreed about Thatcher's relationship to morality. In Extract 5, for example, Kevin Hickson argues that Thatcher did little in terms of moral issues. Matthew Grimley agrees that Thatcher passed few laws that challenged moral permissiveness. Nonetheless, quoting Stuart Hall, he argues that Thatcher's government used distinctly anti-permissive language and that Thatcher presented her government as the answer to a moral crisis.

> **Extract 5** From Kevin Hickson, *The Political Thought of the Conservative Party since 1945*, 2005.
>
> Having defeated the traditional left on the battleground of economics, Conservatives continue to face an array of opponents, such as feminists and gay rights activists, fiercely challenging them in the moral arena.
>
> It is hard to identify what Conservatives concretely achieved in the 1980s in 'remoralising' society. Perhaps the clearest example of Conservatives' 'success' was the incorporation of Section 28 into the 1988 Local government Act, which forbade local authorities promoting homosexuality. Yet such measures have to be viewed in context. For instance, despite their belief in the importance of upholding the value of the family in sex education, the Conservatives' most significant campaign around sex became the promotion of 'safe sex' over fears around AIDS. This was much to the displeasure of moral campaigners outside the Conservative Party, as well as many within, who saw this as a morally neutral message against 'unsafe' sex, when to them the real problem with AIDS was sex outside of marriage in general and gay sex in particular.
>
> As Martin Durham has shown in detail, the Conservative Party under Thatcher kept its distance from external moral campaigning organisations, such as anti-abortion and anti-obscenity groups, many of whom were disappointed to find their favourite social causes not taken up by the government.

> **Extract 6**: From Matthew Grimley, *Thatcherism, Morality and Religion*, 2012.
>
> The moral and religious dimensions of Thatcherism have been overlooked in existing accounts, which have tended to concentrate on what Thatcherism *achieved*, in terms of concrete policy, rather than on what it *represented*.
>
> Of course, it is true that economics were central to Thatcherite policy. It is also true that, as Prime Minister, Margaret Thatcher did little to legislate on morality and the family. The permissive reforms of the 1960s were left intact, and the only Conservative attempts at legislating on morality were Section 28 of the 1988 Local government Act, which banned the promotion of homosexuality in schools, and the clauses of the 1988 Education Reform Act that stipulated the teaching of Christianity in schools (both of which were the result of backbench Lords amendments). But the fact that Thatcher did not legislate to reverse permissiveness does not mean that anti-permissiveness was an unimportant part of her ideology. My argument is that there was more to Thatcherism than the laws it enacted. In order to explore its appeal, we need to look at language as well as legislation – at the words Margaret Thatcher and her associates used.
>
> Some contemporary commentators on Thatcherism did emphasise its moral dimensions. Stuart Hall argued that it was important to explore 'the moral discourses of Thatcherism … They are the site for the mobilisation of social identities and, by appropriating them, Thatcherism has put down deep roots in the traditional, conventional social culture of English society.' Hall also noted the sense of crisis that was so central to Thatcherism, a crisis 'experienced at the popular level in the universal language of popular morality'.

Having read the extracts:
1. Summarise the key arguments of Extract 5 and Extract 6.
2. Select three details from your own knowledge that supports the argument of Extract 5. Write these down as a list under your summaries.
3. Working in pairs, swap your summaries and discuss the lists.
    - Which summary best captured the argument of Extract 5?
    - Which summary best captured the argument of Extract 6?
    - Which details most precisely supported the argument of Extract 5?

Changes in the media

In spite of Thatcher's education laws and campaigns in the right-wing press, there were some significant changes in the way that lesbian women and gay men were presented on television.

In 1985 director Stephen Frears made the film *My Beautiful Laundrette* starring Daniel Day Lewis. One of the main storylines in the film featured a love affair between two gay men and while the film had a modest budget and featured then relatively unknown actors, it was nominated for both the Oscars and BAFTAs. In 1989 the soap opera *EastEnders* screened the first ever gay kiss on British television; *the Sun* newspaper referred to it as 'a homosexual love scene between yuppie poofs … when millions of children were watching'. In the same year the drama *Oranges Are Not the Only Fruit* was broadcast on the BBC, adapted from the semi-autobiographical novel by Jeanette Winterson. It was a lesbian coming-of-age story that presented homosexuality in a positive, sympathetic light and satirised repressive religious attitudes towards gay and lesbian people.

Pop music was also an important way in which LGBT issues came into the mainstream. Boy George and Marilyn, two famous male gay singers, were famed for their androgynous appearance. The electropop duo the Pet Shop Boys' single 'It's a Sin' challenged perceptions about the wrongness of gay desire. Other openly gay bands included Bronski Beat, who became famous for the song 'Small Town Boy' on their album *Age of Consent*. Significantly, these artists appealed to gay and straight young people.

Positive representations of lesbian women and gay men continued into the Major years. The 1992 film *Peter's Friends* was a comedy which centred on a gay man telling his friends that he is HIV-positive. Similarly the hugely popular *Four Weddings and a Funeral* (1994) challenged existing morality by making the point that gay couples could never celebrate their love through marriage. Madonna was also part of this trend, styling herself as 'the world's favorite bisexual' as part of the promotion of her 1992 Girlie Show Tour. Major's government was much less willing to pass laws that discriminated against lesbian women or gay men. Indeed, in 1994 Major made an important symbolic gesture by inviting the actor and gay rights campaigner Ian McKellen to Downing Street. Major was also forced to publicly acknowledge that his 'Back to Basics' campaign (see page 220) was not an attack on homosexuality. Additionally, his government lowered the age of consent between gay men from 21 to 18. Although this did not create complete equality it was recognised as a significant step in the direction of gay rights.

4 Thatcher and feminism

The Thatcher years also saw political divides between conservatives and feminists. In 1978 Thatcher set out her thinking on feminism, stating 'the feminists have become far too strident and have done damage to the cause of women by making us out to be something we are not'. For Thatcher women's rights meant individual equality of opportunity which would allow talented women to earn money, gain promotions and make a difference. Thatcher had little interest in discussion of women's roles, assuming that the nuclear family was no obstacle to the ambition of talented women.

> **Note it down**
>
> This section requires three different kinds of note-taking:
> - First, make a timeline of the important events in order to ensure you have a secure chronology of the period.
> - Second, draw a spider diagram of the ways in which Thatcher's policies toward women either increased or decreased division in the period 1979–97.
> - Third, note down key words and their definitions – you might want to use index cards for this purpose.

Campaigns in the 1980s

During the 1980s, the radicalism of the Women's Liberation Movement of the previous decade (see page 113) led to the development of new organisations and movements. Many campaigned for the rights of the most marginalised women in society. One of the most important figures in the struggle for pay equality for women during the 1980s was the American-born activist Selma James. She became a spokesperson for the English Collective of Prostitutes, an organisation representing sex workers in England. It demanded:

- the de-criminalisation of prostitution
- financial alternatives to prostitution to prevent sex work being the result of poverty
- recognition of the profession
- safety for sex workers.

James was also part of the International Wages for Housework campaign. The campaign had begun in the early 1970s and attracted supporters on the radical left of the women's movement in the 1980s. James and other activists argued that housework was not a choice for most women and was as hard and unfulfilling as most kinds of manual labour that were paid. Women were entitled to be paid for their work as their unpaid efforts actually subsidised **patriarchal society**.

Other feminists pointed to profound problems with Thatcherism. The feminist filmmaker Sally Potter made a series of films including *Thriller* (1979), which dealt with the way in which Thatcherism undermined the traditional role of women. For Potter, Thatcher praised traditionally male-dominated professions such as the finance industry and stigmatised the 'caring professions' which had traditionally, been the work of women. Potter argued that Thatcher treated 'women's work' as part of the problem with modern women. By blaming welfare services for creating a dependency culture, Potter argues, Thatcher was implicitly blaming women for Britain's post-war decline.

> ### The anti-pornography movement
> During the 1980s the Women's Liberation Movement associated the widespread circulation of pornographic images of women in tabloid newspapers and men's magazines with domestic violence and rape. Feminist anti-pornography campaigners argued that pictures of topless women in tabloid newspapers emphasised the submissive role of women and the dominance of men. This, in turn, resulted in violence and was 'propaganda' for male subjugation of women. Labour MP Clare Short campaigned unsuccessfully in the 1980s for a ban on the *Sun*'s page three, which featured topless women every day.

Greenham Common Women's Peace Camp

The Greenham Common Women's Peace Camp was one of the major feminist protests of the 1980s. The campaign was designed to stop US cruise missiles being stationed at the RAF Greenham Common Air Base.

The camp organisers decided to make the peaceful protest women only, partly because they believed that femininity was synonymous with peace and motherhood, but also because they hoped that it would become an arena of politics that was not dominated by men. The protesters held vigils involving tens of thousands of women who surrounded the air base in a human chain. Others engaged in acts of civil disobedience such as cutting through the fences and entering the base. The tabloid and much of the broadsheet press was hostile to the protesters, presenting them as naive idealists and implying that they had abandoned their families and their roles in the home.

Thatcher spoke out against the Greenham Common Women's Peace Camp, declaring that the Greenham Common women should be 'eradicated'. The right-wing press, too, described the Greenham Common protesters as 'mad', 'abnormal' and 'criminal'. The press also implied that the women were unfeminine by stressing the dirt, smell and squalor of the camp. Police evicted most of the protestors in 1984, but a small number stayed until 1987 when the missiles were removed as part of a disarmament deal with the Soviet Union.

Women's rights under Major

John Major's 'Back to Basics' campaign (see page 220) was linked to attempts to blame women, particularly lone parents, for social problems. However, Major's government did pass some significant laws that recognised the rights of women. For example, it criminalised rape within marriage.

Conclusion

For Thatcher, diversity was a threat to social harmony. She believed that new cultures, different lifestyles and different values would lead to social disintegration. However, her own policies, which were designed to promote some values and to undermine others, often caused social and political division. While Thatcher's economic ideas succeeded in replacing Keynesianism and corporatism her moral ideas were less persuasive. By the mid-1990s racism and traditional stigmas surrounding homosexuality were in retreat and there was a new consensus in favour of the equality laws that were passed by Tony Blair's government.

Extended reading: The extent of political and social division within Britain

During the 1980s British society appeared to be more polarised and conflicted than at any other time since the Great Depression. Dr Eliza Filby discusses the extent of these divisions and Thatcher's role in creating them.

When in 1988 Margaret Thatcher uttered her now infamous comment that 'there is no such thing as society' she had handed a gift to her critics. 'There was no such thing as society because Margaret Thatcher had destroyed it' came the reply. But those opposed to Thatcher were perhaps guilty of exaggerating the level of social and political harmony that existed in Britain before 1979. The years commonly known as the post-war consensus (1945–79) were fraught with tension particularly from the late 1960s as the economy began to dip, inflation started to rise and the unions began to flex their power. The 1970s was a decade of intense upheaval and uncertainty with an IMF bailout, the implementation of a three-day week and the Winter of Discontent. Moreover, although Margaret Thatcher would be criticised for giving rise to a culture of individualism, in fact the seeds of this impulse dated back much further to the 1960s when greater affluence and personal freedom triggered a breaking down of old class and gender barriers and associational culture. Deindustrialisation – that is the decline of Britain's Victorian industries and the shrinking of its associated workforce – was one of the most monumental economic changes of the twentieth century. But it had been a long time coming (its origins dated back to the interwar period, if not further) and was therefore a situation that Thatcher may have hastened but certainly did not cause. Not everything can be blamed on one woman or one administration.

When the Conservative government abandoned the post-war commitment to full employment and support for industry, it inevitably led to a steep hike in those on the dole and claiming benefits: one of the main reasons why public expenditure actually increased in the 1980s. The situation of three million people unemployed was one that the government had neither anticipated nor planned and yet it did very little to rectify both in the short or long term. The victims of deindustrialisation were allowed to languish on benefits while the old industrial heartlands became ghost towns. Although the employment figures would improve in the late 1980s, they would never again reach post-war levels. Successive governments would mask the numbers by fiddling the statistics, chiefly by shifting the long-term unemployed onto incapacity benefit as Britain became a nation of dual-wage earners on the one hand and households reliant on benefits on the other. In 1993, those on incapacity benefit stood at three million, exactly the same number that had been on the dole a decade earlier.

Class conflict in Thatcher's Britain reached an intensity not seen since the interwar period. The unionised working class were positioned as a threat to social stability and welfare claimants seen as a drain on the nation's resources as both were cast in direct opposition to middle class interests and prosperity. With the Thatcher government incentivising the middle class to 'opt out' of public services be it through private healthcare, pensions, education or housing, this had the effect of transforming public attitudes towards the welfare state. Gone was the post-war ideal of a universalised system as a right of citizenship as the Thatcher government promoted an alternative concept of a basic safety net on which the poor should not become dependent.

Arguably, the most damaging political divisions of the 1980s were within the left rather than the right. During this decade successive Labour leaders had to contend with the formation

Activity

Having read the essay, answer the following questions.

Comprehension

1. What does Filby mean by the following phrases:
   - 'class conflict'
   - 'popular capitalism'
   - 'universalised system as a right of citizenship'?

Evidence

2. Make a list of the examples of how British society divided during the 1980s based on Filby's essay.

Interpretation

3. Identify the passage in which Filby explains why, in her view, British society was at its most divided during the 1980s.
4. Summarise Filby's interpretation in 25 words or less.

Evaluation

5. Using your own knowledge, write a paragraph explaining how far you agree with Filby's view of British society during the 1980s.

of the Social Democratic Party, splits within the labour movement during the 1984–5 Miners' Strike and managing the conflicting interests of metropolitan socialists in the south (pushing the causes of 1960s identity politics chiefly race, gender and sexual equality) and the traditional industrial class politics of the north. The party's 1983 election manifesto, dubbed the 'longest suicide note in history' by one Labour MP if anything, revealed that it was Labour rather than the Conservatives, who had moved furthest away from the post-war consensus. The SDP-Liberal Alliance positioned itself as the centrist option – the middle way between collectivism and the market – which, if the polls are to be believed, was where most of the British people stood. And yet squabbles within its leadership and its lack of a grassroots structure meant that it never seriously challenged the two main political parties and at election time only had the effect of splitting the anti-Conservative vote. Above all, the 1980s were an ideological age with dogma rather than compromise typifying political culture and debate.

In 1987, the Telegraph journalist T E Utley wrote that there was no such thing as a Welsh, Irish or a Scottish Conservative reflecting the fact that the party's MPs were practically all now located in English constituencies. The Conservatives – once the party of the Union – became in effect a party of South-East England. Great Britain in the late 1990s was a much more divided country than it had been in 1979. The south boomed aided by the deregulation of the City, the growth in the service economy and rising property prices while the north and the Celtic fringe felt the full effects of deindustrialisation. Thatcherism too destroyed one of the key unifying components of the United Kingdom: the unions.

With British working class solidarity eroded so Welsh and the Scots turned to nationalism as the answer. Scottish nationalism, after its setbacks in the 1970s, was once more in the ascendance capitalizing on popular resentment fuelled by high unemployment, the early introduction of the poll tax in Scotland and the southward direction of most of the profits of North Sea oil. Scottish identity positioned itself in direct opposition to Thatcherite individualism as Scots became convinced that only self-governance would save them from this foreign creed.

By the late 1980s the economic debate hinged not on whether Thatcherism was economically credible but whether it was morally just. Thatcher's 'popular capitalism' had not resulted in opportunity for all but an ever-widening gap between rich and poor and a materialist society increasing based on personal consumption and debt. One of the leading critics of the Thatcher's economic revolution was the Church of England who in an extensive report published in 1985 entitled *Faith in the City* revealed the level of poverty and disenfranchisement that existed in Britain. In its scathing assessment, the established Church judged Thatcherism as an unchristian dogma, which had transformed Britain into a 'have and have-not society' and had destroyed the collective ethos, which had guided it since the Second World War. Margaret Thatcher had bulldozed her way through Britain's New Jerusalem in the name of liberty but in doing so, left behind a more individualistic and fragmented society, the ramifications of which are still being felt today.

Dr Eliza Filby, King's College London, author of *God and Mrs Thatcher: The Battle for Britain's Soul* (London: Biteback, 2015).

Work together

Having completed the activity, swap your notes with a partner. Consider:

1 Did you both spot the same evidence in Filby's essay?
2 Has your partner missed anything?
3 Did you agree which passage contained the interpretation? If not, who was right?
4 What was good about your partner's summary of Filby's interpretation?
5 Can you learn anything about Filby's interpretation from your partner's summary?
6 How far did you both agree with Filby's interpretation?

Use these questions to feed back to each other and improve your analysis of the historiography.

Essay technique: Integrating own knowledge

Section C of the exam requires you to evaluate the interpretations offered by the two extracts. You will need to consider the interpretations in the light of your own knowledge of the debate. Therefore, once you have identified the interpretations (see page 182), and worked out the structure of your essay (see page 196), you will need to integrate your own knowledge into your essay.

Imagine you are answering the following question:

> **In the light of differing interpretations, how convincing do you find the view that some of Thatcher's policies were the 'cause of more social division than any other post-war policy' (Extract 1).**
>
> **To explain your answer, analyse and evaluate the material in both extracts, using your own knowledge of the issues.**

You should integrate your own knowledge to support and challenge different aspects of the extract. You can plan this quickly in the exam by annotating the extract; you could use different coloured pens to indicate support and challenge.

As you go through the extract consider the strengths and weaknesses of the interpretation. It is a good idea to make a brief note of your overall judgement at the bottom of the extract.

An example has been done for Extract 1.

Challenge: Beckett acknowledges that Britain was already a divided nation in 1979. Union militancy in 1974 and 1978–79 is a clear indication of social division prior to Thatcher.

Support: Thatcher's policies increased inequality and therefore increased tension and division.

Support: Brixton and Toxteth, 1981.

> **Extract 1** From Clare Beckett, *Thatcher*, 2006.
>
> In 1979, Britain was tired of strikes and hardship, three-day weeks and collective bargaining. Thatcher swept into power without having yet explained or demonstrated her brand of individualistic conservatism. She willingly took personal stands that connected her to the process of change. And the changes caused great hardship among some sections of British society. Her record shows that she did listen and change her policies. The sale of council houses has arguably been the cause of more social division than any other post-war policy. But she said that she wouldn't turn, she said her way was the best way and the only way. So she became absolutely linked with her 11 years of government, years that had seen riots, pitched battles with strikers, record numbers of bankruptcies and war.

Support: Beckett argues that Thatcher took personal stands, rather than seek consensus. She alienated some people in minority communities.

Support: Right to buy divides the working class and takes away right to rent.

Support: The Battle of Orgreave, 1984.

Challenge: The Falklands War created a moment of national unity.

Activity

Using the question on page 214 complete the following activity:

1 Read both extracts and analyse them by looking for:
- the main arguments
- counter-arguments
- evidence
- contrasting arguments between the extracts
- aspects of the extracts that support each other.

2 Make notes on Extract 2 to show how you can support or challenge different aspects of the extract using your own knowledge.

3 Make a brief note of your overall judgement on Extract 2.

4 Make a full essay plan, showing how you will structure your essay, and where you will use the different aspects of both extracts and where you will bring in your own knowledge.

TIP: Own knowledge should be used to support or challenge the interpretations contained in the extracts; it should not dominate the essay.

Extract 2 From Eric Evans, *Thatcher and Thatcherism*, 2004.

A number of riots took place in the inner-city areas of London, Liverpool, Manchester and Bristol. The rarity of such events in twentieth-century Britain was another factor that both alarmed the Tory Party and affronted public opinion, which was more inclined to blame hopelessness and despair born of government policy than it was the intrinsic lawlessness and violence of working-class British youth. Thatcher herself saw matters differently. 'Here' she recalled in her memoirs, 'was the long awaited evidence [for our opponents to argue] that our economic policy was causing social breakdown and violence'. All of this, however, 'rather overlooked the fact that riots, football hooliganism and crime generally had been on the increase since the 1960s, most of the time under the very economic policies that our critics were urging us to adopt'. When she visited the riot area of Toxteth in Liverpool in July 1981, she noted that its housing conditions were not the worst in the city. 'Young people … had plenty of constructive things to do if they wanted. Indeed, I asked myself how people could live in such surroundings without trying to clear up the mess and improve their surroundings. What was clearly lacking was a sense of pride and personal responsibility.'

Work together

Having completed the activity, consider the following questions with a partner:

1 Did you both identify the same arguments and counter-arguments in the extract?

2 Did you agree about which aspect of Extract 2 was the biggest contrast to the main argument of Extract 1?

3 How did your partner's use of own knowledge differ from your own?
- Did they use it to support the same things?
- Did they use it to challenge the same things?
- Did you miss anything that you should note down?
- What can you learn from your partner's approach?

4 Whose use of own knowledge:
- better analysed the interpretations contained in the extracts?
- better integrated own knowledge with the extracts?

Use these questions to feed back to each other and improve your essay planning.

Activity: AS-style question

Historians have different views about the impact on Britain of Thatcher's governments in the years 1979–97. Analyse and evaluate the extracts and use your knowledge of the issues to explain your answer to the following question.

How far do you agree with the view that people in Britain became more socially divided as a result of Thatcher's policies?

4 The effect of Thatcherism on politics and party development

Overview

By the end of the 1980s Thatcherism had profoundly changed the Conservative Party. Increasingly, Tory MPs embraced Thatcher's commitment to the free market, turning their back on the more consensual policies of Heath and Macmillan. Thatcherism also transformed the Labour and Liberal parties. Starting under Neil Kinnock and reaching its full expression under Tony Blair, the Labour Party rejected its traditional commitments to nationalisation, Keynesianism and a growing public sector. Blair rejected the legacies of Harold Wilson and James Callaghan – branding them 'Old Labour'. Blair's 'New Labour' embraced the free market and became 'intensely relaxed about people getting filthy rich'.

Thatcherism became the basis of a new consensus which accepted that:
- business was superior to the public sector
- low inflation was more important than full employment
- the free market was superior to Keynesianism
- the state should fund welfare but work with the private sector to provide public services.

In short, British politics moved to the right during the 1980s and stayed there in the 1990s and beyond.

This chapter examines:
1. Thatcher and the Conservative Party
2. Thatcherism and Labour
3. Thatcher, the SDP and the Liberals.

1 Thatcher and the Conservative Party

Thatcher's downfall in 1989 did not end the Conservative Party's commitment to Thatcherism. Indeed, from 1979 to 1989 she transformed her party.

Note it down

Thatcher's policies, ideas and style had an effect on all the major political parties. Using the 1:2 method (see page x), make notes on the impact of Thatcherism on the Conservative Party, Labour Party and Liberals. Skim the section before you begin to get an overview of the different topics.

Decline of the 'wets'

When Thatcher came to power in 1979 her cabinet was dominated by 'wets', men who had been appointed by Edward Heath. Many of these politicians, such as Jim Prior, Lord Hailsham and William Whitelaw, were committed to the post-war consensus. Thatcher had referred to Conservative politicians who wanted compromise with 'socialism' as traitors in 1978, but she was unable, the following year, to completely exclude moderates from the cabinet.

Moderate MPs like Prior were chiefly interested in preventing economic policies from causing social breakdown. From this point of view he thought that monetarism (see page 37) would be disastrous for Britain because it would lead to rising inequalities, and therefore increased social tension. Many of these '**One Nation Conservatives**' shared a similar upper-class background, having attended elite public schools, served as officers in the army and worked in the City of London. They saw themselves as a part of the natural aristocracy who had a duty to ensure that the poor were provided for.

Thatcherism marginalised the wets in two senses. First, on the whole, traditional 'One Nation Conservative' values were rejected in favour of a commitment to the free market. Second, the influence of upper-class **patricians** declined and, during the 1990s, the party was increasingly dominated by people who were not born rich, but had made their own money.

Wets in government

Thatcher believed that upper-class moderate 'wets' were complacent and weak. From 1979, she excluded 'wets' from key areas of economic policy, promoting Thatcherite 'drys' to important economic posts. Prior was a notable exception. Thatcher initially made him employment secretary. However, he was moved in a cabinet reshuffle in 1981 and was made secretary of state for Northern Ireland, typically seen as 'dumping ground' for ministers who were out of favour. Prior had publicly expressed doubts about monetarism and had a good relationship with several trade union leaders. His demotion was a clear sign that Thatcher was unwilling to change the direction of her policies.

The 1981 reshuffle was described by the press as the 'purging of the wets' with other key moderates sacked:

- Sir Ian Gilmour (Lord Privy Seal)
- Lord Soames (Lord President of the Council)
- Mark Carlisle (Secretary of State for Education and Science).

At the same time, Thatcherites, such as Norman Tebbit, one of Thatcher's keenest and most outspoken supporters, were promoted to important posts.

Rise of the Thatcherites

Following the 1981 reshuffle Thatcherites were increasingly dominant in cabinet. However, it would take two further election victories for Thatcher to win over the majority of the Conservative Party to her ideas. She claimed in 1981 that she was the rebel leader of an establishment party, meaning that she viewed herself as a radical in a party of moderates. By the end of the 1980s her ideas were dominant in the Conservative Party and older consensus ideas were in a minority. This indicates that Margaret Thatcher had a powerful effect on the party and changed it permanently.

Thatcher and Heseltine

One of the 'wets' who survived Thatcher's 1981 reshuffle was Michael Heseltine. He was the secretary of state for the Environment and promoted council house sales in the Housing Act of 1980 (see page 189). He challenged Thatcher in cabinet about the scale of unemployment during the early 1980s and believed that efforts should be made to intervene in the economy in order to relieve the impact in the worst-affected areas.

After the 1981 riots (see page 205) he developed strategies for dealing with unemployment such as **Enterprise Zones** and **Development Corporations** in unemployment black spots. To some extent, these policies resembled traditional corporatism rather than the free-market thinking that Thatcher wanted to promote.

Policy disagreements and Thatcher's dominant personal style alienated Heseltine. Thatcher was sometimes accused of having a **presidential style** of governing. Indeed, she prided herself on being better informed than most of her ministers on key policy areas and often arrived at cabinet with her mind made up on key issues. Heseltine believed that this style was unhealthy; that the cabinet should play an important role in the creation of government policy.

The Westland Affair

Conflict between Thatcher and Heseltine came to a head in 1985 and 1986 in a dispute over the sale of Westland Helicopters. Thatcher and Heseltine disagreed over the future of the company, which was an important British defence manufacturer, leading to Heseltine's resignation.

Heseltine's resignation was largely the result of Thatcher's own 'presidential style'. In most cases she was able to get her own way, but Heseltine, who was ambitious and determined, was unwilling to allow her to stifle the discussion about Westland.

The Westland Affair

In the mid-1980s Westland Helicopters was experiencing serious financial difficulties. Thatcher was opposed to government intervention to save the company and looked to the free market to provide the solution. In November 1985 the US helicopter manufacturer Sikorsky made an offer to buy Westland Helicopters. Heseltine, who was secretary of defence, opposed the bid, believing that it would lead to British dependence on US firms for an increasing proportion of defence equipment. Therefore, Heseltine backed a European consortium which offered to buy Westland Helicopters. Thatcher believed that it was not the role of the state to decide which deal was best, and that Westland's managers should make the decision. In effect, this meant that Sikorsky would buy the company.

Thatcher tried to limit cabinet discussion of Westland, but, in January, Heseltine leaked a letter to *The Times* showing that Westland would lose orders across Europe due to the Sikorsky deal. In response Leon Brittan leaked a second letter, rubbishing Heseltine's claims.

In the end Sikorsky, the US company, bought Westland. Heseltine resigned in outrage and Brittan was sacked for leaking government documents.

Thatcher's fall

Thatcher's fall in 1990 did not mark the end of Thatcherism. Rejecting Thatcher's leadership and the poll tax allowed the Conservatives to keep governing and to push forward with other Thatcherite policies.

The poll tax

By 1990 many Conservatives recognised that Thatcher was unpopular and unlikely to win another election. The party's popularity had declined from its high point in 1987, partly due to Thatcher's introduction of the poll tax (see page 192), her most controversial policy.

The poll tax led to widespread anger and large-scale protests. The All Britain Anti-Poll Tax Federation organised a mass demonstration in Trafalgar Square in March 1990 attended by 200,000 protesters. Despite the heavy police presence the protests turned into a riot.

The poll tax also led to increased tax bills. As the bills increased, taxpayers, who were previously inclined to obey the law, refused to pay, presenting the government with a growing crisis. The policy created extremely bad publicity, as newspapers covered stories of pensioners who could not afford the charge and were jailed. South Yorkshire Police conceded in 1990 that it would be impossible to arrest the tens of thousands of non-payers, demonstrating that the tax was close to being unenforceable.

Thatcher refused to compromise in spite of the problems with the policy. Her uncompromising style, which had been a major asset in the early part of her premiership, led to a growing feeling in the Conservative Party that the only way to ditch the poll tax was to remove Thatcher.

Growing unpopularity

Thatcher's problems mounted during 1990. By November the poll tax was one of many reasons that British citizens were turning against Thatcher's government. The Conservatives were unpopular due to:

- high interest rates (15 per cent), which were draining income from middle-class homeowners
- the recent water privatisation (see page 219)
- party divisions over the amount of powers that were being given to the European Economic Community (forerunner to the European Union)
- Geoffrey Howe's resignation: Thatcher's former chancellor and then her deputy prime minister resigned in protest over Thatcher's anti-European policies.

Thatcher and Europe

Thatcher's attitude to Europe was complex. On the one hand, she was wholeheartedly committed to opening up the free market across Europe. On the other hand, she resented interference from Europe. She feared that European law would force Britain to accept the kind of 'socialist' policies that she had worked hard to roll back.

A further complication was the issue of the single currency. Thatcherites were split on this issue. Some argued that a single currency would help trade and in that sense enable the free market to work more efficiently across Europe. Others argued that keeping the pound protected British independence.

Splits on how far Britain should seek to integrate with Europe were a major problem for the Conservative Party from the late 1980s.

Leadership challenge

In late 1990 Thatcher was extremely unpopular and therefore increasingly vulnerable. Michael Heseltine seized the opportunity and challenged her for the leadership of the party. After the first round of voting Thatcher realised that she had lost the support of her ministers and withdrew.

Significantly, the rejection of Thatcher did not imply a rejection of Thatcherism. The victory of John Major indicated that the Conservative Party wanted to continue with similar policies. Major was the only one of the three contenders not to be associated with the 'wet' faction of the party, and he was the least pro-European. In that sense the party chose the most Thatcherite of the candidates.

The Conservatives under Major

John Major's government continued the mix of free-market policies and policies designed to promote a strong state. However, his government also rethought crucial aspects of Thatcherism, most obviously the poll tax.

Rethinking the poll tax

After taking office as prime minister, John Major moved quickly to deal with the poll tax. In the short term he increased the government's grant to local authorities in order to reduce the 1990–91 poll tax bills by 50 per cent.

At the same time, he appointed Michael Heseltine to design a replacement for the poll tax. Heseltine's council tax re-established the link between local taxation and property value. However, unlike rates, the new council tax had exemptions so that people living alone would pay less than people living in households with multiple wage earners.

The new tax was relatively uncontroversial and much less unpopular than the poll tax that it replaced. However, it abandoned Thatcher's principle that taxpayers should share the burden of government spending in order to make local government accountable.

Privatisation and the public sector

John Major continued Thatcher's policy of privatisation. He completed privatisations that had been initiated by Thatcher, selling off the bulk of the state's electricity companies in 1991, and the remainder in 1995. British Rail was privatised in 1992.

Thatcher created a new consensus that the state had no role in running telecom businesses, car plants, mines, airways or steel mills. The public were less willing to support the privatisation of the railways, water, gas and electricity. In part, there was a feeling that these 'natural monopolies' should stay in state hands, in order to ensure fairness. There were also major problems with the privatisation of these companies. For example:

- Water bills shot up by 40 per cent in the first five years after privatisation.
- Chief executives in privatised water and gas companies received multi-million pound bonuses, in spite of rising bills and neglect of issues such as fixing burst water pipes.
- Privatised utilities, particularly those owned by Railtrack, were often sold at way below the market value, therefore taxpayers did not get the value they deserved from the sales.
- The government continued to subsidise private companies such as the train operators.

Privatisation led to a permanent rolling back of public sector ownership, and a new consensus against nationalisation. However, in some cases, it did not lead to a rolling back of state spending as later privatisations were accompanied by long-term government subsidies.

Economic policy

Broadly, Major's economic policy continued along Thatcherite lines. Major's main economic priorities were growth and low inflation. He used free-market mechanisms rather than returning to Keynesianism or corporatism. Indeed, the National Economic Development Council, which had been the centrepiece of government corporatism in the 1960s and 1970s, was finally abolished by John Major in 1992.

The public sector and welfare

The Major government's welfare policies grew out of the policies that Thatcher had begun in her third term.

The NHS

Major continued to emphasise the Conservative Party's commitment to universal state-provided healthcare. His government implemented the National Health Service and Community Care Act, which Thatcher had introduced in 1990. In essence the Act established an **internal market** in the NHS, in order to ensure that market forces made the NHS more efficient and more responsive to patient (or in Thatcherite terminology 'customer') demand.

PFI

Major's key public sector initiative was the Private Finance Initiative (PFI). Introduced in 1992, this initiative built on the principle established in the 1980s that the state should fund, but not provide public services. PFI established a system whereby private companies would build, manage and maintain schools and hospitals in return for payment from the government. Government contracts were extremely lucrative, and therefore competition to win PFI deals was fierce. Major argued that the private sector was more efficient than the public sector and therefore **outsourcing** the provision of public services to private companies would benefit taxpayers and the people who used public services.

Law and order

Thatcher's law and order policies proved to be influential. Under John Major policing got even tougher and traditional rights were removed.

Concern about acid house and 'rave culture' led to the introduction of the Criminal Justice and Public Order Act (1994). The new law gave the police the power to target 'raves'. The new Act partially removed the traditional right to remain silent after arrest, and criminalised squatting and unauthorised camping.

Finally, the prison population continued to rise under Major (see page 188).

> ### Acid house and rave culture
>
> Acid house is a musical style that emerged in the mid to late 1980s and led to the creation of a new dance culture. The music, which was made with drum machines, samples and synthesisers, was popularised by independent record labels and independent record shops in London and other major cities such as Manchester. A Guy Called Gerald's single 'Voodo Ray' (1988) and KLF's 'What Time is Love?' (1988) were early examples of the new sound.
>
> Acid house also led to the emergence of pirate radio stations, such as Centreforce and Fantasy FM, and to the emergence of super-star DJs and nightclubs such as Heaven and the Wag in London which played the new music. By 1989 acid house was associated with drugs such as LSD (acid), speed and Ecstasy. The period 1988–89 saw the emergence of large-scale 'allnighters' or 'weekenders', which became known as raves (see page 219).
>
> Even before the passage of the Criminal Justice and Public Order Act the police targeted raves. This was reflected in the title of Shut Up and Dance's 1990 acid house album, *Dance before the Police Come*.

Social conservatism

Broadly speaking, Thatcher's social conservatism continued under Major, at least until the failure of his 'Back to Basics' campaign. Major's campaign was an attempt to emphasise what he saw as traditional British values. He defined them as 'self-discipline and respect for the law, to consideration for others, to accepting a responsibility for yourself and your family and not shuffling off on other people and the state'.

The speech was given at the end of 1993 in the context of a larger debate about single mothers. Earlier in the year John Redwood, a right-winger and secretary of state for Wales, had spoken out against 'young women [who] have babies with no apparent intention of even trying marriage or a stable relationship'. Consequently, John Major's remarks were interpreted as a defence of monogamous heterosexual marriage and other so-called 'family values'.

The campaign failed due to a series of Conservative scandals that indicated that Conservative MPs were not as committed to traditional 'family values' as Major's speech implied they should be:

- Conservative minister Tim Yeo's affair and 'love child' were exposed in 1993.
- Steve Norris's five affairs were exposed, earning him the nickname Steve 'Shagger' Norris.
- Further sexual affairs were exposed from 1994 to 1997. The most publicised was Conservative MP Stephen Milligan's involvement in bondage, following his death from **autoerotic asphyxiation**. Additionally, Conservative MP Jerry Hayes was '**outed**' as gay and his relationship with a young man who was below the age of consent was exposed in the press.
- Tory MPs and ministers were also implicated in various financial scandals, including the 'cash for questions' scandal, in which MPs were paid to ask questions in parliament.

Together, the sexual affairs and financial scandals became known as sleaze. Satirist and comedian Armando Iannucci heightened the government's embarrassment by following Conservative ministers, including John Major, around with a man dressed as an eight-foot erect penis, inviting them to 'slap down the Tory sleaze cock'.

Style

Thatcherism was not only a set of ideological positions and a series of policies, it was also a style of governing. Major's style of governing was radically different to that of Thatcher. Whereas Thatcher was accused of being domineering and 'presidential' in style, Major was a much more consensual leader. He tended to try to work with the different wings of his party and seek compromises.

Major summed up his more consensual style by stating he wanted to create 'a country that was at ease with itself'. To some extent this was a recognition that the Thatcher years had been full of conflict and that he wanted British politics to be less divided in order to let the country heal.

The problems of Thatcherism

Major's government was also different to Thatcher's because it faced different problems. Thatcher claimed that Britain's problems had been created by socialism, which had ruined both the economy and the moral character of the nation by creating a dependency culture.

Major's government could no longer blame Britain's problems on the Labour government of the 1970s, or powerful unions. Rather, Major was forced to deal with the problems created by Thatcher. Major had to deal with the problems of privatisation, which lead to rising utility bills and rising rail fares. He was forced to deal with the problem of long-term unemployment, and low public-sector pay. He also had to deal with a recession created by a Conservative chancellor. Therefore, Major's message was radically different from that of his predecessor. Thatcher was clear about who the enemy was and the cause of the problems. Major lacked a clear enemy and a plausible scapegoat, and, other than the poll tax, his party would not allow him to acknowledge Thatcher's mistakes.

Historical interpretation: Major and Thatcherism

John Major clearly continued some aspects of Thatcherism while abandoning or changing others. Therefore the extent to which he continued Thatcher's programme is disputed. Extract 1 argues that Major was a Thatcherite, but not a hardcore one. Extract 2, by contrast, argues that British politics itself changed around 1990, and therefore that Thatcherism lost its original meaning. Major's 'Thatcherism' was therefore undermined by Thatcher's success in tackling the 'socialism' of the 1970s.

> **Extract 1** From Tim Bale, *The Conservative Party: From Thatcher to Cameron*, 2010.
>
> The notion that support for John Major in the 1990 leadership election – or for that matter Heseltine – had less to do with policy and philosophy than it did with personality and background is clearly false: ideology mattered in this contest. Major might not have been a Thatcherite zealot, but he was located towards the right of the Party. As one of his colleagues from the right of the spectrum later put it, 'We knew he wasn't a hard-core Thatcherite, but he was the best we had.' John Major became Tory leader and, as a result, Prime Minister. Yet to some of those who had elected him, he would never be more than a man who owed everything to Thatcher and whose election as leader could be seen as a farewell and rather guilty gift from her to her party.

> **Extract 2** From Robert Saunders, *'Crisis? What Crisis?': Thatcherism and the Seventies*, 2012.
>
> By 1990, most of the enemies Thatcher had fought against since the seventies were slain. Trade union power was broken, corporatism was a thing of the past and Labour had commenced its long march away from socialism. With the fall of the Soviet Union, Thatcher stood triumphant over every foe. In consequence, the appeal of Thatcherism began to change. With the waning of the socialist threat, Thatcherism lost some of its moral and strategic purpose.
>
> All this caused considerable difficulties for Thatcher's successor.
>
> Harassed by her personal devotees, John Major was compelled to prove his 'Thatcherite' credentials without any of the targets against which his predecessor had defined her identity. He could not make speeches attacking the Soviet Union, tame the beast of organised labour, or shield the country from the onset of communism. Instead, he was measured against a set of policy tests – on Post Office privatisation, educational reform and anti-Europeanism – that Thatcher herself would not, as Prime Minister, have passed. In this respect, Thatcherism was a creature of the 'long 1970s', a response to crisis politics which abolished the conditions of its own success. In the 1990s, it was 'Thatcherism' and not Britain that was in crisis: with devastating consequences for the party that Thatcher had led.

Having read Extracts 1 and 2:
1 Summarise the key argument of the two extracts.
2 Select three details from your own knowledge which support the argument of Extract 1. Write these down as a list under your summaries.
3 Swap your summaries and lists with a partner and discuss:
   - Which summary best captured the argument of Extract 1?
   - Which summary best captured the argument of Extract 2?
   - Which details most precisely supported the argument of Extract 1?

What impact did Thatcher's governments have on Britain, 1979–97?

2 Thatcherism and Labour

It is possible that the party that Margaret Thatcher changed more than any other was the Labour Party. In 1997 after four successive election defeats, the Labour Party won a landslide victory but with a manifesto that was radically different from the one written by Michael Foot in 1983. However, some aspects of New Labour were at odds with some of Thatcher's basic convictions.

The Labour left in the 1980s

The Labour Party went through a process of transformation in the 1980s. Indeed, by 1997 the party had abandoned many of its traditional policies. Nonetheless, the change was not wholly brought about as a response to Thatcherism. The New Left, the moderate wing of the Labour Party and the legacy of the Social Democratic Party (see page 224) all played a part in the creation of 'New Labour'.

A jump to the left

Following the defeat of Callaghan in the 1979 General Election there were serious divisions between the left and the right of the Labour Party. As a result of the 1980 leadership election, left-winger Michael Foot became leader of the party.

Foot's 1983 election manifesto proposed:

- unilateral nuclear disarmament (getting rid of nuclear weapons before any other country did with the hope that they would follow suit)
- ending privatisation and re-nationalising recently privatised industries
- leaving the European Economic Community
- a massive increase in spending on social welfare.

The radical left-wing manifesto was one reason for what was one of Labour's worst defeats. Labour MP Gerald Kaufman described it as 'the longest suicide note in history'.

A step to the right

As a result of the defeat, the party's new leader Neil Kinnock and his deputy Roy Hattersley began moving the party to the right. In the mid-1980s they initiated a campaign to expel members of Militant Tendency (see page 191) from the party. Their 1989 policy review, *Meet the Challenge, Make the Change*, ditched many of the policies that the party had adopted under Foot in the early 1980s.

The popularity of the early privatisations and council house sales led Kinnock to question the party's commitment to nationalisation. Nonetheless, he remained committed to improving the welfare state and to the Keynesian policy of '**reflation**' in order to increase levels of employment.

Kinnock resigned as leader following the Labour election defeat of 1992. John Smith continued transforming the party, changing the system by which party leaders were elected. Smith introduced the system of one member one vote, ending the trade union '**block vote**'. This reform was, in part, a response to criticisms that the Labour Party was too close to the unions.

Tony Blair and 'New Labour'

Tony Blair became Labour leader following John Smith's unexpected death in 1994. Blair stated that he was committed to the traditional values of the Labour Party, but wanted to achieve them using new policies. Specifically, Blair wanted to end Labour's commitment to nationalisation. Therefore, the Labour Party conference of 1994 reformed Clause IV, the part of the party's constitution that had justified nationalisation.

Mondeo man

Blair's 'modernisation' of the Labour Party was motivated by research into the changing views of voters. Specifically, Blair wanted to attract the support of 'Mondeo man', a typical working-class Conservative voter. Polling research indicated that a large number of working-class people had benefited from Thatcher's policies and that they supported a low-tax, low-inflation economy in which they could own their own home, rather than rent a council house. However, 'Mondeo man' was also concerned about education and the state of Britain's hospitals.

Blair saw an opportunity to win the support of working-class Conservatives by offering better public services, while not threatening to raise taxes or reverse Thatcher's privatisation policies.

> **Mondeo man**
>
> Also known as 'Essex man', 'Mondeo man' was a phrase invented to describe a type of working-class voter. Typically, this type of voter lived on the outskirts of London, had bought their council house and drove, or wanted to drive, a Ford Mondeo – a mid-sized family car produced from the early 1990s. According to research 'Mondeo man' cared more about his status and personal wealth than about equality – this was reflected in the fact that he wanted a car as a status symbol.
>
> In later years, the Conservatives would strike back by targeting 'Holby City woman'.

Historical interpretation: Thatcher and the Labour Party

Historians have disagreed about the extent to which the Labour Party embraced Thatcherism. All of the extracts acknowledge that the Labour Party changed to some extent as a result of Thatcherism. However, Extract 3 disputes the extent to which the Labour Party ever embraced socialism, and Extract 4 considers the ways in which Blair introduced policies that Thatcher would have rejected. Finally, Extract 5 argues that Blair's approach to politics, and his acceptance of some aspects of Thatcherism, actually had something in common with Old Labour leader Harold Wilson.

Extract 3 From Eric J. Evans, *Thatcher and Thatcherism*, 2004.

A decade of Conservative dominance inevitably altered the agenda of the other political parties. One of Thatcher's major objectives was to destroy Socialism. In the short term, at least, she succeeded. Her triumph should, however, be set in the context of Labour politics. The Labour Party is the only significant political organization in Britain which, since its foundation in 1900, has been remotely interested in promoting socialist policies, and for the most part, its leaders have avoided them like the plague. We might, therefore, legitimately wonder whether Thatcher's anti-socialist crusade was against a real, or an imaginary, dragon.

Nevertheless, the Labour Party emerged from the splits and ideological traumas of the early 1980s a distinctively different party. Ironically, a most significant achievement of Thatcher is one she would be horrified to claim. She provoked a major reassessment within the Labour Party, thus helping to make 'New Labour' not only electable but electorally dominant – albeit more than six years after her own political demise.

Extract 4 From Dennis Kavanagh, *The Blair Premiership*, 2008.

The Thatcher influence was seen in Labour's gradual acceptance of so many policies they had once opposed – privatisation, levels of direct taxation, the use of the free market in public services and changes in industrial relations laws. Indeed the consolidation of the reforms led journalist Simon Jenkins to call Blair and Brown 'Sons of Thatcher'.

This is hardly fair. Would Thatcher or Major have brought in devolution and proportional representation for non-Westminster elections, the minimum wage, the social chapter, the redistributive budgets of Gordon Brown*, sought to enter the single currency or repealed Section 28? Although he accepted much of the Thatcher settlement Blair willingly presided over rises in taxation, public spending and public sector employment.

* Labour Chancellor of the Exchequer

Extract 5 From Jeremy Black, *Britain since the Seventies: Politics and Society in the Consumer Age*, 2004.

Prior to the 1990s, Labour had offered little credible or attractive modernization since the election of 1966. Once Major had lost direction and it looked as though he would not be re-elected, attention had shifted to Labour, increasingly seen as a government in waiting and one that was better led and more coherent than the Conservative government. Under Kinnock, Smith and then, from 1994, with more determination and clarity under Blair, Labour moved away from collectivist solutions based on interventionism and state planning, and prepared to embrace aspects of Thatcherism, not least the marketplace and modest rates of taxation.

Blair's theme was 'New Labour', a different Labour Party eager for modernization, although he ignored the extent to which his attitudes had been prefigured by Harold Wilson in the 1960s. Blair appeared to offer a more appealing vision of life in post-Thatcherite Britain, by championing a society in which the dominance of the marketplace was not to be allowed to undermine social cohesion.

1. Having read Extracts 3, 4 and 5, write a paragraph stating how far you agree, or disagree, with Extract 5. Your paragraph should contain:
- a summary of the extract's argument
- evidence that either supports or challenges that argument
- a concluding sentence in which you analyse the extent to which the argument of the extract is valid.
2. Working in pairs, swap your paragraphs, read them and then write two suggestions about how the paragraph could be improved.

A modern image

Blair's close ally and mentor was Peter Mandelson, who had shaped the party's image since the early 1980s and helped to present Labour as modern and appealing to the middle classes. Blair abandoned Kinnock and Smith's plans to raise the top rate of income tax from 40 to 50 per cent, and the perception that Labour were bad economic managers compared to the Conservatives shifted as Britain entered a new recession under John Major in the early 1990s.

Labour and Rupert Murdoch

Moving to the right helped Blair attract the support of media baron Rupert Murdoch, owner of the *Sun*, *News of the World*, *The Times* and *The Sunday Times*. Murdoch's support helped get Blair's message across.

New Labour's politics

Tony Blair argued for a 'third way' between the extreme free market capitalism advocated by Thatcher, and the Old Labour left. Blair's 'third way' included some Thatcherite elements, as well as policies that had other origins. Blair's Thatcherite policies included:

- a commitment to free markets rather than Keynesianism or corporatism
- a rejection of nationalisation
- continued use of PFI and internal markets in the public sector
- continued welfare reform to tackle the 'dependency culture'
- continued emphasis on tackling crime through police action and longer sentences.

However, Blair was also committed to other priorities that Thatcher had never endorsed. He advocated:

- greater protection of civil liberties by incorporating the European **Bill of Rights** into British law
- limiting the state's right to keep secrets through the introduction of a Freedom of Information bill
- constitutional reform through introducing **devolution** to Scotland and Wales
- greater protection of minority rights by introducing legislation to secure women's rights, the rights of black and Asian people, and LGBT rights, including the repeal of Section 28 (see page 208)
- better regulation of the market to ensure consumer rights
- greater spending on health, education and infrastructure
- greater accountability in local government through the creation of directly elected mayors
- better representation for minority groups and women in politics through mechanisms such as all women shortlists for the selection of parliamentary candidates
- the acceptance of greater union rights and workers' rights through the adoption of the European **social chapter**
- the introduction of a **minimum wage**.

In this sense, New Labour reflected a series of different influences. There were undoubted Thatcherite influences in terms of economic policy; however the stress on civil liberties, the rights of minority groups and women, and the commitment to increased spending on public services were not obviously Thatcherite. Indeed, they reflected a response to some of the inequalities created by Thatcherite policies rather than an acceptance of her whole legacy.

New Labour?

The extent to which Blair changed the fundamental nature of the Labour Party is debated by historians. Certainly, between 1980 and 1983 the Labour Party was dominated by a left-wing leadership. However, traditionally, Labour had always been led by moderates. In the post-war period, all of the party's leaders, except Foot, were moderate. Attlee, Gaitskell, Wilson and Callaghan were all moderates. Most came from the right or centre of the party. Wilson was associated with the Labour left in the 1950s, but as Labour leader he adopted consensus polices. Significantly, Callaghan embraced monetarism prior to Thatcher's election. In this sense, Blair's New Labour could be seen as a return to the tradition of moderate politics that had dominated the Labour Party for the vast majority of its history.

3 Thatcher, the SDP and the Liberals

Thatcherism also had an impact on the Liberal Party and the SDP. The Liberal Party had been a major force in British politics until the 1920s, but had been eclipsed by Labour following 1945.

The Social Democratic Party (SDP) were much newer. The SDP emerged in 1981 as right-wing Labour MPs left the Labour Party in protest at the left-wing policies adopted by Foot. The SDP was created by four former Labour cabinet ministers – Roy Jenkins, Shirley Williams, Bill Rodgers and David Owen. Not only did the new party reject the radical extremes of Labour, it also rejected Thatcherism and attracted one Conservative MP who was on the left of the party.

The SDP–Liberal Alliance

The SDP entered into an alliance with the Liberal Party in 1981. Like the SDP, the Liberals were opposed to what they saw as the extreme policies of the two main parties. The Alliance proposed a series of distinctive policies:

- They advocated radical constitutional reform, including the introduction of **proportional representation**, a bill of rights, a written **constitution** and freedom of information legislation.
- They were the most pro-European of the major parties.
- They supported **co-ownership** rather than privatisation or nationalisation.

The SDP–Liberal Alliance gained a 25.4 per cent share of the vote in 1983, but this resulted in only 23 seats. By 1987 the Alliance had failed to make a major electoral breakthrough and their share of the vote began to decline, leaving them with 22 seats. A merger in 1988 created the Social and Liberal Democrats, which by 1997 was known as the Liberal Democrats. The merger, however, was controversial and David Owen refused to join the new party, remaining head of a smaller SDP.

The impact of Thatcherism

The SDP–Liberal Alliance was also affected by Thatcherism. Its 1983 manifesto retained a commitment to corporatism and a **mixed economy**. By 1987 its position had changed – the party was now in favour of privatisation, and corporatism had been dropped with the exception of an '**incomes strategy**'.

The drift to the right was not fast enough for David Owen, leader of the SDP from 1983. Owen advocated a 'social market economy', which accepted the Thatcherite view that the market was the most efficient way of generating and distributing wealth. However, Owen also wanted to protect the state provision of healthcare and education. He wanted to reform the welfare system so that targeted benefits helped the poorest, without creating a dependency culture. By 1988 Owen's similarity to Thatcher was captured in a joke that he was in fact 'Thatcher with Brylcream' – a reference to his use of the hair product.

Nonetheless, the extent to which Owen was influenced by Thatcher is unclear. Owen had been part of the Callaghan Labour government that had introduced monetarism before Thatcher's election. Moreover, Owen was influenced by some European economies which combined the state and the market. In that sense his growing acceptance of the market may not have been a direct result of Thatcher's influence.

The influence of the 'Owenite' SDP

After 1988 Owen's SDP was increasingly seen as a one-man-band. Therefore, members of the party took new directions. Significantly, a number of former members of the SDP became policy advisors to John Major, while others joined New Labour. Former members of the SDP played an important role devising policies that recognised the need for the state to provide certain forms of welfare within a free market. In that sense, they played an important role between 1990 and 1997 moderating Thatcherite policies and developing the policies of New Labour.

The influence of the Liberals

The Liberal Party also had an impact on politics after Thatcher. The Liberals had been consistent advocates of constitutional reform, and their arguments influenced the direction of New Labour. Traditionally the Labour Party had not been in favour of a bill of rights, freedom of information or voting reform. However, New Labour accepted all of these reforms, at least to some degree. Blair's willingness to consider constitutional reform was a debt to the Liberals and groups like **Charter 88** rather than Thatcher.

Conclusion

The impact of Thatcher on British party politics is disputed. Certainly, the major political parties all embraced the market economy before 1997. However, the extent to which this was due to Thatcher's influence is disputed. Right-wing members of the Labour Party embraced monetarism before the election of the Thatcher government and the SDP also played a role in developing free-market policies that influenced the Conservatives under John Major and the Labour Party under Tony Blair.

Crucially, Thatcher was not the only influence on changing party policy in the years 1979–1997. The New Left's emphasis on the rights of minority groups, and the impact of feminist groups, gay campaigners and black and Asian activists in groups like the Race Today Collective, shifted the political consensus towards greater respect for minority rights. Moreover, the Liberal Party and Charter 88 were crucial in building a consensus in favour of constitutional reform.

Extended reading: The effect of Thatcherism on politics and party development

Party politics were radically different in 1997, when New Labour came to power, from when Thatcher started her premiership in 1979. Historian Jon Lawrence examines Thatcher's influence on these changes.

Historians have spent much time arguing about the balance between ideology and pragmatism in Margaret Thatcher's premiership (1979–1990). But this is to set up a false dichotomy: Thatcher was both ideological and pragmatic. She was an ideologue in the sense that she had a set of strongly held beliefs about what constituted the 'good society' and how politics could help to facilitate its realisation. She was pragmatic in the sense that she knew only to fight political (and industrial) battles that she could win. It was only after her third election victory in 1987 that Thatcher lost this strong intuitive feel for politics (notably on relations with the European Union and on the flat-rate, local community charge or 'poll tax'). By then she had begun to believe the myths about her own infallibility and it made her fallible.

But even those who like to play down the importance of ideology and conviction in Thatcher's politics tend to accept that the political world she vacated in 1990 was radically different from the one she had inherited eleven years earlier. In 1979, public sector enterprises accounted for ten per cent of economic activity and many private firms received state subsidies to retain workers. By 1990 not only had more than fifty public companies been sold or privatised, but the idea that the state should own major companies, or subsidise private-sector jobs, had been driven from the political mainstream. Over the same period, the percentage of houses in owner occupation had risen from 55 to 67 per cent as 1.5 million council houses were sold to sitting tenants at heavy discounts. There was also a sixty per cent increase in the numbers of self-employed workers, while the proportion of the workforce in trade unions fell from 57 to 42 per cent. Perhaps most famously, there was a shift from direct to indirect taxation (i.e. from income and profits to spending). The top rate of income tax fell from 83 to 40 pence in the pound and the base rate from 33 to 25, even though overall taxation hardly changed.

It is hard to believe that all these things would still have happened had Margaret Thatcher lost in 1979 (or, more plausibly, in 1978, if James Callaghan had called an election before the 'winter of discontent', as many expected). Thatcher's record-breaking period in office, coupled with her determination to challenge many of the orthodoxies of post-war public policy, helped tilt Britain decisively towards a more individualist, free-market ('neo-liberal') political settlement. Many of Thatcher's most radical policies, such as the privatisation of the public utilities, may have been improvised in office, but they were wholly consistent with her instinctive radical agenda to reduce the role of the state in everyday economic and social life.

Thatcher believed in a strong but limited state. Unusually, she saw no contradiction between economic liberalism and social conservatism. She argued that if the state intervened less in people's lives the strong ties of family would fill the void, in the process containing capitalism's potentially destructive forces of selfish individualism and acquisitiveness. In her infamous remark about 'society' being a meaningless abstraction, she declared: 'who is society? There is no such thing! There are individual men and women and there are families' (1987). For her, free market economics was about the restoration of the

Activity

Having read the essay, answer the following questions.

Comprehension
1. What does Lawrence mean by the following phrases:
   - 'Third Way'
   - 'Her radical populism helped kill off the old, paternalist style in British politics'
   - 'Economics are the method; the object is to change the heart and soul.'

Evidence
2. Make a list of the examples of Thatcher's impact on the party system in Lawrence's essay.

Interpretation
3. Identify the passage in which Lawrence sets out his view on the extent to which Thatcherism changed party politics in Britain.
4. Summarise Lawrence's interpretation in 25 words or less.

Evaluation
5. Using your own knowledge, write a paragraph explaining how far you agree with Lawrence's analysis of the extent Thatcher changed party politics in Britain.

liberal subject; about freeing individuals to take responsibility for themselves and their families. As she put it in 1981, 'Economics are the method; the object is to change the heart and soul'.

It must be doubted whether Thatcher succeeded in changing 'heart and soul' but she certainly changed British politics fundamentally. Her radical populism helped kill off the old, paternalist style in British politics. By 1990 the Conservative party had been remade in her image. It was less elitist, less landed and much more Eurosceptic. As John Major, Thatcher's successor, found to his cost, traditional Conservative loyalty to the party leader now counted for little when ideological principles were at stake. Thatcher's pragmatic side was forgotten, not least by Thatcher herself. Most damagingly, the party became obsessed by issues that were of secondary importance to voters – notably Europe – and in so doing surrendered the terrain of radical populism to its opponents.

Opposition politics were also radically reconfigured. Thatcher's victory in 1979 deepened historic divisions between Left and Right within the Labour Party culminating, in 1981, in the defection of 28 Labour MPs, and significant numbers of activists, to a new break-away Social Democratic Party (SDP). Paradoxically, the shock of this defection from the right of the party helped halt the rise of the Labour Left as the trade unions swung behind the party leadership. Within six months left-winger Tony Benn's bid to become Labour Deputy Leader had been defeated by the opposition of key trade unions. The high-tide of the Labour Left had passed. But this did nothing to restore Labour's electoral fortunes. In 1983, under the leadership of veteran left-winger Michael Foot, the party only narrowly out-polled an alliance of the SDP and Liberal parties, providing Thatcher with a landslide 144 seat victory on a modest 42.4 per cent poll. Labour then began a long process of 'modernisation' which ultimately led to Blair's 'New Labour' project in the mid-1990s. Initially, the party's new leader, Neil Kinnock, focussed on fighting symbolic battles with radical left-wing groups such as the Trotskyist Militant Tendency, but after the party's third defeat in 1987, he authorised a more radical overhaul of party policy.

But Labour lost again in 1992 in a bitter election fought mainly on questions about Labour's tax plans and its economic competency. Even so, Labour elected its shadow chancellor, John Smith, to succeed Kinnock as party leader. A traditional centre-right Labour politician, Smith was a cautious moderniser deeply sceptical about Thatcherite neo-liberal economics. It was only Smith's untimely death two years later that saw the party leadership fall to Tony Blair. As architect, with Gordon Brown, of the 'New Labour' project, Blair drove through a much more complete accommodation with the market, although in doing so he was not simply embracing the Thatcherite legacy. In fact New Labour looked more towards the dynamic liberalised economies of America, Australasia and Asia for its model than to Thatcher's premiership in the 1980s. They sought to emulate the Clinton 'New Democrats' and the Australian Labor party by embracing globalisation and the free market whilst retaining a strong commitment to state-directed social intervention.

It may be doubted whether the British Labour party would ever have embraced its 'Third Way' without Thatcher's radical premiership, but nonetheless it is misleading to see New Labour as simply a continuation of Thatcherism in disguise. Labour's rehabilitation of interventionist social policies such as the minimum wage and tax credits should be enough to dispel this simplistic argument.

Jon Lawrence is a Reader in Modern British History at Cambridge University. He works on nineteenth- and twentieth-century British social, political and cultural history. He has published a number of books on modern British history including *Electing Our Masters: The Hustings in British Politics from Hogarth to Blair* (2009).

Work together

Having completed the activity on page 226, swap your notes with a partner. Consider:

1 Did you both spot the same evidence in Lawrence's essay?
2 Has your partner missed anything?
3 Did you agree on which passage contained the interpretation? If not, who was right?
4 What was good about your partner's summary of Lawrence's interpretation?
5 Can you learn anything about Lawrence's interpretation from your partner's summary?
6 How far did you both agree with Lawrence's interpretation?

Use these questions to feed back to each other and improve your analysis of the historiography.

Essay technique: overall judgement

Reaching a supported overall judgement is an important part of doing well in Section C. The judgement that you should reach in Section C is similar to the judgement that you should reach in the other sections of the exam (see page viii). However, in Section C, your judgement should be based on an evaluation of the interpretations offered by the extracts, as well as reflecting the overall argument of your essay.

Imagine you are answering the following question:

> In the light of differing interpretations, how convincing do you find the view that 'the Thatcher Revolution brought fundamental changes to British political parties' (Extract 1).
>
> To explain your answer, analyse and evaluate the material in both extracts, using your own knowledge of the issues.

Extract 1 From Earl A. Reitan, *The Thatcher Revolution: Margaret Thatcher, John Major, Tony Blair, and the Transformation of Modern Britain*, 2002.

The Thatcher Revolution brought fundamental changes to British political parties, as they responded to a changing electorate. Thatcher rid the Conservative Party of Tory paternalism; Blair rid Labour of socialism and trade union power. Both parties accepted a strong state, the free-market economy, and a large public sector. The two major parties had to appeal to an electorate where former party loyalties had been homogenized into a broad, moderate center. The Liberal Democratic Party was marginalized to a party of local government.

Thatcher pushed personal leadership to its limits, and eventually paid the price. Major and Blair were cautious leaders: Major because his majority was small, and he wanted to stay in office; Blair because his majority was large, and he did not want defections before the next election. Major could not afford to make enemies, and Blair wanted to be everybody's friend.

Extract 2 From E. H. H. Green, *Thatcher*, 2004.

Thatcher called herself a revolutionary and many of her colleagues termed her and their own policies 'radical'. When she stated that she had 'changed everything' she was referring to the Conservative Party, but it is a description that has been applied to her overall impact. The Thatcher era banished Socialism and saw Conservatism redefined.

The overlaps between New Labour and Thatcherism are apparent. Their roots lay primarily in the perceived necessity for Labour of appealing to the interests of certain social groups. The New Labour approach was often given the shorthand 'third way'. For Gordon Brown, and many of the New Labour leadership, it was a rejection of policy polarity that underpinned their readiness to embrace, what Stuart Hall terms a 'hybrid' economic regime. This helps explain New Labour's enthusiasm for Private Finance Initiatives and the language of 'customers' and 'clients' for those who use public services. Certainly, the language of socialism largely disappeared from the mainstream of British politics.

Your essay plan in answer to the question on page 228 might look like this:

Paragraph	
1 Main argument	**Extract 1:** The Thatcher Revolution brought changes to British political parties: • Conservatives abandon paternalism (Extract 2: she 'changed everything') • Labour abandons socialism (Extract 2: 'the language of socialism largely disappeared') • Lib-Dems marginalised
2 Counter-argument 1	**Extract 2:** Stuart Hall: New Labour is a 'hybrid' – therefore not completely changed.
3 Counter-argument 2	**Extract 1:** Thatcher's style of politics does not persist: 'Major and Blair were cautious leaders'.
4 Counter-argument 3	**Extract 2:** Change is brought about by 'the perceived necessity for Labour of appealing to the interests of certain social groups' (**Extract 1:** 'a changing electorate') rather than Thatcherism.

The focus of your judgement

Your judgement should focus on the specific interpretation raised in the question. In this case, you need to focus on how convincing you find the view that 'the Thatcher Revolution brought fundamental changes to British political parties'.

There is little question that British political parties *did* change, but how they changed and how far this was down to the 'Thatcher Revolution' are the key issues.

Judgements that focus on the specific issue raised by the question are likely to do better than judgements that focus on the general issue of politics from 1979 onwards.

Therefore, you could begin your conclusion like this:

Clear focus on the question —— In conclusion, the view that the 'Thatcher Revolution' changed British political parties is broadly valid. However, the change was not fundamental as Thatcher did not change the style of political leadership and it could be argued that Thatcher was not responsible for these changes at all, but rather that there were key social changes going on in the period. —— Clear argument

This is a good beginning as it focusses on the key interpretation, and therefore focusses precisely on the question. However, the judgement is not supported and therefore cannot be awarded marks at the highest levels. An example of an improved overall judgement can be found on page 230.

Supporting your overall judgement

As in Sections A and B it is important to support your overall judgement. This can be achieved by evaluating the given interpretation. Specifically, you should weigh the given interpretation against the other interpretations you have examined in the essay.

For example, the overall judgement you have just read on page 229 could be improved by adding the following evaluation of the different interpretations:

Direct focus on the question.

In conclusion, the view that the 'Thatcher Revolution' changed British political parties is broadly valid. However, the change was not fundamental. As Extract 2 recognises the Labour Party adopted a '"hybrid" economic regime', that is to say partially Thatcherite, but with aspects of traditional Labour policy. There were 'overlaps between New Labour and Thatcherism' (Extract 1). However, New Labour was a 'third way', and therefore not wholly Thatcherite. Indeed, its support for minority rights, greater protection for civil liberties, constitutional reform and the social chapter were opposed to the Thatcherite agenda. Equally, Thatcher did not fundamentally change the style of political leadership. As Extract 1 argues, Major and Blair were both consensus politicians, unlike Thatcher who was a conviction politician. In this sense, Extract 2 is not wholly correct when it argues that she 'changed everything' in the Conservative Party. It could be argued that Thatcher was not responsible for these changes at all, but rather that there were key social changes going on in the period, like the rise of 'Mondeo man'. In this sense, both main parties had to 'respond to a changing electorate' (Extract 1). Ultimately, there were changes to British political parties, but they were not fundamental as Thatcher did not change the style of leadership of the parties, nor much of what Labour stood for. Moreover, these changes may have been the result of the changing electorate rather than the Thatcher revolution.

Main argument supported by Extracts 1 and 2 is also supported with own knowledge.

Qualifies the main arguments with support from Extract 1, countering a claim made in Extract 2.

Counter-argument from Extract 1 and own knowledge.

The final judgement is supported by a summary of the overall argument, and linked back to the question.

This conclusion is an example of high-level work because it reaches an overall judgement supported by evaluating the interpretations offered by the extracts.

Activity

Plan and then write a conclusion for the question on page 231.

Follow these steps to make a plan:
1 Identify the interpretations offered by the two extracts – remember there may be more than two.
2 Look for contrasting arguments between the extracts, and look for aspects of the extracts that support each other.
3 Make notes on the extracts in order to add own knowledge
4 Note down a brief overall judgement.

Follow these steps to write a conclusion:
1 Start by giving a judgement that focusses on the given interpretation.
2 Support your judgement by weighing up the different interpretations contained in the extracts.

TIPS
- Make sure you refer to both extracts in the conclusion.
- Make sure you use some details from your own knowledge to help weigh up the interpretations from the extracts.
- Use the words 'however', 'nonetheless' and 'therefore' to structure the paragraph.

In the light of differing interpretations, how convincing do you find the view that Thatcherism moved Britain's main political parties to the right (Extract 3)?

To explain your answer, analyse and evaluate the material in both extracts, using your own knowledge of the issues.

Extract 3 From David Coates, *Prolonged Labour: The Slow Birth of New Labour Britain*, 2005.

In terms of party programme and potential government policy, 1997 was less of a watershed moment than all the talk of 'newness' implied. For the electoral realignment of that year was genuinely voter-led, not party-dictated. The rise of New Labour to power in 1997 was much more the product of Labour chasing an electorate that was shaped by ideological forces other than that of Labour itself. New Labour won more through the quality of its market research than through the sharpness of its break with previous political orthodoxies. For in truth, the UK electorate in 1997 was less alienated from Thatcherism as a set of political values than it was from the Conservative Party. That should not surprise us, for Margaret Thatcher had left a very deep shadow on the entirety of UK politics, a deep shadow that her personal departure from power had not rubbed away.

Margaret Thatcher had been one of the few genuinely 'hegemonic' UK politicians of the post-war period. She had understood, as few of her predecessors had, the vital role of ideas in political life, and in consequence had effected what Stuart Hall once called 'the great moving right show': draining the standard language of UK politics of its centre-left content and filling it with her own brand of neo-liberal conservatism.

Extract 4 From Wyn Grant, *Economic Policy: From Old to New Labour via Thatcherism*, 2003.

The direction and content of economic policy was substantially changed after the Conservatives under Mrs Thatcher came into office in 1979. Controlling inflation rather than reducing unemployment became the principal policy objective. By the time of the Major government in 1990, this was expressed in the form of inflation targets, a device retained by Gordon Brown, New Labour's Chancellor from 1997.

Having come to share the basic economic objectives of the Thatcher and Major governments, the Blair believed that sound money and the control of inflation were of prime importance. Direct forms of taxation, particularly the basic rate of income tax, should be restrained. The re-nationalization of privatized industries, even the great public utilities like electricity, gas, water and rail, was abandoned, and further privatizations pursued where possible. Incomes policies were not to be reintroduced and there would be no close relationship with the trade unions or reversion to tripartism. Tony Blair's personal aspiration was to make Labour 'the natural party of business'.

Work together

Having written your conclusion in the activity on page 230, swap it with a partner. Consider the following questions:

1. Does your partner's conclusion begin by focussing clearly on the given interpretation?
2. Does your partner's conclusion mention both of the extracts?
3. Does your partner's conclusion use own knowledge to help evaluate the validity of the interpretations offered by the extracts?
4. Was your partner's overall judgement properly supported by an evaluation of the different interpretations offered by the extracts?
5. Does your partner's conclusion contain anything that you missed?
6. What can you learn from your partner's approach?
7. Whose conclusion better reached an overall judgement?

Use these questions to feed back to each other and improve your writing.

Activity: AS-style question

Historians have different views about the impact on Britain of Thatcher's governments in the years 1979–97. Analyse and evaluate Extracts 3 and 4 and use your knowledge of the issues to explain your answer to the following question.

How far do you agree with the view that Thatcherism moved Britain's main political parties to the right?

Recommended reading

- E. Evans, *Thatcher and Thatcherism* (Routledge, 2013). An insightful and scholarly exploration of Thatcherism, dispelling many of the myths that surround her as a historical figure.

- C. Moore, *Margaret Thatcher: The Authorized Biography, Volume One: Not For Turning* (Penguin, 2013). A fairly even-handed and detailed approach to Margaret Thatcher's career up to 1983 and the Falklands War.

- G. Stewart, *Bang! A History of the 1980s* (Atlantic Books, 2013). A comprehensive economic, cultural and political history of the 1980s, featuring Margaret Thatcher as the focus of the book.

Paper 2

The USA, 1920–55: Boom, bust and recovery

The Big Picture

The story of the USA between the years 1920 and 1955 is one of prosperity followed by depression and a sustained post-war economic recovery.

Boom and crash, 1920–29

After the end of the First World War in 1918, the US economy was booming. Firms were employing new techniques such as mass production to produce commodities such as automobiles and white goods at affordable prices. Advertising was revolutionised, not least through new forms of media such as radio and cinema, feeding a consumer boom.

However, strong areas of poverty and deprivation remained for example within the agricultural sector. Many members of ethnic groups, such as black Americans, experienced continued poverty and discrimination.

The prosperity of the 1920s was unstable, based largely on credit. In 1929 the New York stock market on Wall Street crashed, symbolising both the fragility of the prosperity and the coming of the Great Depression.

There were many tensions in society in the 1920s because of the conflict between old values and new ideas. Prohibition for example was widely circumvented and led to crime; poor immigrants were accused of communism and were subject to a Red Scare; young women were accused of shameless behaviour. It was also a period of violent racism and the emergence of the Ku Klux Klan.

The decade saw developments in culture. The Harlem Renaissance saw black American culture reach out to a white audience, which many hoped would lead to a greater understanding between ethnic groups. It was also the age of mass spectator sports such as boxing and baseball, and the growth of cinema and radio. Literature however reflected a cynicism which seemed justified by the onset of the Depression.

Depression and New Deal, 1929–38

The scale of the Great Depression emphasised how ill-equipped US society was to deal with it. Between 1929 and 1933 US wealth had halved. Millions had lost their jobs and many became hoboes in search of elusive work. Some became bank robbers and outlaws.

Any relief schemes were inadequate to address the scale of the problem. Charities, too, were completely engulfed. President Hoover's measures were insufficient. Indeed the prohibitive Smoot–Hawley Tariff probably made things worse. Hoover was blamed for the extent and persistence of the Depression and shanty-towns or 'Hoovervilles' were named after him.

Hoover's successor, Franklin D. Roosevelt, transformed the role of government. His First New Deal saw measures not only to restore prosperity but also to reform the banks and stock exchange.

Roosevelt attracted many enemies, particularly among big business. He easily won the presidential election in 1936, however, and continued with the Second New Deal which many saw as more radical. His second term was beset with problems – not least his battle with the Supreme Court and the onset of the 'Roosevelt Recession' in 1937. New Deal measures became subsumed by the growing world crisis, and the onset of the Second World War in 1939 saw the USA's economy transformed into a powerhouse.

Impact of the New Deal and the Second World War

During the war the federal government effectively controlled the economy. The period saw improvements in the role and status of women and different ethnic groups although they still faced discrimination.

The New Deal had had a huge impact on the arts, particularly through agencies such as the Federal Writer's Project. Photographers such as Dorothy Lange created a visual archive which symbolised the despair and anguish of the Depression years. The war years brought a new sense of national unity. Hollywood provided effective propaganda celebrating the war effort through documentaries and war films. Radio offered up-to-the minute news.

For those at home, the war years brought unparalleled prosperity. There was full employment with the development of new industries. People increasingly migrated to the cities. Greater employment led to the growth of labour unions.

The transformation of the USA, 1945–55

The USA ended the Second World War as the richest country on Earth. The middle classes – 60 per cent of Americans – had more spending power. They increasingly moved to owner-occupied houses in the suburbs and enjoyed a conspicuous consumption driven by relentless advertising. Poverty did continue, though, particularly for members of ethnic minorities in the South and urban centres.

Within a few years of the end of the war the USA felt itself threatened by communism against which there developed a 'witch hunt'. Senator Joseph McCarthy alleged to have unearthed widespread treason in the State Department, galvanising the USA into an anticommunist crusade. Fears were enhanced by various spy trials and the growth of communism globally.

Hollywood added to these fears. Both science fiction and epic films with religious themes contained anticommunist messages. The cinema itself was in decline however as more people stayed home to watch television. The overwhelming image portrayed on TV was of the white middle class. Black Americans hardly appeared except as stereotypes. However, more black American film and sports stars did appear during the 1950s. Delinquent behaviour among young people was exaggerated.

Various factors supported the development of civil rights but it was a slow process. In 1954, in the *Brown* v. *Topeka Board of Education* case, the Supreme Court ruled that segregated schools were illegal but set no time limits for their integration. The scene was set then for bitter battles. President Eisenhower was reluctant to get involved because he recognised that legislation couldn't change people's hearts.

Key Topic 1 Boom and crash, 1920–29

Overview

In popular mythology the 1920s in the USA saw a period of unparalleled economic prosperity, ending suddenly in October 1929 with the collapse of the New York stock exchange. It was an age of technical innovations and exciting new social and cultural innovations – cinema, radio, jazz music. It was the age of liberated women (nicknamed 'flappers') and young people having fun. Sports stars and film actors became celebrity superstars. There were 'crazes' such as sitting at the top of flagpoles. Charles Lindbergh became a national hero when in 1927 he became the first man to fly solo across the Atlantic.

This picture is far too simple. There certainly was a boom period and the New York stock exchange did indeed collapse. However, these two events are not necessarily connected; the relationship between them is complex. It was an age of tension between the traditional and the new, between those who condemned the immorality of city life and those who favoured new ideas. Not all groups shared in the prosperity. While there was a cultural renaissance for some black Americans, many still lived in poverty and were the victims of racism; women too faced discrimination both at home and in the workplace.

The overarching theme of boom and crash is covered in four sections:
1 The 1920s' economic boom
2 Causes of the Wall Street Crash
3 Changes in society
4 Cultural changes in the 1920s

TIMELINE

1919 January	Eighteenth Amendment – introduction of Prohibition
1920 January–May	Red Scare and Palmer raids
1920 August	Nineteenth Amendment – women could vote in federal elections
1922 September	Fordney-McCumber Act
1924 May	Johnson-Reed Immigration Act
1925 December	*The New Negro* anthology published
1926 September	End of the Florida land boom
1926 October	*The Sun Also Rises* by Ernest Hemingway published
1927 August	Execution of Saccho and Vanzetti
1927 May	Charles Lindbergh's first solo flight across the Atlantic
1929 October	Wall Street Crash

1 The 1920s' economic boom

There was in the 1920s a real feeling of prosperity and optimism among many groups in the USA. It had emerged from the First World War as the most prosperous country on Earth. Many believed that the USA would set an example to the world with its emphasis on technological developments, economic efficiency and minimal government interference in business.

The figures for prosperity appear to speak for themselves.

- Following a brief post-war **recession** in 1920 and 1921, average unemployment never rose above 3.7 per cent in the years 1922–29.
- Inflation never rose higher than 1 per cent.
- Employees were working fewer hours: an average of 44 per week in 1929 compared with 47 in 1920.
- Employees were paid more. The **real wages** of industrial workers rose by 14 per cent between 1914 and 1929, and on average they were two or three times higher than those in Europe.
- There was huge economic growth. Production of industrial goods rose by 50 per cent between 1922 and 1929. **Gross National Product (GNP)** stood at $73 billion in 1920 and $104 billion in 1929. Consumption of electricity doubled, and in 1929 alone $852 million worth of radios were sold.

More industries adopted new manufacturing techniques such as **mass production**. These were underpinned by the development of **management science**, which sought to deploy strategies to ensure goods were produced as efficiently as possible. Advertising grew more and more sophisticated to ensure there was a continuing demand for products. This was made possible in part by the introduction of new mass media such as radio and cinema.

Many Americans had more time for leisure and more money to spend on it. Electrical labour-saving devices, such as vacuum cleaners and washing machines, were introduced and became affordable to more and more people. Motor cars eased travel both to and from work and for leisure pursuits.

Not all shared in the prosperity however. While the industrial sector boomed, agriculture faced difficulties in part because of falling prices and overproduction. Some groups, for example women and black Americans, were largely excluded from the growing economic opportunities.

> ### Note it down
> Use the 1:2 method of note-taking in this section (see page x). For example write down each sub-heading in the left-hand column and a bullet-pointed list of factors relating to each.
>
> You could also begin your collection of index cards (see page xi). Write a term that you need to define (for example, mass production) on the front of the card and the definition on the back. Specialist words are in blue bold type the first time they are used and the definitions may be found in the glossary (pages 492-5). Swap your notes with a partner afterwards to ensure you have covered all the main points.

Reasons for prosperity

The early twentieth century saw the development of mass production, technological advances and marketing techniques which revolutionised industry and impacted greatly on many people's lives, leading to changes in how they managed and spent their money and leisure time. These developments came particularly into prominence in the 1920s as government policies encouraged business to develop with minimal restrictions, fuelling the prosperity of the period. We will consider each of the following factors which created this prosperity in turn:

- government policies
- technological advances
- new business methods
- easy credit
- advantageous foreign markets.

Government policies

There were three **Republican** presidents of the 1920s (Warren Harding, 1921–23; Calvin Coolidge, 1923–29; Herbert Hoover, 1929–33). Each believed in as little government involvement in the running of the economy as possible. The Treasury Secretary from March 1921 to February 1932, Andrew Mellon, believed that wealth filtered down naturally to all classes in society and that, therefore, the best way to ensure increased living standards for all was to allow the rich to continue to make money to invest in industrial development. The basic government policy was *laissez-faire*. This meant the government intervened as little as possible in the economy, allowing the free market to operate with minimal restrictions. However, the picture was not quite as simple as that, and the government did intervene to support business with benevolent policies in three main ways.

High tariffs

The Fordney–McCumber Act, passed in 1922, raised **tariffs** on imported goods to cover the difference between domestic and foreign production costs. In almost every case it became cheaper for American consumers to buy goods produced within the USA than abroad. In effect, this meant that for some products import duties were so high that domestic producers were given an almost guaranteed market.

Tax reductions

The government reduced **federal taxes** significantly in 1924, 1926 and 1928. These reductions mainly benefited the wealthy. During his eight years of office, Mellon handed out tax reductions totalling $3.5 billion to large-scale industrialists and corporations. Despite this, President Coolidge's government actually operated on a surplus; in 1925, this was $677 million and in 1927, $607 million. However, federal tax cuts meant little to people who were too poor to pay taxes in the first place.

Fewer regulations

Economies in government and the attempt to spend less money led to fewer regulations and personnel to enforce them. Laws concerning sharp business practice were often ignored, such as price fixing between companies to prevent fair competition. Where the government did prosecute the offenders usually won on appeal. This lack of regulation could be an important contributor to a company's profits. Many people welcomed less government. However, it should also be remembered that there was, for example, no organisation with the authority to stop child labour in the textile mills of the Southern states. In the 1920s a 56-hour week was common there and wages rarely rose to more than 18 cents an hour.

Technological advances

During this period, technical advances such as mass production, mass access to electricity and developments in transport made possible huge increases in the quantity and variety of products on sale. The motor vehicle and electrical consumer goods industries are particularly striking examples of this. There was a vast extension of leisure activities such as cinema, spectator sport, excursions to the countryside – all made possible by the growth of motor vehicles.

Mass production

Mass production is particularly associated in the USA with car manufacturer Henry Ford whose first assembly line was introduced in his Highland Park factory in 1913 (see box 'Henry Ford and mass production'). The introduction of electricity in the early twentieth century made moving assembly lines possible and manufacturers such as Westinghouse, producing electrical equipment, embraced this technique. Ford, however, developed the concept so everything was subservient to the production line. Workers, for example, were not allowed to take breaks except when designated, so work was repetitive and had to be geared to the speed of the line. Many argued that operatives were turned into robots in this process. However, the result was massive increases in production not just in motor vehicles, but in such industries as clothing manufacture and labour-saving devices. The introduction of standard clothing sizes during the First World War made it possible to mass produce clothing using cheaper materials but based on fashion house designs – there was no copyright on clothing design until the 1950s.

The motor vehicle industry

Of all the developing industries in the 1920s, the growth of the motor industry was perhaps the most dramatic. In 1920 there were 7.5 million automobiles for a population of 106,000,000. By the end of the decade this had risen to 27 million cars on the road, or one for approximately every five people. The industry was the biggest in the USA, dominated by the 'Big Three' firms – Ford, General Motors and Chrysler. It was the largest market for commodities, such as steel and rubber.

Cars were one of the most desirable products among consumers. Asked about workers' aspirations, one official

Henry Ford and mass production

Henry Ford learned engineering as a young man and began his first company in 1903. He was to revolutionise the motor vehicle industry of which he controlled 50 per cent by 1924.

Ford had begun to use methods of mass production long before the 1920s and his famous 'Model T' car had first appeared in 1908. Previously, cars had been only for the wealthy, but Ford wanted ordinary Americans to be able to afford one. The 'Model T' was a basic car with no frills but proved immensely popular. In 1913 Ford adopted mass production techniques which made the price fall and production to rise – by 1914 the price of the 'Model T' came down from $950 to $500. In 1917 his factory moved to Dearborn where his methods came to full fruition – workers tied to the speed of the assembly line and management science strategies such as **time and motion** constantly used.

By 1920 Ford was producing 1,250,000 cars per year, or one every 60 seconds, further improved to one every ten seconds by 1925, when the price had fallen to $290. Petrol, meanwhile, cost between 20 and 25 cents a gallon at a time when average wages in manufacturing industries were in the region of 50 cents an hour.

Ford's factory was clean with excellent safety records and he paid a reasonable wage of $5 per day. However he acted as a dictator to his workforce, would not tolerate **labour unions** and employed a private police force to maintain order.

However, Ford was slow to see the value of choice in products and he began to lose his share of the market as his rivals General Motors and Chrysler expanded. Ford's production fell by 400,000 between 1923 and 1926. In answer to this he decided to introduce a new car, the Model A. In 1927, Ford closed down his factory for five months, laying off 60,000 workers. During this layoff, the factory was retooled for the new Model A vehicle. Unlike Ford, General Motors and Chrysler could introduce new models regularly; they understood that if the market was to remain buoyant, car design had to stay ahead of it and customers had to want to buy the new model rather than keep the old one. This led to sophisticated marketing techniques which saw, for example, the aviator Amelia Earhart launching Chrysler's new Plymouth model at Madison Square Gardens in 1928 and salesmen dressed in seventeenth-century costume to commemorate the first European settlers to America who arrived at Plymouth Rock.

said that 65 per cent are working to pay for cars. In their 1929 study of the residents of 'Middletown', sociologists Robert and Helen Lynd found that one-half of those surveyed possessed an automobile, paying for it mainly on credit, while, by way of contrast, only one-third had bathtubs.

In economic terms, by 1929, the motor industry employed 7 per cent of all workers and paid them 9 per cent of all wages. Detroit, a centre of motor manufacture, expanded 120 per cent between 1910 and 1920. By far the largest industry in the USA, motor manufacture also stimulated many others, as shown in Figure 1. Tyre manufacture, for example, grew 170 per cent in the city of Akron in the second decade of the twentieth century; the Goodyear factories alone had 100 acres of floor space and accounted for sales of over $115 million in 1924.

The motor industry was so important that temporary closure of Ford (see box 'Henry Ford and mass production') was a contributory factor to the recession of 1927. Not only were his workforce laid off, losing $50 million in wages, but the loss of business by companies providing components to Ford created real problems in the economy.

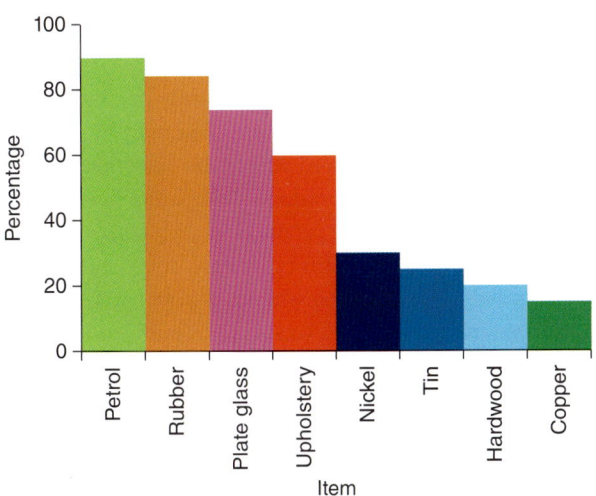

▲ Figure 1: Use of products by the car industry.

Road building

Breaking with the policy of *laissez-faire*, the federal government expended a great deal of energy on road building in the 1920s. The Federal Highway Act of 1921 gave responsibility for road building to central government and highways were being constructed at the rate of 10,000 miles per year by 1929. But this was not enough. New roads could not keep pace with the growth of traffic. Congestion was common, particularly in the approaches to large urban centres. In 1936 the Chief Designer in the Bureau of Public Roads reported that between 25 and 50 per cent of modern roads built over the previous twenty years were unfit for use because of the amount of traffic that was quite simply wearing them out.

Motor vehicles also created the growth of new service industries such as garages, motels, petrol stations and used car salerooms. They gradually changed the landscape alongside the highways of the USA.

Improved transportation also afforded new opportunities for industry. For example, goods could be much more easily moved from factories to their markets. The number of truck registrations increased from less than 1 million in 1919 to 3.5 million by 1929, when 15 billion gallons of petrol were used and 4.5 million new cars were sold.

Electrical devices

Labour-saving devices, for example vacuum cleaners and washing machines, became much cheaper to produce. In 1912, 2.4 million items of electrical goods were sold; in 1929 the figure was 160 million.

However, this trend should not be exaggerated. Much of rural America was still without electricity in the 1920s. Even where electrical power was available, many items we take for granted today were not widely in use. In 1925, for example, Clarence Birdseye patented his freezing process but in 1928 there were only 20,000 refrigerators in the whole country. While there was an industrial capacity to produce millions of electrical goods, by the end of the decade nearly everyone who could afford them or who had access to electricity had them. This meant there was serious overproduction. As we shall see in the next chapter this was to lead to problems in the economy by the late 1920s.

Impact of technological advances on leisure

Technological advances had a huge impact on leisure opportunities in the USA. The growth of motor vehicles enabled people to travel, often for the first time, and the countryside came within reach for urban dwellers. People visited attractions such as Yellowstone National Park and the Grand Canyon and, for those close enough, the seaside. By 1920, 1 million Americans went camping; the city of Denver had opened a 160-acre campsite in 1919 and by 1923 there were 2,000 across the USA. **Tourist courts** developed – cabins where motorists could rest for the night. Families sought accommodation in increasing numbers and hotels became more common. In a *Saturday Evening Post* series of articles, 'Adventures in Automobumming', the writer Sinclair Lewis added a note of caution: 'Always inspect the bathroom with the light on. Look for that ring around the tub.'

The spread of electricity led to most homes owning a radio while more labour-saving devices meant more time for leisure. For those who wanted to go out, 20,000 movie theatres were built in the 1920s (see pages 253–4).

New business methods

This was a period which saw the growth of huge corporations, management science and advertising, which through the exploitation of the new mass media gained great influence. The effect was to make business more efficient and well run, which in turn helped profits.

Growth of huge corporations

Most large corporations, such as Firestone which produced rubber, were manufacturing businesses. They could invest in and exploit the plentiful raw materials of the USA on a vast scale. By 1929 the largest 200 corporations possessed 20 per cent of the nation's wealth and 40 per cent of the wealth generated by business activities. Mergers in manufacturing and mining enterprises trebled to over 1,200 during the decade, leading to even larger business concerns. US Steel, for example, had been created as the Andrew Carnegie Steel Corporation by Andrew Carnegie and was sold to JP Morgan in 1901. It became the world's first billion-dollar corporation and by the 1920s was producing 67 per cent of the USA's steel production.

Large corporations could dominate an industry in various ways.

- They could operate a **cartel** to fix prices. Although this was technically illegal, the government tended to turn a blind eye. They could, as in the case of the petroleum companies, control the entire industrial process. This involved the exploitation of the raw materials, the manufacture of the product, its distribution to wholesale and retail outlets and its sale to the consumer.
- Some organisations, for example US Steel, were so huge that they could dictate output and price levels throughout the industry. They could create **holding companies**. For example, Samuel Insull built up a vast empire based on electrical supply. Eventually he controlled 111 different companies with as many as 24 layers between him and the company actually distributing the electricity. The chain became so complex that even he lost an overall understanding of it. Many businessmen turned up on the boards of directors of numerous companies. The result was that firms supposedly competing with each other were in effect one and the same, with the power to fix output and prices.

It is important to remember that government policies made these developments possible and that they acted against the interest of small business which could not compete. However, many people saw businessmen as heroes who had made possible the great boom period they were enjoying.

Management science

The increased size of businesses meant that they were more complex to manage. This led to the development of different management roles performed by different people in administration. Entrepreneurs like Henry Ford who tried to control all management operations became increasingly old-fashioned. Specialisms developed in production, design, marketing, accounts and finance in ways that had been unheard of in the previous century.

One particularly noticeable aspect of these developments was the growth of business schools: in 1928 there were 89 of them, with 67,000 students. The fact that management science became a respectable occupation for members of the upper middle classes was also an indication that it was becoming increasingly difficult to start one's own company. To rise up the ladder of an established giant offered greater career opportunities than to compete with it.

Advertising and salesmanship

Techniques of advertising developed rapidly during the 1920s. Before then advertisements had mainly comprised of the printed word telling the customer about the attributes of the product. Companies needed to expand demand for their products so they began to hire psychologists to design campaigns and target specific groups such as young women. Lucky Strike for example encouraged women to smoke in public with their cigarettes marketed as 'torches of freedom'. Advertising campaigns began to emphasise slogans, brand names, celebrity endorsements and consumer aspirations. There was a constant need to create demand. The growth in industrial production required a continuous market. It was no longer enough to sell a durable unchanging product that might last the purchaser for life, as Ford had done with his Model T. Now, to fuel the boom, it was necessary for people to buy new things frequently. They had to be convinced that they could not do without the latest model of an electrical appliance or the new design in clothing.

For many consumers advertising techniques worked. Not only did they associate products with a slogan, but they also believed they could not manage without the advertised product. The *Kansas City Journal-Post* was hardly exaggerating when it wrote, 'Advertising and mass production are the twin cylinders that keep the motor of modern business in motion.' By 1929, companies were

▲ 'I am the Playboy' – a classic 1930s advertisement which connected Jordan cars with adventure and excitement. It was one of the first adverts to concentrate on image rather than simply give information about the product. How useful is this for an enquiry into advertising techniques and their effectiveness in the USA in the 1920s? Examine the sales techniques used and the content of the advertisement in your answer.

spending $3 billion annually on advertising, five times more than in 1914. The new mass media, principally cinema and radio (see page 253), brought about a revolution in advertising.

Easy credit

The massive consumer boom was financed largely by easily available credit facilities. People would pay a deposit to secure an item and then pay the rest in regular instalments (this was known as **hire purchase**). The advantage was they could acquire goods before they'd paid for them. The downside was, with instalments they had to pay more than if they'd bought them outright. Moreover if they missed their payments the goods could be repossessed. By 1929 almost $7 billion worth of goods were sold on credit. This included 75 per cent of cars and 50 per cent of major household appliances. One study showed that men earning $35 a week were paying the same amount per month for the family car.

Unfortunately, while the ready availability of credit enabled consumers to buy goods they otherwise could not afford, it often led to problems if the borrowers took on debts they could not repay. Companies, as well as individuals, used easy-credit facilities to finance many of their operations. It seemed that almost everyone was in debt, but at the time there was little concern over this. It was assumed that everyone's credit must be good. Banks and loan companies seemed to be falling over backwards to lend money, often with few questions asked.

Advantageous foreign markets

Reference has already been made to high tariffs that protected US markets (see page 235). However, the government also encouraged businessmen to develop extensive interests abroad, particularly in terms of raw materials that fuelled technological developments. Business corporations bought **oil concessions** in many countries, including Canada, Venezuela, Iraq and the Dutch East Indies. The Firestone Corporation developed a rubber industry in Liberia, while the Guggenheims invested in South America for nitrates, copper and lead. The United Fruit Company had a larger budget in Costa Rica than

> ### Key debate
> #### The reality of 1920s prosperity
> Writing in the early 1930s and returning to the theme in the 1950s, journalist Lewis Frederick Allen doubted the 1920s prosperity was real because too much was being produced and too many shady business practices were allowed. This view was common through much of the twentieth century and into the next, in part because of the mistakes perceived to have been made by leading economic players. Academic Thurman Arnold argued in 1949 that business leaders simply did not understand the workings of the economy in which they operated. In 2009 financier Liaquat Ahamed appeared to support this notion by showing that leading bankers did not understand the interconnectedness of the global economy, making the economies of individual countries somewhat irrelevant. However, more conservative historians such Paul Johnson have argued that the prosperity was real enough to those who benefited from higher wages and better standards of living. As we shall see in future sections, such writers often see the economy as self-righting. They argue that it was government intervention that made the subsequent Depression worse.

Key Topic 1 Boom and crash, 1920–29

the government of that country. Often US investment saw the development of public health schemes and schools in developing countries to provide and maintain a healthy and adequately educated workforce.

Limits to prosperity

Not all groups shared in the prosperity of the 1920s. While industry seemed to enjoy a boom period, the decade saw more problems in agriculture. Life remained hard for many women and even those who appeared to have stimulating jobs were paid less than their male colleagues. Ethnic groups such as black Americans barely benefited from any rise in living standards or expectation of a better life.

Problems for farmers

The years preceding the 1920s had been relatively good ones for farmers. During the war years prices had risen over 25 per cent, and more land had been taken into cultivation. However, after the war, falling demand led to falling prices. For example, wheat prices fell from $2.5 to $1 per bushel. There were several reasons for this:

- **Prohibition** (see pages 248–50) cut the demand for grain previously used in the manufacture of alcohol. In addition, higher living standards meant Americans ate more meat and comparatively fewer cereals.
- The growth of synthetic fibres reduced the market for natural ones, such as cotton.
- At the same time, technological advances meant that more crops could be produced on the same or even a reduced acreage. During the 1920s, 13 million acres were taken out of production. Farm population fell by 5 per cent yet production increased by 9 per cent.
- Greater use of tractors meant fewer horses were necessary and this in turn meant less demand for animal food.
- Ironically, because many farmers became more efficient through mechanisation and new techniques, such as the use of improved fertilisers and better **animal husbandry**, they simply produced too much.

As a result of these factors, possibly as many as 66 per cent of farms operated at a loss. **Wage labourers**, **tenant farmers** and **share-croppers** – in the South, these were mainly black Americans – fared particularly badly. Some farmers grew rich by selling their land for housing and industrial development, but most appeared not to share in any prosperity in the 1920s.

Overproduction

The biggest problem for farmers was overproduction. Too much food meant prices were too low. Farmers were reluctant to underproduce voluntarily because they could not trust their neighbours to do the same. Ideally, they sought guaranteed prices, with the state possibly selling their surpluses abroad for whatever price it could get. American farmers produced so much that there were surpluses despite the rising population.

It was mainly small-scale farmers who went **bankrupt**. They often asked the state for help, as they thought of big business and the banks as being in league against them. government policy was to encourage farms to co-operate together to market their produce. To this end the Agricultural Credits Act of 1923 funded twelve Intermediate Credit Banks to offer loans to co-operatives. However, the measure was of little benefit to small farmers. The last thing they needed was more debt. But large agricultural businesses could afford to take loans to market their produce more effectively, thus squeezing the small farmers even more.

More and more small farmers saw their mortgages **foreclosed** and lost the land their families had farmed for generations. While between 1913 and 1920 the average rate of foreclosure was 3.2 per 1,000, it had risen to 17.4 per 1,000 by 1926. Many farmers naturally became very bitter.

'Agricultural businesses'

The days of the small-scale, self-reliant farmer had already largely passed. In order to survive in the long term, farmers needed to make a profit. The 1920s saw the growth of 'agricultural businesses' – large-scale, well-financed cereal cultivation, ranching and fruit production enterprises – using the techniques of mass production. They required comparatively little labour, except possibly in the case of fruit gathering at harvest time.

Women

Women did not on the whole enjoy improved career opportunities during this period. By 1930, for example, there were only 150 women dentists and fewer than 100 female accountants in the whole of the USA. Although women had been granted the right to vote in August 1920, in 1928 the **League of Women Voters** reported that while 145 women held seats in **state legislatures**, there were only two women among the 435 delegates in the House of Representatives.

There were more jobs for women as clerical workers and salespeople, but overall they tended to remain in comparatively low-paid and often menial jobs; 700,000 women were domestic servants. There were few female industrialists or managing directors. The number of women receiving a college education actually fell by

5 per cent during the decade. Even when women worked in the same job as men, they normally received less money. Despite the image of fun-loving young women nicknamed '**flappers**', women were generally expected to concentrate on marriage and homemaking. It is largely a myth that the 1920s saw more opportunities for women to get to the top in terms of employment opportunities. Less than 2 per cent of judges or lawyers were female.

Black Americans

Black Americans did not share in the prosperity. They made up 10 per cent of the total population, but 85 per cent still lived in the South, itself the poorest region in the USA. There was considerable migration north in search of better opportunities, particularly to the large cities, but here too black Americans faced discrimination in housing and employment. Often they were concentrated in 'ghetto' areas such as Harlem in New York, whose black American population had swelled from 50,000 in 1914 to 165,000 in 1930. Overcrowding and poor living conditions added to their problems in the mainstream economy.

Conclusion: The 1920s' economic boom

While the USA appeared very prosperous during the 1920s, the situation was complex. Government policies favoured business unconstrained by regulations. New production, management and marketing techniques interacted to create business expansion. Many people were better off than ever before and had more leisure time to spend their earnings. However ethnic groups such as black Americans did not share in the prosperity, and employment opportunities were limited for farmers and women. As we shall see in the next section, the prosperity was built on unstable ground and the Wall Street Crash helped trigger its end.

> ### Work together
> Work in pairs or a small group. Go through the ways in which the 1920s:
> - seemed prosperous
> - seemed to have economic problems.
>
> Discuss how far you think the economy was booming in the USA in the 1920s. When you have come to some sort of agreement, you should each write down bullet points summarising your ideas. Having done this, you can compare them and expand on them where necessary.

2 Causes of the Wall Street Crash

In October 1929, the New York stock exchange on Wall Street crashed. It handled about 61 per cent of stocks and shares transactions in the USA. Crashes in other stock exchanges throughout the country and abroad soon followed. While the collapse in Wall Street had been forecast by many financial experts, their warnings had gone largely unheeded. The event was to affect millions of people, most of whom did not even own stocks and shares. The collapse of the stock market may not have caused the ensuing Depression but was clearly a sign that the economy as a whole was in serious difficulties.

There were signs that prosperity was coming to an end. The uneven distribution of wealth, the problems associated with 'get-rich-quick' schemes and indicators in key sectors of the economy showed that the boom was slowing down. Many people had paid for goods on credit and often couldn't afford to take out any more debt or even afford the repayments on what they had bought. Added to this the financial and banking institutions of the USA were often undeveloped and unable to cope with crisis. The banking system, for example, was self-regulated and put its own interests before those of the country. By 1929 the indicators were that supply of goods exceeded demand. The USA could not sell abroad because of high tariffs and the debts owed by many of its trading partners, particularly in Europe. The economy had overheated and the Wall Street Crash was a symptom of this.

> ### Note it down
> This section focusses on the Wall Street Crash and the reasons why it may have happened. You could make notes using a variation on a spider diagram (see page x). You will need a large piece of paper for this because there are a lot of different sections to cover. Draw two spider bodies. Write 'Wall Street Crash' in the centre of one and use the legs to make notes on what this was. Then link it to another circle entitled 'Was the boom slowing down?' Use the legs from this to make notes on: uneven distribution of wealth, instability of 'get-rich-quick' schemes, problems with the banking system, the cycle of international debt and slowdown in the economy.

The Wall Street Crash

The stock exchange on Wall Street collapsed between 24 and 29 October 1929. On Thursday 24 October 1929 a massive amount of selling began on the New York stock exchange. This forced prices down and led to more selling still as **brokers** feared they would be left with worthless stock.

While the volume of trading on Monday was less than that of the previous Thursday, the fall in prices was far more severe. The Dow Jones Industrial Index showed a drop of 38 points on the day's trading, down to 260. Next day, confidence collapsed completely. This was Tuesday 29 October, the day that the stock market on Wall Street crashed.

Altogether, 16,410,030 shares were sold and the Dow Jones Industrial Index fell a further 30 points to 230, a fall of 11.73 per cent. In a few weeks, as much as $30 billion had been lost out of over $100 billion. This represented a sum almost as great as that which the USA had spent on its involvement in the First World War. Table 1 gives some indication of the level of losses.

Source A From *Only Yesterday* by Frederick Lewis Allen (Harper & Row, 1931). This is a classic account of the 1920s in the USA and has been republished many times. Allen is referring to the stock market collapse of 24 October.

> As the price structure crumbled there was a sudden stampede to get out from under. By eleven 'o' clock, traders on the floor of the Stock Exchange were in a wild scramble to sell 'at the market'. Long before the lagging ticker could tell what was happening word had gone out by telephone and telegraph that the bottom was dropping out of things and selling orders redoubled in volume ... Down, down ,down ... Where were the bargain: hunters who were supposed to come to their rescue at times like this? ... There seemed to be no support whatsoever ... Down, down, down. The roar of voices which rose from the floor of the Exchange had become a roar of panic.

What light can be shed on the atmosphere on Wall Street on 24 October 1929 by this piece of descriptive writing?

Table 1: The fall in share price.

Company	Share price on 03/09/1929	Share price on 03/11/1929
American Can	187.66	86.00
Anaconda Copper	131.50	70.00
General Motors	72.5	36.00
Montgomery Ward	137.86	49.25
Radio	101.00	28.00
Woolworth	100.37	52.25
Electric Share and Bond	186.75	50.25

Value of shares

Stock market performance was based on indexes such as the **Dow Jones Industrial Average**. In the 1920s this was based on the performance of 30 of the largest companies quoted on the stock exchange. Points were used rather than prices to indicate trends and average performance. The Dow averaged at 100 points in 1924 and rose to 400 before the Crash of 1929. Its assessment of share value offers a reliable indicator of the performance of the economy.

It is often popularly believed that the Wall Street Crash led to the **Great Depression**. However, many historians have argued that it was simply one sign of a depression already well on the way. Moreover, stock markets had crashed before and have done since without any ensuing economic depression. The Wall Street Crash needs to be seen in the context of an economy which was already in trouble. In the next section we examine these underlying problems in the economy.

Economic problems in the 1920s

While it appeared on the surface that the economy was booming during the 1920s, there were many warning signs that things were not so healthy. These included:

- uneven distribution of wealth
- stability of employment
- the instability of 'get-rich-quick' schemes
- weaknesses of the banking system
- the cycle of international debt
- overproduction and the slowdown in the economy.

Uneven distribution of wealth

Industry and income were all distributed unevenly within the USA, which meant that some regions were much more prosperous than others. In addition, patterns of employment could be unstable, with much unemployment and **underemployment**. As we have seen, some sections of society were better off than others; many women, for example, did not share in the prosperity of the 1920s, nor did ethnic groups such as black Americans.

Income was also distributed very unevenly throughout the country. The Northeast and Far West enjoyed the highest **per capita incomes**; in 1929 these were $921 and $881 respectively. In comparison, the figure for the Southeast was $365. To paint an even gloomier picture, within the region of the Southeast, in South Carolina, while the per capita income for the non-agricultural sectors of the economy averaged $412, that of farmers was only $129. In 1929, the Brookings Institute, a research organisation, found that income distribution was actually becoming more unequal. Its survey discovered that 60 per cent of American families had annual incomes of less than $2,000.

Stability of employment

Employment was often unstable owing to fluctuating demand for goods. Sociologists Robert and Helen Lynd found that, during the first nine months of 1929, of 165 families they surveyed, 72 per cent of the workers had been unemployed at some stage in their working lives. Of these, 43 per cent had been jobless for over a month. This was at a time when there was very little welfare or unemployment benefit and most relief was supplied by charitable organisations.

Workers could not, on the whole, look to labour unions for help. The government did nothing to protect them, and indeed the Supreme Court had blocked attempts by unions to ban child labour and impose a minimum wage for women as being unconstitutional. Many employers operated **'yellow dog' clauses** by which their employees were not allowed to join a union. During the 1920s union membership, which in the early 1920s stood at 4 million, declined overall by 1 million. In 1910, 8.5 per cent of the industrialised workforce was unionised; in 1930 this figure had fallen to 7.1 per cent.

The instability of 'get-rich-quick' schemes

While many people saw easy credit as a strength in the economy, there were also considerable drawbacks. 'Get rich quick' was the aim of many Americans in the 1920s. They invested in hugely speculative ventures and inevitably many lost their money. This situation provided golden opportunities for confidence tricksters and crooks.

In the early 1920s, for example, Charles Ponzi, a former vegetable seller, conned thousands of gullible people into investing in his ventures. He promised a 50 per cent profit within 90 days. When sentencing him to prison, the judge criticised his victims for their greed. Ponzi had not forced people to part with their money. The period saw other more large-scale speculations, notably during the Florida land boom and on the stock exchange in the latter part of the decade.

Land speculation – the Florida land boom

While on bail awaiting trial, Ponzi found employment selling land in Florida. This was a venture well-suited to his talents. Until this time, Florida was a relatively undeveloped state with a small population. In 1910, Miami was by far the biggest city but with a population of only 54,000. With the coming of the motor car, Florida's all-year-round sunshine became accessible to the nation's middle classes and massive interest grew in the state as a paradise for vacations and retirement. This led to a land boom.

Between 1920 and 1925, the population of the state increased from 968,000 to 1.2 million. There were large-scale coastal developments. Parcels of land began to be sold to wealthy northerners on the basis of glossy brochures and salesmen's patter. People began to invest their money in unseen developments, hoping to sell and make a quick profit. Often they paid on credit, with a 10 per cent deposit known as a 'binder'. Success stories abounded to fuel the boom. It was said that someone who had bought a parcel of land for $25 in 1900 had sold it for $150,000 25 years later.

The land boom could be sustained only as long as there were more buyers than sellers. But demand tailed off in 1926. There were scandals of land advertised as within easy access of the sea that was really many miles inland or in the middle of swamps. Then nature played its part, with hurricanes in 1926 killing 400 people and leaving 50,000 homeless. With thousands of people bankrupted, the Florida land boom collapsed, leaving a coastline strewn with half-finished and storm-battered developments.

Stock-market speculation – the bull market

It seemed that few people were prepared to learn the lessons of Florida. As one way to get rich quickly closed so another seemed to open up. In the period from 1927 to 1929 many Americans went 'Wall Street crazy'. Easy credit meant many were able to invest in stocks and shares. They could be bought **'on the margin'** – on credit with loans from their broker. This demand to buy shares is known as a **'bull market'**. Increasingly, people

Key Topic 1 Boom and crash, 1920–29

purchased stocks and shares not to invest in a company but as a speculation. If the price rose shares were sold, so making a quick and easy profit. For a time this seemed to work. Share prices seemed constantly to rise, some spectacularly so. According to the Wall Street Index, stock in the Radio Corporation of America rose from 85 to 420 points in the course of 1928.

> ### The bull pool
> Many 'streetwise' brokers took full advantage of the boom, intending to make as much money as possible before the inevitable collapse. These tended to be the large-scale financiers and bankers. Typically, many of these attempted to inflate prices artificially. William Durant, for example, operated the famous bull pool; he and his colleagues bought and sold shares back and forth to each other, giving the impression of great market interest in a particular issue. Once unwary outsiders began to buy, sending the prices still higher, they would sell, making a huge profit. This selling would cause prices to fall and the outsiders would be left with much depreciated stock. There was little regulation of activities such as insider dealing and it was easy to take advantage of others' naivety.

Weaknesses of the banking system

The banking system was outdated by the 1920s even though the central banking system had only been created in 1913. Twelve regulatory Reserve Banks were headed by the Federal Reserve Board – usually known as 'the Fed' – with seven members appointed by the president. The system allowed banks to regulate themselves without the government having to interfere. However, the Reserve Banks represented the interests of the bankers and so could not be completely relied on to act in the best interests of the nation if there was a conflict of interests. Additionally the Federal Reserve Board wanted to keep the market buoyant so it favoured low interest rates. This fuelled easy credit (see page 239).

While national banks had to join the centralised system, local state banks did not. Most ordinary people's money, particularly in rural and semi-rural areas, was invested in the latter. In the 1920s, there were almost 30,000 banks in the USA. Most were very small and therefore unable to cope with financial problems. If they collapsed their depositors would probably lose virtually all their savings.

The cycle of international debt

The cycle of international debt was at the heart of the economic problems. America's priority was for Europeans to repay the loans they had taken out to finance the First World War. Most Americans thought that the countries should repay their loans. However, most European countries, still suffering from depressed economic conditions arising from the war, could not afford to do so. The prohibitive tariffs made matters worse. European countries could not export their manufactured goods to the USA in great quantities so found it impossible to earn the money to repay the loans.

Overproduction and the slowdown in the economy

The boom was dependent on continuing domestic consumption. High tariffs and generally depressed economies in Europe meant that American producers could sell comparatively little abroad. There were, by the late 1920s, three indicators that the boom was slowing down. This was to have adverse implications for the economy as production was reduced in line with less demand and people began to lose their jobs.

Problems in small businesses

The decade witnessed the growth of huge corporations with considerable marketing power. As a result smaller businesses often faced hard times. During the course of the 1920s for every four businesses that succeeded, three failed. The number of motor vehicle companies, for example, fell from 108 in 1920 to 44 by the end of the decade. Except for high tariffs (page 235), the government was no more prepared to help out failing industrial concerns than it was to help the farmers.

The construction industry

Economic historians tend to agree that the state of the construction industry is generally a good indicator of the overall health of the economy. The mid-1920s saw a great boom in construction, particularly in housing, office building and highways. However, after 1926 demand began to tail off. This led to a fall in demand for building materials, skills such as plumbing and the transportation of building materials. This, in turn, led to higher unemployment in construction-related businesses and had serious knock-on effects on concerns dependent on their custom such as cement and bricks manufacture.

Falling domestic demand

By the late 1920s, production was outstripping demand. The domestic market was becoming flooded with goods that could not be sold. By 1929, stores, with warehouses full of unsold goods, simply stopped ordering more. Electrical goods such as labour saving devices seemed to have reached their peak. Credit seemed exhausted. In the end more people just couldn't afford to buy anything else for themselves or the home. The result was growing unemployment as firms cut back production. Thousands of automobile workers were laid off. More people were in no position to spend on non-essential items. Even though the national unemployment statistics remained low, Irving Fisher, a Yale economist, estimated that in 1929 as many as 80 per cent of the American people were living close to **subsistence**, even when they were in work.

Downward spiral

With growth in the new industries beginning to slow, full-time employment fell and the economy entered into a downward spiral. A fall in income led to a fall in demand, which in turn led to a fall in production that added to unemployment and underemployment. However, the fact that the economy was experiencing problems was concealed by superficial optimism and the frenzy of stock market speculation.

Conclusion: Causes of the Wall Street Crash

The Wall Street stock market crashed in October 1929. However problems in the economy predated this. These included slowdowns in the crucial construction sector, the cycle of international debt limiting trade, and overproduction leading to unemployment and a downturn in demand. The Crash itself reflected weaknesses in the structure of the stock market which prompted unwise practices such as buying on the margin and exploitation by streetwise dealers who operated the bull pool. Also much of the boom was fuelled by a boom in credit which saw comparatively little wealth actually being created.

The Wall Street Crash did not cause the Depression but was a key indicator of its onset.

> ### Work together
> Use the notes you have made during this section (see page 241) to create a list of definitions for the key terms and topics relevant to the causes of the Wall Street Crash. Then share your definitions with a partner. If you think a definition is unclear or needs adding to further, discuss together what needs to be added, agree on the definition and make the changes to your notes.

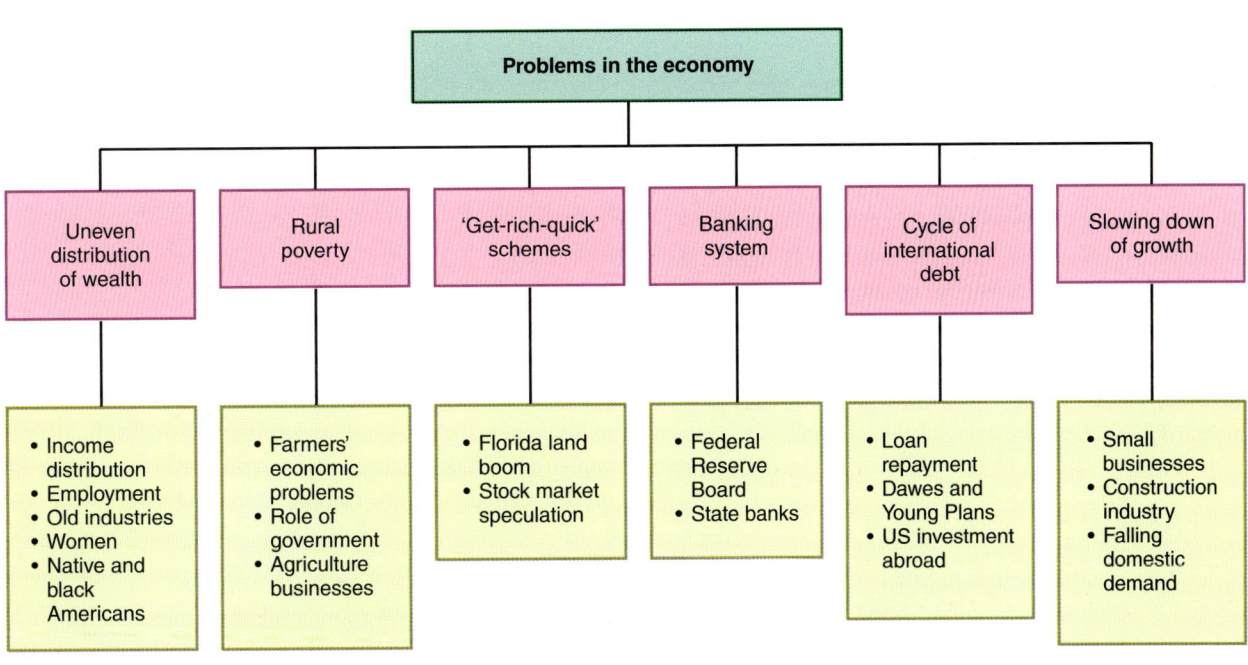

▲ Summary diagram: Problems in the economy.

Key Topic 1 Boom and crash, 1920–29

3 Changes in society

The 1920 census showed more people living in towns than the countryside for the first time in American history: 54 million out of 106 million Americans. However, urban areas were defined as those with a population of only 2,500 plus. Of that 54 million, 16 million still lived in communities of fewer than 25,000 inhabitants. They clung to their rural values such as thrift, hard work and plain living.

Tensions in the 1920s were often, but not always, between those who lived in rural and small-town America and those who lived in cities, whose ways were seen as immoral and sinful. From 1920 to 1930, the numbers of those living in cities of more than 100,000 increased by one-third. Many people viewed this growth of urban living as a real threat to what they saw as the American way of life. Their support for the Republican presidents of the 1920s was part of an effort to turn back the clock.

Tensions included worries about immigration, particularly of people who weren't white or Protestant. It was believed they sought to subvert the American way of life. This led to the so-called **Red Scare** of 1920 and endemic racism throughout the decade. One particularly violent manifestation of this was the emergence of the **Ku Klux Klan**. Prohibition meanwhile saw a vast increase in crime and **gangsterism**. There was also concern that young women were becoming too independent and hedonistic. It seemed to many that the whole structure of society was being attacked.

immigration from southern and eastern Europe in the latter part of the nineteenth and early twentieth centuries led to racist concerns about the survival of the 'Anglo-Saxon' race.

Many people feared immigration from southern and eastern Europe and Asia was a threat to traditional American values and would weaken the USA. This was tied to the idea of **eugenics**, which promoted the inequality of races and believed that too many inferior peoples would threaten the position of the superior white population. Worse, racial intermixing could cause racial degeneration. For this reason many white Americans sought to limit immigration to the USA.

> ### Eugenics
> Eugenics was a scientific theory particularly associated with Francis Dalton which was very influential in the early years of the twentieth century. Borrowing ideas from evolution, it said that the white race was the highest form of human development and other races were inferior and should be kept apart. Many applied this to birth control (see page 251) and limiting immigration of non-white peoples to the USA. It was feared that inferior races bred more quickly and would swamp the whites. One particularly influential racist text was the bestselling *The Passing of the White Race* written by Madison Grant and published in 1916; he argued that any mixing of the races would taint the superior one. The idea led to irrational fears and racist actions.

Immigration laws

In 1921 Congress passed an Emergency Immigration Law. This imposed an annual ceiling on immigration from any European country, limiting it to 3 per cent of the nationals from that country living in the USA in 1911 – which favoured white Protestants whose descendants were more likely to have moved to the USA before that time.

In 1924 this was stiffened by the Johnson–Reed Immigration Act, which banned any immigration from Japan; other Asian groups having been barred earlier. It also set an absolute ceiling of immigration at 150,000 per year, allocated according to the native origins of the existing population. Interestingly, this ceiling did not apply to Mexicans, whom Californian farmers traditionally used as a supply of cheap labour at harvest time.

> ### Note it down
> Use the 1:2 method (see page x) to make notes from this section about the key changes in society. In the first column you could include: immigration and the Red Scare; racism and the Ku Klux Klan; concerns about immorality and new ideas; Prohibition and the rise of crime; the role and status of women and birth control. If you link the overall concept in the first column with the examples in the second column you will be able to see how they fit together - for example, how the Ku Klux Klan was a manifestation of racism; how Prohibition led to a rise in crime; what factors in the role and status of women led to greater demands for birth control, etc.

Immigration and the Red Scare

The USA prided itself on being a land born of immigrants. However, this did not prevent there being laws banning Asians from entry. The truth was that the USA basically welcomed white immigrants, preferably from northwestern Europe rather than from non-white areas. The large-scale waves of

The Red Scare

After the First World War, high inflation caused much industrial unrest. In 1920 food prices had doubled since 1913. It was estimated that during 1919, 4 million workers went on strike. This was one in five of the **labour force**. Many people believed that strikers were led by **communists** who sought revolution in the USA as had happened in Russia in 1917. Fears grew as a general strike brought the city of Seattle to a halt and in Boston the police were striking. Recent immigrants from eastern and southern Europe came to be particularly identified with communism and attempts to overthrow the American system of government.

There were various assassination attempts on high-profile Americans, such as the billionaire John D. Rockefeller. In the period following the First World War and in the wake of the Russian Revolution which imposed a communist government on Russia, there was a Red Scare leading to 6,000 arrests in early 1920. These were known as the **Palmer raids**, named after the Attorney General, Mitchell Palmer, himself an intended target for assassination. Palmer had become very popular through his exposure of 'communist activity' in the USA. He hoped he could use this as a springboard for the Democratic nomination for the presidency in 1920.

However, most of those detained had to be released within a few days due to a complete lack of evidence against them. Palmer announced there was to be a huge communist demonstration in New York on 20 May 1920. When this failed to materialise he looked ridiculous and the Red Scare died away. With it went his hopes of nomination for the presidency.

Sacco and Vanzetti

The case of Sacco and Vanzetti, on the other hand, would not go away. They were Italian immigrants, neither of whom spoke English well. When they were arrested, accused of carrying out an armed robbery near Boston in May 1920, they were found to be carrying guns. They also claimed to be anarchists. Although there was little concrete evidence against them, Sacco and Vanzetti were found guilty and eventually executed in 1927 after years of legal appeals.

There were widespread protests in cities throughout the USA at their executions but in rural America there were many who supported the executions. They were ready to believe that cities were filled with 'foreigners' who would not adopt American ways and who were determined to overthrow the American way of life.

The Ku Klux Klan

Racism was widespread, particularly in small towns and rural areas, against black Americans and other non-white groups. The Ku Klux Klan was an organisation that promoted **white supremacy** and gained considerable support in the Mid-West as well as the South. It had attracted 100,000 followers by 1921.

The Klan was opposed not just to black Americans, but also to Jews, Catholics and foreigners. It attacked ideas it found threatening such as evolution and working on the Sabbath. It also opposed any borrowing from non-'Anglo-Saxon' cultures, for example the popularity of jazz music, which was based in black-American culture.

Undoubtedly, the Klan met a need among many Americans. It gave them a sense of importance, belonging and power. With its secretive language, hoods and robes, burning crosses and violence, it added purpose and glamour to the humdrum lives of the farmers, artisans and shopkeepers who were the mainstay of its membership. It also appealed to the bullying and sadistic instincts in many. Victims could be tarred and feathered, branded and even killed. Plain living, Prohibition and church attendance could now be upheld by terror.

The Klan rapidly collapsed as a mass organisation due to increasing evidence of corruption and exploitation.

- Its leaders were professional fundraisers who controlled all the merchandising members were forced to buy. Robes for example cost $3.28 to manufacture and sold for $6.50. They also owned the Searchlight Publishing Company which monopolised all literature. They even invested in land. All the profits fuelled extravagant lifestyles for the leaders. By the late 1920s members began to realise they were being exploited.
- The leader of the Klan in Indiana, David Stevenson, was a charismatic figure who had built the organisation into a powerful political machine in his state. His downfall was sudden, following the suicide of a woman he had raped. He was convicted of second-degree murder. Stevenson's wickedness also helped to kill off large-scale support of the Klan.
- The organisation was also hurt by revelations of financial mismanagement in Pennsylvania. By 1929 its membership had fallen to 200,000 and it gradually fell from prominence nationally.

Concerns about immorality

Many people connected new ideas, particularly those associated with city life, with vice and immorality. There was widespread distrust of cinema, jazz music and its associated dances, particularly the Charleston and the Black Bottom. Women who wore short skirts, smoked in public and frequented '**speakeasies**' were called 'flappers'. They were generally regarded by more conservative people as shameless. The president of Florida University spoke for many when he complained that 'the low cut gowns, the rolled hose [stockings] and short skirts are born of the devil and are carrying the present and future generations to destruction'.

There were a series of high-profile scandals, such as that which destroyed the career of 'Fatty' Arbuckle, a very popular comedy star. Arbuckle was accused of a sexual attack in which his victim died. Due in part to these scandals, the movie industry agreed in 1922 to self-censorship through an office run by Will Hays. This examined every movie made in Hollywood for any immoral content and also attempted to promote clean living among movie stars. There was concern with the growth of crime and fear that it might spread into rural and small-town areas.

Prohibition

Prohibition illustrates well the contradictions in American society and politics during this period. Supported by those who looked to the government for 'moral regulation' – leading the way to ensure people led clean, wholesome lives – it involved the government interfering in private life to an unprecedented degree.

In 1918 the Eighteenth Amendment banned the sale, transportation and manufacture of intoxicating liquor within the USA. The separate Volstead Act at the same time defined 'intoxicating liquor' as any drink containing more than 0.5 per cent alcohol. Responsibility for enforcement was given to the Treasury. The first Prohibition commissioner charged with implementing the Prohibition laws was John F. Kramer.

Reasons for Prohibition

Prohibition was supported by a variety of interest groups.

- Many women's groups saw alcohol as a means by which men oppressed them.
- Big business saw drunkenness as leading to danger and inefficiency in the workplace, particularly in large factories. The Rockefeller Corporation and Heinz were two examples of large companies that supported Prohibition in the interests of greater workforce efficiency.
- Many religious groups believed alcohol was the work of the devil and was overwhelmingly responsible for sin and wrongdoing.

Supporters of Prohibition tended to be overwhelmingly Protestant, live in small towns in the South and West and, except in the South, vote Republican. Opponents were likely to be urban, of non-northern European ethnic origin, Roman Catholic and vote **Democrat**.

It may seem incredible to us that a nation as large and sophisticated as the USA could even attempt to ban something as commonly available as alcohol. Actually there was surprisingly little opposition to the measure. It had been one of the main policies of the progressive movement. There was a widespread belief that alcohol abuse led to social problems that could only be solved by its abolition. By 1917, 27 states had already passed Prohibition laws and there were 'dry' counties where alcohol was not allowed in several other states. Two factors led to an increased popularity of Prohibition at this time: the first, the impact of war, and the second, disorganisation of the opposition.

1 The impact of war

The First World War gave several boosts to Prohibition. Grain used in the production of alcoholic drinks was needed for food. As a result, many people felt it patriotic to do without alcohol. In 1917 the Lever Act banned the use of grain in the manufacture of alcoholic drinks.

Many of the largest brewers, such as Ruppert, Pabst and Leiber, were of German origin. Their businesses had helped to finance the National German-American Alliance that had supported German interests before the war. During the war, anti-German feeling led many not to buy alcohol from these companies.

Many people believed restrained behaviour in which people did not drink alcohol would be part of the 'brave new world' created after the war. It was felt that alcohol led young soldiers, who were away from home for the first time, into temptation and sinful ways – so best to remove it from their grasp.

2 Disorganisation of the opposition

The forces against Prohibition were not well organised. There was a march and rally in New York City, a parade in Baltimore and a resolution against taking away the working man's beer by the American Federation of Labor. Other than this, there was little protest.

The failure of Prohibition

The Anti-Saloon League (an organisation which supported Prohibition) estimated a $5 million budget would be enough to enforce it successfully. In the event, Prohibition Commissioner Kramer was given $2 million. Although Kramer insisted his department would ensure alcohol would be neither manufactured nor sold in the USA, Prohibition was to be a classic case of a law being passed that was impossible to enforce. There were seven reasons for this.

Geographical difficulties

The USA has 18,700 miles of coastline and land border. Those waters just outside the national limits became known, with good reason, as 'rum row'. Smuggling was so successful that in 1925 the officer in charge of Prohibition enforcement guessed that agents only intercepted about 5 per cent of alcohol coming into the country illegally. In

1924, they seized $40 million worth of alcohol, so the actual volume of business has been estimated at $800 million.

Bootleggers

Chemists could still sell alcohol on doctors' prescriptions. This was naturally open to widespread abuse. Many people known as '**bootleggers**' went into business as producers and distributors of illegal alcohol. The 'King of the Bootleggers', George Remus, bought up various breweries on the eve of Prohibition for the manufacture of medicinal alcohol. He then arranged for an army of 3,000 gangsters to hijack his products and divert them to the illegal **stills** of the big cities. In five years Remus made $5 million.

Industrial alcohol

Industrial alcohol was easily diverted and redistilled to turn it into an alcoholic drink. Illegal alcohol was often called '**moonshine**' because it was manufactured in remote areas by the light of the moon. However, it could equally be made in any old building. There was, of course, no quality control. The dangers for drinkers can easily be imagined and exotic cocktails were often invented to take away the unpleasant smell and taste of materials intended for industrial manufacture. Poisoning from wood alcohol (a simple alcohol made from wood spirit or methanol), although not common, did happen during this period. In one instance, 34 people died in New York City.

Problems for Treasury agents

At the most, 3,000 Treasury agents were employed to enforce Prohibition. They were paid an average salary of $2,500 to shut down an illegal industry whose profits were estimated at $2 billion annually. It is no wonder that many were corrupt. One federal agent was said to have made $7 million selling illegal licences and pardons to bootleggers.

Divisions among supporters

Against this, the 'dry' lobby, while very well organised to achieve Prohibition, was ill-equipped to help enforce it. The Anti-Saloon League, for example, was bitterly divided. Some members sought stricter enforcement laws, believing the League should actually be given power over appointment of officers. Others emphasised education programmes to deter people from drinking in the first place.

Role of government

Some historians have argued that Congress did not do more to enforce Prohibition because it did not want to alienate rich and influential voters who enjoyed a drink. In addition, this was a period of a reduced role by federal government, and most state governments were at best lukewarm in enforcement, particularly where cost was concerned. No one in government seemed to be prepared to say openly that Prohibition could not be enforced because Americans liked to drink alcohol. However, this was nevertheless apparent to many people.

Popularity of 'speakeasies'

As the 1920s progressed, the mood of the nation changed. For many Americans, particularly those living in the cities, their main aim in life became having a good time. Illegal drinking in gangster-run speakeasies became popular with many fashionable city dwellers.

Crime and gangsterism

There is no doubt that Prohibition led to a huge growth in organised crime and gangsterism. Mobsters controlled territories by force and established monopolies in the manufacture and sale of alcohol. These territories and monopolies were defended violently because potentially hugely profitable enterprises were involved. John Torrio, for example, ran most of the illegal alcohol business in Chicago and retired in 1925 with savings of $30 million.

Al Capone, the most notorious of the gangsters and Torrio's chosen successor, became something of a media star. He saw himself as embodying the spirit of free competition and enterprise in the USA. In an age when government interfered little in business, he seemed not to understand that what he was doing was wrong. Capone was a fervent Republican despite the fact that, or perhaps because, this was the party of Prohibition, and Prohibition provided him with his vast profits. When Capone finally went to jail in 1932, for income tax evasion, it was estimated his gang had done some $70 million worth of business. Capone insisted he never forced anyone to enter his speakeasies or drink his liquor. He felt he was primarily a businessman who supplied what people wanted.

Capone was also a man of violence. Where Torrio had often negotiated with rivals, dividing up areas of the city between them, Capone preferred 'turf wars'. Indeed, it was the introduction of an honest police chief in Chicago who prosecuted gangsters and cut bootleggers' profits that led to war between the gangsters as they invaded each other's territory. Gangsters sought both to maximise their profits and extend their territory so there had always been conflict. Threats to cut profits through increased police activity exacerbated this to epidemic proportions in cities such as Chicago. Capone built up an army of 700 gangsters who committed over 300 murders there. On 14 February 1929 five of his men, dressed as policemen, 'arrested' seven of the rival 'Bugs Moran' gang and shot over 100 bullets into them. This became known as the 'St Valentine's Day Massacre'.

Prohibition: For and against

By the end of the 1920s, many people questioned whether Prohibition had been worth it. It had certainly led to an explosion in crime. Between 1927 and 1930 alone, there were 227 gangland murders in Chicago with only two killers ever convicted. If Prohibition helped to create organised crime, it did not die out with its repeal. The gangs found other areas of vast profit such as gambling, prostitution and, later, drugs. Some argue that had it not been for Prohibition such large criminal gangs would not have developed in the first place.

Moreover, illegal drinking made criminals of a good percentage of the population. Interestingly, it had been the working-class saloons that tended to be shut down; the speakeasies that replaced them tended to sell spirits to a wealthy clientele. In this respect Prohibition worked to the detriment of the poor.

However, support for Prohibition remained in many rural areas. While it could take a stranger less than twenty minutes to find alcohol suppliers in big cities, they were very hard to find where the population did agree with Prohibition.

Supporters argued that alcohol consumption fell from an average of 2.6 gallons per person per year in the years before 1917 to one gallon by the 1930s. Arrests for drunkenness fell, as did deaths from alcoholism. There were fewer drunken drivers, therefore safer roads; indeed with the massive expansion of motor transport in the 1920s (see pages 236–7), this could be a significant factor in road safety. Also there were fewer accidents in the workplace, which was important when considering the increasing automation of industrial production with more complex and potentially dangerous machinery.

While many commentators regard Prohibition as a social catastrophe, it is important to remember that these less quantifiable factors show that it did have some positive effects.

End of Prohibition

President Hoover set up the Wickersham Commission in May 1929 to investigate the effectiveness of Prohibition. It reported in fourteen volumes after nineteen months' deliberation that the law could not be enforced. It recognised that many citizens violated it and bootleggers and distributors of alcohol could make enormous profits. It estimated that attempting to enforce Prohibition took up 66 per cent of the entire law enforcement budget. Yet because its members could not agree on the issue, and some thought it morally valid, it hesitated to recommend its abolition.

> **Source B** Humourist Franklin P. Adams made the following comment on the Wickersham Commission report in the *New York World*.
>
> Prohibition is an awful flop.
> We like it.
> It can't stop what it's meant to stop.
> We like it.
> It's left a trail of graft and slime,
> It don't prohibit worth a dime,
> It's filled our land with vice and crime.
> Nevertheless, we're for it.
>
> What criticisms does this poem make of the Wickersham Commission report?

It was President Roosevelt who finally abolished Prohibition in 1933. The Twentieth Amendment made it the responsibility of individual states to decide on the issue. It was an example of federal government cutting its own power rather than an abandonment of Prohibition in total.

Aim
To end manufacture and sale of alcohol for human consumption

Supporters
- Women's groups
- Big business
- Religious groups

Reasons for failure
- Geographical size made enforcement impossible
- 'Bootleggers'
- Easy to redistill industrial alcohol
- Lack of resources for enforcement
- Desires for pleasure among many Americans
- Disagreements among 'dry lobby'

Effects
- Rapid growth in organised crime
- Millions of people became 'law breakers'

▲ Prohibition: A summary.

The role and status of women

Many women were among Prohibition's most enthusiastic supporters. Others however regarded it as conservative and totally at variance with modernising trends in society. It is always misleading to think of 'women' as a homogeneous group. This is why specific women's political parties failed. Women respond to issues as differently as men. However, they did face common issues and discrimination as a result of their gender.

In 1920, the Nineteenth Amendment gave women the right to vote in federal elections but this did not make much difference to the lives of many women. Although women seemed more assertive and 'liberated' their opportunities in society remained limited, for example, they did not generally enjoy improved career opportunities during this period (see page 241).

Legislation moreover did little to help women, although the Sheppard–Towner Act of 1921 did fund healthcare for pregnant women and gave women some control over the clinics it set up. However, some women feared this measure simply reinforced the stereotypical view of women's main role as having lots of children and drew attention away from the need for birth control. Legislation to protect women in the workplace such as the banning of night shift work was similarly attacked. This was because it often meant women simply lost their jobs when they were no longer allowed to work such shifts, meaning they became more economically dependent on men. Despite the efforts of the Women's Party set up by former Suffragist Alice Paul, women never voted as a block and women's movements remained fragmented throughout this period.

While the myth of women as fun-loving 'flappers' undoubtedly contained some elements of truth among the young, it was largely that – just a myth. Surveys found most young women as conservative and traditional as their parents, with ambitions overwhelmingly to get married and have children. In the Middletown survey of 1929 for example, 89 per cent of girls said they'd like a job but would give it up after marriage. A poll at Vassar Women's College found 90 per cent felt they were unprepared for jobs. Colleges focussed very much on domestic skills. One of the female administrators at Vassar College said it should provide 'education for women along the lines of their chief interests and responsibilities, motherhood and the home'.

Key debate
The role and status of women in the 1920s

To a certain extent the focus on flappers conceals the realities for most women in the 1920s. Writing in 2007, Lucy Moore contrasts the post-war opportunities for young women with those of the past and gives examples of how these could liberate them – while including the proviso that most expected to give up work when they married. Other historians have been less sanguine. Writing in the 1990s Michael Parrish argued that even the flappers' movement was a form of exploitation which reinforced gender stereotypes as women seemed to focus on indulgence and beauty rather than serious issues. William Leuchtenberg, in the 1950s, was even more critical, showing that the numbers of women in the workforce and higher education actually diminished during the decade and women had little interest in voting. More recently, however, Lynn Dumenil has redressed the balance, showing how despite the problems they faced, both white and black-American women activists could be influential at state and local level, focussing, for example, on social reforms.

Women and birth control

Margaret Sanger drew attention to the plight of poor women through her work as a nurse. Often lacking any means of contraception, women were forced into dangerous back-street abortions which may have killed as many as 50,000 per year. She began to write articles on contraception. However widespread dissemination was difficult because the Comstock Act of 1873 banned the distribution of both written articles on contraception and items through the US mail. Arrested in 1916 for opening the first contraception clinic in the USA, in 1921 Sanger founded the American Birth Control League.

Many supporters of eugenics supported birth control because they felt the poor should be discouraged from breeding because to do so would threaten race degeneration. This was particularly apposite regarding non-white ethnic groups. Sanger herself began to promote sterilisation for mentally handicapped people, and the birth control movement has undoubtedly been criticised for its associations with eugenics.

Conclusion: Changes in society

Many people, especially those who lived in rural areas and clung to traditional values, worried about developments in US culture which seemed to threaten the established way of life. Most fears were irrational. There was, for example, the idea that immigration from southern and eastern Europe and Asia would threaten US values and indeed the white race, that immigrants from these places might attempt revolution. This was allied to the racism which saw the emergence of the Ku Klux Klan. Prohibition, the ill-conceived attempt to ban the sale of alcoholic beverages, led to a rise in crime but no diminution in the sale of alcohol. Women seemed independent and liberated but their opportunities were in fact limited and most clung to traditional conservative values. The vote did not lead to wholesale changes in the lives and realistic aspirations of women – that was for a later period.

> ### Work together
> First, compare the notes that you have made on this section (see page 246). Add anything that you have missed and check anything that you have disagreed on. Next, divide your paper into two. One of you should extract from your notes the positive aspects of changes in society. The other should note the negative aspects – for example you might consider movement to cities as a positive but the Ku Klux Klan negatively. After you have finished, combine your findings. Are there more positives than negatives? Overall, how would you describe the changes in society during the 1920s?

4 Cultural change in the 1920s

The 1920s were known as the 'Roaring Twenties'. It seemed to be a time of unbounded optimism, a time for youth and fads from crossword puzzles to dance marathons and flagpole sitting. Young women 'flappers' were particularly associated with jazz and dance crazes such as the Charleston and Black Bottom, which in their exuberance and inhibition were very different from the formal dances their parents had been used to, such as the waltz. The 1920s saw an explosion in popular culture. For the first time many people had leisure time and the money to spend on it. There were dramatic developments in media such as radio, cinema and sport. Cinema and sport predated the 1920s of course, but it was the fusion of a new market with improved technologies that enabled them to grow. Advertisers were quick to see how profitable a connection with the new media could be. They developed links which played on the popularity of cultural and sporting celebrities. Cinema in particular brought magic to millions of lives. The darkened 'picture palaces' enabled cinemagoers to dwell in an imaginary world free of everyday cares and aspire to the beauty and lifestyle of stars projected high onto a giant screen.

There were developments, too, in the culture of black Americans with the Harlem Renaissance affording a new respect to their achievements. However it was their music which really crossed over in terms of appreciation – jazz and blues became the mainsprings of American musical culture. Notable bands were led by Count Basie, Duke Ellington and Louis Armstrong. A new generation of writers meanwhile were developing new styles and idioms, although their main themes tended to focus on disillusion and despair, particularly in terms of the stifling morality and material obsessions in American life. They did not share the optimism of the decade.

> ### Note it down
> Using bullet points (see page ix) make notes on the key developments in US culture. Include an example for each key point (for example, flagpole sitting as an example of a fad). Compare your bullet points with those of a partner. Then try to put them together so you are adding each other's information to your own.

The age of 'fads'

The 1920s seemed to many an age of light-heartedness and optimism, symbolised by the massive growth of entertainment and 'fads' – activities that exploded in popularity: some like crossword puzzles retained their popularity while others like flagpole sitting were more fleeting.

The first modern crosswords were published in the *Boston Globe* in 1917, and by 1923 Simon and Schuster published the first book of puzzles – with a free pencil. Such was the craze that the Baltimore and Ohio Railroad placed dictionaries in their trains. Crossword competitions even became a spectator sport. Card games such as mah-jongg and contract bridge became equally popular. For more energetic types there were dance marathons – one Chicago marathon went on for 119 days – roller-skating and rocking horse derbies. There was even an attempt at a 3,400-mile transcontinental race, nicknamed 'the bunion derby'. Fifty-five runners actually accomplished the feat after 84 days' running.

Perhaps the most bizarre fad was flagpole sitting, first begun by a failed boxer 'Shipwreck Kelly' who called himself 'the luckiest fool alive'. In one year, 1929, Kelly spent 145 days atop various flagpoles. One of his emulators, fifteen-year-old Avon Foreman, sat on top of a hickory sapling in his back yard for ten days. In a tribute, the mayor of his home city, Baltimore, said, 'The grit and stamina of your endurance … shows that the old pioneer spirit of early America is being kept alive by the youth of today'.

Jazz was the biggest music craze with its attendant dances such as the Charleston and Black Bottom. To many conservative elements these dances seemed unrestrained and immoral in their level of body contact and free movement. They were particularly associated with the young and 'flappers' who seemed to exercise little moral restraint. Radio and records brought jazz into the home where people were known to push back the furniture to dance to the latest tunes.

The media and sport

The mass media publicised jazz and dancing, both in terms of entertainment in films when sound was introduced and the music through radio and records. The 1920s saw huge developments in media and sport, exploiting the growing income and leisure time available for many people. It was the first real age of mass entertainment.

Radio

Radio grew dramatically from the time of the establishment of the first commercial radio station. KDKA in Pittsburgh was set up in 1920 and by 1922 there were 500 stations dotted across the USA. The first national network, NBC, was set up in 1926 with CBS following in 1927. Some critics argued that invisible energy flying through the air must be dangerous and cited dead birds as evidence. However, for most, the radio brought a new world into people's living rooms. An estimated 50 million people listened to the 1927 boxing match between Gene Tunney and Jack Dempsey. People held 'radio parties' where friends and family could listen together in their home.

Radios weren't cheap. A typical model cost $150, usually paid for on credit. They were often big pieces of cabinet-like furniture. By 1927, 33 per cent of all money spent on furniture was spent on radios. Between 1923 and 1930, 60 per cent of all American families purchased one. Sales grew from $60 million in 1923 to $842 million six years later.

As we have seen radio held huge attraction for advertising and sponsorship which often paid for programmes. In August 1929, for example, the toothpaste company Pepsodent began to sponsor the popular comedy series *Amos 'n' Andy* on NBC; in the next few years the audience for this show would rise as high as 40 million. Programmes ranged across the spectrum from comedies to westerns to detective serials to music and comedy. While some felt the content of programmes should be uplifting and educational, most realised people wanted entertainment – and if it came in the form of serials they would be hooked. The power of radio to broadcast important sporting events should not be forgotten either – it brought the nation together for the first time. Through the power of radio Americans could listen to the same songs, laugh at the same jokes and thrill to the same sporting events at the same time.

Cinema

Cinema was even more significant. While moving picture shows had been around since the early years of the century, often as a novelty feature in a variety show, the 1920s saw their development as possibly the pre-eminent US contribution to world culture. By the 1920s, the cinema industry, centred in Hollywood, Los Angeles, was the fourth largest in terms of capital investment. It employed more people than either Ford or General Motors.

Going to the movies wasn't simply a form of escapism. Often movies were shown in elaborate picture palaces that could hold thousands of customers – in any one day there could be in excess of 10 million people in 20,000 cinemas. The most glamorous picture palaces were on a truly epic scale. The Roxy in New York, which cost in the region of $7–$10 million to build, had three organs, a huge chandelier, a red carpet valued at $10,000 and a 118-piece orchestra.

Movies offered escape, excitement and a chance to imagine oneself in a different world peopled by heroes. Actors became huge stars, the first real celebrities, and included:

- exciting actresses such as Clara Bow, the 'It girl' who symbolised the modern liberated woman, and Theda Bara, the 'vamp' exuding a dangerous sexuality
- action heroes like Douglas Fairbanks
- comic geniuses such as Buster Keaton and Charlie Chaplin.

The first sound film *The Jazz Singer* appeared in 1927; it served to make cinema even more popular.

> **Source C** Sociologist Herbert Blumer led a team which collected data from 2,000 students, published in 1933, in which they discussed their personal impressions of how movies had influenced them (found at https://www.brocku.ca/MeadProject/Blumer/1933/1933_10.html).
>
> Female, 19, white, college sophomore
>
> The impressions which the movies gave me as a child had to be torn down by experience, by reading, and by contact with other people. I thought that only wicked women smoked, that criminals were hard and inhuman and were to be dealt with accordingly. I thought that all society women neglected their children, had parties most of the time, and were untrue to their husbands. I got an idea that divorce was wrong and that people who were in love married and lived happily ever after, in a little rose-covered bungalow. The movies gave me a lot of foolish ideas which my imagination accepted as facts. I think that movies make adjustment to life and understanding of people and their problems more difficult, because of the wrong impressions which they give. The understanding should come first then the movies. Also I think that the movies overemphasize the sex interest, and cause people's minds to dwell on sex out of all proportion to its importance.
>
> Explain in your own words the point this student is making about the influence of movies on her. How valid might this example be within the context of the study which recorded 2,000 responses?

Sport

The 1920s was a golden age for sport both in terms of participation and following. People had more leisure time and sporting heroes attracted huge audiences – particularly in boxing and baseball.

The growth of radio brought national and local matches into people's homes and also helped foster a sense of national community – when, for example, 50 million listened to the Dempsey–Tunney fight on 22 September 1927. Many sports celebrities earned vast amounts from sponsorship deals and advertising. It was estimated that boxer Jack Dempsey made $10 million over the course of his career; baseball player Babe Ruth earned $80,000 just from his baseball salary and may have made 1 million dollars over the course of his playing career.

Baseball

The decade is particularly associated with baseball success, partly because it saw a significant number of supremely gifted players – Babe Ruth and his New York Yankee team-mate Lou Gehrig, for example. The game had been popular since the 1870s because it was easy to play on any patch of waste land but during the 1920s it captured the public imagination to the extent that massive stadia could be built such as West Side Grounds in Chicago. Many historians of the game agree the transformation of the game was largely down to the charisma associated with Babe Ruth. On a more prosaic note however it may be equally due to the introduction of a cork-centred ball that was easier to hit hard. This transferred emphasis away from pitchers to hitters like Babe Ruth – hence the fascination with the spectacular home runs.

1920 saw the formation of the Negro National Baseball League, a testament to the fact that sport was still largely segregated and black American players were excluded from the major league teams. Ironically, black teams toured the USA playing games to mixed crowds. The high point of the season, the East–West All Star game could attract crowds of 30,000. The players earned less than half of the salaries of their white counterparts, and committed themselves to exhausting circuits, some years playing up to three times a day every day. Nevertheless the Negro leagues were among the biggest black-American owned businesses in the USA.

The Harlem Renaissance

On the surface, black Americans gained little in the 1920s. The Ku Klux Klan (see page 247) appeared powerful for much of the decade, labour unions were reluctant to recruit members of ethnic minorities and the **Great Migration** from the South to Northern cities led to conflict and riots. President Harding's bill to outlaw **lynching** failed to pass Congress in 1922 due to the opposition of Southern Senators. Even in urban areas in the North where there were comparatively few black Americans there could be hostility and conflict. Black Americans increasingly were centred in specific areas of cities; one of the most famous in the 1920s was Harlem in New York.

Harlem could represent the ghettoisation or the concentration of black Americans into specific areas with attendant economic and social problems. In 1914, 50,000 black Americans lived in Harlem. By 1930 this figure had risen to 165,000. Of course there were problems, particularly with overcrowding – as an indication of the demand for accommodation, rents doubled between 1919 and 1927 – and poor living conditions. Often as properties fell into disrepair landlords failed to repair them.

However the concentration of so many black Americans into one area led to a flowering of culture – the 'Harlem Renaissance'.

James Weldon Johnson, a black American poet, wrote a very influential essay, 'The Making of Harlem', which appeared in the periodical *Survey Graphic* in 1925; he called Harlem 'a city within a city, the greatest negro city in the world'. The essay was optimistic in tone. He cited individual successes such as 'Pigfoot Mary' who made a fortune from selling fast food on a street corner. He also spoke of the Harlem Renaissance.

Renaissance means rebirth. By this Johnson meant a resurgence of black American culture, a pride in black American life and achievement. Some thinkers such as Alain Locke believed that their history of suffering through slavery and persecution gave black Americans a unique susceptibility to respond to the arts. His poems such as 'The Weary Blues' captured the voices of the residents of Harlem and the small but significant achievements of everyday life. Others were reluctant to portray themselves as victims and sought a specific black American identity and culture. This came particularly through music – jazz, blues and spirituals, which had a depth and intensity that few white Americans could replicate. There was no doubt about the huge popularity of these forms of music and Harlem abounded with clubs where it could be heard and danced to. Alain Locke hoped white appreciation of black American music might lead to greater toleration and even eventual racial equality.

White American interest led to a sanitised version of the music aimed more at white audiences. Notable white jazz musicians included clarinettist Benny Goodman, later known as 'the King of Swing' but spending much of the late 1920s as featured soloist in Ben Pollack's band. Perhaps the precursor of white involvement in jazz music was the 1921 stage musical *Shuffle Along*, whose all-black cast nevertheless attracted largely white audiences. Harlem itself became a place for whites to experience what they no doubt regarded as the exotic – jazz and dancing in clubs such as the Cotton Club and Plantation whose high prices kept out all but the relatively wealthy. These places were also sometimes decorated to reinforce stereotypes, for example as pre-civil war plantations.

Many black Americans resented this influx of whites into their community. Poet Claud McKay called Harlem 'an all-white picnic ground'. Others felt like animals in a zoo and spoke of 'white tourism'.

While one can understand such resentment, there is also the case that exposure to black American culture, however sanitised, aided ethnic understanding. However, the decade saw many black Americans becoming more militant and less tolerant of whites, greater understanding or not. The exponents of this movement were known collectively as 'The New Negro' after the anthology of work edited by Alain Locke in 1925.

Black Americans in the Southern states

Black Americans had been freed from slavery in the South in 1865 after the Civil War. They were protected by the military occupation of the South for ten years. However, when this ended in 1878, states gradually sought ways to disenfranchise them and limit their opportunities. In 1896 segregation was legalised in the court case *Plessey v. Ferguson* which allowed separate but equal facilities in public transport. This led to formal segregation throughout the South where facilities were separate but definitely not equal. The system was commonly known as 'Jim Crow'. It was reinforced not only by legal means but also by white terrorism through lynchings, not merely at the behest of the Ku Klux Klan. The South was a racist society where by the 1920s many black Americans had become apathetic because it was impossible to fight the injustice of the system. Many of course left in the Great Migration to the North.

'The New Negro'

Black American militancy predated the 1920s and can be traced back to the time of slavery. One notable voice was W.E. Dubois (1868–1963) whose magazine *The Crisis* had fought passionately for ethnic rights. Just as there was disagreement about whether black Americans should embrace Western-style culture or celebrate their own identity, there was controversy about whether they should integrate with white society or develop independently and separately. One of the leading exponents of the latter position was Marcus Garvey.

Some black Americans discounted ideas such as 'The New Negro' and Harlem Renaissance; they argued that proponents of these ignored black American achievements up to the 1920s. However the decade did see more black American writers and artists become known to white America such as Alaine Locke, Claud McKay and Langston Hughes, and black American music accepted as one of the great US art forms. Clearly prejudice and injustice went on and there were no moves to end segregation. However if enough white Americans did begin to appreciate that black Americans had a culture worth celebrating this might begin to break down the bonds of prejudice.

Marcus Garvey, 1887–1940

Marcus Garvey believed overwhelmingly in separation between the races. His Universal Negro Improvement Society gained thousands of supporters in the 1920s and encouraged black Americans only to deal with black American businesses. It set up a Black Cross for medical care and the Black Star Shipping Line to carry passengers to African ports. Garvey ran the 'Back to Africa' campaign which encouraged Black Americans to emigrate to the lands from which their descendants had been taken. However, the Black Star Shipping Line went bankrupt and Garvey was jailed for fraud; after this his movement faded. It did nevertheless act as an influence on militant separatist groups such as the Black Muslims in the 1960s.

Literature in the 1920s

While the literary trends in the 1920s reflected a widespread disillusionment with the USA, they led to a renaissance in US writing, much of which is still celebrated today. Writers such as Ernest Hemingway, F. Scott Fitzgerald and Sinclair Lewis (the first American recipient of the Nobel Prize for Literature) came into prominence. Many were exiles, especially in France where the cost of living was low. They hoped to escape the narrow constraints of American society.

Many intellectuals had long complained that the USA was too concerned with materialism and economic growth to appreciate the arts. Following the war, however, they became even more disillusioned – members of 'the lost generation' according to the writer Gertrude Stein – people who had often been involved in the war and could not settle back into an ordered existence. F. Scott Fitzgerald meanwhile coined the phrase 'the Jazz Age' and wrote immensely popular novels such as *The Great Gatsby* about the superficially hedonistic lifestyle of the young that concealed a deep malaise.

Hemingway and *The Sun Also Rises*

This sense of unhappiness is shown in Hemingway's first successful novel *The Sun Also Rises* (1926) in which a group of ex-patriots lead fruitless lives in Paris and elsewhere, drinking, arguing and going off in search of adventure – for example to bullfights in Spain. The hero, Jake Barnes, has been severely wounded in the war and rendered impotent. He symbolises the emptiness of the society Hemingway describes. Interestingly all the protagonists had left either the USA or Britain to escape the stifling monotony and social constraints. While the new lifestyles may have been different, they weren't any better.

Sinclair Lewis and Babbitt

This idea resonated with Sinclair Lewis, who had found considerable success with *Main Street* in 1920, a novel which explored small town life in which the protagonist, while finding life unfulfilling and monotonous returned to it in the absence of anything better. The concept was explored further in *Babbitt*, published in 1925 and examining life in a fictional city, 'Zenith', where one might have expected to find more opportunities for fulfilment. Not so. Babbitt is simply concerned with social status and materialism and it is to this that he returns after a brief attempt at rebellion.

Popular reading

While the literary renaissance resonated with a wide readership, one should not forget however that most people weren't reading Hemingway. They enjoyed popular fiction

Source D First paragraphs of the novel *Babbitt* by Sinclair Lewis. First published in 1922.

> The towers of Zenith aspired above the morning mist; austere towers of steel and cement and limestone, sturdy as cliffs and delicate as silver rods. They were neither citadels nor churches, but frankly and beautifully office-buildings.
>
> The mist took pity on the fretted structures of earlier generations: the Post Office with its shingle-tortured mansard, the red brick minarets of hulking old houses, factories with stingy and sooted windows, wooden tenements colored like mud. The city was full of such grotesqueries, but the clean towers were thrusting them from the business center, and on the farther hills were shining new houses, homes—they seemed—for laughter and tranquillity.
>
> Over a concrete bridge fled a limousine of long sleek hood and noiseless engine. These people in evening clothes were returning from an all-night rehearsal of a Little Theater play, an artistic adventure considerably illuminated by champagne. Below the bridge curved a railroad, a maze of green and crimson lights. The New York Flyer boomed past, and twenty lines of polished steel leaped into the glare.
>
> In one of the skyscrapers the wires of the Associated Press were closing down. The telegraph operators wearily raised their celluloid eye-shades after a night of talking with Paris and Peking. Through the building crawled the scrubwomen, yawning, their old shoes slapping. The dawn mist spun away. Cues of men with lunch-boxes clumped toward the immensity of new factories, sheets of glass and hollow tile, glittering shops where five thousand men worked beneath one roof, pouring out the honest wares that would be sold up the Euphrates and across the veldt. The whistles rolled out in greeting a chorus cheerful as the April dawn; the song of labor in a city built—it seemed—for giants.

How useful would Source D be to a historian conducting an enquiry into the prosperity of the 1920s in the USA?

serialised in the *Saturday Evening Post*, sometimes written by Scott Fitzgerald in less serious moments; in westerns written by Zane Grey and Max Brand whose works sold in their millions; and other pulp fiction by luminaries such as Edgar Rice Burroughs who created Tarzan. One of the most successful magazines was *Reader's Digest* founded in 1922, covering human interest stories, short humorous pieces and condensed fiction for those who didn't have the time or inclination to read complete books.

Conclusion: Cultural change

The 1920s seemed an age of optimism where fads such as flagpole sitting seemed to capture the light-hearted mood. Massive developments in the media and entertainment, notably radio cinema and sport, opened up new worlds for millions. Cinema in particular fed into their fantasies. The popularity of film actors and sports personalities turned people like Babe Ruth, Jack Dempsey, Clara Bow and Theda Barr into celebrity superstars. Black Americans meanwhile enjoyed a renaissance both in terms of their contribution to traditional western arts such as poetry and to ethnic culture through music such as jazz. Jazz and blues indeed crossed over into mainstream US culture. Many writers detected a malaise in American society which fed their imagination. Most Americans, however, read the *Readers' Digest* and popular fiction such as westerns so were either unaware or lacking in sympathy with this development.

Work together

This section offers a good opportunity for you to undertake more research. Working with a partner each pick two of the following: age of fads; media and sport; Harlem Renaissance and the New Negro; literature in the 1920s. Using texts and information from the internet, what more can you find out about these topics? Present your findings to each other.

Recommended reading

F.L. Allen, *Only Yesterday: An Informal History of the 1920s in America* (Penguin, 1938). An entertaining journalistic account from the time of the 1920s in the USA – still in print and readily available.

Bill Bryson, *One Summer: America, 1927* (Transworld Publishers, 2013). Engaging account of all the events of the summer of 1927.

William E. Leuchtenburg, *The Perils of Prosperity* (University of Chicago Press, 1957), especially Chapters 4, 8, 9 and 10. Thorough examination of the 1920s.

Lucy Moore, *Anything Goes: A Biography of the Roaring Twenties* (Atlantic Books, 2008). Entertaining account of the Roaring Twenties with the focus on social history.

Chapter summary

- The 1920s seemed a prosperous decade with developments such as mass production and new business methods boosting industry and government policies favouring business with little regulation.
- Increased pay and leisure opportunities for many people were boosted by development of the car industry and labour-saving devices.
- Not all sectors, for example agriculture, were prosperous, and many groups such as black Americans did not share in the prosperity; employment opportunities were limited for women.
- In October 1929 the Wall Street stock exchange crashed, symptomatic of problems in the economy such as easy credit and 'get-rich-quick' schemes.
- Restrictions on immigration were symptomatic of the endemic racism in white society.
- Prohibition was not only unenforceable but led to an increase in gangsterism and crime.
- Despite a reputation for liberation the role and status of women did not change noticeably.
- There were huge developments in the media and entertainment including sport.
- There was a renaissance in black American culture, particularly associated with Harlem.
- Serious writers such as Scott Fitzgerald and Hemingway remained pessimistic about US society.

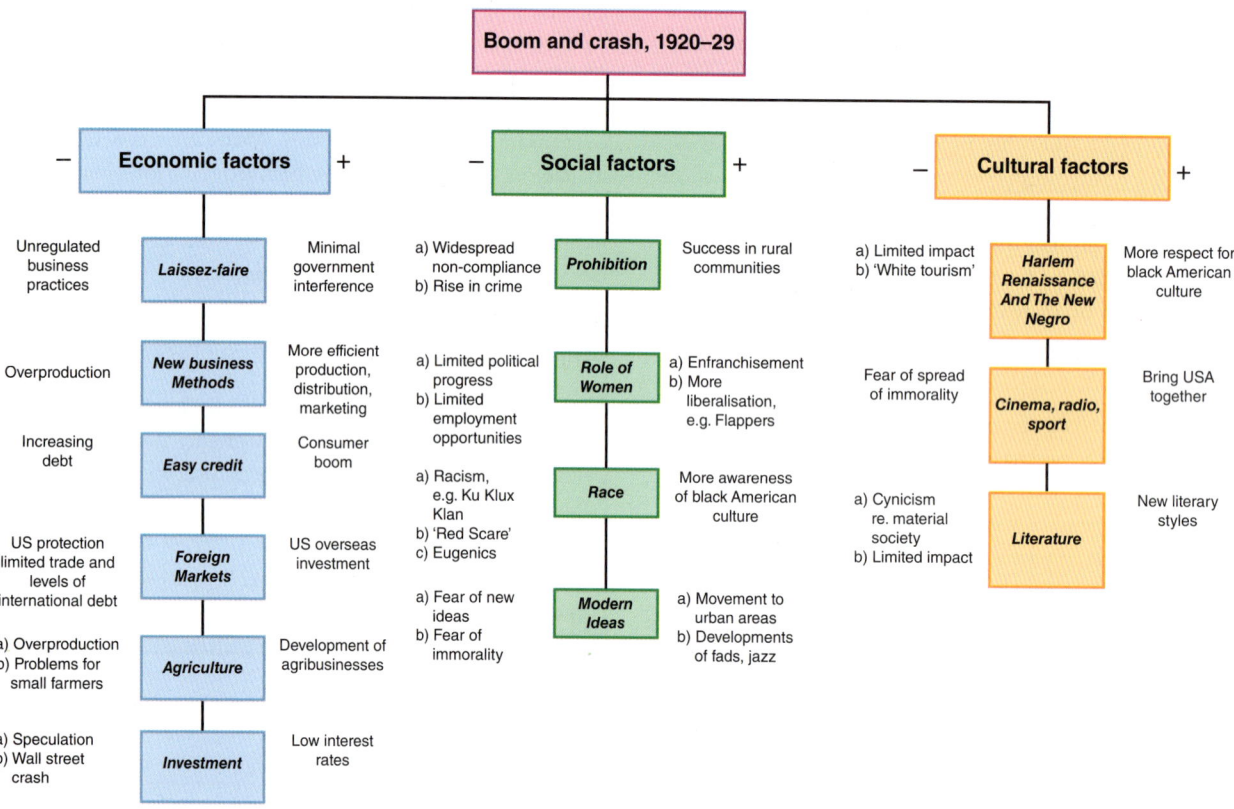

▲ Summary diagram: Boom and crash, 1920–29.

Section A: Essay technique

Focus on the question and understanding the sources

The A level Section A question requires you to deploy a variety of skills. The most important are source analysis and evaluation. In essence, the question asks how much a historian could learn about a specific issue from the two sources. This is a complex task, and requires a range of skills which will be covered in this section and at the end of Key Topics 2–4. These include the ability to:

- understand the focus of the question and the sources (this section)
- structure an essay and write good introductions (Key Topic 2, page 291)
- select information and make inferences from the sources (Key Topic 2, page 292–4)
- place the sources in their historical context (Key Topic 3, page 319)
- evaluate and weigh the evidence of the sources (Key Topic 4, page 345)
- reach and support a final judgement (Key Topic 4, page 349).

The Section A question for AS level is different from that of A level, and some guidance about this is given on page vii. However, you will need to develop very similar skills for the AS exam, therefore the activities will help with the AS exams as well. There are also some AS-style questions in every chapter.

Understanding the focus of the question

In order to answer the question successfully, you must understand how the question works. Below is a typical source-style question (the sources are on page 260). The question is written precisely in order to make sure that you understand the task. Each part of the question has a specific meaning:

'How far' indicates that you must evaluate the extent of something, rather than giving a simple 'yes' or 'no' answer.

The key word here is '**together**'. You must examine the sources as a pair and make a judgement about both sources, rather than separate judgements about each source.

> Study Sources 1 and 2 before you answer this question.
>
> **How far could the historian make use of Sources 1 and 2 together to investigate the extent of prosperity in the USA in the 1920s?**
>
> Explain your answer, using both sources, the information given about them and your own knowledge of the historical context.

This is the essence of the task: you must focus on what a historian could legitimately conclude from studying these sources.

The final part of the question focusses on a specific topic that a historian might investigate. In this case, 'the extent of prosperity in the USA in the 1920s'.

This instruction lists the resources you should use: the sources; the information given about the sources; your own knowledge of historical context that you have learned during the course.

Key Topic 1 Boom and crash, 1920–29 — 259

Source 1 Extract from a speech by Herbert Hoover during the 1928 presidential elections given at New York City, 22 October 1928.

> Our people are steadily increasing their spending for higher standards of living. Today there are almost nine automobiles for each ten families, where seven and a half years ago only enough automobiles were running to average less than four for each ten families. The slogan of progress is changing from the full dinner pail to the full garage. Our people have more to eat, better things to wear and better homes. We have even gained in elbow room, for the increase of residential floor space is over 25 per cent, with less than 10 per cent increase in our number of people. Wages have increased; the cost of living has decreased. The job to every man and woman has been made more secure. We have in this short period decreased the fear of unemployment, the fear of old age; and these are fears that are the greatest calamities of human kind. All this progress means far more than greater creature comforts. It finds a thousand interpretations.

Source 2 Extract from Robert S. and Helen Merrell Lynd's sociological study of Muncie, Indiana, *A New Era in Middletown*, published in 1929. Muncie was chosen because it was felt to be typical of small-town USA.

> Large numbers of people anxious to get their living are periodically stopped by the recurrent phenomenon of 'bad times' when the machines stop running, workers are 'laid off' by the hundreds, salesmen sell less, bankers call in loans, 'credit freezes' [*], and many Middletown families may take their children from school, move into cheaper homes, cut down on food, and do without many of the countless things they desire…
>
> The leading paper offered the following prescriptions for local prosperity: 'The first duty of a citizen is to produce'; and later 'The American citizen's first importance to his country is no longer that of citizen but that of consumer. Consumption is the new necessity'. 'The way to make business boom is to buy.' At the same time that the citizen is told to 'consume' he is told, 'Better start saving late than never. If you haven't opened your weekly savings account with some local bank, trust company or building and loan, today's the day.'
>
> [*] Credit freezes: periods when credit is no longer available.

Overall, all Section A questions ask you to make a judgement about how far two sources are useful to the historian. However, the second half of the question specifies what a historian is focussing on.

The first part of the question sets up the **general task**, which is true of all Section A questions:

'How far could the historian make use of Sources 1 and 2 together to investigate…'

The second part of the question establishes the **specific focus**, for example:

'…the extent of prosperity in the 1920s?'

As you write your essay, you need to focus on both aspects.

How to focus in a source question

In order to maintain your focus in a source question, you can do the following:

- Use the phrases 'Source 1' and 'Source 2' when dealing with the sources so that it is clear which sources you are focussing on.
- Use words such as 'useful' or 'utility' to ensure that you are explicitly addressing the general task.
- Use comparative words and phrases such as 'Sources 1 and 2 disagree' to show that you are using the sources together.

Activity: A focussed introduction

1. Write a short introduction that provides a focussed answer to the question above. See page 291 for advice on writing introductions. Also remember that this is a question about two sources.
2. Having written an introduction, swap it with a partner. Consider:
   (a) Which introduction best focussed on the question? Remember, your introduction needs to focus on the **general task** and the **specific focus**.
   (b) Which introduction best dealt with the sources *together*?
   (c) Which introduction gave the clearest answer to the question?
   (d) What can you learn from each other's approach to the question?

Use these questions to feed back to each other and improve your introductions.

Activity: AS-style questions

(a) Why is Source 1 valuable to the historian for an enquiry into the extent of prosperity in the US in the 1920s?
(b) How much weight do you give the evidence of Source 2 for an enquiry into popular attitudes to the US economy in the 1920s?

Understanding the sources

Understanding the sources is crucial to doing well in Section A questions. The most important aid in this understanding is a detailed knowledge of the period. There are also techniques to aid understanding. Here are a few tips to get you started:

- Read the source word for word – if it helps, read it out loud when you are doing practice questions. This makes it much less likely that you will miss anything in the source.
- Think about the question as you are reading. You will then look out for relevant information within the source.
- Make index cards before your exam of the specific vocabulary for the topic you are studying – for example, 'economy', 'stock market', 'depression'.
- Look up terms and definitions that you don't recognise in practice questions.
- Make index cards of the people who might be quoted in the sources, such as Calvin Coolidge, Herbert Hoover and Henry Ford, and of the documents that might be used as sources on the examination paper. Make notes on who they are and their attitudes to the key issues you have studied.

Comprehension

Comprehension is the most basic source skill. It simply means understanding the source's meaning. You can demonstrate this by:

- **Copying:** writing out the words of the source in your essay.
  TIP: Never copy out too much – just use a few words from the source, incorporating them within the flow of your sentence.
- **Open paraphrasing:** putting part of a source in your own words.
  TIP: Avoid simply rewriting the whole source in your own words.
- **Summarising:** summing up the meaning of the entire source, or a large part of the source, in a single sentence.
  TIP: Summarising can be useful in introductions and conclusions.

These are low-level source skills. They are useful, but you will also want to show off your higher-level skills!

Higher-level skills

Higher-level skills include:

- using the sources together (see page 260)
- making inferences (see page 294)
- analysing sources in their historical context (see page 319)
- evaluating the evidence presented in the sources (see page 346)
- reaching an overall judgement regarding the usefulness of the sources (see page 346).

Activity: Test your understanding

Having read Sources 1 and 2 on page 260:

1. Make a list of words and phrases that you don't understand and look them up in the glossary of this book or online. You should repeat this activity regularly with the sources that you encounter. This will help with many of the sources you will examine as you study the USA 1920–55.
2. Study Source 1. **Copy** the sentence that best expresses examples of the rise in living standards. Make sure you put the quote in quotation marks.
3. **Paraphrase** what Source 2 says about the problems people face in 'bad times'.
4. **Summarise** Source 2 in no more than 30 words to show how the advice people are given for their future prosperity is often contradictory.

Work together

Having completed the activity 'Test your understanding', swap your answers with a partner. Consider:

1. Did you both identify the same words that needed to be defined?
2. Were your partner's definitions clear and accurate?
3. Did you both copy the same bit of Source 1? If not, which quote better summarises the rise in living standards?
4. Is your partner's paraphrase clear? Does it accurately reflect the problems people faced in 'bad times'?
5. Whose summary more precisely expressed the contradictory advice people were offered?
6. What can you learn from the approach of your partner to the two sources?

Use these questions to feed back to each other and improve your analysis of the sources.

Key Topic 1 Boom and crash, 1920–29

Section B: Essay technique

Focus and structure

Your Section B essay, like all of your examined essays, will be judged on how far it focusses on the question, and the quality of its structure. You have probably already got ideas about focussing and structure in Paper 1 (see pages 196 and 229).

Different types of question

Section B questions focus on concepts such as cause, consequence, change/continuity, similarity/difference and significance. These different concepts require slightly different approaches. Here are some examples of these concepts in questions.

This question requires you to explain how far there were problems in the economy.

This question requires you to evaluate how far Prohibition failed. Don't forget it wasn't a complete failure, especially in rural areas.

1. **How far were there signs that the economy was faltering in the second half of the 1920s?**

2. **'The tensions in the 1920s were fundamentally between rural and urban life.' How far do you agree with this statement?**

3. **'Prohibition was a complete failure.' How far do you agree with this statement?**

4. **How far was the Wall Street Crash of October 1929 a significant turning point in the onset of the Depression?**

5. **'The 1920s saw a radical change in the role and status of women.' How far do you agree with this view?**

This question asks you to evaluate how far rural communities with traditional values such as religion and moral lifestyles felt threatened by modern life, particularly in the cities, such as the growth of cinema, jazz, dancing and illicit drinking.

This question requires you to evaluate the significance of the Wall Street Crash in the transition from apparent prosperity to depression.

This question requires you to evaluate how far the lives of women changed and how far they remained the same in the 1920s.

Structuring your essay

Your essay should be made up of three or four paragraphs, each addressing a different factor (see page 40).

However, essays that focus on different concepts will need slightly different structures:

- **Cause essays** require you to explain why something happened. Each paragraph should deal with a different possible cause.
- **Evaluative essays** require you to weigh up the extent of something. Most essays will require you to evaluate at some point, as weighing up is essential to reaching a conclusion. In essays that focus on evaluation, each paragraph should weigh a different factor. For example, if you were dealing with the question, 'How far was the Harlem Renaissance a significant turning point in white Americans beginning to respect black American culture?', you need to consider the impact of the Harlem Renaissance and ask how far it changed the views of white Americans towards the value of black American culture. Most importantly, you need to make a judgement at the end based upon what you have written in the essay.
- **Success or failure essays** require you to evaluate the extent to which something succeeded. Therefore you will need to start by considering the aims in order to establish the criteria for success. You should go on to consider aspects that succeeded and weigh them against aspects that failed in order to reach a conclusion.
- **Continuity and change essays** require you to evaluate the extent of change. Therefore your essay will have to weigh up what changed and what stayed the same.
- **Consequence essays** require you to evaluate which of a range of consequences was most important.

It is crucial to be able to distinguish between the different types of question. Confusing a causes essay with a consequences essay could seriously affect your grade.

Activity: Question types

1. Below are six different Section B style questions. Work out what types of question they are.
   - (a) How far did the lives of black Americans change in the 1920s? [AS]
   - (b) 'Prohibition led to a massive rise in crime in the 1920s.' How far do you agree?
   - (c) 'The economy was real success story in 1920s USA.' How far do you agree?
   - (d) How widespread was prosperity in the 1920s? [AS]
   - (e) 'The most important cause of the Wall Street Crash was easy credit.' How far do you agree with this statement?
   - (f) 'The enfranchisement of women was the most important factor in their gaining more opportunities in the 1920s.' How far do you agree with this statement?
2. Having worked out what types of question you are dealing with, you should now write plans for each question. Use either spider diagrams or bullet-point lists. Make sure your plan reflects the kind of essay that you are dealing with. For example, if you are dealing with a success or failure essay, you should highlight which parts of the plan deal with success and which deal with failure.

Complete one plan at a time, and after each discuss it with a friend.

Work together

Having completed a plan, swap it with a partner. Consider:

1. Did you agree on what type of question you were dealing with? If not, discuss it and work out who was right.
2. Whose plan most clearly focussed on the specific type of question?
3. Did your partner's plan miss anything?
4. Did you miss anything that you should add to your plan?
5. What can you learn from your partner's approach?

Use these questions to feed back to each other and improve your question spotting and planning.

Key Topic 2 The Depression and the New Deal, 1929–38

Overview

The years following the Wall Street Crash saw the onset of a global economic depression. In the USA unemployment estimates varied from one-quarter to one-third of the labour force. Within this figure some groups, such as black Americans and women, fared even worse. President Hoover and the US government were ill equipped to cope with the scale of the economic downturn, although Hoover attempted to intervene more than any of his predecessors. In 1933 the new president Franklin D. Roosevelt promised a New Deal to restore prosperity to the USA. This programme became far more ambitious than simply attempting to end the Depression. Government involved itself more in the lives of people and institutions than ever before. It saw, for example, the first social security measures in the USA and legal recognition of labour unions. The extent to which it actually solved the problems of the Depression is questionable. When it was scaled down in 1937, a new economic downturn occurred.

The overarching theme of the Depression and the New Deal is covered in four sections:
1 The spread of the Depression, 1929–32
2 Hoover's response to the Depression, 1929–32
3 Roosevelt and the First New Deal, 1933–35
4 The Second New Deal, 1935–38

TIMELINE

1929 March	Herbert Hoover becomes president
1929 April	Agricultural Marketing Act
1930 June	Smoot–Hawley tariff
1931 December	Moratorium on foreign debts
1932 January	Reconstruction Finance Corporation
1932 July	Federal Home Loan Bank Act
1932 July	Emergency Relief and Construction Act
1933 March	Franklin D. Roosevelt becomes president
1933 March–September	'100 days' launch of the First New Deal
1935 January	Launch of Second New Deal
1935 July	Wagner–Connery National Labor Relations Act (the 'Wagner Act')
1935 August	Social Security Act
1935 August	Revenue Act
1936 January	Start of Roosevelt's battle with the Supreme Court
1936 November	Roosevelt wins second term of office
1937 February	Judicial Reform Act
1937 June	'Roosevelt Recession' begins

1 The spread of the Depression, 1929–32

No one could have foreseen the scale of the Great Depression in the USA. One historian compared the unemployment figures with casualty lists from the First World War to show their magnitude. In 1933 **Gross National Product (GNP)** was half that of 1929. Most industries suffered decline and the banking system was close to collapse. The human cost was devastating. There was no system of state benefits, and most unemployed had to rely either on their own ingenuity or charity – and charities were close to collapse because of the increased demand and falling

Note it down

In this section try using a spider diagram to take notes (see page x). Draw a circle in the middle of your page with the heading 'The spread of the Depression' inside it. Draw three lines coming out of the central circle that lead to the section headings: Economic impact; Social effects; Gangsters and the rise of crime. Write important points on lines coming out from the section headings and write small points coming out from them. Check page 290 to see if you are on the right track.

revenues. Many of the unemployed became **hoboes**, moving from place to place in search of work. Nowhere in the USA escaped the effects of the Depression. In the countryside, food prices were so low that farmers couldn't afford to harvest their crops. Many lost their farms. Banks were blamed for foreclosing when mortgages couldn't be repaid. This led to a rise in crime and some outlaws like Bonnie and Clyde becoming folk heroes because they robbed banks.

The Depression's economic impact

The Depression had significant economic effects which combined to undermine the confidence of the USA in its ability to recover. The Depression spread throughout the land into almost every sector. However, some new industries did escape its worst effects. In this section we will consider:

- unemployment
- effects on individual industries
- problems with credit and banking.

Unemployment

Unemployment soared, possibly from as much as 3.2 per cent of the **labour force** in 1929 to 25.2 per cent by 1933. This meant that 12,830,000 people were out of work. The Labor Research Association, an organisation that studied trends in employment, complained that these figures were underestimates and that the real figure was nearer 17 million. It was estimated that the national wage bill in 1932 was only 40 per cent of the 1929 figure. By 1933 the Depression covered the whole of the USA.

Unemployment and **underemployment** were spread throughout the country unevenly. New York State alone had 1 million unemployed. In Ohio, 50 per cent of the workforce of the city of Cleveland were unemployed. In Toledo, a staggering 80 per cent were unemployed. However, a military base or university campus could delay the onset of the Depression due to employment opportunities there. Localised circumstances could be significant such as the temporary oil boom in Kilgore, Texas, which ironically led to a glut and collapse of prices elsewhere in that industry. There were also 'Depression-proof' industries such as cigarette manufacture, which shielded Louisville, Kentucky and Richmond, Virginia.

Ethnic minorities and women were particular victims of the Depression.

Black Americans

The magazine *The Nation* reported in April 1931 that the number of black Americans out of work was four to six times higher than white Americans, and that poorly paid jobs traditionally reserved for black Americans, such as those of waiter and lift attendant, were now increasingly being offered to white people. Black-American rural workers were used to depressed conditions. However, employment opportunities in the Northern cities, which had opened up in the 1920s, were now generally closed to them. One study of unemployment in 13 large cities found 52 per cent of black Americans unemployed compared with 31.7 per cent of white Americans. By 1933 the national picture had worsened with 50 per cent of black Americans unemployed compared with 25 per cent of whites. The Depression also slowed the migration of black Americans to Northern cities; during the Depression years 300,000 left the South. Conditions often deteriorated for those who remained, and as we shall see, these were actually exacerbated by New Deal legislation (see page 280).

Native Americans

Native Americans were among the poorest of all Americans. Government policy towards them was based on the Dawes Severalty Act of 1887. This had as its lynchpin the twin notions of **assimilation** and **allotment**. The policy of allotment meant that the old tribal units were broken up and the **reservations** divided into family-sized farms of 160 acres. Surplus land was to be sold off.

The destruction of Native American culture had often left the people listless and apathetic. Allotment had been a failure particularly for those Native Americans who were not farmers by tradition. Moreover, much of the land allocated to them was unsuitable for productive farming. In fact, of 138 million acres owned by Native Americans at the time of the Dawes Severalty Act, 90 million acres had fallen out of their hands by 1932.

Many Native Americans lived in squalor and idleness. By 1926 a Department of the Interior inquiry confirmed that the Act had been a disaster for Native Americans and that the policy of allotment in particular should be reversed. However, nothing had been done to alleviate it. The Great Depression only made matters worse in that Native Americans found it more difficult to leave the poverty-stricken reservations in search of work. It would take a fresh approach during the presidency of Franklin D. Roosevelt, with the Indian Reorganization Act of 1934, to attempt to address their problems (see page 280).

Hispanic Americans

Many Hispanic Americans had predated their white American fellows in the Southwest; the area had been part of Mexico until wrested from that country after war in 1846. However, Hispanic Americans had also been widely recruited throughout the Southwest as seasonal workers to help in agriculture. As the Depression bit, many were repatriated. This took place under the aegis of the Federal Bureau of Immigration and was largely undertaken to cut the budget for relief and free up some jobs for white Americans. Some went voluntarily; there were two trains laid on from San Antonio, Texas in February and August 1930, which together conveyed 7,000 passengers to Central Mexico. Altogether, 400,000 people were repatriated during the Depression years; many were forced to leave following raids in places such as parks where people were living rough. Many of those forced to leave were actually US citizens; some had never lived anywhere but the USA.

Women

Women, particularly those of the working classes, also did badly. Those in unskilled jobs were likely to be laid off before men, and those in domestic service suffered because families could no longer afford to keep them on. Married women often needed to work to keep the family solvent. However, because they had a job, they were often accused of being responsible for male unemployment. It was quite common for them to be dismissed and their work given to men. In 1930 over 75 per cent of American school authorities refused to employ married women. Half of the 48 states had laws banning the employment of married women.

Effects on individual industries

As we have seen, there were some areas that survived the onset of the Depression.

Many business historians, moreover, are keen to emphasise that the period of the Depression was also one of technical innovation; air conditioning, airline travel, colour film and supermarkets were just some of the new ideas introduced in the 1930s. Not everyone suffered equally; some businesses did well at different times, and some were fortunate enough to avoid the Depression altogether, such as the aviation industry.

In the coal industry, production in 1932 was at its lowest since 1904 and the workforce fell by 300,000. Many of those in work were only part-time and wages could be as low as $2.50 per day. Seventy-five per cent of textile firms were losing money, while iron and steel production fell by 59 per cent and US Steel Corporation's workforce was wholly part-time by the end of 1932. Car sales fell from 4,455,178 in 1929 to 1,103,557 four years later.

The average number of people employed in the 'motor city' of Detroit fell by 21.5 per cent between 1928 and 1929. In Toledo, between May 1929 and spring 1932, Willis-Overland, a car manufacturing company, kept on only 3,000 of their 25,000-strong workforce. In similar cases, the number employed by both General Electric and Westinghouse making electrical appliances was more than halved; the only electrical goods not to suffer a significant decline in demand were light-bulbs, which needed to be replaced.

The construction industry, already in decline before 1929, saw the number of newly built residential units fall 82 per cent between 1929 and 1932. Construction contracts were valued at $6.6 billion in 1929 but only $1.3 billion three years later.

With fewer in productive work overall, the growth rate went into decline, from 6.7 per cent in 1929 to −14.7 per cent in 1932, representing a fall in GNP from $203.6 billion in 1929 to $144.2 billion in 1932.

Aviation

The aviation industry developed during the 1930s and seemed impervious to the Depression. Lindbergh's flight across the Atlantic was the spark that set off its commercial growth, which saw $100 million invested in the industry. The Californian company Boeing had so little work during the 1920s that it made furniture to keep it solvent. By 1928 its workforce was over 1,000. In 1930 it produced the first all-metal, low-wing aeroplane, the Boeing 247, which could carry ten passengers with a speed of 155 miles per hour. Cross-continental travel was expensive and initially limited in the main to wealthy businessmen. By mid-decade, however, there were co-ordinated coast-to-coast journeys, and TWA offered non-stop flights from Newark to Chicago; as the busiest airport in the USA, it was fitting that Newark had the first air traffic controllers in 1935. In the same year, the Douglas DC 3 became the first modern airliner with 21 seats and was able to fly 1,500 miles at a cruising speed of 200 miles per hour. The number of airline passengers rose from 474,000 in 1932 to 1,178,858 in 1938 and the number of passenger miles increased 600 per cent between 1936 and 1941. While air passengers comprised only 7 per cent of those taking long-distance trains, clearly the 1930s had seen the introduction of air flight as a major form of transport in the USA.

Problems with credit and banking

Credit had all but vanished. The stock market went into serious decline despite occasional rallies as in December 1929 and April 1930. Bank closures multiplied. There had been 5,000 in the entire period 1921–29, but there were over 10,000 between 1929 and 1933. Most of these were small banks that had overextended lending in the time of prosperity and now could not meet their depositors' demands for their money. When farmers, for example, could not meet their mortgage repayments, the banks had to evict them and take the farms over. In doing so, the banks lost liquid assets in the form of mortgage repayments and gained **bankrupt**, often unsaleable, farms in exchange. As a result, many went bankrupt themselves, often losing their customers' savings in the process.

By 1933, the USA was a land of cash transactions, where those still in work fiercely protected their jobs, credit was tight and no one was prepared to take a risk. It was also a land singularly unable to handle a major depression.

Social effects of the Depression

The human cost of the Depression was enormous. The USA was ill equipped to handle unemployment. There was, for example, no federal unemployment benefit. The **work ethic** was very strong in America and unemployment among the able-bodied was generally held to be their own fault. For this reason alone, the psychological effects of mass unemployment were devastating.

The strain on family life was intense as people fell into unemployment or short-term working, possibly losing their homes or having to sell heirlooms to survive. The number of marriages fell from 1.23 million in 1929 to 982,000 in 1932, with an accompanying fall in the birth rate from 21.2 per thousand in 1929 to 19.5 per thousand in 1932. Suicide rates increased from 14 per 10,000 in 1929 to 17.4 per 10,000 in 1932.

> ### Hoboes
> Many of the unemployed became hoboes. By 1932, it was estimated that there were between 1 and 2 million of them, many of whom lived in shanty towns on the outskirts of settlements. Hoboes were usually given a hard time because people wanted to discourage transients from entering their areas. The Southern Pacific Railroad claimed to have thrown 68,300 of them from its trains. The state of California posted guards to turn them away at its borders, and in Atlanta, Georgia, they were arrested and put into **chain gangs**.

The nature of poor relief varied greatly because it was provided variously by states, local authorities or charities. Most came from charities. In fact, before 1932 no state had any system of recognised unemployment insurance and only 11 operated any kind of pension scheme, with a total outlay of only $220,000, aiding a mere 1,000 people.

At a time when the population was ageing, the majority of elderly people lived below the poverty line. There were very few private pension schemes; in 1925, only 36,000 pensioners were in receipt of benefits from 500 pension plans. This meant old people traditionally had to keep working, live on their savings or rely on their children for support. The Depression meant that, in the main, these options were no longer viable.

▲ Unemployed men waiting for admission to the New York Municipal Lodging House, 1931.
How useful is this source to historians investigating the human effects of the Despression?

The strain on resources

For those who were entitled to relief, there was the added problem that the relief bodies were running out of funds. Charities naturally suffered a decline in revenue during the Depression, at the very time when their funds were most needed. States, too, received less in taxes as unemployment rose. As a result, many had to cut rather than expand their services. In Arkansas, for example, schools were closed for ten months in the year, while teachers in Chicago went unpaid during the winter of 1932–33. The simple truth was that charities could supply only 6 per cent of necessary funds in 1932. In the years 1931 and 1932, when demand was greatest, most states cut their **relief appropriations**. Michigan, for example, reduced funds from $2 million in 1931 to $832,000 in 1932.

The result was that many people went hungry or were starving. *Fortune* magazine estimated in September 1932 that as much as 28 per cent of the total population was receiving no income. This estimate did not include the 11 million farm workers, many of who were in acute difficulties.

Rural poverty

Many farms had their **mortgages foreclosed** when farmers could no longer pay them. Often the auction of foreclosed farm property attracted violence. But there were other ways in which those repossessing property could be thwarted. Local farmers would agree only to bid a few cents and then return the farm to its former owner. Sometimes there was intimidation. In the face of this, two state governors said that payments on farm mortgages could be postponed until circumstances improved.

Poverty in the midst of plenty

The tragedy was that people went hungry in one of the richest food-producing countries in the world. Farm prices were so low that food could not be profitably harvested. In Montana, for example, wheat was rotting in the fields. Meat prices were not sufficient to warrant transporting animals to market. In Oregon, sheep were slaughtered and left to the buzzards. In Chicago, meanwhile, women scoured rubbish dumps for anything edible. Total relief funds in that city amounted to only $100,000 per day, which worked out at payments of only $2.40 per adult and $1.50 per child recipient per week. In 1931, there were 3.8 million one-parent families headed by a woman, with only 19,280 receiving any aid.

Gangsterism

Gangsterism and crime rose during the Depression years. In popular history, the Depression years are often seen as an age of outlaw gangs who robbed banks throughout the South and Midwest. Banks were particularly blamed for foreclosing on farm mortgages or refusing to lend money to see farmers through hard times. Often outlaws were seen as Robin Hood figures but there is little evidence to suggest any shared their ill-gotten gains with the poor and dispossessed. The Clyde Barrow Gang, for example, preferred to steal from general stores and gas stations, whose proprietors were often little better off than the farmers facing dispossession in the communities they served. The gang preyed, therefore, on the very people who may misguidedly have applauded them.

Outlaws such as Clyde Barrow and John Dillinger, who each came to be gang leaders, tended to begin their careers as small-time crooks and graduate to more ambitious projects. Dillinger, a navy deserter, was sentenced to between ten and twenty years' imprisonment for his first offence, after he pleaded guilty. He and an accomplice had robbed a grocery store, escaping with $50. Seething with resentment, he used his years in prison to learn from other inmates, and plan the perfect robberies. After his release in May 1933, having been paroled after nine and a half years inside, he was responsible for at least 24 bank robberies and went by the epithet 'Public Enemy Number One'. Another well-known outlaw, Pretty Boy Floyd, was first incarcerated for the theft of $3.50 from a post office, and Barrow for a similar attack on a gas station. If they wanted to steal large amounts, they had to raid banks, but small stores and gas stations were easier.

Admirers may have thought these outlaws led glamorous lives but the opposite appears to have been the case. All lived lives on the run, with the authorities (notably the FBI) constantly on their heels and the perennial threat that someone they knew would be tempted to cash in on a reward. At one point Dillinger had $10,000 on his head, an unimaginable sum for people caught up in the Depression. Nor did many enjoy the proceeds of their crimes. One store robbery in which a clerk was killed netted the Clyde Barrow Gang $28. What they stole, the outlaws spent – often on protection and bribes.

Many, too, ended their careers in squalid deaths – Pretty Boy Floyd was shot to death in an apple orchard, Bonnie and Clyde died in a Louisiana ambush in May 1934, and Dillinger most famously was caught in an FBI trap outside a Chicago cinema in July 1934. Others faced long stretches in prison. Relatively few escaped justice.

Bonnie and Clyde

Two of the most famous outlaws were Bonnie Parker and Clyde Barrow, the former in particular because of her gender. The Clyde Barrow Gang ranged across the Southwest in the early 1930s, mainly robbing gas stations and stores but gaining notoriety largely for the dozen or so banks they raided. They posed for photographs suggestive of an exciting life charged with sexual allure but in reality they were small-time crooks from appalling backgrounds with a penchant for violence. They were responsible for the deaths of at least nine police officers and weren't concerned if others were killed or injured during their raids. It was the almost clinical execution of two young police officers near Grapevine, Texas in April 1934 which lost them much public sympathy. Bonnie and Clyde were ambushed by a posse of Louisiana and Texas lawmen in Bienville Parish, Louisiana, on 23 May 1934. Together they were shot more than 50 times; there were so many bullet holes in their bodies that the mortician found it difficult to embalm them.

Conclusion: The spread of the Depression, 1929–32

The Depression eventually affected every aspect of the US economy and few industries or areas of the USA escaped its devastation. The human cost was enormous. Millions were unemployed. Many became hoboes travelling in search of work. The impact in rural areas, where overproduction and falling prices continued from the 1920s, led to huge numbers of farm foreclosures for which banks were often blamed. A rise in crime saw many bank robbers applauded as heroes.

Work together

Divide the subheadings in this section between you. Re-read the notes you made under each of the section headings (see page 264), then put them away. Then take it in turns to explain a subheading to your partner. After you have finished each subheading, you can both look at your notes. Discuss what you missed out, and define any terms that either of you found difficult to understand or explain.

2 Hoover's response to the Depression, 1929–33

President Hoover (1929–33) believed that people should be helped to sort out their own problems, but the scale of the Depression defeated him. He did more than any other president to intervene in the economy but many of his measures only made matters worse. The Smoot–Hawley tariff, for example, which was designed to protect US industry, stifled international trade. Hoover did offer a **moratorium** on foreign debts which delayed their collection for 18 months and gave charities monies to disburse to the unemployed in relief. He offered loans to homeowners to help them pay their mortgages and set up the Reconstruction Finance Corporation to loan money to banks and other financial institutions. Finally, he supported the Emergency Relief and Construction Act which gave loans to states to finance public works and reduce unemployment.

However, none of this was sufficient to have any effect. Hoover was widely blamed for the Depression both by those who thought he was exceeding government responsibilities and those who thought he was not doing enough. In 1932 the 'Bonus Army' of **veterans** hoping to receive war pensions early were met with violent dispersal by the same military in which it had served.

Note it down

In this section use index cards as a form of note-taking (see page xi). Here, rather than using them to note definitions, use them to explain ideas. This does not mean that you should stop adding to your glossary of index cards but provides a different way to use them. The overriding issue in this section is why Hoover's policies failed to address the extent of the Depression. The main subheadings are: Hoover's background and beliefs; Federal government policies. For each of his beliefs and policies, put the name or a title on one side of the card and an explanation of the main points on the other side. Bullet point your explanation and use abbreviations if it will help you fit all your notes on one topic onto one card. You can then use these cards for revision.

Hoover's background and beliefs

Herbert Hoover was a self-made engineer who had been involved in various high-profile activities, such as managing relief for refugees during the First World War. He was elected as **Republican** president in 1928 and Americans had very high expectations of his administration. After all, it seemed the economy was booming and, as **Secretary of Commerce** during the 1920s, he was widely believed to have been one of the architects of the prosperity of the 1920s. This changed with the onset of the Depression.

Hoover's beliefs

Hoover's tragedy was that he could not shift from his fundamental beliefs, which he acquired at an early age and never altered. He believed people should be responsible for their own welfare. This attitude was to make him inflexible in his handling of the Depression. He simply did not believe the government should try to solve people's problems. It was the government's job simply to help people solve their problems by themselves. He believed above all in equality of opportunity. He was a self-made man and felt everyone else could be too.

President Hoover worked tirelessly to combat the Depression. He worried constantly and gave generously to charity. He cut his own and state officials' salaries by 20 per cent to help provide revenues for his recovery measures. He well understood the seriousness of the Depression, which overshadowed all but the first seven months of his presidency. In public, however, he had to be optimistic in spite of all the problems. This has led many to argue that he lost touch with reality. 'Hoovervilles' – the shanties where the homeless lived – were named after him, as were 'Hoover blankets' – the newspapers in which they wrapped themselves to keep warm.

Hoover could not bring himself to accept what many increasingly argued was necessary: direct government relief. He continued to believe that the economy had to right itself. 'Economic depression', he said, 'cannot be cured by legislative action or executive pronouncement. Economic wounds must be healed by the action of the cells of the economic body – the producers and consumers themselves.'

The promotion of voluntarism

At first Hoover hoped to persuade businessmen and state governments to combat the Depression through their own voluntary efforts. He called meetings of businessmen in which he implored them not to reduce their workforce or cut wages, but rather to maintain their output and urge people to buy. He encouraged state leaders to begin new programmes of public works as well as continuing with the old.

Hoovervilles

Hoovervilles was the name given to the shanty towns that grew in open spaces on the edge of almost every town and city. At one point there was one in Central Park in New York. They were peopled by the homeless and hoboes seeking work. People lived in squalid conditions with shelters made from any available material, no sanitation and often inadequate water supplies – although where possible they usually sprang up by rivers.

Some Hoovervilles became semi-permanent and well organised. The largest at St Louis, Missouri was financed by private donations and had an unofficial mayor and a church. The one in Seattle ranged over nine acres of public land and was studied by sociologist Donald Roy in 1934; he counted 500 dwellings, with 639 residents, only seven of whom were female. As in St Louis, the Seattle Hooverville had a mayor and system of governance including a police force. It lasted until 1941. The most famous Hooverville was that of the 'Bonus Army' (see page 273).

As the Depression worsened, however, business had little choice but to cut back. Workers were laid off, most investment was postponed and the wages of those still in work were reduced. States also had to reduce their spending (see page 268). The problems were simply too great for **voluntarism** to work, particularly when it went against customary business practice. Bankers, for example, set up the National Credit Corporation in October 1931 with the task of helping failing banks survive. It began with a capital fund of $500 million donated by the major financial institutions. Despite this, with banks continuing to fail at unprecedented rates, the Corporation had spent only $10 million by the end of 1931. Bankers were simply too ingrained in their ways to begin investing in failing concerns. The Corporation faded away, showing again that individual financial concerns would almost always put their own interests before those of their country.

The Depression dominated Hoover's presidency and his government acted tirelessly to address it.

Federal government policies

Although President Hoover eventually intervened in the economy more than any former president, the measures he was prepared to take were wholly insufficient to meet the demands of the economic crisis. Above all, he could not accept the need for direct government involvement, and importantly, neither could his own supporters. This section will look at the measures he took – summarised in Table 1.

Table 1: Government action in response to economic factors, 1929-32.

Year	Economic factors and statistics	Government action
1929	Unemployment 3.2% GDP $103.6 billion GNP $203.6 billion Growth rate 6.7% October: price of shares fell by $14 billion	Agricultural Marketing Act
1930	Unemployment 8.9% GDP $91.2 billion GNP $183.5 billion Growth rate 9.6% Serious drought southeast of the Rockies	Smoot–Hawley tariff $49 million in loans to drought victims
1931	Unemployment 16.3% GDP $76.5 billion GNP $169.5 billion Growth rate 7.6%	Moratorium for 18 months on collection of war debts National Credit Corporation set up with funds of $500 million
1932	Unemployment 24.1% GDP $58.7 billion GNP $144.2 billion Growth rate 14.7%	Federal Home Loan Bank Act Reconstruction Finance Corporation set up with funds of $2 billion Emergency Relief and Construction Act Dispersal by force of 'Bonus Army'

Agriculture

The Agricultural Marketing Act, 1929, established a Federal Farm Board with funds of $500 million to create 'stabilisation corporations'. These were to be given the task of buying, storing and eventually disposing of farm surpluses in an orderly way. However, they had no power to order reductions in production. Huge surpluses in 1931 and 1932 both at home and abroad saw prices fall and the corporations paying above-market values for produce. The Grain Stabilization Corporation, for example, bought wheat in Chicago at 80 cents a bushel while the world price had fallen to 60 cents. By the time it ceased its purchases in summer 1931, it had paid an average of 82 cents per bushel for 300 million bushels while the world price had fallen to 40 cents a bushel.

The Corporation may have been helping farmers but it was also accused of throwing taxpayers' money away. It was buying farm produce at well over the market price and so was seen to encourage farmers to keep producing more when they should have been encouraged to produce less. By 1932 the world price of wheat was between 30 and 39 cents a bushel, less than harvesting costs in the USA. When Congress did propose a bill to subsidise farmers to reduce production, Hoover threatened to veto it because it undermined the principle of voluntary action. In the event, the bill failed without any need for a veto. It was too radical a measure for the time.

The agricultural policy failed mainly, then, for two reasons:

- It was paying American farmers artificially high prices and this could not continue in the long term.
- It treated agriculture as a domestic issue and, therefore, failed to take account of foreign considerations. Without high **tariffs**, there was little point in trying to keep the American price artificially high. The answer to the problem of cheap foreign imports, then, seemed to be even higher tariffs.

Tariffs

The Smoot–Hawley tariff, which came into force in June 1930, was the highest in American history with average duties of 40 per cent on both agricultural and industrial items. It led to most European nations abandoning **free trade** and to even fewer American goods being exported. This was of no advantage to farmers with their huge surpluses. In the years 1929 and 1930 the value of international trade fell in total by $500 million and in 1931 it fell by $1.2 billion. US imports fell from $1,334 million in 1929 to $390 million in 1932 and exports from $2,341 million to $784 million in the same period. Understanding this, farming interests in Congress fought hard against the measure, and it passed the Senate by only two votes. Hoover could have vetoed the bill but chose not to. Although he personally realised it would hurt international co-operation, he allowed himself to be swayed by interests within his own party who felt it was more important to encourage protection.

The repudiation of war debts

Hoover blamed the Depression on Europe but he was probably not entirely correct in doing so. Others have argued that it was the American Depression that spread to Europe and not vice versa. Certainly after the Wall Street Crash, American credit dried up. As we have seen, the Smoot–Hawley tariff made things worse. This led to European countries **repudiating war debts** in the early 1930s.

On 21 June 1931 Hoover announced the USA would postpone the collection of its debts for 18 months if other countries would do the same. This, he hoped, would release monies for investment. It is generally known as the moratorium. In the event, it was too little too late to stop the collapse of European economies.

Interestingly, when the proposed moratorium came up for renewal in December 1932, it was during the period of Hoover's lame duck presidency (the period of time between one president coming to the end of his time in office and a successor taking over). Hoover advised Roosevelt to continue the moratorium. However, Roosevelt, sensing hostility in Congress, agreed to the passage of the Johnson Act. This made it illegal to sell in the USA the securities of any country that had refused to repay its debts. As the stock market was still stagnant, this had little effect except to make European countries even more resentful of the USA. Finland was the only country that continued to pay its debts.

Unemployment relief

As we have seen, unemployment in 1932 was 24.1 per cent and relief agencies and charities could no longer cope with demand. Hoover secured additional amounts from Congress to the tune of $500 million in 1932 to help the various agencies provide relief but this was wholly inadequate to meet the scale of the problem. He set up the President's Emergency Committee for Employment to help the agencies to organise their efforts. But once again he would not countenance direct federal relief, arguing that this destroyed self-help and created a class of people dependent on the government for hand-outs. Even during the severe drought of 1930–31, which saw near-starvation conditions in much of the South, he baulked at direct relief. In the end, Congress allocated a pitifully small sum, $47 million, and even that was to be offered as loans that must later be repaid.

By 1932, with no easing of the Depression, Hoover introduced two more radical measures, which again were insufficient in themselves but marked a significant shift in the level of government involvement.

The Federal Home Loan Bank Act

This measure, passed in July 1932, was intended to save mortgages by making credit easier. Federal Home Loan banks were set up to help loan associations to provide mortgages. However, as the maximum loan was only 50 per cent of the value of the property, it was largely ineffective. It was simply another example of help that failed because it was insufficient to deal with the seriousness of the situation, in this case homes being repossessed.

The Reconstruction Finance Corporation

The Reconstruction Finance Corporation (RFC) was established in January 1932 with authority to lend up to $2 billion to rescue banks and other financial institutions in distress. The new Treasury Secretary, Ogden Mills, said the RFC was 'an insurance measure more than anything else'. It was designed to restore confidence, particularly in the financial system.

Of its loans, 90 per cent went to small and medium banks, and 70 per cent to banks in towns with a population of less than 5,000. However, critics of the RFC pointed to the size of individual loans, not the actual number. They argued that 50 per cent of loans went to the 7 per cent of borrowers who happened to be the biggest banks. Moreover, of the first $61 million committed by the RFC, $41 million was loaned to no more than three institutions. The Central Republican National Bank and Trust Company received $90 million alone – almost as much as the bank held in total deposits at the time.

The clamour for direct relief became so great that in summer 1932 Hoover gave his support to the Emergency Relief and Construction Act. This was the first major legislation to offer relief from the Depression. It authorised the RFC to lend up to $1.5 billion to states to finance public works. This would create temporary employment in local areas while the works were undertaken and improve public facilities such as leisure and sporting facilities. However, to be eligible the states had to declare bankruptcy and the works undertaken had to produce revenues that would eventually pay off the loans. When Hoover agreed to this, many of his erstwhile supporters felt he had gone too far. In 1932 James M. Beck, a former solicitor general, compared Hoover's government to that of Soviet Russia!

Hoover's credibility, which was already severely damaged, was finally destroyed by his role in an event which made him seem cruel as well as unfeeling. This was the treatment of the 'Bonus Army'.

Source A Extract from 'The Bonus Army Invades Washington, D.C., 1932' (found at Eyewitness to History.com). Evelyn Walsh McLean was the wife of the owner of the *Washington Post* and a pillar of Washington society. She describes the scene as the Bonus Army first entered Washington and marched past her elegant mansion.

> On a day in June, 1932, I saw a dusty automobile truck roll slowly past my house. I saw the unshaven, tired faces of the men who were riding in it standing up. A few were seated at the rear with their legs dangling over the lowered tailboard. On the side of the truck was an expanse of white cloth on which, crudely lettered in black, was a legend, BONUS ARMY.
>
> Other trucks followed in a straggling succession, and on the sidewalks of Massachusetts Avenue where stroll most of the diplomats and the other fashionables of Washington were some ragged hikers, wearing scraps of old uniforms. The sticks with which they strode along seemed less canes than cudgels. They were not a friendly-looking lot, and I learned they were hiking and riding into the capital along each of its radial avenues; that they had come from every part of the continent. It was not lost on me that those men, passing any one of my big houses, would see in such rich shelters a kind of challenge.
>
> I was burning, because I felt that crowd of men, women, and children never should have been permitted to swarm across the continent. But I could remember when those same men, with others, had been cheered as they marched down Pennsylvania Avenue. While I recalled those wartime parades, I was reading in the newspapers that the Bonus Army men were going hungry in Washington.

Explain what the impression the auther of Source A had of the Bonus Army. Use examples from the Source to support your answer.

War veterans and the 'Bonus Army'

Congress had agreed a veteran's 'bonus' in 1925. Based on the number of years of service, it was to be paid in full to each veteran in 1945. But, quite understandably, as the impact of the Depression hit them, many veterans said they needed it immediately. A march to Washington was organised to publicise their cause. By 15 June 1932, 20,000 people were camped in the capital, mainly around the Anacostia Flats region. Feeling for the veterans' plight, but insistent that nothing could be done for them, Hoover offered $100,000 to pay for their transportation home. Many refused to budge.

The Secretary of War, determined to move the squatters, called in troops under General Douglas MacArthur. Tanks and infantry not only shifted the squatters, but chased them back to the main camp on Anacostia Flats, where tear gas was used to disperse them. The camp was destroyed, many marchers were injured, and two babies died from the effects of the gas. Americans were horrified at the scenes and whether they were his fault or not, Hoover was blamed. The violent dispersal of the Bonus Army by the military was a major political blunder.

Key debate

Why did the Great Depression last so long?

President Hoover blamed the collapse of the European economies for the onset and continuation of the Depression because they could not repay their debts to the USA. However, historians are more divided. Writing in the 1980s, Charles P. Kindleberger felt the Federal Reserve should have been more prepared to lend money to stricken banks while Robert Sobel argued in 1968 that Hoover should have reformed the whole financial system before it collapsed. Right-wing historians such as Paul Johnson argued in the 1990s that Hoover intervened too much; left alone, the economy would have righted itself. More recently, in the first decade of the twenty-first century, Lee Ohanian and Amity Shlaes have argued that wages were too high, preventing employers from risking expansion in a depressed economy. They agree that government intervention actually prolonged the Depression. Others – for example, historians of the **New Left** such as Howard Zinn – argued the opposite: that the government didn't intervene enough to effectively combat the economic stagnation.

The 1932 presidential election

The USA had been in economic depression for most of Hoover's presidency, and despite his efforts there appeared no end in sight. Hoover was exhausted and was blamed by many for his failed policies (see page 269). Some, such as members of the Communist Party, questioned whether the US system of capitalism could survive and offered extremist alternatives. The **Democrats**, meanwhile, selected a candidate of great charisma who engendered confidence and faith even though he offered little of actual substance in his electoral programmes: Franklin Delano Roosevelt. As expected, Roosevelt won the election despite gaining only 57 per cent of the popular vote. Nevertheless, the USA was about to be changed forever.

Conclusion: Hoover's response to the Depression

Many Americans had high hopes of Hoover as president, but his term of office coincided with the onset of the Depression. While he was prepared to do more than any previous president, the intensity of the economic downturn was too great for his policies to address effectively. Above all, he would not consider direct government intervention. The Depression eventually affected every aspect of the US economy and the financial and banking sectors remained in turmoil. Millions became unemployed. Many became homeless, too, crossing the continent in search of work. Hoover's policies were inadequate to meet the scale of the problem. Although he repudiated foreign war debts, the high tariffs probably made matters worse.

> **Work together**
>
> One of you should take the role of a critic who thinks Hoover didn't do enough to solve the Depression; the other, a critic who thinks he did too much and made things worse. Extract arguments from your notes to justify your relative positions. Then discuss them together. Which side of the debate do you incline to? Which side has the most reliable evidence?

3 Roosevelt and the First New Deal, 1933–35

Following his inauguration, President Roosevelt called Congress into a special session which was to last for 100 days and saw the development of the First New Deal. This resulted in a considerable amount of emergency legislation and the setting up of many 'alphabet agencies'. Many historians have categorised the measures into those intended to bring about 'relief, recovery or reform', but, as we shall see, it is dangerous to assume Roosevelt had a blueprint to transform American life greatly.

The aim of the legislation of the 100 days was largely to restore faith in the US economy. To this end agricultural problems were tackled by the Agricultural Adjustment Act, which paid farmers to produce less, thereby leading to price rises; the banking system was reformed via the Emergency Banking Relief and Glass–Steagall Acts; the stock exchange was regulated to ensure malpractices couldn't occur in future; and industry was helped through the National Industry Recovery Act. In the process Roosevelt acquired many opponents both from the political left and right.

> **Note it down**
>
> Use three index cards headed Agriculture; Banking and finance; Industry. Make notes on each measure discussed in the text on the appropriate card. Compare your cards with those of a partner and amplify what each of you has written.
>
> Use the 1:2 method (see page x) to make notes on alternatives to the New Deal.

The 100 days

Two weeks before his inauguration on 4 March 1933, Franklin Delano Roosevelt addressed a meeting in Miami, Florida. Joseph Zangara fired five bullets at him from close range. All missed their target. Zangara opposed capitalism and sought to kill the man pledged to save it. Fittingly, Roosevelt did go on to save the capitalist system in the USA through his New Deal programme. The New Deal may by no means have been a cohesive programme;

indeed, it often seemed contradictory. It may even be misleading to call it a programme at all. Possibly, it might best be seen as a series of measures to deal with specific crises, with little overall plan. Certainly, it is most easily categorised with the hindsight of history. Historians can look back to see common strands running through the legislation and its implementation. They can see where it led and how its ideas were later developed. There is little doubt that at the end of the New Deal legislation, the USA was changed forever and the role of government greatly increased. However, whether this was intentional is a point for debate.

It is no exaggeration to say that, intentionally or not, at the end of the 100 days the USA had been transformed.

Roosevelt's priority was to create economic improvement, which he attempted not merely through measures to effect recovery but to improve the infrastructure, for example in banking and finance. This was to ensure the system would be modern and sophisticated enough to promote and stimulate a modern economy and, if necessary, able to address any downturn in the future. Roosevelt was very charismatic and used his personality to good effect. He spoke directly to the electorate via the radio in his 'fireside chats' in which he explained his policies. His reassuring voice helped restore confidence and made people feel recovery was on the way.

Agriculture

Agricultural recovery was given a higher priority than industrial recovery. This was for a variety of reasons. Thirty per cent of the labour force worked in agriculture. If agricultural workers could afford to buy more, industry would be stimulated. If agriculture became more profitable, there would be a reduction in farms being repossessed by the banks.

In the long run, the aim of agricultural policies was to make farming more efficient by ending overproduction. This would be done by taking the most uneconomic land out of production so less was produced, thereby raising prices. Agricultural workers who may have been displaced by this process would, it was hoped, move to other jobs perhaps in more urban areas which would be created by other New Deal measures. However, in the short term, farming crises had to be addressed. This was achieved in particular through the Agricultural Adjustment Act.

The Agricultural Adjustment Act, May 1933

Overproduction had been the greatest problem of American agriculture. Neither the McNary–Haugen proposals of the 1920s nor Hoover's Federal Farm Board (see page 271) had addressed this problem. While industrial production had declined by 42 per cent in the

Franklin Delano Roosevelt, 1882–1945

Roosevelt was born into one of the most distinguished and wealthy families in the USA. In 1905 he married his distant cousin Eleanor (see page 301). As a young man he preferred socialising to hard work, but entered politics as a Democrat in the New York Senate. He rose to prominence in national politics largely through his work as Assistant Secretary to the Navy and in 1920 won the nomination for vice-president. However the Republicans won the election. In 1921 Roosevelt caught polio, a debilitating disease which left him crippled but determined to overcome his problems. In 1929, during the Depression, Roosevelt became a reforming governor of New York and implemented policies he would further develop in the White House. In 1931, for example, he set up the Temporary Emergency Relief Act which gave $20 million, financed from an increase in income tax, for work relief during the winter of 1931–32, which was a prototype for the Federal Emergency Relief Act of 1933 (see page 279). Indeed, he appointed many of his New York personnel to positions in the White House – for example, Harry Hopkins as head of the Federal Emergency Relief Administration (FERA). These people, often experts in their field, were known as the 'Brains Trusters'.

Roosevelt served as president no fewer than four consecutive times. He was president during the 1930s when his New Deal transformed the USA and became its war leader during the Second World War when he died still in office. Roosevelt always displayed dynamic energy. Under his leadership, the federal government grew to an unprecedented degree, and in this context it changed American life. Roosevelt is widely regarded as one of the greatest presidents of the USA.

Key Topic 2 The Depression and the New Deal, 1929–38

years 1929–33, agriculture had fallen by only 6 per cent. The main principle behind the Agricultural Adjustment Act was that the government would subsidise farmers to reduce their acreage and production voluntarily. By producing less, the price of food would increase, and so would farmers' incomes.

A new agency was set up called the Agricultural Adjustment Administration (AAA). It would pay farmers to reduce their production of 'staple' items, initially corn, cotton, milk, pork, rice, tobacco and wheat. The programme was to be self-financing through a tax placed on companies that processed food. It was assumed that these companies would in turn pass on the increased cost to the consumer.

Reduction of cotton production was perhaps the most pressing need. At the beginning of 1933, unsold cotton in the USA already exceeded the total average annual world consumption of American cotton. Moreover, farmers had planted 400,000 acres more than in 1932. They were, quite simply, paid to destroy much of this. A total of 10.5 million acres were ploughed under, and the price of cotton accordingly rose from 6.5 cents per pound in 1932 to 10 cents per pound in 1933.

However, it was one thing to destroy cotton but it was far more contentious to destroy food when so many Americans were hungry. Six million piglets were bought and slaughtered. Although many of the carcasses were subsequently processed and fed to the unemployed, the public outcry was enormous.

In fact, the AAA destroyed only cotton and piglets. Drought helped to make the 1933 wheat crop the poorest since 1896, and agreements were reached to limit acreage in other crops in subsequent years, as Table 2 shows.

> **Source B** Extract from Studs Terkel, *Hard Times: An Oral History of the Depression* (Penguin, 1970), quoting C.B. Baldwin, assistant to the Secretary of Agriculture, Henry Wallace.
>
> They decided to slaughter piggy sows. You know what a piggy sow is? A pregnant pig. They decided to pay the farmer to kill them and the little pigs. Lot of 'em went into fertilizer. This is one of the horrible contradictions we're still seeing.
>
> They lowered the supply goin' to market and the prices immediately went up. Then a great cry went up from the press, particularly the *Chicago Tribune* about Henry Wallace slaughtering those little pigs. You'd think they were precious babies. The situation was such, you had to take emergency measures. Wallace never liked it.
>
> Why do you think there was such an outcry about slaughtering pigs?

Table 2: Acreage removed from production.

Year	Acreage removed (in millions)
1933	10.4
1934	35.7
1935	30.3

Total farm income rose from $4.5 billion in 1932 to $6.9 billion in 1935. The percentage of farmers signing up for AAA agreements was high at first – 95 per cent of tobacco growers, for example – and the Act was very popular with farmers.

Faced by drought, Western ranchers sought to bring beef cattle under the protection of the AAA in 1934. By January 1935 the government had purchased 8.3 million head of cattle, in return for which ranchers agreed to reduce breeding cows by 20 per cent in 1937. Overall, it would appear that the AAA worked effectively to deal with the crisis of overproduction, although there were problems.

The Tennessee Valley Authority, May 1933

If the aim of the Agricultural Adjustment Act was to deal with overproduction, the problem the Tennessee Valley Authority (TVA) was set up to deal with in the Tennessee Valley was underdevelopment and poverty. The TVA was one of the most grandiose schemes of the New Deal. It was created to harness the power of the River Tennessee, which ran through seven of the poorest states in the USA. It was hoped that by so doing this region of 80,000 square miles with a population of 2 million people would become more prosperous. The TVA had several major tasks:

- to construct 20 huge dams to control the floods that periodically affected the region
- to develop ecological schemes such as tree planting to stop soil erosion
- to encourage farmers to use more efficient means of cultivation, such as contour ploughing
- to provide jobs by setting up fertiliser manufacture factories
- to develop welfare and educational programmes
- most significantly, perhaps, to produce hydro-electric power for an area whose existing supplies of electricity were limited to two out of every 100 farms.

The TVA effectively became a central planning authority for the region. It was largely responsible for the modernisation and improved living standards that saw its residents increase their average income by 200 per cent in the period from 1929 to 1949.

Banking and finance

Alongside agriculture, a particularly pressing concern was the collapse of the American banking system. By 1932 banks were closing at the rate of 40 per day. In October 1932 the Governor of Nevada, fearing the imminent collapse of an important banking chain, declared a bank holiday and closed every bank in the state. By the time of Roosevelt's inauguration, banks were closed in many states.

The Emergency Banking Relief Act

On 6 March 1933 Roosevelt closed all the banks in the country for four days to give Treasury officials time to draft emergency legislation. The ensuing Emergency Banking Relief Act (EBRA) was passed by Congress after only 40 minutes of debate. Its aim was simply to restore confidence in the American banking system. It gave the Treasury power to investigate all banks threatened with collapse. The Reconstruction Finance Corporation (see page 272) was authorised to buy their stock to support them and to take on many of their debts. In doing so, the RFC became in effect the largest bank in the world.

In the meantime, Roosevelt appeared on radio with the first of his fireside chats. He explained to listeners, in a language all could understand, the nature of the crisis and how they could help. The message on this occasion was simple: place your money in the bank rather than under your mattress. It worked. Solvent banks were allowed to reopen and others were reorganised by government officials to put them on a sounder footing. By the beginning of April, $1 billion in currency had been returned to bank deposits and the crisis was over.

The Glass–Steagall Act

Roosevelt later drew up legislation to put the banking system on a sounder long-term footing. The Glass–Steagall Act of 1933 had the following effects:

- Commercial banks that relied on small-scale depositors were banned from involvement in the type of investment banking that had fuelled some of the 1920s speculation.
- Bank officials were not allowed to take personal loans from their own banks.
- Authority over **open-market operations** such as buying and selling **government securities** was centralised by being transferred from the Federal Reserve Banks to the Federal Reserve Board in Washington.
- Individual bank deposits were to be insured against bank failure up to the figure of $2,500 with the insurance fund to be administered by a new agency, the Federal Deposit Insurance Corporation (FDIC).

Regulation of the stock exchange

To ensure that the excesses of the 1920s, which had caused the Wall Street Crash, were not repeated, two measures were passed:

- The Truth-in-Securities Act, 1933, required **brokers** to offer clients realistic information about the securities they were selling.
- The Securities Act, 1934, set up a new agency, the Securities Exchange Commission (SEC). Its task was to oversee stock market activities and prevent fraudulent activities such as **insider dealing**, as in the bull pool (see page 244).

Economics in government

Roosevelt was a conservative in financial matters and, like his predecessors, he believed strongly in a **balanced budget**. Care was taken to distinguish between the budget for normal government business and that for emergency relief to deal with the Depression. He expected the budget for normal business to balance. He also sought to make all his recovery programmes self-financing and often they began with loans rather than grants. It was hoped that, as money began to be made from the programmes, these loans would be repaid.

The Economy Act, 1933, meanwhile, slashed government salaries and cut ex-soldiers' pensions. Roosevelt, like Hoover, refused to give the veterans their bonus. However, when a second 'Bonus Army' arrived in Washington, Roosevelt greeted them with refreshments and entertainment. His wife was sent to charm them without giving in to any of their demands. As a result of the charm offensive, they departed peacefully.

Industrial recovery

Industrial recovery was a priority for the New Deal. However, it had only limited success due to the scale of the industrial collapse. Although the economy grew 10 per cent per year during Roosevelt's first term from 1933 to 1936, output had fallen so low since 1929 that this still left unemployment at 14 per cent.

The problem was that there was no consensus on how to go about ensuring industrial recovery.

Some businessmen still supported policies of *laissez-faire*; others wanted massive government intervention. Some felt competition should be ended; others believed it to be the keynote to recovery. Again, it is important to note that Roosevelt was in the business of saving the American system of capitalism, not replacing it. This came as a disappointment to many who had hoped for more radical objectives.

Roosevelt's primary aims were to get people back to work and to increase consumer demand. To do this, he needed both to act quickly before the situation got even worse and to gain the co-operation of businessmen. He knew he could achieve little without the latter. Roosevelt was forced to act quickly and under pressure, as Congress was about to pass a measure to restrict the working week to 30 hours with the hope of sharing out the existing jobs. He opposed this scheme because he feared that, rather than raise overall purchasing power, it would simply share out more thinly what already existed. Instead, he replaced it with the National Industry Recovery Act (NIRA) of June 1933. The Act came in two parts:

- the National Recovery Administration (NRA)
- the Public Works Administration (PWA).

The National Recovery Administration

The NRA was set up to oversee industrial recovery. Headed by General Hugh Johnson, it seemed to offer something to all groups involved in industry. Powerful businessmen, for example, benefited from the suspension of **antitrust legislation** for two years. The argument behind this was that if industrial expansion was to be promoted, it was crazy to maintain laws that restricted it. Firms were encouraged to agree to codes of practice to regulate unfair competition such as price cutting, and to agree on such matters as working conditions and minimum wages in their industry.

> **Source C** Extract from the National Industrial Recovery Act (1933).
>
> Declaration of policy
>
> Section 1. A national emergency productive of widespread unemployment and disorganization of industry, which burdens interstate and foreign commerce, affects their public welfare, and undermines the standards of living of the American people, is hereby declared to exist. It is hereby declared to be the policy of Congress to remove obstructions to the free flow of interstate and foreign commerce which tend to diminish the amount thereof; and to provide for the general welfare by promoting the organization of industry for the purpose of cooperative action by trade groups, to induce and maintain united action of labor and management under adequate government sanctions and supervision, to eliminate unfair practices, to promote the fullest possible utilization of the present productive capacity of industries to avoid undue restriction of production (except as may be temporarily required), to increase the consumption of industrial and agricultural products by increasing purchasing power, to reduce and relieve unemployment, to improve standards of labor, and to otherwise to rehabilitate industry and to conserve natural resources.
>
> Summarise Source C in no more than 30 words.

Problems with the codes

Problems with most of the operations of the NRA quickly became apparent. Many of the codes, for example, turned out to be unworkable. This was in part because they were adopted so quickly, often without proper thought or planning, but also because they were often contentious. Many large manufacturers, notably Henry Ford, never subscribed to them and yet small firms complained that they favoured big business. Many small firms found it difficult to comply with all the regulations, particularly the minimum wage clauses. It was hoped, for example, that the firms signing the codes would introduce a minimum wage of $11 for a 40-hour week. Few small firms could afford this.

In March 1934 Congress set up the National Recovery Review Board to investigate whether small firms were disadvantaged by the codes. It was reported that they were indeed placed at a severe disadvantage. Moreover, the codes seemed to favour large companies that could take advantage of them to restrict competition and increase their profits. They could, for example, work together to draw up codes in which they agreed to raise prices while keeping wages low. Some agreed to limit output to raise prices and could therefore afford to cut back on their workforce or pay lower wages.

Unions said that Section 7(a) was too weak for their needs and that many employers, including those who did subscribe to the codes, were still riding roughshod over them. Ford, who did not subscribe to any codes, kept a gang of union bashers on the payroll. Johnson created labour advisory boards to mediate in disputes but, because these were advisory, they had little influence.

The argument that the NRA favoured big business was a particularly persuasive argument. The codes were largely drawn up by representatives from big business, often with the assistance of inexperienced White House officials. One of the first tasks of a newly appointed young government official, for example, was to meet sharp company lawyers to draw up the petroleum codes, even though he knew nothing about the industry.

Ultimately, despite the fanfare, the codes did not help economic recovery. This led Johnson to attempt a 'Buy Now' campaign in October 1933 to encourage people to spend and therefore stimulate production. He also advocated an overall 10 per cent wage increase and ten-hour cut in the working week. Neither was successful.

In reality, the NRA codes looked impressive but they could not bring about an economic recovery. Many critics argued that, in practice, they did little except give large firms the opportunity to indulge in unfair practices – the very opposite of what had been intended. Johnson, a successful businessman himself, believed very firmly in self-regulation by business. There were to be no new government powers over companies. Indeed, the government had agreed to suspend antitrust legislation for two years.

Johnson had made many powerful enemies with his high-handed ways. Roosevelt dismissed him in September 1934. After his departure, some of the codes were relaxed, but the Supreme Court dealt the death blow in May 1935 when it declared the NRA unconstitutional.

The Public Works Administration

The second part of the NIRA set up an emergency Public Works Administration (PWA) to be headed by the Secretary of the Interior, Harold Ickes. It was funded with $3.3 billion and its purpose was 'pump-priming'. It was hoped that expenditure on public works such as roads, dams, hospitals and schools would stimulate the economy. Road building would lead to increased demand for concrete, for example, which would lead the concrete companies to employ more workers, who would therefore have more money to spend, and so on. Eventually, the PWA put hundreds of thousands of people to work, building, among other things, nearly 13,000 schools and 50,000 miles of roads.

It pumped billions of dollars into the economy and was responsible for massive public works schemes, particularly in the West, where it enabled dams to be built to help irrigate former semi-desert land, electricity to be produced and four vast National Parks to be created.

The Civil Works Administration

A further measure to create employment was the Civil Works Administration (CWA). This agency was created in November 1933, with a $400 million grant from the PWA, primarily to provide emergency relief to the unemployed during the hard winter of 1933–34. Although it put 4 million people to work on public works projects, it was closed down in March when the winter was over. However, the FERA agreed to fund more public works projects itself.

However many jobs agencies such as the PWA created, unemployment and attendant social problems persisted and the federal government had to turn to relief measures.

Relief

There were millions of needy people in the USA. One major difference between Roosevelt and Hoover was the willingness of the former to involve the government in direct relief measures. These included the Federal Emergency Relief Act and the Civilian Conservation Corps.

The Federal Emergency Relief Act, May 1933

This Act established the Federal Emergency Relief Administration (FERA). It was given $500 million to be divided equally among the states to help provide for the unemployed. Half the money was to be granted to states for outright relief. With the remainder, the government would pay each state $1 for every $3 it spent on relief.

Roosevelt chose Harry Hopkins to run this programme. He had administered the relief programmes that the President had introduced when Governor of New York. The Act said that each state should set up a FERA office and organise relief programmes. It should raise the money through borrowing, tax rises or any other means. When some states such as Kentucky and Ohio refused to comply, Hopkins simply threatened to deny them any federal monies.

Many states were wedded to the idea of a balanced budget and found expenditure on relief extremely distasteful. It was still felt by many that to be poor was your own fault. Those requiring relief were often treated abominably. One FERA worker reported that in Phoenix, Arizona, over 100 claimants were jammed into a small room in temperatures of over 100 degrees, while an overflow queue was waiting in a nearby garage. In many places there could be interminable waits and delays. Hostile policemen often guarded the long queues of claimants, while uncaring officials completed endless numbers of forms. Even after this, there were usually long delays before any kind of relief was forthcoming.

The bottom line was that states knew Hopkins could not refuse them funds, as the only people who would suffer were those the funds were meant to help – the needy and unemployed themselves. One governor even boasted that he had cut relief spending but still received FERA funds.

In the face of such opposition, the FERA's effectiveness was limited. Its workers were refused office space in some states and often their caseloads were numbered in thousands. Its funds were limited, too. In 1935 it was paying about $25 per month to an average family on relief, while the average monthly minimum wage for subsistence was estimated at $100.

However, although its effects were disappointing, it did set the important precedent of federal government giving direct funds for relief.

The Civilian Conservation Corps, 1933

Unemployment among young people was a huge problem and Roosevelt understood they needed a special programme to afford them both the experience of work and useful training in community service, co-operation and other skills essential to their growth as useful citizens. Unemployed young men between the ages of 17 and 24 (later 28) were recruited by the Department of Labor to work in the Civilian Conservation Corps (CCC) in national forests, parks and public lands. The Corps was organised along military lines, but its tasks were set out by the Departments of the Interior and Agriculture.

The CCC was originally set up for two years but Congress extended this for a further seven years in 1935, when its strength was increased to 500,000. In the period of its life, the CCC installed 65,100 miles of telephone lines in inaccessible areas, spent 4.1 million man-hours fighting forest fires and planted 1.3 billion trees. The CCC gave countless young men, particularly those from the cities, a new self-respect and valuable experience of both comradeship and life in the 'great outdoors'.

Native Americans

The new Commissioner for the **Bureau of Indian Affairs**, John Collier, was determined to reverse government policy towards Native Americans and abolish assimilation.

The Indian Reorganization Act

In 1934 the Indian Reorganization Act finally did away with assimilation along with all the other terms of the Dawes Severalty Act (see page 265). The new Act recognised and encouraged Native American culture. Tribes were reorganised into self-governing bodies that could vote to adopt constitutions and have their own police and legal systems. They could control land sales on the reservations, while new tribal corporations were established to manage tribal resources.

Government policy of recognising Native American culture also came under attack from some quarters. Collier was accused of encouraging Native Americans to 'go back to the blanket'. Many felt that a return to tribal traditions was a backward move. It was argued that they needed assimilation to prosper in American society. Collier also seemed indifferent to Native American resistance to the efforts of big corporations to exploit natural resources on reservation land.

However, Collier did his best to ensure Native Americans could take advantage of New Deal agencies such as the CCC and the PWA – although given the scale of their poverty, the relief these agencies offered was limited. In addition, his work was important in affording a new respect for Native American culture, even if the culture was often misunderstood. As New Deal programmes wound down in the 1940s, Native Americans began to set up pressure groups but often remained among the poorest people in the USA.

Housing

Housing remained an issue because many homeowners were having problems repaying their mortgages, while there was a shortage of public-sector accommodation. The government introduced two measures to try to help.

The Home Owners Refinancing Corporation (HORC), June 1933

This agency helped homeowners in difficulties by offering new mortgages at low rates of interest over longer periods.

The Federal Housing Administration (FHA)

This was established in June 1934 to offer federal insurance to protect the ability to repay low-interest, long-term mortgages taken out by those buying new homes. Clearly, this was an attempt to stimulate the building industry. However, the loans were solely for newly purchased single-family homes; they could not be used to renovate existing properties or for buildings set out as apartments where several people lived.

The FHA therefore did nothing to help the increasingly poverty-stricken inner cities. In fact, one of the agency's unanticipated effects was to encourage the movement to the suburbs. With 65 per cent of new houses costing over $4,000, it was estimated that less than 25 per cent of urban families could afford to take out any kind of mortgage on them. The Act mainly benefited white, middle-class families. Increasingly, inner-city areas tended to be run down and left to poorer ethnic minorities who were forced to rent squalid properties.

> ### Key debate
> #### Was the New Deal a planned programme?
> Michael Parrish, writing in the 1990s, doubted there was any blueprint behind the first New Deal. On the other hand Arthur J. Schlesinger, writing in the 1950s, felt there was a definite overarching aim in saving the capitalist system. More recently William E. Leuchtenburg has tended to agree – the purpose was to preserve the social order. Alternatively, right-wing critics see the New Deal as meddling and making conditions worse. Writing in the first decade of the twenty-first century, both Jim Powell and Burton Fulsom have argued that it prolonged the Depression by ill-advised economic policies. Not only was there no blueprint but the unco-ordinated and economically illogical policies made things worse. Although supportive of the New Deal, Oliver Stone and Peter Kuznick, writing in 2013, conceded that the New Deal was a hotch-potch of measures without ideological underpinning.

Opposition to the New Deal

The New Deal attracted much opposition, from the political right because it was too radical and from the political left because it was not radical enough. In this section the alternatives put forward by some of these opponents are examined.

The right

Many of the wealthy, who had supported Roosevelt in the darkest days of the Depression as the saviour of capitalism, now turned against him when it seemed that capitalism had been saved. This was in part because of the increases in taxes which they argued fell too heavily on them. They also tended to oppose what they perceived as too much government involvement in the economy. This was in part because of the increases in taxes, which they opposed, and also because of what they perceived as too much continued government involvement in the economy. The Republican Party, still associated with its failures during the early 1930s, was rebuilding and preparing for the 1936 election, but it was finding it difficult to field a strong candidate.

Liberty Leaguers

The Liberty League was organised in April 1934 by many conservative Democrats as well as Republicans to promote private property and private enterprise unregulated by law. The Liberty Leaguers attacked Roosevelt throughout the New Deal years and formed the basis of right-wing opposition to him. By July 1936, it had 125,000 members; after Roosevelt's victory in the elections of that year, however, it became less significant.

The left

At the time, Roosevelt was more concerned about threats from the left. This was particularly because left-wing groups might join together to form a third party to challenge him in the next presidential election. The threats varied from those advocating radical schemes such as Old Age Revolving Pensions, Inc. to popular leaders such as Huey Long and Father Charles Coughlin.

End Poverty in California (EPIC)

The novelist Upton Sinclair came up with a scheme whereby the unemployed would be put to work in state-run co-operatives. They would be paid in currency, which they could spend only in other co-operatives. For a time, Sinclair's ideas gained credibility and proved useful recruits for more serious alternative movements as discussed below.

'Share Our Wealth'

In February 1934, Senator Huey Long from Louisiana moved onto the national scene with his 'Share Our Wealth' programme. He advocated that all private fortunes over $3 million should be confiscated and every family should be given enough money to buy a house, a car and a radio. There should also be old-age pensions, minimum wages so that every family would be guaranteed $2,000–$3,000 per year and free college education for all suitable candidates. Long's ideas proved very popular and 'Share Our Wealth' clubs grew to 27,431 in number, with 4.6 million members spread across the states.

Huey Long

As an energetic governor of Louisiana, Huey Long had ordered massive public works programmes – over 3,000 miles of paved highways were built between 1928 and 1933, besides new public buildings and an airport at New Orleans – and ambitious adult literacy schemes. However, he did govern as a dictator and opponents were treated quite brutally by his bully boys.

Long began to talk of joining forces with other radicals to form a third party to oppose Roosevelt in the 1936 presidential election. In 1935, Postmaster General James A. Farley took a secret poll to assess Long's popularity and was shocked to discover that up to 4 million people might vote for him in 1936. This meant that Long might hold the balance of power in the election. The Louisiana Senator was, in fact, gunned down in September 1935. Rumours were circulated by his supporters that Roosevelt's hand was somehow behind the assassination. While these accusations were unfounded, the President must nevertheless have breathed a sigh of relief at the news.

Old Age Revolving Pensions, Inc.

Francis Townsend was a retired doctor who advocated old-age pensions with a difference. Everyone over 60 years of age who was not in paid employment should be given $200 per month on the understanding that every cent of it was spent and none saved. The idea was that this would boost consumption and thereby production and so pull the USA out of the Depression. Moreover, encouraging people to retire at 60 would provide more jobs for the young. Soon Townsend Clubs had 500,000 members and Congress was being lobbied to put the plan into operation. It was, of course, totally impractical. Payments to recipients would have amounted to 50 per cent of national income and an army of bureaucrats would have been necessary to ensure pensioners were spending all their $200. Nevertheless, the level of support showed that the movement had to be taken seriously.

Father Charles Coughlin

Charles Coughlin was a priest whose radio programme, *The Golden Hour of the Little Flower*, was enormously influential during the first half of the 1930s. It regularly commanded an audience of 30–40 million, and listeners contributed more than $5 million per year to his parish in Detroit. In 1934 Coughlin founded the National Union for Social Justice with the aim of monetary reform and redistribution of wealth. Roosevelt was afraid of Coughlin's influence, particularly when a possible alliance with Huey Long was mooted. However, Long was assassinated and Coughlin became increasingly anti-Semitic, blaming Jews for both the New Deal and control of Wall Street. This lost him significant support.

Thunder on the Left

Thunder on the Left is the name given to various political developments that are credited with moving Roosevelt and the New Deal further to the left in 1935 and 1936. Governor Floyd B. Olson of Minnesota, for example, led the Farmer–Labor Party which proposed far-reaching economic reforms. It advocated the state taking control of idle factories to put the unemployed to work, **nationalisation** of public utilities and a postponement of farm mortgage foreclosures.

The impact of the opposition

Roosevelt, meanwhile, had learned of the mood of the country. In the 1934 **mid-term congressional elections**, the Democrats had made gains in both houses, with 69 out of 96 seats in the Senate, the biggest Democratic majority to date. Roosevelt was preparing a second New Deal that was influenced not only by the demands of radical politicians but also by the increasing opposition of big business to his measures.

Conclusion: Roosevelt and the First New Deal, 1933–35

Roosevelt introduced a 'New Deal' to combat the problems the USA faced, in particular to restore faith in the economy and help recovery. In the first 100 days of his administration, he passed much legislation setting up alphabet agencies to address problems in agriculture and industry and to reform the financial institutions. Of these, the NIRA was only partly successful because the problems in industry were so great. Roosevelt attracted hostility from the forces of both the right and left. However, the electorate appeared to endorse his measures as exemplified by the Democrat gains in the congressional elections of 1934.

> ### Work together
> Historians have often debated how coherent a programme the First New Deal was. Working in pairs, one of you should extract from your notes any points that suggest it was a coherent programme and the other extract information that suggests it wasn't. One of you might look at the '100 days', for example, and argue that this was a coherent programme to bring about economic recovery. The other might consider the piecemeal nature of legislation and show how it didn't always work, as with the NRA codes. Each of you should present your findings. When you're finished, come together and re-read your notes. If there are any sections that you found difficult to explain, then add more detail to your notes or work together on a better explanation.

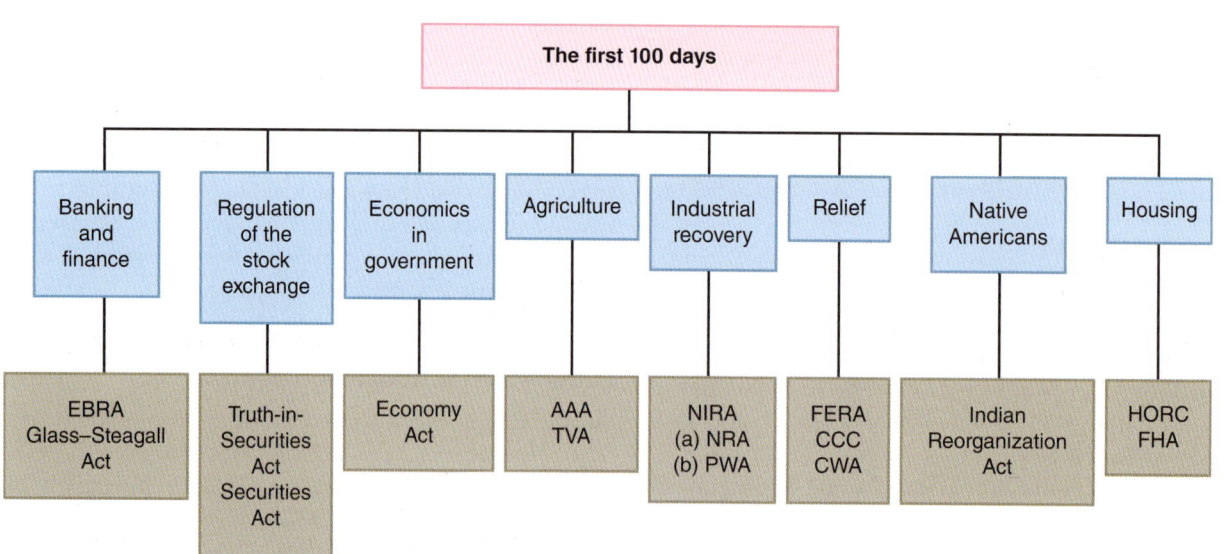

▲ Summary diagram: The first 100 days.

4 The Second New Deal, 1935–38

Many historians have argued that the New Deal seemed more radical in the years after 1935, with Roosevelt genuinely trying to favour the poorer classes at the expense of the rich. They point in particular to the measures that made up the Second New Deal as evidence of this, such as the introduction of social security and the legalisation of **labour unions**.

In the 1936 presidential election Roosevelt won a great victory, yet after this the New Deal was beset with problems. Roosevelt failed to reform the Supreme Court, which found much of his legislation unconstitutional. He was faced with a natural catastrophe in rural areas in addition to ongoing problems from the working of his agricultural legislation. Finally, reductions in federal government spending saw the return of economic **recession**. The New Deal petered out as foreign affairs began to take priority.

> **Note it down**
> You could use either the 1:2 method (see page x) here or further add to your collection of index cards. The important thing is that you note down the main points of each section: why there was the need for a Second New Deal, what was new about the types of measures it included, and why it only enjoyed limited success.

Reasons for the Second New Deal

When the 75th Congress met early in 1935, Roosevelt presented it with a major legislative package. It was called by the contemporary journalist Walter Lippmann 'the most comprehensive program of reform ever achieved in this country by any administration'. Eighty-eight days later, most of Roosevelt's objectives had been achieved. Some measures that he had not particularly supported had also been passed – for example, in the field of labour relations.

Some historians, notably Arthur Schlesinger Jr, have seen the Second New Deal very much as a change in direction. They see the First New Deal as an attempt to reduce business competition in favour of greater co-operation through planning and government guidance. Clearly the AAA and the NRA were examples of this in action (see pages 276 and 278). However, they believe the Second New Deal saw a reintroduction of competition but with regulations about fair play. Examples of this are:

- fair representation for all sides in industry through the National Labor Relations Act (see page 284)
- the Public Utility Holding Company Act that broke up **holding companies** (see page 285)
- a national system of benefits for those groups who could not participate in the system, through measures such as the Social Security Act (see page 285).

Nevertheless, as we will see, in attacking big business, the Second New Deal's bark was always worse than its bite.

Before considering the legislation of the Second New Deal, we need to examine in some detail the motivation behind it and the conditions that made it possible:

- Roosevelt needed to respond to the radical forces described on pages 280–82. He needed to take the initiative from people such as Huey Long, Francis Townsend and Charles Coughlin, to avoid millions of voters supporting politicians with extreme views.
- The climate in the new Congress was for action and Roosevelt wanted to prevent this. He did not wish to surrender the initiative in preparing New Deal legislation. The **Farmer–Labor Party** (see page 282), for example, could rely on possibly as many as 50 supporters in both houses. It was preparing its own programme which would have introduced radical changes. For example, it spoke of minimum hours of work, greater investment in public works, higher taxes for the wealthy and social security. Meanwhile, radical Senators such as Robert M. Lafollette and Robert F. Wagner were preparing their own proposals.
- Roosevelt was increasingly frustrated by the Supreme Court which was beginning to overturn New Deal legislation. He believed it was opposing him. This in itself made him more radical in outlook. He also needed to introduce new measures to replace those such as the NIRA, which the Supreme Court had declared unconstitutional (see page 279).
- Roosevelt was also increasingly frustrated with the wealthy and with the forces of big business, who were opposing him more and more. He was particularly angry when the **US Chamber of Commerce** attacked his policies in May 1935. He believed he had been elected to save American business and he felt let down by its lack of continued support. Moreover, small businesses had benefited little from measures so far adopted. New Deal officials in Washington were becoming aware that small firms had a crucial role to play in economic recovery. Many of the measures taken in the Second New Deal – for example, the Public Utility Holding Company Act (see page 285) – were designed with them in mind.
- Some historians have argued that politics in the USA was becoming more divided and extreme. Roosevelt was seeking the support of the political left.

Legislation

The Second New Deal saw an array of legislation which both continued the work of the first and moved in new directions. Many have seen it as more radical and it certainly intensified opposition from the right. One should however consider its effectiveness and ask what, if anything, it actually changed in the American economy and society.

The Emergency Relief Appropriation Act (ERAA), April 1935

This measure saw the authorisation of the largest appropriation for relief, at that time in the nation's history, to set up new agencies to provide employment through federal works. The $45.5 billion allocated was the equivalent of over $20 billion at 1930 values and well over $400 billion today. It set up the Works Progress Administration (WPA).

The Works Progress Administration (WPA)

The WPA recruited people for public works projects. At any one time it had about 2 million employees and, by 1941, 20 per cent of the nation's workforce had found employment with it. Wages were approximately $52 per month, which was greater than any relief but less than the going rate in industry. The WPA was not allowed to compete for contracts with private firms or to build private houses. However, it did build 1,000 airport landing fields, 8,000 schools and hospitals, and 12,000 playgrounds.

Although it was not supposed to engage in large-scale projects, it did so. Among other things, it was responsible for cutting the Lincoln Tunnel, which connects Manhattan Island to New Jersey, and building **Fort Knox** in Kentucky.

The Resettlement Administration, May 1935

It was decided to merge all rural rehabilitation projects into one new agency, the Resettlement Administration (RA). There were ambitious plans to move 500,000 families from overworked land and resettle them in more promising surroundings elsewhere. This necessitated the agency buying good land, encouraging farmers to move to it and teaching them how to farm it effectively, using modern machinery and efficient techniques.

Overall, the agency only ever resettled 4,441 families so could not be judged a success. The reasons for its apparent failure were partly to do with the costs involved and partly the reluctance of people to move.

The Revenue (Wealth Tax) Act, June 1935

This Act was implemented to pay for New Deal reforms and was perceived by those affected by it to be an attack on the fundamental right of Americans to become rich. Quite simply, the government sought to raise more revenue through taxation and it seemed logical to do this by targeting those who could most afford it.

The Act, drafted by Treasury officials, caused long and heated debate. Many of their original proposals, such as a federal inheritance tax, were defeated. Legislation finally created a graduated tax on corporate income and an excessive profits tax on corporations. The maximum tax on incomes of over $50,000 was increased from 59 per cent to 75 per cent.

In fact, the new taxes raised comparatively little: about $250 million. For example, the laws regulating taxes paid by corporations contained loopholes, which clever lawyers could easily exploit. Only 1 per cent of the population earned more than $10,000 and so the increased income taxes did not raise large amounts of revenue. However, if Roosevelt had taxed the middle classes more, as he was urged to do by more radical colleagues, he would have cut their spending power and thus delayed economic recovery. While the Act did little in itself, it did act as a precedent for higher taxes during the Second World War.

The Wagner–Connery National Labor Relations Act (the 'Wagner Act'), July 1935

Roosevelt was reluctant to become involved in labour relations legislation. There are two major reasons for this:

- There was a mistrust of labour unions in the USA. This was particularly the case among conservative politicians such as the Southern Democrats, whose support he needed.
- He had no more wish to become the champion of unions than to upset big business further – and big business generally loathed unions.

This Act, often known as the 'Wagner Act', was not therefore initiated by Roosevelt. Indeed, he approved it only when it had passed through the Senate and looked likely to become law. Nevertheless, the National Labor Relations Act is generally seen as an important part of the Second New Deal and was a milestone in American labour relations. It was born out of the disappointment with the Labor Board set up under the NRA. It was one thing to allow unionisation but quite another to get employers to accept it and the Board was generally felt to be powerless.

The Act guaranteed workers the rights to collective bargaining through unions of their own choice. They could choose their union through a secret ballot; and a new three-man National Labor Relations Board (NLRB) was set up to ensure fair play. Employers were forbidden to resort to unfair practices, such as discrimination against unionists.

It was the first Act that effectively gave unions rights in law and in the long term committed the federal government to an important labour relations role. However, Roosevelt still did not see it that way and preferred to continue to take a back seat in labour relations.

The Public Utility Holding Company Act, August 1935

There had been many problems resulting from the existence of giant holding-company structures (see page 238), as they were often powerful enough to bribe legislators either to stop legislation that threatened them or to promote beneficial laws. Rates paid to investors were often excessive.

The Public Utility Holding Company Act was quite severe in its operation. It ordered the breaking up of all companies more than twice removed from the operating company. This destroyed the pyramid structure referred to above. It did this by making all holding companies register with the Securities Exchange Commission (SEC), which could decide their fate. Any company more than twice removed from the utility that could not justify its existence on the grounds of co-ordination of utilities or economic efficiency was to be eliminated by 1 January 1940.

The Social Security Act, August 1935

It has already been suggested (see page 267) that the provision made by states for social security was wholly inadequate. For example, only Wisconsin provided any form of unemployment benefit and this was to be paid by former employers as a disincentive to laying off their workers. Roosevelt had long been interested in a federal system of social security. However, what he came up with was both conservative and limited in its provision. Certainly it was not as generous as Townsend's proposal, whose popularity was of concern to Roosevelt and many members of Congress.

The Social Security Act was the first federal measure of direct help as a worker's right and would be built upon in the future. The Act provided for old-age pensions to be funded by employer and employee contributions, and unemployment insurance to be paid for by **payroll taxes** levied on both employers and employees. While the pension scheme was a federal programme, it was anticipated that states would control unemployment insurance.

Limitations of the Act

The Social Security Act was generally inadequate to meet the needs of the poor. Pensions were paid at a minimum of $10 and a maximum of $85 per month according to the contributions that recipients had paid into the scheme. They were not to be paid until 1940 so everyone receiving them had paid something in. Unemployment benefit was a maximum of $18 per week for 16 weeks only.

Assistance programmes for the blind, disabled and families with dependent children were also set up by the Act. However, although states received the same amount per child from the federal government, the amounts paid varied widely; in 1939 Massachusetts paid poor children $61 per month while Mississippi paid $8 per month. Those needing most help, such as agricultural workers, domestic servants and those working for small-scale employers, were actually excluded from the Act. This was because it was felt employers could not afford to pay the contributions and it would in any event cost the Treasury too much to collect them. It was hoped that these workers would be included in the schemes later, once the Act had had time to embed itself.

The importance of the Social Security Act

Although the Social Security Act had serious flaws, it should not be forgotten that it was a major break with American governmental tradition. Never before had there been a direct system of national benefits. But it is important to stress that this was not relief. Roosevelt refused to allow general taxes to subsidise the system. It had to be self-financing. Recipients had to pay into the system. The pensions were not paid at a flat rate but according to how much the worker had contributed previously. Unemployment benefits were low and paid for a very limited period.

Many conservatives argued that even this was too much. It would destroy individual initiative. It would make people dependent on the state. It took powers away from individual states and concentrated them in Washington. Many states compensated for unemployment benefits by cutting back on other schemes of relief. They increased residence qualifications and they made **means-tested benefits** more rigorous. However, despite the limitations and drawbacks, the Act signified a massive break with the traditional role of the federal government. It was also sending out a loud message that it cared about people. It was said that Roosevelt took more satisfaction in this measure than anything else he had achieved on the domestic front.

The Banking Act, August 1935

This Act was intended to give the federal government control of banking in the USA. The Governor of the

Federal Reserve Board, Marriner Eccles, felt that Wall Street exercised too much power in national finance and sought to repeal the 1913 Federal Reserve Act, which governed the American banking system (see page 244). The control of banking was removed from private banks to central government and the centre of financial management shifted from New York to Washington.

Assessing the Second New Deal

The Second New Deal saw an important expansion of the role of federal, state and local government. There was much that was new:

- The banking system was centralised.
- Some of the worst excesses of capitalism, such as the colossal power of the holding companies, were addressed. The attack on unfair competition helped small businesses.
- Labour unions were given a legal voice.
- The Social Security Act created the first national system of benefits, although individual states operated the parts they had control over very differently.
- There was also further development of existing policies, as with the creation of the WPA to aid both relief and recovery.
- The REA helped the process of modernising the rural areas of the USA.

However, not all of the legislation was particularly effective. The Revenue Act of 1935 angered people out of all proportion to its actual effect. Some historians have argued that the Second New Deal differed from the first in that the first was primarily about relief and recovery from the Depression, while the second was about the creation of permanent reforms.

Whatever the merits of individual pieces of legislation, whatever the significance of the Second New Deal in terms of its philosophy, the key element was that the administration was seen to be acting, to be doing something and to be addressing issues and concerns. The Second New Deal continued, of course, to involve itself particularly in everyday issues that were important to those individuals whose concerns probably would previously have been ignored. It was for this reason that the administration could enter the 1936 presidential election with confidence.

Opposition to the Second New Deal

All parties agreed that the 1936 presidential election would be significant. If the electorate voted for Roosevelt for a second term, they would be supporting the changes in the role of government he had made.

In the election, Roosevelt was triumphant. With the smaller alternative parties barely raising a million votes between them, Roosevelt won 60.8 per cent of the popular vote and carried all but two states, Vermont and Maine. The Democrats also appeared to control both houses of Congress. As ever, Roosevelt had offered little in the way of concrete promises in his election speeches but people expected much of him.

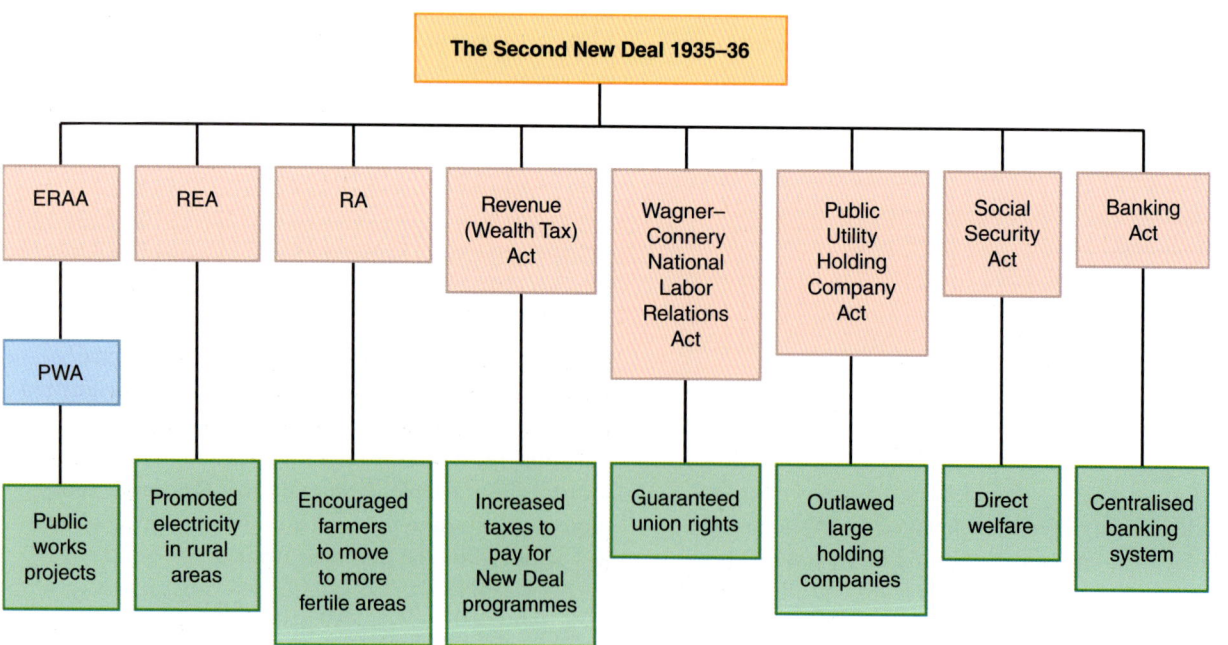

▲ Summary diagram: The Second New Deal, 1935–36.

> **Source D** Extract from Roosevelt's inaugural address, 1937.
>
> In this nation, I see tens of millions of its citizens – a substantial part of the whole population – who at this very moment are denied the greater part of what the very lowest standards of today call the necessities of life ... I see one third of the nation ill housed, ill clad, ill nourished ... We are determined to make every American citizen the subject of his country's interest and concern ... The test of our progress is not whether we add more to the abundance of those who have much; it is whether we provide enough for those who have too little.
>
> Does Roosevelt actually give any concrete promises in this extract? Explain your answer with reference to the source.

Roosevelt had fought the election largely on his personality and the trust ordinary people had in him. He was certainly aided by the disorganisation of his opponents and the fact that the Republicans could not possibly gain support by attacking measures that had benefited so many. Perhaps his victory made him overconfident or even arrogant. Roosevelt faced many problems during his second term including opposition from the Supreme Court and big business, and the limited success of his policies.

The Supreme Court

Given Roosevelt's flexible ideas on the workings of the Constitution, it was perhaps inevitable that he would come into conflict with its guardian, the Supreme Court. Although he had not directly attacked the Court during the election campaign, he felt it was in need of reform. While the Court had supported New Deal laws in the days of crisis, it had increasingly declared legislation unconstitutional as Roosevelt's first term of office came to an end. In the 140 years before 1935, the Supreme Court had found only about 60 federal laws unconstitutional; in 18 months during 1935 and 1936, it found 11 to be so.

Indeed, on one day, 'Black Monday', 27 May 1935, the Supreme Court attacked the New Deal in several ways. For example, it found the Farm Mortgage Act unconstitutional. It argued that the removal of a trade commissioner, which Roosevelt sought, was the responsibility not of the president but of Congress. Most importantly, it found the NIRA to be unconstitutional through the 'sick chicken' case.

The 'sick chicken' case

This was possibly the Court's most serious decision and it motivated Roosevelt into action. The case involved the Schechter Brothers, a firm of butchers in New York who were selling chickens unfit for human consumption. Prosecuted by the NIRA for breaking its codes of practice, the Schechter Brothers appealed against the verdict to the Supreme Court. It decided that their prosecution should be a matter for the New York courts not the federal government, and the poultry code was declared illegal.

In effect, the decision meant that the federal government had no right to interfere in internal state issues. While recognising that the federal government had powers to intervene in **inter-state commerce**, the Court found that it had none to do so in the internal commerce of states.

Moreover, if the federal government could not prosecute individual firms for breaking the NIRA codes, it followed that all the codes themselves must be unconstitutional. This was because they were developed by the federal government but affected individual firms in individual states. The argument went that the executive had acted unconstitutionally in giving itself the powers to implement the codes in the first place. This was because it had no authority to intervene in matters that were the preserve of individual states. Given that the codes were at the heart of the NIRA, it could not survive without them. More significantly, the ruling seemed to imply that the government had no powers to oversee nation-wide economic affairs except in so far as they affected inter-state commerce.

The Judiciary Reform Bill

Roosevelt believed the justices on the Supreme Court were out of touch. Of the nine judges, none were his appointments. He increasingly saw the issue of the Supreme Court as one of unelected officials stifling the work of a democratically elected government, while members of the Supreme Court saw it as them using their legal authority to halt the spread of dictatorship. The scene was set for battle.

On 3 February 1936 Roosevelt presented the Judiciary Reform Bill to Congress. This proposed that the president could appoint a new justice whenever an existing judge, reaching the age of 70, failed to retire within six months. He could also appoint up to six new justices, increasing the possible total to 15. The measure had been drawn up in secret, although, ironically, the idea of forcibly retiring judges had first been proposed by one of the existing members of the Supreme Court in 1913.

Roosevelt gave as the reasoning behind his proposal that the Supreme Court could not keep up with the volume of work and more justices would help. However, everyone knew that it was really a proposal to pack the Court with his own nominees who would favour New Deal legislation.

In the event, the whole thing backfired. It was not a matter of the most elderly justices being the most conservative; in fact the oldest, Justice Brandeis, was, at 79, the most liberal. Nor was the Court inefficient. Chief Justice Hughes could show that the Court was necessarily selective in the cases it considered and that, given the need for considerable discussion on each, a greater number of justices would make its work far more difficult.

Roosevelt had stirred up a hornet's nest. Many Congressmen feared he might start to retire them at 70 next. He had also greatly underestimated popular support and respect for the Court. In proposing this measure, Roosevelt was seen as a dictator. In July the Senate rejected the Judiciary Reform Bill by 70 votes to 20. However, it was not a total defeat for Roosevelt. Justice Van Devanter, who was ill, announced his retirement. The Supreme Court recognised that Roosevelt had just won an election with a huge majority. Most of the electorate clearly supported his measures. Therefore the Court had already begun to uphold legislation such as the National Labor Relations and the Social Security Acts – possibly, as one wag commented, because 'a switch in time saves nine'. As more justices retired, Roosevelt could appoint his supporters, such as Felix Frankfurter, to replace them, but he did not again attempt to reform the Supreme Court.

Opposition to Roosevelt

Roosevelt faced significant opposition from big business and wealthy people who increasingly felt the New Deal had gone too far. Some wouldn't even say his name; they called him 'that cripple in the White House'. Roosevelt himself said that everyone was against him but the electorate. However, the relationship with big business was always difficult. Roosevelt knew the economy couldn't recover without its support and big business may have feared the alternative had the New Deal failed completely. However, they hated the Revenue Act which raised taxes and opposed what they perceived as ever greater government interference.

Republican opponents in Congress were to be joined by more conservative Democrats who also feared the New Deal had gone too far. Roosevelt called for a special congressional session in November 1937 to pass various measures such as an antilynching bill which had been delayed due to the debates on the Judicial Reform Bill. Not one was passed. Roosevelt's opponents in both Houses of Congress issued a 'Conservative Manifesto' in December 1937 calling for lower taxes and antistrike legislation, and warning about the dangers of social security in creating a dependency culture.

Roosevelt was keen to try to ensure more liberal Democrats were elected in the **mid-term congressional elections** in 1938 by touring the country and offering them his support. Unfortunately, mid-term elections are usually concerned more with local issues and Roosevelt's intervention seemed ham-fisted and evidence of a president who was losing authority. By this time it was felt that the New Deal was running out of steam.

The 'Roosevelt Recession', 1937–38

Federal expenditure was cut in June 1937 to meet Roosevelt's long-held belief in a balanced budget. He hoped business had by this time recovered sufficiently to fill the gaps caused by government cutbacks. It had not. The cutbacks led to what became known as the '**Roosevelt Recession**'. Figure 1 shows how unemployment rose, particularly among farm workers, in 1937–38. With the number of unemployed rising from 7,000,000 to 10,390,000 in 12 months, social security payments swallowed $2 billion of the nation's wealth.

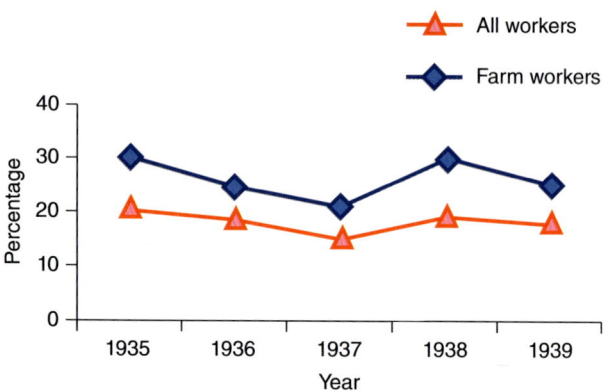

▲ Figure 1: Unemployment, 1935–39.

The same problems of human misery that had been witnessed in the early years of the decade returned in full force:

- In the manufacturing industries, employment fell by 23 per cent and the production of such items as motor cars fell by as much as 50 per cent.
- Overall, national income fell by 13 per cent. Recovery suddenly seemed as far away as ever.

- According to the Federal Reserve Board's index of industrial production, 66 per cent of the gains made during the New Deal years were lost. The fall in this index from 117 in August 1937 to 76 by May 1938 was faster than at any time during the earlier depression of 1929–33.

> **Source E** Extract from *The Personal Side*, edited by Jessie A. Bloodworth in 1939 and based on interviews with families in the 1930s. Here Claud Park had been unemployed, worked for the CWA and was then taken on by the Mississippi Milling Company. However, his hours were reduced.
>
> About two months ago a 25 hour week came into effect … At present his weekly pay checks amount to only $11.75, and his family are again getting behind with the bills. Because of the uncertainty of the working hours it is impossible for Claud to 'fill in' with odd jobs. He feels there is no use to look for more regular work in other factories, for in most of them, work is just as irregular as at the Mississippi Milling Company …
>
> The biggest problem is warm clothing for the children. Claud Jr. and Mary both need shoes, overshoes and winter underwear but so far it has been impossible for the Parks to do more than buy food and pay the rent, gas and electricity bills … She thinks employers don't begin to realise how much hardship they cause by reducing the pay checks of the workers.
>
> How useful is Source E in outlining the problems faced by families during the Depression years?

unions. However, Roosevelt faced defeat when he tried to take on the Supreme Court who had found much of his legislation unconstitutional, and there were continued problems, for example, in agriculture. Government cutbacks in 1937 sparked off the Roosevelt Recession. While continued problems in agriculture were tackled in a Third New Deal, the measures petered out as foreign affairs began to dominate.

> ### Work together
> In this activity you should focus on similarity and difference. Divide a large piece of paper into three. Label the first section 'The First New Deal'. Label both the second and third sections 'The Second New Deal'. In the first section write down the legislation of the First New Deal – for example, the Glass-Steagall Act. In the second section write down legislation of the Second New Deal which is of similar type – for example, the 1935 Banking Act. In the third section note down Second New Deal legislation which is different – for example, the Social Security Act.
>
> When you have completed this task, study the third section in particular. Discuss what was similar and different about the First and Second New Deals.

The end of the New Deal

In the mid-term elections of 1938 the Republicans doubled their seats in the House of Representatives and also made gains in the Senate. Increasingly as his second term drew to a close, Roosevelt was seen as a 'lame duck' president whose New Deal policies had failed to deliver economic recovery to the extent hoped for. Although he was to break with tradition and stand for a historic third (and later a fourth) term of office, this was not known at the time. There were no more New Deal measures passed after January 1939. Increasingly thereafter, foreign affairs began to dominate.

Conclusion: The Second New Deal, 1935–38

The Second New Deal saw an important expansion of the role of federal, state and local government. There was much that was new such as centralisation of the banking system, social security and legal recognition for labour

Recommended reading

Anthony J. Badger, *The New Deal: The Depression Years 1933–40* (Palgrave MacMillan, 1989). This is a standard account of the New Deal, thorough and accessible.

Burton Folsom, *New Deal or Raw Deal: How FDR's Economic Legacy Has Damaged America* (Simon & Schuster, 2009). A highly regarded example of 'New Right' thinking that the New Deal harmed the USA.

Michael Parrish, *Anxious Decades* (W.W. Norton, 1992), especially Part Two. Comprehensive and readable with lots of examples in support of the ideas.

Amity Shlaes, *The Forgotten Man* (Pimlico, 2009), especially Introduction and Chapters 6, 7, 8, 11 and 13. Accessible and well-written argument that the New Deal harmed the USA, with focus on selected individuals.

Chapter summary

- President Hoover's terms of office coincided with the onset of the Depression. While he was prepared to do more than any previous president, the intensity of the economic downturn was too great for his policies to address effectively. Above all, he would not consider direct government intervention.
- The Depression eventually affected every aspect of the US economy and the financial and banking sectors remained in turmoil.
- Millions became unemployed. Many became homeless too, crossing the continent in search of work.
- Hoover's policies were inadequate to meet the scale of the problem. Although he repudiated foreign war debts, the high tariffs probably made matters worse.
- Franklin Delano Roosevelt won the 1932 presidential election. People had great hopes that he could solve the economic problems, not because he had any concrete policies but because he wasn't Herbert Hoover.
- Although there was no blueprint for reform, the first 100 days saw a tide of legislation to address these problems.
- Banking and finance were reformed.
- Alphabet agencies were set up to deal with specific problems – for example, in agriculture, industry, housing.
- States were offered direct relief to distribute among the needy.
- Roosevelt faced powerful opposition both from the right and left. The latter included Huey Long, the influential politician from Louisiana who could have fought Roosevelt in the 1936 presidential election.
- The Second New Deal continued measures for recovery but also introduced emergency relief and, for the first time, social security measures.
- Roosevelt won a decisive victory in the 1936 election.
- His second term was beset with problems, including opposition from the Supreme Court and the Roosevelt Recession of 1937.
- The New Deal failed to bring about sustained economic recovery.

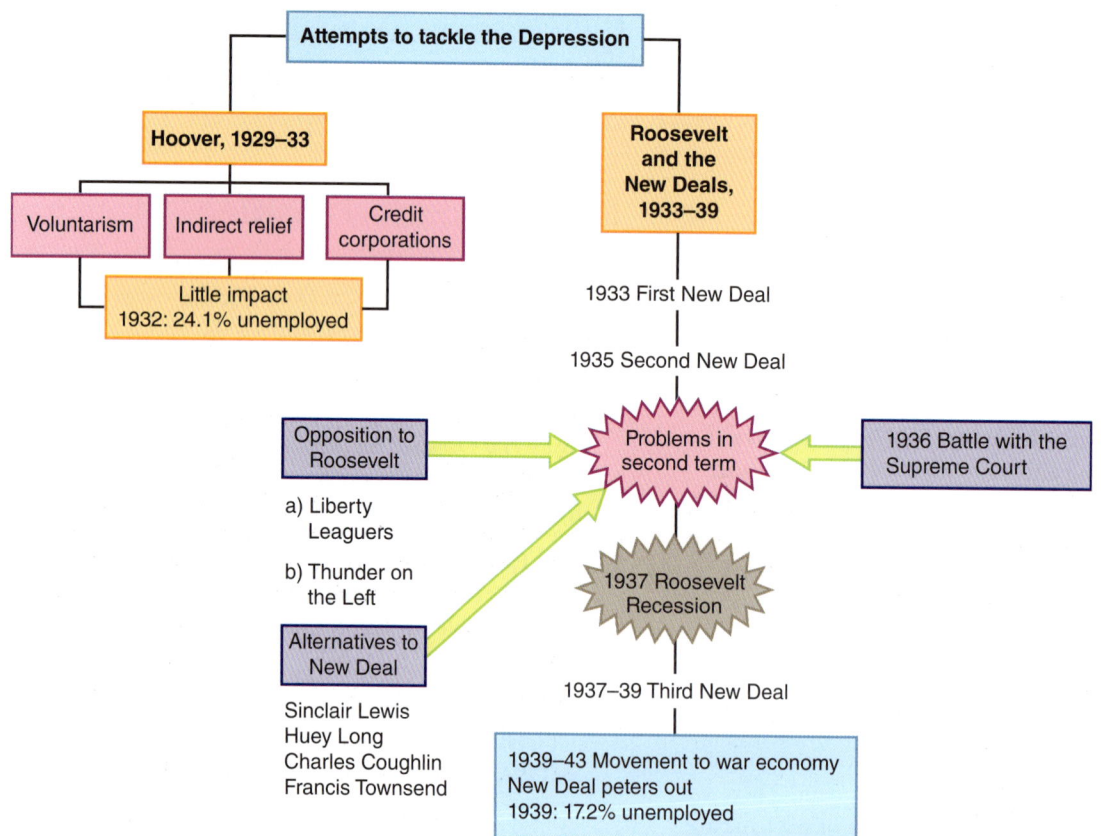

▲ Summary diagram: The Depression and the New Deal, 1929–38.

Section A: Essay technique

Structuring an essay and writing introductions

Well-structured essays will receive higher marks than essays in which the structure is unclear. The structure of your essay should be designed to help you evaluate how far the two sources together are useful to a historian who is investigating a specific topic.

The overall structure of your essay should include:
- an introduction which focusses on the question and sets out the essence of your answer
- a conclusion which summarises your essay in order to weigh up the extent to which the evidence of the sources is useful, and reaches an overall judgement
- the main body which should present a detailed evaluation of the evidence of the sources.

TIP: Remember, the question asks you to consider the sources *together*. Therefore, a structure which analyses Source 1 and then moves on to Source 2 is unlikely to do well. Always try to structure your essay in a way that allows you to deal with the sources together.

Each paragraph should set out an analysis of the usefulness of the evidence of the two sources. Therefore, you need to discuss both sources in every paragraph.

TIP: One way of doing this is to make sure that you discuss both sources in almost every sentence.

For example, imagine you are answering the following question:

> How far could the historian make use of Sources 1 and 2 together to investigate the extent of the Depression in the USA?

An example of how to introduce both sources in an introduction to this question is given on page 292.

Source 1 Oscar Ameringer, an ordinary American citizen, described the situation to a sub-committee of the Committee of Labor in Congress in 1932 (found in L.E. Snellgrove, *The Modern World Sourcebook*, 1984).

> During the last three months I have visited as I have said some twenty states of this wonderfully rich and beautiful country. Here are some of the things I heard and saw.
> A number of Montana citizens told me of thousands of bushels [*] of wheat left in the fields uncut on account of its low price that hardly paid for the harvesting. In Oregon I saw thousands of bushels of apples rotting in the orchards. Only absolutely flawless apples were still saleable – at from 40 to 50 cents a box containing 200 apples. At the same time there are millions of children who, on account of the poverty of their parents, will not eat one apple this winter.
>
> While I was in Oregon, the *Portland Oregon* [newspaper] bemoaned the fact that thousands of ewes were killed by sheep raisers because they did not bring enough in the market to pay freight on them. And while Oregon sheep raisers fed mutton to the buzzards I saw men, women and children walking over the hard roads...
>
> The farmers are pauperized by the poverty of the industrial populations and industrial populations are being pauperized by the poverty of the farmers. Neither has the money to buy the products of the other; hence we have overproduction and under-consumption at the same time and in the same country.

[*] Bushels: old measure of weight.

Source 2 Extract from Studs Terkel, *Hard Times* (Penguin, 1970). In the 1960s the journalist Studs Terkel interviewed people about their memories of the Depression. Jerome Zerbe was a society photographer based in New York.

> Do you remember apple sellers in the city?
>
> No, there were none of those. Not in New York. Never, never. There were a few beggars. You came to recognise then because they'd be on one block one day and one block the next. And finally one day, I saw this pathetic beggar, whom I'd always felt sorry for. This Cadillac drove up. I'd just given him a quarter. And it picked him up. There was a woman driving it. And I thought: well if they can drive a Cadillac, they don't need my quarter. His wife had a Cadillac.
>
> You don't recall bread lines or stuff like that?
>
> I never saw one. Never in New York. If there were, they were in Harlem or down in the Village. They were never in this section of town. There was never any sign of poverty.

Here are three examples of introductions that could answer the question on page 291:

Answer 1

> In Source 1 the author says he has visited twenty states in 'this wonderfully rich and beautiful country'. He says that he saw thousands of bushels of wheat left uncut. This was because the price was so low it hardly paid for the harvesting. This meant the farmers could not make a profit. Source 2 says that there were no apple sellers in New York but there were some beggars. This was due to the Great Depression. But one beggar's wife drove a Cadillac!

Answer 2

> Source 1 is useful to a historian because it is from someone who travelled around the USA. Source 2 is also useful because it gives an eyewitness account of life in New York during the Depression.

Answer 3

> Both Sources 1 and 2 on page 291 are useful to a historian investigating the extent of the Depression although they give different perspectives on the Depression, Source 1 focusses on the wider picture as the author has travelled over the country, while Source 2 focusses on one area of New York City. However, there are problems with both sources. Source 1 relies too much on assertion as in the second paragraph where the author makes a connection between overproduction and underconsumption without evidence in support, while Source 2 offers a skewed picture from a society photographer living in a wealthy part of New York, which may not be typical of the city itself, let alone the entire country.

Activity: Analyse the introduction

Having read the three introductions, in pairs consider the following questions:
1 What skills do the different introductions demonstrate?
2 Which introduction focusses most clearly on the question?
3 Which introduction integrates Sources 1 and 2 most effectively?
4 How could you improve the best of the three introductions?
5 What can you learn from the three samples?

Activity: AS-style questions

1 Why is Source 1 (on page 291) valuable to the historian for an enquiry into the extent of the Depression in the early 1930s?
2 How much weight do you give the evidence of Source 2 (on page 291) for an enquiry into attitudes to poverty during the Great Depression?

Selecting information

Another skill vital for success in Section A is that of selecting the right information from the sources. So what is the 'right' information? It is:

- information that is relevant to the question
- information that illustrates the main point of the source
- information that illustrates the points that you want to make.

In addition to the source material, the exam paper also contains a short description of the source's provenance printed immediately above the source. Selecting the important material from the provenance will also help you do well. You could select information that helps you evaluate the evidence, such as:

- information that would help explain the motives of the writer
- information that helps explain the purpose of the document
- information that helps contextualise the source (see page 319).

TIP: Don't just copy information from the provenance; make sure you use the information to help weigh the evidence that the source presents.

Selection

Imagine you are answering the following question:

> How far could the historian make use of Sources 3 and 4 together to investigate the effectiveness of the New Deal from 1933 to 1939?

You need to think about the focus of the question – here the question is asking you about what these two sources can tell us, as historians, about the effectiveness of the New Deal.

There are problems with oral history; these men are talking about their experiences of the New Deal 30 years on. We don't know if they are relying on memory or speaking with evidence from the period in front of them.

Paper 2 The USA, 1920–55: Boom, bust and recovery

Source 3 Extract from Studs Terkel, *Hard Times* (Penguin, 1970). In the 1960s the journalist Studs Terkel interviewed people about their memories of the Depression. David Kennedy was a member of the Federal Reserve Board.

> There was a very, very serious recession in 37. Marriner [*] spent a good share of his time trying to prove to the public that it was not caused by the Federal Reserve action. Critics said it was...
>
> We really had not made a substantial recovery from the deep Depression of the early Thirties. Unemployment was still very high. The New Deal programs were not stimulating the way people thought. There was sort of a defeatist attitude – that the government just had to do all this for the people. It was not until the war, with its economic thrust, that we pulled out of it. The war got us out of it, not the New Deal policies.
>
> As a matter of fact the policies pursued could have got us into real trouble. It was changing a way of life. You're spending money and going into debt but you're not finding ways and means to explore new projects.
>
> Despite all the programs – PWA, WPA, FSA...
>
> It took care of immediate suffering in part of the areas. I'm not criticising it in that sense. But it didn't pull the thing up so that private enterprise could take its place and replace it.

[*] Marriner Eccles was Governor of the Federal Reserve Board.

Source 4 Extract from Studs Terkel, *Hard Times* (Penguin, 1970). In the 1960s the journalist Studs Terkel interviewed people about their memories of the Depression. Raymond Moley had been one of Roosevelt's earliest advisors but tended to be disillusioned with the New Deal by 1935. In particular he disagreed about relief measures such as unemployment insurance, which he felt would lead to welfare dependency.

> The first New Deal was a radical departure from American life. It put more power in the central government. At the time it was necessary, especially in the farm area of our economy. Left to itself farming was in a state of anarchy. Beyond that there was no need to reorganise in industry. We merely needed to get the farms prospering again and create a market for industrial products in the cities. The second new Deal was an entirely different thing. My disenchantment began then. Roosevelt didn't follow any particular policy after 1936. Our economy began to slide downhill – our unemployment increased – after that, until 1940. This is something liberals are not willing to recognise. It was the war that saved the economy and saved Roosevelt.

Activity: AS-style questions

1. Why is Source 3 valuable to the historian for an enquiry into the causes of the 'Roosevelt Recession'?
2. How much weight do you give the evidence of Source 4 for an enquiry into opposition to the New Deal in the 1930s?

Activity: Selecting from the sources

1. Read the question on page 292 and then the sources above. Make a bullet-pointed list of the information that you would select from Sources 3 and 4 to answer the question.
2. Consider the following questions with your partner:
   (a) Did you both select the same information for the source? If not, whose selections were:
      (i) most relevant to the question
      (ii) most characteristic of the whole source?
   (b) Did you both select the same information from the provenance? If not, whose selections were:
      (i) most relevant to the question
      (ii) most helpful to a historian evaluating the information contained in the source?

Making inferences

Making inferences from sources is one way to demonstrate your understanding of the source and of the period. An inference is a deduction or conclusion that comes from reading between the lines of a source – it's not about what lies on the surface but what's hinted at below. It isn't wild speculation but a conclusion that is drawn from reasoning or evidence. A detailed knowledge of the period is vital to making inferences.

Imagine you are answering the following question:

> How far could the historian make use of Sources 5 and 6 together to investigate to what extent the First New Deal was a coherent programme of reform?

There is a lot of information in Source 5 that is purely on the surface. But beyond that, you can use your own knowledge, to draw out more complex and insightful conclusions, as the annotations below show.

Source 5 Extract from a lecture by Frances Perkins entitled 'Labor under the New Deal' given in 1963. Perkins was Roosevelt's Secretary for Labour from 1933 to 1945.

> Everyone caught the phrase 'New Deal'. It became significant right away. And soon people began to ask just what the New Deal meant. At that time we didn't know. Because the man who had made the statement didn't know himself, I'm quite sure. He had no program. He had some vague ideas but no real plan of what might be done.
>
> Nevertheless as he campaigned you heard reverberations of this same speech. You heard promises to do something about the unemployed but never specifically what he was going to do about them. On one occasion he said, 'We're going to put the unemployed men and women to work.' Not how or where or for whom. He hadn't thought of the Works Progress Administration … Roosevelt campaigned all those months before his election without a specific program in mind. But he knew something would have to be done so the unemployed could go back to work.

Annotations:
- The term 'New Deal' captured the imagination of people but there was no real New Deal programme.
- Roosevelt hadn't yet thought of specific solutions.
- Roosevelt knew something would have to be done to provide employment opportunities.

Source 6 Extract from Roosevelt's speech after having accepted the Democratic nomination for the 1932 presidential election.

> Throughout the Nation, men and women, forgotten in the political philosophy of the government of the last years, look to us here for guidance and for more equitable opportunity to share in the distribution of national wealth.
>
> On the farms, in the large metropolitan areas, in the smaller cities and in the villages, millions of our citizens cherish the hope that their old standards of living and of thought have not gone forever. Those millions cannot and shall not hope in vain.
>
> I pledge you, I pledge myself, to a new deal for the American people. Let us all here assembled constitute ourselves prophets of a new order of competence and of courage. This is more than a political campaign; it is a call to arms. Give me your help, not to win votes alone, but to win in this crusade to restore America to its own people.

Activity: Inferences

Having read the question and example above, you can now practise making inferences from Source 6. Remember:
- Your inferences should help you answer the question.
- Inferences should be informed by your contextual knowledge of the period.

Answer the following question to help you:
1. Given the historical context, why do people seek reassurance about the past?
2. What is Roosevelt actually promising the American people?
3. Explain why he compares the New Deal to a crusade.
4. Compare Sources 5 and 6. Together, what do they imply about the coherence of the First New Deal?

Activity: AS-style questions

1. Why is Source 6 valuable to the historian for an enquiry into the effectiveness of the New Deal in the years 1933 to 1941?
2. How much weight do you give the evidence of Source 5 for an enquiry into the economic impact of the New Deal to 1937?

Section B: Essay technique

Detail and analysis

Paper 2 Section B questions, like Paper 1 Section A and B questions, need to be detailed and analytical. You may have already read the advice on how to write detailed and analytical essays for Paper 1 (see page 79). Now is a chance to practise these skills in the context of opposition to Roosevelt's policies.

Activity: Detail and analysis

Imagine you are answering the following question:

Why was there such widespread opposition to Roosevelt's policies by 1936?

1. Identify the kind of question (see page 259).
2. Make an appropriate plan, writing down the main points of your three or four paragraphs.
3. Next to each of the points, add three supporting details – you could use a different colour if you have one.
4. Write one analytical sentence to conclude each paragraph.

Work together

Having finished the activity 'Detail and analysis', swap your work with a partner. Consider:

1. Did you agree on what type of question you were dealing with? If not, discuss it and work out who was right.
2. Whose plan most clearly focussed on the specific type of question?
3. Were the details that your partner selected the most appropriate to support their points?
4. Could either of you have used detail that better supports the points that you wanted to make?
5. Were all of your partner's sentences truly analytical?
6. What can you learn from your partner's approach?

Use these questions to feed back to each other and improve your use of detail and analysis.

Question practice

1. 'President Hoover did little to combat the Depression.' How far do you agree with this statement?
2. How accurate is it to say that all groups in the USA experienced economic hardship in the early 1930s? **AS**
3. How far did the First New Deal successfully address the effects of the Depression?
4. How successful was the First New Deal in the years 1933–35? **AS**
5. How significant was the Supreme Court in the opposition to the New Deal? **AS**

Key Topic 3 The impact of the New Deal and the Second World War on the USA to 1945

Overview

The impact of the Second World War concealed the failures of the New Deal in terms of economic recovery. However, the New Deal had impacted US society in other ways. It had seen the growth of government and created an infrastructure which would develop significantly further as the USA geared up for war. Women such as Eleanor Roosevelt demonstrated a new assertiveness in gender issues. While the New Deal may not actually have done much to improve the lives of members of ethnic groups, it won the support of black Americans whose voting patterns were largely changed as a result.

As the USA became focussed on war production, unemployment diminished. Women found more job opportunities – for example, in the munitions industries – as men were called on to join the armed forces. Employment opportunities grew for ethnic groups, too, although they continued to face discrimination.

The war saw significant social and cultural changes, not least in Hollywood, which produced patriotic films and propaganda. The emphasis was on unity and national spirit, although this didn't always manifest itself in the way ethnic groups were treated. Discrimination and competition for facilities such as housing led to serious riots.

The USA became prosperous as a result of the Second World War. The period saw a considerable movement to cities and growing assertiveness in women and indeed young people who were either working or in the armed forces. While there was periodic industrial unrest, new industries such as pharmaceuticals grew and the economy developed to such an extent that the prosperity continued when the war was over.

The overarching theme of the impact of the New Deal and the Second World War is covered in four sections:
1. The New Deal and the economy
2. The impact of the New Deal and the war on ethnic minorities
3. Social and cultural changes
4. The war and the economy, 1941–45

TIMELINE

1940 June	Smith Act
1940 September	Selective Service Act
1941 January	War Production Board set up
1941 December	USA entry into the Second World War
1942 January	National War Labor Board set up
1942 January	Office of Price Administration and Civilian Supply set up
1942 February	First Japanese bombing raids on the USA
1942 February	Internment of Japanese Americans living in the West Coast area
1942 October	Office of Economic Stabilization set up
1943 May	Office of War Mobilization set up
1943 June	Smith-Connally War Labor Disputes Act
1943 June	Race riots in Detroit
1944 March	Roosevelt begins his fourth term of office
1945 April	Death of Roosevelt
1945 August	End of the Second World War in Asia

1 The New Deal and the economy

According to Ed Johnson, the Democratic governor of Colorado during the 1930s, the New Deal was 'the worst fraud ever perpetrated on the American people'. While this view may be extreme, it can be argued that, on the surface at least, the actual achievements of the New Deal were rather slender. The national total of personal income stood at $86 billion in 1929 and only $73 billion in 1939. This was despite a population increase of 9 million during the course of the decade. The government seemed reconciled to a permanent unemployment figure of at least 5 million. Wages averaged $25.03 per week in 1929 and $23.86 ten years later.

1940 was a key year in economic terms in that it marked the beginning of **rearmament** and the movement towards a war economy. Its statistics offer some indication of the impact of the New Deal before war production took effect. Good indicators of the impact of the New Deal include unemployment levels and the extent of economic recovery, which this section will look at.

However, the New Deal cannot be judged solely on the economy. Roosevelt spoke of its aims as 'relief, recovery and reform' and it is against these that its success should be judged. It instituted important social changes, such as the introduction of social security, which were to transform the lives of the elderly and vulnerable. It changed the political infrastructure of the USA through the creation of a more powerful executive. Having said this, the New Deal did little to improve employment prospects for women, although there were some notable appointments such as Frances Perkins as Secretary for Labour. The influence of Eleanor Roosevelt was also significant, particularly with regard to social and gender issues.

> **Note it down**
>
> Use the 1:2 method in this section (see page x). If you are revising or organising your notes thematically, you could colour code the different points as to whether they are political, economic or social. This may help you later when trying to answer questions about reasons for the events that you are studying.

The impact of the New Deal on unemployment

In 1933, 18 million Americans were unemployed. In 1939, 9 million were still out of work. The alphabet agencies such as the PWA and the WPA had been created to provide work. The theory was that public works schemes would not only create jobs through the actual ventures themselves, but also stimulate recovery by orders for materials and equipment and provide employment to maintain the facilities that had been created. They would effectively 'kickstart' the economy so that when the employees' time at the agency was complete, they would be able to find a permanent job. The public works schemes would stimulate private enterprise, which would then be able to take on a larger workforce. However, in reality many Americans had left employment in the alphabet agencies to return to joblessness or at best part-time working. Put bluntly, the plan had not worked.

While there was a reduction in unemployment in the early years of the New Deal, it may largely have been the result of people working in the alphabet agencies. The **Roosevelt Recession** of 1937 saw a return to higher unemployment with 19 per cent of the workforce jobless in 1938 (see page 288). The **recession** resulted in part from government reductions in public work schemes and job creation – therefore, it could be argued that the New Deal tended to create temporary jobs working for the government rather than permanent ones in the private sector.

Roosevelt had been warned of this by Chairman of the Federal Reserve Board Marriner Eccles as early as 1937 (see Source 3 on page 293). Eccles advised Roosevelt that federal spending should not be reduced until private enterprise had expanded enough to be in a position to recruit at high levels. However, Roosevelt was more concerned to achieve a **balanced budget** and agreed to cutbacks of $66 million. The result, as we have seen, was a recession in which 1.8 million people lost their jobs between September and December 1939. By 1938 unemployment had risen to 10 million but the damage was done and unemployment did not fall significantly until the onset of the European war.

Most historians agree that the real reason unemployment fell was the amendment of the 1935 **Neutrality Act** in November 1939. This meant **belligerents** could buy from the USA. Within a year there were orders for 10,800 aircraft and 13,000 aeroplane engines.

Economic recovery

If the New Deal had not brought about economic recovery to the extent hoped, it had nevertheless transformed the political and social landscape of the USA. The federal government now took responsibility for people's lives and well-being in ways no previous administrations had. In this way the national infrastructure of the USA was altered by the New Deal.

The differing aims of relief, recovery and reform offer a convenient way of assessing the New Deal. However, they should not be seen as strictly separate. Many measures overlapped. The WPA, for example, offered both relief to the unemployed and a boost to economic recovery through public works schemes. No measure was started solely to address one category. However, as the goals of relief, recovery and reform were used by Roosevelt himself to explain the aims of the New Deal, it may be appropriate to use them for purposes of evaluation.

Relief

One of the greatest achievements of the New Deal was in changing the role of the federal government. This was particularly true of help for the less fortunate members of society. Relief agencies such as the FERA (see page 279) and the WPA (see page 284) were set up to offer hope to millions. There were new departures in governmental responsibilities. The Social Security Act (see page 285) was not strictly a relief measure as it was financed through contributions paid by recipients. However, it did set up a national system of old-age pensions and unemployment benefit for the first time.

It is true that the amounts spent were inadequate for the needs of a population suffering from a prolonged depression. Nevertheless, important precedents were set by this legislation. It could be built on in the future. Never before had the federal government become involved in granting direct relief or benefits. Roosevelt initially saw relief agencies as only temporary expedients until economic recovery was achieved. In offering direct relief, however, he significantly increased the role of the federal government.

This led in turn to a greater role for state and local governments as partners – however unwillingly at first – in many of the programmes.

The effects of the expansion of welfare provision

The growth in expenditure on welfare tells its own story. Before 1930 states spent virtually nothing on relief measures. In 1930 together they spent $9 million. By 1940 this figure had risen to $479 million. A further $480 million was spent on unemployment benefit. Millions of people began to see the federal government as their saviour. It was through social reform that it first directly spoke to them. It was through the provision of relief and benefits that many people first became aware of a president not as a distant figure who meant little to the likes of them, but as someone who was interested in them and who cared about them.

More people took part in presidential elections in the 1930s than had done so previously. In 1920 and 1924 only 49 per cent of the electorate bothered to vote in the presidential elections; in 1928 and 1932 the figure rose to 57 per cent, and by 1936 and 1940 it was 62 per cent. The increase was partly due to the Depression that had destroyed much of what people had previously believed in, and partly due to the programmes of the New Deal which helped them. The provision of relief and benefits helped more and more people feel like they had a stake in their country. It made them feel that they belonged.

Recovery

Economic recovery was sluggish during the New Deal years, in part because many of its measures were contradictory. Roosevelt believed in a balanced budget. He was, therefore, reluctant to spend excessively on federal projects. He failed to see that massive government expenditure might be necessary to offset the reduction in spending in the private sector. This desire for a balanced budget led to a reduction of the budget deficit over the course of Roosevelt's presidency (see Table 1). In 1938 the deficit was lower than the $2.5 billion deficit Hoover had

Table 1: Federal finance deficits.

Year	Deficit (in $ billion)
1932	2.5
1933	1.7
1934	2.8
1935	3.2
1936	4.5
1937	3.1
1938	1.3
1939	3.5
1940	3.6

(Source: US Abstract of Statistics Supplement 1784–1985)

run up in 1932 and over which Roosevelt had criticised him in the 1932 presidential election. Roosevelt had come to power believing in a balanced budget but had come to realise it was no longer possible given the realities of the Depression and the efforts needed to overcome it. It can be seen, therefore, that the deficit rose after the lessons of 1937 and Roosevelt belatedly became converted to the necessity of running a deficit. As events were subsumed by war, the deficit ran to previously unimaginable levels.

Roosevelt was always dubious about the long-term effectiveness of public works programmes. The British economist J.M. Keynes came out of a meeting with him in 1934 very disappointed, saying he doubted the President had really understood what he was saying about how government action could stimulate economic growth. When Roosevelt reversed earlier policy in the wake of the 1937 recession and offered $3.8 billion for public spending, it was not enough to make much of a difference.

It should be remembered that the New Deal was designed to save the capitalist system in the USA not to replace it with a huge public sector. Roosevelt hoped his measures would restore capitalist confidence and expansion. He never questioned the importance of private enterprise and worked to support it. Many New Deal measures favoured big business. For example, the NRA codes were largely drawn up by the representatives of big business (see page 278).

In the later years of the New Deal Roosevelt became annoyed with big business because of its ingratitude for all the New Deal had done for it. However, he never doubted that the answer to economic problems lay largely in the hands of large corporations. Again, it was his faith in capitalism and the **market structure** that led him to maintain his belief in the balanced budget and not adopt a plan of permanent massive state spending. It is interesting to note that the countries that did so, notably Sweden and Germany – albeit in the case of the latter on military expansion – overcame the Depression first. In contrast, by 1939, the USA was the slowest of the major countries to recover from depression. An important lesson taught by the Depression was that the economy was not necessarily self-righting and while governments could kickstart recovery, the economy would fall back into recession if that recovery wasn't real and sustained.

However, the New Deal had transformed the USA in terms of the greater role of government and structures to deal with modern demands.

Reform

The New Deal was, when viewed as a whole, a programme of reform. The reforms were economic, political and social and transformed the national infrastructure of the USA.

Economic reforms

Economic reforms were mainly intended to rescue the capitalist system from its worst excesses and to provide a more rational framework in which it could operate. For example, the banking system was reformed and made more efficient, particularly through the centralisation of banking in 1935 (see page 285). The evils of Wall Street and the holding companies were exposed and reformed. Roosevelt allowed labour unions to take their place in labour relations and reluctantly recognised that the federal government had a role in settling industrial disputes. In this sense the triangular partnership in labour relations between employers, employees and government was created through the work of the National Labor Relations Board (see page 285).

> **National Labor Relations Board v. Jones & Laughlin Steel, 1937**
>
> The National Labor Relations Board (NLRB) had to fight for recognition through its case against Jones & Laughlin Steel, the ninth largest steel producer in the USA. The NLRB accused the firm of discriminating against workers seeking to join a union – in fact, they had fired ten workers in their plant at Aliquippa, Pennsylvania for seeking to do so – and demanded they be reinstated. Not only did Jones & Laughlin refuse, they also took the NLRB to court, arguing it was unconstitutional. The case eventually reached the Supreme Court, where in April 1937 the justices found in favour of the NLRB and deemed it to have legal authority.

> **Source A** Extract from Wendell Willkie's speech accepting the Republican nomination in the presidential election of 1940. In the election Roosevelt carried 38 states and Willkie 10.
>
> When the present administration came to power in 1933, we heard a lot about the forgotten man. The government, we were told, must care for those who had no other means of support. With this proposition all of us agreed. And we still hold firmly to the principle that those whom private industry cannot support must be supported by government agency, whether federal or state.
>
> But I want to ask anyone in this audience who is, or has been, on relief whether the support that the government gives him is enough. Is it enough for the free and able-bodied American to be given a few scraps of cash or credit with which to keep himself and his children just this side of starvation and nakedness? Is that what the forgotten man wanted us to remember?
>
> What that man wanted us to remember was his chance – his right – to take part in our great American adventure.
>
> But this administration never remembered that. It launched a vitriolic and well-planned attack against those very industries in which the forgotten man wanted a chance.
>
> It carried on a propaganda campaign to convince the people that businessmen are iniquitous.
>
> What can be inferred from Source A by a historian evaluating the failure of the New Deal?

Political reforms

Reluctantly, Roosevelt came to realise that the expansion of government he had created was to be permanent. He set up the Executive Office of the President to help manage this expansion and ensure that the federal bureaucracy could cope with the demands being made upon it both at that time and in the future. His attempted reform of the Supreme Court failed (see page 287) but the Court nevertheless became more sympathetic to New Deal legislation, recognising the political realities of the later 1930s. The New Deal also saw an expansion in the functions of state and local government – for example, in terms of welfare provision. The system became more modern and able to address the needs of citizens in the twentieth century.

Social reforms

People increasingly expected that the government would take responsibility for their problems. The Social Security Act and the relief and job creation agencies expanded the role of government considerably.

Key debate
The political and social impact of the New Deal

In the years following the New Deal many historians were supportive. Writing in the 1950s, Carl Degler called it 'a third American revolution' because of the growth in government involvement and the break with **laissez-faire**. However, during the 1960s historians associated with the **New Left** such as Paul Conkin became more critical, arguing that it was too limited in its scope and that it was a missed opportunity for radical change. More recently, right-wing historians such as Amity Shlaes have been more critical still, arguing that it stifled economic recovery. They argue that high wage rates, partly as a result of union activities, discouraged employers from taking on more workers. The emphasis has shifted from the overview to specifics; too much government involvement, in this case the legalisation of labour unions, stifled the private sector's ability to create more jobs.

It is important to repeat that the New Deal should not be judged by targets it did not set itself. It did not intend to change the capitalist structure. Some commentators criticised it as a lost opportunity to bring in a **socialist economic system** with greater equality of wealth and fully centralised planning. They wanted the New Deal to be about these things. Unfortunately for them, it was not. One group who may have hoped for more was women.

Women and the New Deal

Women held more important posts in government during the New Deal era than at any time before or after until the 1990s. Eleanor Roosevelt was one of the most politically active first ladies. As Secretary of Labour from 1933 to 1945, Frances Perkins was only one of many women holding government office, and Ruth Bryan Owen became the first female ambassador (to Denmark) in 1933. Many prominent women had come together through expertise in social work, which was, of course, an asset for designing many New Deal measures. Frances Perkins, for example, had been appointed as Commissioner for the New York Department of Labour by Governor Roosevelt and fought for such policies as factory investigations and shortened working hours for women. As Secretary for Labour in Roosevelt's government, she continued her reform work and, as chairperson of the presidential Committee on Economic Security, helped draw up

Eleanor Roosevelt, 1884–1962

Eleanor Roosevelt expanded the role of the first lady from what had largely been seen as one of fulfilling ceremonial functions and looking elegant, into a more active political role. She did this through manipulation of the media to promote ideas, particularly with regards to social and gender issues. As First Lady, Eleanor built upon her expertise gained as an active helpmeet to her husband. During the First World War she was active in the US Red Cross and often campaigned on Roosevelt's behalf in political contests after he had fallen ill with polio in the early 1920s. She was active when he was Governor of New York State, supporting programmes to help the unemployed and disadvantaged and concerning herself with social issues.

Eleanor was anxious to promote gender issues and ensure women stayed within the workforce. She introduced women-only press conferences in the White House where she gave political opinions on public issues. This indirectly enhanced the role of women in journalism; too often, women had been given the lifestyle and personal interest stories to cover but now they had the First Lady's spin on weighty matters. She also began a monthly feature entitled 'I Want You to Write to Me' for the *Woman's Home Journal* in which readers could submit questions and suggestions about government policies. Within five months of its first appearance, 300,000 women had done so. She also wrote a daily column 'My Day', which was syndicated to 62 daily newspapers.

Eleanor made extensive visits to see New Deal programmes in operation; she has been called 'the president's eyes, ears and legs'. There is no doubt that Roosevelt, because his disability rendered him unable to inspect programmes as much as he would have liked to, took her reports extremely seriously and would often lend his weight to them such as in setting up a model community for coal miners in Arthurdale, West Virginia. Eleanor was also active in the question of **civil rights** and encouraged her husband to consider improving the lives of ethnic minorities – although, as we have seen, he was always constrained by his need for the support of Southern **Democrats**. During the war she promoted the black-American Tuskegee air base, and may have been influential in ensuring its graduates were assigned combat roles.

the 1935 Social Security Act. Unfortunately, when government priorities changed with the onset of war, much of women's influence was lost.

The New Deal itself did little for women. Unlike black Americans, they did not tend to vote as a group. As a result, politicians did not set out particularly to win their support. Much New Deal legislation worked against them:

- In 1933 the Economy Act (see page 277) forbade members of the same family from working for the federal government. A total of 75 per cent of those who lost their jobs through this measure were married women.
- NRA codes allowed for unequal wages (see page 278).
- Some agencies, such as the CCC, barred women entirely.

Women suffered particularly in the professions where, even by 1940, about 90 per cent of jobs were filled by men. There was a strong emphasis from many labour unions that in the job market, men should be the principal wage earners, with women's wages only supplementing this. Where women did find employment – which many had to do to balance the family budget – it tended to be in low-status, poorly paid jobs. On average during the 1930s, at $525 per annum, women earned half the average wage of men.

However, women were to benefit as prosperity returned through the shift to wartime production. It is interesting to consider 1940 as a transition year from the New Deal to 'the arsenal of democracy', which will be covered in the next section.

The economy in 1940

The year 1940 saw rearmament get underway. While the USA would not formally join the war until the Japanese attack on Pearl Harbor in December 1941, Roosevelt had long been worried about the impact of German and Japanese aggression and, while reluctant to join the fighting, openly supported the **Allied powers**. November 1939 saw the removal of the 1935 Neutrality Act which had banned the sale of war materiel to belligerent powers. Soon the USA was swamped with orders for weapons, strictly on a **cash-and-carry** basis. It was also doing significant business with Germany at this time; the Ethyl Gasoline Corporation, for example, helped the Germans develop materials essential for their air war plans. Overall, US investment in Germany increased by 40 per cent between 1936 and 1940.

When Britain began to run out of finance, Roosevelt introduced **Lend-Lease** in May 1940 in which Britain and later the Soviet Union would be 'loaned' weapons until the war was over – and the USA had become, in Roosevelt's words, 'the arsenal of democracy'. In theory, after the end of the war the materiel would be given back. Congress had also allocated $4 billion towards the development of the US Navy in July 1940 and $17 billion towards defence generally in October.

1940 was therefore something of a transition year. The statistics show improvements over the Depression years:

- GNP was up to $113 billion from $68.3 billion in 1933.
- During the same period, the index of industrial production rose from 69 to 126.
- Exports rose from $1.67 billion to $4.02 billion.
- Unemployment halved from 25.2 per cent to 13.9 per cent.

On the basis of these figures, the economy appeared twice as healthy in 1940 as it had been in 1933. If we consider the problems Roosevelt faced when coming to office, that seems no mean achievement – although clearly there were still significant problems. Many historians acknowledge that while the economy had improved over the period 1933 to 1940, the rate of recovery had stalled in 1937.

It may be useful by way of comparison to compare statistics from the New Deal years to the end of the Second World War (Table 2).

Table 2: Personal income and GDP, 1933–40 (figures in $ billion).

Year	Personal income	GDP
1933	46.6	55.8
1934	53.2	64.9
1935	59.9	72.2
1936	68.4	82.5
1937	74.0	90.2
1938	68.4	84.9
1939	72.6	90.4
1940	78.3	100.5
1941	95.3	125.3
1942	122.2	159.6
1943	149.4	192.6
1944	164.9	210.6
1945	171.6	213.1

(Source: *Annual Abstract of Statistics 1789–1945 Supplement*.)

As can be seen from the figures in Table 2, wealth soared in the 1940s; personal income in 1945 was almost four times higher than 1933. Indeed, the whole growth during the New Deal years was small by contrast with the expansion from the 1940s. Clearly, one cannot say what would have happened had the war not intervened and set the economy on the road to recovery. It may have been that more government intervention would have been necessary. However, there was no indication that this would have stimulated long-term recovery, just as the $3.9 billion injection following the Roosevelt Recession had comparatively little effect in remedying it.

Conclusion: The New Deal and the economy

The New Deal petered out as war production intervened. If economic recovery was slow, the New Deal transformed the infrastructure of the USA and paved the way for a vastly enhanced government role during the Second World War. The New Deal did little for women, although more were appointed to high office and Eleanor Roosevelt was a high-profile first lady. Statistics for 1940 show that recovery had stalled somewhat and more government intervention may have been necessary in the hope this would stimulate economic growth.

> ### Work together
>
> Research what historians such as Burton Folsom and Amity Shlaes say about the New Deal. If you don't have access to their books, you can find lectures, podcasts and discussions on various websites. Discuss the following questions:
>
> 1 How valid do you find their arguments?
> 2 How far do you agree that the New Deal harmed the USA?
> 3 How far did the New Deal meet its objectives?
> 4 How successful do you think the New Deal was?

2 The impact of the New Deal and the war on ethnic minorities

The New Deal did little for members of minority ethnic groups, except possibly for Native Americans, whose culture and values were recognised by the Indian Reorganization Act of 1934. There were no specific measures designed to elevate them from poverty, although many benefited from the social security and relief measures. The New Deal did more for Native Americans than past administrations, but critics have argued that it did little for black or Hispanic Americans. However, some New Deal legislation made things worse. Black-American share-croppers were often laid off, for example, when the AAA paid their landlords to produce less. Nevertheless, many black Americans saw Roosevelt as a saviour and their voting patterns shifted. This was because discrimination was fought against by members of the administration, more black Americans were employed by government and there were important measures of support, not least from First Lady Eleanor Roosevelt.

The lives of all groups were changed significantly by the impact of the Second World War. The war benefited African, Native American and Hispanic Americans economically. Ten per cent of black Americans in the South moved north and west to find employment in war production. Discrimination and prejudice remained, however, culminating in significant riots such as in Detroit in 1943. Fifteen thousand Japanese Americans, meanwhile, were interned as enemy aliens.

> ### Note it down
>
> Use the 1:2 method (see page x) to make notes on how ethnic minorities were treated. In the first column, you should include Native Americans, black Americans, Hispanic Americans and Japanese Americans. In the second column, consider how they were treated.
>
> As you make notes, use two index cards to note how each group was treated differently and similarly to the others – for example, the internment of Japanese Americans was unique but all faced discrimination in similar ways.

US entry into the Second World War

The USA had effectively been fighting a war in the Atlantic against German U boats, as they increasingly protected Allied convoys carrying US materiel to help with their war effort. Roosevelt was determined to keep the USA out of the fighting, however. This changed on 7 December 1941 with the Japanese attack on Pearl Harbor aimed at demobilising the US fleet while Japan expanded into the Pacific and Far East. As the USA declared war on Japan, Germany, fulfilling its treaty obligations, declared war on the USA. Had it not been for the attack on Pearl Harbor, the USA may not have entered the war.

Native Americans

The Indian Reorganization Act of 1934 recognised and encouraged Native American culture in a shift from the former policy of **assimilation** (see page 265). Tribes were reorganised into self-governing bodies that could vote to adopt constitutions and have their own police and legal systems. They could control land sales on the **reservations**, while new tribal corporations were established to manage tribal resources. However, many argued that respect for traditional Native American culture and society undermined efforts to modernise and join mainstream society. Indeed, 75 out of 245 tribes vetoed them when asked to vote on the measures.

These measures in no way relieved Native American poverty. Officials did their best to ensure Native Americans could take advantage of New Deal agencies such as the CCC and the PWA to find jobs, but Native American poverty was so great that these measures, for all their good intentions, could have only a very limited effect at best. As New Deal programmes wound down in the 1940s, Native Americans began to set up pressure groups to promote their development but often remained among the poorest people in the USA. In 1943, for example, a Senate enquiry found widespread poverty among Native Americans on reservations.

Native Americans during the war

Native Americans contributed fully in the war effort. At any one time there were approximately 25,000 serving in the fighting forces in unsegregated units, unlike black Americans who were segregated. In the Pacific, Navajos used their own language to transmit radio messages that the Japanese were unable to translate. Many others left the reservations to find work in the burgeoning war industries, often never to return to the traditional way of life.

The New Deal and black Americans

Roosevelt needed the vote of Southern Democrats, who were often racist. A realist, he said, 'I did not choose the tools with which I must work.' Certainly, early in the New Deal, Southern politicians were often his most loyal supporters. Not surprisingly, therefore, the New Deal saw no civil rights legislation. Many measures – the AAA, for instance – worked against black Americans.

Black Americans suffered particularly badly in the Depression, often being the last to be taken on and the first to be fired. Many poorly paid, menial jobs previously reserved for them were now taken by whites. NRA codes allowed for black Americans to be paid less than whites for doing the same jobs. Some black Americans called the NRA the 'Negro-run-around' because it was so unfair to them. The CCC was run by a Southern racist who did little to encourage black Americans to join; those who did faced strict segregation. Antilynching bills were introduced into Congress in 1934 and 1937, but Roosevelt did nothing to support either and both were eventually defeated.

Changing voting behaviour

Despite these negative points, one of the most important political features of the New Deal years was the shift in the voting behaviour of black Americans in the North who were able to vote (less than 5 per cent of black Americans in the South could vote). Traditionally, black Americans voted **Republican** because this was the party that had fought the Civil War in part to end slavery. In 1932, of 15 black-American **wards** in nine major cities, Roosevelt won only four. In 1936, he won nine, and by 1940, all 15. In some black-American areas of cities, notably Harlem in New York, Roosevelt won 85 per cent of the vote. A Gallup poll in 1936 showed that nationally 76 per cent of black Americans intended to vote for Roosevelt. Many black Americans saw him as much a saviour as poor whites did. His portrait hung in many black-American homes.

In 1936 there were 30 black-American delegates to the **Democratic Convention** and, much to the disgust of Southerners, the first black-American Congressman, Arthur Mitchell, delivered the opening speech. We need to look beyond the surface of the New Deal to explain this significant shift of allegiance.

Key Topic 3 The impact of the New Deal and the Second World War on the USA to 1945

Support from Roosevelt's government

Many New Deal administrators showed concern for black Americans and tried to make sure they were included in relief programmes. Eleanor Roosevelt was determined to do all she could to stop racism. She was able to ensure prominent black Americans met the President to explain the racial problems they faced and she herself made a public statement in 1938 when she sat in the 'coloured' section at the Conference of Human Welfare in Birmingham, Alabama. When the black-American singer Marion Anderson was refused permission to sing before an integrated audience at Constitution Hall in Washington in 1939, Harold Ickes, Secretary of the Interior, arranged for her to give a concert in front of 75,000 people, including Mrs Roosevelt, at the Lincoln Memorial. These gestures were significant in giving official respectability to the notion that racism was wrong, and helped black-American leaders to gain confidence in their own struggles. As we will see (page 305) when A. Philip Randolph, head of the black-American trade union, the Brotherhood of Sleeping Car Porters, threatened a march on Washington in 1941 to protest against racism in defence factories, Roosevelt passed Executive Order 8802 outlawing discrimination in the defence industry and setting up a Fair Employment Practices Committee (FEPC) to investigate and prevent such behaviour. Initially, the FEPC had a limited budget and few powers, although it was strengthened in the ensuing years (see page 305).

Moreover, the President did employ more black Americans in government, notably Mary McLeod Bethune at the National Youth Administration (NYA). However, while there were more black Americans in government office, it seems an exaggeration to speak – as some did – of a 'black-American cabinet' addressing race issues. The civil service tripled the number of black Americans in its employment between 1932 and 1941 to 150,000. There was also some unofficial **positive discrimination**, notably again in the NYA where black-American officials were usually appointed in areas where black Americans predominated.

Although there were few official measures specifically to benefit black Americans, there were important gestures of support. There were more black Americans with the ear, if not of the President, then of important figures close to him. Millions of black Americans benefited from relief measures that, even if still favouring whites, gave them more help than they had ever previously received.

Black Americans during the war years

Black Americans demanded better treatment during the war.

Black Americans in the military

In 1941 there were fewer than 4,000 black Americans in the armed forces and only 12 officers. Black Americans rushed to enlist after the declaration of war but were often refused by all-white recruitment boards. Only after pressure from the **National Association for the Advancement of Colored People (NAACP)** (see page 338) did Roosevelt pledge that black Americans would be recruited according to their percentage of the population (10.6 per cent). In effect, this was never attained, although by 1945 there were 1.2 million black Americans in the military. They faced discrimination despite the 1940 Selective Service Training Act which stated that no one should face this when applying for training. Indeed, as in the First World War, the military roles of black Americans were initially limited to non-combat roles such as building installations and ferrying supplies. The Red Ball Express convoy of trucks conveyed half a million tons of supplies and equipment to the advancing First and Third armies in France after D-Day.

It was only through losses in battle that the authorities were persuaded to assign combat roles to black Americans; 17,000 black Americans landed on the beaches on D-Day in June 1944. They distinguished themselves in these roles – although the military itself remained segregated, especially the fighting forces.

Secretary of War Henry Stimson maintained strict segregation in the armed forces, arguing that it was essential to give priority to winning the war and any attempt to turn the armed forces into a social laboratory would hamper this. Many of the wartime committees whose support Roosevelt needed to pass essential wartime measures were chaired by influential Southern Congressmen. Nevertheless, manpower shortages led to 25 warships being integrated and some army training camps outside the South were desegregated.

The home front

The onset of war saw a renewed exodus of black Americans from the South – more than a million moved north throughout the war years. Much prejudice remained; in Akron, Ohio, the centre of rubber-producing plants, black Americans were normally only offered unskilled jobs and faced discrimination in housing, a pattern that was reproduced throughout the centres of industry. Black-American leaders called for a

250,000-strong March on Washington in 1941 to air their grievances.

The threatened march worried Roosevelt, who was fully aware that the Nazis were accusing the USA of hypocrisy by condemning Nazi attitudes towards Jews while openly denying civil rights to black Americans. Roosevelt did what he could. He issued Executive Order 8802 on 25 June 1941 to ban discrimination in defence plants and set up the FEPC to ensure it was carried out. As a result, the black-American workforce in defence plants rose by almost 4 per cent. As time went on, the FEPC had its budget increased to half a million dollars and took on full-time as opposed to part-time employees.

The 'Double V' campaign

In February 1942 the most widely read black-American newspaper, the *Philadelphia Courier*, initiated the 'Double V' campaign – victory against the Axis powers for which black Americans fought courageously both in the armed forces and in war work, and victory over prejudice and discrimination at home. This campaign featured patriotic articles, promotion of the sale of **war bonds**, a weekly 'Double V girl' showing the V for Victory salute and celebrity endorsements including white film stars but always with the reminder that civil rights was long overdue. In a 1942 *Courier* survey, 88 per cent of respondents said civil rights should not be delayed until the end of the war. Moreover, as knowledge of the **Holocaust** in Europe grew and people realised the extremes to which racism could be taken, many Americans began to examine their own racial attitudes. However, there was a long way to go towards racial equality. This is well exemplified by the restaurant in Salina, Kansas which served German prisoners of war (PoWs) but turned away local black Americans.

The Campaign for Racial Equality (CRE) was founded in 1942 and encouraged peaceful protests against segregated facilities. It was left to the 1960s and 1970s to see real progress in race relations in the USA.

Race riots

There was a series of race riots in 47 cities, culminating in three days of violence in Detroit in June 1943 (see page 307) which saw 25 black Americans and nine whites killed, all over whether one housing development should be for white– or black-American families. No one had considered that it could possibly be for both.

In August a serious riot in Harlem left six dead and 600 arrested. The cause was a black American soldier being shot by a white police officer after he had apparently tried to intervene to prevent the arrest of a female. As rumours spread that the soldier was dead, a crowd of 3,000 gathered, and by evening had begun to attack white-owned businesses. At the end of two days, $250,000–$500,000 worth of damage was done and 1,485 stores broken into and looted.

Key debate

The impact of the Second World War on black Americans

In the immediate post-war years many observers, such as the influential journalist John Gunter, noted that the experience of war made black Americans more assertive and prepared to ask the question of why they were fighting for freedom abroad when they lacked it at home. Writing in the 1940s, sociologist Gunner Myrdal felt that with the USA fighting to uphold democratic freedoms during the war, the role and status of black Americans would improve after it. He argued that white consciences must be uplifted by the aims so many of them were fighting for. One could not fight oppression abroad while tolerating it at home.

This view continued and by the 1960s historians were commonly viewing the war years as the catalyst for the civil rights movement. Hence Daniel Snowman, writing in 1968, felt that black Americans had really hoped things would improve as a result of the war and their failure to do so resulted in more determination to effect change. However, there was more pessimism in the 1970s, with Lee Finkle, for example, arguing that the Double V was more a sign of conservatism than militancy – black Americans did not want to appear unpatriotic and the black American media used the Double V to conceal any opposition to the war effort or anger at continued discrimination behind a display of patriotism. More recently, some historians have focussed on the continued discrimination and disappointment. Ronald Takaki, writing in 2000, emphasised the incongruity of the fight for freedom abroad and lack of opportunities at home. Historians agree, however, on the tenacity of black Americans to effect change. Both Snowman and more recently Clarence Taylor show how the threatened march on Washington was the catalyst for Exxcutive Order 8802 prohibiting discrimination in the defence industry.

The Detroit riot, June 1943

The Detroit riot was in many ways typical of the tension and mistrust that existed between the races during the period. Detroit was a major manufacturing centre – the hub of the US automobile industry. By 1943 its population had increased by 30,000 as a result of opportunities for work in war industries. Black Americans faced discrimination at work and in housing; they were excluded from all public-sector housing except the Brewster Housing Project. More industrial expansion brought a demand for more housing. In February 1942 it was decided to accommodate some black American families in the new Sojourner Truth Projects in a white area. Eventually 168 black American families moved, although the first ones had to be protected by the Detroit police and units of the Michigan National Guard.

However, the catalyst for the rioting that left 34 killed was the verbal insults to the girlfriend of a white sailor by a black American. Rumours quickly spread that blacks had raped a white women and whites had attacked a black woman and her baby; as events spiralled, it didn't matter that neither was true. Although it was whites who began the attacks on black Americans, even hauling them off buses, the situation degenerated into black and white mobs attacking each other. Of the 34 killed, 25 were black; 17 of these were killed by police. Three-quarters of the 600 injured were black Americans, as were 85 per cent of the 8,000 arrests.

Change for Hispanic Americans

Hispanic Americans found more employment opportunities as a result of the war but discrimination continued. They worked mainly in agriculture in the Southwest and faced considerable unfair treatment both in the workplace and everyday life. In Texas, for example, 90 per cent of Hispanic-American children were educated in segregated schools where their white teachers often didn't speak Spanish. As the Depression hit, there were moves to deport unemployed Hispanic Americans. In fact, over the course of the 1930s, 400,000 were sent to Mexico, including many born in the USA (see page 266). The Hispanic-American population of Texas fell by as much as one-third while the percentage of Hispanic Americans in the migratory **labour force** of California fell by 10 per cent as they were replaced by migrants. Many Southwestern states, meanwhile, banned Hispanic Americans from public work schemes.

Hispanic Americans and the war

Hispanic Americans volunteered to enlist as enthusiastically as other ethnic groups. It is estimated that as many as 500,000 served in the armed forces, although accurate numbers are difficult because in the segregated armed forces they were classed as white. Some historians have argued that the impact of the war gave many Hispanic Americans a predominantly US as opposed to Hispanic identity.

Hispanic Americans found wartime employment as readily as members of other ethnic groups. They worked on railroads and in shipyards, mines and aircraft and munitions factories, although often at the lowest-paid levels. Nevertheless, 17,000 Hispanic Americans had found employment in the Los Angeles shipyards by 1944, which in 1941 employed none. However, a wartime FEPC study discovered widespread discrimination against Hispanic Americans in oil companies in Houston and copper companies in Arizona where they were denied training and promotion. The **State Department** vetoed a proposed public inquiry on the grounds that it would discredit the USA in Mexico and afford good publicity for Axis agents. In other words, everyone knew discrimination was rife so there was no need to publicise it. Roosevelt agreed and told the FEPC to halt its investigations.

Hispanic Americans and migrants particularly from the US **protectorate** of Puerto Rico in the Caribbean also found plentiful work in the war industries. Some commentators emphasise how this impacted on Hispanic women, who had usually worked as part of a family in seasonal work in agriculture. Now higher wages in war industries afforded them more independence; this caused some tension within more traditional families where women had a lower status and less freedom than men. Hispanic-American women who were bilingual were also in demand in cryptology and communications. The war undoubtedly allowed many to achieve more than their traditional familial expectations.

'Zoot-suiters' and the Los Angeles riots

Young Hispanic Americans faced prejudice in California and particularly in Los Angeles because they were associated with gangs and violence. They tended to wear '**zoot suits**' which were seen as the uniform of lawlessness and immorality. In June 1943 sailors from the Chavez Ravine naval base committed random and widespread attacks on Hispanic Americans in revenge for perceived Hispanic-American violence against sailors. The authorities, both military and civil police, seemed to turn a blind eye while the popular press accused Hispanic Americans of causing the violence. Both the Federal and State governments condemned the attacks but they were allowed to run their course.

Source B In August 1942 the federal government signed the bracero programme with Mexico for the temporary importation of thousands of labourers specifically to work in agriculture and railroads. They would be paid a minimum wage and provided with basic amenities. However, the wage was often less than Hispanic Americans received so there was often resentment if braceros were employed instead of others. They could also be used to break strikes. Braceros tended to live in camps where living conditions were often poor. Often if they left the camp they would be attacked or robbed by locals. However, they could and did protest when treated unfairly. Their treatment in Idaho serves as an example. Often they were given the hardest jobs, such as thinning and harvesting lettuce and beet. They faced chemical pollutants in the fields and often were expected to drink contaminated water. In May 1944 there were a series of strikes which led to the braceros being threatened with jail and deportation. Eventually the strikes were ended by violence by the employers. Braceros learned they had few rights. However, even more were recruited in the post-war years until the scheme ended in 1964. The account that follows tells of how one bracero, known only as Don Jesús, remembered his experiences in the United States (found at http://aztlan.sdsu.edu/chicanohistory/chapter08/c08s07.html).

> Colton was the location for the base of a military squadron but the squadron was not there. The men had been shipped out to Europe to fight in the Second World War, and we were housed there. It was nice and clean there, and we even had a Catholic priest. He saw that most of us were Catholic, and he started to build a small shrine so that we could attend Mass on Sundays. However, not everyone attended to Mass. On Sundays, five buses would also arrive to take us to town to the movies or to drink wine. There was a lot of drinking, and sometimes even fancy women would come to take the money from the braceros and things would get very wild.
>
> Buses arrived early in the day to take us to work. There was about twenty of us per bus. They would take us to some groves to pick oranges. There, we had to put one ladder on top of the other to reach one or two oranges that were way on top of the trees. Sometimes, however, they would take us to Japanese groves, and there the trees were really short but falling over full of oranges. We were given cutters to cut the oranges; but some, in order to go faster, would just pull the fruit from the tree. I did everything as I was told, and it helped me get along with my boss, and thus I soon became a driver. That was a lot easier, and I even had a helper.

Why is Source B useful for studying the impact of the bracero programme on the home front in the USA?

The treatment of Japanese Americans

If other ethnic groups faced discrimination in common, Japanese Americans faced a unique dilemma, that of mass internment. Towards the end of 1941, as US–Japanese relations worsened, 2,000 Japanese labelled subversives were rounded up (along with 14,000 Germans and Italians), although there was no official desire for internment. In fact, General John L. Dewitt, Chief of the Army West Coast Command, dismissed any such talk as 'damned nonsense'. However, increasing fears of a Japanese attack on the West Coast led to calls for internment, even by respected journalists such as Walter Lippmann. Dewitt, responsible for West Coast security, gave in to this pressure, saying it was impossible to distinguish between loyal and traitorous Japanese and therefore all should be locked up.

Between February and March 1942, 15,000 Japanese Americans, many of whom had relatives fighting in the American forces, voluntarily left Dewitt's area of command. However, other areas of the USA refused to accept them. The Attorney General of Idaho, for example, said his state was for whites only. Dewitt decided on compulsory relocation; ten 'relocation centres' were set up throughout the West, where 100,000 Japanese Americans were forcibly sent. They had to leave their property unprotected. Much looting went on in their absence. One source estimated the community suffered losses worth $400 million.

The relocation centres, meanwhile, were akin to prisons with armed guards and barrack-type accommodation. Riots in the camp at Manzanar left two inmates dead. One of the guards said the only thing that stopped him machine gunning them was what the Japanese might do to the American PoWs in retaliation.

By 1944, as fear of Japanese attack receded, the internees began to return home. In December 1944, the Supreme Court forbade the internment of loyal Japanese Americans. Nevertheless, neither their fellow Japanese-American citizens who lived outside Dewitt's West Coast command nor German or Italian Americans had been interned in this way, so ill-feeling among many of those involved remained for some time. Not until 1988 was compensation offered to surviving internees. Ironically, in Hawaii, home to Pearl Harbor and more Japanese Americans than the West Coast of the USA, there was no internment.

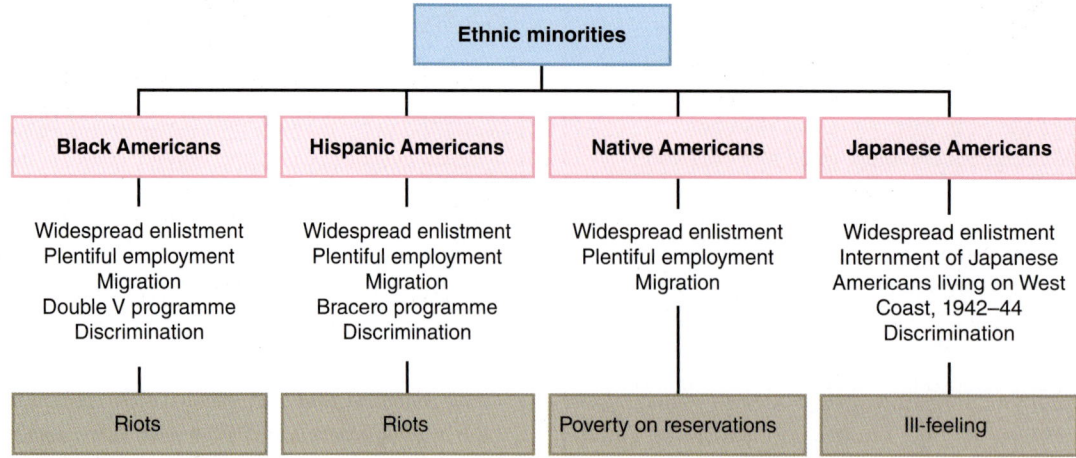

▲ Summary diagram: The war and ethnic minorities.

Conclusion: The impact of the New Deal and the war on ethnic minorities

The New Deal did little for ethnic groups apart from Native Americans, whose culture and right to run their own affairs was recognised in the Indian Reorganization Act of 1934. Nevertheless, ethnic groups did benefit from many New Deal measures, although they still faced discrimination. Many black Americans in particular shifted their political allegiance to the Democrats as a result of New Deal measures. During the war, ethnic groups shared in greater opportunities but were still victims of prejudice and there was a series of riots in 1943. Many Japanese Americans, however, fared worse; they were interned during the war years.

Work together

You should each have index cards showing how each ethnic group was treated differently and similarly. Working in pairs, compare your cards. Discuss in particular how they might be treated similarly. Think about the principles rather than the detail of their treatment.

After this discussion, record any changes to your ideas of how they were treated similarly.

Discuss what you have learned from this exercise in terms of thinking more deeply about principles rather than detail.

3 Social and cultural changes

During the New Deal and war years, writers and artists were encouraged by the federal government to record US life.

The result was a massive archive charting the impact of these times on ordinary people. The war changed people's lives. As the conflict developed, women found greater employment opportunities in the workplace, although equal pay was not widely considered. Their role and status was enhanced due to wartime conditions, although this is rarely seen as a permanent trend. The film industry, meanwhile, devoted much of its energies to producing propaganda and escapist films to ensure morale remained high. The military actually took over much of the Disney studios to produce training films and cartoons both to inform and entertain.

Note it down

As this section covers three different topics, you could use different note-taking techniques for each. For the first section, on the impact of the New Deal on the arts, use a spider diagram (see page x). For the second section, on changes in the role of women, use the 1:2 method (see page x). For domestic propaganda, use bullet points.

The New Deal and the arts

The New Deal encouraged the arts and media not only to create employment but also to record what everyone realised was a significant and possibly unique era. The WPA was given funding to encourage and support writers, artists and musicians to record the Depression era and its impact on people, and to help the artists gain an income. In particular, as a result of its support, US life and culture was recorded and photographed – from detailed guide books to photographs of those whose lives were shattered by the impact of the Depression.

Let Us Now Praise Famous Men

A writer, James Agee, and a photographer, Walker Evans, were commissioned by *Fortune* magazine in 1936 to record the lives of poor **tenant farmers**. They showed the immense dignity of the farmers despite their poverty. Perhaps the magazine was expecting a piece about downtrodden victims. In any event, it refused to publish the work. It did not appear until 1941, when the worst of the Depression was over.

Photography

The period saw the production of intensely moving photographs of victims of the Depression, often commissioned by the Farm Security Administration (FSA) and given without charge to newspapers to publish. Under Roy Stryker, the head of the photography programme of the FSA, talented photographers compiled over 80,000 images of life during the Depression. Notable among the photographers were Dorothea Lange, Walker Evans, Ben Fields and Arthur Rothstein. Lange probably created one of the most iconic photographs in 'Migrant Mother'.

▲ 'Migrant Mother'– an image of Florence Owens Thompson, a destitute worker in a pea-picking camp, not looking into the camera but lost in her own thoughts. Photographed by Dorothea Lange in 1936. What is the value of this photo to a historian investigating the effects of the Depression on families?

The Federal Writers' Project

The Federal Writers' Project was set up under the auspices of the WPA and led by Henry Alsbury, a theatrical producer and journalist, largely to provide employment for authors. It developed into a scheme employing 6,600 of them. In Indiana, for example, 150 were employed at any one time, working between 20 and 30 hours per week.

The work of the Federal Writers' Project was possibly far more significant than originally intended. It compiled works of local and oral history that may not otherwise have been created, including, for example, 2,300 first-person slave narratives, which were subsequently published, accompanied by 500 photographs, as *Unchained Memories*. It was important to hear the voices of the survivors before they were lost. The project's authors also produced a detailed guidebook for each state which included history, culture, photographs and detailed descriptions of every settlement.

The Federal Music Project

Under the auspices of the WPA, the Federal Music Project (FMP) employed musicians to give concerts and held musical festivals. Its remit was wider than simply bringing music to the masses to help them forget their troubles for a while. It also sought to introduce music education into schools and document US music traditions such as the blues. Indeed, it recorded many blues singers who might otherwise have been forgotten, such as Son House. It was particularly successful in education, leading to music programmes in many schools and improving performance among adults.

There was a tension within the FMP, however. Its director Dr Nikolai Sokoloff was very much within the European classical music tradition and sought to promote this. Many found this elitist and at variance with the New Deal idea of promoting the common man. Sokoloff's deputy Charles Seeger was more in favour of making music accessible to everyone and favoured more popular music and the documentation of traditional music.

The project's budget was cut significantly in 1939 and it effectively came to an end, although it was not officially terminated until the WPA itself came to an end in June 1943.

Changes in the role of women

The war saw many women grow in confidence and strength as they had to raise their families without their partners, who were serving in the military. Many commentators, however, feel women still largely supported the traditional family role. Marriage and birth rates rose because people:

- had been putting off marriage during the hard years of the Depression
- wanted to marry and enjoy a brief time of married life before husbands went to war.

The number of marriages rose by 1,118,000 in the years 1940 to 1943. The average age of first-time marriage for women fell from 22.0 in 1940 to 20.1 by the end of the war. The number of children under the age of five rose by 25 per cent. Divorce rose during the war years – albeit at a small level: 1.7 per cent during the 1930s to 2.4 per cent by 1945. However, it was to fall during the later 1940s and early 1950s (see page 325). During the war years, meanwhile, the population of the USA increased by 6.5 million.

The home front

Women had to juggle homecare with work and coping with shortages during the war years. There was tremendous dislocation. Many moved to be near their husbands who were training at the various bases dotted around the USA. Others left to find war work with or without their husbands. There was always a shortage of housing in urban areas and women often had to cope with cramped living conditions and shared facilities. One employee of the War Manpower Commission found that 100,000 women hours a month were being lost in Detroit defence plants so women could do their family laundry.

Women had to take the lead in such necessities as civil defence, recycling, coping with food rationing and so on. Ten thousand women delivered ration coupons. Women grew vegetables in 'Victory Gardens' and joined the Women's Land Army, where they worked on farms to replace men who had been conscripted. In their everyday lives they had to accept shortages as materials were needed for the war effort. Fashions became more austere and plain as less material was allowed, and cosmetics could be hard to find. Often they had to cope with providing food for themselves and their children as well as doing arduous full-time work – which is why many mothers of very young children tended not to work full time if they could avoid it.

To facilitate the growing numbers of young mothers in war work, Congresswoman Mary Norton helped drive the Community Facilities Act of 1941, which provided childcare facilities for workers in defence plants. Demand was much greater than supply, however, and most still relied on relatives to look after small children – or didn't enter the workforce.

Employment

While women found plentiful employment during the war years, they also encountered continuing prejudice and lower pay than their male colleagues. Despite this, employers favoured them because they were cheaper and, even more significantly, not subject to **conscription** into the armed forces. The FEPC tried to prevent discrimination against women in the workplace but there was little attempt to enforce equal pay. Labour unions were reluctant to get involved in equal pay struggles because they largely accepted the mass employment of women as an aberration that would end when peace was restored and their male members came home. An exception to this rule was the United Electrical Workers' Union which fought for equal pay, but by the time its case had been accepted by the War Labor Board, the conflict was over and firms said war conditions no longer applied.

Newspapers ran propaganda articles, such as the story in the *Boston Herald*, on 20 November 1942, about the 19-year-old woman operating a ten-foot crane, in order to boost morale and encourage others to follow.

The numbers of working women grew from 14,600,000 in 1941 to 19,370,000 by 1944, when 37 per cent of all women were working. Many of these were employed in manufacturing, where the percentage of women in the workforce rose from 22 per cent to 32 per cent between 1941 and 1944. More too were employed in munitions production. In January 1942 the director of the Women's Bureau reported that 2,800,000 women were involved in war work. By 1943, 475,000 women were working in aircraft production. By 1945, 300,000 women had joined the female branches of the armed forces, although they were not used in combat. Despite racial and gender prejudice, 300,000 black-American women found work in war-related industries because the demand for labour was so acute. The media devoted considerable efforts to encouraging all groups to find employment in war production and feel confident of victory.

Domestic propaganda: The power and influence of Hollywood

Hollywood responded enthusiastically to the war effort through producing both propaganda films to engender a sense of patriotism and light entertainment, such as musicals and comedy, which offered escapism. Although actors were exempted from combat duty because of their role in making propaganda movies promoting support for the war, many nonetheless volunteered for it. The popular actor James Stewart, for example, served with distinction in the Air Force. Others stayed to make movies. Ironically, those such as the actor John Wayne who made some of the most exciting war movies did not join the military. Actors also were enthusiastic sellers of war bonds, often making nationwide tours to promote them. Dorothy Lamour, a comedy actress famous for appearing in comedian Bob Hope's movies, sold $350 million worth of them. In September 1942 a 'bond blitz' realised more than $800 million after 300 actors had worked 18-hour days promoting them throughout the USA. Actors such as Marlene Dietrich also entertained the troops, often in combat zones. Many worked in the Hollywood Canteen, set up in 1942 by Bette Davis and others to provide free meals and entertainment for lonely servicemen. To be waited on or to dance with a glamorous movie star was a tremendous morale booster.

The Office of War Information was set up in 1942 to co-ordinate efforts to film and record wartime activities. Hence famous directors such as John Ford, John Huston, Frank Capra and George Stevens made morale-boosting documentaries to celebrate the war effort, such as Huston's *Report from the Aleutians* (1943), or propaganda exercises, such as Capra's *Why We Fight* (1942–45). The latter was an attempt to justify the war through powerful attacks on enemy regimes and their brutal aggression. War movies were often more realistic – such as Lewis Seiler's *Guadalcanal Diary* (1943) or William Wyler's *Memphis Belle: A Story of a Flying Fortress* (1944) – because they did not wish to patronise audiences who were either members of the armed forces or their relatives at home.

Movies were also important for escapism and, for this reason, musicals were very popular, particularly if they featured glamorous singers and dancers such as Betty Gable. Popular comedians included Bob Hope and Abbott & Costello. There was also a market for nostalgia with sentimental films portraying an imagined halcyon past such as *Meet Me in St Louis* (1944) and *Yankee Doodle Dandy* (1942). They could also raise morale by showing the home front in a positive light; George Stevens' *The More the Merrier* (1943) took a comic view of the housing shortage while Sidney Lanfield's *My Favourite Blonde* (1942) reflected the tendency to replace gangsters as the villains with Nazi spies. Perhaps the film that represented the war as a moral crusade more than any other was Michael Curtiz's *Casablanca* (1942), with the Nazis as the embodiment of evil and most of the other characters ambivalent until it comes to making a stand against them.

During the war much of the Disney studios were taken over by the military and 90 per cent of its workers became involved in producing training films; indeed, they created 400,000 feet of film and 68 hours of footage. Disney characters were also deployed to improve morale. *Der Führer's Face* starred Donald Duck as an oppressed worker in the vile dictatorship of Nazi Germany. It won the best animation award in the 1943 Oscars. Disney employees also produced humorous insignia for fighting units such as a mosquito riding a torpedo on torpedo boats. Walt Disney, in effect, gave most of his entire operation over to the war effort. His studios were so important that they were afforded military protection.

The power and influence of the media persuaded most Americans that the war was worthwhile, that it was 'a Good War' and that the Axis powers had to be defeated. These years saw a greater celebration of the USA and US values through the media than ever before.

Source C Extract from the memoirs of Alvah Bessie, *Inquisition in Eden* (Seven Seas Books, 1965). Bessie was a Hollywood scriptwriter during the war period.

> There was a great deal of patriotism in Hollywood during the war, much of it even genuine. The stars were busy on bond-selling tours and entertaining troops through the USO; 'back home' there was the Hollywood Canteen (chairman Bette Davis) which was of course made into a film by Warner Brothers...
>
> There was a huge rally for the Red Cross that was held on one of our largest sound stages, and while attendance was not exactly compulsory, your absence would have been noted by captains in charge of each department of the studio. The rally was addressed, haltingly, by Jack L. Warner himself and, in the expected lachrymose manner, by his older brother Harry. There were stars who made speeches, and Major Richard Bong, the ace of the Pacific Theatre of Operations, made a brief appearance ... and a great deal of money was raised.

What are the advantages and disadvantages to a historian of reading memoirs published many years after the time of the events they are describing? Use Source C to provide examples in support of your answers.

Radio

Escapist programmes remained popular on radio but it also became important as a source of up-to-date news. Many stations sent their own war correspondents, who reported from combat zones. Edward R. Murrow's accounts of the Blitz in London were particularly influential in gaining US support for Britain. Evidence suggests they were more influential than newspapers in moulding opinion. Radio also fulfilled a propaganda role with programmes promoting what were perceived as US values such as democracy and equality of opportunity. These programmes included *Lest We Forget* (1943–48). Audiences were informed why the war was necessary in *You Can't Do Business with Hitler* (1942). Radio was for many people their lifeline with the outside world.

Popular music

Popular music played a vital role in improving morale during the war. It was the golden age of swing and jazz, of 'crooners' and sentimental songs. It was the age of the big band led by such luminaries as Glenn Miller, who created a unique nostalgic sound that connected troops overseas with their loved ones at home. Miller himself served in the armed forces and in December 1944 was killed over the English Channel while flying to play concerts for the troops in Paris. Songwriters were quick to connect with war events; within days of the December 1941 attack came 'Remember Pearl Harbor' while 'Hats Off to MacArthur!' (the US commander in the Philippines) was written as the battle for the Philippines was raging in March 1942.

Songs also reflected the emotions of the troops and their loved ones. One real concern that wives and girlfriends may be unfaithful was addressed in the song made famous by the Andrews Sisters, 'Don't Sit Under the Apple Tree with Anyone Else but Me'. Patriotic tunes meanwhile proliferated, especially 'God Bless America', first written by Irving Berlin in 1918 but resurrected to great acclaim in 1939. Artists entertained the troops through the United Service Overseas (USO), often venturing into combat zones. It is estimated that between 1941 and 1947 the USO gave 293,738 performances to 161 million servicemen and women. During the war 702 different troupes were touring.

One of the greatest US singers began his career shortly before war was declared but became a superstar during it. Frank Sinatra was classed as unsuitable for military service and became possibly the first idol of teenagers – called 'bobbysoxers'. When Sinatra opened at the Paramount Theatre in New York on 30 December 1942, the veteran comedian Jack Benny said, 'I thought the goddamned building was going to cave in. I never heard such a commotion.' When Sinatra returned to the same venue in October 1944, 35,000 fans who were refused entrance caused a riot.

The music was so powerful because it captured a mood of nostalgia, of loss and yet of romance that spoke powerfully to those at home and at war. It was evocative of the pleasures of home and domesticity while still speaking of allure and excitement. Many of the lyrics and tunes were banal but powerful for all that for millions far from home.

Conclusion: Social and cultural changes

The war years saw the nation united in the war effort as a result of greater opportunities and effective propaganda. The New Deal had encouraged writers, musicians and photographers to chart US life and this continued through film and radio during the war years. Although women found better-paid employment, they still faced unequal treatment. However, most people were convinced they were fighting a 'Good War' and any sacrifices were worthwhile.

Work together

Historians often talk of turning points, an event or development that changes issues dramatically. The onset of the Second World War was clearly an important turning point in the USA. In pairs, one of you should consider how far it was a turning point for women and the other how far for ethnic minorities.

Be prepared to argue your case to each other. Then discuss whether the Second World War in the USA was a bigger turning point for women or ethnic minorities.

4 The war and the economy, 1941–45

The war years saw the USA emerge as the most powerful nation on Earth, with unemployment insignificant and its industries producing more war materiel than most of its enemies put together. In order to facilitate economic expansion, the government increasingly took control of the economy through the creation of agencies such as the Office of War Mobilization. The war was paid for by greater taxation and war bonds. The war saw considerable dislocation for people with as many as 12 per cent of the population moving to work in war industries. Inevitably, this caused social problems, such as a rise in divorce and crime rates. More secure employment brought a resurgence of union membership and various examples of industrial unrest. The war stimulated new industries, many of which would be in demand in the post-war world. Through the need for armaments, it led to the development of the US **military–industrial complex**.

> **Note it down**
>
> Here you can add to your collection of index cards. This section discusses the impact of the war on the economy. Use your cards to note them and explain their importance. On each card, write the title of the issue: collapse of unemployment; paying for the war; government controls; migration; growing power of labour unions; and new industries. On the back, organise your notes in the following way:
> - **Definition** – a one- or two-sentence summary of the issue.
> - **Reason for it** – why the issue was necessary.
> - **Impact** – the impact of the issue.

The collapse of unemployment

American involvement in war production made the New Deal irrelevant. Between 1941 and 1945 the USA produced 86,000 tanks, 296,000 aircraft and 15 million rifles. Farm income grew by 250 per cent. As more people left the countryside, farms consolidated, grew bigger and production increased by 25 per cent. The former concerns of overproduction and falling prices were negated. Here more was produced because more was required. There were no problems with unsold stock. Prices may have risen considerably but for government controls (see page 314). Unemployment effectively ceased by 1942; in 1944 it stood at 1.2 per cent, having fallen from 13.9 per cent in 1940 (see page 301). In 1944 alone, 6.5 million women entered the labour force; by the end of the war, almost 60 per cent of women were employed. The number of black Americans working for the federal government rose from 50,000 in 1939 to 200,000 by 1944. In the years between 1940 and 1944, 5 million black Americans moved to the cities where a million found jobs in defence plants. GNP, meanwhile, rose from $91.3 billion in 1939 to $166.6 billion by 1945.

Young people in the workforce

Young people increasingly became involved in the workforce; 66 per cent of teenage boys found work in some capacity, with commensurate earnings to spend on items for themselves, predating the usually accepted dates for the invention of 'teenagers' by a decade. The war years saw an increase of 1.9 million teenagers in the workforce. In 1940, 900,000 14- to 18-year-olds were employed and by spring 1944 over 3 million, or one-third, of the age group. Many states had to change their child labour laws to facilitate this.

As a result of employment, teenagers who acquired an income, possibly with absentee fathers serving in the armed forces and mothers in wartime production jobs, often became more assertive. Their elders complained they were losing their deference. They developed their own interests – for example, in terms of popular music (see page 312) and dress, often adopting the zoot suit fashion associated with Hispanic Americans in Los Angeles (see page 306). Of course, many worked only until they were drafted into the military.

Many young people saw education as irrelevant in the uncertainties of the wartime world. The numbers of teenagers in high schools fell from 6.6 million in 1940 to 5.6 million four years later. This led some observers to argue that the biggest problem concerning US youth was not delinquent behaviour but failure to finish high school. This led to a 'back-to-school' drive in 1944, which met with only limited success. Young people not only wanted to contribute to the war effort and were encouraged to do so by employers, but also enjoyed the independence that wages brought them.

Paying for the war

As a result of the costs of the war, the national debt, which stood at $41 billion in 1941, had risen to $260 billion by 1945. The federal government spent twice as much between 1941 and 1945 as it had in the previous 150 years. Roosevelt hoped to pay for much of the war production by increased taxes and the sale of war bonds.

Increased taxation

The highest earners, those with incomes of over $200,000, paid 94 per cent tax. Although the number of taxpayers increased from 7 million in 1940 to 42 million by 1944, the progressive nature of taxation gave a sense of greater equality. The poor grew wealthier during the war years and the rich received a smaller proportion of national income, as Table 3 shows.

Table 3: Percentage of national income taken by the richest 1 per cent of the population.

Year	%
1939	13.4
1944	11.5
1945	6.7

War bonds

War bonds provided 50 per cent of government income and were enthusiastically promoted by celebrities on nationwide tours (see page 311).

Government controls

While the economy grew significantly during the war years, the government was controlling and planning much of it in a way unprecedented in US history.

The government increasingly took control of people's lives. In 1940 the Smith Act was passed, which made it illegal to threaten to overthrow the government. Originally aimed against fascists, it later became associated with the attack on **communists** (see pages 326–31). The Selective Service Act of the same year introduced conscription, initially for men between the ages of 21 and 35, but extended at the outbreak of war to men aged 18 to 45. However, it was in the economy in which the government intervened the most, often employing successful industrialists to run new agencies such as the Office of War Mobilization.

The Office of War Mobilization

The Office of War Mobilization was set up in May 1943 to control production, food prices and rents. Some items – such as meat, sugar and petrol – were rationed. The production of cars for ordinary motorists stopped entirely. Many consumer items, such as clothes, were made from far less material and became simpler in style and other items disappeared from the shops. However, most Americans were comparatively well paid during the war and did not suffer the deprivations of those in other belligerent countries. Although prices rose by 28 per cent during the war years, average wages increased by 40 per cent; people may not have had much to spend these wages on but they could and did save. By 1945, nationally, they had $140 billion in savings. It was the spending power of these consumers that helped to fuel the post-war boom period (see page 325). As one worker said, 'It was a pretty good war if you didn't get shot at.' Average weekly wages almost doubled from $24 to $44.

Other new government agencies included:

- The War Production Board, formed in January 1941, supervised the output of $183 billion worth of weapons and supplies, 40 per cent of the world total. Its task was to facilitate the conversion from civilian to war production, set priorities, allocate resources such as rubber and steel, and prevent production of non-essential items such as nylons by refusing to release materials for their manufacture.
- The Office of Price Administration and Civilian Supply was set up in August 1941 to control inflation. In April 1942 it issued a General Maximum Price regulation which froze prices at March 1942 levels to prevent inflation. It had the power to control all prices (except agricultural commodities) and ration scarce items. Eventually such items as petrol, tyres, coffee, sugar and other foodstuffs were rationed. Almost 90 per cent of food items were subject to price controls.
- The National War Labor Board was set up in January 1942 to settle industrial disputes and determine wages. In July 1942, the Board said wage rises should not normally

> **Source D** Extract from Frederick Lewis Allen, *The Big Change: America Transforms Itself 1900-1950* (Transaction, 1952). Allen was a journalist who was highly respected for his recording of changes in US society. He also wrote the classic *Only Yesterday* (1931) (see page 242).
>
> By the end of 1943 we were spending money at five times the peak rate of World War 1. During the 1930s critics of the New Deal had become apoplectic over annual federal budgets of seven or eight or nine billions, which they felt were carrying the USA towards bankruptcy; during the fiscal year 1942 we spent by contrast over 34 billions, during 1943 79 billions; during 1944 95 billions; during 1945 98 billions…
>
> New plants were built and built fast. The entire automobile industry was diverted from the manufacture of passenger cars into the production of tanks, trucks, weapons. All manner of new products and devices were assigned to American plants to produce in a hurry - ranging from synthetic rubber to radar, from landing strips to proximity fuses, from atrabine [*] and penicillin and DDT to the **Manhattan Project** for the atomic bomb. Always the call from Washington was for speed, speed, speed, and for quantity.
>
> [*] Atrabine: a medicine that can reverse the effect of some poisons and make the heart beat more efficiently during operations.
>
> What can you infer from Source D about the US economy during the war years?

exceed 15 per cent of the January 1941 rates. This was only partially adhered to because there was so much demand for labour. The Emergency Stabilization Act of October 1942 further tried to limit wage rises. Many employers began to offer benefits such as paid holidays, medical insurance and pensions to get round the wage ceilings. Employers who violated the Act could be fined up to $1,000 or imprisoned for up to one year, or both.

- The Office of Economic Stabilization was opened in October 1942 to oversee the work of the agencies responsible for wages and prices.

Migration

In addition to the 15 million servicemen and women who were called up, by the end of the war one in eight civilians had moved to find war work, generally from the South to the North and from East to West. It is estimated that 27 million Americans moved during the war. The population of rural areas fell by 29 per cent as share-croppers and rural labourers found ample work in the urban areas and new centres of war production. It was the biggest migration in US history. The population of California, where there were large numbers of defence plants, rose by 72 per cent during the war years. In actual terms, this meant a net gain of 2 million people. Over 200,000 people moved to Washington DC to find work in government. The result was a huge housing shortage, particularly near defence plants. One solution was to build huge barrack-style facilities which, at their peak, housed 1.5 million people.

Dislocation

The war brought in its wake various social problems. The divorce rate soared from 20 per cent in 1940 to 29 per cent by 1944. There was a rise in youth crime as absent fathers and working mothers often reduced parental control. Often more elderly or conservative people fretted about the first youth 'cult', the 'bobbysoxers', who danced to swing music and idolised 'crooners' such as Frank Sinatra. The increasing number of teenagers in employment saw a commensurate fall in the numbers of high-school students. One million dropped out of education between 1940 and 1944. There was a general fear of the loss of deference among the young. This was true also about servicemen and war production workers who, as we have seen, tended to have lots of money to spend.

The population, meanwhile, rose by 6.5 million between 1940 and 1945, predating the 'baby boom' to be discussed in Chapter 4. 'Furlough' babies were usually the result of servicemen's periods of leave where they were able to meet with wives and girlfriends. Not only did they miss each other but the absence of a loved one in a combat area was also a constant worry, so the relief at seeing them well can hardly be imagined.

The growing power of labour unions

The return of prosperity saw a growth in labour union membership from 10.5 million in 1940 to 14.75 million by the end of the war. Workers became well off; not only did their wages increase due to more opportunities in better-paid industries, but there were unlimited opportunities for overtime, often at higher rates of pay. However, the Economic Stabilization Act had frozen wages as such; workers had to move jobs to get wage increases.

Both the American Federation of Labor (AFL) and the Congress of Industrial Organizations (CIO) supported the war effort and had agreed non-binding pledges to avoid strikes. If industrial disputes could not be amicably solved, they were to be taken to the National War Labor Board, which could help negotiate a binding settlement. In return, the federal government encouraged employers to recognise unions; even Henry Ford did so. The theory was that the unions would control their members by not supporting any strikes while still trying to ensure working conditions improved.

However, in reality the wartime period saw considerable industrial unrest. In 1943, 400,000 coal miners whose union was affiliated neither to the AFL nor the CIO went on strike for 12 weeks, causing their union leader John Lewis to be regarded as a hate figure. On the one hand, it seemed unpatriotic to strike while thousands of young Americans were in combat zones overseas. British journalist Alistair Cooke recorded this among workers in West Virginia in 1942, before the wage controls: 'Mostly we're sore at the guys that strike for an extra ten dollars a week, when the men they draft make thirty dollars a month.' On the other hand, employers were often making huge profits and not passing them on to their workers either through wage rises or improved working conditions.

In June 1943 Congress passed the Smith–Connally War Labor Disputes Act as a response to the miners' strike. It allowed the federal government to take control of any essential industries faced with industrial action. The Act was first used to break a strike by public transport workers in August 1944. They had gone on strike after the FEPC ordered their employers to employ black Americans as drivers. Roosevelt sent 8,000 troops to take over the running of the service if the employees didn't return to work. They acceded and the strike was broken.

Most strikes were unofficial and short, sometimes lasting no more than a few hours. In more protracted stoppages, unions often warned they could not support members taking industrial action because of the no-strike deal and, where employers felt confident enough, they could dismiss the strikers. At the Bell Aircraft company in Marietta, Georgia, members of the electrical department went on strike over the transfer of a popular supervisor; the boss dismissed 70 of them. At the Tire and Rubber Company in Akron, Ohio, 72 employees were expelled from the United Rubber Workers' Union for joining an unofficial strike. Elsewhere, however, such tactics were more successful and employers gave in to strikers' demands to ensure a speedy return to work.

In 1944 two Harvard sociologists, Jerome Scott and George Homas, studied 118 strikes in the Detroit motor industry. The vast majority were related to three factors:

- discipline and working conditions
- what were perceived as unfair company policies
- support for a dismissed colleague.

Elsewhere in February 1944, 6,500 anthracite workers went on strike in Pennsylvania over the dismissal of a colleague while in June 1944, 10,000 struck in the Timken Roller Bearing Company in Canton, Ohio generally over what was perceived as employer intransigence.

Altogether, between Pearl Harbor and VJ Day, there were 14,471 strikes involving 6,774,000 workers, the vast majority unofficial and unsupported by the unions. In 1944 alone 309,000 iron and steel workers, 389,000 automobile workers and 278,000 miners were on strike at various times. Figures in industry estimated that labour efficiency fell by between 20 and 50 per cent during the war years.

Many people were very critical of workers, comparatively safe at home in well-paid employment, taking industrial action while their compatriots were fighting in combat zones across the globe. The end of hostilities saw repressive legislation in the Taft–Hartley Act (see page 328). Nevertheless, there was a precursor to this in the 1943 Smith–Connally Act, which gave the government the powers to seize war production plants if necessary, supervise pre-strike votes and ensure a 30-day cooling-off period took place before any strikes could begin.

The war clearly offered new employment opportunities in new industries which developed as a result of the conflict.

New industries

New industries developed through the demands for war production included advanced electronics, telecommunications, synthetic materials, pharmaceuticals and atomic energy. All of these would be in great demand at the war's end. One example is the growth of the synthetic rubber industry. Following its conquests in the Far East, Japan had cut off 90 per cent of the USA's supply of natural rubber. By 1944 the USA was converting petrol into the production of synthetic rubber. The process was so successful that by 1945, 51 plants were operating and by the end of the war the USA was the largest exporter of synthetic rubber in the world. Similarly, the US pharmaceutical industry grew in part as a result of demand for penicillin. In 1942 the federal government gave 60 companies funding to begin to mass produce a drug that not only saved thousands of lives but also became the most profitable in the world.

Pharmaceutical firm Pfizer, for example, developed a fermentation technique using huge tanks. When they opened their new factory in Brooklyn, New York in March 1944, they produced more penicillin in one month than they had in the whole of 1943.

The growth of the military–industrial complex

The most significant industrial growth was in armaments and weaponry. In 1937 less than 1.5 per cent of national income was spent on defence. As the USA began its rearmament programme, this increased to 10 per cent in 1940; by 1945 it had risen to 50 per cent. In 1940, two-thirds of the steel mills in the USA lay idle. There was, therefore, ample capacity for growth as the occasion demanded. Hence the switch to armaments production came relatively quickly; 33 per cent of the economy was devoted to war production by 1941, and by early 1945 the USA was producing enough to supply 50 per cent of the armaments needs of all its allies. The Soviet leader Joseph Stalin acknowledged at the 1943 Tehran Conference that the war would have been lost without this level of US production.

Initially, war production was achieved by diverting the normal production of existing factories. Hence in the automobile industry, the production of cars and trucks was prohibited and switched to tanks, aircraft and so on. Soon Detroit was producing 20 per cent of aircraft engines. The automobile industry as a whole was producing 20 per cent of all the war production in the USA. During the course of the war, the USA built 300,000 aircraft, 96,000 in 1944 alone.

The war years saw the development of centres of armaments production – naval and aircraft production in the Northwest and California, for example. The population of California increased by 50 per cent during the 1940s but there was also migration to the Northwest to defence plants, for example in Washington State. The Ford factory in Indiana produced more army equipment in 1944 than the whole of Italy.

Inevitably the infrastructure remained so military spending could continue in the post-war years. Many desert areas became associated with military testing and their representatives in Congress sought to continue with this because of the prosperity it brought. People were later to speak of the **military–industrial complex**; it began not in the **Cold War** but during the Second World War when the USA was, indeed, the 'arsenal of democracy'.

Conclusion: The war and the economy

While the war saw greater employment opportunities and a huge economic expansion, it did bring dislocations in its wake. Millions moved to find work in war industries. This led to social problems such as a rise in divorce and crime, particularly youth crime as parental constraints were weakened. New industries developed, notably the manufacture of armaments, but also high-technology concerns which would be in global demand after the war ended. Unemployment collapsed and the USA became an economic powerhouse. The government had direct control unthinkable in previous periods.

> **Work together**
>
> Read this section again carefully. Working in pairs, divide the content into two parts. One of you should take the first half, the other take the second. Each of you needs to read the section for a third time. After you have read it, put your notes and this book away and explain your 'half' to the other person. Note down any areas that you struggled to explain or where the explanation was unclear. These will serve as reminders to revise this section further.

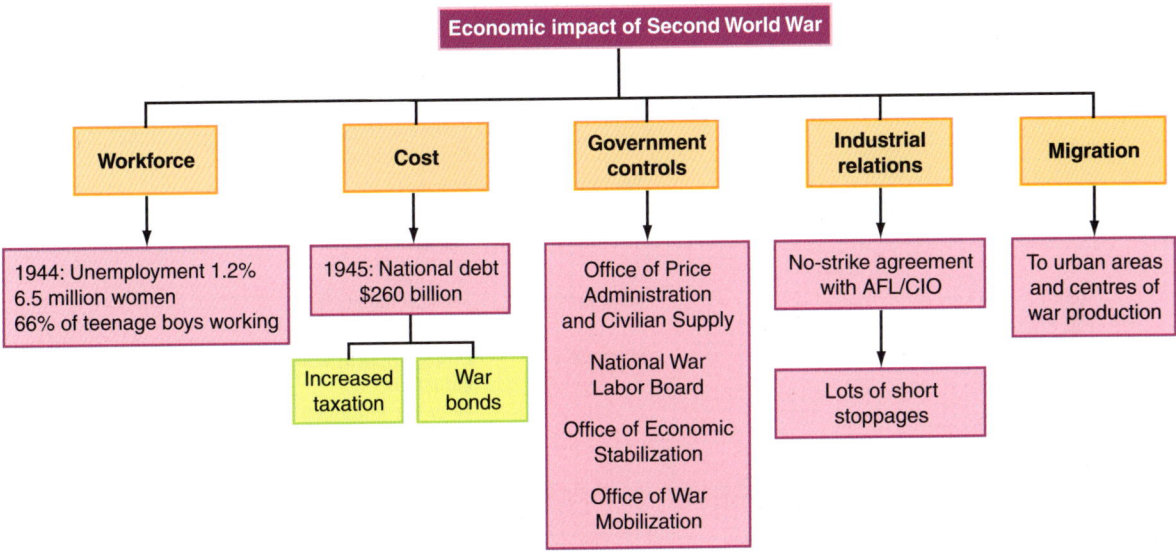

▲ Summary diagram: The economic impact of the Second World War.

Chapter summary

- The New Deal is often judged against its stated aims of relief, recovery and reform.
- It was less successful in effecting recovery but its impact in terms of relief and reform was significant in changing the USA.
- The New Deal did little for women although high-profile appointments were made.
- The year 1940 saw economic improvements stalled until rearmament took effect.
- The Indian Reorganization Act of 1934 saw respect for Native American values, culture and their ability to govern their own affairs.
- Black Americans generally supported the New Deal, although it did little for them as a group.
- African and Hispanic Americans had more opportunities during the war years but still faced discrimination; there was a series of riots in 1943.
- Japanese Americans living on the West Coast were interned as enemy aliens.
- The New Deal encouraged the arts, particularly in terms of reporting and photographing the Depression.
- Women found plentiful work during the war, although were still paid less than men.
- Hollywood improved morale with propaganda and escapist entertainment.
- During the war the government directed the economy through institutions such as the Office of War Mobilization.
- The government paid for the war largely through increased taxation and the sale of war bonds.
- As the economy converted to war production, new industries, notably armaments, developed.
- The Second World War made the USA by far the most prosperous country on Earth.

Effects of New Deal
- Limited economic recovery
- Limited gains for women and ethnic minorities
- Growth in government responsibilities

Effects of the Second World War
- Economic boom as a result of war production
- Plentiful employment for women and ethnic minorities
- Massive growth of government responsibilities
- Media and Hollywood geared to propaganda and morale boosting

More…

Government	Economic controls, FEPC, Smith Act, Selective Service Act, Smith–Connally Act
Employment	Munitions, New industries, e.g. synthetic rubber, pharmaceuticals
Entertainment	Popular music, film, radio, concerts
Migration	Employment in war industries, Housing shortages, Racial tensions

▲ Summary diagram: The impact of the New Deal and the Second World War on the USA to 1945.

Recommended reading

John Morton Blum, *V Was For Victory: Politics and American Culture during World War II* (Harcourt Brace Jovanovich, 1976). Accessible account with a focus on the relationship between politics and culture.

Alistair Cooke, *Alistair Cooke's American Journey* (Allen Lane, 2006). Evocative contemporary account from a leading British journalist of a journey through the USA as it geared up to war production in 1942; published after the author's death.

Ronald Allen Goldberg, *America in the Forties* (Syracuse University Press, 2012), especially Chapter 2. Chapter 2 deals comprehensively with the home front.

Ronald Takaki, *Double Victory: A Multicultural History of America in the Second World War* (Little, Brown & Company, 2000). Very useful for the study of ethnic groups during the war.

Section A: Essay technique

Contextualising the sources

In order to understand the sources properly, you need to place them in the context in which they were written. Specifically, you need to consider the background or environment in which the source was produced. This may sound obvious, but twentieth-century sources were produced by twentieth-century people, and therefore reflect their experiences, beliefs and prejudices at the time they were written. This means that sources are never stand-alone documents – they should be understood within the context of the values and assumptions of the society that produced them.

In essence, your task when contextualising the sources is to try to understand the world in the same way as the writers of the sources. In short, you should try to see things their way. Understanding the context is an important part of evaluating the evidence that the sources contain.

Imagine you are answering the following question:

> How far could the historian make use of Sources 1 and 2 (page 320) together to investigate the contribution of women in the workplace during Second World War?

You have read about the role of women in wartime in this chapter (see page 320). If you wish to remind yourself of this, re-read the chapter or your notes. This is important before embarking on an exercise about context.

One way to contextualise the sources is to begin by asking the question: what issue is this source contributing to? The reason for this is that sources are written for specific purposes. In this case they may have been written for propaganda purposes, and intended to boost morale or offer an example to others.

Here is an example of an attempt to put Source 1 in context:

Source 1 A **newspaper article in the *Boston Daily Record*, Friday 23 October 1943**, written by journalist Joseph Purcell.

Hie From Altar to War Jobs

These amazing 'Women Behind the Men Behind the Guns' are so completely wrapped up in their war work that one bride won't even take time out for a honeymoon. What's more they're not afraid to take on work that requires plenty of 'elbow grease' and Mrs Alice Barnes, 31, of Carlton Ter Watertown and Virginia Brown, 21, of Varnum St Arlington are two attractive examples of that determination.

Mrs Barnes married a storekeeper at the Charlestown Navy yard about a month ago but she didn't let marriage interfere with her splendid record as a drill machine operator. Marriage, she admits, is a pretty important thing, but so, she added, is this war we're fighting and our soldiers are going to get the equipment they need for victory.

So Mrs Barnes smiling from behind a coating of grease and oil told how she got married, reported back on the job a few hours after the ceremony. 'My honeymoon' she grinned, 'can wait until after the war.'

Mrs Barnes operates a machine which bores holes in huge anti-aircraft guns, a job which requires clear thinking and undivided attention.

Annotations:

- *This article was written two years into the war when the USA was approaching the height of its war production.*
- *This is written as an example for others: these 'amazing' women are so dedicated to their work that one didn't take time out for a honeymoon. Their importance to the war effort is emphasised in the phrase 'Women Behind the Men Behind the Guns'.*
- *Although they're not afraid of hard work, they are still attractive.*
- *An example of propaganda. Mrs Barnes is determined that soldiers get the necessary equipment for victory, implying that, with examples like her to follow, the USA will win the war. It also implies again the importance of her job. Without people like her, soldiers may not get the equipment they need.*
- *Mrs Barnes is setting a good example for others to follow.*
- *Despite the dirt and hard work, she is still smiling – an example to others.*
- *Explains what she actually does and the importance and difficulty of the job.*

Key Topic 3 The impact of the New Deal and the Second World War on the USA to 1945

It is crucial to relate your analysis of context to the question. The context for Source 1 (page 319) helps answer the question in the following ways:
- Articles like this attempted to promote the war effort through extolling the work of women.
- Mrs Barnes is singled out as an example for others to follow in terms of putting her job first.
- The emphasis is on victory; women like Mrs Barnes will help US soldiers win the war.
- The mood is upbeat. Mrs Barnes is still smiling despite deferring her honeymoon and doing a hard, dirty job.
- However, we should remember that the article does act as propaganda and give a one-sided view. It does not, for example, talk about how tired women workers might be or the discrimination they might face.

Activity: Seeing things their way

Now try contextualising Source 2 (right).
1. Re-read the question on page 319 – remind yourself of the specific task you are focussing on.
2. Ask yourself the following questions and annotate a copy of the source with the answers:
   (a) What was the purpose of the article?
   (b) What attitudes does it display towards women workers?
   (c) Why does the Brigadier General Kells like women workers?
   (d) How does the article encourage more women to work?
3. Next write a series of bullet points outlining:
   (a) the aspects of the source that are useful for answering the question
   (b) the aspects of the source that are less useful
   (c) a summary of the extent to which the source provides useful evidence concerning the contribution of women in the workforce during the Second World War.

Activity: AS-style questions

1. Why is Source 1 (page 319) valuable to the historian for an enquiry into American attitudes to working women during the Second World War?
2. How much weight do you give the evidence of Source 2 for an enquiry into the changing role of women during the 1940s?

Source 2 Extract from an undated and untitled article submitted to the *Boston Post* by journalist Charles Folsom.

> Right up in the front row overlooking the parade of war are the women – their numbers growing – who work to speed men and munitions through the Boston Port of Embarkation.
>
> These devoted women are no mere spectators. They are part of the show whether in the offices or out doing a man's job. A press tour around the ship and rail terminal, through the vast warehouses, shops, wharf and pier sheds, disclosed what an industrious crew they are. It was easy to understand the enthusiasm of their commander Brigadier General C.H. Kells who likes their work and wants more of them, to release men for sterner duties.
>
> Here is thrill aplenty for the girls, the excitement of sending transport or cargo ships away on time, preparing the shipping lists, making equipment storm proof and bringing up sling loads of goods for ships' booms to hoist into place. An acre of girls keep typewriters clacking, platoons of them charge at freight trains and whisk supplies away on chisel trucks, to stack them up with the fork lift for future shipment.

Work together

Having read Source 2 and completed the activity 'Seeing things their way', discuss the following questions with a partner:
1. Did you both agree on:
   (a) the reasons the author wrote Source 2
   (b) the attitude it displays towards women workers
   (c) why Brigadier General Kells likes women workers?
2. Did you both agree on:
   (a) the aspects of the source that are useful for answering the question
   (b) the aspects of the source that are less useful
   (c) the overall extent to which the source is useful to the historian investigating the contribution of women in the workforce during the Second World War?
   If you disagreed on the answers to any of these questions, try to work out whose answer was better and why.
3. What else would it be useful to know about the source in order to answer the question? Use your discussion to make a three-point list of the ways in which you can use contextual knowledge to improve your essay writing.

Section B: Essay technique

Overall judgement

An overall judgement is as important to a Paper 2 Section B essay as it is to essays in Paper 1. You may have already read advice about the characteristics of a good overall judgement (see page 92). Remember, good judgements are supported, and the best judgements consider the relative significance of the key factors you have discussed in your essay.

Now you can practise writing an overall judgement to an essay concerning the role and status of black Americans during the Second World War.

Activity: detail and analysis

Imagine you are answering the following Section B question:

How far did the lives of members of ethnic minority groups change in the USA during the Second World War?

1. Read the question and work out what type of question it is (see page 262).
2. Make a plan that is appropriate to the specific question. Remember it should consist of three of four main points.
3. Add three pieces of detail to support each of your main points. Remember, use the detail that best supports the points you want to make.
4. Write an analytical sentence to conclude each of your main points.
5. Now write a conclusion to the essay.
   - Start by asserting an overall judgement.
   - Support this by weighing the different main points in your plan.
   - Summarise your overall judgement in the final sentence.

Work together

Having completed a plan in the activity, swap it with a partner. Consider:

1. Did you agree on what type of question you were dealing with? If not, discuss it and work out who was right.
2. Whose plan most clearly focussed on the specific type of question?
3. Did you both begin your conclusion with a clear judgement?
4. Did you both weigh up the different key points to support your judgement?
5. Whose overall judgement was better and why?
6. What can you learn from each other's work?

Use these questions to feed back to each other and improve your essay technique.

Question practice

1. 'The Impact of the New Deal was disappointing.' How far do you agree with this statement?
2. How accurate is it to say that the New Deal was a failure in the years 1933 to 1941? **AS**
3. How far did the New Deal improve the lives of members of ethnic minorities?
4. What was the significance of the Second World War on the role and status of women in the USA?

Key Topic 4 The transformation of the USA, 1945–54

Overview

The USA emerged from the Second World War as the richest country on Earth with unparalleled growth and opportunities for expansion. The federal government gave grants to veterans through the GI Bill of Rights, and opportunities abounded. While some groups feared the prosperity might not last and saved their money, before long these concerns had diminished and a consumer boom developed. This was fuelled by the movement to the suburbs occasioned by affordable housing and the growth in car ownership.

There was, however, a real fear of the spread of communism. This led to an anticommunist witch hunt in the USA led by the House Un-American Activities Committee (HUAC) and Senator Joseph McCarthy. That communist infiltration had taken place was evidenced in several high-profile espionage cases. Fears of communism led to the development of the Cold War and the nuclear age.

The period saw the media, including the growing television network, applauding the nuclear family as the American ideal. It often depicted women simply as homemakers and excluded ethnic groups except as stereotypes. This was slow to change. There were lots of young people – 'baby boomers' – and a market reflecting their interests began to develop.

There was a slow improvement in the role and status of ethnic minorities, although few Native Americans gained from the policy of termination. There were more black American sports and film stars, for example. One significant milestone was the 1954 court case *Brown* v. *Topeka Board of Education* which outlawed separation between the races in public schools. However, white Southerners were to fight tenaciously to maintain segregation and by the 1950s much was still to be achieved on the path to civil rights.

The overarching theme of the transformation of the USA is covered in four sections:
1 Economic transformation
2 The end of post-war euphoria
3 Cultural change
4 The changing status of minorities

TIMELINE

1944	GI Bill of Rights (also known as the Selective Servicemen's Readjustment Act)
1945 April	Death of Roosevelt
1945 August	End of the Second World War in Asia
1947 May	Truman Doctrine speech
1947 June	Taft–Hartley Act
1949 October	China becomes communist
1949 August	USSR explodes its first atomic bomb
1950 February	McCarthy's anticommunist 'witch hunt' begins
1950–53	Korean War
1953 January	Eisenhower becomes president
1954 March	USA explodes its first hydrogen bomb in Bikini Atoll
1954 May	*Brown* v. *Topeka Board of Education*
1954 July	Citizens' Councils formed
1955 March	Southern Manifesto issued

1 Economic transformation

The prosperity resulting from the war continued into peacetime. It was aided in part by the GI Bill of Rights which gave generous grants to 8 million veterans. The USA became the richest country in history. Car ownership rocketed as cars became a status symbol with comfort, speed and new sleek lines. Their growth helped drive the move away from urban centres and into suburbs, where new homes became affordable. Levitt houses (see page 324) were partly pre-fabricated and particularly good value. One downside of the 'white flight' was that urban centres often became decayed and home to the poorest groups in society. The post-war baby boom, growth of employment opportunities and development of affordable housing in the new suburbs led to the development of the nuclear family. At its centre were goods and features that made life comfortable and pleasing. Many goods were paid for with credit and people had to work long hours to maintain their lifestyle. Nevertheless, the growing realisation that the prosperity would continue led to a sense of optimism and strong belief that the USA had the ideal lifestyle.

> **Note it down**
>
> This is another opportunity to add to your themed collection of index cards. In this section there are discussions of economic and social developments. Follow the pattern of providing a definition, notes on the reason for it and on the consequences or impact.

Post-war prosperity

The economic problems that often follow wars were not repeated in the USA in 1945. As we have seen (pages 313–18), the US economy grew significantly during the war. GNP had risen 35 per cent since 1941. The USA had 7 per cent of the world's population but possessed 42 per cent of global income.

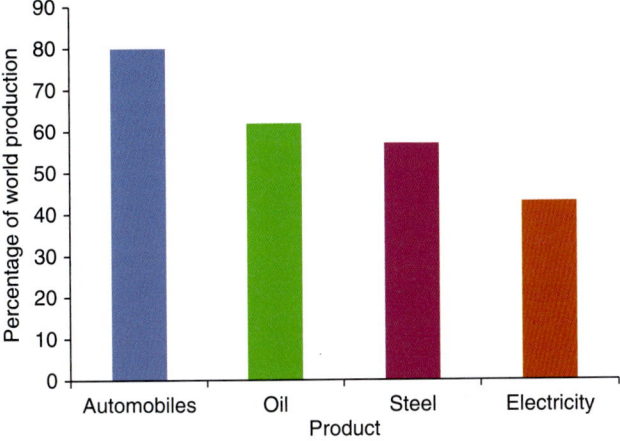

▲ Figure 1: US production as a percentage of world production.

Per capita income at $1,450 was almost twice as high as Great Britain. Urban Americans consumed about 3,000 calories per day, about 50 per cent more than most people in western Europe. The federal government spent more – $36.5 billion in 1948, admittedly significantly less than the $92.2 billion expended in 1945 but considerably more than the $9.4 billion of 1939. This figure was to rise significantly in 1950 with the onset of the Korean War and a massive defence budget in the 1950s and beyond. States, meanwhile, spent more on roads and schools.

Economic expansion created greater employment opportunities in many industries – for example, aircraft production, chemicals and electrical goods. As consumer tastes changed, processed food production made huge gains. Tobacco companies made vast profits and employed many people. As we will see, there was a huge migration to centres of plentiful employment.

Many Americans remembered the pre-war depression, however and, despite the prosperity, many on average earnings of about $3,000 per annum or below tended to live carefully and save where they could. While consumption rose, it was not necessarily conspicuous or wasteful – at least not until, by the late 1940s, it became apparent that the prosperity was going to last. Then the consumer boom gathered apace.

One should note, too, that not all areas of the USA were equally prosperous. Some had a lot of catching up to do. These were mainly in the poorer areas of cities and the South. In 1947, 33 per cent of US homes lacked running water and 40 per cent flush toilets. Many families lived in rented accommodation and could hardly have imagined owning their own property. It was a measure of economic success that by 1960 so many were able to take these things for granted and home ownership had risen from 55 per cent in 1950 to 62 per cent ten years later.

The GI Bill of Rights

The government had passed the GI Bill of Rights (also known as the Selective Servicemen's Readjustment Act) in 1944, offering grants to veterans to improve their education, learn new skills or set up businesses. Eight million veterans took advantage of this measure. All former combatants were to receive $20 per week while looking for work. In fact, less than 20 per cent of the money set aside for this was actually distributed because so many jobs were available for returning veterans. Universities expanded considerably to accept former servicemen whose fees were paid by the government. The University of Syracuse, for example, trebled its number of students. The GI Bill of Rights also offered low-interest home loans that allowed ex-servicemen and their families to move to new houses in the suburbs.

Increasing mobility

The spectacular growth of the car industry led to much greater mobility and the development of suburbs. This meant that many Americans no longer needed to live in crowded towns and cities. The home became very important in terms of privacy and offering a comfortable lifestyle. Even more significantly, it came to symbolise the prosperity of ordinary people because they were owner-occupiers. One day, when the mortgage was paid off, it would be theirs. They weren't spending their wages on rent but investing it in bricks and mortar. It was the lynchpin of the development of the 1950s **middle-class** family.

The growth of the car industry

Sales of new cars rose from 69,500 in 1945 to 6.7 million by 1950. The vast majority were US made; in 1950 there were only 16,000 foreign cars on US roads. Clearly, this led to a great expansion in the car industry dominated by the 'Big Three': Ford, General Motors and Chrysler. Cars seemed to symbolise the confidence of the age; they were sleek, 'gas-guzzling', big and colourful. In 1958 Ford produced a 5.79-metre-long Lincoln model. Choice was paramount, too. In 1961 there were 350 different models on sale. They weren't cheap – a new Chrysler cost $1,300 or about 40 per cent of the average family income – but most were bought on credit. The number of two-car families doubled between 1951 and 1958. As a result, there were more cars in Los Angeles than in the whole of Asia and General Motors was wealthier than Belgium in terms of GDP.

The growth of car ownership also helped develop the facilities associated with them, such as roadside hotels, motels, gas stations and garages. The first Holiday Inn opened in 1952 between Memphis and Nashville in Tennessee. Des Moines in Idaho saw the first McDonald's in April 1955; by 1960 the 228 McDonald's restaurants enjoyed annual sales of $37 million. Road building itself was given a major boost by the 1956 Interstate Highway Act which boosted federal subsidies for road building and developed the infrastructure of US highways. It created a 41,000-mile system, mainly of dual carriageway, designed to eliminate unsafe roads, bottlenecks and other factors that impeded free traffic movement. Interestingly, the bill was intended to create 'a national system of interstate and defence highways' to facilitate speedy evacuation in the event of nuclear attack. However, road-building developments also signified the demise of public transport in the USA. Passenger services on railroads lost an average $700 million per year by the mid-1950s (although this was partly due to the growth of long-distance air travel).

The growth of suburbs

House construction away from urban centres had begun during the war years but expanded rapidly in the years thereafter. In 1944, 114,000 new family homes were built, rising to 1.7 million in 1950. In the decade following 1945, 15 million houses were built, mainly for private purchase. The percentage of Americans owning their own homes rose from 50 per cent in 1945 to 60 per cent by 1960. Many acquired mortgages through the government-sponsored Federal Housing Administration or Veterans' Administration. These offered mortgages of up to 90 per cent of the cost price and interest rates as low as 4 per cent.

The percentage of people living in suburbs grew from 17 per cent in 1920 to 33 per cent by 1960. Critics complained that suburbs lacked variety. Cinema and restaurant managers in urban centres complained of a lack of business as people stayed home. Too often conditions deteriorated in residential inner-city areas as they were left to the poor, often members of ethnic minorities, and they lost funding due to the 'flight of the middle classes' who would have paid taxes to live there. The suburbs, meanwhile, saw the development

Levitt houses

Levitt houses were among the most famous of suburban dwellings. William Levitt (1907-94) has variously been called the 'king' or the 'inventor of suburbia'. While this is going too far, he was nevertheless instrumental in the development of cheap, affordable housing. Levitt was born into a family building firm that operated in the New York area. During the war, he served in the 'seabees' or engineers and, after leaving the forces, simply applied the techniques of building military installations he had learned during the war to commercial construction. His houses came in 27 separate parts to be constructed on site. The parts themselves were manufactured in factories using the techniques of mass production. Before the war, the average builder had constructed five houses per year; in 1947 Levitt built 2,000 on a site in Long Island where the **post-war housing shortage** had been so intense that some people were living in coal sheds. By 1951 this original Levittown had grown to 17,000 homes over 24.283 square kilometres housing 82,000 people. And other developments followed. For example, in Bucks County, Pennsylvania Levitt houses cost $7,990-$15,000, less than houses of similar size elsewhere. When they were being built, they attracted long queues of prospective buyers.

Levitt houses did have their critics. Black Americans were not allowed to buy them and Levitt estates had petty rules such as no shrubs over four feet high. Nevertheless, Levitt has been applauded as the builder who made the dream of a detached home for ordinary Americans a reality.

of new facilities such as the shopping mall. In 1946 there were eight, but over 4,000 by the late 1950s. Here everything could be purchased in one centre arrived at by car. These developments spelled disaster for many small shopkeepers. The development of suburbs as a result of increased prosperity and car ownership effectively changed the lives of millions of ordinary Americans forever.

The consumer society

The growth of suburbs and increasing confidence that the prosperity was here to stay led to a huge consumer boom. Wages generally rose. By 1953 the average family's annual income had reached $4,011. This meant many people had money to spend; in fact, their disposable income rose on average by 17 per cent.

The consumer boom

There was a rapid expansion in consumer items fuelled by incessant advertising – itself a multi-billion dollar industry rising from $6 billion in 1950 to over $13 billion by 1963. By 1960 there were over 50 million televisions in the USA.

Due to the boom in population, baby clothes and nappies were in particular demand. By 1957 nappies alone became a $50 million per year industry. In 1980 historian Landon Jones wrote that 'the cry of the baby was heard across the land' as their numbers grew. Four million babies were born each year between 1954 and 1964. In that year 40 per cent of the population had been born before 1946.

This was possibly the golden age of the American nuclear family. The divorce rate fell from 17.9 per 1,000 marriages in 1946 to 9.6 by 1953. The average age of marriage for females fell from 21.5 years in 1940 to 20.1 by 1956 and within seven months of marriage most women were pregnant.

The amount of leisure time rose, too. One commentator reported that by 1956 many Americans were spending more time watching television than actually working for pay. They were filling their homes with labour-saving devices and **white goods**. By 1951, 90 per cent of American families had fridges and 75 per cent possessed washing machines and telephones – often paid for with credit. The amount of debt increased from $5.7 billion in 1945 to $56.1 billion by 1960. The first Diners' Club cards were introduced in 1950 – made of cardboard. They became plastic in 1955. American Express dates from 1958. Among the new products were frozen and convenience food and TV dinners, long-playing records, electric clothes dryers and Polaroid cameras. All saved time and effort. The introduction of plastics and artificial fibres meant it was easier to keep items clean.

▲ A family of four in 1951 and their food for a year. How useful is this source for a historian investigating the extent of prosperity in the USA in the early 1950s?

Consumption rocketed. With 6 per cent of the world's population in the early 1950s, the USA consumed a staggering 33 per cent of all the goods in the world and controlled 66 per cent of the world's productive capacity. On a more basic level, just the consumption of hot dogs increased from 750 million in 1950 to 2 billion by 1960. A famous photograph showed a typical family with the two and a half tons of food they consumed yearly, including 300 lb of beef, 31 chickens and 8.5 gallons of ice cream (see Source A). Their weekly budget for this amount was $25.

While at first many looked to the example of the 1920s and worried that the prosperity may not continue, as the 1950s developed there seemed no end to the post-war boom and so more and more Americans felt confident that this time it would last. With such confidence at home, the threat most people feared to their way of life was the influence of the USSR, the new foreign enemy.

Conclusion: Economic transformation

As prosperity continued into the 1940s and 1950s, the USA appeared unimaginably wealthy. Most groups seemed to share in the prosperity. The increasing number of cars led to the development of suburbs in which the nuclear family was depicted as the ideal. Their world centred around a home filled with labour-saving devices and white goods. New developments in frozen and convenience food made feeding the family easier while the increasing number of shopping malls made it possible to buy everything under one huge roof. As consumption soared, often fuelled by advertising and easy credit facilities, it seemed that the ideal society had been created in the USA.

Work together

First divide up the trends and evidence for them discussed in this section. This could include growing prosperity, mobility and the consumer boom. Using the recommended reading in this book, your class notes, online research and other independent reading of your own, try to find out more about each of the issues explored here. Share the notes that you have made and make sure that you read them together, explaining any terminology or external events that you have found out about.

2 The end of post-war euphoria

The USA had long been opposed to communism and the House Un-American Activities Committee (HUAC) investigated its spread vigorously in the years after the war, turning its attention to Hollywood and other organisations such as **labour unions**. This was a significant reason for the passing of the Taft–Hartley Act which severely restricted union activity. It was Senator Joseph McCarthy who helped spark the anticommunist hysteria in which ordinary people were accused of communist sympathies and material previously regarded as inoffensive was removed from libraries. McCarthy was brought down by the televised hearings into his accusations that the military had been infiltrated by communists. However, anticommunist fears continued, fuelled in part by spy scandals and the development of nuclear weapons within the USSR.

Fear of the spread of communism and nuclear attack led to the development of a **Cold War** mentality. There were regular anti-attack drills and a massive development of military spending. Some writers have identified the contradictory mentality of huge optimism about economic growth coupled with a fear that nuclear attack and destruction could come at any time.

Note it down

Here use the 1:2 method (page x) with a slight alteration. As usual, note down the 'big points', or headings, in the first column. In the second column write the supporting points in note form. This time add a third column. Here note down any concepts, terms, documents or historical figures that you would like to research further. In this section this could include Senator Joseph McCarthy, Alger Hiss and the Rosenbergs. When you have completed this section, you can then research these points and add the information into this column.

The HUAC and McCarthyism

As we saw in Chapter 1 (page 246), the USA had long been opposed to communism, which it saw as a threat to its way of life. The HUAC was set up by Congress in 1938 to investigate Americans who sympathised with the Nazis, but after the war its focus changed to relentlessly investigate those suspected of supporting communism. In the late

1940s there was a HUAC campaign against members of the Hollywood film community who were accused of making movies with communistic content aimed at brainwashing Americans. This saw, among others, the filmmaker Charlie Chaplin, a British citizen, being forced to leave the USA. While many Hollywood actors, such as Gary Cooper, supported the Committee's investigations, others refused to answer questions. The 'Hollywood Ten', mainly a group of writers and directors, were fired from their jobs and eventually sent to prison for contempt of Congress for refusing to testify before the HUAC. In 1954 a second investigation produced a 'blacklist' of 350 individuals who would not be employed in the film industry.

> **Source A** Extract from an autobiography *Growing Up in Hollywood* by Robert Parrish (Bodley Head, 1976). Parrish was a film director. Here he is referring to attempts to discredit director Joseph Mankiewitz by fellow director Cecil B. DeMille who wanted all directors to sign an Oath of Loyalty. While Mankiewitz was prepared to sign the oath himself, he thought to force people to do so infringed upon their personal liberties.
>
> An interesting organisation called the Cecil B. DeMille Foundation for Americanism was formed. It became the chief source of information for State Senator John Tenney, head of the California Un-American Committee, which then passed the information on to the HUAC in Washington.
>
> Items began to appear in the press suggesting that Mankiewitz was a 'pinko', a '**fellow traveller**' and a 'Communist inspired left wing intellectual who was not adverse to slopping Communist propaganda into his films'. Mankiewitz's credits included *Skippy, Million Dollar Legs, If I Had a Million, Alice in Wonderland, The Gorgeous Hussy, Philadelphia Story* and other pictures which I guess DeMille suspected of having subversive content. A secret Joseph L. Mankiewitz film festival was organised. The pictures were run behind closed doors at DeMille's house with a select audience complete with stenographers, their pencils poised in case *Skippy* or *Alice in Wonderland* or *The Gorgeous Hussy* said anything which could be interpreted as Anti-American.
>
> Why is Source A useful for a historian investigating anticommunism in Hollywood?

As well as investigating Hollywood, the HUAC was suspicious of labour unions and their links to communism. Union leaders were forced to swear that they were non-communist by the terms of the Taft–Hartley Act. Suspicions and fears of communist infiltrators – for example, in labour unions – while subsequently shown to be largely unjustified, were genuinely held by many at the time.

The Taft–Hartley Act

After the war there was considerable labour discontent in part because the government removed wartime price controls before the restrictions on wage rises (see page 315). This led to a period of inflation in which food prices rose by 25 per cent between 1945 and 1947. General Motors employees, for example, demanded wage rises of 35 per cent. In 1946 there was a crippling coal strike and railroad workers also threatened industrial action. Altogether 4.6 million workers, about 10 per cent of the entire **labour force**, went on strike at some point during that year. There were over 5,000 separate strikes.

This unrest helped the Republicans to take control of Congress following the 1946 mid-term elections. They were committed to legislation that restricted union activity. In May, President Truman himself compared the proposed rail strike to the threat to the USA from the attack on Pearl Harbor. He threatened to draft striking railway workers into the armed forces. At the last minute the strike was averted. Many people lacked sympathy with discontented workers because, after the disruptions of wartime, they resented anyone interfering with their ability to lead trouble-free lives. In particular, they wanted the shops to be stocked with the consumer goods they could now afford to buy.

Taking advantage of this mood, Congress passed the Taft–Hartley Act in June 1947, although Truman tried unsuccessfully to veto it. This outlawed the **closed shop** and **secondary strikes** and made union leaders swear that they were non-communist. It also gave the president the power to prevent strikes that he considered to be against the national interest. There would be an 80-day 'cooling-off' period during which a board appointed by the president could investigate the dispute and hopefully settle it without the need for strike action.

It was feared that communists were infiltrating the government as well. After the spy scares (see page 331), the **State Department** was accused of harbouring communist sympathisers. It tended to recruit from the wealthy well-educated classes. This led to some accusations, particularly from working- and middle-class people, that those from privileged positions were seeking to undermine their country to create a society in which everyone is the same. In this sense the campaign against communism could be seen as a class issue where the upper classes were seen to be 'soft' on communism. Certainly, many less well-off members of society supported the view that richer people were more likely to be sympathetic to the very communist ideas which they believed threatened the US way of life.

In 1947 President Truman appeared to fuel these charges by introducing the Loyalty Review Board to check up on government employees. Any found to be sympathetic to 'subversive organisations' could be fired. Within four years at least 1,200 had been dismissed and a further 6,000 resigned. Over 150 organisations were banned, of which 110 were accused of supporting communism.

Organisations such as interest groups that felt they may be at risk from accusations of communist sympathies included the NAACP (see page 338) and the CIO; they purged their memberships of any likely communist sympathisers. On a more individual level, many educators from universities to primary schools were fired on suspicion of having communist leanings. Eleven leaders of the Communist Party were prosecuted under the 1940 Smith Act (see page 314) and sentenced to up to five years in prison. It was argued that their beliefs suggested they would try to overthrow the government in the USA; they had not actually done anything.

The China lobby

The fall of China to the communists in 1949 was unexpected and some felt the State Department could have done more to prevent it. It had grossly underestimated the power of the communists and overestimated that of the nationalists, whom it supported. This led to the creation of a powerful China lobby who campaigned for action against the new communist regime and also a detailed investigation to discover how the USA had come to let it fall. Pat McCarran, a Democratic Senator from Nevada, was a key figure in the Senate Internal Security Subcommittee which tried to persuade people that China had fallen to communism as a result of the work of secret communist infiltrators within the State Department. In particular, the well-heeled figure of Secretary of State Dean Acheson was disliked and distrusted.

Increasingly, the USA was losing confidence in its struggle against the spread of communism. The mood in some quarters was close to paranoia. University teachers who refused to answer questions about their relationship to the Communist Party were fired. In 1949 top US universities simply said that communists were unfit to teach so would never be hired. Within this atmosphere, the stage was set for the emergence of the most notorious anticommunist hunter of all: Senator Joseph McCarthy.

Communism and McCarthyism

Joseph McCarthy was a hard-drinking junior Senator for Wisconsin. On 9 February 1950 he made a speech in which he said the State Department was infested with over 200 spies. Although he hadn't a shred of evidence to back up his claims, and a few days later he readjusted his figure to 57, many listened and believed him.

The speech saw the inauguration of a witch hunt against members of the State Department, other public servants and finally the Army. In 1953 McCarthy was given control of the Senate Committee on government Operations and its subcommittee on Investigations. One of McCarthy's techniques was the use of 'multiple untruth', which meant that his accusations were so complex that it was difficult for anyone to unravel let alone refute them. It is said that McCarthy had access to HUAC and even Federal Bureau of Investigation (FBI) files.

At first McCarthy was highly successful. No one in public life seemed safe from his accusations and he became one of the most popular men in the USA. He gained support from such diverse groups as the veterans' group the American Legion and Christian fundamentalists, many of whom saw communism literally as the work of the Devil. Much of his support was also derived from the less well-educated and less affluent members of society – many of whom, it is often alleged, were more susceptible to simplistic conspiracy theories. These were also the groups that had supported the attacks against the well-off members of the State Department.

McCarthy's downfall

It was McCarthy's aggressive manner and accusations against the military that saw his downfall. Not only did he condemn such highly respected figures as General George Marshall, but in 1954 he also began to investigate the Army as hiding a possible nest of communists. In so doing, he appeared to accuse an institution until recently embroiled in a full-scale war against communism in Korea (see page 330) of supporting communism.

Millions saw the hearings on the new medium of television in December 1954, and they turned against McCarthy because of his bullying tactics; he also appeared at times to be drunk. His audiences saw he was completely bereft of any hard evidence to support his accusations. The Army's attorney, Joseph Welch, stood up to McCarthy when he accused a junior member of Welch's team of having belonged to a pro-communist organisation while at college. He accused McCarthy of attacking people without a shred of evidence in support. President Eisenhower, a former military commander, was critical of McCarthy's investigation of the Army. The tables appeared to turn in particular when McCarthy himself was accused of seeking preferential treatment for one of his aides who had been drafted into the Army. He was censured by the Senate and returned to obscurity until his death from alcoholism in 1957.

▲ Summary diagram: Reasons for the communist witch hunt.

Key debate
The impact of McCarthyism

Most historians have criticised McCarthy over both his personal life and his harmful impact on the USA. James T. Patterson, writing in 1996, mentions his false war record, boorishness and alcoholism. He emphasises how, during the **Red Scare**, free speech was threatened to the detriment of meaningful debate, and how foreign policy initiatives were restricted; there could, for example, be no approaches to communist China during the McCarthy years. Oliver Stone and Peter Kuznick argued in 2013 that McCarthy was a front used by the FBI to destroy the power of the American left, tarring its members with the charge of communism. Conservative historians such as Anna Coulter, writing in 2003, and M. Stanton Evans, writing in 2007, have tried to defend McCarthy, often citing the release of secret government papers known as the Venona project in 1995 as justification that there was a communist conspiracy to infiltrate the US government which McCarthy was right to expose. While this is a hotly contested issue, it is important to be aware that conspiracy theories abound, and it is important to keep within the parameters of informed debate.

Anticommunism and the Cold War context

While McCarthyism may have faded, the USA still felt vulnerable against communist influence at home. It wasn't just Joseph McCarthy who fought against communism. In September 1950 the McCarran Internal Security Act forced all communist organisations to register with the Attorney General and barred any communists from working in defence-related industries. If this may seem reasonable, the Communist Control Act of 1954 made it illegal to communicate communist ideas including by semaphore. In 1954 the city of Birmingham, Alabama, made it illegal even to be seen conversing with a known communist. While the US Communist Party had never attracted more than 100,000 supporters and far fewer actual members, there was, nevertheless, a real fear that if such supporters were in influential positions, they could do untold damage within the USA.

This view appeared validated by various developments that shocked Americans in the years following the Second World War, including the spread of communism within eastern Europe and its success in China.

The development of the Cold War

The result of anticommunism was not only to see 'reds everywhere under the bed' but to feel the USA itself was under attack. This was particularly true when the USSR developed nuclear weapons. People increasingly began to fear nuclear war was likely.

Atomic weapons

In 1949 the USSR exploded its first nuclear weapon. The USA had therefore lost its monopoly on atomic weapons. President Truman said the USA would seek to develop a hydrogen bomb, with as much as a thousand times the power of an atomic bomb. When this weapon was finally tested in Bikini Atoll in March 1954, both sides were entering into an arms race and developing weapons of mass destruction that could, if used, have led to the end of the world.

Military spending

The prospect of other countries developing nuclear weapons meant the USA could be attacked. As a result, the **military–industrial complex** was to develop (see page 316), with defence spending between $40 to $50 billion per year in the 1950s and 90 per cent of foreign aid to US allies going on military spending.

Key Topic 4 The transformation of the USA, 1945–54

Events of the Cold War

The Truman Doctrine

In 1947 Truman had offered the USA's support to countries struggling against communism. The policy was known as the Truman Doctrine or containment because it seemed to imply the USA would stem the spread of communism. The doctrine was first applied in Greece to give aid to the non-communist forces. Greece did not become communist; hence, the first intervention appeared successful.

Marshall Aid

In the following year the USA went further, offering a $13 billion package to help European countries to recover from the effects of the Second World War. This was Marshall Aid, named after the US Secretary of State General George Marshall. A conference of 22 nations was set up to assess their economic needs. The USSR did not attend and refused permission for countries under its sphere of influence to do so.

In the ensuing years two crises emerged in which direct confrontation between the USA and the USSR seemed likely.

The Berlin Airlift, 1948–49

Germany had been divided into four zones of occupation following the end of the war. The capital, Berlin, was also divided, although it lay within the Soviet zone. The Western occupying powers – the USA, Britain and France – relied on Soviet goodwill to travel through its zone to their sectors in Berlin. By 1948 it was clear that the three Western sectors were co-operating and recovery was well on the way through Marshall Aid. In contrast, the Soviet zone remained poor.

In June 1948 the Western zones introduced a new common currency, the Deutschmark. When their leaders tried to introduce it into their sectors of Berlin, Stalin ordered all transport links with the West cut. He believed he could blockade Berlin into accepting communist rule and therefore make the capital part of the future communist East German state.

In retaliation, Britain and the USA organised an airlift of essential supplies to the city under siege. By March 1949, 8,000 tons of supplies were being delivered per day. On 9 May Stalin called off the blockade and things returned to normal. It appeared that in the first great confrontation, the USA had won.

The Korean War, 1950–53

Following the Second World War, Korea was liberated from Japan and divided into North and South. In March 1953 communist North Korea invaded non-communist South Korea. The United Nations sent forces to stop this invasion; the vast majority were American under an American commander, General Douglas MacArthur.

UN forces succeeded in liberating South Korea. However, on McArthur's urging, they then went on to invade the North, ignoring China's warnings of the consequences. China became involved in the war, sending thousands of troops to help the North Koreans. The war effectively became a stalemate for three years. The USA alone lost 27,000 troops and a million Korean civilians died. In 1953 peace was agreed; Korea remained divided into a communist North and non-communist South.

The USA had learned that communism was a global issue and that, if it was to prevent its spread, then a global commitment was necessary. In the early 1950s President Eisenhower spoke of the **domino theory**. While the policy may appear incredibly simplistic, it was nevertheless deeply held and later used to justify full-scale US involvement in the Vietnam War.

Billions of dollars were spent on maintaining a military presence throughout western Europe and southeast Asia, equipping the armed forces, and weapons research and development. Defence establishments were built in otherwise poor areas such as the Southern states; often they were to be found in the areas represented by politicians on the appropriate committees in Congress. Desert areas in Arizona and New Mexico became centres for weapons testing. Many firms followed the military to their new bases, being awarded lucrative contracts to provide weapons, research and equipment. Some historians have argued that this post-war boom in military spending helped to smooth out the former economic inequalities within the USA. California, in particular, benefited from military contracts. One of the knock-on effects was the development of an industry in high technology that was to see it become the centre of the computer industry; the first IBM computer was introduced in 1953.

Fear of nuclear attack

In the 1950s, fear of nuclear attack was real in the USA. Schoolchildren undertook military drills as a matter of course – known as 'duck and cover'. On 14 June 1954, 54 cities took part in a nationwide drill lasting ten minutes in which the streets were supposed to be cleared and everyone sought shelter. While officials pronounced themselves satisfied with the result, they acknowledged, nevertheless, that 12 million would be dead.

The Red Scare

A series of spy scandals in Britain, Canada and the USA further scared the Americans. A British physicist, Klaus Fuchs, was convicted in 1950 of giving nuclear secrets to the USSR. One of his associates, Harry Gold, was arrested on the same charge in the USA. It was felt the USSR had been able to develop its own nuclear weapons so quickly through the infiltration of Soviet agents into the Manhattan Project. US scientists Julius and Ethel Rosenberg were executed for giving away atomic secrets. One Soviet official wrote that they acquired the necessary information about how the atomic bombs were made in the USA and what they were made of in Britain. There was no doubt that communists had infiltrated many branches of US government during the war; the Soviets later claimed that they had 221 operatives spying in the various branches of government.

The Rosenberg case

Julius and Ethel Rosenberg were a husband-and-wife scientist team accused of passing atomic secrets to the Soviet Union. Ethel's brother, David Greenglass, was a soldier working at Los Alamos where the atomic bombs were developed, and passed on secrets to the couple who gave them to Soviet officials. They were convicted largely on Greenglass' testimony, although the subsequent evidence of the Venona papers (see page 329) did confirm the guilt of Julius if not Ethel. Greenglass had implicated the Rosenbergs in a deal to save his own wife from being arrested for her part in the plot. He received a jail term of nine and a half years. Their execution led to an outcry, particularly as they left two small children. The case demonstrated the concern the USA authorities had about infiltration and the determination to show an example.

Source B Extract from Bill Bryson, *The Life and Times of the Thunderbolt Kid* (Broadway Books, 2006). This book is a memoir of the author's childhood in the USA in the 1950s. Here he merges the fear of nuclear attack with rampant consumerism.

> Over 40 per cent of people in 1955 thought there would be a global disaster probably in the form of world war within five years and half of those were certain it would be the end of humanity. Yet the very people who claimed to expect death at any moment were at the same time busily buying new homes, digging swimming pools, investing in stocks and bonds and pension plans and generally behaving like people who expect to live a long time. It was an impossible age to figure.

Why is Source B useful to a historian studying attitudes to nuclear war in the 1950s?

The case of Alger Hiss

It was, however, the trial of Alger Hiss, president of the Carnegie Institute, which really caught the public imagination. Whittaker Chambers, editor of the anticommunist *Time* magazine, accused Hiss of being a communist during his time at the State Department. Hiss had been a key figure at the Yalta Conference at the end of the Second World War. The inference was that he had used his influence there to ensure the USSR's post-war successes. The Yalta Conference had allowed the Soviet Union to extend its influence in eastern Europe and also allowed Soviet citizens to be repatriated.

When Hiss sued Chambers, the latter was able to produce evidence that suggested Hiss had in fact handed over copies of secret documents to the Soviets in 1938. While Hiss' alleged treason was too long ago for him to be prosecuted for it, he was nevertheless found guilty of perjury for lying to the court and sentenced to five years' imprisonment.

Conclusion: The end of post-war euphoria

While there remained optimism about economic growth, there was increasing fear of communist infiltration aimed at destroying the American way of life. This was developed by the HUAC in its investigations and Joseph McCarthy, who first asserted that the State Department was full of traitors. The spy scandals, the fall of China to communism and the Korean War gave credence to these assertions. While McCarthy fell from grace, anticommunist fears continued and led to the development of a Cold War mentality in which Americans both feared nuclear attack and supported the massive growth of the military–industrial complex.

Work together

Consider the following motives for anticommunism: fear of the spread of communism abroad; fear of communist infiltration into the USA; fear of nuclear attack. Working in a group of three, prepare for a debate. Each of you should take one motive. On your own, prepare a case that your motive was the most important. Meet together as a group again and deliver your justifications. Whose case is the strongest?

3 Cultural change

Hollywood, under investigation by the HUAC, sought to prove its loyalty by making a series of Cold War movies about communist infiltration and spies. Such films added to the fear of communism. Science fiction and religious epics also often contained anticommunist messages. TV, meanwhile, grew in power rapidly and threatened the popularity of movies as people increasingly stayed home for their entertainment. Here they constituted a captive audience for the sponsors and advertisers who paid for TV. Advertising was relentless. Often psychologists were hired by advertisers to try to ensure their campaigns had the maximum impact on particular target groups – such as creating messages to make women feel guilty for not buying certain products to please their husbands. Folgers coffee adverts were notorious examples of this.

Women and black Americans faced stereotyping in much of the media. The overwhelming message was that women should be **homemakers** and mothers while their husbands went out to work. However, the drive to maintain the affluent lifestyle often meant that women went to work too. When protests concerning stereotypes drove some programmes featuring black Americans off TV, they became invisible – they simply didn't appear. The overwhelming image was of a white middle-class nuclear family.

Many children grew into teenagers in the late 1950s and a huge market was created for them in popular music and fashionable clothing. Although rock 'n' roll was in its infancy, there were significant fears about the rise in **juvenile delinquency**, fuelled in part by movies that showed youthful rebellion. Despite this, most young people in this period were as conservative as their parents.

> **Note it down**
>
> Draw a spider diagram (see page x) to show cultural changes in the years 1945–55. Label four 'legs' of the spider as follows:
> - Hollywood and the Cold War
> - The growing power of TV
> - Stereotyping in the media
> - The origins of teenage culture.
>
> At the end of the legs, note the impact of each issue. Why is each one important in terms of cultural change?

Hollywood and the Cold War

With Hollywood under investigation by the HUAC, many of its producers sought to demonstrate their credentials as patriotic Americans by both firing those suspected of disloyalty and turning out a raft of movies that alerted audiences to the realities of the Cold War. Of course, many of these were simply thrillers in which the villains shifted from gangsters or Nazis to communist agents. Hence, in Edward Ludwig's *Big Jim McLain* (1952) John Wayne is a HUAC investigator in Hawaii. Playing fast with the reality that they could be and often were jailed for refusing to do so, the villains escape justice by refusing to testify. Movies such as Robert Stevenson's *I Married a Communist* (1950) showed how a former communist's past could catch up with him, while Leo McCarey's *My Son John* (1952) depicted the anguish of parents who suspect their son is a communist spy.

While a plethora of movies showed the Cold War at home through depicting the infiltration of communist agents, others actually depicted Cold War events, such as George Seaton's *The Big Lift* (1950), which dealt with the Berlin Airlift, and Lewis Milestone's *Pork Chop Hill* (1959), about the reality of fighting the Korean War.

Not all movies about the Cold War dealt with the actual events. The 1950s saw a series of science-fiction movies that many critics have seen as thinly disguised warnings of the communist menace. In many of these movies, aliens invade Earth. They lack any individuality; they are all robotic (often literally) and homogeneous – like the American view of communists. Possibly the most frightening was Don Siegel's *Invasion of the Body Snatchers* (1956), in which aliens take over the bodies of people and are all devoid of any individuality or personality. The final scene, in which the hero races onto a busy highway desperately trying to warn people as lorries scream past, had to be reshot to give a more optimistic ending where the hero tells his story in hospital, and his warning is heeded after giant seed pods are discovered.

Hollywood also made epic religious movies during this period, such as Mervyn Leroy's *Quo Vadis* (1951) and Henry Koster's *The Robe* (1953). Some critics have seen these as reassurance that the USA clung to religious belief, unlike godless communists. The Christian evangelist Bill Graham asserted that atheism was masterminded by communists.

To an extent, the Cold War simply provided thrillers with differently labelled villains, and many were unclear as to what secrets were stolen or at threat. They did, however, tap into real fears. Americans felt vulnerable to attack from this alien ideology whose proponents could infiltrate as spies and agents and whose forces had weapons that could threaten their country for the first time.

The growing power of television

In 1954 water officials in the city of Toledo, Ohio began to investigate why there seemed to be huge upsurges in demand during random three-minute periods each evening.

They solved the mystery when they correlated the mass flushing of toilets with commercial breaks on TV. By this time television was a national phenomenon. The number of sets had risen from 60,000 in 1947 to 37 million by 1955; three million were sold in just the first six months of 1950. By 1956 Americans spent $15.6 billion on the sale and repair of TV sets. The TV was the lynchpin of the home. 1954 saw the arrival of TV dinners so the family need not waste precious viewing time eating around the table.

TV advertising

TV stations in the USA were, like radio, always commercial concerns and advertisers adapted to funding programming as readily as they had on radio, sponsoring programmes such as *The Colgate Comedy Hour* and broadcasting adverts in between programmes, often competing to make theirs the most memorable and entertaining. Some programmes could generate income themselves; when in 1955 Walt Disney launched his Davy Crockett series, it was accompanied by sales of $300,000 in tie-in merchandising – including the ubiquitous **fake coonskin caps**.

Popular TV

Popular programmes were viewed by millions. By 1960 it is estimated that TV was the favourite leisure activity of half the population. It is estimated, too, that half the population saw Mary Martin take to the air as Peter Pan in a 1955 spectacular. A regular audience of 50 million watched *I Love Lucy*. Comedienne Lucille Ball broke the stereotypical mould of passive females (see below), being both performer and producer. In 1953 she was awarded an $8 million contract. The irony was that *I Love Lucy* itself was about a dizzy blonde who created comic mayhem wherever she went. Many sitcoms celebrated the American family as the heart of the USA; *Leave It to Beaver,* for example, showed the boy Beaver learning that mum and dad were always right and that life for those outside a family group was uncertain and unpleasant. In this sense family values and the position of the sexes was always reinforced with mum as the homemaker and dad going out to work – such as *The Donna Reed Show*, in which housewife Donna always saved the day with her good sense and quiet manner. TV families, of course, tended to be white and **middle class**; there were few working-class or ethnic groups represented on prime-time TV. Women without husbands were generally seen as unhappy or desperate to find one.

Television became a huge factor in popular culture not only in the USA but throughout the world. Studios grew large and impressive, rivalling those of film, and major actors such as Loretta Young and Ray Milland were recruited to TV.

> **Source C** British film critic Kenneth Tynan visited Hollywood in May 1954. Here, he is writing for *Punch* magazine about the new television studios in Hollywood.
>
> Television City, erected in Hollywood by Columbia Broadcasting System at a cost of twelve million dollars. Shining ... of glass and gadgets, with removable walls and lifts which can carry elephant and mahout [*]. Official handout explains potency of building: 'St Peters in Rome, the Houses of Parliament, the White House in Washington and Radio City in New York are just a few of the public relations force and symbol that well designed buildings can become'. Impressed (why?) to note that Television City had four hundred and seventy five doors. What is more it can also serve as a giant fort and shelter to withstand gamma rays, heat radiation and concussion from a nuclear blast ... Even with all of Los Angeles plunged into darkness, the lights will still shine in Television City.
>
> [*] Mahout: person riding an elephant.
>
> What can you infer from Source C about Tynan's attitude to Television City?

Journalist and broadcaster Edward R. Morrow was concerned that if TV only entertained, it would indeed become the '**opiate of the masses**'. He showed the power of campaigning television with his hard-hitting *See It Now* documentary series. One of its successes was to force the reinstatement of a young USAAF lieutenant who had been told to resign his commission because certain members of his family had suspect political beliefs. It was Morrow, too, who helped expose Joseph McCarthy (see page 328) as a bully who had little evidence to back up his claims.

The stereotyping of women

TV programmes were not the only place where the stereotype of women as homemakers and mothers was created and developed. The media appeared to both create and develop this stereotype. Commentators cite the many periodicals aimed at women such as *Ladies' Home Journal* and *McCall's*, which were full of articles on cooking, fashion, homecare and how to keep your husband happy. Dr Spock, whose hugely influential books on childcare sold over a million every year throughout the 1950s, emphasised the need for a mother's presence and love. Adverts focussed on the woman as housewife and mother. As with TV, the image the media portrayed was usually of white and middle-class women; working-class and ethnic minority women did not feature significantly. Many women's magazines featured articles that emphasised the domestic role of women, although not all would go so far

> ### Women in work
> **Feminist** Betty Friedan conducted research into the subsequent careers of former students of the exclusive all-female Smith College in 1957 and found that 89 per cent were homemakers. However, we should remember that her well-educated, wealthy respondents were hardly typical of women in the USA. Despite the stereotype of women staying in the home, the percentage of women in the labour force did increase in the 1950s from 33.8 per cent in 1950 to 37.8 per cent by the end of the decade. Opportunities for jobs with career-advancement prospects had not noticeably increased. Unions did not generally favour women in the workforce – although they did support a campaign for better working conditions for waitresses.
>
> The biggest increase of women in work was among those who were married – from 36 per cent in 1940 to 60 per cent by 1960. This may have been necessary to help make ends meet. Many commentators have shown that the consumer culture always left people wanting more – the latest model, the newest gadget – and advertising was so persuasive that luxury items became in many people's view necessities. Writing in 1996, historian James T. Patterson concluded that many women in the 1950s sought jobs more than careers, in order to supplement the family income. Clearly, however, this does not negate the effort many were prepared to make to rise in the profession of their choice.

as Mrs Dale Carnegie who asserted in *McCall's* magazine in 1954 that there is 'simply no room for split-level thinking – or doing – when Mr and Mrs set their sights on a happy home, a host of friends and a bright future through success in HIS job.'

The reality behind the stereotype may be more complex. While periodicals may have promoted a particular message, we have little idea how effectively they informed actual relationships. Writing in 2000, historian Nancy Walker showed that even the pervasive view of the periodicals is simplistic. *Ladies' Home Journal*, for example, ran a series of articles entitled 'How America Lives' which did show the wide ethnic and class mix. She argues that the periodicals reflected the complexities of life more than they reinforced stereotypes. The magazine *Redbook*, for example, ran a $500 prize competition in 1960 inviting readers to write on 'Why You Feel Trapped'. They received 24,000 entries. While many women may have accepted a largely domestic role, many others either did not or felt frustrated and unfulfilled by it; the seeds were being sown here for the women's liberation movement of the 1960s.

Hollywood and women

Hollywood was ambivalent about how women were depicted in movies. Often they were shown as passive and vulnerable, waiting for the lantern-jawed hero to rescue them from danger, especially in 'B' movies, but also in westerns such as John Farrow's *Hondo* (1953). In some movies they concluded that the role of homemaker and mother was the most fulfilling for women, such as Charles Walters' *The Tender Trap* (1955). Some movies showed wilful women being tamed – notoriously in Joshua Logan's *Bus Stop* (1956), in which Marilyn Monroe is roped like a steer by her cowboy suitor. However, many movies featured strong women who were protagonists. John Ford often included fiery female leads as in *The Quiet Man* (1952) and showed great respect for the **pioneer women** who often feature as supporting characters in his westerns. Actresses such as Elizabeth Taylor, Bette Davis and Joan Crawford continued to play women who were assertive and dominant. Taylor, in fact, enjoyed some of the most assertive roles of her career in George Stevens' *Giant* (1956) and Richard Brooks' *Cat on a Hot Tin Roof* (1958). Alfred Hitchcock created memorable female characters who aspired to more than domesticity.

Overall, it would be misleading to accept the passive stereotype. Much of the media showed positive role models for women, although there was little obvious signs of the nascent feminism that would come to the fore in the 1960s. The media, moreover, was even more ready to produce stereotypes of black Americans.

The stereotyping of black Americans

Black Americans had long faced crude stereotyping in the popular media, from the warm-hearted but simple 'Mammy' figure to the comic buffoon, portrayed most notoriously by Stepin Fetchit, 'the laziest man in the world'. In *Beulah*, a TV series featuring a 'Mammy' character as a loyal servant, much of the comedy was derived from her efforts to get the foolish but cunning Bill to marry her. Black Americans rarely featured in movies or TV programmes unless the script called for a caricature or a servant. This stereotyping may have shifted slightly in the 1950s but it was more likely to have been replaced by invisibility – black Americans simply didn't appear. After the cancellation of *Amos 'n' Andy*, the next black-American sitcom, *Julia*, didn't appear until 1967.

The NAACP (see page 338) had fought against televising the *Amos 'n' Andy* show. It depicted black Americans as variously indolent, stupid and/or cunning. It arranged a boycott of its sponsor, Blatz Beer, and the producers (CBS) cancelled production in 1952 – although reruns still regularly appeared on other stations, and the series remained on the radio until 1960. The NAACP also succeeded in having 'blackface' scenes cut from TV showings of movies such as Busby Berkeley's *Babes in Arms* (1939).

The stereotypes reflected and perpetuated by the media were far-reaching, with black Americans often shown a lack of respect, especially in the South – adult males being called 'boy' and women 'auntie', and being expected to step out of the way on a crowded sidewalk or stand on public transport while whites sat. The only area in which they had respect appeared to be music, with their white compatriots listening avidly to blues and jazz. In the following decade they were to apply the rhythms to a new hybrid which was to capture the imagination of the young of all ethnic groups: rock 'n' roll.

The origins of teenage culture

Most of the population was young. In 1950, 41.6 per cent of the population was under 24 and, in 1960, 44.5 per cent. Teenagers were increasingly seen as a discrete group with common interests and concerns. As a market developed to cater for their interests, they seemed to look and act differently to their parents. There were increasing concerns that young people were out of control. Evidence was presented of gang fights, teenage drunkenness and disrespectful behaviour toward adults. In 1956 the number of teenage murders in New York rose by 26 per cent over the previous year.

So-called experts from various academic disciplines, particularly psychology, argued that aberrant behaviour could be cured once the problem was recognised. They offered various explanations of delinquency:

- In 1954 psychologist Frederic Wertham published *The Seduction of the Innocent*, which exposed the violence and brutality of comic books that sold in their millions. After this, in fact, the content of comics was moderated but not before 13 states passed laws regulating their publication, distribution and sale.
- Some experts offered the explanation of poor role models, particularly the depiction of rebellious behaviour in movies such as László Benedek's *The Wild One* (1954) and Nicholas Ray's *Rebel Without A Cause* (1955). The former is about a motorcycle gang who terrorise a sleepy town. When asked what he is rebelling against, their leader, played by Marlon Brando, answers, 'What you got?' It was argued that there was a link between violence and rebellion on the screen and in real life.
- Others argued there were too many 'latchkey kids' whose parents were always out at work so exercised little control. The Senate was so concerned that it held hearings on delinquent behaviour throughout the decade.

The reality of teenage behaviour

However, others were not so concerned. Los Angeles police showed that less than one teenage gang in ten actually indulged in violent behaviour. With less than 1 per cent nationally of teenagers ever held up on criminal charges in 1956, Benjamin Fine's 1955 prediction that 1 million teenagers would go through the courts that year was a wild exaggeration.

While the rock 'n' roll music that was to be associated with youth rebellion was beginning at this time, most teenagers still listened to the placid, sedate music of crooners such as Pat Boone, Perry Como and Rosemary Clooney. One of the biggest hit records of 1953 was Patti Page singing 'How Much is that Doggie in the Window?' The first 'cross-over' record where white groups copied the black-American rhythm-and-blues style that became rock 'n' roll was The Crew Cuts singing 'Sh'boom'. The first smash hit was Bill Haley & His Comets' 'Rock Around the Clock', which had appeared in Richard Brooks' film *The Blackboard Jungle* (1955), and went on to sell 16 million copies. Elvis Presley and his acolytes did not come into prominence until later in the decade.

While the year 1951 saw the publication of one of the great novels of teenage angst, J.D. Salinger's *The Catcher in the Rye*, any teenage rebelliousness was for the most part short-lived. Teenagers in the first half of the 1950s may have had more money than their predecessors – the teenage market was reported to be worth $10 billion per year by 1955 – but most were just as conservative and deferential. It should be remembered, too, that one-half of male teenagers during the course of the 1950s were drafted into the armed forces, where discipline and traditional values were vigorously reinforced. Meanwhile, the average age of marriage, young in itself in 1940 at 21.5 years, reduced even lower to 20.3 years; comparatively young women became housewives and mothers. While teenage rebellion was to become a much wider phenomenon as the decade progressed, there were in the early years of the 1950s few real signs of its stirrings – certainly not in middle-class white America.

Conclusion: Culture change

Hollywood stoked fears of communist infiltration with its Cold War movies. More Americans, however, stayed at home to watch TV where commercials depicted an ideal lifestyle with plentiful goods and convenience foods. Women were often stereotyped in the media as homemakers and mothers, although the cinema showed more assertive characters. When they were not shown as stereotypes, black Americans barely appeared at all – especially not on TV. The message was that life was good for the white middle-class nuclear family that made up the backbone of the USA. There were fears about a rise in juvenile delinquency as the number of young people grew but this was mostly unwarranted.

Work together

Imagine you are faced with a Section B exam-style question as follows:

'American society in the 1950s was based on white middle-class nuclear families who lived in the suburbs.' How far do you agree with this statement?

1. Working in pairs, one of you should prepare a response that agrees with the statement and the other one that disagrees with it. Discuss your findings and agree on the information a balanced answer should contain.
2. Each of you should now write out the answer, including a valid judgement at the end based on the evidence you have deployed. Read each other's answers. How similar are they?
3. Each of you should mark your response using the assessment criteria (please refer to the full mark scheme on the Edexcel website), and give reasons for your score using level descriptors and marks.

4 The changing status of minorities

Ethnic minority groups such as Native, Hispanic and black Americans faced differing challenges in the post-war era. They had all contributed fully to the war effort and greater integration in war industries and the armed forces made more people sympathetic to their problems. However, the problems of discrimination remained and it would take later periods to address them fully.

Note it down

Use a spider diagram to note down how the lives of the different ethnic groups changed. At the end of each leg, draw a box in which you note down the factors which remained the same. Note that these may not have been explicitly mentioned in the text. You may need to infer from the text what they were.

Native Americans

During the war, 25,000 Native American served in the armed forces and a further 40,000 worked in war production. This meant many left the **reservations** to live in the same way as other groups in the cities and production centres. Meanwhile, there were concerns that the reservations were no longer viable, that too many Native Americans were living in poverty and that this was no longer acceptable in a wealthy society. Indian Commissioner John Collier had suggested as early as 1941 that reservation life would not be able to accommodate returning servicemen and their families in adequate living standards. The following year he began to hint at a return to **assimilation** (see page 265).

Termination

In 1944 the Indian Claims Commission was set up to offer financial compensation to Native Americans for claims for lost lands – but not to return the lands themselves. The idea was to compensate Native Americans for past exploitation as a prelude to their taking their place as American citizens. As President Truman said, 'With the final settlement of all outstanding claims which this measure ensures, Indians can take their place without special handicaps or special advantages in the economic life of our nation and share fully in its progress.'

However, it was under the administration of President Eisenhower that termination really developed apace. In August 1953 a House Concurrent Resolution, Number 108, announced the termination policy: that the reservations should be broken up and Native Americans encouraged to move to urban areas to live like other American citizens. Native Americans weren't consulted. The idea was effectively that the federal government would absolve itself of any responsibility for Native Americans as a separate group. Their lands would be sold off and the profits distributed among tribal members who would go to urban areas to find work and live as normal US citizens.

Termination began with the sale of valuable lands belonging to the Menominee and Klamath tribes in Wisconsin and Oregon respectively. The whole policy of termination was a disaster from the start. It was a case of the federal government ridding itself of its responsibilities in an attempt to save money, of cutting Native Americans loose without any real effort to acclimatise them to urban life. Many who left the reservations drifted into unemployment and alcoholism and gradually began to move back. By 1960 only 13,000 out of 400,000 Native Americans had moved permanently and only 3 per cent of reservation land had been lost. The policy was abandoned but it left a lasting ill-feeling which would develop in the 1960s into Red Power and more militant Native American action. Hispanics, too, were to develop more militant strategies to combat exploitation in the 1960s, but the 1950s saw a more passive stance.

Hispanic Americans

The bracero programme of contract labour (see page 307) continued until 1964. Possibly as many as 200,000 entered the USA each year between 1950 and 1954. There were plentiful opportunities in the fruit-producing areas of the Southwest where the farmers could hardly meet the demand from increasingly opulent consumers who saw fruit and fruit products no longer as a luxury but as everyday dietary items. Increasing contact between braceros and their compatriots in Mexico saw greater awareness about conditions in the USA and employment opportunities. This led to a huge legal immigration – as many as 219,000 during the 1950s. Illegal immigration must be added to this figure. Employers often preferred to take on illegals because they could avoid red tape and having to meet minimum working standards and wages – although illegal immigrants could still earn ten times as much as they would for the same work in Mexico. As many as 500,000 crossed the border illegally in 1951 alone.

Conditions for legal and illegal workers often remained grim. Hispanic Americans faced discrimination at work and segregation at home. It is ironic that this came at a time when many towns in the Southwest were rediscovering their Hispanic-American past and restoring Hispanic architecture, enjoying its cuisine and applauding its culture and traditions.

Black Americans

The post-war federal governments recognised that change must come in terms of **civil rights** but this was never a priority. Some factors, such as the need to keep the support of Southern **Democrats**, sometimes overrode it. President Truman (1945–52) genuinely wanted to promote equal rights, but his Republican successor Eisenhower (1952–61) was less enthusiastic. He believed it was a task for state and local governments. We will return to the significance of this reluctance when considering the crucial *Brown* v. *Topeka* case (see page 339).

Truman's presidency

Harry S. Truman was the first president since Lincoln to make a significant contribution to the development of civil rights. In September 1946 Truman set up the Civil Rights Committee to investigate racial abuse. In 1947 it published a report, 'To Secure These Rights', which stated bluntly that the USA couldn't claim to lead the free world while black Americans were treated so unequally. It called for laws to prevent **lynching**, the abolition of the **poll tax**, and the FEPC (see page 304) to be made a permanent fixture.

Unfortunately, a coalition of 20 Southern Democrats and 15 Republicans blocked every civil rights measure that was introduced into the Senate – for example, antilynching bills. They often did this by use of the **filibuster**, talking and talking until the bill had run out of time to be considered. One Senator from Alabama summed up their views very crudely: 'I'd rather die fighting for **states' rights** than live on in Truman Boulevard in nigger heaven.' Often these conservatives justified their opposition either by saying that they were upholding states' rights and the issue of race was actually irrelevant, or equating civil rights with communism. Most historians agree that their opposition was fundamentally a result of racism.

The desegregation of the armed forces

One measure that was successfully enacted was Executive Order 9981, passed by Truman in July 1948 to desegregate the armed forces entirely and guarantee fair employment opportunities in the civil service. A Fair Employment Board was set up to replace the FEPC (see page 304), but its impact suffered from underfunding.

While senior military personnel feared the impact of desegregation, it went extremely well. Indeed, by 1950,

Reasons for the progress of the civil rights movement

There were various reasons why civil rights were advanced in the post-war period:

- The NAACP (see below) and the National Urban League both grew dramatically, drawing support from people of all ethnic groups. The number of NAACP local groups increased tenfold during the interwar period and by 1946 they had 600,000 members.
- There was more awareness of the value of black-American culture as a result of the Harlem Renaissance and the popularity of jazz and blues music (see page 335).
- Increasingly, Americans saw the incongruity of racial inequality in a country that promoted freedom and equality of opportunity. This was particularly apposite in the post-war period. The USA had fought against the most racist regime of modern times, and supported decolonisation throughout the world. Communist regimes, moreover, promoted racial equality and could easily criticise the USA for the lack of it. Racial inequality, therefore, made the USA vulnerable to criticism and lacking credibility in the wider world.
- The migration of black Americans away from the South had brought more inter-racial contact, which overall tended to overcome prejudices and ignorance. Politically, moreover, black Americans tended to vote Democrat. This meant the party, outside the South, needed to support civil rights to maintain this support.
- There was a growing black American middle class, particularly in the urban centres, who were voluble and articulate.

the Navy and Air Force were completely integrated. The Army followed during the Korean War, initially where necessity demanded it through the amount of casualties. Even the military training camps in the South were integrated without significant issues. The successful desegregation of the armed forces gave hope for the future.

Eisenhower's presidency

President Eisenhower was less committed to desegregation, although, as we shall see, it became a more significant issue during his administration (see page 341). Eisenhower maintained that legislation couldn't change people's hearts so passing laws to stop desegregation wouldn't work. However, having said this, he was no racist.

Eisenhower's major achievement in terms of civil rights was to facilitate desegregation in Washington DC. Geographically it was a Southern city governed during the 1950s by Congress but with largely segregated facilities. Eisenhower passed Executive Orders desegregating government-run shipyards and veterans' hospitals and tried to encourage integration of schools in the capital, particularly after the landmark *Brown* v. *Topeka* case ruled that schools should not be segregated (see page 339). The city itself was desegregated as the 1950s progressed.

The growth of the NAACP

The NAACP was founded in 1909 to promote the cause of racial equality and in particular to use the law courts to fight for racial justice. While it is most famous in its early years for its campaign against lynching, the NAACP worked in many arenas including the promotion of political rights and equal opportunities in education. As early as 1910, for example, NAACP lawyers successfully sued the state of Oklahoma to make it abolish the 'grandfather clause' it deployed to ensure only whites could vote, while in the post-war period, in 1946, it succeeded in persuading the Supreme Court to rule that transport that crossed state boundaries should not have segregated facilities.

The NAACP and schools

The NAACP realised early on that the quality of schools was crucial to the promotion of equality of opportunity. The 1896 *Plessey* v. *Ferguson* case had allowed segregation and emphasised that facilities must be separate but equal. However, educational facilities in the South were glaringly unequal. In 1930 the NAACP commissioned the Margold Report to investigate the ruling. It reported in 1933. It argued that *Plessey* v. *Ferguson* had been imprecise, poorly thought out and vaguely written. The NAACP sent out researchers to investigate how schools in the South were unequal. Their evidence was stark. The state of South Carolina spent three times more on white schools than black-American schools and 100 times more on school transport. Mississippi spent four and a half times more on white education. Black-American schools were often tumbledown shack-like buildings without facilities. School materials were often dog-eared books that had already served their useful life in white schools. Black-American teachers were usually paid considerably less than their white counterparts. No wonder, then, that in 1946 one-quarter of black Americans in the South were functionally illiterate.

In challenging the separate but equal ruling in education, the NAACP knew it would have to fight a long and difficult battle, but it seemed best to start with higher education. States could hardly argue a case that they provided separate but equal facilities in this sphere when they hardly provided any facilities at all. Within the South no black-American institution could offer PhD study and only two offered any medical education. Any Southern black American wanting to study law, for example, had to leave their state to do so. As early as 1935, the NAACP challenged the decision in Maryland to send a black-American student, Donald Gaines Murray, to train outside the state. This was because the qualification he was awarded elsewhere would not allow him to practise law in Maryland, his home state. It won the case and Murray trained in Maryland. However, Maryland was not in the **Deep South** and rulings there would be more problematic.

In June 1950, NAACP lawyers won two crucial Supreme Court rulings:

- *McLaurin* v. *Oklahoma*: Oklahoma could not maintain separate facilities within its graduate school of education. Prior to this ruling, the school had insisted black-American students be separated in the classrooms, library and canteens. This, it was ruled, disadvantaged them from studying properly.

- *Sweatt* v. *Painter*: The Court ruled that Texas could not offer a separate law school for black Americans that was patently unequal to the ones for white students – it comprised three basement rooms and part-time teachers. Law schools for white Americans were attached to universities and enjoyed full university facilities.

These successes emboldened the NAACP to move on to the question of public schools. Its lawyers wanted to use different cases and different situations to show that separate schools could not be equal.

Brown v. Topeka Board of Education

The NAACP sought people who were prepared to bring cases against inequalities in education. The evidence was manifest: black-American children having to walk miles to poorly resourced schools while schools for whites nearby with better facilities had spare places, the unequal resourcing, curricular limitations and so on. However, it took a brave person to protest. While the NAACP amassed its evidence, would-be plaintiffs were attacked, dismissed from their jobs, had their houses burned and were forced out of their state.

The NAACP decided, of all their cases, to lead with *Brown* v. *Topeka*. Topeka was a town in Kansas. Brown was Reverend Oliver Brown whose seven-year-old daughter Linda had to cross railroad tracks and wait for a bus to get to school on the other side of town while a good white school nearby had plenty of spaces.

The Supreme Court had a new Chief Justice, Earl Warren, who was sympathetic to issues of civil rights. On Monday 17 May 1954 the Court ruled that in the question of education, the notion of 'separate but equal' had no place. This was a monumental decision. Some called it a second American Revolution. Others referred to it as 'Black Monday'. Warren said that, for students, 'segregation' generates a feeling of inferiority 'as to their status in the community that may affect their hearts and minds in a way unlikely ever to be undone'.

The impact of the ruling

Many commentators were wildly optimistic about the ruling, believing it would quickly end segregation in schools. The NAACP chief counsel, Thurgood Marshall, said all

Charlie Houston and the NAACP lawyers

Charlie Houston was born into a wealthy black-American family and became a lawyer after studying at Harvard University School of Law. He knew, however, that this route was not open to most of his compatriots. Many black Americans studied part-time at Howard University, the largest black-American college in the USA. Houston joined this college, becoming vice-dean in 1929. He sought to create a cadre of black-American lawyers who would fight for civil rights and racial equality but knew this could not be achieved through part-time study while maintaining what was often a menial and taxing job to finance it. He therefore abolished part-time study, and insisted his students study full-time, financed by their previous employment. Houston insisted on high standards – some of his students nicknamed him 'Cement Pants' – but he drove himself relentlessly too, travelling the South, for example, to find evidence of inequalities in education. Houston became a full-time counsel to the NAACP in 1935 but by this time he had trained a cohort of excellent lawyers who would both carry the fight for equality through the courts – including Thurgood Marshall, who led the team on *Brown* v. *Topeka* – and train future generations of black-American lawyers.

schools would be desegregated within five years. Others were critical. Some, such as Senator James Eastland of Mississippi, predictably said that communists were behind it. Other critics took solace from the vagueness of the ruling. It did not, for example, address what schools should teach or do. It did not set a deadline. Even when it turned to implementation in May 1955, having given the states a year to prepare, the Supreme Court forbore to implement any deadlines, recognising the difficulties involved. It merely placed the responsibility for implementation on local education authorities within a reasonable time. There were no sanctions for non-implementation. Southern politicians saw this as green light to do nothing. Lieutenant Governor Ernest Vandiver of Georgia said, 'a reasonable time could be one year or two hundred'.

In the event **border states** tended to implement the ruling and states in the Deep South didn't. By the school year 1956–57, 723 school districts were desegregated, involving 300,000 black-American schoolchildren, but 240,000 remained in entirely segregated schools – mainly in the eight states of Alabama, Florida, Georgia, Mississippi, Louisiana, North and South Carolina and Virginia. Most of these states had penalties for any district that did begin desegregation procedures. All followed the lead of Alabama whose legislators declared the *Brown* v. *Topeka* ruling 'null, void and of no effect'. Attitudes were hardening, moreover, and moderate Southern politicians were either having to become more conservative or give way to more extreme colleagues in elections. In the meantime, white Southerners became more anxious to promote their own views on race relations in their region (see Source D).

Black American criticisms

Some black American commentators were critical of the ruling. Writer Zora Neale Hurston said it defamed black-American teachers because it assumed they were giving their students an inferior education, and put black American children at risk from racist bullies. She would have agreed with the President that legislation couldn't change hearts and minds. Others feared that black-American teachers, often inevitably less qualified than their white counterparts, would lose their jobs. Many did. Still others recognised that funding and the quality of educational provision was more important than racial integration. If poor black Americans and poor whites were lumped together in the same schools, they would still be failed in terms of educational provision.

President Eisenhower

President Eisenhower was ambivalent at best about the ruling. He said that it was the job of the Supreme Court to interpret the Constitution and as president he would

---

Source D 'White Dixie's View' from Lew Sadler, published in the *Chicago Defender,* 24 September 1955. Sadler was a white radio announcer from Mississippi.

I've seen many times the mother come home from work, and the kids would hold into the negro woman's legs letting themselves be dragged to the sidewalk and into the car before letting go, because they didn't want her to leave. Does that look like we are allergic to negroes?

The owner of this station [the radio station from which he was a broadcaster] has a brother who owns a [radio] station in Natchez, Miss.[issippi], and when something needs to be done here he will send for James, a Negro who works for the Natchez station, to come here, nearly 200 miles, rather than pull in someone else. Doesn't that sound like we are loyal to a good Negro?

When we need a baby sitter at home we have a Negro women come in rather than white girl. We do not lock up the baby's bank either. Does that sound like we do not trust the Negroes? ... So please do a favour to the South; while you are getting the news try to dig a little deeper and you may come up with something that will enlighten the North to the fact that we have a 'good neighbour' policy of our own.

How effective do you find Sadler's argument that black Americans are treated decently in the South?

Key debate

The significance of *Brown* v. *Topeka Board of Education*

While most historians agree on the importance of this ruling, they emphasise its significance in different ways. Writing in the 1950s and 1960s, C. Vann Woodward argued that the initial response in the South was to 'wait and see'. Panic set in when local courts began to enforce segregation as a result of cases brought by the NAACP. Forty years later, Cottrol, Diamond and Ware tended to agree in that the courts involved themselves in more aspects of life following the Supreme Court's lead. After *Brown* v. *Topeka*, courts were more willing to become involved in political disputes and controversial issues. James T. Patterson focussed somewhat on opposition to the decision and criticised Eisenhower for not giving more overt support. Patterson felt that had he done so, there would have been less opposition. Journalist Adam Cohen has argued that the impact was not on school desegregation as such but on the wider area of civil rights.

accept its decisions. Privately, however, he was furious and blamed Chief Justice Warren in particular. Eisenhower refused to believe legislation could be effective if it went against prevailing opinion – and he recognised that the whites in the South overwhelmingly opposed the ruling to the extent that it could only be implemented through compulsion. He believed the ruling had put back the case of civil rights by 15 years. Eisenhower's policy was initially to do as little as possible to enforce the ruling or antagonise Southern politicians – an attitude that matched that of many Americans. Civil rights simply didn't feature significantly in the presidential election campaigns of either party in 1956.

Integration in entertainment and sport

In the post-war period black Americans had to excel in their field to be accepted. In TV, black-American characters rarely appeared in movies unless the script demanded a stereotype or servant (see page 334). Attitudes were slowly changing, however, largely through the efforts of a few pathfinders.

Entertainment

Black-American music continued to be popular and jazz bands, led by people such as Count Basie, Louis Armstrong and Duke Ellington, seemed to cross the racial divide. Singers Lena Horne and Ella Fitzgerald enjoyed great success. Harry Belafonte was one of the few popular singers who also became significant in the movie industry and helped open the profession to more black Americans through his success. The actress Ruby Dee noted that when she first arrived in Hollywood in 1949, everyone was white, from actors to electricians.

As the 1950s progressed, some very talented black Americans such as Dee, Sidney Poitier and Dorothy Dandridge did feature in more movies but their numbers were few. Having said this, Hollywood was gradually moving beyond the stereotype found, for example, in the Uncle Remus character in Walt Disney's *Song of the South* (1946). Uncle Remus was a noble if simple character who featured in stories originally written in the late nineteenth century. Many black Americans found them patronising in the extreme – and Disney's depiction was faithful to the character in the stories. Some movies went beyond stereotypes such as Elia Kazan's *Pinky* (1949). Overall, however, film producers were reluctant to take risks because of pressure from the HUAC, which equated ideas of racial equality with communism, and declining audiences, due to the onset of TV. They preferred to play safe, not least because Southern audiences made up 20 per cent of cinema goers and would not have welcomed black American heroes.

Sport

In sport, black Americans were represented if they excelled. Hence, Ted Rhodes was the first black American golf player to compete in the US Open, the major US tournament, since John Shipper who had appeared in 1896. There would be no black Americans selected for the Master's Tournament until 1974. Similarly, tennis player Anthea Gibson would win both Wimbledon and the US Championship in 1957 but she had no black-American successor until Arthur Ashe in the 1960s. American football was integrated in 1946 with the first black American starter Bill Willis playing for Cleveland Browns. Other black American players included LA Rams star Woody Strode who subsequently went on to have an acting career. Jackie Robinson was the first major league black American baseball player having signed for Brooklyn Dodgers in 1946 and first performing before an audience of 27,000 (including 14,000 black Americans) the following year. Despite crude racism from opponents, he helped the Dodgers capture the national league pennant and was voted the league's most valuable player. While Chuck Cooper and Earl Lloyd made their basketball debuts in 1950, teams had unwritten quotas of a maximum of four black-American players. In boxing, Sugar Ray Robinson and Floyd Patterson were popular.

It must be emphasised that, particularly in team games, players were overwhelmingly white. Black Americans would be picked because of their overwhelming talent. These people may have been pioneers but the gates to equal opportunity were at best only very narrowly ajar.

The extent of change, 1955

While the prevailing mood in the South may have been 'wait and see' after the 1954 *Brown v. Topeka* ruling, attitudes were hardening. This may have been because local courts, respecting the Supreme Court ruling, were increasingly finding in favour of desegregation – even though judges were putting themselves at risk by doing so. By January 1956 they had upheld the ruling in 19 cases, demanding a prompt start to desegregation or overturning existing laws on segregation. The NAACP had upwards of 170 cases pending.

Southern school boards were finding various ingenious methods to oppose desegregation beyond the penalties already referred to. The most common was to give grants to private schools, which could continue to be segregated. Georgia and North Carolina gave grants to white students to attend private schools. As late as 1959 Prince Edward County, Virginia, did in fact close all its public schools, enabling its white children to attend private segregated ones.

Harry Belafonte, 1927

Harry Belafonte found fame as a singer in the early 1950s and his film-star looks brought him a host of admirers. His long-playing album *Calypso* of 1956 became the first to sell over 1 million copies. Comparatively few of its admiring listeners will have known that the calypso is a Caribbean form of protest against oppression and colonialism. After Hollywood authorities overturned their prohibition on mixed-race romantic plots in 1955, Belafonte went on to make Robert Rossen's *Island in the Sun* (1956), which featured a romance between his character and a white woman played by Joan Fontaine. Although the film was well-received, he was incensed to find all the scenes showing physical contact between him and Fontaine had been cut before release. Twenty per cent of film goers lived in the South and 298 counties throughout the USA still banned mixed-race marriage. The film was banned in Memphis, the legislature in South Carolina threatened a $5,000 fine for any cinema that showed it, and there were widespread protests in the Northern state of Minnesota where parents feared it would spark a rage for mixed-race parties. Fontaine herself received hate mail from all over the USA and feared for her future career.

Belafonte, meanwhile, opened the first black-American-run film company, Harbel Productions, which went on to make highly regarded movies showing black Americans in positive non-stereotypical lights, and recruited black Americans to be trained in all aspects of film production. He is probably the most influential figure in opening up the mainstream film industry to black Americans.

Some authorities passed 'public placement' laws which enabled officials to give racially biased tests to ensure white children went to the best schools. Some states delegated all educational powers to the local boards so every one of them would have to be sued individually for desegregation to take place. The state of Mississippi actually passed a law to make desegregation illegal. Most didn't need to take so drastic a step. By 1964 only 2 per cent of black Americans in the 11 Southern states went to fully integrated schools, and, where schools were integrated, few black-American teachers were allowed to work in them.

Deterioration in relations

The year 1955 saw a deterioration in race relations and violence grew. Of the 11 lynchings in the 1950s, eight took place in 1955. Some of the most horrific murders, including that of schoolboy Emmett Till, took place that year. In 1956, when Autherine Lucy attempted to enrol in the University of Alabama, a riot ensued and she was expelled for misconduct. A mob of 2,000 prevented the desegregation of a school in Clinton, Tennessee and order was only restored when the National Guard arrived in tanks.

These years saw an expansion of the **Ku Klux Klan** with branches in nine Southern states and possibly as many as 20,000 members. There was also an upsurge in thuggish violence from often poor whites. A more invidious reaction was the formation of Citizens' Councils.

Citizens' Councils

Citizens' Councils were groups of influential people, often businessmen and local politicians, who fought integration through economic muscle. Examples of their actions include refusing loans or business to those who supported desegregation. The first such Council was set up in Indianola, Mississippi in July 1954. By 1956 they claimed 500,000 members in 11 states. While officially eschewing violence, they privately condoned or even encouraged it. One of their claims was that the government had been taken over by communists. They supported the Southern Manifesto drawn up by politicians from the Southern states in Congress.

The Southern Manifesto

In March 1956, 22 Southern Senators and 82 of the 106 Southern representatives came up with the Southern Manifesto, which accused the Supreme Court of abusing its powers. It insisted the question of segregation was one of states' rights. It promised, moreover, to fight the decision.

Despite *Brown* v. *Topeka*, civil rights battles had a long way to go in 1955, and the opposition was bitterly entrenched. White Southerners may have been fighting a losing battle but they would fight it to the last.

Conclusion: The changing status of minorities

While the period seemed favourable to civil rights, the events of the early 1950s showed it would be a long battle. Truman favoured an end to segregation but his successor Eisenhower wasn't so keen because he foresaw the problems this would bring. The landmark *Brown* v. *Topeka* ruling outlawed segregation in schools but had no timetable for implementation and eventually prompted both legal and violent reactions.

It might be said that the early 1950s was a period of transition in that black-American role models were appearing in sport and entertainment, but, as with civil rights, there was a long way to go before they would be accepted as equal citizens.

Chapter summary

- The US economy grew significantly during the war and this prosperity continued afterwards.
- The GI Bill of Rights gave grants towards education and setting up businesses to 8 million veterans, who were also offered cheap mortgages.
- The rapid growth in car ownership helped fuel the movement to the suburbs; by 1960, 33 per cent of Americans lived in suburbs.
- The period saw a huge growth in consumerism and in the market for children's goods as a result of the massive 'baby boom'.
- It was the golden age of the nuclear family, which was shown in the media as the ideal lifestyle.
- The HUAC, set up to investigate communism in the USA, turned its attention to Hollywood and many different organisations after the war.
- Senator Joseph McCarthy sparked off a communist witch hunt when he asserted that the State Department had been infiltrated by communists.
- Spy scandals and the development of nuclear weapons within the USSR added to this hysteria.
- The Cold War mentality resulted in a massive development of defence and military spending as the USA increasingly feared nuclear attack.
- Hollywood embraced the Cold War mentality with a series of movies concerning the fight against communist infiltration and events of the Cold War.
- TV grew massively, paid for largely by sponsors and commercials, so advertising was very important.
- Women and black Americans faced stereotyping in the media, although Hollywood often depicted strong female characters.
- Teenagers formed a massively economically valuable culture but teenage rebellion tended to be short-lived in the post-war period.
- Various post-war factors such as changing international affairs and an emerging black-American middle class seemed to make the period favourable for developments in civil rights.
- The success of President Truman's desegregation of the armed forces prompted other measures, but a coalition of Southern Democrats and conservative Republicans in the Senate managed to defeat them all.
- The NAACP increasingly brought cases against discrimination in education and in 1950 the Supreme Court ruled that segregation in higher education should stop.
- In 1954, in a landmark case, *Brown v. Topeka Board of Education*, the Supreme Court ruled that the notion of 'separate but equal' had no place in educational provision.
- Southern states were slow to desegregate and by 1955 were actively opposing it both legally and illegally, often through the use of violence and intimidation.
- The period saw the emergence of several black-American role models in sport and entertainment, but black Americans were still not generally accepted except as stereotypes.
- The year 1955 saw a deterioration in race relations as whites in the South began in earnest their campaigns against desegregation.

Recommended reading

Bill Bryson, *The Life and Times of the Thunderbolt Kid* (Transworld Publishers, 2007). Funny and moving memoir about growing up in the USA in the 1950s.

Eric F. Goldman, *The Crucial Decade and After: America 1945–1960* (Vintage, 1960). Thorough and almost contemporary account of the period.

James T. Patterson, *Grand Expectations: The United States 1945–1974* (Oxford University Press, 1996), especially Chapters 1–6 and 9–13. Well-written and engaging text, accessible and thorough.

C. Vann Woodward, *The Strange Career of Jim Crow*, 3rd revised edition (Oxford University Press, 1974), especially Sections iv and v. The classic account of ethnic relations between black and white Americans in the South; still useful and relevant.

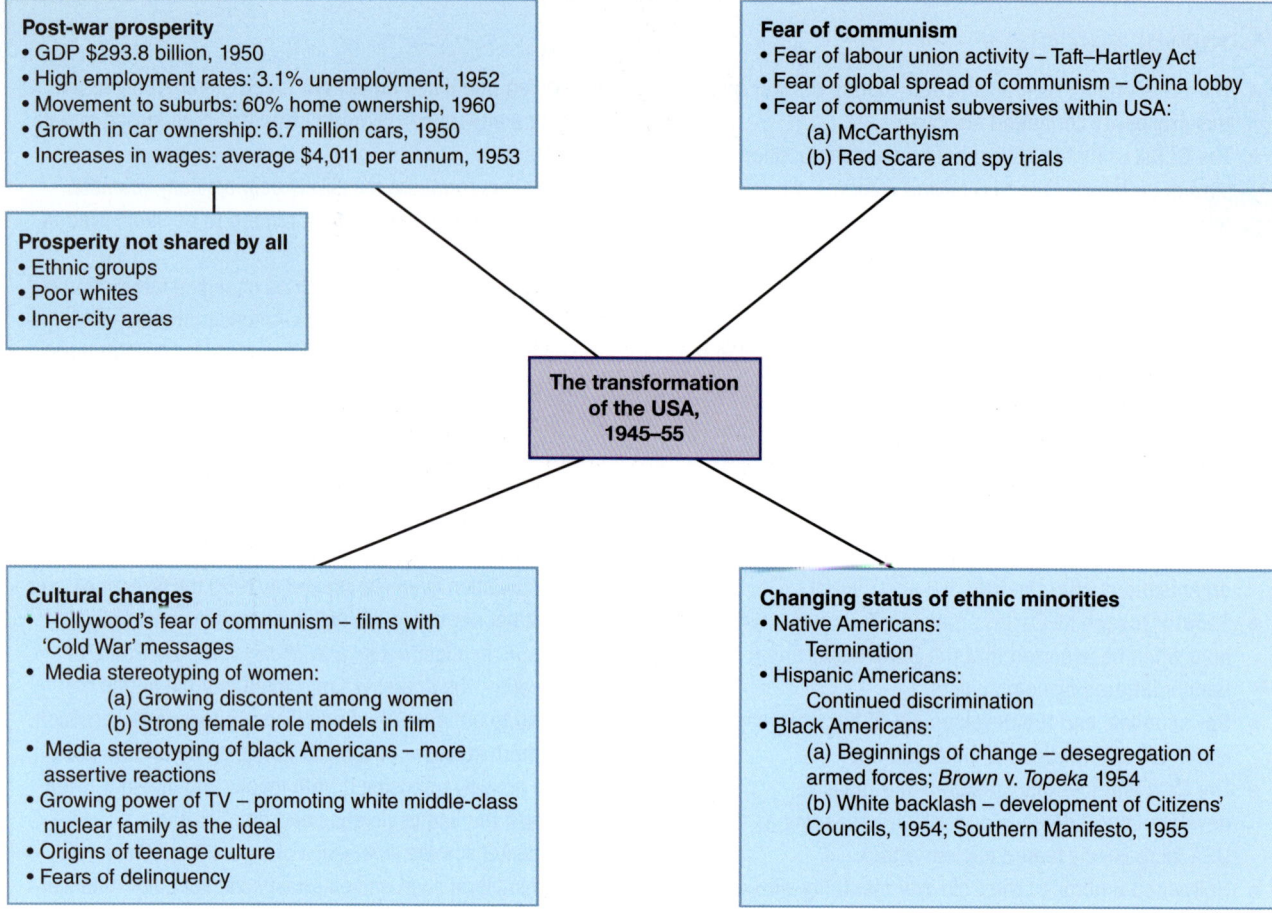

▲ Summary diagram: The transformation of the USA, 1945–55.

Work together

You have reached the end of this unit now. This is a good moment to check through your notes and make sure that they are complete. In pairs, go through the specification and this book. Create a table. In the first column, put the big topic – for example, 'Boom and crash, 1920–29'. In the second column, put the sections – for example, 'The economic boom of the 1920s'. Give the third column the heading 'Notes' and the final column 'Revision'. Now swap folders and complete the following tasks for your partner:

1 Put the notes in order.

2 In the 'Notes' column, tick if your partner has a good set of notes on a sub-topic. Leave it blank if they do not have notes or if they are incomplete. You can also use this column to record the type of notes – for example, class notes, index cards, independent reading.

3 Leave the 'Revision' column blank. As your partner revises, they can then use this column to tick off the sub-topics as they go.

Now swap folders again. This should highlight any areas of strength and weakness in your folders. You can fill in the gaps with further notes, and diversify your notes by doing more index cards, more reading or different types of note-taking. Then you can move on to revision!

Section B: Essay technique

Argument, counter-argument and resolution

The highest marks in Section B of the exam are available for sustained analysis. One way of achieving this is to write an essay that develops a clear argument, then a counter-argument and finally reaches a resolution. This approach is outlined in the activities that support Paper 1 (see page 129). This kind of structure is equally applicable to Paper 2 Section B.

Activity: Argument, counter-argument and resolution

Imagine you are answering the following question:

To what extent did the lives of black Americans change in the post-war period to 1955?

1 Read the question and work out what type of question it is (see page 262).
2 Make a plan that is appropriate to the specific question. Rather than simply picking four relevant factors, develop an argument, a counter-argument and a resolution to the argument.
3 Add three pieces of detail to support each aspect of your essay. Remember, use the detail that best supports the argument you are creating.
4 Write an introduction that sets out the essential aspects of your argument, counter-argument and resolution.
5 Now write a conclusion to the essay.
   - Start by asserting an overall judgement.
   - Support this by writing an evaluative summary of your argument, counter-argument and resolution.
   - Summarise your overall judgement in the final sentence.

Work together

Having written your introduction and conclusion, swap them with a partner. Consider:

1 Did you agree on what type of question you were dealing with? If not, discuss it and work out who was right.
2 Whose plan set out the most compelling overall argument?
3 Which introduction most clearly set out the key claims of the essay?
4 Which conclusion best summarised and evaluated the argument, counter-argument and resolution?
5 What can you learn from each other's work?

Use these questions to feed back to each other and improve your essay technique.

Question practice

1 Why was there so much support for anticommunism in the USA in the post-war period until 1955?
2 How far was the Cold War responsible for the Second Red Scare? **AS**
3 How far did the role and status of women change in the period 1941 to 1955? **AS**
4 How far did the need for affordable housing lead to the development of suburbs in the post-war period?

Section A: Essay technique

Evaluating the sources

Evaluating the sources is essential to doing well in the exam. It means working out how far the sources contain evidence that is useful to a historian doing a specific task.

There are different levels of evaluation, which are rewarded to different extents.

First, your source evaluation must be relevant to the question:

- Source evaluation that is not clearly linked to the question will be awarded marks in the lower levels.
- Sources evaluation that is clearly relevant to the question will be awarded marks in the higher levels.

Second, there is the issue of the criteria you use to evaluate the sources (see Table below).

Level 1	**No criteria** – evaluation is extremely superficial; it does not relate to any criteria.
Level 2	**Questionable criteria** – evaluation is based on criteria, but the criteria are invalid, simplistic or poorly understood.
Level 3	**Formulaic criteria** – evaluation is based on a discussion of the nature, origin and purpose (NOP) of the source.
Level 4/5	**Valid criteria** – at this level, responses will use criteria that reflect the kind of source and the kind of specific task that the question focusses on. In this sense the evaluation will be tailored to the question. At Level 4 the criteria will not be applied rigorously. At Level 5 the criteria will be applied rigorously.

Activity: AS-style questions

1. Why is Source 1 valuable to the historian for an enquiry into American attitudes to racial equality in the 1940s?
2. How much weight do you give the evidence of Source 2 for an enquiry into the status of black Americans in the southern states in the 1940s?

Imagine you are answering the following question:

> How far could the historian make use of Sources 1 and 2 together to investigate the role and status of black Americans in the post-war USA?

Source 1 Extract from *Inside America* by John Gunter, published in 1947. Gunter was a respected journalist with liberal views who had already written books about different areas of the world based on exhaustive research.

> One thing, it would seem, is certain. The days of treating Negroes like sheep are done with. They cannot be maintained indefinitely in a submerged position, because they themselves are now strong enough to contest this position, because the overwhelming bulk of white Americans are, in the last analysis, decent minded and because of education. It is impossible at this stage to halt education among Negroes. But the more you educate, the more you make inevitable a closer participation by Negroes in American life as a whole ... The United States must either terminate education among Negroes, an impossibility, or prepare to accept the inevitable consequences, that is, Negro equality under democracy.
>
> There will never be a 'solution' of the Negro problem satisfactory to everybody. But improvements, no matter how fitful, must continue if American democracy itself is to survive. Discrimination not only contaminates the Negro community; it contaminates the whites as well. There were people in the Middle Ages who thought that the bubonic plague would not spread to their own precious selves. But there is no immunity to certain types of disease. A cancer will destroy a body, unless cured.

Source 2 Extract from *Virginia: A Guide to the Old Dominion*, published in 1940 and compiled by workers of the Federal Writers' Project of the WPA in Virginia (see page 309). These were guide books written as part of the New Deal to record the history, culture, geography and topography of every state.

> In Virginia, as in the entire South, the children of unskilled workers do not go far in school, and uneducated Negroes find only unskilled occupations ... In Richmond, the largest center of Negro population in the state, all street cleaners, garbage collectors and elevator operators in municipal buildings are white...
>
> ... every city and town has a 'street' that serves as the social and business center of Negro life. Here Negroes from every walk of life congregate to purchase from Negro merchants, to ply their trades, to discuss the latest developments in Negro America, or simply to see who else is abroad. Here race pride is triumphant; drug stores, cafes, barber shops, pool rooms, grocery stores, theatres, beauty parlors and garages are operated by and for Negroes. To the uninitiated, the crowd is a group of idlers wasting time in meaningless banter. That banter is however the Negroes' escape from a day of labor in the white man's world. No matter how carefree the outward appearance of Negroes may be, behind their happy dispositions is the imprint of poverty, disease and suffering – birthmarks of a people living precariously, but of a people wholly Virginian.

Simplistic source analysis

Having read the sources, it is clear that both sources think the lives of black Americans need to be improved. Source 2 is more biased against them, however, because it talks about them being unskilled and seeming like a group of idlers. This is a low-level response because there is no indication of why the authors think their lives need to be improved, nor why Source 2 is biased. The evidence offered is very superficial, taking Source 2 at face value in terms of what it literally says without looking for the deeper meaning. You could say that Source 2 is unreliable because it is only about one area of the USA. However, these comments are based on questionable criteria. The source sheds light on a significant area of black American population and can be used to illustrate lifestyle there to which further evidence may be added as to its typicality.

Based on this, here are three basic tips:
- Avoid simply saying 'Source 1 is biased'. Statements like this are very simplistic and are therefore unlikely to get you a good mark.
- Avoid assuming that the only useful sources are eyewitness accounts.
- Avoid assuming that sources relating to only one area aren't very reliable.

Nature, origin and purpose

One way of evaluating the sources is to ask questions about their nature, origin and purpose:
- Nature: what type of source is this?
- Origin: when and where does the source come from?
- Purpose: why did the author write the source?

This approach is a good place to start. However, it can lead to formulaic responses, which are unlikely to gain top marks.

Evaluating sources in their own terms

The best way of evaluating Sources 1 and 2 is to try to understand them in their own terms. Reading the sources in the context of the time is a good way of evaluating their usefulness. By situating the sources in their context, we can argue the following:

- Source 1 argues in favour of improving the role and status of black Americans. It was written in the immediate post-war period when the USA had fought against racist regimes in Europe, when the armed forces were being desegregated and when the expectations of black Americans were rising. Gunter is saying that with the education of black Americans improving, so will their aspirations. Discriminations meanwhile, harms everyone. It has to end if the USA itself is to survive as a democracy.
- Source 2, meanwhile, gives a snapshot at a point in time to argue that, beneath the surface, the role and status of black Americans is unsatisfactory because of their everyday problems. It also emphasises the segregated nature of society with its accent on the phrase 'operated for and by Negroes'.
- Therefore, both sources are useful in the sense that they reflect the limitations in role and status of black Americans while showing in their different ways that the existing position is unsatisfactory.
- However, the two sources do not give the full picture. We do not hear the voices of black Americans themselves nor of whites who favoured segregation and the status quo, nor indeed those who believed that black Americans were happy with an inferior status or were racially inferior to whites.

TIPS:
- Use what you have already learned to help you understand the sources.
- The dates of the sources are often significant. Note, for example, the date of Gunter's book in the immediate post-war period when attitudes might be expected to change. Use what you already know to explore the possible significance of the dates, places and people mentioned in the sources.
- Use your knowledge to situate the sources in the wider debate.

Having read the advice on evaluating the sources on page 346, try to evaluate the sources below in order to formulate an answer to the following question. Use the steps in the activity on page 349 to help you do this.

> **How far could the historian make use of Sources 3 and 4 together to investigate the influence of Joseph McCarthy in the anticommunist witch hunt in the USA in the early 1950s?**

Source 3 Extract from the 'Enemies from Within' speech by Senator Joseph McCarthy in Wheeling, Virginia, 9 February 1950.

> [The growth of communism] indicates the swiftness of the tempo of Communist victories and American defeats in the Cold War. As one of our outstanding historical figures once said, 'When a great democracy is destroyed, it will not be from enemies from without, but rather because of enemies from within.' …
>
> The reason why we find ourselves in a position of impotency is not because our only powerful potential enemy has sent men to invade our shores … but rather because of the traitorous actions of those who have been treated so well by this Nation. It has not been the less fortunate, or members of minority groups who have been traitorous to this Nation, but rather those who have had all the benefits that the wealthiest Nation on earth has had to offer … the finest homes, the finest college education and the finest jobs in government we can give.
>
> This is glaringly true in the State Department. There the bright young men who are born with silver spoons in their mouths are the ones who have been most traitorous …
>
> I have here in my hand a list of 205 … a list of names that were made known to the Secretary of State as being members of the Communist Party and who nevertheless are still working and shaping policy in the State Department.

Source 4 Response by Joseph N. Welch, Attorney for the Armed Forces during McCarthy's investigation into the extent of communist infiltration into the armed forces. On 9 June 1954, McCarthy had accused one of Welch's team, lawyer Fred Fisher, of being a communist because as a young man he had been associated with a leftist organisation, the National Lawyers' Guild. Welch is talking directly to McCarthy.

> You won't need anything in the record when I have finished telling you this.
>
> Until this moment, Senator, I think I never really gauged your cruelty or your recklessness. Fred Fisher is a young man who went to the Harvard Law School and came into my firm and is starting what looks to be a brilliant career with us …
>
> Fred Fisher said, 'Mr. Welch, when I was in law school and for a period of months after, I belonged to the Lawyers' Guild,' as you have suggested, Senator. He went on to say, 'I am secretary of the Young Republicans League in Newton with the son of Massachusetts' Governor, and I have the respect and admiration of the 25 lawyers or so in Hale & Dorr.'
>
> I said, 'Fred, I just don't think I am going to ask you to work on the case. If I do, one of these days that will come out and go over national television and it will just hurt like the dickens.'
>
> So, Senator, I asked him to go back to Boston.
>
> Little did I dream you could be so reckless and cruel as to do an injury to that lad. It is true he is still with Hale & Dorr. It is true that he will continue to be with Hale & Dorr. It is, I regret to say, equally true that I fear he shall always bear a scar needlessly inflicted by you. If it were in my power to forgive you for your reckless cruelty, I would do so. I like to think I am a gentleman, but your forgiveness will have to come from someone other than me.

Activity: Evaluating the sources

1 Having read the sources, try to put them in context by answering the following questions:
   (a) What events were taking place in the USA and elsewhere in terms of the Red Scare at the time McCarthy made his speech in Source 3?
   (b) What debate are the sources contributing to?
   (c) What is the purpose of each author of the sources?
2 Now try to evaluate the usefulness of the sources by answering the following questions:
   (a) What do the sources argue about anticommunism in the USA?
   (b) How similar and different are their arguments?
   (c) How far do the sources reflect the full range of debate over the extent of anticommunism in the USA in the early 1950s?
3 Summarise the extent to which the sources are useful to the historian studying the extent of Senator Joseph McCarthy's influence in the anticommunist witch hunt in the USA in the early 1950s. Make sure you deal with the ways in which they are useful and the limits of their usefulness.

Work together

Having completed the activity 'Evaluating the sources', swap your answers with a partner. Consider:

1 How far did you agree on the context of the sources?
2 How far did you agree on the usefulness of the sources?
3 If you disagreed on the context or the usefulness, what was helpful in each other's approach?
4 Whose summary of the usefulness of the sources was better and why?

Use this discussion to make a note of three ways that you can improve your Section A technique.

Reaching an overall judgement

Having understood, contextualised and evaluated the sources, you should finish your essay with an overall judgement. Reaching a supported overall judgement is an important part of doing well in Section A. Your judgement in Section A is similar to the judgement that you should reach in the other sections of the exam (see page 92). However, in Section A, your judgement should be based on an evaluation of the evidence offered by the sources.

Your judgement should:
- clearly answer the question
- be supported by weighing the evidence of the sources.

In addition to this, the very best essays will distinguish between the levels of certainty of the different aspects of the conclusion.

Imagine you are answering the question on page 348.

Having already read the sources and evaluated them in their context as you did in the activity above, it is possible to reach the overall conclusion as shown on page 350. This is a high-level conclusion as it focusses on the question, reaches a supported judgement and discusses the different levels of certainty of the different claims it makes.

| This focusses directly on the question. | Both sources are useful to some extent in investigating the tactics of McCarthy in the anticommunist witch hunt. Both show his aggression and means of accusation. Both illustrate his assertions about traitors without any supporting evidence. Source 3 demonstrates his bluster, the way he uses an un-named public figure to give weight to his concerns that the USA is under threat from enemies within, and his anger that these traitors are from the wealthy classes. | Contextual knowledge is used to explore the sources' usefulness. |

The sources are used explicitly and together.

The extent to which the sources are useful as a description of McCarthy's tactics is weighed.

However, the bluster which may work to McCarthy's advantage in Source 3 works against him in Source 4. Welch is condemning McCarthy for his bullying tactics in naming Fred Fisher as a communist on live television. His words are intended to shame McCarthy as a bully lacking evidence to support his claims. Both sources show McCarthy lacks evidence to support his accusations. The fact that communism is spreading does not mean it has spread into the State Department as McCarthy asserts. Similarly, the fact that Fisher once joined a leftist organisation does not mean he is a communist. However, neither source really highlights other tactics beyond bluster. They do not, for example, show the research that McCarthy's team undertook or his collaboration with the FBI. Overall, the sources are useful in terms of what McCarthy said and how he said it but not for any wider tactics.

The limits of the sources are summarised.

The uses are also summarised, and a conclusion reached which is supported by the rest of the paragraph.

Work together

Conclusions are made up of a series of claims. A claim is a statement. In the example conclusion above:

1. Count the number of claims made in the conclusion.
2. Do you agree on the number of claims? If not, discuss your different views and try to resolve the disagreement.
3. The different claims deal with a series of issues that are not all certain. List the words and phrases used to describe the different degrees of certainty.
4. Did you both spot the same words and phrases?

Use the list and your discussion to make a note of how you could improve your writing.

Activity: AS-style questions

1. Why is Source 5 valuable to the historian for an enquiry into American attitudes to the role of women in the US in the 1950s?
2. How much weight do you give the evidence of Source 6 for an enquiry into sexual equality in the US in the 1950s?

Source 5 Extract from Betty Friedan, *The Feminine Mystique* (W.W. Norton & Co., 1963). *The Feminine Mystique* was a pioneering work on the dissatisfaction felt by many housewives in the 1950s.

> The problem lay buried, unspoken for many years in the minds of American women. It was a strange stirring, a scene of dissatisfaction, a yearning that women suffered in the middle of the twentieth century in the United States. Each suburban housewife struggled with it alone. As she made the beds, shopped for groceries, matched slipcover material, ate peanut butter sandwiches with her children, chauffered Cub Scouts and Brownies, lay beside her husband at night – she was afraid to ask of herself the silent question – 'Is this all?' ...
>
> They learnt that truly feminine women did not want careers, higher education, political rights – the independence and the opportunities that old-fashioned feminists had fought for. Some women in their forties and fifties still remembered painfully giving up those dreams but most of the younger women no longer even thought about them. A thousand expert voices applauded their femininity, their adjustments, their new maturity. All they had to do was devote their lives from earliest girlhood to finding a husband and bearing children.

Source 6 Extract from Harry Henderson, 'The Mass-Produced Suburbs: How People Live in America's Newest Towns', *Harper's Weekly*, November 1953. Henderson based his observations on extensive visits, observations and interviews in 1950s suburbs.

> The daily pattern of household life is governed by the husband's commuting schedule. It is entirely a woman's day because virtually every male commutes. Usually the men must leave between 7:00 and 8:00 A.M.; therefore they rise between 6:00 and 7:00 A.M. In most cases the wife rises with her husband, makes his breakfast while he shaves, and has a cup of coffee with him. Then she often returns to bed until the children get up. The husband is not likely to be back before 7:00 or 7:30 P.M. This leaves the woman alone all day to cope with the needs of the children, her house-keeping, and shopping. (Servants, needless to say, are unknown.) When the husband returns, he is generally tired, both from his work and his traveling. Often by the time the husband returns the children are ready for bed. Then he and his wife eat their supper and wash the dishes. By 10:00 P.M. most lights are out. For the women this is a long, monotonous daily [routine]. Generally the men, once home, do not want to leave. They want to 'relax' or 'improve the property' – putter around the lawn or shrubbery. However, the women want a 'change'. Thus, groups of women often go to the movies together.

Activity: Write your own conclusion

Imagine you are answering the following question:
How far could the historian make use of Sources 5 and 6 together to investigate the role and status of women in the USA in the 1950s?

1. Put the sources in context:
   (a) What is the significance of the dates of the sources?
   (b) What debate or debates are the sources contributing to?
   (c) How far do the sources agree on the role and status of women in the 1950s?
   (d) Why do you think each source was written?
2. Read the question again.
   (a) Next, write a series of bullet points outlining:
      - the aspects of the sources that are useful for answering the question
      - the aspects of the sources that are less useful.
   (b) Then produce a summary of the extent to which the sources provide useful evidence about the role and status of women.
   (c) Now write the conclusion, remembering:
      - You need to weigh the evidence, and therefore you should use words that help you to do that, such as 'clearly', 'however' and 'nonetheless'.
      - You should weigh the sources *together*, rather than separately. Make sure you use words and phrases that make it clear that this is what you are doing – for example, 'both sources' or 'neither source'.
      - You should try to specify how certain you are about your various concluding claims. Look at the example of a conclusion you have just read and try to use similar words and phrases to show which of your concluding claims are certain and which are less definite.

Work together

Having completed your conclusion, consider:

1. How far did you agree on the context of the sources?
2. How far did you agree on the usefulness of the sources?
3. Which conclusion most effectively weighed the evidence of the sources? How was this achieved?
4. Did both conclusions really consider the sources *together*? How could you improve this aspect of your writing?
5. Which conclusion most effectively expressed the different degrees of certainty? How was this achieved?
6. Which conclusion most effectively focussed on the question?

Paper 2
The USA, 1955–92: Conformity and challenge

The Big Picture

By the early twentieth century, the USA was one of the most prosperous and powerful nations in the world. It suffered a setback during the economic depression of the 1930s, but the New Deal policies of Democrat President Franklin Roosevelt (1933–45) helped to bring the country out of the slump. Previously, the federal government had played a minimal role in the lives of Americans, but Roosevelt greatly expanded government intervention in order to stimulate the economy and assist the poor. He introduced the idea that it was the government's responsibility to provide a welfare safety net for the less fortunate – a revolutionary idea in a nation that traditionally prided itself upon individualism.

Roosevelt also brought the country successfully through the Second World War. However, although the United States emerged from the war as the world's richest and most powerful nation, it faced problems:

- An acute state of tension and antagonism developed between the United States and the next most powerful nation, the Soviet Union. Their 50-year struggle became known as the Cold War.
- Around one-quarter of Americans lived in poverty. Many were non-whites such as black Americans, Native Americans and Hispanic Americans.
- The racism of the white majority was exemplified by the legal segregation of blacks and whites in the Southern states.

Eisenhower's presidency

This unit takes up the story of the United States in 1955 during the presidency of the Republican Dwight D. Eisenhower (1953–61). Eisenhower disliked Roosevelt's New Deal, but because he felt attempts to end the welfare safety net would constitute political suicide, he contented himself with a hands-off approach to domestic affairs. Most Americans seemed content with their reassuring president and an unprecedented affluence that was changing the face and nature of the nation. Those who could afford it moved to the suburbs, leaving the inner cities to impoverished black Americans. Affluent suburbanites were avid consumers who bought all the latest domestic technology that made domestic life easier and the latest cars so that they could travel to work, the shops or on the school run in comfort and style. Eisenhower recognised the importance of such mobility to Americans and promoted a new interstate highway system, alongside which service industries developed.

There was evidence of social change and challenge amid the conformity that characterised suburbia. Young Americans demonstrated rebelliousness primarily through their musical tastes, but the most challenging group was black Americans who, from 1956, gained great publicity for their discontent with Southern segregation.

Kennedy's presidency

In 1961, new president John F. Kennedy called on Americans to reject the stagnation of the Eisenhower years and embrace a 'New Frontier' in areas such as poverty, education and technology. Kennedy's Democratic Party traditionally preferred to focus on programmes to help the poor and the unemployed, but Kennedy's preoccupation with the Cold War limited his domestic achievements.

Johnson's presidency

The second chapter of this unit focusses on events during the presidency of Lyndon B. Johnson (1963–69). Those years were dominated by the protests of students, women and black Americans. Black protests against inequality in the South encouraged Congress to pass laws to end segregation and enable black people to vote. Johnson sought to create a 'Great Society' without poverty and with improved healthcare, housing and education for those who needed it. The mid-1960s were a high point of American liberalism, with a Democrat president and Congress combining to strengthen and enlarge the welfare safety net introduced by Roosevelt. However, concurrent with these unprecedented reforms, Johnson escalated the fight against communism in Vietnam that had been undertaken by the three previous presidents. Much of the student protest was directed against this war. By 1968, a conservative backlash developed; many Americans had grown tired of protests, disorder and Great Society programmes. Their votes carried the Republican Richard Nixon to the White House.

The Nixon, Ford and Carter administrations

The presidencies of Richard Nixon (1969–74), Gerald Ford (1974–77) and Jimmy Carter (1977–81) disillusioned the American public. Nixon was caught attempting a cover-up of the break-in to the Democratic offices in the Watergate building and was forced to resign. When Ford pardoned Nixon, disillusioned voters turned to the Democrat Jimmy Carter. Neither Nixon, Ford nor Carter found the answer to American economic problems, especially inflation. Families struggling with higher prices and less job security tended to blame their president, but external factors such as foreign oil producers raising their prices bore considerable responsibility. Popular dissatisfaction was reflected in decreased voter turnout and negative media coverage of politics. The United States seemed to be a nation in decline, divided by clashing interest groups such as black Americans, Native Americans, women and homosexuals, all demanding their rights.

Reagan's presidency

The fourth chapter looks at the apparent triumph of conservatism in the 1980s. The right-wing Republican President Ronald Reagan (1981–89) worked hard and quite successfully to decrease public acceptance of the Great Society and federal government interventionism. Backed by socially conservative Christians, Reagan criticised new and unwelcome practices such as legalised abortion and campaigns for gender and homosexual rights. However, conservatives could not reverse the social liberalism unleashed since the 1960s. The status of ethnic minorities and women continued to improve, although economic equality seemed impossible to attain. Many, but by no means all, Americans had become more tolerant and inclusive by 1992 and the younger generation remained a constant challenge to the dominant culture.

Key Topic 1 Affluence and conformity, 1955–63

Overview

The United States had emerged from the Second World War (1939–45) as by far the most powerful and wealthy nation in the world. In 1955 it provided the 'good life' for many, but not everyone was satisfied. Some Americans questioned the conformity and consumerism that had come to characterise American society. Others sought greater social, economic or political equality. To a certain extent, these differences were reflected in the presidencies of Eisenhower (1953–61) and Kennedy (1961–63). While Eisenhower appeared satisfied with the status quo, President Kennedy asked Americans to demonstrate greater idealism and activism.

The overarching theme of affluence and conformity is covered in four sections:
1. Urbanisation and affluence
2. Cultural conformity and challenge
3. The civil rights movement
4. Kennedy's New Frontier

TIMELINE

1955	Pennsylvania Levittown constructed
1955	7.9 million new cars manufactured
1955	Senate subcommittee on juvenile delinquency established
1956	The Montgomery bus boycott
1956	William Whyte's *The Organization Man* published
1956	The 'Howl' trial
1957	Vance Packard's *The Hidden Persuaders* and Jack Kerouac's *On the Road* published
1958	J.K. Galbraith's *The Affluent Society* published
1960	John F. Kennedy makes his New Frontier speech
1960	Television ownership reaches 90 per cent
1961	President Kennedy establishes the Peace Corps
1961	Congress funds the moon landing programme
1962	Congress rejects President Kennedy's health care for the elderly bill
1962	Rachel Carson's *Silent Spring* published
1963 April	The Birmingham campaign
1963 August	The March on Washington

1 Urbanisation and affluence

The period 1955–63 was one of unprecedented prosperity for most Americans. With larger homes, more labour-saving devices, more cars and higher salaries than any other people in the world, most Americans felt they lived in a land of opportunity where hard work would improve their standard of living and their social status.

The unprecedented affluence contributed to social and cultural changes such as the rapid growth of **suburbia**, the decline of the cities, the mass production of consumer goods and services, and the increasingly important role of advertising and mass communication in ensuring consumption of the goods that the nation produced. These elements combined to produce what is often characterised as a happily bland consensus, especially under President Eisenhower (1953–61), but there were problems.

Common concerns included:

- the nuclear threat from the **Soviet Union** (in anticipation of an attack, children practised 'duck and cover' under their school desks)
- conformity (critics said that American culture was excessively **homogenised**)
- **consumerism** (Americans led the world in the purchase of material goods such as cars, televisions and household gadgets)
- advertisements (the media and roadside areas were saturated with product messages)
- American youth (most adults felt the younger generation was less conformist and less well-behaved than previous generations)
- race relations (the inferior status of black Americans was particularly pronounced in the South)
- economic inequality (around one-third of Americans were poor and poverty was particularly prevalent among black Americans, **Hispanic Americans** and **Native Americans**).

Note it down

As you read this section, shape your notes into two columns (see the 1:2 method, page x). Put the names of places and people, dates and statistics in one column, and then say in the opposite column what each specific fact tells us about the expansion of the suburbs, the changing nature of cities, the growing ownership and use of cars, service industries and white-collar jobs, and consumerism and domestic technology. For example:

1950: 39.3 million cars	
1960: 73.8 million cars	Demonstrates growing ownership and use of cars

Growing ownership and use of cars

One of the most obvious signs of post-war American affluence was the increasing number of cars on the roads. The purchase of cars had slowed during the economic depression of the 1930s and during the Second World War, when factories geared production to war materiel. Cars were not cheap in 1955; working- and middle-class Americans tended to buy Chevrolets or Fords and they started at $1,300, which was around two-fifths of the average family income. However, with the post-war economic boom, people had more job security and more money to spend. Those who remembered the constraints of the Depression and war years liked to spend their money on new cars. In 1955 alone, 7.9 million new cars were manufactured.

Growing car ownership greatly changed the American lifestyle. Spacious new cars with automatic transmission (instead of gearboxes), equipped with power steering, powerful engines, radios, heaters and air conditioning gave an easy and luxurious drive, demonstrated one's status, and promised mobility and freedom. Long, multi-coloured and decorated with large quantities of chrome and ostentatious tail-fins, most were made in the United States by the Big Three – General Motors, Ford and Chrysler.

The Republican president, Dwight D. Eisenhower, was typically American in that he loved cars. Although Eisenhower disliked excessive federal government intervention in the lives of Americans, he initiated a great highway construction programme. His reasons included the following:

- Upon returning to the United States after the Second World War, Eisenhower described American roads as in 'shocking condition' compared to German autobahns.
- Fuelled by the nation's unprecedented prosperity, car ownership rocketed from 39.3 million in 1950 to 73.8 million in 1960. As Eisenhower told Congress in 1955, an interstate highway system was vital to handle the increased traffic.
- Most Americans agreed with Eisenhower when he said that more cars meant 'greater convenience … greater happiness, and greater standards of living'.

Persuaded by Eisenhower's arguments, Congress authorised the construction of 41,000 miles of interstate highways that opened up the continent to travel and changed American society and culture.

Dwight D. Eisenhower, 1890–1969

Dwight D. Eisenhower was a career soldier who masterminded the Normandy landings in the Second World War. Americans respected him for his wartime achievements, and responded to his genial personality, electing him as their president in 1952 and again in 1956.

He was for the most part a 'hands-off' president, more preoccupied by foreign than domestic policy. A moderate Republican, he did nothing to dismantle the Democrat Roosevelt's New Deal safety net for the elderly and the poor, although he disliked the federal government interventionism that Roosevelt and the New Deal had initiated. His opposition to such interventionism and his lack of empathy with black Americans made him reluctant to respond to black demands for greater equality.

Eisenhower thought it particularly important to balance the national budget. He feared that pressure generated by the military and by big business could lead the federal government to spend so much money on defence during the Cold War that the nation's finances would be destabilised and present a greater threat to the nation's security than communism. It was the Cold War that generated two of his most noteworthy domestic achievements. In 1957 the Soviets launched the first satellite into space, Sputnik. This seemed to demonstrate Soviet technological superiority and it aroused fear and jealousy in the United States. In 1958, Eisenhower responded with the establishment of the National Aeronautics and Space Administration (NASA) and the National Defense Education Act, which promoted the study of science in the United States in order that the nation should not fall behind the Soviets. Eisenhower's other great domestic achievement was the creation of the interstate highway system.

Automobiles and US society

Automobiles reflected and shaped US life and society between 1955 and 1963. They indicated social and ethnic status, gave young people and women a greater sense of freedom, created a new on-the-road culture that led to explosive growth in the service industries, and contributed to suburban growth and urban decline.

Social and ethnic status

The automobile helped reflect and define one's social status. Wealthy white men favoured the most expensive and spacious models such as Lincolns and Cadillacs, while middle- and working-class Americans usually bought Fords and Chevrolets. Cleaning the family car and polishing it with Simoniz car wax became an important ritual in the suburbs, reflecting the increasing level of disposable income and leisure time that middle-class families enjoyed in the 1950s.

The automobile sometimes defined ethnic status. For example, poorer Hispanic American drivers often bought cheap second-hand Chevys, while Cadillacs became a desirable status symbol for the black middle class in the 1960s.

Young people and women

Automobiles reflected and encouraged the desire of young people to gain independence and to escape from parental control. Cars became an important part of dating; the 1953 Kinsey sex survey found that young people had almost as much sex in automobiles as they did in their homes. Young men expressed their individuality by customising their cars in order to emphasise speed and style. They turned respectable, safe family cars into chrome-covered, souped-up 'hot rods' or 'grease machines'.

In some ways, cars helped to free women, such as when they used their cars to visit shopping malls. However, automobiles designed for women reflected traditional attitudes. For example, the 1955 Dodge La Femme came with matching lipstick and shoulder bag, while women could buy clothes in the same fabric that upholstered the Ford Victoria. Sometimes the family car became a source of conflict, as men attempted to assert dominance by monopolising the driving seat.

The on-the-road culture

Cars made life easier and more varied. Americans could get to places faster and more comfortably. They could obtain fast food, watch movies and even attend church from the comfort of their car.

Americans became exceptionally mobile and their new on-the-road culture required cheap accommodation and fast food. In 1952, the modern American motel chain was born when the first Holiday Inn opened near Memphis and by 1960 there were 228 McDonald's. Such roadside motels and restaurants created tens of thousands of jobs in the service industries and also changed the landscape. Large areas of rural America were covered with roads and adjacent motels, restaurants, stores, huge parking lots, neon signs and advertisements.

▲ Los Angeles's 'The stack', a famous clover leaf interchange, completed in 1953.

McDonald's

McDonald's was emblematic of the United States in the 1950s in that it reflected the new on-the-road culture, the rise of service industries that catered to the consumer who wanted speed, efficiency and quality, and the homogenisation of the nation.

The McDonald's story began in 1940 when unsuccessful businessmen Dick and Maurice McDonald opened a drive-in restaurant in San Bernardino, California. They grew anxious that their service was too slow, so they dumped labour-intensive sandwiches and focussed instead upon speedily producing the hamburgers that were easily their most popular product. They substituted paper bags, wrappers and paper cups for the plates and silverware that needed washing, 'disappeared' and got broken. Customers took time choosing condiments, so the brothers put ketchup, mustard, onions and two pickles on every burger. 'Our whole concept was based on speed, lower prices and volume', said Dick.

In 1954 they appointed Ray Kroc as McDonald's **franchise** manager. Kroc opened his first McDonald's franchise in the Chicago suburb of Des Plaines in 1955, by which time McDonald's made $100,000 per annum, a huge sum based upon a $0.15 hamburger. In 1961 Kroc bought out the brothers, considering them unambitious small-timers who made easy profits from his hard work.

Today there are over 30,000 McDonald's in the world, 10,000 of which are in the United States.

White-collar jobs and service industries

The automobile and the resultant on-the-road culture had a dramatic impact on an American economy and workforce that was also undergoing other great changes in the mid-twentieth century:

- An increasingly large proportion of Americans were employed in **service industries** and in associated office-based work. By 1960 there were 7.6 million service workers and the number of **white-collar workers** had grown from 21.2 million in 1950 to 27.2 million.
- In the first half of the twentieth century, a large proportion of American workers were **blue-collar workers**, but new technology left the American economy less dependent upon heavy manual labour in factories and mines in the 1950s. Increased automation decreased the proportion of industrial workers from 39 per cent to 36 per cent of the workforce by 1960.
- By 1960, the 34.8 million service workers outnumbered the 25.6 million manual workers. These statistics were significant in that the fall in manufacturing jobs would lead to economically depressed areas in the old industrial heartlands of the Midwest and Northeast.

Suburbanisation

Perhaps the most important way in which the automobile impacted upon American society was the way in which it enabled people to move from the cities into spacious homes in suburbs that were within an easy drive of work. Left with those who could not afford to move out, cities lost their **tax base** and deteriorated.

The expansion of the suburbs

Suburbs were nothing new; 17 per cent of Americans lived in them in 1920. However, their growth greatly accelerated after the mid-1940s, when 11 million out of the 13 million homes built between 1948 and 1958 were in the suburbs. By 1960, 33 per cent of Americans were suburbanites, mostly middle-class whites in **ranch houses** with double garages, two bathrooms, three bedrooms and large lawns.

What explains the explosive growth of **suburbia**?

First, there had been little house building during the 1930s or the Second World War. This led to a post-war housing shortage so acute that 250 old **streetcars** were sold for use as homes in Chicago. The shortage and easily available mortgages combined to encourage builders to construct more homes. The Federal Housing Administration (FHA) and Veterans Administration (VA) offered house buyers mortgages of up to 90 per cent of the value of a home and up to 30 years to pay them off at a low interest rate (4–4.5 per cent). Between 1944 and 1952, the VA allowed nearly 2.4 million Second World War veterans to purchase homes with virtually no down payment. By 1955, the FHA and the VA provided 41 per cent of all new mortgages, which contributed to the rising percentage of owner-occupied homes (43 per cent in 1940, 61.9 per cent in 1960). Second, land and new homes were cheaper in suburban areas than in cities. Third, increased car ownership and federal highway construction made it easy for suburbanites to commute to work. Finally, faced with inner-city populations of poorer blacks and whites, higher tax rates, noise and congestion, more affluent whites preferred spacious and comfortable homes in racially and economically homogeneous neighbourhoods. This middle-class white exit from inner cities was known as '**white flight**'. As more of the population moved to the suburbs, they were followed by retail services.

Levittowns

The most famous builders in the suburbs were the Levitt brothers, whose developments were known as Levittowns. They began construction on their first development in Hempstead, Long Island, in 1947. Built primarily for young veterans, Hempstead had 17,000 homes, 80,000 residents, seven village greens and shopping centres, nine swimming pools and two bowling alleys. Residents were expected to conform to rules stipulating weekly lawn mowing, no fences and no washing hung out at weekends.

Levittown homes were so popular that when they went on sale, people formed queues to buy them. The Hempstead homes were priced at around $8,000 (only two and a half times the average family income) and they were well-constructed with central heating and built-in closets on 60 x 100 foot lots that were twice the normal size. Most suburban Americans loved their spacious homes with modern bathrooms, gadget-filled kitchens and attached garages.

Levittowns were racially exclusive. Rocks were thrown at a black American family that bought a house in the Pennsylvania Levittown in 1957 and the state authorities had to intervene. It was 1960 before a Levittown house was sold to a black family in New Jersey. William Levitt defended the exclusion of black Americans from Levittowns: 'I have come to know that if we sell one house to a **Negro** family, then 90 or 95 per cent of white customers will not buy into the community. That is their attitude, not ours.'

The changing nature of cities

Government policies, white flight to the suburbs and the black American **Great Migration** northwards contributed to big changes in American cities such as Detroit and Chicago. In these cities, increasing numbers of black people lived together in **ghettos**. This was partly out of personal choice (migrants tended to prefer areas where they already had family or acquaintances) but also because of white racism.

Whites contributed to the growth of large, urban ghettos in several ways:

- They used **restrictive covenants** to exclude black Americans from white neighbourhoods, even though the **Supreme Court** declared these covenants legally unenforceable in 1948.
- Lending institutions, developers and city officials made it difficult for black Americans to buy decent housing. As a result, black tenants paid high rents for poor accommodation in overcrowded ghettos.
- Sometimes whites staged 'housing riots' – as in 1951 in Cicero, Chicago, where several thousand working-class whites used looting and burning to drive out the sole black family.
- In the North, Midwest and West, whites who could afford it fled the nearby overcrowded black ghettos. For example, whites fled Oakland, California, for suburbs such as Hayward. Once in the suburbs, they were unwilling to pay increased taxes to assist inner-city areas. When black pressure for **desegregation** grew during the period 1955–63, Southern whites fled to the suburbs. For example, Atlanta, Georgia was experiencing large-scale white flight by the mid-1960s.
- The policies of the federal government promoted residential **segregation** (see below).

The federal government and the ghettos

Federal government policies played a big part in changing the nature of American cities. First, government policies led to a change in the racial composition of cities. When the FHA distributed billions of dollars of low-cost mortgages from the late 1940s, it openly excluded applicants considered 'risks' because of their income or because they were likely to elicit a hostile reaction from the white majority. These 'risks' were what the FHA described as 'un-harmonious racial or nationality groups', mostly black Americans or Jews. Here, residential segregation was effectively the policy of the United States government.

Second, federally constructed highways enabled suburbanites to commute to city jobs. Federal policies thus bore considerable responsibility for urban decline by allowing the more affluent to move out of the cities to the suburbs. Although Congress authorised the construction of 810,000 subsidised **public housing units** (also known as projects) and the purchase of slum areas for redevelopment in 1949, black Americans bitterly pointed out that 'urban renewal equals Negro removal'. For example, Chicago politicians, businessmen and developers manipulated local

The Pruitt-Igoe project

One famous public housing project was Pruitt-Igoe, in St Louis. The government funded 33 11-storey apartment buildings, constructed between 1954 and 1956. The high-density, high-rise blocks contained 2,800 units that could house 10,000 people. The blocks had laundries, play areas and a 'river of trees'. By 1963, the open spaces had become scrubby and littered, and muggings and rapes were common in the corridors and the elevator that rarely worked. Pruitt-Igoe's architect said, 'I never thought people were that destructive.' By 1965, 30 per cent of the units were vacant and the authorities tore down the project in 1972.

There were many suggestions as to why the project failed. It was said that it had too few facilities, that it was too big, too high-rise and too sterile, and that the housing authorities were starved of money for adequate security and maintenance. Some claimed that as the majority of tenants were single females with their families and/or black, the local authorities did not consider it important to maintain their homes. For example, electricity and water supplies became unreliable. Others pointed out that the development had very poor transport links to the rest of St Louis and that there were very few amenities in the local area.

laws and used federal funds for urban renewal to tear down black neighbourhoods and replace them with commercial buildings or more expensive housing for whites.

Finally, the federal government's attempt to alleviate the black housing shortage was ineffective. Only 325,203 federal housing units were built between 1945 and 1965 and many of them failed, such as the Pruitt-Igoe project in St Louis (see page 358).

Consumerism and domestic technology

Despite the growth of the ghettos, the United States was a land of plenty for many in the period 1955–63, and this economic prosperity generated social and cultural change through the development of the consumer society.

In 1960, average family income gave Americans 30 per cent more purchasing power than in 1950 and suburban Americans in particular rushed to buy cars, labour-saving devices and anything else considered essential and/or fashionable. Must-have domestic technology products such as washing machines, freezers and dishwashers made housewives' lives easier. The ability to buy what Americans wanted when Americans wanted it became an essential part of the 'American Dream'. The mass media (advertising, magazines, radio and especially television) spread this message, not only in advertisements but also in news stories, celebrity profiles and television shows.

Some people hated the impact of the consumer culture on American society. Intellectuals such as David Riesman feared consumerism and runaway materialism were becoming central to the nation's identity and undermining 'traditional American values' such as hard work and careful money management. Harvard economist John Kenneth Galbraith's The Affluent Society (1958) argued that Americans were grossly materialistic and cared little about the less fortunate. Preachers such as the charismatic, conservative evangelist Billy Graham echoed such concerns.

▲ Betty Furness ('The Lady from Westinghouse') became a household name when she appeared in countless advertisements that greatly increased sales of Westinghouse appliances such as refrigerators and fans. These advertisements appeared on TV and in magazines such as the Ladies' Home Journal and the Saturday Evening Post and are a good illustration of the consumer society. What can you infer about American society from this advertisement?

Key Topic 1 Affluence and conformity, 1955–63

The teenage consumer

In 1959, *Life* magazine recorded that teenage consumers had suddenly become 'a major factor in the nation's economy', owning 10 million record players, 1 million TV sets and 13 million cameras, and spending $20 million on lipstick, $25 million on deodorants, $9 million on home perming their hair and over $1.5 billion on entertainment in 1958. They ate 20 per cent more than adults and propped up the ice-cream industry, gobbling 145 million gallons of ice cream per year. The growing number of teenage marriages (one-third of 18- and 19-year-old girls were married) meant that young teenage wives were big spenders on major items such as furniture.

> **Source A** Extract from *Life* magazine's 31 August 1959 article entitled 'A Young $10 Billion Power: The US Teen-age Consumer Has Become a Major Factor in the Nation's Economy.' Here, *Life* describes the expenditure of one Californian teenager.
>
> At 17 Suzie Slattery of Van Nuys, California, fits any businessman's dream of the ideal teen-age consumer. The daughter of a reasonably well-to-do TV announcer, Suzie costs her parents close to $4000 a year, far more than average [*] for the country but not much more than many of the upper middle income families of her town...
>
> Last year $1500 was spent on Suzie's clothes and $550 for entertainment. Her annual food bill comes to $900. She pays $4 every two weeks at the beauty parlour. She has her own telephone and even has her own soda fountain in the house. On summer vacation days she loves to wander with her mother through fashionable department stores, picking up frocks or furnishings for her room or silver and expensive crockery for the hope chest [**] she has already started.
>
> As a high-school graduation present, Suzie was given a holiday cruise to Hawaii and is now in the midst of a new clothes-buying spree for college.
>
> [*] The average family income was around $5,000.
>
> [**] Hope chest: large chest in which young American girls placed items that would be helpful when they became a wife and mother.
>
> How much weight would you give the evidence of Source A for an enquiry into teenage consumer power in the 1950s? Explain your answer, using the source, the information given about it and your own knowledge of the historical context.

Conclusion: Urbanisation and affluence

In 1955 the United States was the world's most affluent nation. That affluence reshaped society; car ownership and federal policies contributed to the growth of suburbs in which consumerism flourished, but also to the growth of inner-city ghettos that demonstrated residential segregation and economic inequality, which was also evident in areas affected by the relative decline of manufacturing industries.

> **Work together**
>
> Working in pairs, test each other's knowledge and understanding of the section 'Affluence and conformity, 1955–63'. Write a test which includes:
>
> - Recall: write five questions testing knowledge of specific facts about American culture, 1955–63.
> - Explanation: write two questions testing understanding of the causes of two changes in American culture.
> - Evaluation: write one question testing understanding of the significance of one of the changes discussed above.
>
> Before answering the questions, discuss what a good answer to an explanation question or an evaluation question should look like, so that you can give each other feedback that will help develop your skills of explanation and evaluation.

2 Cultural conformity and challenge

It has long been argued that America was characterised by greater conformity after the Second World War. Several factors help to explain the increased conformity. Those who experienced the economic depression of the 1930s and the uncertainties of the Second World War, when American men were sent thousands of miles away to fight for their lives, craved economic success and stability. Pressure to conform to identical ideas and practices came from big business, which valued the co-operation and agreement of 'company men', and from advertisements, which encouraged everyone to consume the same goods. A common culture was promoted by the mass media, and this also encouraged conformity. Finally, the period after the Second World War was one of continued international tension with the USSR. Americans believed this danger necessitated national unity and conformity. However, as always, conformity generated challenge, particularly from intellectuals.

> **Note it down**
>
> As you read this section, make notes on the key reasons for conformity. Using bullet points (see page ix), note down the key reasons as headings. Then add supporting detail, such as:
> - key terms
> - statistics
> - key institutions
> - key individuals
> - dates

Suburban conformity

Contemporary characterisations of the Eisenhower years (1953–61) frequently emphasised conformity. For example, writing in 1954, the left-wing literary and social critic Irving Howe said this was an 'Age of Conformity', created by Cold War politics and a **mass society** in which standardisation, co-operation and conformity replaced traditional American values of self-reliance, competition and **rugged individualism**, and in which many Americans worked in increasingly faceless and standardised corporate organisations. In 1960, the poet Robert Lowell wrote of 'the tranquillised 50s'. Contemporary **liberals** argued that Eisenhower's popularity and the general lack of passion for social reform suggested a self-satisfied population (they mocked 'the bland leading the bland'). Critics considered that suburbia and particularly Levittowns (see page 357) best illustrated blandness and conformity.

Similar sentiments about the 'slurbs' or 'Disturbia' were echoed by Presbyterian minister and social critic Stanley Rowland, who wrote in 1956 that everyone in the suburbs 'buys the right car, keeps his lawn like his neighbours, eats crunchy breakfast cereal, and votes Republican' and by sociologist William H. Whyte, whose *The Organization Man* (1956) was a bestseller.

> **Source B** Extract from historian and sociologist Lewis Mumford's prize-winning book *The City in History* (Mariner Books, 1961), in which he lamented the lack of a sense of 'community' in the Hempstead Levittown. Here, he criticises uniformity and conformity in Hempstead.
>
> [A] multitude of uniform, unidentifiable houses lined up inflexibly, at uniform distances, on uniform roads, in a treeless communal waste, inhabited by people of the same class, the same income, the same age group, witnessing the same television performances, eating the same tasteless pre-fabricated foods, from the same freezers, conforming in every outward and inward respect to the same common mold.
>
> In Source B, how does Lewis Mumford use the structure of this sentence and repetition in order to make his point?

The 'organisation man'

In the mid-twentieth century the nature of the American workforce changed. Between 1947 and 1957 the number of salaried middle-class workers rose by 61 per cent. That rise was fuelled by the explosive growth of large corporations that needed specialised personnel to market and manage the corporate product. For example, in a giant company such as General Motors, which employed thousands of **white-collar workers**, scientists would oversee the development of new inventions and designs, marketing analysts would investigate the sales potential of the product, and **management science** experts would co-ordinate the personnel involved in the production.

During the 1950s, critics of American life and society wrote bestselling books about the men who worked in the offices of big corporations and lived in suburbia. Among the most influential of these books were David Riesman's *The Lonely Crowd: A Study of the Changing American Character* (1950), C. Wright Mills' *White Collar: The American Middle Classes* (1956) and William Whyte's critically acclaimed *The Organization Man* (1956), which sold two million copies.

The Organization Man summed up the contemporary criticisms of suburban and corporate America. First, Whyte argued that suburban life promoted 'getting along' and 'belonging'. Second, like Mills and Riesman, Whyte argued that huge corporate enterprises such as General Motors had created a new managerial personality, the 'organisation man' who had to get along with thousands of co-workers. Whyte argued that Americans had increasingly subordinated themselves to the interests and ethos of big organisations that promised security and prosperity. He said that the 'social ethic' of suburbia reflected the corporate 'organisation man'. According to Whyte, the nature of suburban life and the growth of large, bureaucratic organisations threatened the individualism and entrepreneurialism that had made America great.

Writers such as Whyte noted that the pressure to conform began when Americans were young. Many post-war high schools introduced courses on socially acceptable behaviour, while a Californian vocational school informed prospective employers that it socially engineered its graduates into 'custom-built men' with the right attitude to work. Whyte highlighted business organisations' increasing use of **personality tests** to ensure social conformity. It was clear that those who failed to conform to dominant white middle-class values were likely to be ostracised and disadvantaged.

Social change in film and television

By 1960, 90 per cent of American homes had televisions. Polls in the 1960s revealed television as the favourite leisure activity for more than 50 per cent of Americans and it was now a more popular form of entertainment than movie-going. Although movies in particular sometimes challenged the status quo, both television and film frequently served to reinforce contemporary values and to promote conformity. Television was criticised for this.

Criticisms of television

Critics said television had a dangerous influence on viewers because it:

- promoted conformity – 1950s family sitcoms such as *Father Knows Best* (1954–60) and *The Adventures of Ozzie and Harriet* (1952–66) portrayed the domestic bliss of white, middle-class suburban families where mothers invariably stayed at home as the ideal
- promoted consumerism through both non-stop advertisements and programme content – in *I Remember Mama* (1949–56), young family members taught their immigrant parents that consumerism was good
- caused a decline in educational test scores and reading – newspapers and magazines certainly lost sales because of it and *Life* magazine and the *Saturday Evening Post* eventually ceased publication
- made viewers physically inactive and mentally passive.

The main reason why television programmes promoted conformity was because they were designed for maximum mass appeal. Programmes were sponsored by advertisers and a programme that displeased too many people was a waste of the advertiser's money. For example, white racism made it difficult to retain sponsorship for NBC's *The Nat King Cole Show* (1956–57) because Cole was a black American; the sponsors suggested white makeup, but it made the singer look strange. '**Madison Avenue** is afraid of the dark,' said Cole, whose show was soon dropped. The need to keep sponsors happy resulted in predictability and sameness in programming.

> **Source C** In 1961, Federal Communications Commission chief Newton Minow addressed the National Association of Broadcasters. Here, he speaks of frequent predictability and sameness in programming.
>
> > When television is good, nothing – not the theatre, not the magazines or newspapers – is better ... But when television is bad, nothing is worse ... what you will observe is a vast wasteland. You will see a procession of game shows, violence, audience participation shows, formula comedies about totally unbelievable families, blood and thunder, mayhem, violence, sadism, murder, Western bad men, Western good men, private eyes, gangsters, more violence, and cartoons. And endlessly, commercials – many screaming, cajoling, defending. And most of all, boredom.
>
> What do you suppose was Newton Minow's purpose when he made this speech?

> ### Working women in the 1950s sitcom
> A recurring theme in 1950s sitcoms was the undesirability of middle-class women going to work. For example, in a 1955 episode of *The Honeymooners*, the husband is unemployed. When the wife decides to get a job, the husband responds, 'No wife of mine is going to work. I got my pride ... men are the workers in the family.' Similarly, the 1958 'Betty: Girl Engineer' episode of *Father Knows Best* is an excellent example of how young American women in the post-war period were conditioned to believe that the best vocation to which they could aspire was that of wife and mother. When the family's eldest daughter, Betty, hears a vocational lecture at her high school, she decides she wants to become an engineer and plans to spend her spring vacation working with a surveying crew. The college graduate supervisor of the crew tells Betty's father that she would surely be a good engineer. But, he asks, what man would want to come home to see a nice, pretty girl who has been working in the dust and heat? Betty decides that he is right and switches her attention to her date for Saturday night.

Praise for television

Some people disagreed with the criticisms of television. They argued that it was cheap entertainment with programmes that could be watched by the whole family and they rejected the attacks on television's promotion of conformity, insisting that viewers were not passive recipients. They claimed television helped to develop and define a more national culture, decreasing **provincialism** and social divisions, and giving people access to whole new worlds and perspectives, which contributed to a greater understanding of other cultures. They insisted that not all television programmes were mindless. Indeed, some documentaries challenged conformity and prejudice. For example, in his first televised interview in 1957, on *The Open Mind* (1956–present), Dr Martin Luther King Jr presented his ideas about the 'new Negro'. Similarly, news programmes showed challenges to the status quo, such as the black children who tried to enter Central High School in Little Rock, Arkansas, in 1957 (see page 372). Footage of the white victimisation of the black students in Little Rock helped promote positive social change.

Film and social change

Like television, Hollywood often reflected and perpetuated 1950s conservatism and values. Popular western movies and TV shows invariably portrayed heroic men, submissive women and evil '**Indians**'. However, Hollywood also demonstrated the capacity to change and challenge. For example, Hollywood began to change its treatment of sex. This was because it needed to attract audiences at a time when box office receipts were falling due to television – and sex sold. More sexually explicit films such as *Baby Doll* (1956) drew big crowds. Hollywood was able to ignore the **Motion Picture Code** and make such films because public attitudes were liberalising and a 1952 Supreme Court ruling had granted freedom of expression to films. Until 1956, the Code forbade showing interracial marriages, but in 1957 the first interracial movie embrace was shown in *Island in the Sun*. Despite such advances, Hollywood was more conservative on sex than Broadway. For example, the movie *Blue Denim* (1959) was based on a play, but while the 15-year-old girl had an abortion in the play, she kept the baby in the movie and the word 'abortion' was never mentioned.

Hollywood challenges

Movies were beginning to challenge racial stereotypes and attitudes. In the critically acclaimed *The Defiant Ones* (1958), black and white convicts chained together need to co-operate to survive. In director Douglas Sirk's *Imitation of Life* (1959), the final scene of the movie demonstrates that the real heroine is not the white actress (played by Lana Turner) who has achieved fame, but the black mother (played by Juanita Moore) who has devoted her life to the actress' neglected daughter and her own ungrateful offspring who rejects her and tries to pass as white. Clearly, Hollywood was gaining confidence in opposing prejudice. However, moviemaking was a business, and Hollywood had to be careful not to alienate customers. The musical *South Pacific* (1958) is about two interracial romances. It was a big box office hit in most of the United States, but was not well received in the South and nearly caused a race riot on Long Island in New York State. The antiwar movie *Paths of Glory* (1957) helps explain Hollywood's reluctance to engage with challenges to conformity; the movie was critically acclaimed, but did not do well at the box office. Challenging the consensus could be a financial gamble.

Nevertheless, Hollywood sometimes challenged traditional female roles and middle-class conformity. For example, in Sirk's *All That Heaven Allows* (1955), the upper middle-class widow Jane Wyman shocks the country club set when she becomes involved with Rock Hudson, a somewhat **bohemian** gardener who is younger than her. However, even as she rejects middle-class materialism and hypocrisy when she chooses to marry Hudson, it is significant that she does marry again; she still sees her greatest role as that of wife. In *Crime of Passion* (1957), Barbara Stanwyck plays a successful journalist suffocated by suburban life. Desperate for her husband to be 'somebody', she has an affair with his superior. When he refuses to promote her husband, she shoots him dead. While some contemporary critics saw the movie as a **feminist** statement, Stanwyck's villainess does not get away with it; she is turned in by her policeman husband. Hollywood would only go so far in its coverage of nonconformity, as demonstrated in its treatment of teen rebels.

Hollywood's teen rebels

Hollywood's ambivalence about challenging suburban conformity is demonstrated in many movies. In the movie *Rebel Without a Cause* (1955), the charismatic James Dean plays the archetypal teenager struggling with the adult world in mutual incomprehension. The Dean character eventually recognises his father's authority and valuable support. Similarly, *The Blackboard Jungle* (1955) tells of disruptive behaviour in the classroom and some localities wanted it banned. Yet again, Hollywood's sympathy for disaffected youth proved limited; the classroom teacher re-establishes control.

Advertising

Critics of conformity argued that it was promoted by advertisements. Although not a new phenomenon, advertising greatly increased in the 1950s; $5.7 billion was spent on advertising in 1950, but $11.9 billion in 1960. This was mostly due to the rise of television. The consumer society encouraged and was encouraged by the advertising industry, which during the 1950s spent more money than was spent on education.

In 1954, Yale historian David Potter argued that advertising was as socially influential as education and religion, because it dominated the media, shaped popular standards and exercised social control. The advertising industry had such power that it inevitably elicited criticism. In his influential book *The Hidden Persuaders* (1957), journalist Vance Packard argued that advertisements psychologically manipulated consumers. He warned readers about candy targeted at bored children at the checkout and about movie theatre owners whose screens flashed images of Coca-Cola too fast to be seen consciously yet sufficient to remind moviegoers to buy it in the interval. He recounted how research had shown that Marlboro filter cigarettes were considered effeminate until ads associated the brand with Wild West cowboy masculinity and sales rocketed.

Despite Packard-induced panic, research suggested that television viewers often laughed at exaggerated product claims. Furthermore, although the cigarette-manufacturing Philip Morris Company sponsored the most popular TV show, *I Love Lucy*, sales suffered with increasing publicity about the perils of tobacco.

The challenge of teenage culture: Beats and beatniks

While intellectuals lamented conformity in American society, most American adults were anxious about the challenging behaviour of young people. Adults felt that young 'greasers' with cut-off T-shirts, blue jeans and hairstyles such as **pompadours** and **duck-tails** were disrespectful and rebellious, that juvenile delinquency was increasing and that **beats**, **beatniks** and rock 'n' roll (see page 365) constituted a threat to American society and values.

Juvenile delinquency

In response to the general unease, the **Senate** held hearings on juvenile delinquency and newspapers and magazines focussed on the problem in 1955 and 1956. The news magazines *Time* and *Newsweek* recorded the activities of teenage gangs that ranged in size from 10 to 250 and were particularly numerous in the slums of New York and Chicago. Members were frequently from the same ethnic group. They fought each other, stole cars, beat up motorists, demanded 'protection money' from school pupils and even killed. Girls were 'auxiliaries', frequently carrying the boys' weapons (the police hesitated to frisk females) and beating up other girls and motorists.

Experts attributed juvenile delinquency to various factors. Some blamed violence and brutality in comic books (by 1955, 13 states had laws against the sale of comic books, so the industry began to tone down the content). Others said mothers who worked because they were captivated by the consumer culture ignored their child-rearing duties. No doubt many juvenile delinquents sought to gain a sense of status and of 'belonging', to escape from boring and depressing conditions at home and school, and to demonstrate their rejection of the values of their parents and of society. Also, they were subject to peer pressure. One gang member explained that he had to join friends in destroying a Chicago restaurant; if they thought he was 'chicken', he would no longer be able to live in the neighbourhood. Many of these young people were discontented 'have-nots'. In 1955 a gang of 40 gatecrashed a University of Chicago dance, threw bottles, bricks and clubs, stabbed one student in the back and beat up ten others. One gang member explained that college students had asked for trouble because they always acted as if they were better than those who did not go to college.

However, despite adult anxiety, statistics demonstrated no increase in juvenile delinquency and some have attributed that anxiety to traditional generational antipathy and/or nervous adults facing a changing world. For many teenagers, there was little rebellion – only drive-in movies, fast food, old cars and malls. Indeed, many contemporaries complained about a conformist younger generation that seemed to lack the dynamism that had made America great. Most educators considered this a 'silent generation'. There was little to compare to the restlessness and idealism of the next decade, apart from the 'beats'.

The 'beat generation'

The most publicised dissenters from the mainstream culture of 'squares' were the mostly middle-class young 'beats', who rejected materialism, the consumer culture and conformity for a lifestyle characterised by spontaneity, drugs, free love and a general defiance of authority and convention. The first members of the 'beat generation' were a group of Columbia University students that included Allen Ginsberg and Jack Kerouac.

> ### What did 'beat' mean?
> The origins of the phrase 'beat generation' are controversial; Jack Kerouac was certainly important in spreading its use. To most 'beats', the word meant cheated, robbed or emotionally or physically exhausted, although Kerouac said it meant beatitude to him. He thought that the beat generation had disappeared to jails or domesticity by 1957.

Thirty-year-old Ginsberg gained fame and critical acclaim in 1956 after public readings of 'Howl', a poem written under the influence of drugs, which dealt with issues such as drugs, homosexuality and nonconformity. The independent thinkers faced with suffocation in a conformist and materialistic society are introduced in the first few lines of 'Howl':

> I saw the best minds of my generation destroyed by madness, starving hysterical naked,
>
> dragging themselves through the negro streets at dawn looking for an angry fix,
>
> angelheaded hipsters burning for the ancient heavenly connection to the starry dynamo in the machinery of night…

The San Francisco police seized copies and the subsequent trial attracted national attention to 'beats'. Judge W.J. Clayton Horn rejected the obscenity charges:

> The first part of 'Howl' presents a picture of a nightmare world; the second part is an indictment of those elements of modern society destructive of the best qualities of human nature; such elements are predominantly identified as materialism, conformity, and the mechanisation leading to war … It ends with a plea for holy living.

(Quoted in David Halberstam, *The Fifties*, Ballantine Books, 1993)

In 1951, mother's boy, university dropout and US Navy reject (he was honourably discharged on psychiatric grounds for a 'schizoid personality') Jack Kerouac began writing a book about his travels as a young drifter, observing the empty life of contemporary America. The book's excessively long sentences owed much to the rush of sensation Kerouac got from smoking marijuana as he wrote. Ginsberg considered it unpublishable, but eventually, Viking published Kerouac's *On the Road* (1957), after removing much of the description of drug use and homosexual practices. It immediately received critical acclaim; a review in the *New York Times* described it as 'the most beautifully executed, the clearest and the most important utterance yet made by the generation Kerouac himself named years ago as "beat"'.

The influence of the 'beats'

It is difficult to estimate the number of 'beats'. We know of the 150 who became writers and estimates of the others vary from several hundred to several thousand. Acclaimed writers such as Ginsberg and Kerouac were highly influential in literary circles. Initially, the 'beats' were a media sensation, although after 1960 the media rather lost interest. Several 'beat' followers subsequently gained fame for their oppositional stance, including singer-songwriter Bob Dylan, Tom Hayden (see page 400) and Doctor Timothy Leary, a Harvard psychologist who experimented on his students with drugs (see page 402). A somewhat superficial version of 'beats' developed in colleges, where it became fashionable for young people to adopt an anti-establishment attitude. From 1958 they were known as beatniks. Genuine 'beats' had little time for them. Although he became known as 'King of the Beatniks', Kerouac considered beatniks pretentious copycats.

> ### Beatniks
> The word 'beatnik' originated from the word 'Sputnik', the first Soviet satellite in space. The 'nik' section of the word was sometimes added to other words in Cold-War America, such as 'beatnik', and was intended to denote something un-American or even anti-American.
>
> A beatnik could be recognised by some or all of the following characteristics:
> - a 'pad' (apartment) in North Beach, San Francisco, or Greenwich Village, New York City with a mattress, table, lamp, bells, bamboo curtains and a wine bottle or two suspended from the ceiling
> - sandals or barefoot (males)
> - long straight hair, tight jeans, baggy sweaters (females)
> - jazz, sex, drugs (especially marijuana) and swearing
> - critical of materialism, social snobbery, Christianity, the government, cops, politics, employment and patriotism
> - Zen Buddhism
> - coffee-house poetry readings
> - urban black culture vocabulary ('dig', 'cool', 'man', 'split').

The challenge of teenage culture: Music

While juvenile delinquents, beats and beatniks were a minority, rock 'n' roll fans constituted a more widespread challenge to the dominant culture.

Before the arrival of rock 'n' roll in the 1950s, there was no sharply defined 'teenage' music; teenagers swooned over Frank Sinatra, but their parents liked him, too. However, rock 'n' roll was 'young' music. It combined black '**race music**' (rhythm and blues) and hillbilly (country and western). In 1953, Cleveland disc jockey Alan Freed played black artists' rhythm and blues records, christening it 'rock 'n' roll' because the lyrics were frequently focussed on sexual activity. Freed's white, teenage radio audience loved the strong beat and whites such as Bill Haley & His Comets began copying it. Other popular rock 'n' rollers included Chuck Berry, Little Richard and Elvis Presley.

Rock 'n' roll was popular among young people because:

- It added to their sense of group identity – only they could appreciate it.
- With temporary jobs (especially in fast-food outlets) and frequently generous allowances from their parents, teenagers had money to spend on records: $182 million in 1954, $521 million in 1960.

The older generation was less enthusiastic. *Time* magazine compared rock 'n' roll concerts to Hitler's rallies and a psychiatrist described the music as 'a communicative disease ... a cannibalistic and tribalistic kind of music'. Parents feared the impact of rock 'n' roll on their children, because it was often critical of middle-class behaviour and full of sexual longing. The Senate subcommittee on delinquency received a letter that said Elvis Presley was

> *a symbol, of course, but a dangerous one. His strip-tease antics threaten to rock 'n' roll the juvenile world into open revolt against society. The gangster of tomorrow is the Elvis Presley type of today.*

Some white parents feared black culture contaminating their children. The head of the Alabama **White Citizens' Council** said, 'the obscenity and vulgarity of the rock 'n' roll music is obviously a means by which the white man and his children can be driven to the level with a "nigra"'.

Conclusion: Cultural conformity and challenge

While there was a considerable degree of conformity and uniformity in the suburbs, often reinforced by Hollywood and television, there was also considerable discontent and dissent. This was demonstrated by the intellectuals who criticised conformity, the beats, beatniks, fans of rock 'n' roll, and juvenile delinquents. As we shall see in the next section, it was most importantly demonstrated by black Americans who challenged segregation in the South.

Elvis Presley, 1935–77

Elvis was born to poor white Mississippi farm workers in 1935. His father, so poorly educated that he could not spell his own name, spent two and a half years in jail during the economic depression in the 1930s for forging a cheque. When Elvis was 14, his family moved into public housing in Memphis, Tennessee. Most whites hated living in the projects because it put them on the same level as blacks, but it was the best housing the Presleys had ever had and they loved it. Elvis adored movies and could recite the whole script of *Rebel Without a Cause*.

Memphis recording studio owner Sam Phillips – who had said, 'If I could find a white man with a Negro sound, I could make $1 billion' – discovered Elvis. They recorded 'That's All Right' (1954), but Phillips soon sold Elvis to the giant recording company RCA for $35,000.

The handsome young 'Elvis the Pelvis' appealed to young female audiences. They screamed at his movements, which one commentator described as 'strip-teases with clothes on ... not only suggestive but downright obscene'. Presley was filmed from the waist up for his appearance on television's popular family favourite, *The Ed Sullivan Show*.

Elvis and rock 'n' roll certainly revolutionised music. However, while rock 'n' roll sounded revolutionary, it tended to focus on love and annoying social conventions championed by disapproving parents that made life difficult for lovers, rather than on major issues. Elvis himself was big money and quickly became mainstream. His polite manners, devotion to his mother and the gospel songs and romantic ballads he was recording by the end of the 1950s appeased older Americans who had continued to favour easy listening artists such as Nat King Cole and Frank Sinatra.

3 The civil rights movement

Throughout American history, the vast majority of white Americans treated black people as inferior and used varying systems of race control to maintain the supremacy of white people.

By the mid-nineteenth century the Northern states had abandoned slavery but the Southern states sought to continue and expand it. This triggered the American Civil War (1861–65) in which the North defeated the South and ended slavery. The Southern states then introduced a new method of race control, the so-called Jim Crow laws, under which black people were legally segregated from white people in public facilities such as hospitals, railroad cars, restrooms, restaurants and educational institutions.

Black Americans in the South

In 1955, the inferior status of black people in the South was evident in several areas of life.

Social inferiority

The segregation of public facilities demonstrated inferior social status. If a young black American living in a city such as Atlanta, Georgia, wanted 'a day out' downtown, he would have to travel from what racist whites referred to as Atlanta's 'nigger town' at the back of the bus. He could not buy a soda or hot dog at a downtown store lunch counter. If a white drugstore served him, they would hand him his ice cream through a side window and in a paper cup so no white would have to use any plate that he had used. He had to drink from the 'colored' water fountain and use the 'colored' restroom. He had to sit in the 'colored' section of the back of the balcony in the movie theatre. Martin Luther King said that when he was a young man, living under such a system made him 'determined to hate every white person'.

Political inferiority

The inferior political status of black Americans was evidenced by the fact that 80 per cent of them were unable to vote. Southern whites used a variety of methods to obstruct black persons who tried to register to vote. Would-be black voters were often threatened with violence and intimidation. White registrars would close their offices or ask detailed questions on the state constitution or impossible questions such as 'How many bubbles are there in a bar of soap?' An intelligent woman such as Rosa Parks (see page 370) 'failed' the literacy test when she tried to register to vote in Alabama in 1943. When she finally registered in 1945, she had to pay a $16.50 poll tax, a prohibitively expensive sum for many impoverished black Americans.

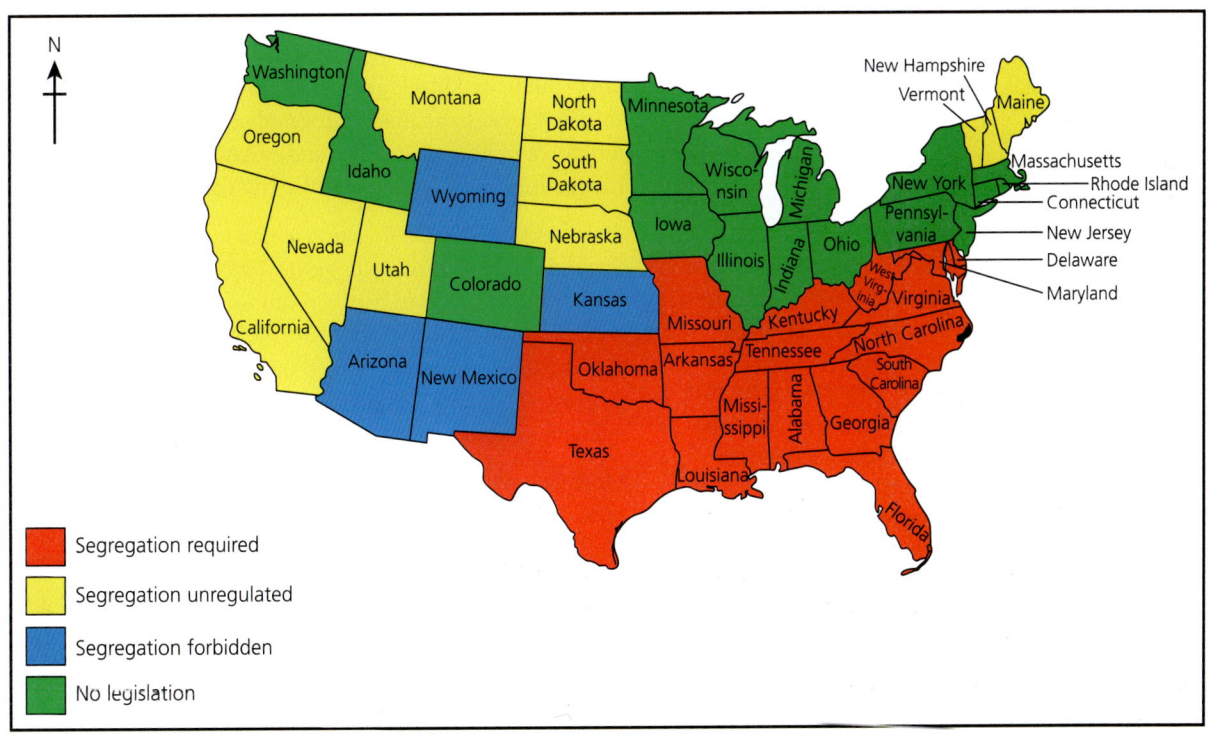

▲ The states in which schools were segregated pre-1954.

Economic inferiority

Despite a slowly growing black middle class that included Martin Luther King and his minister father 'Daddy King', most Southern black people had markedly inferior economic status through working in low-paying jobs, for example as share-croppers and domestics. This inferior economic status owed much to segregated education. Southern states gave black schools far less money than white schools. In 1949 South Carolina spent an average of $179 per annum to educate a white child, but only $43 to educate a black child. Black students had to attend segregated universities in which the teaching staff invariably had fewer qualifications and materials and white university professors. For example, James Meredith sought entry to the white University of Mississippi because his local black college had few teachers with doctorates (see page 392).

Legal inequality

Southern whites used violence and intimidation to maintain their supremacy and there was no protection for black Americans in the law courts. For example, in 1955, 14-year-old Emmett Till wolf-whistled at a white woman. His mutilated body was dragged out of a Mississippi river soon after. His murderers boasted of what they had done but went unpunished.

> **Source D** Extract from journalist William Bradford Huie's article on Emmett Till's murder for *Look* magazine in 1956. Huie paid Till's killers for their story. Here, one of the murderers explains his motivation to Huie.
>
> Well, what else could we do? He was hopeless. I'm no bully; I never hurt a nigger in my life. I like niggers – in their place – I know how to work 'em. But I just decided it was time a few people got put on notice. As long as I live and can do anything about it, niggers are gonna stay in their place. Niggers ain't gonna vote where I live. If they did, they'd control the government. They ain't gonna go to school with my kids. And when a nigger gets close to mentioning sex with a white woman ... I'm likely to kill him. Me and my folks fought for this country, and we got some rights. I stood there ... and listened to that nigger throw that poison at me, and I just made up my mind. 'Chicago boy,' I said, 'I'm tired of 'em sending your kind down here to stir up trouble. Goddam you, I'm going to make an example of you...'
>
> How much weight would you give the evidence of Source D for an enquiry into the situation of Southern black people in 1955? Explain your answer using the source, the information given about it and your own knowledge of the historical context.

By 1955, many black people were ready to protest against their situation. The most significant period of a black civil rights movement that aimed to demolish Jim Crow in the South and to gain social, political and economic equality was about to begin.

> **Note it down**
>
> As you read this section, you might find it helpful to create a table with four columns headed: (1) Date; (2) Event; (3) Causes; and (4) Consequences, and fill in a row of the table for each of the following:
> - The Montgomery bus boycott
> - Little Rock
> - Sit-ins
> - Freedom Rides
> - The March on Washington
> - The Birmingham campaign
> - The Mississippi Freedom Summer.

The Montgomery bus boycott

There was a long tradition of black protest in the United States and it was often led by the National Association for the Advancement of Colored People (NAACP).

The NAACP

When the NAACP was established in 1909, it declared that it aimed to make America's 11 million black citizens economically, intellectually, politically and socially free and equal. The NAACP used several tactics in pursuit of this. In the early 1950s the NAACP newspaper *The Crisis* publicised black grievances, local NAACP branches initiated protests against segregated public places such as lunch counters and theatres, and NAACP lawyers fought inequalities in education and the law courts.

Much of the NAACP litigation aimed to overturn the Supreme Court's *Plessy* v. *Ferguson* (1896) ruling, which had declared the Jim Crow laws constitutional so long as facilities were 'separate but equal'. In 1950, the NAACP won Supreme Court rulings against segregated universities in the South, but its greatest triumph was the Supreme Court's 1954 *Brown* ruling that separate schools in the South were not equal.

However, while *Brown* and other rulings removed all constitutional sanction for de jure segregation, the Supreme Court could only declare that some deed or legislation was against the American Constitution. The Court had no powers of enforcement and its rulings could be ignored. For example, despite the *Brown* ruling, many schools remained segregated. As a result, in practice, the NAACP's litigation strategy rarely brought speedy practical solutions to black American problems. So, the alternative strategy of large-scale community protest was attempted in Montgomery in 1956.

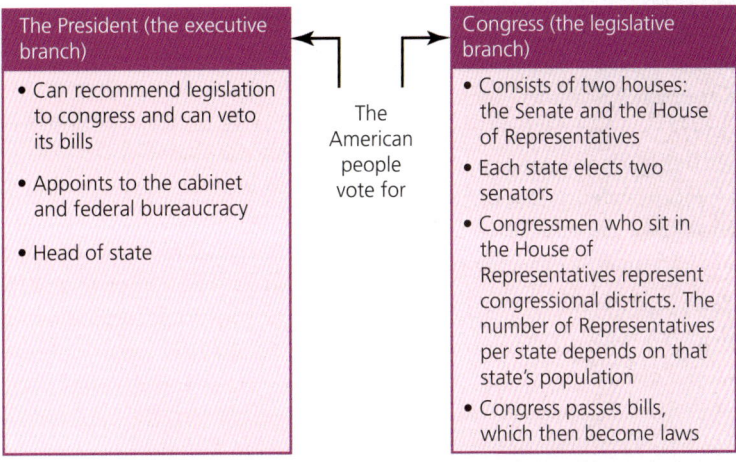

▲ The structure of federal government in the USA.

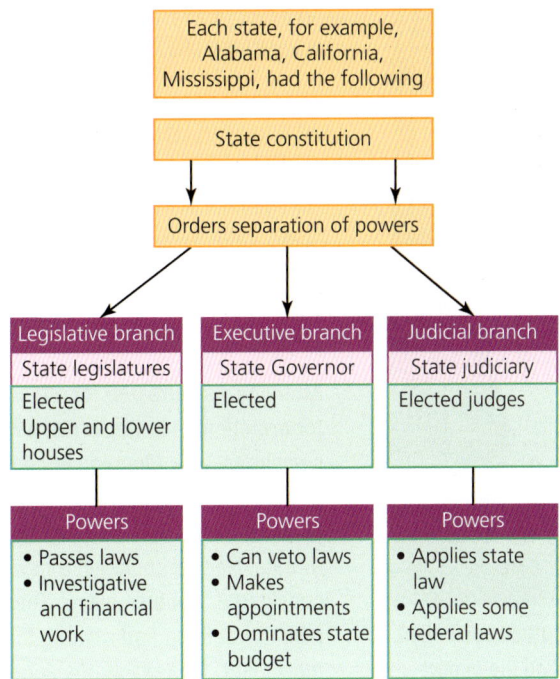

▲ The structure of state government in the USA.

Events in Montgomery

The Montgomery bus boycott is usually seen as the start of the modern civil rights movement. The underlying cause was Montgomery's segregated buses and the behaviour of white bus drivers. When in 1955 a black mother put her two babies on the front 'white' seats in order to free her hands to pay her fare, the driver yelled, 'Take the dirty black brats off the seats', hit the accelerator and the babies fell into the aisle.

Many in Montgomery's black community had had enough. There had long been talk of a bus boycott that would use black economic power to force the white bus company owners to reconsider their policies. The local NAACP branch wanted a court case and when branch secretary Rosa Parks was arrested in December 1955 because she had refused to stand to give a white man her seat on the bus, the NAACP organised a boycott for the day of her trial, assisted by the local black college and the black churches. Parks had been at the front of the 'black section' of the bus, and the system was that if all the seats were full, the black front rows had to be vacated so no white had to stand. Initially, the boycott only sought first-come first-served seating – under that system, Rosa Parks would not have had to vacate her seat in the black front rows. When the city commissioners said no, the black community launched a year-long boycott that sought fully integrated buses upon which anyone could sit anywhere and the employment of black drivers. Twenty-six-year-old Baptist minister Martin Luther King Jr was chosen to lead the boycott, in which most of Montgomery's 50,000 black population participated.

Rosa Parks, 1913–2005

Born in Alabama, the young Rosa Parks went to bed each night clothed, ready to flee if the Ku Klux Klan attacked the family home. It was difficult for Montgomery's black population to obtain an education (whites forced the white head of Parks' school for black children out of Montgomery). However, Parks managed to graduate from high school. During the Second World War, she joined the NAACP, which she said 'was about empowerment through the ballot box'. She considered moving north to Detroit where, she said, 'you could get a seat anywhere on a bus', but race riots there in 1943 made her realise that 'racism was almost as widespread in Detroit as in Montgomery'.

She was an enthusiastic and active member of the NAACP, attending an NAACP leadership training seminar in 1946. She was inspired by the *Brown* ruling in 1954, recalling, 'You can't imagine the rejoicing among black people, and some white people.' She was increasingly ready to make a public stand against white oppression: 'Every day in the early 1950s we were looking for ways to challenge Jim Crow laws.'

After she was arrested for refusing to give up her bus seat for a white man in December 1955, she lost her job as a seamstress in a Montgomery department store, her husband was forced out of his job at a US Army base, their white landlord raised their rent and they received countless death threats. Neither could get a new job because they were considered 'troublemakers'. There was also much male jealousy of Rosa Parks within the Montgomery civil rights movement. As a result, the couple moved to Detroit. During the 1960s, Parks became more militant in her attitudes and admired many aspects of Malcolm X and the **Black Power movement** (see page 391).

Martin Luther King Jr, 1929–68

King was born into a well-educated and relatively prosperous family in a leading Southern city, Atlanta, Georgia. His grandfather and father were pastors of a Baptist church in Atlanta and NAACP activists. Young Martin received poor-quality education in Atlanta's segregated schools and continued to face racial prejudice when he went to college in the Northern city of Boston. In 1954 he became pastor of Dexter Avenue Baptist Church in Montgomery, Alabama.

He gained national attention during the Montgomery bus boycott of 1956 and soon became regarded by white people as the leading spokesman for black Americans. He and his organisation, the Southern Christian Leadership Conference (SCLC), were of great importance in the civil rights movement.

King's campaign in Birmingham (1963) contributed greatly to the passage of the Civil Rights Act (1964) that ended legal segregation in the South, while his campaign in Selma (1965) was vital in the passage of the Voting Rights Act (1965), which made it possible for all black Americans to vote in the South.

After that, King turned his attention to the ghettos of the North, but he made little impact upon the dreadful conditions there. He was assassinated by a white racist in 1968.

The Montgomery bus boycott: Results and significance

- The *Brown* ruling had elicited a white backlash and the establishment of White Citizens' Councils to defend segregation (see below). The Montgomery Citizens' Council organised the opposition to the boycott and used arrests and intimidation to try to frighten leaders such as King. This attracted favourable nationwide attention to the black community's efforts.
- After the NAACP won a legal victory in the Supreme Court ruling against segregated buses in *Browder* v. *Gayle* in November 1956, Montgomery's buses were desegregated.
- Montgomery's black community had demonstrated the potential power of a new mode of activism, **mass direct action,** but it was NAACP litigation and *Browder* v. *Gayle* that ensured the desegregation of Montgomery's buses.
- Only Montgomery's buses were desegregated. Segregation continued in other public places.
- A major new black leader had emerged. King and his inspirational oratory had gained national attention and in 1957 he established the Southern Christian Leadership Conference (SCLC) to continue the fight against segregation.

White racist organisations

Southern whites had long joined organisations to sustain white supremacy. The most famous of these was the Ku Klux Klan. White Citizens' Councils were also influential, but only for a short period during the 1950s and 1960s.

The Ku Klux Klan

The Ku Klux Klan is an armed white racist group established in Tennessee in 1866 after the South's defeat in the Civil War but soon quashed by the federal government (other groups quickly replaced it). The Klan revived in 1915, gaining millions of members across the USA, especially in the cities of the North and Midwest to which black Americans had gravitated during the early twentieth century. The *Brown* ruling revitalised the Klan, but the Montgomery bus boycott suggested it had lost some of its impact; when Montgomery's buses were desegregated, the Klan sent 40 carloads of robed, hooded members through Montgomery's black community, which, instead of retreating behind closed doors as was usual, emerged to wave at them.

The Klan nevertheless persisted in activities such as:

- bombing King's house in 1956 and his motel room during the Birmingham campaign in 1963 (see page 373)
- attacks on Freedom Riders (see page 373) at Birmingham in 1963 (some Birmingham police officers belonged to the Klan)
- bombing a Birmingham church in 1963 (four young girls were killed)
- cross-burnings, church-burnings, beatings, shootings and murders in Mississippi in the winter of 1963–64. The 1964 murder of three civil rights workers – black Mississippian James Chaney, white Congress of Racial Equality (CORE) member Michael Schwerner and white student Andrew Goodman – caused a national sensation and led President Lyndon Johnson to order the **FBI** to go after the Klan: 'I don't want these Klansmen to open their mouths without your knowing what they're saying'
- shooting and killing Viola Liuzzo, a Northern white who participated in the Selma campaign (see page 387).

During the 1970s, Klan membership tripled and violence increased. The Klan remains in existence today.

White Citizens' Councils

The Supreme Court's *Brown* ruling inspired the establishment of the first Citizens' Council, in Sunflower County, Mississippi, in 1954. This inspired white people in Alabama, Louisiana, Mississippi and South Carolina to establish further Citizens' Councils. Similar organisations were set up in other states, with a variety of different names. All of these organisations kept in touch.

Membership of the Citizens' Councils peaked at around 250,000 in 1956. Members were often pillars of the white community – doctors, lawyers, businessmen, politicians and school superintendents. Citizens' Councils:

- made the defence of segregation the main issue of Southern politics
- issued large quantities of racist propaganda, including children's books that described a segregated heaven
- sponsored schools for white children
- subjected civil rights activists (especially the NAACP) to threats and economic pressure. For example, in Yazoo City, Mississippi, 53 black Americans signed an NAACP petition asking the local school boards to integrate the schools. Each of the 53 signatories lost their jobs or were unable to do any business with white people. Two left town and the other 51 removed their names.

The Citizens' Councils differentiated themselves from the lower-class Ku Klux Klan, which was associated with violence. However, some individuals were members of both – for example, Byron De La Beckwith, who in 1963 assassinated Mississippi NAACP activist Medgar Evers.

The Citizens' Councils were in great decline by the 1970s.

The Little Rock crisis, 1957

Soon after the Montgomery bus boycott, a crisis occurred in Little Rock, Arkansas, as a result of the Supreme Court's *Brown* ruling that schools should be desegregated. The city of Little Rock planned to comply with the *Brown* ruling by 1963. Central High School was to be the first integrated school and, encouraged by the NAACP, nine black-American students tried to enter it in September 1957.

Keen to exploit racism to gain re-election, Arkansas governor Orval Faubus ordered the Arkansas **National Guard** to keep the students out. An abusive white mob surrounded the students as they tried to enter the school. Fearing the breakdown of law and order, President Eisenhower reluctantly sent in troops to protect them.

The Supreme Court ruled that any law that sought to keep **public schools** segregated was unconstitutional (*Cooper* v. *Aaron*, 1958) but Little Rock demonstrated that Supreme Court rulings met tremendous resistance in practice. The 'Little Rock Nine' suffered violent attacks in the short time they attended Central High. They were pushed down the stairs and had chemicals and wads of burning paper thrown at them. Faubus closed all of Little Rock's high schools during 1958 and 1959 rather than integrate and got re-elected four times. Central High School was finally integrated in 1960, and other Little Rock schools by 1972.

Little Rock also demonstrated the power of television. On-the-spot TV reporting was pioneered there, and images of black children being spat upon by aggressive white adults gained sympathy nationwide. However, Little Rock confirmed that Supreme Court rulings were insufficient and that other forms of activism were required.

The Birmingham campaign, 1963

In 1963, King's SCLC staged a campaign in Birmingham, Alabama, that sought the desegregation of public facilities and equal employment opportunities. Why did King choose Birmingham? First, it epitomised the horrors of Southern segregation (he described it as 'by far' American's 'worst big city' for racism). Second, he knew Public Safety Commissioner Eugene 'Bull' Connor would mistreat protesters and gain nationwide publicity for Southern bigotry that would hopefully prompt Kennedy into action.

Important groups in the civil rights movement

Many organisations and individuals played an important role in the civil rights movement:

- NAACP litigation won great moral victories such as *Brown* (1954), which inspired activists such as Rosa Parks.
- In 1960, four black college students in Greensboro, North Carolina, began a **sit-in** in a Woolworth's cafeteria. When confused and resentful black waitresses would not serve them, they refused to leave the lunch counter and other students occupied the seats on a rotating basis. This inspired around 70,000 students to participate in sit-ins across the South. Woolworth's was losing money so it soon desegregated all of its lunch counters in the South. The students set up a new organisation, the Student Non-violent Coordinating Committee (SNCC, pronounced SNICK), which organised grassroots activism such as a drive to register black voters in the Mississippi Delta (1961–64). Around 800 Northern volunteers, many of whom were white, participated in the SNCC's **Mississippi Freedom Summer** in 1964, during which 17,000 black people tried to register to vote in Mississippi but only 1,600 succeeded due to Ku Klux Klan violence and the opposition of the white authorities.
- In 1961, the CORE initiated the '**Freedom Rides**', in which an integrated group travelled the South on buses to test Supreme Court rulings against segregated interstate transport (1946) and interstate bus facilities (1960). Black and white riders were beaten up, most famously in Anniston, Alabama. Media coverage exposed Southern white bigotry and prompted Attorney General Robert Kennedy to enforce the Supreme Court rulings.
- Martin Luther King and the SCLC played an important part in the Birmingham campaign and the March on Washington in 1963, both of which contributed to the Civil Rights Act (1964), which ended *de jure* segregation in the South, and in the Selma campaign in 1965, which led to the passage of the Voting Rights Act (1965).

The aim of the direct action of organisations such as the SCLC, the SNCC and the CORE was to force a positive federal government response. It worked. Although Eisenhower had said he would never help enforce school integration, he sent troops to Little Rock. Also, motivated by white violence and the Northern black vote, he promoted the Civil Rights Acts (1957 and 1960) designed to facilitate Southern black voting and school desegregation. Although ineffective, these Acts were the first civil rights legislation for a century. They signalled that the **executive** and **legislative branches** of the federal government (see diagram on page 369) had taken responsibility for black civil rights.

Despite Kennedy's campaign promises, he did nothing at first to help black people. He was irritated by black protests – they provoked white violence and caused international embarrassment for the United States, which claimed to be the world's leading democracy. However, the Kennedy administration responded positively to:

- the Freedom Rides
- black testing of Supreme Court decisions in favour of integrated universities (the Kennedy administration helped James Meredith enter the previously all-white University of Mississippi)
- King's Birmingham campaign.

Events in Birmingham

At first, King struggled to organise demonstrations. Many felt Connor's imminent retirement made protests unnecessary. However, Connor's police and police dogs started attacking the few protesters and King was jailed. Facing bitter accusations that he was a troublemaker, King defended direct action and his provocation of white violence as the best option available to the oppressed in his 'Letter from Birmingham Jail', written partly on prison toilet paper and published worldwide. Once released, he still struggled to mobilise sufficient demonstrators: 'You know, we've got to get something going. The press is leaving,' he said. Controversially, he decided to encourage young black schoolchildren to join the protest marches. Hundreds of them participated. When Connor's high-pressure water hoses tore the clothes off their backs, Birmingham was in the headlines again.

The results and significance of Birmingham

- King's campaign did little to improve the situation in Birmingham itself. No meaningful agreement on segregation was reached and race relations deteriorated. In September 1963 a bomb killed four young black girls attending Sunday school. Black leaders asked King to stay away, saying that they wanted no more 'outside help' or 'outside interference'.
- The publicity generated in Birmingham exposed Southern bigotry at its worst, inspired black protests throughout the South and helped persuade President Kennedy to promote the bill that became the 1964 Civil Rights Act (see page 387) which ended *de jure* segregation in the South.
- Birmingham showed the power of mass demonstrations, which King called 'the greatest weapon' of the civil rights movement.

The March on Washington, 1963

A further great mass demonstration in 1963 was the March on Washington. The march was masterminded by black-American trade union leader A. Philip Randolph, who sought to encourage the federal government to increase black economic opportunities. Organisations such as the NAACP, the SNCC and the SCLC hoped a well-attended march would gain publicity and encourage Congress to pass the civil rights bill, especially as some black Americans were alienated by slow government progress towards equality and were instead turning to violence.

The emotional impact of the March on Washington was great. The civil rights movement presented itself as strong and united. The behaviour of the 250,000 marchers was impeccable. The series of speakers standing before the Lincoln Memorial in the capital reminded the nation of the civil rights movement's domination of the moral high ground. As King pointed out in his 'I have a dream' speech, the speakers and the marchers were calling upon Americans to live up to the ideals of freedom, equality and justice enshrined in their beloved **Declaration of Independence** and Constitution. Many people believe that the emotional impact of that speech and of the march contributed to the passage of the Civil Rights Act of 1964 (see page 387).

Conclusion: The civil rights movement

By 1963 the civil rights movement had forced some change in the South in that the universities, around 10 per cent of schools, interstate transport and some cafeterias were integrated. However, many public places remained segregated despite Supreme Court rulings such as *Brown* that removed all constitutional justification for segregation. Furthermore, Southern black political status remained inferior; approximately three-quarters of black Americans still could not vote. Nevertheless, protests and television had put the inferior social, economic and political status of black people firmly on the national political agenda. What was needed next was congressional legislation to guarantee the equal citizenship of all Americans.

> ### Work together
>
> Looking at the consequences of the activism that you have recorded in your table (see page 368), put the activism used in Montgomery, Little Rock, sit-ins, Freedom Rides, the Birmingham campaign, the March on Washington and the Mississippi Freedom Summer into order of effectiveness. Check with your partner – have you agreed on which forms of activism were the most effective?

4 Kennedy's New Frontier

John Fitzgerald Kennedy was born to a wealthy Boston Irish Democrat family. In his youth, he had little or no grasp of the problems of the poor in the economic depression of the 1930s. He subsequently admitted that he 'really did not learn about the Depression until I read about it at Harvard'. However, that depression had a great impact upon American politics and political parties for the next half-century.

The Democrat President Franklin D. Roosevelt (1933–45) sought to combat the terrible poverty and unemployment of the Depression with his New Deal policies. Roosevelt's New Deal introduced Americans to the idea of unprecedented federal government intervention to aid the poor and stimulate the economy. Roosevelt's Democrat successor President Harry Truman (1945–53) continued Roosevelt's policies with the '**Fair Deal**'. As a Democrat Congressman (1947–53), Kennedy voted for Fair Deal legislation that would help his working-class Boston constituents.

The Republican Dwight D. Eisenhower (1953–61) disliked federal government interventionism. He believed the New Deal and Fair Deal made people too dependent upon the state but he did little to reverse them lest it alienate voters. A Senator during the Eisenhower years, Kennedy announced his presidential candidacy in January 1960 and his campaign emphasised his dynamism in contrast to stagnation and complacency under Eisenhower. His campaign slogan was 'Let's get the country moving again'.

In his speech accepting the Democratic nomination for the presidency in July 1960, Kennedy suggested that in the **New Frontier** of the new decade, Americans should meet new challenges in science, space, international tensions, ignorance, prejudice, poverty and surplus.

> ### Note it down
>
> Using the 1:2 method (see page x), list the challenges Kennedy introduced in his New Frontier speech in one column. Then, as you read this section, put supporting detail on his success/failure in relation to each challenge.

Social welfare and unemployment

In his New Frontier speech, Kennedy had spoken of the challenges of poverty and ignorance, and in a New Frontier legislative programme that leading Republican Senator Everett Dirksen described as 'the New Deal taken

> **Source E** Extract from John Kennedy's July 1960 speech at the Democrat National Convention, in which he accepted the party's nomination for the presidency. Here, he introduces the New Frontier (quoted in Robert Dallek, *John F. Kennedy: An Unfinished Life, 1917–1963*, Penguin, 2003).
>
>> The New Deal and the Fair Deal were bold measures for their generations – but this is a new generation ... Too many Americans have lost their way, their will, and their sense of historic purpose. It is a time, in short, for a new generation of leadership – new men to cope with new problems and opportunities ... I stand tonight [in Los Angeles] facing west on what was once the last frontier ... The pioneers of old gave up their safety, their comfort, and sometimes their lives to build a new world here in the West ... Their motto was not 'every man for himself' – but 'all for the common cause' ... We stand today on the edge of a New Frontier – the frontier of the 1960s – a frontier of unknown opportunities and perils ... The New Frontier of which I speak is not a set of promises – it is a set of challenges. It sums up not what I intend to OFFER the American people, but what I intend to ASK of them ... Beyond that frontier are the uncharted areas of science and space, unsolved problems of peace and war, unconquered pockets of ignorance and prejudice, and unanswered questions of poverty and surplus ... The choice our nation must make [is] ... between the public interest and the private comfort.
>
> Most people consider Kennedy to have been an inspirational speaker. In what ways do you suppose Americans would have found this New Frontier speech in Source E inspirational?

out of a warming oven', Kennedy asked Congress for legislation on several domestic issues, including:

- a new department of urban affairs and housing in order to halt 'the appalling deterioration of many of our country's urban areas' where 70 per cent of Americans lived, and to ensure 'adequate housing for all segments of our population'
- schemes to help the unemployed
- a rise in the minimum wage
- federal financial aid to education
- health insurance for the elderly (medical bills were a major cause of poverty among senior citizens)
- tax cuts to stimulate the economy.

Unemployed, underemployed and unskilled workers

In contrast to Eisenhower, who had vetoed legislation on depressed areas, Kennedy encouraged Congress to pass measures to help with unemployment, underemployment and new skills for workers (the Cold War aroused concerns that the education system produced too few skilled technicians who could work on new weaponry and outer space projects).

The Area Redevelopment Act (1961) granted $394 million to extend employment opportunities in states such as West Virginia. Although poorly funded by Congress, it created 26,000 jobs as well as training programmes that benefited 15,000 people. However, across the nation, 5 million people remained unemployed. Furthermore, Congress refused to re-authorise the Act in 1963 (Republicans resented the focus on key Democrat congressional districts and Southern Democrats were furious with Kennedy over civil rights).

When Kennedy asked for a programme to train and retrain workers unemployed because of increased automation and technological change, Congress passed the Manpower Development and Training Act (1962). By the end of 1962, the administration claimed 351 approved programmes for 12,600 trainees in 40 states. Kennedy declared the Act highly significant, but historians generally agree it had little impact on unemployment because it mainly subsidised officials and private interests who provided the training rather than greatly decreasing the number of unemployed.

Helping the poor

Along with actions to help the unemployed, there were many other measures to assist poorer Americans:

- In the Social Security Amendments Act (1961), benefits for the elderly and disabled were expanded.
- The Minimum Wage Act raised the minimum wage by $0.25 to $1.25 and covered an extra 3.6 million workers. However, half a million of the poorest remained uncovered, including 150,000 laundry women, most of whom were black (the Republicans opposed the 25 cent raise and Southern Democrats had no desire to help black women).
- The national highway system was extended, and this provided jobs in the construction industry.
- The Food and Agriculture Act (1962) gave federal subsidies to farmers, but rural poverty persisted despite administration efforts.
- In the Omnibus Housing Act (1961), Congress granted $5 billion for the extension of existing programmes such as urban renewal and public housing and authorised low-interest loans for struggling middle-income families. However, Congress aimed to get the USA out of recession rather than to alleviate poverty, so the Act was designed to help developers, construction unions and Democrat candidates for office in the cities more than the poor.

- Kennedy used his **executive powers** to focus federal purchasing power and construction projects on areas of high unemployment and to direct the Department of Agriculture to double food distributions to the poor and unemployed. Kennedy's pilot **food-stamp programme** fed 240,000 people at a cost of $22 million annually. He also supported and extended Eisenhower's school lunch and milk programmes so that 700,000 more children could have a hot lunch and 85,000 more schools, childcare centres and camps received fresh milk.

Legislative failures

Most historians consider Kennedy's legislative record unimpressive for two reasons. First, he failed to get congressional support for his major legislative initiatives, which were:

- federal financial aid for elementary and secondary education (rejected in 1961)
- senior citizen health care to alleviate the poverty from which many of the elderly suffered because of medical bills (rejected in 1963)
- a Department of Urban Affairs and Housing to co-ordinate programmes to halt urban decline (repeatedly rejected during 1961–62)
- a civil rights bill to end the Jim Crow laws in the South (stuck in Congress at the time of Kennedy's death)
- tax cuts to stimulate the economy (rejected in 1963).

Second, no major new domestic legislation was passed during his presidency, as would be the case under his successor. Much of what Congress passed was not New Frontier legislation but extensions of existing programmes. However, it could be argued that Kennedy had put health care, urban decline and civil rights legislation firmly on the national legislative agenda.

Kennedy and civil rights

In the 1960 election campaign, Kennedy had promised to aid black Americans and, in March 1961, White House aide Harris Wofford gave a speech focussed on black voting in the South, entitled 'New Frontiers on civil rights'. Kennedy promoted interstate bus and university desegregation, but his measures were invariably reluctant responses to intense black pressure. It was Martin Luther King's 1963 Birmingham campaign (see page 372) that forced Kennedy to fully support a civil rights bill that would end de jure segregation, but the bill remained stuck in Congress at his death.

Kennedy's legislative defeats can be explained by a number of reasons:

- Congress was dominated by Republicans and conservative Southern Democrats who opposed federal expenditure and intervention in education and health insurance.
- Congressmen representing rural areas and small cities opposed expenditure on big cities, while Southerners rejected measures to assist black ghettos.
- Kennedy disliked the congressional bargaining in which Vice-President Lyndon Johnson excelled. He feared unfavourable comparisons and therefore did not use Johnson's legislative expertise. In his first year in particular, Kennedy relied upon inexperienced aides to promote his legislative agenda.
- The disastrous US-backed invasion of **communist** Cuba (April 1961) confirmed Kennedy's belief that national security took priority over social and economic reforms. Sixty-three per cent of voters agreed with Kennedy that national security was the most important issue facing Americans.

The Peace Corps

In his New Frontier speech in July 1960, Kennedy had challenged Americans to deal with 'unanswered questions of poverty and surplus'. He made little progress in dealing with poverty in the United States, but in 1961 Kennedy established his Peace Corps to help impoverished countries in Africa and Asia.

Kennedy described the Peace Corps as an organisation that allowed Americans to fulfil their responsibilities to 'world development' and 'world peace' by means of young volunteers sent to help poorer nations help themselves through teaching and technical aid. Although he insisted that the Peace Corps was not an instrument of 'propaganda or ideological conflict', in private he expressed the hope that it would counter Soviet propaganda that depicted the United States as selfishly exploiting weaker nations, and also show that American national values were superior to Soviet values.

Kennedy's inspired choice to head the Peace Corps was his brother-in-law Sargent Shriver, a tireless, idealistic, charismatic, well-travelled businessman who attracted quality staff. Thousands volunteered and those who got through the tough training programme (22 per cent failed) went off with minimal allowances to live and work alongside the nationals of the country to which they were allocated. Between 1961 and 1963, the Peace Corps sent volunteers to 44 developing countries that requested aid.

Kennedy and the Cold War

Kennedy believed that communism was dangerously expansionist and he was determined to oppose it. During his years in Congress, the Soviets took over eastern Europe (1944–48), China became communist (1949) and communist influence increased in many other areas. Kennedy fully supported the US war against communism in Korea (1950–53) and President Eisenhower's opposition to communism in Vietnam. As president, Kennedy opposed communism in many areas, including Cuba, Vietnam, less developed nations and space.

Cuba

In 1959 left-wing revolutionaries led by Fidel Castro overthrew a pro-American Cuban government. US–Cuban relations deteriorated during 1960 because Castro sought to end the American stranglehold over the Cuban economy. Cuba was only 90 miles from Florida and the Eisenhower administration decided that this was a communist threat too close to the United States. Eisenhower therefore planned US support for an invasion by anticommunist Cuban exiles that would overthrow Castro. Kennedy executed the plan in 1961, but the invasion at the Bay of Pigs failed ignominiously. Afterwards, Kennedy wrote to Richard Nixon, the Republican whom he defeated in the 1960 presidential election:

> It really is true that foreign affairs is the only important issue for a president to handle, isn't it? I mean, who gives a shit if the minimum wage is $1.15 or $1.25, in comparison to something like this?

Another Cuban crisis occurred in 1962 and this time Kennedy was perceived to be the victor when he forced the Soviets to remove missiles from Cuba.

Vietnam

Kennedy greatly escalated the US involvement in Vietnam that Truman and Eisenhower had initiated. When Eisenhower left the White House, there were just under 1,000 American military and civilian advisers there; when Kennedy died, there were nearly 20,000 'advisers', many of whom were engaging in combat.

Less developed nations

From the late 1940s, many new nations emerged in Africa and Asia. Most were former colonies that were granted their independence by colonial powers. For example, the United States gave the Philippines independence in 1946. Kennedy called less developed nations the 'lands of the rising peoples' and encouraged them to align with the USA in the Cold War. His Peace Corps was a success in this area.

Space

The USA and the Soviet Union both sought to demonstrate their technological superiority in space, and Kennedy ensured an eventual US triumph through the first landing on the moon (see page 378).

Although cynical critics within the United States derided 'Kennedy's Kiddie Korps' as a lot of kids bouncing around the world in Bermuda shorts, 71 per cent of Americans approved of the Peace Corps, tens of thousands volunteered and both political parties attested to its success when they voted to finance it for the next half-century. Many volunteers impressed their host nations and improved the US image there. Significantly, though, this was a New Frontier that owed much to Kennedy's desire to compete in the less developed nations, which he considered to be the next great Cold War arena.

The space programme

In May 1961 President Kennedy was convinced that something had to be done about a series of American Cold War humiliations:

- In October 1957 the Soviets sent the first satellite into space ('Sputnik' or 'fellow traveller') and boasted incessantly about their lead in achievements in space.
- In November 1957 a US satellite launch failure made worldwide news (British newspaper headlines included 'Oh, What a Flopnik').
- In April 1961 the Soviet Yuri Gagarin orbited the Earth. American journalists reminded Kennedy he had pledged to energise the US space programme and asked why the Soviet Union was the first country to send a human into space.
- In April 1961 the US-supported invasion of Cuba failed.

Kennedy needed a success in space to help restore faith in his leadership and the New Frontier spirit and he told Congress in May 1961 that he wanted to land a man on the moon before the end of the decade. He said it would demonstrate American superiority and bring valuable international prestige, especially in the 'battles for minds and souls' in the new Cold War arena of the less developed nations. Kennedy spent a great deal of time justifying the $40 billion cost of a moon landing ($225 for each American). In a 1962 speech, he echoed his July 1960

New Frontier speech about the challenge of 'uncharted areas of science and space', saying such difficult goals tested and measured a nation's greatness. However, his real preoccupation was a Cold War triumph. Privately, he told NASA chief James Webb he was not interested in space – only in beating the Soviets.

Despite considerable opposition to the moon programme, it could be argued that Kennedy eventually won the argument. By 1965, 58 per cent of Americans favoured the moon project and in 1969 the United States proudly landed the first man on the moon to international acclaim. Here, at least, it could be said Kennedy opened a New Frontier, although once again it was primarily in the Cold War.

Environmentalism and the expansion of the National Park system

In a 1961 speech, Kennedy described river and stream pollution as alarming and Congress responded with the Water Pollution Control Act Amendments, which built upon previous legislation. Similarly, the establishment of the Cape Cod National Seashore in 1961 followed on from the establishment of the first national seashore in 1953. Kennedy also supported a wilderness bill, but it failed to pass under him.

Marine biologist and conservationist Rachel Carson's book *Silent Spring* (1962) was a major factor in triggering the environmentalist movement in the United States. Carson's book detailed the adverse impact of pesticides upon the environment. The book infuriated the chemical companies but generated a favourable popular response. Kennedy responded to Carson's concerns by inviting her to attend the White House Conference on Conservation (May 1962) and to testify about pesticides before Kennedy's Science Advisory Committee. That committee's report (May 1963) supported her claims. Kennedy's reaction to environmentalist concerns was encouraging, but it was under Johnson and Nixon that the federal government gave a meaningful response to environmentalist concerns and expanded the National Park system (see page 398).

Conclusion: Kennedy's New Frontier

On the one hand, although Kennedy's 1960 campaign had held out the promise of change, none of his major reforming initiatives (the tax cut, federal aid to elementary and secondary education, the urban affairs and housing department, senior citizen health care and civil rights) became law in his presidency, and despite his promises about poverty he did little to overcome it. On the other hand, it could be argued that Congress was unco-operative and that at least he helped prepare the way for Johnson's great reforming programmes by placing important issues on the national agenda (see page 376). The Peace Corps and his commitment to landing a man on the moon could count as New Frontier successes, although both owed much to Kennedy's Cold War preoccupation. Perhaps he was right to put 'peace and war' above the health and welfare of individual Americans, although it should be noted that his Cold War policies have also come in for considerable criticism.

Work together

Using President Kennedy's aims as stated in his July 1960 New Frontier speech as topic titles (see page 375), one of you could argue that a particular policy was a success and the other could offer the opposing argument that it was a failure. You could toss a coin to decide who gets to argue for what!

Chapter summary

- During the period between 1955 and 1963, Americans became more suburban, mobile, consumerist and conformist.
- Television and advertisements helped increase conformity and consumerism.
- Some young people challenged conformity through rock 'n' roll, others through being 'beats'.
- Suburban expansion contributed to urban decay and impoverished black American ghettos.
- Black Americans challenged the status quo with an increasingly effective civil rights movement.
- The Eisenhower era was seen as complacent and conformist, but John F. Kennedy promised change.
- Due to his preoccupation with the Cold War, Kennedy opened a New Frontier in space and in less developed nations.
- Kennedy managed no landmark legislation, although Congress added to existing programmes.
- The situation of the poor in the United States did not greatly improve under Kennedy.

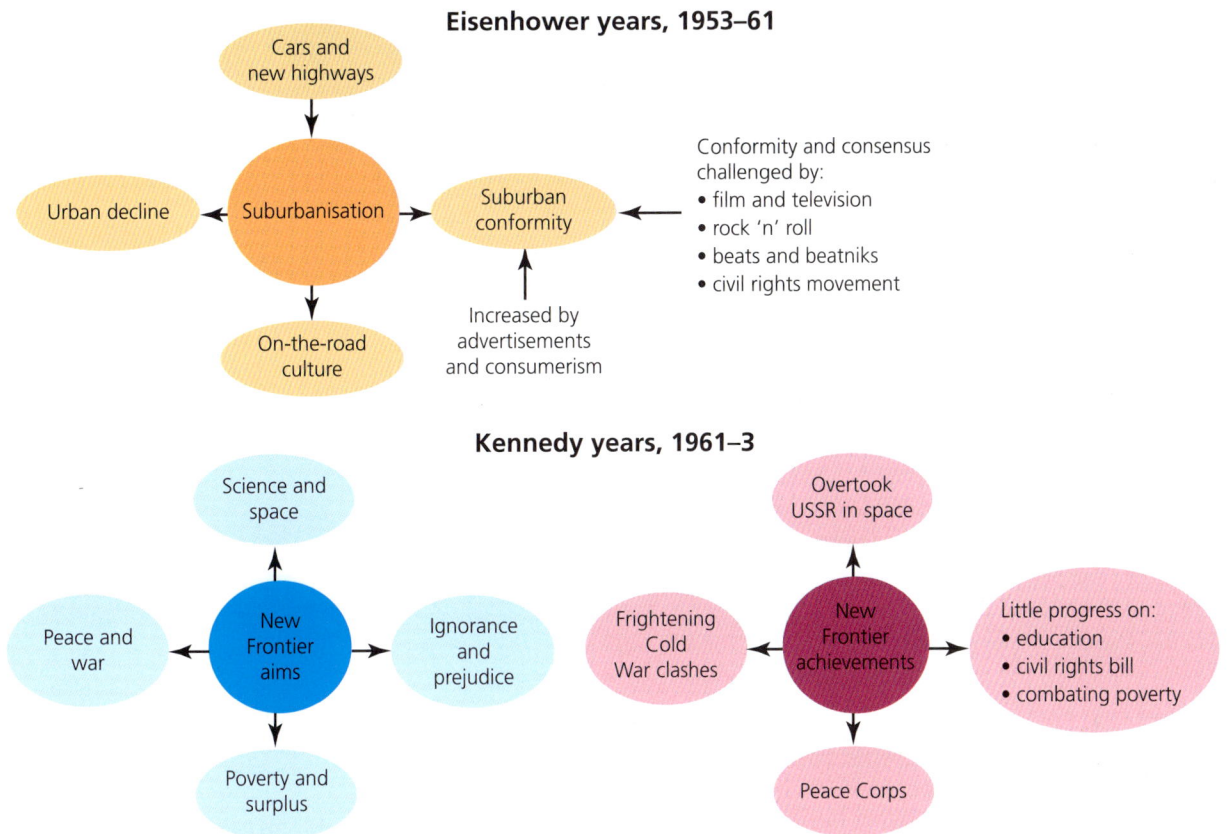

▲ Summary diagram: Affluence and conformity, 1955-63.

Recommended reading

Jean-Christophe Agnew and Roy Rosenzweig (eds), *A Companion to Post-1945 America* (Blackwell, 2006). Chapter 2 makes interesting points on race, Chapter 5 gives a good overview on the mass media from 1945, Chapter 14 investigates changing attitudes to sexuality.

Robert Dallek, *John F. Kennedy: An Unfinished Life, 1917–63* (Penguin, 2003). A very balanced and highly detailed account of Kennedy's life and achievements by an outstanding American historian.

Adam Fairclough, *Better Day Coming: Blacks and Equality, 1890–2000* (Penguin, 2001). A lively study by one of Britain's leading historians on the black struggle, often using biographical details to illuminate black problems and responses.

David Halberstam, *The Fifties* (Random House, 1993). Many people find biographies the best way to generate enthusiasm in and comprehension of a historical period. In this easy-to-read account by a journalist who is lively but nevertheless accurate on the historical detail, biographies are effectively used in order to humanise and enliven the text and to illustrate general trends.

James T. Patterson, *Grand Expectations: The United States, 1945–74* (Oxford University Press, 1996). Another outstanding American historian, with a more readable style than Dallek. This makes an excellent introduction to the course and gives brief but useful introductions to many of the contemporary writers who are likely to turn up in the source section of your exam.

Section A: Essay technique

Focus on the question and understanding the sources

The A level Section A question asks you how much a historian could learn about a specific issue from two given sources.

In order to answer the A level Section A question you will need to be able to:
- understand the focus of the question and understand the sources (this section)
- structure an essay and write good introductions (Key Topic 2, page 416)
- select information and make inferences from the sources (Key Topic 2, pages 417 and 419)
- place the sources in their historical context (Key Topic 3, page 447)
- evaluate and weigh the evidence of the Sources (Key Topic 4, page 479)
- reach and support a final judgement (Key Topic 4, page 482).

The Section A question for AS level is different from that on A level, and some guidance about this is given on pages vi–viii. However, you will need to develop very similar skills for the AS exam, therefore the activities will help with the AS exams as well. There are also some AS-style questions in every chapter.

Understanding the focus of the question

In order to answer the question successfully, you must understand how the question works. Below is a typical source-style question (the sources are on page 381). The question is written precisely in order to make sure that you understand the task. Each part of the question has a specific meaning.

'How far' indicates that you must evaluate the extent of something, rather than giving a simple 'yes' or 'no' answer.

They key word here is '**together**'. You must examine the sources as a pair and make a judgement about both sources, rather than separate judgements about each source.

> Study Sources 1 and 2 before you answer this question.
>
> **How far could the historian make use of Sources 1 and 2 together to investigate suburban conformity in the USA in the years 1955–63?**
>
> Explain your answer, using both sources, the information given about them and your own knowledge of the historical context.

This is the essence of the task: you must focus on what a historian could legitimately conclude from studying these sources.

The final part of the question focusses on a specific topic that a historian might investigate. In this case, 'suburban conformity in the USA in the years 1955-63'.

This instruction lists the resources you should use: the sources; the information given about the sources; your own knowledge of historical context that you have learned during the course.

Source 1 Extract from historian and sociologist Lewis Mumford's prize-winning book *The City in History* (Mariner Books, 1961), in which he lamented the lack of a sense of 'community' in the Hempstead Levittown. Here, he criticises uniformity and conformity in Hempstead.

> [A] multitude of uniform, unidentifiable houses lined up inflexibly, at uniform distances, on uniform roads, in a treeless communal waste, inhabited by people of the same class, the same income, the same age group, witnessing the same television performances, eating the same tasteless pre-fabricated foods, from the same freezers, conforming in every outward and inward respect to the same common mold.

Source 2 In 1961, Federal Communications Commission chief Newton Minow addressed the National Association of Broadcasters. Here, he speaks of frequent predictability and sameness in programming.

> When television is good, nothing – not the theatre, not the magazines or newspapers – is better ... But when television is bad, nothing is worse ... what you will observe is a vast wasteland. You will see a procession of game shows, violence, audience participation shows, formula comedies about totally unbelievable families, blood and thunder, mayhem, violence, sadism, murder, Western bad men, Western good men, private eyes, gangsters, more violence, and cartoons. And endlessly, commercials – many screaming, cajoling, defending. And most of all, boredom.

Overall, all Section A questions ask you to make a judgement about how far two sources are useful to the historian. However, the second half of the question specifies what a historian is focussing on.

The first part of the question sets up the **general task**, which is true of all Section A questions:

'How far could the historian make use of Sources 1 and 2 together to investigate…'

The second part of the question establishes the **specific focus**, such as:

'… suburban conformity in the USA in the years 1955–63?'

As you write your essay, you need to focus on both aspects.

How to focus in a source question

In order to maintain your focus in a source question, you can do the following:

- Use the phrases 'Source 1' and 'Source 2' when dealing with the sources so that it is clear which sources you are focussing on.
- Use words such as 'useful' or 'utility' to ensure that you are explicitly addressing the general task.
- Use comparative words and phrases such as 'Sources 1 and 2 disagree' to show that you are using the sources together.

Activity: A focussed introduction

1. Write a short introduction that provides a focussed answer to the question on page 380. See page 416 for advice on writing introductions. Also remember that this is a question about two sources.
2. Having written an introduction, swap it with a partner. Consider:
   (a) Which introduction best focussed on the question? Remember, your introduction needs to focus on the **general task** and the **specific focus**.
   (b) Which introduction best dealt with the sources *together*?
   (c) Which introduction gave the clearest answer to the question?
   (d) What can you learn from each other's approach to the question?

Use these questions to feed back to each other and improve your instructions.

Activity: AS-style questions

1. Why is Source 1 valuable to the historian for an enquiry into public attitudes towards suburbia in the 1950s?
2. How much weight do you give the evidence of Source 2 for an enquiry into public attitudes to the media in the 1950s?

Understanding the sources

Understanding the sources is crucial to doing well in Section A questions. The most important aid in this understanding is a detailed knowledge of the period. There are also techniques to aid understanding. Here are a few tips to get you started:

- Read the source word for word – if it helps, read it out loud when you are doing practice questions. This makes it much less likely that you will miss anything in the source.
- Think about the question as you are reading. You will then look out for relevant information within the source.
- Make index cards before your exam of the specific vocabulary for the topic you are studying – for example, 'suburban', 'Levittowns', 'mass society', 'rugged individualism', 'conformity'.
- Look up terms and definitions that you don't recognise in practice questions.
- Make index cards of the people who might be quoted in the sources, such as William Whyte, David Riesman, Lewis Mumford and C. Wright Mills and the documents that might be used as sources on the examination paper. Make notes on who they are and their attitudes to the key issues you have studied.

Comprehension

Comprehension is the most basic source skill. It simply means understanding the source's meaning. You can demonstrate this by:

- **Copying:** writing out some of the words of the source in your essay.
  TIP: Never copy out too much – just use a few words from the source, incorporating them within the flow of your sentence.
- **Open paraphrasing:** putting part of a source in your own words.
  TIP: Avoid simply rewriting the whole source in your own words.
- **Summarising:** summing up the meaning of the entire source, or a large part of the source, in a single sentence.
  TIP: Summarising can be useful in introductions and conclusions.

These are low-level source skills. They are useful, but you will also want to show off your higher-level skills!

Higher-level skills

Higher-level skills include:

- using the sources together (see page 380)
- making inferences (see page 418)
- analysing sources in their historical context (see page 447)
- evaluating the evidence presented in the sources (see page 479)
- reaching an overall judgement regarding the usefulness of the sources (see page 482).

Activity: Test your understanding

Having read Sources 1 and 2 on page 381:

1. Make a list of any words and phrases that you don't understand and look them up in the glossary of this book or online. You should repeat this activity regularly with the sources that you encounter. This will help with many of the sources you will examine as you study the USA, 1955–92.
2. **Extract** from Source 1 short phrases that you could use as quotations to prove that Mumford sees Hempstead as characterised by uniformity and conformity.
3. **Paraphrase** what Source 2 says about commercials on television.
4. **Summarise** Mumford's complaints in Source 1 in no more than 25 words.

Work together

Having completed the activity 'Test your understanding', swap your answers with a partner. Consider:

1. Did you both identify the same words that needed to be defined?
2. Were your partner's definitions clear and accurate?
3. Did you both extract similar short phrases from Source 1?
4. Is your partner's paraphrase clear and accurate?
5. Whose summary more precisely expressed Mumford's complaints?

Use these questions to feed back to each other and improve your analysis of the source.

Source 3 Extract from an interview with Leonard Evans conducted in November 2014. During the 1960s Evans was the principal and football coach of a black school in McKinney, Texas. He later became the district's first black teacher to work at a school for whites. He recalls life in McKinney in the 1960s.

> I have seen a whole lot of difference in the years that I've been here. Growing up, McKinney felt 100 percent segregated, but people were used to it. When you get in a habit of doing things, we didn't consider it bad. Because it's something you'd do every day. That is one of the reasons we didn't have much problems with race relations: we were trained by our parents what we could do and what we couldn't. When we wanted a hamburger, we would go to the North Side Pharmacy lunch counter. You could stand right there and see the cook make it, but you couldn't sit down on the stool. They didn't make yours no different than the other persons, but when they got through making it, and wrapping it up, they handed it to you, you paid the money and you went on out of the store.

Activity: AS-style questions

1. Why is Source 3 valuable to the historian for an enquiry into the status of black people in the Southern states in the early 1960s?
2. How much weight do you give the evidence of Source 4 for an enquiry into the problems facing black students in the Southern states in the early 1960s?

Source 4 Extract from H. Rap Brown's autobiography *Die Nigger Die!*, published in 1969. Brown went to high school in the late 1950s. Initially, Brown went to an all-black high school in Texas, before moving to an integrated high school in Baton Rouge, Louisiana. Here he recalls his experience of integrated education.

> America's a bitch. America says you got to have money to live and to get money you got to have a job. To get a job, you got to have an education. So along comes a Black man and he gets a worse than inferior education so he can't qualify for a job he couldn't get because he was Black to begin with and still he's supposed to eat, keep his family together, pay the rent and buy an Oldsmobile [*].
>
> There was this blood [**] I grew up with named J.S. He was a smart dude, particularly in math. The teachers had to tell J.S. he was smart, 'cause it was so obvious. But they made a point of letting him know that being smart wasn't enough if your hair was uncombed, your clothes a little dirty, your skin a little ashy and your manners not the best. In other words, you may be smart, but you black!
>
> White people got hung up on integration. Segregation was the problem and the elimination of segregation was the solution, not integration. It was the unequal nature of segregation that Black people protested against in the South, not segregation itself. Separate but equal is cool with me. What's the big kick about going to school with white folks?

[*] Oldsmobile: a beaten-up outdated car.
[**] Blood: a person who is part of your group.

Section B: Essay technique

Focus and structure

Your Section B essay, like all of your examined essays, will be judged on how far it focusses on the question, and the quality of its structure. You have probably already got ideas about focussing and structure in Paper 1 (see pages 40–41).

Different types of question

Section B questions focus on concepts such as cause, consequence, change/continuity, similarity/difference and significance. These different concepts require slightly different approaches. Here are some examples of these concepts in questions.

This question requires you to explain the **causes** of conformity.

1 Why were so many Americans willing to conform to contemporary values in the 1950s?

2 'Between 1955 and 1963, the main consequence of increased car ownership was the growth of service industries.' How far do you agree with this statement?

This question asks you to evaluate the **consequences** of increased car ownership.

This question requires you to evaluate the extent of **change/continuity** in American society and culture after rock 'n' roll became popular.

3 How far can the popularisation of rock 'n' roll be considered a turning point in American society and culture in the years 1955–63?

4 To what extent did television and movies both promote conformity in the years 1955–63?

This question requires you to evaluate the **similarity/difference** between television and the movies with regard to conformity and challenge.

This question requires you to evaluate the **significance** of the Montgomery bus boycott for the development of the civil rights movement in the years 1956–63.

5 How significant was the Montgomery bus boycott in the black American struggle for equality?

Structuring your essay

Your essay should be made up of three or four paragraphs, each addressing a different factor (see page 40).

However, essays that focus on different concepts will need slightly different structures:
- **Causes essays** require you to explain why something happened. Each paragraph should deal with a different possible cause.
- **Consequence essays** require you to evaluate which of a range of consequences was most important.
- **Continuity and change essays** require you to evaluate the extent of change. Therefore your essay will have to weigh up what changed and what stayed the same.
- Many essays are **evaluative essays**. They require you to weigh up the extent of something, such as **change and continuity**, **similarity and difference**, **significance** or **success or failure**. An example of an essay that requires you to evaluate success or failure would be:

To what extent were Kennedy's policies successful?

A success or failure essay requires you to establish the criteria for success – and you could use Kennedy's aims. His aims, as set out in his July 1960 New Frontier speech, could be used to structure your essay so that your paragraphs would probably be:

Paragraph 1 – science and space

Paragraph 2 – peace and war

Paragraph 3 – ignorance and prejudice

Paragraph 4 – poverty and surplus.

Within each of those paragraphs you would weigh up the extent of success or failure. For example, in the science and space paragraph, you could point out that in his lifetime, there was no sign that he had overtaken the Soviets in the space race – so he was not immediately successful. However, you could point out that after his death, thanks to his policies, the Americans were the first to land on the moon – so he had eventual success.

It is crucial to be able to distinguish between the different types of question. Confusing a causes essay with a consequences essay could seriously affect your grade.

Activity: Question types

1. Below are five different Section B style questions. Work out what types of question they are.
   (a) How did the increased popularity of television impact upon Americans in the years 1955–63?
   (b) What explains the growth of suburbia in the years 1955–63? **AS**
   (c) How far did American cities change between 1955 and 1963?
   (d) To what extent did the Interstate Highways Act (1956) represent a turning point in the US economy and US society in the years 1955–63?
   (e) To what extent did both rock 'n' roll fans and the 'beats' offer a serious challenge to American society in the years 1955–63? **AS**

2. Having worked out what types of question you are dealing with, you should now write plans for each question. Use either spider diagrams or bullet-point lists. Make sure your plan reflects the kind of essay that you are dealing with. For example, if you are dealing with a success or failure essay, you should highlight which parts of the plan deal with success and which deal with failure. Complete one plan at a time, and after each discuss it with a friend.

Work together

Having completed a plan in the activity, swap it with a partner. Consider:

1. Did you agree on what type of question you were dealing with? If not, discuss it and work out who was right.
2. Whose plan most clearly focussed on the specific type of question?
3. Did your partner's plan miss anything?
4. Did you miss anything that you should add to your plan?
5. What can you learn from your partner's approach?

Use these questions to feed back to each other and improve your question spotting and planning.

Key Topic 2 Protest and reaction, 1963–72

Overview

Expressions of discontent with the status quo became far more common during the 1960s, a decade noted for the exceptional number of protests in the United States. In this 'decade of protest', dissatisfied groups included black Americans, Hispanic Americans, Native Americans, students, women, hippies and homosexuals.

Ethnic minority protesters demanded improvement in their social, economic and political status. Some of them sought it through integration, others hoped to attain it through separatism. Student protests targeted several issues, including the escalation of US involvement in the Vietnam War. The first notable protest by gay men took place in 1969. It was directed at the harassment perpetrated by New York City police. Hippies rejected the materialistic values of the consumer society; their protests took the form of opting out rather than the demonstrations favoured by the other dissatisfied groups.

President Lyndon Johnson had long been optimistic that the affluent society could be even better. His Great Society policies aimed to end poverty and racism. However, his attempts at reform, coupled with large numbers of protests, combined to generate a conservative backlash from those whom Johnson's successor, President Richard Nixon, described as the 'great silent majority'.

The overarching theme of protest and reaction is covered in four sections:

1. Civil rights
2. Johnson's Great Society, 1964–68
3. Protest and personal freedom
4. Reactions to the counter-culture, 1968–72

TIMELINE

1963	Betty Friedan's *The Feminine Mystique* published
1963	President Kennedy assassinated; Lyndon Johnson becomes president
1964	President Johnson introduces his Great Society
1964	Civil Rights Act
1964	Johnson elected president
1964	Berkeley Free Speech Movement
1964–68	Annual summer riots in the ghettos
1965	Malcolm X assassinated
1965	Martin Luther King's Selma campaign
1965	First US ground troops sent to Vietnam
1965	Elementary and Secondary Education Act
1965	Medicare and Medicaid set up
1965	Voting Rights Act
1965	Watts riots
1965	Department of Housing and Urban Development established
1965	Cesar Chavez and United Farm Workers agree to join grape pickers' strike
1966	Meredith March Against Fear in the South
1966	National Organization of Women established
1966	Martin Luther King's Chicago campaign
1966	Black Panthers established
1966	Demonstration Cities Act
1967	Hippies' 'Summer of Love'
1968	Tet Offensive in Vietnam
1968	Martin Luther King assassinated
1968	Fair Housing Act
1968	Riots at the Democratic National Convention in Chicago
1968	Republican Richard Nixon elected president
1969	Stonewall riots
1969	Woodstock music festival
1969	Media exposure of the My Lai massacre in Vietnam
1970	Student riots at Kent State University
1970	Nixon re-elected in a landslide victory

1 Civil rights

The 1964 Civil Rights Act gave the **federal government** the legal tools to end *de jure* **segregation** in the South. Racial discrimination was no longer enshrined in law and public transport, universities, hospitals, playgrounds, libraries, museums, privately owned theatres, movie houses, restaurants, gas stations and hotels were to be desegregated by 1965. The Act forbade discrimination in employment on grounds of race, religion and sex and established an Equal Employment Commission.

Congress passed the Act because of:
- the activism of civil rights organisations such as the **NAACP**, the SCLC, the CORE and the SNCC (see page 373)
- the sympathetic response of Northern whites to the civil rights movement
- the feeling that it would be a suitable tribute to the assassinated President Kennedy, who had introduced the bill
- President Johnson's commitment to civil rights and his persuasion of Congress.

The Act helped revolutionise the South in that many public places were desegregated. However, racism could not be legislated out of existence; although the Act supported the **Supreme Court**'s ruling that schools should be desegregated, 68 per cent of Southern black schoolchildren still attended segregated schools in 1968. Although that statistic improved dramatically by 1973, when nearly half of black children attended majority white schools, a process of re-segregation began after that year.

The greatest weakness of the 1964 Civil Rights Act was that it did little to facilitate black voting in the **Deep South**. The problems faced by would-be black voters were demonstrated during Martin Luther King's Selma campaign.

The Selma campaign, March 1965

The situation of black Americans in the South was always worse in Deep South states (see map on page 367) such as Mississippi and Alabama, where white racists traditionally maintained even stricter control than in other Southern states.

Selma, Alabama had a population of 29,000, half of whom was black. However, despite an SNCC campaign, only 23 were registered voters. King therefore organised a campaign against **disfranchisement** in Selma, because he knew Sheriff Jim Clark would react violently to protest. As Birmingham had demonstrated (see page 373), King worked hard to ensure that black American protest should be non-violent but sought to elicit white violence in order to demonstrate white racism at its worst. King aimed to expose white brutality and black disfranchisement in Selma in the hope that it would force Congress to respond to President Johnson's request for voting rights legislation.

When King led would-be voters to try to register, whites threw venomous snakes at them, a trooper shot a youth trying to shield his mother from a beating and Sheriff Clark clubbed a black woman. When the Selma authorities jailed King for his demonstrations, he wrote a highly effective letter in which he said, 'This is Selma, Alabama. There are more **Negroes** in jail with me than there are on the voting rolls.' It was published in the *New York Times*.

The SCLC and the SNCC organised a march from Selma to the state capital Montgomery in order to further publicise their cause. When state troopers attacked the marchers with clubs and tear gas, black activists christened this 'Bloody Sunday'. 'Bloody Sunday' made worldwide headlines and prodded Congress into passing a Voting Rights Act (1965) that transformed the South.

The Voting Rights Act, 1965

The Voting Rights Act disallowed the literacy and constitutional interpretation tests that Southern white registrars traditionally used to stop black voter registration (see page 347). The power of Southern white registrars was decreased with the establishment of federal registrars.

The Voting Rights Act was a great success; by 1968 even Mississippi had 59 per cent of its black population registered to vote. Once registered, black people gained a voice in who represented them in local, state and federal government. As a result, the number of black Americans elected to office increased sixfold from 1965 to 1969, then doubled from 1969 to 1980. In 1969, Charles Evers became the first black man to be elected as mayor of Fayette, Mississippi. Fayette was a small town, but in 1973 two major Southern cities – Raleigh, North Carolina, and Atlanta, Georgia – elected black mayors. The Voting Rights Act ensured that from 1965 onwards, elected officials would pay more attention to the needs of the black population. King's campaign had contributed to great and positive change in the South.

King's changing priorities

Soon after Selma, the Watts ghetto in Los Angeles erupted. This caused King to change his priorities and to turn his attention to the **ghettos**.

> **Note it down**
>
> As you read this section, use a spider diagram (see page x) to make notes on the attempts of Martin Luther King, Malcolm X, the Nation of Islam and the Black Power movement to improve ghetto life. Colour code each attempt to signify degree of success – for example, great success (green), some success (orange) and failure (red).

Ghetto problems

Ghetto residents faced many problems:

- Housing was invariably poor and white prejudice made it difficult for black Americans to move elsewhere. Furthermore, many were too poor to consider moving.
- Poor-quality education made it hard to break out of the poverty cycle. In the early 1960s, only 32 per cent of black students graduated from high school, compared to 56 per cent of whites. Black people constituted 11 per cent of Americans but 46 per cent of the unemployed. This was because of poor education and the decreased number of jobs for unskilled workers due to increased automation. Chicago had 50–70 per cent black youth unemployment.
- The vast majority of policemen were white and racist.

The problems of the ghettos led to ghetto riots and increased black radicalism in the years 1964–68.

The Watts riots, 1965

Black Americans rioted in some big city ghettos in the summer of 1964, but the first large-scale ghetto riot was in Watts in Los Angeles. In August 1965 black mobs crying 'Long live Malcolm X' (see page 390) set fire to several blocks of stores in Watts. The rioting had a great impact on Martin Luther King. He told the press this had been 'a class revolt of underprivileged against privileged … the main issue is economic'. He began defining 'freedom' in terms of economic equality, called for 'a better distribution of the wealth' of America and planned his Chicago campaign.

> ### Black Americans in the North, Midwest and West
>
> Prior to the mid-1960s, most black Americans in the South considered it preferable to live in Northern cities such as New York, Midwestern cities such as Chicago and Western cities such as Los Angeles. Although white racism had led to **de facto segregated** housing and inferior ghetto schools that damaged employment opportunities, there were two main reasons why life in the North, Midwest or West seemed better. First, black people outside the South had the vote. As a result, there were two long-serving black Congressmen in the US House of Representatives. William Dawson represented a Chicago ghetto from 1943 to 1970, and Adam Clayton Powell represented New York City's Harlem ghetto from 1945 to 1971. Second, black Americans suffered less discrimination in public places. Rosa Parks said that she was attracted by the prospect of life in Detroit because black people could sit where they wanted on buses (see page 370).

The Chicago campaign, 1966

King staged a campaign in Chicago for two reasons. First, although the Civil Rights Act of 1964 ended *de jure* segregation in the South, *de facto* segregation and social and economic inequality continued in the ghettos. Second, many ghetto residents believed that the moderate civil rights leaders did not understand their problems and were no help in solving them. As a result, many were turning to radicalism and violence. Fearing that this would alienate whites and prevent further federal support, King hoped his Chicago campaign would encourage black ghetto residents to reject radicalism and violence and support the moderate wing of the civil rights movement.

Chicago's population of 3 million included 700,000 black Americans who suffered unemployment, housing and education problems in the ghetto. During the Chicago campaign, Martin Luther King's family became temporary ghetto residents from July to September 1966. His family found that their relationships deteriorated dramatically in the stifling heat of a small apartment without parks or pools in which to cool down.

King's campaign aimed to draw attention to the appalling living conditions in the ghetto and the difficulties facing any black family that tried to move out. In order to demonstrate and publicise the housing issues, King led reporters around rat-infested ghetto apartments that lacked heating for freezing winters or air conditioning for boiling summers, and led marches into white districts where black people could not buy or rent homes. The marchers were met with white abuse and violence. After two months of publicity, marches and protests, Mayor Daley made an agreement with King that the housing situation would be improved and King left Chicago in the belief that some progress had been made. However, Mayor Daley reneged on the agreement after King left Chicago.

The Chicago campaign's significance

Many Northern whites who had supported King's Southern campaign sympathised with Chicago whites who knew that if blacks moved into white working-class areas such as Cicero, property values would fall and schools would decline. Furthermore, helping the ghettos would cost taxpayers money and white Americans were unwilling to pay for improvements.

Not surprisingly, King's Chicago campaign achieved little. It alienated whites and despite a $4 million federal government grant for Chicago housing and a legacy of community action, many black Chicagoans lapsed into apathy. Several SCLC workers remained in Chicago after King left, but one said, 'I have never seen such hopelessness … A lot of people won't even talk to us.' Some turned to the **Black Power movement** (see page 391), which contributed to King's increasing disillusionment and conviction that further progress was unlikely.

Nevertheless, King persisted. He sought to broaden the movement by uniting all the impoverished groups in his Poor People's Campaign. He wanted black Americans, **Hispanic Americans**, **Native Americans** and poor **Appalachian whites** to come together to camp out in Washington DC in a civil disobedience campaign that would draw national attention to their poverty. However, he soon admitted his idea 'just isn't working. People aren't responding'.

In March 1968 a white racist assassinated King in Memphis, Tennessee.

King's achievements

King's achievements were great. He played a vital role in the demise of *de jure* segregation in the South through his protests, inspiration and organisation. His exceptionally impressive rhetorical skills and ability to inspire helped to ensure the success of the Montgomery bus boycott (see page 370), after which he was recognised by many as the leading spokesman for black Americans. Although his SCLC was poorly organised and ineffective at first, other protesters recognised his publicity value and those involved in the **sit-ins** and **Freedom Rides** sought and gained his support. It is to King's credit that he was willing to be led as well as to lead. His belief in the effectiveness of mass protest and his manipulation of white violence switched the emphasis of black activism from the NAACP's litigation strategy to mass action and turned the antisegregation principles enshrined in *Brown* (see page 339) into reality. His influence peaked in 1963 with his speech at the March on Washington and his Birmingham campaign, both of which played a big part in encouraging Kennedy to support what became the 1964 Civil Rights Act. His Selma campaign was key in the passage of the 1965 Voting Rights Act.

Obviously, King did not achieve the crucial legislation of 1964–65 alone. Protesters, other civil rights organisations, churches, local community organisations and thousands of unsung field workers also played a part. The federal government, especially the Supreme Court and President Johnson, played a vital role, as did the white extremists who aroused moderate white sympathy (President Kennedy joked that 'Bull' Connor was a hero of the civil rights movement). The other black organisations were frequently critical of King. After the Montgomery bus boycott, NAACP leader Roy Wilkins felt that King had taken too much credit, and the SNCC resented his 'top-down leadership', believing it more effective to empower ordinary people. Nevertheless, King's contribution to the transformation of the South was extremely important.

> **Source A** Extract from Ella Baker's recorded interview with Gerda Lerner, December 1970. Baker worked for the SCLC but felt she was disregarded because she was neither male, nor a minister, nor a Ph.D. She encouraged the students to establish the SNCC and warned them against adults taking over their movement. Here, she explains why she preferred to empower the people rather than to rely upon a leader.
>
> I have always felt it was a handicap for oppressed people to depend so largely on a leader, because unfortunately in our culture, the charismatic leader usually becomes a leader because he has found a spot in the public limelight. It usually means that the media made him, and the media may undo him. There is also the danger in our culture that, because a person is called upon to give public statements and is acclaimed by the establishment, such a person gets to the point of believing that he IS the movement. Such people get so involved with playing the game of being important that they exhaust themselves and their time and they don't do the work of actually organising people.
>
> How much weight would you give to the evidence of Source A for an enquiry into contemporary views about Martin Luther King? Explain your answer, using the source, the information given about it and your own knowledge of the historical context.

King failed to achieve anything significant in Chicago, but ghetto problems were great and long-standing. After 1965, Congress did little more to help black people, but Presidents Johnson and Nixon supported **affirmative action** programmes designed to remedy the effects of past discrimination and to combat current discrimination in employment and higher education. Under Nixon's Philadelphia Plan (1969), the federal government pressed companies with federal government contracts to ensure non-discriminatory employment practices, while universities gave ethnic minority students places even if their test scores were lower than those of white candidates.

Affirmative action proved to be of great significance and assistance to aspirational black Americans in the quarter-century after King's death. He had repeatedly called for affirmative action, so it could be argued that King played an important part in the introduction of such programmes.

In comparison to more radical activists such as Malcolm X and some of the advocates of Black Power (see page 391), Martin Luther King was a moderate. However, in his challenge to the nature and structure of American society, he had been a revolutionary – and, in the South, a successful one.

The impact of King's assassination

The impact of King's assassination was both positive and negative:

- Within weeks of King's assassination in 1968, Congress was shamed into passing a Fair Housing Act. The Act prohibited racial discrimination in the sale or rental of housing and required the Department of Housing and Urban Development 'affirmatively to further the purposes' of fair housing. However, white resistance made it difficult to enforce and discrimination in housing continued.
- The SNCC had always feared that King's 'top-down leadership' distracted from the need to empower black communities at grassroots level, but while the civil rights movement seemed leaderless at the national level without King, black activists continued to work effectively at local level.
- The executive and judicial branches of the federal government continued to aid black Americans, mostly through the promotion of affirmative action.
- The immediate aftermath of the assassination was terrifying. It provoked major riots in over 100 cities across America. Forty-six people died, 3,000 were injured and 27,000 arrested. A total of 21,000 federal troops and 34,000 National Guardsmen restored order following $45 million worth of damage to property across the nation.
- It encouraged followers of Black Power (see page 391) in their belief that King's relative moderation was not the best way forward.

The significance of Malcolm X

Malcolm X was significant in that he drew national attention to the terrible problems of the ghettos of the North and encouraged the black militancy demonstrated in the rise of the Black Power movement and the ghetto riots of 1964–68.

Malcolm X's background

Malcolm Little was born to a struggling Midwestern family in 1925. Although a bright boy, he subsequently recalled his teacher telling him to forget his ambition to be a lawyer as it was unrealistic for a 'nigger'. He left school at 14 and moved from Nebraska to Boston. Like many black American males, he worked as a shoeshine boy and railroad porter. His more profitable career as a drug dealer, burglar and pimp resulted in his incarceration in 1946.

While in jail, Malcolm joined the Nation of Islam (NOI), a black American religion that became very popular in the ghettos.

▲ Malcolm X.

The Nation of Islam

The NOI was established in 1930 and led from 1934 to 1975 by Elijah Muhammad, a self-styled prophet of Allah. The NOI differed from orthodox Islam in believing that:

- Allah originally created people black
- the evil scientist Yakub created other races
- whites would rule the world for several thousand years until Allah returned and ended their supremacy.

With temples in black ghettos in cities such as Detroit, New York and Chicago, the NOI offered black Americans an alternative to the white man's Christianity. The NOI urged:

- the separation of blacks and whites
- black economic independence through growing food, producing manufactured goods and owning stores
- the development of an independent black nation
- pride in black culture and history in the schools it established in cities such as Detroit
- religious commitment and a puritanical lifestyle without alcohol or extramarital sex.

The religious teachings of the NOI impressed Malcolm. It taught him the white man was the devil – 'a perfect echo', he said, of his 'lifelong experience'. Its emphasis upon the importance of black culture and history gave him the sense of racial pride and identity that he needed. As he told the NOI's Philadelphia temple a few years after his release from jail, 'We are a lost people. We don't know our name, language, homeland, God, or religion.'

After his release, Malcolm became a minister in the NOI and by the 1950s, he was its most effective preacher and recruiter. He and the NOI first gained national attention through a television documentary, *The Hate that Hate*

Produced (1959), which introduced white Americans to Malcolm's bitter characterisation of them as the enemy.

The impact of the NOI

While estimates of committed members vary from 25,000 to 250,000, the NOI had widespread influence by 1969. The NOI:

- increased divisions between blacks and whites and among blacks (Malcolm attacked Martin Luther King for humiliatingly begging for access to the white-dominated world and urging helpless black Americans to 'turn the other cheek')
- contributed to the rise of the Black Power movement, the achievements of which are controversial (see page 393)
- often had a transformational impact (in 1975, the *Washington Post* praised its impact on 'thousands of black derelicts, bums and drug addicts, turning outlaws into useful, productive men and women').

The NOI certainly transformed Malcolm X, although he left in 1964 because of Elijah Muhammad's corruption and refusal to allow him to join the Birmingham campaign (see page 373). 'We spout our militant rhetoric', said Malcolm, but 'when our own brothers are … killed, we do nothing.' It was probably a NOI gunman who assassinated Malcolm in 1965.

Malcolm X's aims, methods and achievements

Like Martin Luther King, Malcolm aimed to improve black lives through sermons, speeches and writings to advertise problems and encourage change. However, their methods were very different.

While King sought integration, Malcolm favoured **separatism** ('I'm not interested in being American, because America has never been interested in me'). Malcolm believed black people could regain their self-esteem through control of their own social, economic and political lives. As the NOI taught that whites were evil, it made sense to live separately from them.

Malcolm rejected King's advocacy of non-violence, arguing that it disarmed the oppressed. He mocked the Christian 'turn the other cheek' philosophy, saying only a fool would tell his followers to love the white enemy who treated the black population so badly. He felt such Christian teachings were 'criminal' in that they encouraged white violence against submissive blacks. If whites treated black protesters badly, 'the Negroes themselves should take whatever steps are necessary to defend themselves'.

Contemporary assessments of Malcolm's achievements varied. Newspapers and magazines such as the *New York Times* and *Time* printed critical obituaries describing him as a racist and a demagogue. Black integrationists were critical; the NAACP's leading lawyer Thurgood Marshall said Malcolm achieved nothing. Black baseball player Jackie Robinson pointed out that while Martin Luther King and others put their lives on the line in Birmingham, Malcolm stayed in safer places such as Harlem. The NOI derided him after his death. Future NOI leader Louis Farrakhan dismissed him as a 'cowardly hypocrite dog who is worthy of death'.

Malcolm was probably right in claiming that the fear he generated among whites helped the passage of the civil rights bill. However, his greatest significance lay in that he:

- drew early attention to Northern ghetto problems
- contributed to the growing pride in being black
- inspired a new, assertive generation of black Americans such as Stokely Carmichael and influenced the development of the Black Power movement.

Black Power and the Black Panthers

The Black Power movement developed in the mid-1960s. Black Power meant different things to different people. Cleveland Sellers of the SNCC said, 'There was a deliberate attempt to make it ambiguous … [so that] it meant everything to everybody.' Most white people associated Black Power with violence, but for many black people it meant political and social independence and in particular racial pride. Martin Luther King said, 'The Negro is in dire need of a sense of dignity and a sense of pride, and I think black power is an attempt to develop pride.'

Black Power advocates

A Black Power advocate could believe in one or more of these:

- violence
- armed self-defence
- separatism
- alliance with victims of colonialist oppression in the less developed nations
- 'not … black supremacy … exclusion of whites … advocacy of violence and riots' but 'political power, economic power, and a new self-image for Negroes' (the SNCC's Floyd McKissick)
- 'an attempt to develop pride' (Martin Luther King)
- black working-class revolution
- black capitalism.

Black Power developed for several reasons. First and most importantly, it was due to ghetto problems such as poverty, poor housing, poor schools, discrimination and police brutality. Second, it owed much to the influence of Malcolm X. Third, most ghetto residents agreed with Malcolm that organisations such as the NAACP and the SCLC were too slow to help and insufficiently focussed on ghetto issues. Fourth, the SNCC and the CORE became disillusioned by the slow progress towards equality and by the lack of federal protection in the **Mississippi Freedom Summer** (see page 373), and elected radical leaders such as Stokely Carmichael. It was Carmichael who first popularised the phrase 'Black Power' during the Meredith March of 1966.

The Meredith March

James Meredith was the first black American student to enter the University of Mississippi. In 1966 he planned to march through Mississippi to encourage black voter registration and, he told reporters, to challenge the 'overriding fear that dominates the day-to-day life of the Negro in the United States … particularly Mississippi'. After Meredith was shot by a white man and hospitalised, Carmichael's SNCC and King's SCLC took up the March. Carmichael was arrested for putting up a sleeping tent in a field and when released he furiously urged the burning of 'every courthouse in Mississippi'. While King's followers chanted 'Freedom Now', Carmichael's cried 'Black Power'.

The Meredith March was highly significant. First, it drew national attention to the deep divisions within the civil rights movement. For example, it was widely reported in the press that Carmichael had insisted upon the exclusion of whites from the march but that King had refused to agree. Second, although the phrase 'Black Power' was not new, the Meredith March gave it national prominence. Third, as the respected black newspaper the *Chicago Defender* said, 'This is a new day … the doctrine of passive resistance as preached by Dr King is ebbing … [There is a new] determination to meet fire with fire.' Fourth, the march brought Carmichael to the attention of white people and to the forefront of the black struggle.

Stokely Carmichael

In his book *Black Power* (1967), Carmichael set out what he saw as the characteristics of the Black Power movement. He wrote that non-violence was foolish when faced with 'someone [white] bent on destroying you'. He urged black Americans to 'close ranks' and reject interracial protest. Instead, he emphasised solidarity with anticolonial movements in the less developed nations. Carmichael envisaged eventual integration, but only when black Americans could be accepted as real equals.

However, it was the Black Panthers rather than Carmichael who were the most famous advocates of Black Power.

The Black Panthers

The Black Panthers, one of the most radical of black organisations, called for a revolution in American society. Founded in 1966 in Oakland, California, by Huey P. Newton and Bobby Seale, the Black Panthers said they were 'the heirs of Malcolm X'. Their ten-point platform included full employment, decent housing, 'education that teaches us our true [black] history', worldwide working-class struggle, **reparations**, **self-determination**, an end to police brutality and improvements in the ghetto.

Despite having only around 5,000 members in 30 loosely affiliated urban **chapters** in cities such as Oakland, Boston, New Orleans, Chicago and Kansas City, the Black Panthers had a considerable impact. Their newsletter had a circulation of around 250,000 by 1969.

Ghetto programmes

The Black Panthers won support among many ghetto residents with their practical help. They had over 40 clinics advising on health, welfare and legal rights. Their achievements in this area were often impressive. For example, they ran breakfast programmes for thousands of poor black schoolchildren and raised awareness of sickle cell anaemia, a disease that disproportionately affected black people. In 1969, the Black Panthers set up their first Liberation School, a summer school for black children in Berkeley. The curriculum in these schools was designed to generate knowledge of and pride in black culture and history. Other schools followed in cities such as Philadelphia and New York.

Police brutality

A major Black Panther aim was to combat police brutality. They stockpiled weapons for self-defence and tailed the police in the hope of exposing their brutality (violent shootouts resulted). In 1967, Black Panthers surrounded and entered the California state legislature to protest repressive legislation. Such actions, coupled with their paramilitary uniforms, weapons and rhetoric (Seale would cry, 'Power to the People … The revolution has come … Time to pick up the gun' at rallies), made the Black Panthers appear strong and fearless to those who had long been oppressed.

However, such actions antagonised the white authorities and not surprisingly the Black Panthers were targeted by the police and the **FBI**. Out of the many court cases against the Black Panthers, the most famous was the case of the Chicago Eight, who were arrested for conspiring to incite a riot at the **Democratic National Convention** in Chicago in 1968 (see page 410). Bobby Seale was one of Chicago Eight charged in 1969. He was jailed and, after his release, he left the Black Panthers in 1974. In that same year, Newton fled to Cuba in order to avoid frequent arrest. While Seale eventually became a media celebrity (he wrote a bestselling cookbook, *Barbecu'n with Bobby* in 1988), Newton was shot dead in 1989 in Oakland by a drug-dealing member of a rival group.

Evaluating the Black Panthers

Opposition from the police and the Nixon administration and their own internal divisions dramatically decreased Black Panther influence and dynamism by the early 1970s. However, they had caught the popular imagination, perhaps because they attracted so much media attention. Indeed, it has been suggested that they were little more than a temporary media phenomenon. Although whites usually reviled them, the Black Panthers were popular in the black community. Polls indicated that a majority of black Americans sympathised with the Black Panthers and black nationalism. In contrast, the **approval rating** of the NAACP among the black population dropped from 80 per cent in 1963 to just 20 per cent in 1969. Black Panther popularity was due to the highly practical help offered in the ghetto programmes and to the assertiveness that demonstrated and aroused black pride.

The decline of Black Power

By the early 1970s the Black Power movement had fizzled out. Suggestions for the decline include that it:

- was always relatively ill-defined and poorly organised
- was unrealistic in thinking America was ripe for revolution
- was sexist and alienated its female supporters
- lost the white liberal funding that supported the SNCC and the CORE before their switch to radicalism (the SNCC excluded white members in 1966, the CORE excluded them in 1968)
- attracted the hostility of the white authorities, who pursued and silenced Black Power leaders.

However, the movement had a lasting impact.

The significance of Black Power

There is no doubt that the Black Power movement contributed to growing black pride. The movement raised black American morale, especially by encouraging college courses on black history and culture. Black Power failed to solve ghetto problems, but they were probably insoluble given white unwillingness to fund improvements.

There is considerable disagreement over the impact of Black Power in relation to violence. What most black Americans considered to be self-defence, most white Americans perceived as violence. While some suggest that self-defence and/or violence alienated whites and damaged the previously effective civil rights movement so that it was unable to achieve much after 1965, others point out the impossibility of progress in dealing with the ghetto problems. Some argue that the Black Power movement played a part in encouraging some white support for affirmative action.

Black Power helped to inspire radical Native Americans (see page 442), women (see page 403) and Hispanic Americans (see below). Interestingly, though, the most prominent Hispanic American of the 'decade of protest' was Cesar Chavez, a man more like Martin Luther King than Malcolm X or Stokely Carmichael.

The work of Cesar Chavez

Mexican Americans worked and lived mostly in states bordering Mexico (Arizona, California, New Mexico and Texas). By 1968, around 80 per cent lived in urban ghettos where they suffered from high unemployment, segregated schools, poor housing and police discrimination. In the first half of the twentieth century, middle-class Mexican Americans established civil rights organisations such as the League of United Latin American Citizens (LULAC). By the early 1960s they had won some important local victories on **segregation**, police brutality and voter registration. However, unlike the NAACP, they did not gain great support, attention or political clout. Many Mexican Americans were poorly educated, were not US citizens and hoped for an eventual return to Mexico, so they avoided organisations such as the LULAC and mainstream US politics. This was particularly the case with horribly exploited Mexican farmworkers in California, many of whom were illegal immigrants fearful of being sent back to Mexico and even greater poverty.

California's San Joaquin Valley was a rich farming area where migrant Mexican-American farmworkers earned the minimum wage or less for planting and harvesting the vegetables and fruits that fed America. Many spent whole days bent at the waist because their employers gave them short hoes. Their health was further jeopardised by the powerful disinfectants with which the crops had been sprayed. The workers had no protection from federal or state authorities; they were not voters, so politicians ignored them.

Chavez's United Farm Workers

In 1962, Arizona-born Cesar Chavez (1927–93), a former migrant labourer and veteran civil rights activist, formed the first union of farmers set up since the Depression and the sole union controlled by Mexican Americans. In 1965

> ### Young Mexican-American activists
>
> A good example of the greater pride and purposefulness encouraged by Chavez and the UFW was Mexican-American student activism in east Los Angeles in 1968. The students demanded more:
>
> - college preparatory lessons
> - Mexican-American history lessons
> - bilingual lessons
> - Mexican-American teachers, administrators and councillors
> - Mexican food in school cafeterias.
>
> When those demands were ignored, over 10,000 students walked out in protest. These 'blowouts' soon spread to other high schools in the Southwest.
>
> These students began to call themselves 'Chicanos'. They organised the First National Chicano Youth Liberation Conference in Denver in 1969, which was followed by the establishment of the La Raza Unida Party (LRUP) in Texas in May 1969. The LRUP did not last long, because it was only able to win electoral victories where there was a large, concentrated Mexican-American population. However, it won representation on school boards and city councils in several Texan towns, such as Crystal City and Eagle Pass. More importantly, it demonstrated the increased Mexican-American activism that owed so much to Chavez and the UFW.

his small United Farm Workers (UFW) joined a strike started by Filipino farmworkers against California's San Joaquin Valley grape growers. Chavez organised non-violent demonstrations, including an inspirational 300-mile march to the state capital, with banners showing pride in Aztec and Catholic culture. In 1966, with the help of white middle-class **liberals** such as Senator Robert Kennedy, the UFW organised a national boycott of table grapes, supported at its peak by 17 million Americans. In 1970 the growers finally agreed to sign union contracts, but the triumph was somewhat short-lived. Grower opposition, mechanisation and rising immigration weakened the UFW so that by the late 1980s, members harvested only 10 per cent of the grapes.

For many, then and now, Chavez was a hero; his religiosity, encouragement of Catholic Church support, emphasis on non-violence and ability to inspire made *Time* magazine liken him to Martin Luther King. He gave ethnic Mexican workers their first positive and successful American role model. He and the UFW:

- contributed to the eventual passage of exceptionally worker-friendly legislation in California
- helped galvanise Mexican Americans and Mexican immigrants into activism
- played an important part in stimulating a civil rights movement that inspired formerly quiescent Mexican Americans throughout the Southwest to a greater ethnic pride and purposefulness. That in turn led local and national government to pay greater attention to Mexican-American needs.

Conclusion: Civil rights

The civil rights movement had several areas of focus. In the South, civil rights activism made a vital and successful contribution to the end of *de jure* segregation and black disfranchisement through the Civil Rights Act of 1964 and the Voting Rights Act of 1965. That legislation revolutionised and greatly improved black lives. The movement in the South was dominated by Martin Luther King, who emphasised the importance of non-violence in black protest.

The ghettos constituted another area of focus in the civil rights movement. Ghetto problems were given great prominence in the early 1960s by Malcolm X and this was important in generating the Black Power movement. Many of the participants in this movement rejected non-violence, arguing that black people were entitled to defend themselves. Neither King, nor Malcolm, nor the Black Power movement managed to improve ghetto conditions. However, Malcolm and the Black Power movement were important in generating greater black pride.

The black civil rights movement helped to inspire other ethnic minorities, such as Mexican Americans.

> ### Work together
>
> Work with a partner. One of you should identify positive aspects of the civil rights movements of 1963–72, the other the negative aspects. After you have finished, combine your findings. Overall, would you say that the civil rights campaigns of the period were more of a success than a failure?

2 Johnson's Great Society, 1964–68

President Lyndon Johnson personally experienced poverty in his youth and in a May 1964 speech, he introduced his dream of a **Great Society** in America that would be characterised by:

- the end of poverty
- racial equality
- educational reform
- modern housing
- the end of urban decay
- a renewed sense of community
- environmentalism
- peace with other nations.

Americans had already demonstrated readiness to respond to an idealistic president who repudiated the selfishness and complacency of the 1950s. Furthermore, after Kennedy's assassination, many welcomed Johnson's optimism and positivity about what America could achieve. With a 75 per cent approval rating in the polls, Johnson persuaded Congress to enact an exceptional quantity of reforming legislation that impacted upon millions of lives.

> **Note it down**
>
> Look at the summary of Johnson's Great Society dreams from his May 1964 speech. Using the bullet points as side headings, create a table with columns headed: Aims; What Johnson did; How successful. Fill in the table as you read the chapter.

Civil rights laws

One aspect of the Great Society of which Johnson dreamed was racial equality. The civil rights bill was stuck in Congress at Kennedy's death but when Johnson insisted that the best way to honour Kennedy's memory was to pass it, Congress agreed. The Civil Rights Act of 1964 ended legally enforced segregation in the South but did not ensure that black people throughout the South could vote. Martin Luther King's Selma campaign drew attention to this and Johnson and Congress responded with the Voting Rights Act (see page 387).

The 'open housing law', 1968

Johnson supported integrated housing. He argued that 'imprisoning the Negro in the slums' was immoral and exacerbated racial tensions. However, whites opposed integrated housing, sometimes because of racism but mostly because black movement into white neighbourhoods made property values fall. Johnson received his worst-ever hate mail over his plea for integrated housing and Congress repeatedly rejected his appeals for legislation until Martin Luther King's assassination.

After King's assassination, Congress felt it had to respond with a legislative tribute. The 1968 Fair Housing Act prohibited discrimination in the sale or rental of housing, but proved difficult to enforce in the face of determined white opposition.

Johnson's achievements

The Civil Rights Act and the Voting Rights Act transformed black American lives in the South. Johnson also used his **executive powers** to help black Americans. For example, an Executive Order of 1965 required any institution receiving federal funding to employ more non-whites. This accelerated the spread of affirmative action (see page 389), opinions of which varied. Liberals praised it as greatly helping minorities in education and employment, while conservatives criticised it as discriminating against whites and demeaning blacks.

Although the situation of many black Americans remained dire, Johnson had helped improve their social, political and economic status through his civil rights legislation, affirmative action policies and War on Poverty (see page 396). 'I think Johnson was the best we ever had', said civil rights activist Bayard Rustin.

> **Source B** Extract from Johnson's speech before Congress, March 1965, in support of the voting rights bill.
>
> Rarely are we met with a challenge ... to the values and the purposes and the meaning of our beloved Nation. The issue of equal rights for American Negroes is such an issue ... The command of the **Constitution** is plain ... It is wrong – deadly wrong – to deny any of your fellow Americans the right to vote in this country ... A century has passed, more than 100 years, since the Negro was freed. And he is not fully free tonight ... A century has passed, more than 100 years, since equality was promised. And yet the Negro is not equal ... [The protests of the American Negro] have awakened the conscience of this Nation ... He has called upon us to make good the promise of America. And who among us can say that we would have made the same progress were it not for his persistent bravery, and his faith in American democracy?
>
> Which of Johnson's words in Source B do you suppose were designed to appeal to the consciences of his audience?

Poverty and unemployment

For Johnson, the end of poverty was the most important element of his Great Society. In January 1964, he declared an 'unconditional war on poverty'. A group of University of Michigan social welfare experts predicted in 1962 that it would be relatively easy to end poverty with a $2 billion annual budget. Others rightly judged this unrealistic.

Johnson persuaded Congress to pass an Economic Opportunity Act (EOA) in 1964, boasting that 'for the first time in all the history of the human race, a great nation … is willing to make a commitment to eradicate poverty among … the forgotten fifth'. The EOA established an Office of Economic Opportunity (OEO) to co-ordinate the War on Poverty and in February 1965 Johnson proudly informed Congress of progress:

- Forty-four states had antipoverty programmes, and six more soon would have.
- Fifty-three Job Corps centres providing job training were receiving thousands of applications daily.
- Members of 25,000 families on welfare were receiving work training.
- Thirty-five thousand college students were on work-study programmes, under which poorer students could earn federal funding through part-time work.
- Thirty-five thousand adults were learning to read and write.
- Ninety thousand adults were enrolled in basic education programmes.
- Neighbourhood Youth Corps in 49 cities and 11 rural communities were giving young people jobs to help them stay in education or receive training.
- Eight thousand Volunteers in Service to America (VISTA) were assisting groups such as needy children, Native Americans and migratory workers.
- Over 4 million were receiving Aid to Families with Dependent Children benefits.
- Loans were being given for small businesses and rural development – for example, $17 million was distributed in rural loans in 1968.

Johnson's achievements

Contemporary assessments of the success of the War on Poverty varied, usually according to the political stance of the assessor.

Some OEO-financed programmes were greatly praised. Two acclaimed programmes were:

- Head Start, which was designed to enable poor pre-school children to catch up with other children before beginning school. Nearly 1 million disadvantaged children enrolled in the programme during Johnson's presidency.
- Upward Bound, which linked higher-education institutions to poorer students with college potential. Around 50,000 disadvantaged students participated in the programme each year during Johnson's presidency.

Other antipoverty measures were also of benefit – for example, the extension of Kennedy's **food-stamp programme** through the Food Stamp Act (1964) and the 35 cent rise in the minimum wage.

However, statistics that suggested improvement to some were criticised by others. Johnson boasted that the percentage of Americans in poverty was falling (it fell from 17 per cent in 1965 to 11 per cent by 1972) and that federal expenditure on the poor had increased from $13 billion in 1963 to $20 billion in 1966. However, critics said this level of federal expenditure on the poor was excessive and pointed out that it cost more to put a ghetto youth into the Job Corps than into Harvard. In sharp contrast, liberals complained that the War on Poverty was underfunded. Their complaints were unrealistic; Congress and taxpayers would not have agreed to further expense.

Johnson failed to eradicate poverty. For example, one-third of non-white families still lived below the **poverty line**, with unemployment and **infant mortality rates** nearly twice those of whites. He deserves credit for drawing attention to poverty and for his efforts to improve the situation, but invites criticism for making politically unrealistic promises and for weaknesses in the planning and implementation of his antipoverty programmes (see page 397), which even his aides subsequently admitted.

Education

Johnson's Great Society promised improvements in education; 'nothing matters more to the future of our country', he said. In 1964 he highlighted the problems:

- Fifty-four million Americans had never finished high school.
- Eight million had under five years of schooling.
- One hundred thousand high-school graduates with proven ability could not afford to enter college.
- Schools were overcrowded and run down and there was a shortage of good teachers.

As Congress felt education should be under local control, presidents rarely obtained funds for it. However, emphasising that America spent 'seven times as much on a youth that is gone bad' as on one who stayed in school, Johnson persuaded Congress to double federal expenditure on education to $8 billion. Two important acts channelled the money towards the poorest states and the poorest children: the Elementary and Secondary Education Act (ESEA) and the Higher Education Act (HEA).

The ESEA, 1965

Opinions of the effectiveness of the ESEA vary. In an example of flaws in the planning and implementation of Johnson's antipoverty programmes, critics pointed out that while he saw the ESEA as an antipoverty programme, local officials made sure it never was; in 1985, the National Institute of Education estimated that half the expenditure had gone to children living *above* the poverty line. Defenders responded that 6.7 million poor children benefited, that assistance to those above the poverty line was essential to make the measure politically acceptable and that there was nothing wrong with helping *all* American children.

Critics pointed out that the preoccupied President paid little attention to how the legislation worked in practice and that it was difficult for the federal government to extend its reach into local school districts. However, liberals rejoiced that the law reinforced the principle of federal aid to schools and helped galvanise state governments into greater investment in education.

The HEA, 1965

The HEA aimed to help poorer students and 11 million of them benefited from the $650 million it provided. By 1970, 25 per cent of college students received some financial aid from the HEA, helping the number of students rise from 15 per cent of 18- to 22-year-olds in 1950 to 34 per cent in 1970 and 52 per cent in 1990. Most people praised the Act for greatly increasing opportunities for students, especially those from low-income families. The HEA also helped poorly funded black colleges.

Johnson's achievements

By the end of Johnson's presidency, millions of children had benefited from federal aid to education, the percentage of those with a high-school diploma rose, the shortage of teachers had been ended, new buildings had been constructed and the accessibility of a college education had increased. His biographer Robert Dallek concluded (in *Flawed Giant: Lyndon Johnson and His Times: 1961–73*, Oxford University Press, 1999), 'If his educational reforms did not lead to a Great Society, they have at least made for a better society. It is an achievement for which Johnson deserves the country's continuing regard.'

Housing and urban problems

Johnson envisaged a Great Society with an end to urban decay and urban housing problems. American inner cities were characterised by poverty, poor schools and housing, pollution and congestion. Congress accepted several of Johnson's suggestions for improvement.

First, the new government department of Housing and Urban Development (HUD) was established in 1965. HUD co-ordinated the various programmes to combat housing shortages and decay in the urban areas where over two-thirds of Americans lived.

Second, Johnson suggested that Chicago, Detroit, Houston, Los Angeles, Philadelphia and Washington DC be designated 'demonstration cities' or 'model cities', in which the local community and all levels of government would work on the lack of cheap housing, good transportation and recreational facilities, and on slum clearance. Congress passed the Demonstration Cities Act (1966), but at $1.2 billion the programme was underfunded. Johnson estimated the total cost at $2.4 billion, but the *New York Times* said New York City alone needed $6 billion. Senator Robert Kennedy criticised model cities as 'a drop in the bucket', insufficient to deal with this 'central problem of American life', while the *New York Times* claimed the model cities failed because members of Congress demanded something for their particular constituents, so that the six cities became 150 cities and the money was spread too thinly to be effective.

Third, Johnson tried to improve ghetto housing. His Omnibus Housing Act (1965) financed rent supplements and $8 billion worth of low- and moderate-income housing in the ghettos. Through federal loans and his famed powers of persuasion, Johnson was successful in encouraging builders to construct reasonably priced housing. However, the ghettos remained dire and white taxpayers remained unwilling to help. So, in 1968 Johnson focussed on obtaining an end to discrimination in housing. This would cost taxpayers nothing but hopefully alleviate the overcrowding in the ghettos. He told Congress:

> Minorities have been artificially compressed into ghettos where unemployment and ignorance are rampant, where human tragedies and crime abound, and where city administrations are burdened with rising social costs and falling tax revenues. Fair housing practices, backed by meaningful federal laws that apply to every section of the country, are essential if we are to relieve the crisis in our cities.
>
> (Quoted in Robert Dallek, *Flawed Giant: Lyndon Johnson and his Times: 1961–73*, Oxford University Press, 1999)

Congress responded with the Fair Housing Act (see page 395).

Johnson's achievements

Housing was one of the major causes of ghetto discontent. Four-fifths of the Detroit ghetto rioters arrested in 1967 had jobs paying over $120 weekly, suggesting that it was housing and alienation rather than poverty that caused their dissatisfaction. However, taxpayers did not want to fund large-scale improvements and opposed integrated housing. Although Johnson tried, the minority housing problem was surely too great for any one president to solve.

> ### The environment
> Rachel Carson's book *Silent Spring* (1962) aroused national interest in environmental dangers and Congress responded to Johnson's requests. During his presidency, legislation to protect the landscape included the Wilderness Act (1964), which protected 9.1 million acres of federal land, and the Highway Beautification Act (1965), which decreased billboard advertising and eliminated junkyards. Johnson added 50 new areas to be administered by the National Parks Service and expanded existing ones. Three new National Parks were set up during his presidency: Guadeloupe Mountains National Park in Texas, North Cascades National Park in Washington State and Redwood National Park in California.
>
> Environmental legislation such as the Water Quality and Clean Air Acts (1965) and the Clean Water Restoration Act (1966) gave the government the authority and the responsibility to act forcefully against air and water pollution. With these measures, Johnson began the environmental and safety regulations that subsequently triggered great debate over the scale of federal government interventionism. Despite powerful opponents, his regulations have generally remained, suggesting that the advantages outweighed the disadvantages.

Medicare and Medicaid, 1965

The elderly had always constituted a large proportion of America's poor and healthcare was a major cause of their poverty. **Democrats** such as Johnson had long advocated federal financial support for healthcare, but conservative Americans insisted that subsidised or free healthcare smacked of **communism**. Four successive Congresses had refused to help the large proportion of over 65s who had no private health insurance. However, with Democrat majorities in both houses of Congress and Johnson's legendary powers of persuasion (some said bullying), Congress established **Medicare** and Medicaid in the Social Security Act of 1965.

Medicare provided federally funded health insurance for over 65s and those with disabilities, regardless of their income or existing medical conditions. In 1966, 19 million Americans enrolled in Medicare. Under the provisions of Medicaid, the federal government gave financial assistance to states to help them provide medical assistance to residents who could not afford essential medical services. Within a single year, Medicaid increased the amount spent by the federal and state governments on healthcare for poorer citizens from $1.3 billion to over $2 billion.

Johnson's achievements

Johnson rightly boasted that he had produced 'a healthcare revolution'. Medicare helped lift millions of elderly Americans out of poverty and within a decade became so popular that no president dared to oppose it lest he alienate the powerful 'grey vote'.

However, there were problems. First, there were gaps in coverage (for example, eyeglasses). Second, both Medicare and Medicaid proved far more expensive than Johnson anticipated. For example, because the legislation allowed hospitals and doctors to set the fees, total Medicare costs rocketed from $3.5 billion in 1966 to $144 billion by 1993. In 1965 around 5 per cent of the **GNP** was spent on healthcare, but over 15 per cent by 1990. Third, although one-fifth of the population benefited from Medicare and Medicaid by 1976, the problem of reasonably priced care for all Americans remained.

Conclusion: Johnson's Great Society

Johnson found himself torn between 'the woman I really loved – the Great Society' and the 'bitch of a war' against communism in Vietnam, a legacy from his three predecessors that he greatly expanded.

In his January 1966 State of the Union address, Johnson said America could afford both the Great Society and the war, but the War on Poverty became a casualty of the war in Vietnam. By 1966 there was a growing belief that his Great Society had run out of steam in the face of financial reality. The Vietnam War precipitated inflation and tax rises, making the Great Society unpopular. In 1967, Missouri's governor told Johnson there was 'no great public support for your Great Society programmes'. Congress demanded, and Johnson agreed to cuts in Great Society programmes. President Kennedy's brother-in-law Sargent Shriver claimed, 'Vietnam took it all away, every goddammed dollar. That's what killed the war on poverty. It wasn't public opinion.' Between 1965 and 1973, $15.5 billion was spent on the Great Society and $120 billion on Vietnam. Some said the Great Society was an unrealistic dream; Richard Nixon described the War on Poverty as a 'cruel hoax' because taxpayers were never going to grant unlimited funds to help the poor.

Johnson's Great Society achievements have always been controversial and assessments of them depend upon the political stance of the person making the judgement. Johnson greatly increased the role and expenditure of the

▲ Johnson, in the front to the right, promoted his Great Society vision at an address to graduates of the University of Michigan, 1994. Why do you suppose President Johnson chose to attend a graduation ceremony?

federal government in areas such as education and welfare, which liberals approved and conservatives disapproved. Conservatives lamented that Johnson's social welfare programmes increased dependency, while liberals lamented that the War on Poverty failed to end poverty and had little impact on American cities and even less on rural areas. Conservatives criticised the expense of the Great Society, while liberals criticised Johnson for not going far enough, saying much of what he did was symbolic rather than substantive. Johnson certainly never managed to do as much as he had hoped, repeatedly saying: 'So little have I done, so much have I yet to do.'

For many of the poor, elderly, sick and unemployed, Johnson made a considerable difference. His achievements would surely seem miraculous, if only he had not promised so much more. Critics say his broken promises led to disillusionment with government and politics and damaged liberalism, while supporters are awed by aspirations and efforts that went far beyond what any other president conceived and attempted, with the possible exception of Johnson's hero Franklin D. Roosevelt.

> ### Work together
> There is a great deal of legislation and a great many statistics to learn about Johnson's Great Society. Create index cards (see page xi) with the name of an Act on one side and an explanation on the other, and also cards with statistics on one side and an explanation of what they provide evidence for on the other. Test each other on the contents of those cards.

3 Protest and personal freedom

While the 1950s was a decade many considered characterised by consensus, conformity and stagnation, the 1960s was a decade of change and protests. The black civil rights movement helped inspire other protesters such as students, women, gay men and lesbian women, and those opposed to the Vietnam War.

Women's protests focussed initially upon inequality in employment and then expanded to target sexism. By the end of the 1960s, lesbian women and gay men were increasingly vociferous about discrimination. The largest group of protesters were students. Their targets included the restrictive practices of the university authorities, black inequality and the Vietnam War. It was the Vietnam War that generated the most protests. Student protests against the war were frequently fuelled by fears of the **draft** as well as by opposition to US policies in Vietnam. Students were not the only antiwar protesters; in 1969, in particular, older Americans participated in protests.

> **Note it down**
>
> Create a table to fill in as you read this chapter.
>
> | | Aims | Methods | Achievements |
> |---|---|---|---|
> | Student protest | | | |
> | Women's movement | | | |
> | Gay rights movement | | | |
> | Hippies | | | |

Student protest

The targets of student protesters included the college authorities, conformity, **materialism**, war and racism. Unprecedented numbers of students protested in the 1960s because of some or all of the following reasons:

- President Kennedy encouraged idealism. In his July 1960 speech (see page 375), he had urged Americans to face the challenges posed by issues such as peace and prejudice. Many students took up his challenges and demanded peace in Vietnam and an end to prejudice against ethnic minorities. In his **inaugural address** in 1961, he said, 'Ask not what your country can do for you; ask what you can do for your country.' For many of the young, change and improvement seemed possible in their optimistic, affluent society led by this charismatic and idealistic young president.
- The civil rights movement gave practice and inspiration to many student protesters.
- Students resented college authorities who treated them as children and supported an unjust war in Vietnam.
- The rocketing student population decided it could protest without risk because everyone else seemed to be protesting, there was safety in numbers and students had no jobs to lose or families to support.

The SDS and the New Left

One of the most influential student organisations was Students for a Democratic Society (SDS). SDS was established in 1960 by Tom Hayden and other University of Michigan students who were inspired by the **socialists** of the 1930s, the beat generation (see page 365) and student participation in the civil rights movement (see page 387).

In 1962, representatives of SDS, the SNCC, the CORE and the Student Peace Union met at Port Huron, Michigan. They called upon students to change the political and social system, to liberate the poor, the ethnic minorities and all enslaved by conformity, and to support a peaceful foreign policy. SDS emphasised the potential of the individual, currently stifled by the impersonal nature of the big universities, bureaucracy and the centralisation of all power, and called for 'participatory democracy' and a '**New Left** … consisting of younger people' to awaken Americans from 'national apathy'.

> **Source C** In 1962, Tom Hayden was the main author of the Port Huron Statement, which set out the ideas espoused by SDS. Here, the manifesto expresses unease with affluence, racial inequality and **Cold War** militarism.
>
> We are people of this generation, bred in at least modest comfort, housed now in universities, looking uncomfortably to the world we inherit … We begin to see complicated and disturbing paradoxes in our surrounding America. The declaration 'all men are created equal…' rang hollow before the facts of Negro life in the South and the big cities of the North. The proclaimed peaceful intentions of the United States contradicted its economic and military investments in this Cold War status quo … While two thirds of mankind suffers undernourishment, our own upper classes revel amidst superfluous abundance.
>
> How much weight would you give the evidence of Source C for an enquiry into the attitude of young people toward American society in the early 1960s? Explain your answer using the source, the information given about it and your own knowledge of the historical context.

SDS first gained national attention with its April 1965 anti-Vietnam War demonstration in Washington DC. Possibly as many as 25,000 marched, but the march did nothing to halt President Johnson's continued escalation of the war. However, that demonstration was not the first student protest to hit the headlines. Student radicalism had first gained national attention in December 1964 at the University of California at Berkeley.

Berkeley's Free Speech Movement

The leader of the December 1964 protests at the University of California at Berkeley was Mario Savio. Savio had participated in the SNCC's Mississippi Freedom Summer and black voter registration campaign (see page 372) and wanted to raise money for the SNCC. However, the university authorities did not allow fundraising and political activity on campus. This prompted thousands of Berkeley students to protest against this infringement upon their constitutional right to free speech. They occupied the administration building until the police ejected them and made 800 arrests. This student movement became known as the Berkeley Free Speech Movement (FSM). Its slogan was 'You can't trust anyone over 30'. The students gained considerable support from the Berkeley teaching staff, so the university backed down and allowed political discussion and activities on campus. However, there was another flare-up in 1965 when a student was arrested for displaying the word 'fuck'.

The FSM triggered nationwide student protest. Students criticised their universities as impersonal, bureaucratic and excessively regulatory (the **age of majority** was 21 so universities served **in loco parentis**) and demanded a say in university government. Antiwar students disliked universities undertaking (paid) research for government defence agencies.

Antiwar protests

Student antiwar sentiment pre-dated the escalation of the Vietnam War. Established in 1959, the Student Peace Union staged a protest outside the White House in 1961 against the testing of nuclear weapons. It had 3,000 members by 1962.

The Vietnam War led tens of thousands more students into antiwar activism. In May 1964, 1,000 Yale University students staged a protest march in New York City. During 1965, many universities held 'teach-ins' with antiwar lectures and debates; 20,000 participated in a Berkeley teach-in. The protests frequently led to disorder. For example, in 1965, 8,000 marchers (mostly from Berkeley) clashed with the Oakland police and vandalised cars and buildings. The largest antiwar protest to date was staged by SDS in Washington DC.

The Vietnam War

At the Geneva Conference in 1954, the French colonialists agreed to exit Vietnam, which was to be temporarily divided into a **communist** north and a non-communist south. In defiance of the Geneva agreements, President Eisenhower made the division permanent when he created and supported the anticommunist 'state' of 'South Vietnam'. Determined to sustain this anticommunist state, Kennedy sent 20,000 American 'advisers' to South Vietnam. Some engaged in combat with the communists. Johnson began bombing communist North Vietnam in 1964 and dispatched the first American ground troops to South Vietnam in 1965. By 1968, there were over 500,000 US soldiers there. Some had volunteered, some had been drafted.

Fear of the draft motivated some antiwar protesters, while the more idealistic opposed the American bombing that caused Vietnamese civilian casualties and believed that the Vietnamese should be left to decide upon their form of government. Ironically, the president who dreamed of creating the Great Society became one of America's most hated leaders because of his Vietnam policies.

In 1967, the New Left's National Mobilization Committee to End the War (the Mobe) organised a demonstration in Washington as part of the Stop the Draft Week. Over 100,000 attended the march, chanting 'Hell no, we won't go'. Draft cards were publicly burned across America. Several thousand Berkeley radicals tried to close down the Oakland draft headquarters. Faced with 2,000 police who attacked them with clubs, the demonstrators retaliated with cans, bottles, smoke bombs and ballbearings placed on the street to stop police horses. High on drugs, some vandalised cars, parking meters, newsstands and trees. By 1968, many other protests were violent; the main targets were campus administration buildings and the offices of the **Reserve Officer Training Corps (ROTC)**. Students resented the military attempting to recruit promising graduates through these offices. Across the nation, many of these offices and buildings were burned or bombed. The trigger for many of the protests in 1968 was events at Columbia University in New York City.

Columbia University protests

In 1968, students at Columbia University had multiple grievances. They opposed the university's involvement in weapons research; as this research assisted the government, the students felt the university was supporting the Vietnam War. There was also controversy about the relationship between the university and adjacent Harlem and its black and Hispanic populations. Since 1958, Columbia

University's expansion programmes had led to the eviction of several thousand Harlem residents from properties owned by the university. In 1968 the university planned to construct a gym in a public park. The Harlem population would be able to access the gym, but through a separate door. Students interpreted this as a segregationist policy and opposed the construction of 'Gym Crow', although defenders said that the separate door was necessary because the gym was situated on a hill.

These grievances generated protests in which 1,000 of Columbia's 17,000 students participated. Students seized five university buildings and covered the walls with pictures of Malcolm X and communist heroes such as Karl Marx and Che Guevara. The police used clubs and made 692 arrests. The university shut down for that term and abandoned the gym and many defence contracts. Hundreds of similar occupations followed across the USA.

Assessment of the student protest

Some protesters achieved their aims. Student civil rights activists played an important part in the dismantling of the Jim Crow laws and in the establishment of courses on black history and culture in the universities. Student complaints about the university authorities were redressed, as seen with the relaxation of the controls on free speech and political activism in Berkeley and the ending of the defence contracts at Columbia. Many people believe that the antiwar protests helped persuade Johnson to halt escalation and Nixon to end the war.

Some protesters failed to achieve their aims. The opposition of SDS and the New Left to American materialism proved ineffective. Veterans of SDS and the New Left complained that their worthwhile ideas about the consumer culture were discredited by the **counter-culture**'s selfishness and excess (see below).

Assessments of student protest invariably depend upon the political stance of the assessor. Some people credit the student protesters with improving the quality of American life, particularly for ethnic minorities, and with ensuring the US withdrawal from Vietnam. Others believe that student protest promoted violence, offered little that was constructive and damaged the great American liberal tradition. Many contemporary Americans disliked protesters and the counter-culture, and this contributed to a conservative reaction that helped gain the **Republican** Richard Nixon the White House in the election of November 1968.

The counter-culture

Some define the 'counter-culture' as including all those who protested against the dominant culture, such as **feminists**, those opposed to the Vietnam War, the Black Panthers (see page 391) and the **hippies**. Others focus solely on hippies when they consider the counter-culture. The hippies certainly seem to best illustrate a movement that adopted an alternative lifestyle to that of the dominant culture.

The roots of this hippie counter-culture lay in the beat generation (see page 365), with its spontaneity, drugs, free love and general defiance of authority and convention. The hippie counter-culture rejected American society's emphasis on individualism, competitiveness and materialism, preferring communal living and harmony. In their uniform of faded blue jeans, they listened to music that reaffirmed their beliefs, singing 'We Shall Overcome' by Joan Baez, 'All You Need is Love' by the Beatles and antiwar songs.

In the mid-1960s, a group of alienated young people moved into San Francisco's Haight-Ashbury area, wearing 'alternative' clothes such as Indian kaftans, attending '**happenings**', smoking and selling cannabis, adopting new names such as Coyote and Apache, and growing their hair. Perhaps as many as 100,000 hippies visited Haight-Ashbury, which became a centre of a **bohemian** lifestyle and was re-christened 'Hashbury' because of the popularity of **hash**. Two events in San Francisco in 1967 gained national attention. The first was the 'Human Be-in' that took place in Golden Gate Park in January. Thousands of young people met to celebrate personal freedom, communal living and environmentalism. Allen Ginsberg (see page 365) and Dr Timothy Leary were among those attending. The second was the 'Summer of Love', which attracted tens of thousands of followers of the counter-culture from all over America. *Time* magazine noted that every major city had 'hippie enclaves' and estimated that there might be around 300,000 hippies.

Woodstock

The greatest counter-culture happening was the Woodstock rock festival in New York State in 1969, which was attended by 400,000 people. Its favourite slogan was 'Make love not war'. One enthusiastic participant recalled how 'everyone swam nude in the lake, [having sex] was easier than getting breakfast, and the pigs [police] just smiled and passed out the oats [drugs]'. The acts were led by Joan Baez, Jefferson Airplane and Jimi Hendrix. Hendrix's performance of the American national anthem, 'Star Spangled Banner', attracted criticism from those who interpreted his use of amplifier feedback and distortion to make a sound like exploding bombs as an antiwar statement.

Sex and drugs

The common contemporary consensus was that hippies enjoyed premarital and extramarital sex more often and more openly than previous generations. In 1967, Republican politician Ronald Reagan told reporters that student protesters' activities 'can be summed up in three words: Sex, Drugs and Treason'. A favourite hippie drug was cannabis, which induced relaxation and happiness. Some graduated to the stronger LSD, a synthetic drug that produced colourful hallucinations and inspired much psychedelic art and some rock music. Some preferred heroin, which was far more addictive and physically damaging. Some liked to combine several addictive substances, such as alcohol, cocaine and barbiturates. Harvard University professor Dr Timothy Leary discovered hallucinogenic mushrooms on a visit to Mexico, openly advocated drug use in his *Psychedelic Review* and advised students to 'Turn on, tune in, drop out'. Harvard fired him.

The Diggers

Many hippies were content to listen to music and experience communal living. Others wanted more. For example, the Diggers of San Francisco sought a social revolution and the end of **capitalism**. They organised free music concerts and distributed free food, medical care and transportation. In a happening in December 1966, they paraded a coffin through the streets of San Francisco, carrying signs saying 'The Death of Money'. In October 1967, they proclaimed the 'Death of Hippie' and rejected the counter-culture, which they said had been taken over by the media.

The significance of the hippies

The hippie movement had faded by the mid-1970s, but it had influenced American society. Hippies drew attention to and popularised Eastern philosophy and religion, health foods and environmentalism, and contributed to the liberalisation of attitudes towards sex and drugs. They also helped trigger the conservative reaction that brought Richard Nixon to the White House.

Overall, the impact and significance of the hippies was of less importance than that of those who protested against the Vietnam War and racial and gender inequality.

The growth of the women's movement

Women's activism grew dramatically in the 1960s because of persistent inequality, other protest movements and the influence of Betty Friedan.

Inequality

The economic inequality of women was pronounced. Increasing numbers of women worked after the Second World War. By 1963, most of them were in low-paid jobs such as waitresses, cleaners, shop assistants or secretaries. Educated women were expected to choose 'female occupations' such as nursing and teaching, which conformed to traditional stereotypes of women as providers of nurture and care. Many employers were sexist. In the mid-1960s, Congresswoman Martha Griffiths scolded an airline that had fired stewardesses when they married or reached age 32: 'You are asking … that a stewardess be young, attractive and single. What are you running, an airline or a whorehouse?'

Statistics demonstrated inequality in employment opportunities in the early 1960s; for example, women constituted 80 per cent of teachers but 10 per cent of principals, and only 7 per cent of doctors and 3 per cent of lawyers.

Gender inequality was often enshrined in law and practice. Eighteen states refused to allow female jurors, and six said women could not enter into financial agreements without a male co-signatory. Schools expelled pregnant girls and fired pregnant teachers. Some states prohibited married women from accessing contraception. Daniel Patrick Moynihan, a leading figure in President Nixon's administration, admitted that 'male dominance is so deeply a part of American life the males don't even notice it'.

Not surprisingly, increasing numbers of articulate middle-class women agitated for equal pay, equal opportunities and equal respect in the 1960s.

The activist tradition among women

The women's movement did not appear out of the blue in the 1960s. Established in 1916, the National Women's Party was still active, particularly in demanding an **Equal Rights Amendment (ERA)** to the Constitution in order to guarantee gender equality. Long influential in the Democratic Party, labour movement activists helped persuade President Kennedy to establish his Commission on the Status of Women. Although Kennedy's commission called for equal pay, it also suggested special training for marriage and motherhood and rejected demands for the ERA.

The impact of other protest movements

Other protest movements encouraged women's activism in the 1960s. First, they showed that protests could bring desired results, such as legislative reform. Second, their sexism inspired a reaction. Women faced discrimination and sexual harassment in civil rights organisations such as the SNCC and SDS. 'Women made peanut butter, waited on table, cleaned up and got laid. That was their role,' confessed one SDS male. In 1964 women constituted 33 per cent of SDS members but only 6 per cent of the leadership. Although SDS approved a pro-women's rights resolution, the accompanying debate was characterised by male ridicule of and contempt for gender equality. Having been politicised by organisations such as SDS, some disillusioned women moved on to campaign for women's rights.

Some antiwar protesters became feminists. In early 1968, hundreds of women attended an antiwar meeting in Washington then marched to Arlington National Cemetery and staged a mock 'Burial of Traditional Womanhood'.

Betty Friedan and domesticity

In 1963, Smith College graduate and suburban housewife Betty Friedan drew attention to the dissatisfaction of many middle-class housewives with domesticity.

Women's magazines, films and advertisements in the 1950s frequently promoted domesticity as the norm and the ideal. Girls were encouraged to play with dolls, to emphasise their femininity and to play down their intellectual capacity. Some women took refuge in tranquillisers (the quantity taken doubled between 1958 and 1959) or alcohol.

Friedan wrote about what she described as 'the problem that has no name' in *The Feminine Mystique* (1963). She said women were imprisoned in a 'comfortable concentration camp', taught that 'they could desire no greater destiny than to glory in their own femininity'. That destiny required focussing upon the needs of their children and husband rather than upon their own needs. Friedan urged women to break out of the 'camp' and fulfil their potential through education and work. Her bestselling book tapped a reservoir of discontent, especially among college students.

The establishment of the NOW

In 1966 Betty Friedan and others formed the National Organization for Women (**NOW**) because they were unhappy when the government's Equal Employment Opportunities Commission (EEOC) refused to enforce **Title VII** of the 1964 Civil Rights Act, which banned discrimination in employment on the basis of sex as well as race. The NOW aimed to monitor the enforcement of the legislation and to demand an amendment to the Constitution that affirmed women's right to equality in all areas.

> **Source D** Extract from *The Feminine Mystique* (Penguin, 1963) by Betty Friedan. Here, she explains the dissatisfaction of suburban housewives with the contemporary emphasis upon the merits of domesticity.
>
> The problem lay buried, unspoken, for many years ... It was a strange stirring, a sense of dissatisfaction, a yearning that women suffered in the ... [mid] twentieth century ... Each suburban wife struggled with it alone. As she made the beds, shopped for groceries, matched slipcover material ... chauffeured Cub Scouts and Brownies, lay beside her husband at night – she was afraid to ask even of herself the silent question – 'Is this all?'
>
> ... There was no word of this yearning in the millions of words written about women, for women, in all the columns, books, and articles by experts telling women their role was to seek fulfilment as wives and mothers ...
>
> The proportion of women attending college in comparison with men dropped from 47% in 1920 to 35% in 1958. A century earlier, women had fought for higher education; and now girls went to college to get a husband. By the mid-fifties, 60% dropped out of college to marry, or because they were afraid too much education would be a marriage bar ...
>
> American girls began getting married in high school ... Girls started going steady at 12 ... an advertisement for a child's dress ... in the *New York Times* in ... 1960, said: 'She Too Can Join the Man-Trap Set.'
>
> How much weight would you give the evidence of Source D for an enquiry into American women's attitudes in the early 1960s? Explain your answer, using the source, the information given about it and your own knowledge of the historical context.

> **Source E** The NOW held its founding conference in Washington DC in October 1966. There it produced a Statement of Purpose. Here, the Statement explains why the organisation is needed.
>
> [The NOW aims] to break through the silken curtain of prejudice and discrimination against women in government, industry, the professions, the churches, the political parties, the judiciary, the labor unions, in education, science, medicine, law, religion, and every other field of importance in American society. There is no civil rights movement to speak for women, as there has been for Negroes and other victims of discrimination. The National Organization of Women must therefore begin to speak.
>
> What does this extract from the NOW's Statement of Purpose suggest about contemporary male attitudes to the abilities and role of women?

The NOW used a variety of tactics including:

- Litigation – for example, the NOW represented Lorena Weeks, who said that the Southern Bell company had contravened the 1964 Civil Rights Act when it denied her application for promotion to switchman because a woman would not be able to lift a weight of 30 pounds. Weeks and the NOW lost the initial case in 1966, but were victorious in 1969 after several appeals.
- Political pressure – for example, the NOW produced a Bill of Rights for Women (1968) that sought the enforcement of Title VII, equal access to education and employment, maternity leave, federally funded childcare to assist working mothers and reproductive rights (the NOW was the first national organisation to endorse the legalisation of abortion).
- Public information campaigns – for example, in 1967 the NOW helped gained national attention for the flight attendants' fight against sexist airline advertisements such as 'I'm Debbie, Fly Me'.
- Protests – for example, in 1970 the NOW organised a national women's strike for equality. An estimated 100,000 women gave the strike active support. Thousands marched with 'Don't iron while the strike is hot' banners. Some protesters dumped their children on their husbands' desks.

Airlines versus stewardesses

In 1963, all flight attendants were female and airlines fired them for getting married or when they were 32 years old. A flight attendants' union was established to publicise this situation; for example, during a 1963 press conference a 35-year-old stewardess asked, 'Do I look like an old bag?'

A combination of factors kept the airlines' treatment of the stewardesses in the news in 1965. First, the House of Representatives held hearings on the treatment of the stewardesses, which further increased public support for their cause. Second, the federal government's EEOC began to implement Title VII of the 1964 Civil Rights Act. In its first ruling on the issue, the EEOC found Northwest Airlines guilty of illegal discrimination in firing a stewardess for getting married, but this ruling was not enforced. As a result, 1966 saw the first of a series of court battles in which the airlines faced the stewardesses, who had the support of the EEOC and the NOW.

Eventually, the stewardesses won. In 1968, some of the major airlines agreed that stewardesses could marry and in 1970 a federal court ruled against marriage bans and age restrictions (*Sprogis v. United*). In 1972 an appeal court ruling enabled men to become flight attendants.

From women's rights to women's liberation

The women's rights movement in the early and mid-1960s sought equal rights and opportunities in work. The late 1960s saw the development of the women's liberation movement, which put a new emphasis upon publicising and opposing sexist oppression and cultural practices that objectified women. The movements overlapped.

Among the leading radicals were Jo Freeman, Shulasmith Firestone and Ti-Grace Atkinson.

Jo Freeman, Shulasmith Firestone and Ti-Grace Atkinson

Jo Freeman was an excellent example of the connection between the protest movements of the 1960s. She served on the FSM committee at Berkeley and was one of the 800 arrested in December 1964 (see page 401), and she worked on voter registration for the SCLC in Alabama, Mississippi.

In 1967, Freeman and Shulasmith Firestone attended a National Conference of New Politics in Chicago. Conference director William Pepper said that their resolution on gender equality did not merit floor discussion: 'Move on, little girl. We have more important issues to talk about here than women's liberation.' This inspired Freeman to produce a newsletter, *Voice of the Women's Liberation Movement*, which encouraged the formation of women's liberation groups nationwide.

The first national meeting of women's liberation activists was held in Chicago, where Freeman lived. Freeman said the women's liberation movement was a 'younger branch' of the women's movement that 'prides itself on its lack of organisation … Eschewing structure and damning the idea of leadership … thousands of sisters around the country are virtually independent of each other'. She saw the women's liberation movement as complementary to the older organisations such as the NOW.

Support for 'women's lib' was generated through Freeman's newsletter and through '**consciousness-raising**' meetings in colleges and in the community. These meetings sought to raise awareness of gender inequality and to encourage activism to combat it. Awareness certainly increased; in 1960, one-quarter of women polled said they felt discriminated against, but after consciousness-raising, it had reached two-thirds by 1974.

Shulasmith Firestone and Ti-Grace Atkinson were excellent examples of 'women's libbers' whose opposition to male domination went too far for many members of the NOW. The experience at the National Conference of New Politics inspired Shulasmith Firestone to establish a women's liberation group in New York City, the New York Radical

Feminists, which held consciousness-raising meetings focussed upon the issue of male subordination of females. In her book, *The Dialectic of Sex* (1970), she suggested solutions such as in vitro fertilisation to free women from their biologically determined position in society.

Ti-Grace Atkinson was an early member of the NOW, but left the organisation in 1968 because she considered it insufficiently radical. She set up a group called The Feminists in New York City. Atkinson argued that the sexual revolution (see page 407) had benefited men more than women as it had given them easier access to women's bodies. She was critical of marriage (which she likened to slavery) and pornography.

Disunity in the women's movement

Women activists frequently disagreed over tactics and issues:

- Some members of the NOW felt that the beliefs of Shulasmith Firestone and Ti-Grace Atkinson and the dramatic demonstrations of some supporters of 'women's lib' made the American public less sympathetic. For example, in 1968, a group of over 100 women disrupted the swim-suited parade at the Miss America pageant in Atlantic City with a stink bomb and crowned a live sheep 'Miss America'. They threw bras, girdles, curlers, false eyelashes, wigs and other 'women's garbage' into a 'freedom trash can', singing,

    Atlantic City is a town without class,

    they raise your morals and they judge your ass.

- Some women activists disagreed over the demand for legalised abortion.
- Breakaway groups such as the Radicalesbians resented the lack of support from the NOW for lesbian women.

However, despite the disunity, the women's movement proved more lasting than most 1960s protest movements. Its effectiveness was demonstrated by the response of the federal government.

> ### Where did 'Ms' come from?
> Women's libbers began to use the prefix 'Ms' in protest against the 'Miss' and 'Mrs' differentiation that had no counterpart for unmarried and married males. Gloria Steinem published *Ms*, a magazine that explored issues such as female sexuality and the **glass ceiling**.

▲ A women's liberation march in the late 1960s. Would Betty Friedan have agreed with the sentiments expressed on this poster?

The government response

President Johnson responded favourably to feminist lobbying with a 1967 executive order banning gender discrimination by federal contractors. The NOW monitored enforcement, fighting over 1,000 discrimination cases and winning $13 million in back pay for women by 1971.

The Democrat-controlled Congress was sympathetic to women's demands. Title IX of the Education Amendments of 1972 prohibited sex discrimination in educational institutions receiving federal funds. More significantly, both houses of Congress agreed to the Equal Rights Amendment (ERA) in that year. However, President Nixon opposed the ERA and abortion. He vetoed the 1971 Child Development Act, which would have established the national system of childcare centres for poor working mothers that feminists had long sought. Nixon believed mothers should stay at home and feared the cost of the system. However, he recognised gender equality was an increasingly important political issue, worried that only 3.5 per cent of the people whom he appointed to office were women, and did nothing to stop the EEOC taking enforcement increasingly seriously.

The Supreme Court was supportive of women's rights in rulings such as *Weeks* v. *Southern Bell* (see page 405) and *Reed* v. *Reed* (1971). In the latter, the Supreme Court ruled that Idaho's insistence that 'males must be preferred to females' with regard to the administration of the estates of the deceased was unconstitutional and that laws differentiating men and women had to be 'reasonable not arbitrary'.

Sexual liberalisation

While groups such as students, women and black Americans protested publicly against establishment values, many Americans privately disregarded social norms through sexual behaviour that defied convention and upset conservatives.

Anxieties about sexual liberalisation were nothing new; conservatives in the 1920s had bemoaned women with short skirts and 'loose morals'. However, exceptional changes in attitudes in the 1960s constituted a sexual revolution with increased acceptance of casual premarital sex, abortions, homosexuality and extramarital relations. The proportion of unmarried couples living together increased dramatically. The number of couples who cohabited rose dramatically:

- 1955 – around 250,000
- 1960 – 500,000
- 1970 – nearly 750,000
- 1980 – around 2 million.

Similarly, the percentage of single white women who had had sex was around 25 per cent in the mid-1950s, but more than double that by 1972. The percentage of babies born to unmarried women also rose. These changes were rapid. In 1969, 74 per cent of women said they believed premarital sex was wrong; by 1973 it was only 53 per cent.

Popular culture reflected the change. In 1963, a New York City television station cancelled a programme on 'A Sexual Revolution', while the married couple in the popular *The Dick Van Dyke Show* (1961–66) were assigned separate beds separated by a nightstand. In a flashback episode about their son's birth, the word 'pregnant' was considered unsuitable for use. However, by 1968, the Broadway show *Hair* celebrated sexual freedom. The naked cast on the stage caused a sensation that helped trigger increasing nudity and graphic depictions of sexual activity in mainstream entertainment.

What explains the sexual revolution?

The sexual revolution had its roots in slowly changing attitudes after the Second World War, when sensationalist book covers and *Playboy* (first published in 1953) increasingly emerged onto the open shelves rather than from under the counter and the **Kinsey Reports** (1948–52) generated greater and more open discussion of sex. Shocked but fascinated, Americans learned from Kinsey that:

- 68 per cent of American males and 50 per cent of American females had engaged in sex before marriage
- 37 per cent of males and 13 per cent of women had had at least one homosexual experience
- 8 per cent of males and 4 per cent of females had had some kind of sex with animals.

Kinsey's report both reflected and hastened the liberalisation of sexual behaviour. The pace of change speeded up even more after 1960, when the widespread availability of the first oral contraceptive for women ('the pill') liberated many women from fears of pregnancy at a time when many groups were demanding greater freedom and change. Armed with the pill and influenced by the rights revolution and the counter-culture, women began to insist upon their right to express their sexuality as they saw fit, unrestricted by old conventions.

Conservatism, birth control and abortion

Long-standing conservatism about birth control and abortion had held back sexual liberalisation. It was 1965 before the Supreme Court ruled in *Griswold* v. *Connecticut* that married couples could not be refused contraception and 1974 before doctors could no longer refuse birth control to unmarried adults for 'moral reasons'. Abortion was illegal until 1973, so women sought backstreet practitioners, or used bleach douches or inserted coat hangers. In the early 1960s, one Chicago hospital treated over 5,000 women patients for abortion-related complications.

The impact of sexual liberalisation

As a result of sexual liberalisation, sex was 'discovered', explored and given saturation coverage by popular culture. More importantly, many individuals felt that sexual liberalisation had freed them from a stifling Victorian moral code. Increasing numbers of Americans felt free to cohabit and have children outside marriage. Liberals saw the period as characterised by an upward trajectory toward ever-greater freedom, but conservatives bemoaned the 'permissive society' as contributing to the breakdown of the traditional family unit.

The origins of gay rights

The history of gay rights is an excellent example of the domination of conservatism and consensus in the 1950s and the impact of the rights revolution in the 1960s.

American culture had long been **homophobic**. In the post-Second World War era, same-sex sexual activity was illegal and homosexuals were considered perverted and commonly expelled from universities or fired from jobs. The American Psychiatric Institute classified homosexuality as a mental illness until 1974.

Gay men had been involved in nationwide community building, lobbying, publishing and networking since the Second World War but had struggled to gain acceptance. In 1951 a group of homosexual men in Los Angeles established the first Mattachine Society to promote greater tolerance. In Mattachine Societies in several cities in the 1960s there was much discussion of emulating the black civil rights movement and the Black Power movement. However, as yet the authorities remained intolerant, as demonstrated in New York City.

The Stonewall riots

Gay men had long suffered **entrapment** at the hands of the New York City police. In 1969 homosexuals at the Stonewall Inn in Greenwich Village fought back against police harassment, triggering five days of rioting in which hundreds participated. This has often been seen as the birth of gay rights. Although gay life in America did not begin with the Stonewall riots, what was new in the late 1960s was increased gay group consciousness and assertiveness and slowly changing public attitudes. However, gay rights such as the legalisation of homosexual acts and freedom from discrimination had not yet been attained.

Lesbian assertiveness

The protest movements of the 1960s played an important part in the development of lesbian assertiveness. For example, Kate Millett participated in CORE activism (see page 372), then joined the NOW committee in 1966. She then moved to more militant groups such as the Radicalesbians and the New York Radical Women. In her book *Sexual Politics* (1970), she criticised the patriarchal nature of American society and argued that the traditional family upheld sex-based oppression. Another early member of the NOW, Ti-Grace Atkinson (see page 405) was perhaps the first person to use the phrase, 'Feminism is the theory, lesbianism is the practice.'

The relationship between the NOW and vociferous lesbians was initially tense. Many NOW members feared that equating women's rights with lesbianism would damage their cause, but from 1971 the NOW began to acknowledge lesbian rights as a feminist issue.

Conclusion: Protest and personal freedom

While the 1950s was perceived as a decade of conformity and stagnation, the 1960s unleashed a pent-up desire for change on the part of ethnic minorities, students, hippies, women and homosexuals – even President Johnson sought to transform American society. Some of the demand for change was motivated by idealism, some by a whole group's exasperation with inequality, and some stemmed from a more personal focus on the rights of the individual. The 1960s saw real change, sometimes through legislation, sometimes through new attitudes. The United States would never be the same again.

> **Work together**
>
> Look at what your partner has written in their table from the activity on page 400 about the achievements of the movements of students, women, gay men, lesbian women and hippies. Are you in agreement over their successes and failures?

4 Reactions to the counter-culture, 1968–72

Californian Richard Nixon served in Congress (1947–53) and then as Eisenhower's vice-president (1953–61). After defeat in the 1960 presidential election and in the 1962 Californian **gubernatorial** election, he retired from politics, telling the media they would no longer have Richard Nixon to kick around. *Time* magazine said, 'Barring a miracle, Richard Nixon can never hope to be elected to any political office again.' However, the protesters, the counter-culture and events in 1968 provided that miracle.

While protesters and the counter-culture made headlines throughout the 1960s, life went on as normal for those whom Nixon described as 'the great **silent majority**' or **Middle America**. The silent majority regarded radicalism, protests, violence and the counter-culture with ever-increasing horror and helped ensure Nixon's election to the presidency in November 1968.

> **Note it down**
> Create two spider diagrams (see page x) to show the reasons why Richard Nixon appealed to the silent majority in: (1) 1968; and (2) 1972.

The rise of the 'silent majority'

When Richard Nixon accepted the Republican nomination for the presidency in August 1968, he talked about those whom he would soon christen the silent majority. He was not the first to use the phrase 'silent majority' but he popularised it after a speech in November 1969 in which he asked 'the great silent majority of my fellow Americans' to support his Vietnam policies. From his speeches, it is clear that Nixon's silent majority were those who did not protest against the war (Nixon spoke of the 'vocal minority' who did), participate in riots or adopt a counter-cultural pose. When Nixon talked to advisers, he used the term 'Middle America' interchangeably with the 'silent majority'.

The rise of the silent majority owed much to exasperation with riots and protests and to events during 1968 that suggested that the United States was a nation in crisis. These events included the Tet Offensive, the assassination of Martin Luther King and the riots that followed, the Miss America pageant (see page 406) and the Democratic National Convention in Chicago.

> **Source F** In his acceptance speech at the Republican National Convention in Miami in August 1968, Richard Nixon described the silent majority or Middle America.
>
> As we look at America, we see cities enveloped in smoke and flame. We hear sirens in the night. We see Americans dying on distant battlefields abroad. We see Americans hating each other; fighting each other; killing each other at home. And as we see and hear these things, millions of Americans cry out in anguish. Did we come all this way for this? Did American boys die in Normandy [*], and Korea [**], and in Valley Forge [***] for this?
>
> Listen to the answer to those questions. It is another voice. It is the quiet voice in the tumult and the shouting. It is the voice of the great majority of Americans, the forgotten Americans – the non-shouters; the non-demonstrators. They are not racists or sick; they are not guilty of the crime that plagues the land. They are black and they are white – they're native born and foreign born – they're young and they're old. They work in America's factories. They run America's businesses. They serve in government. They provide most of the soldiers who died to keep us free. They give drive to the spirit of America. They give lift to the **American Dream**. They give steel to the backbone of America. They are good people, they are decent people; they work, and they save, and they pay their taxes, and they care … This, I say to you tonight, is the real voice of America.
>
> [*] Normandy: American troops fought against the Germans in Normandy during the Second World War.
>
> [**] Korea: American troops fought against communism in Korea (1950–53).
>
> [***] Valley Forge: American troops spent the winter of 1777 at Valley Forge during the American War of Independence.
>
> Why is Source F valuable to the historian for an enquiry into reactions to the protests and the counter-culture? Explain your answer, using the source, the information given about it and your own knowledge of the historical context.

Tet and the impact of events in Vietnam

By the end of 1967 there were over 500,000 American troops in Vietnam. The war was becoming increasingly unpopular among Americans, so the Johnson administration launched a public relations offensive which claimed that America was winning the war.

During the Tet holiday in January 1968 the Vietnamese communists launched their great Tet Offensive on South Vietnam. Although American and South Vietnamese forces eventually re-took South Vietnam's cities, American media images showing communists overrunning the South Vietnamese capital suggested a 'credibility gap' between what Johnson was saying about winning the war and what was actually happening. Exhausted by the war and public hostility to his policies, Johnson said he would not stand for re-election but would focus on ending the war. The silent majority did not want to lose the war but hoped that America could somehow achieve the 'peace with honour' that the Republican presidential candidate Richard Nixon promised.

Assassinations: King and Kennedy

The second crisis was the assassination of Martin Luther King by a white racist in March 1968. The assassination provoked major black riots in 100 cities in which 41 died, 3,000 were injured, 27,000 arrested and $45 million worth of property was damaged. It took 21,000 federal troops and 34,000 National Guardsmen to restore order. The silent majority was tired of black rioting and feared that America had become a divided country in which political dialogue had been replaced by acts of violence. This seemed to be confirmed a few weeks later by the assassination of Democratic presidential candidate Robert Kennedy and then by events at the Democratic National Convention.

The Democratic National Convention, Chicago

In August 1968 the Democrats met in Chicago for their National Convention to choose their presidential candidate. The Mobe (see page 401) and the **Youth International Party** (Yippies) called on young people to come to Chicago to demonstrate contempt for the American political process by disrupting this convention.

The silent majority watched in horror as:

- around 30,000 members of the New Left (see page 400) arrived in Chicago, spreading rumours that they were going to put LSD in the city's water supply
- Chicago's Mayor Daley mobilised around 12,000 police and banned marches
- the Yippies produced their candidate for president – 'Pigasus', a squealing young pig
- the media revealed students having sex in public and provoking the police (calling them 'pigs', blowing marijuana smoke in their faces, throwing bags of urine at them and giving them the finger). Removing their badges and nameplates, the police retaliated with clubs and gas. According to a British journalist, 'the kids screamed and were beaten to the ground by cops who had completely lost their cool … They were rapped in the genitals by cops swinging billies [clubs]'.

Polls recorded 56 per cent approval of police actions against the protesters, while one Congressmen accused radicals of wanting 'pot instead of patriotism' and 'riots instead of reason'. Chicago confirmed, and sometimes caused, many voters' support for the presidential candidate for law and order in 1968, Republican Richard Nixon.

The appeal of Richard Nixon

By the time of the 1968 presidential election, many Americans craved law and order and a return to the good old days before all the disruptions and changes. Although never personally popular, Richard Nixon was a moderate Republican, associated with the peace and prosperity of the Eisenhower years. He appealed to Middle America, to the silent majority of law-abiding, hard-working patriots. He attracted voters tired of radicalism, change and Great Society programmes, especially as he promised to bring 'peace with honour' in Vietnam.

Nixon narrowly defeated the Democratic candidate Hubert Humphrey in 1968. He was re-elected in a landslide victory in 1972, assisted by the impact of events during 1969 and 1970 that further alienated conservatives.

Woodstock and the counter-culture

Middle America continued to observe the counter-culture with incomprehension and fear. While the young people who flocked to happenings such as the Woodstock music festival in 1969 (see page 402) saw liberation and freedom, Middle America saw anarchy. They worried about youthful behaviour and role models such as rock stars Janis Joplin, Jim Morrison and Jimi Hendrix, all of whom died from drug overdoses within a ten-month period in 1970–71. Even more worrying than Woodstock and rock stars was increased student radicalism and violence.

Student radicalism and violence

As the 1960s wore on, some student protesters became more militant and violent. In 1969–70, there were over 2,000 bombings or attempted bombings; 56 per cent were by students, 19 per cent by black extremists. There are many examples of violent student behaviour:

- Radical students blew up University of Colorado buildings because scholarship funds for black students were frozen.
- Anticapitalist students in San Diego, California, set fire to banks.
- Kent State students demanded the admission of more black students and the abolition of the ROTC (see

below). In a six-hour battle with the police, seven students were shot, 13 injured and 600 arrested, after which Ohio's governor called in the **National Guard**.
- A pro-Black Panthers demonstration set Yale Law School library books on fire.

Much of this continuing student unrest was due to the Vietnam War.

The impact of events in Vietnam and at Kent State

Nixon's first term as president was dominated by the ongoing war in Vietnam. Antiwar protests continued because even as he withdrew American troops from South Vietnam, he increased the bombing to ensure a strong negotiating position in the peace talks.

In 1969, tens of thousands of protesters of all ages joined the nation's largest ever antiwar protest, the **Moratorium**. However, many Americans disliked protesters; polls showed that 84 per cent thought student protesters and black militants were treated 'too leniently'. Nixon's deputy attorney general thought students constituted the majority of the protesters: 'We just can't wait to beat up those … kids'.

When Nixon extended the bombing to the communist supply trail in Cambodia in spring 1970, antiwar protests erupted in over 80 per cent of American universities. Police and National Guardsmen clashed with students, most famously at Kent State, Ohio.

Kent State

Kent State students rioted in the central business district and firebombed the ROTC building. Some held a peaceful protest rally at which panicked National Guardsmen fired indiscriminately, killing four and wounding 11. Days later, two more students were killed and 12 wounded at Jackson State, Mississippi, when police opened fire on the women's dormitory. Perhaps it was because the Jackson State students were black that there was far less attention from the press (and also from historians ever since).

After Kent State, some Americans felt the government was deliberately murdering dissenters, but Middle America agreed with Nixon's criticisms of 'these bums … blowing up the campuses'. Over half of Americans blamed the students for what happened at Kent State.

The end of the protests

Nixon hated protests and decreased their number by depriving radical students of federal scholarships and loans, adjusting the draft so fewer students felt threatened, secretly monitoring disruptive groups and keeping protesters busy and broke with court actions (10,000 were arrested in Washington in spring 1970). Although the courts threw out most of the cases because they violated civil rights, the protests were dying out by 1971.

Nixon's success in dealing with the protesters, coupled with Woodstock, Kent State and the Democratic National Convention in Miami Beach in 1972, increased his appeal and confirmed Middle America's support for him in the presidential election in 1972.

The Democratic National Convention, 1972

Middle America watched the Democratic National Convention in horror. Some long-haired young delegates expressed support for the communist cause in Vietnam and nominated communist China's leader Mao Zedong as the Democratic Party's candidate for vice-president. New party rules ensured the selection of the left-wing George McGovern as the Democratic Party's candidate for the presidency and many of the silent majority considered McGovern to be the candidate of the counter-culture. He wanted to legalise marijuana and abortion, and give $1,000 to every American to decrease poverty. The **party's platform** called for the 'equitable distribution of wealth and power' and 'the right to be different'. Many delegates demanded the recognition of gay rights.

This leftward movement of the Democratic Party helped increase Richard Nixon's appeal in 1972.

Nixon's appeal in 1972

When Nixon stood for re-election in 1972, he once again appealed to the 'great silent majority', by now even more exasperated with the counter-culture and protest than in 1968.

In the election, Republicans played on conservative fears of McGovern, calling him the '3As' candidate: 'acid, abortion and amnesty'. Nixon and Vice-President Spiro Agnew's campaign focussed on pot, permissiveness, protest, pornography and patriotism. Agnew asked voters if they wanted to be ruled by a democratically elected president or a 'disruptive, radical and militant minority'. Voters responded with a decisive repudiation of the counter-culture and the protests; Nixon won by a landslide, with 60.7 per cent of the popular vote. Traditional American values had been reasserted. The left had become increasingly extreme, and reaction had set in on the right.

Nixon's attack on the Great Society

Nixon's rhetorical campaign attacks on the expense of the Great Society assisted his electoral appeal and his victories in 1968 and 1972, but Democrat control of Congress and his own moderate, pragmatic Republicanism ensured that he left it basically intact.

Welfare and antipoverty programmes

During the 1968 presidential election campaign, Nixon said he wanted to save taxpayers' money by eliminating the more wasteful, inefficient Great Society programmes and by reforming what he called the 'welfare mess'. He told his advisers that the American people were 'outraged' by the welfare system, 'and, in my view, they should be'. Polls in 1968 revealed that 84 per cent of Americans believed 'there are too many people receiving welfare money who should be working'. After the Great Society raised awareness of entitlements, the number of Americans receiving Aid for Dependent Children (AFDC) rose from 3 million in 1960 to 8.4 million by 1970. One in nine children, and one in three black children, were on welfare.

President Nixon attacked Great Society programmes and principles from several angles:

- He successfully shrank the OEO (see page 396), closed 59 Job Corps centres and cut federal housing programmes.
- He tried to reform the welfare system. Polls showed that 80 per cent of Americans believed over half of those on welfare could get a job if they wanted, and Nixon hoped he could make welfare recipients work through his Family Assistance Plan (FAP). Conservatives liked three aspects of the FAP: first, welfare recipients would only have received $1,600 per annum; second, there were work requirements; third, the number of bureaucrats who administered the system was decreased. Liberals disliked those provisions, but were pleased that the plan would have made 13 million more Americans eligible for federal aid. That in turn alienated conservatives. There were so many criticisms of Nixon's FAP that Congress rejected it.
- Nixon vetoed the 1971 Child Development Act, which would have provided free childcare to enable poor mothers to work. He said it was too expensive and smacked of communism.

However, having been brought up in poverty, Nixon was basically sympathetic to the poor. Despite all his anti-Great Society campaign rhetoric, he increased federal expenditure on education, private healthcare, social security, Medicare and Medicaid, and actually spent more on social programmes than Johnson.

School desegregation and affirmative action

The Great Society was to have been characterised by racial equality. In pursuit of this, Supreme Court rulings in 1971 and 1973 supported the bussing of students from one neighbourhood to a school in another neighbourhood in order to end *de facto* segregation of schools. However, Americans opposed bussing by eight to one, and Nixon attacked it as 'wrenching' children from their families. When the Justice Department began to respond to the Supreme Court's ruling, Nixon told them to 'Knock off this crap. Do only what the law requires and not one thing more.' He was initially unsuccessful in his attempts to slow down school desegregation, but his appointment of conservative Supreme Court justices led to rulings that eventually ended bussing.

Nixon claimed to dislike affirmative action (see page 389), which he described as reverse discrimination, but in practice his administration gave minorities considerable help. For example, he put pressure on federal contractors to employ more minority workers. As so often with Nixon, there was a gap between what he said and what he did. In many ways, his record on race was quite impressive. His promotion of affirmative action helped ensure its entrenchment in federal government agencies and contractors for many years to come.

The role of the media in influencing attitudes

Richard Nixon's two presidential election campaigns suggested a nation deeply divided between those who wished the nation to remain the same and those who campaigned to change it. Exhaustive media coverage of the divisive protest movements and disorder and occasional challenges to social norms on television and in film affected attitudes toward issues such as race, war, government and family.

The environment

Nixon said in his first term that 'people don't give a shit about the environment', and reassured blue-collar workers that, 'In a flat choice between smoke and jobs, we are for jobs.' However, dramatic incidents, such as the spontaneous combustion of Ohio's polluted Cuyahoga River, contributed to rising concern. Nixon produced impressive environmental legislation on endangered species (1969), clean air (1970) and coasts (1972), established the Environmental Protection Agency (1970) and created 642 parks.

Film, television and challenge

Sometimes, television and film promoted conservative values. For example, John Wayne made the movie *The Green Berets* (1968) in support of the war. It did well at the box office, suggesting silent majority support for US efforts in Vietnam. However, the black comedy movie *M*A*S*H* (1970), although ostensibly about the Korean War, was clearly critical of militarism and the Vietnam War and it too was very popular. In another tale of opposites, the family-friendly movie *The Sound of Music* (1965) was incredibly popular, while *Easy Rider* (1969), which celebrated drug taking, sexual liberalisation and the counter-culture, was not. Much depended on the quality of the film; *Bob and Carol and Ted and Alice* (1969) traced sexual liberalisation in Los Angeles and was a big critical and commercial hit. Hollywood offered more challenges to traditional values than television in this period, and such challenges no doubt contributed to change.

The news media and civil rights

Coverage of the civil rights movement, and especially of white mistreatment of black people in Birmingham (see page 373), helped change Northern white attitudes to Southern segregation and contributed to the passage of the 1964 Civil Rights Act. Similarly, repeated showings of the violence of Bloody Sunday (see page 387) helped ensure the passage of the Voting Rights Act. However, media coverage did not always promote a positive change in attitudes; images of ghetto riots helped turn many against further aid for black Americans after 1965.

The news media and the impact of events in Vietnam

Media coverage of the Vietnam War challenged the government's position and veracity and many people believe it changed the public's supportive attitude to an antiwar stance through coverage of:

- the Tet Offensive
- the My Lai massacre
- the publication of the **Pentagon** Papers.

The Tet Offensive

Before the Tet Offensive in early 1968 (see page 409), the government was publicly optimistic about the war and the media was generally supportive. However, when media coverage of Tet showed communists overrunning the South Vietnamese capital, America's most trusted television reporter, Walter Cronkite, felt he had been misled: 'What the hell is going on? I thought we were winning this war.' The war and especially Tet increased the 'credibility gap' between what the government claimed and what was actually happening. This made the media more critical of and confrontational towards the government. Vietnam made a significant number of reporters keen to challenge 'official' sources, which helped generate a more cynical public attitude toward politics and politicians.

The My Lai massacre

Soon after Tet, 347 unarmed South Vietnamese civilians were beaten and killed by American soldiers at the South Vietnamese village of My Lai. The army wanted to cover up such atrocities in order to protect the reputation and morale of its forces. However, investigative journalist Seymour Hersh's exposure of the My Lai massacre was picked up by the major newspapers in late 1969.

Polls suggested that the extensive coverage of the massacre did not change people's attitude to the war; while it shocked those who were already antiwar, others felt this was simply how war was. After all, the North Vietnamese also killed civilians. However, it has been argued that the coverage did help change some people's attitude to the war in that it made them think that if the war was turning American boys into killers of civilians, then it was time to get out.

The Pentagon Papers

In 1971, the *New York Times* further challenged the reputation of the government by publishing the Pentagon Papers, leaked Defence Department documents that revealed American leaders misleading (some said lying to) Congress and the public over the escalation of US involvement in the Vietnam War.

The news media and other protest movements

Protests and the counter-culture made interesting news and the media covered them at length. While the media might ridicule movements such as feminism, it gave them a national platform and aroused awareness, which could change attitudes. For example, television coverage of the chemical-saturated Cuyahoga River in Ohio spontaneously bursting into flames in 1969 helped increase environmental awareness and generate legislation (see page 412).

Sometimes, media coverage simply reaffirmed existing positions, as with the reactions to My Lai. Other times, media coverage was such that it provoked countervailing attitudes. The media gave hippies coverage out of all proportion to the numbers involved; reporters and television cameras flocked to cover happenings in San Francisco in 1967 and there was disproportionate coverage of the roughly 10,000 counter-cultural communes established between 1965 and 1975. That coverage helped convince Middle America that the time had come to challenge the counter-culture.

Conclusion: Reactions to the counter-culture

By 1968, and even more so by 1972, many Americans had had enough of protest, the Great Society and the counter-culture. This led them to elect Richard Nixon as president. Nixon managed to decrease the number of protests but he failed to demolish all the Great Society programmes; indeed, he did much to preserve the social policies of his Democrat predecessors. However, although a moderate Republican in practice, Nixon's harsh electoral rhetoric contributed to the increasing polarisation of American society and politics.

Work together

This section covers multiple divisions between liberals who sought change and conservatives who opposed it. Make a date list covering all the events included in this chapter. Take it in turns to offer the opposing conservative and liberal viewpoints on each event or issue. Be sure to include the Democratic National Conventions at Chicago (1968) and Miami Beach (1972), the elections of 1968 and 1972, Woodstock, Kent State, welfare, bussing, affirmative action, My Lai, hippies, feminism, gay rights and student protests.

Chapter summary

- President Johnson's ambitious Great Society programmes helped the poor but could not defeat poverty.
- The 1960s was a decade of protests that improved the situation of students, black Americans, Mexican Americans, women and homosexuals.
- The civil rights movement contributed to the legislation that ended segregation and black disfranchisement in the South.
- The controversial Black Power movement drew attention to continuing black problems and helped increase black pride, but alienated white Americans.
- Students constituted the largest group of antiwar protesters. Many believe the protests contributed to the end of the Vietnam War.
- Some young people 'dropped out' and adopted the counter-culture.
- The 1960s saw greatly changing attitudes towards sexual behaviour.
- The liberalism and change that dominated the 1960s generated a conservative backlash and bitter divisions.
- The Vietnam War also encouraged bitterly opposing viewpoints.
- By 1972, American politics and society were characterised by a discord and unease that sharply contrasted with the years 1955-63.

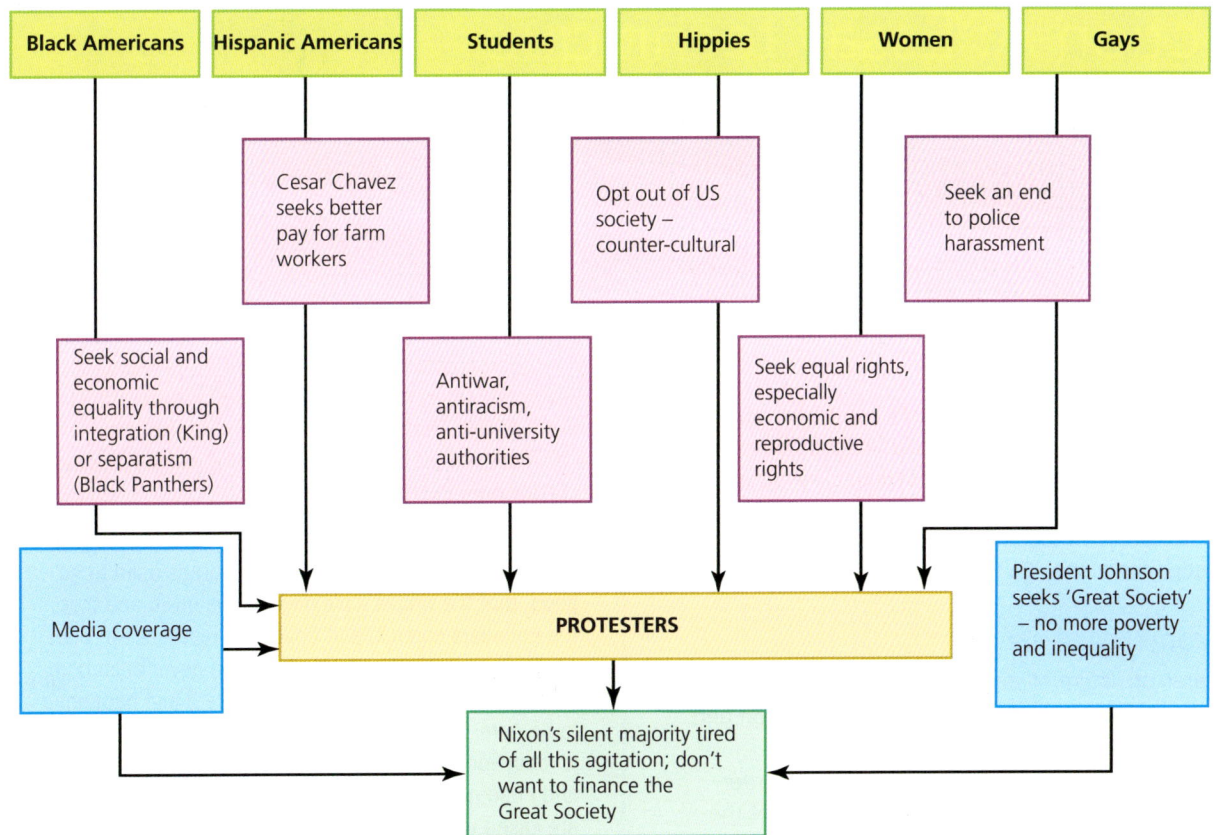

▲ Summary diagram: Protest and reaction, 1963–72.

Recommended reading

Robert Dallek, *Flawed Giant: Lyndon Johnson and his Times, 1961–73* (Oxford University Press, 1998). Contains balanced and detailed treatment of the passage and impact of the Great Society legislation.

David Garrow, *Bearing the Cross: Martin Luther King, Jr., and the Southern Christian Leadership Conference* (William Morrow, 1986). A very detailed biography of King. Plentiful use of contemporary sources gives a real 'feel' for the period.

Michael Heale, *The Sixties in America: History, Politics and Protest* (Edinburgh University Press, 2001). A good, easy read on the 'decade of protest'.

Manning Marable, *Malcolm X* (Penguin, 2011). The most recent and the most acclaimed biography of Malcolm.

Vivienne Sanders, *Race Relations in the USA 1863–1980* (Hodder Education, 2006). An A-level textbook that explains the background to our period.

Vivienne Sanders, *Politics, Presidency and Society in the USA, 1968–2001* (Hodder Education, 2008). An A-level textbook that covers much of our period and helps to bring it alive through brief biographical studies and interesting anecdotes.

Section A: Essay technique

Structuring an essay and writing introductions

Well-structured essays will receive higher marks than essays in which the structure is unclear. The structure of your essay should be designed to help you evaluate how far the two sources together are useful to a historian who is investigating a specific topic.

Overall structure

The overall structure of your essay should include:
- an introduction, which focusses on the question and sets out the essence of your answer
- a conclusion that summarises your essay in order to weigh up the extent to which the evidence of the sources is useful, and reaches an overall judgement
- the main body, which should present a detailed evaluation of the evidence of the sources.

TIP: Remember, the question asks you to consider the sources *together*. Therefore, a structure that analyses Source 1 and then moves on to Source 2 is unlikely to do well. Always try to structure your essay in a way that allows you to deal with the sources together.

Paragraph structure

Each paragraph should set out an analysis of the usefulness of the evidence of the two sources. Therefore, you need to discuss both sources in every paragraph.

TIP: One way of doing this is to make sure that you discuss both sources in almost every sentence.

For example, imagine you are answering the following question:

> How far could the historian make use of Sources 1 and 2 together to investigate the reasons for the Montgomery bus boycott?

On page 417 are three examples of introductions that could answer this question.

Source 1 Extract from Martin Luther King's speech to a Montgomery Improvement Association meeting at the First Baptist Church in Montgomery, Alabama, on 31 January 1956. The feeling that King was the 'star' of the boycott was developing. Here, King refuses to take credit/responsibility for the boycott:

> Some of our good white citizens told me today that the relationships between whites and coloreds used to be good, that the whites have never let us down and that the outsiders came in and upset this relationship. But I want you to know that if M.L. King had never been born this movement would have taken place. I just happened to be here. You know there comes a time when time itself is ready for change. That time has come to Montgomery, and I had nothing to do with it ... We are a chain. We are linked together, and I cannot be what I ought to be unless you are what you ought to be.

Source 2 Extract from Roy Wilkins, the NAACP leader, writing after the 1956 Montgomery bus boycott, which Martin Luther King had claimed signalled the emergence of the 'new Negro'. Wilkins was jealous of and frequently antagonistic toward King and his ideas. Here, Wilkins rejects King's claim that the boycott saw the emergence of a 'New Negro'.

> The Negro of 1956 who stands on his own two feet is not a new Negro; he is the grandson or the great grandson of the men who hated slavery. By his own hands, through his own struggles, in his own organised groups – of churches, fraternal societies, the NAACP and others – he has fought his way to the place where he now stands.

Activity: AS-style questions

1. How much weight do you give the evidence of Source 1 for an enquiry into black American attitudes to segregation in the late 1950s?
2. Why is Source 2 valuable to the historian for an enquiry into the origins of the Civil Rights movement in the mid–1950s?

Answer 1

> Source 1 says that 'there comes a time when time itself is ready for change'. This means that the people of Montgomery had had enough of the Jim Crow laws. It also says that it was not 'outsiders' such as Martin Luther King himself who upset race relations in Montgomery. It was written by Martin Luther King, who was the head of the Montgomery Improvement Association, which orchestrated the boycott. Source 2 is from Roy Wilkins, the head of the NAACP. He says there was no 'new Negro', and that black Americans had a long tradition of organisations and that this culminated in the Montgomery bus boycott.

Answer 2

> Source 1 is useful to a historian because it sets out Martin Luther King's view of why the Montgomery boycott took place. Source 2 is also useful because it suggests that the boycott took place because black Americans had a long tradition of organising to fight for equality.

Answer 3

> Taken together, both sources are a useful reminder of the contemporary controversy over the reasons for the Montgomery bus boycott. Older civil rights activists such as Wilkins sought to emphasise the traditions and role of 'the NAACP and others' (Source 2), while others emphasised the role of Martin Luther King and the 'new Negro', contributing to the criticisms that prompted King's disclaimer that he 'just happened to be here' (Source 1). While both sources have the disadvantage of being somewhat self-justifying explanations, Wilkins is of more use to the historian investigating the reasons for the boycott in that he reminds us of the 'organised groups' that have played a part in past and present black activism.

Activity: Analyse the introduction

Having read the three introductions, in pairs consider the following questions:
1 What skills do the different introductions demonstrate?
2 Which introduction focusses most clearly on the question?
3 Which introduction integrates Sources 1 and 2 most effectively?
4 How could you improve the best of the three introductions?
5 What can you learn from the three samples?

Selecting information

Another skill vital for success in Section A is that of selecting the right information from the sources. So what is the 'right' information? It is:

- information that is relevant to the question
- information that illustrates the main point of the source
- information that illustrates points you want to make.

In addition to the source material, the exam paper also contains a short description of the source's provenance printed immediately above the source. Selecting the important material from the provenance will also help you do well. You could select information that helps you evaluate the evidence, such as:

- information that would help explain the writer's motives
- information that helps explain the document's purpose
- information that helps contextualise the source (see page 447).

TIP: Don't just copy information from the provenance, make sure you use the information to help weigh the evidence that the source presents.

Selection

If you were answering the Montgomery bus boycott question on page 416:

- You need to think about the focus of the question – here the question is asking you about what these two sources can tell us, as historians, about the reasons why the boycott occurred.
- Remember the historical context: Wilkins' NAACP was an old, respected organisation that had done a great deal for black Americans, while the 'new boy' Martin Luther King seemed to be getting a great deal of credit and publicity during and after the boycott.

Activity: Selecting from the sources

6 Make a bullet-pointed list of the information that you would select from Sources 1 and 2 to answer the question on page 416.
7 Consider the following questions with your partner:
   (a) Did you both select the same information for the source? If not, whose selections were:
      (i) most relevant to the question
      (ii) most characteristic of the whole source?
   (b) Did you both select the same information from the provenance? If not, whose selections were:
      (i) most relevant to the question
      (ii) most helpful to a historian evaluating the information contained in the source?

Making inferences

Making inferences from sources is one way to demonstrate your understanding of the source and of the period. An inference is a deduction or conclusion that comes from reading between the lines of a source – it is not about what lies on the surface but what is hinted at below. It isn't wild speculation but a conclusion that is drawn from reasoning or evidence. A detailed knowledge of the period is vital to making inferences.

Imagine you are answering the following question:

> **How far could the historian make use of Sources 3 and 4 to investigate the role of the media in influencing attitudes to the Vietnam War in the years 1968–69?**

There is a lot of information in Source 3 that is purely on the surface. But beyond that, you can use your own knowledge to draw out more complex and insightful conclusions, as the annotations below show.

Source 3 Extract from President Lyndon Johnson's 1 April 1968 speech to the National Association of Broadcasters (*Public Papers of the President: Johnson 1968*, pages 482–483). The day before, he had announced his withdrawal from the presidential election race, saying that he planned to spend the remainder of his presidency focussing upon bringing peace in Vietnam. Here, he reflects upon the relationship between the media and war.

> As I sat in my office last evening, waiting to speak, I thought of the many times each week when television brings the war into the American home. No one can say exactly what effect those vivid scenes have on American opinion. Historians must only guess at the effect that television would have had during earlier conflicts on the future of the nation: during the Korean War, at the time when our forces were pushed back there to Pusan [*]; or World War II, the Battle of the Bulge [**], or when our men were slugging it out in Europe or when most of our Air Force was shot down that day in June 1942 off Australia.

[*] US troops were sent to oppose communism in Korea (1950–53). Early in the war, the communist forces drove the US forces to Pusan, at the southernmost tip of the Korean peninsula.

[**] The Battle of the Bulge represented a great setback in the US effort in the Second World War.

Annotations:

- Johnson seems to be suggesting that the television coverage focussed on the more unpleasant aspects of the war.

- In his speech the night before, Johnson had said that he would not stand for re-election to the presidency but would spend the remainder of his term focussing upon trying to bring peace in Vietnam. It seems that as he was waiting to make that speech he was thinking about the relationship between television coverage, the war and his own resignation. Clearly, he sees television as incredibly influential and as having played a part in ending his political career.

- Johnson is clearly suggesting that if there had been coverage of previous wars in the way that the Vietnam War was covered, then those previous wars would have been far more unpopular, and probably had some dire effect on American national security.

Below is an example of how you could develop the inferences annotated around Source 3 into a paragraph in answer to the question on page 418.

> In his speech to the National Association of Broadcasters on the day after he announced he would not be standing for re-election, President Johnson clearly implied that television broadcasters greatly influenced public attitudes to the Vietnam War through their negative coverage – a point he had made in private many times before. He suggested that their coverage had been unpatriotic. Similar coverage of wartime 'vivid scenes' (obviously of death and destruction) would probably have turned Americans against previous wars that Johnson considered vital to national security, such as the Second World War and the Korean War. Johnson pointed out that in both wars there were dreadful crises for American forces, such as at Pusan, the Battle of the Bulge, and in the air off Australia in 1942. Johnson in effect asked what would have happened to the nation's security if media coverage had made the United States stop fighting after those crises.

Source 4 Extract from Michael Arlen, *Living Room War* (Syracuse University Press, 1969). Arlen was a television critic who wrote for *The New Yorker*. Here, Arlen describes what American television viewers saw of the Vietnam War.

> [What] a television viewer of the war [usually] saw at least for the first two thirds of its duration was a nightly stylised, generally distanced overview of a disjointed conflict which was composed mainly of scenes of helicopters landing, tall grasses blowing in the helicopters' wind, American soldiers fanning out across the hillside on foot, rifles at the ready, with now and then (on the soundtrack) a far-off ping or two, and now and then (as a visual grand finale) a column of dark billowing smoke off a mile away invariably described as a burning Viet Cong ammo dump.

Activity: Inferences

Having read the question on page 418 and example on this page, you can now practise making inferences from Source 4. Remember:
- Your inferences should help you answer the question.
- Inferences should be informed by your contextual knowledge of the period.

Answer the following questions:
1. From your knowledge of the period and the evidence of Source 4, what do you suppose prompted Michael Arlen to write his book on the *Living Room War*?
2. Arlen mentions a 'visual grand finale'. What does this imply about the nightly television coverage?
3. Compare Sources 3 and 4. Together, what do they suggest about the role of the media in influencing attitudes to the Vietnam War?

Work together

Having completed the activity on inferences, consider the following questions with your partner:
1. Did you both make the same inferences from Source 6?
2. If you differed, look at the source again, discuss your points of view and try to work out which inferences are more likely to be correct.
3. How can the inferences that you have made help you answer the question?

Having discussed these questions, make a bullet-point list of three things that you can do to make sure you use inferences effectively in Section A questions. Review the list with your partner.

Activity: AS-style questions

1. Why is Source 5 valuable to the historian for an enquiry into the impact of television on American politics in the late 1960s?
2. How much weight do you give the evidence of Source 6 for an enquiry into the impact of television news on attitudes to the Vietnam War in the late 1960s?

Source 5 Extract from Martin Luther King's *Where Do We Go from Here*, published in 1967. The book was the last that King wrote. It reflected the experience of the Chicago Campaign, in which King had seen first-hand the conditions of the Northern ghettos.

> Exploitation is possible because so many of the residents of the ghetto have no personal means of transportation. It is a vicious circle. You can't get a job because you are poorly educated, and you must depend on welfare to feed your children; but if you receive public aid in Chicago, you cannot own property, not even an automobile, so you are condemned to the jobs and shops closest to your home. Once confined to this isolated community, one no longer participates in a free economy, but is subject to price fixing.
>
> The Chicago Urban League have documented a 10–20 per cent 'color tax' which applies to virtually every product purchased in the segregated community. This is especially true of housing. As adults my neighbours pay more rent in the substandard slums than the whites pay for modern apartments in the suburbs.

Source 6 Extract from Elaine Brown's *A Taste of Power: A Black Woman's Story*, published in 1992. Brown was a leading member of the Black Panther Party and worked closely with Huey P. Newton and Bobby Seale, the founders of the party. She was head of the Black Panther Party from 1974 to 1977. In this extract she describes the initiation of the Survival Programs of the late 1960s.

> Huey was accelerating the progress of our Survival Programs. To push the momentum he ordered Bobby to take charge of all the Survival Programs. In one stroke, he changed the course of the party. Bobby's giant food giveaways gained tremendous support for all our other Survival Programs. Even middle-class blacks, previously reluctant to support or be identified with the Party, began to endorse it and making contributions. As Bobby's spirits and leadership reached the other chapters, support for the party's free food programs grew by leaps and bounds. We expanded our free clinics and preventative medicine projects – through which we placed the deadly blood disease peculiar to blacks, sickle-cell anaemia, on the agenda of America's medical profession. We implemented new ideas, such as a shoe program – renting a factory and manufacturing shoes to give away to our people. The confused police and FBI had to regroup, bury their old assault plans, and invent new tactics to attack us.

Activity: AS-style questions

1. Why is Source 5 valuable to the historian for an enquiry into Martin Luther King's final campaigns?
2. How much weight do you give the evidence of Source 6 for an enquiry into the changing nature of the Black Panther Party in the late 1960s?

Section B: Essay technique

Detail and analysis

Paper 2 Section B questions, like Paper 1 Section A and B questions, need to be detailed and analytical. You might have already read the advice on how to write detailed and analytical essays for Paper 1 (see pages 56 and 79). Now is a chance to practise these skills in the context of the USA, 1955–92.

Activity: Detail and analysis

Imagine you are answering the following question:

'The Black Panthers achieved little of note.' How far do you agree with this view?

1. Identify the kind of question (see page 384).
2. Make an appropriate plan, writing down the main points of your three or four paragraphs.
3. Next to each of the points, add three supporting details – you could use a different colour if you have one.
4. Write one analytical sentence to conclude each paragraph.

Work together

Having finished the activity on detail and analysis, swap your work with a partner. Consider:

1. Did you agree on what type of question you were dealing with? If not, discuss it and work out who was right.
2. Whose plan most clearly focussed on the specific type of question?
3. Were the details that your partner selected the most appropriate to support their points?
4. Could either of you have used detail that better supports the points that you wanted to make?
5. Were all of your partner's sentences truly analytical?
6. What can you learn from your partner's approach?

Use these questions to feed back to each other and improve your use of detail and analysis.

Question practice

1. How far was Betty Friedan responsible for the growth of the women's movement?
2. How accurate is it to say that Johnson's Great Society programme of 1963–68 was a failure? **AS**
3. To what extent was the situation of Americans who lived in poverty improved in the years 1963–72?
4. How significant was the growth of 'the silent majority' in US politics in the years 1968–72? **AS**

Key Topic 3 Social and political change, 1973–80

Overview

During the presidencies of Eisenhower (1953–61), Kennedy (1961–63) and Johnson (1963–69), many Americans experienced unprecedented and apparently ever-increasing affluence. The United States had by far the strongest economy in the world and was way ahead of its nearest rivals in the production of manufactured goods. The majority of Americans were confident that the federal government served the nation well.

However, there were dramatic changes in the years 1973–80. These were years of political and economic crisis. President Nixon (1969–74) was forced to resign because of conduct unbecoming of the nation's leader. Presidents Gerald Ford (1974–77) and Jimmy Carter (1977–81) both failed to get elected for a second term because they seemed unable to cope with inflation and recession. Furthermore, it seemed as if economically dynamic Japan or West Germany might replace the United States as the world's leading economic power. Many Americans were convinced that the age of affluence was over, although in reality Americans on average still had the best standard of living in the world.

The years 1973–80 were not devoid of progress. Women, black Americans, Native Americans, gay men and lesbian women continued their campaigns to gain more rights. These campaigns necessitated great struggle and there was an ominously growing conservative backlash against such challenges to the status quo. Nevertheless, although workers' rights were being eroded, other groups were successful in the fight for their rights.

The overarching theme of social and political change is covered in four sections:
1. The crisis of political leadership
2. The impact of economic change on society
3. Changing popular culture
4. The extent of progress in individual and civil rights

TIMELINE

1973	The Paris Peace Accords end the US involvement in the Vietnam War
1973	Watergate burglars convicted
1973	Supreme Court legalises abortion in *Roe v. Wade*
1973	Native Americans occupied Wounded Knee
1973	OPEC embargo on the sale of oil
1973	War Powers Act
1974 July	Supreme Court rules against bussing (*Milliken v. Bradley*)
1974	President Nixon resigns
1975	Indian Self-Determination Act
1975	Omnibus Energy Act
1976	Congress passes Hyde Amendment
1976	Carter defeats Ford in the presidential election
1977 Jan–Feb	Exceptionally bad weather causes a fuel crisis
1977	United Mine Workers' strike
1978	Supreme Court upholds affirmative action
1978	Pro-gay Miami ordinance defeated
1978	Antigay Californian Proposition defeated
1978	Ethics in government Act
1978	Congress guts Carter's energy programme
1979	Birmingham, Alabama, elects a black mayor
1979	Iranian fundamentalists seize American hostages
1980	Carter's attempted rescue of Iranian-held American hostages fails
1980	Supreme Court rules in favour of Hyde Amendment
1980	Alaska Lands Act
1980	Reagan and conservatives triumph in presidential/congressional elections

1 The crisis of political leadership

The greatly increased power and prestige of the presidency during the twentieth century owed much to increased US involvement in international affairs. The president's role as **commander-in-chief** increased his importance during wars, especially the lengthy **Cold War**. This caused unease and jealousy in **Congress**, which sought to limit presidential power. The unpopularity of the Vietnam War and President Nixon's involvement in the Watergate scandal provided an opportunity for Congress to do this.

Neither Congress nor successive presidents appeared able to solve the nation's economic problems in the period 1973–80 and this, combined with Watergate, led many Americans to perceive the period as characterised by a crisis of political leadership. It was Watergate that shocked Americans most; for the first time in American history, a president was forced to resign.

> **Note it down**
>
> Create a spider diagram (see page x) with 'Crisis of political leadership' in the centre. As you read this chapter, add names, dates and statistics that illustrate the crisis to the diagram. You could use colour coding to differentiate presidents.

The impact of Watergate on politics and the presidency

The Watergate building was an office block in Washington DC. Its name came to symbolise corruption, illegality and abuse of power under President Richard Nixon.

In 1972, Nixon's Committee to Re-elect the President (CREEP) hoped to gain electoral advantage through the acquisition of Democratic Party secrets; in pursuit of this, the CREEP organised two illegal break-ins into the **Democratic National Committee** headquarters in the Watergate building, in order to install electronic surveillance devices. The first burglars were apprehended within the **Democrat** offices on 17 June 1972 and arrested.

Nixon's initial reactions were mixed. On the one hand, he seemed unconcerned: 'I think the country does not give much of a shit when somebody **bugs** somebody else.' He complained to aides that the Democrats had long bugged **Republicans** but 'they never got caught … every time the Democrats accuse us of bugging, we should charge that we were being bugged and maybe even plant a bug and find it ourselves … everybody's trying to bug everybody else, it's politics'. On the other hand, he quickly moved to try to cover up the administration's involvement in the break-in. It is uncertain whether the President knew about the break-in, but he was involved in the attempted cover-up from the first.

Within days of the discovery of the second break-in, Nixon and his aides discussed using the **CIA** to stop the **FBI** investigating the CREEP's financing of the break-in. This was a clear attempt to obstruct justice. When the CIA refused to co-operate, the President tried to pay the burglars to keep quiet: a further **obstruction of justice**. Despite these attempts, the Watergate burglars were convicted in January 1973. When the **Senate** began an investigation into the Watergate affair in February, public opinion turned increasingly against the Nixon administration. The President's **approval rating** sank to 17 per cent, Vice-President Spiro Agnew was forced to resign over tax evasion and accepting bribes, and Nixon's own finances were investigated.

The Watergate tapes

Like Kennedy and Johnson, Nixon had tape-recorded conversations in the White House. Great pressure from Congress, the press and public opinion forced him to release some of his tapes. In July 1974, the **Supreme Court** ruled that he had to release all of them. When the tapes revealed that Nixon had ordered the cover-up, the House of Representatives moved to **impeach** him. The charges included:

- obstruction of justice (through participation in the cover-up)
- abuse of power (by using government agencies such as the FBI, the CIA and the **IRS** against his political enemies).

To avoid impeachment, Nixon resigned in August 1974 and Vice-President Gerald Ford became president. Nixon was the first president forced to resign while in office and he left the White House in disgrace. Previous presidents had engaged in illegal activities, but Nixon did more of them and more frequently; 25 of his aides and associates were jailed. Nixon himself was pardoned by his successor, President Gerald Ford.

The significance of Watergate

The Watergate scandal impacted upon US politics in a number of ways. First, it had an important impact on the Republican Party. Nixon was a moderate Republican, but he and his policies were discredited by Watergate. Following Nixon's resignation, more right-wing Republicans such as Ronald Reagan dominated the party.

Second, Nixon's presidency adversely affected the prestige and power of the presidency. Long concerned by the increasing power of the president during the twentieth century, Congress enacted several laws to limit presidential power and avoid another Watergate. Among them were the War Powers Act (1973) designed to limit presidential power to take the nation into war, and the Ethics in government Act (1978) that, among other things, made it easier for a special prosecutor to investigate alleged presidential wrongdoings. These measures demonstrated that Congress was jealously guarding against any further increase in the power of what Democrats called the '**Imperial Presidency**'. The revulsion generated by Nixon and Watergate prompted Presidents Gerald Ford (1974–77) and Jimmy Carter (1977–81) to try to differentiate and distance themselves from Nixon with a new style of leadership.

▲ Nixon boarding the White House helicopter shortly after resigning as President, in the wake of the Watergate scandal. Do you think Nixon had any reason to give his famous V-for-victory sign in this photo?

Source A Extract from the *Gettysburg Times*, 29 January 1970. The *Gettysburg Times* was printed in a small Pennsylvania town and its circulation was not large. Here, the journalist writes about President Nixon changing the appearance of 'the White House police'.

President Nixon's August idea of European-style formal dress garb for White House police has bloomed in late January – to a cold reception from some critics.

The new $95 outfits ordered for about 100 policemen are described by the Secret Service as 'a white cream tunic, made out of elastique, with a double-breasted cut, three buttons, a stand-up collar, gold nylon trim and a vinyl cap.'

Nixon apparently was pleased by the uniforms since he had four of the police in their new outfits at the front door of the White House when British Prime Minister Harold Wilson arrived for a state dinner Tuesday night ...

Some critical comments from bystanders ... ranged from ... 'They look like extras from a Lithuanian movie' ... [to] 'Nazi uniforms'.

Nixon's suggestion for new uniforms came last summer after he noticed the palace guards and policemen during his European tour.

How much weight would you give the evidence of Source A for an enquiry into public perceptions of President Nixon in 1970? Explain your answer, using the source, the information given about it and your own knowledge of the historical context.

Ford, Carter and a new style of leadership

Nixon had emphasised the ceremonial aspects the presidency, most famously with the White House guards (see Source A on page 424), but his two successors played down the ceremonial in an attempt to suggest a new leadership style.

Gerald Ford was a respected and popular Congressman from 1948 to 1973. He accepted the vice-presidency after Spiro Agnew's resignation, with the self-deprecatory joke that he was '**a Ford not a Lincoln**'. When Nixon resigned, Americans were desperate for a 'regular guy' in the White House. They thought they had one when pyjama-clad president-elect Ford picked up his own newspaper off his front porch and waved to the press. Some Americans related to his family (his lively and outspoken wife was photographed pushing him fully clothed into the **Camp David** pool).

Carter, too, rejected excessive formality. After he was sworn in as president, he and his family walked down **Pennsylvania Avenue** – an unprecedented and highly informal gesture. Carter sold the presidential yacht and wore casual clothes for a televised broadcast.

The decreased formality failed to stop near-constant criticism of Ford's and then Carter's leadership. After a brief honeymoon period with the press and public, Ford's popularity with Congress, the media and the American people plummeted because he pardoned Richard Nixon. The pardon ensured there were no further proceedings against the disgraced president for his involvement in Watergate, but many Americans believed that Nixon should be put on trial as the other Watergate conspirators were.

Ford v. Congress and the media

Ford sought to demonstrate to the Democrat-controlled Congress that this was a new style of leadership in that he wanted to work in partnership with them. He volunteered to be the first president since Lincoln to testify before Congress (about the pardon). However, the pardon irreparably damaged relations.

It was probably the general loss of respect for the presidency after Watergate, Ford's informality and the fact that he had not been elected president that combined to make the media decide that Ford was fair game for disrespectful coverage. The media enjoyed making fun of him. Lyndon Johnson's joke that he had played **football** once too often without a helmet was frequently cited. Ford was shown falling over on ski slopes and stumbling down a plane ramp; one network showed the latter 11 times in one newscast. A *New Yorker* magazine cover showed him as Bozo the Clown. A right-wing New Hampshire newspaper christened him 'Jerry the Jerk'.

Ford's frequently indecisive leadership did not help. For example, when he changed his position on taxation, the *New York Times* said, 'President Ford has not turned the economy around … but at least he has turned himself around.'

Ford v. Carter in 1976

In the 1976 presidential election, Ford was defeated by the Democrat Jimmy Carter. The election seemed to confirm that there was a crisis of political leadership. First, Carter's emphasis upon being an outsider who had never been part of the corrupt Washington scene contributed to his victory. Second, a poll revealed that 76 per cent of people believed Ford lacked 'presidential quality', and 80 per cent said the same of Carter.

The leadership of President Carter

There was much criticism of Carter's leadership style. There were criticisms of his micromanagement, his inability to establish a productive relationship with Congress, what some considered to be a joint presidency with his wife and his apparent inability to cope with crises:

- News of Carter's micromanagement leaked out in 1979 with the story of how in his first six months as president he reviewed all requests to use the White House tennis courts.
- Although a Democrat, Carter's relations with the Democrat Congress were poor. The House Speaker said Carter 'didn't seem to understand' the need to master the legislative process.
- The media made much of the influence of his wife, referring to her as 'Mrs President'.
- By December 1977 polls revealed that only 18 per cent of Americans had 'a lot' of confidence in Carter and it was commonly asked, 'Can Carter cope?' By 1980 he had the lowest-ever approval rating of any president. He seemed incapable of dealing with the most pressing contemporary issues, the economy, the energy crisis (see page 430) and the Iranian hostage crisis.

The impact of the Iranian hostage crisis

In January 1973 President Nixon signed the Paris Peace Accords, which ended the Vietnam War. Although the public welcomed this American exit from Vietnam, there was a growing fear that the USA was losing its international primacy. Problems with Iran seemed to confirm this.

In 1978 Islamic fundamentalists led a successful revolution against the repressive, pro-American shah of Iran. In 1979, Iranian militants stormed the US embassy in Tehran and took 60 Americans hostage in protest against Carter allowing the Shah to receive cancer treatment in the USA. American humiliation increased when Carter tried but failed to negotiate the hostages' release then sent helicopters on an unsuccessful rescue mission in 1980. One helicopter broke down upon entering Iranian airspace, another got lost in a sandstorm and a third developed hydraulic problems. The commanders and President Carter agreed to abort the mission, but then one of the helicopters crashed into a US transport aircraft. Both burst into flames, eight American airmen died and four were badly burned. Eventually, Carter's painstaking diplomacy won the release of the hostages, but only after the United States had a new president. By the November 1980 presidential election, the general feeling was that Carter was a poor leader who messed up everything. By 1980, a poll revealed that only 18 per cent of Americans rated him 'a very strong leader'.

The Iranian hostage crisis impacted upon the 1980 presidential election and upon the future direction of American society and politics; in combination with Carter's apparent inability to solve the nation's economic problems, it contributed to Carter's defeat by the conservative Republican Ronald Reagan. The 'great communicator' Reagan came across as warm, genial and optimistic about American international and domestic capacities, in contrast to the earnest, moralistic Carter who told Americans that they were suffering crises of confidence and spirit. In 1980, 47 per cent of registered voters simply stayed at home; many were poor and/or unemployed and would normally have been expected to vote Democrat but were disillusioned with politics and with the leadership of Jimmy Carter.

Growing political disillusionment

Polls indicated increasing disillusionment with politics:

- Percentage of Americans who felt that government will 'do what is right most of the time': 1969 – 56 per cent; 1979 – 29 per cent.
- Percentage of Americans believing government officials were 'smart people who know what they are doing': 1969 – 69 per cent; 1979 – 29 per cent.
- Percentage of Americans who felt that US affairs were run for the benefit of a few big interests rather than all the people: 1969 – 28 per cent; 1979 – 65 per cent.
- Percentage of Americans who agreed that the 'people running the country do not really care about what happens to you': 1966 – 26 per cent; 1977 – 60 per cent.

Disillusionment with presidents was nothing new. For example, **liberals** had mocked Eisenhower and his fellow Americans ('the bland leading the bland'). However, the Vietnam War caused the 'credibility gap' that damaged faith in Johnson and the presidency (see page 409); then Watergate and the pardon exacerbated the situation. Media coverage of Ford's falls demonstrated growing disrespect. Disillusionment with politics increased under Carter, when roughly half of the electorate felt alienated from the political process and never bothered to vote. 'Why don't people vote? Because it doesn't make a difference', said a welfare worker. The turnout in presidential elections (54 per cent in 1976, 53 per cent in 1980) confirmed the alienation of a significant proportion of the electorate, some of whom were turning to single-issue politics, such as environmentalism.

Environmentalism's political impact

There had always been Americans concerned to preserve wilderness areas and conserve resources. However, by the 1970s the environment became an important political issue due to publicity (see page 412), increased awareness that the Earth's resources were finite and the desire to experience wilderness and parks. In 1969, 1 per cent felt the environment was the greatest domestic problem, but 25 per cent did by 1971. Membership of environmental organisations grew (see Table 1) with middle-class liberals joining old organisations such as the Sierra Club or new ones such as the National Resource Defense Council. Edward Abbey's novel *The Monkey Wrench Gang* (1975) attracted a great deal of attention. The *New York Times* said his story of protesters using sabotage in opposition to those who were damaging the environment made Abbey 'an underground cult hero'. Environmentalism was strengthened by the revelation that Love Canal, near Niagara Falls, was so full of industrial waste that it caused disproportionate numbers of miscarriages and birth defects in the local population, which was relocated *en masse* in 1978.

The political implications of environmentalism lay in the fact that:

- the environmentalist lobby gained such strength that many politicians were encouraged to pass environmental legislation
- industry and economic growth provided employment but could damage the environment.

Table 1: Membership of environmental organisations.

Year	Number of members
1960	125,000
1970	1 million
1980	2 million
1990	6.3 million

Environmentalist legislation

Some environmentalist legislation had been passed under Kennedy (see page 377), and even more under Johnson (see page 398) and Nixon (see page 412). The Environmental Protection Agency (EPA), established by the Nixon administration in 1970, asked American car manufacturers to cut down on exhaust emissions. In compliance with the EPA regulations, the manufacturers introduced catalytic converters and unleaded gasoline in 1975, cutting car pollution by 75 per cent. In 1976, Congress passed the Toxic Substances Control Act.

Carter was the first successful presidential candidate to campaign on environmentalism. He obtained legislation to prevent chemicals from polluting the environment, expand National Park and wilderness land (the 1980 Alaska Lands Act set aside one-third of the state as wilderness), renew the Clean Air and Clean Water Acts (see page 398), and seek alternative sources of energy. However, Carter's ambitious energy programme (see page 431) failed to get through Congress intact because Americans hated paying more for petrol.

Carter's impressive achievements were insufficient for environmentalists and upset the traditionally Democratic labour unions. Workers in industries that generated a great deal of pollution believed that environmentalists threatened their jobs. Many sported bumper stickers saying 'If you're hungry and out of work, eat an environmentalist.'

A political minefield

Environmentalism had become a major political issue that aroused passionate emotions. It caused:

- intra-party conflict (the Democratic Party contained middle-class liberals who favoured environmental legislation and blue-collar workers who did not)
- inter-party conflict (as the party of big business, Republicans were often less concerned about the environment than Democrats)
- a conservative backlash, evident during Ronald Reagan's 1980 presidential election campaign when Reagan claimed that air pollution in Los Angeles was 'substantially controlled' (he then found that his plane could not land there because of smog)
- surprising unanimity in states whose dependence upon manufacturing made them feel threatened by environmentalism (for example, Michigan politicians of all parties opposed legislation that would damage Detroit's car industry)
- tension between the federal government and several states (for example, the 1979–81 'Sagebrush Rebellion').

The 'Sagebrush Rebellion'

Under the National Wilderness Preservation System set up by Congress in 1964, the federal government controlled vast tracts of land in Southwestern states such as Arizona. Much of the land was desert, covered with sagebrush plants. The 'Sagebrush rebels' were mostly businessmen. They demanded state control over National Wilderness land so that economic activities such as mining, ranching and real-estate development could take place. They criticised the adverse economic impact of federal government land conservation policies.

Conclusion: The crisis of political leadership

The protest movements of the 1960s reflected and generated a more critical view of American society and politics. Then, the combination of the credibility gap over Vietnam, the Watergate scandal, Ford's inconsistency and his pardon of Nixon, and Carter's apparent inability to cope created growing voter disillusionment and a sense of a nation in crisis. This in turn was exacerbated by economic and international problems. Sometimes, the criticism of the nation's political leaders could be considered unfair. As will be seen in the next section on economic problems, the world was changing and the challenges of leadership were greater.

Work together

Check your partner's spider diagram on the crisis of political leadership. Have you both written down the same names/dates/statistics to illustrate the crisis? If not, explain your inclusion of different details.

2 The impact of economic change on society

After the Second World War, the United States was the world's wealthiest nation. However, by the 1960s there were worrying economic trends. First, while the United States still led the world in manufacturing industries that employed many Americans, those industries were in decline. Second, the expense of the Vietnam War and to a lesser extent of the **Great Society** raised the **federal government deficit** from $1.6 billion in 1965 to $25.3 billion in 1968, leading to inflation and a weakened dollar.

By 1973 other countries seemed poised to overtake the USA as the world's leading economic power. The American economy suffered from inflation (mostly due to rising oil prices and federal government overspending), a **balance of trade** deficit and a weakened currency. All of this impacted upon the lives of Americans, many of whom had an insatiable appetite for the consumer goods and oil (for cars and heating) that they now struggled to afford.

> **Note it down**
>
> You could use either the 1:2 method (see page x) here or add to your collection of index cards. Either way, note down the causes of economic change (rising inflation, the oil crisis, the impact of foreign competition), then give an explanation of the impact of that change.

The effects of inflation

Inflation was a potential problem for the vast majority of Americans. Gerald Rafshoon, Assistant to the President for Communications, told Carter:

> It is impossible to overestimate the importance of the inflation issue … It affects every American in a very palpable way. It causes insecurity and anxiety. It affects the 'American Dream'.
>
> (Quoted in Julian Zelizer, *Jimmy Carter*, Times Books, 2010)

During 1973–80, Americans experienced unprecedented inflation (see Table 2). Inflation was in or near double figures for much of the decade. It made everything more expensive: mortgages, loans, food and energy. During July 1974 alone, prices rose by 3.7 per cent. A 1978 poll showed that 63 per cent of Americans considered inflation their greatest concern.

Table 2: Average inflation rate, 1955–92.

Year	Average inflation rate
1955	0%
1963	1.24%
1973	6.16%
1980	13.8%
1992	3.03%

> When you are revising the years 1955–92, study this table and explain the reasons for the variation in the percentages.

As the cost of living rose at a yearly average of 8.2 per cent between 1973 and 1983, inflation greatly affected family incomes. The hardest hit were those in the areas of declining manufacturing output known as the **Rust Belt**. Increasing numbers previously accustomed to well-paid manufacturing work found themselves unemployed.

Unemployment and service jobs

Across the nation, unemployment rose throughout the decade. For example, it was 6.5 per cent in December 1974 but 8.9 per cent by May 1975. The increase in unemployment was due to two main factors. First, other countries were producing manufactured goods at lower prices and often superior quality. Second, there was increasing mechanisation in American industry; men were replacing machines. These factors combined to decrease employment opportunities in occupations such as car manufacturing in Detroit and steel production in Pennsylvania. It was difficult to find alternative employment, apart from within the service industries. Service jobs constituted 60 per cent of employment opportunities in 1970 but 70 per cent by 1980. However, many were low paid. Although the federal minimum wage rose from $2.10 an hour in 1975 to $3.35 per hour in 1981, it failed to keep pace with rising prices. Many mothers had to work in order to maintain the usual family income; 38 per cent of women worked in 1960, 43 per cent in 1970 and 52 per cent in 1980.

▲ Figure 1: Percentage of the US labour force unemployed, 1953–95.

Poverty and homelessness

Poverty increased as the 1970s wore on. The proportion of US citizens living below the **poverty line** grew from 11.2 per cent in 1974 to 12.5 per cent in 1976 and included 50 per cent of all black female heads of household. The numbers eligible for the **food-stamp programme** grew from 18.5 million in 1976 to 20 million in 1980. Black family incomes were particularly hard hit, because black workers were disproportionately represented in unskilled occupations.

Homelessness became an increasing problem. By the early 1980s politicians and the press recognised that the USA was experiencing a homelessness crisis. Estimates of the total number of homeless people in 1980 vary from 200,000 to 1 million.

Reasons for homelessness

There were several reasons behind the increased number of homeless people:

- During the mid-1970s, the number of institutions for the mentally ill decreased. There were two reasons. First, the American Association for the Abolition of Involuntary Mental Hospitalization campaigned to give these people greater personal freedom and independence. Second, these institutions increasingly struggled for financial survival. A 1973 federal district court ruled that patients in mental health institutions had to be paid for their labour, but that unpaid labour had helped keep the institutions running. Conservatives wanted to decrease expenditure on such institutions and were reluctant to make up for the shortfall, so some were forced to close. Many former residents ended up on the streets and homeless.
- As a result of continuing urban renewal policies (see page 375), many inner-city 'skid row' hotels that had housed the exceptionally poor were demolished. Those who had formerly obtained shelter in such hotels struggled to find alternative accommodation.
- Rising unemployment (see Figure 1) led some people into depression, despair and life on the streets. Budget cuts and lower welfare benefits contributed to the sense of hopelessness.
- The number of homeless women increased because of declining marriage rates and the increased number of single mothers. The lack of support from a partner and feeling that the authorities were unsympathetic led many to simply give up and live on the streets.
- The increased use of crack cocaine in the inner cities resulted in addicts spending all their money on the drug and unable to afford regular living accommodation.

The oil crisis and the end of cheap energy

Dramatic rises in the price of oil resulted in an energy crisis that had an adverse impact on family incomes and industry during the 1970s.

In the three decades after the Second World War, the United States went from energy self-sufficiency to an energy deficit situation. With 6 per cent of the world's population, Americans consumed one-third of the world's oil production. Roughly 30 per cent of the oil Americans used had to be imported, mostly from the Middle East. The resulting American economic vulnerability was exposed when Nixon's support of Israel in the **Yom Kippur War** (1973) led to an Organization of Petroleum Exporting Countries (**OPEC**) oil embargo on the United States. The end of the embargo was followed by a 387 per cent hike in the price of oil that greatly damaged the American economy (except for the US oil companies). Americans now paid around 30 per cent more for heating oil and petrol.

Several dramatic events illustrated the seriousness of the energy crisis during the decade:

- In 1974, a strike by 100,000 independent truckers demanding lower fuel prices brought the nation's roads to a standstill for 11 days and left stores with empty shelves.
- In the exceptionally harsh winter of 1976–77, a natural gas shortage forced the closure of schools and factories, especially in the Eastern USA. Fuel stations closed on Sundays or cut their hours in order to conserve supplies, and long queues developed at the petrol pumps. The first American energy riot occurred in Levittown, Pennsylvania, when truckers barricaded expressways; 100 were injured and 170 arrested in two nights of violence.
- In late 1977, 165,000 United Mine Workers began a three-month strike. The consequent coal shortage led to school closures and shortened working weeks in the Eastern USA.
- In 1979, half the nation's petrol stations were without fuel. Those that had it were charging 50 per cent more than the year before. Drivers queued for petrol on specified days, often for several hours.

The significance of the energy crisis

The end of the era of cheap energy hit Americans' standard of living. Probably one-third of the alarming rise in prices was due to the increased cost of oil. Cheap oil had been vital to post-Second World War prosperity and economic growth, helping industry and accelerating socially transformative suburbanisation (see page 357) and **consumerism**.

The energy crisis provided politicians with an apparently insoluble problem, but voters wanted them to 'do something about it'. One obvious way to decrease energy consumption was to raise taxes on oil, but voters disliked increased energy prices. The inability of politicians to solve this conundrum contributed to the growing political disillusionment.

From 1973, many private citizens tried to save fuel, turning down the thermostat and joining carpools. In 1977, President Carter suggested that thermostats be adjusted so that heating was at a maximum 18°C in winter, and air conditioning would only kick in at 26°C in summer. Government buildings led the way in implementing these suggestions and some factories cut hours. However, Americans still consumed frightening quantities of fuel.

The impact of foreign competition

In combination with the energy crisis, foreign economic competition contributed to a sense of national decline from the mid-1970s.

Although the United States still produced 25 per cent of the world's manufactured goods in the 1970s, American companies struggled against technologically superior rivals in Germany and Japan. Such foreign competition led to increased unemployment and a **trade deficit**. By 1978–79 the annual US trade deficit was around $40 billion.

The impact of foreign competition was demonstrated in the automobile industry. Inexpensive and well-made Japanese car imports were extremely attractive to American consumers. Japanese companies had 23 per cent of the US automobile market by 1981. American car companies were slow to adapt. Even as sales of American cars fell, manufacturers continued to produce 'gas guzzlers' that used a great deal of fuel, while Japanese cars were smaller and more economic. Chrysler lost billions and needed a controversial $1.5 billion government bailout in 1980. The number of permanent jobs in the automobile industry fell from 940,000 in 1978 to 500,000 in 1982. In the car manufacturing city of Detroit, unemployment reached 24 per cent by 1980.

Americans reacted uneasily to foreign competition. Some attacked Toyotas with sledgehammers, United Auto Workers asked President Carter to restrict Japanese car imports and some sported 'Buy American: the job you save may be your own' bumper stickers – all to no avail. Many American companies moved production abroad or bought finished products from foreign manufacturers for whom labour was cheaper and less assertive (see page 428).

Nevertheless, although Americans felt economically squeezed, the United States remained easily the world's most affluent society with a far higher **GNP** than its nearest rivals.

A nation of hamburger flippers

US economic problems led the **AFL-CIO** to describe the US as 'a nation of hamburger stands, a country stripped of industrial capacity and meaningful work ... A service-economy ... a nation of citizens busily buying and selling cheese-burgers'. While this is clearly an exaggeration, the union leaders had correctly identified a long-term economic trend: the decline of skilled manufacturing jobs and the increasing dependence of American workers on low-paid, insecure jobs in the **service industry**.

The response of the government

Voters were unimpressed by the federal government response to the economic problems of 1973–80. Ford had various ideas for improving the economy. He asked Americans to voluntarily cut their mileage by 5 per cent and stop throwing out food, and he distributed red-and-white WIN ('Whip Inflation Now') buttons. America liked his buttons but rejected his suggestions. He cut federal expenditure and asked Congress to approve a tax rise. When that made him unpopular, he proposed a tax cut, which the Democrat-controlled Congress made larger than he thought wise. In the long run, the tax cut and 1975 Omnibus Energy Act (domestic oil prices were allowed to rise slowly so consumption decreased) helped bring the economy out of recession.

Carter's responses to rocketing inflation, increasing unemployment and rising energy prices pleased no one. He adopted standard methods for handling inflation such as decreasing government expenditure (for example, he froze federal workers' wages) and urging voluntary wage and price controls in the private sector. Blue-collar workers who traditionally voted Democrat disliked Carter's focus upon inflation rather than unemployment, his voluntary wage guidelines and his criticism of striking miners in 1977, and considered him unsupportive over the minimum wage. The business community distrusted Carter; they feared his energy proposals (see below) would damage industry and worried about the impact of mounting trade deficits on the dollar, which had slumped on the world currency markets. All of this added to the growing sense of crisis and of failure of presidential leadership. In many ways, Carter was unfairly judged; his support for his **Federal Reserve Board** chairman's tough stance on inflation (he curbed the money supply) led to revival under Reagan.

Carter and the energy crisis

Carter tried harder than any other president to solve the energy crisis. He wanted to end dependence on the unstable Middle East, and in April 1977 his energy programme suggested:

- oil conservation – for example, through cutting down on travel
- the development and use of alternative sources of power, especially nuclear power, coal and solar energy
- higher taxes on large automobiles to encourage Americans to buy smaller models
- greater insulation in homes and workplaces.

Although Carter's proposed energy legislation got through the House of Representatives, it met insuperable opposition in the Senate. This was because:

- Carter had drawn it up with insufficient consultation and lobbying.
- States where automobiles and natural gas and oil were produced opposed the programme.
- Voters did not want to pay higher taxes in a period of high inflation or change their lifestyles.

In 1979 OPEC raised oil prices (see page 430) and Carter called again for actions to reduce dependence on foreign oil.

> **Source B** Extract from President Carter's televised speech, 15 July 1979. The President felt that there was much that was wrong with America, but that it could be solved by the confidence and unity that could be effectively tested in a new approach to the energy crisis.
>
> It's clear that the true problems of our nation are much ... deeper than gasoline lines or energy shortages ... inflation or recession ... All the legislation in the world can't fix what's wrong with America ... [It is] a fundamental threat to American democracy ... a crisis of confidence ... We can see this crisis in the growing doubt about the meaning of our own lives and in the loss of a unity of purpose for our nation.
>
> The erosion of our confidence in the future is threatening to destroy the social and political fabric of America ... We've always believed in ... progress ... Our people are losing that faith, not only in government itself but in the ability as citizens to serve as the ultimate rulers ... of our democracy ... In a nation that was proud of hard work, strong families, close-knit communities, and our faith in God, too many of us now tend to worship self-indulgence and consumption ... The symptoms of this crisis of the American spirit are all around us ... Two-thirds of our people do not even vote. The productivity of American workers is actually dropping ... there is a growing disrespect for government and for churches and for schools, the news media, and other institutions ...
>
> These changes ... [came] upon us gradually ... [through years] filled with shocks and tragedy ... the murders of John Kennedy and Robert Kennedy and Martin Luther King Jr ... the agony of Vietnam. We respected the presidency as a place of honor until the shock of Watergate ... ten years of inflation began to shrink our dollar and our savings. We believed that our nation's resources were limitless until 1973, when we had to face a growing dependence on foreign oil ...These wounds are still very deep ... Looking for a way out of this crisis, our people have turned to the federal government and found the ... gap between our citizens and our government has never been so wide ... In little more than two decades we've gone from a position of energy independence to one in which almost half the oil we use comes from foreign countries, at prices that are going through the roof. Our excessive dependence on OPEC has already taken a tremendous toll on our economy and our people ... It's a cause of the increased inflation and unemployment that we now face. This intolerable dependence on foreign oil threatens our economic independence and the very security of our nation. The energy crisis is real.
>
> Public reaction to the speech was initially positive, but then became negative. Looking at the content of Source B, what can you find that (1) initially attracted Americans and (2) then turned them against Carter?

Congress responded to some of Carter's suggestions. The Energy Security Act (1980) offered loans and incentives to promote the search for and use of alternative energy, including synthetic fuels, alcohol fuels and biomass energy. However, Carter's suggestion that nuclear power was one route to US energy independence became particularly unpopular after a nuclear meltdown at Pennsylvania's Three Mile Island reactor in 1979 mobilised environmentalists. They staged nationwide protest marches demanding that all nuclear facilities be shut down.

Overall, Carter failed to get Americans to agree on how to solve the energy crisis, but at least he contributed to greatly increased awareness of the importance of energy conservation; per capita consumption of energy decreased by 10 per cent between 1979 and 1983.

Conclusion: The impact of economic change on society

Although America remained the world's leading economic power and most affluent society, the combination of federal government overspending, foreign competition, excessive oil consumption and rising oil prices hit family incomes and damaged the confidence that life would continue to get better that had characterised America in the 1950s.

Work together

Revise your notes on the government response to the economic changes of 1973–80. Do you and your partner agree on the effectiveness of the government measures?

3 Changing popular culture

The media claimed that there was a cultural revolution in the 1960s, a decade when television and particularly Hollywood presented anti-establishment and anti-authority themes, just as in the 1950s (see page 363). However, it could be argued that a cultural revolution was even more in evidence in popular culture in the 1970s than in the 1960s. The dramatically increased commercialisation of sport led to more cheating and violence, while music, movies and television suggested a bitterly divided society.

> **Note it down**
>
> In the 1970s popular culture became increasingly diverse, reflecting the experiences of an increasingly fragmented society. As you read this section, focus first on the different areas of culture: popular sport, music etc. Second, within each area, note down (1) key examples of popular culture; (2) the way they reflect changes in US culture; and (3) which groups were involved with different aspects of the culture. Use a note-making strategy that you feel best allows you to complete this task.

Business interests in sport

Before the 1970s, many Americans felt sport reflected all that was good about the '**American Way**'. They felt both were characterised by the capacity for hard work, equal opportunities for advancement and frequent success. They believed that team games and team spirit correlated with good citizenship and fostered a sense of community and that all sports strengthened character.

The commercialisation of sport dated from the mid-nineteenth century, but it accelerated in the twentieth century and particularly in the 1970s, when many argued that the over-commercialisation of sport encapsulated all that was bad in the American character, especially excessive greed.

By 1973, colleges, teams and athletes earned vast sums from spectators, corporate sponsors and TV rights. The sums increased further between 1973 and 1980. The amount received by the **National Football League (NFL)** for TV rights rose from $188 million in the period 1970–73 to $646 million in 1978–82. Corporate sponsorship increased dramatically in the 1970s because there was so much more sport on TV and corporate advertisers could target the increasing number of armchair spectators. Overall, American television viewers preferred sports programmes to everything else on TV apart from movies. While 90 per cent of men watched sport on television, 'only' 75 per cent of women did.

One of the clearest signs that sport was all about money was an acceleration of the trend whereby teams such as **football**'s Oakland Raiders dumped their supporters and traditional homes and moved to another city. Raiders' owner Al Davis had failed to get the city of Oakland to finance stadium improvements, so in 1980 he decided to move the team to Los Angeles. The *Los Angeles Times* noted, 'Sports business is rough-and-tumble competition business. Self-interest rules.'

Another famous example of business interests invading sports was the New York City Marathon. Entrepreneur Fred Lebow took control of the marathon in the 1970s. He changed the nature of the New York Road Runners Club, which administered the marathon, from a volunteer organisation facilitating the athletic interests of its members to a business enterprise. He increased the marathon's attractiveness to corporate funding by raising the number of participants.

Athletes and profits

Athletes began to demand a greater share in the profits generated by sport and resented restrictions on their ability to earn more money. For example, John Mackey of the Baltimore Colts sued the NFL in order to gain greater bargaining power over salaries and movement from one club to another. Mackey and the NFL players' union won their case in 1976. Labour disputes, lawsuits, walkouts and strikes characterised team sports during the 1970s. It was commonly thought that this was a legacy of 1960s' challenges to authority, especially as many of the players such as John Mackey who led the fight against traditional labour practices in sport were black Americans who drew on the traditions of the civil rights and **Black Power movements**.

Cheating and violence

Sport was such big money that the numbers tempted to cheat greatly increased. In the 1970s, the rise in investigative journalism led to much exposure of what seemed to be an ever-increasing amount of corruption. Players themselves spilt the beans to make money. It was estimated that one-third of the US Olympic team used steroids in 1968 and 68 per cent by 1972. In 1980 University of New Mexico coaches were found falsifying athletes' grades in order to keep mediocre students who earned the university gate-money.

Violence in sport was nothing new but it increased due to the money at stake in the 1970s. One social commentator wrote that violence was endemic in sport because it 'makes good television'. In a 1978 football game, a New England Patriot bumped into Oakland Raider Jack Tatum and suffered two fractured vertebrae, which left him a quadriplegic. In his autobiography *They Call Me Assassin* (1980), Tatum said he did not feel guilty or sad about his opponent's fate, because it was 'what the owners expect of me when they give me my paycheck'.

Commercialisation was clearly changing the nature of American sport and some felt it caused change in music, too.

The fragmentation of popular music

Popular music both mirrored and influenced contemporary society. In the 1970s the fragmentation of popular music into new genres and the related battles over commercialisation and 'pure' musical forms suggested a society bitterly divided over the merits of **materialism** and conformity.

Rock, pop and commercialisation

The rock culture that developed in the late 1960s rejected easy-listening and pop music. Although born in the mainstream and dominating it by the 1970s, rock claimed to be opposed to **mass society**; rock was 'good', serious music, whereas pop was 'bad', trivial music. Rock culture perceived itself as anti-mass culture, with superior, authentic music full of feeling and creativity and uncorrupted by commerce and fashion; pop had inferior, over-commercialised, unoriginal music, the consumption of which manipulated buyers. Rock was aware of the social implications of musical production and consumption; pop lacked awareness and was corrupted and conformist. Rock rejected the ethical compromise and capitulation that characterised pop.

New genres and fragmentation

Although rock dominated the music industry in the 1970s, older categories such as rhythm and blues and country and western remained popular and new sub-genres such as heavy metal, punk, disco and hip-hop acquired fans. The disco boom began in 1974 and by 1976 there were around 10,000 discotheques in the United States. The first disco hit to reach the charts was Gloria Gaynor's 'Never Can Say Goodbye' (1975). Gaynor's fame was eclipsed by Donna Summer, whose 'Love to Love You Baby' reached number two in the charts in 1976. By the end of 1976, the pop charts were full of disco records, such as Hot Chocolate's 'You Sexy Thing' and the Bee Gees' 'You Should Be Dancing'. Rock fans despised disco music as formulaic, attributing its 'death' by 1979 to record companies saturating the markets with low-quality, standardised products. Heavy metal, punk, hip-hop and singer-songwriters lasted longer.

Heavy metal

Originally a British-led phenomenon, heavy metal and its exceptionally loud volume was popular in America. The most successful American heavy metal band in the 1970s was Grand Funk Railroad. Heavy metal was ignored by radio and the press, which gave it the outsider status that perhaps explains its success. Lacking radio play, heavy metal performers focussed on live shows characterised by noise and the phallic guitar thrusts that provoked the nickname 'cock rock' (there were no women artists in heavy metal). Heavy metal is often associated with the occult, as demonstrated by Alice Cooper, a group that wore makeup and engaged in showy animal rituals. By 1976, the group had eight gold or platinum albums, including the 1973 album *Billion Dollar Babies*, which reached number one in the charts. Although the members of Alice Cooper were ex-athletes, the spandex, high-heeled boots and makeup in which they performed challenged traditional gender roles.

Punk

American punk rock developed in the mid-1970s. Punk rockers such as The Ramones rejected the pompous and pretentious elements of the dominant rock culture. Punk rock aimed to shock, so The Ramones used Nazi symbols and played songs with titles such as 'I Don't Care', 'I Don't Wanna Be Tamed' and 'Now I Wanna Sniff Some Glue'. Punk rockers believed commercialisation had destroyed American music and that the biggest and most popular bands had sold out to money and become corrupted. Punks, such as the California-based group The Dead Kennedys, rejected elaborate instrumentation and their songs were often anti-establishment, with a political message. The Dead Kennedys 'Holiday in Cambodia', for example, was critical of well-meaning middle-class students. The band's name was chosen to reflect the death of American idealism. Their aggressive realism and political radicalism attracted a loyal following among working-class young people and left-wing students.

By the end of the 1970s punk was metamorphosing into new kinds of music, such as no wave and new wave.

No wave emerged in the underground clubs of downtown New York, where bands such as the Contortions and DNA flourished. Like punk, it rejected commercialism. Indeed, the influential no wave band Teenage Jesus and the Jerks refused to perform songs lasting more than 30 seconds in order to reject a commercial sound.

New wave bands took punk in a more commercial direction. Combining punk guitars with disco drum machines, the new wave band Blondie took the new sound into the mainstream, with their number-one single 'Heart of Glass' in 1979.

Hip-hop

Hip-hop began in New York City's Harlem ghetto in the early 1970s. This black urban youth culture comprised rapping, DJing, graffiti, beatboxing and breakdancing. As a black musical form, hip-hop had its roots in the black tradition of talking to music. From 1968, the Last Poets put rhythmic, rhyming speech against the funky sounds of Kool and the Gang. While there had always been talking in soul music, Harlem street poets such as Gil Scott-Heron were more politically conscious and lamented ghetto conditions. By the late 1970s, hip-hop had spread to urban centres across America.

Many people consider The Sugarhill Gang's 'Rapper's Delight' (1979) the first hip-hop record; initially it just scraped into the pop Top 40, but eventually sold over 2 million copies. Purists criticised the group as pre-fabricated and felt that hip-hop lost some of its real character after 'Rapper's Delight' alerted the mainstream media to its existence.

The first supposedly 'rap' record to reach number one in the pop charts was Blondie's 'Rapture'; lead singer Debbie Harry tried to be respectful of hip-hop, but purists saw this as yet another example of white exploitation of a black musical tradition. Rap as sung by black Americans inevitably included topical themes; an early recorded example was 'How We Gonna Make the Black Nation Rise' (1980) by Brother D and Collective Effort.

Singer-songwriters

Singer-songwriters gained great kudos in the 1970s because they were 'authentic'; they wrote their own music and were singing from the heart. The lyrics written and sung by artists such as Carole King and Carly Simon were frequently highly personal. Simon's recordings sometimes suggested a **feminist** influence, although the popular 'Nobody Does It Better' (1977) was a straightforward love song. Although Bruce Springsteen wrote and sang romantic songs, in his appearance and lyrics he and his 'heartland rock' represented the forgotten man 'born down in a dead man's town' in the old, declining industrial areas, where he cannot find a job. Springsteen was a native of New Jersey, a state where a high proportion of manufacturing jobs were lost. His songs frequently refer to Rust Belt unemployment and other aspects of working-class life.

▲ Bruce Springsteen performs in the late 1970s. What point do you suppose he was trying to make when he performed in his vest?

Music in the 1970s: Conclusions

A considerable amount of the popular music in the 1970s reflected a society in which many of the young sought in varying degrees to differentiate themselves from other young people and adults. While many of the young still liked more traditional forms of music such as easy listening and country and western, different tastes and attitudes contributed to the continuation and proliferation of multiple musical genres. Basically, music reflected a wide variety of tastes and lifestyles, as did film and television.

Contradictions in film and TV

Film and television offered a mixture of escapism and exploration of social and political tensions during the 1970s. Escapism was usually more lucrative at the box office, but films and television that explored and reflected rising violence, racial conflict and political corruption also did well, so that one critic contended that the political energies of the 1960s were channelled into the arts in the 1970s and contributed to a cinematic rebirth. To a lesser extent, the same could be said of television.

Television and social consciousness

Ridiculed as the 'Hillbilly Network', CBS cancelled series such as the popular and long-running *The Beverly Hillbillies* (about a backwoods family that discovered oil and suddenly found themselves with a great deal of money and a residence in Beverly Hills) and turned instead to 'social consciousness' programmes such as *All in the Family* (1971–79). Its central character was Second World War veteran and blue-collar worker Archie Bunker who ranted at black people, feminists, homosexuals and hippies (although Archie's liberal creators meant him to be a rather ridiculous bigot, many in **Middle America** agreed with him). The show topped the ratings from 1971–76. All the 1960s tensions were covered in this ground-breaking series: abortion, sexuality, the Vietnam War, racism and women's liberation.

Two series on independent-minded women were very popular; *Maude* (1972–78) had a feminist central character, while the heroine of the popular *Mary Tyler Moore Show* (1970–77) was a 30-something, single, intelligent working woman facing invariably less intelligent and sexist males in the workplace.

Pressure from organisations such as the Gay Activist Alliance forced TV networks into more sympathetic portrayals of homosexuals; for example, the made-for-TV movie *A Question of Love* (1978) was about a lesbian mother's child custody case.

The origins of America's racial tensions were explored in ABC's mini-series *Roots* (1977), black American writer Alex Haley's story of the enslavement of his ancestors. A record-breaking 100 million viewers tuned in for the last episode – nearly half the American population. Racism was also reflected in a new movie genre, Blaxploitation.

Blaxploitation movies

Between 1969 and 1974, independent black filmmakers and studios made what became known as Blaxploitation films, with black casts and action-packed adventures in the **ghettos**. Blaxploitation movies were a result of:

More sex and violence

From 1934, the motion picture industry engaged in self-censorship; the Production Code Administration monitored the content of movies to ensure that they did not encourage socially unacceptable behaviour. In 1968 the Code was abandoned in favour of a film rating system that guided moviegoers as to the likely content of movies. The end of the Code in 1968 contributed to more sexually graphic movies in the 1970s – most famously *Last Tango in Paris* (1973), which is explicit even by today's standards. In another indication of changing attitudes, a porn movie, *Deep Throat* (1972), was a massive hit among ordinary filmgoers.

On television, several series were titillating rather than explicit. Critics called such programmes 'jigglevision' because breasts and buttocks could be seen moving. Others christened it 'Tits & Ass Television'. A good example was the popular series *Charlie's Angels* (1976–81), which had three private investigator heroines. One critic dismissed it as 'an excuse to show 60 minutes of suggestive poses by walking, talking pinup girls'. One of the stars, Farrah Fawcett-Majors, said, 'When the show was number three, I figured it was our acting. When it got to be number one, I decided it could only be because none of us wears a bra.' When citizen group campaigns against television violence led to a decrease in 'hard action', one network executive responded, 'If violence goes down, sex will go up.' It did. The most sexually explicit programme was ABC's 1977 comedy series *Soap*.

Contemporary academic studies indicated a strong link between violence on TV and the rising crime rate; a group of youngsters who had seen the 1974 TV movie *Born Innocent* committed a rape identical to one in the movie. Violent films included *The Godfather* (1972), *The Texas Chainsaw Massacre* (1974) and *Taxi Driver* (1976). Contemporary anxieties about increasing crime help explain the popularity of the vigilante hero in *Death Wish* (1974) and its four sequels.

- black dismay about the bland black characters in mainstream movies
- Hollywood's awareness that, as black people constituted 30 per cent of the audience in city cinemas, Blaxploitation films would make money
- greater black awareness generated by Black Power (see page 391).

Blaxploitation movies were characterised by black heroes overcoming corrupt whites and by the depiction of black and white women as sex objects, suggesting that this genre owed much to feelings of emasculation in the ghettos. These movies aroused tensions within the black community. Some middle-class black critics rejected the violence, drug dealing and gangsters of the 60 or so Blaxploitation films. They claimed that the smash hit *Superfly* (1972) contributed to a dramatic increase in cocaine use among ghetto youths, and that this glamourisation of ghetto life distracted blacks from the collective political struggle.

Movies and political issues

The eminent film critic Pauline Kael considered the 1970s a 'Golden Age' of movies. Many films of this time dealt with social disorder and political corruption. Released while Watergate was a national obsession, *The Conversation* (1974) explored the privacy and responsibility issues facing a surveillance expert. Watergate itself was the subject of the highly popular *All the President's Men* (1976), the story of the *Washington Post* reporters who exposed the scandal. Its director Alan J. Pakula also covered the theme of corruption in American national politics in *The Parallax View* (1974). *Chinatown* (1974) told of corruption at a local level when big business gained a stranglehold over Los Angeles' water supply during the 1930s, while *The China Syndrome* (1979) focussed on the attempted cover-up of the near-meltdown of a nuclear plant; current environmentalist debates were reflected in such explorations of the issue of public good versus private greed.

Although there was little from Hollywood on Vietnam, racism, the rise of feminism and the gay subculture, the small number of films that were produced were frequently of exceptionally high quality. For example, *The Deer Hunter* (1978) began with a moving, authentic depiction of Pennsylvania steelworkers, and then traced the ruin of their lives through service in Vietnam.

Pure escapism?

Many films were escapist entertainment. *American Graffiti* (1973) and *Grease* (1978) looked back affectionately to teenage life in the 1950s and were great box-office hits, as were Woody Allen's hymns to New York City and his own neuroses, *Annie Hall* (1977) and *Manhattan* (1979).

Science-fiction films such as *Star Wars* (1977) and *Close Encounters of the Third Kind* (1978) were optimistic in tone and very popular. However, the message of some sci-fi films was downbeat. *Soylent Green* (1973) was set in a future world of environmental disaster, mass poverty and ghettoisation, in which a small privileged male elite reduced women to the status of slaves. *Logan's Run* (1976) echoed similar environmentalist themes. Such films were often popular because they reflected contemporary concerns.

Science fiction was also popular on television, with series such as *The Incredible Hulk* (1978–82). *Fantasy Island* (1977–84) – where one's wishes came true – was classic escapist fare, reflecting how by the mid-1970s viewers were tiring of 'social consciousness'. This was when 'jigglevision' (see page 436) and crime shows such as *Hawaii Five-0* (1968–80) and *Starsky and Hutch* (1975–79) became popular. Two series about idealised families, *The Waltons* (1971–81) and *Little House on the Prairie* (1974–83), were particular favourites. Television followed the movies in presenting an idealised view of the 1950s, with the long-running sitcom *Happy Days* (1974–84).

Contradictions in movies and TV: Conclusions

During the 1970s film and television, much like pop music, became increasingly fragmented. Many movies and television programmes were escapist, allowing audiences to get away from current political and social tensions. However, movies and television also reflected contemporary anxieties and issues. A great deal of science fiction played on contemporary concerns about issues such as the environment and the message of many of these films was that there could be no escape from inevitable disaster. Similarly, the popularity of 'cops-and-robbers' television programmes surely owed much to fears about rising crime. Movies and television were no more capable of escaping contemporary reality than were the news media.

Developments in news media

The expansion of investigative journalism was the most important of several developments in news media in the 1970s. It was inspired by the Vietnam War (see page 401), the credibility gap (see page 413) and Watergate. The exposure of Watergate had made *Washington Post* reporters Woodward and Bernstein national heroes. Although the exposure of scandal and corruption was nothing new (it had been christened 'muck-raking' by President Theodore Roosevelt in the early twentieth century), the war and Watergate encouraged countless aspirational journalists to seek another career-making scandal. Evaluation of the role of the news media in and after Watergate varied. Some believed journalists played an essential role in maintaining American democracy. Others feared that Watergate encouraged journalists to make big scandals out of the relatively trivial and felt the war and Watergate had given the press an exaggerated sense of its own importance in politics.

A second and related development in news media was the expansion of television news coverage. In an unprecedented development, a news programme became the most successful programme in American history. First aired in 1968, the magazine-style CBS News programme *60 Minutes* was fixed in the 7pm Sunday evening slot from 1976 and viewing figures rocketed. *60 Minutes* led the way in several investigative journalism innovations such as hidden cameras and 'gotcha journalism' – surprise visits to the subjects of investigation. Critics attacked the programme as breeding a cynical attitude to national life and politics.

Another much-criticised development was the increased incidence and popularity of 'happy talk' – additional and (some would say) meaningless comments inserted into news programmes, usually in the form of a highly informal conversational style between journalists. Al Primo took his Philadelphia *Eyewitness News* format to ABC's New York news programme in 1968 and stations across America copied his style. As reporters in the field talked to studio anchors, purists carped that newsmen were becoming personalities, and that their physical appearance and facility with banter seemed more important than their journalistic skills and the news itself.

A fourth development was the increased importance of previously marginalised groups, such as women, in the news. Women became more prominent in programme content (the 1973 'Battle of the Sexes' tennis match between Billie Jean King and 55-year-old former champion Bobby Riggs was televised) and programme presentation. The **NOW** (see page 404) campaigned for more women on television and the development of the special reports on current issues in the 1970s increased opportunities for women such as Barbara Walters, who joined *ABC Evening News* in 1976.

Finally, the news media paid far more attention to sexual issues in the 1970s.

Conclusion: Changing popular culture

The changes in popular culture in the 1970s did not come out of the blue; there was a long history of commercialisation in sport and music, of ever-increasing sex and violence and the exploration of social and political tensions in television and film, and of muck-raking in journalism. However, the pace and awareness of cultural change seemed to increase during these years and this would contribute to a conservative cultural backlash by the 1980s.

> **Work together**
>
> You could listen to some of the recordings or watch some of the movies and television programmes mentioned in this section. You could then discuss what they seem to suggest about popular culture in the period.

4 The extent of progress in individual and civil rights

The 1960s was a decade of rights-consciousness and contagious protests; black American demands for equal rights encouraged students to demand greater rights from university authorities and to oppose the **draft**, and inspired Mexican Americans, Native Americans, women and homosexuals to demand their rights. The protesters gained some of what they sought and ensured that the rights of minorities and women remained high on the political agenda in 1973.

In the years 1973–80, desired advances were not always attained or admired. Many in Richard Nixon's 'great **silent majority**' were tired of demands for rights that seemed to threaten their own.

> **Note it down**
>
> Notes on the issue of progress (like that of success/failure) lend themselves to a chart that shows the position at the start of a given period and then at the end. As you read this chapter, summarise the situation in 1973 for black Americans, Native Americans, women, workers and homosexuals, and then note any changes in subsequent years. Finally, fill in summaries of their situation in 1980, giving your assessment of the degree of progress achieved by each group.

The political and social impact of *Roe* v. *Wade*

In 1973, the Supreme Court legalised abortion in *Roe* v. *Wade*, one of the most divisive rulings in American history.

Abortion before *Roe* v. *Wade*

Before 1973, abortion was a crime in 30 states and legal in certain cases in 20 states. For example, in 1967 Colorado became the first state to allow abortions in cases of rape, incest or a threat to the woman's health. By 1972, 13 other states had a similar law, including California, Oregon and North Carolina. In the 30 states where abortion was a crime, many women risked backstreet abortions (see page 407). By the 1960s, college students could usually have safe abortions performed by sympathetic doctors but poor women lacked such access. Many feminists considered the right to abortion the most important of women's rights; one said, 'We can get all the rights in the world … and none of them means a doggone thing if we don't own the flesh we stand in.' From 1971, the National Abortion Rights Action League lobbied state legislatures for the legalisation of abortion.

Roe v. *Wade* ruling

The case of an impoverished Texas woman who did not want to bear a child that would grow up in poverty led to the Supreme Court's *Roe* v. *Wade* (1973) ruling. The Court said that women could abort in the first 13 weeks when a foetus could not sustain life on its own. The ruling was politically and socially divisive. While feminists, women who feared unplanned pregnancies, liberals and organisations such as the NOW and Planned Parenthood were thrilled, conservatives were outraged.

Opposition to *Roe* v. *Wade*

Conservative organisations such as the National Right to Life Committee, set up in 1967 by the Catholic Church to oppose abortion, campaigned against *Roe* v. *Wade* in the courts, in elections and in the streets. Anti-abortion activists proved highly effective fundraisers and recruiters. They used methods such as mass mailings containing highly emotive language. One 1978 anti-abortion mailing contained graphic pictures and pleaded, 'Stop the baby killers … Abortion means killing a living baby, a tiny human being with a beating heart and little fingers … killing a baby boy or girl with burning deadly chemicals or a powerful machine that sucks and tears the little infant from its mother's womb.'

Perhaps the single most influential opponent of abortion and women's rights was Catholic lawyer and mother of six Phyllis Schlafly, 'Sweetheart of the Silent Majority', who among other things campaigned for women's skirts to be two inches below the knee. She was representative of a resurgent social conservatism that was closely associated with the Republican Party. Republican representative Henry Hyde led Congress in the passage of a law that banned the use of federal funds for abortion. In 1977 the Supreme Court (by now more conservative) ruled Hyde's measure constitutional, and extended the ban on federally funded abortions to military and Peace Corps personnel. *Roe* v. *Wade* had played a big part in mobilising the social conservatism that revitalised the Republican Party and would contribute greatly to 'culture wars' in the 1980s (see page 458).

Women's rights

Women's rights had increased since the early 1960s:

- Women had gained greater freedom in their sexual lives and the right to abortion.
- Attitudes towards women and work had changed. For example, over two-thirds of female college students agreed that 'the idea that the woman's place is in the home is nonsense'.

However, feminists failed to achieve economic equality. Despite the 1963 Equal Pay Act, professional women still received on average 73 per cent of the salaries paid to professional men and most women remained in the lowest-paid jobs. Sixty-six per cent of US adults classified as 'poor' were women. Furthermore, feminists failed to obtain the Equal Rights Amendment (ERA) and encountered increasing conservative opposition.

The Equal Rights Amendment (ERA)

Feminists sought an ERA to the Constitution to guarantee equal rights under the law. The proposed amendment said:

- Equality of rights under the law shall not be denied or abridged by the United States or by any state on account of sex.
- Congress shall have the power to enforce, by appropriate legislation, the provisions of this article.
- This amendment shall take effect two years after the date of ratification.

The Democrat-controlled Congress voted overwhelmingly for the ERA in 1972. Liberals were delighted, but opponents said it would lead to gay marriages, women in combat, unisex toilets and the end of the nuclear family. Phyllis Schlafly established a 'Stop ERA' organisation in 1972 that attracted 50,000 members. When 20,000 feminists met in Houston, Texas, for a National Women's Conference in 1978, Schlafly's counter-rally drew 8,000 supporters. She said, 'The American people do not want the Equal Rights Amendment, and they do not want government-funded abortion, lesbian privileges, or … universal … childcare.' Many conservative states agreed with Schlafly and the ERA never obtained the assent of 75 per cent of the states that was necessary for an amendment to the Constitution, even though the issue remained high on the political agenda during the 1970s.

Opposition to women's rights

The advances in women's rights mobilised ominous conservative opposition. Seventy per cent of those contacted by the National Right to Life Committee turned out to vote in the congressional elections in 1978 (twice the national average) and 50 per cent of them donated at least $25 to the Committee. The conservative campaign against abortion affected the 1980 congressional elections; several liberals were defeated, including George McGovern (see page 411). The social conservatives continued to gain strength. In 1979, San Diego housewife and bestselling author Beverly LaHaye established Concerned Women for America (CWA) to fight against the ERA and abortion. It had 500,000 members by the mid-1980s. LaHaye and her supporters wanted women to stay at home, look after the family and not deprive men of possible employment.

Clearly, women had not yet achieved equal rights and the issue had polarised American society. Women's rights were frequently challenged by conservatives, as were workers' rights.

Workers' rights

By 1973, American labour unions had the **collective bargaining rights** gained in the Wagner Act (1935) and many members received the benefits won by unions in the late 1940s and 1950s, including health insurance, life insurance, paid vacations and pensions. Non-union members had few such rights, but legislation guaranteed a minimum wage and maximum working hours.

In 1973, unions appeared powerful. Over 19 million Americans belonged to unions in 1970 and there were many strikes:

- After the largest public employees strike in American history in 1970, when 200,000 postal workers went on strike, the federal government approved their collective bargaining rights, although not their right to strike.
- 1.8 million employees were affected by strikes and lockouts in 1974, when 31.8 million working days were lost.
- In 1977, the United Mine Workers' 109-day strike led to a fuel shortage that caused lay-offs and school closures.

However, it was becoming clear that the labour unions were in decline. The 19 million unionised Americans constituted only 27.4 per cent of non-agricultural workers. This percentage was way below that of most other industrialised nations, where workers often had more rights than American workers. For example, the Supreme Court had ruled **common situs picketing** illegal in 1951 and Congress (which had demonstrated anti-union sentiment in the 1947 Taft–Hartley Act), rejected successive presidents' call for legislation to make it legal. When President Ford introduced a bill to allow it but with restrictions in 1975, business opposition was so great that Ford vetoed his own bill in order to appease right-wing Republicans.

Reasons for the decline of unions and workers' rights

While unions retained the right to strike in 1973–80, workers' rights were threatened for several reasons.

First, employers naturally disliked unions and public opinion was often anti-union because of:

- anticommunism (employers frequently and successfully associated union membership with **communism**)
- corruption scandals (the leader of the mob-dominated transportation workers' Teamsters Union was jailed in 1967)
- the belief that unions and strikes damaged the nation's economy.

Second, unions were traditionally strongest in the heavy and manufacturing industries that slowly declined after the Second World War. After the war, the proportion of **white-collar** and service workers in the American labour force increased (see page 357). Between 1973 and 1980, 80 per cent of new private-sector jobs were in low-paid service/retail areas. These workers were often temporary or part-time and therefore harder to unionise.

> ### Wagner Act and Taft–Hartley Act provisions
>
> The pro-union Wagner Act (also known as the National Labor Relations Act) of 1935 guaranteed the right of workers to organise and required employers to bargain with recognised union representatives. The Act prohibited discrimination against union members, refusal to bargain and management sponsorship of company unions. Agricultural workers were exempted from the Act's provisions.
>
> The anti-union Taft–Hartley Act (1947) authorised the president to call for a 'cooling-off' period before a strike could be called, banned closed shops (where all workers in a workplace had to be members of a union) and secondary boycotts (boycotting goods of companies hostile to unions), allowed states to pass 'right-to-work' laws that limited collective bargaining, and made union leaders swear that they were not communists.

Third, the great post-war economic growth area was the South. This growth owed much to the **interstate** highway system, the growing use of air conditioning to combat the hot climate and the anti-union traditions of the South. When the South's economy boomed, the unions failed to attract large numbers of members.

Fourth, in the 1970s, businesses tried to lower costs in the face of increasing foreign competition and a domestic market decreased by high unemployment and high inflation. As jobs were hard to come by, businesses could squeeze unions. Employers threatened to move their plants to areas where labour costs were lower and employees more amenable. For example, RCA moved its production of televisions to Mexico in 1980. There was a great wave of plant closures in the late 1970s, particularly in high-paying jobs in the steel, textile and automotive manufacturing industries. Thirty-eight million industrial jobs were lost in the 1970s, mostly in the Rust Belt. Firmly allied to a Republican Party that contained many anti-union politicians such as California's governor Ronald Reagan, corporate America lobbied ever more effectively. This combination of economic problems and increasing conservatism in national politics decreased union power and effectiveness. That contributed to an average 2 per cent yearly fall in workers' **real income** between 1973 and 1981, so that by 1981 it was at 1961 levels.

Fifth, following 1965 immigration legislation, an influx of foreign workers willing to work for lower wages undermined American labour, including Cesar Chavez's United Farm Workers (see page 393).

Sixth, workers often lacked unity. Unions and minorities clashed over their rights, especially over **affirmative action**. President Nixon had ensured affirmative action in federal hiring and contracting (see page 389), but organised labour declared it unfair. In 1975 a federal judge ruled against the Detroit Police Department's 'last hired, first fired' seniority principle. This ruling protected recently hired black officers. Faced with losing their jobs, some white officers protested in the streets: 'Talk about rights; we've got no rights.'

Non-unionised workers

Those who were not unionised and worked in low-waged or part-time employment had few rights. Their vulnerability to employer abuse increased if they were first-generation or illegal immigrants. The 1970s saw the revival of **sweatshops** in the garment industry in New York City and Los Angeles where such people were employed. Many were women, and most women workers suffered discrimination (their wages were 61 per cent of men's in 1960 and still only 65 per cent in 1985) and sexism (ad man F. William Free penned 'Cigarettes are like women. The best ones are thin and rich' for the American Tobacco Company in 1970).

Gay rights

In 1973, homosexuals often suffered employment discrimination and public hostility and humiliation. Homosexuality was considered a mental illness that could be cured. The authorities harassed bars and restaurants that served homosexual customers. However, the Stonewall riots (see page 408) generated growing **gay pride** and political militancy in the 1970s. For example, the New York Gay Liberation Front, established in 1970, urged gays to 'come out' proudly. Some did, and gay rights obtained several victories in 1973–80.

Public attitudes were changing and progress was made in noted centres of gay life:

- San Francisco passed an ordinance banning employment discrimination on grounds of sexual orientation in 1972. New York City followed in 1979.
- In 1973, the NOW finally endorsed gay rights.
- In 1974, the American Psychiatric Association removed homosexuality from its list of psychological disorders.
- In 1978, Californian voters resoundingly defeated Proposition 6, which would have rescinded a 1975 law that protected homosexual teachers from discrimination and given school districts authority to fire gay teachers who publicly endorsed homosexuality.
- In 1980, the Democratic **party platform** supported equality for all, regardless of sexual orientation.

However, there were also setbacks in a decade that saw the rise of the **Religious Right** and a conservative backlash. In 1977–78, Baptist ministers Jerry Falwell and Tim LaHaye gained national attention in a successful battle against a Miami pro-gay rights ordinance. That Miami defeat generated greater assertiveness among gay-rights activists in major cities, most famously in San Francisco. San Francisco's Castro area was becoming a totally homosexual community, with bars, restaurants, political organisations and public celebrations for gay men and lesbian women.

Overall, though, progress remained relatively slow. In 1980, millions of homosexuals remained in the closet, fearing ridicule, harassment, job loss and losing custody of their children. Politicians remained fearful of promoting gay rights, homosexuals were portrayed unsympathetically in the media and there were public debates over whether they were fit to be teachers or to hold positions of responsibility. Homosexual activity remained illegal (although rarely prosecuted) in many states.

Native American rights and the impact of Red Power

After centuries of mistreatment by whites, Native Americans joined in the rights revolution of the 1960s. Their campaign continued in the 1970s.

TIMELINE

Native American history

1700s	Europeans settle and conquer North America, treat Native Americans as inferior and take their lands
1800s	Native American tribes confined to reservations on land whites do not want
Roosevelt (1933–45)	Roosevelt promotes Native American culture and control over reservations and attempts to alleviate economic problems
1944	National Congress of American Indians (NCAI) established. It sues state and federal governments over discrimination in employment and education and treaty-breaking in relation to land and resources
1946–1978	The federal government's Indian Claims Commission distributes $800 million compensation for lost lands
1950s	The federal government encroaches upon reservations and tribal self-government rights
1960s rights revolution	Increased Native American assertiveness elicits federal government assistance:

- Johnson appoints a Native American to head the **Bureau of Indian Affairs** (BIA)
- Johnson's 1968 Civil Rights Act contains an 'Indian Bill of Rights' designed to protect Native Americans from corrupt or tyrannical tribal officials and from state government attempts to exercise criminal or civil jurisdiction over Native Americans on reservation land without consultation with the tribe
- Native Americans are among the greatest beneficiaries of Johnson's War on Poverty (see page 396), gaining access to better health services, housing, education, welfare and poverty benefits, and employment

Native Americans in 1973

In 1973, half the 700,000 Native American population lived short, hard lives on **reservations** with unemployment that ranged from 20 per cent to 80 per cent (depending on the natural resources and physical location of the reservation), a 44-year life expectancy (the national average was 64) and exceptionally high rates of suicide and alcoholism. Those living in cities invariably had low-paying jobs and poor housing and schooling. While many Native American problems resulted from the poverty and sense of dislocation consequent upon their loss of land over the centuries, their historic land treaty rights were frequently ignored. Native Americans had been granted US citizenship after the First World War, but most wanted the right to tribal self-government in order to preserve their culture and identity. Under self-government, a tribe could regulate tribal land, taxation, resources and individual behaviour.

Inspired by the Black Power movement, a Red Power movement developed. The NCAI's director defined Red Power as 'the political and economic power to run our own lives in our own way' and the National Indian Youth Council's president said, 'We do not want to be pushed into the mainstream of American life.' Red Power militants used organisations, occupations and litigation to achieve these aims.

Organisations

The most militant Native American organisation was the American Indian Movement (AIM), which was established in 1968 in Minneapolis-St Paul, the largest Native American ghetto. With 40 **chapters** across the USA and Canada, the AIM worked to improve ghetto housing, education and employment and also attracted members from the reservations. The AIM's methods included:

- stressing positive imagery – for example, by opposing names such as the 'Washington Redskins'
- monitoring police racism (the Native American population in Minneapolis jails subsequently fell by 60 per cent)
- establishing survival schools such as the Heart of the Earth Survival School in Minneapolis, which, from 1972, instructed urban children in Native languages and culture
- organising marches to publicise the need for compensation for US government violations of nineteenth-century treaties with Native Americans, such as the 1972 'Trail of Broken Treaties' from San Francisco to the BIA in Washington DC.

Occupations

Occupations gained great publicity, as demonstrated by the Native American occupation of the Pine Ridge Reservation village of Wounded Knee (1973), where members of the Sioux tribe had been massacred in 1890.

In February 1973, around 300 Sioux occupied Wounded Knee to publicise reservation problems: over 50 per cent unemployment, exceptionally high suicide and alcoholism rates, and a 46-year life expectancy. The trigger event for their occupation was inequality in legal rights; the indictment for manslaughter of the white killer of Wesley Bad Heart Bull could have led to his release within a decade, but when Wesley's mother protested, she was arrested on a charge that could have led to 30 years' incarceration.

The AIM-inspired occupation force demanded:

- free elections of tribal leaders (many Pine Ridge Reservation residents disliked authoritarian tribal president Richard Wilson)
- the review of all treaties, especially the 1868 treaty that concerned the tribe's land rights.

When hostages were held at gunpoint, heavily armed federal forces quickly besieged Wounded Knee and two Native Americans were killed. After 71 days, peace was agreed and the federal government promised an investigatory commission. The commission said that the 1868 treaty between the tribe and the federal government was superseded by the federal government's power to take land, but the occupation generated some federal government sympathy.

Litigation

Native American lawyers gained some successes in the law courts. For example, the federal government traditionally leased mining rights on reservations to private companies and Native Americans gained little, but in 1973 the Northern Cheyenne of Montana won a federal court victory enabling them to renegotiate mineral contracts. After 50 years of protest, controversy and litigation, coal mining on Navajo and Hopi reservation lands ceased in 2005.

The federal government and Native Americans

Congress responded to Native American activism with the Indian Self-Determination and Education Assistance Acts (1975), which gave tribes control over federal aid programmes and reservation education. Some Native Americans felt the legislation promised more than it delivered, primarily because it was insufficiently funded. Others said it increased Native American influence over federal actions and Native American financial and organisational resources. Some argue that the educational provisions were successful (especially in the growth of community colleges) and that the Educational Assistance Act paved the way for other helpful laws such as the Indian Health Care Improvement Act (1976), in which Congress granted $1.6 billion to help improve the availability and delivery of healthcare for Native Americans.

Native American litigants had similar mixed feelings about Supreme Court decisions:

- In *US* v. *Wheeler* (1978), the Supreme Court affirmed the right of a federal court to try a Native American who had already been tried by his tribe. While the Court recognised the 'unique' **sovereignty** of Native American tribes, it said it was 'limited'.
- In *Oliphant* (1978), the Supreme Court limited tribal authority over non-Indians and **Indians** of other tribes on reservations.
- While the American Indian Religious Freedom Act (1978) recognised rights to practise Native American cultural traditions, such as the use of the hallucinatory drug peyote, an increasingly conservative Supreme Court greatly weakened the Act in 1990.
- Decisions in 1979 resulted in the restoration of 1,800 acres to Narrangansetts in Rhode Island and $100 million compensation to the Sioux for 'dishonourable dealing' in the acquisition of the Black Hills in South Dakota (the Sioux rejected the money and demanded the land instead).

Native American rights in 1980

By 1980 Red Power had contributed to a greater awareness of Native American rights to **self-determination** and land. However, treaty rights were still frequently ignored and, although reservation Native Americans had greater self-government, most remained economically disadvantaged. Land rights lost over the centuries would never be restored and half the Native American population remained on unproductive reservation land. The economic status of Native Americans, like that of black Americans, remained greatly inferior to that of white people.

The status of black Americans, 1973–80

In 1973 all black Americans had the vote and *de jure* **segregation** (see page 387) had ended. However, *de facto* **segregation** and economic inequality indicated continuing inferior status.

Economic status

One-third of black Americans and one-half of black American children lived below the poverty line. The black **infant mortality rate** of 19 per cent was higher than that in some developing nations. One-third of black workers had low-status, low-skilled jobs in low-wage occupations. Average black earnings were one-half that of whites. Black Americans constituted 12 per cent of the US population but 43 per cent of arrested rapists, 55 per cent of those accused of murder and 69 per cent of those arraigned for robbery – statistics that owed much to inferior economic and social status. Ghetto crime, poverty and unemployment remained problems that even black mayors could not solve.

On the positive side, black Americans benefited from Great Society programmes. Although Nixon criticised many aspects of the War on Poverty and 'all that welfare crap', **social security** and welfare payments doubled during his presidency and he and the Supreme Court promoted affirmative action to end economic inequality. The Supreme Court ruled in favour of affirmative action (*Griggs* v. *Duke Power Company*, 1971), while Nixon ensured that over 250,000 companies with federal contracts employed a fair proportion of minority workers. Nixon's support for affirmative action encouraged universities to use positive discrimination on behalf of minority applicants. Affirmative action helped make one-third of black Americans middle class by 1980, but a white backlash developed. Marine veteran Alan Bakke challenged the University of California at Davis for rejecting his application to medical school while accepting minority candidates with lower grades. In *Bakke* v. *Regents of the University of California* (1978), the Supreme Court gave qualified support for the university's affirmative action, on the grounds of the importance of diversity in the community rather than as a remedy for past discrimination.

Educational status

White opposition to integrated education demonstrated continuing black social inequality. In 1971 the Supreme Court ruled it time for the full implementation of school **desegregation** (*Swann* v. *Charlotte-Mecklenburg*), specifying the **bussing** of black and white children to each other's schools as the way to achieve racially mixed schools. When the US courts endorsed the bussing of children to schools that were often a long distance from the students' homes, Nixon spoke out against wrenching children from their community.

Despite Nixon's opposition, the percentage of Southern black American children in segregated schools fell from 68 per cent to 8 per cent during his presidency. However, *de facto* segregation proved harder to combat in the North, where the white backlash against bussing was demonstrated in Boston:

- Irish-Americans staged protest marches and **sit-ins** to demonstrate their opposition to school integration in 1974.
- Irish-American Senator Ted Kennedy had to flee and hide from an Irish-American antibussing mob because he had advocated bussing (while sending his own children to private school).
- The pro-bussing *Boston Globe* employed sharpshooters to defend its building.

Opposition to integrated schools caused private school numbers to rise across America (Boston's **public schools** contained 45,000 whites in 1974 but only 16,000 by 1987) and **white flight** to accelerate (6 per cent of the population moved to the suburbs in the 1970s). After Nixon appointed four conservatives to the Supreme Court, it ruled that Detroit schoolchildren should not be integrated through bussing (*Milliken* v. *Bradley*, 1974) and the Democrat Congress legislated against bussing in the Education Act of 1975.

> **Source C** Extract from Supreme Court Justice Thurgood Marshall's dissent to the Supreme Court ruling in *Milliken* v. *Bradley*. Here, he criticises the majority's opinion that bussing should not be used to integrate the children of the predominantly black Detroit schools with the children of the predominantly white suburban schools:
>
> This court recognised [in *Brown*] … that remedying decades of segregation in public education would not be an easy task. Subsequent events, unfortunately, have seen that prediction bear bitter fruit … the Court today takes a giant step backwards … [The state of Michigan has] engaged in widespread purposeful acts of racial segregation in the Detroit School District … **Negro** children have been intentionally confined to an expanding core of virtually all-Negro schools immediately surrounded by a … band of all-white schools … [The *Milliken* ruling will increase segregation in Detroit when] white parents withdraw their children from the Detroit city schools and move to the suburbs to continue them in all-white schools … [and guarantee] that Negro children in Detroit will receive the same separate and inherently unequal education in the future as they have been unconstitutionally afforded in the past … Today's holding, I fear, is more a reflection of a perceived public mood that we have gone far enough in enforcing the Constitution's guarantee of equal justice than it is the product of neutral principles of law.
>
> What can you infer about Supreme Court rulings from Source C?

Political status

The Supreme Court sometimes acted to ensure equal political status, ruling that no redrawing of political boundaries should leave ethnic minorities worse off in terms of political representation (*Beer v. United States*, 1976). Some states went further, creating districts in which black American voters were grouped together to help ensure the election of black officials.

More black Americans were elected mayors of major cities, such as Detroit (1973), Los Angeles (1973), Washington DC (1974) and Birmingham (1979), and over 20 black Americans representing congressional districts with predominantly black populations sat in the US House of Representatives from 1973 to 1980. However, the limitations of black progress were demonstrated in that black candidates rarely won white votes; as a result, only 1 per cent of elected officials were black in 1980. The sole black American Senator in the US Congress in this period was Edward William Brooke III, who represented the liberal state of Massachusetts from 1967 to 1979.

Conclusion: The extent of progress in individual and civil rights

Contemporary commentators noted a 'rights revolution' in the 1960s, but black Americans, Native Americans, women and homosexuals had not achieved equality by 1973. As a result, campaigns for women's rights and minority rights continued in the period 1973–80. During that time, the campaigns for Native Americans and gay rights became far more assertive than in the previous decade. Women, homosexuals, Native Americans and black Americans continued to gain more rights in the period 1973–80. Women gained greater **reproductive rights**; homosexuals won some victories against discrimination; Native American tribal sovereignty and land rights had a fair amount of support from the federal government. However, all the groups that sought equality faced frequent difficulties in sustaining and expanding their rights in the face of conservative opposition. Indeed, workers' rights were being increasingly threatened.

> **Work together**
>
> Examine your partner's table (see page 438) on changes in the position of black Americans, Native Americans, women, workers and homosexuals. Explore whether you both came to the same conclusions about the extent of progress and, if you disagreed, see if you can attain consensus.

> **Chapter summary**
>
> - After Vietnam, Watergate and two rather weak presidents (Ford and Carter), many Americans were disillusioned with politics.
> - Some Americans focussed their political activity on one issue, such as environmentalism.
> - Americans suffered from inflation, expensive energy and declining competitiveness in international markets.
> - Although still the world's richest nation, America felt the pinch and the government seemed unable to solve the problem.
> - Some contemporaries worried about the commercialisation of sport and popular music.
> - Some good-quality movies and TV programmes covered contemporary issues, whereas others were simply escapist.
> - Women's reproductive rights increased but their economic rights seemed unenforceable.
> - Supreme Court support for abortion rights triggered a conservative backlash.
> - Workers' rights were eroded in the face of a struggling economy and rising conservatism.
> - Greater assertiveness of gay men and lesbian women gained increased liberal support for gay rights.
> - Native Americans gained more self-government but remained economically disadvantaged.
> - Some black Americans benefited from affirmative action but the economic and social status of most remained inferior.

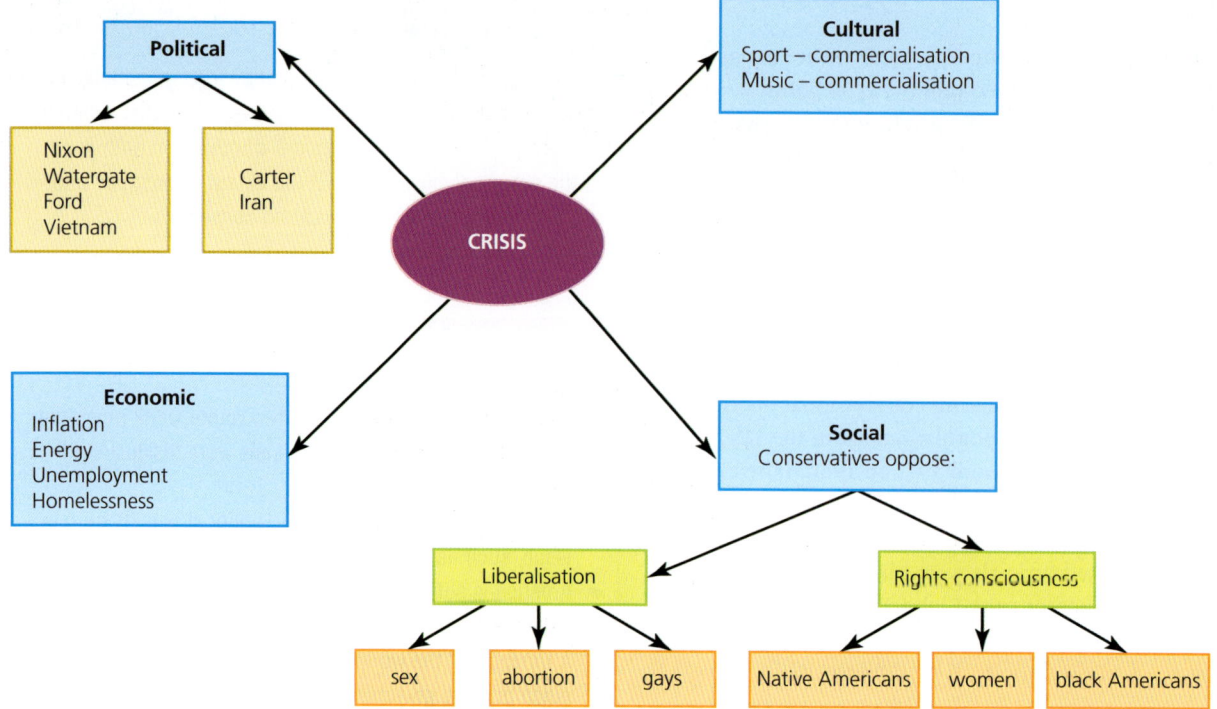

▲ Summary diagram: Social and political change, 1973–80.

Recommended reading

Reebee Garofalo, *Rockin' Out: Popular Music in the USA* (Pearson Prentice Hall, 2005). An easy read, with an accompanying CD. There are separate chapters on rock 'n' roll, the fragmentation of popular music, punk and disco, MTV (see page 467) and rap and metal.

Kathryn Jay, *More Than Just a Game: Sports in American Life since 1945* (Columbia, 2004). This is far more analytical than most 'sports history'. It covers our whole period and gives particularly interesting insights into the fight for equality by black Americans and women.

James Patterson, *Restless Giant: The United States from Watergate to Bush v Gore* (Oxford University Press, 2005). Another scholarly, well-substantiated and well-written volume in the *Oxford History of the United States* series. This covers the 1973–92 section of our syllabus.

Steven Ross, *Movies and American Society* (Blackwell, 2002). This has chapters on how movies reflected and shaped American society under Eisenhower and Reagan, on issues such as colour and Vietnam.

Melvin Small, *The Presidency of Richard Nixon* (Kansas University Press, 1999). A relatively balanced account of Nixon's presidency.

Section A: Essay technique

Contextualising the sources

In order to understand the sources properly, you need to place them in the context in which they were written. Specifically, you need to consider the background or environment in which the source was produced. Although the second half of the twentieth century might not seem so long ago, people frequently had very different experiences, beliefs and prejudices from those with which we are familiar. This means that sources are never standalone documents – they should be understood within the context of the values and assumptions of the society that produced them.

In essence, your task when contextualising the sources is to try to understand the world in the same way as the writers of the sources. In short, you should try to see things their way. Understanding the context is an important part of evaluating the evidence that the sources contain.

Imagine you are answering the following question:

> How far could the historian make use of Sources 1 (see page 448) and 2 (see page 449) together to investigate black American progress toward social and economic equality with whites in the years 1964–74?

You have read about *de jure* and *de facto* segregation and about the depiction of black Americans in the movies. You might want to remind yourself of what you have read by looking at those sections (page 443 onward) or your notes again.

One way to contextualise the sources is to begin by asking the question: what debate is this source contributing to? The reason for this is that sources are written to contribute to ongoing discussions. For example, during the 1960s and the 1970s there was much discussion in the United States about:

- the extent to which the economic status of black Americans was improving
- whether discriminatory practices against black Americans in public places in the North and the South had been improved by the provisions of the 1964 Civil Rights Act
- the extent to which film and television influenced the behaviour of Americans
- whether Blaxploitation movies were a help or a hindrance to black Americans.

Naturally, there was much that was written between 1964 and 1974 that would have contributed to one or more of these debates. Working out (1) to which debate a source is contributing, and (2) to which side of the debate the source is more sympathetic, can help you evaluate the evidence the source contains.

On page 448 it an example of putting a source in context.

Source 1 Extract from the reports of the weekly **New York-published entertainment magazine, Variety**, on reactions across the United States to the 1968 movie *Guess Who's Coming to Dinner?* The movie featured Spencer Tracy and Katharine Hepburn as a highly educated, upper-middle-class white couple, whose daughter plans to marry a highly educated, middle-class black American, played by Sidney Poitier. Here, *Variety* reports on reactions on 27 February 1968 in the Southern city of Atlanta, Georgia, and 12 March 1968 in the Northern city of Cincinnati, Ohio.

Variety magazine was published in New York, one of the most liberal of American cities, as demonstrated by the gay and feminist activism there.

[When the movie studio Columbia chose to have the Atlanta premiere of] *Guess Who's Coming to Dinner?* at the northside Capri Cinema rather than at a downtown [cinema] ... it meant that hordes of Negroes plus hippies of both races flocked into the community of Buckhead to see the record-breaking ... film on miscegenation.

Clearly, most black moviegoers in Atlanta usually attended the movie theatre in the area where they lived – the downtown or inner-city area.

Undoubtedly many residents were shocked by this unusual influx, and last week their anger was expressed by Lamar Q. Ball, the segregationist editor of the *North Side News*. 'Never in your life have you Northsiders ever seen such a crowd in Buckhead. For three nights in one incomprehensible row!' he said in a front-page editorial. 'Blacks and mulattos [*] in part of the line outnumbered whites ... The subject of the picture is what attracted these hordes, many of whom have become contemptuous of their [segregationist] elders for denouncing those [integrationists] who are willing to destroy the white race just by encouraging moron Negroes to vote' ... he approvingly quoted ... [a woman who said,] 'This is nothing to be brought out in the open for sound-minded people to view in a theatre, shoulder to shoulder with perverts.'

This was written after the 1964 Civil Rights Act ended de jure segregation in Southern cities such as Atlanta, but Ball is still blatantly racist and pro-segregation in his news publication, which some Atlantans are obviously buying.

This is a disparaging reference to the 1965 Voting Rights Act that enfranchised black Americans throughout the South.

Ball's viewpoint is obviously a minority one. Reviews in the general press were favourable in Atlanta ... [and] business at the Capri has been outstanding.

Columbia's *Guess Who's Coming to Dinner?* ... got a record-making and rock-throwing reception in southern Ohio cities 26 miles apart.

The Cincinnati ghetto erupted in a riot in 1967.

In Cincinnati – which had riots last summer – the picture is jamming the 3,000-seat Albee with mixed race audiences setting record grosses...

In Hamilton, robed Klansmen picketed the Court Theatre, Wednesday night. Next came counter-picketing and window smashing of nearby stores and a filling station. Damage $1,840. No arrests.

The Ku Klux Klan was clearly still active and engaging in intimidation in the North in 1968.

[*] Mulattos: those with black and white ancestry.

It is crucial to relate your analysis of context to the questions. The context for Source 1 above helps answer the question on page 447 in the following ways:

- It shows that in a large Southern city, Atlanta, and a large Northern city, Cincinnati, there are mixed views on the movie and also, as the Atlanta section makes clear and the Cincinnati section implies, on miscegenation. This suggests that progress was being made, but slowly.
- The positive attitude of *Variety* towards what the movie seemed to reveal about race relations was perhaps affected by the fact that it was published in a liberal city, for a nationwide audience. In choosing Ball and the woman with stage experience to quote, *Variety* has chosen two racists lacking in any subtlety ('moron' and 'perverts'), which serves to discredit extremist views more than if some racist had opposed the film on, say, the grounds of supposed concerns about disorder.
- On the other hand, the reviews seem quite balanced in what they say about audience reaction, because both positive and negative reactions are covered.

Therefore, Source 1 is useful to the historian studying black American progress toward equality with whites in that an interracial marriage seems to have been acceptable to at least some of the many Americans who flocked to see the movie. Furthermore, *Variety* seems to be making a balanced, careful report on audience reactions. However, there are limits to the usefulness of Source 1. First, we only have two cities here. Second, someone might be quite happy to see interracial relationships in a movie but unwilling to have a black neighbour or have a close member of the family involved in an interracial relationship. Third, one wonders whether the nature of the magazine has affected what has been written about this apparent black American progress towards social equality.

Source 2 Extract from Alvin F. Poussaint, 'Blaxploitation Movies: Cheap Thrills That Degrade Blacks', published in *Psychology Today*, Volume 7, Number 9, February 1974. Poussaint was a black American medical practitioner, specialising in psychiatry, and he participated in the civil rights movement.

> Black youth in Brooklyn dramatically increased their use of cocaine after the movie *Super Fly* glamorized the narcotic ... 'blaxploitation' films have their heaviest impact on black youths ... [they] glorify criminal life and encourage in black youth misguided feelings of machismo that are destructive to the community as a whole ...
>
> Negative black stereotypes are more subtle and neatly camouflaged than they were in the films of yesteryear, but ... blacks are [still shown as] violent, criminal, sexy savages ...
>
> Many cast members try to dismiss the possibility that blaxploitation films have a negative effect on audiences. They assert that movies ... have no lasting effect on theatergoers ... [But] movies of any type are seldom mere entertainment because they teach cultural values and influence behavior ...
>
> Movies have lied to us before. The movies were at least partially responsible for teaching blacks and whites that ... [black Americans] were lazy, happy-go-lucky, thieving, sexually promiscuous, and mentally inferior ...
>
> In the 1960s blacks developed a new pride and self-consciousness ... And the white establishment gained a lucrative yet untapped market. Among the first to discover the black market was the movie industry ...
>
> Some blacks and whites argue that such films are psychologically beneficial to the black viewer ... [because they] show the black man or woman as a hero ... youthful black audiences seem to support [this argument] ...
>
> Given the perennial unemployment among blacks in all fields, we should not be quick to condemn the black artists who take part in the production of these films. But we should be aware of the source of the economic rip-off, the white movie industry.

Activity: Seeing things their way

Now try contextualising Source 2 above.

1 Re-read the question on page 447 – remind yourself of the specific task you are focussing on.
2 Ask yourself the following questions and annotate a copy of the source with the answers:
   (a) Is there anything about the author that might have influenced the writing of Source 2?
   (b) Which debate is Source 2 likely to be contributing to?
   (c) The source may reflect the views of a specific group of black Americans – which group?
   (d) Does the source reflect the views of black Americans across the nation?
   (e) Who wrote the source?
   (f) Why was the source written?
3 Next, write a series of bullet points outlining:
   (a) the aspects of the source that are useful for answering the question
   (b) the aspects of the source that are less useful
   (c) a summary of the extent to which the source provides useful evidence concerning black American progress towards equality with whites in the years 1964–74.

Work together

Having read Source 2 and completed the activity 'Seeing things their way', discuss the following questions with a partner:

1 Did you both agree on:
   (a) the reasons the author wrote Source 2
   (b) the debate that Source 2 is addressing
   (c) the extent to which Source 2 might reflect the views of black Americans across the United States?
2 Did you both agree on:
   (a) the aspects of the source that were useful for answering the question
   (b) the aspects of the source that are less useful
   (c) the overall extent to which the source was useful to the historian investigating black American progress toward equality with whites in the years 1964–74?
If you disagreed on the answers to any of these questions, try to work out whose answer was better and why.
3 What else would it be useful to know about the source in order to answer the question?

Activity: AS-style questions

1 Why is Source 1 (page 448) valuable to the historian for an enquiry into American attitudes to the status of black Americans in the late 1960s?
2 How much weight do you give the evidence of Source 2 (above) for an enquiry into the portrayal of black Americans in pop culture in the 1970s?

Section B: Essay technique

Overall judgement

An overall judgement is as important to a Paper 2 Section B essay as it is to essays in Paper 1. You may have already read advice about the characteristics of a good overall judgement (see page 92). Remember, good judgements are supported, and the best judgements consider the relative significance of the key factors you have discussed in your essay.

Now you can practise writing an overall judgement to an essay concerning growing political disillusionment in the years 1973–80.

Activity: Overall judgement

Imagine you are answering the following question:

To what extent was growing political disillusionment in the years 1973–80 due to Watergate?

1 Read the question and work out what type of question it is (see page 384).
2 Make a plan that is appropriate to the specific question. Remember it should consist of three or four main points.
3 Add three pieces of detail to support each of your main points. Remember, use the detail that best supports the points you want to make.
4 Write an analytical sentence to conclude each of your main points.
5 Now write a conclusion to the essay.

- Start by asserting an overall judgement.
- Support this by weighing the different main points in your plan.
- Summarise your overall judgement in the final sentence.

Work together

Having completed a plan in the activity, swap it with a partner. Consider:

1 Did you agree on what type of question you were dealing with? If not, discuss it and work out who was right.
2 Whose plan most clearly focussed on the specific type of question?
3 Did you both begin your conclusion with a clear judgement?
4 Did you both weigh up the different key points to support your judgement?
5 Whose overall judgement was better and why?
6 What can you learn from each other's work?

Use these questions to feed back to each other and improve your essay technique.

Question practice

1 To what extent was progress made in individual and civil rights in the years 1973–80? **AS**
2 'Popular culture invariably reflected political and social tensions in the United States in the years 1973–80.' How far do you agree with this statement?
3 'Pop culture became escapist during the 1970s.' How far do you agree with this statement? **AS**
4 'Inflation adversely affected the living standards of almost all Americans during the 1970s.' How far do you agree with this statement?
5 How accurate is it to say that, in the years 1973–80, the women's movement achieved a great deal? **AS**

Key Topic 4 Republican dominance and its opponents, 1981–92

Overview

At the end of the 1970s, political and social conservatives combined in a formidable coalition that put the conservative Republican Ronald Reagan in the White House from 1981 to 1989. Reagan spoke out in favour of the traditional family values beloved by the social conservatives, and promised the lower taxes and decrease in government interventionism sought by the political conservatives.

On the one hand, the 1980s seemed to demonstrate the triumph of conservatism, with the popular Reagan as president and well-supported campaigns against abortion, homosexuality, and sex, violence and drugs in popular culture. However, youth culture continued to challenge traditional values, and popular culture often seemed dominated by sex and violence. Furthermore, despite frequently successful conservative opposition, ethnic minorities, women, gay men and lesbian women continued to make progress towards equality.

The overarching theme of **Republican** dominance and its opponents is covered in four sections:
1. New directions in economic policy
2. The Religious Right and its critics
3. Cultural challenge
4. Social change

TIMELINE

1980	President Reagan elected
1981	National debt stands at $1 trillion
1981	New cable channel MTV airs music videos non-stop
1982	Equal Rights Amendment finally defeated
1983	*A Nation at Risk* published
1985	Parents Music Resource Center established
1985	Hollywood star Rock Hudson dies from AIDS
1986	Nancy Reagan hosts 'Just Say No' (drugs) rally at White House
1986	President Reagan's speech to the Knights of Columbus
1986	Californian voters approve 'English-only' proposition
1987	Water Quality Control Act
1987	Senate rejects Robert Bork
1987	500,000 march in New York City to demand gay rights in federal funds for AIDS research
1988–89	Over 70,000 anti-abortionists arrested for blocking access to abortion clinics
1989	National debt at $2.6 trillion
1990	President Bush and Congress raise taxes
1992	Los Angeles race riots
1992	Clinton defeats George H.W. Bush in presidential election
1992	'Year of the Woman'
1992	Carol Moseley Braun elected to the Senate

1 New directions in economic policy

Born in 1911 to a struggling family in small-town Illinois, Ronald Reagan's employment history (**sportscaster**, Hollywood actor and TV star) made him a relaxed, effective public speaker and contributed to his subsequent reputation as the 'great communicator' of politics.

Reagan's Hollywood career lasted from 1937 to 1964. At the height of his popularity in movies, federal and state taxes took 91 per cent of his income. This created his intense loathing of taxation, which he considered a disincentive to work (in some years he refused offers to make more than two movies a year because the high taxation rate made it unprofitable). His resentment of high taxation caused him to become a committed and politically active Republican.

Reagan was elected governor of California from 1967 to 1974, impressing many as handsome, charming, reassuring, self-effacing and lacking greed for power. Many voters responded to his persuasive and repeatedly articulated calls for cuts in:

- taxation
- '**big government**'
- crime
- welfare payments (he claimed to know of '**welfare queens**' who collected multiple welfare cheques and drove around in Cadillacs).

Reagan believed in **supply-side economics**, which emphasised economic growth through low taxation and less government regulation. During his presidency, these economic beliefs were known as **Reaganomics**.

Reagan defeated Carter in the 1980 presidential election primarily because of Carter's poor record but also because lower taxes and the end of big government appealed to many and because he seemed more decisive, optimistic and likely to gain foreign respect for the United States.

> **Note it down**
>
> As you read about President Reagan, create a table. In the left-hand column, explain what Reagan's policies were. In the right-hand column, make notes on the impact of each policy on particular groups. The different groups are: the rich; business owners; the elderly; the poor; the labour unions; and the unemployed. When you get to Section 2, you can add: the unemployed; women; homosexuals; and ethnic minorities.

The impact of Reagan's policies on workers and their families

Reagan came to the White House determined to move the United States in new and conservative directions in economic and social policies. He wanted to cut taxes, reduce the size and role of the **federal government**, cut public spending and minimise welfare state arrangements where possible. Some anti-'big government' conservatives wanted a total demolition of welfare safety nets but despite his campaign rhetoric, Reagan knew it would be political suicide to cut programmes such as **social security** and **Medicare** (see page 398), because elderly voters were a powerful bloc. Reagan recognised that he would not be able to totally dismantle the **Great Society** but that he could begin to reverse it. His policies adversely affected many workers and their families through their incomes, employment rights, education and environment.

Family incomes

In spring 1981, Reagan persuaded **Congress** to agree to most of his budget requests. Congress agreed to reduce the budget of 212 federal programmes, most of which had aided the working poor. Among their number were food stamps, student loans and **child nutrition programmes**. Reagan's budget reduced the level and range of benefits for 'safety net' programmes such as Aid to Families with Dependent Children (AFDC). Of the 13 million children living below the **poverty line** in 1984, many were the offspring of single mothers who depended heavily upon AFDC. The majority of those women were black Americans, and conservatives believed that AFDC encouraged promiscuity, irresponsibility and the break-up of the traditional family.

Reagan's 1981 cuts in individual and corporate taxes benefited the rich rather than the poor and the subsequent tax rises that Reagan called 'revenue enhancements' hit the less wealthy hardest. Consequently, his tax and social programme policies increased the gap between rich and poor during the 1980s:

- The share of the national income of the wealthiest 1 per cent rose from 8 per cent to 15 per cent.
- The average income of the poorest decreased by $1,300 per annum.
- The number of homeless people increased from 200,000 to 400,000.

Left-wing critics bitterly compared Nancy Reagan's $25,000 wardrobe for the first inauguration with the 500,000 whose names Reagan deleted from the list of the registered disabled. New York's **Democrat** governor Mario Cuomo said, 'At his worst, Reagan made the denial of compassion respectable.'

The years 1981–83 were particularly hard on workers and their families, with double-digit inflation and 10 per cent unemployment (around 50 per cent in the **Rust Belt**). Average family income plummeted under Reagan. It recovered in 1987 but only to 1973 levels. Only half of America's families maintained their standard of living in the 1980s, usually because both parents worked.

> **Source A** Extract from the memoirs of the Democrat Speaker of the House of Representatives, Tip O'Neill (quoted in Thomas P O'Neill, Jr., with William Novak, *Man of the House: The Life and Political Memoirs of Speaker Tip O'Neill*, Random House, 1987). Here, O'Neill recalls a January 1986 meeting with President Reagan.
>
> > When I complained that [the unemployment rate of] 7 percent was still too high, the president replied that the figure would be lower if members of the armed services were counted in the work force. While this was true enough, it had always been true – and had nothing to do with the topic at hand.
> >
> > Then he started a familiar song. 'Those people out there can get jobs if they really want to,' said the president. 'I'm told about the fellow on welfare who makes phone calls looking for work. On the third call they offer him a job, and he hangs up. These people don't want to work.'
> >
> > I couldn't believe he was still spouting this nonsense, and I exploded. 'Don't give me that crap!' I said. 'The guy in Youngstown, Ohio, who's been laid off at the steel mill and has to make mortgage payments – don't tell me he doesn't want to work. Those stories may work on your rich friends, but they don't work on the rest of us. I'm sick and tired of your attitude, Mr. President. I thought you would have grown in the five years you've been in office, but you're still repeating those same simplistic explanations.'
>
> How far would you trust Tip O'Neill's recollections of this meeting in Source A?

Reagan and education

Reagan's Secretary of Education commissioned a study that exposed the dreadful state of public education; *A Nation at Risk* (1983) highlighted declining test scores and poorly equipped schools that had produced around 23 million functional illiterates. Conservatives blamed the permissive society; liberals blamed the lack of federal funding and old-fashioned teaching methods. Reagan made no attempt to improve the quality of education received by American children. He considered the Department of Education, set up by President Carter in 1979, an unsuccessful example of big government. He tried but failed to abolish it, although he managed to reduce its staff by 25 per cent and to cut its programmes savagely. Like most conservatives, he felt that schools were best managed at the local level, so he decreased education block grants to the states by 63 per cent. States struggled to make up the shortfall. As a result of Reagan's policies, the education of those whose parents could not afford to send them to private schools suffered.

Employment rights and deregulation

Reagan's policies were pro-business and anti-labour:

- He opposed the minimum wage and obstructed congressional attempts to increase it, which further widened the gap between rich and poor.
- He was hostile to unions. For example, in 1981, 12,000 air-traffic controllers ignored the 'no-strike for federal employees' clause in their contracts and went on strike for higher wages. The president had the power to fire federal employees who ignored the clause, but no one really expected any president to do so. However, Reagan fired them all and called in the military to do their jobs while new controllers were trained. **Liberals** and labour leaders were horrified at this attack on workers' rights. However, conservatives were impressed, especially when the number of strikes plummeted as major companies followed Reagan's anti-union policies.
- He appointed over 400 conservatives to the judiciary. Their rulings in the late 1980s made it harder for women, minorities, the elderly and the disabled to sue employers over employment discrimination.

Reagan believed the economy would benefit from lightening the regulatory burdens on industry and business. He therefore cut the staff of regulatory agencies by an average 25 per cent but failed to differentiate between stifling economic regulations and regulations that protected the environment and health and safety. There was a 50 per cent fall in prosecutions for illegal disposal of hazardous waste, which adversely impacted upon the environment. His regulatory agency appointees ensured that bodies such as the Occupational Safety and Health Administration made decisions in favour of business and against labour, so that workers had decreased protection against accidents and unhealthy working conditions. The number of personnel in the Consumer Product Safety Commission was cut by 38 per cent, so the Commission was less active in ensuring that the products that consumers purchased were safe products. Deregulation policies such as these disadvantaged many workers and families.

Congressional and public resistance

Reagan did not always get what he wanted. Sometimes Congress tempered his conservatism. When Reagan was informed that the fund from which social security payments came would be bankrupt by 2000, he suggested almost immediate cuts in benefits for early retirees but backed down when faced with near-unanimous congressional outcry. Although Congress accepted his 1981 budget, his later budgets were substantially rewritten and Congress was unco-operative over many of his attempts to reduce the size of the federal government. For example, although he vetoed the renewal of the $18 billion Clean Water Act (he said it was too expensive), Congress overrode his **veto** of the virtually identical 1987 Water Quality Control Act.

Sometimes public opposition was significant. Most Americans valued social security, Medicare and veterans' benefits, so Reagan left them basically intact, along with school lunches and Head Start (free breakfast for poor schoolchildren). The Department of Agriculture's attempt to save money by having ketchup and pickle relish substitute part of the vegetable portion in federal-subsidised school lunches was publicly ridiculed then dropped.

Economic successes in the Reagan years

Reagan's policies did not always impact adversely on workers and the family:

- His massive defence expenditure brought prosperity to regions with defence and aerospace industries, such as the West Coast.
- His tax reform bill of 1986 simplified the tax code, increased taxes on corporations and **capital gains**, lowered the top rate of taxation from 50 per cent to 28 per cent, and raised the bottom rate of taxation from 11 per cent to 15 per cent. The Democrat Speaker Tip O'Neill told the House of Representatives that a vote for Reagan's major tax reform bill of 1986 was 'a vote for the working people of America over the … well-financed corporations'.
- Following the **recession** early in Reagan's first term, the United States experienced its longest-ever period of economic growth in peacetime. Between 1980 and 1988 inflation fell from 13.5 per cent to 4.7 per cent, unemployment fell from 7 per cent to 5.2 per cent and 16 million new jobs were created. This economic growth was mostly due to the **tight money policies** of Carter appointee Paul Volcker at the **Federal Reserve Board**, to whom Reagan gave full support, and to external factors such as the fall in oil prices consequent upon the discovery of new oil sources.

On the other hand, Reagan's tax cuts and defence expenditure led to a budget deficit that would cause great problems for future American workers and their families.

The budget and trade deficits

Although Reagan had emphasised reductions in federal expenditure during his campaigns, he failed to balance the budget because his tax cuts decreased federal government income and his defence expenditure skyrocketed. 'Defence', he said, 'is not a budget item.' Reagan had criticised the $1 trillion national debt in 1980–81 as 'mortgaging our future and our children's future' but it tripled to more than $2.6 trillion on his watch. Federal expenditure increased from $699.1 billion in 1980 to $859.3 billion in 1987 and even non-defence expenditure increased. The budget deficit in **constant dollars** was over five times that of his predecessors, prompting Congress to pass the Balanced Budget and Emergency Deficits Control Act (1985), which tried to ensure a future balanced budget through spending cuts.

The USA remained an economic giant; with 5 per cent of the world's population, it produced 25 per cent of its goods in 1990. However, Reagan left it economically weakened with a massive budget deficit and a huge national debt. He financed his tax cuts and weapons purchases with money borrowed from Japan and Germany. In 1984 he joked, 'I'm not worried about the deficit. It's big enough to take care of itself.' Democrat Walt Rostow called Reagan 'a good-time Charlie. "Nothing bad is going to happen on my watch. Screw the future"'.

Although Reagan bore great responsibility for the nation's economic problems, it was not all his fault:

- Polls confirmed that the majority of Americans did not want to reduce spending on social programmes such as social security and Medicare, and Congress was determined to defend them. Those social programmes contributed greatly to the federal budget deficit.
- American consumers naturally preferred to buy cheap imported goods rather than domestic products made more expensive by higher labour costs, and this contributed to the growing **trade deficit**, financed by borrowing from abroad.

The growth of the trade deficit

In the mid-1980s the USA went from being one of the world's largest creditor nations to the world's largest debtor nation. Such a deficit allowed for a higher standard of living in the 1980s but some future generation would have to pay for the borrowing and the interest accrued upon it.

The United States began the 1980s with a positive trade balance in manufactured goods, but as the decade progressed this quickly developed into a negative trade balance. This owed much to changing patterns of consumer spending, which rocketed because of the rise of new discount stores such as Walmart (see Table 1). These discount stores boasted that they were the friend of the consumer because they made low-cost but good-quality goods widely available. However, these cheap goods were made for the most part in low-wage foreign factories, which contributed to the loss of manufacturing jobs in the United States as well as to the trade deficit. That deficit rose from $38 billion in 1982 to over $150 billion per annum by the second half of the decade. On average, during every week of the Reagan–Bush years (1981–92), American consumers spent around $2 billion more on imported goods than foreigners spent on goods made in the United States.

Table 1: The growth of Walmart.

Year	Number of stores	Number of employees	Sales
1975	125	7,500	$340.3 million
1987	1,198	200,000	$15.9 billion

Government action

Many Americans felt that the government should do something about the trade deficit, so the Reagan administration persuaded Japanese manufacturers to voluntarily limit their exports to the United States in 1981. The Japanese responded by opening manufacturing plants within the United States, which gave employment to thousands of Americans. The government also imposed a 25 per cent tariff on imported trucks and a 3 per cent tariff on imported cars.

Nevertheless, the trade deficit continued to grow. The annual trade deficit with Japan passed the $50 billion mark in 1985, so that by the late 1980s and early 1990s many Americans were accusing Japan of launching an economic offensive against the USA.

Reagan's legacy

Although President Reagan made some Americans feel better about their country, for others there was much to lament in his legacy. He did little about the mounting trade deficit. He dramatically increased the national debt. His policies on taxation, welfare, education, labour and deregulation had an adverse effect upon workers and their families. Future generations would have to pay for his policies. Indeed, this began just months after Reagan left the White House; his deregulation of the savings and loan industry led to risky loans and when the bubble burst in 1989–90, $132 billion of taxpayers' money was used to bail out savings and loan institutions.

Reagan had a dramatic influence on the economy and government of the United States. 'We made a difference', he said. He created a new public philosophy; it was now generally considered unwise and undesirable to continue to increase expenditure on social welfare. Even liberal Democrats in Congress had to admit that major new domestic expenditures were out of the question, partly because of Reagan's creation of this new public philosophy and partly because he had left the federal budget in such a state.

The significance of Bush's decision to raise taxes

The son of an affluent Connecticut banker and Senator, George H.W. Bush made his fortune in oil in Texas. He had a strong sense of civic duty and served in Congress, then as an ambassador, then CIA chief. A discreet and loyal vice-president to Ronald Reagan from 1981–89, Bush was elected president primarily because of Reagan's endorsement and his own 'no more new taxes' promise.

Lower taxes versus balanced budget

Bush's presidential campaign was based on contradictory promises; he pledged a decrease in the $2.7 trillion deficit, upon which $200 billion interest was being paid annually, but also promised no new taxes. Once elected, he agreed with Congress in November 1990 that taxes must rise.

Bush's decision to raise taxes was highly significant:

- It signalled his belief that the federal government had spent beyond its means so that, despite his campaign promise 'to make kinder the face of the nation, he did nothing to help workers worried about family incomes.
- It demonstrated the difficulties facing a democratic nation living beyond its means. Politicians in search of votes made promises they could not keep.
- Coupled with Bush's failure to vigorously promote a conservative social agenda, it infuriated conservative Republicans who dominated the 1992 Republican Convention and weakened Bush's bid for re-election.
- In conjunction with the other problems facing workers and their families, the tax rise caused many voters to reject Bush. A poor campaigner, Bush lost to the charismatic Bill Clinton in the 1992 presidential election. Bush seemed helpless and uninterested in the face of recession, while workers felt that Clinton could 'feel their pain'. The nation seemed to be swinging back to the left, electing a Democratic president and a Democratic Congress.

Problems for American workers in the Bush years

The recession that began in 1990 hit workers and their families hard. Losing money, the Big Three car manufacturers fired 60,000 workers, while large corporations fired middle managers. By summer 1991 unemployment hit an eight-year high of 7.8 per cent. The popular perception was that the Bush administration was of little help to the American worker. The administration's closure of 31 major military bases from 1991 cost 70,000 people their jobs and many rightly feared that Bush's promotion of the North American Free Trade Agreement (NAFTA), which would eliminate all barriers to trade and investment between the United States, Canada and Mexico, would lead to the relocation of American industry and the loss of American jobs. The President's social and fiscal conservatism caused him to veto:

- family and medical leave legislation
- a civil rights bill to counter racial discrimination in employment
- a bill that he said would give the unemployed excessive benefits.

Conclusion: New directions in economic policy

Reagan's new directions in economic policy were highly significant. He dramatically widened the gap between the rich and the poor and left a massive federal deficit to his successors. That deficit ensured that the federal government would struggle to return to the interventionism that arose in the Great Depression and culminated in Johnson's attempts to create the Great Society. President George H.W. Bush was anxious about the federal deficit and recognised that taxes had to be raised, but failed to rein in government spending and to balance the budget. The national debt soared from $1 trillion in 1980 to nearly $3 trillion in 1989 and to $4 trillion in 1993. Despite Republican criticisms of the extravagance of the Great Society, the United States began the 12 years of Republican presidential rule as the world's leading creditor and ended it as the world's largest debtor.

Work together

Look at your tables (see page 453) that sum up this section. You could use smiley (or not) faces to sum up whether the impact was beneficial to each particular group – not forgetting to differentiate between opinions as to what was beneficial for a particular group. For example, if an individual's welfare payments were cut under Reagan, that individual would not be happy, but the Reagan administration would!

2 The Religious Right and its critics

Reagan's presidential election victories of 1980 and 1984 were largely due to his policies on taxation and the role of government, and to his opposition to 1960s permissiveness and his advocacy of traditional family values. Reagan's social conservatism won him the support of the large group of right-wing voters who mobilised in the late 1970s to oppose the social changes that had occurred since the 1960s. This group was known as the **Religious Right** and it was the strongest grassroots movement in late-twentieth-century America.

> **Note it down**
> Continue the table that you used for taking notes on Section 1 (see page 453).

The beliefs of the Religious Right

Religious Right campaigners sought to promote a socially conservative agenda. The Religious Right leadership included Catholics such as Phyllis Schlafly (see page 439) and conservative Protestants such as Beverly LaHaye (see page 440), whose 500,000-strong Concerned Women for America membership far outnumbered the membership of the liberal National Organization of Women (**NOW**) by the mid-1980s. Schlafly, LaHaye and their followers disliked the **counter-culture** that had developed in the 1960s and sought conformity to 'traditional family values'.

The Religious Right had great political and social importance. First, it increased the polarisation of American politics and society in what some called 'culture wars'. It did this through its campaigns to promote traditional family values. The Religious Right insisted that those values could be maintained if women were homemakers who never had abortions, extramarital affairs or pre-marital sex, and recognised the male as the head of the family.

Second, the Religious Right affected the outcome of presidential elections. Many in the Religious Right voted for Reagan in 1980 and 1984 and George H.W. Bush in 1988 in the hope that they would promote traditional family values and oppose abortion, homosexuality and drug taking.

The promotion of traditional values

The Religious Right promoted their belief in traditional values through:

- organisations
- the media
- support for conservative politicians.

> **The Religious Right**
> The Religious Right opposed:
> - feminism, which they blamed for damaging paternal authority and weakening the family
> - divorce (divorce rates doubled between 1965 and 1985 from 25 per cent to 50 per cent of all marriages)
> - mothers going out to work (they lamented that fewer than 50 per cent of women were full-time **homemakers**, believing this adversely affected family life)
> - the Equal Rights Amendment (see page 403)
> - drug taking
> - abortion and *Roe* v. *Wade* (see page 438) (there were four abortions for every ten births between 1974 and 1977)
> - sexual liberalisation (roughly 500,000 unmarried couples lived together in 1970, and around 1 million by 1980)
> - unmarried mothers, many of whom relied on welfare payments (the percentage of children born to unmarried mothers rose from 11 per cent in 1970 to 18 per cent in 1980 and 28 per cent in 1990)
> - homosexuality
> - popular culture's preoccupation with sex
> - pornography
> - the teaching of sex education in schools (even as they worried about increased teenage pregnancy rates).

An excellent example of the use of these various methods was Baptist minister Jerry Falwell, whose social conservatism was demonstrated in his opposition to smoking, drinking and rock 'n' roll, and in his advice that women should follow what the Bible said about submission to their husbands. Falwell's long-running *Old Time Gospel Hour* was broadcast on 225 TV stations and 300 radio stations each week during the 1980s. He described the Baptist '**Moral Majority**' organisation that he established in 1978 as 'pro-life, pro-family, pro-morality and pro-American'. He said the Moral Majority were 'going to single out those people in government against what we consider to be the Bible, moralist position'. In 1980 he helped raise millions of dollars for Ronald Reagan's presidential campaign and some estimated that his Moral Majority registered around 2 million voters.

Falwell disbanded the Moral Majority in 1989, but other organisations appeared. For example, the Christian Coalition was established in 1989 in order to lobby the government to enact socially conservative measures. By 1992, it boasted 150,000 members and claimed to control the Republican Party in several Southern states.

Republicans and the promotion of traditional values

From the first, the Religious Right looked to conservative politicians to promote traditional values and the Republican Party quickly responded. The relationship between the Religious Right and conservative politicians was first forged after the **IRS** threatened to end federal tax exemptions for racially segregated Christian schools in 1978. This energised evangelical, fundamentalist Protestants. They constituted an important voting bloc, particularly in the South. Congressional Republicans responded to these voters' concerns and stopped the IRS implementing the policy.

Reagan and the Religious Right

The most influential of the politicians associated with the Religious Right was Ronald Reagan. During his presidential election campaign in 1980, he emphasised his disgust at 1960s excesses and permissiveness and his opposition to feminism and the Equal Rights Amendment (see page 403). Despite his divorce in 1952 and his difficult relationships with two of his four children, Reagan was the apostle of the nuclear family and his 1984 presidential election campaign 'Morning Again in America' advertisements played on traditional family values. Although he rarely attended church, he supported school prayer (the **Supreme Court** had ruled against it in 1962) and criticised the federal courts for not allowing **creationism** to be taught in schools (some extreme religious conservatives believed in creationism and opposed the teaching of **Darwinism**). He told an audience of evangelical ministers that he was a **born-again Christian**. The Religious Right grew disappointed with Reagan during his presidency. Although he said he wanted constitutional amendments to ban abortion and restore prayer in **public schools**, he could not get the necessary two-thirds majority in Congress and the Religious Right felt he did not try very hard on these issues. He failed to endorse the Family Protection Act (see box) and Congress did not pass it.

> ### The Family Protection Act
> This proposed legislation called for the prohibition of abortion, the restoration of school prayer, tax breaks for wives and mothers who stayed at home, tuition tax credits for children attending private schools, single-sex sports at school, parental censorship of reading materials in schools, and the denial of teenage access to contraception unless parents were notified. It never became law.

> **Source B** Extract from a telephone speech by President Reagan to the Annual Convention of the **Knights of Columbus**, who were meeting in Chicago in 1986. Here, he reassures them that he shares their socially conservative beliefs and he points out that his judicial appointments will help promote traditional values.
>
> I know you feel deeply that nothing affects fundamental morality more gravely than assaults [such as abortion] upon the sanctity of life itself ... [I believe] all human life is sacred [and] ... the family is likewise sacred; something the Knights of Columbus have understood from the first ... later this year, our Domestic Policy Council will report to me on ways federal programs could be restructured to strengthen families and promote family values ... And just yesterday I announced our most recent family initiative, a dramatic undertaking intended to bring to an end one of the worst social evils besetting our country – drug abuse ...
>
> In many areas – abortion, crime, pornography, and others – progress will take place when the federal judiciary is made up of judges who believe in law and order and a strict interpretation of the **Constitution**. I'm pleased to be able to tell you that I've already appointed 284 federal judges, men and women who share the fundamental values that you and I so cherish, and that by the time we leave office, our administration will have appointed some 45 per cent of all federal judges.
>
> How much weight do you give the evidence of Source B for an enquiry into President Reagan's promotion of 'traditional values'? Explain your answer using the source, the information given about it and your own knowledge of the historical context.

However, Reagan helped promote traditional values through a highly successful judicial strategy that constituted a most important victory for social conservatism. His successful nomination of nearly 400 conservative judges 'Reaganised' the judiciary, and helped compensate for his failure to win congressional approval for his conservative social agenda.

By the end of his presidency, Reagan had appointed over 50 per cent of the federal judiciary. The election of George H.W. Bush as his successor ensured that three-quarters of federal judges were conservative Reagan or Bush appointees by 1992. Reagan's judicial strategy was exceptionally successful and any assessment of his effectiveness in imposing his agenda on the country must take this into account.

The Religious Right and the Supreme Court

Despite Reagan's appointment of conservative justices, the Religious Right was often displeased with the Supreme Court, especially over school prayer and its refusal to overturn *Roe* v. *Wade* (see page 438). However, the Court was becoming more conservative on many issues. For example, it frightened liberals with several decisions that seemed to be chipping away at *Roe* v. *Wade* and abortion rights.

The campaign against abortion

In its campaign against abortion and the Supreme Court's *Roe* v. *Wade* decision, the Religious Right promoted its values in several ways and to great effect:

- It used emotive mailings (see page 439) and slogans.
- It used 'reformed' sinners to advertise its causes. For example, former feminists were encouraged to tell people that they had renounced feminism.
- It enlisted the support of Republican politicians who sought their votes. Even moderate Republicans felt they had to oppose abortion. Earlier in his career, George H.W. Bush had been pro-choice like his wife, but he had changed his stance to please conservative Republicans and said in his 1988 election campaign that 'abortion is murder'.
- It appropriated civil rights movement tactics, including 'rights' language that emphasised the rights of the unborn child (its opponents emphasised the rights of the mother), and Operation Rescue's sit-ins.

Operation Rescue

From 1987, many anti-abortion activists joined the militant organisation Operation Rescue. Its slogan was 'If you believe abortion is murder, act like it's murder.' Regional branches were set up across the nation. Initially, Operation Rescue staged peaceful sit-ins to block access to abortion clinics in New Jersey and New York, but members became increasingly involved in illegal activities such as trespassing on the property of clinics. The organisation gained nationwide attention during the 1988 Democratic National Convention in Atlanta, Georgia, when over 1,200 members were arrested for staging disorderly protests outside abortion clinics. During 1988-89, nearly 50,000 members were arrested and jailed.

The federal government and abortion

The Religious Right was often disappointed by the federal government's stance on the abortion issue in the Reagan–Bush years. For example:

- Following Justice William Brennan's retirement from the Supreme Court in 1990, the Religious Right hoped that President Bush would nominate a known pro-lifer, but he nominated David Souter, whose views on abortion were unknown.
- In 1981, President Reagan appointed Sandra Day O'Connor to the Supreme Court, which upset the Religious Right because of her record of sympathy towards women in need of abortions.

On the other hand, the Religious Right was sometimes encouraged by federal government actions. For example:

- President Reagan persuaded Congress to fund 'chastity clinics' where women would be encouraged to avoid sex.
- Reagan's judicial appointments resulted in several Supreme Court rulings that hindered abortions. For example, in *Webster* v. *Reproductive Services of Missouri* (1989), the Supreme Court ruled that Missouri could deny women access to public abortion facilities. Chief Justice Rehnquist, who had been appointed by Reagan, said, 'Nothing in the Constitution requires states to enter or remain in the business of performing abortions.'

Basically, the divisions over abortion within the various branches of the government reflected the divisions among the public. This was demonstrated after *Webster*; the Religious Right hoped that many states would follow Missouri's example and deny women access to public abortion facilities, but only three states did so. Furthermore, in *Webster*, the Supreme Court did not overturn *Roe* v. *Wade*. Indeed, *Roe* was reaffirmed by the Court in a 1992 ruling that abortion was constitutional (*Planned Parenthood* v. *Casey*). That decision disappointed the Bush administration, which then declared support for an anti-abortion constitutional amendment. However, the Democratic Congress refused to agree to such an amendment.

The campaign against homosexuality

Along with its opposition to abortion, the Religious Right and most of Middle America opposed homosexuality. Although Catholics and Protestants had a history of frequently deeply uneasy relations, Religious Right leaders appealed to both when they opposed gay rights as part of their campaign for a return to 'traditional moral values'.

Opponents of homosexuality were first energised by the campaign for gay rights (see page 407) and antigay groups such as the Traditional Values Coalition and the Umbrella Voice sprang up (they supported Reagan in 1980). The campaign against homosexuality then gained further strength from the mid-1980s with the spread of **AIDS** (see page 468).

Among the leading campaigners against homosexuality were:

- **televangelist** Pat Robertson. In 1966, Baptist minister Robertson set up *The 700 Club*, a Christian news and television programme that is still running. Robertson promoted traditional values, such as writing to donors that the 'socialist' feminist agenda encouraged 'women to leave their husbands, kill [abort] their children, destroy **capitalism** and become lesbians'. In 1988 he declared himself a Republican presidential candidate, but lost to George H.W. Bush. He did not help his cause by publicly praying for God to divert a hurricane from Virginia to New York (New York had far more voters than Virginia). In 1989 he established the Christian Coalition, which lobbied against gay rights and abortion, and was pro-school prayer
- Concerned Women for America (see page 440)
- Pat Buchanan. In 1992, George H.W. Bush won the Republican presidential nomination but allowed defeated Republican rival Pat Buchanan to deliver the opening speech at the National Convention. Buchanan said that the Democrat presidential candidate Bill Clinton and his vice-presidential candidate Al Gore constituted the 'most pro-gay and pro-lesbian ticket in history'
- Jerry Falwell and his Moral Majority (see page 458)
- televangelist Jim Bakker and his PTL ('Praise the Lord') Club (in 1988, Bakker was indicted and convicted for large-scale fraud and conspiracy).

Campaigners against homosexuality had support in the courts and at state level; in 1986 the Supreme Court upheld a Georgia law that criminalised sodomy, and 24 other states and Washington DC had similar laws against what they called 'deviant sexual intercourse', even in private. Traditional attitudes died hard.

The success of the campaigns

The Religious Right's campaign against abortion was the most successful of its campaigns. Through pressure on the courts and the legislatures, it made access to abortion more difficult. The success of its campaign is attested by the current problems facing those seeking an abortion in conservative states.

While the Religious Right could help arouse intense emotions over abortion with its claim that it was protecting the life of the unborn, there was no such issue of 'murder' in the campaign against homosexuality. The ultimate ineffectiveness of this campaign is attested by the current successes in the courts over the issue of same-sex marriage. Even less effective was the campaign against drugs.

Nancy Reagan's 'Just Say No' campaign

The Religious Right believed that the nation had a huge drug problem in the 1980s – so much so that some people called drug-taking 'the American disease'. Many contemporaries found the statistics frightening:

- Recreational drug use had tripled since the 1970s (a 1987 survey revealed that half of all citizens under the age of 45 had smoked marijuana at least once).
- Around 40 million Americans (nearly one in six) used illegal substances.
- 375,000 babies were born addicted to cocaine or heroin.
- There were around 12,000 drug-related deaths annually (this was far fewer than the 200,000 alcohol-related and 300,000 tobacco-related deaths).

The federal war on drugs had a long history, beginning in 1914, when the Harrison Act defined all drug users as criminals. That law remained in operation for the rest of the century. During the presidencies of Ronald Reagan and George H.W. Bush, the federal government's war on drugs focussed upon eradicating foreign supplies at source, halting their importation and arresting dealers and users. Thousands of small-time users and dealers were sent to prison, but despite the vast expenditure on the drug war in the Reagan and Bush years, cocaine and other street drugs became cheaper and more widely available.

The growth of the drug problem

In 1985, barely 1 per cent of Americans surveyed counted illicit drugs as a major national problem. Their main concerns were economic and foreign policy issues. However, by 1989, over 50 per cent of those surveyed said that drug use was the gravest threat to national security. There were four reasons for this change. First, the inexpensive cocaine derivative 'crack' became widely available. Even poor ghetto inhabitants could afford crack, which served as a means of temporary escape or social mobility for black Americans and **Hispanic Americans** who could make fortunes selling it. Second, media coverage of drug use increased. Stories of crack addicts staging robberies in order to finance their addiction and newborn babies writhing in agony from crack withdrawal made frightening yet compulsive reading. Third, the **Cold War** was winding down in the mid- to late-1980s and some contemporaries felt that that drug war was replacing the Cold War as the major national security issue in the minds of Americans. Fourth, the President and First Lady placed a great deal of emphasis on the drug problem (their children subsequently admitted having used drugs in the 1960s and 1970s).

'Just Say No'

Stung by criticism of her extravagance (see page 454), First Lady Nancy Reagan turned to charity work. Supported by her husband, she launched the antidrugs 'Just Say No' campaign. She obtained a great deal of media coverage from visiting nurseries that treated 'crack babies'. She told reporters that what she had seen 'would make the strongest hearts break'. The Reagans condemned drug use as immoral and criminal and claimed that the best prevention and cure came from the promotion of religious values, harsher school discipline and the strict enforcement of antidrug laws. In 1986 the President ordered that federal workplaces be 'drug-free' and called for routine urine testing on workers in 'sensitive' jobs involving 'public health and safety' or 'national security'.

In 1988 Congress passed the Drug-Free Workplace Act, which declared that universities and contractors that received federal government money had to maintain a 'drug-free workplace'. Critics described this outbreak of urine testing as 'jar wars'.

By 1990, federal and state expenditure on the enforcement of drug laws was over $10 billion per annum. Most of the money was spent on law enforcement and imprisonment. Around 750,000 Americans were charged each year with the violation of drug laws (mostly marijuana). Some contemporaries thought that the money and effort would have been better spent on rehabilitation or on the poverty that often underlay the problem. The drug seizures had little impact on availability or price and the Reagan war on drugs was basically futile. Reagan's successor George H.W. Bush continued the Reagan administration's concentration upon law enforcement, and was equally unsuccessful.

With drugs, as with homosexuality and traditional family values, the Religious Right did not succeed in fending off the challenges to the social conformity that they desired. However, the Religious Right did succeed in generating culture wars that exacerbated political divisions.

The growth of bitter political divisions

The combination of the backlash against the counter-culture and 1960s permissiveness and the disagreements over the role of the federal government in providing a welfare safety net produced increasingly bitter political divisions from the 1980s. There were divisions:

- between Republicans and Democrats over traditional moral values and big government
- among Republicans over traditional moral values
- among Democrats over big government.

Republican intra-party divisions

Intra-party divisions were often as bitter as inter-party divisions. For example, George H.W. Bush suffered frequent attacks from within the party for being insufficiently conservative. In 1988, Reagan aide Pat Buchanan and televangelist Pat Robertson were among those who said Bush was more 'eastern establishment liberal' than rugged individual, a Texan who was 'all hat and no boots'. Bush went on to win that election, but conservative Republican attacks contributed to his defeat in 1992.

During the 1992 campaign, former Reagan aide and rival for the Republican nomination Pat Buchanan attacked Bush again and promised that if he were the Republican candidate, he would wage a 'culture war' against liberal influence in government, education, churches and Hollywood. Buchanan had considerable support from Republicans disillusioned with Bush's tax hike and his lack of total enthusiasm for the Religious Right social agenda (Bush said he would not mind having a gay cabinet member). Buchanan wounded Bush by portraying him as an insincere conservative. Bush allowed Buchanan to make the opening speech at the 1992 Republican National Convention and the self-styled 'pitbull of the right' spoke for the Religious Right when he attacked 'radical feminism', 'abortion on demand' and 'homosexual rights', saying:

> There is a religious war going on in this country. It is a cultural war as critical to the kind of nation we shall be as the Cold War itself. This war is for the soul of America.
>
> (Quoted in Rhys Williams (ed.), *Cultural Wars in American Politics*, Aldine, 1997)

Democrat intra-party divisions

The divisions within the Democratic Party were far less bitter. Old-style Democrats still hankered after Great Society policies, but recognised that more centrist 'New Democrats' were more electable. New Democrats such as Bill Clinton advocated a balanced federal government budget and decreased federal government interventionism. For example, Clinton said the era of big government was over and that he wanted to 'end welfare as we know it', so that it would 'cease to be a way of life'.

Inter-party divisions

The bitterest divisions were the inter-party divisions, as demonstrated in the struggle over Reagan Supreme Court nominee Robert Bork. Most Republicans approved of Bork, but Democrats loathed him because he had:

- attacked some liberal Supreme Court decisions
- defended a Connecticut law that would have denied contraceptives to married couples
- opposed abortion

▲ Nancy Reagan with 'Just Say No' teenagers.

- claimed women's rights were not included in the **Fourteenth Amendment**
- criticised the principle of racial equality.

Black organisations such as the **NAACP** and women's organisations such as the NOW worked hard to stir up vociferous popular opposition to Bork and engaged in exceptionally aggressive lobbying of Senators, which contributed greatly to the **Senate** rejection of Bork.

Bitter political divisions: Conclusions

Fuelled by the increasingly strident media and **sound-bite communications**, the culture wars and the debate over big government led to increased (and ongoing) partisanship and gridlock in Washington. This was much in evidence during the presidency of Bill Clinton (1993–2001) when the inability of the President and Congress to agree upon federal expenditure led to federal government shutdowns in 1995 and 1995–96. In the last years of his second term, Clinton found it difficult to focus on the government of the nation because of the Republican attempt to have him **impeached** over his denial of an affair with White House intern Monica Lewinsky. This Republican pursuit of the President was in part a reflection of the bitter culture wars. All this was a far cry from the atmosphere of content, unity and consensus in Washington in the Eisenhower years.

Conclusion: The Religious Right and its critics

The Religious Right had mounted a formidable counter-offensive against the social changes and challenges that had developed since the 1960s. However, it proved unable to turn the clock back; homosexuals were not reverting to the closet nor abortions to the back streets, the number of divorces and single-parent families continued to rise, and drug-taking and sexual liberalisation proved unstoppable. Disillusioned by the ineffectiveness of most of its campaigns, the Religious Right seemed to have lost momentum by 1992. However, the culture wars that it had helped generate continued to divide Americans.

Work together

Take it in turns to argue in favour of Religious Right beliefs and actions, and then to give criticisms of them.

3 Cultural challenge

Despite the apparent strength of conservatism in the White House, the Supreme Court and Religious Right campaigns, challenges to the dominant culture continued in the years 1981–92 – so much so that it could be argued that there was no longer a 'dominant culture' in the United States and that neither side was victorious in the culture wars.

Many young Americans continued to challenge the more traditional, conservative culture through their behaviour and choice of music. While women and ethnic minority activists were relatively subdued, homosexuals dominated the headlines through the AIDS crisis.

All these dissenting groups demanded a more tolerant society and their preferences were often catered for by the music industry, television and Hollywood, which continued to give a platform to alternative lifestyles and cultural challenge. American society was becoming increasingly fragmented, a trend that was hastened by technological advances that made entertainment a less communal experience.

> **Note it down**
>
> Divide your page(s) into three columns. As you read this section, put the challengers in the first column, what their challenge was in the second, and factual evidence (names, dates and statistics) about the challenge in the third.

> **Sub-genres of metal**
>
> - Death metal focussed on death – for example, the Florida group Death's debut album was *Scream Bloody Gore* (1987).
> - Black metal focussed on the occult and was anti-Christian, but American black metal groups such as Morbid Angel failed to break into the US charts.
> - White metal focussed on Christian themes – for example, the Orange County band Stryper's *To Hell with the Devil* platinum album of 1986.
> - Lite or pop metal usually focussed on love; the combination of romantic content and MTV videos that focussed on male crotches and bare chests appealed to females – for example, Bon Jovi's bestselling, suggestively titled *Slippery When Wet* album (1986).
> - Speed/thrash metal rejected romantic themes and dealt with issues such as justice and the environment – for example, the multiple-Grammy-Award-winning group Metallica, especially in their *... And Justice for All* (1988) album.

Trends in youth culture

In 1981–92, popular culture remained an ideological battlefield. Social conservatives grew particularly anxious about the content of rap and metal music. That music was central to a disaffected youth culture that challenged conservatism over issues such as sexual and social freedoms, drug-taking and race.

Heavy metal

Heavy metal was first popular among young, white males in the early 1970s (see page 434). Within a few years it seemed in decline, but then it revived, and dominated youth culture in the 1980s. Popular performers included Van Halen and, from 1983, Los Angeles groups such as Dokken, one of whose dominant themes was males victimised by a femme fatale. Radio was uninterested in heavy metal, but the video music channel MTV played a vital role in promoting it, so that heavy metal's market share of popular music rose from 8 per cent in 1983 to 20 per cent in 1984. That provoked the opposition of the Religious Right and other conservative groups such as the Washington-based pressure group the Parents Music Resource Center (PMRC).

In 1985 the PMRC successfully pressured MTV to cease its promotion of metal with its explicit lyrics and sexually explicit and violent videos. However, as heavy metal became even more popular, MTV created a weekly late-night programme devoted to it, *Headbangers' Ball*. That after-hours slot decreased the number of complaints and the programme soon averaged 1.3 million viewers weekly, becoming MTV's most popular show. In 1988, 11 of the 50 bestselling albums were metal, although this popularity caused it to lose its outsider status. It became more mainstream and commercial-sounding, which contributed to its fragmentation into several sub-genres.

The heavy metal scene attracted alienated young white male fans. Few women or black Americans were part of the heavy metal scene. However, the great and continuing black influence on, and popularity in, American music was demonstrated when, by 1990, black pop and rap were overtaking heavy metal at the forefront of youth culture.

Rap

Hip-hop had its roots in the gang cultures of the South Bronx and Harlem **ghettos** (see page 435). First commercially recorded in 1979, hip-hop's rap music covered topical and controversial themes such as 'How We Gonna Make the Black Nation Rise?' (1980). The cover of the black separatist New York group Public Enemy's *It Takes a Nation of Millions to Hold Us Back* album (1988) seemed to show incarcerated black Americans, a reference to the disproportionate number of young black males in jail.

Rap revealed generational and class divides in black music. It was ignored by black radio, which one rap publicist blamed on the 'buppies' (black urban professionals) who dominated the medium. It was variously criticised by many older black Americans as:

- bigoted (groups such as Public Enemy made anti-Semitic comments)
- sexist (Ice Cube attributed the lyrics in his 1980 hit album *AMERIKKKA's Most Wanted* to the black masculinity crisis – he sings that he has made the 'neighborhood hussy' pregnant, so 'What I need to do is kick the bitch in the tummy')
- violent (one 1988 hit rap song was 'Fuck Tha Police' by N.W.A., which stood for Niggaz With Attitude).

In response to such criticisms, a few women such as Queen Latifah and Salt-N-Pepa became rappers and male rap groups started a Stop the Violence campaign in 1988.

By the late 1980s, rap artists such as MC Hammer and Vanilla Ice demonstrated how rap was becoming mainstream. Rap was the focal point of several movies about ghetto life and a white rapper group sang 'Proud to Be Black'.

Popular music on trial

A group of wives of influential Washington politicians established the PMRC, motivated they said by lyrics that 'are sexually explicit, excessively violent, or glorify the use of drugs and alcohol'. While they were particularly critical of heavy metal, they also cited songs such as Prince's 'Nikki' and Madonna's 'Like a Virgin'. The music industry pointed out that it would be hard to police and rate lyrics like movies. First, there were thousands of recordings each year, compared to around 300 movies. Second, lyrics could be misinterpreted. John Denver pointed out that radio stations refused to play his 'Rocky Mountain High' (a hymn to his beloved Colorado) because they thought he was singing about drugs. Undeterred, the 'Washington wives' mobilised their husbands in the Senate, which began investigating the PMRC's accusations in 1985. The influential music magazine *Rolling Stone* said, 'Beneath the save the children rhetoric is an attempt by a politically powerful minority to impose its morality on the rest of us.'

By 1988 the PMRC had added fascination with the occult and suicide as dangers that popular music presented to the minds of American youth. The music industry finally accepted a voluntary rating system because of great pressure from Washington and the publicity resulting from several highly publicised suicides. For example, the suicide note of two Chicago teenagers contained the lyrics of Metallica's 'Fade to Black'. Metallica responded by saying that many young people said their music *stopped* them killing themselves.

Madonna

Madonna began her career singing disco, with hits such as 'Holiday'. She then became a pop star, renowned for her music videos. Madonna's music sold exceptionally well; she had 12 top-ten hits in a row between 1984 and 1987. In her videos and performances she always pushed at (some felt beyond) the limits of public acceptability. She used controversy to generate sales; all her albums went platinum.

There were three main controversies over Madonna. One was the sexuality in her videos, performances and public addresses. She talked a great deal about sex, promoted safe sex in her interviews, distributed condoms at her concerts and performed at AIDS benefits. She was the main target of the PMRC's concerns about sexuality in music. Susan Baker, a founding member of the PMRC, complained that Madonna was teaching young girls 'how to be porn queens in heat'. 'Justify My Love' (1990) was the video that most upset the PMRC, because it hinted at homosexuality and group sex. This was the first video officially banned by MTV, which helped make it the bestselling music video ever.

A second and related controversy concerned Madonna's supposed objectification of herself in early videos such as 'Like a Virgin' and 'Material Girl' (both 1984). However, she argued that she was in control of her image. Some feminists agreed with her and felt that she was demonstrating female empowerment in her videos, in which women took the dominant role over men. Other feminists felt that the videos were akin to pornography (most feminists decried pornography as exploiting women).

The third great area of controversy was her use of religious iconography, most famously in a 1989 Pepsi advertisement in which she sang 'Like a Prayer'. The song's video contained religious symbols such as the cross and a dream scene about making love to a saint. That upset the Religious Right and Pepsi dropped their sponsorship.

In many ways, Madonna was the embodiment of youth culture in the 1980s in her chafing at conventionality and advocacy of sexual liberation, gay rights (she frequently declared herself bisexual) and women's rights.

Madonna and her sexuality constituted one main PMRC target. Other targets included:

- Jello Biafra, leader of the Dead Kennedys, who was arrested in 1986 for distributing harmful material to a minor – a young Los Angeles girl had bought the group's *Frankenchrist* album, which contained a poster picturing ten penises and vulvae. Although the group and their label were found not guilty, the legal costs nearly ruined them
- 2 Live Crew, whose album *As Nasty As They Wanna Be* (1990) was the first recording to be declared legally obscene in a federal district court (one of the tracks, 'Me So Horny', was about sex in a wide range of positions). The group was acquitted and the Supreme Court refused to accept a challenge to the ruling
- Ice-T, whose song 'Cop Killer' brought controversies about the relationship between rap and violence into the headlines. The song encapsulated black discontent with the 'not guilty' verdict on police who beat up fleeing black American suspect Rodney King. Critics included President George H.W. Bush and Vice-President Dan Quayle. Conservatives and police organisations across America called for a boycott of the company behind the song and Ice-T agreed to delete it from the Body Count album in future, raising the question as to the extent to which cultural challenge was influenced by financial considerations.

Non-oppositional youth culture

Not all young people were disaffected. Many participated in non-oppositional manifestations of popular culture. They were fans of sport or mainstream movies and some seamlessly developed into what *Time* magazine christened 'yuppies' (young, upwardly mobile urban professionals). Yuppies liked making money, BMWs, designer casual gear, gourmet food, high-tech sound equipment, jogging, high-fibre diets and natural-fibre clothes. A Berkeley study of yuppies concluded that American individualism had left the community-conscious citizen behind and morphed into the 'economic man'.

The popular TV show *Family Ties* (1982–89) was about two ex-hippie and liberal parents with a young Republican son and a highly materialistic daughter, both believers in Reaganomics (see page 452). *Family Ties* demonstrated the increased fragmentation of American society, a trend accelerated by new developments in technology.

The impact of technology on popular culture

Technological change accelerated in the years 1981–92 and impacted upon popular culture in that:

- cable television, remote-control devices, **videocassette recorders (VCRs)** and portable CD technology helped revolutionise entertainment in that they all gave the individual consumer greater choice
- personal computers revolutionised the way Americans produced, received and exchanged information.

Personal computers

In the 1960s and 1970s, computer use was mostly confined to government agencies and big businesses, but, from 1981, IBM sold small desktop personal computers (PCs) for use in the office or at home. This constituted the start of a computing revolution. The young Bill Gates recognised the market for 'user-friendly' software to operate the new PCs. In 1983, his company Microsoft launched its Word and Windows programmes controlled by a 'mouse'. With this user-friendly software, nearly one-quarter of American households possessed a personal computer by the early 1990s. They used them to word process, manage their finances and play games. During this period, Microsoft's employees rocketed from just three to almost 6,000. By 1992, annual Microsoft revenue exceeded $1 billion and Bill Gates was the richest person in the world.

Remote-control devices

Most new TVs were operated by hand-held remote control. This new technology enabled viewers to 'channel surf' in order to avoid advertisements and increased the individual's choice as to what was to be viewed. This new trend for personalised entertainment also owed much to the development of the videocassette recorder (VCR).

VCRs

VCRs were invented in the 1960s but only became popular in the 1980s because mass production made them cheap and the Supreme Court ruled that recording television shows for home use was not a violation of copyright law. By 1990, three-quarters of all households owned a VCR. Along with the recording of TV shows, possession of a VCR enabled viewers to rent feature films from video stores and to play games. Here again, the opportunities for personalised entertainment were increased by the new technology.

Cassettes and CDs

Before the 1970s Americans who wanted to hear a particular piece of music usually played vinyl records on frequently bulky record players. However, during the 1970s cassettes became popular. Customers could buy pre-recorded cassettes or record music onto blank cassettes and play them on tiny portable players such as a Sony Walkman or on a boombox (also known as a ghetto blaster). Then, in the late 1970s, the compact disc (CD) came on the market. Supposedly offering better sound and easier use than records and cassettes, and certainly more resistant to wear, the CD was portable and offered the option of entertainment solely for one. Indeed, it could be argued that the new technology contributed to the fragmentation of American society. Americans could now access the entertainment that they wanted when they wanted.

The growth of cable television and the influence of MTV

Along with home video technology, the development of cable television further increased opportunities for personal choice and individualised entertainment. President Reagan's deregulation of television in the early 1980s encouraged a dramatic expansion in cable services and the quantity of available channels (the number rose from five or six to several hundred). By 1990, 90 per cent of American homes had cable service. Whereas over half of Americans had watched an *I Love Lucy* episode in the 1950s, cable television contributed to the fragmentation of American society when it catered to markets divided and defined by age, education, gender, race and socioeconomic status. Speciality cable channels targeted different groups:

- Starting in 1979, ESPN focussed on coverage of sports.
- C-SPAN, established in 1979, offered exhaustive coverage of federal government activities.
- Created in 1980, Cable News Network (CNN) gave 24-hour news coverage; its 1987 human interest story of 18-month-old Jessica McClure, stuck down a well in Texas, brought it national attention. Its 1991 coverage of the **Gulf War** brought huge audiences, because it was the only news station with reporters inside Iraq.
- Reverend Pat Robertson's Family Channel reached 50 million homes and showed his programme *The 700 Club* (see page 461) several times each week.
- Home Shopping Network advertised consumer products.
- Disney targeted children aged six to 14 years with programmes such as cartoons and re-runs of *The Adventures of Ozzie and Harriet* (see page 362).
- MTV aired non-stop music from 1981.
- Pornography was more widely available.

As cable television was not subject to Federal Communications Commission (FCC) guidelines, there was far more sex and violence. A 1990s study said that there was a profanity once every six minutes on over-the-air television, but every two minutes on cable.

MTV

The most significant cable channel of the 1980s was MTV, the first 24-hour music video cable channel and the most influential music outlet yet. Eight-five per cent of its predominantly white, suburban audience was aged between 12 and 34 years. It was the fastest-growing cable channel ever, and the most effective way for a record to obtain a national audience; it had 23 million viewers by 1982. From 1981–83, MTV presented 24-hour music, mostly rock. While it inspired the development of other music video channels, such as Black Entertainment Television (BET) and The Nashville Network, which offered country music, MTV remained the giant among them.

Racism and sexism

Initially, MTV's choice of music was much criticised in the popular press. Black artists were rarely shown and one employee admitted on air that this was because MTV did not want to alienate the small-town Midwest. However, when Michael Jackson's popularity soared, MTV showed his videos, such as his huge hit 'Thriller' (1982).

Along with racism, MTV was charged with sexism. In its early years, in particular, MTV focussed on appealing to young white men; as a result, women were objectified in videos such as Van Halen's 'Hot for Teacher' (1984) and Robert Palmer's 'Addicted to Love' (1985) in order to encourage young male viewers to continue watching.

Some women retaliated with feminist themes. In Donna Summer's 'She Works Hard for the Money', a single working mother who is exploited in the workplace and unappreciated by her selfish children joins in an exhibition of female solidarity in the streets. Cyndi Lauper's 'Girls Just Wanna Have Fun' (1984), considered a feminist anthem, contributed to one of her ten MTV music video award nominations. Madonna made a great deal of money by objectifying herself in early videos such as 'Like a Virgin' and 'Material Girl' (both 1984 – see page 465), which greatly excited young male purchasers and female wannabes, raising questions as to who was exploiting who.

Overall, while conservatives viewed MTV as a bad influence on American youth, young Americans enjoyed the music and the videos, and the sense of empowerment that came with an oppositional stance.

The impact of the AIDS crisis

Homosexuality acquired an increasingly prominent place on the national agenda in the 1980s for two reasons. First, the Religious Right waged a great antihomosexual campaign (see page 461). Second, the spread of AIDS impacted on the lives of homosexuals, drug users and haemophiliacs, public perceptions of gays and the campaign for gay rights.

Acquired immunodeficiency syndrome (AIDS) can be transmitted through sexual activity, contaminated needles and blood transfusions. Scientists identified the human immunodeficiency virus (HIV) in 1984 but could offer no cure. The impact of AIDS upon a sufferer's life was terrifying; it was a virtual death sentence and victims were socially ostracised. Most of those who had AIDS were young, gay men. Around 5,500 Americans had died from it by 1985, and over 46,000 by 1989. In 1989 there were over 80,000 confirmed cases and possibly ten times more who were infected.

Because AIDS mostly struck male homosexuals and intravenous drug users, Middle America associated it with immorality. Antihomosexual sentiment was already strong and AIDS further fuelled it. Some conservatives claimed the 'gay plague' was God's punishment for sexual deviancy: 'The poor homosexuals,' said Pat Buchanan (see page 461). 'They have declared war on nature and now nature is exacting an awful retribution.'

Initially, the AIDS scare encouraged many gay men to remain in the closet (in 1985, three-quarters of Americans said that they did not know any homosexuals). However, the anxiety generated by AIDS soon impacted upon and accelerated gay rights activism. In 1987, the newly established ACT UP (AIDS Coalition to Unleash Power) followed up the first **gay pride** parade in New York City with a demonstration that demanded equal rights and more research into AIDS.

President Reagan and AIDS

After President Reagan's movie actor friend Rock Hudson died from AIDS in October 1985, Reagan asked Surgeon-General C. Everett Koop for a report on the problem. Koop's report suggested three remedies ('one, abstinence; two, monogamy; three, condoms') and called for sex education in schools, even at elementary level. However, Reagan refused to advocate the use of condoms or to speak to Congress to get funding to help investigate and find cures for the disease. Indeed, his budget required a cut in AIDS research. Reagan's inaction had the support of conservatives such as Phyllis Schlafly, who like Reagan opposed the advocacy of condoms and sex education. As a result of social conservatism, HIV infection was far greater in the United States than in western Europe, which promoted advertisements about safe sex and needle exchanges.

The Ryan White Care Act

Federal government assistance for AIDS sufferers probably owed more to individuals such as the Indiana teenager Ryan White than to ACT UP. A haemophiliac who contracted AIDS through a blood transfusion, White became a highly articulate and persuasive national spokesman for AIDS sufferers. He helped change public perceptions of AIDS and after he died in 1990, Congress passed the Ryan White Care Act. This granted $220 million to help victims of a so-called 'gay plague' that killed others along with gay men.

Controversial issues in film and TV

The AIDS crisis and attitudes toward homosexuality constituted one of the many controversial social issues that bitterly divided Americans and were explored in film and television in the period 1981–92.

▲ Ryan White returning to school, having been excluded after his AIDs diagnosis. What can you infer from this photo about attitudes towards the AIDs epidemic in 1986?

Key Topic 4 Republican dominance and its opponents, 1981–92

Source C Extract from a speech by gay activist Vito Russo at an ACT UP demonstration in Albany in May 1988. Here, Russo expresses his frustration at the response from the government, the media and heterosexuals to the AIDS crisis.

> You know, for the last three years, since I was diagnosed, my family thinks two things about my situation. One, they think I'm going to die, and two, they think that my government is doing absolutely everything in their power to stop that. And they are wrong, on both counts.
>
> So, if I'm dying from anything, I'm dying from homophobia. If I'm dying from anything, I'm dying from racism. If I'm dying from anything, it's from indifference and red tape, because these are the things that are preventing an end to this crisis. If I'm dying from anything, I'm dying from Jesse Helms [a deeply conservative Republican Senator]. If I'm dying from anything, I'm dying from the President of the United States. And, especially, if I'm dying from anything, I'm dying from the sensationalism of newspapers and magazines and television shows, which are interested in me, as a human interest story – only as long as I'm willing to be a helpless victim, but not if I'm fighting for my life.
>
> If I'm dying from anything, I'm dying from the fact that not enough rich, white, heterosexual men have gotten AIDS for anybody to give a shit.

How much weight would you give to the evidence of Source C for an enquiry into attitudes toward homosexuality in the years 1981–92? Explain your answer, using the source, the information given about it and your own knowledge of the historical context.

Homosexuality

Audiences remained wary of films and television series on homosexuality. In 1981, NBC considered a sitcom called *Love, Sidney*, about a homosexual artist who is the surrogate father to a female friend's child. However, NBC got cold feet; according to one reviewer, 'The very idea of a gay man coming into our homes so close, offended so many people that NBC relented ... [Sidney became] just a strange, sad little man who doesn't date much.' Due to pressure from the Religious Right, Hollywood was also reluctant to deal with homosexuality in the years 1981–92. The movie *Longtime Companion* (1989) was the first widely released movie to deal with AIDS. It received great critical acclaim but audiences were not large; the box-office receipts were under 1 per cent of the receipts of the year's top grosser, the escapist adventure film *Indiana Jones and the Last Crusade*.

Sex

President Reagan felt there was too much sex and violence on TV, but his deregulation policies (see page 467) so weakened the Federal Communications Commission (FCC) that the sex and violence continued and increased. The sexually explicit and violent content of film also increased in this period.

Continuing sexual liberalisation and the old adage that 'sex sells' inevitably led to more explicit sex in films such as *Basic Instinct* (1992) and in television series. In 1988 the Planned Parenthood Federation of America bought full-page newspaper and magazine ads that pointed out, 'They did it 20,000 times on television last year, but nobody used a condom.' The teen-drama series *Beverly Hills, 90210* (1990–2000), which was very popular with pre-teens, associated being sexually active with being 'cool'. A common theme in sitcoms such as *The Fresh Prince of Bel-Air* (1990–96) was that being a virgin was highly embarrassing for a teenager. Frank discussions of adult sexual behaviour was the norm on talk shows such as *The Jerry Springer Show* (1991–present).

Occasionally, the sex went too far, as in the highly controversial *The Last Temptation of Christ* (1988). The depiction of Jesus Christ fantasising about marriage to and sex with Mary Magdalene greatly upset the Religious Right. Conservatives such as Concerned Women for America (see page 440) organised opposition. They promoted letter-writing campaigns, street protests and picketing. Such campaigns were frequently effective; some movie chains refused to screen the movie and, although critically acclaimed, its box-office receipts barely covered production costs.

Violence

Both Hollywood and television were criticised for gratuitous violence in the years 1981–92. Movies that contained a great deal of violence included *RoboCop* (1987), *Die Hard* (1988) and *The Silence of the Lambs* (1991).

The Silence of the Lambs raised the issue of when and if extreme depictions of violence were acceptable; the movie received great critical acclaim but nevertheless made some critics uneasy (the movie ends with the escaped criminal saying that he is 'having an old friend for dinner', a humorous reference to cannibalism that some considered inappropriate).

The movie *Die Hard* and NBC's television series *The A-Team* (1983–87) raised the issue of whether cartoonish violence was acceptable. *The A-Team* was the fourth most popular television programme during 1983; some claimed that its violence was similar to that of Tom and Jerry cartoons in that no blood and gore resulted from the violence, but others felt that it was likely to have an undesirable influence upon the 7 million out of 42 million viewers who were aged between two and 11.

Cable television showed graphically violent feature films. In 1988, Senator Paul Simon of Illinois came across a gory movie murder scene in the 1974 movie *The Texas Chainsaw Massacre* as he channel-surfed in his hotel room. Simon persuaded Congress to pass an Act in 1990 that exempted the broadcast and cable networks and programme producers from antitrust laws if they decided to work together to come up with a common set of standards regarding violence. The ineffectiveness of the measure was attested in late 1992 by President-elect Bill Clinton, who told *TV Guide* that the networks and producers should be 'deglamorizing mindless sex and violence'.

War

War was a favourite theme for many moviegoers and television viewers. There were a number of antiwar films – for example, *Platoon* (1986) and *Born on the Fourth of July* (1989), the latter based on the memoirs of disabled and disillusioned Vietnam War veteran Ron Kovic. However, there were many more movies that lauded militarism and male assertiveness and had regressive depictions of women, reflecting the conservative revival of the Reagan years. In *Rambo* (1985), a Vietnam veteran rescued American prisoners of war in defiance of the Vietnamese, who were presented as subhuman. The male leads in *Stripes* (1981) and *An Officer and a Gentleman* (1982) were moulded into admirable individuals by the Army, while the female lead in the latter simply wanted to capture an officer husband.

The role of women

While Hollywood churned out several pro-feminist films in the 1970s, a considerable number of 1980s films promoted the 'good mother' as opposed to the independent woman. Most notable among them was *Fatal Attraction* (1987), in which a single career woman seduces and nearly destroys a happily married man until the 'good mother' manages to kill her off. Men in American movie theatres cheered the killer mom on with cries of 'Kill the bitch'.

A major explanation of Hollywood's frequent conformity to the currently prevailing conservative values lay in the desire to maximise revenue; faced with the new threat from cable, it was sensible to follow mainstream culture in order to be sure of an audience. Pre-Reagan, Goldie Hawn had been Private Benjamin in the 1980 film of the same name, whose army career enabled her to reject a womanising husband at the end of the movie. In *Overboard* (1987), she was tamed by her he-man husband. The few strong-minded women in films of the era tended to be strong in defence of their families, as in *Terms of Endearment* (1983). Abortion was 'bad' in several movies of the Reagan era, such as *Another Woman* (1988) and *Criminal Law* (1989).

Several television series covered the tensions faced by women in relation to work and family:

- *Roseanne* (1988–97) was about a struggling working-class woman who worked hard in a variety of under-skilled jobs and then came home and had to do all the housework. 'I wanted to send a message about how much we mothers really do', said the star and scriptwriter of the show, Roseanne Barr. *Roseanne* was the most-watched television show in the United States in the years 1989 and 1990.
- The third most-watched show in 1991–92 was *Murphy Brown* (1988–98). In that year, Murphy, a successful TV journalist, became a single mother. In an excellent example of the perceived influence of television, Murphy's motherhood triggered an intervention from Vice-President Dan Quayle, who said in May 1992 that America suffered from 'a poverty of values', that 'bearing babies irresponsibly is simply wrong', and that Murphy Brown 'doesn't help matters' by 'mocking the importance of fathers, by bearing a child alone'. Quayle's speech triggered a national debate.

- The long-running series *Cagney and Lacey* (1982–88) explored the difference between two female detectives: one home-loving and with an idealised family; the other ambitious, single and with multiple partners. Although heralded for its portrayal of strong competent working women, the series reflected social conservatism in that the single detective Cagney was invariably less content and stable than the married detective Lacey who, with some struggle and tension, managed to combine work and motherhood.
- Another long-running series, the sitcom *Cheers* (1982–93), was affectionately centred upon a womanising bartender, but pitted him initially against a critical woman who longed for career success. However, her successor simply sought family life, preferably with a rich man.

Controversial issues in film and television: Conclusions

Like music, movies and television reflected the widely differing tastes and values of the American population. Many movies and television programmes were pure escapism, although even the escapism was often highly controversial; for example, the attitude to sex in *The Fresh Prince of Bel-Air* and the violence in *The A-Team* disturbed a considerable number of Americans. Entertainment inevitably reflected the great changes that had taken place in American society between 1955 and 1992. While considerable numbers of Americans still believed in the generally accepted values of the mid-twentieth century, those values had been successfully challenged, leaving American society deeply divided.

Conclusion: Cultural challenge

The 1980s was a decade of culture wars in which social conservatives attempted to hold the line against multiple challenges to their values. The challengers included many young Americans in their choice of music and entertainment and the many Americans who favoured sexual liberalisation. Such challenges were reflected in the treatment of controversial social issues in film and television and were facilitated by technological developments such as the growth of cable television, which enabled the individual to choose forms of entertainment in line with their individual tastes and values. It was perhaps the challengers who won; by 1992, the Religious Right seemed disheartened and disillusioned, recognising that even the staunchest supporters in the federal government could not turn the clock back to their idealised vision of the 1950s.

> **Work together**
>
> This section has examined various aspects of the culture wars of the 1980s. In order to ensure that you have enough material to answer an exam question on this topic:
>
> 1. Look back at the headings throughout this section which list the key topics that are being covered.
> 2. Now write a single-sentence summary of each topic, making sure you link each to the culture wars.
> 3. Using your notes, pick three specific details – these could be statistics or the names of television shows, music groups or films – to support each point.
> 4. In pairs, look at each other's summaries and answer the following questions:
>   - (a) Did your summaries agree on the main features of the culture wars?
>   - (b) Did your partner have enough specific detail to support the key points they made?

4 Social change

In 1955, the political, legal, economic and social status of ethnic minorities and women was markedly inferior to that of white men. The civil rights movement had inspired multiple campaigns for equality in the 1960s; these generated considerable advances in the status of black Americans, Hispanic Americans, **Native Americans** and women.

It is tempting to see a straightforward upward trajectory towards ethnic and gender equality, but progress was often resisted and sometimes halted by conservatives, especially in the 1980s. Furthermore, while some members of ethnic minority groups and some women felt that there had been insufficient change, others felt that the changes that had occurred were undesirable. One thing everyone agreed upon was that the status of ethnic minorities and women *was* changing.

> **Note it down**
>
> As you read this section, create a table in which you record the status of women, black Americans, Native Americans, Hispanic Americans and homosexuals in 1955, 1963, 1973, 1981 and 1992. You will find material for 1981–92 in this section, but you might need to refer back to your notes on previous chapters for the other dates – that will be useful revision.

The changing status of ethnic minorities

In the years since 1955, the status of ethnic minorities had changed for the better. Nonetheless, by 1992 racial inequality was still a significant feature of US society. Andrew Hacker's influential book *Two Nations* (1992) claimed that 'a huge racial chasm' remained between black and white. The same was true in terms of equality between whites and Hispanic and Native Americans.

Political status

Between 1981 and 1992, the political status of ethnic minorities changed for the better as black Americans and Hispanic Americans became increasingly well represented in government and politics.

Black Americans

President Reagan appointed a black cabinet member, and Colin Powell headed the **Joint Chiefs of Staff (JCS)** under President George H.W. Bush. More black candidates were elected to political office. In 1988, Jesse Jackson made a serious run for the Democratic nomination for the presidency and was the front runner until controversy erupted over his anti-Semitic remarks. During the 1980s, NAACP lawyers won hundreds of cases that led to changes to congressional districts and voting systems that assisted the election of thousands of black officials by the 1990s. The number of black Congressmen increased from 45 in 1990 to 69 in 1992. Major cities continued to elect black mayors. For example, Chicago elected a black mayor in 1984 and Philadelphia followed suit in 1988. Increased black influence was also demonstrated in the rejection of Robert Bork's nomination to the Supreme Court (see page 462).

However, improvements in black political status had limits. Black Americans rarely won statewide elections; in 1992 the sole black governor was Douglas Wilder of Virginia (1990–94), and the sole black Senator was Carol Moseley Braun from Illinois (only the second black American elected to the US Senate in the twentieth century). In that many white voters simply did not want to be represented by a black candidate, black political status remained unchanged.

Hispanic Americans

The political status of Hispanic Americans also changed and improved in the years 1981–92. Journalists and Hispanic leaders called the 1980s the 'Hispanic decade' because of the increasing number and politicisation of Hispanic citizens. Hispanic American organisations such as the League of United Latin American Citizens (LULAC, established in 1929) and the Mexican American Legal Defence and Educational Fund (MALDEF, established in 1968) became much more effective in their lobbying. For example, the LULAC and the MALDEF helped persuade Congress to make the Immigration Reform Control Act (1986) more sympathetic to the status of **undocumented aliens**. President Reagan appointed the first Hispanic cabinet member in 1989 and the number of Hispanic Americans in the US House of Representatives rose from five in 1970 to ten in 1980 and 17 in 1992.

Native Americans

While many blacks and Hispanics sought equal political status within an integrated political system, many Native Americans preferred **separatism**. In 1990 one in four Native Americans lived on a tribal reservation. Tribes had become far more assertive over **sovereignty** and land rights and, in the years 1981–92, their activism focussed upon lobbying and litigating over those issues. This activism was often effective; for example, the Supreme Court supported Native American tribal sovereignty and tax powers in *Merrion* (1982). However, the issue of where Native American sovereignty was superseded by state or federal authority remained problematic; for example, in *Duro v. Reina* (1990), the Supreme Court ruled that tribal courts did not have criminal jurisdiction over someone who was not a member of the tribe, but that tribes

> *also possess their traditional and undisputed power to exclude persons who they deem to be undesirable from tribal lands … Tribal law enforcement authorities have the power if necessary, to eject them. Where jurisdiction to try and punish an offender rests outside the tribe, tribal officers may exercise their power to detain and transport him to the proper authorities.*

Like other ethnic minorities, Native Americans had put their rights and status firmly on the national agenda since the 1960s, while not yet attaining all that they sought. *Duro* demonstrated that full tribal sovereignty was not possible within the United States.

Status in the legal system

By 1992, black and Hispanic Americans were quite well represented in police departments but there was continuing racism in law enforcement and the legal system. For example, after a high-speed car chase in Los Angeles in 1991, white police caught up with black suspect Rodney King and were filmed beating him up. Riots erupted in Los Angeles when an all-white jury found the police innocent; 55 died, 2,300 were injured and riots followed in Atlanta, Birmingham and Chicago.

In 1992 it was found that the Sheriff's Department of Volusia County, Florida, stopped a disproportionate number of black and Hispanic American drivers on the portion of the **interstate** highway that ran through the county. Although black and Hispanic Americans constituted only 5 per cent of the drivers on that portion of the road, they constituted 70 per cent of those stopped by the police, and were stopped for far longer periods than white drivers were.

Another issue was the disproportionate number of black males in jail. A common black viewpoint was that this denoted unequal black status and that the police unfairly victimised black Americans. While white conservatives insisted that black Americans were more likely to commit crime, white liberals pointed out that poor education and a high unemployment rate contributed to black involvement in crime, drugs and gang turf wars.

Asian Americans were equally convinced of racism within the legal system after a case that began in 1982. Chinese-American Vincent Chin was clubbed to death in Detroit by two white car workers who thought he was Japanese and culpable for car industry layoffs (see page 431). Asian Americans were disgusted when the killers' sentence was a mere three years' probation.

Although Native American tribes had increased powers of law enforcement on **reservations** after 1974 (see page 472), they remained caught between their cultural traditions and the dominant legal system, as in 1990 when the Supreme Court ruled that states could deny employment to peyote users because peyote was an illicit drug not part of an essential religious practice (Native Americans customarily used peyote for religious experiences).

Economic status

With the exception of Asian Americans, ethnic minorities remained on average poorer than white Americans. Statistics demonstrated the continuing inferior economic status of black, Hispanic and Native Americans:

- Between 1970 and 1990, roughly 30 per cent of black Americans lived in poverty.
- Black Americans were more than twice as likely to be poor than white Americans.
- Black unemployment was twice that of whites and opportunities were decreasing for some; two-thirds of adult black males in Chicago's South Side were employed in 1960, but only one-third by 1990.
- In 1990, the median black household income was $24,000, compared to $40,100 for whites.
- The average net worth of black Americans in relation to white Americans sank from one-eighth in 1970 to one-fourteenth by 2000.
- Around one-quarter of Hispanic Americans lived below the poverty line.
- Native American income was less than half the national average.

On the other hand, a growing black and Hispanic middle class confirmed the changing economic status of some members of ethnic minority groups. This owed much to federal government policies, such as **affirmative action** (see page 389).

Affirmative action

Affirmative action was solidly entrenched in the major corporations and universities by 1992. It helped increase the number of ethnic minority students attending college. The proportion of black high-school students who went straight to college increased in the 1980s and 1990s. In 1983, only 38.2 per cent of black high-school students enrolled in colleges immediately after graduating from high school, compared to 55 per cent of white high-school students. By 1992, 51.5 per cent of black high-school graduates enrolled directly in college, although this was still lower than the 63.9 per cent of white students. Similarly, the number of Native Americans with a college education increased by 20 per cent between 1970 and 1990, while the percentage of Hispanic Americans with some college education increased by one-third.

Increased educational opportunities ensured a rise in ethnic minority incomes. Average black income rose by nearly 20 per cent between 1981 and 1992 (see Figure 1). The average Hispanic income in constant dollars rose from $10,524 in 1975, to $16,674 in 1981, and to $28,822 in 1992.

Affirmative action helped change the economic status of ethnic minorities by enhancing their employment opportunities, but it elicited a conservative reaction. The battle between conservatives and liberals over affirmative action was illustrated in 1989–91 when the increasingly conservative Supreme Court limited the scope of affirmative action programmes in *City of Richmond* v. *Croson Company* (1989). The Supreme Court ruled against Richmond City Council's policy, which guaranteed that a minimum of 30 per cent of the value of city contracts would go to minority-owned firms. The Democrat-controlled Congress retaliated with a civil rights bill that provided new legal remedies for anyone who suffered workplace mistreatment (1990), but President Bush vetoed it, claiming that it would lead to frivolous lawsuits and force businesses to set racial hiring quotas. Probably because he was anxious to improve his image with women and minorities after the Clarence Thomas confirmation battle (see page 477), Bush accepted a modified version of the bill in 1991.

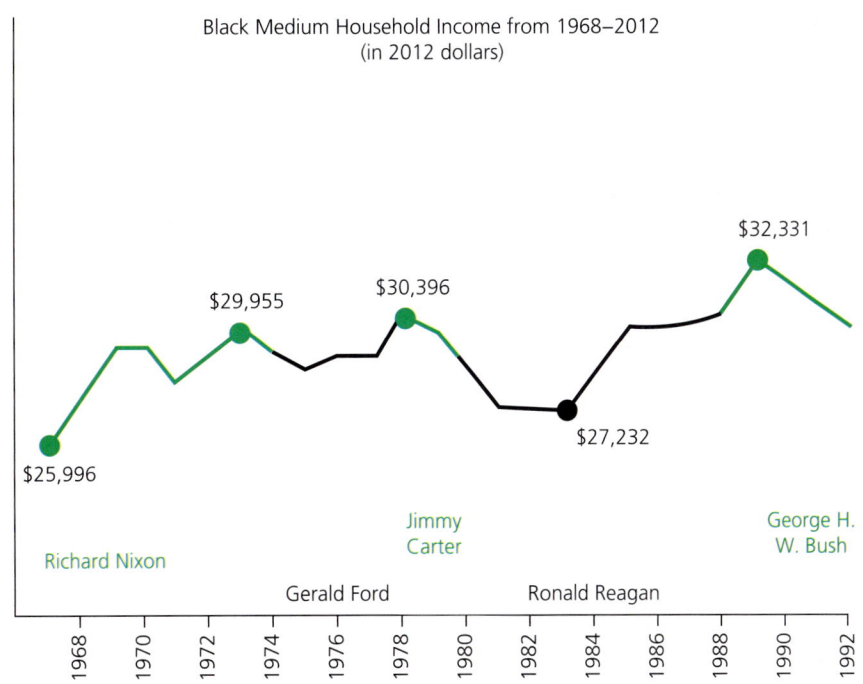

▲ Figure 1: Black median household income, 1968-92. (Source: US Census Bureau, *Current Population Survey, Annual Social and Economic Supplements*.)

Social status

During the period 1981–92, there was much evidence of advances in racial tolerance and integration, but also of intolerance and **segregation** (see below).

The extent of racial tolerance and integration by 1992

By 1992, half the black population lived in neighbourhoods that were more than 50 per cent white and the number of interracial marriages and cohabitants was slowly rising. Southern school **desegregation** peaked in 1988, when 43 per cent of black schoolchildren attended schools that were more than 50 per cent white.

On the other hand, 9 per cent of black Americans continued to live in *de facto* **segregated**, overcrowded and impoverished inner-city ghettos where life expectancy was lower (see Table 2) and schools remained poorly funded.

Table 2: Black American life expectancy.

Year	Average age at death for black Americans	Average age at death for white Americans
1960	63.6	70.6
1970	64.1	71.7
1980	68.1	74.4
1990	69.1	76.1

Continuing white opposition to integration demonstrated that black people's social status remained inferior. Furthermore, white opposition to integrated schools ensured that Southern schools slowly became re-segregated after 1988. Hispanic Americans also suffered from white opposition to integration; between 1968 and 1995, the proportion of Hispanic Americans in mostly minority schools rose from 55 per cent to 74 per cent.

The role of the federal government

Since the mid-twentieth century, the federal government had tried to remedy mistreatment and prejudice with varying degrees of effort and effectiveness. However, conservatives such as President Reagan frequently opposed measures that would lead to further integration.

Reagan supported a constitutional amendment to outlaw bussing (see page 412) and when the Democrat-controlled Congress rejected the proposal, his administration refused to press lawsuits to enforce it. When the Supreme Court ruled in 1984 (*Grove City College* v. *Bell*) that the only area of Grove City College that required compliance with antidiscrimination laws was its financial aid programme, Congress retaliated with a 1988 Civil Rights Restoration Act that Reagan vetoed. Congress then overrode his veto. The Act stipulated that recipients of federal funds must comply with civil rights laws in all areas.

Reagan had more success with the courts than with Congress, due to his 'Reaganisation' of the judiciary.

Key Topic 4 Republican dominance and its opponents, 1981–92

Most of the 368 federal judges whom he appointed were young white males. Of the rest, only seven were black, 15 Hispanic and two Asian. Increasingly conservative courts were unlikely to promote integration and racial tolerance.

Tolerance

Throughout the 1980s, there remained much evidence of both prejudice and racial tolerance:

- In 1986 Californian voters expressed their decreased tolerance of the Hispanicisation of the state in approving **Proposition 63** (the 'English is the Official Language of California Amendment' to the Californian constitution) by two to one, although in 1989 the Los Angeles School Board agreed to bilingual education.
- Both Chief Justice William Rehnquist (1985) and President Reagan (1988) made derogatory remarks about 'inferior' Native American culture, but Congress demonstrated respect in the Native American Grave Protection and Reparation Act (1990), which enabled Native Americans to retrieve remains of their ancestors from museums and universities.
- The Smithsonian Institute's National Museum of Art's show 'The West as America: Reinterpreting Images of the Frontier, 1820–1920' rightly emphasised white mistreatment of Native Americans, but it infuriated conservatives and led some Republicans to threaten to cut the museum's budget.
- White audiences enjoyed watching *The Cosby Show* (see below) about a black family, but were less enthusiastic about television depictions of romantic relationships between black and white Americans. In 1989, the cancellation of *The Robert Guillaume Show* owed much to audience inability to cope with the concept of an interracial relationship.

Conservatives were not the only threat to tolerance of ethnic minority assertiveness. The liberal historian Arthur Schlesinger Jr's *The Disuniting of America: Reflections on a Multicultural Society* (1991) lamented the 'cult of ethnicity' as divisive. White anxiety about national disunity limited the tolerance of some whites toward ethnic minority assertiveness. Some members of ethnic minorities also considered minority assertiveness a barrier to integration; this was an important part of the reasoning behind Supreme Court Justice Clarence Thomas' opposition to affirmative action.

The impact of black American success

It could be argued that black success in politics, business, sport and popular culture produced inspirational role models for black Americans and overturned stereotypes of black inferiority.

White Americans certainly admired and enjoyed watching black artists and athletes. *The Oprah Winfrey Show* (1986–2011) became a phenomenal success. This talk show, with its celebrity interviews, self-help advice, book recommendations and coverage of controversial social issues, was the number-one daytime show for two decades and an estimated 48 million Americans watched it every week. *The Cosby Show*, about a black physician and family man with a lawyer wife and exceptionally well-behaved children, was the top-rated sitcom for most of the late 1980s (over 30 million American households watched it in 1986 and 1987). A high proportion of musical superstars were black Americans, including Michael Jackson, Prince and Whitney Houston. Nineteen of the 50 top albums of 1985 were by black artists, and eight out of the top 12 in 1986. Black sports stars such as basketball's Michael Jordan were national heroes. In 1992 Jordan earned $21 million from endorsements, appearance money and royalties that attested his nationwide appeal. Black athletes dominated team sports in the 1980s. In 1986, 63 per cent of top **football** players, 33 per cent of baseball players and 75 per cent of basketball players were black.

During the 1980s, the production and consumption of traditional black American foods led to success for black American companies such as Glory Foods. Established in 1989, Glory Foods sold traditional dishes such as corn bread mixes, okra and beans. Its products were available nationwide in supermarkets. Jerry Rubin was another business success story. In the 1960s, he had participated in antiwar protests, helped found the Yippies (see page 410) and joined the **Black Power movement** (he was one of the Chicago Eight – see page 392). In 1980, he became a Wall Street stockbroker and quickly established the Business Networking Salons, which organised parties that enabled professionals and entrepreneurs to network.

A positive or negative impact?

Overall, black American successes in business and politics had a positive and inspirational impact, especially upon the aspirational black middle class. Jesse Jackson demonstrated that a black American could stage an impressive run for the Democratic nomination for the presidency. He attracted considerable white support at the Democratic National Convention in Atlanta in 1988, when he came second to the eventual candidate Michael Dukakis (Dukakis got 2,876 votes, Jackson 1,218).

White Americans had little problem in accepting and often idolising successful black Americans in sport and popular culture, but it did not necessarily make them more willing to accept black neighbours or to support initiatives to help the ghetto poor. It was the latter upon whom black successes in sport and popular culture impacted most. Black ghetto youths idolised sports stars such as Michael Jordan rather than politicians and businessmen.

Some argued that black sporting success confirmed the historic white prejudice that blacks were natural athletes and that this only served to reinforce white prejudices that blacks were physically aggressive and lacking in intellect. While there were many successful black athletes, there were few black people in sports management. The first black baseball manager was appointed in 1975, but when Cito Gaston became a Major League baseball manager in 1989, he was still only the fourth black American to do so. While Michael Jordan argued that participation in athletics helped black students to become more connected to academic studies, some sociologists claimed that many black schoolchildren neglected their studies in order to concentrate upon sporting success.

Just as there were arguments as to whether black sporting successes had negative or positive impacts, there was also continued controversy as to whether or not the changing status of women was desirable.

The changing status of women by 1992

Women's status changed between 1955 and 1992 – not enough for liberals and too much for conservatives. Women's gains and prospects were threatened by the conservative backlash, the strength of which was demonstrated in effective opposition to the Equal Rights Amendment (see page 439), a lost cause by 1982. However, women were guaranteed most of the rights that the ERA would have guaranteed through federal government actions such as:

- the Civil Rights Act of 1964
- Title IX of the Education Amendments of 1972, which protected Americans from gender discrimination in educational programmes
- multiple court decisions
- decrees by the federal bureaucracy.

Still, some women felt their status remained inferior in politics and the workplace, and that their **reproductive rights** were being eroded by resurgent social conservatism.

Women and work

The Religious Right blamed feminism for the rising percentage of women in the workforce (see Table 3), but it was the financial calculation that getting a job best served their families' well-being that lay behind the increasing number of working women.

Table 3: The number of women in the workforce.

Year	Percentage of women in the workforce
1960	38
1970	43
1980	52
1990	57.8

The economic status of women was improving but remained inferior to that of men, so groups such as the NOW campaigned for equal pay and job opportunities. Although women's wages were rising (they were 62 per cent of men's wages in 1980 but 72 per cent in 1990), they remained markedly unequal. Furthermore, women held fewer executive and managerial positions and less than one-fifth of doctors and lawyers were women. Continuing inequality reflected both sexism and many women's desire to interrupt their careers to have children.

Sexual harassment

While sexual harassment had long been rampant in the workplace, tolerance of it decreased as women became more assertive and the federal government more supportive. In 1980, the Equal Employment Opportunity Commission (EEOC) stated that sexual harassment was a form of sex discrimination, prohibited by **Title VII** of the 1964 Civil Rights Act. The Supreme Court agreed in *Meritor Savings Bank* v. *Vinson* (1986). This enabled women to take legal action over sexual harassment in the workplace so that by 1991 the number of sexual harassment cases filed annually reached 6,000. The issue of sexual harassment dominated the media in 1991 due to the Tailhook Association scandal.

> **The Tailhook scandal**
>
> The Tailhook Association aimed to support those involved in naval aviation. At its annual convention in Las Vegas in 1991, it was alleged that over 100 Navy and Marine officers sexually assaulted and sexually harassed around 80 women. Rear Admiral Duvall Williams led the investigation, but the Assistant Secretary of the Navy, Barbara Pope, heard him say, 'A lot of female Navy pilots are go-go dancers, topless dancers or hookers'. This led to another investigation, and over 100 resignations (among them Rear Admiral Williams) and demotions.

Reproductive rights and social conservatism

Like ethnic minorities, women had to fight not only to gain but to retain rights in the face of social conservatism. Although *Roe* v. *Wade* (1973) (see page 438) seemed to guarantee women's reproductive rights, a series of Supreme Court rulings pleased the anti-abortion lobby. These included *Webster* v. *Reproductive Services of Missouri* (1989) (see page 460) and *Planned Parenthood of Southeastern Pennsylvania* v. *Casey* (1992). The latter ruling upheld a Pennsylvania state law that required women to undergo counselling and then wait 24 hours before the abortion. However, the Court struck down the Pennsylvania provision that a married woman had to produce 'a signed statement that she has notified her spouse that she is about to undergo an abortion'. Justice Sandra Day O'Connor persuasively argued that the many women who were victims of physical and psychological abuse at the hands of their husbands would have good reasons not to tell them about an abortion.

The *Planned Parenthood* case highlighted several issues. First, O'Connor was the first female Supreme Court justice. When Reagan appointed her in 1991, it demonstrated the changing status of women in that even a socially conservative president felt he ought to appoint a woman to the Supreme Court. Second, O'Connor's arguments demonstrated the importance of female representation in giving the female viewpoint in the federal government. Third, the case served as a reminder that decisions about women were made by a federal government dominated by elderly, white men.

Women in politics

Women constituted roughly half of the US population but in the years 1981–92 they remained dramatically under-represented in government at all levels, from state legislatures to the federal government. There was some progress in the **executive branch**. Once Gerald Ford became the first modern president to appoint a woman to the cabinet, most of his successors felt compelled to do likewise. When President Reagan failed to appoint a single woman to his cabinet, he was roundly criticised.

In some ways, the choice of Geraldine Ferraro as the Democratic Party's vice-presidential candidate in the 1984 presidential election campaign seemed a giant step forward. However, some sexist responses suggested women were nowhere near attaining equal political status. The *Denver Post* asked, 'What if she is supposed to push the button to fire the missiles and she can't because she's just done her nails?' and Vice-President George H.W. Bush's wife dubbed Ferraro 'something that rhymes with witch'.

There was some progress in the **legislative branch**, to which increasing numbers of women were elected. However, in 1979–80 there were still only 16 Congresswomen and no female Senators. The numbers had improved by 1991–92, with 28 Congresswomen and two Senators, but a real turning point came in 1992, thanks primarily to President George H.W. Bush's nomination of Clarence Thomas to the Supreme Court.

The impact of Clarence Thomas

Back in 1969, black Congresswoman Shirley Chisholm declared that 'in the political world I have been far oftener discriminated against because I am a woman than because I am black'. That racism was less acceptable than sexism was evident in the 1991 confirmation hearings of Clarence Thomas, a black American who was accused of sexual harassment by black law professor Anita Hill. The dismissal of Hill's testimony by the 96 per cent male Senate revitalised women campaigners who had been relatively quiet amid the prevailing conservatism of the era. In combination with the Democrat focus upon the under-representation of women in Congress and declaration that 1992 was the 'Year of the Woman', the Thomas case prompted unprecedented numbers of women to stand for local, state and national office in 1992. As a result, the number of women elected doubled; in the new Congress in January 1993, there were 47 women out of a total of 435 members of the House of Representatives and seven women among the 50 Senators. However, 47 Congresswomen and seven Senators still constituted a dramatic under-representation.

The impact of women in the workplace

Social conservatives, including members of the Religious Right, emphasised what they perceived as the negative impact of women in the workplace. They asserted that working women took men's jobs. Furthermore, they claimed that working mothers could not look after their families properly and that women in the workplace contributed to the destruction of the family through higher divorce rates and 'latch key kids'. *Newsweek* magazine lamented divorce rates and wondered whether working 'supermums' were damaging their kids.

Table 4: The percentage of marriages ending in divorce.

Year	Percentage of marriages ending in divorce
1955	23
1960	22
1970	33
1980	52
1990	49

On the other hand, liberals and organisations such as the NOW argued that employment opportunities had a positive impact upon women, helping them to fulfil their potential and achieve satisfaction. Whatever one's ideological stance, it was difficult to deny that the increasing number of waged women had a dramatic impact on family finances, helping many American families maintain their standard of living during the 1970s and 1980s. This is not to say that women were uniformly enthralled by participation in the workplace – the impact upon the many who were doing the 'double shift' (paid work and housework) was frequently negative: 'I need a wife' was a common joke among American working women.

The impact of women in politics

The impact of women in politics grew greater between 1955 and 1992. More women served on state legislatures and in the US House of Representatives. Martha Griffiths (see page 403) inspired other Congresswomen; she played a vital part in getting Congress to pass the Equal Rights Amendment (see page 439). Women in Congress were important in the passage of legislation that helped women, such as the Child Support Recovery Act (1992), which was designed to ensure that delinquent fathers paid child support, and the 1988 Women's Business Ownership Act, which gave financial aid to women to help them establish businesses. In 1992 Dianne Feinstein, who had been San Francisco's first female mayor, and Barbara Boxer were both elected to the Senate as California's two Senators. Both would subsequently become highly influential figures.

Conclusion: Social change

There is no doubt that the status of ethnic minorities and women had changed for the better since 1955 and that in many ways it continued to do so in the years 1981–92. However, the battle for equality was not yet won, as shown in many areas, such as the re-segregation of schools and the continuing disparities in economic status between white men and others.

President Reagan and the Religious Right would have felt more comfortable in the society and politics of 1950s America. They tried to turn the clock back to a time when abortion was illegal, middle-class women knew that their place was in the home, homosexuals kept quiet, affirmative action was unheard of, popular culture was not full of sex and violence and the federal government gave far less help to the disadvantaged.

Reagan and the Religious Right did not manage to turn the clock back, but it could be argued that they slowed it down. They strengthened conservatism in society and government. However, they were unable to silence advocates of equality such as feminists, homosexuals and ethnic minorities, who proved able for the most part to hold on to the advances made since the 1960s.

> ### Work together
> Debate the extent of the improvements in the status of ethnic minorities and women. One of you should take a positive stance, the other a negative stance.

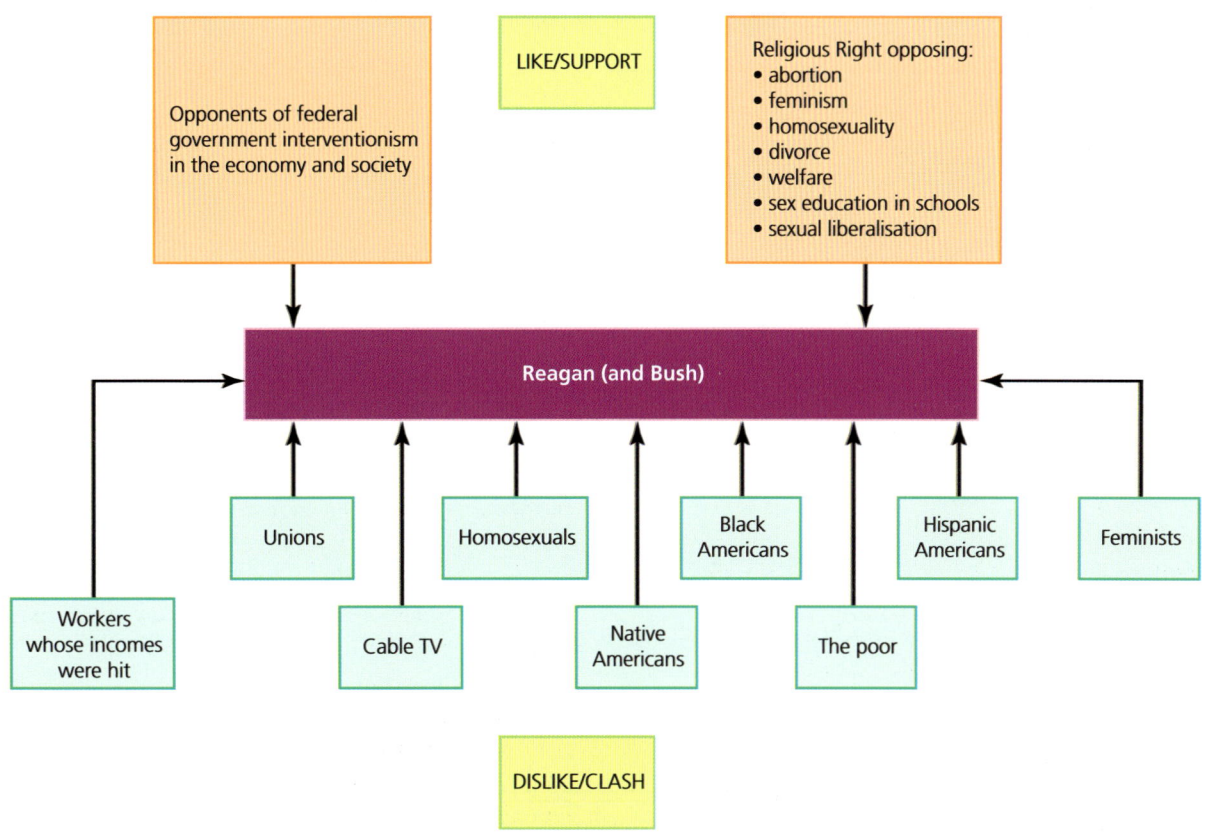

▲ Summary diagram: Republican dominance and its opponents, 1981–92.

Key Topic 4 Republican dominance and its opponents, 1981–92

Chapter summary

- President Reagan's economic and deregulation policies favoured business and impacted adversely upon workers and their families.
- Reagan tripled the federal government deficit through his expenditure on defence and tax cuts for the wealthy.
- The Religious Right voted for Reagan and George H.W. Bush in the hope that they would promote their conservative social agenda.
- The Religious Right opposed abortion, divorce, welfare, working women, homosexuals, drugs, sexual liberalisation, and sex and violence in popular culture.
- Some young people subscribed to a disaffected youth culture, which challenged conservatism over issues such as sexual and social freedoms, drug-taking and race.
- Technology affected culture, generating more options for individual choice in entertainment.
- The AIDS crisis generated a national debate on homosexuality and exacerbated the culture wars.
- The rights of women, ethnic minorities and homosexuals had increased by 1992, but conservative opposition was strong and threatened regression.
- Generally, women and ethnic minorities remained economically, politically and socially inferior in status to white males.

Recommended reading

Michael Schaller, *Right Turn: American Life in the Reagan–Bush Era, 1980–1993* (Oxford University Press, 2007). A lively and detailed account of these years.

Michael Schaller and George Rising, *The Republican Ascendancy: American Politics, 1968–2001* (Harlan Davidson, 2002). A very clear explanation of the beliefs, policies and actions of Reagan, Bush and the Religious Right.

Stephen Tuck, *We Ain't What We Ought to Be: The Black Freedom Struggle from Emancipation to Obama* (Belknap Press of Harvard University, 2010). Students usually find Tuck one of the most accessible of academic historians. This book is an interesting read and a good survey of black history and the most recent research on it.

Section A: Essay technique

Evaluating the sources

Evaluating the sources is essential to doing well in the exam. It means working out how far the sources contain evidence that is useful to a historian doing a specific task.

There are different levels of evaluation, which are rewarded to different extents.

First, your source evaluation must be relevant to the question:
- Source evaluation that is not clearly linked to the question will be awarded marks in the lower levels.
- Sources evaluation which is clearly relevant to the question will be awarded marks in the higher levels.

Second, there is the issue of the criteria you use to evaluate the sources (see table).

Level 1	**No criteria** – evaluation is extremely superficial; it does not relate to any criteria.
Level 2	**Questionable criteria** – evaluation is based on a criteria, but the criteria is invalid, simplistic or poorly understood.
Level 3	**Formulaic criteria** – evaluation is based on a discussion of the nature, origin and purpose (NOP) of the source.
Level 4/5	**Valid criteria** – at this level responses will use criteria that reflect the kind of source and the kind of specific task that the question focusses on. In this sense the evaluation will be tailored to the question. At Level 4 the criteria will not be applied rigorously. At Level 5 the criteria will be applied rigorously.

> Imagine you are answering the following question:
>
> How far could the historian make use of Sources 1 and 2 (page 480) to investigate attitudes towards the role of women in the 1980s?

Activity: AS-style questions

1. Why is Source 1 valuable to the historian for an enquiry into the status of women in the 1980s?
2. How much weight do you give the evidence of Source 2 (page 480) for an enquiry into attitudes to women in America in the 1980s?

Source 1 Extract from Susan Faludi, *Backlash: The Undeclared War Against American Women* (Broadway Books, 1991). Faludi wrote a great deal about feminism in the 1980s. Here, she explores how Hollywood reacted to the social conservatism of the 1980s and portrayed strong or complex women unfavourably, particularly in the movie *Fatal Attraction* (1987).

'Punch the bitch's face in', a moviegoer shouts ... 'Kick her ass', another male voice pleads from the shadows. The theatre in suburban San Jose, California, [has] every seat taken, for this Monday night showing of *Fatal Attraction* in October 1987. The story of a single career woman who seduces and nearly destroys a happily married man has played to a full house here every night since its arrival six weeks earlier...

'I don't get it really', says Sabrina Hughes, a high-school student who works the Coke machine and finds the adults' behaviour 'very weird' ... 'Sometimes I like to sneak into the theatre in the last 20 minutes of the movie. All these men are screaming, "Beat that bitch! Kill her off now!" The women, you never hear them say anything. They are all just sitting there, real quiet.'

Hollywood joined the backlash ... [and followed] the 'trends' the eighties media flashed at independent women – and reflected them back at American moviegoers ... 'I'm 36 years old!' Alex Forrest, the homicidal single career woman of *Fatal Attraction*, moans. 'It may be my last chance to have a child!' ... Rising financial insecurity ... fostered Hollywood's conformism and timidity.

Source 2 Extract from interviews with Adrian Lyne, the British-born director of the Hollywood movie *Fatal Attraction* (1987) (quoted in Susan Faludi, *Backlash: The Undeclared War Against American Women*, Broadway Books, 1991). Here, Lyne expresses satisfaction that his movie was the second-top-grossing film of 1987 in the United States and that his wife has never worked.

> It's amazing what an audience-participation film it's turned out to be. Everybody's yelling and shouting and really getting into it. This [*Fatal Attraction*] is a film everyone can identify with. Everyone knows a girl like Alex … [Unmarried career women] are sort of overcompensating for not being men. It's sad, you know, because it kind of doesn't work … You hear feminists talk, and the last ten, twenty years you hear women talking about fucking men rather than being fucked, to be crass about it. It's kind of unattractive, however liberated and emancipated it is. It kind of fights the whole wife role, the whole childbearing role. Sure you got your career and your success, but you are not fulfilled as a woman …
>
> My wife has never worked. She is the least ambitious person I've ever met. She is a terrific wife. She hasn't the slightest interest in doing a career. She kind of lives this with me, and it's a terrific feeling. I come home and she's there.

Simplistic source analysis

Having read the sources, it seems clear that Adrian Lyne and his movie are hostile towards feminism. So, you could say that 'Adrian Lyne is biased against feminism'. However, this would be a low-level response, because it is not clear why you consider Source 2 biased. Additionally, it is not clear how this statement answers the question.

You could say that 'when the sources are talking about a movie, they are not useful – there was no Alex Forrest and these events did not happen'. However, that would be based on questionable criteria; although *Fatal Attraction* was 'only' a movie, millions of Americans saw it. The fact that it was the year's second-highest grosser and that large-scale 'audience participation' occurred suggests that some members of the audience did not find what some considered to be its antifeminist theme unacceptable. So, the criteria that 'it is only a movie' is not appropriate to the sources.

Based on this, here are two basic tips:
- Avoid simply saying 'this source is biased'. Statements like this are very simplistic and are therefore unlikely to get you a good mark.
- Avoid assuming that the content of popular culture (such as movies) does not constitute useful evidence for our period.

Nature, origin and purpose

One way of evaluating the sources is to ask questions about their nature, origin and purpose:
- Nature: what type of source is this?
- Origin: when and where does the source come from?
- Purpose: why did the author write the source?

This approach is a good place to start. However, it can lead to formulaic responses, which are unlikely to gain top marks.

Evaluating sources in their own terms

The best way of evaluating sources is to try to understand them in their own terms. Reading the sources in the context of the time is a good way of evaluating their usefulness. By situating the sources in their context, we can argue the following:

- First, the sources are useful in that both present the socially conservative attitudes towards the role of women that became prominent in the United States in the Reagan era. In both sources, there is evidence of male antipathy towards 'independent women'. In this age of the Religious Right, there was considerable opposition to 'career women' like Alex Forrest and there were men like Adrian Lyne who preferred a 'terrific wife' who 'hadn't the slightest interest in doing a career'. The film's popularity, with 'every seat taken' and enthusiastic 'audience participation', suggests that the movie's unpleasant, frustrated career woman theme resonated with audience attitudes – or at least with the attitudes of some males.
- Second, both sources usefully remind us that not everyone in 1987 was a social conservative who felt that the role of a woman should be that of homemaker. Sabrina's comment that the women 'are all just sitting there, real quiet', suggests that there might be a difference in the sexes' attitudes. That seems to be confirmed by the author of Source 1 (page 479) – while she does not reveal her attitude towards women in this extract, the title of her book (*Undeclared War*) suggests some sympathy for women who faced this hostile attitude to any 'strong and complex' behaviour.
- Third, there are limitations in the usefulness of the sources. By no means all Americans went to the movies and it may be that those Americans who did go to see *Fatal Attraction* were those most likely to sympathise with the film's attitude to women. At the time this movie was made, organisations such as the NOW were successfully litigating against gender discrimination in employment and equal employment opportunities had considerable support in the federal government. This provides us with the main argument that these sources are not really useful for the historian investigating attitudes toward the role of women in the 1980s; neither source covers the attitude of those who felt, like Betty Friedan, that women should be free to play the economic and social role of their choice.

Having read the advice on evaluating the sources, try to evaluate the sources below in order to formulate an answer to the following question.

> **How far could the historian make use of Sources 3 and 4 together to investigate the impact of successful black Americans in the period 1981–92?**

Source 3 Extract from *Out of Bounds* (Zebra Books, 1989), the autobiography of Jim Brown, a record-breaking football player in the NFL, 1957–65. Here, he expresses his frustration with contemporary black athletes' attitude toward less fortunate black Americans.

> When I look at the black stars today, I wonder if they ever study history. How do they think they got the position they're in? Blacks who came before them paved the way ... A lot of them ... spoke out, provoked some thought, took some damn chances, instead of saying, 'Hey, I got mine. Everything is cool.' If we had done that, the guys today would be starting from scratch.
>
> And that is my crucial point: it's thirty years later, but everything is not cool. If blacks start taking their gains for granted, future generations will have serious trouble ... I want them to wake up. To look around, realise the struggle is only beginning ... I look at athletes today, black and white ... They're Very Nice, Very Rote, everyone says they're Wonderful. Maybe so. But I can't help thinking they're not that wonderful. They won't say a word about South Africa [*]. It's the worst country there is. They have apartheid. They're terrorists, killing people in the name of white superiority. These Wonderful Guys, particularly when they're at the peak of their visibility, are the ones who can get people's attention. Why don't they speak up?

[*] At this time, white South Africans dominated South Africa's politics and economy, and the social inferiority of South Africa's black majority was enshrined in law through a system of racial segregation known as apartheid.

Source 4 Extract from Reverend Jesse Jackson's address to the Democratic National Convention, San Francisco, 17 July 1984. Jackson's 1984 campaign for the Democratic presidential nomination won black Democrat votes and also had considerable white Democrat support. Here, he challenges black ghetto youths to be optimistic and ambitious. Quoted in Clayborne Carson *et al.* (editor), *The Eyes on the Prize Civil Rights Reader*, Penguin, 1991, page 708.

> I have a message for our youth. I challenge them to put hope in their brains and not dope in their veins. I told them that like Jesus, I, too, was born in the slum, and just because you are born in the slum does not mean the slum is born in you, and you can rise above it if your mind is made up. I told them in every slum there are two sides. When I see a broken window, that is the slummy side. Train some youth to become a glazier; that is the sunny side. When I see a missing brick, that is the slummy side. Let that child in the union and become a brick mason and build; that is the sunny side. When I see a missing door, that is the slummy side. Train some youth to become a carpenter; that is the sunny side. And when I see the vulgar words and hieroglyphics of destitution on the walls, that's the slummy side. Train some youth to become a painter, an artist; that is the sunny side.

Activity: Evaluating the sources

1. Having read Sources 3 and 4, try to put them in context by answering the following questions:
   (a) What statistics demonstrate the success of black American sports stars in the years 1981–92?
   (b) To which debate are the sources contributing?
2. Now try to evaluate the usefulness of the sources by answering the following questions:
   (a) What do the sources suggest about the impact of successful black Americans?
   (b) How similar and different are their arguments?
   (c) How far do the sources reflect the full range of debate over the impact of successful black Americans in the period 1981–92?
3. Summarise the extent to which the sources are useful to the historian studying the impact of successful black Americans in the period 1981–92. Make sure you deal with the ways in which they are useful and the limits of their usefulness.

Reaching an overall judgement

Having understood, contextualised and evaluated the sources, you should finish your essay with an overall judgement. Reaching a supported overall judgement is an important part of doing well in Section A. Your judgement in Section A is similar to the judgement that you should reach in the other sections of the exam (see page vii). However, in Section A, your judgement should be based on an evaluation of the evidence offered by the sources.

Your judgement should:
- clearly answer the question
- be supported by weighing the evidence of the sources.

In addition to this, the very best essays will distinguish between the levels of certainty of the different aspects of the conclusion.

Imagine you are answering the question above on page 481.

Having already read the sources and evaluated them in their context as you did in the activity on page 481, it is possible to reach the following overall conclusion. This is a high-level conclusion as it focusses on the question, reaches a supported judgement and discusses the different levels of certainty of the different claims it makes.

The conclusion opens with a clear focus on the question

Here the usefulness of the sources is considered in the light of the careers of the two authors.

The evidence of both sources is weighed in the light of the values and concerns of the society from which it is drawn in order to reach a judgement.

> Taken together, Sources 3 and 4 are useful to the historian as they show a range of ways in which successful black people impacted on American society in the period 1984–89. First is the obvious fact that Source 3 is written by a sportsman turned writer, whereas Source 4 is a speech from a senior figure within the Democratic Party – one of the two parties of government in the US. But more than this a historian can infer that both have a wide social impact. Jim Brown's autobiography clearly addresses politics and history as well as sport. Equally, Jackson's speech shows the breadth of his impact. Jackson was born in the South, yet his speech focuses on the experience of black people in the slums. From the description he gives the historian can infer that he is discussing ghettos in the North, no doubt reflecting his experience in SCLC's 1967 Chicago campaign. Source 3 claims that black sports stars no longer have a political impact. However, read in context, this may not be the case. During the Reagan years mainstream culture became more individualistic. Black sports stars might not have been talking about politics in the 1980s, but the source recognises they are still stars 'at the peak of their visibility', indicating that they have a significant media profile. In this sense Source 3 implies that black sports stars in the 1980s had a different impact to the stars of the previous generation rather than no impact at all. Finally, taken together the two sources have one major limitation: neither gives any clue to the impact of successful black women in the 1980s. Therefore, while the sources are useful to a historian as evidence of the breadth of black men's social impact, the sources are much less useful in terms of the light they shed on the cultural impact of successful black women.

The conclusion distinguishes between different levels of certainty, beginning with what is obvious and moving to what can be inferred.

An inference about the meaning of Source 4 is linked to the context of Jackson's background, civil rights work and the general distinction between conditions in the North and the South.

Finally, the conclusion considers a major limitation of the two sources and reaches an overall judgement reflecting the balance of the argument.

Work together

Conclusions are made up of a series of claims. A claim is a statement, in this case about the usefulness of the sources for investigating the impact of successful black Americans in the period 1981–92. In the example conclusion above:

1 Count the number of claims made in the conclusion.
2 Do you agree on the number of claims? If not, discuss your different views and try to resolve the disagreement.
3 The different claims deal with a series of issues that are not all certain. List the words and phrases used to describe the different degrees of certainty.
4 Did you both spot the same words and phrases?

Use the list and your discussion to make a note of how you could improve your writing.

Imagine you are answering the following question and carry out the activity on page 484:

> How far could the historian make use of Sources 5 and 6 to investigate the culture wars of the 1980s?

Source 5 Extracts from statements to Congress at hearings on whether records should be labelled with warnings about sexually explicit, violent or otherwise disturbing (to some) content in order to protect children. Here, Senator Paula Hawkins, and Susan Baker and Tipper Gore of the Parents Music Resource center, express concern and suggest remedies (quoted in Robert Dallek, *John F. Kennedy: An Unfinished Life, 1917–1963*, Penguin, 2003):

> [Statement of Senator Paula Hawkins] Much has changed since Elvis' seemingly innocent times. Subtleties, suggestions, and innuendo have given way to … descriptions of often violent sexual acts, drug taking, and flirtations with the occult.
>
> [She showed album covers, including heavy metal band WASP's *Animal (F**K LIKE A BEAST)*, and Van Halen's 'Hot for Teacher' video.]
>
> … I still hear art is art, and in America artists are supposed to be free to express themselves …
>
> [Statement of Susan Baker of the PMRC] Some say there is no cause for concern. We believe there is. Teen pregnancies and teenage suicide rates are at epidemic proportions today … Rape is up seven percent … There certainly are many causes for these ills in our society, but it is our contention that the pervasive messages aimed at children [in recordings] which promote and glorify suicide, rape, sadomasochism, and so on, have to be numbered among the contributing factors.
>
> [Statement of Tipper Gore of the PMRC] We are asking the recording industry to voluntarily assist parents who are concerned by placing a warning label on music products inappropriate for younger children due to explicit sexual or violent lyrics … A voluntary labelling is not censorship … [The PMRC] is not advocating any federal intervention or legislation whatsoever.

Source 6 Extract from the statement of Frank Zappa before Congress, in the September 1985 hearings on record labelling (quoted in Robert Dallek, *John F. Kennedy: An Unfinished Life, 1917–1963*, Penguin, 2003). Zappa was a critically acclaimed and versatile musician, equally at home with rock or classical music. He was a passionate believer in free speech, and highly critical of contemporary society and politics. Here, he gives his opinion of the PMRC:

> The PMRC proposal is an ill-conceived piece of nonsense which fails to deliver any real benefits to children, infringes the civil liberties of people who are not children, and promises to keep the courts busy for years, dealing with the interpretational and enforcemental problems inherent in the proposal's design … The PMRC's demands are the equivalent of treating dandruff by decapitation.
>
> No one has forced Mrs Baker or Mrs Gore to bring Prince or Sheena Easton into their homes. Thanks to the Constitution, they are free to buy other forms of music for their children. Apparently, they insist on purchasing the works of contemporary recording artists in order to support the personal illusion of [their right to control the composer or performer] … Taken as a whole, the complete list of PMRC demands reads like an instruction manual for some sinister kind of 'toilet training programme' to house-break all composers and performers because of the lyrics of a few.

Activity: AS-style questions

1. Why is Source 5 valuable to the historian for an enquiry into American attitudes to the influence of popular culture on America in the 1980s?
2. How much weight do you give the evidence of Source 6 for an enquiry into American attitudes to the influence of popular music during the 1980s?

Activity: Write your own conclusion

1 Read the question, the sources and the information about the sources on page 483.
2 Put the sources in context:
   (a) What is the significance of the location of those making statements in the sources?
   (b) What debate or debates are the sources contributing to?
   (c) How far do the sources agree about warning labels on records?
   (d) Why did the Senate hold these hearings?
3 Read the question again.
   (a) Next, write a series of bullet points outlining:
      - the aspects of the sources that are useful for answering the question
      - the aspects of the sources that are less useful.
   (b) Then produce a summary of the extent to which the sources provide useful evidence concerning the culture wars of the 1980s.
   (c) Now write the conclusion, remembering:
      - You need to weigh the evidence, and therefore you should use words that help you to do that, such as 'clearly', 'however' and 'nonetheless'.
      - You should weigh the sources *together*, rather than separately. Make sure you use words and phrases that make it clear that this is what you are doing – for example, 'both sources' or 'neither source'.
      - You should try to specify how certain you are about your various concluding claims. Look at the example of a conclusion you have just read and try to use similar words and phrases to show which of your concluding claims are certain and which are less definite.

Work together

Having completed your conclusion, swap it with a partner. Consider:

1 How far did you agree on the context of the sources?
2 How far did you agree on the usefulness of the sources?
3 Which conclusion most effectively weighed the evidence of the sources? How was this achieved?
4 Did both conclusions really consider the sources *together*? How could you improve this aspect of your writing?
5 Which conclusion most effectively expressed the different degrees of certainty? How was this achieved?
6 Which conclusion most effectively focussed on the question?

Use this discussion to make notes on how you can improve your Section A technique.

Section B: Essay technique

Argument, counter-argument and resolution

The highest marks in Section B of the exam are available for sustained analysis. One way of achieving this is to write an essay that develops a clear argument, then a counter-argument and finally reaches a resolution. This approach is outlined in the activities that support Paper 1 (see pages 116, 129 and 153). This kind of structure is equally applicable to Paper 2 Section B.

Activity: Argument, counter-argument and resolution

Imagine you are answering the following question:

To what extent were the campaigns of the Religious Right successful?

1. Read the question and work out what type of question it is (see page 384).
2. Make a plan that is appropriate to the specific question. Rather than simply picking four relevant factors, develop an argument, a counter-argument and a resolution to the argument.
3. Add three pieces of detail to support each aspect of your essay. Remember, use the detail that best supports the argument you are creating.
4. Write an introduction that sets out the essential aspects of your argument, counter-argument and resolution.
5. Now write a conclusion to the essay.
   - Start by asserting an overall judgement.
   - Support this by writing an evaluative summary of your argument, counter-argument and resolution.
   - Summarise your overall judgement in the final sentence.

Work together

Having written your introduction and conclusion, swap them with a partner. Consider:

1. Did you agree on what type of question you were dealing with? If not, discuss it and work out who was right.
2. Whose plan set out the most compelling overall argument?
3. Which introduction most clearly set out the key claims of the essay?
4. Which conclusion best summarised and evaluated the argument, counter-argument and resolution?
5. What can you learn from each other's work?

Use these questions to feed back to each other and improve your essay technique.

Question practice

1. 'The economy, society and politics of the United States were revolutionised in the Reagan era (1981–89).' How far do you agree with this statement?
2. How accurate is it to say that, in the years 1981–89, the Religious Right succeeded in promoting traditional values? **AS**
3. To what extent did the status of women (you could substitute Native Americans or ethnic minorities or black Americans) change between 1955 and 1992 (you could substitute between 1981 and 1992)?

GLOSSARY

Paper 1: Britain transformed, 1918–97: Themes

1973 oil crisis Reduction in oil production and raising of prices by the Organization of Petroleum Exporting Countries (OPEC) in October 1973; they wanted to punish Europe and America for supporting their enemy, Israel, in the 1973 Yom Kippur War. This had a devastating effect on Western economies, which were dependent on supplies of cheap oil.

Abdication Resignation of a monarch; specifically relating here to the resignation of Edward VIII in 1936.

Affiliated members Trade union members who support the Labour Party through the donation of part of their membership dues to the party.

Anarchist Person who does not believe in organised government.

Appeasement The policy of offering concessions to aggressive states to avoid conflict; specifically relating here to the policy of seemingly giving in to Hitler during the late 1930s in the hope he would be satisfied with his existing gains.

Armistice Ceasefire coming into force on 11 November 1918 to end the hostilities during the First World War.

Artisan working class Skilled, educated workers who could command better wages and had a higher social status than unskilled labourers.

At the point of delivery At the time one receives medical treatment.

Attendance allowance Allowance for those looking after people who need constant care.

Austerity Name given to the period of continued rationing and shortages after the Second World War.

Balance of payments The difference in value between imports and exports. If a country is importing more than it exports, it had a balance of payments deficit.

Battle of Britain Aerial Second World War battle over Britain between the RAF and German *Luftwaffe*.

Black market Illegal buying and selling.

Black Panthers Radical black paramilitary group of the 1960s and 1970s.

British Medical Association (BMA) Professional organisation representing doctors and surgeons.

British Transport Commission Government body responsible for administering the country's transport network.

Budget deficit When a government spends more than it receives in income.

C1s The category for the skilled working classes in sociological criteria.

Child-centred learning Learning based on the psychology of how a child learns and how to engage him/her in active involvement in learning.

Child Poverty Action Group Pressure group that campaigns against poverty.

Citizen's arrest Arrest by a citizen as opposed to a policeman.

Coalition Merging of different political parties to form a government.

Cold War From c.1946 to c.1987, the USA and the Soviet Union were antagonists in a war that was 'cold' in that neither directly attacked the other. Their enmity was caused by opposing ideologies. The USA believed in a multi-party state with a capitalist economy, while the communist USSR favoured a single-party state and a state-controlled economy.

Collective security An alliance of nations pledged to defend one another against aggressors.

Collectivist Someone who believes in the welfare of the community over that of the individual.

Communism Political philosophy that favours a state-controlled economy and the equal distribution of wealth among the population.

Conscription Compulsory military service for a period of time.

Consumer credit Credit available for the purchase of consumer goods.

Consumerism The pursuit and acquisition of consumer goods.

Corporal punishment Physical punishment – for example, caning in schools.

Corporatism Organisation of society on behalf of common as opposed to individual interests.

Cultural assimilation Process by which an outsider adopts the majority lifestyle and values.

Currency reserves Foreign countries and foreign banks often keep large quantities of each other's currencies. This might be in the form of bank notes or debt issued by the government such as treasury bonds (the government equivalent of an IOU). The more in debt a country is, the more power a holder of these reserves can have over it. If all the reserves are sold in a short space of time, it will cause the value of that currency to rapidly decrease, having a damaging effect on the economy of the country it is issued in.

Deferential Term given to the traditional respect shown by lower members of society for those in classes above them.

Demobilisation The return of conscripted soldiers to civilian life at the end of the war.

Direct grant schools Schools directly funded by the government.
Direct taxation Taxes taken directly from pay packets.
Disarmament Getting rid of weapons and military forces.
Dole Unemployment benefit paid for by the taxpayer.
Dominions Self-governing former colonies that nevertheless retained close ties to Britain.
EEC The European Economic Community, the trading block of European states that eventually became the EU.
Emergency Powers Act Passed in 1920, it gave the government the right to use the powers in the Defence of the Realm Act during peacetime but required parliament to meet before it was implemented.
English Bar Register of lawyers in England.
Episiotomy Operation to aid difficult childbirth.
Etonians People who go to Eton Public School.
Eugenics Discredited theory of racial and class inequalities.
Fabians/Fabian Society Organisation of moderate socialists.
Fascist Member of a political movement characterised by extreme nationalism and racism.
First-past-the-post Election system where the candidate with the most votes is elected irrespective of whether he/she has a majority of votes cast.
Flapper Term used to describe fun-loving, unmarried young women in the 1920s.
Free trade Trade without import and export duties.
Full employment An economic goal for unemployment to be virtually non-existent and almost all the potential workforce employed.
GDP Gross Domestic Product: one way to measure the wealth of a country based on the value of how much it produces.
Gendered Relating to gender; specifically here that many occupations were reserved for men, and women found it very difficult to be employed in them.
General strike A strike of the key workers in a national workforce, bringing most of the economy to a halt.
German zone of occupation Area directly occupied by the Germans during the Second World War.
Gestapo Secret police in Nazi Germany.
GNP Gross National Product: the aggregate value of the goods and services produced in a country.
Gold Standard A fixed exchange rate for currencies based on the value of gold.
Great Depression The severe economic downturn in the early to mid-1930s resulting in mass unemployment.
Great Exhibition An exhibition in 1951 celebrating British manufacture.
Heavy industry Industries such as coal mining, iron and steel.
Home Rule Self-government.

Honours list The bi-annual award of knighthoods and peerages to public figures.
Hung parliament Where no single party has a parliamentary majority.
IMF International Monetary Fund, founded to lend money to countries in financial trouble.
Incitement to mutiny A criminal offence where one encourages soldiers not to obey orders or to rebel against their officers.
Indirect discrimination When a stipulation – for example, in a job interview – is applied to everyone but in reality could only be met by a small minority of applicants.
Infant mortality Death rate of small children.
Injunction Court order banning people from doing specific things.
Interest rate The cost of borrowing money.
Knighthood An award bestowed by the crown. Knights are referred to as 'Sir'.
Labour exchanges Job centres where people signed on for unemployment relief and which provided details of job vacancies.
Labour movement A general term for members of the working class engaged in politics, either in trade unions or political parties.
League of Coloured People British civil rights organisation founded in 1931 with the aim of racial equality throughout the world.
League of Nations International organisation established after the end of the First World War to keep peace between nations; a forerunner to the United Nations.
Left wing Political tendency supporting ideas such as socialism or more social welfare.
Lend-Lease Agreement Agreement by which the USA 'lent' Britain the materiel to fight the Second World War on the understanding that it would be repaid afterwards.
Light industries/manufacturing Production of goods such as household appliances.
Local government register List of people eligible to vote in local elections.
Locked out Locked out of one's place of work by one's employer over an industrial dispute.
Lower middle class People such as semi-professionals – for example, clerks and craftsmen.
Luftwaffe German air force.
Marginal tax The percentage of tax applied to the range of one's income.
Mass Observation Organisation that surveyed public attitudes during the mid-twentieth century.
Mass picketing Protests outside places of work where strikes are taking place, designed to prevent non-striking employees from getting into work.

Materialism The prioritising of material objects and consumer spending; emphasis on the value of possessions.

Maternal mortality rates Death rates of women in childbirth.

Means test An assessment of a person's income, carried out before they were entitled to any welfare payments. Claimants who were considered to have sufficient incomes to survive on were not eligible.

Merchant shipping Commercial shipping – for example, freighters.

Meritocratic Promotion based on ability.

Middle classes White-collar and professional classes.

Miners' institutes Social clubs for miners in the small mining towns in Wales and England.

Ministry of Information The official government ministry that communicated essential information to the public about rationing, bombing, blackouts and war work.

Minority government Where the ruling party has more seats than any one other political party, but can still be outvoted by a coalition of opposition parties. A minority government must either form a coalition or have agreements with other parties to vote its legislation through parliament.

Mixed economy An economy composed of private enterprise and nationalised industries.

Moderate left Socialists who favour social reform and equality, but do not advocate revolution or radical change to achieve them.

Monetarism The economic belief that the goal of government should be to keep inflation to a minimum. This can be achieved by reducing the amount of money in circulation in the economy. Cuts to welfare and an increase in interest rates are ways that governments can reduce the money supply, but this often leads to an increase in unemployment.

Morganatic marriage Marriage where the offspring cannot inherit.

Motion of no confidence A vote in parliament against the government. If the vote is passed, the government normally has little choice but to resign.

National Executive Committee of the Labour Party Governing body of the Labour Party.

National Government A coalition of political parties that places national interest above party politics. Britain saw a series of National Governments between 1931 and 1945, which were largely dominated by the Conservatives.

National Health Insurance Insurance taken directly from pay to provide sickness benefit if necessary.

National Minority Movement (NMM) Established by the Communist Party of Great Britain in 1924. Its goals were to introduce more radical, revolutionary ideas into the moderate trade union movement. Its first conference in January 1925 included 615 delegates, who represented over half a million workers.

Nationalisation State ownership of industrial and commercial concerns.

Nazi Germany Germany ruled by Hitler, 1933–45.

Official Secrets Act Law by which information sensitive to British security may not be divulged.

Paris Peace Conference The meeting of Allied war leaders at the end of the First World War to decide the shape of the post-war world.

Passenger-kilometres The number of passengers multiplied by the distance travelled.

Paternalist A hierarchical view of society that sees the upper classes as benign 'parents' to the lower classes, knowing what is right for them and acting in their best interests; and where employers are concerned for the welfare of their employees in a fatherly fashion.

Peerage The title of 'Lord' with a seat in the House of Lords.

Piece rate Special rate of pay based on how much is produced.

Political consciousness Awareness of political issues.

Political levy Charge to union members that support the Labour Party.

Poor Law guardians Local committees that managed the Poor Laws and workhouses.

Post-war consensus The broad agreement on issues between all the main political parties in the post-war period.

Poverty line The line based on economic criteria between those in poverty and those not.

Pre-fabricated homes Homes that are manufactured on site from ready-made units.

Preventative healthcare The practice of helping patients to manage their diet, fitness and overall wellbeing to prevent illness from occurring in the first place.

Private member's bill Bill brought by MPs in a personal capacity, i.e. not necessarily sponsored by their party or the government.

Public Assistance Committee The local committee appointed to administer the means test.

Public assistance institutions Former workhouses in the 1930s. Many had been converted to cater for the elderly and the sick.

Public works schemes Government job creation schemes, such as building work, designed to give the unemployed jobs.

Rastafarianism Religious sect based in the Caribbean.

Rearmament Re-arming with weapons and building up armed forces.

Recession A cyclical downturn in the economy, resulting in unemployment and economic hardship.

Repatriation Removal to one's country of origin.

Rote learning Learning facts through continual repetition.

Russian Civil War A three-year war in Russia (1918–21) following the communist seizure of power, fought between the Bolsheviks and their opponents. Britain became involved on the side of the anticommunist forces.

Russian Revolution The overthrow of the Russian Provisional government in October 1917 by the communist Bolshevik Party, resulting in civil war and a wave of terror against enemy classes (the former aristocracy and the middle class). It led to the establishment of the Soviet Union in 1922 under the communists.

Safe seats Constituencies where a particular party is most likely to be re-elected.

Second-wave feminism The women's liberation movement of the 1960s and 1970s, so called because first-wave feminism in the early twentieth century had brought political equality with the gaining of the vote but little progress in other spheres.

Sedition Treason against the government.

Self-financing A scheme that is self-financing does not normally require money from the government or taxpayer to make it work.

Sexual revolution A period of rapid change in attitudes and beliefs about sexual behaviour and morality.

Shop stewards Local union representatives in workplaces, who grew increasingly powerful during the post-war period because they could call spontaneous strike action.

Short-hour contracts Part-time working.

Siege economy An economy in which imports and exports are controlled and export of capital is limited – for example, to protect the value of the currency.

Skiffle A British version of 1950s rock 'n' roll, modelled on Elvis Presley and Chuck Berry.

Social mobility Movement between different classes.

Socialist An individual who believes that the wealth generated by capitalism should be evenly and fairly distributed among the working people who create it.

Soviet Union In 1922 Russia became known as the Union of Soviet Socialist Republics, the USSR or the Soviet Union.

Speculative boom Boom in investment in the hope that the economy will grow but not based, for example, on actual orders.

Stagflation A compound of 'stagnation' and 'inflation', when prices rise despite a slowdown in the economy.

State of emergency Emergency or crisis situation announced by the government.

Stop-go economics Term given to the economic policy of the Conservative government 1951–64, which involved adopting measures to slow growth when the economy grew too quickly and then as it slowed relaxing them to enable it to grow again.

Superpower rivalries Post-war rivalry between the USA and the Soviet Union.

Sympathetic strikes Strikes undertaken by unions who are not involved directly in the dispute but who show solidarity with workers who are.

System-built Method of building from pre-fabricated components.

Tariffs Custom duties.

Technocratic class Technical experts.

Think-tank Group of experts who come up with new ideas.

Tick An informal agreement with a local shopkeeper to have goods and pay for them later.

Total war The mobilisation of the entire population to win the war.

Trade union movement Membership and organisation of trade unions, designed to improve members' working conditions and pay.

Trades Union Congress (TUC) Organisation of different trades unions to speak and act on their behalf.

Treaty of Versailles Treaty signed in July 1919 to end the First World War.

U-boats German submarines.

Unemployment insurance Money taken out of wages to provide an income in the event of subsequent unemployment.

United Nations International peacekeeping organisation founded in 1945; successor to the League of Nations.

Unofficial strikes Strikes not sanctioned by the union leadership.

US Congress Legislative body of the USA.

USSR See Soviet Union.

Victorian Poor Laws Social welfare laws during the Victorian period, based largely on the workhouse.

Wall Street The financial centre in New York.

Welfare institutions Government and charitable organisations responsible for distributing benefits to the poor.

White Paper Document outlining government policy on an issue.

Women's liberation movement Movement advocating female equality in all areas of life.

Women's suffrage movement The campaign in the late nineteenth and early twentieth century to secure votes for women in Britain.

Workhouses Prison-like institutions that destitute individuals and families were sent to and given shelter in return for working.

Paper 1: Britain transformed, 1918–97: Historical interpretations

Apartheid A system of racial segregation, in which people were separated and forced to live apart. Only people legally classified as 'white' were entitled to citizenship rights.

Autoerotic asphyxiation The sexual practice of restricting your own breathing whilst masturbating in order to heighten sexual arousal.

Basic rate of tax The lowest rate of income tax.

Bill of Rights A law that legally defines the rights of citizens, making them defensible in courts.

Block vote A large number of votes that are cast by one person or one organization.

Budget deficit The annual debt of a government.

Charter '88 A pressure group founded in 1988 to campaign for greater protection of civil liberties in the UK.

Closed shop Where people in a particular industry must belong to a union.

Consensus politician A member of the government who believes in the post war political and economic consensus that lasted from the 1940s to the 1970s.

Constitution The fundamental rules of government, which define the powers of the different parts of government and the rights and duties of citizens. A constitution can be partially or wholly written, or entirely unwritten.

Conventional forces The parts of the armed forces that are non-nuclear.

Co-ownership An economic arrangement where workers own shares in their business, allowing them to play a role in directing the company.

Corporation tax A tax on business.

Deflationary Policies that tend to reduce government spending.

Deregulation The process of abolishing or weakening the rules that govern the behavior of organisations, usually businesses.

Development Corporations government organisations designed to stimulate economic growth in specific regions or parts of the economy.

Devolution The process of decentralizing power to the regions. In the 1980s and 1990, debate about devolution referred to the transfer of powers from the government in London to democratically elected assemblies in Scotland and Wales.

Enterprise Zones Regions of the country in which the government allowed business special advantages such as lower rates of tax, in order to stimulate economic growth.

Exchange Rate Mechanism (ERM) As a member of the European Community, Britain became part of the ERM in 1979. It was a system to make the values of Europe's currencies stable in relation to one another. This was the first step towards creating a single currency, the Euro.

Falklands War A conflict between Argentina and the United Kingdom over the Falkland Islands. The conflict lasted for around 10 weeks, beginning in April 1982.

HIV Human immunodeficiency virus – the virus that causes AIDS.

Incomes strategy A policy designed to control levels of pay, usually across a number of industries or the whole economy.

Interest rate This is the cost of borrowing set by the Bank of England. If it rises, mortgages and loans become more expensive to repay. Monetarists saw it as an effective way of taking excess money out of the economy.

Internal market A mechanism designed to make the NHS function more efficiently. It divided the NHS up into purchaser and providers. In theory the arrangement was supposed to raise standards by making providers compete for business from purchasers.

Irish Republican Army (IRA) aka The Provisional IRA A paramilitary organization dedicated to ending British rule of Northern Ireland. From 1969, the IRA defended Republican areas from paramilitary attacks. In 1971 they started a bombing campaign and were designated terrorists by the British government.

LGBT (lesbian, gay, bisexual, and transgender) LGBT was a term adopted by people identifying as lesbian, gay, bisexual and transgender. The term replaced the term 'gay community' in order to emphasize the diversity of sexuality and gender identity.

Meritocratic Where people are promoted because of their skill, not their social background. In the stock market of the 1980s, many upper class traders who had once dominated the industry were forced out by educated working class stock brokers who were far better at trading.

Minimum wage The lowest legal rate of pay.

Monetarism Monetarism is the economic philosophy that the main goal of a government's economic strategy should be to bring down inflation. Monetarists believe that inflation is caused by an excess of money circulating in the economy.

National Front An extremist political party founded in 1967. The Party is committed to ending immigration of black and Asian people, and forced repatriation of Britain's black and Asian citizens. In addition to standing for election the NF organised marches and some members were associated with violence against black and Asian people.

Natural monopolies An industry that is most efficiently organised around one supplier. Water, electricity and gas are often regarded as natural monopolies as competition is difficult to organise.

Glossary

One Nation Conservatives A form of conservatism that emphasises the need for governments to act pragmatically to ensure social cohesion. One Nation Conservatives also believe that the rich have a duty to look after the interests of the poor.

Outed Usually meaning that a person preferring to keep their sexuality private has been named as gay or bisexual. 'Out' can also mean a person who has publically proclaimed their homosexuality or bisexuality, as in 'out and proud'.

Outsourcing The practice of employing another organisation to deliver services on behalf of another. During the 1980s the term was used to describe employing private companies to deliver services that had once been delivered by the government.

Owner occupation A form of home ownership in which the resident of the house owns the property.

Patriarchal society A form of social organisation in which men dominate women.

Patricians Senior members of the Conservative Party. In the context of the 1970s and 1980s Patricians tended to be associated with the One Nation wing of the party.

Picket A form of direct action in which people protest outside a place associated with their grievance.

Presidential style A type of leadership in which a leading member of the government acts like a president, without having the constitutional authority to do so. The term is often used to describe British prime ministers who work independently of their Cabinet.

Proportional representation A term used to refer to a variety of voting systems that attempt to ensure a close link between the proportion of votes cast for different political parties and the proportion of seats won.

Rates The taxes that home owners paid to the local council based on the value of their homes. A reduction in rates favoured wealthier home owners.

Secondary action Strike action in one sector of the economy in support of industrial action in another sector.

Secondary picketing Picketing of locations not directly related to the industrial dispute. For example workers in dispute with a car manufacturer might picket the car showrooms that sell the cars.

Sinn Fein Irish Republican political party that campaigns for a united Ireland. The party was associated with the IRA.

Social Chapter Also known as the European Social Charter, the Social Chapter is a European treaty guaranteeing rights to health, education and minimum standards in employment across most of Europe.

Top rate of tax The highest rate of income tax.

Trotskyites Revolutionary socialists who follow the arguments of the Russian Revolutionary Leon Trotsky. During the 1970s many small, radical Trotskyite parties emerged on the fringes of British politics.

Underclass A group of people with an extremely low social and economic status. The underclass are considered to have a lower status than the working class.

VAT Value Added Tax is a tax not on people's pay but on the things they buy. VAT is added onto the price of most household goods. Because it increases prices it can temporarily boost inflation, and it affects poorer people more than wealthier ones.

Wets Moderate Conservatives who were cautious about or critical of Thatcher's radical policies. The 'Wets' were associated with the consensus policies of Edward Heath in the period 1972–4. The 'Wets' were contrasted with the 'Drys', who supported Thatcher's radical policies.

Paper 2: The USA, 1920–55: Boom, bust and recovery

Allied powers The powers fighting Germany and its allies in the Second World War.

Allotment Policy by which each Native American family was given a plot of 160 acres to farm. This went against the traditional Native American idea of common land ownership.

Animal husbandry The breeding and raising of animals in agriculture.

Antitrust legislation Laws to break down trusts. Trusts were companies that worked together to control manufacture, supplies and prices to ensure other firms could not compete, thus guaranteeing maximum profits for themselves.

Assimilation The idea that Native Americans should adopt American lifestyles and values. Their traditional lifestyles would disappear.

Balanced budget Where government expenditure should not exceed its income.

Bankrupt When firms or individuals have insufficient money to pay their debts.

Belligerents Countries fighting in war.

Blackface Where white performers wear black makeup to portray African Americans, often in crude stereotypical fashion.

Bootleggers People who make alcohol illegally to sell.

Border states States lying between Northern and Southern ones, such as Arkansas, Maryland, Missouri and Kansas.

Brokers People who buy and sell stocks and shares.

Bull market Stock market where there is lots of confidence and lots of buying and selling.

Bureau of Indian Affairs Government agency dealing with Native Americans.

Carnegie Institute Organisation set up in 1922 for research and scientific discovery.

Cartel A group of companies agreeing to fix output and prices in order to reduce competition and maximise their profits.

Cash-and-carry The sale of goods to belligerents who are also responsible for transporting them.

Chain gangs Groups of convicts chained together while working outside the prison – for example, in digging roadside drainage ditches.

China lobby Influential group of politicians, journalists and business interests who wanted US involvement to defeat the communist government in China and restore it to non-communist rule.

Civil rights Rights for citizens such as voting, non-discrimination and equality of opportunity.

Closed shop Where people in a particular industry must belong to a union.

Cold War From c.1946 to c.1987, the USA and the Soviet Union were antagonists in a war that was 'cold' in that neither directly attacked the other. Their enmity was caused by opposing ideologies. The USA believed in a multi-party state with a capitalist economy, while the communist USSR favoured a single-party state and a state-controlled economy.

Communist A believer in economic equality and a state-controlled economy.

Conscription Where people are called up to join the armed forces.

Cross-over Where a film or piece of music is popular enough to cross from the African-American to other ethnic markets.

Deep South The Southernmost states – for example, Alabama, Florida, Georgia, Louisiana, Mississippi, North and South Carolina and Virginia – which clung to traditional ways, including racial segregation, most tenaciously.

Democrat The political party, or supporter of that party, that supports more government intervention and traditionally appeals to a wider cross-section of society than the Republicans.

Democratic Convention Meeting of delegates to decide the Democratic presidential candidate.

Domino theory A theory first elucidated in the post-war period that if one country fell to communism, its neighbours would follow, falling like a stack of dominoes.

Dow Jones Industrial Average An index showing how shares in the top 30 large companies have traded on the Wall Street stock market.

Eugenics A commonly held belief derived from spurious scientific evidence, which has since been completely discredited, that the different races were unequal and whites were superior.

Fake coonskin caps Caps very popular with children, modelled on the type of fur cap Davy Crockett is supposed to have worn.

Farmer–Labor Party Left-wing party proposing far reaching reforms such as nationalisation of public utilities and the state taking over idle factories to find work for the unemployed.

Federal taxes Taxes paid to the federal government in Washington, as opposed to local or state taxes.

Fellow traveller Name given to a suspected supporter of communism.

Feminist Someone who supports equal rights and fair opportunities for women.

Filibuster Where politicians talk endlessly until a bill they oppose runs out of time for consideration.

Fireside chats Roosevelt's radio addresses to the electorate. Such was his warmth and charisma that it felt

Glossary

like he was speaking to people in their living rooms; hence the term 'fireside chats'.

Flapper Name given to young women leading lives devoted to frivolity and enjoyment.

Fort Knox Home of the US gold reserves in Kentucky.

Free trade Trade without import or export duties.

Furlough Period of leave from the military.

Gangsterism The growth of gangs of criminals.

Government securities Bonds and bills issued by the government to raise revenue.

Grandfather clause Where people could only have the vote in a state if their grandfathers had; this was used to disenfranchise African Americans whose grandfathers would have been slaves.

Great Migration In the first half of the twentieth century, several million African Americans left the rural South, with its racially segregated public places and limited economic opportunities, for great Northern cities such as New York, Midwestern cities such as Chicago and Western cities such as Los Angeles.

Gross National Product (GNP) The total value of goods and services produced in a country.

Hire purchase The practice of buying items on credit after paying a deposit.

Hoboes People who wandered around the USA in search of work.

Holding companies Where one huge company obtains a controlling interest in smaller companies across all the levels of production, distribution and sales, in order to control the market.

Holocaust Attempted extermination of Jews and other groups by the Nazis during the Second World War.

Homemakers Mothers who stay at home to look after their families, rather than going out to work.

Insider dealing Unfair practices on the stock market – for example, brokers getting together to bring the price of stocks up or down.

Inter-state commerce Trade between different states.

Ku Klux Klan Racist group advocating white supremacy. It adopted methods of terror to intimidate other groups such as African Americans and Jews. During the 1920s it was particularly prevalent in the Southern and Midwestern states.

Labour force People in employment.

Labour unions US term for trade unions formed to look after the interests of their members.

Laissez-faire An approach where the government deliberately avoids getting involved in economic planning, thus allowing free trade to operate.

League of Women Voters Organisation founded in 1920 to help women become more involved in politics and public affairs.

Lend-Lease Scheme whereby the USA loaned war materiel initially to Britain, and later to the USSR, until the war was over.

Lynching Illegal hangings, often used by the Ku Klux Klan as a means of terror.

Management science The application of technological and scientific ideas to running a company successfully – such as time and motion where the amount of time it should take to complete a process in manufacturing is timed and subsequently monitored. The aim is to use scientifically proven methods to run the company.

Manhattan Project Code name given to the programme within the USA to develop nuclear weapons.

Market structure The way in which the capitalist system works through supply and demand.

Mass production The process of making large numbers of the same item using machinery and conveyor belts.

Means-tested benefits Where the level of welfare benefits received is based on the recipient's income.

Mid-term congressional elections Elections that take place every two years, half way through the president's four-year term of office.

Middle class The increasingly affluent social group that typically moved into the suburbs and enjoyed the post-war consumer boom. They were widely regarded as the lynchpin of 1950s society.

Military–industrial complex Term given to the relationship between the US military and the industrialists who supply it with materiel.

Moonshine Illegally manufactured alcohol.

Moratorium Term given to Hoover's offer to postpone debt repayment for 18 months.

Mortgages foreclosed Loss of home, farms etc. when mortgages could not be paid.

National Association for the Advancement of Colored People (NAACP) An organisation seeking to improve the lives of black Americans.

Nationalisation State ownership of industrial and commercial concerns.

Neutrality Acts Acts passed in the 1930s forbidding the sale of arms to any nations fighting in war.

New Left School of historians critical of the New Deal for not adopting more radical changes.

Nuclear family Family unit of father, mother and children with other family members living elsewhere.

Oil concessions Involvement in foreign oil industries on favourable terms.

On the margin On credit (specifically of the purchase of stocks and shares).

Open-market operations Buying and selling of government securities on the open market to control the monetary supply.

Opiate of the masses Device to keep the lower classes subdued, based on the analogy of opium which makes users lethargic.

Palmer raids Mass arrests of suspected revolutionaries in 1920.

Payroll tax Tax paid by employers for each of their employees.

Per capita income Income per head of the population.

Pioneer women Women who moved to live on the Western frontier of the USA in the nineteenth century.

Poll tax A tax levied on would-be voters, which made it harder for black people (who were usually poorer) to vote.

Positive discrimination Process by which members of one group are deliberately favoured over those of others.

Post-war baby boom Massive growth in the numbers of children born after the Second World War.

Post-war housing shortage The housing shortage in the USA after the Second World War, caused by the collapse of private building during the war due to shortages of materials.

Prohibition The banning of the manufacture, transportation and sale of alcohol for consumption.

Protectorate An area under US 'protection', heavily influenced by the USA.

Pump-priming Expression used to suggest government spending would lead to economic growth.

Real wages The value of wages in terms of how much they will actually buy.

Rearmament Rearming the military in preparation for a future war.

Recession Downturn in the economy.

Red Scare Attack by the US authorities who feared a communist revolution, on people suspected of left-wing sympathies.

Relief appropriations Public money earmarked for relief purposes.

Republican One of the two main political parties; they tend to favour wealth, business and a limited government role in the economy, supporting ideas such as *laissez-faire*.

Repudiating war debts Where countries ceased repaying their war debts.

Reservation An area allocated for a specific group of Native Americans to live.

Roosevelt Recession Downswing in the economy associated with Roosevelt's cutbacks in government spending in 1937.

Secondary strikes Where workers strike in support of others in an industrial dispute.

Secretary of Commerce Government minister responsible for trade.

Share-croppers Farmers who rented land and were paid by the landowners a percentage of what they produced.

Socialist economic system A system of sharing wealth more evenly with more public ownership of economic concerns.

Speakeasies Illegal clubs where alcohol was sold.

State Department Federal government department responsible for foreign affairs.

State legislatures The law-making bodies of individual states.

States' rights The rights of specific states according to the Constitution.

Stills Place where illegal alcohol was made.

Subsistence Just enough income to live on.

Tariffs Import and export duties.

Tenant farmers People who rented the land they farmed.

Time and motion A system in which production techniques are allocated set times for completion and production targets laid down on this basis.

Tourist courts Cabins for motorists to rest for the night; early motels.

Underemployment Short-time working.

US Chamber of Commerce Non-governmental organisation responsible for speaking for business in the USA.

USSR Union of Soviet Socialist Republics; the Soviet Union.

Veteran An ex-serviceman.

Voluntarism The notion that business and state government should solve the Great Depression through their own voluntary efforts.

Wage labourers People who worked for wages.

War bonds Loans to pay for the war, to be redeemed after victory.

Wards Electoral districts in the USA.

White flight The movement of white Americans away from inner-city areas and into the suburbs.

White goods Household appliances such as refrigerators and washing machines.

White supremacy The racist idea that white people are superior to members of other ethnic groups.

Work ethic The feeling that people should work hard and the unemployed should go out and find a job. It derived from the notion that how well one worked was a sign of one's worth, both personally and socially.

Yalta Conference Conference of Allied war leaders in February 1945 to discuss the post-war world. The Soviet leader Stalin insisted that eastern European countries must have governments friendly to the USSR.

'Yellow dog' clauses Clauses by which employees had to agree not to join a labour union.

Zoot suits Fashion trend favoured by Hispanic Americans during the 1940s, featuring long jackets, trousers baggy at the top and tight at the bottom, chains and wide-brimmed fedora hats.

Paper 2: The USA, 1955–92: Conformity and challenge

'A Ford not a Lincoln' Ford was saying he was not of the calibre of President Lincoln, and playing on public familiarity with cars: Fords were the cars of ordinary Americans, Lincolns were expensive, prestige cars.

Affirmative action Programme to give members of previously disadvantaged minorities a headstart in areas such as education and employment; also known as positive discrimination.

AFL-CIO (American Federation of Labor and Congress of International Organizations) The central organisational body of American labour unions.

Age of majority Age at which an American legally becomes an adult.

AIDS Acquired immunodeficiency syndrome is the result of a sexually transmitted disease. It is acquired through the exchange of bodily fluids, especially blood and semen. It strikes down the body's natural defence system, making it vulnerable to other diseases.

American Dream The belief that all Americans have the freedom and opportunity to make themselves economically successful through hard work.

American Way What Americans perceived to be their national characteristics of democracy, equality of opportunity and hard work.

Appalachian whites Many of those who lived in the Appalachian mountain range were impoverished. They were often disparagingly referred to as 'hillbillies'.

Approval rating American pollsters continually monitor the percentage of the population that approves of the performance of the president.

Balance of trade It is economically important for a country's exports to be of greater value than its imports, otherwise there is an unfavourable balance of trade that damages the nation's economy.

Black Power movement Vaguely-defined 1960s black American movement that meant different things to different people – for example, black separatism, black pride, black economic self-sufficiency, black violence, black nationalism, black political power, black domination.

Beats Young American intellectuals in the late 1950s who rejected materialism, consumerism and conformity.

Beatniks A more superficial version of a 'beat'.

Big government Republicans traditionally accuse Democrats of being the party of large-scale federal interventionism that costs money and makes government less efficient.

Blue-collar workers Persons engaged in manual labour.

Bohemian Relaxed, non-materialistic, unconventional lifestyle.

Born-again Christian A Christian who has discovered their faith or had it refreshed and revitalised by some crisis experience.

Bugs Secret listening devices to eavesdrop on others.

Bureau of Indian Affairs Federal agency that oversees Native American welfare and reservations.

Bussing The transportation of students to schools outside their neighbourhood in order to ensure that the schools are multi-racial.

Camp David Presidential mountain retreat in Maryland.

Capital gains Profit from the sale of property or an investment.

Capitalism A system of free trade and an economy unregulated by the government.

CIA (Central Intelligence Agency) Federal government agency with particular responsibility for monitoring foreign threats.

Chapters Local branches of a national movement – for example, of the AIM or the Black Panthers.

Child nutrition programmes Federal government programmes to help ensure that poor children get some decent meals.

Cold War From c.1946 to c.1987, the USA and the Soviet Union were antagonists in a war that was 'cold' in that neither directly attacked the other. However, they engaged in competition over armaments and allies. Their enmity was caused by opposing ideologies. The USA believed in a multi-party state with a capitalist economy, while the communist Soviet Union favoured a single-party state and a state-controlled economy.

Collective bargaining rights The right to form a union and negotiate with employers.

Commander-in-chief The American Constitution gives the president great potential power in wartime as head of the US armed forces.

Common situs picketing An entire construction site could be picketed even though the union's dispute might be with only one out of many contractors there.

Communism A political philosophy that favours a state-controlled economy and the equal distribution of wealth among the population.

Communist A believer in economic equality and a state-controlled economy.

Congress The American legislature (similar to Britain's Parliament), consisting of the Senate and the House of Representatives. Voters in each American state elect two Senators to sit in the Senate and several Congressmen or Congresswomen (the number depends on the size of the state's population) to sit in the House of Representatives.

Consciousness-raising Meetings of women to raise awareness of gender discrimination, common in the USA from the late 1960s.

Constant dollars To make comparisons between dates more meaningful, economists factor in changes in the cost of living or the value of the currency etc.

Constitution The rules and system by which a country's government works. The USA has a written constitution.

Consumerism Obsession with the acquisition of material goods.

Counter-culture Lifestyle and beliefs in opposition to the mainstream dominant culture, such as those of hippies.

Creationism A biblical account of the origins of the Earth and the life that is on it. Believers in creationism reject Darwinism.

Culture wars 1980s struggle between social conservatives and those with more liberal attitudes on issues such as sexuality and abortion.

Darwinism Charles Darwin promoted the theory of evolution.

Declaration of Independence In 1776, the American colonists declared their independence from Britain in a document much revered by Americans. Its declaration that 'all men are created equal' encouraged groups such as black Americans to demand equal rights.

Deep South Southernmost states of the American South, such as Mississippi, Georgia and Alabama, which were more socially and politically conservative than those in the Upper South, such as Arkansas.

De facto **segregated** Segregated in fact although not in law.

De jure **segregation** In the Southern context, the legal segregation of black and white people.

Democrat A supporter of one of the two main US political parties. The twentieth-century Democratic Party usually favoured government intervention and expenditure to help the disadvantaged.

Democratic National Committee The national co-ordinating body for the Democratize Party.

Democratic National Convention Convention to choose or confirm the Democratic Party's nomination for the presidency.

Desegregation The ending of the segregation of the races – for example, by integrating educational institutions.

Disfranchisement Being deprived of the vote.

Domestics Workers in private households – for example, cooks and maids.

Draft Compulsory call-up to serve in the nation's armed forces (known as conscription in Britain).

Duck-tail In 1950s America, hair tapered at the back of a male's head so that it resembled a duck's tail.

Entrapment When law enforcement officials create an artificial situation to entice known criminals to commit a crime and get arrested.

Equal Rights Amendment (ERA) Congress passed the ERA in 1972. Designed to ensure that women's equality in employment and education was enshrined in the American Constitution, it never became law because it was never ratified by a sufficient number of states.

Evangelist In the twentieth-century American context, some would say a more fanatical and/or enthusiastic Protestant who tended to be socially conservative and took the Bible very literally.

Executive branch The presidency is one of the three branches of the federal government. The president oversees the implementation of legislation and, as commander-in-chief, has responsibility for the armed forces and defence.

Executive powers As head of the executive branch of the US government, the president has to implement legislation through the federal bureaucracy. Although Congress has to grant the executive the money, the president has a great deal of purchasing power if, for example, he wishes to make companies with federal contracts pursue equal employment opportunities.

Fair Deal President Truman's programme to help groups such as schoolchildren, the sick and workers.

FBI (Federal Bureau of Investigation) Federal agency that deals with crime.

Federal Government The USA is a federation of many separate states (for example, the Northern state of New York and the Southern state of Alabama) that have considerable power over local issues such as voting and education. The federal government has three branches: the president (the executive), Congress (the legislature) and the Supreme Court (the judiciary).

Federal government deficit Cumulative amount by which the government has overspent over the years. Foreign investors frequently buy up the nation's debt, as the Japanese did with the US debt in the 1980s.

Federal Reserve Board Governs the Federal Reserve System, which helps implement the government's monetary policy and oversees the Federal Reserve Banks.

Feminist Advocate of equal political, social, economic and legal rights for women.

Food-stamp programme Food stamps provided by the federal government to aid the poor in feeding their families. They were piloted by President Kennedy and then became a national programme with President Johnson's Food Stamp Act (1964).

Football American football, as opposed to soccer.

Fourteenth Amendment Passed in 1868, this said that all citizens had equal protection under the law and were not to be deprived of life, liberty or property.

Franchise Big companies such as McDonald's allow individuals to open and operate a store under licence. The individual and the company share the profits.

Freedom Rides Integrated groups of civil rights activists rode together on interstate buses across the South, in defiance of and in protest against continued segregation on interstate buses.

Gay pride 1970s campaign by homosexuals to emphasise self-worth in the face of continued discrimination and prejudice.

Ghettos In the United States, impoverished areas populated by ethnic minorities.

Glass ceiling Feminists commonly spoke of an invisible barrier to the rise of women to the top positions in employment.

GNP (Gross National Product) The aggregate value of the goods and services produced in the country.

Great Migration In the first half of the twentieth century, several million black Americans left the rural South, with its racially segregated public places and limited economic opportunities, for great Northern cities such as New York, Midwestern cities such as Chicago and Western cities such as Los Angeles.

Great Society President Johnson said he wanted to create a US society free from the racism and poverty that were particularly prevalent in the urban ghettos.

Gubernatorial Pertaining to a governor – for example, of a state.

Gulf War Forces of the United States and its allies liberated Kuwait after an Iraqi invasion in 1990–91.

Happenings Large events such as concerts for members of the counter-culture.

Hash Marijuana, also known as pot and weed.

Hippies Young people (often students) in the 1960s who rejected the beliefs and fashions of the older generation and favoured communal living, free love and recreational drugs.

Hipsters Followers of non-mainstream fashions.

Hispanic Americans Residents of the United States; they or their ancestors came from Spanish-speaking countries in the Caribbean, Central America, Latin America or the Philippines.

Homemakers Mothers who stay at home to look after their families, rather than going out to work.

Homogenised Made things undifferentiated, all the same.

Homophobic Prejudiced against homosexuality.

Impeach Under the American Constitution, Congress has the power to bring an errant president to trial in a process called impeachment.

Imperial Presidency During the Cold War, presidential power increased so much that some commentators thought the president was becoming like an Emperor; hence 'Imperial'.

Inaugural address Speech made to the nation by a new president upon first taking office.

Indians Prior to the 1970s, Americans referred to Native Americans as 'Indians'.

Infant mortality rate Estimated number of infant deaths for every 1,000 live births.

In loco parentis In the parental role.

Interstate Between the various US states.

IRS Internal Revenue Service (federal government tax department).

Jim Crow laws Jim Crow was an early 1830s comic, black-faced minstrel character developed by a white performing artist that proved to be very popular with white audiences. When in the late nineteenth century the Southern states introduced laws that legalised segregation, they were known as 'Jim Crow laws'.

Joint Chiefs of Staff (JCS) The heads of the US Army, Navy and Air Force.

Judicial branch The federal government has an executive branch (the president), a legislative branch (Congress) and a judicial branch (the Supreme Court). The Supreme Court rules on whether or not actions and laws are in line with the American Constitution.

Justice Department Federal government department that monitors the enforcement of national laws.

Juvenile delinquency Criminal behaviour of the young.

Kinsey Reports In 1948, Doctor Alfred Kinsey, an Indiana University entomologist, brought out his first book on American male sexuality; a second, on female sexuality, followed five years later. Both were bestsellers.

Knights of Columbus A Catholic service organisation.

Labour unions Associations of workers who bargain with employers over pay and conditions, and sometimes organise strikes over those issues. More commonly known as trade unions in Britain.

Legislative branch Congress is one of the three branches of the federal government. All laws have to be passed by Congress.

Liberalism In the American context, tolerance and/or approval of federal government interventionism to help the disadvantaged and campaigners such as civil rights activists and feminists.

Liberals American liberals favour federal government intervention in order to ensure racial equality and help for the disadvantaged.

Madison Avenue Headquarters of the American advertising industry, in New York City.

Management science The application of technological and scientific ideas to running a company successfully – such as time and motion (where the amount of time it should take to complete a process in manufacturing is timed and subsequently monitored). The aim is to use scientifically proven methods to run the company.

Mass direct action In the context of the civil rights movement, when large numbers use non-violent methods such as sit-ins, strikes and boycotts in protest against existing practices.

Mass society Intellectuals decried American society in the 1950s as characterised by mass standardisation, co-operation and conformity.

Materialism Obsession with wealth and valuable objects.

Medicare Federal health insurance for the elderly and the disabled.

Middle America Ordinary Americans, neither rich nor poor; often small-town or rural residents, sometimes manual workers or service workers. Also known as the 'silent majority'.

Mississippi Freedom Summer A 1964 campaign by civil rights organisations such as the SNCC and the CORE, aimed at empowering Mississippi's black population through voter registration.

Moral Majority Religious Right organisation.

Moratorium In this context, suspension of normal activities to facilitate nationwide anti-Vietnam War protests.

Motion Picture Code Hollywood's system of self-censorship, in operation from 1930 to 1968.

NAACP (National Association for the Advancement of Colored People) Civil rights organisation, primarily concerned with black Americans.

NASA (National Aeronautics and Space Administration) Federal government agency responsible for research into and exploration of space.

National Guard Armed forces reservists, maintained by the state, but the president can call them up in a crisis.

Native Americans The indigenous population of North America.

Negro Until the late 1960s, black and white Americans referred to black Americans as Negroes.

New Deal President Roosevelt's programme to bring the US out of economic depression. It required government intervention in and expenditure on issues such as poverty and employment.

New Frontier President Kennedy's programme of challenges for the American people to meet in the areas of science and space, peace and war, ignorance and prejudice, and poverty and surplus.

New Left Student movement of the early 1960s, which sought greater racial and economic equality and an end to social conformity.

NFL (National Football League) Organisation that oversees the top American football teams.

NOW (National Organization of Women) Organisation that campaigns against gender inequality.

Nuclear family Traditional family, with mom, pop and kids.

Obstruction of justice A criminal offence wherein an individual makes investigation of potentially criminal acts difficult.

OPEC (Organization of Petroleum Exporting Countries) Organisation that co-ordinates the price and production policies of oil-producing countries.

Party platform The promises and policies set out by the Democratic or Republican parties, usually before elections.

Pennsylvania Avenue Major Washington DC thoroughfare, on which the White House is situated.

Pentagon Building in Washington DC that is the headquarters of the Department of Defense.

Personality tests Tests used by employers to reveal whether prospective employees will fit in with the prevailing ethos and work well.

Poll tax A tax levied on would-be voters, which made it harder for black people (who were usually poorer) to vote.

Pompadour Male hairstyle, with hair brushed up high from the forehead.

Poverty line Imaginary and arbitrary line, drawn by the federal government, below which an American is considered to be in poverty.

Proposition 63 Voters approved the proposition that 'English is the official language of California'. The proposition directed the California legislature to preserve the role of English as California's common language and prohibited it from passing laws that diminished the status of English.

Provincialism Lacking awareness of and empathy for other, different areas and lifestyles.

Public housing units Housing for the disadvantaged, subsidised by the federal government. Also known as 'the projects'.

Public schools In the United States, government-funded schools.

Race music Rhythm and blues, mostly associated with black composers and performers.

Radical feminism Feminism that focusses on patterns of male domination within society.

Ranch houses Long, single-storey homes that became popular in mid-twentieth-century America.

Reaganomics President Reagan's economic philosophy, which emphasised low taxes and deregulation, which it was thought would stimulate the economy.

Real income Income after taking into account the effect of inflation on purchasing power.

Recession Period of slowdown in economic growth; contributes to unemployment.

Religious Right Large and influential group of voters that developed in the late 1970s. Their beliefs were a reaction to the counter-culture of the 1960s and included opposition to abortion, bussing and homosexuality. Those with similar conservative beliefs but less religiosity were known as the New Right.

Reparations Compensation.

Reproductive rights The right to use family planning and to have an abortion.

Republican Supporter of one of the two main political parties. Twentieth-century Republicans tended to favour business interests and opposed government interventionism.

Reservations Lands allocated to Native American tribes in the nineteenth century after their own traditional habitat was taken over by white people. Most tribes had their own reservation.

Reserve Officer Training Corps (ROTC) College-based programme for training officers for the United States armed forces.

Restrictive covenants Legal agreements that stopped 'undesirables' such as black Americans and Jews living in certain buildings or areas.

Rugged individualism Many Americans believed their country's dynamism had been shaped by individuals who conquered wilderness areas previously inhabited only by Native Americans.

Rust Belt Term popularised in the 1980s to describe areas of the Midwest and Northeast that had traditionally hosted great manufacturing industries but were now in decline.

Segregation The separation of people because of race (for example, separate housing, schools and transport).

Self-determination The freedom of a group or nation to make their own choices and form of government – for example, black American control over black Americans.

Senate Upper chamber of the bicameral US legislature, Congress. Senate consent is needed for the passage of laws and for many important presidential appointments.

Separatism In this context, the black desire to live as independently as possible from white Americans.

Service industry Industries such as hotels, motels, restaurants and petrol stations.

Share-croppers Poor Southern farmers who worked the land for a landowner and shared the crops with him as payment for use of his land.

Silent majority Also known as Middle America. President Nixon popularised the phrase in the early 1970s, to describe those who did not protest against the Vietnam War or the status quo; the quiet, hard-working bedrock of American life and values.

Sit-ins Black Americans occupied seating in segregated restaurants and refused to move as a protest against segregation.

Social security President Roosevelt introduced social security payments for the unemployed and the elderly.

Socialists Political group that opposes massive disparities in wealth.

Sound-bite communications Snappy phrases and sentences designed to catch the audience's attention.

Sovereignty In the Native American context, the right to self-government on reservations.

Soviet Union In 1922 Russia and all its republics became known as the Union of Soviet Socialist Republics, the USSR or the Soviet Union.

Sportscaster Radio or television commentator on sport.

Sputnik First satellite into space, sent up by the Soviet Union.

Streetcars Trams.

Suburbia Residential area that encircles cities.

Supply-side economics Focussing on the supply rather than the demand in an economy. In practice, this means government should concentrate on achieving inflation-free economic growth, rather than on unemployment and providing welfare safety nets.

Supreme Court The judicial branch of the federal government, consisting of nine justices nominated by the president and accepted by Congress. The Court rules on whether actions or laws are constitutional. It has no powers of enforcement.

Sweatshops Small factories where workers are poorly paid and work in poor conditions.

Tax base Taxpayers within an area such as a city.

Televangelist Preacher who uses television to reach a larger audience.

Tight money policies Decreasing the money supply and raising interest rates to combat inflation.

Title VII Section of the 1964 Civil Rights Act that banned discrimination in employment on the basis of sex and race.

Trade deficit When the value of a nation's imports is greater than that of its exports.

Underemployment When a worker wants to work full time but can only find part-time opportunities.

Undocumented aliens Illegal residents of the United States, usually Mexican Americans.

Veto To stop something from happening – for example, stopping a bill from becoming an Act.

Videocassette recorder (VCR) Machine that records television programmes onto cassettes.

Welfare queens Phrase popularised by Ronald Reagan. It refers to the fact that between 1980 and 1990 the number of single mothers rocketed due to more divorces, more unmarried mothers and greater awareness of available benefits. The phrase constituted coded racism because black Americans constituted around 10 per cent of the population but nearly 50 per cent of those receiving Aid to Families with Dependent Children.

White Citizens' Council Southern white supremacist groups established in response to the Supreme Court's *Brown* ruling (1954), which declared segregated education unconstitutional.

White-collar workers Those who work in offices.

White flight As the twentieth century progressed, increasing numbers of white Americans left the cities to minority groups and migrated to the suburbs.

Yom Kippur War War between Israel and neighbouring Arab states in 1973.

Youth International Party Also known as Yippies. Radical student group that wanted to show contempt for the political system at the Democratic Party Convention in Chicago in 1968.

INDEX

Abdication Crisis 12, 14
abortion 74–5, 94, 102, 113, 114, 407, 477
    legalisation in the US 438–9
    and the religious right 460
AfricanAmericans *see* black Americans
agriculture
    in the USA 240, 271, 274, 275–6
AIDS crisis 208, 464, 468–9
appeasement policy 13, 14
Asian Americans 473
Attlee, Clement 12–13, 16, 123
    government of 15–16, 25, 57
    welfare state 62–3
aviation industry 266
Baldwin, Stanley 8, 9, 12–13
    and Churchill 14
    economic policy 28
banks
    in the United States 244, 266–7
    and interwar Britain 9, 25, 30
    and the New Deal 277, 285–6
Barrow, Clyde 268, 269
baseball 254
Beatles 145
Beatniks 365
Belafonte, Harry 342
Benn, Tony 22, 37
Berlin Airlift 330
Bevan, Aneurin 16
Beveridge Report 60, 62, 82
Bevin, Ernest 16, 46, 48
birth control 74, 77, 111, 113, 251, 407
black Americans 233, 241, 247
    Black Power Movement 370, 389, 390, 391–3, 476
    and civil rights 233, 337, 338–42
    and the Depression 265
    Harlem Renaissance 252, 255, 256
    and the New Deal 302, 303–4
    and the Second World War 304–6, 308
    in the Southern states 255, 367
    status of 443–5, 472, 473, 474–6
    stereotyping of 334–5
    see also civil rights movement
Blair, Tony 169, 179, 222, 223, 224
Bork, Robert 462–3
Bowie, David 146
British Empire 34, 118
BUF (British Union of Fascists) 10–11, 120
Bush, George H.W. 456–7, 460, 462, 474
Butlin's 158–9
Callaghan, James 19, 20, 22–3, 36, 37, 85, 162, 224
    and industrial relations 50, 52
    Ruskin speech 86–7
    welfare policies 65
Capone, Al 249–50
car industry
    in the USA 236–7, 324, 430
car ownership
    in Britain 130, 158, 161–4
    in the USA 322, 324, 355–7
caravanning in Britain 160–1
Carmichael, Stokeley 392
Carter, Jimmy 353, 422, 424, 425–6, 453
    and the energy crisis 430, 431, 432
Chamberlain, Neville 12, 13–14
Chavez, Cesar 393–4
childbirth 75
China lobby 327
Churchill, Winston 15
    and immigration 123
    in the interwar years 28–9, 43
    premiership 14, 17
cinema
    in Britain 99, 141–4, 210
    in the USA 233, 253–4, 308, 311, 413, 436, 437
    blaxploitation movies 436–7
    controversial issues 469–70
    Hollywood and the Cold War 332
    Hollywood and women 334
    and social change 363
civil liberties in Britain 187–8
civil rights movement 233, 337, 338–42, 367–74, 387–94
    Birmingham campaign 372–4
    Chicago campaign 388–9
    and Johnson 395
    Little Rock crisis 372
    Montgomery bus boycott 368–71
    and news media 413
    Selma campaign 387, 389, 395
    and student protest 402
    Watts riots 388
    White Citizens' Councils 372
class (Britain)
    and car ownership 163
    and education policy 82
    and the NHS 73
    and political parties 4–5, 28
    and social change 94, 96–9
    and spectator sports 156
    and spy films 143
    Thatcher and 'class war' 200–3, 212
    and tourism 157–9, 161
    and women 107, 112–13
Clinton, Bill 457, 462, 463
Cold War 15, 329–31, 355, 423
    and Hollywood 332
    and Kennedy 377
collective security 12–13
communism
    anticommunism and the Cold War 329–31
    in Britain 7, 8, 10–11
    antiracist campaigns 120
    and postwar Europe 32
    Red Scare in the USA 246–7, 326–9, 331
    and the Vietnam War 401
consensus politics (Britain) 2, 15, 16–17, 170
Conservative Party (Britain) 2
    in 1918 5
    interwar years 7, 10
    and Major 218–21
    postwar consensus 15, 16–17
    and state welfare 64–5, 66
    and Thatcher 170, 216–218
consumerism
    in Britain 98, 106, 112, 133, 137–8
    in the USA 233, 325–6, 354, 359–60
contraception *see* birth control
Cook, Arthur 44
Coolidge, Calvin 235
corporatism 34, 185
Coughlin, Father Charles 281–2
counterculture 402–3, 409, 410, 414
cricket 156
crime in the USA 249–50, 268–9
Cuba 377
customer service in Britain 159
defence policy under Thatcher 186
deflation (Britain) 26–7
Detroit riot (1943) 306
divorce 110–11, 325
domestic violence 114
DouglasHome, Sir Alec 19, 83
drug abuse 402, 461–2
economic challenges (Britain) 2, 25–41
    consumer boom 33
    IMF crisis 22, 35, 37, 66
    interwar 8, 25–31
    postwar 32–7
    Second World War 31–2
    see also Great Depression (192934)
economic challenges (USA) 232
    1920s 232, 233–41
    New Deal 232–3, 274–89, 290
    postwar economic change 322–6, 428–32
    Second World War 313–17

Wall Street crash 29, 241–5
Eden, Anthony 17–18
education
    in Britain 80–92
        comprehensive schools 83–7
        Education Act (1944) 82–3
        ethnic minorities 120
        policy and reform (191843) 80–2
        progressive education 86–7
        secondary schools 81–2, 82–3
        Thatcher reforms 193
        universities 87–9, 120
    in the USA
        and civil rights 338–40, 341–2, 444
        and Johnson's Great Society 396–7
        Reagan's policies on 454
Eisenhower, Dwight D. 328, 352–3, 355, 374, 422, 426
    and the civil rights movement 337, 338, 340
employment
    in Britain 46–7
        and living standards 132–3
        migrant workers 119
        in the NHS 75
        Second World War 46, 134–5
        women 46, 106–7, 109, 110
        and youth culture 150
    in the USA
        decline of workers' rights 440–1
        postwar 357
        Reagan's policies on 454–5
        service jobs 428, 431
        and the Wall Street crash 243
        and women 240–1, 310, 476–7, 478
        young people 313
environmentalism 412, 426–7
ERM (Exchange Rate Mechanism) 176
ethnic minorities *see* immigration (Britain)
European Economic Community (EEC) 21, 22
Fabian Society 11, 69, 82
Falklands War 200
Falwell, Jerry 441, 458
fascism 10–11, 120
Festival of Britain 136, 137
Festival of Light 104
film *see* cinema
financial services (Britain) 178
Firestone, Shulasmith 405–6
First World War
    in Britain 4, 5, 7
        class and social change 97
        economy 25
        and ethnic minorities 118
        and women 106–7
    and the USA 4
        Prohibition 248

war debts 272
flapper girls 111–12, 247
food
    in interwar Britain 133
        wartime rationing 61, 133, 134, 135
Foot, Michael 22, 207, 224
football 155, 156, 157
Ford, Gerald 422, 424, 425
Ford, Henry 236
Friedan, Betty 404
gangsterism 249–50, 268–9
GCHQ, banning of union membership at 187
Germany 12, 13, 14, 63
ghettos 358, 387, 392
GLC (Greater London Council) 190, 191–2
Gold Standard 9, 10, 14, 28–9
Great Depression (192934)
    in Britain 29–30, 45, 60, 97
        and family life 112
        and living standards 132–3
        and popular culture 142, 155–6
    in the USA 232–3, 264–74
Greer, Germaine 114, 115
greyhound racing 155
Harding, Warren 235
Harlem Renaissance 252, 255, 256
Healey, Denis 22, 36, 37
healthcare
    in Britain 68–77
        in 1918 68
        ethnic minorities 120
        interwar 69–70
        mental health 75
        Second World War 71
        tuberculosis 69–70
    and Johnson's Great Society 398
    see also NHS (National Health Service)
Heath, Edward 20–1, 36
    economic policy 20, 21, 36
    education policy 85, 88, 89
    industrial relations under 20, 21, 37, 50–1, 52
    and Thatcher 170, 171
Heseltine, Michael 217
Hispanic Americans
    and the Depression 265–6
    postwar era 337
    and the Second World War 208, 306–7
    status of 472, 473, 474, 475
    United Farm Workers 393–4
Hiss, Alger 331
Hitler, Adolf 12, 13
hoboes 267
holidays 130, 157–61
homelessness 429

homosexuality 94, 100, 102, 208–10, 408, 441
    in film and TV 469
    and the religious right 460–1
Hoover, Herbert 232–2, 235
    and the Depression 269–73, 274, 279
        War Veterans and the 'Bonus Army' 273
Hoovervilles 270
hospitals (Britain) 68, 69
housing
    in Britain 9, 133, 135–7
        Thatcher reforms 189–90
    in the USA 357–8
        and Johnson's Great Society 395, 397
        New Deal 280
        postwar 324–5
HUAC (House UnAmerican Activities Committee) 326–9, 332
hunger marches (Britain) 30
IMF crisis (Britain) 22, 35, 37, 66
immigration (Britain) 94, 118–28
    black community and Thatcher 204–6
    black radicals 125–6, 202
    Commonwealth and 'new Commonwealth' immigration 122
    discrimination 119
    education and health 120
    and the First World War 118
    Immigration Acts 124–5
    multiculturalism 125, 127, 205
    race relations law 126
    and reggae 146–7
    and Thatcher 204–6
    working rights 119
immigration (United States) 246
    see also black Americans
incomes
    in the USA 323, 453–4
India 14
industrial relations (Britain) 2, 42–5, 47–53
    Dagenham sewing machinists' strike 109
    General Strike (1926) 8, 42, 44–5, 48
    Heath government 20, 21, 37, 50–1, 52
    Industrial Charter 48
    interwar years 42
    Thatcher governments 185–6, 200–3
    war years 47–8
    Wilson governments 20, 21, 50, 52
    'winter of discontent' 52–3, 200
industry
    in Britain 25, 26, 27
        cars 162
        employment in 47, 132–3
        interwar years 42–3

Index 501

nationalised industries and privatisation 174–5, 190
   postwar nationalisation 31, 33, 34
   and technology 36
   in the USA
      and the Depression 266
      motor vehicle industry 236–7, 324
      and the New Deal 277–9
      and the Second World War 316
inflation
   in Britain 2, 21, 25, 36
      and monetarism 172
      and Thatcherism 177
      and welfare spending 65
   in the USA 234, 428
Iranian hostage crisis 425–6
Ireland 4
Japanese Americans
   and the Second World War 307, 308
Jenkins, Roy 102, 125
Johnson, Lyndon B. 353, 389, 407, 426
   Great Society 395–9, 412, 428
Joseph, Sir Keith 20, 37, 64, 65, 174
Keeler, Christine 19
Kennedy, John F. 18, 353, 374–8, 422
   assassination of 410
   and civil rights 372, 373
   and the Cold War 377
   and the Peace Corps 376–7
   space programme 377–8
Keynes, John Maynard 29, 32
Keynesianism 184, 185
King, Martin Luther Jr 371, 372, 373, 374, 376, 387–90, 394
   assassination of 410
Korean War 16, 330
Ku Klux Klan 247, 255, 342, 370, 371–2
Labour Party (Britain) 2, 4, 7, 16
   in 1918 5
   consensus politics 15
   education policies 83
   and local government 190
   and the National Government 9, 10, 12
   and Thatcherism 213, 222–4
Lady Chatterley trial 102
law and order in Britain 171, 186–7, 219
Lawrence, Stephen 206
Lawson, Nigel 174, 176
League of Nations 12
Lend Lease 32, 135, 300
Levitt houses 324, 357–8
Liberal Party (Britain) 2, 4–5, 225
liberalism and the liberal society 98–104
Liberty League 281
literature in the USA 256–7
living standards in Britain 132–40
Lloyd George, David 5, 7, 28, 59
local government (Britain) 190–2
Long, Huey 281

Longford, Lord 103, 104
McCarthy, Senator Joseph 233, 326–9
McDonald's 357
MacDonald, Ramsay 7–8, 9, 10
   and Churchill 14
   see also National Government (Britain)
Macmillan, Harold 18–19, 35, 83
   Conservative welfarism 63
   economic policy 18, 34
   'Night of the Long Knives' 18
   Wolfenden Report 102
Madonna 465, 466
Major, John 169, 176, 179, 202, 205, 210, 211
   and the Conservative Party 218–21
   economic policy 219
Malcolm X 389, 390–1, 392, 394
management science 235, 238, 361
Manhattan Project 331
Marshall Aid 32, 330
media
   in Britain 99, 100, 130, 187
   in the USA 412–14, 436–8
Meredith, James 392
military spending
   Britain 13, 14, 31–2
military–industrial complex
   in the USA 316, 329
miners' strikes (Britain) 44, 48, 51
   and Thatcher 200–3, 213
monetarism 37, 66, 172
Moors murderers 103
Mosley, Oswald 11
Muggeridge, Malcolm 103, 104
mugging 187
Munich Agreement (1938) 13
Murdoch, Rupert 224
music 144–7, 205, 252, 253, 312, 434–5
   African American 340–1, 435
   challenges of popular music 465–6
   Federal Music Project 309–10
   heavy metal 434, 464
   punk 147, 434–5
   rap 465
   reggae 146–7
National Assistance Act (Britain) 15, 63
National Government (Britain) 2, 3, 4, 9, 10–14
   economic policy 10, 30–1
   welfare provisions 59–60
National Insurance Acts (Britain) 15, 63, 64
National Parks (United States) 378
Native Americans
   and the Depression 265
   and the New Deal 280, 303
   postwar era 336–7
   rights 442–3
   and the Second World War 308
   status of 472–3, 475

Nazi Germany 12, 13
New Cross fire 204–5, 206
New Deal 232–3, 274–89, 290, 352
   Agricultural Adjustment Act 274, 275–6
   and the arts 309–10
   Farmer–Labour Party 283
   Glass–Steagall Act 274, 277
   impact of
      and the economy 296–302
      and ethnic minorities 302–4
   industrial recovery 277–9
   opposition to 280–2
   and the 'Roosevelt Recession' 288–9, 302
new towns (Britain) 137, 138
NHS (National Health Service) 15, 16, 57, 63, 71–7
   challenge of medical advances 76–7
   creation 70, 71–2
   development and spending 72
   impact of 73–6
   internal market 219
   Thatcher reforms 192
Nixon, Richard 353, 389, 409, 410, 411–12, 414, 422, 438
   Watergate scandal 423–4
NOI (Nation of Islam) 390–1
Northern Ireland 207
Notting Hill riots (1958) 123
nuclear weapons 329, 330
oil crisis (1973) 25, 36, 51, 430–2
Open University 88
Orgreave, Battle of 201
Owen, David 225
Parks, Rosa 370
Philby, Harold 'Kim' 19
photography 309
Pizzey, Erin 114
popular culture
   in Britain 130, 141–52
      acid house and rave culture 219, 220
      cinema 99, 141–4, 210
      music 144–7
      radio 147–8
      television 103–4, 148–9
      youth culture 150–1
   in the USA 252–7, 361–6, 464–71
      postwar 332–6, 433–8
poverty
   in Britain 63, 133, 138–9
   in the USA 233, 268, 354, 375–6, 429
      black Americans 444
      and Johnson's Great Society 396, 398–9
      Nixon's antipoverty programme 412
Powell, Enoch 126
Presley, Elvis 366
privatisation policy in Britain 174–5, 190, 219

Profumo affair 19, 94
Prohibition 248–50
quality of life changes (Britain) 130–68
    leisure and travel 130, 155–64
    living standards 132–40
    popular culture 130, 141–52
racism in Britain 118–20, 121, 123
radio 147–8, 156, 253, 312
railways in Britain
    the Beeching axe 163
Rape Crisis Centres 114
Reagan, Nancy 461, 462
Reagan, Ronald 353, 402, 453–6, 469, 475
    and the religious right 459, 478
Red Clydeside 43
regional policy (Britain)
    Special Areas Act 30–1
Reith, John 147
religion
    in Britain 103–4
    religious right in the USA 441, 458–63, 468, 470, 478
Ridney, Nicholas 20, 201
roads in Britain 162, 163–4
Roosevelt, Eleanor 301, 304
Roosevelt, Franklin D. 274–89, 352
    and the New Deal
        economic impact of 296–302
        First 274–82
        Second 283–9
Rosenberg case 331
Rowbotham, Sheila 113
Russian Civil War 43
Sagebrush Rebellion 427
Sands, Bobby 207
Scargill, Arthur 51, 201
Scottish nationalism 213
SDP (Social Democratic Party) 213, 224–5
Second World War
    in Britain
        Churchill's premiership 14
        cinema 142, 143
        economic policy 31–2
        and education 82
        employment changes 46, 134–5
        healthcare 71
        and immigration 121
        industrial relations 47–8
        Mass Observation 98, 142
        Phony War 14
        rationing 61, 133, 134, 135
        total war 14
        and university education 87, 88
        welfare provisions 60–2
        and women 108, 112
    in the USA 233
        and black Americans 304–6
        and the economy 313–17
        entry into the war 303
        GI Bill of Rights 323
        labour unions 315–16
        and LendLease 32, 135, 300
        migration and dislocation 315
        Office of War Mobilization 314
        social and cultural changes 308–12
sex scandals (Britain) 19, 94, 99
sexuality/sexual liberalisation 100–2, 208–10, 407–8
    in films and TV 469–70
    and Madonna 465, 466
    see also homosexuality
Smith, John 202
Smoot–Hawley tariff 232, 269, 271–2
social change
    in Britain 9, 94–128
        and class 94, 96–9
        and education 84, 89
        and the liberal society 98–104
        see also quality of life changes (Britain); women
    in the USA 471–8
        interwar years 246–52
        New Deal and the Second World War 308–12
Social Security Act (USA) 285, 297–8
Soviet Union 8
space programme (United States) 377–8
sport
    and black Americans 341
    spectator sports in Britain 155–7
    in the USA 254, 433–4
spy scandals (Britain) 18–19
state intervention
    meanings of 185
    and Thatcher 169, 184–8
stock market
    and the Wall Street crash 243–4
stopgo economics 34
Stopes, Dr Marie 111
strikes see industrial relations (Britain)
student protest 400–2, 410–11
suburbs, growth of 324–5, 354
Suez Crisis 17–18
Supreme Court (United States)
    and the New Deal 287–8
    and the religious right 460
Taft–Hartley Act 328
taxation
    in Britain 16, 172, 174
    and the New Deal 284
    in the USA 313–14, 456–7
technology
    in Britain 36, 46
    and popular culture 467–8
    in the USA 236–8
television
    in Britain 103–4, 148–9
    cable television and MTV 467–8
    in the USA 332–3, 362–3, 413, 436
    controversial issues 469–70
Thatcher, Margaret 21, 169–231
    Bruges speech 184
    and `class war' 200–3
    and conviction politics 70
    economic policies 25, 37, 169, 170–83
        1981 budget 173
        consequences of 177–8
        Lawson boom and bust 176–7
        legacy of 179, 180–1
        supply side economics 174–5
    education policies 85, 88
    election of (1979) 2, 22
    fall of 218
    and feminism 210–11
    and immigration 204–6
    industrial relations policy 53
    and Northern Ireland 207
    personal beliefs 170–1
    politics and party development 169, 216–28
    and the public sector 169, 189–93
    and sexuality 208–10
    and state intervention 169, 184–8
    welfare policies 65
    and women in politics 109–10
Thomas, Clarence 474, 477–8
tourism 157–61
trade
    British 27–8, 32
    deficit in the USA 430, 456
travel 161–4
Truman, Harry S. 337
unemployment
    in Britain
        insurance 58–9
        interwar 9, 11, 30, 60, 132
        postwar 35, 47
        and Thatcher 178
    in the USA 328, 454
        and the Depression 265, 267, 272
        and Kennedy 374–5
        and the New Deal 279–80, 297–8
universities 87–9, 120
urbanisation in the United States 354–9
Vassall, John 19
Versailles, Treaty of 13
Vietnam War 377, 398, 409–10, 426
    antiwar protests 401
    media coverage 413
violence
    Battle of Orgreave 201
    in films and TV 469–70
    football hooliganism 157
    and young people 151
voting rights (Britain) 2, 5
voting system (Britain) 16
wages
    in Britain 47, 119

in the USA 234
Wall Street crash 29, 241–5
Watergate scandal 423–4
Webb, Sidney and Beatrice 11
welfare state (Britain) 15, 57–78
    Beveridge Report 60, 62, 82
    establishment 57, 62–3
    healthcare 68–77
    rightwing challenges to 57, 64–5, 66
    Thatcher reforms 192–3, 212
    welfare provision in the interwar years 58–60
Whitehouse, Mary 94, 103–4
Williams, Ivy 107
Wilson, Harold 224
    economic policies 19, 35–6
    education policy 85
    governments 19–20, 21–2
    industrial relations 20, 21, 50, 52
    welfare policies 64, 65
women
    in Britain 94, 106–15
        Dagenham sewing machinists' strike 109
        employment opportunities 46, 106–7, 108, 110, 132
        Equal Pay Act 110
        family life and personal freedom 110–15
        feminism and Thatcher 210–11
        and the NHS 74–5
        in politics 108, 109
        and Second World War 108, 112
        Sex Discrimination Act (1975) 110
        voting rights 2, 4, 5, 106
    feminists and the women's movement 113–14, 402, 403–7, 439–40
    in the USA 332, 333–4, 356, 362
        in the 1920s 247, 251
        and the Depression 266
        and Eleanor Roosevelt 301
        in films and television 470–1
        and the New Deal 300
        in politics 240, 478
        reproductive rights 477
        and the Second World War 310–11
        and work 240, 310, 476–7, 478
workhouses 58, 68
World Disarmament Conference 12
youth culture 150–1, 332, 335–6, 364–6
    in the 1980s 464–7
    juvenile delinquency 364
    young people and cars 356
Zircon affair 187

The Publishers would like to thank the following for permission to reproduce copyright material.

Photo credits

pp. 2–3 © Tupungato/Fotolia; **p. 7** Library of Congress Prints and Photographs [LC-USZ62-8054]; **p. 11** Mary Evans / Marx Memorial Library; **p. 12** ©2003 Credit:Topham / AP; **p. 13** Library of Congress Prints and Photographs Division [LC-DIG-ggbain-23679]; **p. 14** © Lucian Milasan/Fotolia; **p. 21** © Bettmann/CORBIS; **p. 28** Library of Congress Prints and Photographs Division [LOC_ LC-DIG-npcc-23727]; **p. 30** © Mary Evans Picture Library / Alamy; **p. 32** © jelwolf – Fotolia.com; **p. 45** Brooke/Topical Press Agency/Getty Images; **p. 51** Fox Photos/Hulton Archive/Getty Images; **p. 53** ©PA Photos / TopFoto; **p. 57** © Tony Baggett/Fotolia; **p. 61** © Hulton-Deutsch Collection/CORBIS; **p. 75** Mary Evans Picture Library/GULLIVER PHOTOS; **p. 81** Otto Ohm Collection / IBL / Mary Evans; **pp. 94–5** © Rawpixel/Fotolia; **p. 100** © Bettmann/CORBIS; p. 101 © Jeff Morgan 12 / Alamy; **p. 109** Bob Aylott/Keystone/Getty Images; **p. 111** Library of Congress Prints and Photographs Division [LC-USZ62-118338]; **p. 114** Fairfax Media/Fairfax Media via Getty Images; **p. 122** © Illustrated London News Ltd/Mary Evans; **pp. 130–1** © acceleratorhams/Fotolia; **p. 134** © chrisdorney/Fotolia; **p. 136** © Simon Balson / Alamy; **p. 143** ©TopFoto; **p. 145** ©TopFoto; **p. 151** © chriskemp/Fotolia; **p. 155** Kurt Hutton/Picture Post/Getty Images; **p. 156** © Brian Jackson/Fotolia; **p. 157** ©PA Photos / TopFoto; **p. 158** © drhfoto/Fotolia; **p. 159** © Trinity Mirror / Mirrorpix / Alamy; **p. 160** rehtse_c/Thinkstock; **p 162** © Trinity Mirror / Mirrorpix / Alamy; **p. 164** Library of Congress Prints and Photographs Division [LC-DIG-matpc-15804]; **p. 169** © Tim Graham / Alamy; **p. 171** Library of Congress Prints and Photographs Division [LC-DIG-ppmsc-03266]; **p 173** © davispics/Fotolia; **p. 218** © jorisvo/Fotolia; **pp. 232–3** Hulton Archive/Getty Images; **p. 236** Library of Congress Prints and Photographs Division [LC-USZ62-111278]; **p. 239** Image Courtesy of The Advertising Archives; **p. 256** Library of Congress Prints and Photographs Division [LC-USZ61-1854]; **p. 267** Popperfoto/Getty Images; **p. 275** Library of Congress Prints and Photographs Division [LC-USZ62-11190]; **p. 300** © World History Archive / Alamy; **p. 309** © Atomic / Alamy; **p. 325** Why We Eat Better, 1951 (b/w photo), Henderson, Alexander (1831-1913) / Hagley Museum & Library, Wilmington, Delaware, USA / Bridgeman Images; **p. 339** © Bettmann/CORBIS; **pp. 352–3 & 356** JOHN BRYSON/The LIFE Picture Collection/Getty Images; **p. 355** © Stocktrek Images, Inc. / Alamy; **p. 359** CBS Photo Archive/Getty Images; **p. 366** © Pictorial Press Ltd / Alamy; **p. 370** Don Cravens/The LIFE Images Collection/Getty Images; **p. 371** Rolls Press/Popperfoto/Getty Images; **p. 390** Library of Congress Prints and Photographs Division [LC-USZ62-115058]; **p. 399** © CORBIS; **p. 406** ©The Image Works / TopFoto; **p. 424** Rolls Press/Popperfoto/Getty Images; **p. 435** © Lynn Goldsmith/Corbis; **p. 462** © Bettmann/CORBIS; **p. 464** SNAP/REX; **p. 467** © Bettmann/CORBIS

Acknowledgements

Philip Larkin: verse from *Annus Mirabilis*, in *The Complete Poems of Philip Larkin* (Faber and Faber, 2012); Betty Jerman, 'Squeezed in Like Sardines in Suburbia' (*The Guardian*, 19 February 1960); Earl Aaron Reitan, *The Thatcher Revolution: Margaret Thatcher, John Major, Tony Blair, and the Transformation of Modern Britain, 1979–2001* (Rowman & Littlefield, 2002); Jeremy Black, *Britain since the Seventies: Politics and Society in the Consumer Age* (Reaktion, 2004); Studs Terkel, *Hard Times: An Oral History of the Depression* (Penguin, 2001); Account of a bracero, known only as Don Jesús (http://aztlan.sdsu.edu/chicanohistory/chapter08/c08s07.html); article by Joseph Purcell (*Boston Daily Record*, 23 October 1943); Lew Sadler, 'White Dixie's View from Lew Sadler' (*Chicago Defender*, 24 September 1955); Allen Ginsberg, extract from 'Howl' (1956); Thomas P. O'Neill, Jr. with William Novak, *Man of the House: The Life and Political Memoirs of Speaker Tip O'Neill* (Random House, 1987); *Variety* magazine, March 1968; Alvin F. Poussaint, 'Blaxploitation Movies: Cheap Thrills That Degrade Blacks' (*Psychology Today*, Vol. 7 No. 9, February 1974); Vito Russo, speech delivered at ACT-UP demonstration in Albany, May 1988 (http://www.actupny.org/documents/whfight.html); US Census Bureau, *Current Population Survey, Annual Social and Economic Supplements*; Jesse Jackson, quoted in Clayborne Carson et al. (ed.), *The Eyes on the Prize Civil Rights Reader* (Penguin, 1991).

Every effort has been made to trace all copyright holders, but if any have been inadvertently overlooked, the Publishers will be pleased to make the necessary arrangements at the first opportunity.